Jim Mandeville

Team RBS member Jack Nicklaus, winner of 18 professional major championships.

Introduction

It is an honour for RBS to present *The World of Professional Golf 2004*, the golf annual founded 38 years ago by Mark H. McCormack.

Mark was a friend, and I was saddened last year by his passing. I was pleased therefore that the McCormack family has decided to continue the publication of this annual in Mark's memory.

As an international company headquartered in Scotland, the home of golf, we have enjoyed a long association with the game, and in the case of the R&A and the Open Championship that association goes back for over 100 years. More recently, we have deepened our involvement with golf in both the U.S. and Europe. The annual represents a terrific record of professional golf around the world and it is both informative and definitive; enjoy!

Fred Goodwin
Group Chief Executive

The Royal Bank of Scotland Group

Presents

The World of
Professional Golf
Founded by
Mark H. McCormack
2004

An IMG PUBLISHING Book

An IMG PUBLISHING Book
Editor: Bev Norwood
Contributors: Steve Eubanks, Andy Farrell, Donald (Doc) Giffin, Marino Parascenzo, Robert Sommers

First published 2004
© IMG Operations, Inc. 2004

Designed and produced by Davis Design

ISBN 1-878843-39-7

Printed and bound in the United States of America.

Contents

Foreword
(Written in 1968)

It has long been my feeling that a sport as compelling as professional golf is deserving of a history, and by history I do not mean an account culled years later from the adjectives and enthusiasms of on-the-spot reports that have then sat in newspaper morgues for decades waiting for some patient drudge to paste them together and call them lore. Such works can be excellent when insight and perspective are added to the research, but this rarely happens. What I am talking about is a running history, a chronology written at the time, which would serve both as a record of the sport and as a commentary upon the sport in any given year — an annual, if you will....

When I embarked on this project two years ago (the first of these annuals was published in Great Britain in 1967), I was repeatedly told that such a compendium of world golf was impossible, that it would be years out of date before it could be assembled and published, that it would be hopelessly expensive to produce and that only the golf fanatic would want a copy anyway. In the last analysis, it was that final stipulation that spurred me on. There must be a lot of golf fanatics, I decided. I can't be the only one. And then one winter day I was sitting in Arnold Palmer's den in Latrobe, Pennsylvania, going through the usual motions of spreading papers around so that Arnold and I could discuss some business project, when Arnold happened to mention that he wanted to collect a copy of each new golf book that was published from now on, in order to build a golf library of his own. "It's really too bad that there isn't a book every year on the pro tour," he said. "Ah," I thought. "Another golf fanatic. That makes two of us." So I decided to do the book. And I have. And I hope you like it. If so, you can join Arnold and me as golf fanatics.

Mark H. McCormack
Cleveland, Ohio
January, 1968

Mark H. McCormack
1930 – 2003

In 1960, Mark Hume McCormack shook hands with a young golfer named Arnold Palmer. That historic handshake established a business that would evolve into today's IMG, the world's premier sports and lifestyle marketing and management company — representing hundreds of sports figures, entertainers, television properties, artists, musicians, writers, celebrities and prestigious organizations and events around the world. With just a handshake Mark McCormack had invented a global industry.

Sean McManus, President of CBS Sports, reflects, "I don't think it's an overstatement to say that like Henry Ford and Bill Gates, Mark McCormack literally created, fostered and led an entirely new worldwide industry. There was no sports marketing before Mark McCormack. Every athlete who's ever appeared in a commercial, or every right holder who sold their rights to anyone, owes a huge debt of gratitude to Mark McCormack."

Mark McCormack's philosophy was simple. "Be the best," he said. "Learn the business and expand by applying what you already know." This philosophy served him well, not only as an entrepreneur and CEO of IMG, but also as an author, a consultant and a confidant to a host of global leaders in the world of business, politics, finance, science, sports and entertainment.

He was among the most-honored entrepreneurs of his time. *Sports Illustrated* recognized him as "The Most Powerful Man in Sports." In 1999, ESPN's Sports Century listed him as one of the century's 10 "Most Influential People in the Business of Sport."

Golf Magazine called McCormack "the most powerful man in golf" and honored him along with Arnold Palmer, Gerald Ford, Dwight D. Eisenhower, Bob Hope and Ben Hogan as one of the 100 all-time "American Heroes of Golf." *Tennis* magazine and *Racquet* magazine named him "the most powerful man in tennis." Tennis legend Billie Jean King believes, "Mark McCormack was the king of sports marketing. He shaped the way all sports are marketed around the world. He was the first in the marketplace, and his influence on the world of sports, particularly his ability to combine athlete representation, property development and television broadcasting, will forever be the standard of the industry."

The London *Sunday Times* listed him as one of the 1000 people who influenced the 20th century. Alastair Cooke on the BBC said simply that "McCormack was the Oracle; the creator of the talent industry, the maker of people famous in their profession famous to the rest of the world and making for them a fortune in the process … He took on as clients people already famous in their profession as golfer, opera singer, author, footballer, racing car driver, violinist — and from time to time if they needed special help, a prime minister, or even the Pope."

McCormack was honored posthumously by the Golf Writers Association of America with the 2004 William D. Richardson Award, the organization's highest honor, "Given to recognize an individual who has consistently made an outstanding contribution to golf."

Among McCormack's other honors were the 2001 PGA Distinguished Service Award, given to those who have helped perpetuate the values and ideals of the PGA of America. He was also named a Commander of the Royal Order of the Polar Star by the King of Sweden (the highest honor for a person living outside of Sweden) for his contribution to the Nobel Foundation.

Journalist Frank Deford states, "There have been what we love to call dynasties in every sport. IMG has been different. What this one brilliant man, Mark McCormack, created is the only dynasty ever over all sport."

Through IMG, Mark McCormack demonstrated the value of sports and lifestyle activities as effective corporate marketing tools, but more importantly, his lifelong dedication to his vocation — begun with just a simple handshake — brought enjoyment to millions of people worldwide who watch and cheer their heroes and heroines. That is his legacy.

1. The Year in Retrospect

It would be hard to find a bigger sports story in 2003 than Annika Sorenstam's appearance at the Bank of America Colonial. Not only were the Thursday and Friday rounds of the Fort Worth, Texas, event the most publicized of the year, the story challenged the Iraq war on the front pages of most newspapers and led almost every televised newscast in America and Europe at least once during the week.

The mechanics of the story were simple:

Not long after 13-year-old Michelle Wie tried and failed to qualify for the Sony Open in Hawaii, Sorenstam attended a Callaway Golf media luncheon in late January at Arnold Palmer's Bay Hill Club in Orlando, Florida, during the annual PGA Merchandise Show. One of the reporters, Jeff Shain of the *Miami Herald*, asked Sorenstam what she thought of Wie's attempt to play with the men, and club professional Suzy Whaley's upcoming start in the Greater Hartford Open, a spot Whaley earned by winning a PGA sectional championship in Connecticut. Sorenstam said she thought it was great. Shain then asked, "Would you ever consider doing that?"

She answered with 15 words that launched the biggest sports frenzy of the year. "If I got an invite, I would say yes in a heartbeat," Sorenstam said.

On the short ride back to her home at Lake Nona Golf Club, Sorenstam and her manager, Mark Steinberg of IMG, talked about the implications of those 15 words. "I told her it's not going to be a question of whether or not you can get in; it's going to be a question of which one you're going to choose," Steinberg said. "Requests and exemption letters came in immediately."

The Colonial, a PGA Tour event that had once been close to the major championships in stature, with a history forged from the hardscrabble work ethic of Ben Hogan, was one of the tournaments that offered Sorenstam an exemption. The event had lost a bit of luster over the years, falling between the Masters and Jack Nicklaus' Memorial Tournament. Tiger Woods left it off his schedule; Ernie Els chose to pass up Colonial to play in London; Davis Love took the week off to go to his daughter's horse show, and Masters champion Mike Weir spent the week in Canada. Vijay Singh committed to play the Colonial, but withdrew after winning the week before in Dallas. Sadly, this was no longer the tournament that Hogan built. As famed Fort Worth journalist and author Dan Jenkins put it, "The Colonial tournament had drifted deeper down in the mindset of people in the last few years, and this was something that would bring it back."

The good folks of Fort Worth got more than they bargained for when Sorenstam accepted their invitation.

The first signs that this was something special were the media requests. Within two weeks of announcing that Sorenstam would play, tournament officials were flooded with three times the normal requests for credentials. By the first of March, they decided to double the size of the media center. By the Masters, it was obvious an even bigger tent and additional parking would be needed. Probably not since Colonial hosted the U.S. Open in 1941 had there been this much interest in the club or the tournament.

Callaway Golf, Sorenstam's longtime club sponsor, developed an advertising campaign around "playing with the boys," and every Title IX and women's rights advocate in the country hopped on the Annika bandwagon. By the time she arrived for a Monday practice round, Sorenstam had become "Annika," a one-name international star, the best female golfer in the world becoming the first woman to compete in a men's golf event in 58 years, since Babe Didrikson Zaharias in Los Angeles in 1945, and a hero to little girls everywhere.

"Truthfully, none of us knew what to expect," said her husband, David Esch. "Not even Annika." What they didn't expect were the thousands of people who showed up to support her. "Go Annika" buttons sold out before the first shot of the tournament was struck.

Aaron Barber and Dean Wilson, the professionals who drew Sorenstam as a group to play together in the first two rounds, bought two of the buttons. "I think it will be great to play alongside her and watch how someone like her handles herself in this situation, in this tournament, that is so unique," Wilson said. As it turned out, Sorenstam could not have asked for two better companions. "Those guys were supportive and made me feel really welcome," she said. "I don't know what would have happened if I hadn't played with them, but they sure made this week more special."

By her tee time on Thursday, the frenzy had hit a fever pitch. Parking lots that had never filled at Colonial were teeming before noon. The gallery stood 10 to 12 deep down the fairway awaiting her arrival. As Barber said, "I was walking next to her as we walked down to the 10th tee, which was our first hole, and the crowd started going crazy. I guess it would be like playing in front of a sold-out Super Bowl or something. It was an electric atmosphere that I've never come close to experiencing in golf before."

"We met on the putting green five to 10 minutes before our tee time," Wilson said. "It was just crazy. I didn't expect that many people. I walked up to her and I said, 'Are you ready for this?' And in her neat, shy little voice she said, 'I don't know.' She looked so terrified. I thought, 'This is cool.' She wasn't too proud to show that she was nervous, and that it was a bit overwhelming."

When she hit her first drive down the middle of the 10th fairway, the crowd erupted in cheers, and Sorenstam gave a huge smile and a playful wobble as she walked off the tee. It was the first of many coming-out moments for her.

The criticism of Sorenstam, and to some extent the LPGA Tour she dominated, was that she, and it, lacked charisma. The best female golfer in the world went a long way toward dispelling those notions with her performance at Colonial. When she made her first birdie at the 13th, her fourth hole, her fist-pump reaction harkened everyone back to the late 1970s when Nancy Lopez's disarming personality and infectious smile lured legions to the ladies' game.

"My opinion changed, because I think she handled herself very well," said Angela Stanford, a Fort Worth native and LPGA player who finished second in the playoff in the 2003 U.S. Women's Open and who was critical of Sorenstam's decision to play with the men. "She always was pretty standoffish toward me, and made me feel kind of nervous. But she was so friendly to everybody there, and she interacted with the crowd. A lot of people said she should act on the LPGA Tour the way she did at Colonial, and I second that. I think she's done a better job on our tour after that."

In the end, charm and crowd support gave way to shaky putting. Despite finishing the week tied for third in driving accuracy and tied for 53rd (better than middle of the pack) in greens hit in regulation, Sorenstam finished last in putting. That statistic produced rounds of 71 and 74, four more strokes than it took to play over the weekend.

Afterward, Sorenstam said all the right things. "I've learned a lot and experienced a lot. It's been wonderful," she said. "I'm glad I did it, but this is way over my head. I wasn't as tough as I thought I was. I've got to go back to my tour where I belong."

ANNIKA SORENSTAM

EVENT	POSITION
Safeway Ping	T-3
Kraft Nabisco Championship	2
The Office Depot	1
Takefuji Classic	T-2
Michelob Light Open	6
Nichirei Cup World Ladies	1
Bank of America Colonial	MC
Kellogg-Keebler Classic	1
McDonald's LPGA Championship	1
Giant Eagle Classic	T-2
ShopRite Classic	T-14
U.S. Women's Open	4
Evian Masters	T-17
Weetabix Women's British Open	1
HP Open	3
John Q. Hammons Hotel Classic	T-10
Safeway Classic	1
Samsung World Championship	4
Mizuno Classic	1
ADT Championship	2

Sorenstam's one-week foray to the PGA Tour had the desired effect: She drew attention to her outstanding abilities and, as a result, attracted new fans to the LPGA Tour, where she once again dominated. She won six times on the LPGA and seven times around the world. Two of the wins were majors — the McDonald's LPGA Championship and the Weetabix Women's British Open. Those wins moved her over another milestone, as she became only the sixth woman in history to compete the career Grand Slam. It could have been better than that. Two ill-timed swings, one with a pitching wedge at the Kraft Nabisco Championship (where she finished second) and the second with a four wood at the final hole of the U.S. Women's Open (where she finished fourth), were all that kept Sorenstam from winning all four of the women's major championships in the same year. "I realized that the Grand Slam is possible," she said later. "It was pretty close."

While 2003 didn't quite match Sorenstam's 13-victory season in 2002, she got off to a fantastic start, finishing second in the Kraft Nabisco and winning by four strokes the following week at The Office Depot. As a sign of Sorenstam's dominance, she won even though she wasn't hitting the ball well. "What wears on me more than anything is I'm not playing my best," she said after the victory over Se Ri Pak, Pat Hurst and Heather Bowie in Tarzana, California. "I hit a lot of good shots, then I hit something out of the blue. That's not a very comfortable feeling."

In the seven weeks after making that statement, Sorenstam tied for second in the LPGA Takefuji Classic in Las Vegas, was sixth in the Michelob Light Open at Kingsmill, first at the Nichirei Cup World Ladies in Japan, missed the cut at the Bank of America Colonial, won again at the Kellogg-Keebler Classic in Illinois, and beat Grace Park in a playoff in the season's second major event, the McDonald's LPGA Championship. She had four victories and made history by the second week of June. It appeared to be another record-setting year.

Her biggest disappointment of the year was her failure to capitalize on an opportunity at the U.S. Women's Open. Sorenstam was the favorite through 71 holes when she needed only a par on the reachable par-five 18th to ensure a playoff berth with Stanford, Kelly Robbins and Hilary Lunke. A birdie would guarantee Sorenstam her third U.S. Women's Open title. Standing the middle of the fairway, she had only 236 yards to the flag, perfect four-wood distance.

When she came out of the shot, sending the ball into the right trees, there was a collective gasp from the gallery. The ball landed beyond the trees and the scorer's tent, and next to the portable toilets, which set up the most dramatic situation of the week as Sorenstam pleaded her case for a favorable drop. She didn't get it, and was left with a 40-yard shot under trees and over a bunker. "There was hardly any grass. It was dirt," she said. "I didn't expect the ball to shoot so high, and it hit the branch and then went into the bunker." From there, she hit a poor bunker shot to 15 feet and missed her par putt and the playoff.

"It's going to take a while to get over this," Sorenstam said. "But at the end of the day it's just a golf tournament. Right now, I just want to forget this week. I'll charge my batteries and be ready when I need to. But right now, I feel like being grumpy."

Her mood brightened considerably one month later when she won the Weetabix Women's British Open to complete the career Grand Slam. It was her 46th career title and second major victory of the year. "It's not just this year. Since last year, I've played in eight majors and had a chance to win seven of them," she said. "It's been that close. We're talking one or two or three shots."

Her LPGA career victories Nos. 47 and 48 came in the autumn when she held off Beth Daniel by a stroke at the Safeway Classic and lapped the field with a nine-stroke victory at the Mizuno Classic for her second win of the year in Japan. In the season-ending ADT Championship, she shot 71 to lose by one stroke to Meg Mallon. It was hard for Sorenstam to be upset. "I'm going to let go of this in a heartbeat," she said of her loss to Mallon. "This year has been too great to look back and say that this was a big disappointment. I'm very happy with my year. It's been fabulous in so many ways. Not a lot of things are going to make me unhappy right now."

Sorenstam led the LPGA money list for the sixth time and had worldwide earnings of $2,159,050, more than $500,000 ahead of runner-up Se Ri Pak. She won Player of the Year honors again in a contest that wasn't close. The only reason she didn't win the Vare Trophy for lowest stroke average was that she didn't play enough rounds to qualify. Her career titles put her in the World Golf Hall of Fame in October, one month after she was the emotional leader of the victorious European team in the Solheim Cup at home in Sweden and one month before holing a 39-yard wedge shot from a bunker for eagle at the ninth hole of the Skins Game, a shot that gave her the overnight lead and allowed her to finish second to Fred Couples with five skins and $225,000. "I've played with a lot of fine players," defending Skins Game champion Mark O'Meara said after being shut out this year. "I would have to put Annika at the top of the list."

As the year drew to a close, no one could question that Sorenstam was golf's biggest newsmaker. The long-term impact of her Colonial appearance was still open for debate. Not long after Sorenstam's appearance, Jan Stephenson accepted a sponsor's invitation to play in a Champions Tour event, where she tied for last. Michelle Wie, the 13-year-old sensation, accepted invitations to play in events on the Canadian Tour and the Nationwide Tour. She missed the cuts by a mile in both. Whaley missed the cut at Hartford, and the same was true of Laura Davies in Korea and Sophie Gustafson in Japan. Only Se Ri Pak made the cut, in a Korean event.

The first eye-raising issue on the LPGA Tour in 2003 arose, not at a golf tournament, but at the Super Bowl, when Gustafson, Sweden's second-best player behind Sorenstam, made her first public appearance with her new boyfriend, Ty Votaw, the Tour's commissioner. Votaw refused to discuss his personal life, but the LPGA's Board of Directors discussed it during their annual meeting in January.

"We had a meeting and the matter was discussed openly and honestly," said board chairwoman Marguerite Sallee. "There is 100 percent support for Ty. It is one of those matters that is certainly gray. It would be different if he were seeing one of his reports at the office of the LPGA. What matters is how it is handled, and I think Ty has behaved with grace and dignity."

The public could instead focus on the golf being played by Sorenstam and the others. Se Ri Pak won three times (second only to Sorenstam on the LPGA Tour) and staked a claim to first-in-line for the throne in women's golf if Sorenstam should retire for motherhood, which the 33-year-old Swede hinted might come sooner rather than later.

Pak's first victory came at the Safeway Ping, the event where Sorenstam shot her historic 59 in 2001. The Korean star shot 64 in the final round to beat Grace Park by two and a group including Sorenstam by four, saying at the time, "I thought I had to shoot a low score, like eight under, to have a chance, because I knew Annika would go low again." Sorenstam did not go low, but Pak's comments proved a point: No matter who was leading or how well the field was playing, there was always one player on everyone's mind.

Shortly after her victory in Phoenix, Pak was asked if she was ready to play with the boys at Colonial. She laughed and said, "No, I'm not good enough. Not yet."

Pak finished second to Sorenstam at The Office Depot before winning her second title of the year at the Chick-fil-A Charity Championship. The next week she tied for eighth in the Michelob Light Open at Kingsmill before hitting a month-long lull where she didn't post a top-10 finish. She came back with a strong fourth-place tie at the Wegmans Rochester event in late June, but failed to follow it up with a good showing in the event she won as 20-year-old, the U.S. Women's Open. Her next top-five finish was in Canada at the BMO Financial Group Canadian Women's Open when she finished in fifth, six shots behind Beth Daniel.

Then came the event that proved to be symbolic of the pecking order in women's golf, the Weetabix Women's British Open. Pak and Sorenstam were tied after 71 holes and seemed destined for a playoff until Pak hit her tee shot into one of the many crater-deep bunkers that dot the landscape at Royal Lytham and St. Annes. Sorenstam won with a par.

There were plenty of bright spots for Pak, however, including a 10th-place finish in a Korean men's event, the best finish of any of the crossover artists. She finished second to Sorenstam on the LPGA money list (and second worldwide with $1,611,928) and second in stroke average, although Pak won the Vare Trophy because of the number of rounds she played. She won again at the event she seems to own, the Jamie Farr Kroger Classic. "I guess I'm just relaxed on this course," Pak said after winning for the fourth time. "You have to play smart, and I know what to do. I have a lot of confidence."

She also had age on her side. As Pak put it, "I'm only 26. I've got a long way to go."

There were plenty of young challengers who could make that same claim, including Grace Park, who only won once, but who contended deep into many weekends through the year. Park finished third in worldwide money with $1,417,702 and set some lofty goals for her future. "I want to be the best," she said. "That's a big goal, but I think I can get there."

Hee-Won Han won back-to-back at the Sybase Big Apple Classic and the Wendy's Championship for Children and finished fifth in worldwide money, which meant that three of the top five earners in women's golf hailed from Korea, a trend that didn't sit well with some. Jan Stephenson was one who didn't like what she was seeing from the influx of Korean players. In a November interview in which she admitted that her comments would probably get her in trouble, Stephenson told *Golf Magazine* that "the Asians are killing our tour." She went on to accuse Korean players of being rude, selfish and failing to speak English to their pro-am partners, even though "most of them can speak" the language. The comments stirred a controversy on the LPGA, and Stephenson backtracked after the quotes became public.

Stephenson's comments weren't the only criticisms the Korean players received in 2003. After several complaints about possible rules violations — including Korean fathers giving advice to daughters during their rounds and possibly improving lies in the rough — Votaw called a meeting with his Southeast Asian contingent and explained their responsibilities as players and ambassadors of the women's game. Some were miffed, including Pak, who said, "It's unfair to make this about Korean players. If some players are doing wrong things, they should be singled out, not put in a group with others who have done nothing wrong."

Votaw also had a chat with Danielle Ammaccapane after she gave a tongue-lashing to Michelle Wie for some perceived etiquette violations during their first two rounds together at the U.S. Women's Open. It was easier to forgive a 13-year-old for stepping in someone's line than it was to give a pass to a 38-year-old who behaved so badly the USGA said it "could refuse her application next year."

The Ammaccapane-Wie showdown drove home another point Votaw had tried to make. All year he talked about the "five points of celebrity" and how accessibility and congeniality were just as crucial to the LPGA Tour's continued success as making birdies. Fortunately, a few of the tour's winners were naturally gifted in that area. Among them was the year's first major championship winner, Patricia Meunier-Lebouc, a delightful Frenchwoman whose bubbly personality and self-effacing charm won over fans who couldn't pronounce her name before she won the Kraft Nabisco Championship in a down-to-the-wire duel with Sorenstam.

Meunier-Lebouc led by three strokes at the beginning of the final round, lost the lead to Sorenstam at the 12th, and regained it with a birdie at the 13th. When the Swede failed to birdie the final hole, Meunier-Lebouc two-putted for a one-stroke victory. She then said, "Golf is what I do; it is not who I am," a refreshing statement from an athlete of any gender or nationality. Then she said of her win, "It's wonderful. I really was feeling that maybe it's my day. I deserve it."

Another major winner who deserved all the praise was Hilary Lunke, a smiling blonde from Medina, Minnesota, who became a hero to the short-hitting housewives in the world when she held off Sorenstam in regulation play and beat Kelly Robbins and Angela Stanford (another player who had the "five points of celebrity" down pat) in a playoff at the U.S. Women's Open. Lunke won it on the strength of her short game, one-putting more greens than anyone by a big margin, and making a tough 15-footer on the final hole of an 18-hole playoff to beat Stanford by a single shot.

"I didn't have 100 percent of my ball-striking," Lunke said after wearing out five, seven and nine woods all week, "but I had 155 percent of my putting." Later, she won the hearts of everyone when she said, "We just bought a house last week; so this is good timing. Now we can pay for it." In a year of major upsets, Lunke's win could have been the biggest.

While she didn't win a major, Sophie Gustafson had a surprisingly good year considering the whirlwind of publicity surrounding her relationship with the commissioner. Gustafson won three times on the Evian Ladies European Tour, including victories in the Irish Open and back-to-back in the HP Open and the BT Ladies Open. Her fourth win of the year (and only victory in the United States) came in October at the Samsung World Championship in Houston when Gustafson shot a final-round 64 to leap past Sorenstam and Rachel Teske.

That U.S. victory wasn't without controversy. Standing over a 30-foot putt on the 14th green at the TPC at The Woodlands, Gustafson appeared to take her stance and sole her putter, which is the technical definition of "addressing the ball." When the ball began rolling down an embankment and came to rest eight feet away, many assumed Gustafson should have been assessed a one-stroke penalty. When an official was called to the green, Gustafson claimed she had not grounded her putter. "The ball had stopped on the top of the slope," she said. "I knew that it could move, and so I never grounded my club. Then it started not to actually move, but to wobble. Probably three to five seconds later, it started to roll down the slope."

Some, including television commentators, disagreed, but as Juli Inkster, who was playing in the group with Gustafson, put it, "If Sophie said she didn't ground her club, then she didn't ground her club. I wasn't really looking at it, but you have to give her the benefit of the doubt. She's a straight arrow."

Gustafson was third in the world in total victories with her four, three wins behind Sorenstam and six behind the winningest player in professional golf in 2003 — Yuri Fudoh of Japan.

Those unfamiliar with the Japan LPGA Tour probably never heard of Fudoh, and even those who followed golf closely in 2003 probably would have guessed Ernie Els or Annika Sorenstam led the world in victories. But Fudoh won 10 times. Her best finish in the United States (in one of her infrequent appearances) was a tie for 20th in the U.S. Women's Open.

ERNIE ELS

EVENT	POSITION
Mercedes Championships	1
Sony Open in Hawaii	1
Caltex Masters	2
Heineken Classic	1
Johnnie Walker Classic	1
WGC Accenture Match Play	T-33
Dubai Desert Classic	2
Bay Hill Invitational	T-38
Masters Tournament	T-6
MCI Heritage	T-10
Shell Houston Open	T-17
Volvo PGA Championship	4
Memorial Tournament	T-13
U.S. Open Championship	T-5
Buick Classic	T-11
Barclays Scottish Open	1
The Open Championship	T-18
The International	T-6
PGA Championship	T-5
WGC NEC Invitational	T-17
BMW International Open	T-17
Omega European Masters	1
Dunhill Links Championship	2
WGC American Express Championship	T-12
HSBC World Match Play	1
Chrysler Championship	T-34
Tour Championship	17
Nedbank Golf Challenge	17
Ernie Els Invitational	1

Men also played golf in 2003, and many of them did quite well. Ernie Els was one. He captured four titles on three continents in the first two months of the year (including back-to-back PGA Tour events in Hawaii), and looked to be on his way to a career year. At Kapalua, playing in the Mercedes Championships against the winners from 2002, Els shot 31 under par and won by eight strokes. He then won on Oahu at the Sony Open with a 47-footer for birdie in a playoff with Aaron Baddeley to become the first since Steve Jones in 1989 to win the first two events of the U.S. season.

A week later, Els kept the streak alive with a victory at the Heineken Classic in Australia, and he came within one fatigued tee shot of making it four in a row. At the Caltex Masters in Singapore, Els led China's Zhang Lian-wei by one stroke on the final hole. A pushed tee shot forced Els to chip out and hope to make par off a wedge, which he hit to five feet. Meanwhile Zhang almost holed his nine-iron approach and made birdie. When Els missed the five-footer, Zhang, a former caddie from Guang-Zhou, became the first Chinese golfer to win a PGA European Tour co-sponsored event.

Els made up for that a week later back in Australia when he won the Johnnie Walker Classic by 10 strokes — his fourth win in five starts. Then Els pulled one of the oddest stunts in recent memory. A couple of days before Arnold Palmer's Bay Hill Invitational, Els was playing around in the garage of his Orlando home when he took several swings at a heavy punching bag. The resulting wrist injury kept Els out of The Players Championship and nagged him the remainder of the year.

Still, Els won four more times, including the Barclays Scottish Open at Loch Lomond the week before heading to southern England to defend his title at the Open Championship. "I have a lot more faith in my ability these days," Els said after the Scottish victory. "When I've played close to my best, I've won pretty convincingly."

He was not near his best in his defense at Royal St. George's, and tied for 18th, the only major championship in which he was not a contender. He tied for sixth at the Masters and tied for fifth at the U.S. Open and the PGA Championship.

Els won convincingly in Switzerland when he rallied from two strokes behind to take the Omega European Masters by six over Michael Campbell. And he did well at the HSBC World Match Play at Wentworth (where he also owns a home), when he won his fifth World Match Play title to equal the victory record held by Gary Player.

Els captured the European Order of Merit title and led all male golfers in worldwide wins. He capped off the year with a win at his own tournament, the Ernie Els Invitational, in George, South Africa. It was Els' second week of good play in George, the first coming in September when the big man battled Tiger Woods to a draw in the Presidents Cup and elevated his hero status among the home crowd.

In America Els finished ninth on the money list, but was fourth in scoring average, three-tenths of a shot behind the leader, Woods. A good illustration of the kind of year Els had was the records he set. His 31-under-par score at the Mercedes Championships set a PGA Tour scoring record in relation to par. Three weeks later he shot 29 under par at the Johnnie Walker Classic and set the all-time scoring record in relation to par on the PGA European Tour.

His $7,604,342 in worldwide earnings was second only to Vijay Singh, and while he finished the year with eight new trophies, Els left the world wondering just how good he could have been in 2003 if that punching bag hadn't hit back.

TIGER WOODS

EVENT	POSITION
Buick Invitational	1
Nissan Open	T-5
WGC Accenture Match Play	1
Bay Hill Invitational	1
The Players Championship	T-11
Masters Tournament	T-15
Deutsche Bank - SAP Open	T-29
Memorial Tournament	T-4
U.S. Open Championship	T-20
Buick Classic	T-13
100th Western Open	1
The Open Championship	T-4
Buick Open	T-2
PGA Championship	T-39
WGC NEC Invitational	T-4
Deutsche Bank Championship	T-7
WGC American Express Championship	1
FUNAI Classic at Walt Disney World Resort	T-2
Tour Championship	26
Target World Challenge	2

Another player who battled injury successfully in 2003 was Tiger Woods, who struggled to recover from off-season knee surgery and won five titles, his fifth consecutive Player of the Year crown and his fifth straight Vardon Trophy for the lowest scoring average. Woods missed the first five weeks, but when he did return at the Buick Invitational, he did so in a big way, winning by four strokes even though he struggled to find the fairways at Torrey Pines. Aaron Oberholster, who led briefly, summed up what many were thinking when he said, "When Tiger Woods is shooting 66 and can't find earth with his driver, if he does find earth with driver or three wood, he's going to awfully hard to beat. Nine fairways in two days and he's eight under par! Okay, he's good. News flash. The guy's a beast. He's still in another league from Ernie."

Phil Mickelson started a controversy with his comments in the March issue (out in February) of *Golf Magazine*: "In my mind, Tiger and I don't have any issues between us. Well, maybe one. He hates that I can fly it past him now. He has a faster swing speed than I do, but he has inferior equipment. Tiger is the only player who is good enough to overcome the equipment he's stuck with."

Mickelson endorsed Titleist and Woods was affiliated with rival Nike, so there was a commercial edge to Mickelson's words. Many wondered why Mickelson would step over the line, break an unwritten rule, and criticize another player's equipment. Was it because Mickelson was in love with the new technology, and Woods was not? Woods hardly reacted to the back-handed compliment, leaving it to Nike to respond indirectly in its advertising.

After Woods started with the victory, Mickelson had nothing but praise. "He's just an impressive player," Mickelson said. "It isn't easy to step in and out of competition, and yet he never gives anything back. I know I like to play a couple of tournaments and work my way into a competitive mindset. He's able to walk in and out of it at will."

Two weeks later Woods won his second event of the year, the WGC Accenture Match Play, becoming the first to win all of the World Golf Championships events. David Toms, who lost in the final, was impressed and dejected at the same time. "I didn't give up, but you have to play great to beat Tiger, even when he isn't," Toms said. "When he plays well, he wins. It's that simple. We all know it. I'm just glad he doesn't play 25 tournaments a year."

Woods became only the fourth ever to win the same event four consecutive times when he won the Bay Hill Invitational by a record 11 shots despite suffering from a severe stomach virus. "If I wasn't in contention, I wouldn't have gone. There's no way," Woods said, after being up all night before the final round. "It was a joke. Every single tee shot hurt, because my abs were obviously sore from last night, and I continued on while I was playing. The night was long, and the day was probably even longer. That being said, I'm happy with the way I played." The victory added to the legend as Woods joined Young Tom Morris, Walter Hagen and Gene Sarazen as the only players to win the same event four years running.

He won again in Chicago at the Western Open, and won for a fifth time at the WGC American Express Championship in Atlanta. Woods finished third in the world in earnings with $7,400,288 and broke one of the most impressive records in the history of the game at the Tour Championship in Houston, when he made the 36-hole cut and finished in the money for the 114th consecutive event, breaking the mark of 113 set by Byron Nelson in the 1940s. "It's a great record, a greater record than a lot of people realize," Jim Furyk said. "He's playing against very deep fields filled with talent, and it only takes one bad round to push you over the cut line."

Woods admitted that the streak involved a little luck, such as the 2003 Masters where he had to save par from a greenside bunker at the ninth hole to play the weekend, but he was quick to add, "You've got to work your butt off, too." To those who might argue that the streak was tainted because it involved some tournaments that had no cut, Davis Love offered the best observation. "Go back and look and he wouldn't have missed the cut if there had been one," Love said. "And the World Golf Championships events, all he does is win those. You probably can't count those against him."

While he didn't win any majors in 2003, Woods contended into Sunday at the Masters and was a couple of funky bounces at Royal St. George's away from hoisting the claret jug at the Open Championship for a second time. Late in the autumn he battled Ernie Els into the darkness of night at the Presidents Cup, and a few days later got engaged to Elin Nordegren. Not a bad year.

VIJAY SINGH

EVENT	POSITION
Mercedes Championships	T-4
Sony Open in Hawaii	T-20
Phoenix Open	1
AT&T Pebble Beach National Pro-Am	T-28
Bay Hill Invitational	T-20
The Players Championship	MC
Masters Tournament	T-6
Shell Houston Open	T-9
HP Classic of New Orleans	T-11
Wachovia Championship	T-2
EDS Byron Nelson Championship	1
Memorial Tournament	T-4
U.S. Open Championship	T-20
Buick Classic	T-18
100th Western Open	11
The Open Championship	T-2
Buick Open	T-8
The International	T-2
PGA Championship	T-34
WGC NEC Invitational	T-6
Deutsche Bank Championship	4
Bell Canadian Open	T-6
John Deere Classic	1
Dunhill Links Championship	T-16
WGC American Express Championship	T-2
HSBC World Match Play	T-3
FUNAI Classic at Walt Disney World Resort	1
Chrysler Championship	2
Tour Championship	T-5
Nedbank Golf Challenge	3
Office Depot Father-Son Challenge	T-4
Target World Challenge	7

The only professional golfer who made more money than Els or Woods was Vijay Singh, who had the best and worst year of his career. Singh won four PGA Tour events, contended in every major championship (although he didn't win one) and earned $8,499,611 around the world. In so doing, Singh dislodged Woods from a spot he had occupied for five consecutive years. Woods held the record for most years in a row atop the World Money List, holding the spot from 1998 through 2002. Tom Watson was the only other player to lead the world in earnings for more than three consecutive years. Watson led from 1977 through 1980, and while Jack Nicklaus took the title a total of seven times, he never led the World Money List more than three years in a row.

He won the third event of the PGA Tour season — the Phoenix Open — and threw down the gauntlet to the youngsters on tour. "A person's age is only a number," said Singh, age 40, after his first win. "I see all these young players coming out and playing so well. But they don't have the experience. I see guys my age or older, and I know nobody wants it more than me. I really don't believe they have seen my best stuff yet. I expect to compete until I'm 50. Sam Snead won out here when he was 52. I get mad when I don't win, because I feel I'm as good as anybody."

He proved that point with his second victory at the EDS Byron Nelson Championship in May, followed by two more late-season wins at the John Deere Classic and the FUNAI Classic at Walt Disney World Resort. In addition, Singh finished second five times and contended until late in the week at both the Masters and Open Championship. His 18 top-10 finishes in 27 starts led the world. Only Woods, who had 12 top-10s in 18 starts, matched Singh's top-10 percentage.

Singh did all this on the strength of his new strength. After turning 40, Singh built a large gym on one side of his home in Ponte Vedra Beach, Florida, and he rededicated himself to working out longer and harder, which was saying a lot for a guy who wrote the book on long practice hours. "I'm making up for lost time," Singh told *Golf World* at the end of the year. "I'm 40, but I'm not 40. I didn't always have the benefit of the best coaching. I didn't know what I was doing, really didn't know my swing until I was 27 or 28, maybe even 30."

Equally impressive was how well Singh played given the public relations nightmare when he was quoted as saying he hoped Annika Sorenstam would miss the cut at Colonial. Mix all the off-course drama with the fact that Singh finished second to Woods in scoring average, victories and all-around statistics, and it probably should not have come as a surprise when Singh finished second to Woods in the Player of the Year voting by both the players and the Golf Writers Association of America. Woods also won on the PGA of America points system. "I'd be lying if I told you I wasn't disappointed about that, but that was out of my control," Singh told *Golf World*. "It was still my most gratifying year."

DAVIS LOVE

EVENT	POSITION
Bob Hope Chrysler Classic	T-12
AT&T Pebble Beach National Pro-Am	1
Nissan Open	T-49
WGC Accenture Match Play	T-17
Ford Championship at Doral	T-12
Honda Classic	T-2
The Players Championship	1
Masters Tournament	T-15
MCI Heritage	1
HP Classic of New Orleans	T-16
Wachovia Championship	T-29
FBR Capital Open	T-7
U.S. Open Championship	MC
The Open Championship	T-4
CVS Charity Classic	T-5
The International	1

PGA Championship	MC
WGC NEC Invitational	3
John Deere Classic	T-27
WGC American Express Championship	T-40
Chrysler Classic of Greensboro	MC
FUNAI Classic at Walt Disney World Resort	T-5
Chrysler Championship	T-6
Tour Championship	T-5
Target World Challenge	1

From a playing standpoint, Davis Love could have said the same thing. After a career lull that produced only two wins in five years and many questions about his desire, passion and drive for the game, Love rededicated himself to a stringent work routine in 2003, and won four times on the PGA Tour and five times overall. The first victory of the year came in his second start when he captured the AT&T Pebble Beach National Pro-Am, ending a 44-tournament winless drought in the only tournament he had won between 1998 and 2003. Love won the Pebble Beach event in 2001, breaking up what would have otherwise been a 100-tournament winless run. "If you come here thinking it's going to be wet, it's going to be windy and cold, you've got to play with amateurs, it's going to take six hours, you've already lost," Love said. "It definitely is a week for a good attitude, and that fits for me."

He played well at the Honda Classic, but lost to his pal Justin Leonard. What no one saw coming was the 64 Love fired in the final round of The Players Championship to win his second title of the year and vault onto everyone's top tier of players to watch in 2003. Only four other players — Jack Nicklaus, Hal Sutton, Fred Couples and Steve Elkington — had won The Players Championship more than once, and only one of those, Couples, did it with a final-round 64. It seemed fitting that Couples would witness Love's final round in 2003.

"Davis can rip up a golf course," Couples said. "And right now, he's driving it 300 yards dead straight, and he's putting well. That was the easiest 64 you'll ever see. It was the best round of golf I've ever seen played."

A few weeks later, Love won again at the MCI Heritage. He finished third on the PGA Tour money list, fourth in worldwide earnings with $7,333,146, and seventh in scoring average, which made 2003 one of his best years on the golf course. It was also one of his worst off the course.

In the early summer, Love was driving his truck down by a fishing cabin near his home on St. Simons Island, Georgia, in search of his wife's brother-in-law, Jeff Knight, who also worked for Love in the family business. As he got to the cabin, Love saw Knight's truck and sensed that something was terribly wrong. Inside the cabin, he found that Knight had taken his life. Knight was the subject of an FBI investigation for having embezzled funds from Love's accounts. That had put a strain on the family, but in the tragic outcome Love's worst fear was realized.

Love went winless for three months in the summer. Then he lapped the field in The International, winning by such a large margin he could have picked up and walked in after 16 holes on Sunday and still won in the modified-Stableford format. Afterward, Love choked up as he dedicated the victory to his wife.

Love capped off his year by holding off tournament host Tiger Woods to win his second Target World Challenge.

MIKE WEIR

EVENT	POSITION
Phoenix Open	T-9
Bob Hope Chrysler Classic	1
AT&T Pebble Beach National Pro-Am	T-3
Nissan Open	1
WGC Accenture Match Play	T-17
Ford Championship at Doral	T-14
The Players Championship	T-27
BellSouth Classic	MC
Masters Tournament	1
Wachovia Championship	T-18
Memorial Tournament	3
U.S. Open Championship	T-3
100th Western Open	T-3
The Open Championship	T-28
The International	T-54
PGA Championship	T-7
WGC NEC Invitational	T-23
Bell Canadian Open	10
WGC American Express Championship	T-28
HSBC World Match Play	T-5
Chrysler Championship	T-13
Tour Championship	T-19
PGA Grand Slam	2
Target World Challenge	T-4

Not everything in 2003 involved tragedy or controversy. For the first time in over 30 years, four first-timers won the major championships. At the time, Mike Weir's win in the Masters Tournament seemed surprising. He was a short hitter on a long, wet golf course geared toward big bombers. Forget that Weir was one of the most accurate iron players in the game. The Bob Hope Chrysler Classic and the Nissan Open (two events Weir won before arriving in Augusta) weren't quite the Masters, and Weir's game wasn't ready for the rigors of the expanded 7,200-yard Augusta National golf course.

All that changed by Sunday. When Weir made an uphill six-footer for par at the final hole to force the first Masters playoff in 13 years, he moved from "good player" status onto the "great champion" stage. His three-putt bogey to beat Len Mattiace in the playoff seemed anticlimactic.

Not only did that confirm Weir as the best Canadian golfer ever, he leapt past a struggling Phil Mickelson to become the best left-handed player in the game. Weir didn't win again after the Masters, but he had the best major championship record of any player in the world. He finished third in the U.S. Open and tied for seventh in the PGA Championship. He also finished fifth on the PGA Tour money list, sixth in the world in earnings with over $5.6 million, and he had the third lowest stroke average on the PGA Tour.

To call 2003 a breakout year for Weir wouldn't do it justice. He won the Bob Hope Chrysler Classic by playing smart and conservative and holding off 49-year-old Jay Haas (who also had his best year in over a decade), and he won at Riviera through pure Hogan-like shotmaking. By winning at Augusta, Weir became the most popular figure in Canada, replacing The Great One, Wayne Gretzky, as the standard-bearer athlete for the nation. "It's pretty nice," Weir said. "A lot more than I expected."

Weir wasn't the only winner in Augusta. Hootie Johnson, the embattled chairman of Augusta National Golf Club, stood his ground and insisted that his private club would remain private and all male as long as the members saw fit. In January that position seemed untenable, and many (notably the editors of *The New York Times* and Martha Burk, the chairwoman of the National Council of Women's Organizations) viewed Johnson as a boor. Who would have believed that Johnson would come out a winner, and Howell Raines, the *Times* editor-in-chief, would be forced to resign over this and other scandals? And who would have thought that Burk, who had blustered and bullied her way onto every television network in the country while playing the Augusta issue for all it was worth, couldn't muster enough protesters to fill up the Washington Road Hooters?

To call the protest "small" would be kind. No more than 40 bused-in antagonists with signs and tee shirts slogged their way through a field. They were protected by 120 police and sheriff's deputies (three for every protester) and witnessed by upwards of 100 journalists, who struggled to find those cogent enough to be interviewed. There was a one-man Klan rally and an Elvis impersonator to put the episode into perspective.

Martha Burk left quietly, and golf fans probably forgot about the membership of Augusta National as soon as they realized that watching a tournament on television without commercial interruptions was pretty neat.

JIM FURYK

EVENT	POSITION
Mercedes Championships	T-6
Sony Open in Hawaii	T-33
AT&T Pebble Beach National Pro-Am	T-5
Nissan Open	T-32
WGC Accenture Match Play	T-9
Ford Championship at Doral	2
Honda Classic	T-5
The Players Championship	T-4
Masters Tournament	4
MCI Heritage	T-10
Wachovia Championship	MC
EDS Byron Nelson Championship	5
Bank of America Colonial	T-5
Memorial Tournament	T-24
U.S. Open Championship	1
Buick Classic	T-22
100th Western Open	T-3
The Open Championship	MC

Buick Open	1
PGA Championship	T-18
WGC NEC Invitational	T-6
Deutsche Bank Championship	T-13
WGC American Express Championship	T-12
Las Vegas Invitational	13
Chrysler Classic of Greensboro	T-46
FUNAI Classic at Walt Disney World Resort	T-12
Tour Championship	8
WGC World Cup	T-5
PGA Grand Slam	1

There were plenty of commercials in the U.S. Open telecasts, along with a number of corporate tents and official licensees. There wasn't a lot of drama. Jim Furyk won his first major title the way he lived his life: quietly, methodically, and without a lot of flair. As Tiger Woods said, "Jim grinds you into the ground. That's his style, and it works pretty well for him."

It worked pretty well at Olympia Fields, a golf course on a train line 45 minutes outside of Chicago, that hadn't hosted the U.S. Open since 1928. Furyk set 36- and 54-hole scoring records for the Open, and held a three-stroke lead after three rounds in the 60s. The only chance of drama was if Furyk had a meltdown on Sunday, which was about as likely as a meteor hitting nearby Gary, Indiana. "He's not going to give it back," Woods said. And he didn't. With two birdies and four bogeys (the last coming on the final hole when Furyk three-putted with tears in his eyes), the man with the quirkiest swing in golf matched 72s with Australian Stephen Leaney and won by three.

"I love being in front and hitting solid shots and trying to put the ball in the fairway, put the ball in the middle of the greens, and put pressure on the other guy to hit the shots," Furyk said. "I'm thankful that this week was my week and today was my day. Things just fell into place for me this week, and I think that's part of it. I played very, very well. I had a lot of control over my swing and my emotions this week. I hit the ball where I wanted to, and I knocked in some great putts."

Those words aptly described Furyk's season. He won again at the Buick Open, put together 15 top-10 finishes, and finished the year fifth in world-wide money ($5.6 million), fifth in World Ranking (up from 13th) and fifth in PGA Tour scoring average. "I'm no better a player today than I was yesterday, just because I won the U.S. Open," he said. "But you hit definite levels in your career, and this is a big step."

Furyk won again in the four-man finale, the PGA Grand Slam of Golf. To say his game had reached another level was an understatement.

If Weir and Furyk winning the first two major championships of the year came as a surprise, the final two threw the golf world into a collective state of shock. On the links of Royal St. George's along the southern coast of England, a Hooters Tour veteran playing in his first major championship pulled the upset of the century, and became the first man since Francis Ouimet in 1913 to win the first major he ever played. Ben Curtis of Kent, Ohio, was ranked 396th in the world when he went on a mid-round birdie tear in the final round of the Open Championship and finished with one of the par saves of the year, holing a breaking eight-foot par putt at the 72nd hole to upset Thomas Bjorn, Vijay Singh, Davis Love, Tiger Woods, Sergio Garcia, Nick Faldo and everyone else in the field.

Not only was Curtis a no-name, he had never had a top-10 finish. He was only in the field by virtue of a 13th-place finish in the Western Open, and the only people in Sandwich who knew his name were the ones he had played with in his 13 previous PGA Tour starts and his fiancée.

"Guys win major championships out of the blue and this is one that was won out of the blue," said Bjorn, who was leading Curtis by two through 15 holes on Sunday before failing to get out of a bunker at the 16th (double bogey) and missing the green at the 17th (bogey). "I should have fought everybody off," Bjorn said. "It was a funny feeling, because we thought we were going to fight off Tiger or Davis or Vijay all day, and then it was just the two of us, and he came out ahead."

Curtis Strange, a commentator on the Open for ABC Sports, called it "the greatest upset in the history of golf, and maybe in all of sports." Strange didn't give Curtis much of a chance even as he stood over the eight-footer at the 18th. "He's not going to win," Strange said, "but he can make this and feel pretty good about what's he's done here this week."

Curtis told those crowded in for his press interview afterwards, "Right now many people are probably saying, 'Well, he really doesn't belong there,' but I know I do and that's all that matters."

If Ben Curtis winning a major championship weren't screwy enough — Curtis Stranger, as one tabloid headline put it — the final major of the season added another name to Bjorn's list of guys who "win major championships out of the blue." This time it was 34-year-old Shaun Micheel, ranked 169th in the world, who upset golf's order by beating the strongest field of the year in the PGA Championship. Micheel, another Hooters Tour graduate, finished off with the shot of the year, a 175-yard seven iron that came within a couples of inches of falling in the hole for eagle. "It was an absolutely perfect, perfect number," Micheel said. "I knew it was pretty close. I had to ask somebody how close it was. I saw it was only two inches, and I figured I could make that one."

It was the first time since 1969 that players who did not have a major victory previously won all four of the men's major championships.

The birdie on the final hole at Oak Hill Country Club in Rochester, New York, gave Micheel an even-par 70 on his round for a four-under 276 total, two strokes better than Chad Campbell. "It's kind of scary, really," Micheel said. "A year ago, I was trying to win the B.C. Open, and up until a month or two ago, I was trying to keep my card. I really can't believe this happened to me."

Campbell, the runner-up to Micheel, finished with a significant victory of his own in The Tour Championship.

There were plenty of other stories worthy of note in 2003 including Kenny Perry, Jay Haas, David Toms, Charles Howell, Justin Leonard, Brad Faxon, Bob Tway, Peter Jacobsen, Fred Couples and Chris DiMarco.

Phil Mickelson ranked third in driving distance for the year, averaging 306 yards off the tee, but ranked 189th in accuracy, failing to hit 50 percent of the fairways. The result was a winless season, a drop to 38th on the money list, and from second to 15th on the Official World Golf Ranking. This year Mickelson also tried out as a pitcher for the baseball minor league Toledo Mud Hens. His 65 miles-an-hour fastball left Lefty without a baseball offer, and without much direction.

Mickelson's slump was news because his talent seemed so boundless, and everyone thought he would snap out of it soon. The spectacular freefall of David Duval finished its second full year with no parachute in sight. Duval fell from No. 1 in the world in 1999 to 238th by the end of 2003. He made only four cuts for the year and only broke the top 30 one time. He finished 211th on the money list and failed to break par in the final six months of the season.

"There are some things I'm still figuring out and working on," Duval said. "I'll be happy to address them when I've worked through them and feel comfortable with where I am."

Because of his precipitous collapse, Duval wasn't on captain Jack Nicklaus' Presidents Cup team, which was just as well. Former PGA Tour commissioner Deane Beman put a playoff clause in the rules of the first Presidents Cup to ensure a winner and differentiate the event from the Ryder Cup. But Nicklaus and International captain Gary Player were having none of it.

After the Americans and Internationals dueled to a three-day tie in what everyone agreed was some of the finest and most compelling golf of the year, and after Tiger Woods and Ernie Els continued the battle for three extra holes on the South African coast, holing putt after crucial putt to extend the event further, Nicklaus and Player agreed to end it, as darkness was covering the golf course. "We came halfway around the world to do something for the betterment of golf," Nicklaus said. "Is there any doubt in anybody's mind we accomplished that?"

On the European front, Els won the Order of Merit going away in part because it looked as though the PGA European Tour would produce a different winner every week Els wasn't playing. Darren Clarke, who won the WGC NEC Invitational, was second to Els on the Order of Merit. Padraig Harrington and Fredrik Jacobson, who each won twice, were third and fourth on the list, closely followed by Ian Poulter, Paul Casey, Lee Westwood, Thomas Bjorn, Brian Davis and Phillip Price.

Europe produced 24 different winners in 2003 and none of them were Colin Montgomerie or Sergio Garcia. Montgomerie and the Spanish sensation struggled with their games most of the year. While Montgomerie won the Macau Open on the Asian PGA Tour, his best in Europe was two top-five finishes. Garcia won his second Nedbank Golf Challenge title in South Africa, but didn't make much of a dent in Europe.

Their absence left the door open for winners such as a former caddie from China (Zhang Lian-wei) and Europe's first Korean winner (K.J. Choi) along with the usual complement of Swedes, Danes, Brits, Scots, Kiwis and Africans. Zhang won again in his homeland, taking the Volvo China Open, and Choi won in Korea at the SK Telecom Open. They joined Harrington and Arjun Atwal as the only players to win on both the European and Asian Tours, while Els was joined by his compatriot Retief Goosen and young Australian Adam Scott as the only winners in both Europe and America.

Nick Price, at age 46, maintained a No. 12 ranking to provide Southern Africa with three players among the world's elite, and 23-year-old Trevor

Immelman won twice on the home circuit. Scott was in a group of prominent Australians including Stuart Appleby, Robert Allenby, Peter Lonard and Stephen Leaney.

American Todd Hamilton won four tournaments in Japan but left to successfully compete for a place on the 2004 U.S. PGA Tour. Toshimitsu Izawa won back-to-back events and led the money list. Hirofumi Miyase, Shingo Katayama and Hideto Tanihara also each won twice, and Shigeki Maruyama had a victory in America.

One of the best stories in 2003 was the resurrection of Westwood, who had fallen from third in the world to 182nd on the Official World Golf Ranking. Westwood won three times in 2003, twice in Europe at the BMW International Open and the Dunhill Links Championship. "There were times when I thought about putting the clubs away and calling it a day," Westwood said of his two-year drought and spectacular fall in form. "But that would have been an easy thing to do. I just enjoy winning and being in the lead with my name on the leaderboard and in front of people. I have worked for three years to get back to here." By the time he won a third time at the Nelson Mandela Invitational in South Africa, Westwood had clawed his way back to 65th in the world.

If there was any multiple winner of 2003 that proved to be a bigger surprise than Westwood, it had to be the only man to win a U.S. PGA Tour event after joining the Champions (formerly the Senior) Tour. Craig Stadler hadn't sniffed a victory since Tiger Woods was wearing glasses in calculus class. The man known as The Walrus had fallen into that 40-something Neverland of those who were playing out their eligibility and looking forward to their 50th birthdays. He had been on tour since Gerald Ford was president and, with a dozen victories, was counting the days until he made his Champions Tour debut.

Stadler won in his fourth start after joining the old guys in June. "I wanted to win early," he said after capturing the Ford Senior Players Championship. "I wanted to come out and just tell myself — and pretty much a lot of people — that I can still play good, still play well consistently."

A week later, something magical happened. He traveled to Endicott, New York, for the B.C. Open as a favor to the sponsor, who had given his son, Kevin, an exemption the last two years. Four days and one nine-under-par 63 later, Stadler became the first to win a senior event one week and a regular event the next. "It's like la-la-land here the last two weeks," Stadler said. "As bad as I was playing on the West Coast in the spring, I'm playing that good now, and I have no rhyme or reason for it. I was pretty much hating everything about golf. I was kind of waiting until I turned 50 to see what would happen, and all of a sudden I learned how to play again. It's the magical number. Get a good bottle of wine, turn 50, and you start putting well. It's an amazing thing."

He won twice more on the Champions Tour, at the Greater Hickory Classic and the SBC Championship, making 2003 the best year of Stadler's career since he won three tournaments including the Masters in 1982 and was Player of the Year. "I probably had more confidence in 1982 than I do now," he said. "That was a magical year. Winning breeds winning. The more you win, the more you expect to be there. It's fun now, that's for sure."

The game was fun for a lot of middle-aged guys in 2003. Peter Jacobsen,

49 and last seen kissing a trophy and hoisting a check in 1995, won the Greater Hartford Open after posting two top-10 finishes in Houston and Hilton Head. Fred Couples had an inspiring victory in the Shell Houston Open. Scott Hoch was the winner of the Ford Championship at Doral. Jay Haas didn't win, but had two seconds (Bob Hope Chrysler Classic and The Players Championship), a tie for fourth in Houston and a handful of fifth-place finishes, including one at the PGA Championship. His year was capped in grand fashion when he went 2-1-1 in the Presidents Cup and thumped Stephen Leaney 4 and 3 in singles.

And there was Kenny Perry, who at age 43 had never won more than one tournament a year and seemed to enjoy amateur drag racing and coaching his son's high school golf team as much or more than playing golf. Perry won the Bank of America Colonial (Annika's event), the Memorial Tournament and the Greater Milwaukee Open, and was a leading contender deep into the weekend at both the U.S. Open and Open Championship.

"Experience," Haas said of the resurgence. "There's nothing like it."

The final, and perhaps best, story of the year was at once the saddest and also the most heart-warming. On January 15, Bruce Edwards, Tom Watson's caddie for three decades, was diagnosed with amyotrophic lateral sclerosis, ALS, commonly known as Lou Gehrig's disease. For reasons unknown, the cells of Edwards' cerebral cortex were dying at a rapid clip. With medication to retard the symptoms, he would lose control of his speech and fine motor skills within a year to 18 months. Within two years — five years at the outside — he would be dead.

Watson, the winner of eight major titles, immediately took care of all Edwards' medical expenses and became the most visible spokesman for a disease that claims 100,000 lives a year. He launched a website (www.driving4life.org), and spoke passionately and emotionally about Edwards' courage. The world took notice when Watson shot 65 and shared the first-round lead in the U.S. Open. The crowd at Olympia Fields shouted "Broooce" on every tee, and they gave the duo a standing ovation after every holed putt.

The crowds didn't forget what Watson was playing for when he won the Senior British Open, recapturing the 36-year-old magic at Turnberry, site of his duel with Jack Nicklaus in 1977, and the JELD-WEN Tradition, where he birdied the final hole to beat Tom Kite, Gil Morgan and Jim Ahern. "I promised Bruce I was going to win for him before it was over," Watson said after his final win of the year. "Today, as he said, it was the first of many. I hope he's right."

When Watson finished second in the Charles Schwab Cup Championship, he wrapped up the season-ending $1 million prize given by Schwab to the most consistent player of the year. At the awards presentation he donated the entire check to ALS research.

"If you can measure a man's success by the friends he's had, then I've been very successful," Edwards said, his speech slurred and slowed from the disease. "Everybody has to leave this earth. If I go in a year or less, I've lived a wonderful life. If I leave, I've had a friendship with one of the greatest golfers in the world. We've had a lot of wins, a lot of rounds. I remember Tom saying, 'The game is a game of moments, and I want my share.' Well, not only did he have his share, but I had my share."

The Royal Bank of Scotland Group

Presents

The Major Championships

2. Masters Tournament

So much for Masters chairman Hootie Johnson's course changes turning Augusta National Golf Club into a long-hitter's paradise. In the final nine holes of the 2003 Masters Tournament (that time on Sunday afternoon when CBS announcers tell us the "tournament begins"), the two players battling to own the most sought-after green jacket in the world were a soft-spoken, short-hitting left-hander from Canada, and a softer-spoken and equally short-hitting journeyman from Ponte Vedra Beach, Florida, with two career wins in a decade of professional starts.

Who would have believed it? Mike Weir and Len Mattiace slogging around a rain-drenched course and slugging it out one short drive at a time? The Masters wasn't supposed to be like this. With the new-and-improved (and soaking wet) golf course playing every bit of its 7,290 yards, this was supposed to be either another major title for Tiger Woods, who with three early season victories, had his sights set on becoming the first to win three straight Masters, or it was going to be a breakout week for one of the young bombers. Throw in the fact that the first round was a washout, creating a couple of 12-hour days on Friday and Saturday, and it was easy to see why good money rested on guys like Woods, Phil Mickelson, Ernie Els or Davis Love. Conventional wisdom said that if you couldn't hit the ball 300 yards on the fly, you might as well be ready for an early exit.

Weir, ranked 39th in driving distance (out of 49 players left in the field on the weekend) proved the old Harvey Penick adage. A good putter was, indeed, a match for any man. "I'm no bomber, that's for sure," Weir said. "I have to make my wedge game work for me and rely on my putting and chipping and course management skills. I'm not going to have power on the golf course. But I felt like if you're consistent, you have a good putter in your hand, that's the great equalizer."

Weir used his great equalizer to roll in a six-foot par putt on the 72nd hole for a four-under-par 68 and a 281 total to send him back to the 10th tee for the first Masters playoff in 13 years. One anticlimactic bogey later, Weir became the first Canadian to win a major championship and the first left-hander to don a green jacket. The feat left Weir dazed and almost speechless. "It was an incredible day," he said. "I couldn't ask to play much better."

The same could also be said for the man Weir beat in the playoff. Mattiace played 17 career-making holes on Sunday. Starting the final round five strokes back and an hour ahead of the leaders, Mattiace, owner of the 2002 Nissan Open and FedEx St. Jude Classic trophies and a reputation as one of the truly good guys in the game, rolled in putt after crucial putt to reach eight under par for his round, and build a two-shot lead with one hole to play. The fact that he bogeyed the final hole to shoot 65 didn't faze him. Mattiace still called it "my best Sunday ever."

"I gave it my all today," Mattiace said. "And what I mean by that is that I didn't get out of focus. I was right there. My caddie and I, we were focused on each shot. And I did a great job of that, of focusing on each shot, looking and hitting. That's all you can ask for."

Well, it wasn't all he could have asked for. Mattiace had to wait and watch and hope that Weir didn't make every putt. "I knew that there was a very good chance for a playoff," Mattiace said. "If Mike made a bogey or something coming in, then so be it. But if he made a birdie, so be it as well. But I was expecting the playoff."

He was right. Weir kept making par after gritty par until finally, on the last hole of regulation, he stared at an uphill 45-footer for birdie. Putt goes in: Weir wins. Two-putt: Playoff. Three-putt this hole, and it would haunt Weir the rest of his career. Just ask Scott Hoch. There are no givens at Augusta National.

Weir had the advantage of watching his playing companion, third-round leader Jeff Maggert, putt on almost the same line. Maggert missed, but gave Weir a good "read" of the green. After Maggert tapped in and moved off, Weir studied the lengthy putt, and then hit it directly on line … rolling … rolling … and then stopping six feet short.

"I wouldn't wish that second putt on 18 on anybody," Weir said. "That was as nerve-wracking as it gets. It was just a gut-wrenching day, a lot of comeback putts that I needed to make and was able to make. To do that coming down the stretch knowing what a great score Len had today, that's what I'm really proud of."

In classic Augusta National tradition, the six-footer wasn't two inches off Weir's putter when the crowd jumped to its feet. When the ball found the center of the hole, the cheers were deafening. For his part, Weir looked like an inmate who had just had his sentence commuted. It wasn't over yet.

The last time two players strode to the 10th tee for extra holes, it was Nick Faldo versus Raymond Floyd back when the other George Bush was President and a high school kid with glasses named Tiger Woods was learning to drive his father's Impala. Faldo won that match with a birdie on the second hole.

This time, it was over in an ugly hurry. Weir three-putted the 10th green from 40 feet for his first bogey of the day. That was all he needed after Mattiace made the cardinal error of hitting his approach shot left with a six iron. With a pine tree and a glass-slick incline in front of him, Mattiace chopped his third shot across the green. Weir then gunned his birdie effort seven feet past, which gave Mattiace another chance. He rolled his par putt 18 feet long and left, prompting a "patron" (which is Augusta-speak for gallery member) to say, "Three worst words in golf: You're still away."

Mattiace missed his 18-footer and tapped in for a double bogey. That gave Weir two putts from seven feet. He used them both, tapping in from four inches for the victory. Weir raised both arms to the crowd. Then, sitting in the front seat of a golf cart on his way back to the wood-paneled basement of the Butler Cabin for a chat with Hootie Johnson and Jim Nantz of CBS, the first-time major champion put his head in his hands and sobbed while his father hugged him and said, "Just let it out."

Those weren't the final tears of the day. Back at the clubhouse, Mattiace tried to answer a few questions outside the media center before the awards ceremony, but he broke down and buried his face in a towel. "It was just the whole day," Mattiace said. "We try to build up to a certain level, a certain focus and a certain intensity. My wife will tell you that Sunday night I have to crash. I guess that's what I did. The intensity was so high, and with the emotions of playing today and executing and shooting a great score, it all just came out."

Weir was more succinct in describing his emotions. "Unbelievable," he said. "Just unbelievable."

Weir's tap-in bogey for victory (the first over-par playoff win in Masters history) wasn't the first unbelievable moment of the week. Who would have thought that Woods would come within one greenside bunker shot of missing his first 36-hole cut since 1997, and then rally into contention only to blow his chances with a mental error early in Sunday's round?

And who (other than his wife and Mom) would have dreamed that Jeff Maggert would lead this Masters by two strokes with 16 holes to play only to give those shots back (plus two more) with penalties that ranged from the ridiculous to the sublime? Or that a big-hitting amateur named Ricky Barnes would contend through three rounds? Or that a year after announcing his retirement from play at Augusta National, Arnold Palmer would be back playing with his aging Army still intact? Or that for the second year in a row, a few days of rain would make the world's prettiest golf course look like a mud-wrestling video?

Or — and this had to be the kicker — that the first left-handed Masters champion, and only the second southpaw ever to win a major (behind Bob Charles), would not be Phil Mickelson? Certainly Mickelson wouldn't have believed that. He said as much before the first round. "I'm going to leave that one unanswered," Mickelson said when asked who he thought would be the next left-handed player to win a major; but then he answered it anyway. "I think we all know the answer to that."

Yes, this one was wild and wooly. There were lights on the practice range (a first for Augusta National), televised coverage of the opening nine and no television commercial interruptions (both firsts). Elvis even made an appearance. But in the end, this Masters boiled down to what it always comes down to: The man with the hot putter finished on top. And when the rain clouds cleared and the tournament was finally underway, all the hoopla and extra-curricular distractions that plagued this tournament for the better part of a year were finally (and mercifully) put aside.

From the time the club re-opened its doors after its annual summer respite, one name and one story hung over Augusta National like a bad thunderstorm. You couldn't even talk University of Georgia football in the community without someone mentioning Martha Burk, the chairperson of the National Council of Women's Organizations, a group no one had heard of before Burk picked a fight with Augusta National's Johnson over the inclusion of women in the club's membership.

It all started in June 2002 when Burk sent a letter to Johnson objecting to the club's male-only membership and demanding that Augusta National "open the membership to women now, so that this is not an issue when the tournament is staged next year." Johnson responded with a letter of his own in which he informed Burk that he "found your letter's several references to discrimination, allusions to sponsors, and your setting of deadlines to be both offensive and coercive. Any further communication between us would not be productive." In case anyone missed his point, Johnson put out a statement to the press that said, "We will be bullied, threatened, or intimidated ... at the point of a bayonet."

This thrust Burk and Johnson into the middle of a media frenzy that would last upwards of nine months. During that time, *USA Today* would publish a list of Augusta National members, their ages and occupations, and *The New York Times* would run so many stories on the subject that their own reporters would rise up in protest. The Girl Scouts of America and Junior League were cited as examples of private single-gender clubs that also shouldn't be forced to integrate at the point of a bayonet, and Debbie Schlussel, a vocal supporter of Johnson, even dragged a restaurant chain into the fracas. "Hooters is a public establishment, but they don't allow male waiters," Schlussel said. "I don't see (Burk) protesting that."

In July of 2002, at the Open Championship in Britain, of all places, Tiger Woods was foisted into the scrum when he said of Augusta National's membership, "They're entitled to set up their own rules the way they want them. It would be nice to see everyone have an equal chance to participate if they wanted to, but there is nothing you can do about it. It's unfortunate, but it's just the way it is." That prompted the *New York Post* to put Woods on its back page under the headline, "Hypocrite – Two-Faced Tiger Says Augusta Has 'Right' to Ban Women." The fact that the club did, indeed, have the legal right not to include women in its membership was irrelevant. By February the story had defied all logic and reason and had become a circus-like distraction for both the tournament and the city of Augusta, Georgia.

Lines were clearly delineated by tournament time. Television sponsors were granted relief from their commitments, and corporate entertainment in Augusta was off by 40 percent. Meanwhile, those who petitioned Richmond County and the city of Augusta for protest permits included Burk's NCWO, an anti-Burk protester from Tampa who printed buttons saying, "Honk If You Love Hootie," and 39-year-old J.J. Harper, the self-proclaimed "Imperial Wizard of the American White Knights of the Ku Klux Klan," an organization that, to everyone's knowledge, had one member.

Thankfully, it rained for three days. Monday's practice round was a complete washout, and Tuesday wasn't much better. The weather that had kept Georgia temperatures mild all winter had also produced one of the wettest springs on record. Freshly lain red oak mulch turned to odiferous mud, and the first fairway appeared more suited for rafting than golf. By midday Tuesday, a lot of people were wondering if the golf course was going to be playable.

That question was answered late Wednesday. No one could play, at least not on Thursday. For the first time in its history, the first round of the Masters was a complete washout. Thursday passed without a single shot. That meant early times on Friday with the hopes of getting 36 holes completed in a single day. Everyone knew it was impossible. If it had rained again on Friday, the tournament could have run into Monday or Tuesday of the following week, throwing a wrench into everybody's schedule. As rain peppered the white veranda on the old plantation clubhouse, only one thing seemed certain: This was going to be a long week.

The lights came on (literally) at 6:30 a.m., an hour before the first tee time and fully 40 minutes before sunrise on Friday morning. For the first time in its 70-year history, Augusta National installed incandescent floodlights around the practice range, making the place look more like a parking lot than the practice ground at one of the world's most prestigious golf tournaments.

"We've played under the lights before in places like Disney and Las Vegas, but never at Augusta," Jeff Sluman said.

This came on the heels of Johnson striking an unapologetic tone in his pre-tournament press conference, telling one reporter, "If you have a question, I'll answer it, but don't lecture me." He went on to say, "There may well come a time when we include women as members of our club. However, I want to emphasize that we have no timetable and our membership is very comfortable with our present status … Going forward, our club will continue to make its own decisions, and we will continue to make what hopefully is a major contribution to the game of golf and to charity."

Their contribution that Friday was the longest day in Masters history. Because of the large number (94) of players in this year's field, it was virtually impossible for everyone to complete two rounds in a day. They teed off in threesomes off both nines, which worked fine for nine holes, but when the first group off No. 10 made the turn, they had to wait 40 minutes on the first tee. That back-up caused the first round to run toward the six-hour mark.

It was a hard day to keep up with the scores and the grinding pace of play. All eyes were on Woods, who was paired with Barnes, the U.S. Amateur champion, a strapping blonde who looked more like an All-American football player than Arizona's best golfer since Phil Mickelson. When Barnes hooked his opening tee shot into the pine straw, Woods offered some encouraging words. "He came up to me and said, 'Relax. Things are going to be okay. It's going to be a long day,' and that was kind of reassuring," Barnes said. The advice worked. Barnes hooked a four iron off the pine needles and onto the first green. "I hit a great recovery shot and he came up to me and said, 'See.' And I was like, 'Okay.'" One hole later, Barnes hit a six iron to one foot for his first birdie in a professional major championship.

By the middle of the afternoon Barnes was on his way to being a crowd favorite. With only a handful of players under par and even fewer close to the 60s, Barnes hit one swashbuckling shot after another, pounding drives past Woods and putting on a display that had a lot of observers comparing him with a young Arnold Palmer. He hit a pitching wedge to one foot for a birdie on the seventh, followed by a hooked tee shot and bogey on the par-five eighth. He made another birdie on the 13th after laying up in front of Rae's Creek and hitting a lob wedge to a foot. Three-putts from 75 feet gave him another bogey at the 16th. Barnes came back with a 35-foot birdie putt at the 17th and a fine six-iron approach from the pine straw to seven feet for birdie on the 18th.

Although it was tough to separate the first and second rounds because of how the day was compacted, Barnes was clearly the star of the day. His 69 turned out to be one of only three opening rounds in the 60s, and only one stroke worse than first-round leader Darren Clarke, who had one bogey (at 11) and an eagle (at 15) on his way to a 34-32 round of 66. Sergio Garcia also provided some fireworks, chipping in twice for pars before going on a four-birdie second-nine tear that moved him to three-under-par 69 to round out the first-round leaders.

Weir had three birdies and a bogey in his opening 18 holes, a steady performance that left him tied for fourth somewhere in the middle of the longest day. He hardly missed a beat as he grabbed a quick sandwich and prepared for the rest of his afternoon. "I feel good," Weir said. "I'm hoping to keep playing the way I'm playing. I'm hitting a lot of good iron shots."

The same could not be said for Woods, who watched Barnes make a handful of birdies while making none of his own. Woods shot 76 in the first round, his worst starting performance in the Masters since turning professional, and the first time he had gone 18 holes in a major without a birdie since the first round of the Open Championship at Carnoustie in 1999. "I didn't hit the ball all that bad," Woods said. "I didn't make any putts, and had a couple of bad breaks. I'm still not out of this thing. I just need to play a decent round. It doesn't have to be a great round. I just need to make some putts."

If it was any consolation, Woods' 76 was two-tenths of a shot lower than the average score for the field, making this both the slowest and highest scoring first round of any Masters since 1988. Ernie Els, another pre-tournament favorite, shot 79, which tied Bernhard Langer and David Duval, both of whom had their worst Masters opening rounds ever. Sandy Lyle joined the worst-first-round club with an 82, which made him low man in his group. Tommy Aaron and Charles Coody, the other two members of Lyle's threesome, shot 92 and 83 respectively. As they limped into the clubhouse for their short lunch break, Lyle said, "They're going for a power nap." Then, when asked if he was looking forward to the second round of the day, Lyle said, "I don't think so. Not really, no."

He wasn't alone. Jack Nicklaus shot 85, his highest score ever in the Masters by four strokes, and one shot worse than Arnold Palmer, who proved that coming out of Masters retirement wasn't such a bad idea after all. Both Palmer and Nicklaus wrote letters to Johnson asking the chairman to reconsider his decision (made in 2002) that past champions wouldn't be invited back to play after their 65th birthdays. Johnson listened and rescinded the policy. After Friday, Nicklaus wasn't sure he'd made the right decision. Running into Palmer in the locker room during lunch, Nicklaus said to his old friend and rival, "Why'd you have to write that darned letter?"

Late in the day the players marched out into the mud for as many holes of the second round as daylight would allow. First-round leader Clarke wasn't thrilled about it. When asked if he was looking forward to a second round on Friday, Clarke patted his ample midsection and said, "Does it look like it?" By sundown it didn't. Clarke was puffing like a man who smokes big Cuban cigars (which he does). His last two holes were bogeys, which he said he would love to attribute to fatigue, "but not really. Just made a couple of mistakes." Still, he was pleased with his play over the day. "Overall if somebody would have said, 'You're four under after 28 holes,' I would have bit their hand off last night," Clarke said.

Weir was also thrilled to be finished. When the day was over, he led the Masters by two strokes at six under par through 30 holes thanks to three straight birdies on the second nine (his third nine of the day). "On 13 I made a really nice putt, maybe 20 feet from behind the hole," he said. "At 14 I was just over the green and chipped in," for his second birdie. "And at 15, I hit a nice wedge shot in there to six feet and made that one."

The lights came on again around the clubhouse and driving range around 8:00 p.m., but not many players were anxious to stay around. Saturday was going to be another long day.

In addition to a two-shot lead, Weir teed off Saturday with the advantage of having only six holes left in his second round. Some players had as many as 12 holes to complete before learning if they had made the 36-hole cut, and if they were lucky enough to slip into the final 36, they had another 18 holes on Saturday afternoon.

Weir started on the short par-four third hole early Saturday morning and played his final six holes in even par for 68. Clarke didn't fare as well, finishing the final eight holes of his second round in plus two to shoot 76. Garcia fared even worse, shooting 78 in the second round, nine shots worse than his first-round number. Mickelson snuck in with a 70 in the morning light to move into a tie for third place at one-under 143 with Barnes, who continued to dazzle the crowds with one big shot after another.

The biggest surprise of them all, however, was the dramatic way Woods finished his second round. Hovering on the cut line at five over par through 33 holes, Woods made a great birdie at the seventh. "That's when I was able to say, 'Okay, now I've got it,'" he said. "I could birdie eight, and make a run at number nine and be in solid shape. Well, then I bogey eight from the middle of the fairway, flair a tee shot out to the right on nine, pull it in the bunker, and all of a sudden I'm looking at possibly missing the cut." Woods had to get up and down from the left greenside bunker with very little green between his ball and the hole in order to play the weekend. The fact that he hit the sand shot of his life and drained the five-footer for par should have surprised no one. But as Woods' mother, Kultida, said afterward, "He makes me too nervous."

At the end of a long and confusing two rounds, the Masters leaderboard looked like this:

Mike Weir	70-68 - 138	Jeff Maggert	72-73 - 145
Darren Clarke	66-76 - 142	Ernie Els	79-66 - 145
Phil Mickelson	73-70 - 143	Jonathan Byrd	74-71 - 145
*Ricky Barnes	69-74 - 143	K.J. Choi	76-69 - 145
David Toms	71-73 - 144	Nick Price	70-75 - 145
Paul Lawrie	72-72 - 144	Charles Howell	73-72 - 145
Jose Maria Olazabal	73-71 - 144	*Hunter Mahan	73-72 - 145
Vijay Singh	73-71 - 144	Billy Mayfair	75-70 - 145
Brad Faxon	73-71 - 144	Phil Tataurangi	75-70 - 145
Jim Furyk	73-72 – 145	John Rollins	74-71 - 145

*Denotes amateurs

Sometime during the lunch break between the second and third rounds, 30 women in tee shirts, along with no more than 10 professionals from the Rainbow PUSH Coalition, showed up at a rally that Martha Burk originally estimated would draw 900 to 1,500 people and "shut Augusta down." The media-to-protester ratio was five to one, which is why the Elvis impersonator and the guy with the sign that read "Woman, Fix My Dinner" got airtime and print coverage.

In the end, there were more interesting people in Bob Estes' gallery than at the protest. Jesse Jackson didn't come (although he had promised to "stand shoulder-to-shoulder" with Burk), but a guy from Atlanta named Dave Walker did. Walker was a pro-war protester who carried a sign that said, "Give War A Chance." A group called People Against Ridiculous Protests planted the most pointed sign on the premises. It read simply: "Look At All The Ridiculous People." That summed up Saturday outside the gates.

Inside the ropes, things were more interesting. Within a span of four hours Woods went from struggling to make the cut and seemingly out of the tournament, to one of the favorites with 18 holes to play. He did this with six birdies in the only bogey-free round of the day. He started on the second nine and got things rolling in a hurry. After a routine par at the 10th, he rolled in a 50-footer for birdie at the 11th, which was the hardest hole on the course on Saturday, averaging 4.469. "When I made that putt I got some positive momentum," Woods said. "I said, 'You know what, let's just keep things going.'"

He did just that, two-putting for birdies at the 13th and 15th holes to go out in 33. He two-putted again for birdie at the second before rolling in a 20-footer for birdie at the par-three sixth. He followed that with another birdie at the seventh. Suddenly, the world's No. 1 player was right back in contention. If he had birdied the eighth or ninth or both, then he might have been in the final pairing on Sunday. As it was, he made pars coming in for a 66, tying Maggert for low round of the day.

"This tournament, we all know anything can happen on the back nine," Woods said. "You just need to get yourself in position. Even though I'm now, what, four back? That's not inconceivable. That's for sure."

Maggert, who turned out to be the tournament leader at the end of the third round after eight birdies and a double bogey (at the 11th hole), agreed with Woods' assessment. "If you look at the leaderboard now, it would be tough to say that Tiger's not one of the players you've got to worry about," Maggert said. He then backtracked, saying no, he wouldn't be worrying about Tiger. "There's nobody out there I can control tomorrow but myself," Maggert said. "I need to play well and hit good golf shots. If I do that, I'll have an excellent chance."

Maggert took only 21 putts and made only two pars on his second nine that included a hook into the water on the 11th and three consecutive birdies at the 16th, 17th and 18th. "Sometimes you get in a rhythm with the putter and the hole looks as big as a coffee can," he said. "I hit some decent shots close to the hole and started rolling them in. Course management and ball-striking make up for length any day. They make a big thing of length when we play on big golf courses. But I feel like I'm a strong player in all parts of the game, other than maybe I don't hit the ball as far with my driver. Certainly, accuracy, my short game and my putting make up for that."

Any other day Weir could have said the same. But Saturday afternoon, Weir's putter abandoned him. "My round was a little disappointing today," Weir said after making six bogeys and three birdies for a 75 to drop him two strokes behind Maggert. "But I'm still in the last group tomorrow and still have a great chance to win if I play a really solid round. I'm really looking forward to it."

Clarke was not, having continued his slide from 66 to 76 to 78 and out of contention.

With one round to play and the tournament back on track, the leaderboard at Augusta National looked like this:

Jeff Maggert	66 - 211	Len Mattiace	69 - 216
Mike Weir	75 - 213	Ernie Els	72 - 217
Vijay Singh	70 - 214	Mark O'Meara	70 - 217
David Toms	70 - 214	Rich Beem	71 - 217
Phil Mickelson	72 - 215	Paul Lawrie	73 - 217
Jose Maria Olazabal	71 - 215	K.J. Choi	72 - 217
Tiger Woods	66 - 215	Nick Price	72 - 217
Jim Furyk	71 - 216	Fred Couples	69 - 217
Jonathan Byrd	71 - 216		

Few may have noticed when Mattiace birdied the second and third holes on Sunday. After all, he started the day six strokes back, and he had seven players with a combined total of eight major titles and six green jackets between him and the top of the leaderboard. So when Mattiace birdied the eighth to inch a little closer, everyone gave a polite smattering of applause. It was always good to have a dark horse running well the first few furlongs. But no one gave Mattiace much of a chance, not with Woods, Singh, Olazabal, Mickelson and Toms ahead of him.

All eyes were squarely focused on the final three groups of the day. Woods and Olazabal led the way, with Singh and Toms right behind them. Bringing up the rear were Maggert and Weir, who seemed almost forgotten, and certainly underestimated. The last time Weir was in the final group in a major was the 1999 PGA Championship, when he played with Woods and shot an 82, a round where he said he "learned a lot" by watching the way Woods conducted himself. Maggert had played well in several majors, but had never been able to come through with a victory.

Woods, Mickelson and Weir inched a little closer to Maggert's lead when all three birdied the second hole. Maggert made a good up-and-down par on the first and a routine par on the second. There appeared to be nothing wobbly in the leader's game. One hole later, the freakiest event of the week would turn this one on its head.

Rule 19-2:b of the *Rules of Golf* reads: "If a competitor's ball is accidentally deflected or stopped by himself, his partner, or either of their caddies or equipment, the competitor shall incur a penalty of two strokes."

Maggert pulled a two-iron shot from the third tee into the fairway bunker, which wasn't that big a deal. He only had sand wedge to the green on a hole where the tees had been moved up to entice players to go for the green on their tee shots. But Maggert tried to play it smart. He hit his ball in a good spot to approach the pin, even though the lip of the bunker was a tad high. It still shouldn't be a problem. What he didn't count on was catching the wedge a touch thin, and having the ball ricochet off the lip and hit him in the chest. "I tried to get out of the way," he said. "But I guess my reflexes aren't what they used to be."

He wasted no time assessing the penalty, holding up two fingers in Weir's direction to let him know that this was going to be a whopper. To his credit, the next shot did, indeed, find the green, and Maggert two-putted for seven. "The golf tournament wasn't anywhere close to being over at that point," he said. "I was playing well and putting well. I knew I could make birdies and come back."

He did just that, making birdies at the fifth and 10th to climb back into contention with eight holes left. But disaster struck again at the par-three 12th. Maggert's nine-iron shot sailed long and right and into the top of the back bunker. From there he hit two balls into Rae's Creek and took an eight, a quintuple bogey if anyone cared to count. The fact that he came back with three more birdies on the second nine to finish alone in fifth place was almost forgotten. When the day was done, Maggert had shot 75 with five birdies and no bogeys. His only over-par scores were a seven and an eight. "My scorecard today looked more like a telephone number than a golf score," he said with a half-hearted smile. "But this golf course can do that to you."

Woods also found trouble at the third, just not with the rulebook. Woods was one of the players the committee had in mind when they set the tees forward. He had just birdied the second to pull within three of the lead, and he needed to make something happen to get the momentum flowing. The green was only 320 yards away. He thought about hitting a two iron, but his caddie, Steve Williams, talked him into a driver. "I made a mental blunder," Woods later admitted. "It's the player's call, and ultimately I made the wrong decision."

He blew the shot into the pine trees right of the green. With no stance, no swing and nowhere to go, Woods turned his wedge upside down and hit his second shot left-handed. The ball rolled into a tight lie in front of the green. From there, he hit a pitch long and over the green, chipped back, and two-putted for a double-bogey six. "It cost me a lot," he said. "A lot of momentum. I should have hit iron. Hindsight is 20/20."

Still, Woods thought he had a chance. "I birdied nine. I figured if I could go out and shoot 30 on the back nine, you never know. And I just didn't do it." Woods shot even-par 36 on the second nine for a 75 on the day and a 290 total, nine shots out of the playoff.

Meanwhile, Mattiace rolled in a "bomb" from 50 feet on the 10th and reached the par-five 13th in two. Now, he was more than a dark horse. "That was the best drive I hit all week," Mattiace said of his drive at the 13th. "I hadn't gone for the green all three other days. I hit a beautiful four wood. It's funny because I hit a great shot and the ball was one yard from going in the creek, so it's crazy stuff. It stayed up and then the putt was just the way I saw it. That was a great feeling. All week I've been practicing the four wood off of a right-to-left lie, practicing it, waiting to hit it. When I finally had it, I said this is what I've been practicing all this time for, and I executed it."

When the putt fell at the 13th, Mattiace held a share of the lead. Another birdie at the 15th, followed by a crucial 15-footer for birdie at the 16th gave Mattiace a two-shot cushion over Weir. If he could par in, he would shoot 64. One more birdie and he would equal the course record (which was set by Nick Price in 1986, long before the course was lengthened and a "second cut" of rough was added).

He parred the 17th, but pushed his drive into the trees on the 18th and made bogey. "I kind of hit a flare-out drive to the right, not a very good drive," he said of his tee shot on the final hole. "I was totally blocked out to go for the green, so I pitched out and set myself up for a little nine iron. I just turned the nine iron over a slight hair to go to the back of the green, and I had about a 35-footer down the hill, which looked like ice to me." He left the first putt short, but made the second putt for bogey and a round of 65 for his 281 total.

That set up the showdown with Weir, who hung in with birdies at the second and sixth on the front, and two more birdies on the par-fives on the second nine (13 and 15) to set up the crucial two-putt par at the 18th. "To go bogey-free at Augusta National on Sunday, I can't ask for more than that. Once it all soaks in, I'll realize how special it is," Weir said. He made comeback par putts on the 16th and 17th before arriving on the final tee knowing he needed to make par.

"I had 195 yards to the hole from the fairway up the hill," Weir said of his play at the 18th. "So I had a four iron into the green, which is no easy task. I was trying to hit a low shot to land it below the hole and run it up there. The other day I hit a four iron to the top and it ran over the back of the green. I didn't want to have that downhill putt. From the sounds of the crowd it sounded like it almost got up there and then came back down. Then I really watched Jeff's putt closely. He gave it a pretty good rap, and I thought I did too. I was really surprised to see it come up that far short. That was a really hard putt to judge, and I'm really happy to make that one, obviously, to get into the playoff."

Weir finished with 68 for his 281 total to match Mattiace. Mickelson was third at 283 and Furyk fourth at 284, both finishing with 68s. Then came Maggert with his 75 and 286, followed by Els and Singh at 287.

Of the playoff Weir said, "The feeling was intense pressure for sure. But I saw the difficulty Len was in, and I knew I needed to do my job and try to make that birdie putt. Len's such a great putter, even though he was behind the tree and hit it 25 feet, the odds of him making that putt were pretty good. He shot 65 today. And I wanted to bear down. The shadows from the trees were just coming across the green and it's tough to really pick up the subtleties in the breaks there. But after he missed his bogey putt, I wanted to finish it off in style. Luckily the par putt didn't run too far past."

After breaking down in sobs, Mattiace pulled himself together and tried to be philosophical about his loss. "One of us was going to lose," he said. "I was okay with that. I gave it my all today. This proves to me that I can do some good stuff."

Almost entirely lost in the drama of the playoff was the fact that Mickelson birdied the final hole to finish alone in third place. "It's better than finishing fourth," Mickelson said of another top-five finish in a major championship without a victory. "But there's really no consolation out there. Heading into the week I was very calm and I felt very ready to play. I'm feeling very comfortable in the major championships now. I just know that if I go out and play I'm going to have a shot on Sunday, and it's fun to have a chance at winning."

Mike Weir and Len Mattiace couldn't have agreed more.

3. U.S. Open Championship

The normally insidious U.S. Open Championship rough, while still punitive, wasn't anywhere close to the depths at Pebble Beach in 2000; and the golf course, Olympia Fields Country Club in suburban Chicago, while long enough at 7,190 yards, was not as long as Bethpage Black in 2002. Not a single player lodged a complaint to the press about the golf course, which might have been a first for the United States Golf Association, especially in the U.S. Open.

The greens, while contoured, were soft and receptive, the fairways were reachable and mowed at a respectable 3/8 of an inch. If you missed a fairway by a foot or two, you only had to negotiate $1\frac{1}{2}$-inch rough. It wasn't until you really hit one offline that you got into the $3\frac{1}{2}$-inch rough, and even then it was manageable. Throw in perfect weather and just a breath of wind, and it was easy to see how this 103rd rendition of America's national golf championship might have been considered a kinder, gentler U.S. Open where birdies and fist-pumping histrionics were to rule the day.

A strange thing happened on the way to the prize-giving ceremony. Jim Furyk, a grinder whose play more closely resembled Hale Irwin than Tiger Woods, posted a two-birdie, four-bogey final round of 72 for an eight-under-par 272 total and a three-stroke victory almost devoid of drama. If not for Sunday being Father's Day, and the fact that Furyk's dad, Mike, a golf professional and his only coach, was there to witness the victory, this one might have gone down as the dullest national championship in more than a decade.

Furyk wouldn't have wanted it any other way. "I love being in front and hitting solid shots and trying to put the ball in the fairway, put the ball in the middle of the greens, and put pressure on the other guy to hit the shots," Furyk said. "I'm thankful that this week was my week and today was my day. Things just fell into place for me this week, and I think that's part of it. I played very, very well. I had a lot of control over my swing and my emotions this week. I hit the ball where I wanted to, and I knocked in some great putts."

He did all of those things with the fastidiousness of an accountant. Furyk's pre-shot routine was once described as "a study in obsessive-compulsive behavior," followed by a swing that made Ed Fiori's and Miller Barber's swings look downright conventional. David Feherty, a CBS television analyst, summed up Furyk's swing when he said, "It looks like an octopus falling out of a tree." David Toms called him "a modern-day Scott Hoch," which could be interpreted a number of ways. Furyk couldn't have cared less, except for how the victory vindicated the swing and the style of play his dad taught him as a child.

"He's always been my teacher," Furyk said of his father. "He's taken a lot of criticism along the way, which I never heard, because no one is going to criticize a junior player, but he took a beating as my teacher in teaching me my swing. That I made it on tour was kind of his validation. And this is just a step forward that's something we can share together."

It wasn't until the final hole, with a four-shot lead, that Furyk let the thoughts of his father seep into his conscious. That's when his emotions got the best of him. Tears in his eyes, Furyk three-putted for bogey on the final hole. "Having my dad here, I had a hard time telling him 'Happy Father's Day' because I knew I'd get choked up," Furyk said. "I knew it would be a big day, not only for me from a career standpoint. I knew he was going to be out there, my mom was going to be out there, and my wife was going to be out there. What I've done as a person, and as a golfer, I owe to my family. They've done a lot for me, made a lot of sacrifices for me, and allowed me to be here. It's a special moment."

The week was full of special moments, even if the golf course lacked the typical U.S. Open buzz. An almost hour-long train or bus trip from downtown Chicago, and closer to Michael Jackson's childhood home in Gary, Indiana, than Wrigley Field, Olympia Fields had a lot of people scratching their heads. Rich Skyzinski, former editor of the now-defunct USGA magazine *Golf Journal*, called the selection of Olympia Fields, which hadn't hosted a U.S. Open since 1920, "out of the blue." He went on to say, "this course wasn't on anybody's short or long list."

Once it made it onto the list, however, the USGA did their best. Senior Director of Rules and Competitions Tom Meeks said, "After working on this golf course for five years, I don't know how we could have made it more difficult and still kept it fair." Fairness was a big issue after the criticism the USGA received for the greens at The Olympic Club in 1998 (with four-footers running 20 feet past the hole), Southern Hills in 2001 (where the 18th green became a putt-putt contest for eventual winner Retief Goosen and losers Mark Brooks and Stewart Cink), and for the forced carries at Bethpage Black (where Nick Price said "half the field couldn't reach the fairways"). When some people questioned whether Olympia Fields met the USGA's exacting standards for identifying the best players in the world, Meeks replied, "I wouldn't say this is the easiest rough I can remember, but it's definitely not the hardest, either."

The course yielded 353 birdies and 10 eagles in the opening round, and 24 people broke 70 while only two failed to break 80. Those were not typical U.S. Open opening-round scores, but then, without a relative docile course set-up, we might not have been treated to the best golf story of the week, and one of the best sports stories of the year.

At 1:28 in the afternoon under a cloudless sky, the gallery seated around the tee at the par-four 10th offered a polite smattering of applause for Game No. 46, which included Angel Cabrera, Scott Verplank and the man everyone came to see, 53-year-old Tom Watson, playing on what the USGA said would be his last "special invitation."

If Watson were to play in another Open, it would be through qualification. If his caddie, Bruce Edwards, were to loop in another Open, it would be through a miracle of God. Edwards, who at 46 had been with Watson in one of the most enduring player-caddie relationships, had complained of pain and loss of grip pressure in his hands early in year. Watson insisted that he go to a doctor. The diagnosis was amyotrophic lateral sclerosis, Lou Gehrig's disease, a steadily degenerative and fatal nerve disorder.

By the time the 1:30 p.m. starting group teed off on the 444-yard 10th, the thousands in attendance and millions watching on television knew about Edwards' condition and Watson's commitment to his longtime friend. The

USGA had offered a golf cart to Edwards, who promptly turned them down. "I want to walk with him," Edwards said. He would walk every step. But what Edwards didn't know, and what the crowd could have never expected, was how the day would play out.

If there had been a shank on his three wood, Watson would have found it with his opening tee shot. The ball went low and right, into the first cut of rough. From there he tried to snap-hook a four wood onto the front of the green, but the ball slid right, he chipped to 12 feet and hit what he termed "a terrible putt, an awful putt for bogey." He hit another terrible putt on his second hole after reaching the green with his approach. The ball scooted past the hole, and he was left with a downhill eight-footer. When that putt found the cup, Watson almost skipped to the hole. Maybe this was a sign of good things to come.

Holing an eagle from the fairway is never a bad thing, but when you're struggling with your putter, it's a double whammy. Not only do you get a couple of shots back, you do it without having to stand over a putt. That's what happened to Watson on the 454-yard, par-four 12th, his third hole of the day. "I hit a perfect drive," Watson said. "And I hit a six iron right at the hole, and I said, 'Well, I hope that's close.' All of a sudden the arms go up … field goal. Bruce said, 'You holed it.' That completely changed my round."

One over par was now one under, and Watson was on a roll. At the 16th, his seventh hole of the day, he made a 15-footer for birdie to move to two under par, and at the first hole (his 10th) he hit a sand wedge to 10 feet and made that putt for birdie to move to three under. By then the crowd had swelled, and the electricity of the moment could have lit the Sears Tower. By the time they reached the tee at the long, par-three seventh, the scene looked more like a Cubs game than a golf tournament. Shouts of "Come on, Tom!" and "Brooooce!" echoed through the trees. No one on the premises could have missed it. Something epic was underway.

Watson knew he still had work to do. With the pin cut 210 yards away on the far right edge of the green behind a bunker, he hit a cut four iron that didn't really cut. The ball landed in the middle of the green, leaving him a 45-footer for birdie. He and Edwards read it from every angle, and Watson made what appeared to be a great stroke. The ball broke two feet and looked like it was going in when it stopped on the front edge of the hole, seemingly defying gravity. A groan went out from the crowd, but a second later the ball fell in and the place went wild. Watson chased after the putt and gave the ball a two-fisted point when it fell in for birdie. He was four under with two holes to play.

Long before Watson rolled in the birdie at the seventh, Brett Quigley had taken his shoes off and played from the creek on the same hole. He had walked away with bogey at the par-three, but came roaring back with six consecutive threes on the back nine, including birdies at the 12th, 13th, 14th and 16th and pars at the par-threes (15th and 17th). A two-putt par at the 18th gave Quigley the clubhouse lead at five-under 65. With a touch more magic, Watson could match or beat that score.

The old warrior found the touch again at the eighth when he hit a nine iron to 20 feet and rolled that putt into the back of the hole for another birdie. No one could remember a more uproarious Thursday crowd at a U.S.

Open than the one following Watson by the time he reached the ninth tee. "The crowd helped me," he said. "They willed me to make par on the last hole. I felt them pulling for me."

He hit a "lousy" shot at the final hole, a pushed seven iron that landed in the greenside bunker. "I only had about 60 feet of green to hit to, and I missed the whole green," Watson said. Edwards replaced the divot, tossed his man a sand wedge, and trotted to the side of the green. He, too, still had work to do. On the way, the crowd was screaming, "Hole it, Tom!"

The moment reminded Watson of another delicate little wedge shot he'd had 21 years before. That one was from the rough behind the 17th green at Pebble Beach. Edwards had been on the bag that day, and as he had handed Watson his wedge, the caddie had said, "Get it close." Watson was having none of it. "Get it close?" he said. "I'm going to make it." Back then he did hole it. And as he ran across the green with his arms in the air, Watson had interrupted his celebration to point an "I told you so" finger at Edwards. It was a moment seared in golf history.

Now, he was faced with another delicate wedge shot from a bunker with the crowd screaming, "Hole it! Hole it!" Watson didn't hole it, but he hit a good shot to eight feet. Edwards grabbed the rake and smoothed the sand, just as he had done thousands of times before. He then helped his man read the eight-footer and held the flag while Verplank and Romero tapped in and cleared the stage. Watson labored over the putt for what seemed like an eternity, but when the ball hit the center of the hole, the roar was deafening.

Only then did Watson cry. Arm-in-arm with Edwards, the two men shared one of the most compelling stories of the year in all of sports.

"After being with him since 1973, I didn't start getting emotional until he did," Watson said. "He started to crack a bit early in the back nine, and he kind of shed a tear there. The last few holes, there were quite a few tears there from both of us. And it was quite a memory for me, to be able to play the last few holes in the U.S. Open, my favorite tournament, most difficult to win, with my friend and caddie for 30 years, Bruce Edwards. It's a memory that I will ...", and the tears came once more. Finally, he said, "If I shoot 90 tomorrow, I don't care."

Neither did Edwards, who was a profile in courage throughout the week. "If you can measure a man's success by the friends he's had, then I've been very successful," Edwards said. "Everybody has to leave this earth. If I go in a year or less, I've lived a wonderful life. If I leave, I've had a friendship with one of the greatest golfers in the world. We've had a lot of wins, a lot of rounds. I remember Tom saying, 'The game is a game of moments, and I want my share.' Well, not only did he have his share, but I had my share."

None was more special than the embrace from his friend after the magical round that Thursday. With one round in the books in the U.S. Open, the leaderboard looked like this:

Tom Watson	65	Jim Furyk	67
Brett Quigley	65	Tom Gillis	68
Justin Leonard	66	Mark Calcavecchia	68
Jay Don Blake	66	Ian Leggatt	68
Stephen Leaney	67		

Ernie Els summed up the situation nicely on Friday when he described Olympia Fields: "Last year at Bethpage, the USGA overcooked it. This year, they undercooked it." One professional even compared this U.S. Open set-up to the John Deere Classic.

Okay, it wasn't Quad Cities, but there had never been a U.S. Open with more two-day rounds in the 60s. A total of 62 scores of 60-something were posted in the first two days. Among those who were making a mockery of par was Woody Austin, the journeyman former bank teller who had lost to Davis Love in a playoff at the MCI Heritage, but who was best known for knocking himself unconscious in 1997 after missing a short par putt and whacking himself in the head with the putter. Austin had broken 70 only one time in 11 previous U.S. Open rounds, and had a championship scoring average of 73.9 going into the week. He helped that average considerably on Friday with a seven-birdie, one-bogey 64, a score that was one shy of the U.S. Open single-round record.

"I had no idea (about the record), honestly no clue whatsoever," Austin said. "I was simply going through my mode of trying to get back in the game. I was trying to get back in the tournament." He did that with seven birdies in 14 holes between the second and 15th, after a three-putt bogey at the first. "After the three-putt on the first hole I settled myself down," he said. "I just put the ball exactly where I was supposed to put it on the greens. I didn't make any downhill sliders. I put the ball below the hole and I had so many chances all day."

That seemed to be the story of the day. Even if Austin had "no clue whatsoever" about the scoring record, it didn't matter by late afternoon. Vijay Singh, fresh out of the frying pan from his comments concerning Annika Sorenstam, shrugged the boo-birds off his shoulder and shot a championship-record 63, matching the U.S. Open single-round mark of Johnny Miller (1973, Oakmont), and Jack Nicklaus and Tom Weiskopf (1980, Baltusrol).

"I hit a lot of drivers out there," Singh said. "That wasn't my plan when I started off on Monday or at practice, but I started to swing a lot better and the ball was kind of going where I was aiming, so I said why not go ahead and be aggressive on the golf course, and I shot a good number."

He hit a perfect tee shot on the par-five first hole and hit his second shot just short of the green. When his chip shot went in for an eagle three, he was two under after one hole and had a jumpstart on a great round. Another great drive and a nine-iron approach to 10 feet set up a birdie at the second. He was three under after two.

After a sloppy bogey at the third, he hit an eight iron to 10 feet on the fourth and made another birdie. But he gave it back with an errant tee shot and three putts for a bogey at the par-five sixth, a hole that gave up four eagles and 57 birdies on Friday. Singh's six was one of only 16 bogeys on the hole all day. He parred in on the front nine before catching fire on the back.

A 30-footer on the 10th got him back to three under, and an 18-footer on the 11th moved him to four. He made a 10-footer at the 13th, a six-footer at the 14th and a 20-footer at the 15th to shoot only the third 29 in U.S. Open history. The only hiccup on the back came at the 14th when a spectator suggested that Annika Sorenstam would have holed her second shot from the fairway had she played it from the same spot as Singh. He had words with the man (a conversation Singh denied in his post-round interview), and Chicago's finest asked the spectator to watch the rest of the third round on television from an off-site location.

Not only did Singh deny his words, he forgot about some of the birdies he had made. "I wasn't aware I was making all those birdies," he said. "I was playing a hole at a time, so I started off and made a good putt on 10, and then kind of got the momentum going and I birdied 11 and three more after that. I was hitting it close, and feeling good about my game, so I wasn't emotionally concerned about the score; I was just playing my game, and enjoying it."

Asked if he realized how special his round was, Singh said, "It would have been better if I did it on Sunday. There are two more days to go. I'm going to focus on what I'm going to do tomorrow, and try to forget this round."

Remarkably, as good as Singh's round was, it didn't give him sole possession of the lead. Furyk went out early with Phil Mickelson and Darren Clarke. He made birdies on the first, sixth, 13th and 14th and had one of the few bogey-free rounds of the tournament. Even more impressive was the fact that the four birdie putts he made were from two, four, 10 and eight feet. As Furyk later said, it was "probably my best round to date in a U.S. Open. I had total control of the golf ball. I put it in play and hit a lot of greens."

He hit 17 greens to be exact and only missed one by a couple of feet. Furyk's four-under-par 66 tied him with Singh at 133, the two lowest 36-hole totals in U.S. Open history, breaking Nicklaus's record from 1980 at Baltusrol.

But where Nicklaus (and later T.C. Chen, Lee Janzen and Tiger Woods, who had equaled Nicklaus's 36-hole record) opened substantial leads through 36 holes, this one remained a race. Jonathan Byrd shot 66 to enter the weekend two shots back and tied at 135 with Stephen Leaney, who added 68 to his Thursday 67. Justin Leonard, Fredrik Jacobson, Eduardo Romero, Nick Price and the player everyone was watching, Tiger Woods, were tied at 136, three off the pace.

Woods birdied the first hole from a greenside bunker when his 15-footer found the hole. He got the crowd revved up by rolling in a 50-footer for birdie at the par-three fourth. He followed that up with a bogey at the fifth after misjudging his approach and leaving it short of the green. One hole later he got the shot back with a two-putt birdie at the sixth. When he hit a six-iron approach to two feet on the ninth for his fourth birdie of the round, everyone knew who was moving up the leaderboard.

The only other mistake Woods made was at the 11th, where he pulled a seven iron into the rough left of the green and had to hack it out 12 feet past the hole. That putt stayed low and left for Woods' second bogey of the day. He added two more birdies on the back when he hit pitching wedge to three feet at the 13th and sand wedge to eight feet at the 16th.

Woods summed up his round and his attitude. "It's a little bit easier to score when you're in the fairway," he said. "I just needed to get the ball in play. From there you can go ahead and decide if you want to get aggressive or play conservatively. And there's nothing wrong with making pars in the U.S. Open."

About the only players who weren't able to shoot under par on Thursday were the first-round leaders. Watson didn't hit enough fairways, and made a double bogey at the 12th to shoot 72, while Quigley limped in with 74. "I hope this is my bad round," Watson said. "The golf course is there for the taking. It was not as difficult as you would normally expect a U.S. Open course to be because of the softness of the greens. Some of pins were in more dangerous positions today, and I expect they'll be in more precarious positions tomorrow. You see some of the dots for tomorrow, and we're going to have some fun ones."

Through two rounds, the leaderboard shaped up like this:

Vijay Singh	63 - 133	Tiger Woods	66 - 136
Jim Furyk	67 - 133	Eduardo Romero	66 - 136
Jonathan Byrd	66 - 135	Nick Price	65 - 136
Stephen Leaney	68 - 135	Tom Watson	72 - 137
Justin Leonard	70 - 136	Robert Damron	68 - 137
Fredrik Jacobson	67 - 136		

In some other years, rounds of 69 and 75 in the U.S. Open would put a player on the leaderboard. This year, those results sent you home. Steve Flesch, Adam Scott, Tim Clark, Stuart Appleby, Tom Gillis and Jose Maria Olazabal were among the players at 144 who didn't make the 36-hole cut. For two rounds the field averaged 72.293, another 20-year U.S. Open low. Soft greens, short rough and little wind the first two days made the course seem, if not easy, "less difficult," as Furyk put it. "You never call a U.S. Open course easy," he said. "But some are more difficult than others."

Furyk found Olympia Fields to be just to his liking. After his first practice round on Monday he had told his father he liked the course. "It fits his eye," Mike Furyk said. "The holes set up perfectly for the way he shapes the ball."

Furyk continued to shape the ball perfectly on Saturday as he methodically picked his spots and played the kind of fairways-and-greens game that usually wins major championships. After starting the third round with four straight pars, Furyk split the middle of the fifth fairway with a driver and hit a seven iron to four feet for birdie. On the next hole he put to rest any questions about his length off the tee when he boomed a drive past the 350-yard mark and had only a five iron into the green on the 555-yard, par-five sixth.

He pushed his second shot a tad and the ball landed in the greenside bunker, but Furyk was always a master in the sand. He blasted out to two feet and sank the putt for his second birdie of the day. At the ninth, he added another birdie with a driver and pitching wedge to six feet. When that putt fell, so did another milestone. Furyk joined Tiger Woods and Gil Morgan as the only players in history to reach 10 under par in the U.S. Open. The fact that Furyk did it with 27 holes to play had a number of people wondering just how low the scores could possibly go.

Two bogeys and two birdies on the second nine (including a 40-foot birdie putt at the 15th that provoked the most emotional display of the week from Furyk), and the leader finished with 67 and a 54-hole U.S. Open scoring record of 10-under-par 200.

"I don't know if I had any expectations," Furyk said in typical fashion. "My goal was to go out and play a solid round of golf, and put myself in position for Sunday. I did that. Mission accomplished."

The position was probably better than he expected. After starting the day tied for the lead with Singh and three ahead of Woods, Furyk ended with a three-shot lead over Australian Stephen Leaney and five shots clear of Singh and Nick Price.

Singh struggled, shooting 72 after his 63 on Friday. He missed putt after critical putt on the back nine to shoot 38. "I was hitting good shots," he said. "I had two bad shots and had a bad break on my lie on 18, but that's the way it goes."

The biggest drama of the day came when Nick Price birdied five of his first six holes to jump into the lead by two strokes. Price had been lurking after rounds of 71 and 65, but he caught fire early when a 20-footer fell for birdie at the first hole. Always considered a great ball-striker, Price could still get on a roll that reminded people why he was once the No. 1 player in the world. He hit a three wood and pitching wedge to eight feet on the second and made that putt, and followed it up with a five iron, nine iron to 10 feet for another birdie at the third. When his eight-iron shot at the fourth stopped six feet away and that putt fell, Price took sole (albeit temporary) possession of the lead.

He extended that lead to two shots when he hit driver, five iron into the center of the green at the par-five sixth and two-putted from 25 feet for his fifth birdie. That was when the good times came to a screeching halt. Price hit the wrong club on the seventh hole and his ball plugged in the greenside bunker. He felt fortunate to make bogey from there. Another bogey on the ninth, followed by two more at the 11th and 12th, and the lead was gone. Price shot 69 and entered the final round tied with Singh for third place at five-under 205.

If Price's charge provided some temporary drama, the other big story on Saturday was the charge that never came. A sign of how Tiger Woods' day would go came early. On the first hole, he was about to make contact with his second shot of the day when someone in the gallery whistled, the sort of shrill noise that stops traffic. Frustrated, he dropped his club and shouted. But it wasn't whistlers that kept Woods from contending on this day; it was his putter. Woods had 35 putts and shot 75.

"I didn't play that poorly, that's the funny thing," Woods said. "I hit a lot of good shots, but I made nothing today. I could never get a feel for the line. I left every putt on the low side short, and the only putt I made, I said, 'just hit it three feet by,' and it went in the hole."

Stephen Leaney thought the greens were just right, but having played most of his competitive golf in Europe and Australia, he was accustomed to slightly slower putting surfaces. "The pin placements were difficult," he said. "You didn't have a lot of flat putts, even if you hit it to 10 feet."

Leaney hit to three feet on the first hole for the first of five birdies on his round. A six iron to six feet on the fourth marked the second birdie, and a nine iron to five feet on the ninth set up another birdie and a first-nine 32. He gave all those shots back in two holes. He pulled a five-iron approach at the 10th, caught a terrible lie in the rough, bladed his third shot over the green, hacked his fourth shot on, and two-putted for double bogey. A three-putt for bogey one hole later dropped Leaney back to even par on his round.

To his credit, he hung in there and hit some great shots coming in. A six iron to 20 feet on the 15th set up his fourth birdie of the day, and a stellar seven-iron shot that looked like it might go in the hole at the 18th set up an easy birdie for a two-under 68 and sole possession of second place at 203.

"You don't plan to have a chance to win — I guess you don't think that far ahead that you're thinking about winning the tournament," Leaney said. "You just want to get in position to win. And I've been pleased that I've been able to concentrate day-by-day, and not get too far ahead of myself. I haven't thought about winning the tournament at all this week, until just now. I'm only three shots back, but I'm not going to worry about winning unless I have a chance to win with a few holes tomorrow. I know that in the past to win tournaments you have to follow a lot of steps, and one of those steps is to stay in the present and just try to take one step at a time. That's what I have to draw on, and that's what I'm going to try to be thinking about."

With 18 holes to play, this was the leaderboard:

Jim Furyk	67 - 200	Eduardo Romero	71 - 206
Stephen Leaney	68 - 203	Jonathan Byrd	71 - 206
Nick Price	69 - 205	Mark O'Meara	67 - 207
Vijay Singh	72 - 205	Mark Calcavecchia	67 - 207
Dicky Pride	66 - 206	Billy Mayfair	67 - 207
Ian Leggatt	68 - 206		

Jim Furyk had never led by three strokes entering the final round of any tournament, much less the U.S. Open. And while he had been steady since joining the PGA Tour in 1994, there was a big difference between winning the Las Vegas Invitational and the Argentine Open and capturing your nation's national championship.

"I'm excited about the day," Furyk said. "I would always rather have the lead. I have to shoot that much less to go out and win this golf tournament." When asked if he had thought about what winning a major championship would mean to him, he said, "No, I don't like to put the cart before the horse."

All business, barely a smile, Furyk looked no different on Sunday morning than he did on Wednesday night. But inside was a churning volcano. Furyk could never remember being so nervous before a round of golf. He was so concerned about it that on the way to the golf course he mentioned his nervousness to his father.

"You're nervous?" Mike Furyk said. "That's good. If you're not tight, you're not going to win."

"This tight?" the son asked.

"This tight," answered his father.

It had been that way between the Furyk men for years. Mike caught immeasurable grief for the quirkiness of Jim's golf swing. But less was more in Mike Furyk's model. When Jim was nine years old, Mike told him how it was going to be. "I'll drop you off at tournaments, but I won't really follow you, because golf has a lot of pressure, and all I can do is add a lot of pressure by being there," he said. "There's nothing I can do out there. You have to do it for yourself."

Mike broke that rule only a few times, and only then when his son insisted on having him there. On one occasion, Jim hit a good drive on a par-five hole, but pulled his second shot into the rough. When he looked back at his dad, hoping to get a little help, Mike had another chat with him. "I said to him, 'If you think you're going to play the game and never hit a bad shot, you might as well get out of the game right now,'" Mike said. "'I know you're trying harder than anybody out here, and that's good enough for me. The next time you hit a bad shot and look for me, I'm not coming out again.' He never did look for me again. He understood that whatever he did, I was satisfied with him."

Those lessons served Furyk well as he teed off on Sunday. He hit a perfect three wood on the first hole and made a routine par, which extended his lead to four strokes. Leaney found the rough and started his day with a bogey six. Leaney came back with a solid birdie at the second, followed by another bogey at the third, and another birdie at the fourth. Through four holes, Leaney was even par without making a par, while Furyk had made nothing but pars. Two more bogeys by Leaney coupled with a steady diet of pars by Furyk, and the lead was five with nine holes to play.

That's when the rest of the field starting packing it in. Furyk might not have won any majors prior to this week, but everyone knew what kind of closer he was. "I consider myself a very hard worker and a guy that can grind it out in tough conditions," he said. "If I get over par early in a tournament, I won't just throw in the towel and make a plane reservation. I'll try to come back, squeak it out and make the cut. That's just me; that's how I grew up. I work hard, and I'll grind it out."

Those who might have had a chance at catching the leader shot themselves in the feet. Singh had three bogeys and one double bogey on the first nine. He shot 78 and finished tied for 20th. Price bogeyed the first hole and never got his putter working. He shot 75 to tie for fifth with Ernie Els, David Toms, Fredrik Jacobson and Justin Rose at 280.

The best round of the day went to one of the hottest players of the year. Kenny Perry, a back-to-back winner at Colonial and Memorial, shot 67 to reach red figures. He finished at 279 and tied for third with Masters champion Mike Weir.

Furyk would have to make some monumental mistakes to lose this one, an unlikely prospect given how well he was controlling his swing and his emotions. "I bogeyed 10," he said. "I hung a three wood out to the right and got too close to the bunker, so I laid up with a pitching wedge, hit my 60-degree wedge too hard, about 25 feet behind the hole, and two-putted for bogey.

"On 12, I pulled my driver a little bit and hit it in the short cut on the left. I think my best shot of the day was the second shot I hit there. I rifled a five iron right at the stick. I was licking my chops and thinking about how good a shot it was, and it landed four yards short of the green, and ended up 40 yards from the pin. So I went from my best shot of the day to really struggling to make bogey."

Furyk came back with a solid birdie from three feet at the 14th to keep the lead at five over Leaney, which made the bogey at the par-three 17th seem trivial. "I flew a three iron over the 17th green, and I just physically can't do that," Furyk said. "I can't figure out how the ball went so far. I pitched it short, and the first putt went six feet by. I was a mess at this point. But I knocked in a six-footer, made the bogey and went to the 18th tee."

At the final tee, with a four-shot lead, he asked his caddie what to hit.

Knowing that his man was fueled by adrenalin and seeing how far he had just hit a three iron on the previous hole, the caddie told Furyk to go with the three iron again. "I thought, 'You know what, that's a heck of a play,'" Furyk said. "I couldn't believe how far the three iron went, and I ended up hitting a seven iron to the back of the green.

"And then I lost it emotionally. The concentration was gone. I knew that I could pretty much do anything on that green and win the golf tournament. I knocked the first putt pretty far by, but had an uphill putt coming back, and couldn't focus on that second putt. I just wanted to get the golf tournament over with, and win."

He did just that, tapping in for a three-putt bogey and a three-stroke win. His 272 total matched the 72-hole scoring record set by Jack Nicklaus in 1980 and matched by Lee Janzen in 1993 and Tiger Woods in 2000, but Furyk couldn't have cared less that he let another record slip away with those final two bogeys.

"My wife and I were reading the names on the trophy on the 18th green during the presentation," Furyk said. "From a professional standpoint, that's the most special thing about it; my name will be on that trophy forever with some unbelievable names in golf. You can't take that away from me now. It's a special feeling."

4. The Open Championship

The Open Championship had seen its share of obscure winners since its founding back in 1860, a year before the American Civil War, but in the era beginning with the end of the Second World War, it seems safe to say none so surprising as Ben Curtis, a 26-year-old former Ohio Amateur champion playing not only his first year on the PGA Tour but his first national championship as a professional.

It seems equally safe to say that no one — well hardly anyone — had ever heard of Curtis until after he had played 36 holes or realized he had any kind of golf game.

All, that is, but Vijay Singh, who had been paired with him in the last round of the Western Open two weeks earlier. Singh shot 66 that day and placed 11th. Curtis shot 68 and tied for 13th, which assured him a place in the Open Championship field.

Singh had been impressed. Speaking to his wife, Ardena, Vijay said of Curtis, "He's no pushover. This guy can play."

Considering the developments at Royal St. George's Golf Club in July of 2003, Singh's comment seemed prophetic. Curtis was indeed no pushover. Curtis won the Open while four of the game's best players bumbled their way to second through fourth places. Over the last four testing holes, only Curtis holed a putt of any length, while Thomas Bjorn played them in four over par, Tiger Woods in two over, and Singh and Davis Love in one over.

Curtis played them in two over as well, but facing a breaking eight-foot putt to save par on the 18th, he rolled it in. The par four saved him; it held his total score to one under par, just enough to beat Bjorn and Singh by one stroke. With a round of 69 and a total of 283, only Curtis, the game's 396th ranked player, had beaten the formidable par.

Situated on England's southern coast beside the town of Sandwich, just across the English Channel from France, Royal St. George's had been transformed into a man-sized course since the 1993 Open, when Greg Norman, the swashbuckling Australian, won with a score of 267, 13 strokes under par, and beat Nick Faldo by two strokes.

Galleries that week had been treated to a scoring circus. Besides Norman and Faldo, 21 others shot under Sandwich's 72-hole par of 280, both Faldo and Payne Stewart shot 63s, and Norman shot 64. Ernie Els, playing in his third Open, shot four rounds in the 60s and finished seven strokes out of first.

In the years since, Sandwich had been lengthened and toughened. The club added nearly 250 yards to its length, stretching it from 6,860 yards in 1993 to 7,106 in 2003, tees had been repositioned to set up different angles into fairways, and a hot and dry summer had baked those fairways hard as a blacksmith's anvil.

Add the predictably unpredictable bounces on that heaving, tumbling land that kick even the well-placed drive into unplayable positions, and in Sandwich the field found a course that tested the imagination, the shot-making skills, and the patience and resolve of the world's premier players.

It surprised them as well.

Where 23 men had shot under 280 in 1993, not one approached that score in 2003. Par had been raised from 70 to 71 through a revision of the fourth hole, and at the end of four days, only Curtis broke the new par — by one bare stroke. Bjorn and Singh tied for second at even-par 284, and Woods and Love tied for fourth at 285.

Well into that last round, any of four other men could have won, but each of them failed.

Bjorn could have won, but three strokes ahead of Curtis with four holes to go, he played them in four over par. He lost every one of those strokes over the 15th, 16th and 17th holes, and two of those on the 16th alone, a par-three of 163 yards. He bunkered his tee shot and needed three shots to escape. Two shots rolled back into the bunker almost at his feet.

Woods could have won, but he overshot the 15th green, under-clubbed on the 17th, and bogeyed them both. Singh could have won, but he bunkered his tee shot on the 16th as well, and needing birdies, he could do no more than par the two closing holes.

Love could have won, but two strokes behind Bjorn, the leader after three rounds, he shot 39 on the first nine through a combination of loose iron play and timid putting, and while he struggled back, once again he left key putts short and fell into a tie for fourth, alongside Woods.

At the time he won, Curtis had played only 13 tournaments since he joined the PGA Tour — none of them major championships. He may have been the most unexpected winner of this championship since 1886, when David Brown won with a score of 157 for the 36 holes.

According to debatable legend, Brown had been busy following his craft as a chimney sweep when officials, charged with filling out the field, called him from someone's chimney, gave him a bath, dressed him and sent him to play at Musselburgh. So far as we know, after he collected his prize money, Brown climbed back up the chimney and completed the job.

Curtis had no such background, but like Brown, he had been a first-class golfer. He grew up in Ostrander, Ohio, about 30 miles north of Columbus, and lived in a house alongside the Mill Creek golf course, built, owned and run by his grandfather. His father, Bob Curtis, served as greenskeeper at the time Curtis won.

Ben began playing about the time he learned to walk, went through junior ranks, became very good at it, and moved on to Kent State University, where he earned All-America recognition.

He reached the semi-final round of the 1999 United States Amateur but lost to David Gossett, the eventual champion, at Pebble Beach, and was selected to play for the United States in the 2000 World Amateur Team championship, in Munich. Later in the year he turned to professional golf.

A man of honor, he disqualified himself from his first attempt at the U.S. PGA Tour, in 2000, because he thought he might have taken a wrong drop. He qualified on his third try, joined the 2003 Tour, then won a place in the Open field by his finish in the Western Open. Otherwise he would have been in Kent, Ohio, helping plan his wedding to Candace Beatty, who was there in Sandwich with him.

That the 2003 Open would be different became obvious from the start. Woods, who expected to win every tournament he entered, started with a seven on a par-four hole; Jerry Kelly made an 11 on the first as well; 48-

year-old Norman, playing in only his third tournament of the year, shot 69; Els began the defense of his 2002 championship with 78, effectively shooting himself out of it; both Jim Furyk, the U.S. Open champion, and Mike Weir, who had won the Masters, shot 74s; Steve Elkington, loser to Els in the 2002 playoff, shot 86 and withdrew, and Colin Montgomerie fell down before breakfast and hurt his right hand so badly he withdrew on the eighth hole. It had been quite an opening day.

When it ended, the field looked up and saw Hennie Otto in first place. A 27-year-old South African who would rather have played rugby but followed the money instead, Hennie shot 68, three under par on a course where holding a ball on the fairway could become a severe challenge. Perfectly placed drives often caromed off knobs into heavy rough.

Statistics claimed Woods hit only three fairways that first day, but those are misleading figures. He hit at least half the 14 fairways on driving holes, but the uneven ground kicked his ball into trouble. Good shots often brought poor results, but players of this caliber should know how to cope.

Furthermore, the day began rainy and ended windy. A fresh breeze swept in from the southwest at 20 to 25 miles an hour and often gusted to more than 30. Players unfamiliar with the course found the wind as troubling as capricious bounces.

A veteran of difficult conditions, Norman often aimed at a spot 30 or 40 yards left of a fairway and allowed the wind to carry the ball back into play. Younger players struggled with themselves to take such risks.

As a consequence, only five players scored under par that day. Aside from Otto, at 68, and Norman at 69, Love played quite a steady round of three birdies and a lone bogey on the 18th and shot 69, and S.K. Ho, a 29-year-old Korean playing in his first Open, shot 70, along with the Swede Fredrik Jacobson. Seven others matched par 71, and Ben Curtis shot 72, along with five others.

Although he finished among the 16 men who shot 73, Woods caused the major frenzy of the day when he pushed his first drive so far over the heads of forecaddies and marshals alike lining the first hole and so deep into matted grass it remained hidden until hours later when another marshal stepped on it. Woods believed it was the first lost ball of his professional career.

Driven back to the tee in a cart, Woods teed up another ball and hit it just as badly, but he found this one, hacked it across the fairway into more rough, pitched onto the green, and two-putted from 15 feet for his seven. With 71 holes still ahead of him, Woods played the rest of the round in one under par, still a viable threat.

Kelly struggled even harder than Woods, although he did find his drive in deep rough. He took nine more shots to reach the green, often moving the ball no more than a yard or two, and once on, holed a putt from 30 feet to avoid shooting an even dozen. Hacking through the grass, though, he injured a finger and withdrew.

Montgomerie had to give it up as well. Leaving his hotel to have breakfast with friends, he felt raindrops, looked up, stumbled over a step, fell forward, thrust out his right hand to break the fall, and injured his wrist. He tried to play, but gave up, afraid he might cause more damage if he played on.

Montgomerie fell at about 7:30 that morning. By then, Otto had been on the course for an hour. He had climbed out of bed at 4 o'clock to make his 6:30 starting time. A man of passion, Otto had once snapped the shafts of every one of his clubs and dumped them into a river, but he played calmly and serenely through the first round, even though he looked as if he might have fallen to two over par after four holes.

Els began just before 2 o'clock, grouped with David Toms, the 2001 PGA champion, and Shigeki Maruyama, the good-natured Japanese golfer who had tied for fifth at Muirfield in 2002. All three played dismal golf. Maruyama shot 83 and Toms played only a little better, shooting 80. Neither figured in the championship.

Els had been having a good year. He had looked especially sharp in winning the Barclays Scottish Open the week before the Open, the third tournament he had won on the European Tour, and he had won twice in the United States as well. But after an enthusiastic greeting from the gallery gathered by the first tee, he played loose golf and stumbled home in 78.

His first hole should have been a clue. He drove into the rough, his second shot reached the green, but his 40-foot putt died halfway to the hole, and he missed the second. He scrambled to save par on the second, birdied neither the fourth nor the seventh, two highly vulnerable par-fives, and after driving so close to the green of the fifth a birdie seemed certain, he slunk away with another par. He dropped a stroke on the eighth, a par-four of 455 yards, where he drove into the right rough, hit his approach even farther right, pitched on with his third, rammed his first putt against the back of the hole, and stared as it stubbornly refused to fall. Another bogey on the ninth, and Els had gone out in 40.

Still playing shabby golf, Els began the homeward nine with a string of three-putt bogeys, came back in 38, and at the end of the day found himself 10 strokes behind a fellow South African few at Sandwich had heard of before noon.

Els' uninspired golf couldn't match Norman's confident, attacking game — controlling the ball and playing his shots low so they would bore through the wind.

His play of the fourth stood out. His drive settled in the fairway below the level of the green, 194 yards away. With the wind in his face, Greg rifled a low four iron that hit short, scooted onto the green, ran directly at the flagstick, and died within a foot of the hole. An easy eagle three.

Norman said later he had four options with that shot.

"I could have hit a five iron, landed it on the front of the green and let it bounce once and stop, hook it to the front with a six iron, or tried to fly it on top by cutting a high four iron and holding it against the wind. It made more sense to me to hit it about 165 to 167 yards and let it go. It was just a half four-iron shot, really."

With his birdie on the fourth, Norman reached the turn in 33 strokes, three under par. When he played another four iron to about five feet and birdied the 11th, a 242-yard par-three, he had moved to four under par. If he could hold on, he would shoot 67. Instead, he lost two strokes and came back in 36. Still, Norman had turned in a remarkable round under trying conditions.

"It was a very difficult day," he said. "If I'd been given a 69 before I went to the first tee, I'd have more than settled for it."

This was the leaderboard after the first round:

Hennie Otto	68	Tom Watson	71
Greg Norman	69	Fred Couples	71
Davis Love	69	Charles Howell	71
S.K. Ho	70	Thomas Levet	71
Fredrik Jacobson	70	Mathias Gronberg	71
Gary Evans	71	Scott McCarron	71

Otto's reign didn't last. Allowed to sleep in before his 11:26 starting time the next morning, he showed none of the sharpness of his first round, shot 76, yet landed softly. He fell no further behind than fourth place, alongside six others, a group that included Kenny Perry, who had won three of the last four tournaments he had played, Thomas Levet, a loser to Els in the 2002 Open playoff, Sergio Garcia, a gallery favorite, and Curtis, who shot his second 72. All seven tied at 144.

The lead belonged to Love, at 141 after a solid round of 72. With 73, Ho tied for second place at 143 with Bjorn, who had opened with 73 and added 70 in the second round.

Woods added 72 to his opening 73 and at 145 tied for 11th, along with Singh and three others. Both men would be in contention until the very end. Els shot 68, which jumped him into a tie for 16th place, but Norman lost his touch and shot 79, fully 10 strokes over his opening 69, and fell into a tie for 35th.

At least he survived for the last two rounds. The 36-hole cut fell at 150, an unusually high figure for the times. Even so it caught Jim Furyk, who only a month earlier had won the U.S. Open, David Toms, Gary Wolstenholme, the Amateur champion, Ricky Barnes, the U.S. Amateur champion, Justin Rose, the young man who at 17 had nearly won the 1998 Open, and sadly, David Duval, who had played such wonderful golf at Royal Lytham and St. Annes two years earlier. Suddenly no longer able to play at this level, Duval shot 83-78–161 and missed by 11 strokes.

Once again Sandwich demonstrated there would be no reprise of 1993. Not only had Els shot the lowest round of the day, just eight others broke par and 11 more shot 71. Only Els had shot in the 60s, just the fourth in two rounds. Nevertheless, the course could be beaten.

Among those at 70, Mark Roe opened with six consecutive threes, added one more on the second nine, along with a two, but ruined his round with an eight on the 14th. Paul Casey had shot 85 in the first round, but he went out in 31 in the second and came back in 40. Scott McCarron shot into the lead briefly by birdieing five holes on the first nine, offset by bogeys on the first two, and shot 33. It all evaporated coming in, though, and McCarron shot 74, with a seven on the 17th.

The field had averaged 75.15 strokes. If the Royal and Ancient Golf Club had meant to create a formidable course, one where par meant something, it certainly succeeded here. Sandwich may have been the toughest playable course within memory. Carnoustie in 1999 had been a terror, but it had been made severe with bridle-path fairways and wheat-field rough. Sandwich may have produced quirky bounces, but its wider fairways fed into short rough, and for the most part, the deep stuff caught only the poorly played shots.

Love looked to be in serious trouble only once. He had played steady golf through the first six holes, then birdied the seventh, the easiest hole on the course — it gave up 125 birdies and eight eagles through the first two rounds — and had another on the ninth.

Out in 34, two under par, he had lost those strokes by bogeying three of the first four holes on the homeward nine. Usually a high-ball player, Love tried to punch a shot into the 10th but pushed it enough that the ball tumbled into a greenside bunker, costing him one stroke.

A five iron to 10 feet set up a birdie on the 11th, but he three-putted the 12th from about 30 feet, and trying to play a safe drive on the 13th, he pulled his tee shot into knee-high grass and lost another stroke.

Now, standing on the 14th tee and looking at the out-of-bounds stakes, he chose to play safe and drive with his three iron once again. And again, instead of splitting the center of the fairway, his ball drifted right, caught one of those dreaded slopes, and headed toward Prince's.

Love saw the ball scoot right, but then heaved a sigh of relief as the marshal signaled that all was well. He learned later that the ball had hit squarely against one of the stakes, rebounded to safe ground, and settled on a little tuft of grass.

His had been a remarkable stroke of luck. Had his ball slipped between those stakes, he'd have had to play another shot from the tee — his third — and most likely score no better than seven. As it was, he made his par five, played the next four holes in one over par, and took over first place.

Finding Ho in second place surprised the gallery as much as seeing Curtis so close behind. After Ho had played the first seven holes of the opening round in even par, someone asked Els what he knew of him. Els offered only the obvious: "He has a shorter surname than mine."

He had also played 36 holes in three fewer strokes than Els and rested in second place, alongside the fiery Bjorn, who the previous day had cost himself a two-stroke penalty. Failing to recover from a greenside bunker alongside the 17th, Bjorn slashed at the sand, a rules violation since his ball still lay in the sand. It would cost him dearly later in the week.

Ho played the game with far less passion. He came from Korea, where his father owned a driving range in Pusan, on the southeast coast. Since Korea had so few professional tournaments, Ho played the Japanese Tour, where he ranked 17th in money winnings. Preparing for the Open, he flew to Christchurch, New Zealand, so he could practice playing in the wind — obviously a judicial move considering his 70 in the blustery opening round. He started even more strongly in the second, but his game unraveled on the second nine.

Off just before noon, Ho birdied the third, the first of the par-three holes, then played two strong shots onto the fourth green and holed the putt for an eagle three. Four under par for 22 holes, he had taken the lead.

Perhaps his nerves frayed at the thought, but he lost strokes on the eighth and ninth but still turned for home in 35, one under par. Only solid putting kept him going, especially a long one of perhaps 30 feet that saved a par three on the 16th, and he came back in 38.

In contrast to the opening round, Woods teed off late in the day, as usual before a huge gallery that lined up three and four deep along the first fairway wondering if he would go with his driver once more or play a safer club. Woods chose discretion, played a three wood, and this time kept his ball visible. Safely past the first, he pitched to about 10 feet and birdied the second and added two more on the fourth and seventh, the two defenseless par-fives.

He had begun the day two over par, and now, with three birdies, he stood one over par for 25 holes and had closed in on the leaders. It wasn't to last, though. He overshot the ninth by a great distance and bogeyed, overshot the 10th as well but holed a 30-footer to save par. Then he played the 12th.

Perhaps not Sandwich's easiest hole, at 381 yards it is the shortest of the par-fours. Its green had none of those deep and dangerous pot bunkers, but it was long and narrow and fell away at the sides. Woods' approach caught the slope on the right, rolled to the bottom of the incline, and settled on the green's collar.

Taking his putter, Woods rolled the ball up the incline three feet past the hole. Stepping up to the ball, he rolled it three feet past once again. Another try gained some ground, but still the ball hadn't touched the hole. Then he tapped it in.

He claimed — with a smile — that since his ball had rested on the green itself, "Technically it had been a three-putt." Actually, it had been a four-putt.

No matter, he had taken six strokes, and when he bogeyed the 17th, he had shot 72 and lagged four strokes behind Love with 36 holes to play. The Open still lay within his reach.

These were the second-round leaders:

Davis Love	72 - 141	Marco Ruiz	71 - 144
S.K. Ho	73 - 143	Alastair Forsyth	70 - 144
Thomas Bjorn	70 - 143	Tiger Woods	72 - 145
Ben Curtis	72 - 144	Vijay Singh	70 - 145
Hennie Otto	76 - 144	Scott McCarron	74 - 145
Sergio Garcia	71 - 144	Mathias Gronberg	74 - 145
Kenny Perry	70 - 144	Chad Campbell	71 - 145
Thomas Levet	73 - 144		

Woods played one miracle shot and Garcia played another, three men shot 67s, the lowest rounds of the week, but one was disqualified, and Bjorn inched to the top of the leaderboard by shooting 69 and replacing Love.

Bjorn had been but one of eight men who shot in the 60s, while 11 others shot 70 and nine more shot 71. A total of 28 men had either matched or broken Sandwich's par.

In what seemed the most significant move of the day, Woods finally gave his fans what they yearned for by playing the first nine in 31; Nick Faldo caused a frenzy by shooting 67, and Pierre Fulke, a stocky, 5-foot-8 Swede, shot his own 67 a few hours later.

Mark Roe shot 67 as well, but unfortunately he had committed a fatal sin. Because he and Jesper Parnevik, his playing companion, had neglected to switch scorecards, they had recorded each other's scores on their own cards. Both men were disqualified under rule 6-6d — *Wrong score for hole.* It reads: "The competitor is responsible for the correctness of the score recorded for each hole on his card. If he returns a score for any hole lower than actually taken, he shall be disqualified. If he returns a score higher than actually taken, the score as returned shall stand."

Furthermore, because Decision 6-6d/4 deals specifically with this situation, the R and A had no wiggle room; despite pleading from other players and the R and A's soul-searching, the ruling stood. The mix-up could have been corrected simply by switching the names on the scorecards, but no one noticed until after both Roe and Parnevik had signed their scorecards and walked off.

Otherwise it had been a normal, unpredictable day. The sun blazed down, sending temperatures into the high 70s, unfamiliar territory for the natives, the wind had calmed during the second round and remained gentle throughout the third, and yet no one had taken Sandwich by the throat. After his blistering opening nine, Woods stumbled back in 38, shot 69, and climbed into a tie for third place, at 214, with Singh, Perry, Garcia and that fellow Curtis.

Bjorn shot 69 as well and took over first place at 212, when Love turned in another 72 and fell to second at 213.

While Curtis shot 70, his best round of the week, Ho slipped to 72 and dropped into a tie with Philip Price at 215. Price had shot 69, one of eight rounds in the 60s that day, and 11 more shot 70, one under par. By then only Bjorn, Singh, Perry and Fredrik Jacobson had played two rounds under par.

Just when someone believed he had taken a grip on Sandwich, the strokes he had won evaporated through unpredictable bounces, putts that broke in two or three different directions and escape-proof bunkers. Els made up no ground by shooting 72, and Otto continued falling back by shooting 75 and dropping into a tie for 27th with Phil Mickelson, who appeared lost with rounds of 74, 72 and 73.

In one of the day's improbable episodes, Nick Faldo had observed his 45th birthday on Friday but celebrated on Saturday by tearing around Sandwich in four under par so early in the day only three men had finished before he posted his 67. Since the course had been strengthened substantially in the 10 years since he and Payne Stewart set the course record at 63, he could be said to have broken his own record.

Out in 34, two under par, Faldo took the adventurous route home. He parred only the 12th, 15th and 16th and bogeyed the 10th and 13th, but he took back those lost strokes with birdies on the 11th, where his four-iron tee shot settled within 20 feet of the hole, and the treacherous 14th, where he played a 60-yard pitch-and-run to eight feet.

He drove his galleries to frenzied cheering by birdieing the two closing holes with classic iron play — a three iron to four feet on the dangerous 17th, then a seven iron to eight feet on the 18th. His finish brought back memories of a past decade when Faldo had been the game's best, most reliable player.

Meantime, off hours later than Faldo, Woods began slowly, missing the first green but chipping close for an easy par four, then two-putted both the second and third. For two days now the galleries had waited for Woods to break out and play as he had so often before. Now he brought those galleries to life on the fourth, the first of the par-fives.

A big drive placed him within a five-iron shot of the green. He ripped it within 20 feet of the hole, then ran the putt home for an eagle three.

Two more pars and then Woods came to the seventh, the second of those vulnerable par-fives. Another big drive, then a pitch from 150 yards that bounced along the edge of the green, then tumbled into a bunker. A superb bunker player, Woods dug it out, and as the gallery gasped, his ball ran along the ground and dived into the hole. A second eagle three. When the ball fell, the roar of the crowd must have been heard across the golf course.

Now four under, he birdied the ninth and turned for home in 31, five under par, good enough to move into first place, two strokes ahead of both Bjorn and Singh.

When he was at his best, Woods had been nearly invulnerable once he took the lead, but here the strokes slipped away again. He missed the 11th green and three-putted the 13th from 30 feet, losing two strokes, then almost made them up on the 14th. On the green with two big shots, he read his 20-footer perfectly. His ball broke left as it approached the hole and looked as if it might miss by a foot, but then it swung right and died looking over the back lip. A birdie there, but he lost two more strokes over the last four holes, came back in 38, and shot 69, his best round. But he didn't lead the championship.

Nor did Love, who played loose golf over the first nine, three-putting the first and fifth holes. Davis took one stroke back by holing from six feet on the seventh, but he gave it back on the eighth, where he rolled his first putt 12 feet past and missed coming back. Out in 38, by then he had fallen from first place into third.

Love had played dull golf, to be sure, but he had won three tournaments earlier in the year and had the experience to bounce back. Curtis, on the other hand, had never been in this situation and looked as if he had gone as far as he could go. Three bogeys and a lone birdie and he too had gone out in 38, about what everyone expected.

But he had not been expected to run off five threes on the second nine and come home in 32. He birdied the 10th and 15th, then added another at the 17th, which gave up strokes grudgingly. Short of the 18th green with his approach, he ran his third shot within three feet of the hole. Facing the kind of putt that makes strong men quiver, Curtis rolled it in as coolly as if he had been on the practice green. With 70, he stood only one over par for 54 holes and left the impression he might just possibly finish well the next day — perhaps even contend.

Love, though, dropped another stroke by bunkering his tee shot on the 11th and missing a six-foot putt, but a drive and one iron onto the 14th green and a 30-foot eagle putt saved his day. Davis closed with four solid pars and shot 72, one over for the day, even par for 54 holes.

Singh played a strange round. Starting with five straight pars, he made only two more the rest of the day. He either birdied, eagled or bogeyed the other 11 holes, and when he pieced together this debris, he had shot 69 and claimed a share of third place.

Then there was Garcia. Woods had played the first of the day's two miracle shots by holing from the bunker on the seventh. Garcia played the other, saving the most ridiculous par of the championship.

Effervescent as ever at the start, Garcia turned grim when he bogeyed the second hole and turned even grimmer by committing the sin of taking a six at the seventh, where birdies were common and eagles frequent. He won back those strokes by birdieing the 10th and 14th, a far more testing hole than the seventh, and moved to the 17th at even par. Here he played a hole that defies belief.

First, he pulled his drive into knee-deep grass and took a violent swing, hoping to pitch toward the distant green. As he swung into the ball, everyone looked up, expecting to see a ball in mid-flight. Instead, they saw nothing; Garcia had only driven his ball deeper into the grass. Now began a frenzied search for a ball lying no more than three or four feet from its original position. Garcia and his caddie gingerly parted stands of grass, but still the ball remained hidden. They must have looked for two or three minutes before Sergio found it. Now taking the shorter route, he chopped at it again, and this time flew it onto safe ground on the fairway near a spectators' crosswalk about 60 yards short of the green.

Lying three now, in danger of dropping two strokes, Garcia drew a lofted club, played a pitch-and-run that hit short, ran onto the green and darted directly at the hole. While Sergio stared and the gallery drew its breath, the ball slammed against the flagstick and dropped into the hole. A bizarre par four.

Garcia flung his arms heavenward and broke into an expansive grin, and the gallery whooped and yelled. Lucky or not, the shot saved Garcia's skin. With 70, he tied four others for third place.

While Woods, Garcia and Curtis, too, had warmed the galleries, Bjorn had played what at a glance appeared a dull though efficient round that could have been three or four strokes better. He had eagled the fourth, holing from 15 feet, bogeyed the fifth, birdied the seventh, and then run off 11 straight pars.

Even so, his had been a frustrating day. One after another makeable putt had looked into the hole and glided past. As each putt missed, he stared and smiled a rueful smile, then moved on to the next hole. No fits of temper that matched his impulsive slash at the sand in the first round.

At the end he had moved into first place, leading by one stroke over Love with just 18 holes to play.

The third-round leaderboard:

Thomas Bjorn	69	- 212	Philip Price	69	- 215
Davis Love	72	- 213	S.K. Ho	72	- 215
Tiger Woods	69	- 214	Pierre Fulke	67	- 216
Vijay Singh	69	- 214	Gary Evans	70	- 216
Kenny Perry	70	- 214	Peter Lonard	70	- 216
Sergio Garcia	70	- 214	Fredrik Jacobson	70	- 216
Ben Curtis	70	- 214			

By the time the fourth round opened, it had become clear that low scores depended on picking up strokes on the first nine, because the homeward nine would not yield. For example, Woods had played the first nine in five under par through the first three rounds, but the second nine had cost him six precious strokes. Curtis, by contrast, had played the first nine in three over par and the second in two under. At the end of the day, Curtis had played the first nine in one under and the second in even par while Woods had played the first nine in six under and the home nine in eight over.

Sandwich had indeed turned into an unexpectedly stern test of the game. Where in 1993 a score of 67 hardly caught anyone's attention, in 2003 we had three, and only two of those counted. But as the final round began, more than one man started out as if he might lower the course record.

Padraig Harrington ran off four straight birdies, Darren Clarke birdied three of the first four holes, Norman stood two under after seven, and Faldo birdied the fifth and eagled the seventh — three under. Of those, only Faldo mattered. Harrington shot 69 and tied for 22nd; Clarke shot 74 and tied for 59th, and Norman, who had thrilled the galleries with his opening 69, shot 68 this day, but tied for 18th place at 290. This had been a very good championship for Greg.

It hadn't been bad for Otto, either. After his opening 69, Otto had played dull golf through the next two rounds, then sprang back to life with 69 in the last and climbed into a tie for 10th place. Brian Davis shot 68, which, along with Norman's, was the best score of the day and jumped him into a tie for eighth, alongside Fredrik Jacobson, at 286, three strokes behind Curtis.

After his eagle on the seventh, Faldo had nothing left, shot 70, and at 287 tied for eighth with Kenny Perry.

While a few had played well, others had not. Ho slumped to 77 and dropped into a tie for 28th, and Garcia, two strokes behind Bjorn as the day began, birdied only two holes, bogeyed five, shot 74, and joined Otto in the 10th-place tie.

Even though Curtis had never before played under this kind of tension, he carried himself as if he had spent his life playing championship golf. Instead of wilting under the pressure, he thrived. From the first tee he lashed a drive that drifted into the short rough, pitched to five or six feet, and walked toward the green with long, ground-eating strides so common to those raised in the country. Then he holed the putt.

With the birdie, he had caught Love and closed within a stroke of Bjorn. From then on the Open turned into a dogfight as Love, Bjorn, Woods, Singh and Curtis struggled to defeat this unyielding course that tested every shot in their arsenal and every ounce of their character.

Two-putt pars on both the second and third holes, then a two-iron second to 20 feet and a seeing-eye putt that never looked like anything but falling and Curtis had another birdie on the fourth. Two under now, he had passed Bjorn, who by then had missed the first green and bogeyed.

Ben's pitch missed the fifth green and his chip rolled six feet past the hole, but facing another of those putts that must be holed, Curtis rolled it in and added to his credentials as a contender.

Now the gallery began taking him seriously. He had been applauded before, but only as a game young man in over his head, yet showing unexpected determination. From what he had shown this day, some saw him as a potential winner and urged him on.

Another par on the sixth, and Curtis moved on to the seventh, where he must birdie or lose a stroke to the field. Drawing back his three wood, he drilled a drive into playable position in the short rough and followed with a seven iron to the front of the green. His first putt just missed falling for an eagle three, so he took his birdie and added a routine par on the eighth. Three under for the day, two under for the championship, Ben looked as if he could run away from the field.

Now Curtis ran off three straight birdies that put him in command of the championship. He might have made it four had his putt on the eighth rolled a touch farther instead of stopping inches short. One hole later, left with an awkward lie in the short rough right of the ninth fairway, Curtis pitched inside two feet, went out in 32, and dipped four under for the round.

Not through yet, he pitched to 20 feet and birdied the 10th, then played a five iron to 15 feet and birdied the short 11th. Curtis had putted beautifully; he had played those 11 holes in six under par and led the field by two strokes. Still, seven tough holes lay ahead.

Meanwhile, as Curtis piled up the birdies, Love had been playing shabby golf. He had gone out in 39, and although he settled himself on the home nine, his closing 72 wasn't nearly good enough.

All the while, Woods remained the most dangerous player within reach of Curtis, capable of golf others only dreamed of. He barely missed holing from 30 feet on the first hole, played a nice running shot into the second and came away with another par, then birdied three of the next four holes. His birdie on the fourth showed just what he could do. Bunkered with his second shot, he pitched out to 10 feet and holed for the birdie four, then barely missed an eagle on the seventh. With the birdie, he stood two under par for the distance.

By then Singh had dipped to three under and taken over first place, followed by Bjorn, Woods and Curtis.

The tension had been building throughout the afternoon as first one player made a move and fell back, then another. No one could quite grasp who would come out on top. Eventually, every one of them tossed away strokes like confetti at a parade.

Woods made no further headway and threw it away with loose approaches to the 15th and 17th, and Singh played the last 11 holes in three over par, losing his chance.

Playing behind Singh and Woods, Bjorn had bogeyed the first hole by overshooting the green, but he birdied the third, added another at the fourth with a long drive, a 200-yard five iron and two putts, and still another at the seventh. At that moment, he, Singh and Curtis all stood at three under par, but from the eighth through the 11th Bjorn missed a series of makeable putts that could have made the difference.

Curtis, too, lost his touch. Missing fairways, missing greens, and missing holeable putts, he bogeyed the 12th, 14th and 15th. Safely past the 16th, Ben played a six-iron approach that carried to the front of the 17th green's false front and rolled back off. One more bogey, his fourth in six holes, and he had fallen back to one under par. He had squandered all but two of the strokes he had won over the first 11 holes. When his approach scooted over the 18th green and his chip glided eight feet past coming back, it looked like the end. Instead, he read the putt correctly and played the shot as if he had no nerves at all. It dropped for the par and his 69. He had finished the 72 holes in one under par.

Nevertheless, he had fallen three strokes behind Bjorn.

Then Bjorn fell apart. His breakdown began with a drive into a fairway bunker that cost him one stroke on the 15th and climaxed on the 16th, the hole that ruined him.

He had played cautiously throughout the day, aiming his approaches for the middle of the greens, but watching Love play a neat draw into the 16th that settled left of the hole, he tried to play a similar shot. It was a big mistake. The hole had been cut close to the right side near the edge of a gentle slope above a bunker. Bjorn's ball hung right of the hole, took the contour of the ground, and rolled into the bunker.

Perhaps he tried to play too good a shot, but his first try stopped short of level ground and rolled back to his feet. His second fell short again, and as the gallery groaned, it, too, tumbled back, but this time into a deep depression, either a footprint or the equivalent of a divot in the sand. As the ball fell back into the sand once again, Bjorn simply stared.

He made it out with his third attempt and holed the putt, but he had taken five shots to play a par-three hole, wasted two precious strokes, and fallen into a tie with Curtis.

Curtis had been watching on a television set in a temporary cabin near the practice ground, where he had been warming up for a possible playoff. He continued warming up after Bjorn bogeyed the 17th as well and fell a stroke behind, and he continued even after Bjorn parred the home hole, where he needed a birdie to tie.

With that, Ben Curtis had won the 2002 Open Championship. In winning, Curtis had shown character as well as shot-making skill. He improved his scoring each day and saved his best until the last with a closing 69. Sandwich gave up only 24 rounds in the 60s — 25 if we count Roe's — and Curtis's closing round was among them. Only Greg Norman, Brian Davis and Hennie Otto broke 70 twice.

Curtis had actually won the championship on the second nine of the third round and the first nine of the fourth. Since he had closed his third round with 32, when he shot another 32 going out the last day, he had played his last 18 holes in 64. He finished with 37 strokes on the home nine — just good enough.

5. PGA Championship

After four grueling days on a golf course that looked more like a U.S. Open venue than the one that hosted this year's Open, the 85th PGA Championship came down to the 72nd hole, and wasn't decided until Shaun Micheel hit the shot of the year. Where Micheel's seven-iron shot from the first cut of rough on Oak Hill Country Club's 18th hole ranks among the great shots in major championship history will be open for debate. What is inarguable is that it was the best shot of 2003 and the best of the 34-year-old Micheel's until-then-undistinguished career.

The champion recounted the hole this way: "I just tried to trust my swing," Micheel said. "From what it looked like from the tee, I got a pretty nice bounce. Could have bounced left or maybe even straight and gone into the primary cut, but it got just enough of a bounce right. The ball was sitting up. The first cut of rough this week, the ball just sits up magnificently. It's in great condition. I was in a pretty good spot there. I had 162 yards to the front, a little bit into the wind and a little bit left-to-right with a perfect lie."

The hole was cut 13 paces from the front edge, leaving Micheel 175 yards. He hit a seven-iron shot that never left the flag. "It was an absolutely perfect number," Micheel said. "I knew it was pretty close. I had to ask somebody how close it was. I saw it was only two inches, and I figured I could make that one."

The birdie on the 18th gave Micheel an even-par 70 on his round for a four-under-par 276 total, two strokes better than runner-up Chad Campbell, who was playing alongside Micheel, and who had hit his approach 18 feet beyond the hole. A birdie by Campbell and a miscue by Micheel, and the outcome could have been different. As it was, Campbell made par for a 72 and 278 total, and Micheel became only the seventh player to make the PGA Championship his first PGA Tour win, and the seventh to win this major in his first appearance. He also rivaled British Open champion Ben Curtis as an unlikely major championship winner.

But it wasn't like Micheel was a straight-out-of-college rookie with an outstanding amateur career (such as Jerry Pate in the 1976 U.S. Open) or a way-down-the-list alternate who shocked the crowd with his prodigious length (John Daly). This championship was Micheel's 164th start since earning his PGA Tour card in 1994. Before that he had spent three years in the hinterlands of the Asian, Hooters and Nike Tours before landing a steady job on the PGA Tour. "It's kind of scary, really," Micheel said. "A year ago I was trying to win the B.C. Open, and up until a month ago, I was trying to keep my card. I really can't believe this happened to me."

The feeling was mutual. Watching at the family home in Collierville, Tennessee, Shaun's father, Buck, said, "I've seen him on a roll a couple of times at the club, but never in a tournament. His putter saved him." Buck's point was well taken. Even though the final seven iron was the most memorable shot of the tournament, Micheel's putter saved him. He averaged 28.7 putts per round, and was third in the field in greens hit in regulation with an average of 12 per round. That combination resulted in 21 birdies, the most all week, a surprise to everyone, including Micheel, who came into the week ranked 181st in putting.

"I always seem to battle myself," Micheel said. "I may not be the most patient person, but at least I kind of plod my way around the golf course. I've had a lot of tournaments where something negative just creeps into my head at the wrong time. It's amazing, you think the words 'three putt,' and the next thing you know, you've got a six- or seven-footer, and you three-putt the hole. I just wish that I could turn that around into something positive. I wish I could think, 'Wow, I'm going to make this putt,' and actually make it."

Micheel didn't think he was going to make everything, but he didn't believe he would three-putt either. "I think that you can look back in history, the major champions, the guys that win the majors, they play golf a certain way," Micheel said. "Maybe that's why they don't win 20 regular tour events where it takes 20 under to win. I seem to play to the fairway, and I play to the middle of the green. Some tournaments you can't do that. You cannot do that at the Bob Hope Chrysler Classic where it takes 30 under to win. Those tournaments are not good for me."

If Micheel's golf game were a paint color, it would be primer gray — nothing flashy, and certainly no distinguishing characteristics. After the third round, Micheel had to answer questions about how fans were going to tell the two co-leaders apart in the final round. "I guess I'll have to call him in the morning to make sure we don't dress alike," Micheel said.

That sort of dry humor (and a game that matched it) was perfect for this particular set-up at Oak Hill, a course that Tiger Woods called, "the toughest, fairest course we've ever played." Others weren't so kind in their comments about the famous course in the Rochester suburb of Pittsford, New York. "I don't know why you have to make it unplayable," said Steve Flesch, who opened with 79, came back with 70 and missed the cut by one stroke. "There is a lot more to playing golf than hitting it down the fairway. This is not golf. I just think it's kind of a chicken way of setting up a golf course." Mark Calcavecchia said, "One week of this is okay, but if we had a steady diet of this stuff, you'd see a bunch of guys in the hospital or at the back doctor or with broken wrists." Jerry Kelly, who shot 78 and 75 and went home early, asked rhetorically, "Do you need to see carnage to have a great champion? I don't think so."

The brunt of the criticism concerned the rough, which had been thickened and lengthened. It wasn't exactly what the PGA of America had in mind, but as Kerry Haigh, director of tournament operations, said, "Two and a half or three weeks ago, we were struggling to get the rough to grow, it had been so dry. We consciously tried to get it boosted to make it championship rough." The "boost" included a heavy dose of fertilizer. "We got over three inches of rain the first 10 days of August," Haigh said. "Once you're into the championship, you don't want to be bailing hay. The grass was wet, the heavy mowers were just laying it over, not cutting it."

Hand mowers were brought out, but it was too little, too late. As Paul Azinger described it, "You hit it in the rough, your hopes are gone. If the hole is a three wood, five iron, you're better off hitting the five iron first, keeping it in the fairway and then trying to hit the three wood on the green. It's really, really hard, but I think it's very, very fair. This place is claustrophobic. You know if you miss, there are places where it's a disaster. Any miss, you're not going to reach the green in two."

Woods concurred with that opinion. "Carnoustie wasn't fair. This is fair, but this is by far the hardest we've ever played," Woods said. "I mean, the wind hasn't blown yet, and we've gotten kind of lucky. If it would have blown around this course, over par would have won this tournament easily."

As it turned out, only three players broke par for the week in relatively calm conditions — the other was South Africa's Tim Clark at 279 — and the field averaged 74.31 on the par-70 layout. There were 4,700 pars for the week and a whopping 3,554 bogeys, double bogeys and higher scores. Almost all of that over-par play was attributable to the rough. From spots other than the fairway, the course played an average of nine shots harder than it did if your ball found a closely mown area. As Tom Watson put it, "You're not supposed to reward anybody for hitting it in the rough at a PGA Championship."

Even the winner thought it was tough. As he was accepting the Wanamaker Trophy from PGA executive director Jim Awtry, Micheel said, "Can I please come back and play after you've mowed it?" That brought a hearty laugh from the gallery, all of whom had witnessed the best in the world struggle to advance the ball. Later on Sunday night, Micheel said, "I showed up on Tuesday to play a practice round and saw how difficult this golf course was. I was just trying to make the cut. That was my main goal, and I probably would have been happy with that."

Five days after that first exposure to Oak Hill, Micheel looked at his name engraved alongside the likes of Ben Hogan, Byron Nelson, Jack Nicklaus and Tiger Woods and he broke down. "I don't think there's anything left," he said. "I spit it all out there in the rough. It's all in the golf course."

The winner wasn't the only one who left everything out on the course. From the opening gun, this one had all the markings of a slugfest. The only thing missing were the marquee heavyweights. Woods opened with 74, followed with 72 and two 73s, and never contended on the weekend. His name never appeared on the first page of the leaderboard. "I just didn't drive very well, and put myself under a lot of pressure because of it," Woods said. "It didn't matter what club I hit off the tee, I couldn't keep it in play. I just need a little more trust in my swing. I feel pretty good stepping over it, and as soon as I come down, I just don't trust it, but that is just the way it goes sometimes."

This was Woods' first year without a major title since 1998, and it extended his "did not win" streak to six consecutive majors, a laughably small number considering he had won eight professional major titles coming into the week, which was one more than Arnold Palmer won in his career. But the public's unrealistic expectations of Woods were understandable. The streak he put together from the summer of 1999 through the middle of 2002 was unparalleled. As a result of that high bar, anytime Woods didn't win, especially in a major championship, it was news. "Tiger made us think it was easy to win majors," Hal Sutton said. "It's not."

Compounding the "Tiger slump" talk were persistent tales of knee trouble — Woods underwent arthroscopy knee surgery in December of 2002 and admitted to cutting back on his practice schedule to protect the knee — and speculation that the breakup with long-time teacher Butch Harmon had led to some changes in Woods' swing. Harmon fueled many of those stories by saying things like, "I see a lot more of a Mark O'Meara's influence now in Tiger's swing. It's a lot rounder now than I would like to see. When he was playing his best golf, the swing was more up and down."

Woods admitted to having some difficulties with his swing. "I'm just not matching up," he said. "With the longer clubs, I'm getting behind even more. I'm hitting the outside of the ball, and when you do that, you can't shape it, can't hit shots, can't do anything."

With four victories through the first of August, everyone agreed that "can't do anything," might have been a bit of a stretch. But Woods' struggles in the 2003 majors created a lot of talk. By the end of the week, he was 12-over-par 292 and tied for 39th, his worst finish in a major since turning professional late in 1996. "This year has been frustrating, since I've been there with a chance going into the weekend every week except this one," he said. "It just hasn't happened, but that's the way it goes."

What was a bit surprising, however, was how many great players failed to take advantage of Woods' off week. Of the pre-tournament favorites, the best finish by Phil Mickelson, Vijay Singh or Davis Love was a tie for 23rd by Mickelson. Love, who won The Players Championship, led the money list going into the week and had talked all year about rededicating himself to win a major and the Player of the Year title, shot 74 and 75 and missed the cut. Singh had a good opening round and was hovering at two over par before shooting 79 on Sunday to drop into a tie for 34th at 291.

Mickelson was a different story. He opened the week with a four-under 66 to share the lead with Rodney Pampling. "I did a number of things well," Mickelson said. "I felt like I putted it well and drove it pretty good off the tee. The misses I had, I missed on the side of the fairway or in the rough that I wanted to miss on, and it left me with a chance to save par. I just hit some good iron shots, too.

"Spending time with (teacher) Rick Smith has helped. We spent time about a month ago, and I could see things turning around. I am starting to feel very confident in certain aspects of my game, especially off the tee. I'm going to miss tee shots, but if I can miss them on the proper side, I can be okay and maybe salvage par."

Mickelson got off to a good start, birdieing the 10th hole (his first of the day) after hitting driver, sand wedge to 15 feet. A routine par from the fairway on the 11th was followed by a three iron off the tee and into the rough on the 12th. But he missed the fairway on the "right side," and was able to hit a seven iron to four feet for his second birdie of the round. That was followed by four steady pars before Mickelson made his first bogey at the long, difficult 17th. But at the 18th (the second hardest hole of the week), Mickelson hit driver into the fairway and six iron to 15 feet for his third birdie in nine holes. He followed that up with birdies at the second (four wood, eight iron to 20 feet) and the par-five fourth (driver, four wood, chip to one foot) before pushing his drive on the ninth and failing to get up and down for his second bogey of the day.

He wasn't too high or low on his round. "Everybody wants to get off to a good start," he said. "It's tough to play catch-up at major championships because the courses seem to progressively get more difficult as the week goes on. You want to take advantage of it on Thursday and Friday. But it's

Thursday right now, and there's a lot of golf left."

No one had to quote Mickelson's words to co-leader Pampling. The last time Pampling lead a major, he made history. It was the 1999 Open Championship, and after taking the first-round lead, Pampling became the first to lead after day one in a major and miss the cut at the end of day two. "Obviously, it's the first day, and there's still three more days to go, but it's a nice position to be in, that's for sure," he said this time.

Pampling made birdies at the 13th and 14th (his fourth and fifth holes of the day), and missed four other short putts on the back nine. He made a 10-footer for birdie at the first hole and another birdie putt of similar length on the eighth before throwing in one final par for what turned out to be as perfect a round as anyone had on this course. "The fact that I didn't make a bogey, that's definitely a bonus," Pampling said. "Any time you can do that in the majors, it's certainly going to hold you in a good position."

Billy Andrade was also in good position after coming perilously close to failing to qualify. Andrade played well in the final weeks of July and had to wait for Larry Nelson to withdraw before being extended an invitation. He made the most of it, shooting three-under-par 67, his lowest opening round in 14 PGA Championship appearances and the second-lowest score he ever had fired in this tournament (he shot 66 in 2001). "I am absolutely tickled to death to be here," Andrade said afterward. "To be the seventh alternate in the week, and to have the opportunity to get a phone call on Monday saying that I'm in the tournament, I have to thank Larry Nelson personally for having a bad hip. I guess there's some reason why I'm here. There are reasons that we don't know about. When you're seventh alternate you don't think that you have a shot. So I'm here for a reason, and I'm going to try to seize this opportunity and seize the moment."

Another player hoping to seize the moment was Masters winner Mike Weir, who was making his own bid for Player of the Year honors. Two major titles should do it. Weir opened with a 68. "For me at Augusta, the golf course played very long, but my wedge game was very good and I drove it well and putted great," Weir said. Then, echoing the theme of the week, he said, "You have to hit it in the fairway. That's the bottom line, no matter how far you are hitting it, you have to be hitting the fairways."

Somewhere lost in the chatter of past major wins and close ones that got away, a player no one other than his pregnant wife and a few faithful friends followed shot a quiet 69, and answered questions in front of four reporters before heading out alone to the range. "I missed the first three fairways, but thank God I've got a putter in my bag this week," Micheel said. "I made a few bad swings out there, but I made some critical putts. I really like the set-up."

After the first round, the leaderboard looked like this:

Phil Mickelson	66	Shaun Micheel	69
Rodney Pampling	66	Michael Campbell	69
Billy Andrade	67	Fred Funk	69
Mike Weir	68	Tim Herron	69
Lee Janzen	68	Aaron Baddeley	69
Vijay Singh	69	Kevin Sutherland	69

As predicted, the course got firmer, faster and tougher on Friday, and the scores went up accordingly. Mickelson followed his 66 with a less-than-stellar 75. "I really thought that today was a day I was going to be able to take advantage of some good play and make some birdies," Mickelson said. "Certainly the scores have gone back, and we've seen a lot of guys struggle today, but we also see a number of guys at one over par. There are a lot of guys keeping it around par, and that tells me that it's a pretty fair test of golf."

Exactly eight players were at one-over-par 141 or better. Of those, only Micheel posted two rounds in the 60s. His 68 on Friday included four birdies in his final five holes. The streak started at the fifth (his 14th hole) where he hit a nine iron to three feet and rolled the putt in for birdie. At the par-three sixth, he hit a six iron into the center of the green 20 feet from the hole and made that putt for his second consecutive birdie. After a routine par on the seventh, he hit seven iron to eight feet on the ninth and made that to take what was looking like a two- or three-over-par round and turn it into the lowest score of the day, and one of only three rounds in the 60s.

"Today was much different than yesterday," Micheel said. "Yesterday I was thankful to have my putter in the bag, and today I couldn't seem to buy a putt in the beginning. I was a little bit more nervous than I thought I was going to be. I had some nice shots. Actually, the first five or six holes, I didn't really mis-hit a shot, and I was three over par, which is about what the majors seem to do to you. You lose your focus for just a little while, and you're three over par.

"The key to any golf tournament, but especially this week, the way the golf course is set up, is to hit the ball in the fairway. We can't emphasize that enough. I've never seen rough this deep, actually. I've played in only two U.S. Opens prior to this, but I don't recall ever seeing anything like this. I saw them out mowing the other day, and all they were doing was sticking it straight up. When I played my practice round on Tuesday, I thought to myself, 'This could be a long week.' Fortunately, yesterday some of the fairways I did miss were on a couple of the shorter holes that I could pitch out on and make some nice pars to settle down.

"With this golf course, you need to be on top of your game. I think Phil Mickelson said yesterday that not too many people come from behind in a major championship, and when you play this golf course, you see what he means. I played a nice round that last 12 holes, and I'm obviously going to think about that tonight and think about some of the other rounds I've played really well earlier this year, and hopefully build on that."

Micheel came into the week 169th in the World Ranking with a career-best finish of tied for third at the 2002 B.C. Open, where he shot 74 on Sunday to lose to Spike McRoy the same weekend that Ernie Els was winning a four-way playoff in the Open Championship at Muirfield. Those stats didn't bode well for Micheel's chances, especially with Mike Weir lurking only two shots back and Els three behind with 36 holes to play.

"I'm not in too bad a position," Els said after a four-birdie, two-bogey and one-double-bogey round of 70. "I really wanted to get to red numbers by the end of the day, and I almost did that. I have two rounds to go and I am here for the weekend. I have a chance. Already we have seen the greens firm up a little bit, and it doesn't look like it's going to rain again, so it will be tough to go under par."

After two rounds, the leaderboard looked like this:

Shaun Micheel	68 - 137	Phil Mickelson	75 - 141
Mike Weir	71 - 139	Adam Scott	69 - 141
Billy Andrade	72 - 139	Tim Herron	72 - 141
Rodney Pampling	74 - 140	Chad Campbell	72 - 141
Ernie Els	70 - 141		

Of all the players within a handful of shots of the lead going into the weekend, no one would have predicted the outcome. Campbell, a player who had dominated the Hooters and Nike Tours and who was expected to do great things despite having never won a PGA Tour event, shot the low round of the tournament on Saturday, a 65 that moved him to the top of the leaderboard. But Micheel stuck with him, shooting 69 to keep his streak of under-70 scores alive at three. The two players, both winless and remarkably similar in appearance and demeanor, would be in the final pairing.

"It's funny," Micheel said. "Everybody thinks I'm Chad Campbell. It's unbelievable. I don't remember who it was, but someone came up to me and said, 'Great playing' at such and such a tournament. I just said, 'Okay.' It didn't dawn on me until later, but it's amazing how everybody thinks Chad and I look alike. I think I'm a litter bit lighter ... at least that's what I claim in my bio.

"The pairing tomorrow, I think, is going to be great. I hope that we can both communicate with one another and that we both play well. I'm excited. Hopefully, he's excited to play with me, because I think we pretty much have the same type of games. We both hit the ball pretty straight. We both, I think, hit a lot of greens. We are both out here trying to win a major championship, so it ought to be fun."

Fun wasn't the first word that came to most people's minds when they considered what Micheel must have been going through. But those who knew him best thought the reaction was perfect. "I don't let him feel sorry for himself, or get down on himself," said Micheel's wife, Stephanie, a domestic relations attorney in Memphis. "I used to have to pump him up a lot more. He made four cuts his first year out here (1994) and realized he was in over his head, and there have been a lot of tough times since then, particularly on the Asian Tour." Micheel's caddie, Bob Szczensny, thought his man had a chance because of a critical round a month before when Micheel finished 10th at the Greater Hartford Open and secured his 2004 PGA Tour card. "Shaun's been extremely calm," Szczensny said. "Part of that is because he's always been a bubble guy, and this year, he locked up his card pretty early. That probably freed him up to relax, not worry about things so much."

It also helped that he didn't have Woods or any other top-ranked player breathing down his neck. Els shot another even-par 70, as did Mike Weir, but other than those two stars, the first page of the leaderboard had reporters scrambling for their media guides. Tim Clark shot 68 to enter the final round four shots back, while Alex Cejka, a Czech-born naturalized German last seen contending at the 2001 Open Championship, shot 68 to draw within five shots of the lead. A pair of 40-something stalwarts, Fred Funk and Jay

Haas, made appearances on the leaderboard, as did Loren Roberts and Charles Howell. Not a shabby group of leaders, but certainly not what everyone expected.

With one round to play, this was the leaderboard:

Shaun Micheel	69	- 206	Alex Cejka	68	- 211
Chad Campbell	65	- 206	Billy Andrade	72	- 211
Mike Weir	70	- 209	Charles Howell	70	- 212
Tim Clark	68	- 210	Fred Funk	70	- 212
Ernie Els	70	- 211	Vijay Singh	70	- 212

Weir and Els were the favorites, even though they started the final round three and five strokes back, respectively. Both had major championship trophies and both were in the midst of multiple-win seasons. They were veterans having great years. When the pressure of Sunday rolled around, conventional wisdom said Micheel and Campbell would wilt, and one of the wily winners from the past would rise to the top.

So much for conventional wisdom. Els seemed poised to take charge early. Out two groups ahead of the leaders, he birdied the fourth hole to pull a shot closer, but gave it back with bogeys at the sixth and seventh. He came back with birdies at the eighth and ninth to pull within three shots of the lead. By then, the leaders were well into their rounds and the pressure was mounting. If Els were to make a move, it needed to be early in his second nine. Instead, he hit an eight iron right of the 10th green and made bogey, and then pulled a pitching wedge left of the 12th green. When his pitch shot from the rough at the 12th jumped 20 feet past the hole and the putt for par hung on the lip, Lanny Wadkins, watching from the CBS broadcast booth, said, "That's the way Ernie's week is going to be — a little short."

"I played a different game plan today," Els said after finishing with 71 for a 282 total and a tie for fifth place with Haas. "I was really quite conservative off the tee, and I took a lot of two irons and put it in play. And that's just the way you have to play this golf course. I wasn't all that sharp with my fairway irons today, and that cost me the golf tournament."

Weir's round was much the same. After scrambling all week, the struggles he was having with his golf swing finally caught up with him. "I think if I sit back and analyze it, you're trying to go to the well too many times with poor ball-striking," the Masters winner said after a dismal 75 left him at four-over-par 284 and tied for seventh with Funk and Roberts. "Today, it kind of caught up with me."

That left Clark and Cejka to challenge the leaders. And while they are both fine players, the prospect of Alex Cejka making a run isn't as daunting as seeing Ernie Els climb up the leaderboard. Of course, none of it might have mattered. By the time they got halfway through their round, this one was purely match play, with some of the most pressure-packed ball-striking in recent major championship history.

Micheel birdied the first hole after splitting the middle of the fairway. "Hitting that fairway was key," he said. "That's a tough shot for me, a right-to-left hole with a left-to-right wind. That's always been just a really difficult shot. I had a nice comfortable six iron into the green. It was just a shot that I was trying to get onto the green, in the middle of the green, just to kind of get my round going. I was able to make a nice smooth swing and it went the perfect distance."

Campbell bogeyed the first after hitting what he termed "just a bad three wood" right of the fairway. He pitched out, hit his third shot to 15 feet, and missed the par putt.

After rolling in the short birdie at the first, Micheel missed the second fairway. "I don't really like that tee shot, either," Micheel said. "There's a tree that hangs over the edge, and I was just trying to hit a four iron out there in the fairway to leave me a pitching wedge in. Unfortunately, I had to pitch out. I had about 120 yards, and I hit it 10 feet and thought I made the putt, but it just slid by."

Campbell missed the fairway as well. "I just didn't hit fairways," he said. "I had just a terrible lie on two — Shaun and I both did. We could barely get it back to the fairway and we were only about five feet off of it." Campbell was able to get up and down for par to get one of the two shots back he had lost at No. 1. He gave that back and then some at the par-three sixth where he hit a seven iron over the green. "I just hit the wrong club," Campbell said. "I thought the wind was right-to-left and it ended up being down. I should have hit eight iron. It was just dead where that pin was today."

Compounding the error was the fact that Micheel birdied the sixth. "Again, I had perfect yardage," he said. "It was just a perfect eight iron. I left myself a pretty difficult putt, even though it was only four and a half feet. I really studied that one pretty hard." He made it for another two-shot swing. Suddenly, the lead was three.

Both players bogeyed the seventh after missing the fairway, but Micheel gave another one back with a poor tee shot at the eighth. The lead was two, which was where it would remain through the next four holes. It wasn't until the 13th that things got really interesting again. Campbell made a birdie to pull within one. "I hit two iron, five iron, nine iron to about three feet, just above the hole, and made a good putt," he said. But, for the second time in the round, he gave it back one hole later and then some. After driving his ball in the fairway bunker, Campbell hit his second shot fat and failed to get up and down for par. Meanwhile, Micheel hit driver on the par-four and two-putted from 35 feet for birdie. The two-shot swing extended the lead back to three.

One hole later there was another two-shot swing, this time in Campbell's favor. "I hit it just short of pin-high on the left with a six iron and just made a great putt, probably 25 feet," Campbell said. Micheel three-putted for bogey, and the lead was back to one shot.

Micheel made up for his error with a clutch 35-footer for birdie at the 16th after driving the ball in the right rough. "I was fortunate that if you do miss the fairway and the wind is a certain direction, you can get the ball on the green," he said. "Somehow, the two times that I was in the rough, the grass was growing towards the green, and you've got to have that." The lead was two, with two holes to play.

A poor bogey by Micheel after a pulled approach on the 17th set up the drama at the 18th. One hole to go, a lead of one shot, it doesn't get much more gut-wrenching. Micheel hit a good shot in the first cut on the left, and Campbell hit a good shot in the middle. Campbell played first and hit his approach a touch long. But he had a makeable birdie putt. That's when Micheel hit his miracle seven iron.

"I knew I had to hit a good shot," Campbell said. "That was obviously before he hit his. I didn't know how close he was. I didn't know it was an inch. I was thinking maybe four or five feet, at least have to make a putt and maybe I could get there and make a birdie. Maybe something else would happen. That was a great shot. He played great all day."

Campbell ran his birdie putt past the hole and made a great par putt coming back for 72 to finish alone in second place at 278, one shot clear of Clark, who shot 69, and two ahead of Cejka (69).

As for Micheel, prior to the seven iron-to-two-inches finale at Oak Hill, he was most famous for saving the lives of an elderly couple when their car plunged off a 30-foot embankment and into a lake in North Carolina in 1993. "No one else could get down to where they were," Micheel said. "So Doug (Barron) and I were left trying to help. I didn't want to test my swimming skills with clothes on, so I stripped down to my boxers and we managed to pull them out.

"I lost the tournament that week because I kept hitting it in the water the last few holes. It was kind of ironic."

If that incident didn't shake him, a 175-yard shot on the final hole of a major was a walk in the park. "It was breathtaking," Stephanie Micheel said through tears after it was over. "I can't think of a better way for this to end."

6. The Players Championship

Fred Couples called it the "the best round of golf I've ever seen played." Pretty heady stuff from a guy who was once the No. 1 player in the world, played in 75 major championships, and won this tournament twice. But that wasn't all Couples had to say about the final-round 64 that his buddy, Davis Love, shot on a cold, windy afternoon to win The Players Championship at the TPC at Sawgrass in Ponte Vedra Beach, Florida. "Davis can rip up a golf course," Couples said. "And right now, he's driving it 300 yards dead straight, and he's putting well. That was the easiest 64 you'll ever see."

Couples wasn't alone in that analysis. "That 64 is one of the best rounds ever," said veteran Jay Haas, who played in the final group and wound up finishing second to Love, six strokes behind, along with Padraig Harrington. "A 64 here in the summer with no wind and the greens rolling at a seven on the Stimpmeter would be impressive." The fact that the temperature never hit the 60-degree mark on Sunday, the greens were hard and fast, and swirling Atlantic wind gusts hovered around 15 miles an hour added more than a measure of credibility to the praise being heaped on Love. "He just kept piling up birdies," Harrington said. "I'd like to go back and see it on TV myself." Even those who played great had nothing but good things to say about Love's round. Jim Furyk shot 69 to finish tied for fourth and said, "I played my heart out, but I didn't see seven or eight under par in my bag today."

The caddies even got in on the praise. Joe LaCava looped for Couples in 1996 when his man shot 64 to win. Witnessing Love's round firsthand was a bonus. "It was every bit as good as Fred's round in '96," LaCava said. "You didn't even think about Davis making a bogey. Fred's eight under was on harder, faster greens, but Davis had to deal with more breeze."

Love's 64 might have looked the same on the scorecard as the one Couples fired seven years before, but the perspective of both players was certainly different. When Love won his first Players Championship in 1992 he was a 28-year-old long-ball hitter with "potential" stamped on his forehead, while Couples was 31 and a month away from winning the Masters and becoming the No. 1 player in the world. The two of them represented the new faces of golf in the pre-Tiger era. The golf world expected a lot. Unfortunately, Couples wouldn't win another major and would only capture five more titles in the next decade. Love would win one major, the PGA Championship in 1997, but would have to carry the label as one of golf's classic underachievers, a wealth of natural talent that never fully panned out.

"It was important to win in 1992, and I felt it then," Love said. "I think now it's made it even harder for me to win, because I have a much better appreciation for how important this is to the players, and to the game of golf. It is a very rewarding win."

While the eventual margin was six strokes, it was closer than that. Love started the final round two shots behind Haas and Harrington and tied with Couples and Craig Perks at 207. A birdie at the par-five second didn't do much for his cause, as all the leaders birdied No. 2. Where he made his move was on the difficult par-three eighth. A four iron to 10 feet set up the first of what would turn out to be five consecutive birdies, which gave Love a three-stroke lead. Three more pars set up the shot of the tournament at the par-five 16th. After pulling his three-wood tee shot into the pine trees, Love hit the six iron of his life, a high draw in a wind that seemed to come from four different directions. The ball stopped on the front of the green, leaving him 10 feet for eagle. When that putt fell while Haas was making bogey on the 15th, this tournament result was decided.

"I joked that every time I hit it in the right rough at 16 that you're better off in the left trees than in the right rough," Love said. "I hit it and thought, 'Oh gosh, here we go.' As long as you're not up against a tree, you are better off over there. I've seen a couple of guys hit it there and have an easy lay-up. It's almost impossible to get a good lay-up out of that right rough. When I saw it laying over there clean without a tree in the way, I knew I could knock it on the green. It was a straight six iron, 197 yards. It really wasn't that difficult a shot except for the fact that there was a big lake on the right, and you had to miss that, but other than that, it was a straight six iron."

Two routine pars (if such things are possible on the 17th and 18th at the TPC at Sawgrass) gave Love the most decisive victory of his career, a total of 271, 17 under par, on rounds of 70, 67, 70 and then 64. "It was obviously an incredible round of golf," Love said. "I'm as thrilled as I can be. Six birdies and an eagle in those conditions was not what anybody was expecting. It was my best job of hanging in there and doing the things that I do well for 18 holes. I don't think I've ever done a better job. If that's what the back nine of a major championship feels like with a lead, at least I know how it feels now. It was an eerie feeling to grab the lead, and have to play that nine holes of golf in those conditions was very nerve-wracking."

His other rounds weren't bad either. It wasn't like Love came out of nowhere. He shot the opening 70 to trail Harrington by three. The 67 on Friday moved him one shot closer to the lead, and another 70 on Saturday kept him within two and in the next-to-last group on the final day. But no one expected a 64. "You know I shot 62 once at Greensboro in pretty bad conditions," Love said. "I had a hole-out and made a bunch of putts — not to take anything away from Greensboro — but this round of golf, yeah, I'll remember it the rest of my life."

Not only did the 64 tie the lowest final round in Players Championship history (a record Couples held alone before witnessing Love's round), Love was the only player in the field who didn't make a bogey on Sunday. He was also one of only seven who went all week without a three-putt.

The fact that he never led until the second nine on Sunday seemed irrelevant in the end. This victory was as solid as any in his career. "It's something I've been building up to the last few months," Love said. "I've been building up for this and been improving. I had the best attitude I've had in a long time."

Love wasn't a favorite when the week began, despite the fact that he had won in handy fashion at the AT&T Pebble Beach National Pro-Am. It was no surprise that Tiger Woods was considered the pre-tournament player to watch. He had won three times and was coming off one of the most dominating performances of his career at Arnold Palmer's Bay Hill Invitational, where he won by 11 shots, becoming the third player in PGA Tour history to win the same event for four consecutive years. If not Woods, Ernie Els, who had four worldwide victories and was attempting to come back from a wrist injury (he hurt himself hitting a heavy punching bag in his garage), looked like a solid favorite. Lightning would have to strike for Love to win.

That's exactly what happened on Thursday, with lightning, wind and rain so intense that even those in the clubhouse felt threatened. The course had already absorbed 15 inches of rain in the six days leading up to the tournament, and some questioned whether this final round of thunderstorms that suspended play midway through the first day would leave the course unplayable. "Twelve days ago this course was unplayable," said Rocco Mediate, whose home is at the TPC at Sawgrass. "It was so wet the superintendent told me the rough on the ninth hole was nine inches high."

Thankfully the maintenance crew mowed before Thursday, and Mediate along with Skip Kendall, Jay Haas and Bob Tway finished their rounds before play was suspended. All four shot 68 to lead in the clubhouse when the sun set. That score might have held had Padraig Harrington not come in with seven holes left. Harrington started on the 12th on Friday, and played the final seven holes in two under to finish the first round at 67 and later tied with Couples for the lead.

Harrington didn't have time to ponder that position. By the time he signed his card and had a quick lunch, it was time to tee off for the second round. Five birdies and one bogey later, he had shot a second-round 68, finished 26 holes for the day and led the tournament at 135, nine under par. "It was a long, hard day," Harrington said. The Irishman handled the tough course with style, rolling in putts on the second, fifth, ninth, 11th and 12th holes, with his only bogey coming at the short par-four third. "I stayed focused all the way through, and it's just when I finished that I realized how much it was taking out of me."

"I've been coming here for five years, and every year I've gained a little bit," Harrington said. "After the early results of the year, I sat down and had a look at some of my notes from previous years and how I was doing at the same times. I compared things, and the results were pretty similar, but I've got to say I'm quite a bit ahead of other years in all aspects of my game. I certainly feel like I've done some good work with my swing over the winter, and I've done a good bit of work on my short game and putting. Everything seemed to have stepped up a little bit from previous years. I'm very happy. It's a good position to be in, really can't be better."

Harrington's lead was two strokes over Love, Perks and Kendall, but Love entered the weekend with a great deal of confidence. He played 36 holes on Friday and showed a level of maturity and patience that had been noticeably absent from his game in recent years. After a rugged round of 70 in soggy conditions where he said, "everybody got a few squishy shots," Love started his second round on the second nine and made birdies on the 10th and 11th. He struck the ball well for six more holes and made solid pars, before making a terrible mistake on the 18th. A pushed approach with a seven iron left him with virtually no shot. He made a gallant effort, but the ball only moved about five feet. "I barely got it out of the deep rough into the fringe," he said. "I had like a 50-foot putt, knocked it six feet by, and missed it coming back. I said to myself walking off there, 'You've hit two bad shots really, maybe three bad shots all day, and got no breaks, so maybe you can get a break on the front.'"

That break came on No. 1, Love's 10th hole of the day. After hitting a good drive, he hit a wedge a little long, leaving himself 30 feet for birdie. He ran that putt almost six feet past the hole and made the par putt coming back. "After I made that par putt on one, I played pretty confidently," he said. "I hit every putt feeling like I was going to make it."

He almost did make them all. On the par-five second hole, he hit the green with his second shot, rolled his eagle putt five feet past, and made the comebacker for birdie. He followed that up with a 15-footer for birdie at the third. He then caught another of the breaks that had eluded him earlier. A two iron off the tee on the fourth flew a little left and onto the hill that guards the fairway. The ball could have easily hung up in the rough and left him with no shot at the green. Instead, it took a good hop and bounded back into the fairway. From there Love hit a pitching wedge to 10 feet and made his third birdie in a row. Another good drive and an eight-iron approach at the fifth led to his fourth birdie in a row, and a two iron, nine iron to five feet on the sixth made it five in a row.

"I hit it pretty good the whole 36 holes," Love said. "I had a few bad shots, but I think with soft conditions and some of the squirty lies, you're going to hit a few bad ones. But I hit the ball pretty well. It was a nice run, and then I hit a bad tee shot at eight (which led to a great up-and-down par). At nine I hit kind of a squirter lay-up, got in the edge of the rough, and didn't get a birdie putt. But I made a nice putt for par at nine. It was a nice putting nine, and a pretty solid day except for a couple of swings."

The surprise of the tournament had to be Haas, but then Haas had been something of a surprise all season. At age 49, Haas was having his most successful year in almost a decade. He had finished second to Mike Weir at the Bob Hope Chrysler Classic and had been in contention deep into the weekend almost every week, a shock for a guy who was supposed to be tuning up for the Champions Tour. "I get a lot of grief from my friends," Haas said. "I'm in the locker room reading the newspaper with my glasses on and they just call me 'Old Man.' But, hey, I'm thrilled. If I wasn't playing good, they wouldn't be talking to me."

Haas had come in under the radar with rounds of 68 and 70 the first two days, nothing earth-shattering but good enough to earn him a late tee time on Saturday. Ahead of the leaders on a sunny, cool day, Haas got a confidence boost when he rolled a couple of long ones close to the hole. "I started off a little shaky," he said. "I had long two-putts at one, four and five, and made about a 10-footer at two, but after that I started to play well, hit a lot of good shots, had a real nice stretch right in the middle of the round, and overall played about like I did on Thursday. I felt real comfortable out there."

He was comfortable enough to post a bogey-free 67. "I've played here 20 times, and this is the best I've played by far," Haas said. "I can't explain it. On this golf course, you would think experience is a big factor, and it is, but there's a lot of young guys up there too, and one middle-aged guy. You know, I feel like I'm capable. I came within a swing or two at the Bob Hope, but if I'd had a steady diet of missing cuts and losing every tournament by 20 or 30 strokes then I wouldn't be very confident. I'm certainly not overconfident, but I feel good about the way I'm playing. Just as a golfer, no matter what age, I feel good about my game."

Haas had reason to feel good. Harrington came within 90 seconds of missing his tee time on Saturday after choosing to warm up at the far end of the range. "I went to the lower practice area because the green there is particularly fast, and I expected the greens to speed up a bit from yesterday," he said. "I did my preparation 10 minutes away from the first tee really. I was cutting it a little tight, but no worries."

The hustle at the first tee didn't seem to affect him. Harrington parred the first hole and made a routine birdie at the second. He then kept pace with a steady diet of pars until the seventh, where he found the greenside bunker with his approach, leaving him a long third shot. "I had about a 25-yard bunker shot, something like that," Harrington said. "I was feeling particularly confident actually about getting up and down. Just hit a bad shot." The shot in question was a thin screamer that flew over the green and into the high stuff behind the gallery. "It was one of those bad shots that you can't recover from," Harrington said. "Sometimes you hit those on the golf course. I hit it over the green and could only try to put it 20 feet away from the hole." His fourth shot rolled 23 feet by, and he two-putted for double bogey.

To his credit, Harrington didn't let the troubles at the seventh ruin his round. "You can never expect for everything to go smoothly," he said. "That's golf. When you're leading the tournament, you have to expect a few knocks. That was just one of them." Harrington came back with a great up-and-down for par from an edgy lie in a bunker on the eighth, and hit another great bunker shot from 40 yards on the par-five 11th. That shot stopped nine feet from the hole, and Harrington made the putt for birdie. Another birdie at the 16th capped off a two-under-par 70 to leave Harrington in a tie with Haas atop the leaderboard at 11-under 199. Love and Perks also shots 70s to move to nine-under-par 201, along with Couples who added a 69.

There appeared to be a good score out there for the taking on Sunday, despite cold drizzle and healthy wind gusts. Robert Allenby put on his rain suit and promptly shot his best round of the week, a 65 that put him in the clubhouse at 278. Kirk Triplett also has his low round of the week and his only round in the 60s. A 67 before the winds picked up gave Triplett a 280 total and left him tied for eighth with Scott Verplank.

As great as those rounds (along with Love's) were, a few players surprised the crowds by failing to make anything resembling a charge. Among them was Tiger Woods, who had gotten progressively better each of his first three rounds. After an even-par 72 that he called "pretty good," Woods shot respectable scores of 70 and 68 to enter the final round at 204, and five shots off Haas and Harrington's lead. Had he gone out with a few early birdies and posted a 64 or 65 of his own, who knows what might have happened. As it was, Woods could never get any putts in the hole. After missing his second four-footer of the round, this one seemed to be out of his reach. He finished the day with 72 for a 282 total. That put him in a six-way tie for 11th place. "I didn't play that bad," Woods said afterward. "I hit a lot of good shots and a lot of good putts, but nothing went in."

Darren Clarke would have loved that problem. Clarke couldn't find the fairway on Sunday. From the second hole on, he struggled to reach the greens from awkward lies in the rough. Were it not for a stellar short game, Clarke wouldn't have been close to the 71 he shot to finish tied for sixth with Campbell at 279.

Jim Furyk, a local Ponte Vedra Beach resident who had more than his share of experience on the course, ground out a four-birdie, one-bogey 69 to tie Allenby at 278, which cleared the stage for the final two groups.

Two hours and five of Love's birdies later, this one was all but over. Haas, who had putted fearlessly all week, finally remembered how hard this game can be. He missed a makeable par putt at the third and three-putted for bogey at the fourth. When Love birdied the eighth and ninth, Haas went from leading the tournament to trailing by two.

The same applied to Harrington. After driving the ball perfectly for most of the week, the Irishman sprayed a couple of tee shots on the opening nine that resulted in bogeys. By the time he reached the ninth tee, he was playing catch-up on a day when it looked like Love wasn't going to stumble, even as the rain and wind intensified.

"I just didn't let the weather affect me," Love said. "I was nervous about it for sure, because we saw the rain. Obviously, I sat in the parking lot all morning and watched it rain. I knew it was softening up and going to be a squishy, mud ball kind of day, and then combine that with the amount of wind and cooler temperatures, and it was a big change, a blustery day, and certainly not the kind of day you wanted to play the 17th and 18th holes in."

By the time he reached 17th tee, this one seemed in the bag. Barring a catastrophe on the two hardest closing holes in tournament golf (which wasn't out of the realm of possibility), Love had this one wrapped up. When his tee shot on the 17th found dry land in the middle of the green, the crowd on the hillside erupted. They had seen the eagle at the 16th from their perch, and they knew that the shot at the 17th clinched it. Two putts and a dry-land, three-wood tee shot at the 18th did, indeed, seal the deal.

"I was trying as hard as I could not to look at the scoreboards," Love said. "Obviously, with all the mechanical and manned leaderboards, it's hard to miss them, but I was trying not to look at what Jay and Padraig were doing, trying to stay focused on what I was doing, playing each shot and picking targets and not worrying about the score. Shoot, I was just trying to win. I would have taken double bogey, double bogey on those last two holes if that's what it took to win. I challenged myself coming off of nine that it would be nice to have a five-shot lead with two to play. When I got on the 17th green after I putted my putt up there, I started looking at the leaderboard real hard, adding it up, and I saw that I did have a five-shot lead. That was really a good feeling."

He also hoped it would be a springboard for bigger things throughout the remainder of the year. "I certainly don't expect to shoot 64 every day for the rest of my life, but I fully expect that now, if I keep doing this, stick with it, I can do anything I want to do as long as I'm prepared," he said. "I'll be prepared (for the Masters) and I'll do my best. I might win and I might not, but at least now I'm back to where I was when I was picked as a guy that had a chance to win at Augusta. I wasn't picked as that guy the last couple of years."

With that, Love took his crystal trophy and climbed behind the wheel of his 45-foot Prevost motor coach (which served as both his mode of transportation and his lodging for the week). If there was anything better than driving the big rig back to Sea Island to see his family, it was doing so with the biggest win and best round of his career under his belt.

7. HSBC World Match Play

The more things change, the more they stay the same. So it was at the HSBC World Match Play Championship, under new sponsorship, with a new qualification system and for the first time in 40 years without its founder, the late Mark H. McCormack. But for the traditionalists, much was familiar about this sunny, English autumnal week at the Wentworth Club in Virginia Water, Surrey, not least the recent tradition that Ernie Els usually walks away with the spoils.

Even from the start of the week the focus was on whether Els could equal the record number of victories in the tournament, which stands at five. Gary Player had set the mark originally after winning his fifth title in 1973, only the 10th time the event had been staged. Two decades later, Seve Ballesteros won his fifth title in 1991, although the Spaniard's great period of domination had been between 1981 and 1985 when he won four times in five years.

Both Player and Ballesteros, along with other former champions such as Bob Charles, Nick Faldo, Sandy Lyle and Ian Woosnam were invited to play in the Pro-Am on Wednesday and they were in reminiscing mood afterwards. "It has always been a great thrill for me to participate in this event," Player said. "We are inundated with medal events around the world and it was a great idea of Mark McCormack to have us playing man-against-man in a match play tournament on a great course at a great time of year. It didn't matter where I was in the world, I eagerly awaited my invitation to this event and never, ever, did not come as far as I can remember unless I was ill."

Player participated in perhaps what is still the most famous match in the tournament's history. It came in only the second year, in 1965, when he played Tony Lema in the semi-finals. Lema had been the Open champion the previous year, while Player was the reigning U.S. Open champion. At 6 up after 18 holes, Lema put his arm around Player as they walked off to lunch and said, "Never mind, you'll get invited back next year."

"I thought to myself, 'Well, thank you, but in the meantime I've got a bit of news for you,'" Player recalled. "We went into the clubhouse and all the press were around Tony saying, 'You've beaten Gary Player.' I didn't have any lunch. I went to practice, got to the first hole and lost that. That's golf." From 7 down with 17 to play, Player mounted what remains the biggest comeback the event has seen and finally won at the 37th. The next day he beat Peter Thomson in the final to win his first title.

For the 20th playing of the tournament in 1983, a number of past champions were invited and the first round was expanded to 16 players with the matches reduced to 18 holes. The draw pitched Ballesteros against Arnold Palmer, and the aging American was 2 up with two to play. It became one of the great Seve dramas. He won the 17th and, short of the green in two at the 18th, chipped in for an eagle before winning at the third extra hole. One of Ballesteros' favorite memories was beating Sandy Lyle in the 1982 final at the 37th hole. "It was raining like hell, but I managed to hit a driver and a three wood at the first and holed the putt from about 35 feet," he said.

There was also his second final against Bernhard Langer in 1985. "I won the match on the 14th and I tried to shake his hand but he was walking away. He didn't know the match was over. He wanted to continue and I had to say, 'Bernhard, sorry, but I don't think we have to play any more.'"

Ballesteros added, "As Gary said, this is a fantastic tournament and match play has always been very special for everybody. It is more dramatic, more aggressive and I think it is more interesting after you play medal golf the rest of the year. Match play demands a lot of desire, a lot of determination and will power." Even in defeat, Ballesteros could astonish, as when he made seven twos at the short holes against Els in a second-round match in 1994. That was Els' first match in the tournament. He won the title at his first three attempts and collected 11 straight victories before losing a match, to Vijay Singh in the 1997 final.

Following his victory in the Open Championship in 2002, Els added his fourth World Match Play title a few months later to come within breathing distance of Player and Ballesteros. "Seve has done so much for the European Tour and obviously his performances in the Ryder Cup make him the best match player in my book," Els said. "And second would be Gary Player because of all the records he has here. Those are two of the icons of the sport and I'm working myself hopefully up to that level, and by the time I'm done, hopefully I'll be up there."

Player has never made a secret of his admiration for his younger compatriot. "Ernie has such a magnificent swing," Player said. "He is such a fine young man and I'm delighted he has the desire to travel and to be an international player. Now he's going to the gym as well. The world is at his feet. He's got as much potential, I believe, as Tiger Woods. It depends on his desire."

Under the new qualifying criteria for the tournament, Els was exempt as the defending champion, as was Tiger Woods as the world No. 1, although as with some of his countrymen, he was unavailable despite the first prize being raised to £1 million. The remainder of the field came from a points list compiled from performances in the major championships. After a curious year in the majors, the list of qualifiers was not quite what might have been expected. But Els said, "There are some new faces, but the criteria were laid down at the start of the year, and everybody that's here proved themselves in the majors.

"There are some well-known players, some who have been regulars here, who are not here, but they didn't play well enough in the tournaments that counted," Els continued. "New sponsor, new criteria, I think you have to go with it."

For only the second time in the event's history there was no British or Irish player and the three Europeans in the field only got in due to others withdrawing. But that did not stop the knowledgeable Wentworth gallery from supporting the event, with each day's crowd up on the previous year and Friday, Saturday and Sunday not far short of record figures, welcoming news for HSBC in the sponsor's first year.

Although there were no "home" players, there were two players staying at home. Els and Thomas Bjorn both live near the 16th hole of the West Course. Els had a bye in the first round, along with major winners Mike Weir, Ben Curtis and Shaun Micheel. Bjorn, who was the runner-up at the Open Championship, faced Len Mattiace on the opening day.

Mattiace, who turned 36 the previous day, was the journeyman professional who only lost in a playoff to Weir at the Masters in April. He had sneaked in a practice round at Wentworth when he was in England for the Open in July and was so taken with the event that he suggested it would be a fascinating experiment if for one year every tournament was match play rather than stroke play. "I think players would develop differently and different personalities would come out," the American said.

Winning the last two holes before lunch put Mattiace 3 up, but it was over a quick meal that Bjorn sat down with his caddie, Billy Foster, and his sports psychologist, Jos Vantisphout. "We were all thinking similar things, but Billy and I said our thoughts and then we left it to the wise man to decide what to do," Bjorn said. "I was worrying about the match and what Len was doing, instead of focusing on getting the ball in the hole."

As statement of intent, Bjorn's drive at the first hole in the afternoon, measured officially at 385 yards, was emphatic. It was downwind and the ball scampered down the valley and up the other side, leaving him only a wedge to the green. A par was good enough to win the hole, as it was at four of the first six holes. The strong wind, on a day otherwise blessed with autumnal sunshine that suggested some of the traditions of the tournament remained, made conditions particularly tricky with the course, often soggy at this time of year, still running hard and fast due to the lack of rain.

Experience of the layout was important, and Bjorn and Singh were the only two players on the opening day who had played in the event before. As Mattiace struggled, the Dane won six holes on the front nine and the momentum of the match had swung irrevocably. Bjorn, who won 4 and 3, relied on his Ryder Cup experience and also enjoyed the support of the gallery. "There is no experience like the Ryder Cup, and the more match play you've played, the easier it is when you are in these situations," he said. "I felt like I live here," Bjorn added, smiling, of the crowd's encouragement. "I've played Lee Westwood and Monty here before, and I know how difficult it is to play against people who are well supported."

Singh, chipping in at the first and holing from 40 feet at the second, never let up against Germany's Alex Cejka. He might have tied the record-winning margin in the event, and in the process eased the pain of an 11-and-10 drubbing by Mark O'Meara of which he had been on the wrong end, but eventually Singh had to settle for an 8-and-7 win. At the age of 40, Singh produced some of his best golf in 2003 and eventually overtook Woods to lead the U.S. money list, but the years were catching up in one way. Although he won the title in 1997 from the first round, the Fijian was slightly miffed at not being given a bye into the quarter-finals. As the world No. 3, one place behind Els, and one of only three members of the world's top-20 present, Singh thought the seedings should have been based on the world rankings.

The match between Chad Campbell, the runner-up at the U.S. PGA Championship, and Fredrik Jacobson, a flamboyant young Swede, was a repeat of past American college encounters and might well have been a future Ryder Cup singles. But it never lived up to the billing. Campbell was 5 up after 10 holes, again at lunch, and then won four of the first five holes of the afternoon. As the American holed from 30 feet on the second green, Jacobson must have suspected it was not his day, and Campbell won 6 and 5.

Tim Clark, the South African who was third at the PGA, was never ahead against Australian Stephen Leaney, the U.S. Open runner-up, until the 10th hole in the afternoon. He went ahead with a par there, then the next four holes were halved until Clark won the 15th and 16th, where he holed a birdie putt from 10 feet to claim a 3-and-2 victory.

The next opponent for Clark, the No. 64 in the world, was the world No. 2 and the No. 1 seed, Els. It was Ernie's 34th birthday and at 5 up with six to play, it was looking like an easy day. But Clark, showing little respect for his countryman, then won the next four holes. Els had to hole a five-footer at the 17th for a half and then won the 18th with a birdie for a 2-hole victory that came as a relief in the end. "You have to take your hat off to Tim," Els said. "He showed so much character in coming back. I had a couple of shocking holes, but he responded and hit some great shots. It was a hell of a match and maybe it's what I needed for the weekend. I had everything easy and then all of a sudden I had to hit some shots under the gun, and I felt I responded in a positive way."

When Micheel lost to Singh at the second extra hole, it was the second time in less than 24 hours he had been robbed. The winner of the PGA Championship two months earlier was in his rented house having dinner when burglars stole $2,000 in cash, credit cards and his driver's license. "It was quite frightening," said the American. "I guess people are more brazen about that sort of thing round about here, but it wasn't the greatest start to my Match Play participation." The welcome he received on the course from the large gallery was more friendly, but after waiting two hours for the police to arrive, he had not got to bed until 3:30 a.m.

Perhaps surprisingly, Micheel had been 3 up until Singh, a former PGA champion himself, won the last hole before lunch. He went 3 up again with an eagle at the fourth in the afternoon, but the match suddenly shifted gear when Singh made four birdies in five holes between the sixth and the 10th. Despite not being his usually consistent self off the tee, Micheel birdied the short 14th and the 16th, with a fine eight iron out of a fairway bunker, to take the lead again. Both players made a mess of the 17th hole, but the notorious par-five proved fatal for the newcomer to the West Course. Micheel first drove out of bounds on the left, then hit another drive into the trees on the right. His next shot crossed the fairway and was also out of bounds.

Both birdied the 36th hole and parred the 37th, but at the 38th, the short second, Micheel's tee shot found a bunker and he failed to get up and down. It was a sad way for such a fine match to end. "It was a battle of attrition," Micheel said. "I didn't get much sleep last night, but you play on adrenaline and the desire to win. I took Vijay to the wire and it's disappointing to have the opportunity to win and not to do so." The compensation for all his troubles was the £90,000 prize money. "Any time you win a match like that," said Singh, "you feel for the other guy."

Wins for Curtis and Bjorn set up a semi-final clash between the formerly unknown American who claimed such a dramatically unexpected victory in the Open Championship at Royal St. George's and the Dane who squandered his chance to win on that extraordinary day in July by taking three shots to escape from a bunker on the 16th hole. "I can understand why people will look back to the Open," Bjorn said, "but that's long gone for me. I lost the Open, but it doesn't matter who I lost it to. I don't have any unfinished business with Ben Curtis. I will be very determined to win the match but not because of the Open. I have to feel like I'm playing the best player in the world, stick my head down and play my game."

Bjorn did just that in beating Weir 5 and 4 in a match in which he was never behind and only even for three holes. Curtis lost three of the first four holes to Campbell, but found his game soon enough to come home in 32, with an eagle at the 18th giving him a 1-up advantage at lunch. Putting as he had so smoothly at Sandwich during the summer, five birdies and no bogeys helped the 26-year-old from Kent, Ohio, to a 5-and-3 win over Campbell.

"I'm really thrilled," said Curtis, who had not finished better than 13th before he won the Open nor better than 30th since. "I know in my heart that I truly deserved to win the Open. You want to do well and prove to everyone you deserve it, but I will try not to think about that tomorrow. You can only do your best."

Curtis was ranked 396th in the world before he won at Sandwich, but his preparation had been meticulous. So it was this week, although there had also been time to take his new bride, Candace, his parents, her parents and her brother on a sightseeing trip around London. He had also thought he might take his family down to the scene of his summer triumph, but there had not yet been time and he was hoping there wouldn't be.

Bjorn went 4 up after 15 holes, but Curtis showed his fighting qualities by getting back to all square at the 10th in the afternoon. The Dane went 2 up again at the 13th, then the next two holes were exchanged before Bjorn drove so far into the trees at the 16th that he was up against a garden fence. He lost that hole and had to hole a six-footer at the next to remain 1 up, but when Bjorn found the green at the 18th in two and Curtis thinned his third out of a bunker, the American conceded.

Bjorn admitted fatigue was beginning to play its part. "Today was always going to be the tough day and I did get tired," Bjorn said. "Tomorrow I'm sure adrenaline will get me through. I'm up against the star of the field and a friend of mine, and I'm under no illusion about how difficult it will be." Curtis had enjoyed the tournament and added, "The crowds were very good to me. It's nice that people want to root for their Open champion."

"Ben has got a great career ahead of him," Bjorn said. "His career has taken a massive change. Other guys who win majors build up to it, but this guy has gone straight into it. That's difficult, but he's a good enough player to win tournaments."

Els and Singh were meeting for the fourth time, with Els having the advantage after winning their meetings in the 1996 final and the 2002 semi-final. Although he said he had had a quiet evening celebrating his birthday, Els was more scrappy than is usually the case in the morning. Although his only dropped shots were at the 13th and the 15th, following the latter, he was 4 down. He promptly turned the situation around with a record run of eight consecutive holes won, beating the streak of seven by Lema against Player in their 1965 epic.

Els drove into a bunker at the 16th, but an exquisite eight iron to three feet set the recovery in motion. He birdied each of the last three holes of the morning, holing from 15 feet at the 17th and Singh missing from five feet at the last for a half. Els' birdies at the short second and the par-five fourth kept the run going, but he was also helped by bogeys from Singh at the first, the third and the fifth. The Fijian managed to halve the sixth, but immediately lost the seventh to be 5 down.

The quality of the match around the turn was terrific, with Singh birdieing the eighth and the 11th, and the 10th halved in birdies and the 12th in eagles, where both men were putting from four feet. At the 10th it became clear Els would not be denied. Singh chipped in for his two, but then Els holed a putt from 27 feet for the half and had the good grace to smile sheepishly. "I gave it a whack and it went in," Els said after winning 5 and 4. "I had to stand my ground because Vijay was coming back, and I was really pleased with my second shot at the 12th to not lose that hole.

"I was trying to find a swing all morning and finally found a good feeling on the 18th tee, and I took that with me to the afternoon. I knew I had to try something because Vijay was really dominating me, but I don't know what he had for lunch because he seemed to lose his rhythm in the afternoon."

This was also the day Els was confirmed as the European Order of Merit winner when Darren Clarke pulled out of the Madrid Open, an event he had to win to keep his challenge alive. Els had let it be known he would play in the Volvo Masters at Valderrama if he needed to and last-place money there would leave Els out of reach, so Clarke had to concede.

There was no such turnaround in the final, on the chilliest day of the week, as Els led from the third hole. He lunched comfortably at 3 up, despite Bjorn winning three out of four holes early in the back nine, and reached 6 up in the afternoon when Bjorn got lost in the trees at the ninth and bogeyed the 10th.

An early finish was delayed, however, when Bjorn holed from 18 feet on the 12th for an eagle and then holed in one at the 14th. It was only the third ace ever in the event and the first at the uphill, 179-yard 14th. "Follow that," Bjorn told Els, who could not, his attempt at the half pitching not far away but running over the back of the green.

"It was an unbelievable shot," said Els. "I was looking at his swing and the divot and they looked perfect. It will be the shot people remember from this week." Bjorn won a £37,000 car from Toyota Land Cruiser, but when Foster said he had always wanted such a vehicle Bjorn handed over the keys to his caddie, who had made the crucial switch in club selection from the three iron Bjorn had wanted to hit to the successful four iron. Bjorn also went on to collect the £400,000 runner-up prize, but after his collapse in the Open at Sandwich and two playoff defeats, it was another disappointing Sunday for the Dane.

"It has been a season of near-misses, but I have learned a lot this week," he said. "I just need to improve a little bit in every category. I don't need a lot, but more consistency would help. I wasn't as tired today as yesterday and I probably didn't have to play my absolute best to win, but there is no shame in losing to this guy. They don't come any better and he knows how to handle things in this tournament. He never gets too hard on himself. He is too tough a cookie to get through."

Els, a gentleman to the last, never let it get that far, or even as far as the 16th green, which is near his house on the grounds. Instead, when he looked like losing the 15th, he holed a curling, right-to-left, 25-foot putt to leave Bjorn with only a short walk to his own house by the 16th tee, where both finalists' children, who are friends and go to the same school, had spent most of the day playing together.

Els was left to lift the new Mark McCormack Trophy and pocket the £1 million first prize. It was the biggest check ever handed over by a sponsor in any country outside Els' native land. If anyone was experienced at playing for a seven-figure sum it was Els, as he won $2 million at the Sun City tournament last year.

"It is an obscene amount of money," Els admitted, "but I am really comfortable about it. It certainly makes you think out there, but I've spent enough now. I'll put it in the bank. I've got kids to feed."

In claiming his record-equaling fifth title, Els extended his run in the event to 18 wins in his 22 matches. "I really love this championship and to join Gary and Seve is illustrious company," said Els after his seventh win of the season. Echoing Player from a few days earlier, Ballesteros, who followed the match every step of the way for BBC Television, said Els had, "more ability and talent than Tiger Woods. If he really wants to be No. 1, he can be."

"I hold Seve in the highest regard and he has given me a lot of quiet advice over the years," Els said. "He says I need to get mentally tougher. It was difficult today playing against a good friend. You want to be in that certain mood, but it's tough against someone like Thomas. We are such good friends, but I played well tee-to-green, even if my putting stroke let me down at times. The course was totally different to how it usually is in October, so we had to play some different shots, but the greens were in magnificent shape. This is a wonderful championship with so much history. I'm not one for records, but I've got the opportunity to do something next year, and hopefully I'll be healthy and ready to play."

8. American Tours

In an era of personal trainers, limber backs, 400-yard drives and teenage phenoms, the 2003 PGA Tour could have been subtitled "Revenge of the Gray Hairs," as players over age 40 made a resurgence. It started early when Rocco Mediate (41) finished second in the season-opening Mercedes Championships, and Vijay Singh (40) beat John Huston (42) at the Phoenix Open. A week later, Jay Haas (49) went down to the wire before losing to Mike Weir in the Bob Hope Chrysler Classic. "All of a sudden, guys were saying, 'Wait a minute, if these guys can play like that, I can too,'" Haas said.

Scott Hoch won again at age 47, and in one of the more emotional comebacks on tour in 2003, Fred Couples returned to win in his 43rd year, just two years after hinting that he might hang up the spikes and call it a career. Singh won three more times and finished second five times including in the Open Championship in Britain. He broke Tiger Woods' string of having led the money list for four consecutive years. That might not have come as a great shock given how hard Singh worked and how ageless his game seemed. But no one saw Kenny Perry coming.

At age 42 Perry was one of many players whose midsection had expanded as his hairline regressed. He seemed destined to play out his 40s as a ceremonial competitor or, as he put it, "a pretty good player who can still compete a little bit." That was before Perry won three times in 2003, including back-to-back wins at the Bank of America Colonial and Jack Nicklaus' Memorial Tournament. He also finished tied for third in the U.S. Open, tied for eighth in the Open Championship and tied for 10th in the PGA Championship, the best record of his career by a mile.

Davis Love, not quite 40 but on a comeback at 39 after a two-year lull, was even more impressive, with four PGA Tour victories including The Players Championship. His other wins were in the AT&T Pebble Beach National Pro-Am, MCI Heritage and The International, plus he won the unofficial Target World Challenge.

The older winners just kept coming. Bob Tway, who holed out from a bunker to beat Greg Norman in the 1986 PGA Championship, an event that looks as old as *Citizen Kane* when viewed on videotape, came on to win the Bell Canadian Open at age 44. The man Tway beat in a playoff in Canada was no youngster. Brad Faxon (42) didn't win in 2003, but he was second three times and had eight top-10 finishes.

Even Tommy Armour (43) got into the act. The great grandson of the Silver Scot had a little silver of his own by the time he won his first victory in 13 years at the Valero Texas Open. Not only did Armour win in Texas, he did it with an all-time tour scoring record of 26-under-par 254.

By the time John Huston won the Southern Farm Bureau Classic at age 42, he felt like a spring chicken. After all, Peter Jacobsen, who hadn't won a tournament since Woods was a freshman at Stanford, captured the Greater Hartford Open title and probably was Comeback Player of the Year at age 49. But Jake wasn't the oldest winner of the year. Craig Stadler (50) became the first to win a PGA Tour event after joining the Champions Tour when he fired a final-round 63 at the B.C. Open.

Meanwhile, Woods was not to be forgotten. The world's best player had another stellar year despite coming back from knee surgery. He won five times, becoming the first to win five or more tournaments a year for five consecutive years. He also won the Vardon Trophy for a fifth consecutive year and captured his fifth straight Player of the Year crown. The most impressive accomplishment of Woods' year came when he teed off in the Tour Championship in October. With that start, Woods broke Byron Nelson's half-century-old record for consecutive cuts made at 114. And while he didn't win any major championships, Woods contended deep into the final round at the Masters and was a couple of bounces away from capturing his second Open Championship.

U.S. PGA Tour

Mercedes Championships—$5,000,000
Winner: Ernie Els

As if coming off a year where he won his third career major championship and captured six titles around the globe weren't enough, Ernie Els kept rolling by winning the season-opening Mercedes Championships by a record eight strokes. Els posted a 31-under-par 261 total and broke the PGA Tour's 72-hole scoring record of 29 under par (set by John Huston at the 1998 Hawaiian Open and equaled by Mark Calcavecchia at the 2001 Phoenix Open).

"When is Tiger coming back?" Els asked on Saturday night, as he pounded practice range balls. Tiger Woods, who beat Els in a playoff to win the 2000 title, was recovering from arthroscopic knee surgery, which suited the winner just fine. "For some reason, I don't miss him this week," Els said.

Even after winning the Open Championship in Britain, Els admitted to suffering from Tiger-on-the-brain syndrome. He was still hung over from the 2000 season when he finished second in three majors, and was runner-up to Woods five times. "He shot us all down, especially me," Els said. "I was trying to downplay it all at the end of that year, but I think it was still taking its toll on me."

His performance at the Plantation Course at Kapalua in Maui, Hawaii, went a long way toward vanquishing those memories. Els played the par-fives in 16 under par, and made birdie or eagle on 32 of 72 holes, the final one coming when he tapped in for birdie at the par-five 18th on Sunday with the scoring record well in hand. "In the long term, that might mean something to me," he said. "Right now, it doesn't mean much. It's something to tell (his children) Samantha and Ben."

Samantha Els was the first to greet her father after his victory. Els smiled as the three-and-a-half-year-old put a lei around his neck, but his expression was more one of relief than exhilaration. As great as his play was, this one wasn't a complete cakewalk. When K.J. Choi rolled in a 12-footer for birdie on the par-three 11th, the lead was only one shot. But Choi three-putted the 13th and 14th greens for bogeys, while Els made two more birdies at the 12th and 14th to put it out of reach.

"I was playing a little tentative," Els said. He turned it around on the 12th hole, when he blasted a tee shot 373 yards and almost drove the green on the par-four. "That tee shot was the key to the round," he said.

Even if he wasn't thinking of Woods, Els hit some tee shots with his new Titleist 983k driver that had others using words like "Tiger-length." He averaged 306 yards off the tee for the week (the longest in the field), and on the final four holes averaged 342.2 yards with the driver.

"It makes me feel very, very comfortable at the moment," Els said of the way his game has taken shape. "I can go out there and really think about trying to play well. I really look forward to the year now. This is really a perfect start, something I needed."

Choi finished at 23-under-par 269 and tied for second with Rocco Mediate despite a poor putting display in the final round. Playing in the final group with Els, the stocky Korean missed a six-footer for birdie on the fourth hole and an eight-footer for eagle on the fifth. When his three-footer for par lipped out on the sixth, Choi appeared to be done for the day. Still, he hung on and made a game out of it until the two three-putts.

"I was having all kinds of trouble putting," Choi said. "I just couldn't read the breaks today. In order for me to become a better player, those are the kinds of things I have to overcome."

Through one week at least, it looked like Els had overcome all the things that might stand in his way. "I don't see a problem with Ernie challenging Tiger for the next however many years," Mediate said. "I certainly think Tiger would love for that to happen. He likes to be pushed."

Els wouldn't take that bait. "I'm not trying to send a message to anybody," he said. "I'm just trying to prove to myself that I can play well. Let's see where it takes me."

Sony Open in Hawaii—$4,500,000
Winner: Ernie Els

At the Sony Open in Hawaii at Honolulu's Waialae Country Club, Ernie Els became the first player in 14 years to win the first two events of the PGA Tour season. To accomplish this (and become the first since Steve Jones in 1989), Els had to shake a testy bulldog named Aaron Baddeley from his trouser legs. "I thought the kid would go away," Els said. "Then, the last four or five holes, he started swinging great."

Els' prediction of a Baddeley meltdown wasn't a bad guess. The 21-year-old was best known for winning back-to-back Australian Opens as a teen-ager before contracting "the hooks" and falling off. With a rebuilt swing and a short game that produced 40 one-putts in 72 holes, Baddeley impressed Els and everyone else as he drained a 12-foot putt on the 72nd hole to finish at 16-under-par 264 and tie with Els.

That putt came after two incidents on the 17th which looked as though they might taint the outcome. First, Baddeley rolled a birdie effort three feet past the hole. With his ball close to Els' line, the young Aussie asked if Els would like the spot moved. Els declined, and promptly yanked his putt into Baddeley's mark, which kept it from going in. "He spotted it with an English pound," Els said. "I had to laugh at myself, because it was such a total amateur mistake, with all due respect to the amateurs out here. I'm sure he was kind of laughing inside."

Moments later, when Baddeley stroked his three-footer, a spectator slammed the door of a portable toilet, and Baddeley made his worst putt of the week. It hit the lip of the cup and spun out. The two walked off the 17th with pars.

On the 18th green they had to call an official to determine who was away. When the official deemed Els' putt a few inches longer, the Big Easy made a great stroke, but the ball didn't take the break. He tapped in for par and watched as Baddeley drained the 12-footer to force extra holes.

Both players birdied the par-five 18th, the first extra hole, so they went to the 10th, a par-four Els had birdied in regulation when he drove the green. Armed with a driver again, Els hit a high hook — the kind of shot Baddeley had battled through two unsuccessful years. Els' ball landed in the rough where a lady picked it up and started to put it in her purse before officials descended on her. "I was a little disappointed I had to drop it," Els said. "She had put it in a very nice lie for me."

The lie didn't matter. Els had no play at the pin. He did all he could, which was to punch the ball beyond the hole, leaving himself over 40 feet for birdie. Baddeley, who had driven his ball into the greenside bunker, blasted out to 15 feet.

Just when it appeared that Baddeley would win his first start as a PGA Tour member, Els rolled the putt into the hole. Baddeley, who took a few extra seconds to collect himself, left his attempt a quarter of an inch short. "You can almost not believe it," Els said. "That was quite something. I was just trying to stay alive, and all of a sudden, I win the tournament."

Baddeley handled the outcome as well as could be expected. "It was a heck of a putt," he said. "I'm disappointed, because I had a chance to win. But I'm happy, because I made Ernie work for it."

"I know exactly what it feels like," Els said. "You come so close, you grind so hard. I know it's disappointing. Unlucky for Aaron, but he's going to win a lot of titles."

Phoenix Open—$4,000,000
Winner: Vijay Singh

The only concession Vijay Singh seemed willing to make to the calendar was the belly putter he used so deftly to shoot 23-under-par 261 and take home his second Phoenix Open title at the TPC of Scottsdale. Of course, Singh won his first Phoenix title in 1995 by putting with his eyes closed. "That was a feel thing," said the veteran, one month shy of his 40th birthday with an even dozen PGA Tour victories to his credit. This time, he kept his eyes open and let his experience do the rest.

"A person's age is only a number," Singh said after defeating John Huston by three strokes. "I see all these young players coming out and playing so well. But they don't have the experience. I see guys my age or older, and

I know nobody wants it more than me. I really don't believe they have seen my best stuff yet. I expect to compete until I'm 50. Sam Snead won out here when he was 52. I get mad when I don't win, because I feel I'm as good as anybody."

He was better than everyone else on Sunday, and that was saying something. Harrison Frazar set the tone early in the week when he opened the tournament with a nine-under-par 62. Tim Petrovic followed the lead with 63 on Friday, and David Toms got into the act with 63 on Saturday. Frazar still held the lead going into Sunday, but there was no doubt this was going to be a birdie-fest.

Singh got off to the fastest start, rolling in birdie putts on five of the first six holes to take the lead. "It was a dream start for me," he said. "I birdied one and two, and then birdied four, five and six. You do something like that when you're just one or two back to start, and you're definitely going to have good momentum."

That momentum resulted in 29 on the first nine after he made a short putt for birdie at the ninth, and reached 22 under par for the tournament with an uphill 12-footer for birdie at the 11th. Singh's lone error came at the par-three 12th, where he hit his approach into the back bunker and failed to get up and down. He made up for that one on the next hole when he reached the par-five 13th in two and two-putted for birdie. The same on the 15th. He hit one more errant shot on the 17th when he chose driver ("Wrong club," he later said) off the tee and hit it wide right. But Huston, the closest pursuer, couldn't make up any ground. Ten minutes after Singh's scrambling par at the 17th, Huston also took out driver and hooked his tee shot in the water.

"I think that's when I knew I was safe," Singh said. "When I drove off 18 and knew Huston had made bogey on 17. I can handle a three-shot lead. I was quite happy with that."

Huston finished alone in second place with 67, while Frazar shot 69 to finish tied for third with Petrovic, Robert Gamez and Retief Goosen at 265. "I knew Vijay had played really well on the first 11 holes or whatever," Huston said. "But still, you can make up some ground out here the last few holes, or you could lose some ground. You've just got to stay patient and do your own thing."

Singh had a slightly different philosophy, one that will continue to suit him no matter what his age. "When you're making putts and hitting it close, you can have a good score," he said. "That's what I did on the front side. I think that's what won the golf tournament."

Bob Hope Chrysler Classic—$4,500,000
Winner: Mike Weir

This Bob Hope Chrysler Classic looked like one of the more entertaining scenes out of the movie *Tin Cup*. You had three guys who looked nothing like the athletes that leap between the practice tee and fitness trailer on the PGA Tour these days. Throw in a 49-year-old veteran going for broke on the last hole only to see his dreams disappear in the shimmering waves of an artificially colored pond, and the result was one of the most fun-to-watch golf events of the winter — exactly the sort of thing Bob Hope would have wanted at PGA West in La Quinta, California.

Mike Weir won the 90-hole event, birdieing the last three holes to shoot a 30-under-par 330 total and nip Jay Haas by two strokes. It was a lot closer than that. If the tournament had been 72 holes, Tim Herron would have won by four. When the wind blew on Sunday, Herron struggled with a 38 on the first nine and lost the lead to Haas, who had set the tone of his week in the second round when he shot 61, the lowest round of his 28-year career and the best ever by a 49-year-old on the PGA Tour. Herron responded one day later with a 61 of his own — the lowest score by a fat man since the fitness trailer opened in the 1980s.

Weir never shot anything lower than 64 (which he did on Thursday), but his 25-under-par 273 total after Saturday's fourth round was good enough to get him in the final threesome, where he seemed like the odd-man-out until the par-four 16th.

Herron had regained a share of the lead with Haas after an eagle at the par-five 14th, while Weir was a shot behind. At the 16th, Herron hit his tee shot into the sand and then pushed his second shot into a rock outcropping well right of the fairway. That led to an unplayable lie and a drop in the gravel. His fourth shot found the water in front of the green. Herron's first shot from grass was his sixth from the drop area. Three blows later, he tapped in for an eight. When both Haas and Weir birdied the 16th, the swing was five strokes.

Haas took a one-shot lead into the final two holes and played conservatively to the center of the green on the par-three 17th. What he could have never expected was the 40-footer Weir would make for birdie to reach 29 under par. The two were tied with only the par-five 18th to play.

Weir hit first and drove his ball into the right rough and onto a questionable downhill lie. From there, he would have to lay up. "My only option, really, was to lay up," he said afterward. "If I hit 10 balls from there, I might be able to get one on the green, but I felt I could lay it up to 80 or 90 yards, my wedge shot is right into the wind, and I had the back I could play into."

He executed the plan to perfection, laying up to 85 yards and hitting wedge to nine feet.

Haas, however, was a victim of his own length. His tee shot was well over 300 yards, which left him 193 yards to the flag. "I was almost too close," he said. "I'd almost rather go in there with a five wood or something where I could stick it up in the air. I was between a four and five iron, and I took the four. I mis-hit it a little bit, but I was a little surprised it didn't carry."

When Haas's shot found the water, par was all he could hope for. When that didn't materialize and Weir drained the nine-footer for birdie, the Canadian-filled gallery in Southern California erupted in cheers, and Haas was left to ponder what might have been. "I'll look back, I guess, and think about what could have been," he said.

Haas might have had a sleepless flight home, but Weir thought the runner-up made the right call. "That was a no-decision for Jay there, too," the winner said. "It's a definite go from where he was. I would have done the same thing."

The third member of the group, Herron, made eagle on the final hole to finish in a tie for third with Chris DiMarco at 16-under-par 334. He, too, spent some time thinking about what could have been. "In hindsight," he said of his escapades, "I think I could have beaten an eight."

AT&T Pebble Beach National Pro-Am—$5,000,000
Winner: Davis Love

Every winner can point to at least one good break during the week. For Davis Love, who won 13 times in his first 11 years on the PGA Tour only to see the well run dry after 1997, those breaks were rare. Love had won only two tournaments in five years when he found himself leading the AT&T Pebble Beach National Pro-Am on the Monterey Peninsula in California going into a final round. He made a game of it, losing the lead on the first nine to Mike Weir, then gaining it back when his tee shot on the par-three 12th hit the foot of a photographer and rolled to within five feet of the hole. The birdie putt gave Love the lead again, and gave his confidence a much-needed shot in the arm.

"That's probably as nervous as I've ever been playing a round of golf," Love said. "I don't know if it was because I was playing with (amateur partner) Wayne Gretzky, or just that it had been two years since I won. It just seemed like whenever I would make a mistake this week, it would force me to get back to a positive. This was one of the biggest wins ever for me."

The break at the 12th wasn't Love's only test of the day. Four holes later he missed an eight-foot par putt at the same time Tom Lehman was holing a sidehill 20-footer for birdie at the 17th. The two-shot swing gave Lehman a share of the lead. He threatened to take the lead outright until his four-footer for birdie on the 18th slid past the hole. "That green has been trashed by the saltwater," Lehman said. "That's not nearly as much grass on that green as the rest, so it was quicker. It went right through the break."

Lehman was disappointed with the green at the 18th, but not with his game. Like Love, Lehman has been in a drought since his breakout year of 1996. His play at Pebble Beach changed that, at least in his mind. "I feel like my game is the best it's been in a long time," he said. "I really am hitting the ball more like I used to. It became quite evident to me at the beginning of the season that if I start making a few putts, I'm going to be a factor in some tournaments this year."

Love agreed with that assessment, so much so that he paid a little too much attention to what Lehman was doing. "I did a good job of not watching the leaderboard, but I was watching Tom Lehman," Love said. "I guess that's just as bad. I was watching him probably too much."

Fortunately for Love, he didn't watch Lehman's putt at the 18th. "I figured I needed to make eagle to win, birdie to tie," he said. With that thought in mind, Love hit two perfect shots to within 20 feet on the 18th. A routine two-putt birdie was good enough for the victory. Love shot 72-67-67-68 for a 274 total to win by one stroke over Lehman and by two over Weir and Tim Herron. Lehman finished with 67, while Weir shot 68 and Herron, 66.

Love's previous victory in the middle this dry spell also came at Pebble Beach in 2001, which Love attributed to the attitude he brings to this event. "If you come here thinking it's going to be wet, it's going to be windy and cold, you've got to play with amateurs, it's going to take six hours, you've already lost," Love said. "It definitely is a week for a good attitude, and that fits for me."

As for the break Love caught on the 12th, he tossed the ball to the photographer after making the four-footer for birdie. "If we hit somebody in the head, we give them the ball," he said. "I felt like if you hit a guy in the foot and it comes back on a green and you make birdie, he at least deserves the ball — maybe more."

Buick Invitational—$4,500,000
Winner: Tiger Woods

First-round leader and PGA Tour rookie Arron Oberholser might have been considered prescient Thursday night at the Buick Invitational in San Diego were his predictions not so, well, obvious. "When Tiger Woods is shooting 66 and can't find earth with his driver, if he does find earth with driver or three wood, he's going to be awfully hard to beat," Oberholser said. "Nine fairways in two days and he's eight under par? Okay, he's good. News flash. The guy's a beast. He's still in another league from Ernie (Els)."

Indeed, while Els was on the other side of the world winning his fourth tournament of the year by 10 strokes, Woods was reminding everyone why he was still the No. 1 player despite a two-month break to recover from arthroscopic knee surgery. After rounds of 70 and 66 where he "couldn't find earth" off the tee, Woods did, indeed, make some adjustments and start hitting fairways. The result was a 68 on Torrey Pines' famed South Course on Saturday and a one-shot lead over Brad Faxon going into the final round.

But Faxon wasn't the player in the final group everyone came to see on Sunday. Two shots off the pace and the only player to shoot in the 60s every one of the first three days stood Phil Mickelson, a San Diego native who started the year with the No. 2 world ranking.

From the five-deep galleries that showed up on Sunday, everybody in Southern California came hoping for a smackdown. Faxon jokingly considered wearing a striped referee's jersey. "A friend of mine suggested it, and if I could have pulled it off without alienating sponsors I probably would have done it," he said.

If this had been a fight, Faxon would have stopped it after Woods hit a 231-yard four iron to three feet on the 11th and tapped in for a birdie, or when the four iron he cut around a tree from 200 yards out of deep rough on the 15th landed within 15 feet. The tournament wasn't over until Woods tapped in at the 18th for 68 and a 272 total, four clear of Carl Pettersson, five ahead of Faxon, and six in front of the fourth-place tie involving Mickelson, Oberholser and Briny Baird.

"He looked like he'd been playing for weeks in a row," Faxon said. "Every part of his game was on. It's hard to imagine someone playing any better."

Woods was thrilled by the victory, but even happier to be playing pain-free for the first time in months. "I know I answered my questions," he said. "Mine was whether this knee would hold up for 72 holes, and would it be sore." He answered most of those questions on his first competitive swing of the week and his first shot in a tournament since December 12. "I snapped my leg," he said. "I saw where my spike had slipped in the ground and there was no pain. Last year, that shot would have been unbelievably painful."

It was the first of many tee shots he hit with a purpose. "My competitive feeling on the golf course came back," he said. "It was a successful week."

Faxon and Mickelson both limped in with 72s on Sunday.

"He's just an impressive player," Mickelson said of Woods. "It isn't easy to step in and out of competition, and yet he never gives anything back. I know I like to play a couple of tournaments and work my way into a competitive mindset. He's able to walk in and out of it at will."

Nissan Open—$4,500,000
Winner: Mike Weir

Mike Weir had to wonder when he would stop being considered the underdog. He won the 2000 WGC American Express Championship in Spain, where Tiger Woods was supposed to cap off his best year ever with a successful title defense. When he won the Tour Championship in 2001, he was the spoiler to Ernie Els. Even this year's Bob Hope Chrysler Classic was a surprise to some. That was supposed to go to 49-year-old Jay Haas. So Weir shouldn't have been surprised when he was the underdog in the Nissan Open at Riviera Country Club in Pacific Palisades, California, even after making up a seven-shot deficit and forcing a playoff with long-hitting Charles Howell.

"It sucks," Howell said after losing to Weir on the second playoff hole. "That is my general thought. I never at any point thought I wasn't going to win the tournament."

Seven strokes behind after rounds of 72, 68 and 69, Weir said he was thinking about "playing solid and trying to shoot a really good number. But I can't say winning was on my mind."

Weir did all that, shooting 66 for a nine-under-par 275 total, and then waiting for an hour for a playoff. After some questionable decision-making and putting that was almost painful to watch, Howell couldn't have been more accommodating. He shot 73 for his 275 total.

On Riviera's short par-four 10th (315 yards), Howell attempted to drive the green, which he had done easily in the pro-am. "I hit it about four feet and made eagle," he said. His tee shot on Sunday was wide right, and the ball nestled under a tree. From there he had to hit a low punch shot to a shallow green. The ball ran into the back bunker, and he failed to save par.

Two holes later, Howell drove his ball into perfect position on the left side of the fairway, but missed the green right. With the pin cut only four paces on the right side, he again failed to save par. "That one at 12 bugged me," he said. "I had a great drive with that fairway playing into the green. I only had seven iron to the green, and made a bad swing. I certainly wasn't going at that flag."

His final mistake in regulation came at the par-five 17th. Having fallen into a tie with Weir, Howell hit a huge drive, but pushed a three wood to the short side of the green with the pin cut only three paces from the fringe. His pitch from the rough got hung up in the fringe, and he two-putted for par. Another par at the 18th took them to extra holes.

The two halved the 18th, the first playoff hole, with pars, which sent them back to the 10th, a hole they played very differently. Weir, who has never been mistaken for a long hitter, laid up to 75 yards with a fairway wood, while Howell, one of the longest in the game, blasted driver right for the second straight time on the short par-four. The ball landed in a greenside bunker, which left him with a long sand shot and little room for error.

Weir played first and hit his wedge to nine feet. Howell hit a brilliant sand shot to five feet. "I would put that shot up against anyone," he said. Unfortunately for Howell, his poor putting eclipsed his questionable shot selection. After Weir made the nine-footer for birdie, Howell never touched the hole with his five-footer. For the second time in five weeks Mike Weir walked away a winner.

"This is the type of golf course where length isn't an issue," Weir said. "And I think that's something that needs to be looked at, the way courses are set up. You have to really work the ball around here and play smart, and hit it on the right side of the holes. Just the subtleties of this course, the little rolls, the gentle slopes. There are a lot of nice little doglegs where you have to shape the ball. And that, in my mind, is the way golf should be played."

WGC Accenture Match Play—$6,000,000
Winner: Tiger Woods

It shows the state of affairs in golf when the only criticism the golf media can muster is that Tiger Woods didn't win by a big enough margin in the Accenture Match Play, one of the World Golf Championship events at the La Costa Resort in Carlsbad, California. Woods defeated Carl Pettersson (2 and 1), K.J. Choi (5 and 3), Stephen Leaney (7 and 6), Scott Hoch (5 and 4) and Adam Scott (19 holes). But Woods didn't pulverize David Toms in the final. He won 2 and 1 over the 36-hole match, but he bogeyed three of the closing holes to let Toms climb out of a 5-down deficit.

"I didn't give up, but you have to play great to beat Tiger, even when he isn't," Toms said. "When he plays good, he wins. It's that simple. We all know it. I'm just glad he doesn't play 25 tournaments a year."

The two times Woods has made it to the finals (he lost to Darren Clarke in 2000), the event has drawn its largest television ratings. The fact that this was his first win and the last of the WGC events he needed to round out his trophy case, made it the must-see event of the week. In 112 competitive match-play holes, Woods lost only 18, three of those coming late on Sunday to Toms, who kept it close until an errant tee shot on the 17th.

"He's swinging at the ball as good as I've seen him swing in a while," Toms said. "He's very much in control. The only time he seemed to get off out there, he'd get out of rhythm every once in a while when he tried to hit it hard. But when he played within himself, he had a lot of good shots."

Toms made it to the final by defeating Anders Hansen (3 and 1), Chris Riley (1 up), Alex Cejka (1 up), Jerry Kelly (4 and 3) and Peter Lonard (1 up).

If the lack of marquee names on either side of the bracket seemed surprising, it shouldn't have. Every year a large number of big-name players make early exits. This time around, Ernie Els, four victories and 40,000 miles into a marathon winter of golf, lost to Phil Tataurangi on the 20th hole of the first match, prompting the loser to say, "This stuff happens in this format.

A year ago, I might have dug a hole over something like this, but I made mistakes, and I'll learn from them. I like the changes they made to the course, but that doesn't mean I'll be back. In fact, I'm pretty sure I won't be. My love affair with La Costa might be over."

Those making early exits with Els included Retief Goosen (beaten by Jay Haas), Sergio Garcia (losing to defending champion Kevin Sutherland) and David Duval (who lost to Justin Rose in one of the better 20-hole matches).

At least Woods and Toms kept it interesting. Saturday's match between Woods and Scott had everyone marveling over how similar the two players' swings looked. The humble Toms' win over the affable Kelly was the feel-good match of the week. The fact that Woods won the final surprised exactly no one, not even the champion.

Woods wouldn't come out and say he expected to win, but he didn't have to. "I'm starting to feel good," he said. "That's no doubt about that. I was on a tear, a streak from 1999 into 2000. It kind of rolled over. I started putting the pieces together again at the end of last year. At the PGA Grand Slam I started playing better. My practice sessions at home, I was starting to work on some things that I know I used to do in my golf swing that I haven't been able to do because of my leg, and things started to come together. I'm pretty excited about that."

Chrysler Classic of Tucson—$3,000,000
Winner: Frank Lickliter

At age 33, balding, with the remnants of a goatee on a face that fits his nickname, Frankie the Blade, Frank Lickliter looked awfully silly wearing the conquistador hat the good folks of Tucson substitute for a trophy. But after wandering through the wilderness of a swing change that produced four months of missed cuts, Lickliter would have put on a tutu if that were what it took to win. "This is validation that I know I'm going in the right direction," Lickliter said after cruising through the Chrysler Classic of Tucson in 19-under-par 269. "It gives me faith in myself."

Lickliter shot 63 in the second round for the lead and never lost it. That's not to say this was a runaway. Chad Campbell, who shot 63 on Saturday, made seven birdies in the final round and drew a share of the lead when he holed an eight-footer for birdie at the 665-yard 15th. He quickly gave it back with a three-putt bogey at the 16th, but stayed within a stroke when both players parred the 17th.

That's when play was suspended for 49 minutes because of rain and lightning. "I'm surprised they waited so long," Lickliter said. "When I was on the 17th tee, I saw a string of lightning go across the sky."

Both players denied it, but the long wait seemed to have had an impact on their swings. Both Lickliter and Campbell pulled their drives into the water on the 465-yard, par-four 18th, the hardest hole on the course. Campbell played first to the green and hit his third shot to 25 feet. That's when Lickliter hit what he called "the best iron shot I hit all week," a five iron that never left the flag and stopped four feet beyond the hole. "That shot was just an example of what I've been learning. I had nothing but positive thoughts when I made that swing," Lickliter said.

Campbell missed his par putt, which meant Lickliter could have two-putted from four feet to win. The fact that he made the putt extended the final margin to two shots, and kept his bogey-free final round intact. Lickliter finished with 69, while Campbell posted a 67 for his 271 total.

It was Lickliter's second career win, and the $540,000 paycheck moved him to 12th on the money list, a statistic that he hoped would move him out of also-ran status and back into the Masters. "I know I'm on the right road," he said. "If I keep doing what I'm doing, everything else will take care of itself."

Ford Championship at Doral—$5,000,000
Winner: Scott Hoch

It's not every day (or night) that the eventual winner of a PGA Tour event is jeered on the second hole of a playoff, as Scott Hoch was in the Ford Championship at the Doral Resort in Miami. It's not every day that a player stops play on his 20th hole of the day because of darkness. The last time a tournament was stopped at sundown, tour officials suspended play well past dark in 2001 at Hilton Head. This time, the eventual winner made the call.

"I saw the green, and I saw the hole, but you couldn't read the green, at least I couldn't," Hoch said of his nine-footer on No. 1, the second extra hole he was playing with Jim Furyk. "I got my eyes fixed, but my doctor didn't give me night vision."

Hoch's caddie, Damon Green, thought the putt broke right. From what Hoch could see, he thought it might move left. "That was one of the reasons that I didn't putt, because I don't want to be standing over a putt that I'm unsure about, especially when I can't see to make it," Hoch said.

The decision was met by catcalls from some of the Miami faithful who had stayed for the playoff after Hoch and Furyk made barn-burning pars on the 18th to finish with 17-under-par 271s. Furyk was first to finish in regulation, flying his second shot so far over the final green it landed in the grandstands. After a drop, he made a miraculous save for a 68. Ten minutes later, Hoch was long and right, and got a similar drop from the same stands. He, too, made a great par, and the playoff started a little after 6 p.m. The only problem was that the sun goes down in Miami about 6:24 in early March.

Hoch and Furyk made it through one playoff hole without incident, although Furyk pulled his tee shot into a bunker and flew a nine iron from 140 yards into the fifth row of the bleachers. "Who says I only have warning-track power," he said. "Circle the bases." After another drop, Furyk made another great save to tie Hoch and take this one more inning.

That's when Hoch called it a day. After struggling to reach the par-five first hole with his third shot after driving his ball into an old footprint in a bunker, Hoch looked at his nine-footer and called PGA Tour official Slugger White over for a conference. "There's absolutely no gamesmanship involved here," Furyk insisted. "And it's not a question of him having to ask me what I want to do." Hoch had the right to call play due to darkness. He invoked that right, and heard about it from the fans.

"I know they wanted to see us finish today, and I'm sorry that they can't," Hoch said. "But when you can't see, you've got to wait. And I can't see in the dark."

The decision proved to be the correct one. The next morning, Hoch saw that the putt did, indeed, break right. He hit it in the back of the hole for birdie, halved the hole with Furyk, and moved back to the 18th, where he split the middle of the fairway with his drive and hit a nine iron to 10 feet.

Furyk pulled his drive into the same bunker he had found the day before, hit his approach to 25 feet and missed the putt. When Hoch drained the 10-footer for birdie, all was forgiven from the spectators.

"Scott played great," Furyk said. "There's not much I could do. Three pathetic drives in the playoff. Now I wish Scott had tried that putt in the dark last night."

At age 47, Hoch became the oldest PGA Tour winner since Tom Watson won the Colonial at 48, a statistic that was not lost on the winner. "This is very, very big," Hoch said. "Under these conditions early in the morning, to hit those shots, that felt great. You always wonder if this is going to be your last win. When you get up in the mid-40s and upper-40s, it has to creep in your mind. Am I good enough to win? It's getting harder and harder."

Honda Classic—$5,000,000
Winner: Justin Leonard

What a way to impress your in-laws! Justin Leonard and his wife Amanda were three weeks clear of their first wedding anniversary before her parents witnessed their new son-in-law strike a golf ball in person. When the PGA Tour stopped for the Honda Classic at Palm Beach Gardens, Florida, a few miles from their home, Leonard got a dozen passes for his extended family, and then set a high bar, shooting a five-under-par 67 on Sunday morning for a tournament record 24-under-par 264 total and a one-shot victory over Davis Love and Chad Campbell.

The winner teed off in the morning, but not because he was hopelessly down the leaderboard. Leonard was one shot back after rounds of 63, 70 and 64. The PGA Tour got everyone on the course by 10 a.m. to beat the predicted afternoon thunderstorms.

Campbell roared in with 65 for a share of second place and Tim Herron shot 64 to finish alone in fourth at 266.

In the end, Leonard made the crucial putts and Love didn't. "He did what he had to do," Love said. "He only hit a few bad shots, and made some great up-and-downs, so I feel like he won it. I knew what I had to do. I had to shoot six or seven under to win, and I just didn't do it."

Instead Love shot 69 despite getting off to a rousing start with birdies at the first and third holes to take a two-stroke lead. Leonard also birdied the first, but stayed two back until Love bogeyed the par-three sixth after Leonard rolled in a 15-footer for birdie. The two-shot swing knotted the pair at 19 under par. Leonard followed with birdies from four feet at the eighth, one foot at the ninth and two feet at the 11th, typifying what was a birdie-fest week on the Sunset course at the Country Club at Mirasol.

Arthur Hills designed the course for older members who own their own golf carts. The best players in the world demonstrated as much. Rounds of 69 and 70 missed the cut, and there were 18 rounds of 64 or better. Adam Scott shot 62 on Sunday and finished tied for 65th, while Chris Riley, playing in the final group with Love and Leonard, finished the tournament at 269, never held the lead, and finished in a seven-way tie for 14th.

Love eagled the ninth to take a one-shot lead again, but Leonard's birdie at the 11th squared the two for a second time. When Love failed to birdie the par-five 15th after playing the par-fives in 14 under par for the week, Leonard took the lead for good with another deft up-and-down for birdie. One hole later, Leonard missed the green with a seven iron, giving Love another chance. But the third-round leader pulled an eight iron into a greenside bunker. "That's the one I'm going to kick myself over," Love said. "After that, I was forcing it at 17 and 18."

"I made a couple more putts than he did, and a couple of key up-and-downs to where the last couple of holes didn't make much of a difference," Leonard said.

Fortunately for everyone, the rain held off until the final putt fell, but just barely. "It was getting pretty ugly out there," Leonard said. When it finally came, eight inches of water fell on the course as Leonard and his in-laws shared a victory toast. "The only problem is, I set the bar pretty high," Leonard said. "Now, they are going to expect me to come down here and win every year. I'll have to try to soften their expectations."

Bay Hill Invitational—$4,500,000
Winner: Tiger Woods

So much for the knee giving him trouble. On a day when a lot of guys might have withdrawn, Tiger Woods struggled through a stomach virus to win his fourth consecutive Bay Hill Invitational by a record 11 strokes at Arnold Palmer's Bay Hill Club in Orlando, Florida.

Woods became the third player in PGA Tour history to win the same tournament four years in a row. Walter Hagen won the PGA Championship 1927-1930, and Gene Sarazen won the Miami Open 1926-1930 (no tournament in 1927).

"If I wasn't in contention, I wouldn't have gone. There's no way," Woods said, after being up all night with nausea. "Every single tee shot hurt, because my abs were obviously sore from last night, and I continued on while I was playing. The night was long, and the day was probably even longer. That being said, I'm happy with the way I played."

The way he played was four-under-par 68 on Sunday for a 19-under-par 269 total that included playing the last 44 holes without a bogey, a performance so dominant that he more than doubled the five-stroke lead he took into the final round. "He was ready to play," said Brad Faxon, who played the final round with Woods and tied for second with Kirk Triplett, Kenny Perry and Stewart Cink. "As sick as he felt, I don't think if he felt great he would have played much better than that. When he's got a seven- or eight-shot lead, he's not going to throw up all over himself."

Woods wondered if he would even be able to play, and he considered going to a hospital. "I thought about going in," he said. "But the problem is not checking into the hospital; it's checking out. I wanted to get some fluids in me, but I was afraid of getting in there and not being able to leave."

Fortunately for him, the weather was wet and cool, so he was able to keep himself hydrated. The soggy course conditions also kept anyone from making a serious move. He knew that pars would do the trick. "I saw that Faxon wasn't swinging all that well," Woods said. "I knew if I could keep making a lot of pars, put a whole bunch of pressure on these guys, then they would have to play some kind of special round to catch me."

He was tested early. After sitting on his bag through most of what was normally his warm-up session, Woods hit a weak cut shot off the first tee that landed in the rough. He then plopped onto his golf bag and sat with his head down for a couple of minutes before slowly walking down the fairway. A ginger par on the first hole was followed by a missed green on the second, a mediocre chip and a testy 15-footer for par. When that putt fell, Woods seemed to find something deep inside himself that allowed him to keep going. Another 12-footer for par on the third kept the momentum in place. After that, he hit fairways and greens, and let the rest of the field fall away.

Woods' 11-shot margin of victory was the largest in the 25-year history of the tournament and one of the five largest in his career, behind such milestones as his 15-shot U.S. Open win in 2000 and the 12-shot thumping he put on the Masters field in 1997. He also won the 2002 PGA Grand Slam by 14 and the 2000 WGC NEC Invitational by 11.

"It was mind-boggling watching the way he played," Cink said. "That was just an incredible performance."

The Players Championship—$6,000,000
Winner: Davis Love

See Chapter 6.

BellSouth Classic—$4,000,000
Winner: Ben Crane

By the first week of April 2002, the PGA Tour had seven first-time winners. By that same week in 2003, they were still looking for their first. That ended on the first week of April, when Ben Crane put together the best weekend of the year to come from nine back and win the BellSouth Classic by four strokes at the TPC at Sugarloaf in Duluth, Georgia.

"I'm so thankful I played great," Crane said after capping off rounds of 64 and 63 with an eagle at the par-five 18th hole. "I'm a little numb still."

That will happen to you when you struggle to make the cut and then finish strong, playing the last three holes in three under par to reach 16-under-par 272 and win by four. Crane's early rounds of 73 and 72 left him so far back in the pack that his 64 on Saturday was played several hours before CBS televised the event. It did move him into a tie for seventh place, within six shots of leader Lee Janzen and within four of runner-up Bob Tway.

Janzen struggled on Sunday. He bogeyed three of the first five holes. His tee shot on the sixth wound up behind a tree and he had to punch out, leading to the cardinal sin of professional golf — a bogey on a par-five. Janzen shot 40 on the first nine, and Tway, who went out in 33, seemed in control, four shots clear of the field.

Suddenly, out of what seemed to be nowhere, Crane's name leapt onto the leaderboard. He shot 34 on the first nine, which put him five shots behind Tway. A two-putt birdie on the par-five 10th got his momentum rolling. He followed it up with a seven iron on the par-three 11th that led to a five-foot putt for his second birdie in a row. Crane drove the green on the par-four 13th and two-putted for his third birdie on four holes. On the par-three 15th he hit another excellent shot that led to a fourth birdie from six feet. The longest putt he had to make came on the 16th when he rolled in a 20-footer for his fifth birdie of the second nine.

"It kind of got me excited," Crane, who is the excitable kind, said of his birdie binge. "I worked so hard not to look at the leaderboard all day."

He finally took a peek at the leaderboard after making par at the 17th, and saw that Tway was one over on his second nine. "I kind of wanted to have an idea what I needed to do on 18," Crane said. "I looked at my caddie and he said, 'Well, if you make par, I think we're all right.' So, I just stepped up there and ripped a driver, and it went all the way down to the bottom."

Steve Jones and Chris DiMarco were watching on television in the locker room as Crane pulled out driver on the 18th tee. "Wrong club," DiMarco said. The tee shot went 375 yards, bounding down the hill. Crane had a seven-iron second shot into the 576-yard, par-five hole. He hit it 18 feet, and rolled in the putt for eagle.

"When you hit it there, you've got to go," Crane said. "If you hit it on top of the hill, and you have a one-shot lead, you lay up." When the eagle putt fell, Crane flipped his putter in the air and let out a yell.

Tway gave it a try at the 18th as well, but his ball found the water, leading to a bogey and a final round of 71. He finished alone in second place at 276, four behind Crane, and one shot clear of Retief Goosen, Jay Williamson and Hank Kuehne. "I looked up and saw that (Crane) was at 14 under, and I said, 'Gee, he must have birdied some holes quickly,'" Tway said. "It must have been a fabulous round. I'll have to watch the replay and see how he did it."

Masters Tournament—$6,000,000
Winner: Mike Weir

See Chapter 2.

MCI Heritage—$4,500,000
Winner: Davis Love

This win was as ugly as his Players Championship victory was flawless, but when you're a five-time winner of an event, as Davis Love became when he outlasted Woody Austin in a four-hole playoff in the MCI Heritage at the Harbour Town Golf Links at Hilton Head Island, South Carolina, aesthetics aren't always going to be to your liking.

For a guy who had won once in almost five years, Love surely turned things around in the early months of 2003, taking three titles in four months, and jumping into the lead on the money list with just under $3.7 million before the first of May. The victory at Hilton Head had a little bit of everything, including some good breaks, some bad breaks, and more bad shots at sundown than you'll see in a "Gunsmoke" rerun.

For a while this looked to be Ernie Els' tournament all the way. Els started the final round four strokes behind third-round leader Stewart Cink, but with four birdies and an eagle on the first nine, Els grabbed the lead and showed no signs of letting go. He hit every shot perfectly, and when Cink struggled with his accuracy off the tee, Els appeared in command. Then, on the par-four 16th, Els tried to hit driver around the corner of a dogleg. Instead, he pounded the ball straight through the fairway, off the cart path and out of bounds. He re-teed and made a double bogey to create an eight-way tie for the lead with Austin, Hal Sutton, Chris Riley and David Gossett among others.

Els continued his implosion on the par-three 17th, when he hit his tee shot over the green and failed to get a par. Another bogey on the 18th gave Els a final-round 69 for a 274 total, three strokes out of the playoff. "I'm dumbfounded," Els said of his shot at the 16th. "It's the only shot I missed all day. One bad break and that's the tournament."

Sutton was the next to fall. His approach to the 18th drifted left and plugged in the greenside bunker. He blasted out to 20 feet and missed his putt for par, which left him at 272, tied with Gossett, Riley and Geoff Ogilvy, but one stroke out of the playoff. "I don't want to sound like sour grapes," Sutton said, "but I got a bad break. I had to be aggressive with that bunker shot. I couldn't hit the flop shot I wanted."

Love would have joined them as well had it not been for a great shot at the final hole. After pushing his approach and missing the green from 145 yards, Love told his brother, Mark, who always caddies for him at the Heritage, that he was going to hole the chip. Seconds later, the deft little shot rolled 30 feet across the putting surface, clanged off the flag, and fell in for a birdie. Love gave Mark an I-told-you-so point before raising his fist to the cheering crowd. With four Heritage trophies (and tartan jackets in his closet), Love had a boisterous fan base on the island.

Woody Austin saw it all. He had a chance to win the tournament in regulation, but missed his birdie effort at the 18th after a great approach that flew right over the flag. That would prove to be the story of the next hour. Austin would have three more chances to end it with his putter, but each time he pulled, pushed, misjudged or otherwise mis-hit the ball with his long putter. On the second playoff hole, he missed a three-footer for par that would have ended it. He swears he wasn't returning the favor from the first playoff hole when Love made bogey from the middle of the 18th fairway after Austin had pulled his tee shot into the yacht parking area known as Calibogue Sound.

Both players made messes of the 17th, where they each missed the green and made bogey. Finally, with the sun behind the neighboring mainland, Love decided to "quit screwing around." He hit a perfect six iron from the middle of the 18th fairway, and the ball hit the flagstick before dropping to within tap-in range.

"There were a lot of bad shots out there," Love said. "It was a lot like my win at Pebble Beach; I just gutted it out."

Shell Houston Open—$4,500,000
Winner: Fred Couples

The lasting memory from the 2003 Shell Houston Open wasn't the prodigious tee shots that the winner hit all week, or the birdie he made at the 18th to extend the margin of victory to four, or the cheering crowd who made Redstone Golf Club sound like a Texans home game. The image of the week was when Fred Couples pulled the visor over his face and broke down in sobs after capturing his first victory in five years.

"I mumbled a few things, then basically I wanted to get out of there," Couples said. "I needed to regroup a little bit. It's really different. I haven't won in five years. Heck, I haven't really played in five years. A year ago, I was miserable. My swing was getting worse and worse. I'd play, and I'd chop it around."

The tears weren't for the victory or for the 21-under-par 267 he had posted to beat Mark Calcavecchia, Stuart Appleby and Hank Kuehne. They were for his wife, Thais, and his children, GiGi and Oliver. Thais had told him to get off the couch and rededicate himself to golf, or retire, that the half-hearted measures he was putting forth on the golf course weren't helping. She had set up a meeting between Couples and swing coach Butch Harmon, and pushed him out of the house and back onto the practice tee. "It's all a question of motivation for Fred," said 49-year-old Jay Haas, who threatened on the weekend but finished fifth with a 272 total. "Thais probably said, 'Get your butt out there and show them what you can do.' You watch him on the range and you wonder, how can this guy not win every week, or be threatening every week?"

In years past, Couples had the excuse of an injured back. He almost didn't play because of a problem with his back before the tournament, but electrotherapy and the warm humid Houston air kept his muscles loose enough to play. He led after each of the first three rounds, but the last round was a lot closer than the final scores would lead you to believe.

Calcavecchia was one stroke behind when the day began, and he made up that with two straight birdies to start. At the fourth, Calcavecchia found the water and Couples made birdie for a two-shot swing. Calcavecchia made up a shot one hole later with a 21-foot birdie. The shakiest moment for Couples came at the seventh when, for the second day in a row, he pulled a six iron into the water and made double bogey. That knotted the two friends again.

Couples could have folded, especially after hitting his tee shot at the par-three eighth to 60 feet after Calcavecchia hit his shot to within two feet. But Couples made a perfect putt, rolling the ball in from across the green for birdie. He threw his putter and visor in the air as the crowd went wild. One hole later, Couples regained the lead with an 11-foot birdie.

A bogey at the 10th by Couples knotted the two again at 17 under, and Calcavecchia took the lead outright with a two-putt birdie at the par-five 12th. A bogey by Calcavecchia on the 13th squared things again, but Couples had other problems to worry about. Appleby was taking possession of the lead after his fourth birdie on the second nine. A bogey at the 16th dropped Appleby one shot back as Couples and Calcavecchia both birdied the 15th.

Another concern was Kuehne, who started the final round two shots back, but found himself alone atop the leaderboard after birdies at the 10th, 15th,

16th and 17th. But the big-hitting Texan got greedy on the 18th and pulled his tee shot into the water from where he made bogey. "I just hit a bad shot," Kuehne said. "No excuses."

Couples watched it all in typical nonplussed style. "Calc went nuts, then Kuehne went nuts, then Appleby," he said. "It was a lot of fun to be a part of it."

It was especially fun after Couples birdied the 14th, 15th and 16th, the last coming after a six iron rolled to within inches of the hole. "That was the shot of the round," Couples said. "I didn't know how close it was. The people were going crazy."

"That's the best I've ever seen Freddie play," Calcavecchia said. "I will take out of this week that I know I am going to win again, eventually."

Calcavecchia made bogey on the 17th after taking off his shoes and hitting a miraculous recovery shot from the hazard's edge to within 17 feet, and then leaving the putt a quarter of a turn short. That, plus Couples' birdie at the 18th, opened up the margin to four shots. Couples finished with 67 for his 267 total, while Kuehne shot a closing 67 for his 271 total to tie Appleby, with 69, and Calcavecchia, 70.

"I feel honored to win again," Couples said. "I played a very, very good round of golf."

HP Classic of New Orleans—$5,000,000
Winner: Steve Flesch

Can a winless former Rookie of the Year feel a victory coming the moment he walks out of his hotel? "I don't want to say it was one of the those *Caddyshack* deals," said Steve Flesch after coming from behind to beat Bob Estes on the first playoff hole in the HP Classic of New Orleans. "I just had one of those feelings."

Part of that feeling came from the comfort level Flesch had gained with his new belly putter. "Hey, if it's good enough for Freddie Couples, it's good enough for me," he said. The other part was the 20 mile-per-hour winds whipping over his head as he warmed up. "If you throw wind or rain or some funny element in, it helps everyone else's chances," he said. "Today it helped me. I'm always trying, but sometimes I just think that there is no way I can win. Today, for some reason, I just knew from the first hole."

Flesch trailed third-round leader (and sentimental favorite) Scott Verplank by seven strokes when the day began. Verplank never lived in New Orleans, but his college roommate and best friend, Tommy Moore, was a native son of the Bayou and former teaching professional at the host course, English Turn Golf and Country Club. Moore passed away at age 34 from a rare blood disorder. As was his custom, Verplank had dinner with Tommy's widow and kept the memory of his friend alive throughout the week. He also played fantastic golf, shooting a course-record 63 on Friday after opening with 65. A 67 on Saturday made Verplank look unbeatable. His closest competition was Bob Estes, who had been the model of consistency with three 66s, but this tournament was Verplank's to lose.

Verplank did just that, holding on to a slim two-shot lead through 15 holes despite some shaky putting, but made bogey on the 16th after almost driving the par-four hole. His sand wedge approach plugged in a bunker. Two holes later, he pushed his tee shot into a fairway bunker on the long par-four finishing hole and hit an approach into the fifth row of the grandstands right of the green. "I should have tried to play it from the martini glass it landed in," Verplank said of his situation at the 18th. A drop, a long pitch, a poor chip and two putts later, Verplank walked away with a double bogey and 74 on his card. "I just played bad," he said. "I don't know what else to say. I had plenty of opportunities to get a little distance, and I didn't make the putts."

That left the battle up to Estes and a charging Flesch, who got off to a strong start and pulled to within a stroke of the lead with a birdie at the par-five 15th. He then made two crucial par saves at the 16th and 18th, the latter coming after finding the same fairway bunker Verplank would struggle with later in the afternoon. Flesch's 65 for a 21-under-par 267 total was on the board for almost an hour before the rest of the field finished. Flesch was hitting balls when Verplank fell apart and missed the playoff by a shot, and Estes made a miraculous up-and-down from a plugged lie in the greenside bunker at the 18th for 69 to force extra holes.

They went back to the 18th, the hardest hole on the course, especially in a gusting wind. Flesch pulled his tee shot, but was able to hit the green wide right, leaving himself 35 feet for birdie. Estes hit a good shot and was half that distance. The good feelings Flesch had experienced all day kept flowing as he stood over the 35-footer.

"When I walked onto the green, I didn't feel like I needed to read the putt," Flesch said. "Something inside me was saying, 'You're going to make it anyway.' I remember reading the putt, but I don't remember what I read. I just knew I was going to make it. That's the only way to describe it. I got over the putt, and I just tried to go through my routine, but I don't even remember hitting it. It got over that ridge and 15 feet from the hole I knew it was in. I didn't overanalyze it. I let instinct take over. And here I am."

Estes hit a good putt to halve the hole, but it never got high enough. "His was a perfect putt," the runner-up said. "I just never got mine high enough, so it never had a chance."

Wachovia Championship—$5,600,000
Winner: David Toms

The triple-bogey eight which David Toms took on the final hole of the Wachovia Championship was still worth a million dollars and a return to the winner's circle.

Toms shot 10-under-par 278 in the debut of the Wachovia Championship in Charlotte, North Carolina, at the Quail Hollow Club, which had not hosted the PGA Tour since the Kemper Open left in 1979. That was good enough for a 73 and a two-shot victory over Vijay Singh, Robert Gamez and Brent Geiberger. The margin was six strokes when Toms teed off on the final hole. "My game plan was to make a birdie and finish off in style," Toms said. "I went from being in total control and picking my targets to trying to hang on and finish."

It was an unnecessary moment of greed in search of a superfluous birdie that led to this comedy of errors. His tee shot went 50 yards off line, and into trees so thick there was some question about whether it was out of bounds. Toms chipped out, but the ball rolled through the fairway and into a hazard. A drop, a penalty, a lay-up and a four-putt from 45 feet mercifully ended this one. "I thought my caddie was going to putt for me in a second," Toms said. As for the razing he was bound to get in the locker room, Toms approached the matter philosophically. "They're going to realize that I played a great round of golf until that last hole," he said. "And they're going to stick it to me a little bit for that way I finished. But that's fine. I can take it. I've got the trophy and that big check."

Gamez was the first to offer both praise and a little needle. "You just let your guard down," he said of how something like that could happen. "And 18 is not a hole you can let your guard down on. But he obviously putted well all week."

Toms' putting and ball-striking were superb through most of the week. Rounds of 70, 69 and 66 gave him a five-shot lead going into the final round. No one got closer than three shots until the debacle at the 18th. "For guys who don't quite have the ability of a Tiger Woods or an Ernie Els or a Phil Mickelson, it doesn't quite come as easy," Toms said. "I can't be off and win golf tournaments. I have to be playing my best golf."

That was Toms' way of explaining his 11 top-five finishes in a winless streak that had extended to 41 tournaments prior to this win. "I finally got that monkey off my back," he said. "It will be a week that I'll remember for a long time, just because of the way I played golf. It wasn't a fluke that I won, because I felt like I played great golf all week."

EDS Byron Nelson Championship—$5,600,000
Winner: Vijay Singh

The most telling moment of the week in Dallas came after the first round when a PGA Tour official announced the arrival of Vijay Singh in the media center at the EDS Byron Nelson Classic. "They don't (care)," Singh said.

The comment came a few days after Singh was reported to have said to a golf writer for The Associated Press that not only did he find it inappropriate for Annika Sorenstam to play on a sponsor's exemption at the Bank of America Colonial, he hoped she missed the cut, and would withdraw if he were paired with her. Singh said that he had not been quoted accurately. Three days later, he hoisted the championship trophy and accepted congratulations from Nelson on a fine week of golf.

Such is life for the hardest working man in golf. Playing as if the media firestorm never happened, Singh birdied the 15th and 16th holes in the final round to win by two strokes over Nick Price. Earlier rounds of 65, 65 and 69 gave Singh a one-shot lead over Jeff Sluman entering the final round. Sluman's putting was off on Sunday, but it wouldn't have mattered. Singh played spectacular golf all day, holding off charges by Price, Robert Allenby and Scott Verplank, all three of whom shot 65 in the final round.

Price was the most serious contender. After Singh pulled a tee shot on the 10th hole and made bogey, Price birdied the 13th and took the lead. A three-putt bogey at the 15th, followed by Singh rolling in a 28-footer on the same hole a few minutes later, reversed the standings. "Vijay is a straight-up person," Price said afterward. "You always know where you stand with him. He sure got crucified this week. It just shows you how strong the guy is that he can come back and play the way he did and win. I certainly have a lot of admiration for him."

Singh was semi-animated in victory. "I've wanted to win this tournament for a long time," he said after tapping in for 66 and a 15-under-par 265 total. "I finally did it."

He also seemed at ease in discussing his round. "I hit one bad shot all day," Singh said. "Actually two. I hit the wrong club on No. 2, and a bad drive on No. 10. The key shot was hitting a good drive on No. 12 after hitting the bad drive on No. 10." The shot on the 12th led to a sand wedge approach to two feet and a tap-in birdie. The final birdie, on the 16th, came after Singh hit his second shot on the par-five into the greenside bunker and blasted out to six feet.

After his 13th career victory, Singh said, "I've just won the Nelson, and I'm not going to the Colonial. It has nothing to do with the controversy. I've played four straight tournaments, and I need a break." He said he had promised his wife, Ardena, that if he won, he would take the next week off.

"I can't trust you guys, even talking to you, I can't trust you," Singh told the press. "That's how bad it's become ... When I get to a tournament, I totally close out everything that I can. I guess that's why I have been able to play so well in my career. A lot of things went on in my life, and I just focus on what I have to do, and golf is what I need to do."

Bank of America Colonial—$5,000,000
Winner: Kenny Perry

The Bank of America Colonial, a tournament shrouded in the legend of Ben Hogan, could be summed up in 2003 very easily: Annika Sorenstam missed the cut and stole the show, while Kenny Perry won the tournament and still couldn't be picked out of crowd at a local Hooters restaurant. "I'll probably be remembered as the guy who won Annika's event," Perry said, "but that's okay with me."

Sorenstam, playing on a sponsor's exemption, became the first female in 58 years to tee off in a PGA Tour event, which turned the otherwise so-so week in May into the biggest golf media circus of the year. The tournament at Colonial Country Club in Fort Worth, Texas, had so many requests for media credentials they had to expand the size of the media center and bring in reinforcements from the tour to help with the reporters. Crowds for the first two days exceeded those that saw the U.S. Open the last time it was contested at Colonial in 1941. And barely anyone noticed when Perry, the soft-spoken, affable professional from Kentucky, jumped into the lead with a 64 on Friday, 10 shots better than the score Sorenstam posted that same day.

Ten thousand people saw Sorenstam's 74; a couple of hundred saw Perry's 64. But that seemed to be fine with everyone. Sorenstam shot 71 on Thursday in what was, without a doubt, the most eagerly anticipated and watched opening round of a golf tournament in years, maybe ever. She missed just one fairway and had 11 birdie putts of 30 feet or shorter. The fact that she only made one of them seemed beside the point. This was as pressure-packed a round of golf as anyone had ever played, and Sorenstam did herself, and all her fans, proud.

"Best round all year, man, woman or child," said Scott Verplank, one of two dozen players who watched Sorenstam's round from the locker room. "I'm totally impressed. If she came here to get better, she got better today."

"You never see that many guys watching golf in the locker room," said Jay Williamson, who was among those doing just that. "We're sitting up there, and she's making it look easy."

It didn't look so easy on Friday when her ball-striking wasn't quite up to the standards of the first round and her putting continued to give her fits. After the five-over-par 145 missed the cut by four strokes, Sorenstam shed a tear or two, and then told the huge press gathering, "I'm glad I did it, but this is way over my head. I've got to go back to my tour where I belong. I'm very thankful and honored to have been here, but I know where I belong. I'm going to go back to my tour with all the experience I've gained and win golf tournaments."

The next day, Perry shot a course-record 61 and took an eight-shot lead into the final round. A day later, he removed all drama with an easy 68 for a tournament-record 19-under-par 261 and a six-shot victory over Justin Leonard.

The margin would have been greater had Leonard not done a little record-setting of his own. With one hole to play, Leonard was 10 under par on his round, which had the CBS announcers offering the prospect of a 59. Leonard thought about it, too. "I was trying to hit the ball a foot from the hole (on 18)," he said. "That was a mistake. I was trying to hit it close and it didn't work out."

He missed the green and made bogey to tie Perry's record 61 from the day before. But even the cheers for Leonard couldn't rattle the 17-year veteran. "I can't say enough how I felt this week," Perry said. "I was very calm, very relaxed. It was easy. Normally, I'm stressed out and under a lot of pressure, but for some reason, I was able to defeat those demons and feel relaxed and play some great golf."

Memorial Tournament—$5,000,000
Winner: Kenny Perry

When you mention back-to-back winners on the PGA Tour, names like Ernie Els and Tiger Woods or maybe Vijay Singh or Jim Furyk come to mind. Kenny Perry doesn't make the short list. But the Franklin, Kentucky, native went a long way toward rectifying that when he won his second event in as many weeks in Jack Nicklaus's Memorial Tournament at Muirfield Village Golf Club in Dublin, Ohio.

Perry came back from winning the Bank of America Colonial, a tournament where a player who missed the cut (Annika Sorenstam) got more attention than one who set a new course (61) and tournament (261) record (Perry), to win with an impressive week of shot-making against Furyk, Woods, Els, Davis Love, Mike Weir and the rest of the best. His 65-68 opening rounds gave him a one-shot margin going into the weekend. A 70 on Saturday widened the gap to two, and a 32 on the first nine on Sunday allowed him to put it on cruise control for the final two hours.

That turned out to be a good thing. Perry, who had never won back-to-back events in his 17-year career, ran out of gas on the closing stretch, limping in with five bogeys for 40, an even-par 72 and a 275 total. All that did was cut the margin of victory to two shots, and give the winner something to talk about afterward. "The tank was empty," Perry said. "There's no doubt, I'm mentally and physically exhausted. The two weeks have been exhausting. I never experienced the press and the people pulling for me like I did this week, all of the phone calls."

It might have been close if Perry hadn't come out so strong on Sunday. He rolled in a 20-footer for birdie on the second hole and birdies on both front-nine par-fives. He missed a four-footer for birdie on the third, and capped off the side by hitting a 163-yard eight iron out of a sand-filled divot to a foot at the ninth. When that putt fell, the tournament was effectively over.

"That front nine was probably the best nine I played in a long time," Perry said. "I shot some good rounds last week, but to shoot 32 on that nine through those winds and conditions really set up this victory for me."

He was also philosophic about his two-week hot streak. "I always knew I could win out here," he said. "I was not pushing the right buttons at the right time, it seemed like. Mentally and emotionally now I'm so much calmer on the golf course. I just feel relaxed for some reason. I feel like when I get into the heat of the shot I'm able to slow down, my heart rate slows down. I slow everything down. I slowed my swing down and I was hitting terrific golf shots."

That sentiment was echoed by the best in the world. "He is playing beautifully," said Woods, who shot 65 on Sunday (low round of the day) to finish tied for fourth with Vijay Singh at 279. "If my memory serves me correct, the tournaments he has won he has set records. Last week was a joke to shoot that at Colonial. You never see scores like that, and to do it here, back-to-back, with the wind blowing as hard as it has, he has put up some good numbers."

Third-place finisher Mike Weir, who also shot 65 on Sunday for a 278 total, agreed with Woods' assessment. "He's playing fantastic," Weir said of the winner. "When he gets hot, he can really go after it and go low. He's just in a nice groove right now."

Nice is the right word for Perry, whether you're talking about his game or his personality. "We had a strong field this week, and that excites me to be able to beat the best," he said. "I'm very competitive. Even though I always felt I didn't have the talent that these guys had, I always felt I had the heart and soul and guts to play."

FBR Capital Open—$4,500,000
Winner: Rory Sabbatini

The real winner was the weather in the FBR Capital Open in Potomac, Maryland. By the time Rory Sabbatini arrived on the Monday of U.S. Open week to finish off his most consistent tournament of the year and pick up his second career PGA Tour victory, three inches of rain had fallen in 24 hours, adding to the 28 days of precipitation the TPC at Avenel had received in the last month. It was a sloppy slugfest in front of only a few spectators. But none of that seemed to bother Sabbatini, who took the 36-hole lead with rounds of 68 and 66, and then napped on Saturday as the water kept rising.

On Sunday, rested and ready, Sabbatini shot another 68 to take a one-shot lead over Nicholas Fasth into the new week. There were a few interesting runs on Monday, the first coming from Padraig Harrington, who birdied the third and seventh holes to pull even with Fasth at 11 under par (one back), but that was as close as either of the Europeans got.

Harrington bogeyed the eighth, double-bogeyed the 10th, and never got closer than within two shots of the lead again, while Fasth made double bogey on the eighth and followed it up with a triple-bogey six on the par-three ninth after his tee shot hit a rock wall and ricocheted into the hazard behind the green.

The only remaining contender was Duffy Waldorf, who apparently closed to within two shots of the lead with a birdie at the 12th. But, not so fast. Telephone lines at the USGA lit up after Waldorf tapped down a ball mark that was apparently on his line while his ball was off the green. Waldorf initially denied that he had broken any rule, telling a PGA Tour rules official that "I would have missed the green by 50 yards if I'd hit it over that mark," but a later review in the television compound showed it differently. Waldorf assessed himself two strokes and fell into a tie for second.

Waldorf wouldn't have won anyway. Sabbatini did away with all challenges by holing a 60-foot eagle chip at the par-five 13th. "I hit a great chip, and it worked absolutely perfectly," Sabbatini said. "It's not often that you hit shots like that, that come off like you want and react like you want. That was definitely a confidence booster, and that kind of settled me down a little bit."

Newly settled down after the eagle, Sabbatini made a birdie at the 15th and hit a seven-iron approach to three and a half feet for another birdie at the 16th. That was enough to slam the door. His closing 68 and 270 total was four better than Waldorf, Joe Durant and Fred Funk.

"It's been a long time since I've had this feeling," the winner said. "It's great to finally get that second win. It's been really a roller-coaster ride this whole week."

U.S. Open Championship—$6,000,000
Winner: Jim Furyk

See Chapter 3.

Buick Classic—$5,000,000
Winner: Jonathan Kaye

It took nine years, four car wrecks, one surgery and a two-month suspension for displaying his PGA Tour money clip in an inappropriate (below his belt buckle) manner — and 30 holes in one day on an injured knee — but Jonathan Kaye finally lived up to his playing potential with a one-hole playoff victory in the Buick Classic at Westchester Country Club in Harrison, New York. He made a four-footer for birdie on his 29th hole of the day to force a playoff with John Rollins, and then beat Rollins on the same hole with a 12-footer for eagle.

Kaye beat a field that included Tiger Woods, newly crowned U.S. Open champion Jim Furyk, Retief Goosen, Ernie Els, Fred Couples and Sergio Garcia, all of whom were within three strokes of the lead at one point. Furyk held the first-round lead with 66, giving him thoughts of joining Els (1997) and Hale Irwin (1990) as the only players to win at Westchester the week after winning the U.S. Open. Furyk finally returned to earth on Friday with 73. He never stopped smiling as he finished the week tied for 22nd.

Woods hit the ball as well as anyone on the waterlogged golf course (seven inches of rain in the three weeks leading up to the tournament), and the six-inch rough suited his the-tougher-the-better style of play. It wasn't the tee-to-green performance that cost the world's No. 1. He took 31 putts in the third round and missed more putts inside 10 feet than he did in all of 2000. Still, Woods shot 67-69-71-70 for a 277 total and ended the week tied for 13th place, six strokes behind.

Kaye, who finished his third round early Sunday morning (a 68 that left him tied for the lead with Rollins and Skip Kendall), then hobbled around on his injured knee for 18 more holes, birdieing the fourth, fifth and seventh before bogeying the par-five ninth. He made up for that mistake with a six-foot birdie putt at the 14th and a two-putt birdie from 30 feet at the par-five 18th. The final putt from four feet was to shoot 67 and 13-under-par 271 and force the playoff. Rollins also finished with 71, and Joey Sindelar was third at 273 after posting a final 68. Tied for fourth at 274 were Garcia, Kendall, Fred Funk and Jay Haas.

The strained knee came about on Saturday when Kaye slipped off a water cooler on the course. He didn't think anything about it until Sunday morning when he found it hard to walk. By the time he rolled in the last putt to force extra holes, the pain was gone.

The playoff started and ended at the 18th. Rollins missed the fairway and had to lay up short of the green. Kaye hit a perfect tee shot and hit a three iron to 12 feet. When he rolled in the eagle putt, he raised his fists in the air and shouted, "I told you so," to his caddie, Rich Caniglia.

He wouldn't say if that message was for Caniglia, or for the rest of us.

"He's not too concerned about what other people think of him," Caniglia said. "I think that helps him in the long run. He just goes about his business. He knows where he wants to go and what he wants to accomplish. This is a start."

FedEx St. Jude Classic—$4,500,000
Winner: David Toms

In his first victory of the year at the Wachovia Championship, David Toms had the luxury of four-putting for an eight on the last hole to win by two. He could afford no such shenanigans in the FedEx St. Jude Classic at the

TPC at Southwind in Memphis, Tennessee. Toms started the final round one stroke behind Sweden's Richard S. Johnson, but the former PGA champion made a terrible swing off the first tee and made bogey from the right trees. "I didn't say, 'Oh, here we go again,' or anything," Toms said. "I said, 'Let's continue to play.' I birdied the next four holes in a row, and that was the key."

The four consecutive birdies moved Toms into a share of the lead with Lee Janzen and Nick Price, and another birdie at the eighth gave him the lead outright. Janzen gained another temporary share of the lead with birdies at the 10th and 11th, and Price birdied the 15th, 16th and 17th (well ahead of the leaders) to regain a spot atop the leaderboard.

Toms birdied the 12th to separate himself once more, but he followed it up with a bogey at the 13th. That brought the man Ryder Cup captain Curtis Strange called "tougher than an English steak" to the 231-yard, par-three 13th, a downhill monster with water on the right and a pin cut in the sucker right corner. "After I bogeyed 13, I wanted to go for the pin and make it back up," Toms said. "But you can't do that. So I played the shot like I was supposed to, way out to the left side of the green."

That play left Toms with a 51-footer for birdie, a putt that broke twice and had to traverse a healthy ridge before reaching the hole. Johnson, playing with Toms, called it, "the best putt I've ever seen." The shot moved Toms to 19 under par. He never gave up the lead again.

"It was one of those putts I'll remember for a long time, because, obviously, winning the golf tournament, that was a big part of it," Toms said. "It's a putt I could have three-putted very easily. To make it, that helped tremendously."

At the 528-yard 16th, Toms hit a five iron from 233 yards onto the green and within 10 feet of the hole. When that eagle putt fell, it was all but over.

Price tried to put some pressure on the leader behind him, but he went for a closely tucked pin on the final hole and found the water. His closing bogey gave Price 62 for the day and 267 for the week, good enough for sole possession of second, one stroke ahead of Johnson, Bob Estes and Fredrik Jacobson. "I didn't put any brakes on today," Price said. "I can't play much better than the way I played this weekend. If I'd not shot 73 on Thursday, I might have had a realistic chance."

Price needed every birdie just to stay close. Toms had an eagle, eight birdies and three bogeys, enough for a 64 and a 264 total and a three-shot margin of victory. "I knew if I played my game, I was going to be there in the end," he said. "I felt good about my game even after I bogeyed the first hole. That's what I'm doing a lot better now than I did early in my career. I wouldn't say I'm the guy to beat, but I definitely like my chances."

100th Western Open—$4,500,000
Winner: Tiger Woods

The week began with Tiger Woods complaining about hot-faced drivers. It ended with Woods plucking another record from the books while demolishing the field in the 100th Western Open at Cog Hill Golf and Country Club in suburban Chicago. He became the first player in PGA Tour history to win four tournaments a year for five straight years. Ben Hogan, Lloyd Mangrum and Tom Watson had four-year runs with four or more wins, but none of them averaged 303 yards off the tee while saying some other guys were playing with non-conforming hot drivers. And none of those others shot 21-under-par 267 in the Western Open, a tournament that was a major in Hogan and Mangrum's day, and one that Woods turned into a rout despite a couple of rain delays. Woods had rounds of 63, 70, 65 and 69.

When Sunday's second storm blew through Cog Hill and sent the players scurrying to the locker room, the leaders had played their 63rd hole of the week and Woods held a 10-stroke lead. The final margin was five over Rich Beem and equaled the tournament record set by Scott Hoch in 2001. Jim Furyk, Mike Weir and Jerry Kelly tied for third place, seven strokes behind. Woods summed up his dominating performance by saying, "The things I've been working on are starting to come together. Any time you win, you've got to feel pretty good about it."

Woods certainly had a lot to feel good about in Chicago. With an early trip to Britain for the Open Championship on his itinerary, Woods shucked any talk about a slump by opening with a course-record 63 and leading wire-to-wire. In addition to finding most of the fairways (and hitting his driver only 20 percent of the time), he only needed 104 putts for 72 holes.

This came after Woods had stirred the pot with his claims that certain players were taking advantage of technology and knowingly playing with clubs that do not conform to USGA specifications. "They know who they are, and we know who they are," he said. But PGA Tour commissioner Tim Finchem said, "I don't believe any player is knowingly playing with a non-conforming club." This was after Finchem announced that the tour would offer voluntary testing of drivers in 2004 "to protect the manufacturers and give the players comfort in the knowledge that their equipment is conforming." Woods called the development "a good start." He then took all the remaining drama out of the week by running away from the field.

Beem tried to make a game of it with three birdies and an eagle in the first five holes of his Sunday second nine (after the rain delay) to pull to within five strokes. Woods had set the tone in the final round with five birdies and only one bogey through his first 11 holes. He needed just 13 putts in that stretch including an 18-footer at the seventh after a pushed tee shot and miraculous recovery that produced the first fist-pump of the day.

After the rain delay, Woods parred the 12th and 13th, and then missed a six-inch putt for par at the 14th. It was only his second bogey of the day (the other one came at the fourth) and his first short miss of the week. But all that did was keep Hoch's tournament record intact. Pars the rest of the way gave Woods his 38th career PGA Tour victory.

"Rich (Beem) got it going on the second nine and made it interesting," Woods said. "I knew that if he birdied out, I would have to make some pars coming in in order to win the tournament. I was able to do that." Then he added, "This is certainly a shot of confidence, no doubt about it. Hopefully, all the things I've been working on will come together a little more at the Open than they did this week."

Greater Milwaukee Open—$3,500,000
Winner: Kenny Perry

After shooting his second 66 for a one-stroke victory in the Greater Milwaukee Open, Kenny Perry summed up his startling late-career success (three victories by the second week in July) the way he answers most questions: with a story. "You know, I play a bunch now with my son, Justin, who is 17," Perry said after making birdies on the final two holes for a 12-under-par 268 total to win by one stroke over Heath Slocum and Steve Allan. "I see a lot of me in him, or a lot of the way I used to be. One bad shot, and he's done. He just beats himself up, like I used to. I keep telling him it's so much mental out here. And it's only golf. Forget it and move on."

That's what Perry did at Brown Deer Park golf course after reaching 12 under par with a birdie at the 11th hole and then three-putting the 12th after standing in the fairway with a wedge in his hand. He also shrugged it off and moved on after making double bogey at the 13th from the middle of the fairway with a nine iron to the green. That debacle came from pulling the ball into the bunker, blasting out and three-putting.

All this bloodletting turned a one-shot lead into a three-shot deficit to Allan, who also was in the process of shooting 66. But Perry never got down and never gave up. He came back and birdied the 15th to get one of the shots back. Then he got a little help from Allan, who bogeyed the 17th. Then Perry rolled in a 20-footer for birdie at the 17th to regain a share of the lead. He hit an approach to the par-five 18th over the green and into the rough. From there, Perry chipped the ball perfectly, leaving himself an uphill three-footer for birdie and the victory.

"When I saw the chip, I pretty much expected him to win," said Allan, who was on the range hitting balls in the hopes of a playoff. "He's a good putter."

"He'd been putting well all day," said Slocum, who was playing with Perry. Slocomb had stayed close, but he knew that a birdie at the 18th probably wouldn't be enough. "I expected Kenny to make it."

And make it he did. "I blasted out of that stuff and I had three-footer straight uphill," the winner said. "What kind of putt would you like to win a golf tournament but straight in under the hole uphill?"

The putt fell, Perry had his third victory of the year, the 17th of his career, and a lot of explaining to do. "I don't know why all of a sudden I'm winning golf tournaments," he said. "It's just my time, and I believe in my heart that I'm going to win. I always thought I would win here. I really did. I just play so well here year after year. I felt like it was going to be my time."

Having Slocum and Allan chasing him, along with Brett Quigley who shot 65 to finish fourth at 270, gave Perry a moment of pause. "I knew I had nothing to lose," he said. "And those guys are fighting to win their first."

Perry knows what it's like having that kind of pressure on you. He used to beat himself up and tell himself he wasn't that good. Now, he takes it all in stride. "I guess I've opened some eyes, including my own," he said. "The only person who ever thought I could be this good was my dad. He believed in me more than me."

B.C. Open—$3,000,000
Winner: Craig Stadler

While the big cats were away, an aging Walrus came out to play. Craig Stadler, who turned 50 on June 2, won as many tournaments in six weeks after celebrating that birthday as he did in during all of his 40s. The first came at the Ford Senior Players Championship. He then traveled to Endicott, New York, for the B.C. Open as a favor to the sponsor, who had given his son, Kevin, an exemption for two years. Four days and one 63 later, the elder Stadler became the first ever to win a senior event one week and a regular tour event the next.

"It's like la-la-land here the last two weeks," Stadler said after making birdie on the last hole to reach 21-under-par 267 and beat Alex Cejka and Steve Lowery by one stroke. "As bad as I was playing on the West Coast in the spring, I'm playing that good now, and I have no rhyme or reason for it. I was pretty much hating everything about golf. I was kind of waiting until I turned 50 to see what would happen, and all of a sudden I learned how to play again. It's the magical number. Get a good bottle of wine, turn 50, and you start putting well. It's an amazing thing."

Starting the final day eight shots behind Lowery, Stadler relaxed and fired at the pins early and often. He birdied six of his first nine holes, starting with a 29-footer for birdie at the first and tap-ins at the third and fifth. When he rolled in a breaking 48-footer for birdie at the seventh, the crowed erupted, and the race was on.

"I didn't even consider coming from eight shots back," Stadler said. "I just wanted to go out and make some birdies early and shoot a good round."

He did just that, while Lowery struggled to find the fairways. With the leader making a lot of scrambling pars and very few birdies behind him, Stadler chipped in for his sixth birdie at the ninth, and then rolled in a 38-footer for another birdie at the 12th. That tied him for the lead. "Once the putt went in on 12, there was a little different mindset," he said. "I thought I might have a chance at this thing."

Another birdie at the 15th to move to 21 under par knocked Lowery, who three-putted the 12th for bogey, out of the lead for the first time since Thursday.

Stadler's only blemish came at the 17th, when he pushed an iron shot into the bunker at the par-three, blasted to 10 feet and missed his par putt. He quickly made up for it with a sand wedge to six feet and as solid a putt as he had hit all week on the final hole for the final birdie of the day to complete his round of 63, nine under par.

Lowery stayed within a shot, although he wasn't striking the ball well enough to have much of a chance. The real threat was Cejka, who birdied the 16th to gain a share of the lead and made a solid two-putt for par at the 17th. A birdie at the short final hole would give the German his first American victory. But, just has he had done the day before, Cejka pulled his tee shot on the 18th into the water hazard. After a drop, he gave himself a decent putt at par, but the ball stopped an inch short of the hole.

"I just turned it a little bit too much," Cejka said of his drive. "It just caught the edge. The putt was good. I thought I had it. It just broke in the end too much."

"I didn't even consider the fact that he might make bogey on 18," Stadler said. The winner had been staying loose on the driving range when Cejka stumbled at the last. "Golf is a fickle game," Stadler said. "I was just trying to go out and make some birdies. I certainly didn't plan on shooting six under on the front nine, but I had a couple of chip-ins and I made a bunch of bombs. I missed a couple of short ones, but the long ones all went in. That doesn't happen very often, so it sure is fun when it does."

Greater Hartford Open—$4,000,000
Winner: Peter Jacobsen

Buoyed by seeing Craig Stadler win again at age 50 and fearful of getting beat by a girl, Peter Jacobsen brought out his A-game at age 49 for lighting-in-a-bottle four rounds in the Greater Hartford Open. Jacobsen shot three-under-par 67 on Sunday for a 266 total after carrying a one-shot lead into the final round. That proved to be good enough for a two-stroke victory over playing partner Chris Riley, who hit two balls out of bounds during his final-round 68. Todd Fischer closed with 65 to take third place alone at 269.

"Definitely my best golf is behind me," Jacobsen said on Friday night after rounds of 63 and 67 gave him a one-shot edge going into the weekend. "I realize that. But that doesn't mean I can't play well for four days and possibly win a tournament."

This was said after Jacobsen showed the proper deference to a 36-year-old mother of two who shot 153 and missed the cut. Suzy Whaley became the first woman to qualify for a PGA Tour event in 58 years by winning a PGA of America sectional championship, but some of her thunder was stolen earlier in the year when Annika Sorenstam accepted a sponsor's exemption to play in the Bank of America Colonial. Still, Whaley smiled her way around the course and didn't embarrass herself. "I had the best time," she said afterward. "I absolutely loved every minute of it."

The same could be said for Jacobsen, who played the weekend like it was an outing in his Golf Channel television show, "Unplugged." Fist pumping, joking and shaking hands with members of the gallery, Jacobsen was one part stand-up comic and two parts rejuvenated golfer. He shot 69 on Saturday to maintain a one-shot lead over Riley, who rallied with a third-round 63 after an opening 75.

Riley admitted to being excited by the size of the gallery following the final group on Sunday. That might have accounted for the tee shot on the first hole that flew out of bounds and a second errant out-of-bounds ball later in the round. "You can't hit two balls out of bounds on Sunday and win an event," he said. "You know how the crowds are here in Hartford. They're just huge. Maybe I got a little caught up in the moment."

He calmed himself down enough to make an eagle at the par-five 15th to pull back to within two of the lead. Jacobsen answered with a birdie on the 17th to keep the margin at two and stroll up the 18th with a victory in hand. His 67 gave Jacobsen a 266 total and a winning check for $720,000, almost 10 times the size of his biggest previous high.

"When I was 30 years old, I thought I should have won every week," he said. "You think you're going to do it again and again. It doesn't happen that way. I think it makes this victory that much sweeter. I think I'll appreciate it more."

Buick Open—$4,000,000
Winner: Jim Furyk

Late Sunday afternoon, you could find out all you needed to know about the Buick Open in Grand Blanc, Michigan, by looking at the driving range. It was empty except for a few volunteers who were closing up. What made that unusual was that Tiger Woods, Geoff Ogilvy, Briny Baird and Chris DiMarco were all in the clubhouse with scores of 19-under-par 269, which was only two strokes shy of the lead, and the leader had a couple of holes to play. Normally, hitting a ball or two to keep the back warm just in case would have been prudent. When the leader was Jim Furyk, the rest of the field knew they might as well empty their lockers. This one was all but over.

"That fellow drives it straighter than a cable wire," said Neal Lancaster, who played with Furyk in the final round. Furyk hit 42 of 56 fairways and played nearly mistake-free golf en route to a final-round 68 and a two-shot win. He missed only one green on Sunday, the last one, which didn't really matter because he avoided the water and got up and down for a 21-under 267 total and his second victory of the season.

"This is definitely my best year," Furyk said. "Early in the week, my ball-striking was mediocre at best, but I did what I needed to do with my short game to score. As the week went on, I was striking the ball better, and I had a lot of confidence. I got gradually better with each day."

That gradual improvement led to rounds of 68, 66, 65 and the closing 68 in which Furyk never flinched when Woods' name inched up the leaderboard. The 65 gave him a one-shot edge over Carl Paulson with 18 holes to go, but it was Woods that everyone was watching. "Jim is one of the best thinkers out here," said Furyk's caddie, Mike "Fluff" Cowan, who also spent two glorious years as Woods' first looper. Of his current boss, Cowan went on to say, "And he doesn't frighten easily. He doesn't frighten at all."

According to Shotlink, the gadgetry the PGA Tour has installed to tell viewers everything they ever wanted to know about distance and accuracy, Furyk made 321 feet of putts throughout the week, while Woods, who hit a lot of fairways and his fair share of greens, finished the week zero for 13 in putts outside 25 feet.

Woods made enough inside 25 feet to shoot two 69s and a 65 in the first three rounds, and 66 on Sunday. "I really didn't make anything all day, and I still shot 66," Woods said. "I could have had something really low. If I don't lip out four or five putts, it is a ho-hum 62 or even a 61. I thought I needed 63 to give me a really good chance, and it just didn't happen."

Ogilvy had the best final round among the leaders with 65, Baird shot 66 and DiMarco, 67.

Woods was right about what number he needed. A 63 would have nipped Furyk by one. As it stood, however, the U.S. Open champion did what he often does when he's in the lead: he played fairways-and-greens kind of golf. "Every time I made a mistake, I came right back and hit good golf shots to put it away," Furyk said. "I'm proud of that."

The International—$5,000,000
Winner: Davis Love

Davis Love knew what was at stake. With no clear domination on the PGA Tour this year, there was a chance that Love, Mike Weir, Jim Furyk or Vijay Singh might win the Player of the Year title. Even Kenny Perry had a chance.

With that and a lot of other personal matters on his mind, Love put forth his most impressive performance of the year, building a large lead in the first two rounds of The International in Castle Pines, Colorado, and slamming the door on any challengers with three birdies in his first four holes on Sunday. He finished the modified-Stableford event with 46 points, 12 more than Retief Goosen and Singh, who tied for second place. Love could have picked up and walked in after the 15th, taking the maximum (double bogey) on the last three holes, and still won by three. The rest of the players on tour hadn't been beaten this badly by anyone except Tiger Woods in years.

"Obviously, the first two rounds set the tournament up for me," Love said of compiling a tournament-record 36 points. "All I had to do was play good on the weekend and not make any big mistakes. I basically won it with my putter the first two days."

Love added five points to his total on each of the final two days, which was enough for the 12-point margin.

If there ever was to be any drama on the final day, Love eliminated it with a 25-foot birdie putt on the first hole. He then three-putted the second for bogey, but rebounded with a 15-footer for birdie at the third and a four-footer for birdie at the fourth. That gave him a 15-point lead over John Rollins, who would finish alone in fifth with 31 points.

"I knew I had to get off to a good start today," Love said. "That was the challenge for me. I made nice putts at one and three, and then hit a good shot into four."

Singh made a move with birdies at the seventh, eighth and 10th holes, but he was playing for second place. He had that position locked up until Goosen rolled in a six-footer for eagle at the par-five 17th. Singh birdied the 17th to reach 35 points, but a bogey at the 18th dropped him back into a tie with Goosen.

After the final putt fell (Love bogeyed the 16th, birdied the 17th, and bogeyed the 18th, not that it mattered), the winner got choked up as he dedicated the win to his wife, Robin. Her sister's husband, Jeff Knight, had committed suicide in the midst of an FBI investigation into alleged fraud and embezzlement from Love.

"It's been a strain for her, and then to have in the last two or three weeks — I don't want to say too much — some really mean things said about her that are completely untrue is just not fair because she's a good person," Love said. "She's been very strong, not only for the family, but in our business, because my brother-in-law ran our whole family office. She's been very patient and supportive. I've been able to go back and play golf. It was a tough thing to have happen in the middle of my best year, and she picked up the pieces for me so I could keep going.

"Contrary to popular rumor," Love said, "I'm not getting divorced, and we are not unhappy, and we're doing very, very well at home."

PGA Championship—$6,000,000
Winner: Shaun Micheel

See Chapter 5.

WGC NEC Invitational—$6,000,000
Winner: Darren Clarke

With a cold Guinness and a fine Cuban cigar that he admitted was "highly illegal over here," Darren Clarke summed up how he planned to spend the rest of his Sunday evening after winning the WGC NEC Invitational at Firestone Country Club in Akron, Ohio. "Oh, I don't think there will be any time for food tonight," he said. "Food is highly overrated."

So is exercise if you look at Clarke, who weighed in at just over 250 pounds before this tournament, despite some early season vows that he would slim down after becoming fatigued at the Masters. "Darren got confused," said friend and fellow Irishman David Feherty. "He went looking for the fitness van and found the fatness van." He put all his girth behind him at Firestone, matching Tiger Woods' 65 on Thursday and then coming back with rounds of 70, 66 and 67 for a 12-under-par 268 total and four-stroke victory over Jonathan Kaye.

"Darren just played perfect," Kaye said after shooting 70 on Sunday. "He made one mistake that I saw all day. He kind of flubbed a chip on the fifth hole, but he was so far ahead then that he had the opportunity to make a few errors."

Clarke only had a one-shot lead going into the final round, but he extended that pretty quickly when he hit a six iron to three feet and made eagle at the par-five second while Kaye was making bogey. "Enough said," Kaye said. "You hate to give up three shots in one hole."

The lead stretched out to five strokes through 13 holes, despite the chip at the fifth. With no one making a move, Clarke was able to survive a couple of bogeys at the 15th and 16th before cruising in with a final birdie at the 18th to stretch the margin back to four shots. "I got five shots ahead and didn't know what to do," he said. "Today, I felt very calm. I had a day where I was very comfortable, knew exactly what I was trying to do, and things went my way. It's great to see progress not only in my long and short games, but from the mental side as well. It's great to see everything culminate and end up with a win again."

Woods made a brief charge after struggling to find the fairways on Friday and Saturday. He made an eagle and two birdies to close to within two shots of the lead through nine holes, but consecutive bogeys at the 12th and 13th doused Woods' chances. "I just couldn't get anything going," Woods said after finishing with 70 for a 274 total and a share of fourth place with Chris Riley. Davis Love was one stroke ahead in third place alone.

With Clarke sucking all the drama out of the outcome, a lot of attention turned to Open Championship winner Ben Curtis, who not only lived in nearby Stow, Ohio, but who got married the Saturday night of the tournament. He shot 64 on Thursday and was the first-round co-leader with Sergio Garcia, a development that could have caused a delay of the approximately

6:00 p.m. wedding on Saturday had he not shot 76 on Friday. With an 11:40 tee time on Saturday, Curtis shot 72 before being whisked away by local police at 4:25 p.m. He made it to the church on time, and then celebrated until a little after three in the morning, a night that made his 70 on Sunday even more remarkable.

It was also the kind of night Clarke expected to have on Sunday. "I've yet to decide where this will take me," Clarke said of the private jet awaiting him at the airport. "But the opportunities are wide open."

Reno-Tahoe Open—$3,000,000
Winner: Kirk Triplett

One week after withdrawing from the PGA Championship because of a bad back, and one day after struggling through some twinges in the lumbar region on his way to a one-over-par 73, Kirk Triplett summed up the status of his health this way, "When the putts go in, nothing hurts."

That was easy to say Sunday after Triplett had one-putted 13 greens and shot a course-record 63 for a 271 total to come from five strokes behind and win the Reno-Tahoe Open in Nevada by a whopping three strokes over Tim Herron. "In the back of my mind, I was thinking I would show up, shoot 74 and 75, and go hang out with the kids on the weekend," Triplett said. Instead, he shot 67 and 68 in the first two rounds, leaving him a stroke behind Herron at the halfway mark. The pain he had felt a week before came back on Saturday, and at 41, Triplett knew he needed to take it easy. He cobbled together a 73 on ginger swings and a lot of Advil. He was five back and several groups ahead of the leaders when the day began.

"I knew I had an outside shot going into today, but you don't have a 63 in your mind realistically," Triplett said. "I had tremendous support from all the folks in the gallery out there hollering. Every couple of holes I could see someone I knew. It was just very comfortable for me out there."

Triplett went to college at nearby University of Nevada where he got a degree in geological engineering. The only earthquake he studied on Sunday was one of his own making. He birdied eight out of 11 holes, including four in a row that began with a 10-footer on the third. Then he two-putted the par-five fourth after reaching the green. The next two birdies came from 23 and 10 feet. When he made the turn, he had caught Herron at 13 under par.

The lead became Triplett's alone after he hit a 170-yard approach at the 10th to two feet and rolled in the short one for yet another birdie. He followed that up with a 17-footer for birdie at the 11th, and another birdie from seven feet at the 13th. The only makeable putt he missed came at the 17th where a 13-footer hit the hole and spun out. By then he didn't need it. Herron followed every birdie he made on the front with a bogey. He got within two shots of Triplett when a 20-foot chip on the 13th found the hole for birdie, but that was as close to the lead as he would get. Herron finished with 71 for a 274 total.

"When I got to 14, I knew he was running," Herron said of the noise he heard up ahead. "I heard a lot of screams ahead of me. I felt like I missed an opportunity, but the guy did shoot a 63."

He also equaled the tournament record of 271 set by John Cook in 2001 and equaled by Chris Riley and Jonathan Kaye in 2002 (Riley won in a playoff). The paycheck, $540,000, put Triplett over the $10 million mark in career earnings. "That number," he said, "I can't wrap my arms around it. I was taking geology courses over at UNR, because I thought that maybe I could get on as a geological engineer or petroleum engineer and make $50,000 a year, which was a great starting salary in 1985."

Beating that by a factor of 10 in one week validated his career choice and took a little of the hurt away at not making the field in Akron, Ohio, this same week. "Maybe," he said, "I was supposed to be in Reno."

Deutsche Bank Championship—$5,000,000
Winner: Adam Scott

It was not surprising that an Aussie with a swing so similar to that of Tiger Woods that even golf coach Butch Harmon could hardly tell them apart would win a PGA Tour event, and Adam Scott did in the Deutsche Bank Championship at the TPC of Boston in Norton, Massachusetts.

"It's difficult winning in America, not just being a foreigner, but a young player," said 23-year-old Scott. After a couple of quick birdies in the opening round, nobody got closer than three shots to Scott, who added a five-under-par 66 to earlier scores of 69, 62 and 67 for a 264 total and a solid four-shot victory over Rocco Mediate.

After watching Justin Rose, a fellow young star from the European Tour, shoot 63 to take the opening-round lead, Scott came out with 62 on Friday to open up a four-stroke advantage. His 67 on Saturday kept the lead at three, and he never let anyone get closer. A simple up-and-down for birdie on the par-five second hole extended the lead to four, and by the time he holed a 30-foot chip for birdie at the seventh, the lead was six.

"I feel relieved more than anything," Scott said. "Only one or two young guys have done well here. Sergio for one and, of course, Tiger. Justin (Rose) and I have been talking about it. We had a head-to-head battle (at the Alfred Dunhill Championship) three years ago, my first win, and that day we said, 'Let's make this a habit.' It hasn't happened since."

He wasn't sure it was going to happen this week. After missing the green badly and making bogey at the 11th, he hit a poor drive on the 12th at the same time that Mediate was making a four-birdie run. "When I bogeyed 11 I asked my caddie, 'How do we stand?'" Scott said. "He said Rocco was 15 under, and I felt like that was a little bit of a shock. I felt like I was way out in front, but I was only three. It was time to knuckle down and really bury it."

Two great par saves at the 12th and 14th followed by a six-footer for birdie at the 15th locked this one up. "He's as good as you can get," said Mediate, who finished with 65. "At his age, we've got our hands full."

Rose was alone in third place, one stroke further back at 269.

This was a new Labor Day weekend event on the PGA Tour schedule, with the Tiger Woods Foundation as the tournament charity. Woods was not a factor at the end, finishing tied for seventh, nine strokes behind at 273.

Bell Canadian Open—$4,200,000
Winner: Bob Tway

There was a nostalgic Sunday duel between a couple of 40-somethings in the Bell Canadian Open at Hamilton Golf Club in Ancaster, Ontario. The winner was Bob Tway, a 44-year-old who won the 1986 PGA Championship. He beat another aging warrior, Brad Faxon, 42, in a three-hole playoff, which meant that, no matter what, the PGA Tour was going to have its eighth over-40 winner of the year.

"It's really a special win," Tway said after shooting eight-under-par 272 and winning with a bogey on the third extra hole. "I've been coming to Canada for a long, long time. This is a national championship, and it means a lot. I've always thought of it as a bigger tournament than a normal stop."

Other players didn't share Tway's feelings. Only three in the top 20 came to this playing of Canada's national Open: Mike Weir, Vijay Singh and Adam Scott. According to Weir, a Canadian, "Timing is a big part of it. Tiger's new tournament (Deutsche Bank Championship) with a Monday finish leading up to this had an effect." Those who chose to stay home missed a gem. Hamilton hadn't hosted this event since Tommy Armour won in 1930. At 6,946 yards, it was supposed to be too short, but proved anything but. "This is another wake-up call that we don't need to go everywhere and stretch the tees back 80 yards," Faxon said.

Distance wasn't the issue this week, just as it isn't on most courses the players praise. The winner was the one who made the most putts and had the fewest mistakes. Tway proved to be that person, hitting a 35-yard chip at the 17th to three feet, and holing a 25-foot par putt at the 18th to finish the day with 66 to be first in the clubhouse at 272.

Faxon had his putter working well. He birdied the 13th with a seven-footer, the 14th with a 43-footer and the 15th with a 10-footer to get to eight under par with three holes to play. After a routine par on the 16th, Faxon almost fell out of the lead when he missed the fairway at the 17th, but the putter saved him again. He rolled in a 10-footer to remain tied with one hole to play. He had a chance to win in regulation, but his 45-footer for birdie at the last hole stopped six inches short. He finished with a 67.

In the playoff, both players parred the 18th the first time through. They moved on to the 17th, where Tway made par from the rough and appeared to cede the advantage to Faxon, who found the bunker with his second shot and hit one of the most spectacular shots of the week, a 55-yard blast to four feet.

"The shot he hit out of the bunker was incredible," Tway said. "It's incredible if it's a practice round. It's the hardest shot there is. The only saving grace for me was that he was above the hole and couldn't hit that putt with any speed. So it kind of meandered off to the right on him a little bit. I think he hit a good putt."

Faxon agreed. It was a tough four-footer that stayed right all the way. "It's a hard putt," he said. "I thought it was going to break a little left; it never did. I'd love to have it again."

One hole later Faxon made it easy on Tway by missing the fairway at the 18th and leaving himself with a difficult approach. The shot went 60 yards and landed in a hazard. When his putt for bogey missed the hole, all Tway needed was two putts for bogey to win his first event in almost seven years.

"I didn't get down between wins as much this time as I did during my last dry spell," Tway said. "But you know, my wife, Tammie, always tells me there's only one happy guy out here every week. This was my week. It isn't easy, but the reason I keep doing it is the reason we all keep doing it. We still love it."

Tom Pernice was third, one stroke behind at 273. K.J. Choi and Hidemichi Tanaka tied for fourth at 274, one ahead of Vijay Singh and Fred Funk.

John Deere Classic—$3,500,000
Winner: Vijay Singh

According to locals in Silvis, Illinois, the best way to break a long summer drought is to have the PGA Tour in town for the week. What could be an addendum to the *Farmer's Almanac* was validated the second week of September as players in the John Deere Classic almost needed outboard motors to finish. It took an extra day and a 16-under-par 268 total for Vijay Singh to emerge from the muck as the winner.

"You have got to deal with it," Singh said of the weather that ranged from soggy to miserable. "We all like to complain sometimes just for the sake of complaining, but in the end, you go out there and play."

Singh would love to have played on Saturday after shooting 66 and 68 and trailing J.L. Lewis by four strokes, but that was not to be. No one struck a shot. A total of 84 players made the 36-hole cut, too many to play 36 holes on Sunday, so the PGA Tour made another cut, eliminating 18 players. The applicable rule in the handbook reads: "In an effort to achieve (a 72-hole event) by Sunday, 36 holes may be played on Sunday following a reduction of the field to the score which has the closest number of professionals to 60."

"It's way too early to make that decision," said Andrew Magee, one of the players sent packing. "Chances are we're going to have to finish on Monday, anyway, so what's the hurry to send us home Saturday morning? Why not keep us around and see what it looks like Sunday morning? There are a lot of bad decisions out here, but nobody has to answer for them like the players do. On top of everything else, I think it's a slap in the face of the John Deere people."

Magee turned out to be right on one point. They did indeed have to finish on Monday, which prompted Paul Azinger to quip, "We need a new committee on this tour — the Stupid Rule Committee." Singh played 23 holes on Sunday before sunset. In that time he had overtaken Lewis by one stroke and was tied with Chris Riley, who shot 66 and was even par through three holes of the final round when play was called.

Singh made four birdies in the final 13 holes to run away from Riley, Lewis and Jonathan Byrd, who all tied for second place. The bogey-free 65 and 268 total were good enough for a four-shot victory, as Lewis and Riley both had even-par 71 final rounds and Byrd finished with 68.

None of the distractions seemed to bother Singh. "If I play well," he said, "I have no worries about what can go wrong."

84 Lumber Classic of Pennsylvania—$4,000,000
Winner: J.L. Lewis

After Hurricane Isabel washed out Friday's second round of the 84 Lumber Classic of Pennsylvania and forced a 36-hole Sunday finish, J.L. Lewis, who trailed Cameron Beckman by three strokes at the halfway mark, played like a bottle of vintage wine. Although 43 years old, Lewis got better and better as the afternoon went on.

On the Sunday morning, Lewis shot 68 on the rain-softened Nemacolin Woods Resort's course at Farmington in the hills of western Pennsylvania. That dropped Lewis seven shots off Beckman's lead after the youngster posted a course-record 64.

The lead and the course record lasted less than four hours. Lewis got into a rhythm unlike any he had ever experienced. He shot 31 on the first nine of the fourth round (his 19th through 27th holes of the day) to reach 17 under par and pull to within one stroke of the lead. Beckman, Stuart Appleby and Frank Lickliter were then tied for first place. Lickliter shot 32 on his third nine of the day and Appleby had 64 in the third round.

Lewis took the lead for the first time when he reeled off four straight birdies at the 11th through 14th holes to get to 21 under par with four holes to play. He fell back into a tie with Appleby and Lickliter when he made bogey at the 15th, but he regained the lead with a short birdie putt at the par-five 16th. All he had to do was par in for a one-stroke victory. He made a routine par at the 17th, but pushed his tee shot at the 18th into some high rough. He hit a perfect wedge shot to 20 feet and sank the putt for a new course-record 62 for a 266 total and a two-shot victory over Appleby, Lickliter and Frank Petrovic.

"At my age, to be able to do it is a feat," Lewis said. "It's a lifetime experience, you know."

Lewis said he learned about winning this week from losing to Vijay Singh the week before. "I led the tournament every day," he said of the John Deere Classic. "The fourth round I didn't play as well as I'm capable, but I learned a lot. I watched Vijay, and he won it easy. Nobody put any heat on him, really. But what I noticed most is, he didn't put any heat on himself."

One guy who did put some heat on himself, again, was unofficial tournament host John Daly, who was sponsored by 84 Lumber. Daly, who appeared despondent, withdrew in the middle of the second round when his hands began trembling. "When I saw him sitting down and his caddie ran over to me, I just called for an official," said Steve Flesch, who was paired with Daly. "I knew what was going on. It surprised me that he lasted that long. He got over his tee shot the hole before — which he birdied — and his caddie was shaking his head like, don't hit it. His driver was just wobbling from the shakes. When I went over and saw him, he was upset and he was trembling."

That pattern had become all too familiar for Daly in 2003. With his latest wife under indictment for money laundering, the man whose troubles are never far from the surface went into another spiral that included 10 missed cuts and five withdrawals in the span of 23 events.

"Even yesterday he didn't look good," Flesch said. "He was shaking, listless, distant is the best word I can describe. He'd have an eight-footer and run it four feet past, and he'd kind of step over and putt like he's playing with his buddies. I know that's John's style, but he just looked like he was somewhere else."

Valero Texas Open—$3,500,000
Winner: Tommy Armour

Maybe it was the name. Carrying around the legend of the Silver Scot, your grandfather and namesake, every time you sign an autograph or endorse a check has to be a burden, especially when you're trying to make a living as a professional golfer. There had to be some reason for Tommy Armour's winless streak to have extended to 366 starts over 13 years and eight months. But in the shadow of the Alamo, in San Antonio at the Valero Texas Open, Armour finally achieved a PGA Tour victory.

Armour, 157th on the 2003 money list and going nowhere fast, turned his career around in a big way at LaCantera Golf Club. Not only did he win his first event, he did so by shooting 26-under-par 254, the lowest score ever recorded on the PGA Tour. Defending champion Loren Roberts shot the same score he did the year before at LaCantera (261) and lost by seven strokes, tied for second place with Bob Tway.

To top it off, Armour bogeyed the last hole. "He was lapping the field," Roberts said. "It was something to watch."

That's about all anyone could do. Armour shot 64 on Thursday, but trailed by three as LaCantera gave up plenty of low numbers throughout the week. A 62 on Friday moved Armour three ahead. He followed that with 63 on Saturday to run away. The closest pursuer after 54 holes was Duffy Waldorf, who was six strokes back after a 62 of his own. Waldorf cut the lead down to three with birdies on the first three holes, but that was as close as anyone got. "It was Goldilocks conditions," Waldorf said. "Not too soft, not too hard, just right."

Waldorf finished with 67 for a 262 total, good enough to win almost any week on tour, except this one. He placed fourth. Roberts shot 62 to vault into a tie for second with Bob Tway, who said, "It would have been a pretty good tournament except for Armour. I felt I played very good and I'm sure a lot of other people did, too. To play this well and lose by seven shots is pretty amazing."

"I had a chance to play decent on Saturday and just really didn't do it on the back nine," Roberts said. "I think if I could have put up four under on the board or something, and come out with a 62 today, I think that might have put a little more pressure on him. But Duffy birdied the first three holes out of the gate and he didn't crack. It was his tournament to win."

Armour wasn't sure how to explain the difference between his previous history and his record-setting week. All he could say was, golf isn't everything. "I take it seriously, but it's not the end-all," Armour said. "You only get one trip around in life. Golf is just something that I love to do."

WGC American Express Championship—$6,000,000
Winner: Tiger Woods

You couldn't blame the small group of reporters (those able to find Woodstock, Georgia) for asking Player of the Year questions. After all, the last time Player of the Year, Vardon trophy and the money title were up for grabs in October, Monica Lewinsky was an unknown White House intern. So you had to forgive the scribes who persisted in asking Tiger Woods who he would vote for, and what criteria he would use to make his decision.

It should have surprised no one that after Woods put "number of wins" and "the money title" high on his list, he went out and won his fifth tournament of the year and moved back to his familiar No. 1 spot on the yearly earnings sheet. "It's what he's done throughout his career, so I don't know why we should be surprised," said Charles Howell of Woods' grind-to-the-finish win in the WCG American Express Championship.

Through the first weekend in October, Woods had earned $6,278,746, padded his cushion at the top of the Official World Golf Ranking, and made his fifth straight bid for Player of the Year. He did it with a closing 72 on the rough-hewn, 15-month-old Capital City Club's Crabapple course, a sprawling Fazio design in the middle of rural Georgia where the greens were, according to Woods, "harder and faster than Augusta National" and the Bermuda rough was so thick and high only the USGA could love it.

Woods opened with 67 and shot a 66 on Friday that playing companion Rocco Mediate called, "so good it was silly." That gave Woods a five-shot cushion going into the weekend on a course were birdies were sparser than the gallery. In front of dozens of spectators, Woods shot 69 on Saturday to keep the lead despite a 64 by Vijay Singh, who then trailed by two strokes.

The fact that Woods reached eight under par with 18 holes to play was, in and of itself, a testament to his dominance. The top 70 players in the world averaged 74.08 on this course. "This week required almost a U.S. Open mentality," Woods said, "and having to play conservative isn't bad. You have to be precise. You don't have to go out there and shoot 66 every day to have a chance to win the tournament."

A two-over-par 72 on Sunday was enough. Singh cut the lead to one early, but the iron play that had been so precise the day before wasn't quite as good. He bogeyed the ninth and 10th holes from the middle of the fairway, and Woods was able to cruise home with a six-under-par 274 total and the two-shot win over Singh, Tim Herron and Stuart Appleby.

"I wasn't really concerned with Tiger," said Singh, who matched Woods' 72. "I was trying to put something together myself and I didn't. Terrible."

Singh remained $171,000 behind Woods in earnings after the weekend, but after the impressive victory on a course that had most of the world's best shaking their heads, Woods was clearly back in the Player of the Year race. "It's still up for grabs," Woods said. "If (Mike) Weir or Furyk or Vijay win the Tour Championship, they have a chance at the Player of the Year or money title, or both. Davis, too. A lot can happen at that last tournament."

True, but the rest of the contenders entered the homestretch in a familiar position: chasing Tiger Woods.

Southern Farm Bureau Classic—$3,000,000
Winner: John Huston

With 70 of their elite brethren trudging through the rough and struggling for bogeys at the WGC American Express Championship, John Huston and Brenden Pappas put on the best show in golf about 400 miles west in the muggy delta of Mississippi, at Madison in the Southern Farm Bureau Classic. With a two-stroke lead over Hidemichi Tanaka and Paul Stankowski going into the final round, Huston lipped out of a couple of birdie putts and reached a couple of par-fives in two, and then had to hold off Pappas, who shot 62 and came within one ill-timed bogey of gaining a playoff.

Huston had a feeling some one would make a run. Two 66s and a 68 had given him an edge with 18 holes to play, but enough players were close and the Jack Nicklaus-designed Annandale Golf Club was soft and receptive, so anyone could make a charge.

The only taker was Pappas, who got progressively better every round after an opening 72. A multiple winner in his native South Africa, Pappas did well on the former Buy.com (now Nationwide) Tour, but had yet to experience the Sunday pressure of being in contention on the PGA Tour. This week did little to prepare him. The crowds were pleasant enough, but more people were at the Ole Miss football game and the State Fair (in Madison the same week) than saw this playing of Mississippi's only tour stop. Throw in the fact that this was the only event on the 2003 PGA Tour not televised anywhere, and it was easy to see how Pappas could confuse this for old home week on the Vodacom Tour.

He got off to rousing start on Sunday, shooting five-under-par 31 on the first nine to reach 14 under par and make up three shots on Huston. "I rolled in a 30-footer for eagle on No. 5 and I knew the way I felt — the way I was going — the game was on," Pappas said.

The putter stayed hot. Pappas rolled in putts from between five and 50 feet on the second nine, making five birdies between the 10th and 15th. When the 20-footer for birdie at the 14th fell, Pappas had pulled into a tie for the lead. When the 28-footer on the 15th found the cup, Pappas held the lead outright. Another birdie from 13 feet at the 17th extended the lead to three shots, and had people pulling out their calculators and whispering the tour's magic number of 59.

The good things came to an end on the final hole when Pappas pushed his tee shot into a bunker. He caught a bad break in that the ball nestled a foot from the lip and an overhanging tree limb blocked his view to the green. He took his only escape route, but his pitch shot was too hard and it landed in ground under repair. A free drop, a lay-up, a mediocre pitch and two putts later, Pappas put down his only bogey of the day. It would prove costly.

"Standing on the 15th tee I was thinking, 'I've had a lot of disappointments. It would be nice to have one go the other way,'" Huston said. It did. Huston hit the laser irons that had been his bread and butter for almost 20 years, knocking the flag down on three consecutive holes. He made birdies on the 15th, 16th and 17th, with the longest putt being five feet. That gave him the luxury of a lay-up on the par-five 18th for a routine two-putt par, a final round of 68, a 268 total, and a one-stroke win over Pappas.

"When I bogeyed 18, I basically gave him that ray of hope to win the tournament," Pappas said. "When I woke up this morning I told my wife, if I shoot 10 under, the chances are I'll probably finish second. It wasn't a prediction, just a statement. It turned out to be right on the button."

Las Vegas Invitational—$4,000,000
Winner: Stuart Appleby

Because he had been in contention so many times — including a playoff in the 2002 Open Championship won by Ernie Els and two runner-up finishes in the waning days of the 2003 season — it seemed incongruous that Stuart Appleby hadn't won a PGA Tour event since 1999. But that was a fact. Another fact that seemed counterintuitive was Appleby's position on the money list. With a swing that looked like a model of efficiency and a work ethic and temperament that had top-10 written all over it, Appleby's 53rd position in earnings didn't seem right, nor did the fact that he was staring headlong at missing the Tour Championship for the third year in a row.

But that was before he set the desert ablaze with 36 birdies and two eagles in the 91-hole assault-on-par known as the Las Vegas Invitational. Appleby finished regulation with 35 birdies and a five-round total of 31-under-par 328, and then polished off Scott McCarron with a 15-footer for birdie on the first extra hole, a playoff made possible by missed 15-footers for birdie from both players on the final hole of regulation. Appleby's scores were 62, 68, 63, 66 and a final-round 69. McCarron, who added 66 to earlier rounds of 69, 62, 64 and 67, had a shorter putt than Appleby in the playoff, but it missed left.

"As soon as I saw (the putt in the playoff), I thought I could make it," Appleby said. "As it was going to the hole, I thought, 'It's a little slow, a little left,' but it dropped in."

Appleby raised a clinched fist in the air when the final birdie hit the hole, basking in the knowledge that the $720,000 would move him into the top 10 on the money list and get him back into both the Tour Championship and the Mercedes Championships in 2004. He was also thinking about the breaks he caught at the par-three 17th hole in both rounds on the weekend. On Saturday, his ball flew left of the 17th green and seemed destined to find a pond. But the ball stayed on the bank between the putting surface and the water. Recalling Fred Couples' triumphant recovery in the 1992 Masters after receiving a similar break at the 13th, Appleby made a great chip and putt for par in the third round, and then repeated the performance on Sunday. In the final round, the ball appeared to defy gravity, hanging on the edge of nowhere just long enough for Appleby to chip on and two-putt for bogey.

That left Appleby tied with McCarron, who missed a birdie putt on the 13th after a car squealed its tires in a nearby parking lot as he was preparing to putt. "I heard it, and it broke my concentration," the runner-up said. "Things like that happen when you lose." You also see your closest competitor catch a lot of good breaks when you lose. "Stuart's ball stays up on 17 twice," McCarron said. "It was just his turn to win."

Good breaks aside, the winner still had to shoot some impressive numbers. His opening 62 tied for the low round of the week. Unfortunately, there were 10 other 62s, including one by McCarron in the second round. Appleby came back to take a one-shot lead over Steve Flesch into the final round.

Flesch's putter went south on Sunday, and he shot 74 to finish tied for sixth at 334. Appleby's bogey at the 17th dropped him to two under on his final round, but he still had one last chance to end it in regulation. When the birdie putt at the final hole slid by, he tapped in for 69, his worst round of the week. But that didn't affect his attitude in the playoff. Once he had hit the approach to 15 feet, he walked up the green with a world of confidence. "As soon as I saw that putt, I thought I could roll it in," Appleby said. "I had a feeling that I could make it quite easily. It was only about four to eight inches of break."

He did, indeed, roll it in, which put the pressure back on McCarron to make his putt of similar length and line. "I thought I'd made it when I hit it," McCarron said. "I was very surprised. But that's the way it goes."

McCarron walked away disappointed, but ready to take a break from the game. "I'm on vacation," he said as he was leaving the scene. "See you guys at the Bob Hope in 2004."

Appleby, on the other hand, was happy to have a couple of events left, including the Presidents Cup and, with his new spot on the money list, the Tour Championship. "This is certainly good momentum going into those events," he said. "Winning is obviously what we're trying to do out here. A lot of things come with it. Holing that putt on the last hole makes a lot of other great things happen."

Chrysler Classic of Greensboro—$4,500,000
Winner: Shigeki Maruyama

Trying to figure out who's the best Japanese golfer to compete in the United States is difficult. Isao Aoki was the first Japanese to win a U.S. PGA Tour event when he holed a wedge from the fairway to beat Larry Rinker in the 1983 Hawaiian Open, and he dueled Jack Nicklaus until the final hole of the 1980 U.S. Open at Baltusrol. But Aoki never played in the U.S. full time. The same was true for Jumbo Ozaki, who won even more than Aoki, but rarely ventured out of Japan.

Most observers will give the current award to Shigeki Maruyama, who won the 2003 Chrysler Classic of Greensboro by five strokes over Brad Faxon and, in so doing, became only the fourth player on the PGA Tour of any nationality to win at least one tournament in each of the last three seasons. He was already the first Japanese player to win a tournament on the American mainland. His victories at the Greater Milwaukee Open in 2001, GTE Byron Nelson Classic in 2002 and now the Chrysler Classic of Greensboro solidified his spot.

The other players who won at least one event in each of the past three years were Tiger Woods, Justin Leonard and Jim Furyk. "I'm really happy to be one of those players, to be listed with the big names," Maruyama said. "This big win gives me a lot of confidence."

The way he won was also a confidence booster. Maruyama putted like a maniac all week, averaging a career-best 25.3 putts for the four rounds. He shot 65 and 64 the first two days, and took a five-shot lead into the weekend. A third-round 70 by Maruyama allowed Faxon to cut the margin to three. When Maruyama got up and down for birdie at the par-five 15th to extend the lead to four shots with four holes to play, everyone, including Faxon, knew that this one was over. Maruyama closed out with one more birdie for 67, a 266 total, and the five-stroke victory.

"That's some low scoring," Faxon said. "Some pretty good golf. It's not just going to happen; you've got to hit good shots, and you've got to make a lot of putts, and he made a lot of putts."

Maruyama, who had been battling a neck injury all season, agreed with that assessment. "I wasn't expecting this kind of week," he said. "My putting was the big thing. This was the best putting week of my whole life. A couple of weeks ago I was just trying to get to 125 on the money list. After this win, I can see the Tour Championship. That would be a big chance."

FUNAI Classic at the Walt Disney World Resort—$4,000,000
Winner: Vijay Singh

Vijay Singh did all he could do; he won his fourth title of the year and all but locked up the 2003 money title. "I feel like if I take the money title, I have a good chance of winning Player of the Year," Singh said after shooting 23-under-par 265 in the FUNAI Classic at the Walt Disney World Resort to win by four strokes over Tiger Woods, Scott Verplank and Stewart Cink. "If I don't (win the money title), there's no chance."

By announcing that he would play in Tampa and at the Tour Championship (the final two stops on the schedule), Singh, who left Lake Buena Vista, Florida, $250,000 ahead of Woods in official earnings, set himself up to win the title he covets most: the one with a dollar sign in front of it. "That's my goal," Singh said. "If I get the job done, I should win it."

He certainly got the job done at Disney World. He shot 64 and 65 to take a one-stroke lead into the weekend, and effectively nailed the door shut when he hit every fairway on Saturday en route to a 69. So confident was Singh with his golf swing that, in shooting a final-round 67, he hit driver on holes where most other players were hitting irons and fairway woods. When he reached the par-five 10th hole on Sunday with his second shot and two-putted for birdie, the tournament was effectively over. His closest challenger, Cink, came up short on the par-five hole and failed to get up and down. Singh got to 23 under par with a 40-footer for birdie at the 12th, while Cink failed to convert an eight-footer for birdie at the 11th.

"It does not surprise me at all that it was Singh who went out there and took it," Cink said. "He's on top of his game, and I knew he was not going to make too many bogeys."

Even Singh's putter, which had been the bane of his game for years, appeared to cooperate. According to his caddie, Dave Renwick, "His putting has been a boost all year. He's picked up a few shots at each tournament, and that's all he's needed."

Of the second-place finishers, Woods had the most productive final round. He started out with a bogey at the first hole but didn't sniff an over-par score after that. Six birdies and an eagle later, he tapped in for 65 and a 19-under 269 total. When Cink and Verplank both missed short birdie chances at the final hole, Woods stayed in a tie for second place.

But the questions afterward weren't about the 65 or the second-place finish. Nor were a lot of folks interested in the 55-year-old record Woods tied when he survived his 113th consecutive 36-hole cut, matching Byron Nelson from the 1940s. All those speaking to Woods wanted to hear was what he thought about possibly losing the money title for the first time in five years, and how that would affect the Player of the Year vote.

"It's important, but it's not that important," Woods said of the money title. "If he has it wrapped up, so be it. Anybody would rather have Player of the Year than the money title." And Woods seemed well on his way to making his fifth straight claim to that coveted title. He locked up the Vardon Trophy for lowest stroke average, and he would later break the 36-hole cut record at the season-ending Tour Championship. "It's a great record, a greater record than a lot of people realize," Jim Furyk said of the consecutive cuts streak. "He's playing against very deep fields filled with talent, and it only takes one bad round to push you out of the cut line."

Woods admitted that the streak involved a little luck, but he was quick to add, "You've got to work your butt off, too." To those who argued that the cut streak was illegitimate because it involved tournaments that had no cut, Davis Love offered up the most poignant observation. "Go back and look and he wouldn't have missed the cut if there had been one," Love said. "And the World Golf Championships events, all he does is win those. You probably can't count those against him."

Indeed, the consecutive cuts streak survived the Palmer, Nicklaus and Watson eras before Woods arrived on the scene. He also left Disney World having extended his record number of weeks atop the World Ranking, a record Singh would like to see end soon. "I give myself five years," Singh said. "It's going to be really hard to get Tiger from the No. 1 spot. He's playing well every week. I just have to match that and play better than that in the next few years. We'll have to wait and see."

Chrysler Championship—$4,800,000
Winner: Retief Goosen

The Chrysler Championship had more plotlines than a Tom Clancy novel. First, there was the Player of the Year question, which went unanswered, as Vijay Singh finished second and locked up the money title, but failed to pick up his fifth victory of the year. Then there was the other end of the money spectrum; since the Tampa, Florida, tournament was the last full-field event of the year, a slue of players were vying to keep their places on the PGA Tour. Pat Bates, Glen Hnatiuk and Esteban Toledo made it by a hair. Per-Ulrik Johansson, Dicky Pride and Mark Wilson did not. They left with a trip looming to the final stage of the qualifying tournament.

And Retief Goosen won the tournament, shooting 69, 66, 67 and 70 for 12-under-par 272 total and a three-shot cushion over Singh and a four-shot margin over Briny Baird. For Goosen, the gold at the end of the rainbow would be a trip back to Maui for the 2004 Mercedes Championships, a trip he hasn't missed since his breakout victory in the 2001 U.S. Open. This time, he took charge on Friday with a five-under-par 66 to stretch his lead to two strokes. He extended it to three with 67 on Saturday. When Singh made a run with a couple of early birdies, Goosen responded with a seven iron to 15 feet for birdie at the 13th and two of the best shots of the week to reach the par-five 14th in two. When he two-putted for birdie, the lead was back to three, which is where it remained.

"Once I'm out there, I just want to get as far ahead as possible," Goosen said. "Luckily, it happened for me again this week."

Singh knew that he would have to make birdies coming in to have a chance, which was no easy task on the tough Cooperhead course at the Westin Innisbrook Resort. When birdies at the 16th and 17th failed to come close, Singh knew his day was done. "Goosen is too good a player to mess up," he said.

Goosen's 73 on Sunday the week before at Disney World left him 26th on the U.S. money list and in danger of losing a spot in the season-ending Tour Championship. That, coupled with a burning desire to take his wife and seven-month-old son, Leo, to Maui in January were the reasons Goosen chose Tampa over the European Tour and the Volvo Championship at Valderrama. "If I would have had a good round last week, I might have gone back to Europe," Goosen said.

He also attributed his late-season return to winning form on a readjustment of his priorities. "I have put golf second and really focused on the family side of life," he said. "As a result, I feel like I've learned a lot about my game."

Tour Championship—$6,000,000
Winner: Chad Campbell

The first week of April, *Sports Illustrated* put Chad Campbell on the cover of its special Golf Plus addition and labeled him as "the next big thing." Pretty heady stuff for a guy whose biggest claim to fame was 13 victories and three Player of the Year titles on the Hooters Tour. The biggest thrill there came when his Player of the Year trophy was presented by the Hooters Girl of the Year. Seven months after that magazine cover, however, Campbell was still winless in the big leagues and had fallen behind such upstart stories as Ben Curtis and Shaun Micheel.

That changed in Houston when Campbell played 27 holes in 17 under par over the weekend to make up five shots on second-round leader Charles Howell, and then run and hide from the field with a series of steady pars. His 16-under-par 268 included a 68 on Sunday and the best round of the tournament by a mile — a 61 in the third round. In the process Campbell became the first to make the Tour Championship his first PGA Tour win.

"A 61?" said Chris Riley, who was Campbell's college roommate at UNLV. "I didn't see that out there. I saw a 66 or a 67, not a 61. But Chad has dominated at every level. He dominated in college, dominated the Hooters Tour, and dominated the Nationwide Tour. He's a top-tier player."

Howell, who witnessed Campbell's weekend eruption, said, "In a good way, he's a very boring golfer, which is what you want to be. Fairway, green, and then he hits his putt and it either goes in or stops right next to the hole. Fairway, green, putt. Fairway, green, putt. When a guy like that is on, you've got to make a bunch of birdies to beat him."

Howell couldn't put together the birdie barrage he needed, even though he kept it close with a series of birdies in the middle of the final round. But a final-round 70 after three straight 67s wasn't quite good enough. A fourth straight 67 would have forced a playoff, but as happened throughout much of the year, Howell's putter abandoned him late on Sunday.

Campbell going out in 31 on Sunday didn't help. By the time the two made the turn, the lead was five. After Howell's charge sputtered, Retief Goosen picked up the mantle, pulling within two shots through 11 holes, but could get no closer. A final-round 69 left Goosen alone in third place at 272, one behind Howell, who birdied the last hole from a foot to take sole possession of second at 271. Riley finished fourth with 273.

"It's nice to get the first one under my belt," Campbell said. "I'm glad to not have to answer those questions any more. Hopefully this will make the next time I get in that situation even easier. Obviously, after yesterday it was kind of hard to follow up a good round with another good one. I was able to get off to another good start on the front nine today. And I was able to have a little cushion on the back nine, which made it easy."

The other players knew Campbell was a force to be reckoned with. "He's been threatening for a while," said Vijay Singh, who finished tied for fifth at 276 and atop the season-ending money list. "He's a very aggressive player. When he gets it going, like this week, there's no stopping him. We will hear a lot more from Chad Campbell. That is not the end of it."

WGC World Cup—$4,000,000
Winner: South Africa

The South African "B" Team brought their "A" game to Kiawah Island, South Carolina, and held on after a shaky one-over-par 73 on Sunday for a 13-under 275 total, good enough for a three-stroke victory over England's Paul Casey and Justin Rose. Trevor Immelman and Rory Sabbatini wouldn't have been paired for South Africa had Ernie Els and Retief Goosen been available, but when they shot 63 in the third round to open up a seven-stroke lead, the pair proved that there is some real depth of skill in their country.

"I normally don't watch the leaderboard much," Immelman said. "But with seven shots, it just kind of felt funny. I needed to keep an eye on what was going on."

What was going on was a charge by the United States team of Jim Furyk and Justin Leonard. The Americans cut the lead to three strokes on the first nine in the alternate-shot format, but failed to make any substantive putts all day. A bogey, triple-bogey run on the 12th and 13th holes ruined any chances the Americans had. They finished with 75 for a 284 total and a tie for fifth place with Ireland's Padraig Harrington and Paul McGinley.

"It was frustrating today," Leonard said. "We played solid enough on the front, but could get nothing to go in." Then came the disaster when Leonard missed a relatively easy par putt at the 12th, and Furyk followed with a hooked tee shot into the water at the 13th. "We played 17 real solid holes without any putts going in," Furyk said. "I got loose on one tee shot and we ended up making a triple bogey. Other than that, we played well."

Sabbatini said before the final round that he would "take 18 pars right now and run." They weren't quite so fortunate, making two birdies and three bogeys, which was still good enough. England actually had a better week-end, following up their 66 on Saturday with a five-under 67. Two 73s by England in the opening rounds proved to be the difference. "South Africa were 10 ahead of us at the beginning of the day, so we weren't realistically looking at them," Rose said. "We could look at second, and if South Africa had a nightmare round we could be there."

The nightmare never came, and Immelman and Sabbatini cruised in with three final pars to take South Africa's second World Cup title in three years. "Obviously, you can never really say you've got it in the bag," Sabbatini said. "I was pretty certain with four holes to go that we had ourselves in a really good position. If we stuck with what we were doing and didn't make any blatantly stupid errors out there, we were fine."

Special Events

CVS Charity Classic—$1,200,000
Winners: Jeff Sluman and Rocco Mediate

He couldn't say he wasn't warned. Tournament host Billy Andrade had already been told that the team of Rocco Mediate and Jeff Sluman was going to be hard to beat. The warning had come from no less an authority than Mediate himself. "He did; he told me that," Andrade said. "He said every time they play together, they shoot lights out. They go out and birdie everything. He said that. I guess they backed it up."

Sluman and Mediate shot a tournament-record 57 at Rhode Island Country Club. After trailing Nick Price and Scott McCarron by two strokes, Sluman and Mediate went on a birdie tear, recording seven straight threes between the second and eighth holes. The run included six birdies and an eagle at the par-five eighth. After a par at the ninth, Sluman birdied the 10th, Mediate the 11th, Sluman the 12th and Mediate the 13th. Sluman made another birdie at the 15th, and Mediate picked up his last birdie at the 17th. Needing one more birdie to close the door, Sluman rolled in a putt at the 18th for the 14-under-par 57 and a two-day total of 22-under 120.

"I told Billy, you guys are making a mistake," Mediate said. "Jeff and I play well all the time when we play together."

Brad Faxon and Andrade finished second, following their 63 with a 58 to miss a playoff by one stroke. Dudley Hart and Chris DiMarco were third at 122 after rounds of 63 and 59, and the Quigleys, Dana and Brett, came in with 62 after a 61 in the first round to place fourth.

Price and McCarron couldn't make any putts in the second round after leading with an opening 61. They closed with 66 for a 127 total, tied for seventh place.

Franklin Templeton Shootout—$2,400,000
Winners: Jeff Sluman and Hank Kuehne

One week after dislodging John Daly from his four-year perch atop the PGA Tour's long-driving statistics, Hank Kuehne showed he had a putting touch to go with the long ball as he rolled in a five-footer for birdie on the second extra hole to win the Franklin Templeton Shootout. "It's nice to be able to stand up here and do what you have to do to win," Kuehne said after he and his partner, Jeff Sluman, beat the teams of Chad Campbell/Shaun Micheel and Brad Faxon/Scott McCarron.

Sluman and Kuehne started the final round four strokes behind. The closing format was a scramble, which suited their games perfectly. They began their move when Kuehne made a birdie putt at the 10th hole, followed by Sluman rolling in an eight-footer for birdie at the 11th. They made birdies at the 12th, 13th and 14th to climb within a shot of the lead. Then, on the 17th, Kuehne missed the green with his second shot, but Sluman laid up in front of the green. Sluman followed that up with a deft wedge shot to six feet, and Kuehne drained the putt. A par at the 18th gave the team a round of 60 and a total of 23-under-par 193.

Just as was the case in August when he hit the shot of the year on the 72nd hole of the PGA Championship, Micheel was the hero of his group, rolling in a 10-footer for eagle at the 17th and following it up with another birdie putt of 15 feet at the 18th for a final-round 61 and a spot in the playoff.

The final group joined the playoff when Faxon's putter got hot. He and McCarron birdied the 14th, 15th, 16th and 17th holes, and had a makeable birdie putt at the 18th that Faxon let slide a little low and left. They tapped in for their 193 and went back to the 18th tee for overtime.

This first time through, Faxon and McCarron hit their first bad shot of the day. After 18 holes of scramble format, the transition to alternate shot for the first hole of the playoff was a little tough. McCarron hit a good tee shot, but Faxon pull-hooked the approach into the water. They made bogey and were eliminated when Kuehne/Sluman and Campbell/Micheel made pars.

One hole later, with yet another format, Kuehne ended it. Back to the 18th a second time, the four remaining players played best-ball, which worked to Kuehne's advantage. He hit a huge drive, which left him with little more than a flip wedge to the final hole. The shot stopped five feet away, and he rolled the putt in for a birdie to end it. Afterward, he couldn't stop praising Sluman and the way their games complemented each other.

"I couldn't have found a better partner, period," Kuehne said. "Together we make a good combination."

Callaway Golf Pebble Beach Invitational—$300,000
Winner: John Daly

It seemed ironic, given his history with Callaway Golf, that John Daly's second professional victory of 2004 would be in the Callaway Golf Pebble Beach Invitational. Daly, who was taken on by Callaway Golf founder Ely Callaway as a reclamation project, severed ties with the company after failing to live up to his promises to stop drinking and gambling. This, after Callaway had loaned Daly money to pay off his gambling debts.

Daly's three-under-par 69 moved him to nine-under-par 279 for the week. Jim Thorpe and Bo Van Pelt also shot 69s in the final round to tie for second at 280, one clear of third-round co-leader Michael Muehr, who closed with 71.

Daly was the most consistent player of the week at Pebble Beach, California. He opened with 69, followed it up with 68, and his one bad round (everyone had one during the week) was 73 in the third round. Thorpe's big number was a 77 in the second round, which he bracketed between two 67s before his closing 69. Van Pelt's opening 74 was followed by a 64 before closing out with rounds of 73 and 69.

Janice Moody was the low woman of the week, and the only female who finished under par. Her 283 total beat Carin Koch by seven shots and Emily Klein and Natalie Gulbis by 13.

UBS Cup—$3,000,000
Winner: United States and Rest of the World Tied

Not long after captains Jack Nicklaus and Gary Player ended the Presidents Cup in a tie, captain Arnold Palmer led his team of Americans to a come-from-behind tie at the UBS Cup on Sea Island, Georgia.

The matches — with a United States team of six players ages 50 and older and six between the ages of 40 and 49 taking on a Rest of the World team of similar makeup — were close all week. The Rest of the World led by one point going into the final-day singles, but the Americans gained a tie quickly when Hale Irwin made nine birdies and routed Bernhard Langer 7 and 5. U.S. Senior Open winner Bruce Lietzke put the U.S. ahead with a 6-and-5 win over Barry Lane. When Mark O'Meara beat Ian Woosnam 6 and 5, it looked like the Americans might run away with a victory.

The Rest of the World rose to the challenge. Tony Jacklin went down to the wire before defeating Palmer 1 up, and Nick Faldo beat 2002 Ryder Cup captain Curtis Strange 2 up to give the Rest of the World a one-point lead.

For a while it seemed that every match would come down to the 18th hole. Tom Watson dueled Colin Montgomerie to a draw after both missed birdie putts at the final hole, and Des Smyth beat Craig Stadler 1 up. When Bill Longmuir beat Rocco Mediate 1 up, it appeared that the Rest of the World had rallied to victory. Their lead was 11-9, and they needed only 1½ points to claim the UBS Cup.

Brad Faxon started the U.S. rally with an 18-foot birdie putt on the par-three 17th for a 2-and-1 win over Carl Mason. That was followed by Hal Sutton's win over Vicente Fernandez to tie the matches at 11 points each.

It all came down to the final two matches, which went to the final hole. Raymond Floyd was one down to Rodger Davis standing on the tee at the long, difficult par-four 18th. Floyd rallied with a two-putt par to win the hole after Davis failed to get up and down from a greenside bunker. That kept the matches level at 11½ with one match remaining on the course.

Eduardo Romero had Scott Hoch 2 down through 14 holes. Hoch got one back with an eagle at the par-five 15th, and he hit a spectacular bunker shot at the 17th to save par and keep the match alive. One down with one to play,

Hoch found the green at the 18th and two-putted for par. Romero missed the green to the right, and hit a pitch to eight feet.

It all came down to one putt. The rest of the players held their breath as Romero made what appeared to be a good stroke, but the putt missed the hole. Romero lost the hole and his match with Hoch ended in a draw. As a result, three days of matches finished in a 12-12 tie, and the U.S. retained the UBS Cup.

"There were a lot of matches that changed on the 18th hole," Hoch said. "After I saw Raymond had halved his match, it was huge. So that gave me a little inspiration or pressure, however you want to look at it."

PGA Grand Slam of Golf—$1,000,000
Winner: Jim Furyk

Even after shooting nine-under-par 135 and winning the PGA Grand Slam of Golf by a whopping eight shots, U.S. Open champion Jim Furyk couldn't help but pay deference to the man who wasn't there. "I guess we're all glad Tiger wasn't here," Furyk said of five-time defending champion Tiger Woods, who had become such a mainstay of this event that some people in Poipu Beach had never seen this tournament without him. "I think we all want to play against the best players in the world, and that's undeniably Tiger right now, but this is a great field."

It's billed as the most prestigious field in golf, because of the qualification requirements. Featuring the winners of the four major championships, this was the first time in the event's 21-year history that all four players were first-time major champions, and the first time in five years that there were no fill-ins either because a major winner couldn't make it or because one player had won more than one major title. This time around, Furyk won easily. Mike Weir, the Masters winner, finished second at 143, while Cinderella winners Ben Curtis (Open Championship) and Shaun Micheel (PGA Championship) were over par for the two-day event.

While the change in players was refreshing, the competition wasn't any closer than it was in the years Woods dominated. Furyk ran away with it, shooting 67 on Friday to take a five-stroke lead into the final round, and maintained that margin through the first nine. When he birdied the 10th, the lead was six, and when he hit a five iron to six feet for birdie at the 12th, this one was effectively over. "At one point we were playing for second place unless something crazy happened," Weir said. "You never know in this game, but as well as Jim was playing, he wasn't gong to mess that up."

Furyk added one more birdie at the 14th, bringing his two-day birdie total to 11, while the other three players had a combined 14 birdies. "I kind of got out to a big lead, and just kept the ball in play in between the trees, and got it done," Furyk said. "I played solid. I struck the ball very, very well Friday, and today I found a way to get in the hole and made some putts."

Weir tried to make it close. He birdied the second to pull within four shots, and got it to within four again with another birdie at the sixth, but that was as close as anyone came.

Office Depot Father-Son Challenge—$1,000,000
Winners: Hale and Steve Irwin

It came down to one putt, an 18-footer on the 17th green with the greatest golfer of all time assuming his familiar crouch and staring down the line like a predator stalking its prey. But at age 63, Jack Nicklaus didn't make the big putts as he once did. This was no exception. After watching his son Jackie miss, Nicklaus hit a good putt that came up a couple of inches short.

The Nicklauses needed that birdie to tie Hale and Steve Irwin, who birdied the 18th in front of them to close out a final round of 61 in the Office Depot Father-Son Challenge at Champions Gate Golf Club outside Orlando, Florida. The Irwins came in at 21-under-par 123 in the two-day event, one stroke clear of the Nicklauses, who birdied the final hole to shoot 62 and finish at 124. Larry and Josh Nelson finished third with rounds of 63 and 62.

The Irwins' 61 equaled the low round of the week. Craig and Kevin Stadler shot 61 on Sunday after opening with a 65, and first-round leaders Bernhard and Stefan Langer followed their opening 61 with a 65 to tie for fourth with the Stadlers, Tom and David Kite, and Vijay and Qass Singh.

This was the Singh's first Father-Son event, and the father couldn't have been prouder. "It was my first competition with him, and really the highlight of my year," Vijay said. "I know he enjoyed it, but I think I enjoyed it more. He's my baby, and it was an honor to play with him."

The rules were modified to allow grandfathers to play with their grandsons, enabling Arnold Palmer to play with his grandson, Sam Saunders. They shot 65 and 67.

Target World Challenge—$5,000,000
Winner: Davis Love

Sporting a goatee and a newly revamped putting stroke, Davis Love appeared to have run away from the field in the Target World Challenge at Sherwood Country Club in Thousand Oaks, California. His lead was three strokes over K.J. Choi after a third-round 63. Host Tiger Woods was nine strokes back. When Love birdied two of the first five holes, his lead was stretched to seven, and it appeared that Love could practice his victory speech.

Then Woods went on a tear. Ten strokes down with 10 holes to play, Woods tapped in for a birdie at the ninth to start the charge. He parred the 10th and then made five birdies in a row. Love lipped out two par putts and then was long on the par-three 12th and three-putted for double bogey.

"I got into a rhythm on the back nine and just got it going," Woods said.

Love had no such luck. "I felt like I was letting someone back into the tournament," he said. "I just didn't know who."

When Woods rolled in a birdie at the 15th, he was only one stroke behind. "I thought 65 was realistic, but not to win," Woods said. "When I saw Davis at 13 under, I figured if I shot 29 on the back, that would put me at 11 under, and at least I would make him work for it. When I birdied the 15th, I thought if I could birdie the last three holes I would have a chance to win the tournament."

That was not to be. Woods pushed his tee shot into a creek at the par-five 16th and had an 18-footer for par. He missed birdie efforts the last two holes and finished with 65 for a nine-under-par 279 total.

The lead stayed at one shot until Love reached the 16th. Playing conservatively, Love pulled his third shot 45 feet left of the hole, leaving himself a difficult downhill, sidehill putt. When he stroked the putt, the ball barely crested the hill before turning down and into the hole. "When it got up there about 10 feet away, I knew it was in," Love said. "And that made me very excited, because I didn't have a second putt."

The lead was two strokes with two holes to play, but it wasn't over until Love blasted out of a greenside bunker at the 18th to within three feet for par and a closing 72. His 277 total earned him the largest payday of his career, $1.2 million, and the honor of being the only two-time winner of this event, having also won in 2000.

"It was fun competing, rather than to have a six- or seven-shot lead and hanging on," Love said. "Tiger proved even if he's not playing good, in crunch time he can shoot the best round of the week in the worst conditions."

Nationwide Tour

What started as a developmental tour for aspiring professionals had, by the end of 2003, become home to a lot of professionals who couldn't quite make it on the PGA Tour, but who found they could make a decent living on the Nationwide Tour. Tjaart van der Walt, a consistent winner on the Southern Africa Tour, finished 23rd on the Nationwide money list and made $175,967, not enough to lease his own jet, but good enough to bring van der Walt back for another season in America.

Daniel Chopra will be back as well. Chopra played 22 events in 2003 and held a spot in the top-20 — to qualify for the 2004 PGA Tour — until the final week of the season when he was nudged aside by Tommy Tolles, who took the final qualifying spot. Chopra finished 21st on the money list with $178,799, missing by $1,164.

For the second straight year, the Nationwide Tour started out in Australia where Joe Ogilvie, an Austin, Texas, resident and Duke University graduate, won with a five-under-par 279 total. The $90,000 winner's check got Ogilvie off to a good start. He led the Nationwide money list for most of the summer and extended that lead with another win in Hershey, Pennsylvania, at the Reese's Cup Classic. "I won twice out here in 1998, but those were my only two good tournaments all year," Ogilvie said. "This is, by far, the best golf I've played."

He also felt confident that his four-shot win at Hershey Golf Club would prime him for a return trip to the PGA Tour, where Ogilvie spent most of his time from 1999 through 2002. "This golf course really prepares you for the PGA Tour, because you never really can feel comfortable out here," he said. "You can't let your guard down, and you can't lose your patience."

Ogilvie kept his patience and his cool, and led the money list until the final week of the season, even though he didn't win again. After the Nationwide Tour Championship in Prattville, Alabama, Ogilvie dropped to second on the money list behind Zach Johnson, who won the Rheem Classic early in the season and the Envirocare Utah Classic late in the summer.

When Johnson shot a final-round 68 in Prattville to finish third, he won the money title with a total of $494,882. It was Johnson's ninth top-three finish, which broke a Nationwide Tour record. He also led the tour in scoring average at 68.97, putts-per-green-hit-in-regulation at 1.699, and all-around statistics. Johnson was also second in birdies per round, averaging 4.77 under-par holes for 80 rounds.

But Johnson would have given up the money title to do what Tom Carter did. Carter was the only player of 2003 to earn the PGA Tour's "battlefield promotion" by winning three times. He captured the Samsung Canadian PGA Championship in early July, and then followed it up with a win at the Price Cutter Charity Classic and another victory in Canada at the Alberta Calgary Classic. By the first of September Carter had a PGA Tour card in hand.

The other multiple winners of the year were Chris Couch and Guy Boros. Couch won his first event in September when he shot a final-round 69 for a 14-under-par 274 total in the Oregon Classic and then rolled in a five-foot birdie putt on the first extra hole to beat third-round leader Jason Bohn. It was an emotional win for the former University of Florida golfer, who had lost his mother to cancer only five months before. "I felt like Mom was up in heaven watching down on me today," he said. "It was a good feeling to win for her. I wanted to win so bad I could taste it."

After the first victory, Couch was able to relax and focus on his primary objective: getting on the PGA Tour. "Every win is important, because it gives you five years of great status," he said. "I go from conditional status to fully exempt status with the win. But now I've got to play solid the rest of the year to reach my ultimate goal."

He had locked up that goal by the time he arrived in Alabama, but Couch moved from ninth on the money list to fourth when he shot 18-under-par 270 to win the Tour Championship by three strokes. "This is more than I could ever imagine," he said. "I started off the year so bad. I've worked hard for this. It hasn't hit me yet, but I'm sure it will tomorrow."

The other two-time winner of the year, Boros, who bore a striking resemblance to his famous late father, Julius, won his first title of the year on the shores of Lake Erie, which seemed appropriate given the number of times Guy accompanied Julius to the lake for golf and fishing. "If I had to win one on this tour, this would be it," Boros said after rolling in a 12-footer on the final hole to shoot 13-under 275 and win the Lake Erie Classic in Western New York by one shot. "This is like a second hometown for me. I started coming here 35 years ago with my dad. I'm sure he's in heaven doing a little dance right now."

If Julius did a little dance after Guy's first win, he held a heavenly ho-down when his son captured the Dayton Open in late July to secure a spot in the top 20 and ensure a PGA Tour card for 2004. Boros finished the year 14th on the money list with $210,461.

A victory didn't guarantee a place on the PGA Tour. Scott Gutschewski won the Monterey Peninsula Classic late in the year, but finished 26th on the money list with a shade over $172,000. James Oh, Roger Tambellini, Jeff Klauk, Michael Long and Brett Wetterich all won tournaments in 2003, and all failed to advance.

There were also some familiar PGA Tour names who earned another trip in 2004. Blaine McCallister, a longtime PGA Tour veteran, won the Northeast Pennsylvania Classic in early June and finished the season a solid 12th on the money list. Bo Van Pelt also earned his way back with a win at the Omaha Classic and a fifth-place finish on the money list. And Tripp Isenhour got a return trip when he won the BMW Charity Pro-Am in South Carolina and went on to finish eighth on the money list with $262,646.

The BMW event was unique, not in the fact that Isenhour won it, but because it featured the winner of 18 professional major championships. Jack Nicklaus played for the first time on the Nationwide Tour and for the first time with all four of his sons. Nicklaus shot 70 for a total of 283, 14 shots off Isenhour's total.

"It was a better round, but not competitive enough," Nicklaus said. "The boys and I enjoyed the week. Steve and I have played together probably 20 times, and this is the first time we've ever won something." (Team Nicklaus won the pro-am portion of the event.) "We'll be back next year," Jack added. "It's always nice to come back and defend."

If the Nicklaus clan wasn't enough of a draw, the Nationwide Tour also had among its ranks the longest hitter in professional golf. Victor Schwamkrug, a former Long Driver of America participant, led all tours in driving distance for the year with a 339.30 average, 15 yards longer than Hank Kuehne, who won the long-drive crown on the PGA Tour. Schwamkrug didn't come close to earning his PGA Tour card, finishing 90th on the money list, but as he said, "People come out to watch me hit the ball a long way. I'm not going to disappoint them."

Canadian Tour

Following the pattern of the PGA European Tour and the Southern Africa Tour, the Canadian PGA Tour had 11 different winners in 12 events in 2003. They also had a large worldwide representation among those winners. A Swede, a few Canadians and an American or two all captured titles, as well as an amateur from Vancouver. There were also some players from South Africa and Australia who didn't win, but who played exceptionally well throughout the year. If 2003 showed anything, it was that the Canadian Tour has evolved into an international circuit for aspiring young stars.

The only two-time winner was Rob Johnson of Terre Haute, Indiana.

Anders Hultman of Sweden got things off to a rousing start with four rounds in the 60s and a two-stroke victory in the TravelTex.com Canadian Tour Classic in Austin, Texas. Hultman was tied with Michael Harris of Troy, Michigan, after three rounds, but both players were three shots behind Austin resident Joe Ogilvie. Ogilvie couldn't hold on. A closing 74 dropped him into a four-way tie for second place which included Harris. Hultman was the only player to break par all four days and one of only five players to shoot a sub-70 score on Sunday.

Rain dampened the second event, also sponsored by TravelTex.com, with a deluge that shortened it to 36 holes. Rob Johnson shot 65 and 69 to win by two strokes over Mark Johnson of Helendale, California, and Harris, who had his second runner-up finish in as many weeks.

Another breakout winner emerged in the third week when Erik Compton, a University of Georgia standout who failed in two attempts to earn his U.S. PGA Tour card, shot a final-round 63 to walk away with the Michelin Guadalajara Classic in Mexico. Compton's 270 total was four better than David Hearn, who shot 64 on Sunday, and Antonio Maldonado from Queretaro.

Compton showed a lot of heart in the final round, which was a pun he had heard many times. "Every week," he said. "It stops being funny after a while." Compton is the only golfer on any professional tour who has been the recipient of a heart transplant.

Derek Gillespie of Oshawa, Ontario, shot 66, 67, 67 and 65 to run away with the Corona Ixtapa Classic of Mexico. The winning margin was eight strokes over Jim Salinetti of West Palm Beach, Florida, who led after an opening-round 65 and only trailed by two going into the final round. A 71 on Sunday erased all hope for Salinetti, who made a testy putt on the final hole to take second place.

In the fifth week, the Canadian Tour finally made its debut in Canada at the Northern Ontario Open where a new winner also made his debut. Mario Tiziani was the only player to shoot four rounds in the 60s. His closing 68 and 271 total was good enough for a six-shot thumping of the Australian duo of Tony Carolan and David McKenzie. Carolan shot 69 in the final round while McKenzie shot 70 to share second at 277.

The city of Oshawa took another title in week six, although it wasn't from the same player. This time Oshawa native Jon Mills won the MTS Classic in abysmal weather, shooting rounds of 72 and 71 on the weekend. He had posted rounds of 67 and 65 on Thursday and Friday to open up a three-shot lead over Dave Christensen. The lead was cut to two when Christensen shot 71 on Saturday to Mills' 72, but that was as close as anyone got. Christensen shot 75 on Sunday, while Mills cruised in with a 71 for a 275 total, three clear of Bryan DeCorso of Guelph, Ontario.

One week later in Edmonton Johnson became the only two-time winner of the year on the Canadian Tour when he won the Telus Edmonton Open by two strokes over Calgary's Dustin Risdon. Johnson took the lead in the second round with a 64 and held it through the weekend with rounds of 71 and 69. Stuart Anderson of Edmonton shot 66 to move into a four-way tie for third with Dave Christensen, Jason Enloe of Dallas and Australian Scott Hend at 276.

Patrick Damron of Orlando, Florida, became the seventh different winner of the year when he edged out Robert Hamilton and Richard Zokol in the

Victoria Open. Damron led from the opening round after a 63. He extended that lead with a 67 on Friday, and while he gave a few shots back with a 71 on Saturday, a 68 was good enough for a one-shot win over Hamilton and British Columbia's Zokol.

One week later the tour had its only amateur winner of the year when James Lepp of Vancouver ran away from the field in the Greater Vancouver Classic. Lepp led from the opening round and closed with 67 for a 269 total and a five-stroke margin over Nathan Fritz and Mark Johnson.

Not only was the tour trotting out different winners almost every week, the scores those winners were shooting showed a great deal of depth in the Canadian Tour fields. Nick Watney of Fresno, California, proved that point with rounds of 66, 67, 68 and 67 for a 268 total and a five-stroke win in the Lewis Chitengwa Memorial. South Africa's Alan McLean had the low round of that tournament on Sunday when he fired a 64 to finish in a three-way tie for second with Derek Gillespie and Mexico's Alex Quiroz at 273.

At the Bay Mills Open Players Championship a week later, Tampa's Rodney Butcher finished the week at 10-under 278 and won the biggest first-place check of the year (C$37,600). Jon Mills finished second at 283, two better than Australian David McKenzie and three clear of Brad Sutterfield of St. George, Utah.

In the final event of the year — the two-man match-play Casino de Charlevoix Cup in Pointe-au-Pic, Quebec — Bryn Parry and Alex Rocha held off a strong field from both the Canadian and Quebec Tours.

Tour de las Americas (South America)

The Tour de las Americas was filled with new winners in 2003, as well as a few old faithfuls who made the most of their returns to South America. The first week of the season saw Argentina's Rafael Gomez retain his Caribbean Open title with a final-round 69 for a total of 13-under-par 275 and a three-stroke edge over Jamaica's John Bloomfield.

"Truthfully, after playing so many great holes, I struggled, not hitting the ball the way I wanted at the finish," Gomez said. "The main thing is, I got the job done. Last year I had the misfortune of breaking the trophy replica of my victory, so I promised my family I would win again so we could have another trophy. I'm overjoyed to be able to keep that promise."

A Yank won in the second week. Charles Warren could afford a double bogey on the final hole of the Samsung Panama Open after his nearest challenger, fellow American Ken Duke, plunked a ball in the water at the 16th hole and failed to get up-and-down. That mistake by Duke gave Warren a four-shot lead, which he needed. A double bogey at the 18th left him with a final round of 71 and a four-under 284 total, enough for a one-stroke edge over Duke.

"You never know what to expect at the beginning of a new season," Warren said. "It worked out good from my point of view; everyone was in the thick of things for the first 10 or 11 holes, and then I made three birdies (at the 11th, 12th and 13th), which kind of separated me from the pack, so those were really big. I'm really happy. This is a great way to start 2003."

Duke agreed. "I played well all week and only three-putted once during four rounds, which was great considering the wind and how fast the greens here are," he said. "I made that one major error at the 16th, and it cost me. Luckily, I managed to birdie the 18th and that was a sweet way to end what in all respects for me was a good start to the new season."

Speaking of good starts to the season, 21-year-old Andres Romero had a spectacular start to his year when he broke the tournament record in the Cable & Wireless Panama Masters with a 14-under-par 274 total. His four-stroke victory could have been better. Romero had a four-footer for birdie at the final hole for a course-record 64, but he three-putted. "I guess I got too emotional," he said. "I just wanted to get finished." It was his lone bogey of the day and one of only two for the week. "I'm still sort of stunned," he said. "This is my first big win, something I've dreamed about for a long time. I'm not sure I believe it yet."

European Challenge Tour player Sebastian Fernandez was the fourth different winner in as many weeks. Fernandez rolled in a short par putt on the first playoff hole to win the Costa Rica Open. But rather than being elated by his win, Fernandez was torn. His best friend on tour, Cesar Monasterio, held a five-shot lead with nine holes to play before collapsing with six bogeys to fall into a tie. Monasterio made another bogey in the playoff to lose.

"I'm saddened for my friend Cesar," Fernandez said. "He had so much to gain by winning. Maybe that added too much pressure. Of course winning this important title is great. So far my visits to Central America have been very successful, but I'd have preferred winning in a different way this week."

Daniel Vancsik felt pretty good about his playoff win one week later in Guatemala City. Vancsik finished the Telefonica CA Guatemala Open tied with Jean Abbate at 10-under-par 274 and then rolled in an eight-footer for birdie on the first extra hole. South Africa's Michael Kirk and Ireland's Damien McGrane had birdie putts of reasonable length on the final hole to join the playoff, but both missed to share third place at 275. Vancsik also missed a birdie putt on the final hole from 12 feet that would have won outright. But he forgot about the miss and jumped for joy as he rolled in the winning eight-footer.

"It's wonderful," he said. "I hit the ball perfectly over the final stretch." That's how James Hepworth felt when he shot a final-round 66 for a 13-under 275 total to win the Amex Los Encinos Open by three strokes over fellow Englishman Sam Walker and Italy's Francesco Guermani. "Clearly, I'm delighted," Hepworth said, "especially as I did not lose my nerve coming down the stretch and played well all the way. This was a great experience."

Octavio Gonzalez made it seven different winners the third week in May when he won the Acapulco Fest Invitational. The 33-year-old from Puebla birdied two of the final three holes for a 67 and a four-stroke victory. "Playing against this level of international competition and coming out on top is very satisfying," Gonzalez said. "I was very nervous at the beginning. After I double-bogeyed the seventh to fall two back, I really had to work very hard to try and get my game back on track."

After a long summer respite, the tour resumed in mid-November in grand style with Angel Romero shooting a tournament-record 15-under-par 273 in the Bancolombia American Express Open. The wire-to-wire victory included a final-round 69 and not much in the way of a challenge. Mexico's Juan Salazar shot 67 to finish second at 278, two strokes clear of third-place finisher Miguel Guzman.

"I played much as I'd hoped to play," Romero said. "Very regular golf."

Andres Romero became the only repeat winner of the season when he took the Medellin Open with another tournament record 19-under-par 269 total. "I don't think I really missed a shot," Romero said after clipping Venezuela's Carlos Larrain by one stroke after Larrain shot a course-record 62 in the final round. "When you are playing like that, you really begin to believe you can win."

Someone who always believed he could win was Paraguay's Carlos Franco, who joined an elite group when captured his second straight American Express Trump Brazil Open. Only Mario Gonzalez, Billy Casper, Roberto de Vicenzo and Vicente Fernandez had won Brazil's top tournament back-to-back before Franco's victory. This one wasn't easy. It took two extra holes and a near eagle for Franco to defeat Eduardo Argiro, but when his iron shot at the second extra hole for eagle lipped out, Franco had a mere tap-in putt for the win.

Argiro also came out on the losing end at the season-ending Mexican Open. After missing a birdie putt at the final hole to finish the week at nine-under-par 279 and tied with American Jeff Burns, Argiro could do nothing but watch as Colombia's Eduardo Herrera shot 70 for a 278 total and a one-stroke victory. "I made only one mistake today, blocked my drive at 16 but was able to save par," Argiro said. "I'm really very satisfied with my work today, even if it turned up one shot light in the end."

9. European Tours

The story out of Europe in 2003 was the number of different winners, 30 in 38 events. For most of the year it looked as if a hot streak was one victory, and if your name wasn't Ernie Els, you had to step aside. One of the exceptions to that rule was a young Swede named Fredrik Jacobson, who won the Omega Hong Kong Open the last week of 2002 (which counted as a European win in the 2003 season) and won twice more at the Algarve Open de Portugal in April and the season-ending Volvo Masters at Valderrama. On the world stage, while rising to the No. 17 ranking, Jacobson tied for fifth in the U.S. Open, tied for sixth at Royal St. George's in the Open Championship, and posted third- and eighth-place finishes at the FedEx St. Jude Classic and Western Open respectively. He was also one of captain Seve Ballesteros' few bright stars on the Continental squad at The Seve Trophy, making him the most accomplished Swedish male in the game.

Ian Poulter, Paul Casey and Lee Westwood also won twice each in Europe. Poulter took the Celtic Manor Wales Open and the Nordic Open. Casey won the ANZ Championship (an Australasian event that also counted as official money in Europe) as well as the final Benson and Hedges International Open, which ended its run when a law banning tobacco sponsorship of sporting events took effect. Westwood was the winner of the BMW International Open and the Dunhill Links Championship. Those victories put Jacobson, Poulter, Casey and Westwood at fourth, fifth, sixth and seventh on the Order of Merit, over a million and a half Euros behind Els, the winner.

Els showed that he could win anywhere and everywhere. After capturing two victories in Hawaii on the U.S. PGA Tour, the big South African won the Heineken Classic and the Johnnie Walker Classic in Australia. Els could have made it five in a row. He was leading by one stroke standing on the final tee at the Caltex Masters in Singapore when he pushed his drive into the woods and made a bogey to lose to Zhang Lian-wei of China. Els also finished second in Dubai, where once again he lost by a single shot. By the time he returned to his Orlando home for the Florida swing of the PGA Tour, Els had an Order of Merit lead that he would not relinquish. He finished with €2.9 million.

An ill-advised swing at a punching bag in his garage couldn't stop Els from dominating in Europe. The week before traveling to southern England to defend his title at the Open Championship, Els picked up his third European win at the Barclays Scottish Open. His fourth came the first week of September when Els won the Omega European Masters. A month later Els won his fifth HSBC World Match Play title at Wentworth. But just as impressive as his European wins and Order of Merit title were the margins of his victories and the miles he logged in between. Els' four stroke-play victories on the European Tour were by a total of 22 strokes. Only one of the victories was close. Nick Faldo came within a stroke of forcing a playoff at the Heineken Classic. Other than that, Els' victory margins were 10, five, and six.

The man who finished second on the Order of Merit was no slouch. Darren Clarke won another World Golf Championships event, the NEC Invitational, becoming the only one other than Tiger Woods to capture two titles. Clarke rebounded and rededicated himself to the game. He quit smoking cigars, hit the gym instead of the pub, lost 20 pounds, and won €2.2 million. What he didn't do was win anywhere in Europe. A string of good finishes gave Clarke hope that his future would be bright in both Europe and the world.

Padraig Harrington won the 2002 BMW Asian Open (which counted for 2003) and the Deutche Bank - SAP Open in 2003, and he played consistently enough through the year to finish third on the Order of Merit with over €1.5 million.

Another player who was able to look at the bright side of life in 2003 was Westwood. After plummeting from third in the world to 182nd on the Official World Golf Ranking, Westwood won twice in Europe. "There were times when I thought about putting the clubs away and calling it a day," Westwood said of his two-year drought. "But that would have been an easy thing to do. I have worked for three years to get back to here."

Europe produced a Chinese winner in 2003 (Zhang) and a winner from India (Arjun Atwal) as well as the usual cadre of contenders from such countries as Sweden, Holland, Spain, South Africa, England, Ireland and Wales. But nowhere among the winners were two of the tour's stalwarts, Scotland's Colin Montgomerie and Spain's Sergio Garcia. Montgomerie did have a victory on the Asian PGA Tour in the Macau Open and Garcia won the year-ending Nedbank Golf Challenge in South Africa.

PGA European Tour

South African Airways Open—£500,000
Winner: Trevor Immelman

See African Tours chapter.

Dunhill Championship—£500,000
Winner: Mark Foster

See African Tours chapter.

Caltex Masters—US$900,000
Winner: Zhang Lian-wei

See Asia/Japan Tours chapter.

Heineken Classic—A$2,000,000
Winner: Ernie Els

See Australasian Tour chapter.

ANZ Championship—A$1,750,000
Winner: Paul Casey

See Australasian Tour chapter.

Johnnie Walker Classic—£1,000,000
Winner: Ernie Els

See Australasian Tour chapter.

Carlsberg Malaysian Open—US$1,100,000
Winner: Arjun Atwal

See Asia/Japan Tours chapter.

Dubai Desert Classic—€1,778,110
Winner: Robert-Jan Derksen

Were it not for some well-founded apprehensions and words of caution coming out of the U.S. Department of State, Tiger Woods would have filled out the field at the Dubai Desert Classic, and Robert-Jan Derksen, a former four-time Dutch Amateur champion, would have stayed home in Amsterdam. But, with war less than two weeks away and the United Arab Emirates situated within missile range of Baghdad, Woods opted not to make the trip, and Derksen found himself in the field.

Five days later, Derksen rolled in a four-footer for a final-round 65, a total of 17-under-par 271 and a one-stroke victory over Ernie Els. To say the Dutchman was overjoyed would be an understatement. He left the final green in tears. "This is the biggest shock of my life," he said. "Unbelievable."

Everyone in attendance echoed those sentiments. Derksen came into the week ranked 593rd in the world and had never finished in the top 10 on the PGA European Tour. In fact, he had only been out for three weeks in 2003 after his sixth trip through the qualifying tournament. Even after shooting 67 on Saturday to pull within three of Els, nobody outside his parents and a few Dutch expatriates living the desert high life in Dubai paid much attention to Derksen. He still remained unnoticed when he pulled within two shots of the lead with a birdie at the 11th on Sunday.

Then the most remarkable 20 minutes of the week turned this tournament upside down. Derksen reached the par-five 13th with his second shot, but was left with a 65-foot putt for eagle. When that putt fell while Els was making double bogey from a sandy lie in the rough at the 12th, the lead switched. Els went from two up to two down.

Els came roaring back with a birdie at the 13th after hitting a 400-yard tee shot, and he followed that up with a birdie at the 14th to regain a share of the lead. Derksen didn't fold. He hit two good shots to the right of the green at the par-five 18th and hit a delicate pitch to four feet, setting up the final, dramatic birdie. After rolling the putt in and breaking down in sobs, Derksen waited to see if Els could top his birdie and force a playoff.

The South African hit a booming drive and a perfect three iron, but the ball released through the green and into the high grass at the back. From there, he hit a fluffy pitch to 20 feet and missed his birdie putt. "I couldn't hit two better shots than the two I hit into 18," Els said. "But what can you do? One guy comes out of the pack and beats you. He played well, so it's one of those things."

Derksen viewed it as one of those things that could change his life forever. The €291,994 winner's check was more than he had made in his career. "Before this year, I never thought I could win," he said. "But I started believing in myself a bit more this year. I needed a bit of luck. That is what I got today."

Qatar Masters—€1,400,200
Winner: Darren Fichardt

Outside of South African Darren Fichardt, whose three-foot birdie putt on the first extra hole was good enough for his second career win, no one in Doha seemed pleased by this year's Qatar Masters. For starters, 50 players dropped out before the tournament began because of the skirmish taking place a couple of hundred miles away between Saddam Hussein's Iraq and Coalition Forces and the fact that 30,000 American troops were stationed on the Qatar-Iraq border. Scotland's Andrew Coltart summed up the feelings of many when he said, "I have a wife and family at home, and if anything happens to me in a war zone, I'm not insured."

Those who made the trek to Doha Golf Club had to deal with sandstorms and a "second cut" that infuriated 35 players. Even with the late withdrawals, a full field was entered for the first two rounds, and after battling the elements, 89 were within 12 strokes of the lead. That forced tournament director David Williams to add a second cut, lowering the cut number from low 70 and ties to low 50 and ties. Tour rookie Simon Wakefield, one the 35 given a €2,000 check and sent packing, called the decision, "Absolutely scandalous. They're messing with our livelihood. I stood on the last tee three over and thought I only had to make a par. If I get to the end of the year, and I'm €1,000 short of keeping my card, I'm not going to be happy."

Fichardt was happy, not only that he didn't fall below the second cut line, but because his wife, a psychologist, had chastised him into making the trip. "Don't be a wimp," Natasha Fichardt told her husband. That turned out to be the most sage advice of the week, as Fichardt shot 71, 69 and 66 to share the lead with James Kingston (68, 67, 71) with one round to go. Both players shot uninspired 69s on Sunday in the midst of a sandstorm. They signed for 13-under-par 275 totals before trudging back to the 18th tee for a playoff.

Kingston hit his second shot into the greenside bunker at the 581-yard par-five, while Fichardt found the green. Fichardt two-putted from 40 feet for birdie while Kingston missed a six-footer that would have kept the playoff alive. "After playing 72 holes, a playoff over just one hole is always hard," Fichardt said. "I thought James was going to make a birdie. But as it turned out, it was my day today."

Madeira Island Open—€600,000
Winner: Bradley Dredge

There's no better feeling than an eight-stroke lead with one hole to play, unless you count the feeling you get from the round of 60 that puts you there. Bradley Dredge enjoyed the euphoria of both when he shot 12-under-par 60 on the Santo de Serra course at Santa Cruz, Madeira, to take an eight-shot lead into the final round of the Madeira Island Open. A 71 on Sunday for a 16-under-par 272 total kept the margin at eight over Fredrik Andersson, Brian Davis and Andrew Marshall.

"It feels wonderful," Dredge said. "I have waited a long time for this, so I will savor it for a few weeks. Going out in the third round and shooting 60 made it so much easier for me, and although I made a few errors, I knew my game was in good shape."

Dredge bogeyed his first hole on Sunday, but rectified that mistake with a birdie at the third. He then birdied the seventh, bogeyed the eighth, and made two more birdies at the par-five 11th and par-four 13th before enjoying his victory a little too soon and making bogey at the 18th for his 71.

Dredge was the highest-ranked player in the field on the Portuguese island at 70th, and he became the sixth first-time winner on the European Tour in 2003, joining Robert-Jan Derksen (Dubai Desert Classic), Trevor Immelman (South African Open), Mark Foster (Dunhill Championship), Fredrik Jacobson (Hong Kong Open) and Zhang Lian-wei (Singapore Masters) as a first-timer.

"When I was asked if I had thought about holing a winning putt, when I was a 15-year-old I never imagined it would be from four inches and having about eight putts from there," Dredge said. "That's a pretty good feeling."

Seve Ballesteros had a fiery confrontation with tournament director Jose Maria Zamora after Ballesteros was given a slow-play warning by official John Grant. According to Ballesteros, the wind was a mitigating factor to his deliberate play, but Grant said he didn't care. "That was a very rude way to answer someone like myself," Ballesteros said. "It broke my concentration. I am the only star here this week who has won a major. For the people of Madeira, it is important I play well and make the cut."

Zamora refused to back down. "Seve's group finished 27 minutes behind those in front," the tournament director said. "Why should we allow them to spend 20 minutes more than the rest of the field?"

Algarve Open de Portugal—€1,250,000
Winner: Fredrik Jacobson

With one victory under his belt (the European Tour's season-opening 2002 Hong Kong Open) and an injured wrist that finally felt like it had healed, Fredrik Jacobson reacquainted himself with tournament golf for the first time in three months at the Algarve Open de Portugal. The wrist and Jacobson's game were little worse for the wear. He opened with 64 at Vale do Lobo to take the first-round lead, and despite a disappointing 76 in the second round, he came back strong on the weekend to pick up his second career victory and his second victory in six starts.

"I went to see a doctor in Sweden, but they couldn't find anything serious in the X-rays," Jacobson said of his ailing wrist. "It's probably a bit of inflammation. It's still there a little bit now, but I can't rest it any longer."

A 71 on Saturday gave the Swede a one-stroke lead going into the final round, but he quickly lost that by shooting 38 on the first nine. He dug the hole a little deeper with a bogey at the 12th. Then Jacobson came charging back with a birdie at the 15th while a cadre of challengers struggled to finish. Jacobson regained the lead when he hit his second shot just short of the green at the par-five 17th and pitched in for an eagle.

Ahead by two with one hole to play, Jacobson made a sloppy bogey at the 18th that proved meaningless when his playing partner and nearest competitor, Brian Davis, failed to convert a birdie putt. Jacobson shot even-par 72 for a 283 total, one better than Davis (70-71-71-72), Bradley Dredge (69-73-74-68) and Jamie Donaldson (72-71-73-68).

Second-round leader Greg Owen had a lackluster weekend, shooting 76-73 to finish alone in fifth at 285, while James Kingston and Richard Sterne shared sixth at 287.

Canarias Open de Espana—€1,750,000
Winner: Kenneth Ferrie

For the seventh time in four months, the European Tour produced a first-time winner. This time it was Kenneth Ferrie, who shot a closing 69 for a 22-under-par 266 total and then birdied the second extra hole to win a three-way playoff with Peter Lawrie and Peter Hedblom and take the Canarias Open de Espana. More remarkable than the first-time winning streak was the absence of European stalwarts on the leaderboards.

With the noteworthy exception of Ernie Els, who was then the hottest player in the world, none of the usual European leaders had sniffed a victory in 2003. Sergio Garcia, a perennial favorite in Tenerife, had dropped from the fourth-ranked player in the world to No. 11. Colin Montgomerie had fallen further from 10th to 19th, and Bernhard Langer had plummeted from 16th to 42nd. Lee Westwood, once fourth in the world and European Order of Merit winner, came to Spain ranked 246th.

"The gap between the European Tour and the U.S. Tour is wider now than it ever has been," said columnist and television commentator David Feherty, himself a former European Tour winner. "The difference between the two tours is so stark. Compared to the big show you see in American golf, the European Tour looks like a cottage industry."

If the performance at Golf Costa Adeje was any indication, a new crop of 20-somethings was ready to make a run on the cottage. Ferrie, a 24-year-old in his second year on tour, played like a veteran, putting together rounds of 67, 65 and 65 before closing with a birdie to shoot 69 and join the playoff at 266. He then birdied the 18th again in the playoff, along with both Lawrie and Hedblom.

All three marched back to the 18th tee again for a second playing. This time Lawrie hit his second shot through the green, and Hedblom missed the green to the right. Ferrie hit a second shot to 12 feet. He missed the eagle putt, but it didn't matter. When Lawrie and Hedblom failed to save pars, the victory belonged to the Englishman.

Italian Open Telecom Italia—€1,100,000
Winner: Mathias Gronberg

Trailing by three and searching for his first victory since the summer of 2000, Sweden's Mathias Gronberg "found his form" as they say, in the Italian Open Telecom Italia, a well-paying but second-tier event on Europe's spring schedule. Gronberg shot 65 on Sunday to make up three strokes and win by two over third-round leader Ricardo Gonzalez, Colin Montgomerie and Jose Manuel Lara. "I feel great about the way I played," Gronberg said. "It's nice to know I remember how to win."

The Swede shot 68 on Saturday to trail Gonzalez by three with Pierre Fulke another two behind. That deficit was made up quickly when Gronberg reeled off three straight birdies at the third, fourth and fifth holes. He added another birdie at the par-four seventh to gain a share of the lead. When his eagle putt at the 514-yard, par-five 11th fell for the second straight day, Gronberg had the lead for the first time.

Lara, who was one group ahead of Gronberg, eagled the par-five 16th to gain a share of the lead. They remained tied for the better part of an hour as Lara bogeyed the 18th at the same time Gronberg made a bogey at the 15th. That allowed Montgomerie to join the group at 15 under par. But Gronberg came back with another eagle at the 16th from the fringe to take a two-shot lead. That's the way they finished. Gronberg's 17-under-par 271 earned him €183,330, but more importantly, he felt he had rediscovered his winning ways.

Equally thrilled was Montgomerie, who matched Gronberg's final-round 65 to finish at 273 and tied for second with Lara, who also shot 65, and Gonzalez, who posted a 70. "I needed to get back some confidence," Montgomerie said. "I feel very comfortable here, and respected again. Today has given me a lot of confidence to go into the three big tournaments coming up. I'd lost my confidence in America for two months."

For the second time this season, Seve Ballesteros erupted at tour officials. This time he was disqualified after refusing to accept a one-stroke penalty for slow play. He signed for a 75 when he should have had a 76.

European Tour official John Paramour was on the receiving end of Ballesteros' tirade, and the Spaniard didn't limit his comments to this incident. Ballesteros said, "This is a personal problem that comes from (executive director) Ken Scofield and all of his staff. This tour is a dictatorship. There is no freedom. So when someone goes against the system he is in the sights at all times. Most of the players are against the regime, but they are afraid to speak out."

Paramour, calm as ever, explained the situation. "Ballesteros and (Gregory) Havret were found to be approximately 12 minutes out of position after the fifth hole. On the 14th tee, Seve was allowed 50 seconds to hit the tee shot, but took 64 seconds. On the 16th tee, where he was permitted 40 seconds, he took 51 seconds. I informed him after both those shots that each was a bad time."

Mitchell Platts, director of public relations for the European Tour, shook his head before offering the following statement: "We have every confidence in John Paramour, and we know he has the full confidence of the tournament committee."

Benson and Hedges International Open—€1,596,860
Winner: Paul Casey

The buzz at The Belfry had little to do with the golf, even though Paul Casey's 71 in less-than-stellar conditions was good for a four-stroke victory over Padraig Harrington. Nor was there much emotion because this was the last playing of the tour's oldest event, the Benson and Hedges International Open, a consequence of Britain's ban on tobacco sponsorship of sporting events. No, the big news was about Seve Ballesteros.

Through the week, Ballesteros was vilified for comments after receiving a slow-play penalty in Italy and for changing his scorecard to a score lower than the one he had. As Bernhard Langer put it, "There is no reason for Seve to act the way he has acted. We have rules, and we must obey those rules. Otherwise, you have 150 guys out there arguing, and where would we end up? It's not proper."

Ballesteros shot back on the BBC: "I have to say I am disappointed in some of the players and some of the media. They have formed an opinion based on one side. I think that is very unfair."

Ken Scofield, the executive director of the European Tour and the main target of Ballesteros' rage, called the comments "unfortunate" and speculated that they stemmed from "frustration at a very sad decline entering its seventh year."

Casey stayed out of the controversy and went about the business of winning his third career tournament. Tied for the lead with Padraig Harrington and Stephen Scahill after three rounds, Casey had an up-and-down final round that included some early bogeys, a couple of crucial birdies in the middle and some steady pars to finish. He was still tied with Harrington at the turn, but the lead reached two strokes when Casey rolled in a 25-foot birdie putt on the 11th while Harrington was three-putting for bogey at the 12th. Casey padded the lead with a 12-footer for birdie at the 12th, and the lead stretched to four when Harrington made another bogey at the final hole. Casey's 71 gave him an 11-under-par 277 total, while Harrington's 75 left him at 281.

For Casey, the key to winning his first event in his home country was the time he spent in his second home in Arizona. "The big thing was playing a lot of golf in Scottsdale before I came back to Europe," Casey said. "I played almost every day for several weeks. I always felt I had a game to win on courses like this, and I consider myself quite a good wind player."

Casey earned €262,227 and vaulted into the second spot on the Order of Merit behind Ernie Els. Harrington moved to third in the Order of Merit after earning €174,818 for second place. Rolf Muntz, Paul Lawrie and Stephen Scahill tied for third place at 282.

Deutsche Bank - SAP Open—€2,700,000
Winner: Padraig Harrington

There had already been plenty of warning. Tour officials had announced weeks before the Deutsche Bank - SAP Open that the Gut Kaden course in Hamburg had experienced a few problems. Snow in April and a fungus akin to root-rot left the greens looking like dustbowl Oklahoma, and left the European Tour with no option but to implement preferred-lies rules on the fairways and the greens.

"All you can do is hit a solid putt, and if it bounces off-line, it bounces off-line," said Tiger Woods, the winner of three of the last four Deutsche Bank - SAP Open events and runner-up in the other. Woods finished nine strokes behind, but hit as many greens and more fairways than the winner. He said the difference was "the putts started off on line, but didn't quite end up there. I played well. I only had three bogeys the entire week. I hit good putts, but they didn't go in. Overall I'm pleased with the way I played."

The winner was Padraig Harrington, who got off to a great start, shooting 65 to share the lead with Retief Goosen. Two days later, after rounds of 66 and 70, Harrington held a two-stroke lead over Goosen with one round to play.

That should have been enough, especially after playing the first 17 holes on Sunday in three under par. But Harrington found himself trailing by one shot after Thomas Bjorn went on a nine-birdie run for a 63 and 269 total, 19 under par. It could have been a 62, but Bjorn's eight-footer on the final green hit one of the bumps and bounced away.

Harrington knew what he had to do, and he did it masterfully. After reaching the green on the par-five hole with his second shot, he made a good stroke on his 45-foot eagle putt, but the ball hit a bump and bounced six inches into the air, coming to rest 15 feet short. Bad thoughts crept into Harrington's head as he prepared for his birdie putt. When it went in for 68 and a 269 total for a spot in a playoff, Harrington felt the momentum shift in his favor.

"It would have been a real dent in my confidence had I missed," Harrington said. "In fact, the question of 'What am I going to say?' crossed my mind more than once. I hit a good putt, though. That was very satisfying. I walked off that green feeling like I had proved something."

One hole later (the 18th again) Harrington proved something again with an eight-footer for birdie to win the playoff. "This is a step up the ladder for me," the winner said. "But I still have another step to make if I am to win a major."

Volvo PGA Championship—€3,500,000
Winner: Ignacio Garrido

With the noteworthy exceptions of the Open Championship and the HSBC World Match Play, Britain has no bigger golf tournament than the Volvo PGA Championship. Which is why it was such a big deal when Ignacio Garrido, who hadn't had a top-30 finish since 1997, won with back-to-back birdies on Wentworth West Course's par-five 18th. The first birdie, from the front edge of the green, was for a seven-under-par score of 65 and an 18-under 270 total, good enough to catch third-round leader Trevor Immelman and force a playoff. The second came when he hit a deft pitch from the right rough to three feet and made the putt for the victory.

Garrido was as shocked as anyone, saying that he had undergone some "very big changes" in his golf swing and could "feel the results coming."

Nothing in his game after the 1997 Ryder Cup at Valderrama hinted at this kind of breakout performance. "By the time I settled down and realized what was going on, I had won," he said.

He won by virtue of a 66-65 weekend and a little help from Immelman, who showed signs of nerves with his putter on Sunday. Immelman snatched the lead from Darren Clarke on Saturday with a 64, the low round of the tournament, that left him three clear of Garrido and Ernie Els, who was coming back for a second time after a wrist injury. Immelman missed several short birdie efforts early in his final round, and despite making five birdies and one bogey in the first 17 holes (with three of the birdies coming after the 14th), he needed a birdie at the final hole to force a playoff.

The South African almost went one better. His 60-footer for eagle nipped the edge of the hole before rolling a few inches past. The tap-in birdie gave Immelman a closing 68 and a share of the lead.

One hole later, Immelman's putter deserted him again. After Garrido pitched to three feet and seemed certain to make birdie, Immelman stroked another eagle putt, this one coming up five feet short. When he missed his birdie effort, Garrido had his second career victory.

"Playing in the Ryder Cup and my previous victory were the highlights of my career, but I think this is better than those," Garrido said. "Winning this tournament is far more than I thought I could achieve."

Celtic Manor Resort Wales Open—€2,112,185
Winner: Ian Poulter

Not even a bout of tonsillitis and a couple of inopportune bogey runs could stop England's Ian Poulter from completing his wire-to-wire victory in the Celtic Manor Resort Wales Open. Poulter battled his heath and his game on Sunday, taking penicillin for the nagging case of tonsillitis that had plagued him all week before shooting an up-and-down, two-under-par 70 for an 18-under-par 270 total and a three-stroke victory over Jonathan Lomas, Darren Fichardt and Jarrod Moseley.

Despite the three-stroke margin, the outcome was uncertain until the final hole. Poulter had led by three after 65 and 67 in the first and second rounds. He extended his margin to six strokes through 13 holes on Saturday, only to make two bogeys and a double bogey. He finished with a birdie for 68 to keep the margin at two over Phillip Price.

Price struggled on Sunday, shooting 74 for a 276 total and a share of seventh place. Leading by three with four holes to play, Poulter made bogeys on the 15th and 16th holes to allow Moseley (who shot a course-record 63 on Saturday and had four birdies in his first 11 holes on Sunday) to get within a stroke. At the 18th, Moseley stumbled. Needing a birdie to tie, he pushed his tee shot into the trees on the 554-yard par-five and made a bogey six. He finished with 69 and a 273 total. That allowed Poulter to relax and make a birdie of his own at the last to extend the margin to three with his 70 for a 270 total. Fichardt and Lomas both shot 68s for their 273s.

"I feel on top of the world right now," Poulter said. "I had no expectations at the start of the tournament. After my pro-am I went back to my room and fell asleep for two hours, which shows you how drained I was. But to then shoot 65 in the first round, feeling as bad as I did, was very pleasing. Today, I hit a couple of silly shots at the end of the back nine, but I am delighted to have finished the job."

Daily Telegraph Damovo British Masters—€2,105,520
Winner: Greg Owen

The first-time winners kept popping up. This time it was England's Greg Owen who hoisted a European Tour trophy for the first time. With a closing 71 at the Forest of Arden Golf Club in Warwickshire, Owen finished the week at 14-under-par 274 and three strokes clear of Christian Cevaer and Ian Poulter in the Daily Telegraph Damovo British Masters.

A pair of 68s gave Owen a share of the lead with David Lynn at the halfway mark, and Owen jumped ahead of the pack with 67 on Saturday. He entered the final round four clear of Poulter, who had the low round of the tournament on Saturday when he put together a 10-birdie 63.

Poulter cut the lead to two on the first nine on Sunday, but no one got any closer. When Owen rolled in his final putt for par for 71, the margin was three. Poulter shot 70, and the Frenchman Cevaer shot 68 to share second place at 277.

Darren Clarke, who struggled with his swing in the first two rounds, shot 66 for a 280 total and a share of fourth place with Robert Rock and Anthony Wall. "The first two rounds I hit the ball worse than I have all year," Clarke said. "The last two I hit it exactly as I have all year. There's nothing more I can do tee-to-green."

Justin Rose, who was using this event as a tune-up for his first U.S. Open, shot a final 67 after a couple of lackluster rounds Thursday and Friday. His 284 total left him in a six-way tie for 24th place, not the kind of showing Rose had hoped to have. "I still need a little more work," he said. "My swing is not in the slot to hit iron shots at the flag. It's not precise enough yet."

Aa St. Omer Open—€400,000
Winner: Brett Rumford

Make that nine first-time winners in 16 events, the best start for first-timers in two decades on the PGA European Tour. This time it was Brett Rumford, a 25-year-old Australian who was most known for losing a three-stroke lead on final nine of the 2001 Ericsson Masters in his homeland, who found his way to victory, shooting 67 for a 269 total, 15 under par, and a wire-to-wire triumph at the Aa St. Omer Open in Lumbres, France.

"I am proud of myself for playing some good golf," Rumford said. "I didn't want to reflect on it (Ericsson Masters), but I led by three over quite a strong field in Australia and let it slip in the final round. My game went on a slide ever since that tournament. Right now I just want to enjoy this week, as I have waited so long for it."

Granted Rumford won in a week when Europe's best were at the U.S. Open, but that didn't take away from the course-record 64 he shot on Thursday to take a two-stroke lead that he would not relinquish. Rounds of 70 and 68 kept the lead at three going into the final day.

By the time he made his first birdie at the fourth hole on Sunday, Rumford's lead had shrunk to a single stroke thanks to a quick start by England's Ben Mason, who birdied three of his first five holes before a bogey at the eighth halted the charge.

"Ben came at me early, and he holed some good putts," Rumford said. "Not much was happening from my side, so I had to dig deep and stay in the present and play the golf I had been playing all week."

The leader made a birdie at the seventh to extend the margin back to three, but he almost blew it when his tee shot at the ninth came close to going out of bounds. "I was extremely lucky, but those are the breaks you need if you are to win the golf tournament," Rumford said after saving par from the trees. "Fortunately, it went my way this week."

Birdies at the 10th, 12th and 13th opened up a six-shot lead, and Rumford cruised in with four pars and a bogey (at the 17th) to win by five strokes over Mason, who shot 69 for a 274 total and also felt good about his week. "I made a good start, put a bit of pressure on Brett, but he responded very well," Mason said. "This continues the learning curve. Last group on the final day is always nice and hopefully many more to come."

Diageo Championship at Gleneagles—€1,719,309
Winner: Soren Kjeldsen

By the middle of June it looked as though the parade of first-time winners on the European Tour would never end. This time it was Soren Kjeldsen of Denmark who joined countrymen Soren Hansen, Thomas Bjorn and Steen Tinning as one of the Great Danes of Europe. Kjeldsen cruised in with a final round of 72 for a nine-under-par 279 total and a two-stroke victory over Alastair Forsyth in the Diageo Championship at Gleneagles.

"The year has been good to me so far, and with this tournament now, it's been a fantastic year," the winner said. "I can't ask for anything more. I hung in there and it was fantastic."

Fortunately, he had a big margin going to the final round, thanks to scores of 68 and 67 on Friday and Saturday. With a five-shot lead over Forsyth, Kjeldsen got off to a shaky start when he missed a six-footer for par. He got a birdie at the second, but gave it back with a bogey at the third. When Kjeldsen bogeyed the eighth while Forsyth was rolling in an eight-footer for birdie at the ninth, the lead that had once seemed insurmountable was down to two.

The margin remained at two after Kjeldsen birdied at the 11th while Forsyth was two-putting for birdie at the par-five 12th. It stayed close until Kjeldsen holed a 30-footer for birdie at the par-three 14th. That extended the lead to three strokes with four holes to play. Things turned bleak for both on the tee at the 15th. Kjeldsen hit his shot well to the right and in the trees. He punched out, hit his third shot to three feet and saved par. Forsyth was not as fortunate. From the left rough he missed the green badly to the right, chunked his third to 20 feet, and failed to convert his par putt. With that, Kjeldsen's lead was extended to four.

Forsyth birdied the 16th and 18th holes, but it was too little too late. His closing 69 and 281 total left him alone in second place, one better than Paul Broadhurst and two clear of a resurgent Colin Montgomerie, who called the week "important" and said, "I'm continuing to make progress."

The same could be said for the winner, who was as entertaining in his interview as he was on the course. "I'd dropped a few shots on the front nine, so when I came back to the 10th tee, I told myself that if I came home in 34, I would put some pressure on the others," Kjeldsen said. "The birdie at 14 and the up-and-down at 15 were absolutely a turning point. I figured if I could shoot 34, they would have to shoot four under on the back nine to beat me, which was pretty tough with the pressure and the finish of the tournament, and that is the way it turned out.

"It was a hard day, but it was a fantastic feeling to sit here with this trophy. I felt before this that I had to get more into contention and I felt that the other Danes who had won were more in contention than I was in tournaments, so I had to be there or thereabouts on Sundays."

Open de France—€2,500,000
Winner: Philip Golding

The Open de France provided for the emergence of another unlikely first-time winner. This time it was 40-year-old Philip Golding, a journeyman who held the record for most trips through the European Tour qualifying tournament (16), who emerged victorious. A final-round 69 for a 15-under-par 273 total put the Englishman one shot clear of David Howell and two ahead of Justin Rose and Peter O'Malley.

It was an impressive performance from a man who had never had a top-five finish. An opening 66 gave Golding the first-round lead, but Howell caught him when Golding shot 70 and Howell came back from an opening 71 to shoot 65. Golding reclaimed a one-shot edge on Saturday with a 68 to Howell's 69. O'Malley was also one stroke back after shooting 66 on Saturday, which set up a final-round showdown.

Howell claimed the lead early with a birdie at the third hole while Golding was making bogey at the second. Golding put together an impressive mid-round run of four birdies between the eighth and 14th holes to reclaim the lead and extend it to two strokes. But a bogey at the 16th dropped the lead to one. Then he had to watch as Howell, playing directly ahead of him, birdied the short, water-strewn par-five 18th to shoot 69 and finish at 274.

"I saw David had birdied the last, so I said to my caddie, 'Four to win,' which is what you dream of," Golding said. "I trusted my swing, hit the fairway, and then hit a six iron 167 yards over the water. I tried not to think of my family. I knew they would be going mental every time I holed a putt, and I knew I'd get emotional if I thought of them."

He didn't hole his eagle putt, but a routine two-putt for birdie was enough for the win. "The guys who drew encouragement from Malcolm's (Mackenzie) win here last year will now be saying, 'If Phil Golding can win, so can I.'"

Howell's final birdie wasn't quite good enough for the victory, but it put him one stroke clear of O'Malley, who birdied the final hole to shoot 70 and tie for third with Rose, who was coming off a tie for fifth place in his first

U.S. Open, but who had to endure a few oddities in Versailles. The first was a one-shot penalty on Thursday when Rose stepped on his golf ball while searching for it in the rough. Then on Saturday, Rose hit a hook into a water hazard after a photographer snapped a shot in his backswing. As if these problems weren't enough, Rose suffered from a bad cold that had him sneezing and wheezing his way around to a 65 on Sunday. "It was a good show," he said. "Not quite good enough, but I'm pleased."

Smurfit European Open—€2,887,500
Winner: Phillip Price

He left himself a little work — a self-inflicted injury when a three-foot putt at the 17th hole spun out, resulting in his only three-putt of the day — but Phillip Price rose to the occasion and birdied the 18th to win the Smurfit European Open by one stroke over Alastair Forsyth and Mark McNulty. In the process, Price beat one of the strongest European fields of the year, shooting 70 for a 16-under-par 272 total and earning an even greater measure of respect from his peers.

"I suppose I'm a bit short on titles, and it has bothered me a little bit that I haven't won more often, especially in big tournaments," Price said. "But I classify this as a big tournament, and to win here is just fantastic."

Price was in charge for most of the week, shooting 66 in the first round at The K Club in Dublin, Ireland, site of the 2006 Ryder Cup, to share the lead with Forsyth, and a 69 on Friday to take the top spot outright. He extended the lead to three with a 67 on Saturday, and seemed in control, even after Darren Clarke made an eagle on the fourth hole on Sunday to temporarily gain a share of the lead at 14 under. Price made a birdie at the fourth to reclaim the outright lead, which he never gave up until the three-putt at the 17th.

"If I had holed my putt for par on the 17th, I probably could have coasted down the last, but I left myself a bit of work to do," the Welshman said. And he came through. From the center of the final fairway, Price hit his approach through the green and into the first cut of rough. He then took a sand wedge and chipped to two feet. When that putt fell, Price had his third career victory. "I hit the chip to two feet, which was pretty good," he said. "It was a relief to see the putt go into the middle of the hole."

Both McNulty (who, at 49, was looking to become the oldest winner on tour) and Forsyth (who found himself one shot short of a victory for the second week in a row) shot 68s to share second place. Gary Evans also shot 68 to finish in fourth at 275, and Eduardo Romero shot 68 as well to tie for fifth at 276 with Darren Clarke, who shot 71 despite his early eagle.

Barclays Scottish Open—€3,240,447
Winner: Ernie Els

In the early weeks of the year Ernie Els looked unbeatable. Then he ran headlong into a punching bag. While playing around in his Orlando, Florida, garage, Els took a swing at a punching bag and injured his wrist. In that instant, what could have been a career-defining year looked like a technical knockout. He withdrew from The Players Championship and missed the Deutsch Bank - SAP Open (and a much anticipated match-up with Tiger Woods) when the wrist flared up again. So it was quite rewarding for the Big Easy to return to the European Tour and pick up his fifth worldwide win with a wire-to-wire victory at the Barclays Scottish Open at Loch Lomond.

Els cruised in with a two-under-par 69 for a 17-under-par 267 total and a five-stroke trouncing of the field. Phillip Price, fresh off his third career win in Ireland the week before, tied for second with Darren Clarke. The South African took charge with a 64 on Thursday to open up a three-shot lead. He followed it up with two 67s to stretch the lead to five, which is where it remained for most of the final day.

The last round was a bit up and down. Els bogeyed the second hole after missing a short putt, but came back with a 10-footer for birdie at the par-five sixth. He made another birdie at the ninth from seven feet and a third at the 11th, before making a bogey at the 12th, another birdie at the 14th and a final bogey when a three-footer spun out of the hole at the 16th. By then it was a moot point. Clarke nibbled into the lead with an early birdie, but he gave it back with a bogey at the ninth and back-to-back bogeys at the 11th and 12th. He rallied for three birdies in his final six holes, but it was too little too late.

"It was a day where I didn't swing the club very well," Clarke said. "I had a few opportunities at the start to make some birdies, to make a dent in his lead, but I didn't make them."

The prevailing wisdom was that it wouldn't matter. Els seemed ready to do whatever was necessary to win. "I think deep down I probably felt Ernie was uncatchable today," said Price, who had five birdies and two bogeys in his final-round 69. "I felt like I was really trying just to get second place."

Els had no such thoughts. In the eight European stroke-play events he had participated in prior to defending his title at the Open Championship, Els had carded three victories, two seconds, one fourth, one fifth and a sixth, and was 101 under par for the year. "I leave (the week) with a lot more confidence than I have ever had going into a major," the winner said. "Although the Open will be a new week, I have a lot more faith in my ability these days. When I've played close to my best, I've won pretty convincingly."

That was certainly the case at Loch Lomond. "I was pleased with the way I coped today," Els said after his closing 69, his worst round of the week. "It is never easy to lead from start to finish, and today I wasn't as comfortable on the greens. I had a little battle within myself, and I'm proud to have overcome that."

The Open Championship—€5,685,750
Winner: Ben Curtis

See Chapter 4.

Nissan Irish Open—€1,800,000
Winner: Michael Campbell

Heartbreak comes in bunches — at least that's what Thomas Bjorn said after being handed his second straight down-the-stretch loss, this time in a playoff to Michael Campbell at the Nissan Irish Open. It was the second time in as many weeks that Bjorn had failed to convert a third-round lead into a victory, the first coming when he took three to get down from a greenside bunker on the 70th hole of the Open Championship. The loss in Ireland wasn't quite as dramatic or as devastating, but it was still a loss.

At the Open Championship it was Ben Curtis who came out on top after Bjorn failed to birdie the final hole. A week later at Portmarnock, it was Campbell who birdied the first playoff hole to knock Bjorn out. Still, the loser seemed to take the proper perspective. "I came here with one thing on my mind, and that was to prove I was doing the right things with my golf," Bjorn said afterward. "Nothing will make up for last week until ... if ... I win a major, but the 64 on Thursday showed me I am doing the right things."

Bjorn led by two after that 64, but he followed it up with a 74 that dropped him three strokes behind Campbell. Campbell shot 71 on Saturday to let Bjorn back into the mix. The two shared the lead with 18 holes to play. Both shot 71s on Sunday to finish at 11-under-par 277. They were joined by Peter Hedblom, who birdied the 14th, 15th, 16th and made a 25-footer for birdie at the 18th to shoot 68 on Sunday for a 277 of his own.

The playoff started on the 18th, a well-bunkered, 411-yard par-four with a progressively narrowing fairway. All three players hit the fairway. Bjorn played first and hit his approach to 20 feet. Hedblom was second and hit his shot 15 feet beyond the flag. That set up the shot of the tournament. Campbell, who hadn't won an event since the 2002 Smurfit European Open at The K Club, also near Dublin, and who had only broken into the top-50 once all season, hit his second shot to one foot. When Bjorn and Hedblom failed to convert, Campbell tapped in for the victory.

"Michael hit a great shot in," Hedblom said. "We needed to make birdie, but couldn't come up with the putt."

Campbell said he couldn't feel sorry for Bjorn this week. The week before was another matter. "I was out there to win," he said. "Last week I felt sorry for him. It's amazing when you see a friend going for his first major. I felt sick inside watching the last nine holes. The best thing he did this week was play. If he had been at home he would have had too much time to think about things."

Scandic Carlsberg Scandinavian Masters—€1,900,000
Winner: Adam Scott

Although it's hard to tell their swings apart from a distance, no one has ever confused Adam Scott with Tiger Woods on the final day of a tournament. But that might change with more finishes like Scott's final-round 69 in the Scandic Carlsberg Scandinavian Masters at Barseback Golf Club in Malmo, Sweden. Tied with Maarten Lafeber at the end of three rounds, Scott opened up a three-shot cushion with birdies at the 11th and 12th and cruised in for a 277 total, 11 under par, and a two-stroke win over Nick Dougherty.

Scott had missed the cut in his three previous starts and six of his last nine before arriving in Sweden. "I feel free now to go the PGA Championship and just play," Scott said of his upcoming trek to Rochester, New York. "I don't have any pressure on me, and this takes a bit of weight off my shoulders. I can go there with nothing holding me back."

A 67 on Saturday put Scott in the final group with Lafeber, but Scott quickly took the lead as Lafeber limped in with 75. That left the door open for Dougherty, who finished second to Scott in the 2002 Qatar Masters. This time the Englishman never mounted a charge. Scott bogeyed the 14th to allow Dougherty to get within two, but Scott came back with birdies at the 15th and 16th to pull away. Dougherty matched Scott's 69 for a 279 total and second place, two clear of Robert Karlsson, Andrew Coltart and Luke Donald.

While a lot was made of Scott's ball-striking and the striking resemblance his swing has to that of Woods, it was the youngster's putter that saved him in Sweden. Scott played the entire week without three-putting a single green. "That made a huge difference," he said. "I feel if I don't three-putt, this is where I should be at the end of the week, and I'm very happy. It was a real relief to go out and play well today. I managed to keep myself calm, but there were some really crucial times when I had to hole some putts to keep myself in front, and I was pleased I managed to do that."

He was also pleased by the position the win put him in with a special team event coming in November. "This win will get me into the running for the Presidents Cup," Scott said. "I would still like to make that team."

Nordic Open—€1,600,000
Winner: Ian Poulter

One week before the final major championship of the season, the recovery of Colin Montgomerie seemed complete. The big Scot had shown glimmers of brilliance at varying times throughout the year, but he also had some terrible disappointments, like pulling out of the Open Championship after injuring his hand. It wasn't until the weekend in Copenhagen that Montgomerie had a real shot at winning for the first time in more than a year. He didn't quite get the job done, missing a 15-footer on the final hole that would have forced a playoff with Ian Poulter in the Nordic Open, but there was no mistaking the seven-time Order of Merit winner's return to form.

"I didn't quite get the momentum and didn't have feel with the putter," Montgomerie said after tapping in for a closing 68 and a 267 total, one more than Poulter, who closed with 66 after shooting 65 in third round. "I left too many short this week, including the one on the last hole for the tie," said Montgomerie.

Montgomerie's 65-64 run on Friday and Saturday (the best back-to-back scores the Scot had strung together in more than 12 months, even though Simon's Golf Club in Copenhagen, Denmark, is considered one of the easiest tests on the European Tour) vaulted him into a tie for the lead with Soren Hansen, who shot a course-record 62 on Saturday. The two held a one-shot edge over Poulter going into the final round.

EUROPEAN TOURS / 161

On Sunday Montgomerie had six birdies, but two bogeys where he failed to convert par-saving putts of 18 and 15 feet cost him the chance at a title. Poulter had six birdies as well, but he had no bogeys, which proved to be the difference. Poulter's 22-under-par 266 was the best aggregate of his career, and the win was the fifth of his career and second of 2003, the first coming in June at the Wales Open.

Hansen couldn't keep the momentum going on Sunday. He shot 69 and tied for third place with Stephen Gallacher and Gregory Havret at 20-under-par 268.

BMW Russian Open—€400,000
Winner: Marcus Fraser

Australia's Marcus Fraser and Austria's Martin Wiegele started the final round of the BMW Russian Open tied for the lead at 15-under-par 201. In a situation similar to the one that would transpire a few hours later with Shaun Micheel and Chad Campbell in the PGA Championship, Fraser and Wiegele battled their way around the Le Meridien Moscow course, swapping the lead back and forth until the final hole. Wiegele went one up with a birdie on the 15th, but bogeyed the 16th to fall back into a tie. Both players parred the 17th, and both had birdie putts on the 18th. Wiegele's putt from 50 feet was unrealistic at best, and most speculated that he would be lucky not to three-putt. When the putt came within an inch of falling in for birdie, Wiegele fell to his knees in agony.

Fraser missed his birdie effort at the 18th as well, so both players shot 68 for 19-under-par 269 totals. They returned to the 18th for the playoff where both made birdie the first time through. The second time down the same hole, Wiegele missed the fairway and the green and failed to get up and down for par. That allowed Fraser to two-putt for par and earn an immediate promotion off the Challenge Tour and into the ranks of European Tour winners in this co-sponsored event.

"It was the most pressure I have ever played under," the 25-year-old Fraser said. "Now it feels great, but when I was out there it wasn't all that pleasant."

Peter Harmon shot 66 to finish alone in third at 272, two clear of Jose Manuel Carriles, Tim Milford, Andrew Coltart and Graeme Storm who tied for fourth at 274.

BMW International Open—€1,800,000
Winner: Lee Westwood

With most of the Europe's best back from their two-week jaunt to America (where no European fared well in the PGA Championship but a European stalwart, Darren Clarke, won the WGC NEC Invitational), it was time to resume some semblance of normalcy. In most people's book, that did not include Lee Westwood breaking his three-year winless drought with six late birdies and a final-round 66 at the BMW International Open, but that's what happened.

Westwood, who missed the cut in Rochester and tied for 46th in Akron where there was no cut, trailed Robert Karlsson by three strokes going into the final round and stood four behind Karlsson with nine holes to play. The 30-year-old Englishman rattled off birdies at the 11th, 12th and 13th holes to move into contention as Karlsson struggled to find the fairways. A string of three more birdies on the 16th, 17th and 18th coupled with a Karlsson implosion put Westwood on top. A chip-in birdie at the 17th put him two ahead of Alex Cejka with one hole to play. The birdie at the 18th for a 19-under-par 269 extended the margin of victory to three over Cejka.

After the final putt fell, Westwood put his head in his hands and sobbed. "I'm fairly emotional," Westwood said. "It has been more than two years since I won. This is a big moment. There were times when I thought about putting the clubs away and calling it a day. But that would have been an easy thing to do. I battled it out, and, hopefully, this is one of many rewards.

"I just enjoy winning and being in the lead with my name on the leaderboard and in front of people. I have worked for three years to get back to here, and there was no reason not to enjoy it."

Karlsson's demise began with a three-putt on the 10th for a bogey that seemed to unnerve him. Afterward he found only two fairways coming in and shot 74 for a 274 total and tie for eighth place.

Omega European Masters—€1,600,000
Winner: Ernie Els

Ernie Els continued his winning romp around the world in Switzerland, when he rallied from two strokes behind to win the Omega European Masters by six over Michael Campbell. Els' final-round 65 included consecutive birdies from the first through fourth holes to overtake Eduardo Romero, the third-round leader, who struggled with his putter. When Romero added to his troubles with a bogey at the sixth, Els extended the lead with a fantastic par on the fifth after getting relief from a bench and some advertising signs.

"I made the perfect start today to do something special with four birdies, but that was a career path at the fifth," Els said. "What a hole that was. From being two behind and all of a sudden I was ahead, and although I lost a bit of rhythm after my brilliant start, I felt like I kept everything together."

Indeed he did. Els reached the par-five first hole in two to set up the first birdie. Then he hit his approach to five feet for a birdie at the second to gain a share of the lead. At the par-three third, his tee shot stopped 12 feet away and he kept the momentum going when that putt fell. The birdie at the fourth was from 15 feet, and the par at the fifth came after two drops and a curling 20-footer that found the back of the hole. He had one bogey (a three-putt at the eighth), but made up for it when his second shot found the putting surface at the par-five 15th and he two-putted for another birdie. He finished it off with a birdie at the 17th and a par at the 18th.

Els played the last 13 holes in two under to finish at 17-under-par 267 and pick up his sixth worldwide victory of the year over Campbell, who shot 66 to finish alone in second at 273.

Romero shot 74 to finish in third at 274. "I putted terrible," the Argentinean said. "Nothing happened for me today. I tried my hardest to win, but it was not to be."

Trophee Lancome—€1,800,000
Winner: Retief Goosen

Even though he struggled off the tee in the final round, Retief Goosen never lost his poise or the lead in the Trophee Lancome in Paris, finishing off a wire-to-wire victory with a 70 for a 18-under-par 266 total, four better than Paul McGinley.

It was a lot closer than it looked. Goosen jumped out to the first-round lead with a 63 that was one stroke off the course and tournament record, but his scores got progressively higher though the week. He shot 65 to open up a five-shot lead over McGinley and a 68 on Saturday to allow the Irishman and 2002 Ryder Cup hero to pull within three.

Goosen birdied his first hole on Sunday from 10 feet, but couldn't find the fairway for several holes after that. He birdied the fifth from the rough, but bogeyed the sixth when another tee shot went awry. He made another birdie at the par-three eighth from eight feet to reach 19 under. He bogeyed the 11th from the rough, and McGinley, who birdied the fifth, eighth, 10th and 11th, pulled within one stroke.

Goosen hit his tee shot on the par-three 12th to 14 feet and made the putt for birdie, and followed it up with another birdie at the 15th while McGinley was making bogey. On the par-five 16th, the Irishman made a double bogey to hand Goosen the title, even though the champion made two bogeys on the closing three holes.

"I was really struggling all day," Goosen said, "especially with my driver. It's been a great week here with my family, but a tough one on the golf course today. I struggled with my swing, and I think I used all of the golf course to get the job done."

Despite his erratic finish, McGinley finished alone in second at 270, one clear of Raphael Jacquelin and Ian Poulter, and two ahead of Hennie Otto and Nicolas Colsaerts.

Linde German Masters—€3,000,000
Winner: K.J. Choi

For Korean K.J. Choi the Linde German Masters was supposed to be an opportunity to gain some experience on the European Tour. "I would have been happy with a top-10 finish before I came here," said Choi, a two-time U.S. PGA Tour winner. "A win is very rewarding."

Choi made the best of his first start on the European continent, shooting 67 for a 26-under-par 262 total and a two-stroke victory over Miguel Angel Jimenez. "I am so happy to have won this tournament after having been invited to play," Choi said. "This week the impression of Germany for me has been wonderful."

The former weight-lifting champion carried a one-shot lead into the final round after opening with 63 and following it up with rounds of 68 and 64. Jimenez was his closest pursuer after bracketing a 62 on Friday with a pair of 67s.

Choi lost the lead early in the final round when he bogeyed the third hole, but he regained it when he holed out a wedge shot from the fairway for eagle at the par-four fifth. Another birdie at the seventh extended the lead, but he ran into trouble again at the 12th and walked away with a bogey to allow Jimenez to close to within one stroke. The 39-year-old Spaniard, looking for his first victory of the year, birdied the fourth, fifth and seventh, but dropped to two behind with a bogey at the 11th. He still had a chance to catch Choi until the Korean hit a spectacular second shot at the par-five 13th. The ball stopped 12 feet from the hole, and Choi rolled in the putt for his second eagle of the day.

From then on it was a battle for second place. Jimenez birdied the 13th and made a 20-footer for birdie at the 18th to shoot 68 and finish the week at 264, one ahead of Ian Poulter and Niclas Fasth. "I played very well and I am pleased with my showing the whole week and the whole tournament," Jimenez said. "I didn't make any real mistakes today. I tried my best to catch K.J., but he just beat me in the end, and that is golf."

Anders Hansen, Darren Clarke and Carlos Rodiles finished in a tie for fifth at 268, but no one came close to challenging Choi in the final holes. "Now, I have a five-year exemption over here," Choi said with great surprise. "So, I plan to play more."

Dunhill Links Championship—€4,281,240
Winner: Lee Westwood

The spectacular collapse of Lee Westwood was one of European golf's great mysteries. How had Europe's former No. 1 player, the first man to dislodge Colin Montgomerie from his Order of Merit throne, fallen into such a sustained slump? How could he have gone from fourth in the world to 248th? More importantly, could he claw his way back?

With a closing 67 for a 21-under-par 267 in the Dunhill Links Championship over the three-course rota of the Old Course at St. Andrews, Carnoustie and Kingsbarns, Westwood won for the second time in 2003, only a month after winning the BMW International Open. The endless hours of work with David Leadbetter were beginning to pay off. He played 72 holes with only one bogey and defeated Ernie Els by one stroke in the celebrity pro-am that was once the Dunhill Cup team event.

Westwood parred the Road Hole and the final hole on the Old Course to hold off a formidable field that included Els, Vijay Singh, Darren Clarke and Retief Goosen. That followed on the heels of Westwood's course-record 62 at Kingsbarns on Saturday, a round that included the Englishman's first competitive double eagle when a four-iron shot from 218 yards found the hole on the par-five ninth.

"As soon as I hit my second at the ninth, I knew it was a great shot," the winner said. "It probably started two yards right of the flag. There was not much wind, and it's quite cold. It landed just short of the slope and ran up there and skipped on."

The two carried over to Sunday when Westwood had five birdies in a six-hole stretch in the middle of his round and five closing pars into the wind. "A month ago you'd have never thought it," Westwood said. "It just shows you how quickly you can turn it around."

Westwood had to par the final two holes because of some spectacular home-stretch play by Els, who birdied the 17th by making a 35-foot putt and then birdied the 18th after hitting a fantastic pitch through the Valley of Sin to within four feet. Els' closing 64 secured second place with a 268 total, two clear of Raphael Jacquelin and three ahead of Maarten Lafeber and Darren Clarke.

"When the putt went in on 17, I thought, 'yes, big Ern,'" Els said. "And the shot at the last will stay with me for a long time. All in all, it was a fun week."

Westwood echoed those sentiments. "It's just incredible," he said of his recent resurgence. "It has been some turnaround for me since the start of the year, and even in the last eight weeks. Having made a double bogey on the last hole to miss the cut at the PGA Championship, I was having doubts about my ability to come back."

Dutch Open—€1,000,000
Winner: Maarten Lafeber

On the heels of a solid performance at the Dunhill Links Championship, Marten Lafeber kept his game rolling in his homeland and became the first Dutchman since the Truman administration to win the Dutch Open. He did so with solid putting and the best weekend of any player in the field.

Rounds of 67 and 69 on Thursday and Friday left Lafeber three off the pace set by Soren Hansen, the hottest Dane on tour this season. Lafeber cut into Hansen's lead on Saturday when the Amsterdam native fired a six-under-par 64 to pull within one stroke and earn a spot in the final Sunday pairing.

Hansen extended his lead with birdies at the second and third holes, almost holing his approach at the third. He bogeyed the eighth to let Lafeber climb back to within a shot, and followed it up with a bogey at the ninth while Lafeber was making birdie. That two-shot swing proved to be the difference. Once Lafeber had the lead, he never gave it up. Hansen made another run with birdies at the 14th and 16th, but he needed a birdie on the 18th to force a playoff. When Hansen failed, Lafeber had the luxury of two putts from four feet for the win. Lafeber finished with 67 for a 13-under-par 267 total, one clear of Hansen, who shot 69, and a hard-charging Mathias Gronberg, who finished with 65.

"It feels incredible," Lafeber said. "I played really solid and managed to get the putts in. I was so glad not to have to make that birdie putt on the last hole, as the tension was building over the last few holes. I wanted to win so badly that last few months, and to win this tournament means so much to me. It is incredible, a dream come true."

"I am happy for Maarten," Hansen said. "It has been due for a long time, and now it will be interesting to see how he does in the future, because he is a very good player and he played very well today. I made a mistake on the eighth and ninth, but I managed to get it back over the back nine, so that I played myself into it on the 18th. Unfortunately, I have not bettered par on that hole all week, which is a shame."

Gronberg gained a temporary share of the lead after rolling in his sixth birdie of the day at the 15th, but he pushed his eight-iron approach at the

16th and gave up a stroke with a bogey. He did make birdie at the 18th, however, to gain a share of second place. "I wasn't even thinking about winning," Gronberg said. "I was hoping to play maybe five or six under, but would have taken a top-five before the day started."

Lafeber's first career victory made him the first Dutchman since Joop Ruhl in 1947 to win his country's national Open. "To win in your home country is incredible, especially when it is your first one," Lafeber said. "It is one of the hardest tournaments for me to win because people expect you to do well and win. Now I have done it. I am very, very relieved the victory is finally there. I knew everybody wanted me to win, and the support I have had this week has been incredible."

HSBC World Match Play—£2,300,000
Winner: Ernie Els

See Chapter 7.

Turespana Mallorca Classic—€400,000
Winner: Miguel Angel Jimenez

Miguel Angel Jimenez felt good about his finish in the inaugural Turespana Mallorca Classic. He had struggled early in the week, shooting an opening-round 72 on the par-70 Pula Golf Club course to trail the leaders by eight strokes. He made progress in the second round with 67 to close to within five of the lead with one round to play. Then he spent some time working on his swing in front of a full-length mirror, and had some good feelings on the putting green before his final round. When he shot 65 for a 54-hole total of 204, Jimenez thought he had done well for himself, maybe a top three or even a runner-up finish. With that, he went to the locker room, took a shower, changed into his jeans, and watched the final holes on television.

Jose Maria Olazabal appeared to have the tournament locked up. He had gotten to eight under par in the middle of his final round and held a three-stroke lead with five holes to play. A bogey at the 15th cut that lead to two, but as Jimenez said, "Olazabal had been solid all week." There was no need to think he couldn't close this one out.

Then the unthinkable happened. Olazabal, two up with two to play, hit his tee shot out of bounds on the 17th and took a double bogey. The lead was gone. He and Jimenez were tied with one hole remaining.

"After I changed into my jeans, the tournament director told me of the situation, and I went to get ready for a playoff," he said. "I thought there would at least be a playoff, but that is golf for you."

Olazabal found the green at the 18th with his approach, but because of the configuration of the putting surface, he had to chip his third shot over a ridge. The ball stopped 12 feet beyond the hole, and Olazabal missed his par effort, handing Jimenez his first win since the 1999 Volvo Masters.

"Just imagine how I feel right now," Olazabal said after his double bogey, bogey finish left him at even-par 70 for his round and 205 for the tournament. "The tournament was mine when I was standing on the 17th tee, but

I just didn't know how to catch it. I wanted to play my tee shot on 17 open, to the left, but I over-cut it and it went out of bounds. Then 18 was very difficult. I hit a three iron pin high, but to the right, and when I got to the ball I couldn't putt it. So I had to play a chip, but missed the putt coming back."

Jimenez felt sorry for the way his friend and fellow countryman finished, but he was also thrilled at breaking a three-year winless drought. "It feels great to have won again, and it is nice to have done it in front of a Spanish crowd in Mallorca," Jimenez said. "I think the difference in my form recently has all been down to attitude on the course. Sometimes we have to realize that we are only human, and human beings miss putts and fairways, and there's nothing we can do about that. You can't put pressure on yourself all day long.

"I knew that I could hit the ball well, but my attitude towards my own game has changed. I feel at ease, relaxed and comfortable on the course now."

Telefonica Open de Madrid—€1,400,000
Winner: Ricardo Gonzalez

In a testament to the adage "never give up, especially at golf," Argentina's Ricardo Gonzalez overcame the will to quit after a bogey at the second hole of the final round left him seven shots back, and mounted one of the biggest charges of the year, rallying with eight birdies in a 12-hole stretch to win the Telefonica Open de Madrid by one stroke over Padraig Harrington, Marten Olander, Nick O'Hern and third-round leader Paul Casey.

"After three-putting the second, I thought the tournament was over," Gonzalez said. At that point he might have been right. Despite a stirring 66 on Saturday, the Argentinean entered the final round six strokes behind Casey, who had led from the first day. "I was seven behind and the will had left me. I didn't have any motivation, but then I started to play well, the door opened, and the light switched on for me."

It started with a birdie at the fourth and didn't end until he drained a 30-footer for par at the 16th while Casey was making another bogey. That gave Gonzalez a two-shot lead as he stood on the 18th tee. He admitted to succumbing to nerves on the final hole, leaving his approach in a greenside bunker and failing to get up-and-down for par, but he still shot a six-under-par 65 and finished the week at 270. Harrington and Olander were already in the clubhouse at 271, which meant that only Casey and O'Hern, playing together in the final group, had a chance of catching him. When both failed to convert birdie putts on the final green, Gonzalez had his second career victory.

The win also moved him up to 43rd in the Order of Merit, which qualified him for the season-ending Volvo Masters. "That is the best round I played all year," the winner admitted.

Harrington also played well, equaling Gonzalez's final-round 65 after shooting two-over 73 on Friday. Also making a final-round charge was Spanish favorite Sergio Garcia, who was looking for his first win on any tour in 2003. Garcia opened the week with a strong 64, but had been plagued by putting woes ever since. Two rounds of 71 left Garcia seven shots back. He pulled to within two with two to play, but rather than birdieing the final two holes to force a playoff, he bogeyed the 17th and 18th to shoot 67 and finish in a four-way tie for sixth.

Volvo Masters Andalucia—€3,500,000
Winner: Fredrik Jacobson

It wouldn't be a stretch to say that Fredrik Jacobson had the most underrated year of any player on any tour. He finished in the top five in two majors and won twice on the European Tour, while still flying so far under the radar he wasn't even the most talked-about Swede of the year. Still, after a dramatic finish and a four-hole playoff victory in the season-ending Volvo Masters Andalucia at Valderrama, the 28-year-old Jacobson positioned himself as the leading Swede who isn't named Annika.

"I am into all the majors now, and I want to get into the Ryder Cup," Jacobson said after competing his third victory in the dark. He said he planned to split his time between Europe and the U.S. PGA Tour in 2004.

In the season-ending event in the Spanish coastal village of Sotogrande, Jacobson led from the first round. His 64 gave him a two-shot advantage, which he maintained with a 71. Another 71 on Saturday allowed Carlos Rodiles to close the gap and enter the final round tied with Jacobson at 10-under-par 206. Through 16 holes on Sunday Jacobson seemed in command. He took a one-shot lead to the tee at the 17th, which remains the most ticked-up hole in professional golf.

This time Jacobson discovered what all the fuss was about. Just as Tiger Woods did at the 1999 WGC American Express Championship, Jacobson hit what appeared to be a perfect third shot into the 17th green. But the ball bounced forward, stopped, and then slowly trickled off the front of the green and into the water. This prompted an uncouth round of applause from the gallery on the hillside behind the green, as Rodiles (a Spaniard) benefited most from Jacobson's misfortune. Rodiles made birdie and Jacobson made double bogey. Not only did the lead change, Jacobson went from one up with two to play to two down with one hole remaining.

The Swede never gave up. He hit a nine iron from 145 yards to within a foot of the hole at the 18th and made birdie while Rodiles failed to save par from the back of the green. Both signed for scores of 70 and 276 totals, and went back to the 18th tee for the playoff.

Jacobson kept the drama high, pulling his tee shot near a tree, but he hit a miraculous eight iron into the first cut of rough in front of the green. He got up and down and watched Rodiles miss his birdie putt, which put them back on the 18th tee together for a third time as darkness approached.

This time, it looked as though Rodiles would put it away. He hit a six iron to six feet, while Jacobson missed the green to the right. But a deft up-and-down by Jacobson and a pushed putt by Rodiles took this one to a third extra hole. They moved to the 10th where both players made birdie. Finally, with darkness upon them, Jacobson won with a par on the 18th after Rodiles hit his tee shot behind a tree and had to play backward into the fairway.

"It was a really, really tough battle out there with Carlos," the winner said.

"It has been quite unbelievable the way the story went up and down with my leading for a while, then Carlos going in front. It was quite hard to stay in the battle." .

The Seve Trophy—€2,200,000
Winner: Great Britain & Ireland

It seemed fitting that in a year when Seve Ballesteros, the legend for whom The Seve Trophy was created, found himself embroiled in one controversy after another, that the tournament that bears his name would end on a disquieting note.

Taking a 10-8 lead into the singles matches on Sunday, Great Britain & Ireland captain Colin Montgomerie got the match-ups he had hoped for and a break that he didn't expect. Moments before the matches were to begin, Montgomerie was handed a gift when Thomas Bjorn had to withdraw because of a neck injury. Had the injury been reported a few minutes earlier, it would have been up to Montgomerie to nominate a player to sit out and take a halve. But because the injury wasn't reported until Bjorn was about to tee off, the match was conceded and Paul Casey won a point without taking a swing.

"It is a recurring injury," Bjorn said. "It just popped up at the wrong time. I am obviously very disappointed for myself and also very disappointed for my teammates, because we felt we got a little bit of momentum going yesterday. When I woke up this morning, I felt a little something, but I did all the physio stuff I normally do, and everything appeared to be okay. But when I went down to hit some balls on the range it just got worse and worse, and it got to the state where there was nothing I could do."

That put the matches at 11-8. When Montgomerie eliminated fellow-captain Ballesteros 5 and 4, the GB& I team was within two and a half points of retaining the cup. Europe didn't pick up a point until late in the day when Ignacio Garrido defeated Paul Lawrie 3 and 2 to make it a 12-9 contest. When David Howell rolled in a birdie putt on the 18th to beat Alex Cejka 1 up, victory for GB&I seemed all but assured.

Fredrik Jacobson gave the Continentals a glimmer of hope when he trounced Lee Westwood 3 and 2 in a match where the Swede never trailed. Jacobson went undefeated for the week, proving to be one of Europe's best young prospects for the future. Unfortunately, Jacobson's heroics were too little too late for Ballesteros' team. Moments after Jacobson's win, Justin Rose closed out Raphael Jacquelin 3 and 2 to put the GB&I team within a half-point of victory.

Then the controversy erupted. On the third green of his match with Padraig Harrington, Jose Maria Olazabal had a 12-footer for birdie. He also had what he believed to be a couple of old ball marks on his line. As he went to repair the marks Harrington took exception, claiming that they might not be ball marks. Olazabal repaired the marks anyway, prompting Harrington to call for an official ruling. When referee Tony Gray arrived on the green, the marks had already been repaired, so he could not make a ruling.

Insulted that his integrity had been questioned, Olazabal picked up his mark and conceded the hole to Harrington. That proved significant as Harrington hung on to halve the match and win the final half-point the GB&I team needed to retain the cup. It was a bizarre ending to a bizarre year that saw Ballesteros erupt on two separate occasions, once when he was warned for slow play and another when was penalized a shot for the same offense. In the latter incident, Ballesteros refused to accept the penalty and was disqualified for signing an incorrect scorecard.

"We had a difference of opinion," Olazabal said. "I'm not going to waste any more time talking about it."

Harrington elaborated a little more. "I fully believe that Jose thought they were pitch marks," he said. "I was not clear. I was 50-50, so it was possible he was 100 percent right. It was a disagreement of opinion. This is not worth losing a friend over, not for a half-point, not for a point, not for anything. My reaction put Jose in a very difficult position, and he did the honorable thing in his eyes and conceded the hole. Not that I wanted him to."

The captains tried to dampen the controversy with conciliatory speeches afterward. "It has been a great week," Montgomerie said. "Everybody got something out of it. Everyone on my team contributed at least a half-point, which is excellent, and I couldn't have asked anything more from any of them."

Ballesteros agreed to an extent. "It has been a great week here," he said. "The only problem we have had is the result. I have already told my players to get practicing for next year."

Omega Hong Kong Open—US$700,000
Winner: Padraig Harrington

See Asia/Japan Tours.

Challenge Tour

Johan Edfors of Sweden finished on top of the Challenge Tour Order of Merit despite losing a playoff at the Grand Final at Golf du Medoc in Bordeaux. Edfors lost out to a brilliant seven-iron shot by Spain's Jose Manuel Carriles at the first extra hole of the season-ending tournament. But the 28-year-old Edfors had earlier won the Stanbic Zambia Open as well as the Fortis Challenge Open in The Netherlands to earn playing rights on the PGA European Tour for 2004.

Edfors, who was in his fifth season on the Challenge Tour, will join seven players as rookies on the main circuit. The others were fellow Swede Martin Erlandsson, Martin LeMesurier, Jamie Elson and James Hepworth, all from England, Scotsman Scott Drummond, Argentinean Sebastian Fernandez and Martin Wiegele of Austria.

The seven other qualifiers who earned promotion to the European Tour after finishing in the top 15 on the Order of Merit will all be returning to the main circuit. The experienced Carriles was joined by countryman Ivo Giner, as well as Swedes Peter Hanson and Michael Jonzon, and Englishmen Stuart Little, Robert Coles and Ben Mason.

Australia's Marcus Fraser earned immediate promotion to the European Tour when he won the BMW Russian Open, an event co-sanctioned with the main circuit. It was Fraser's third victory on the 2003 Challenge Tour after wins at the Nykredit Danish Open and the Talma Finnish Challenge, the latter coming just two weeks before his playoff win in Moscow over Wiegele.

Another Australian, Brett Rumford, who lost his European Tour card in 2002 and failed to regain it by only one shot at the qualifying tournament, also benefited from winning a co-sanctioned event at the Aa St. Omer Open. European Tour members Bradley Dredge and Miguel Angel Jimenez won the other two co-sanctioned events, while Darren Clarke also appeared as a winner on the Challenge Tour after supporting a new tournament in his native province, the Benmore Developments Northern Ireland Masters. His prize was a mere 878,597 euro less than his check for winning the WGC NEC World Invitational a few weeks previously.

Two of the most impressive debut seasons on the Challenge Tour were produced by Elson and LeMesurier. Elson, 22, is the son of Pip Elson, who won the Sir Henry Cotton Trophy as the Rookie of the Year on the European Tour in 1973. After playing college golf in the United States, Elson represented Great Britain and Ireland in the Walker Cup in 2001 before turning professional in March 2003.

He won in only his third appearance on the Challenge Tour at the Volvo Finnish Open and had another six top-10 finishes to finish 10th on the Order of Merit. "I'm delighted to have made it," said Elson. "I feel a certain amount of pride because I only turned professional in March and didn't know what to expect when I did.

"But my first win made me believe I could get onto the European Tour this season, and I think the Challenge Tour has taught me so much and will stand me in good stead for next year. I suppose I'm following in my dad's footsteps. Obviously he taught me how to play and it would be a great achievement to emulate his first year on the European Tour."

LeMesurier, who finished second on the Order of Merit, had an even more dramatic start when the 27-year-old won the Tessali - Metaponto Open in his first appearance. He then finished second, fourth and eighth before winning again at the Clearstream International Luxembourg Open, a sequence which spanned only six weeks.

10. Asia/Japan Tours

The days of cut-and-dried outcomes of the races for No. 1 on the Japan Tour seem to be long gone. During the formative quarter-century of the circuit, it was a major upset when the top player to finish the season atop of the money standings was not Masashi (Jumbo) Ozaki or, before his remarkable run began, Tsuneyuki (Tommy) Nakajima or Isao Aoki. After Ozaki won his last seasonal title in 1998, that leading position was held by four different players — in order, Naomichi (Joe) Ozaki, Shingo Katayama, Toshimitsu Izawa and Toru Taniguchi.

Izawa broke that pattern in 2003, but it was far from a predestined occurrence. Izawa got a huge boost toward clinching the No. 1 spot he seized just three tournaments before the end of the season when American Todd Hamilton, who was enjoying his finest of 11 years on the Japan Tour, passed up the final two events. Hamilton, who racked up four victories and held the No. 1 spot through most of the season, passed up his chances of garnering that honor for 2003 and returned to America to participate in the qualifying tournament for the PGA Tour. His decision paid off. He tied for 16th when the nerve-wracking, 108-hole grind ended in Florida and will compete, along with Japan's Hirofumi Miyase, as an exempt player on the 2004 PGA Tour. Miyase just made the qualifying 30 and ties, finishing tied for 28th.

His performances on the 2003 tour marked an impressive rebound for the 35-year-old Izawa, who had gone without a victory the year after his record money-winning season in 2001, when he won ¥217,934,583 off five victories. He dropped to 14th in the standings that year. Izawa won the 13th and 14th titles of his career back to back in July to establish his challenge to Hamilton, whom he slipped past at the Dunlop Phoenix in late November. Taniguchi, the 2002 leader, was a winless non-contender in 2003 and tumbled to 34th on the money list.

Besides Hamilton and Izawa, only two other players — Miyase and Katayama — won more than once on the 2003 Japan Tour as nine players landed titles in Japan for the first time. One of them — Hideto Tanihara — won twice during the year, but the second victory was in the Japan/Asia Okinawa Open, the kickoff tournament of the 2004 Japanese season. Like Izawa, Katayama and Miyase won twice on the 2003 circuit. Katayama wound up fourth on the money list after placing first, then second, then third in the preceding seasons. He included the Japan PGA Championship among his victories. Izawa won the Japan Tour Championship and Hamilton the Japan PGA Match Play. Keiichiro Fukabori took the Japan Open.

Three overseas players were among the nine first-time winners. Andre Stolz of Australia took the season-opening Token Homemate Cup, Yeh Wei-tze of Taiwan the ANA Open and Jyoti Randhawa became the first Indian winner ever in Japan with his victory in the Suntory Open. The only other overseas victors in 2003 were Thomas Bjorn of Denmark, who won the rich Dunlop Phoenix for a second time, and Brendan Jones of Australia, a first-time winner in 2002. The ninth first-time winner was Tetsuji Hiratsuka, whose victory in the season-ending Golf Nippon Series jumped him into second place on the money list, some ¥13 million behind Izawa.

Older players had their days, too, particularly 48-year-old Masahiro (Massy) Kuramoto, who joined an exclusive group of worldwide players when he shot 59 in the opening round of the Acom International and went on to his first victory on the Japan Tour in eight years and his 29th official title. Kiyoshi Murota, also 48, ran away with the Mitsui Sumitomo Visa Taiheiyo Masters and Naomichi Ozaki, at age 47, bagged the Bridgestone Open title. The incredible Masashi Ozaki, now 56, nearly joined them. He finished second to Yeh Wei-tze by a stroke in the ANA Open and lost in a playoff to Kuramoto in the Acom International the following Sunday.

The Asian PGA Tour enjoyed its ninth season, and if anyone was tempted to stamp it a coming-of-age year, there was good reason. The heroics and history were attracting attention worldwide.

India's Arjun Atwal had a coming-of-age year of his own. He won twice, taking the Carlsberg Malaysian Open and the Hero Honda Masters, and realized two dreams: He won the Order of Merit (becoming the tour's first career $1 million winner) and he went to the United States and qualified for the PGA Tour. In the Order of Merit race, Atwal beat out China's remarkable Zhang Lian-wei, himself a two-time winner and a powerful figure in the emerging golf in his country. In winning the Asian-European co-sponsored Caltex Masters, he nipped the rampaging Ernie Els, ranked No. 2 in the world, with a birdie on the final hole. Zhang also won the Volvo China Open.

The Far East got its own version of the Ryder Cup at Mission Hills Golf Club in China, the inaugural Phoenix Dynasty Cup presented by Visa, with the Asians scoring a runaway win over the older, wiser, favored Japanese. Among other attention-getters in 2003: Thai amateur Chanin Puntawong, 16, tied the single-round record (in relation to par) with an 11-under-par 61, and Taiwanese amateur Lo Shih-kai became the youngest player, at age 14 years and 275 days, to make the cut on the tour.

Others dropped by to leave their mark. There was Korea's Choi Kyung-ju, better known as K.J. Choi on the U.S. PGA Tour, taking the SK Telecom Open. American John Daly, of grip-it-and-rip-it fame, charged down the final nine of the Kolon Cup Korean Open for his first win since 2001. Scotland's Colin Montgomerie won the Macau Open late in the season, just barely keeping alive his streak of at least one victory a year since 1989. And Ireland's Padraig Harrington took the Omega Hong Kong Open in December, laying on a bit of what he called "fat over the winter" for world ranking points.

Phoenix Dynasty Cup

It started with the Ryder Cup in 1927 — the beginning of international team competition in professional golf. This was the United States vs. Great Britain, and later Great Britain-Ireland, then Europe. Next came the Presidents Cup in 1994, the United States vs. International, a team from the rest of the world. As golf grew and spread around the world, it was just a matter of time until the idea would take root in the Far East. Introducing the Phoenix Dynasty Cup Presented by Visa — Asia versus Japan.

The Dynasty Cup was played at Mission Hills Country Club, the gleaming resort outside Shenzhen, China. Mission Hills was already internationally known as the site of the 1995 World Cup of Golf.

On paper and in the view of most observers, the Japan Tour — much older and with the more experienced golfers and ostensibly deeper in talent — was the favorite. Hsieh Min-nan, Asia's non-playing captain, said as much before the teams reached Mission Hills. "We are a growing tour and still rank behind the U.S. PGA Tour and the Japan Tour," he said. And then he added, "But when we win — and yes, I am confident of victory — it will give the Asian PGA Tour a better profile."

Much to everyone else's surprise, Asia didn't merely win the inaugural Phoenix Dynasty Cup. After splitting the opening day's alternate shot matches, 3-3, Asia won 5-1 in the better-ball matches, and 8½-3½ in singles. Add it up and that's a walloping 16½ to 7½ margin.

"I was surprised by the margin of victory," Hsieh conceded, "but it shows that the Asian players are very good."

It wasn't hard to find the source of Hsieh's bright outlook. In gauging his team's strength, he noted two recent impressive Asian Tour successes. China's Zhang Lian-wei beat Ernie Els, then ranked No. 2 in the world, in the Caltex Masters, and India's Arjun Atwal ran off from Retief Goosen, No. 5 in the world, in the Carlsberg Malaysian Open. "I was really impressed with our players' performances," Hsieh said, noting in the head-to-head competition their "… stunning golf and cool composure. Their victories will increase the team's chances of winning the first Dynasty Cup and raise the confidence of the other team members."

Then he noted another edge his team had. "The Asian players are also familiar with the World Cup course at Mission Hills," he said. "We may also gain a slight advantage over Japan as our players are well into the season on the Asian PGA Tour. In contrast, the Japan Tour has yet to tee off."

Isao Aoki, captain of the Japan Tour team, considered these factors and said, "They may have a little advantage over our players. However, I've got a team made up of veterans and young players, and we would like to bring the first Dynasty Cup back to Japan. It's going to be a great event."

There was this about the Phoenix Dynasty Cup and its role in the world of golf: "It will be great for Asian golf," said Jyoti Randhawa, one of three Indian players on the Asian team. "The Ryder Cup has helped make the game popular in Europe and the United States and I think something similar will happen here, with the best players in Asia taking on the top Japanese players."

Zhang Lian-wei, China's top player, had a similar opinion. "The Dynasty Cup will definitely raise the awareness of golf on mainland China," he said. "Tiger Woods played an exhibition match at Mission Hills a couple of years ago and there were big crowds there to see him. The Dynasty Cup is a big event for China and I expect good galleries."

There was nothing left to do, then, but tee it up. The Phoenix Dynasty Cup was played in a Ryder Cup format, with alternate shot (foursomes) the first day, better-ball (four-ball) the second, and singles the last day.

On the first day, there was no hint of the runaway Asian victory. Hsieh led off the alternate shot with Chinese stars Zhang Lian-wei and Liang Wen-chong, and it was a memorable debut for Chinese golf. They promptly delivered a squeaker of a 1-hole victory over Japan's Nobuhito Sato and Hajime Meshiai. The Japanese won the ninth hole, and squared the match on Meshiai's 30-foot birdie putt at the 17th. But Sato's poor drive at the 18th handed the hole and the win to Asia. Japan drew level immediately, Hiroyuki Fujita and Katsumasa Miyamoto taking the Indian pair of Arjun Atwal, one of Hsieh's aces, and Jeev Milkha Singh, 3 and 1. Then Japan took the lead, 2-1, on Taichi Teshima and Keiichiro Fukabori's 1-hole win over Lin keng-chi and Kang Wook-soon. It seemed the prognosticators were right. The Japanese were already proving to be too much.

Suddenly things were reversed, thanks to a ball. The Thai pairing of Thongchai Jaidee and Prayad Marksaeng were 2 down at the turn and slipping. "I didn't have any feeling using Thongchai's ball," Prayad said. "That was why we decided to switch to my regular ball and started to play better. I told Thongchai to simply concentrate on his putting." And the Thais bounced back for a 2-and-1 win over Toru Suzuki and Katsunori Kuwabara. This squared the match at 2-2. Then it was Japan's turn again. Tsuneyuki Nakajima and Tomohiro Kondo led all the way in a 2-and-1 win over Thammanoon Srirot and Thaworn Wiratchant. "We kept saying, 'We can do it, we can do it,'" Nakajima said, and Japan was leading, 3-2.

Then Hsieh's strategy paid off handsomely. His final pairing for the day was Jyoti Randhawa, No. 1 on the Asian Tour, and Korea's Charlie Wi. "I was very nervous, much more than I expected," said Wi, who had never played alternate shot before. "We went 2 down immediately, but I told Jyoti to play it one hole at a time." Then they ran off three straight birdies from the 14th for a 2-and-1 victory over Kiyoshi Murota and Yasuharo Imano, squaring the day at 3-3.

"The score line shows that the Asian team is very good," said Aoki. "We knew that the players would be nervous on the first day, so it's good to have three points in the bag."

Hsieh was equal parts joy and relief. "We had a bad start, and I was worried after the first nine holes," he said. "But we fought back very well. Asia has every reason to feel proud today."

The Phoenix Dynasty Cup took a stunning turn in better-ball on the second day. What was looking like a real struggle turned into a complete rout. Hsieh stuck with his same pairings for the better-ball the next day, and was re-warded with a stampede. Asia spotted Japan a 1-point lead on an easy Nakajima-Meshiai 3-and-2 win over Thammanoon and Thaworn. Then Asia swept the next five matches without trailing.

Thongchai chipped in for an eagle at the par-five second hole, and that put him and Prayad ahead to stay in a 2-and-1 win over Miyamoto and Suzuki. The match was square. Asia surged into the lead when Lin and Kang, beaten the day before, took no chances this time. They logged six birdies to run away from Sato and Imano, 4 and 3. Then came Randhawa's blistering display. Partnering Charlie Wi, Randhawa notched eight birdies for another runaway, this one 5 and 4 over Teshima and Kuwabara. Two points down, two to go.

Chalk up one more, this from the Indian pairing, Atwal and Singh, redeeming their first-day loss against Fujita and Fukabori, 2 and 1. And Asia's eighth point came from the Chinese pairing, Zhang and Liang, 2 and 1 over Murota and Kondo.

"Our players who started later in the day got a huge boost as the early pairings started off strongly," Zhang said. "It was really good to see the blue numbers showing up for Asia."

It was a tough day for Aoki, the Japanese captain. He was frustrated. "The Asian side looked to have come up with some good combinations," he said, "and it doesn't help with our players struggling to adapt on these greens. I felt so much stress watching the players on the course. It must have been even worse for them."

But now he had a new and different problem.

"Our players," he said, "need to play well on the front nine tomorrow to have a chance."

Asia, the underdog in many eyes, now led by 8-4 and needed only 4½ points from the 12 singles matches the next day to pick up the first Phoenix Dynasty Cup.

Asia's Hsieh was all but bursting at the seams. "Before the tournament, people told me that the Japanese had an 80 percent chance of winning," he said, "but now I'm 80 percent confident that we can do it tomorrow."

As it turned out, Hsieh wasn't over-confident. He was under-confident.

Prayad Marksaeng, first out for Asia in singles, got the first point in such dramatic fashion, it must have seemed like a bell tolling for Japan. Prayad was 1 down to Taichi Teshima through the 12th. Then he birdied the 13th from 50 yards and holed a 30-foot putt for another birdie at the 15th to go 1 up. At the 16th, Teshima lost his ball in the woods and drove his third shot into a hazard and conceded the hole. They halved the 17th, and Prayad had a 2-and-1 win. "After finding out I was first out, I knew it was my responsibility to get the first point for the team," Prayad said. "I attacked whenever I had the opportunity, but it was always very tight against Teshima. It feels really good to be part of this winning team."

Kang Wook-soon got the next point with ease, a 4-2 romp over Toru Suzuki. Asia had two of the 4½ points. They were stalled for a moment when Kiyoshi Murota thumped Lin Keng-chi, 6 and 5. Charlie Wi got the point back emphatically, whipping Hajime Meshiai, 4 and 3. Asia's fourth point came from Jyoti Randhawa, 2 and 1 over Hirofumi Miyase, who replaced an ill Keiichiro Fukabori.

It fell to Thammanoon to clinch the Phoenix Dynasty Cup. No one was more eager. "After losing my opening two matches, I was determined not to lose a third time," Thammanoon said. "I just kept telling myself, 'I have to win, I have to win.'" And this he did, dropping a 30-foot birdie putt on the 15th for a big 4-and-3 win over Hiroyuki Fujita for Asia's decisive point.

Asia rolled through the singles, 8½-3½, to wrap up the lopsided win. The Asians didn't merely win, they dominated. Of the eight winners, Prayad trailed for three holes, Randhawa for four. The other six never trailed. Kang and Thammanoon both led for the last 12 holes; Wi, Liang and Zhang for the last 13, and Singh, with a birdie at No. 1, for 17.

"My players tried their best, but it was unfortunate that the result ended this way," said a dejected Aoki. "Our players were depressed after losing, but this experience will make them stronger for future events."

It was more than just a victory for the Asian golfers. It was validation of their tour. Randhawa put it best for everyone, saying, "We have really shown that Asian golf has come of age."

Asian PGA Tour

Caltex Masters—US$900,000
Winner: Zhang Lian-wei

Ernie Els was on a roll. It was more like a landslide. It was late in January and he already was looking for his fourth consecutive victory, a streak that began in the last tournament of 2002. In fact, he was within one hole of getting it in the Caltex Masters, which launched the 2003 Asian PGA Tour. Alas, sooner or later, golf will cool even the hottest golfer. But the scriptwriter hadn't been born yet who would even suggest that Els' streak would end the way it did here.

Els' run had started with the Nedbank Challenge in South Africa in December, and then he took his first two starts of 2003 on the U.S. PGA Tour — the Mercedes Championships and the Sony Open. Now late January found him at Laguna National in Singapore, in the Caltex Masters, co-sponsored by the Asian PGA Tour and the PGA European Tour. It didn't seem to matter to Els, the No. 2-ranked player in the world, where he played or when. He was on his way to making history. The next thing he knew, he had become a footnote to it: The man who finished second to the first Chinese (and the fifth Asian) ever to win on the European Tour.

Zhang Lian-wei dropped a four-foot birdie putt at the final hole to pluck the Caltex Masters from Els' grasp. After rounds of 68-71-69, he closed with a two-under-par 70 for a 10-under 278 total. He really hadn't expected the win.

"I was pretty pumped on the front nine, but I couldn't catch Ernie," Zhang said. "I managed to keep up with him on the back nine and stay one shot behind him, but I really felt that I was aiming for a top-three finish. It was only on the last hole when I sensed I had a chance."

Heavy storms plagued the tournament, forcing part of the first day over into the second, and the second into the third, but when everything finally settled, this much was clear: Daniel Chopra shot 65 in the first round and faded to a 77, and Els took over and led Zhang by three in the second, then by two going into the fourth.

Els might have won except for stumbling home in the third round. He was leading by five, then bogeyed the last two holes, missing the green at the 17th and misclubbing himself at the 18th and missing a five-foot par putt. Even so, he came out of the third round leading by two. But the warning signs were up. "There are some guys really close to me," he said, "so I've got to try and play the way I have been and hope for the best."

Els did — until the final hole. He was leading Zhang by a stroke coming to the 18th. Then he put his tee shot into the right rough. He hit his approach to the front of the green, chipped to five feet, but missed the par putt and shot 73. Zhang, on the other hand, lofted a graceful nine-iron approach from 136 yards over two bunkers to within four feet of the cup. Then he holed the birdie putt. He had won.

"Its always tough to lose like this," Els said, "but it has happened before and it will probably happen again. It's just one of those things."

Zhang, of course, was not quite that calm. Sometime after golf came to China in the early 1980s, Zhang gave up track and field to become a caddie, so that he could learn to play golf. In a comparatively short time, he was struggling on the world stage. And now this. "I'm so delighted," he said. "This time, I am so happy."

Carslberg Malaysian Open—US$1,100,000
Winner: Arjun Atwal

Arjun Atwal could sit back and contemplate his victory in the Carlsberg Malaysian Open with some satisfaction. He had opened with a stunning 62, he led wire-to-wire, finished at 24 under par, and won by four strokes. "This win kind of makes me believe in myself a bit better," he said.

If he still had any hidden doubts, he had only to check his scorecard. Through 72 holes, against a combined Asian and European tour field — it was a co-sponsored tournament — there was only one blot on his entire card, a double bogey in the third round. Not only that. He erased a ghost. In the 2000 Malaysian Open, he led after two rounds but let it get away. Not this time.

This was Atwal's second victory on the European Tour, and to lock it up he had to hold off South Africa's Retief Goosen, a former U.S. Open champion who closed to within one stroke three different times in the final round. Goosen had to settle for a tie for second with American Brad Kennedy. Atwal shot 62-65-67-66, for a 24-under 260 total at the Mines Resort at Kuala Lumpur. Good as it was, the 62 was only worth a tie for the first-round lead with Sweden's Fredrik Andersson. They would have shared the course record except that the round was played under the lift-clean-place provision because of heavy rains. Andersson would fall away, but others took up the chase of Atwal.

A kind of moment of truth arrived for Atwal two days later, when the rain-interrupted second round was completed Saturday morning. He shot the 65 and led at the halfway point (it would be by three over Goosen when the disjointed rounds were finally completed). Then he remembered the Malaysian Open of 2002. He also led that one after the second round, but a third-round 75 ended his hopes for a victory and knocked him back to a tie for fourth. Would that ghost haunt him? Atwal answered with a 67 in the third round, wrapping up the final 10 holes on Sunday.

In the final round, Atwal turned back Goosen in a head-to-head battle. Goosen started the final round two strokes behind Atwal. Goosen birdied the first and fifth holes to close within a stroke, but Atwal answered with a birdie of his own at the next hole. Goosen got to within a stroke again with a birdie at the 10th, but he watered his tee shot at the 13th. "That was a terrible two iron, and that was a bit of a turning point," Goosen said. Actually, it pretty much rolled out the red carpet for Atwal.

Then came the 18th. Atwal put his approach on the fringe of the green. Then he chipped in for a birdie three and a 66 for the four-stroke win over Goosen and Kennedy.

"It was fun," Atwal said. "I was on top of my game. I felt really comfortable all week. There didn't seem to be anything wrong with my game."

Myanmar Open—US$200,000
Winner: Lin Keng-chi

Taiwan's Lin Keng-chi was a bit rasher than most golfers, but he said it anyway. Before the final round of the Myanmar Open, Lin, who was tied for the lead at the time, simply announced that he intended to win. And so he did. Lin faced a stiff challenge down the stretch, but he turned it back and picked up his fifth Asian PGA Tour victory by a comfortable three strokes.

"I stuck to my own game, and it worked," said Lin, a regular on the Japan Tour who got into the tournament on a sponsor's invitation. He had reason to be confident. He was the Asian Tour's first Order of Merit winner in 1995, when he won three times with iron play so accurate they called him "Lin the Pin." He turned back all comers in the Myanmar Open with his 67-69-70-69–275, 13 under par at Yangon Golf Club. Thailand's Thongchai Jaidee, the defending champion, birdied the last two holes to finish second.

At the end, Lin's earliest threat was American Jason Knutzon, a rookie on the Asian Tour, but not for long. They were tied for the lead at 10 under par going into the fourth round. But while Knutzon was self-destructing his way to a 78, Myanmar's Aung Win, who started the day three shots behind, picked up the chase. Win, playing with Lin and Knutzon, birdied the first hole, and if that got the home fans excited, his move down the stretch really got them stirring. He made a tournament of it, catching Lin with birdies at the 12th and 13th. But Lin was up to the final challenge, and Win was not.

Lin fired back with two birdies over the last three holes while Win suffered expensive bogeys at the 14th and 18th. "The pressure was intense, especially when I dropped a shot," said Win, who closed with a two-under-par 70 and slipped to a tie for third with South Africa's James Kingston. Still, Win had made a good showing. Six shots off Lin's lead at the halfway point, he closed the gap to three with a 67 in the third round.

Lin had staked his claim in the first round. A late starter, he birdied five of his last nine holes to tie Kingston for the lead at 67. "I won here two years ago," an encouraged Kingston noted, "and it's a good chance for me this year." But 72 in the second round nudged him off to one side. Lin led at the halfway point by a stroke over Thongchai and India's Mukesh Kumar. "I'll be playing my own game out there tomorrow," Kumar said.

Unfortunately, it was a 76. For Lin Keng-chi, the Myanmar Open was as much a reunion as a tournament. "I'm feeling pretty relaxed here, playing with old friends," he had said. And if he overstayed his welcome by winning, they hoped he would be as relaxed in a couple weeks. He would be playing with — not against — his old pals as the Asian Tour team in the inaugural Dynasty Cup against the Japan Tour.

Phoenix Dynasty Cup
Winner: Asia

See beginning of chapter.

Royal Challenge Indian Open—US$300,000
Winner: Mike Cunning

In idle conversation, Mike Cunning might have found himself in something of a trivial question: How could a guy clinch an Order of Merit title without having won a tournament? The answer of course is by having enough high finishes. But he canceled out the question at the Royal Challenge Indian Open late in March with a new one: How can a guy come from practically nowhere and simply run off with a tournament? And the answer is: birdies, lots of birdies.

Cunning rang up an 18-under-par 270 total at Delhi Golf Club for a five-stroke victory over Canadian Rick Gibson, runner-up for the second straight year. It was Cunning's first victory on the Asian PGA Tour, and it was a high point in an interesting career. He had started out in tennis, but switched to golf in his youth. "I had no wheels, no speed," he explained. He played the U.S. PGA Tour in 1992, then went to Asia and won three times in 1994. Then he joined the Asian PGA Tour when it was formed in 1995, and in 1997 he became the first non-Asian to top the Order of Merit, and he did it without winning. It was simple addition: He had 11 top-10 finishes.

Cunning was no real threat through the first two rounds, and was two off Jyoti Randhawa's lead going in the final round. He exploded out of the starting gate with three straight birdies, then made two more birdies but offset them with two bogeys for an outward 33. He came home with a fury. He hammered out five birdies over the last six holes for an eight-under-par 64 and a five-shot victory — on a card of 69-69-68-64 — that was much tougher than it looked.

The 33 at the turn still left him a stroke behind South African James Kingston, who bolted into the lead with a double eagle at the par-five eighth hole. But Kingston couldn't keep pace. He bogeyed the 11th and 16th, clearing the way for Gibson to finish second.

Whoever left early from this tournament missed a heck of a show. There were new faces atop the leaderboard in each round, but none of them Cunning's. Myanmar's big-hitting Zaw Moe, a regular on the Japan Tour, took the first-round lead with a course-record, nine-under-par 63 and said simply, "It was one of those days." Gibson took second place with 65 fuelled by two eagles. And India's Arjun Atwal, winner of the Carlsberg Malaysian Open a month earlier, posted a 69 that included a four-putt from 25 feet. "That," he said, "was quite unbelievable."

Thailand Open—US$150,000

Winner: Edward Loar

The 2003 Thailand Open gave the world of golf a peek at two promising futures — one belonging to Edward Loar, a young American professional in his second season on the Asian PGA Tour who scored his first victory in a runaway, and the other belonging to Chanin Puntawong, a 16-year-old Thai amateur who didn't threaten, who barely made the cut, but who tied an Asian PGA Tour record with a tidy 61.

Chanin, latest in the line of exciting Asian youngsters, squeaked through the cut right on the number (two-under-par 142), then in the third round ran off seven straight birdies at one point and needed just 24 putts in the 11-under-par 61 at the par-72 Krisada City Golf Hills. That left him three strokes behind Loar's third-round lead.

"My goal was to make the cut," said Chanin. "But now I am in contention. I have nothing to lose by playing aggressively in the final round." Then he closed with an 81 and tied for 47th. That returned the attention to Loar and the chase, and also to the fierce heat. With early April temperatures hitting near 100 degrees, the tournament may have been a question of survival as much as golf.

Loar, shooting 67-66-67-69–269, 19 under par, made a bit of history of his own — the first left-hander to win on the Asian Tour. He opened the tournament two shots off Ted Oh's lead. Korea's Oh, an early Asian whiz kid who played in the 1993 U.S. Open as a 16-year-old amateur, this time drew attention with a 65 and a one-shot lead over American Scott Taylor. "But I'm not reading too much into today," said Oh. "It's just the first round." Prudent thinking. A 74-73 finish would drop him to 31st.

In the second round, Loar (66) was in a three-way tie for the lead at 11-under 133 with Thongchai Jaidee (66), trying to become the third Thai to win the Thailand Open in its 37-year history, and Australian Jason Dawes (65), in his first full season on the tour. Loar's approach was simple: Take advantage of Krisada's inviting space. "There's plenty of room, and my strategy tomorrow will be to keep busting it and making a few putts," said Loar, who was averaging over 300 yards off the tee.

Dawes, a shorter hitter, would depend on accuracy. "I don't hit it as far as Thongchai or Loar," he said, "but I'm hitting my irons well and putting well." But that wouldn't be enough against Loar.

In the third round, Loar posted six birdies and was nicked for only one bogey in the 67 on his way to a three-stroke lead over Chanin and Dawes. Chanin, through the courtesy of the 61, now had a chance to become the youngest ever to win on the Asian Tour. The distinction at the moment belonged to Korea's Kim Dae-sub, who was 17 years and two months old when he won the 1998 Korean Open as an amateur.

Loar, playoff runner-up in the 2002 Myanmar Open, was too strong. He pulled ahead on the front nine. He birdied the second hole, eagled the fourth, and then also eagled the seventh, hitting a sensational four-iron shot out of a fairway bunker to two feet. "That probably clinched the victory for me," he said. Wilting a bit in the heavy heat, he bogeyed twice on the back, but still won by five over Dawes.

"This is awesome," Loar said. "My first win as a professional — and it's special."

Maekyung Open—US$400,000
Winner: Chung Joon

Korea's Chung Joon finally learned how to win, and India's Amandeep Johl found a new way to lose.

It was the Maekyung Open early in May, and one of the two would be scoring his first win. Chung, 31, was doing his best to hold on. Johl, 32, was doing his best to catch him. It came down to the final hole. Johl needed a birdie to win, a par to tie and force a playoff. And then the gods took over. It had to be the gods. How else to explain this one?

Johl, trying to get to a pin cut back-left at the 18th, hung his approach shot out slightly to the right. Golfers have hit many things — walls, carts, spectators' heads. But a photographer's tripod? The tripod was off the right edge of the green, presumably out of a golfer's way. But the ball hit it anyway and caromed back off the green, and Johl had come that close. No birdie, no par, but a bogey, and Johl lost again.

On the other hand, Chung, who led from the second round, finally won, but he didn't back into this victory and he didn't tip-toe in either. Posting five birdies and two bogeys, Chung finished with a strong three-under-par 69 at Korea's Nam Seoul Country Club for a one-stroke win over Johl, who closed with 67.

"This is unbelievable," said Chung, who shot 70-68-68-69 for a 13-under-par 275 total. "I've messed up in the final rounds on numerous occasions, but it did not happen today." His best Asian Tour finish was a tie for fourth in the 1998 Indian Open.

The question was, was the pressure too much for Korea's Kang Wook-soon? He opened the Maekyung Open with a 67 for a two-stroke lead, then sank out of sight. Defending champion Eddie Lee, who won the event as a 19-year-old amateur in 2002, started with a par 72 and never was a threat.

Chung leaped to his opportunity in the second round with a 68 that gave him a two-stroke lead over a field that had seven Koreans in the top nine after 36 holes. Among them, tied for sixth, was Ted Oh, the tour's Rookie of the Year in 2001. Chung was encouraged. He had missed the cut in his previous two events, but now some solid iron play gave him five birdies — three in a row from the 14th — and only one bogey.

Chung started hot in the third round, getting a birdie at the first hole and an eagle three at the fourth, followed by a birdie at the fifth. Then he ran into a series of bogeys, and just when it seemed he was headed into his usual late-tournament fold, he birdied three of the last five holes for 68 and a three-stroke lead over Johl and Korean Choi Yoon-soon. Johl, meanwhile, bogeyed two of the first three holes, but eagled the 16th for a 69. Then came the dramatic final round.

Johl was hardly resigning himself to defeat and Chung wasn't giving up. Johl eagled the par-five fourth hole and birdied the 11th and 12th to catch Chung. But Chung birdied the 13th to edge in front again. Both birdied the 15th, and then Johl tied it again with a birdie at the 16th. And so at the 18th, Johl needed a birdie to win, a par to tie, but first he had to hit the green. He hit a camera tripod instead.

SK Telecom Open—US$400,000
Winner: K.J. Choi

At home in Korea, he's Choi Kyung-ju, but in the West, he's K.J. Choi. No matter. As Shakespeare might have said, a Choi by any other name plays as beautifully. And so Choi, Korea's most famous golfer and a two-time winner on the U.S. PGA Tour, came home to Seoul late in June to win the SK Telecom Open. Not that it was a cakewalk. Choi led the first round of the rain-shortened tournament, then had to rebound to win in a playoff. Oddly enough, he must have been the only guy in the field who hadn't planned on winning it.

"I did not come here trying to win," said Choi. He didn't explain the puzzling statement, but perhaps that was his way of explaining that he simply wanted to play in his homeland to salute the opening of the Baekahmvista Country Club course. Countryman Shin Yong-jin probably wished Choi had stayed away. Choi led the first round, Shin went ahead in the second, and Choi, with a stunning series of putts, tied him in the third and final round, then beat him on the second hole of a playoff. Choi shot 64-69-68, and Shin 68-64-69 to tie at 15-under 201.

Former U.S. Open champion Corey Pavin, whose last victory was in 1996, made one of his best showings since, shooting 67-68-68 to finish third, two strokes out of the playoff. Pavin interrupted an all-Korean show. Yang Yong-eun, with 67-66, tied Choi in second place at the halfway point, and Park Young-soo, with 70-64, was just a stroke behind. They tied for fourth with Kim Tae-bok, four shots behind.

Choi, 33, last won in Korea in 1999 and joined the U.S. PGA Tour in 2000, so in case anyone had forgotten him, he reintroduced himself to the homefolks with fireworks. Starting the first round at No. 10, he birdied his first three holes. "I got off to a great start, and managed to keep it going," Choi said. "The fans were great and really lifted me."

He birdied all four par-fives, had nine birdies overall, and one bogey for his 64 — which became the course record and which would be tied by Shin and Park. In the second round, Shin raced to six straight birdies at one point, and added two others for a bogey-free 64 and a one-stroke lead on Choi. "It will be an honor for me to play in the final group with Choi," Shin said. And then he turned prophet. "A 67 should be good enough to take the title," he said.

Uncanny. Shin was precisely right. The problem was, he shot 69 and Choi 68 to tie him. Choi, a former weightlifter, showed he was muscle with a touch. Trailing Shin by a stroke with two holes to play, he had to hole a 15-foot putt to stay on his heels. Then this series: A 10-foot birdie putt at the 18th to tie Shin in regulation, a seven-footer at the first playoff hole to stay alive, and finally a 10-footer for birdie and the victory. And anyone who thought this was a lark for the homeboy-turned-U.S. tour star was very much mistaken. "The pressure was on me," a relieved Choi said. "The pressure today was as much as when I won twice on the U.S. PGA Tour last year."

Mercuries Masters—US$300,000
Winner: Lin Wen-ko

The Asian PGA Tour, off since late June, resumed in mid-September with the Mercuries Masters, and it couldn't have come at a better time for Thailand's Thongchai Jaidee. "I'm feeling good," said Thongchai, a former paratrooper with the Royal Thai Army. "I spent a lot of time working on my fitness and my game during the summer break."

But it all went for naught. Well, not totally for naught, because Thongchai did finish second. But for one of the tour's ranking stars, after leading for three rounds and part of the fourth, finishing second was a decided come-down. Thongchai came that close to winning only to have Taiwanese Lin Wen-ko filch it from him in the final round. Lin managed this despite staggering down the stretch, which indicates that Thongchai was uncommonly off his game.

"This was incredible," said Lin, age 27, so obscure that he was not even listed in the tour's player directory. "There is no way I expected to win. I was so lucky."

This was Lin's first win as a professional, and if he was lucky, he was lucky for four rounds. This was not a weak field at the Taiwan Golf and Country Club. American Edward Loar, the Thailand Open champion, and India's Amandeep Johl, the Maekyung Open runner-up, were among those who missed when the cut came in at four-over-par 148. Other Asian veterans challenged briefly but fell back, among them Thailand's Thammanoon Srirot and Thaworn Wiratchant, both from the winning Dynasty Cup team. So lucky Lin, never more than two strokes off Thongchai's lead in each of the first three rounds, shot 70-69-68-73—280, eight under par. Thongchai seemed bound for the winner's circle with 68-70-67, but a final-round 76 did him in.

Thongchai, the Asian Order of Merit winner in 2001 and second in 2002, got off to a shaky start. He bogeyed three of his first four holes in the first round, then fought back with five birdies and an eagle at the 335-yard fifth hole, where he drove the green and holed an eight-foot putt. "I'm swinging the club nicely at the moment and if the putts continue to drop, I've got a chance to win," he said. Lin could say the same, but apparently no one was paying attention. He started the second round with three straight birdies to trigger a first-nine 31, but a double bogey at his 16th cost him the lead and left him with a 69 and one stroke behind Thongchai. In the third round, Lin birdied the last hole for 68 and was second to Thongchai by two strokes, but Thai veteran Thammanoon Srirot, four shots off the lead, was considered the real challenger.

Lin started the last round two shots behind, but was two ahead at the turn on a two-under-par front nine. Lin was three ahead when Thongchai bogeyed the 10th. Then the pressure got to Lin. He bogeyed three straight from the 14th to drop back into a tie. Then Thongchai made a fatal error. He bogeyed the par-three 17th. He parred the 18th, but now steady, so did Lin. "I forgot about the three bogeys," Lin said. He had his victory.

Kolon Cup Korean Open—US$400,000
Winner: John Daly

There's the old expression that if a guy didn't have bad luck, he'd have no luck at all. The remark was tailor-made for John Daly, the grip-it-and-rip-it flawed hero or anti-hero — depending on one's view — of American golf. It seems he had calmed his various demons, at least for the moment, and he had found a new wife. After the bad choices, this one was the love of his life. Then in the summer of 2003, she was arrested and indicted on drug charges. After all this, surely the fates owed him something. Whether it was the fates or Daly himself, that "something" was the Kolon Cup Korean Open, his first victory since the 2001 BMW International Open in Germany.

Daly didn't lead until the second nine of the final round, when a burst of birdies launched him to a four-under-par 68 and a one-stroke win over Thailand's Thaworn Wiratchant. Scotland's Simon Yates was third, one stroke further back. It was a tough-won victory. In fact, it was a tough tournament for all. The par-72 Woo Jung Hills Country Club proved to be one of the toughest tests on the Asian PGA Tour. Daly shot 73-69-72-68–282, a mere six under par. Of the 67 finishers, only eight broke the par of 288. Daly and Yates were the only players with two rounds in the 60s.

The Kolon Cup Korean Open was distinctive for another reason. After Annika Sorenstam was invited to play in the U.S. PGA Tour's Colonial, it seemed to be fashionable to have a woman golfer in the field for the novelty and the draw. Suzy Whaley won a spot in the Hartford Open, and Michelle Wie, amateur whiz kid of 13, played by invitation in Canadian Tour and Nationwide Tour events. (None of them made the cut.) Accordingly, England's Laura Davies, a power on the American LPGA Tour, was invited. "I'm not suggesting I'll go out and win," said Davies, the first woman to play in an Asian Tour event, "but I'm hoping to make the cut and certainly not make a fool of myself. I'll be going out there with some expectations." She shot 78 and 77 and missed the cut by four strokes.

Daly had to work his way slowly up the leaderboard. Korea's Ted Oh, former teenage amateur whiz and now 27, carded six birdies and suffered only one bogey for a 67 in the first round, which was suspended because of darkness. When it was completed the next morning, Oh was the first-round leader by a stroke over countryman Lee Sun-ho. Daly bogeyed the 16th and double-bogeyed the 17th for 73 and was six back. Lee, with birdies at the 15th and 17th, took the second-round lead with 72–140, and found himself crowded by five guys only two back, including Daly (69). The cast changed again for the third round. China's Liang Wen-chong, seeking his first victory, was about to take the lead alone, but he bogeyed the 16th and 17th and shot 70 and tied Thaworn (71) atop the leaderboard with three-under 213. Daly was now just a stroke behind, and Thaworn became the man he was chasing.

In the final round, while Liang was soaring to 77, Thaworn was steady, and Daly was on a wild ride. He posted seven birdies and three bogeys for his 68. He broke away with a burst of three straight birdies from the 11th, and got another at the 15th. Thaworn also birdied the 15th but could only par in from there. The fates, for a change, had smiled on Big John.

Macau Open—US$250,000
Winner: Colin Montgomerie

Golf is the cruelest game. Take Scott Barr, an unknown Australian and a teaching professional at Singapore Country Club, who failed to win his playing card on the Asian PGA Tour. The Macau Open was only his second Asian Tour event. When he took the lead in the second round, the question was — who was he? Then he held it through the third round, and then was still holding on late in the fourth, and they were about to call him the winner. He got all the way to the final hole. And there? Enter Colin Montgomerie.

Montgomerie, No. 1 in Europe for seven straight years from 1993, was running out of time. His impressive string was leaking away. Beginning in 1989, he had won at least once somewhere in the world each year, a 14-year streak. He was still winless in 2003, and he had only two events left — the Macau Open here in mid-October, and two weeks later, the Volvo Masters in Spain. He was down to the 11th hour. Worse, he trailed all the way in Macau until the final hole. There, he caught Barr, then beat him on the first hole of a playoff.

Montgomerie, now age 40, ranked 41st in the world, was playful when he arrived at Macau. Asked what his chances of winning were, he smiled. "My chances of doing well here," he said, "depend on all the other competitors playing badly."

That's not the way things started out. Montgomerie racked up seven birdies — four in a row from his fourth hole — against two bogeys for a 66. That tied him for second place, three behind the course-record 63 posted by Adam Fraser, a little-known Australian who made it through the Asian Tour's qualifying tournament in the spring. Montgomerie was delighted with his 66. "I feel I've got my game now," he said. "Unfortunately, it's at the end of the year. I wish it was the start of the year."

In the second round Montgomerie posted 72. While Fraser's magic faded into 77, an even lesser-known Aussie, Barr, stepped up. Barr shot 67 for a two-stroke lead on Thailand's Thaworn Wiratchant after 36 holes. Montgomerie had drifted five off the lead. "It's unfortunate," Monty said. "But never mind — that is golf." He shot 67 in the third round, but couldn't get any closer than three strokes to Barr, who raced to three birdies over the final four holes for a 69. So Barr led Montgomerie and American Jason Knutzon by three going into the final round. "I need something like a 66 tomorrow," Monty said. Not quite.

A 72 took Knutzon out of the running in the final round, and Montgomerie spent the day chasing Barr, who was on the verge of one of the most unexpected wins in Asian Tour history. Barr led him by three with six holes to play. Then Barr bogeyed the par-five 13th and Montgomerie birdied — a two-shot swing. Barr missed a birdie from six feet at the 16th. At the par-five 18th, both caught the bunker to the right of the green. Barr blasted out and left himself 20 feet from the pin. He made his par for a par 71. Montgomerie finessed an exquisite splash to a foot and birdied for a 68. After 72 holes, Montgomerie was finally in the lead, if only tied for it.

The playoff went back to the 18th. Montgomerie reached the green in two, but Barr caught the greenside bunker again. Barr's attempt at a delicate bunker shot came down short of the putting surface, and he chipped to a foot. His par was secure, but Monty two-putted for his birdie four — and for his first victory of 2003.

Sanya Open—US$200,000

Winner: Marcus Both

Marcus Both, a 24-year-old Australian and a rookie on the Asian PGA Tour, came to the inaugural Sanya Open unknown and unnoticed. He hovered just off the lead in the first three rounds, and then he came to the final hole facing a crucial putt. "The longest one in my life," he said. It was all of four feet. More to the point, it was for the victory. He holed it for what was a fitting finish.

Both had raced to five straight birdies on the last nine and held on for a one-stroke victory over the trio of Singapore's Mardan Mamat, South Africa's Hendrik Buhrmann and Taiwan's Chen Yuan-chi. None of the three led at the end of any round. Both didn't lead either, until the end. Trailing by three strokes at the start of each round from the second, Both shot scores of 68-70-70-67 for a 13-under-par 275 total, and he was stunned. "I can't tell you what I'm feeling right now," Both said. A number of golfers could say the same.

All told, it was a cracking introduction for the Sanya Open, a late addition to the October schedule, designed to promote tourism at Hainan Island, a tropical area off the southern tip of China. The resort's crown jewel was the par-72 Yalong Bay Golf Club designed by Robert Trent Jones, Jr.

Taiwanese veteran Wang Ter-chang, 41, seeking his first top-10 finish of the season, tied the course record in the first round with 65. "The record was on my mind, but I didn't play solidly enough coming in," Wang said. He led by one stroke over American Greg Hanrahan.

A 76 in the second round took Wang out of the running. American Andrew Pitts played the last 12 holes in eight under par for a 64, the new record, and a tie for the lead with Sweden's Stephen Lindskog, who eagled the 18th for a 68. They were at 135, one stroke ahead of Hanrahan and Australia's Scott Strange.

In the third round, at the 18th hole, Hanrahan fired a seven iron to four feet and birdied for 69, an 11-under 205 total and a two-stroke lead. At age 45, Hanrahan was a pioneer of the Asian PGA Tour. The Sanya Open was his 156th event out of 164 stroke-play tournaments in the tour's history. His best finish was second place in the first year, 1995. Victory here was not exactly beckoning. Nine players, including Both, were within three strokes of him.

Hanrahan exited with 75. Over the final nine holes, the lead changed hands five times, and eight players were in contention. Then up stepped Both. "I hung in there on the first nine (even par)," he said. "But from the 12th, I hit some great wedge shots close for three easy birdies, and holed a long putt from 20 feet at the 15th to keep the run going. Before I knew it, I had five in a row and was in the lead." Both got a scare at the 18th. He left his approach shot a dangerous 45 feet short and knocked his first putt four feet past. And so he faced the "longest putt" of his life coming back.

As news of Both's victory was reported across the world, there were those in the press who held that Marcus was merely the second Both to gain international prominence in golf. The first was his cousin, Andrew, the noted golf writer of the Australian Associated Press who covers the U.S. PGA Tour.

Hero Honda Masters—US$300,000
Winner: Arjun Atwal

The Hero Honda Masters was beginning to look like a Singh family reunion (minus the godfather, Vijay). First there was Jeev Milkha Singh, 32, Asian PGA Tour veteran and the first Indian to qualify for the U.S. Open in 2002. He was trying to break a four-year victory drought. He was heading that way in the first two rounds and then his putter turned sour, and so another Singh took over — Digvijay Singh — no relation, age 30 and pretty much an unknown. Digvijay wasn't merely seeking his first Asian Tour win. This was the first time he had even led a tournament, that being in the third round.

Everyone knows what happens to unknowns carrying the lead into the final round for the first time. It did happen to Digvijay, and there to pick up the pieces along with the victory was Indian star Arjun Atwal. The US$48,450 first prize made him the first to top a career $1 million in winnings on the Asian Tour. It was his sixth Asian Tour victory and his second of the year, after the Carlsberg Malaysian Open in February.

"That was nice," said Atwal, 31, "but winning here and sealing the Order of Merit was foremost on my mind." He did have the Order of Merit all but sealed. It was early in November, and he was $126,000 ahead of China's Zhang Lian-wei with four events to go. The thought could soothe him after the fright of staggering down the Delhi Golf Club's final stretch. But Atwal did wrap it up, shooting 69-71-70-71 for 281 total, seven under par, for the one-stroke victory over Mexico's Pablo Del Olmo, American Gary Rusnak and India's Jyoti Randhawa, who happens to be Digvijay Singh's brother-in-law.

Back to the Singhs: Jeev, a four-time Asian Tour winner and now a regular in Japan, raced to a two-stroke lead with 66 in the first round. A 72 in the second left him with a one-stroke lead over a trio that included the other Singh, Digvijay, who dogged his heels with superb golf, hitting every fairway and 15 greens in regulation for 68. Vijay Kumar, the 2002 Indian Open champion, was also in that tie for second with 71, but would have been the solo leader except for a triple bogey out of the bushes at his last hole (No. 9). "Apart from that," Kumar said, "I played really solid."

In the third round, Digvijay leapfrogged into the lead immediately — his first lead ever — dropping a 10-foot putt for an eagle three at the first hole. He stayed in the lead the rest of the day, shooting 68 for a one-stroke lead and a case of nerves. "I won't deny having some butterflies in my stomach," he said, thinking ahead to the fourth round. The butterflies got a little too frisky. The next day, he blew to a 78 and tied for 10th.

While Digvijay was wobbling, Randhawa slipped into the lead, but a double bogey at the 13th tripped him up. That was the opening Atwal needed. Back at the par-five eighth, Atwal had holed a thumping 50-foot putt for an eagle to go to nine under, but proceeded to bogey four of the next five holes. Then, with Randhawa out of the way, he pulled himself together and birdied the 14th and 17th and saved par with a 10-foot putt at the 18th for the decisive stroke he needed.

Atwal couldn't remember when he had played so badly and still survived. "It was perhaps the first time my ball-striking was so bad en route to a victory," he said. "But my putting was immaculate."

Volvo China Open—US$500,000
Winner: Zhang Lian-wei

China is a land rich in ancient folk tales. This could be a modern one: Zhang and the Magic Nine Iron.

The last time China's Zhang Lian-wei won — this was only in January — he was modestly hoping to finish second or third. That was in the season-opening Caltex Masters, when he didn't dare presume he could beat front-running Ernie Els. But he did, and on the final hole, no less. Now, in mid-November, the Volvo China Open had come to his homeland, where golf was growing and he was its No. 1 player — and therefore was also No. 1 in the pressure cooker.

"There's more pressure on a Chinese player when he is playing in his national Open," Zhang said. "You can feel the excitement . I don't mind that sort of pressure. In fact, I think I play better under those conditions."

Almost not, however. Zhang shared the lead in the first round, trailed by one through the second when Korea's Choi Gwang-soo tied the course record with a 64, and led by two through the third round. The final round was the tale of the Magic Nine Iron.

Zhang won in Singapore with the nine iron. At the final hole, with Els having difficulty, Zhang lifted a nine-iron shot over two bunkers to four feet from the cup, setting up the winning putt. This time, it was the fourth round again, but at the 16th hole, after some shaky moments. And this time, he lobbed his nine-iron shot from 129 yards, out of heavy rough, to within six inches of the cup. "My shot of the week," Zhang said. And just in time. He had been leading by five down the final stretch, but a sudden attack of nerves nearly wiped it out. He bogeyed the 13th and 14th holes, and saw his lead shrivel to one when Thailand's Thaworn Wiratchant birdied the 15th and 16th ahead of him. So the tap-in at the 16th bumped Zhang's lead back up to two strokes, which was the margin he started the day with and the margin he won by.

And so Zhang, fighting the discomfort of a cold, had the fifth victory of his career, playing the par-72 Shanghai Silport in 67-69-69-72–279, 11 under par, and winning by two over Thaworn. Zhang started the final round two up on Australia's Unho Park and immediately doubled the lead when he birdied the first hole and Park bogeyed. The wind was up and the pins were tough, so no one could really put any real pressure on Zhang, except for Thaworn.

"When I made the turn, I didn't think I had a chance," Thaworn said. "But after the birdies on 15 and 16, I knew I was close." But he missed a birdie from six feet at the 17th, and it became huge when Zhang recovered.

"I knew I was getting tight on the back nine after my two bogeys," Zhang said. Then came the nine iron at the 16th. "For sure, the best shot I hit this week," he said. "The lie wasn't good, but I struck it perfect." Zhang had finished third in the first China Open in 1995, tied for fourth in 2000 and tied for fifth in 2002. This time — the tap-in at the 16th, the cruise home and the tale of the Magic Nine Iron had been told again.

"I've been trying to win this for the past nine years," Zhang said. "There is so much pressure. I'm very, very happy now. I'm very relieved."

Acer Taiwan Open—US$300,000
Winner: Jason Dawes

It wasn't so much that Jason Dawes, a 30-year-old Australian, came out of nowhere to take the Acer Taiwan Open — and in a walk, no less. The real surprise was that anyone could win at all in those winds that whipped Sunrise Golf Club at Tao Yuan. The raw facts: In the comparatively agreeable first round, 15 player shot the par-72 course in the 60s and 26 others broke par. Ah — but over the next three rounds, the only sub-par scores were four 70s, and no two by any one player. Dawes was the only one to break par for the tournament, posting 68-70-73-73 for a four-under-par total of 284, and he won by a cushy eight strokes over India's Jeev Milkha Singh. The brutal truth came as early as the halfway point: A whopping 10-over 154 made the cut.

The tournament was a scorekeeper's worst dream, with one round after another blown over into the next day. So Dawes had the clubhouse lead with his 68 when the first round was suspended on Thursday. He was three shots behind Singh and his 65 after the round was completed Friday morning. Thai veteran Thammanoon Srirot was second at 66, and he was even par and in the running through the sixth hole when the second round was suspended. He completed the round Saturday and was out of the running with an 85.

The winds were interrupted by a little history in the person of Taiwanese teenage amateur Lo Shih-kai. Shooting 73-75–148, he became the youngest ever to make the cut in an Asian PGA Tour event. Lo was 14 years and 275 days old, replacing Thai amateur Prom Meesawat, who made the Thailand Open cut at the age of 16 years and 133 days. "I'm glad I made the cut," Lo said, "as it shows that I have progressed from last year." But he hadn't progressed quite far enough. He also became the youngest ever to get disqualified for signing an incorrect scorecard. Justin Rose was another disappointed player. Rose, amateur hero in the 1998 British Open and pre-tournament favorite, never got going and tied for 14th.

The one thread running through all this was the notion that Dawes wouldn't hold up. Nothing in his resume suggested otherwise. Dawes, in his first full season, had joined the tour through the qualifying tournament, and his best finish was second in the Thailand Open in April, seven months earlier. He was looking much better in this disjointed Taiwan Open. He posted four birdies and two bogeys for a 70–138 and a two-stroke lead on Taiwan's Chen Chung-cheng after 36 holes. It was still a race when the third round was suspended, finding them tied at four under. All that changed dramatically Sunday morning. Dawes wrapped up a third-round 73, and Chen an 80. So Dawes was leading by five going into the final round, but over Scotland's Simon Yates. From there, it was a cakewalk. Yates soared to an 81, and Singh, after middle rounds of 80 and 77, managed to wring a day's-low 70 out of the course. Dawes, meanwhile, was making another comfortable 73 for the eight-stroke win.

"It was extremely surprising," Dawes said. "I don't really want to say it, but it just seemed so easy out there today. Maybe it's because I'm a little older and wiser now."

Omega Hong Kong Open—US$700,000
Winner: Padraig Harrington

For a while, the Omega Hong Kong Open in December was looking like a class reunion from the European qualifying tournament, the way the November "graduates" were frolicking on the leaderboard. But it took a masters degree to conquer Hong Kong Golf Club, and the man with the credentials was none other than Padraig Harrington, the easy smiling Irishman. It was a kind of double victory for him. The tournament was the third-from-last event on the 2003 Asian PGA Tour and the first on the 2003-2004 European Tour.

It was a cruel finish for South Africa's Hennie Otto. He had birdied three of the last four holes for a 65 and was the early leader at 10-under-par 270. But along came Harrington. He had inched into the lead on the front nine, slipped coming in, then birdied the 17th and 18th to edge Otto by a stroke.

"The Far East suits me — I like the greens here," said Harrington, who shot 67-69-67-66–269, 11 under par. "I went out there at the start of the day expecting to do well. I knew that a lot of people would have to shoot low to keep up with me."

But that wasn't apparent until late in the tournament. First came the qualifying reunion. In the first round, England's Richard McEvoy, 24, who won the European qualifying a month ago, raced away with birdies on the 14th, 15th and 18th holes to an eight-under-par 62 and a four-stroke lead. Scotland's Steven O'Hara, another graduate, tied for second behind him at 66. "To start off like that in my debut is just amazing," McEvoy said. He was more amazed in the second round, when he shot a 68 that kept him comfortably in the lead by three, this over the defending champion, Sweden's Fredrik Jacobson.

The string ran out on McEvoy in the third round. He shot 74. But Sweden's Christopher Hanell, another qualifying graduate, jumped up to take his place. Hanell shot 65 to go one up on Harrington and Thailand's Prayad Marksaeng, who both three-putted the 18th for bogeys and 67s. "No blemishes on the card," Otto said. "It feels great to be up on the leaderboard. I'm loving it." McEvoy and O'Hara got knocked aside by 74s, but European stars Darren Clarke (69) and Thomas Bjorn (65) kept the pressure on. Harrington was hot. He holed a bunker shot for an eagle at the 12th and drained a 20-footer for a birdie at the 17th. But the bogey at the 18th stung. "I feel I have missed a bit of an opportunity," he said.

Harrington almost missed another in the final round. He edged into the lead with a three-under first nine, then hit a shaky stretch. At the 10th, he lost his tee shot and bogeyed. He birdied the 12th but gave the stroke back with a bogey at the 14th. Up ahead, Otto was tearing up the course, getting birdies at the 13th, 15th, 16th and 17th. It turned out he'd need one more. But he missed a five-footer at the 18th. "I knew I needed that one to have a chance of winning," he said.

Harrington made a prophet out of him. After a brilliant par save at the 16th, Harrington birdied the last two holes for the win. The victory meant more than money. The tournament was rich with world ranking points, and Harrington was taking an eight-week winter vacation.

"I needed a few points in the world rankings," he said, sounding like a bear heading for hibernation, "to have a bit of fat over the winter."

Volvo Masters of Asia—US$500,000
Winner: Thongchai Jaidee

Mix the weariness of long distance travel and the depression of disappointment and what do you get? If you have the heart of Thongchai Jaidee, the answer is a championship. The Thai star had all the reasons for a half-hearted effort — who could blame him? — but somehow turned them into the biggest win of his career in the Volvo Masters of Asia at Bangkok Golf Club.

Disappointment? Jaidee, 34, had gone to the United States to take a crack at the PGA Tour's qualifying school. He didn't make it. Then he had arrived at Bangkok Golf Club from halfway around the world that December Wednesday, the day before the Volvo Masters began. And from there, chasing front-running Ted Purdy, he slowly but surely made his way to the head of the class.

"I would like to thank the Thai fans," Thongchai said. "It has been a great week. After the first round, I really didn't think I had a chance. I felt tired because of the rush to make it here. I had no feelings. But things felt much better on the second day."

Early on, the tournament — the championship of the Asian PGA Tour — belonged to Purdy, 30, a former American college star who won the Hero Honda Classic when he joined the Asian Tour in 1997. He staked his claim to the Volvo Masters in the first round, making birdies on the last five holes for a scorching nine-under-par 62 and a three-stroke lead. "It's so nice when everything you hit finds the middle of the hole," Purdy said.

In the second round, he got up-and-down at the only two greens he missed, and shot 66 for a 14-under 128 and a five-stroke lead. India's Randhawa Jyoti had warned that Purdy was going to run away with the tournament if someone didn't get busy. That someone turned out to be Taiwan's Lin Keng-chi. Lin fired a 65 in the third round, catching Purdy, who had to scramble to a cooling 71.

Thongchai, meanwhile, had come to life. After opening with a jet-lagged 71, he bounced back with 65 in the second round. "I had a good 10 hours of sleep last night," he said. He greeted the round by holing a bunker shot for an eagle on the par-four first hole. He was seven behind Purdy going into the third round, and a 65 left him just one behind going into the fourth. "I'm in a good position, but I think I need a really low round to win," Thongchai said. "Perhaps a 63."

Actually, a 65 for a 19-under 265 total did it. He won by one stroke over Lin. Purdy closed with 74 and dropped to a tie for seventh. India's Arjun Atwal, who did make it through the American qualifying, returned with Thongchai on Wednesday and locked up the Asian PGA Tour's Order of Merit title. Atwal finished a distant 57th, but it was enough to keep him ahead of China's Zhang Lian-wei, who needed to do much better than his 32nd place. All that, however, was secondary in Thongchai's big week.

"I feel very proud to have won in Thailand," Thongchai said. "This is definitely the best win of my career."

Japan Tour

Token Homemate Cup—¥100,000,000
Winner: Andre Stolz

Unheralded Andre Stolz scored his first victory outside of his native Australia and New Zealand when he captured the season-opening Token Homemate Cup on the Nagoya course of Token Tado Country Club in early April. Sticking close to the lead all week, Stolz came from a stroke back with a one-over-par 71 in Sunday's final round to win by a shot with his 278.

The Aussie's victory sidetracked the bid of 38-year-old Tsuyoshi Yoneyama for his first win since 1999 on the circuit. Yoneyama, who enjoyed by far his best season that year with his only three victories in his 16 years on tour, never trailed through the first three rounds of the Token Cup. He roared off in front with 63 Thursday, though it only gave him a one-stroke lead over Toru Suzuki and two over Stolz. He slipped to 72 Friday, but retained a share of the lead with Craig Jones (66-69) and Ted Purdy (68-67). With his first of three consecutive 71s, Stolz was just a shot behind at 136 with Yasuharu Imano (68-68), Tetsu Nishikawa (68-68), Nobuhito Sato (70-66) and Azuma Yano (69-67).

Yoneyama and Stolz distanced themselves from the field Saturday with wind-blown 71s, Yoneyama edging a stroke in front of Stolz with his 206. Four players tied for third at 209. The Australian seized the lead with two early birdies Sunday and hung on to first place the rest of the way despite two back-nine bogeys. With 72, Yoneyama tied for second at 279 with Tadahiro Takayama (69) and Nobuhiro Masuda (70).

Tsuruya Open—¥100,000,000
Winner: Hirofumi Miyase

Hirofumi Miyase failed to maintain a narrow lead in the final round of the Tsuruya Open, but made up for it in the subsequent three-way playoff. The 32-year-old parred the first extra hole to defeat Hisayuki Sasaki and Takashi Kanemoto and land the fifth title of his 13-year career, his first since 2000.

Miyase had a lot of ground to make up after the first round at Sports Shinko Country Club at Kawanishi when Frankie Minoza, the Philippines veteran, opened with an eight-under-par 63. Miyase shot 68 and rested in 20th place, then soared to the top Friday with 62, the week's best score. At 130, he sported a four-stroke lead over Kanemoto (67-67) and five over Brendan Jones (67-68) and Kiyoshi Murota (66-69).

The race tightened Saturday when Miyase produced just a one-under-par 70 for 200. Jones shot 66 and took over second place at 201. Shinichi Akiba was at 202, also firing 66, and Kanemoto was three behind after a 69. Sasaki made the biggest move Sunday, making three birdies on the last six holes for 65 and his 270. Kanemoto reached the playoff total with 67 as Miyase closed with 70 for his 270.

The Crowns—¥120,000,000
Winner: Hidemasa Hoshino

Hidemasa Hoshino picked off his first victory, staging a strong finish to win by three strokes on the Wago course at Nagoya Golf Club the first week of May. Trailing by a stroke after 54 holes, Hoshino stirred up a three-under-par 67 Sunday for 270. Toshimitsu Izawa, the leading money winner in 2001, also shot 67 Sunday and tied for second at 213 with Taichi Teshima (71) and Zaw Moe of Myanmar (68).

Hoshino sat seven strokes off the pace after the opening round when Tomohiro Kondo blazed around Wago in 62 strokes, which gave him a mere one-shot lead over Hiroyuki Fujita and two over Teshima. After 36 holes, though, Hoshino trailed by just a stroke after a 64 for 133. The top positions were bunched as Kondo (70), Teshima (68) and Peter Teravainen (65) led with 132s. Moe (67), Shigemasa Higaki (64) and Fujita (70) shared the runner-up position with Hoshino.

Teshima (70) and Fujita ((69) moved in front Saturday at 202, but led Hoshino (70), Tsukasa Watanabe (68) and Toru Tanaguchi (69), the 2002 tour leader, by just a shot after 54 holes. Hoshino then prevailed Sunday.

Fujisankei Classic—¥110,000,000
Winner: Todd Hamilton

A rejuvenated Todd Hamilton ended five frustrating seasons with a resounding five-stroke victory in the Fujisankei Classic. It was a precursor of a big year to come for the veteran American who had campaigned in Japan for 10 seasons and landed seven titles, but hadn't come up with a victory since winning the now-defunct Jun Classic in 1998.

The 37-year-old Hamilton, an Illinois native who played his college golf at the University of Oklahoma, began the tournament smartly with 67, but had to take a back seat to the ageless Masashi (Jumbo) Ozaki that day. The 56-year-old Japanese great, winner of 92 titles on the Japan Tour, opened in front with nine birdies and a seven-under-par 64, which was matched early the next day when Ryoken Kawagishi finished a round that was suspended by darkness Thursday after a rain delay. When Hamilton repeated his 67 and Ozaki slipped to 73, the American went ahead to stay Friday. Kawagishi shot 71 and Murota 70 to share second place.

Hamilton fattened his margin to four strokes Saturday, shooting a no-bogey 65 on the Kawana Hotel golf course at Ito. Little-known Shigeru Nonaka slipped into second place with a 67, and Ozaki bounced back with the same score to tie for third five back with China's Zhang Lian-wei and Tetsuji Hiratsuka.

Hamilton wrapped up the victory Sunday with his fourth straight round in the 60s, a 68, for a 17-under-par 267. Nonaka (69) and Hiratsuka (68) were the runners-up.

Japan PGA Championship—¥110,000,000
Winner: Shingo Katayama

Shingo Katayama, the most consistent player on the Japan Tour in the 2000s, avenged one of his 2002 disappointments and added a major title to his already impressive record when he won the Japan PGA Championship at Miho Golf Club in mid-May. The colorful Katayama, he of the cowboy hats, edged South Korea's S.K. Ho (also known in Asia as Hur Suk-ho) by a stroke in the championship, which he had lost to Kenichi Kuboya in a play-off the previous year. It was his 13th victory in nine years on the circuit, all of them since 1998.

Toru Suzuki, a six-time winner in Japan, held sway through the first three rounds at Miho. He began with a five-under-par 67, good for a one-shot lead over Takao Shimada, Eiji Mizoguchi and Todd Hamilton, coming off his Fujisankei victory the preceding Sunday. On Friday, Suzuki, sparked by an early eagle, posted a 66 and broke away to a four-stroke lead over Katayama and Ho, who both followed first-round 71s with matching 66s for their 137s.

Suzuki maintained his lead Saturday, shooting 67 for 200. Katayama and Ho shaved a stroke off his margin when they matched 66s for the second straight day, then battled for the title Sunday as Suzuki was fading to a 75 and a fourth-place finish with 275. Katayama caught fire in the middle of the round Sunday, running off four birdies en route to a 68 and the victorious total of 271. Ho shot 69 to finish second at 272, a stroke in front of Tsukasa Watanabe.

Munsingwear Open KSB Cup—¥120,000,000
Winner: Hirofumi Miyase

Hirofumi Miyase became the season's first multiple winner when a strong finish gave him a three-stroke triumph in the Munsingwear Open KSB Cup at Kobe's Rokko Kokusai Golf Club. Just a stroke off the lead after 54 holes, Miyase shot the day's best round, 68, for his winning, 13-under-par 275. Coupled with his victory a month earlier in the Tsuruya Open, it gave the 32-year-old six wins in his 13-year career.

The week's best scoring came in the opening round. Go Higaki, inspired by a hole-in-one, and Katsumasa Miyamoto fired potent 64s to lead the field by two strokes. Higaki, a winner just once in his decade on the circuit, aced the 11th hole after running off six birdies on the front nine. Six players, including week-long contenders Taichi Teshima, S.K. Ho and Takashi Kanemoto, were at 66. Teshima, 35, the 2001 Japan Open champion, birdied three of his last five holes Friday for 69–135 and slipped into a one-stroke lead over Kanemoto (70).

Teshima had an inconsistent 71 with five birdies, four bogeys, but retained a share of first place Saturday at 206, overtaken by Ho, who shot 67, the day's top round. Miyase shot 69 to move within a stroke of the lead, then jumped in front early with birdies on the first three holes Sunday. He offset three later bogeys with four birdies for the winning 68. Ho shot 72 and was the runner-up at 278, one stroke in front of Teshima and Mitsuhiro Tateyama.

Diamond Cup—¥110,000,000
Winner: Todd Hamilton

Todd Hamilton followed Hirofumi Miyase's lead in the Diamond Cup. Just as Miyase did in winning the Munsingwear Open the previous week, Hamilton lingered just off the lead for three rounds, then closed brightly with a sparkling, seven-under-par 65 to score his second win of the season and ninth of his long career in Japan. He posted a 12-under-par 276, three better than runner-up Steve Conran of Australia in the three-year-old tournament.

The American produced a bogey-free 67 in Thursday's opening round at Oarai Golf Club, and he and four others trailed leader Tsukasa Watanabe by a stroke. Also at 67 were Hidemasa Hoshino, The Crowns winner in May; Daisuke Maruyama, Yeh Wei-tze of Taiwan and Mamoru Osanai. The next two days belonged to 43-year-old Kiyoshi Maita, whose only victory in his 18 years on the tour came in the 2000 Suntory Open. Four strokes off the lead after 18 holes, Maita came up with a bogey-free 67 and inched a stroke in front at seven-under-par 137. Watanabe (72) and Katsunori Kuwabara (70-68) were next and Hamilton shot 72 for 139. Rain interrupted Saturday's round as Maita remained in front at 209, two ahead of Hamilton (72), Maruyama (71) and Katsuyoshi Tomori (70).

Par was not good enough for the veteran Sunday as Hamilton put a win beside the earlier one in the Fujisankei with the day's best round. He had seven birdies in the solid round, breaking away with a run of three in the middle of the round. Conran had a 66 to grab second place, one stroke ahead of Tomori and Maruyama.

JCB Classic Sendai—¥100,000,000
Winner: Katsuyoshi Tomori

One wouldn't have thought it had been eight years since Katsuyoshi Tomori won on the Japan Tour from the way the 48-year-old veteran handled his game en route to victory in the JCB Classic Sendai at Shibata's Omotezao Kokusai Golf Club. Tomori brought home the bacon for the first time since he won the 1995 Japan Match Play Championship with an impressive, 20-under-par 264, finishing two strokes in front of Yusaku Miyazato, his only serious challenger and popular native son in Miyagi Prefecture. It was Tomori's sixth win dating back to 1987.

Tomori shaped a pair of 64s to go with two 68s during the tournament. He rang up six birdies over his first nine holes of the opening round on his way to the first 64 and trailed only India's Jyoti Randhawa, who racked up eight birdies for a 63 Thursday then shot himself in the foot Friday with a 75. Tomori moved in front Friday with the first 68 for 132 and a two-shot margin over Fiji's Dinesh Chand.

The second 64 Saturday virtually clinched things for Tomori, the bogey-free round staking him to a five-stroke lead at 196 over Miyazato (65) and Tadahiro Takayama (64). Miyazato came up with a 65 Sunday, but it merely tightened the final margin as Tomori shot his second 68 for the victorious 264. Shingo Katayama placed third with a closing 65, but was five strokes behind the winner.

Mandom Lucido Yomiuri Open—¥100,000,000
Winner: Hideto Tanihara

Bad weather disrupted the Mandom Lucido Yomiuri Open two weeks later, but it may have been a blessing in disguise for Hideto Tanihara. Dense fog and a threatening typhoon wiped out the opening round, forcing officials to reduce the tournament to three rounds and Tanihara was three strokes in front of the field when he reached the concluding 54th hole. It gave the unheralded 24-year-old his first victory and made him the third man to break the ice in 2003.

Tanihara began his surprising performance at Nishinomiya with a seven-under-par 65 Friday at Yomiuri Country Club, set up when he birdied his first two holes and eagled the fifth. His start overshadowed those of two of Japan's top stars — 56-year-old Masashi (Jumbo) Ozaki and Toshimitsu Izawa, 2001's leading money winner — who shot 66s and shared second place with Taiwan's Hsieh Chin-sheng.

The remarkable Ozaki, who won his 94th official title in 2002, went after the 95th Saturday, shooting 68–134 and slipping a stroke in front of his younger brother Naomichi (71-64), Kiyoshi Maita (68-67) and Kiyoshi Sunairi (67-68). Tanihara took a 71 and was two back at 136 with Izawa (70) and Hidehisa Shikata (68-68).

The final round belonged to Tanihara, who ran off five birdies on the first nine and went on to a 64, notching the three-stroke victory with a 16-under-par 200. Nobuhito Sato closed with 65 and jumped into second place as Ozaki shot 71 and dropped to fourth.

Gateway to the Open Mizuno Open—¥100,000,000
Winner: Todd Hamilton

Todd Hamilton continued the finest of his 11 years in Japan with a come-from-behind victory in the Gateway to the Open Mizuno Open. The win, his third of the season and 10th in Japan, strengthened his hold at the top of the circuit's money list and gave him a bonus — a spot in the field of the following month's Open Championship.

The American, who lives in Texas, was up and down through the weekend at Kasaoka's Setonaikai Golf Club. His opening 70 put him four shots behind Tadahiro Takayama, who surprised with a no-bogey 66 Thursday and led by a stroke over Toshimitsu Izawa. Steve Conran of Australia and Mitsuo Harada started with 68s. Hamilton surged in front Friday. Undaunted by a driving rain, he matched Takayama's 66, ripping off seven birdies against a lone bogey to go a stroke ahead of Tetsuji Hiratsuka and Kiyoshi Maita.

The rains continued Saturday as Izawa, coming off a disappointing season after reigning as No. 1 in 2001, shot 68 for 206 in his quest for his first win since late in 2001. That jumped him ahead of Hamilton, who slipped to 73–209 and into a fourth-place tie behind Yoshitaka Yamamoto (207) and Yeh Wei-tze (208).

None of the top three fared well Sunday, especially the veteran Yamamoto, who absorbed a horrendous 83. Hamilton, though, was sharp on the gusty day. Three birdies in a row starting at the fifth hole moved him ahead and he went on to shoot 69 for a 10-under-par 278. Australia's Brendan Jones also shot 69 Sunday and took second place at 279, a stroke in front of Izawa, who struggled to a 74, Hiratsuka (71) and Nobuhito Sato (70).

Japan Tour Championship—¥120,000,000
Winner: Toshimitsu Izawa

Experience told Toshimitsu Izawa to forget about his bad finish the preceding Sunday in the Mizuno Open — and he did with rewarding emphasis. The 35-year-old Izawa, who had endured a winless season in 2002 after capturing the money title the previous year in resounding fashion, scored his first victory in 20 months, landing the important Japan Tour Championship and the Shisido Hills Cup the first week of July. He nosed out David Smail and Tadahiro Takayama by a stroke with his 14-under-par 270. Interestingly, the event is just four years old and Izawa won the inaugural in 2000.

Smail, in the hunt all week, opened the tournament at Shisido Hills Country Club with 66 and shared first place with Katsumasa Miyamoto as Izawa settled for a one-under-par 70. Izawa then charged up the leaderboard Friday with a 10-birdie 63, making four of the birdies on his first six holes. He wound up tied for the lead with Taichi Teshima, who went without a bogey for a second straight day and shot 65 for his 133. Takayama was a stroke back after a 66.

Izawa eased a shot in front Saturday with a 68–201. Teshima had 70 and dropped into a third-place deadlock with Takayama (69) as Smail, whose 67 matched the day's low score, took over the runner-up spot at 202. It was a fight to the finish among Izawa, Smail and Takayama, Izawa prevailing with 69 and Takayama (68) joining Smail (69) in the runner-up slot. Although his failure to win the previous week in the Mizuno Open cost him a trip to the Open Championship, he picked up a worthwhile perk with the Tour Championship victory — a berth in the NEC Invitational in Akron, Ohio.

Woodone Open—¥100,000,000
Winner: Toshimitsu Izawa

Toshimitsu Izawa found himself on a roll when he played in the renamed Woodone Open at Hiroshima Country Club. Fresh from his first victory in 21 months in the Japan Tour Championship the preceding Sunday, Izawa maintained the pace with another win, although, in what had been the Juken Sangyo Open for many years, he had to do it in a playoff. It ran his career total to 14 titles.

Masahiro Kuramoto, a faded star now age 47, who was one of the Japan Tour's leading players in the 1980s, regained a moment of glory in the first round of the tournament, shooting a seven-under-par 65 to lead Izawa and Dinesh Chand of Fiji by a stroke. However, Kuramoto, whose last of 32 victories came in 1995, began to tail off Friday. He shot 70 for 135, falling a stroke behind the high-stepping Izawa, who put up a 68 for 134. Kuramoto shared second place with Tatsuhiko Takahashi (69-66), but was not a factor after that.

Izawa held onto his one-stroke lead Saturday. He birdied the first two holes and had four other birdies, but took three bogeys for 69 and 203. Toru Suzuki and Katsunari Kuwabara, with 67s, were at 204. Kiyoshi Murota, who was another stroke back Saturday, shot 70 Sunday to tie Izawa, who slipped to par 72 for his matching 275 total. Izawa ended the playoff at the second extra hole, becoming the season's first back-to-back winner. It was just the second playoff of the year.

Sato Foods NST Niigata Open—¥50,000,000
Winner: Katsumasa Miyamoto

Katsumasa Miyamoto ended a dry spell at the Sato Foods NST Niigata Open. After finishing eighth on the Japan Tour money list and winning twice in 2001, Miyamoto went winless in 2002 and hadn't seriously challenged during the first four months of the current season. At Toyoura's Nakamine Golf Club, he began the tournament in front and ended there, picking off a one-stroke victory with his 17-under-par 271, his fifth win over a six-year period.

Miyamoto launched his title bid with a seven-under-par 65 Thursday, one better than the efforts of little-known Koumei Oda and Hideto Tanihara, the Yomiuri Open winner in June. Miyamoto stayed close the next two days, as the lead on Friday reverted to the unlikely Yoshiaki Mano and Hisashi Sawada, who had 134s, Mano shooting 66 and Sawada 67. Veteran Hideki Kase stood at 135 and Miyamoto at 136 after a 71, sharing fourth place with Keiji Sakamoto.

Miyamoto remained two behind after Saturday's round. He shot 69 for 205, leaving him two strokes back of Mano (69), Kase (68) and Tsuyoshi Yoneyama, who surged into contention with 65, the day's best round. None of them could cope with a pair of 66s Sunday. One, the product of eight birdies and two bogeys, gave Miyamoto his victory total, and the other jumped American Gregory Meyer into second place, one stroke behind the winner and one ahead of Mano, a rewarding finish for a player who was 126th on the 2002 money list.

Aiful Cup—¥120,000,000
Winner: Taichi Teshima

Flush with victory, Katsumasa Miyamoto made a strong run at two in a row in the Aiful Cup, but eventually lost in overtime to Taichi Teshima at Koymatsu's Twin Fields Golf Club. Teshima, who had made a couple of bids earlier in the season, birdied the first extra hole of a playoff to post the third victory of his career and first since winning the Japan Open in 2001.

The 35-year-old controlled the lead most of the way after overtaking first-round leaders Hidehisa Shikata and Koki Idoki, who opened with 65s, Idoki was in quest of the fourth title of his 20-year career and first since 1993. Teshima shot 67 and Miyamoto 68 the first day, then Teshima took command Friday with a flawless, eight-birdie 64 for 131. Miyamoto matched that round and settled into second place, one stroke back. Idoki fell four off the pace with 70–135.

Teshima retained a three-way share of the lead when he shot 70 Saturday for 201, joining Shikata (68) and Tetsuji Hiratsuka (67). Miyamoto dropped back into a fourth-place tie when he shot 72–204. Miyamoto came up with a sparkling 65 Sunday to overtake Teshima at 19-under-par 269 and force the playoff, but his par on the first extra hole wasn't good enough.

Sun Chlorella Classic—¥130,000,000
Winner: Brendan Jones

Brendan Jones' game flourished on the weekend and it reaped him the dividend of victory in the Sun Chlorella Classic. A back-to-back pair of 68s pulled him into a three-way tie for first place after 72 holes at Sapporo Bay Golf Club, and he won the year's third playoff in a four-tournament stretch on the first extra hole over Taichi Teshima and Daisuke Maruyama. The 27-year-old Australian had won his first tournament on the circuit in the rich Philip Morris event the previous autumn.

Jones had ground to make up every day. Toshinori Muto came out of nowhere Thursday to lead the tournament with 68, two strokes in front of runner-up Kazuhiro Kinjo. Jones was bunched in a six-way tie for third with Teshima and Maruyama at 71. The deadlock was at the top after Friday's round. Muto shot 72 and Teshima, Maruyama and S.K. Ho 69s to all card 140s. Jones was four back after his 73 that day.

The Australian recovered with 68 Saturday, but remained four behind as Maruyama matched the 68 for 208 and Azuma Yano joined him with a 66. They led Teshima (70), Kinjo (69) and Hajime Meshiai (67) by two shots. The 280s were products of Jones' second straight 68, Teshima's 70 and Maruyama's 72.

Hisamitsu-KBC Augusta—¥100,000,000
Winner: Soushi Tajima

Soushi Tajima made an impressive breakthrough on the Japan Tour with his victory in the Hisamitsu-KBC Augusta tournament at the end of August after a two-week opening on the schedule. Tajima became the fourth first-time winner, leading from start to finish and winning by four strokes, the second largest margin on the 2003 tour to that point in the season.

Tajima's run to the title began with a splash as he blistered the course with an eight-under-par 64. The 26-year-old, competing in his third season on the Japan Tour, birdied six of his first nine holes on his way to a two-stroke lead over Dinesh Chand and a three-shot advantage over five players, including Naomichi (Joe) Ozaki. Chand, of Fiji, who pursued Tajima closely all week, overtook him with a 68 Friday as Tajima was carding a 70.

Tajima regained sole possession of the lead Saturday when he shot 68 and Chand took 69. Hisayuki Sasaki moved into third place at 214 with a 66 and tied Chand for the runner-up position Sunday with 69 to Chand's 70–273. Tajima raced away to his four-stroke victory with a six-birdie, one-bogey performance for a 19-under-par 269.

Japan PGA Match Play—¥80,000,000
Winner: Todd Hamilton

Todd Hamilton won the Japan PGA Match Play for a second time, a repeat of his first victory on the Japan Tour. Nine years after he won the Match Play title in an 8-and-7 runaway, Hamilton won the 36-hole title match again, this time at Tomakomai's Nidom Classic course by a 3-and-2 score over New Zealand's David Smail in one of the few all-foreign-player finals in the history of the 32-man event. It was his fourth victory of the season and 11th in as many seasons in Japan.

The toughest of Hamilton's five matches came in the semi-finals when he squeezed out a 1-up victory over Hirofumi Miyase. He advanced to that match in the following sequence: 3-and-2 over Kiyoshi Murota, 3-and-1 over Kim Jong-duck, and 5-and-3 over Toru Taniguchi.

Smail followed a more difficult path to the finals. Dinesh Chand took him to 19 holes before bowing in the opening round. Smail then won 2 up over Tsukasa Watanabe, 2-and-1 over Hiroyuki Fujita, and 4-and-3 over Tetsuji Hiratsuka, before losing to Hamilton.

Suntory Open—¥100,000,000
Winner: Jyoti Randhawa

Another country was heard from on the Japan Tour when Jyoti Randhawa captured the Suntory Open the second week of September. Randhawa became the first Indian to claim a title when he posted eight-under-par 276, two strokes ahead of runner-up Paul Sheehan at Sobu Country Club in a tournament that has had eight winners from overseas.

The lead changed hands after each of the first three rounds. Masayuki Kawamura started out in front with a six-under-par 65, two in front of Hiroyuki Fujita and three ahead of Randhawa and three other players. Fujita took over Friday when he shot 66 for 133 and Kawamura took 69 for 134. Randhawa and Sheehan were three back at 136.

The overall scoring soared Saturday. Surprisingly, a par round boosted the Indian player two strokes into the lead with 207, and Australian Sheehan moved into second place at 209 despite taking a two-over-par 73 that day. Sheehan caught Randhawa at the fifth hole Sunday, but Randhawa regained the lead with a birdie at the eighth hole and hung on for his two-stroke victory.

Phil Mickelson came to Japan for the tournament, but didn't fare any better than he did in America during the season. He finished in a tie for 18th with a two-over-par 286 total.

ANA Open—¥100,000,000
Winner: Yeh Wei-tze

David defeated Goliath again. Coming down the stretch in the ANA Open, Yeh Wei-tze, a man with no victories on the Japan Tour, was battling Masashi (Jumbo) Ozaki, a man with 94 of them, including eight in that very tournament. Yet, the Taiwanese player prevailed on the Wattsu course of Sapporo Golf Club, making a birdie on the final hole to edge Ozaki and Tsuyoshi Yoneyama by one stroke with his 11-under-par 277. He was the sixth first-time winner of the season. Two years earlier, countryman Lin Keng-chi took the ANA title.

Taichi Teshima, the Aiful Cup winner in August, and Ryoken (Ricky) Kawagishi, a successful veteran, shared the first-round lead with 65. Paul Sheehan, the previous week's runner-up, had a 66, and Yeh was among five players at 67. Yeh followed the 67 with a 66 to jump four strokes into the lead at 133. Teshima (72) and Sheehan (71) were at 137 as Kawagishi shot himself out of contention with 78.

Yeh lost just a stroke off his margin when he shot par 72 Saturday for 205. Ozaki and Yoneyama elbowed their way into a second-place tie at 208, Ozaki carding a 67 and Yoneyama a 69. Five others were another stroke back.

Yeh, admittedly nervous Sunday in the presence of the legendary, 56-year-old Ozaki, still managed a par 72 for 277 and the one-shot victory over defending champion Ozaki and Yoneyama.

Acom International—¥120,000,000
Winner: Masahiro Kuramoto

Even with a 65 in the opening round, Masahiro Kuramoto couldn't carry his fast start in July's Woodone Open on to victory, something that had eluded the 48-year-old veteran since the 1995 Suntory Open. Eight tournaments later, he dazzled the field and Japanese fandom when he began the Acom International with a 59, the lowest score ever recorded on the Japan Tour and one of just a handful around the world. Even though that record start gave him a five-stroke lead, Kuramoto had to survive a three-way playoff before ending his victory drought with his 29th official and 33rd overall career win.

Although he came back to earth Friday, Kuramoto maintained sizeable leads through the next two rounds. A second-round 69 for 128 left him three strokes ahead of runner-up Shinichi Yokota (67-64) and five in front the Yusaku Miyazato (69-64) and Steve Conran (68-65) in third place. A third-round 70 for 198 bumped his margin back up to four over Miyazato and five ahead of five others.

One of those five was Masashi (Jumbo) Ozaki, coming off a near-miss in the ANA Open the previous Sunday. Eight behind in a tie for 14th place was Katsumasa Miyamoto. Eighteen holes later, both of those men had caught Kuramoto and brought on a playoff. Kuramoto shot 73 Sunday while Ozaki produced a 68 and Miyamoto a 65. The playoff ended quickly when both Ozaki and Miyamoto bogeyed the first hole and Kuramoto won with a par.

Georgia Tokai Classic—¥120,000,000
Winner: Nozomi Kawahara

First-time winners became almost commonplace in the late season on the Japan Tour. Nozomi Kawahara became the fourth ice-breaker in a six-tournament stretch — and seventh of the year — when he eked out a one-stroke victory in the Georgia Tokai Classic in early October. With his 13-under-par 275, Kawahara finished one stroke ahead of Shingo Katayama and Tsuyoshi Yoneyama, two veterans with multiple wins on their records.

Soushi Tajima, the KBC Augusta winner earlier in the season, started after a second 2003 victory with a 67 that gave him the first-round lead. Just a stroke back were Daisuke Maruyama, Hideto Tanihara, Satoru Hirota and Takashi Kanemoto. Kawahara opened among a dozen players with 69s. Tajima faded Friday, and Maruyama became the front-runner with the 66 he fashioned despite a double bogey at Miyoshi Country Club's par-three 16th hole. The 134 vaulted the winless, 10-year veteran three strokes ahead of Kawahara, who grabbed the runner-up spot with 68–137.

Although inconsistent, Kawahara took over the lead Saturday. He produced a 69 out of seven birdies, two bogeys and a double bogey for a 206 total that put him a stroke in front of Maruyama, who slipped to 73, and Katayama and Ryoken Kawagishi, who had 69s. The 33-year-old Kawahara repeated the 69 Sunday and nailed the victory despite a bogey on the final hole.

Japan Open—¥120,000,000
Winner: Keiichiro Fukabori

Keiichiro Fukabori picked the right time and place to end a long victory slump — the Japan Open — and he did it brilliantly. Trailing by five strokes entering the final round, Fukabori conjured up a sparkling, seven-under-par 64 Sunday and walked off with a two-stroke victory, the most important by far of the four on his record.

The 34-year-old veteran started fast at Tochigi's Nikko Country Club. He joined Ryoken Kawagishi and Hidemasa Hoshino in first place with 66, but fell four off the pace Friday when he floundered with a 75. Tatsuhiko Takahashi added a 70 to his first-round 67 to take sole possession of the lead Friday at 137. Kawagishi, with 72, and Daisuke Maruyama (70-68) trailed by a stroke, and Hoshino, four-time Open champion Tsuneyuki (Tommy) Nakajima and visiting Australian Craig Parry, the 1997 winner, were another shot back.

Yasuharu Imano made his presence known Saturday. He jumped from four back to two ahead with a 66 for 207 and a three-stroke lead over Parry (71), Maruyama (72) and Kawagishi (72). Fukabori actually lost ground Saturday. His 71 left him at 212 with the five-stroke deficit that he made up plus some Sunday with the 64 and his 276 total. Imano could manage just 71 and finished second with 278. Thailand's Prayad Marksaeng was third at 281.

Bridgestone Open—¥110,000,000
Winner: Naomichi Ozaki

The Ozaki brothers age well. Just like his oldest brother, Masashi, who is still contending and winning in his mid-50s, Naomichi (Joe) Ozaki showed that he still had plenty of game when, at age 47, he scored a playoff victory over Australian Paul Sheehan in the Bridgestone Open at Sodegaura Country Club in Chiba in late October. It was Ozaki's first victory since the 2000 Japan Open and his 30th victory on the Japan Tour, a total that no doubt would have been even greater if he hadn't campaigned full-time on the U.S. Tour for several seasons in his prime years. Interestingly, both Masashi (1988 and 1997) and his other brother, Tateo (1986), were past Bridgestone winners.

Two players who had been frequent but frustrated contenders earlier in the season — Daisuke Maruyama and Tetsuji Hiratsuka — shared the first-round lead with 65s amid a flurry of low scores. Ozaki was among five players who shot 66. One of them — Hiroyuki Fujita — advanced into a first-place tie Friday, shooting 67 to join Maruyama (65) at 132, but the day's big noise came from veteran Hajime Meshiai, who broke the course record with a 63 that jumped him into fourth place after an opening 71. The 49-year-old Meshiai, the tour's leading money winner in 1993, had an eagle, eight birdies and a bogey in the round that broke Hsieh Min-nan's 21-year-old record. Sheehan held third place with 67–133.

Maruyama remained tied for first place for the third straight day Saturday. He shot 67 for 199 and was joined at the top by Sheehan, who fired 66. Hideto Tanihara matched Meshiai's record score and climbed into third place at 201. Ozaki staked out fourth place with 67–202, setting himself up for the run at the title Sunday. He shot 65 and Sheehan 68 in the final round for their 267s. Ozaki took the victory when he birdied the par-five 18th, the second hole of the playoff.

ABC Championship—¥120,000,000
Winner: Shingo Katayama

Shingo Katayama kept alive his bid for a second money title when he blitzed the field in the ABC Championship (formerly the Philip Morris) the first weekend of November. Katayama, No. 1 in Japan in 2000, jumped into third place in the 2003 standings behind Todd Hamilton and Toshimitsu Izawa with his nine-stroke victory at the ABC Golf Club in Tojo thanks to its ¥24 million first prize.

Katayama started and finished with eight-under-par 64s and was only out of the lead after the second round when Tetsuji Hiratsuka, a frequent contender during the season, shot a dazzling 63 for 132 and led him by a stroke. Katayama regained the lead the next day when he mustered a 68 for 201 and went two strokes in front of Katsumasa Miyamoto (64) and Hiroyuki Fujita (66). He sensed the victory that day, remarking that "I've got the same vibe I had at the end of the 2000 season," when he won three of the season's last four tournaments to annex the money title.

His second 64 Sunday left the field in his dust. Miyamoto shot 71 but held onto second place at 274, nine behind Katayama and his year's best victory margin with his 265. Izawa, Hiratsuka and Tsuyoshi Yoneyama finished another stroke back, as Fujita shot 73 and fell into a sixth-place tie with Zaw Moe.

Mitsui Sumitomo Visa Taiheiyo Masters—¥150,000,000
Winner: Kiyoshi Murota

Kiyoshi Murota struck a blow for the oldest players with his resounding, six-stroke victory in the prestigious Mitsui Sumitomo Visa Taiheiyo Masters in early November at Gotemba. In striking parallel, the 48-year-old Murota succeeded Tsuneyuki (Tommy) Nakajima, who also was 48 when he won the Taiheiyo Masters in 2002. It was the sixth tour victory for Murota and three of them came during the most recent three seasons. Murota broke this one open when he shot a course-record 62 in the third round to go six strokes in front, his winning margin as things turned out.

Murota's move came at the expense of Ben Curtis, who made a strong bid to put the Taiheiyo Masters on his record to go with his surprising Open Championship in July. Making his first strong showing since the Open at Royal St. George's, Curtis led for two days. The 26-year-old American started off Thursday with eight birdies and a 65, finishing a stroke in front of Murota and Masashi (Jumbo) Ozaki. Then he doubled the gap when he shot 69 for 134. Ozaki was at 136 with Azuma Yano, Tomohiro Kondo and Toshimitsu Izawa. Murota was another stroke back after a 71.

Then came the course-record 62 as Murota soared in front by six strokes with 199. He racked up 10 birdies in posting his best score ever on tour and picking up a ¥1 million bonus for the feat. Curtis shot 71, which was good enough to put him in the runner-up position with 205.

Murota admitted to a few jitters on the back nine in the final round, but even though he shot a one-over-par 73, he was never threatened. Curtis also shot 73 and dropped into a three-way tie for second with Hiroyuki Fujita and Kim Jong-duck. Murota's winning total was 272.

Dunlop Phoenix—¥200,000,000
Winner: Thomas Bjorn

As is so often the case, players from the usually strong contingent of international stars, lured to the Dunlop Phoenix by its hefty purse, dominated the action as the Japan Tour headed down the stretch. In the end, it was a second Dunlop Phoenix triumph for one European Ryder Cupper and bitter disappointment for another. Denmark's Thomas Bjorn came from three strokes off the pace to take away a victory that appeared to be in the hands of Spaniard Sergio Garcia.

For three days, Garcia had held or shared the lead as he sought to put a weak season behind him with his first victory of the year. It all came apart in Sunday's final round when a poor performance on the greens — 39 putts — contributed heavily to a seven-over-par 78 and plummeted him from a three-shot lead into sixth place in the final standings, four behind Bjorn. The Dane, who had beaten Garcia in a playoff at Phoenix Country Club in 1999, needed only a 71 for his winning, 12-under-par 272. Daisuke Maruyama shot 70 to take second place with 274, and Lee Westwood, a four-time winner in Japan, jumped into a third-place tie with American David Gossett and Tetsuji Hiratsuka.

Garcia was sailing along nicely for three days, comfortable on a course where he had finished second twice — the playoff loss to Bjorn in 1999 and in 2002 behind Kaname Yokoo. The first day, he shot 66 and shared first place with Hank Kuehne, the long-hitting American, and Jun Kikuchi of Japan. Garcia moved in front by a stroke Friday when he added a 65 for 131. Bjorn and Maruyama also had 65s that day and were tied for second. Then, on Saturday, with 67–198, Garcia widened his margin to three strokes over Bjorn and five over Toshimitsu Izawa before the roof fell in on him Sunday.

Even though he, too, had a bad final round of 77, Izawa slipped ahead of Todd Hamilton in the money race. He tied for ninth while Hamilton tied for 26th.

Casio World Open—¥140,000,000
Winner: Katsumune Imai

Not to be outdone by the Americans, the Japan Tour opened its doors to a leading player on the U.S. LPGA Tour — Sweden's Sophie Gustafson — and her presence in the Casio World Open partially overshadowed a brilliant performance by Katsumune Imai, until that week winless on the circuit. The sideshow ended when Gustafson missed the cut by six strokes and Imai had the stage to himself over the weekend as he rolled to a seven-stroke victory. He was the eighth first-time winner of the season.

While the attention was on the LPGA star Thursday and Friday, Imai was building a four-stroke lead with a pair of seven-under-par 65s. He had an eagle and five birdies in the first one Thursday, starting off two strokes in front of Dinesh Chand, Soushi Tajima and Koki Idoki. Everything was going right for Imai on the Kaimon course of Ibusuki Golf Club at Kagoshima. He made a hole-in-one on the par-three fourth hole in the process of shooting the second 65 Friday. Four back then was Jyoti Randhawa, the Suntory Open winner in September, who posted 68-66 for the 134.

Imai increased his lead to five strokes Saturday, clicking out a bogey-free 67 for 197. Tajima, like Randhawa a first-time winner in 2003 (KBC Augusta), roared into the runner-up spot with a torrid 64–202. Randhawa had 69–203.

Imai went unchallenged Sunday, firing a solid, six-birdie 67 for his winning 24-under-par 264, matching the low 72-hole score of the season, posted by Katsuyoshi Tomori in the JCB Classic Sendai. Shingo Katayama came up with a 66 to join Brendan Jones in second place at 271.

Golf Nippon Series JT Cup—¥100,000,000
Winner: Tetsuji Hiratsuka

Good things happens to those who wait — or something like that. Tetsuji Hiratsuka proved the point in the season-ending Golf Nippon Series JT Cup, the limited-field tournament to which only the season's winners and leading money winners are invited. Hiratsuka was a consistent challenger through the season, so much so that, even without a victory, he was fourth on the money list going into the finale. His patience paid off at Tokyo's Yomiuri

Country Club, where he led most of the way and equaled the year's best 72-hole score with a 16-under-par 264.

Hiratsuka joined three others — David Smail, Kiyoshi Murota and Taichi Teshima — atop the leaderboard the first day with 66. Leading money winner Toshimitsu Izawa trailed by a stroke. Teshima inched into the lead Friday with his five-under-par 65 for 131, a stroke ahead of Smail (66) and Izawa (65).

Hiratsuka, who shot 68 and dropped to fourth place with 134, then moved ahead to stay Saturday with a sizzling 63 that included two eagles. At 197, he had a three-shot lead over Izawa (68) as Teshima had to settle for a par 70 and 201. Hiratsuka was steady and unchallenged Sunday. He shot a bogey-free 67 for 264, the winning score for the second week in a row in Japan, and became the year's ninth first-time victor.

Izawa matched the 67 to take second place and clinch the season's money title with ¥135,454,300. Hiratsuka advanced to the No. 2 position with the winner's prize money of ¥30 million giving him earnings of ¥122,227,033 for the year. Todd Hamilton, whose four victories were tops for the season and who led the money standings for much of the season, forfeited his shot at No. 1 when he elected to return to America to play in the qualifying rounds for the 2004 PGA Tour. He qualified. Japan's loss.

Asia/Japan Okinawa Open—¥100,000,000
Winner: Hideto Tanihara

It wasn't a warning so much as an announcement. Watch out world, here comes Hideto Tanihara.

Well, it wasn't much, even as announcements go, but it came from the heart when Tanihara, Rookie of the Year for 2003 on the Japan Tour, trailed through three rounds then emerged in the final round to take the year-ending Okinawa Open. It was the second victory of the year for the 26-year-old Tanihara, and having stuffed it into his bag, he issued his proclamation.

"This victory," Tanihara said, "will give me a three-year exemption in Japan, and that will give me the opportunity to play abroad."

The win capped a sensational rookie year. Tanihara scored his first victory in the Yomiuri Open in June, and he had seven other top-10 finishes before taking the Okinawa Open, which was jointly sponsored by the Japan and Asian PGA Tours for the second year. So it would seem that he would be heading out for points east, west, south and north at his first opportunity.

Meantime, he could savor a victory that — for a rookie — was of near-epic proportions. Tanihara hung around, three strokes off the lead, through the first three rounds, playing the par-72 Southern Links Club in 66-76-68. Then as challengers fell away in the final round, he notched a strong 69 for a nine-under-par 279 and a comfortable three-stroke win over a crowd of seven topped by a disappointed Hiroshi Goda, who led the second and third rounds.

Tanihara showed the patience and class of a tested veteran against a quality field of tested veterans. First came the mighty Masashi Ozaki, age 56, turning back time to shoot a stunning nine-under 63. "I was relaxed, positive and aggressive throughout the round today," he said. The magic didn't last. He blew to a 79 in the second round. He would bounce back, but he had left himself too far out of it.

The tournament belonged to Goda, who shared the lead in the second round (74–139) and owned it outright by a stroke (68–207) in the third. His inspiration isn't likely to find its way into the instruction books. "My shoulder was hurting yesterday," Goda said, "but I slept well after drinking sake. This morning I was fine." Sake happens to be a Japanese liquor. But he backslid to a 75 in the final round and settled into the crowd at second place. Other challengers also fell short. Korea's Charlie Wi made two bogeys early then birdied 10 of his next 14 holes and shot 64 to join that runner-up jam. Ozaki started the day just two off the lead, but struggled to a 74 and finished ninth. It was Tanihara to center stage, and he was a model citizen from the school of playing 'em one at a time.

"When I started this morning (three off the lead), I never thought of winning this tournament. I kept playing to the center of the green. And when I looked at the scoreboard on 15, only then did I realize I was ahead." He was even par on three birdies and three bogeys through the 10th, then birdies at the 11th, 14th and 15th got him three ahead and on his way to the comfortable victory.

"Winning," Tanihara said, "is certainly a nice present for the New Year."

11. Australasian Tour

They raised the storm warnings as Typhoon Ernie approached the Australian coast.

More to the point, this was Ernie Els, the "Big Easy" by way of South Africa. Give him a ball, a peg to put it on and some ground to stick the peg in, and he can win anywhere. This was especially true early in 2003. He was playing Monopoly. He wasn't leaving much for anybody else. And so the alarm was raised when he arrived for a brief visit to Australia. Els had already won the first two events on the U.S. PGA Tour — the Mercedes Championship and the Sony Open — on successive weeks. After a runner-up finish in the Caltex Masters in Singapore, he headed for Australia, where he won two more.

His first stop was the Heineken Classic in the first week of February. England's Paul Casey created an early stir, and then Nick Faldo challenged. Meanwhile, Els, the defending champion, trailed by 10 strokes after 36 holes and still trailed after 54. A charge in the final round brought him a second consecutive Heineken Classic title.

"I didn't think I had much of a chance," Els said. "This game is quite amazing sometimes."

It got even more amazing two weeks later in the Johnnie Walker Classic. Maybe embarrassing is a better word. Els simply ran away with it by 10 strokes for his fourth victory in five starts in 2003. "The way I'm playing now," said easy-smiling Ernie, "is some of the best golf I've ever played."

The Australasian Tour started with the Holden New Zealand Open which ended with a case of nerves that fortunately wasn't fatal for New Zealand's Mahal Pearce. Pearce started the final round two strokes off the lead and built up such a cushion that he could double-bogey the final hole and still win by two strokes for the first victory of his career.

Casey, frustrated at the Heineken Classic, made his mark at the ANZ Championship, a Stableford-style event. Scoring was in points, but if it had been stroke play, he still would have won comfortably. The victory was particularly tasty for Casey. He recalled the critics, who decided he was a bust for not cashing in big when he first came out on the PGA European Tour. Said Casey, "This probably answers a few critics out there."

At the Jacob's Creek Open, Australian fans got a taste of the confusion that perplexed American fans for a while. There was a Joe Ogilvie in the field. But didn't they mean Ogilvy? Well, no. That was an Australian golfer named Geoff Ogilvy; this one was Joe Ogilvie. The distinction became clearer established when Ogilvie, the American, turned back this challenger and that, and won by a stroke. The tournament and the Clearwater Classic the following week were co-sponsored by the Australasian Tour and the Nationwide Tour, the developmental circuit of the U.S. PGA Tour. Ogilvie noted, "Our whole life is pretty much sheltered in America. It's great for us to come over here and play a course like this."

If Ernie Els' two victories were the highlight of 2003, then Robert Allenby's win in the MasterCard Masters was the icing on the cake. First, it was a tribute to Allenby's fortitude that he could even finish. He was suffering from the flu, badly enough that he even lost his hearing for a while. So it was hardly surprising that he blew a two-stroke lead with nine holes to play and ended up in a four-man playoff. And the playoff is Allenby's specialty. He ran his career playoff record to a stunning 8-0. Said Allenby, almost as an afterthought, "It seems like I'm all right when it gets down to finishing things off."

In the Australian PGA Championship, the early money was on such luminaries as Greg Norman, celebrated native son, and Rich Beem, the 2002 American PGA champion. But it was Peter Senior, the little Aussie with the big broom putter, now 44, who plucked the coveted title. But only just. He led much of the way, but had to struggle to bring it home. "I was leaking a bit of oil at the end," Senior said, "but I hung on."

And at the Australian Open late in December, the last event of 2003, Peter Lonard fittingly won on the last hole. Chris Downes, an Australian of promise, seemed about to win. Then so did American Rickey Barnes, the U.S. Amateur champion of 2002, winless and frustrated since turning professional six months earlier. Seven different players had a chance in the final round. Lonard squelched them all when he dropped a nine-foot birdie putt at the 18th hole.

"It was," said Lonard, "a wonderful way to finish the year."

Holden New Zealand Open—NZ$700,000

Winner: Mahal Pearce

If happiness is being able to double-bogey the final hole and still win by two strokes, then New Zealand's Mahal Pearce was the happiest man in the country when the 2003 Australasian Tour got underway with the Holden New Zealand Open the third week of January.

Pearce, who started the final round two strokes behind the leader, Australia's Chris Downes, built up such a head of steam that he was leading by four heading into the final hole. Then he stumbled to a double-bogey six and still beat Australia's Brett Rumford by two strokes. Pearce, notching the first victory of his career, played the par-72 Auckland Golf Club in 69-70-69-70– 278, 10 under par.

Downes was the favorite heading into the last round, after a sensational eagle three at the 17th in the third round. He reached the 17th green with a driver and a seven iron, and coolly rolled home a 15-foot putt for the eagle. It gave him a three-under-par 69 that was even better than it seemed.

"It was pretty gusty out there, and the greens got bumpy in the afternoon, so I'll definitely take a 69," said Downes, taking a two-stroke lead over Pearce and New Zealand's Gareth Paddison. Downes fell to 75 in the final round, and Pearce made his move.

Behind Rumford, the runner-up by two, were Downes and Australian Nathan Green tied at 281. Aussie Wayne Grady, co-runner-up with Greg Norman in the 1989 Open Championship (behind winner Mark Calcavecchia), and New Zealand's Michael Campbell were in a logjam tie for ninth.

Heineken Classic—A$2,000,000
Winner: Ernie Els

First, England's Paul Casey was getting the game of his early promise warmed up. Then Nick Faldo, now 45, was in charge, getting his old game back. But in the end at the Heineken Classic, here came the guy with the easy gait and the gentle smile — Ernie Els.

Els, the defending champion, trailed by 10 strokes after the second round, by three after the third, and didn't lead until the last round, but he needed some help — a clutch putt here, a bounce off a spectator there. And so he rang up a seven-under-par 65 in the final round for a one-stroke victory. Now 2003 was beginning to look like his year. He came to the Australasian Tour with back-to-back victories to lead off the U.S. PGA Tour, the Mercedes Championship and the Sony Open in Hawaii, and after a runner-up finish in the Caltex Masters in Singapore, now a repeat in the Heineken Classic. Els posted 70-72-66-65—273, 15 under par. This was his third victory in five starts, and also his 10th victory worldwide in just over 13 months.

"I made some good saves coming home," Els said. "I'm happy with the way I played. I was a little tired, but I seemed to get some energy the last few days."

Casey jumped out with a seven-under-par 65 in the first round, for a one-stroke lead over Spain's Santiago Luna. Just two back were England's Warren Bennett and Gary Evans and Australians Peter Fowler and Peter Lonard. "I saw all of Melbourne's lovely weather today," said Casey. "I think I did pretty well, considering the elements." The elements consisted of clouds and light wind early, then a drenching rain late in the morning that forced a 90-minute delay. Els bogeyed his first hole before the suspension hit. "I had a very shaky start," Els said. "I was lucky not to bogey the second. I tried to rebound during the rain delay, but there were so many changes of weather."

Greg Norman, the big local favorite, was all but out of the running with a first-round 73. "I putted terribly," Norman said. He wouldn't threaten the rest of the way.

Casey shot 67 in the second round for a two-stroke lead at the halfway point, leaving Els 10 shots behind. "I don't know if I've overplayed myself a bit," said Els, playing for the fourth straight week. "But I've lost my rhythm again." Faldo, hanging close from the start, broke through with a 65 for a one-stroke lead in the third round. Said Faldo, 45 and winless since 1997, "It will be great to go out and show them that there's still plenty of the old Faldo in me." There was, but there was a little too much of Els.

It all came down to the final holes. At the 16th, Els drove into the rough, then put his approach on the edge of bunker. He putted all the way across and off the green. He made the putt coming back, saving par from 15 feet. He saved par again from four feet at the 17th, and at the 18th, his tee shot hit a spectator and ended up near the ropes instead of heavy rough. He put his approach into a bunker, but he blasted out to four feet and made that putt, too, for a par. He also made eight birdies along the way for the 65.

Lonard, playing with Faldo in the last pairing, was tied for the lead after 17 holes. But at the 18th, he pushed his drive into a tent area, then hit his second into a bunker and bogeyed for 68 and a tie with Faldo (69) for second place, a stroke behind Els. Faldo needed a birdie at the final hole to force a playoff, but put his approach through the green and against an advertising sign.

"I didn't think I had much of a chance — particularly the way I played Thursday and Friday," Els said. "But somehow I got through. This game is quite amazing sometimes."

ANZ Championship—A$1,750,000
Winner: Paul Casey

England's Paul Casey would have won the ANZ Championship no matter which way it was counted. Under stroke play, Casey's 71 in the final round would have given him a two-stroke victory over Australians Stuart Appleby and Nick O'Hern. But the tournament was played under a modified-Stableford scoring system, and so he beat them by four points.

Casey got a grip on this victory in the third round, when an eagle sparked him to a six-point lead going into the final round.

The modified-Stableford system, popularized by The International on the U.S. PGA Tour, scores eight points for a double eagle, five for an eagle, two for a birdie, zero for a par, and minus one for a bogey and minus three for anything higher. Australia's Peter Fowler led off the tournament with nine birdies and a bogey for 17 points on the oceanside course of the New South Wales Golf Club near Sydney. It was an encouraging start. "It's hard work to continue playing, but my game's coming together," said Fowler, 43, winless since the 1993 BMW International on the European Tour. He led by a point over fellow Aussie Stuart Appleby, who made eight birdies and no bogeys for 16 points.

Australia's Brendan Jones leapfrogged into a share of the lead with 14 points on Friday with an eagle and six birdies, but hurt himself with three bogeys. His 22 points overall tied him with countrymen O'Hern, Nathan Green and Terry Price. Casey, a former Arizona State University player in the United States, surged into the lead with a 21-point third round sparked by an eagle at the fifth hole. He led Appleby by six points, 39-33. "I'm going to go out there and just try to attack the golf course again — try and make as many birdies as I can," Casey said. "I think this format suits me. I wish every week was like this."

Casey attacked again in the final round, getting five birdies, but the course fought back and cost him four bogeys. So he logged six points for a total of 45, to beat Appleby and O'Hern by four. "The first win was tough," said Casey, who won the 1991 Scottish PGA. "This shows the first wasn't a flash in the pan, and it probably answers a few critics out there."

Johnnie Walker Classic—£1,000,000
Winner: Ernie Els

It was all but embarrassing. Ernie Els simply ran away with the Johnnie Walker Classic by 10 strokes — his fourth victory in five tournaments in 2003. And when he'd wrapped it up, he managed a sheepish smile and an exercise in understatement. "The way I'm playing now," said the easy-going

South African, "is some of the best golf I've ever played. The whole package is good at the moment."

Everyone knows how it goes with golf. The good turns bad so fast. So Els was careful while at the same time trying to explain how he was dominating everywhere he went. He had opened the 2003 season winning the Mercedes Championships by eight strokes with a record 31-under-par total. Then he took the Sony Open in Hawaii, and after a second place in the Caltex Masters, he repeated as champion in the Heineken Classic. Now he had win No. 4, the Johnnie Walker Classic, and it was only mid-February.

Els just roared through the tournament, shooting 64-65-64-66–259, 29 under par at Lake Karrinyup Country Club at Perth. That broke the European Tour 72-hole record in relation to par, the 27 under shot by Jerry Anderson in the 1984 European Masters. The Johnnie Walker Classic was co-sponsored by the European, Australasian and Asian Tours. So Els also broke the Asian record of 26 under set by Jeev Milkha Singh in the 1996 Phillip Morris Asian Cup.

Not that Els or anyone else really noticed, but Australia's Stephen Leaney and Andre Stolz matched Els' closing 66 and tied for second at 269, 19 under par. Retief Goosen, the 2002 Johnnie Walker Classic winner, tied for fourth with a global cross-section — Australia's Robert Allenby, England's Justin Rose, New Zealand's David Smail and France's Jean-Francois Remesy.

From the start, things were going so well for Els that he permitted himself a little fantasy. "I must admit I was thinking some silly stuff there," Els said. "It was just for a split second, and I came down to earth on No. 11, making bogey there. That kind of settled all those silly thoughts." The silly thoughts he was thinking in the first round were of shooting 60. He began after streaking to seven under par in his first seven holes, logging an eagle, five birdies and a par. The 60 disappeared, so he settled for 64 and a one-stroke lead over England's David Lynn. That was the closest anyone would get to him. It was all over but the explanations.

Els said it was this simple: "This week, everything went right. I had a great time. The greens are soft, the wind stayed away, and I could just go out there and attack the golf course."

Jacob's Creek Open—A$1,000,000
Winner: Joe Ogilvie

The Jacob's Creek Open came to the Kooyonga Golf Course, near Adelaide, opening what might have been part of a new day in global golf. The tournament was co-sponsored by the Australasian Tour and the Nationwide Tour, the developmental circuit of the U.S. PGA Tour. This was the start of a five-year arrangement, and to this extent, at least, it represented the further linking of tours around the world.

Joe Ogilvie won the Jacob's Creek Open, and this was the American Joe Ogilvie, who played the U.S. PGA Tour for four years, and not Geoff Ogilvy, the Australian, a member of the U.S. PGA Tour. The important name to Joe Ogilvie: Winner. Two more victories or finishing in the top 20 on the Nationwide money list would put him on the PGA Tour in 2004.

Ogilvie established himself early, shooting a five-under-par 66 in the first round to tie Australia's Marcus Fraser at a stroke off the lead shared by Australian Jarrod Moseley and American Roland Thatcher at 65. In the second round, Thatcher shot a one-over 72 in the strong winds. "I think the golf course was punishing us for doing the damage we did on the first day," he said. At that, he didn't get badly hurt. But he wouldn't get the lead back, either.

It was Ogilvie's tournament the rest of the way. He and Fraser shot 70s in the second round to tie for the halfway lead at six-under 136. Then Ogilvie took over from there. With Kooyonga getting more resistant by the day, a par 71 for a 207 total was enough to get him the third-round lead by two strokes over Australia's Shane Tait (67). The field spread out from there. Moseley, with 71, was a stroke further back, and Thatcher (74) slipped a further stroke behind.

Ogilvie then wrapped it up with a one-over 72 in the final round for a five-under 279 total and a one-shot victory over Tait (71). It was Ogilvie's third career victory on the Nationwide Tour. Australia's Peter Senior, gritty veteran of both Europe and the United States, finally surfaced with a 69 to join a three-way tie for third with New Zealand's Mahal Pearce (66) and Canada's David Morland (68) at two-under-par 282.

Clearwater Classic—A$1,000,000
Winner: Ryan Palmer

The only smart way to play with the lead, Ryan Palmer figured, was to play as though you were not leading. "I've got to go out as if I'm two or three behind," Palmer said. "I've got to stay aggressive. I don't want to get too protective. That's when you can get into trouble."

That was after Palmer took a three-shot lead through the third round of the Clearwater Classic, a co-sponsored Australasian and Nationwide Tour event. Palmer went warily into the final round, cruised to a 68, and in just his second Nationwide Tour start, scored his first victory. He shot a 17-under-par 271 total on the Clearwater Resort course for a three-stroke victory over Australia's Andre Stolz, who closed with 68. American Kevin Johnson shot 67 and finished third.

American Joe Ogilvie, who won the Jacob's Creek Open the week before, looked like a good candidate to make it two wins in a row when he opened the tournament with a five-under-par 67 and a share of the first-round lead. "I holed a lot of four- to-seven-footers for par, but I missed a little one for my bogey," said Ogilvie. "It was a round that could have been even par as well as five under." A 73 the next day took him out of the running for a second straight victory.

Palmer, a former Texas A&M University player, rocketed to the top of the leaderboard in the second round with a course-record nine-under-par 63. That put him at 12-under 132 and gave him a four-stroke lead. "I've shot 63 before," Palmer said, "but to do it in a Nationwide Tour event in only my second start makes it very special for me. It's been an exciting day."

Palmer, who missed the cut in his first Nationwide start the week before, was about to find even more excitement. He shot 71 the next day to take a three-stroke lead into the final round. It's a moment of truth for a rookie.

That's when Palmer decided to play the last round as though he were trailing instead of leading. And that's exactly what he did. A tidy four-under 68 carried him comfortably to the three-stroke win.

"I was expecting some good things to come out of this week," Palmer said. "It's gone a lot better than even I thought it would."

MasterCard Masters—A$1,250,000
Winner: Robert Allenby

Maybe golf ought to enact the Allenby Provision. Anytime Robert Allenby is in a playoff, they ought to concede it to him and then everyone can just go home. Allenby, the spindly Australian, struck again in the MasterCard Masters. All he did was beat Adam Scott, Craig Parry and Jarrod Moseley, stretching his playoff record to an amazing 8-0. And in the process of getting there, he led or shared the lead from the second round while at the same time having to soldier on under a cold and a bad case of the flu, the wretched misery of which caused him to lose his concentration now and then, and even his hearing. But it was all worth it. Allenby had gone two years without a victory.

The tournament in December was pretty much his to win or lose. He led from the second round on, holding a two-stroke lead at the halfway point and a two-stroke lead after 54 holes. It seems he was lucky even to get through the third round. First, the Huntingdale jinx struck again. He hit his opening tee shot into the trees on the left. "Every year," he said, "I always hit it into those trees, so I guess I was expecting to hit it one day in there." The self-fulfilling prophecy cost him dearly, a double bogey. He also had three bogeys, but notched five birdies for his 72. Under the circumstances, the ragged round was a standout performance. The flu-wracked Allenby was all but dragging himself around Huntingdale "If you lose your concentration at any given time," he said, "it's very easy to hit some off shots, and that's what happened a few times." Concentration? He even lost his hearing for two holes.

The final round was a steeplechase. Scott shot 64, Parry 67, Moseley 69 and Allenby 71 to tie at 11-under 277. So Allenby had them just where he wanted them — in a playoff. Allenby and Scott birdied the first extra hole, knocking out Parry and Moseley, who had parred. At the second, true to the very special script the gods have written for him, Allenby lofted his nine-iron approach to three feet. Scott, who had driven into a bunker, did well just to get a seven iron to the green. Scott had a long birdie try, and missed it. Allenby had that three-footer, and made it.

"It seems like I'm all right," Allenby said, "when it gets down to finishing things off."

Australian PGA Championship—A$1,000,000
Winner: Peter Senior

The 2003 Australian PGA Championship was notable for a number of reasons. There was, for example, Jean Van de Velde, the tragicomic hero of the

1999 Open Championship, trying to make a comeback from a serious knee injury. And wisecracking Rich Beem, the 2002 U.S. PGA champion. And then there was Greg Norman, most notable in the press for having a pro tennis player for a caddie. While everyone was otherwise occupied, there was Peter Senior, the bouncy little 44-year-old Aussie, sneaking in under the radar for his first Australasian Tour victory since 1997. After leading comfortably most of the way, Senior, who won this Australian PGA in 1989, got to the barn just in time to win by a stroke over Rodney Pampling.

But what a week it was for Senior. "My confidence has been boosted with how I've been playing," he said, after tying for the first-round lead with Steve Collins on eight-under-par 64 at the Hyatt Regency resort course at Coolum. "I made some birdies on difficult holes, and that got me on my way. I hit it to six or seven feet about eight or nine times." He'd taken advantage of a calm day and a course with rain-softened greens. Eight players shot 67, and more than half of the 156-man field finished at par or better.

Collins shot 73 in the second round, leaving Senior to lead all alone, and that he did. Senior shot 65 in the second round for a five-stroke lead at the halfway point. "I thought I could birdie every hole," Senior said, and the spirit was still with him in the third round, when he dropped a 50-foot putt for a birdie at the 18th to keep his five-stroke margin with a 69 in changing winds. "If I happen to win on Sunday," the little Senior offered, "you won't see a happier chappie."

At the final counting, American Chip Beck, another guy in search of his game, tied for 14th at seven-under 281. Van de Velde closed with 75, his only round out of the 60s, and tied for 20th with Norman, who also shot a final-round 75. Far back in the field were two big names — Steve Elkington, at par 288, and American Stewart Cink, who started 71-67 and finished 76-78 for a 292 total.

As for Senior, he just did happen to win. His five-shot lead just drained away. He bogeyed the last two holes — three-putting the 18th — for a 73 and the one-stroke win. "I was leaking a bit of oil at the end," the happy Senior admitted, "but I hung on."

Australian Open—A$1,500,000
Winner: Peter Lonard

The Australian Open at Moonah Links closed out 2003 on the Australasian Tour. Promising Australian Chris Downes almost won. It was looking like his championship through the first three rounds. Ricky Barnes, the 2002 U.S. Amateur champion, almost broke through after turning professional six months earlier. There was one crazy dash for the finish line, when any one of seven players could have won. Peter Lonard got there first with his very last chance — a birdie at the final hole.

"It was," said Lonard, with a shrug and a grin, "a wonderful way to finish the year." Indeed — a wonderful way to finish a tournament too. The birdie at the 18th in the final round gave Lonard a three-under-par 69 for a nine-under total of 279 and his first victory since the 2002 Australian Masters. He won by a stroke over Downes and another Aussie, Steven Leaney, who also was runner-up to Jim Furyk in the U.S. Open.

Downes led or shared the lead through the first three rounds, beginning with an especially impressive five-under 67 in the first round, when only 30 of the 123 starters broke par in worsening weather. Stuart Appleby, one of the international Aussies, shot a hot-cold 69. He birdied his first four holes, bogeyed the next two, then had three birdies and two bogeys over the last 10 holes. The chase got really crowded in the third round. Downes, who was tied with defending champion Stephen Allan after two rounds, shot 71 to take the lead. Leaney (68) was a stroke behind, and seven others, including Allan and Barnes, were tied a further stroke back.

The final round was played in wind and rain, and the chase was on. At one point, seven players held a share of the lead, including Barnes, who was enjoying his finest hour. He had missed the cut in all six PGA Tour events he played since turning professional in July. This wouldn't be his break-through, but it was his best finish as a pro. A closing 73 tied him for ninth at five-under 283. Among other prominent players in the hunt, Robert Allenby tied for sixth and Stuart Appleby for 11th.

Coming down the final stretch in lousy weather, it was a battle between Lonard and Leaney. Both had shot the first nine in even par. Lonard then caught Leaney with a birdie at the 15th. Leaney had a chance to retake the lead at the 17th, but his birdie putt lipped out. Then Lonard finished brilliantly. At the 18th, he lofted his approach to nine feet and made the birdie for the lead. This left Leaney one last gasp — an 18-foot birdie putt of his own to force a playoff. But his putt pulled up short and left. Lonard had his Australian Open.

"To be part of Australian golf history for the rest of time is something special," Lonard said. "You look through the list of winners, it's a catalog of the best golfers of all time. I'm privileged to be a part of it."

12. African Tours

It was a great year for South Africans, especially for Ernie Els, currently the best player on the continent. Els, ranked third in the world, won eight times on five continents in 2003, making him the runaway leader among the men. His only win in his homeland came over Christmas in his own tournament, the 36-hole Ernie Els Invitational, where he shot a round of 60. His other victories were in America (two), Europe (three), Australia (one) and Asia (one).

Retief Goosen, the seventh-ranked player in the world and the second-best South African in the game today, won in both America and Europe, but failed to capture a title in his homeland, while Rory Sabbatini, South Africa's sweet-swinging wonderboy, won on the U.S. Tour but didn't do much at home either. Zimbabwe's Nick Price did not win, but remained among the world's best with a No. 12 ranking. South Africa's Tim Clark, ranked 67th in the world, also did not win.

Like so many other international golfers, Africa's best seem destined to abandon their home tour for the pot of gold that has become the U.S. PGA Tour. Even those who did play well in Africa in 2003, such as Trevor Immelman, who won twice, unequivocally stated that their ultimate goals were to play in the U.S. "Of course that's the objective," Immelman said after taking both the South African Airways Open and the Dimension Data Pro-Am. "The best players in the world play in America. To be able to compete at that level is what every golfer wants."

Immelman, age 23 and ranked 75th in the world, came to America towards the end of the year and teamed with Sabbatini to win the WGC World Cup for South Africa.

South Africa also was the host to the 2003 Presidents Cup, held at the Links at Fancourt near George. Spectators turned out by the tens of thousands to watch Gary Player and Jack Nicklaus lead the International and American squads to a draw in what many thought was the ultimate coming-out party for this bi-annual team event. The fact that it ended without a winner was irritating to some watching at home half a world away. For those who witnessed Tiger Woods and Ernie Els battle into the darkness, there was no other outcome that seemed acceptable. As Els said, "This is the biggest sporting event in the history of South Africa. Everybody loved it."

While Els and Goosen were raking up worldwide wins, the Sunshine Tour, which runs most of the professional events in South Africa, produced a plethora of different winners. With the exception of Immelman, the tour had a different winner every week, including some familiar names, like Des Terblanche, Nic Henning, Desvonde Botes and Hennie Otto, and some new ones, like Tyrol Auret, Dion Fourie and Johan Edfors.

Lee Westwood and Simon Hobday won the unofficial Nelson Mandela Invitational. It was Westwood's third victory of the year after two winless seasons and a drop to 182nd in the World Ranking. "You draw confidence from any time you win a tournament, playing well and hitting a few good shots coming down the stretch," Westwood said. "This is no different."

Sergio Garcia hoped some of that same confidence carried forward for him. Garcia went winless in America and Europe in 2003, but won late in the year at the Nedbank Golf Challenge. "It feels great," Garcia said after holding off Goosen in a final-round duel. "Hopefully, this will give me a boost going into next year."

South African Airways Open—£500,000
Winner: Trevor Immelman

Trevor Immelman grew up in Cape Town, playing at Erinvale Golf Club, which made victory there even sweeter in the South African Airways Open. It was an emotional victory because of that, and because the 23-year-old Immelman's father, Johann, is the tour's commissioner. Trevor won in a playoff over Tim Clark, the highest-rated South African in the field at No. 58, since compatriots Ernie Els and Retief Goosen were off in Hawaii at the Mercedes Championships.

Immelman, ranked 102nd in he world, shot 67 in the final round to tie Clark at 14-under-par 274 and won on the fist playoff hole, the 18th, when he hit a nine iron to within two inches of the hole. Clark, who closed with 69, knew where he had lost the tournament. In the third round, he held a three-shot lead over Jean Hugo and a seven-shot edge over Immelman before taking a quadruple-bogey nine on the par-five 16th, a meltdown that included four wedge shots from the edge of the green. When Immelman birdied the same hole, it was a five-stroke swing.

Clark held a two-shot lead with three holes to play, but Immelman birdied the 16th and 18th to get in the clubhouse first at 274. When Clark's birdie efforts failed to fall on the final three holes, it was back to the 18th for the playoff and the dramatic ending.

Hugo, who played alongside Clark in the final group, struggled in the final round. His 73 left him tied for third with Bradford Vaughan, Tjaart van der Walt and Bobby Lincoln at 277.

Dunhill Championship—£500,000
Winner: Mark Foster

Trevor Immelman came within one shot of matching Ernie Els' feat of back-to-back victories. While Els was holding off Aaron Baddeley in a playoff in Hawaii for his second consecutive U.S. PGA Tour win, Immelman was losing the Dunhill Championship in Johannesburg to an eagle in the Southern Africa Tour's first six-way playoff. Mark Foster was the victor, holing a 40-footer for eagle on the second extra hole.

Foster started the final round three shots behind leader Bradford Vaughan before making four straight birdies on the sixth through ninth holes to gain a share of the lead with nine to play. Vaughan had a chance to put it away, but he missed numerous short putts over the final nine holes. That allowed Immelman, Doug McGuigan, Anders Hansen and Paul Lawrie to join the fray. Lawrie had the low round of the day, finishing with a flurry of birdies for a 65 to be first in at 15-under-par 273. Immelman was next in after making a birdie at the 18th for a 67 and a share of the lead.

McGuigan appeared to have it under control late in the day. He forged a two-shot lead through 16 holes, but gave it all back when he hit his approach shot in a greenside bunker at the 17th and took two strokes to get out. That led to a double bogey, which gave new life to a host of players. McGuigan parred the 18th for a 68 to join the group at 273, along with Hansen, who shot 69 on Sunday. Vaughan was last in with a 71.

Foster, who struggled with a stomach virus the final day, showed the hot hand in the playoff, making a birdie on the first extra hole and an eagle on the second to put this one away.

As for the 23-year-old Immelman, he thought he should have won this title outright. But he wasn't complaining about a victory and a second in the first two weeks of the year. He also wasn't interested in any further comparisons to Els. "I don't see myself as the next Ernie," he said. "I've got to do my own thing. I've been put on this planet to play golf, and I want to be the best that Trevor Immelman can be."

Dimension Data Pro-Am—R2,000,000
Winner: Trevor Immelman

When Trevor Immelman held off Ernie Els, Darren Clarke and David Frost to win the Vodacom Championship in 2000, everyone predicted great things for him. Three years later, he appeared to be living up to those expectations. With a final-round of 71 at Gary Player Country Club, Immelman held on to win the Dimension Data Pro-Am and take home his second Southern African title in three weeks.

Immelman seemed to have this one well in hand after rounds of 67, 68 and 65 left him three shots clear of American Bruce Vaughan and seven ahead of fellow South African Andrew McLardy. That's where it stayed through most of the first nine. But McLardy put together a string of birdies in the middle of his round to move within three of the lead, while Vaughan added a couple of birdies on the back to stay close. When Vaughan birdied the 15th, the lead was down to two. Immelman then bogeyed the 16th to cut his margin to one. McLardy joined the party with another birdie on the 17th to move within one of the lead as well.

Both McLardy and Vaughan had birdie putts on the 18th to tie, but failed to convert. That gave Immelman a little breathing room. He two-putted for par at the last for a 17-under-par 271 total and a one-stroke victory. McLardy shot 65 to share second place with Vaughan, who shot a closing 69, at 272, while Nick Price surged into the fray with 66 for a 274 total and fourth place.

The victory put Immelman atop the Southern Africa Order of Merit going into the season-ending Tour Championship.

Southern Africa Tour Championship—R2,000,000
Winner: Hennie Otto

After shooting 64 on Friday to take a three-shot lead into the weekend and following it up with a 68 on Saturday to extend his lead to six, Hennie Otto had to be feeling pretty good about his chances in the Southern Africa Tour Championship. A few quick birdies on Sunday and Otto should have been able to put it on cruise control.

What no one expected was the hottest player in South Africa to birdie seven of his first nine holes to go out in 29. But that's what Trevor Immelman did. Suddenly, this one was a horserace. Immelman, who was coming off two victories and a second in the previous three weeks, trailed by seven at the start of the final round, but pulled to within two at the turn.

It remained there, as Otto made two birdies on the front nine and three birdies and one bogey on the back for a closing 68 and a 17-under-par 271 total. Immelman matched Otto's back-nine 34 for a course-record 63, but that wasn't good enough. The 23-year-old South African finished alone in second at 273, six shots clear of third-place finisher Craig Lile, who shot 70.

Mark McNulty and Mark Mouland shared fourth at six-under-par 282, while James Kingston and Titch Moore were tied for sixth at 283.

Immelman led the field in birdies for the week with 24, but he also made nine bogeys, which ultimately cost him a shot at the title. Still, he won the Southern Africa Order of Merit title, finishing well ahead of second-place earner Mark Foster.

Stanbic Zambia Open—€100,000
Winner: Johan Edfors

The weather won this one. With rain falling by the bucketful for most of the week and the third round canceled due to severe thunderstorms, Johan Edfors shot a spectacular 66 in a constant downpour for a nine-under-par 206 total and a four-stroke victory in the Stanbic Zambia Open.

"I love the rain," the Swede said after making up five strokes on second-round leaders Scott Drummond, Desvonde Botes, Travis Fraser and Sebastian Fernandez. Edfors then extended his cushion to four with the best score of the final day by a mile. "For some reason I always play well in the rain," he said.

The leaders certainly didn't play well. Botes shot 79 to fall into a tie for 17th at 216. Fernandez did a little better, shooting 78 to finish in a tie for 12th at 215, while Fraser couldn't wait to get off the course. He shot 88, the highest score of the tournament by six strokes.

That left the door open for Edfors, who made two birdies and one bogey on the first nine, before putting together three consecutive birdies at the 10th, 11th and 12th. At the par-five 13th, he hit a beautiful second shot to within five feet of the hole and was looking at an easy eagle putt when the skies opened up again.

Play was suspended for an hour, and when it resumed, officials scrambled to dry the greens. The putting surfaces were like sponges, which was great for approach shots, but not so good for putts. Edfors missed his eagle attempt at the 13th, but tapped in for his fourth birdie in a row to take sole possession of the lead. Two more birdies at the 17th and 18th extended the margin to four over Michael Kirk and five over third-place finisher Scott Drummond.

FNB Botswana Open—R250,000
Winner: Trevor Fisher

Club professional Trevor Fisher, a 23-year-old in his first full year on the Southern Africa Tour, was never far from the lead in the FNB Botswana Open, which he considered "great" since his previous best finish was a tie for 10th in the 2002 Vodacom Players Championship. A 67 on Thursday put Fisher one shot off Sean Farrell's early lead, and a 68 on Friday moved him into a tie for the lead with Farrell with one round to play. Des Terblanche, the most experienced of the leaders, was only one back going into Saturday's final round, which made him the favorite to take the title.

For a while Terblanche appeared to have control. He was six under par through 12 holes, enough to overtake the leaders and open a two-stroke cushion. Then Terblanche made one bad swing. He pushed his approach at the 13th into a greenside bunker and the ball plugged under the lip. One failed attempt to get out of the sand led to a double bogey, and just like that, Terblanche and Fisher were tied at 12 under with five holes to play.

That's when the club professional caught fire. Fisher reeled off birdies at the 14th and 15th to take a one-shot lead, as Terblanche also birdied the 15th. The lead stayed at one as both players parred the 16th. Then Fisher put it away with a five iron on the par-three 17th that hit just short of the hole and stopped five feet away. He made the putt for birdie while Terblanche missed the green to the right and made bogey.

Terblanche birdied the 18th to shoot 67 and finish at 203, but it was too little too late. Fisher two-putted for par at the final hole for 66, a 201 total and a two-stroke victory.

"I can't believe it," Fisher said. "This means so much to me." More than anything, the win meant a two-year exemption on the Southern Africa Tour. "It's great to not have to play those pre-qualifying rounds anymore," he said. "I just wanted to have fun out there, leading a tournament for the first time in my career. The win was a real bonus."

Limpopo Industrelek Classic—R300,000
Winner: Marc Cayeux

With rounds of 68 and 64 and a one-stroke lead going to the final round, Marc Cayeux tried not to think about becoming only the second to win the Limpopo Industrelek Classic more than once. When he birdied five of his first seven holes to extend the lead to three, Cayeux relaxed and cruised to victory.

"I'm very proud of the way I played this week," Cayeux said after closing with 65 for a 197 total, three clear of Tyrol Auret, who shot 67, 66 and 67.

Auret rolled in a birdie putt at the 10th to cut the lead to two, but Cayeux responded with birdies at the 12th, 14th and a 20-footer for birdie from the fringe at the 15th that extended the lead to four with three holes to play. That allowed Cayeux to make bogey on two of the last three holes and still win by three strokes for his second victory in this event, the first coming in 2000. Hennie Otto was the only other player to have won the Limpopo Industrelek Classic twice (1999 and 2001).

The three birdies on the second nine got Cayeux to 21 under par before he pushed his tee shot into a greenside bunker at the par-three 16th for his first bogey. By then it didn't matter. The lead was three when he pulled his approach into the left rough at the 18th and made his second bogey in three holes, but Auret bogeyed the final hole as well.

Sean Ludgater equaled Cayeux's 65 to finish third at 202, while first-round leader Sean Farrell closed with a 69 for fourth at 203.

Capital Alliance Royal Swazi Sun Open—R250,000
Winner: Des Terblanche

With two top-10s in as many weeks (including a runner-up finish to Trevor Fisher at the FNB Botswana Open) and a modified-Stableford format that rewarded a lot of birdies, Des Terblanche felt pretty good about his chances going into the final round at the Capital Alliance Royal Swazi Sun Open. He had led from the start, posting 13 points in the first round and 18 in the second to lead by three points with one round to play. A few more birdies on Saturday and Terblanche should be able to break his three-year winless drought on the Southern Africa Tour.

The birdies weren't all that plentiful in the final round. Terblanche struggled with his putter and assembled only eight points through 13 holes. He gave three of those back when he pushed his tee shot into the water at the 14th and took double bogey. "I played solid, but I just didn't make any putts," Terblanche said. "It was really a grinding day."

Meanwhile, Brazilian Adilson da Silva was going on a birdie binge that wouldn't end until he was in the clubhouse with 36 points, 15 in the final round. He picked up six points with three consecutive birdies at the seventh, eighth and ninth, six more with another streak of birdies at the 12th, 13th and 14th, and four more with birdies at the 17th and 18th. His only lost point of the day came when he bogeyed the 16th. While Terblanche was going through his troubles at the 14th, da Silva was sitting in the clubhouse with 36 points.

Terblanche finished with only five points in the final round, but still had a chance. The 18th was the first playoff hole, and both players missed the green. When Terblanche chipped the ball to a foot, the pressure was on da Silva. The Brazilian had spent a little too much time in the locker room and not enough on the putting green before the playoff. His nine-footer for par didn't come close. Terblanche rolled in the one-footer for par and the win.

Devonvale Championship—R200,000
Winner: Hendrik Buhrmann

With a one-shot lead going into the final round and three birdies to start his Saturday, Hendrik Buhrmann appeared poised to capture the Devonvale Championship. That was before Marc Cayeux and Shaun Norris went on birdie binges that almost ruined Buhrmann's day.

Cayeux had four consecutive birdies on the first nine to stay close to Buhrmann, who also rolled in a five-footer for birdie at the seventh to keep the lead at three over Cayeux and four over Norris. The leader stumbled on the 10th, hitting a three wood behind a tree and making his only bogey of the week. Buhrmann recovered with birdies at the 11th and 12th that extended the lead to four, but Cayeux came back with birdies at the 12th, 14th and 15th to cut the lead to one.

Norris also mounted a late charge with birdies on three of his last four holes for a final-round 65 and a 17-under-par 199 total. Cayeux was looking to better that, but he bogeyed the 16th to give Buhrmann a two-shot edge with two holes to play. A birdie at the 17th by Cayeux didn't gain him any ground. The leader rolled in a short birdie putt right behind him to keep the lead at two. That gave Buhrmann some breathing room, which he needed. He missed the green at the 18th and made a bogey to shoot a final-round 67 for an 18-under-par 198 total and a one-shot win over Cayeux and Norris.

Des Terblanche knew what he was doing as well. The big South African continued his good play in the homeland with rounds of 67, 66 and 67 for a share of third with Justin Hobday at 200.

Canon Classic—R200,000
Winner: Tyrol Auret

With three birdies in his final four holes of regulation and two critical putts in successive visits to the 18th green, Tyrol Auret picked up his first win on the Southern Africa Tour with a one-hole playoff victory over Warren Abery in the Canon Classic. The win came on a day when Auret had the lead, lost it, and gained a share of it again on the final green, before ending things with a 24-foot birdie putt on the first extra hole.

"It feels great," the winner said after rounds of 65, 68 and 67 for a 13-under-par 200 total at Bramble Hill Golf Club in Fancourt. "If you keep knocking on the door long enough, it's going to open sometime. My putter was hot all week, but especially in the final round. The putts I made were just phenomenal. It was just meant to be."

That didn't appear to be the case with one hole left to play in regulation. After starting the final round with a one-shot lead over Abery, Auret fell behind in the middle of the round, but clawed his way back with birdies on the 15th and 17th. Still he trailed Abery, who was six under on his round through 17 holes, by two as they stood on 18th tee. Abery three-putted the 18th for bogey and a round of 66, while Auret, staring at a 36-footer for birdie, rolled the putt in the center of the hole to force a playoff. It was a two-shot swing no one saw coming.

Back on the 18th for extra holes, Abery hit his approach over the flag and off the back of the green, while Auret hit it pin high and 24 feet left. Abery hit a good chip and left himself a reasonable look at par, but he never got a chance to hit the putt. Just as he had done only minutes before, Auret rolled his birdie putt in the back of the hole to put an exclamation point on his victory.

Brett Liddle had the low round of the final day, 64, after taking temporary command of the lead with six birdies and an eagle through his first 12 holes. Liddle's putter cooled in the closing holes, and he finished the tournament at 202 and in fifth place, one shot behind Grant Muller and Justin Hobday.

Royal Swazi Sun Classic—R200,000
Winner: Nic Henning

Nic Henning had been there before, but it had been awhile. It was in 1999 that Henning held off Irish star Darren Clarke in a playoff to win his last title at the Vodacom Players Championship. So when Henning broke a three-way tie for the lead at the Royal Swazi Sun Classic with birdies at the second, fourth, fifth and sixth holes in the final round, everyone wondered if the lanky South African would remember how to put a tournament away.

Henning wondered the same. A birdie at the 12th gave him a three-shot lead over Mark Murless and a four-shot cushion over Andre Cruse. The only person who could stop Henning from winning was Henning, which is what almost happened.

Armed with a three-shot lead with two holes to play, Henning hit a solid approach shot into the 17th and promptly three-putted from 15 feet for bogey after Murless made birdie. Suddenly, the lead was one with the par-three 18th ahead. When Henning pushed his tee shot at the final hole into a greenside bunker, he couldn't stop the bad thoughts from creeping into his head. He had made a bogey at the third after a poor bunker shot, and was lucky to make par at the seventh after thinning a shot from a greenside bunker there. "I stood over that last bunker shot and said to myself, 'Well, there's nothing left to do. Just finish it off,'" Henning said.

That's what he did. The bunker shot took one hop and landed in the hole for a birdie two to cap off a final-round 67 and an 18-under-par 198 total, two better than Murless (who two-putted the final hole for par and a round of 69) and three clear of Cruse and Andre van Staden.

"It was a long finish, those last two holes," Henning said. "The bogey at 17 was pure nerves, because I hadn't won for a while before this. My seven-iron approach just made it over the water guarding the green, but the ball was in a hole. I didn't hit a bad third; it finished about 15 feet away. But then I went and three-putted. Thank goodness I didn't have to putt at the last."

Parmalat Classic—R200,000
Winner: Desvonde Botes

Nothing cures an ailing back like a victory. At least that's what Desvonde Botes said after winning the Parmalat Classic by two strokes. Botes shot a final-round 70 that included three late bogeys and one double bogey as wind gusts on Silver Lakes swirled at 20 miles an hour. A few dropped shots late in the day didn't matter as Botes birdied the final hole for a nine-under-par 207 total, two better than James Kingston and five clear of Nic Henning and second-round leader Andre Cruse.

The win was Botes' first after being sidelined for six months with back problems. "Last year was horrible," he said. "I've had the back problem on and off for most of my career. It's called a hernia of the disc, and it just requires a lot of stretching."

Botes stretched his way to victory thanks to some clutch early birdies and help from Cruse, who led by two strokes going into the final round after a

64 on Friday. Cruse couldn't hit the fairway in the final round. He shot 41 on the first nine and fell from contention. By the time he tapped in his final putt, Cruse had shot 76 and fallen into a tie for third with Henning at 211.

That opened the door for Botes, who came through with a 32 on the first nine that was capped by a spectacular greenside bunker shot on the par-five seventh. From a plugged lie with little green to work with, Botes blasted the ball to six inches and made the putt to reach 11 under and take a three-shot lead.

Botes made bogey at the 10th and double bogey at the 12th after hitting his second shot in the water hazard guarding the green. He followed that up with a bogey at the par-three 13th to fall into a tie with Kingston at seven under. "I just had to tell myself to forget about the drops and focus on my game again," Botes said.

He did just that, coming back with a two-putt birdie at the par-five 14th and a five-footer for birdie at the 15th. When Kingston made bogey at the 14th, Botes' lead was back to three. He made another bogey when he hit yet another approach into the water at the 17th, but rebounded with a closing birdie to extend the margin of victory to two.

Seekers Travel Pro-Am—R200,000
Winner: Chris Williams

The inaugural Seekers Travel Pro-Am wasn't supposed to be a marathon, especially given the brutal Dainfern heat that had professionals and amateurs chugging water. But that's how it turned out as 44-year-old Chris Williams and rookie Jason Jackson slugged it out for six extra holes in the longest playoff in Southern Africa Tour history before Williams put away the victory with a par on the par-five 17th after Jackson hit his second shot in the water.

It was an anticlimactic ending to one of the most riveting rounds of the season. At the beginning of the day Jackson trailed second-round leader Thabang Simon by five strokes after Simon's course-record round of 61. Williams was six back, while Ashley Roestoff was three off the lead.

Simon stumbled out of the gate with a double bogey on the first hole and never recovered. He limped in with 78 to finish at 210 and in a tie for 16th place.

That left the tournament wide open. Jackson, a recent graduate of Arkansas State who said his main objective "was to make the cut this week," birdied the second, third, fourth, eighth and ninth holes to take the lead at 12 under par. Williams was close behind. He birdied the second, third, fourth, sixth and ninth holes to get to 11 under. This was far from a two-man race. As many as eight players were within three shots heading into the final nine.

When Jackson flubbed a chip and made bogey at the 11th, there was a two-way tie for the lead. When he double-bogeyed the 14th after taking two to get out of a greenside bunker, Williams was alone at the top.

Jackson charged back with an eagle at the par-five 15th to reach 13 under, while Williams was sitting the clubhouse at that same number after a final-round 65. All Jackson needed was a par at the 18th to force a playoff. A birdie would win it for him outright. He sprayed another approach shot into a bunker and had to make a 15-footer for par to keep from falling out of the lead. When that putt fell, Jackson was in with 66 and a 13-under-par 203 total. Roestoff had a similar 15-footer at the 18th, but his was for birdie to shoot 68 and join the playoff. That putt also found the bottom of the hole.

The playoff began at the 18th hole, and all three players made par. The second time down the 18th, Roestoff hit his second shot over the green and made bogey to be eliminated as both Williams and Jackson made pars.

Another trip down the 18th produced two birdies. Then the pair moved on to the first hole where they made pars again. Pars at the second sent the playoff to the 17th, where Jackson made eagle earlier. This time through he pushed his second shot into the pond. After Williams reached the green in two, Jackson hit another ball in the water from the drop zone to remove all drama. Williams three-putted for his par.

Bearing Man Highveld Classic—R200,000
Winner: Dion Fourie

After a three-year hiatus from the Southern Africa Tour, Dion Fourie returned with a splash, birdieing three of his final four holes for a final-round 68 and a one-stroke victory in the Bearing Man Highveld Classic. It was a dramatic ending to birdie-filled day.

Fourie, who came back to golf after realizing that a desk job wasn't for him, trailed 20-year-old Divan van den Heever by three strokes going into the final round. When van den Heever failed to make any birdies on the first nine, five players charged into a tie for the lead at 13 under par. Among them was Ashley Roestoff, who moved into a share of the lead with two birdies and then took the lead alone with a birdie at the par-five 10th to reach 14 under.

Roestoff, who lost in a playoff the week before at the Seekers Travel Pro-Am, fell away with bogeys at the 13th and 14th. He finished with 71 for a 13-under-par total of 203. For a while that looked like a good number. Rookie Albert Kruger shot 67 on Saturday and was thrilled to sit in the clubhouse at 203 and watch the rest of the field take a shot at his score. Tyrol Auret was next in at 203 under when he finished with 66.

Thirty minutes later, a new benchmark was set when Desvonde Botes birdied the 17th and parred the 18th for a 65 and 14-under-par 202 total. The only players on the course with a chance to beat that score were van den Heever and Fourie.

"It was getting quite ridiculous with all the names on the leaderboard," Fourie said. "I felt like we were trying to force the birdies to come, and that's when I said to my caddie that we just needed to chill out and they would come on their own."

Moments after that discussion, Fourie rolled in a 15-footer for birdie at the 15th to get back to 13 under. He reached 14 under when his birdie putt at the 16th found the hole, and when he hit his second shot at the par-five 17th to 12 feet, the tournament seemed to be his. He missed the eagle, but tapped in a birdie to get to 15 under, which is where he finished, with a 201 total.

Van den Heever could have forced a playoff after making a 12-footer for birdie at the 15th and hitting his second shot at the 17th to within eight inches of the hole for an eagle. He found the bunker with his second shot at the 18th and failed to make a par. His 72 left him tied with Botes at 202.

Platinum Classic—R500,000
Winner: Doug McGuigan

After a series of disappointments that included losing the Nashua Masters three years ago when Mark McNulty fired a 61, and then losing again this year in a six-way playoff at the Dunhill Championship, Doug McGuigan had to be thinking "Here we go again," as he saw his name fall from the top spot in the final round of the Platinum Classic.

This time Ashley Roestoff threatened to keep McGuigan winless. After starting the final round tied with Alan Michell and two ahead of Roestoff, McGuigan played his first four holes in one under par, only to fall a shot down to Roestoff, who began his final round with four consecutive birdies.

McGuigan battled back with four birdies in the next eight holes to tie. Roestoff lipped out a chip shot for birdie at the 12th, and both missed birdie putts inside seven feet on the 13th.

McGuigan missed an opportunity to take the lead at the par-three 17th after Roestoff flew his tee shot over the green and bladed a chip shot 40 feet below the hole. Even though his ball was sitting perfectly in the fringe, McGuigan hit his chip shot 10 feet beyond the hole and missed his par effort after Roestoff two-putted for bogey.

At the 18th, McGuigan hit his approach 40 feet below and left of the hole, while Roestoff was 25 feet away. "On the 18th green, I thought I should just get my 40-foot putt close to the hole and try to make a playoff," McGuigan said. "But, fortunately, it went in."

The putt for birdie at the final hole gave McGuigan a final round of 67 and a 17-under-par 199 total, one better than Roestoff, who missed his birdie putt at the 18th and finished with 66.

Nelson Mandela Invitational
Winners: Lee Westwood/Simon Hobday

Lee Westwood and partner Simon Hobday shot a best-ball 64 to finish at 15-under-par 273 and win the Nelson Mandela Invitational by two strokes over Tim Clark and Hugh Baiocchi.

"You draw confidence from any time you win a tournament, playing well and hitting a few good shots coming down the stretch," Westwood said after capping his third victory of the year with birdies at two of his final three holes. "This is no different."

It was Hobday's second Nelson Mandela Invitational title and he couldn't have been happier. "It feels great to win it for a second time," Hobday said. "The wind was blowing here, but otherwise this is a very relaxing tournament to play in, and I've always had great company playing in the event."

Andrew Coltart and John Mashego finished in third at 276, one clear of Omar Sandys and John Bland.

Presidents Cup
Winner: United States and International Teams Tied

The United States and International teams had played to a 17-17 tie in the Presidents Cup after four days, then three extra holes by their designated playoff competitors, Tiger Woods and Ernie Els respectively, as darkness was arriving over the Links Course at the Fancourt Hotel and Country Club in George, South Africa.

The team captains, Jack Nicklaus and Gary Player, discussed among themselves and with their teams what they should do next, considering that all had other plans and the charter airline flight to America was scheduled for later that night. After a cell phone call to Tim Finchem, the PGA Tour commissioner, Nicklaus proposed that the event be declared a tie, with Jack's American team, as the defending champion, retaining the cup. The Internationals wanted to continue playing instead.

Nicklaus countered that the teams be declared co-champions, and that was it, as Nicklaus and Player raised their right arms with hands clasped.

"We came halfway around the world to do something for the betterment of golf. Is there any doubt in anybody's mind we accomplished that?" Nicklaus said. "If Gary and I violated the agreement we signed about producing a winner through a playoff, so be it. We made our views known before we even came here, and that hasn't changed. Not necessary."

"What difference does it make, where the cup goes?" added Nicklaus, who figured that regardless of the outcome, the trophy was bound for PGA Tour headquarters in Ponte Vedra Beach, Florida.

The Americans had to rally for 7½ of 12 available points in the singles matches on the final day because they had been swept 6-0 in Saturday's fourball (better-ball) matches. The Internationals led 3½ to 2½ after the alternate-shot matches on the first day. The United States took 7 of the 10 points on Friday, with both fourball and alternate-shot matches, to carry an American lead of 9½ to 6½ into the third day. The Saturday sweep put the Internationals in front 12½ to 9½.

With 17 of the world's top 22 players competing, the Sunday pairings looked like some of the best match-ups of the year. In the first match out, U.S. Open champion Jim Furyk downed Masters winner Mike Weir of Canada, 3 and 1. A few minutes later, the Americans were within one point as Jerry Kelly held on to beat Tim Clark of South Africa, 1 up, in the first of four matches that would go to the final hole, a reachable par-five with a green that looked like the burial ground for two elephants and a humpback whale.

The Internationals rallied with K.J. Choi of Korea smothering Justin Leonard 4 and 2, and Peter Lonard of Australia whipping Fred Funk 4 and 3.

The surprises for the United States turned out to be Charles Howell, who won his singles match 4 and 3 over Adam Scott of Australia and who went 3-2-0 for the week (and might have gone undefeated if not for having to play Tiger Woods' errant tee shots in the alternate-shot format), and Jay Haas, the oldest man in the field at 49, who thumped Stephen Leaney of Australia on Sunday and extended his record to 2-1-1. With those two points in the bag, the Americans looked to their big guns to close the deal.

But Phil Mickelson went 0-5 for the week, losing in the singles 2 and 1 to Retief Goosen of South Africa. Then David Toms lost his fourth match

Masters Tournament

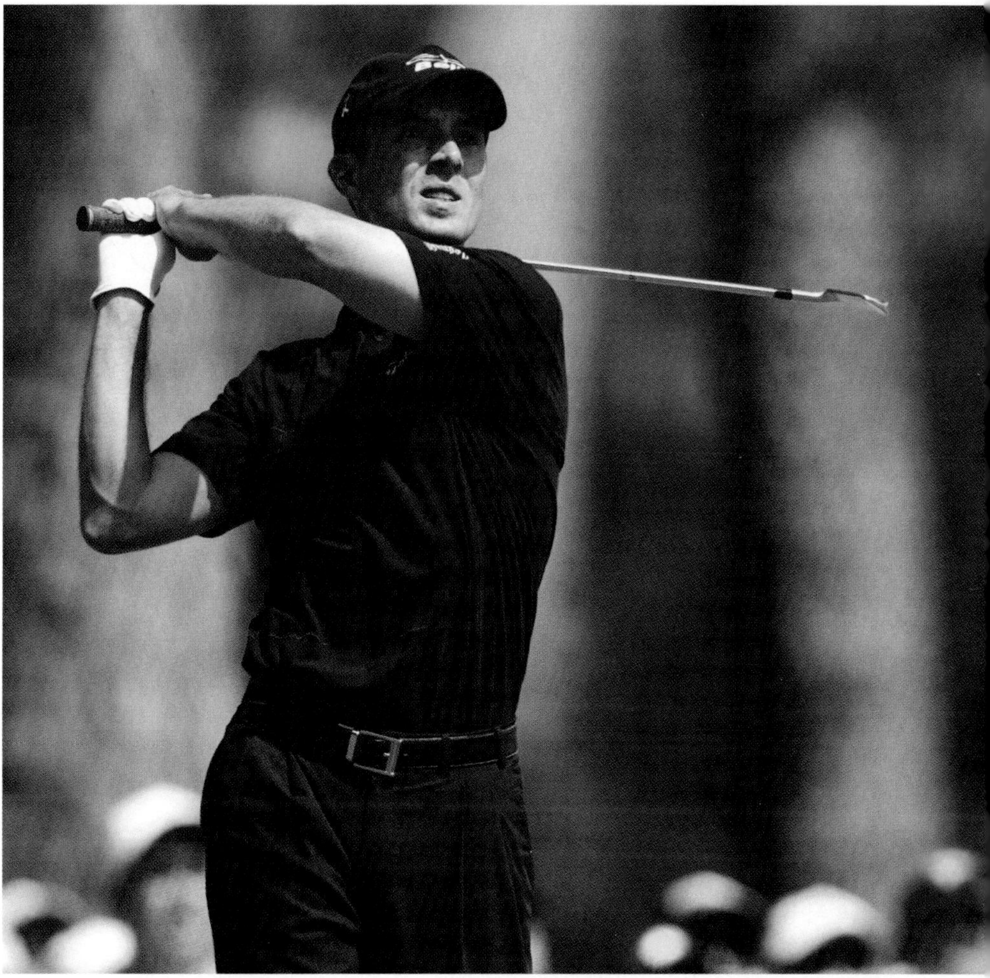

Getty Images

Harry How/Getty Images

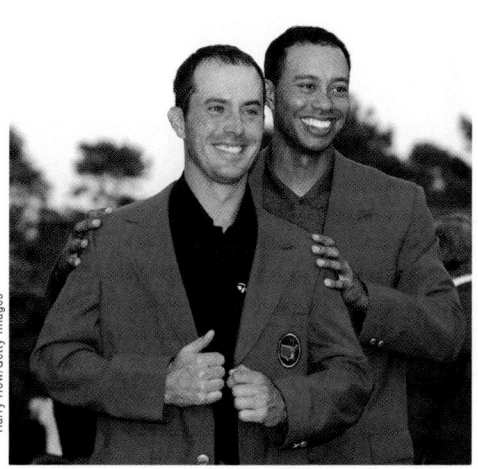

Mike Weir had three victories by April, including the Masters Tournament, to become the world's best left-handed golfer. Tiger Woods (left) presented the champion's green jacket.

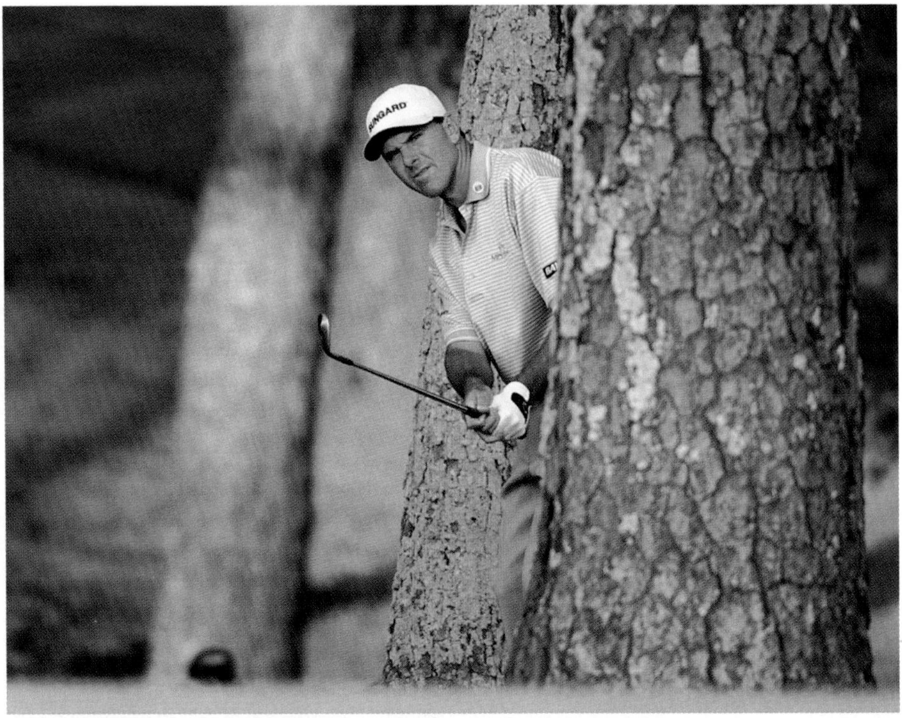

Harry How/Getty Images

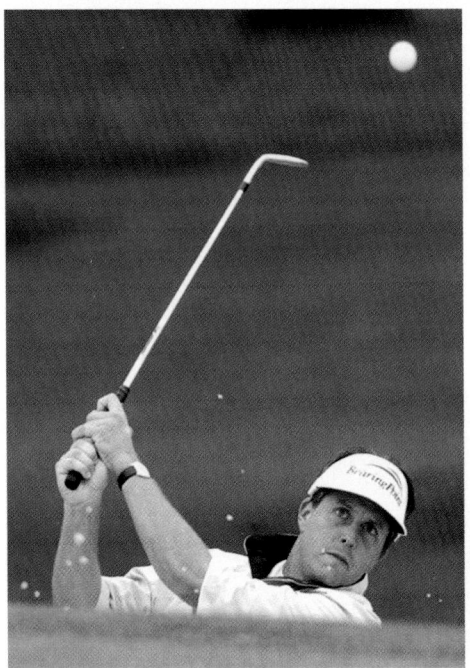

A 65 in the final round put Len Mattiace in a Masters playoff, where he found trouble in the trees.

Harry How/Getty Images

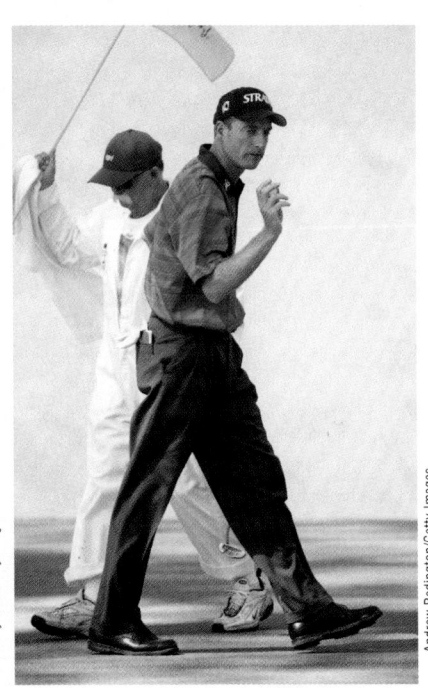

Phil Mickelson was third, two shots back.

Andrew Redington/Getty Images

Jim Furyk took fourth place.

Harry How/Getty Images

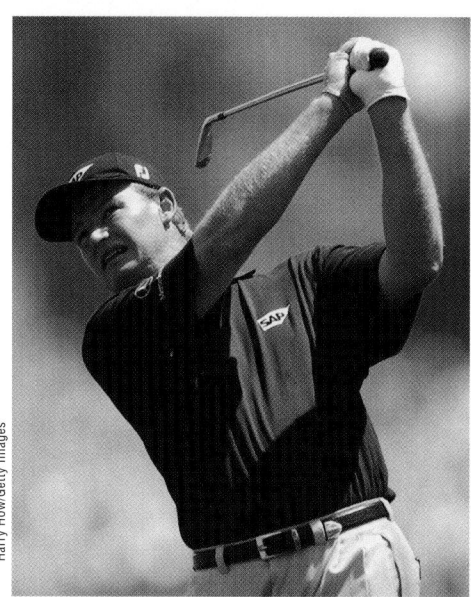

Ernie Els began with 79 and tied for sixth.

Harry How/Getty Images

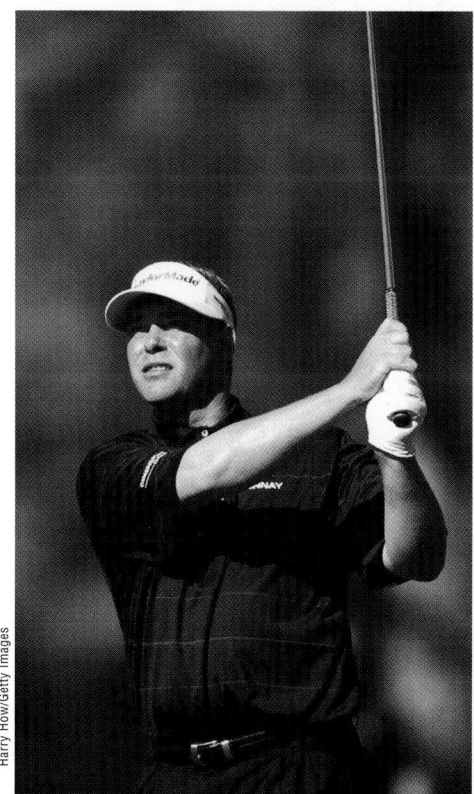

Starting with 66, Darren Clarke fell to 28th.

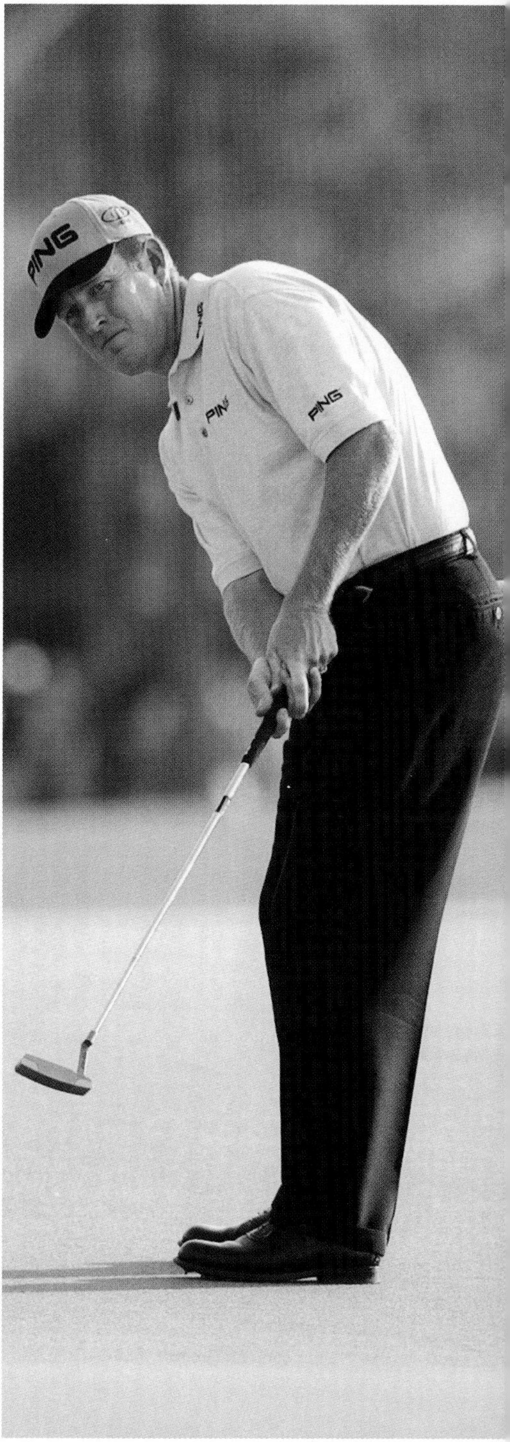

Harry How/Getty Images

Jeff Maggert had a 66-75 weekend to be fifth.

Jim Furyk won the U.S. Open Championship by three strokes and set scoring records.

Phil Inglis

Stephen Leaney took second place.

Phil Inglis

Masters champion Mike Weir tied for third.

Michael C. Cohen

Bruce Edwards and Tom Watson were emotional favorites.

Michael C. Cohen

Kenny Perry shot 69-67 for a share of third.

Michael C. Cohen

With a final 78, Vijay Singh tied for 20th.

The Open Championship

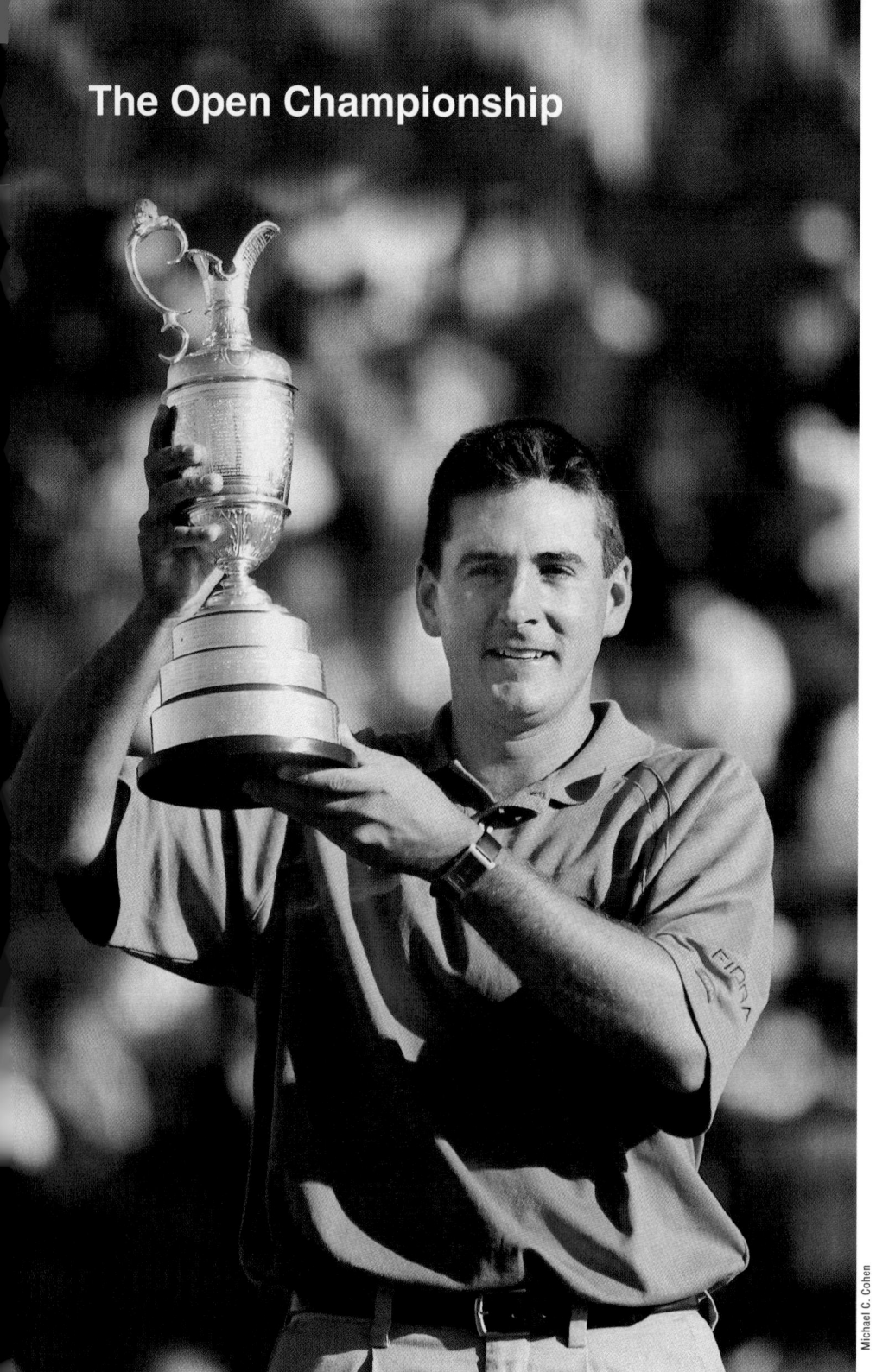

One of the most surprising major winners ever, Ben Curtis took home the claret jug.

Phil Inglis

Vijay Singh started with 75 and tied for second.

Michael C. Cohen

Thomas Bjorn led with three holes to pla

Phil Inglis

Davis Love was two strokes behind.

David Cannon/Getty Images

Tiger Woods lost a ball on his opening tee shot.

Andrew Redington/Getty Images

Mark Roe was disqualified, along with Jesper Parnevik.

PGA Championship

A seven-iron shot from 175 yards to within two inches of the hole enabled Shaun Micheel to win the PGA Championship by two strokes.

Michael C. Cohen

Michael C. Cohen

Michael C. Cohen

Chad Campbell was the runner-up.

Michael C. Cohen

Tim Clark finished 68-69 for third place.

Michael C. Cohen

Tiger Woods was 16 strokes behind.

Michael C. Cohen

Alex Cejka overcame a poor start to be fourth.

Michael C. Cohen

Ernie Els played steadily and tied for fifth.

With four victories, Vijay Singh had official PGA Tour earnings of over $7.5 million.

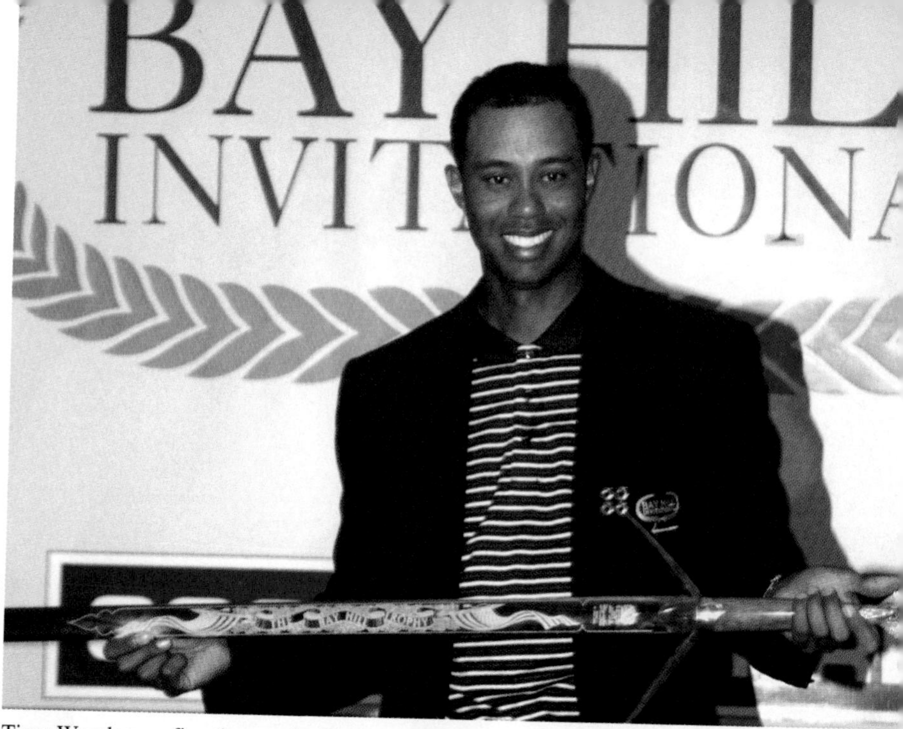

BAY HILL
INVITATIONAL

Tiger Woods won five times to be Player of the Year and got his fourth consecutive Bay Hill title.

Davis Love had four PGA Tour wins.

Jim Furyk climbed to No. 5 worldwide.

Mike Weir had a great year overall.

Chad Campbell won the Tour Championship.

Phil Mickelson had no victories.

Kenny Perry won three, including Milwaukee.

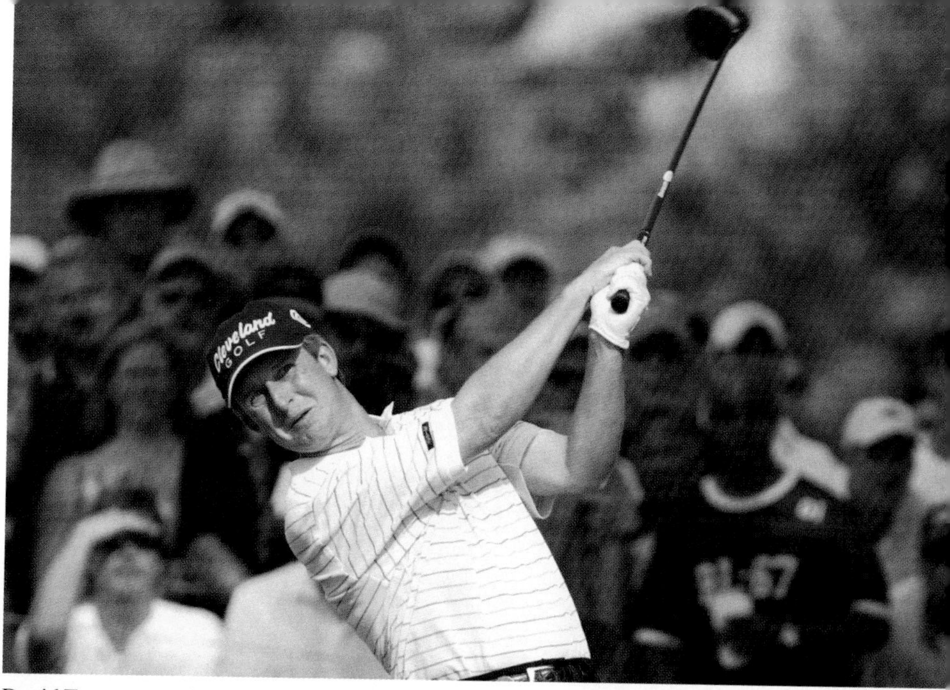

Michael C. Cohen

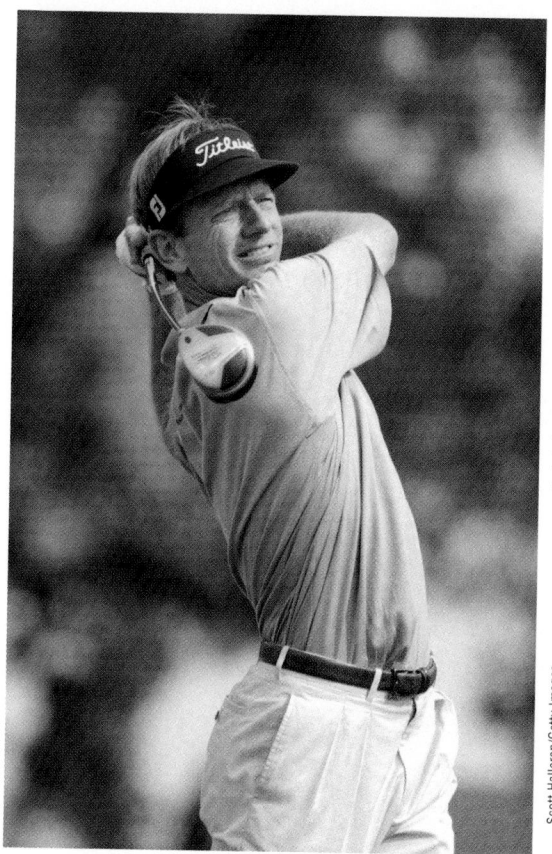

David Toms won twice, at Charlotte and Memphis, and held the ninth spot in the World Ranking.

Michael C. Cohen

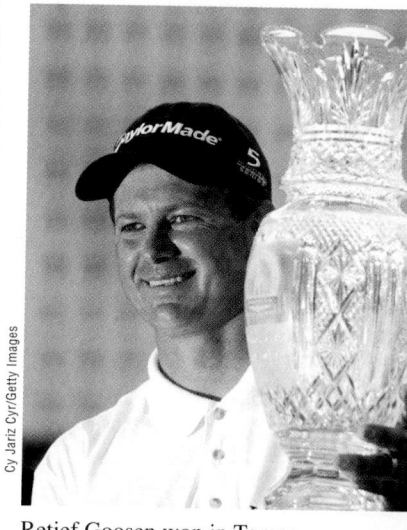

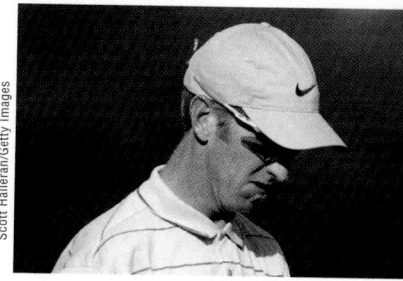

Brad Faxon rose from No. 48 to No. 22 in the world.

Cy Jariz Cyr/Getty Images

Retief Goosen won in Tampa.

Scott Halleran/Getty Images

David Duval had a dismal year.

Charles Howell was ranked No. 18.

Stuart Appleby took the title in Las Vegas.

Bob Tway was the Bell Canadian Open champion.

Robert Allenby won in Australia.

Chris DiMarco earned $2.7 million worldwide.

Jeff Gross/Getty Images

Peter Jacobsen won again at age 49.

Michael C. Cohen

Justin Leonard won the Honda Classic.

Scott Halleran/Getty Images

Jonathan Kaye was the Buick Classic winner.

Matthew Stockman/Getty Images

Age 46, Nick Price held a No. 12 world ranking.

Andy Lyons/Getty Images

Scott Hoch won the Ford Championship.

Jeff Gross/Getty Images

Fred Couples was a popular winner in Houston.

The Players Championship

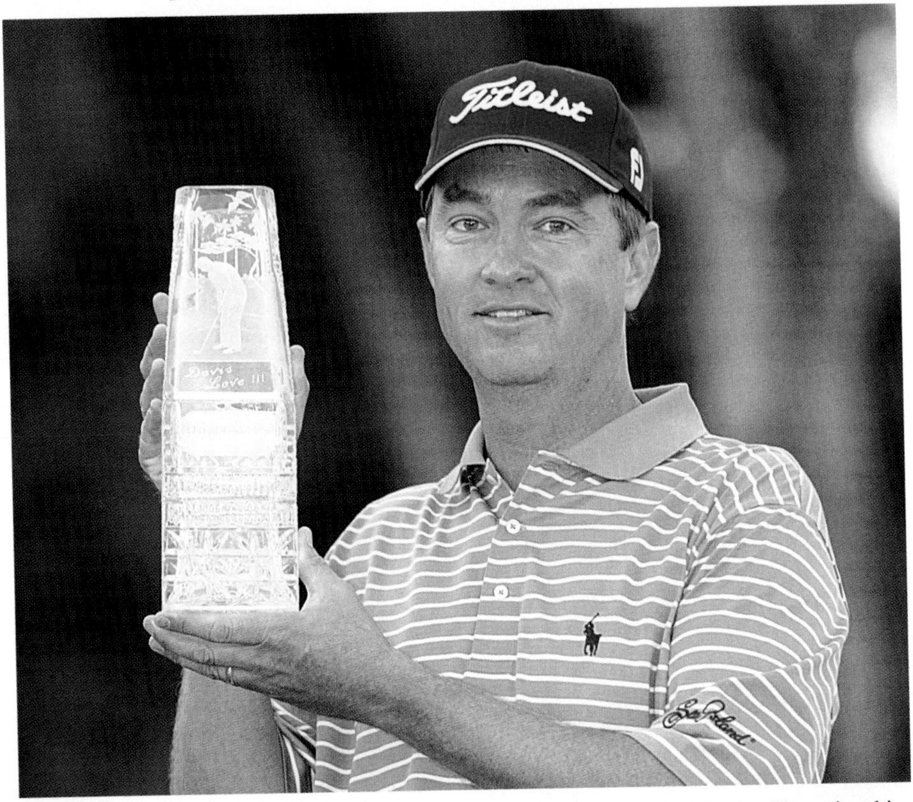

Jamie Squire/Getty Images

With 64 in the final round, Davis Love was a six-stroke winner in The Players Championship.

Jamie Squire/Getty Images

Jamie Squire/Getty Images

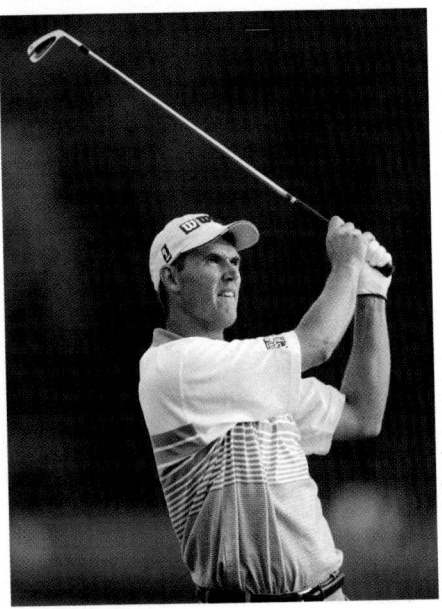

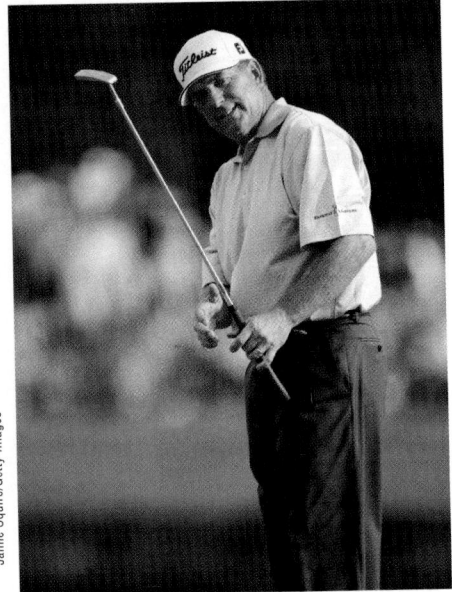

Padraig Harrington (left) and Jay Haas both finished with 72s and shared second place.

of the week when Vijay Singh of Fiji whipped him 4 and 3. It took Woods to stop the bleeding, which the world's No. 1 golfer did with a 4-and-3 win over Els.

The shot of the day came in the next match when Chris DiMarco, playing in his first international team event, hit a near-perfect eight iron to five feet on the difficult par-three 17th and rode the birdie to a 1-up victory over Stuart Appleby of Australia. Choked up beyond words afterwards, DiMarco call the shot, "the best I've ever hit in my life given the situation."

Kenny Perry and Nick Price of Zimbabwe went at it like two seasoned warriors. They halved only two of the final 10 holes, and the point was decided in the American's favor when Price missed a 15-footer for birdie on the final hole and broke his putter over his knee in disgust. Embarrassed, Price hid the putter under his arm as he congratulated Perry on his 1-up victory and 4-1-0 record for the week.

The teams were knotted at 16½ points each with one match left on the course. It came down to Davis Love and Robert Allenby of Australia. When Allenby found waist-high weeds on the 16th, Love took a 1-up lead which he maintained after a routine par on the 17th. All Love needed was a halve on the par-five 18th and the cup would remain with the Americans. A thin four-iron shot was followed by a weak wedge shot, and Love lost the hole, halving the match with Allenby and bringing the score to 17-all.

Unlike the Ryder Cup, where ties go to the defending champion, the rules of the Presidents Cup stated that the tie would be decided in a playoff between one player from each team, whose names had been sealed in envelopes since the start of the week. To the surprise of no one, the names turned out to be Woods and Els.

They played the 18th, first and second holes, sinking putt after crucial putt to keep the matches alive. "One of the most nerve-wracking moments I've ever had in golf," Woods said of his 15-footer on the third extra hole. After that, Nicklaus told Woods what the captains had in mind, if Els should also hole his putt. When Els made the 12-footer, Els said it was "probably the first time I've ever felt my legs shaking a little bit."

And so the Presidents Cup ended. "A perfect decision," said Woods, who had been in the chorus of players who disliked the playoff format from the beginning.

Nedbank Golf Challenge—US$4,060,000
Winner: Sergio Garcia

By the end of 2003, Sergio Garcia needed a confidence-booster and he found it at the Nedbank Golf Challenge, where he achieved his only victory of the year in a playoff with Retief Goosen. Garcia had finished 95th on the U.S. PGA Tour and 49th on the PGA European Tour money lists, far from the standard of play that Garcia expected and that others expected of him. "It's a great feeling to do this, especially after a year in which I have struggled to get my swing right, and it looks like I got it right," the 23-year-old Spaniard said.

Garcia posted scores of 68, 66, 70 and 70 for a 14-under-par 274 total over the Gary Player Country Club course in Sun City. He entered the final round leading by one stroke over Goosen, and lost the lead after shanking his approach shot to the first hole. He bounced back with birdies on the third and fourth holes, but trailed Goosen by one with five holes to play. They were tied after Goosen bogeyed the 14th, then both had pars on the remaining holes of regulation. Garcia won the title and the $1.2 million first prize with a birdie on the first playoff hole, the par-three 16th. He also won in a playoff on the same hole in 2001.

Hassan II Trophy—US$350,100
Winner: Santiago Luna

A good year for Santiago Luna was made even better by a victory in the Hassan II Trophy with $50,000 and a very valuable jeweled dagger as prizes for the champion. Luna repeated his 2002 victory in the event at Dar-es-Salam Golf Club in Rabat, Morocco. He also won in 1998.

With scores of 68, 70 and 69, Luna entered the fourth round with a six-stroke lead over Joakim Haeggman and Nicolas Colsaerts. Luna won with ease, shooting 70 for a 277 total, 15 under par, and Haeggman shot 68 to place second, four strokes behind at 281. Mark Roe was third at 282 after a closing 66, and Colsaerts shot 70 for fourth at 283.

Before coming to Morocco, Luna, who had three top-10 finishes earlier in the year in Europe, made the cut in his last six starts to keep his player's card. "I had a great end of the season," Luna said, "and it seems Morocco has always been lucky for me. Golf is like that, and so is life itself. Last year, I finished badly and had to fight to retain my card. This year the reverse has happened."

Ernie Els Invitational—R234,280
Winner: Ernie Els

In golf, eight generally is not a number held in high regard; for example, an eight scored on a single hole is known as a "snowman" for the two circles in the number, one atop the other. But eight was a lucky number in this year's Ernie Els Invitational, a 36-hole charity event in December over Fancourt Resort's Outeniqua and Montagu courses.

This was the eighth playing of the tournament and Els, the host, finally won. His margin was eight strokes and it was his eighth victory of the year worldwide. Els shot 65 in the first round but was joined in the lead by Bobby Lincoln. It was no contest in the second round as Els shot 60 while Lincoln soared to 68 and no other player in the field shot lower than 67. Els had a 125 total while Lincoln was second at 133 and last-year's winner, Louis Oosthuizen, was third at 136.

Senior Tours

Since its inception, the Champions Tour (formerly the Senior PGA Tour) has had a few dominating players each year who had multiple wins and a lot of momentum. Don January, Arnold Palmer, Chi Chi Rodriguez, Jack Nicklaus, Lee Trevino, Hale Irwin, Gil Morgan, Bruce Fleisher, Larry Nelson and on and on. The players even came up with their own Wild West jargon to describe their dominant players. "There's a new sheriff in town," they would say. One expected Irwin or Nelson to step up to the first tee wearing spurs and a holster, a nickel-plated revolver glistening in the sun.

But 2003 was different despite the addition of notables such as Craig Stadler and Ben Crenshaw.

Stadler probably had the biggest impact on the 2003 season. Winless on any tour since 1996 and 11 years removed from his last multi-win season, Stadler won in only his fourth start as a senior at the Ford Senior Players Championship. A week later Stadler shot a final-round 63 at the B.C. Open and became the only player ever to win a PGA Tour event after winning as a senior. "It's like la-la-land here the last two weeks," Stadler said. "I have no rhyme or reason for it. I was kind of waiting until I turned 50 to see what would happen, and all of a sudden I learned how to play again. It's the magical number. Get a good bottle of wine, turn 50, and you start putting well. It's an amazing thing."

He won twice more on the Champions Tour for a four-victory season and a level of achievement that that he hadn't experienced since winning the Masters and three other events in 1982. "Winning breeds winning," he said. "The more you win, the more you expect to be there. It's fun now, that's for sure."

Stadler tied Carl Mason from the European Seniors Tour for the most wins by a senior in 2003, but neither won the money title. That honor went to one half of the best story of 2003.

Tom Watson came out in January with renewed purpose and a sense of urgency in his game. For good reason. On January 15, his caddie of 30 years, Bruce Edwards, was diagnosed with amyotrophic lateral sclerosis, Lou Gehrig's disease. With the proper medication to retard the degenerative effects of the disease, Edwards would lose his speech and most of his gross motor skills within a year. Within two years, five at the outside, he would be dead. Watson wanted to win for his friend and raise money for research. He formed a website, www.driving4life.org, and he spoke with great passion and conviction about Edwards and the battle to find a cure to his disease.

Watson and Edwards struck a poignant pose at the U.S. Open when Watson shot a 65 and shared the first-round lead. Even after he faded to a tie for 28th, the memory everyone had was of caddie and player embracing again at the national championship. Watson almost won the U.S. Senior Open, but couldn't quite catch Bruce Lietzke. But a month later he returned to Turnberry, site of one of the greatest duels in major championship history when Watson beat Jack Nicklaus in the 1977 Open Championship. This time, Watson beat Mason for the title.

Edwards wasn't on the bag in Scotland. Cold weather and extended travel accelerate the effects of the illness. So when Watson won the JELD-WEN Tradition, there was a sense of a mission accomplished. "I promised Bruce I was going to win for him before it was over," Watson said after his final victory of the year. "Today, as he said, it was the first of many. I hope he's right."

When Watson finished second to Jim Thorpe in the Charles Schwab Cup Championship, he won the money title and wrapped up the $1 million prize given by Schwab to the most consistent player of the year. At the awards presentation he donated the entire check to ALS research. There wasn't a dry eye in the house.

Thorpe finished second on the money list with two victories. He joined Hale Irwin at that number. Lietzke also had two wins, but that was it for multiple winners in 2003. John Jacobs won a major title, the Senior PGA Championship, and players such as Jay Sigel, Gil Morgan, Allen Doyle, Doug Tewell, Don Pooley, Wayne Levi and D.A. Weibring all won once, making 2003 one of the most diverse and exciting seasons in the history of senior golf.

Champions Tour

MasterCard Championship—$1,500,000
Winner: Dana Quigley

On a week when the greatest legends of the game were playing some of their best golf in years, it seemed fitting that the Iron Man of the Champions Tour, a guy who spent his pre-age 50 days selling sweaters and reading about people like Tom Watson, Jack Nicklaus, Larry Nelson and Arnold Palmer, would beat all those players and 30 more to win the season-opening Master-Card Championship in Hawaii. "The hits just keep on coming," Dana Quigley said after shooting 67 for an 18-under-par 198 total and his eighth career victory as a senior.

Quigley birdied the last three holes at the windless and defenseless Hualalai Golf Club on the Big Island of Hawaii to overtake Nelson by two strokes, and beat third-round co-leader Fuzzy Zoeller by three. Zoeller, Nelson and Quigley started the final round tied for the lead at 131. Nelson had the most up-and-down day. He eagled the par-five seventh, but still trailed Zoeller, who also rolled in an eagle putt there. Then Nelson made a bogey at the eighth, a double bogey at the ninth, and another eagle at the 10th to claim the lead before making bogey at the 12th. Nelson capped his round with a couple of late birdies at the 16th and 17th for a 69 and 200 total. Quigley took the lead for good with a birdie at the 14th and extended the margin to two by matching Nelson's birdies at the 16th and 17th and adding one more at the 18th.

"Every part of my game is clicking," Quigley said. "I'm putting better than ever. I'm dedicating myself this season to becoming one of the best putters out here. I felt when I came out here I'd be ready to play, and I was." In his sixth season on the Champions Tour, Quigley has become known as a man who never takes a day off. "My season never ends," he said. "My friends think I'm crazy, but this is my life. My passion for golf, you cannot believe it. People call it work, but it's not work for me. I love playing golf."

Zoeller bogeyed the 11th and 14th holes to shoot 70 and finish third at 201, while Tom Watson matched Quigley's closing 67 to tie for fourth with Stewart Ginn at 203.

Royal Caribbean Golf Classic—$1,450,000
Winner: Dave Barr

In the 1980s, Mike Weir found inspiration by watching fellow Canadian Dave Barr compete on the PGA Tour, winning two times in a respectable if not distinguished career. In 2003 it was Barr who was inspired. One week after watching Weir win the Bob Hope Chrysler Classic, Barr birdied his final four holes to shoot 67 for a nine-under-par 207 total and a one-stroke victory in the Royal Caribbean Golf Classic in Key Biscayne, Florida. It was Barr's first win in 16 years, and the first ever for a Canadian on the Champions Tour.

"It's been a long time," Barr said after capping his round with a 35-footer for birdie to finish ahead of Gil Morgan and Bobby Wadkins. "That's a lot of grinding. It's great to win, but I certainly didn't expect to win the first one of the year. To win this one is a great surprise."

Through 14 holes, Morgan and Wadkins were battling for the lead, and Barr seemed to be lost in the group. Wadkins had eight birdies and two bogeys in the 14 holes, but he added two more bogeys to his card before the end of the round. Morgan was three under par for the round and nine under for the tournament with only a few holes to play, but his putter kept him from putting it away, and his driver abandoned him on the final hole.

"I struck the ball well enough," Morgan said. "But I didn't make any putts. I had at least six putts inside 10 feet, and I don't think I made any of them. My putter was the culprit today."

Barr stayed close, but considered his chances slim. "The idea of winning after 14 holes didn't seem feasible," he said. "Bobby had been making a lot of birdies, and I guess I got caught up in his draft, like a NASCAR race."

The Canadian made a birdie at the 15th after hitting an eight iron to five feet. He added another birdie with a four-footer at the 16th. He made a 35-footer for birdie at the 17th and another from an equal distance at the 18th. Suddenly, the guy who didn't have a chance was tied for the lead with Morgan and one clear of Wadkins.

Morgan only needed a par at the 18th to force a playoff, but his tee shot drifted left and into a water hazard. After taking a drop, he hit a three wood from 245 yards through the green, chipped to six feet, and missed his par putt. Wadkins had a seven-footer for birdie, which would have also forced a playoff, but that putt crept low as well.

Suddenly, Barr, a conditional qualifying graduate who wasn't sure how many events he would play, was the winner at 207, with Morgan and Wadkins tied for second one shot back. Morgan finished with 70 and Wadkins, 68.

"The way I was thinking, just get it close for two putts," Barr said. "At that point, I had had a good tournament. You're not really thinking about making it."

Speaking of not thinking, on Friday Fuzzy Zoeller agreed to a promotional piece for a Miami television station. The segment was to have Zoeller giving a golf lesson to a reporter on the sixth hole. Zoeller didn't think twice when the crew asked him to hit a couple of shots for some full-speed footage. As a result, he was disqualified for practicing on the golf course between rounds. "If the finger is to be pointed at anyone it should be the Champions Tour, not Fuzzy," said PGA Tour spokesman Bob Combs. "We put him in a difficult situation."

"I know I wasn't supposed to hit shots on the course," Zoeller said. "I thought everybody had gotten the okay. I guess I shouldn't be so nice."

ACE Group Classic—$1,600,000
Winner: Vicente Fernandez

A mighty wind blew through Naples, Florida, over Valentine's Day weekend, just the kind of weather Vicente Fernandez remembered from his boyhood days in Argentina. The 56-year-old felt so at home that he shot a four-under-par 68 in the worst of the weather on Sunday, sinking a 60-footer on the final green for a 202 total and a three-stroke victory in the ACE Group Classic.

"It was one of the best rounds I've played under these circumstances from tee to green in these weather conditions," Fernandez said. It was his first win on the Champions Tour since 1999, and provided a rebound after personal tragedy led to a 31st place finish on the 2002 money list. In a 12-month span, Fernandez lost his mother, brother-in-law, an aunt and his longtime coach. When his caddie, Brian Deasy, was diagnosed with cancer, it was almost too much for the affable Fernandez. "That has been with me off the course," he said. "I've tried very hard not to put them on the course during my play, because I'm very emotional. Before I hit my last putt, I started thinking about them."

Fernandez led wire-to-wire after opening with a 66 and following with 68. That left him tied with former Tampa club professional Jay Overton, who followed his 71 with a 63. Overton struggled to find fairways and finished with 72 for a 206 total and a share of fourth place with Gil Morgan and Tom Purtzer.

Des Smyth, making his Champions Tour debut, had the low round of the final day, shooting 66 to tie Tom Watson for second at 206. But no one came close to Fernandez, who carried a one-stroke lead into the final two holes and extended it to three with a 10-footer at the 17th and the bomb at the 18th.

Verizon Classic—$1,600,000
Winner: Bruce Fleisher

After a couple of hiccups on a hole that seemed to have his number, Bruce Fleisher finally got even with the 415-yard, par-four 18th at the TPC of Tampa Bay, and gained his 16th career Champions Tour victory at the Verizon Classic. Fleisher, who lost this event in 2002 to Doug Tewell when he failed to find the fairway on the final hole, had more trouble when he found the water at the 18th early Sunday morning while completing the rain-delayed second round. The bogey left him one stroke behind Hale Irwin, where he remained through 16 holes of the final round.

Then Fleisher got an unexpected break. Irwin, the all-time winningest senior, hit his tee shot to the 213-yard, par-three 17th to within 20 feet. Fleisher hit a great shot to seven feet. Irwin blew his first putt five feet past, and missed the par effort coming back. When Fleisher made his birdie, the lead shifted in his favor.

All that was left was negotiating the 18th. This time Fleisher hit a great tee shot and found the center of the green with his second. He didn't make his birdie putt, and Irwin had a chance to force a playoff. His 13-footer for birdie narrowly missed the hole, and Fleisher had exacted his revenge. "It's a course where you have to drive the ball in play," he said. "It takes a lot of patience."

Fleisher hit every green in his final-round 67 and 205 total.

Irwin shot 69 to finish second at 206, a finish that left a sour taste. "It's not just that I lost, but because of the manner that I didn't take care of business," Irwin said. "For me, the story line comes down to a very poor week of putting. All in all, I can't fault the way I struck the ball, but, oh my goodness, what a frustrating week putting. I three-putted 17. I had a birdie putt then ended up three-putting. That's horrible. Absolutely horrible."

"It's hard to believe," Fleisher said. "I think when you beat Hale, it's a little more satisfying than just winning. We all know that he's the best out here. I've said that all along. He just doesn't let up. He doesn't make mistakes. He did on 17, which is rare. He opened the door for me, big time."

MasterCard Classic—$2,000,000
Winner: David Eger

David Eger, a former PGA Tour employee, joined the elite group of winners by capturing the MasterCard Classic in Lomas Altas, Mexico, for his first professional victory in his second season on the Champions Tour. Eger, the 1988 U.S. Mid-Amateur champion and former director of tournament operations for both the U.S. Golf Association and the PGA Tour, birdied three of the last four holes, including a four-footer at the final hole, for a 65 and a 12-under-par 204 total. He then had to watch as Bruce Lietzke and Eamonn Darcy tried birdie putts to tie him for the lead. When both putts failed to drop, Eger got his first lead of the day.

"Winning hardly ever entered my mind," Eger said. "I never led until the end. I didn't have time to think about the rewards or consequences. I just played golf."

Eger had the low round on Sunday, but he was almost matched by Hale Irwin, who also missed a birdie putt at the 18th that would have forced a playoff. Irwin shot 66 and finished tied for second with Darcy, Lietzke and Tom Jenkins, who all shot 70 on Sunday for totals of 205. The biggest loser was Lietzke, who held the lead for most of the round before his putter abandoned him. When the final birdie effort failed, all Lietzke could say was, "I'm very disappointed. At the beginning of the day, I thought the tournament was mine. But I kept messing up the putts of 10 to 12 feet."

As disappointed as Lietzke was, the week offered a reminder that golf is not the be-all and end-all of anything. On Friday night Walter Hall, Butch Sheehan, Bobby Walzel, Rodger Davis, Bob Gilder and Jim Thorpe went to dinner at an Argentine restaurant in Mexico City. Seated near the front door, they were greeted by a couple of gunmen who robbed them of their wallets and watches.

"A guy approached me and said, 'Give me your watch,'" Hall said. "I said, 'Excuse me?' The next thing I know, he pulls out a gun, cocks it, and puts it against my forehead. It took me about five seconds to get that watch off. There's no such thing as a life-and-death putt when you've had a loaded gun pointed at your head. Birdies and bogeys don't matter. It took about 30 seconds and they were gone. No one tried to be a hero, and nobody got hurt."

All were shaken by the ordeal, even those who weren't there. As Gilder put it, "It was later, when you had time to think about what could have happened, that you kind of realized how scary the whole thing was."

SBC Classic—$1,500,000
Winner: Tom Purtzer

The SBC Classic was shortened to 36 holes, but that didn't dampen the sweetness of Tom Purtzer's victory. It was a first for the 51-year-old, who had always been one of the classic ball-strikers in the game but who had always struggled on the greens. His three PGA Tour victories were considered underachieving for a man with his talents, and his winless rookie year on the Champions Tour in 2002 was a disappointment. But he put all that discontent behind him with one big putt on the final green at Valencia Country Club in Valencia, California.

Trailing Gil Morgan by two strokes with one hole to play, Purtzer hit a perfect drive and a good 255-yard, three-wood second shot into the 546-yard par-five hole. His ball rested on the front fringe of the green, 58 feet from the hole. Morgan tried to avoid the trouble on the right with his second shot, and as a result pulled his three-wood approach into the rough. From there he hit a nine-iron third shot to 30 feet.

"I've seen strange things happen before on this course, so I wasn't ready to quit," Purtzer said. "I wanted to make a three and get to nine under (135)." That's what Purtzer did when he rolled the putt into the hole for eagle and a round of 68. "I hit it on the line I wanted, but it broke so much that it's just in the hands of the golf gods," he said. "It's one of those deals that you watch it disappear and then you go, 'That didn't just happen.' You can't believe it."

If Purtzer couldn't believe it, imagine how Morgan felt. Morgan charged his 30-foot birdie putt seven feet past the hole and missed the comebacker for par. He shot 71 for a 136 total. "It was a pin I'd never seen before," Morgan said. "I left myself a tough 30-footer."

Purtzer shot 67 in the first round to trail Morgan by two strokes. There were five lead changes in the final round, with Purtzer pulling ahead with four consecutive birdies between the fourth and eighth holes. But Morgan reclaimed the lead with birdies on the first three par-fives before the bogey at the 18th. "I never expected Gil to back up," Purtzer said. "He just doesn't do that."

Toshiba Senior Classic—$1,550,000
Winner: Rodger Davis

This one went to one of the good guys. Australian Rodger Davis, one of the best-liked and respected players on the Champions Tour, broke through with his first victory when he fired a 68 for a three-day total of 16-under-par 196 at the Toshiba Senior Classic in Newport Beach, California.

"The great part happened this morning," Davis said. "At least 25 guys came up to me and said, 'Keep it going, Rodger.' That meant a lot."

It also meant a lot for Davis to be able to put an unpleasant episode behind him. Two weeks before, Davis was one of six players robbed at gunpoint in Mexico City.

Davis also felt that fate had shined on him in the form of an instructor who gave him a short-game tip before the first round. "One of Dave Pelz's guys was standing near the chipping area, and my caddie asked him to take a look at me," Davis said. The instructor, who never told Davis his name, told the Australian to move the ball back in his stance a few inches. The tip was worth at least two shots a day. "If you think you can chip, it takes pressure off your irons," Davis said. "You can have a crack at a couple of flags. You can take a chance and know you can get up and down if you miss." As for the tip, Davis chocked it up to fate. "If I had been there five minutes later, it probably wouldn't have happened," he said.

What happened to Davis were rounds of 65 and 64 and a two-shot lead. He extended that lead to four with a 68 on Sunday. Larry Nelson finished second after a 67 left him at 201, one stroke clear of Jose Maria Canizares, John Jacobs and defending champion Hale Irwin.

"I think a lot of people thought they might be able to catch Rodger," Nelson said. "I thought I needed a 64 or 65 to have a chance, but that wouldn't have been enough. I would have needed a 63 just to tie. Too tough."

Nelson was among those happy to see Davis take his first win in America to go with 29 international titles. "When he came out, we thought it would just be a matter of time before he won," Nelson said. "But you don't really know. Sometimes before a guy turns 50 you don't see him for a couple of years. Between 48 and 50 a lot of things can happen."

"I'd won everywhere else I played," Davis said. "This just seals it off."

Emerald Coast Classic—$1,450,000
Winner: Bob Gilder

In previous years, the knock on the Champions Tour was that the same guys won every week. If the first eight weeks of 2003 were any indication, that criticism could be chunked into the nearest water hazard. Bob Gilder put on a birdie display that rivaled anything seen in years, and became the eighth straight first-time winner of 2003. With rounds of 66, 64 and 63, Gilder set a tournament record at the Emerald Coast Classic in Milton, Florida, with a 17-under-par 193 total and a four-stroke victory over Leonard Thompson, Vicente Fernandez and Larry Nelson.

Gilder shared the second-round lead with Tom Watson, and 10 players began the final round within three shots of the lead. Gilder separated himself with three birdies to start his round, while Watson started with bogey, par, bogey. By the time they made the turn, this event was Gilder's to lose, and he would have had to botch things badly to let it get away.

"It was really fun, because I wasn't nervous," Gilder said. "I felt in control. You only get nervous when you're not playing well."

Thompson led after the first round with a 63, but his 68 on Saturday dropped him one behind Gilder. All three runners-up shot 66 on Sunday while Watson struggled all day, finishing with 74 for a 204 total and a tie for 15th place. It was another Florida disappointment for Watson, who remained winless in the Sunshine State for his entire career.

Liberty Mutual Legends of Golf—$2,250,000
Winner: Bruce Lietzke

The oldest event in senior golf, the Liberty Mutual Legends of Golf, moved to a new location in Savannah, Georgia, and crowned a new champion, Bruce Lietzke, the ninth different winner of the year. Lietzke took a one-shot lead over Dana Quigley into the final round and held on to win with a 71 for a 10-under-par 206 total. "I had the lead and I birdied the first hole," Lietzke said. "I really should have been able to stretch that lead out, and I just couldn't do it."

Fortunately, he didn't need to. Quigley also shot 71 to tie for second with David Eger while Bob Gilder and Hubert Green finished another stroke back at 208.

In his final round, Lietzke hit every green except the third (where he saved par), but didn't make a putt longer than 10 feet. "I was pretty disappointed in that," he said. "But I'm real happy to be the 2003 champion. I'm surprised that 71 won. I gave the tournament away in Mexico, and had thoughts of that on the back nine today. This feels good not to give a tournament away."

The low round on Sunday went to Bobby Wadkins, who bettered his opening 75 by 10 shots and tied for sixth with Doug Tewell and Morris Hatalsky at 209.

Bruno's Memorial Classic—$1,400,000
Winner: Tom Jenkins

The media center was abuzz with activity the day before the opening round of the Bruno's Memorial Classic in Hoover, Alabama. Unfortunately, golf was not the hot topic. The reason was the presence in the pro-am of newly named Alabama football coach Mike Price, who was playing in his second Champions Tour pro-am in three weeks, and who was answering questions about reports of an affair with a strip club dancer during the Emerald Coast Classic.

When Price was fired on Saturday after having never coached a game for the Crimson Tide, the normally festive event took on a somber air. The 30,000 fans at Greystone Golf Club were looking for a distraction and they found it in a final-round showdown including Tom Jenkins, Bruce Fleisher and Hale Irwin. Jenkins, the long shot of the group, cruised in with an easy victory, shooting 67, 66 and 67 for a 16-under-par 200 total and a three-stroke victory over Fleisher, who closed with 70. Irwin, the leader by a stroke going into the final round, limped in with 73 to tie for third with Jim Colbert at 205.

"It was a great day," Jenkins said after posting four straight pars to finish his round. "It's always a great feeling to go head-to-head with those guys and beat them."

The victory might have been sweeter if Irwin and Fleisher had played better down the stretch. Irwin never led after the third hole. He bogeyed the third and fourth, and then missed short putts for par on the 13th and 14th. His only birdies were on the par-fives where he reached the greens in two shots. "It was just one of those days," he said. "If I hit it close, I missed the putt. I never seemed to get my feet under me. I seemed to be left-footed all day. Nothing against left-footed people, but I'm right-footed."

Fleisher stayed in contention through the 15th, when Jenkins missed a three-foot putt that would have given him a two-shot lead. On the 16th, Fleisher missed a five-footer for par, extending Jenkins' lead to two strokes. He made another bogey at the 18th. "At 18 I was just trying to save face," Fleisher said. "I hit about an eight-footer for bogey. What a game. It's humbling."

Kinko's Classic of Austin—$1,600,000
Winner: Hale Irwin

No one had to remind Hale Irwin of the last time he whiffed a putt in competition. It was in 1983 at the Open Championship in Britain. Irwin, leading at the time, left a birdie putt hanging on the lip of the hole. In frustration, he took a jabbing stroke, and missed. He lost by one stroke.

Those recollections came flooding back in Austin, Texas, when Irwin, in a midst of what appeared to be another final-round meltdown (his fourth of the season), did it again: He whiffed a two-inch tap-in at the sixth hole in the final round of the new Kinko's Classic of Austin. This time, it didn't cost Irwin the title. He held on to birdie the final hole for a 73 and an eight-under-par 208 total, enough to tie Tom Watson and force a playoff, which Irwin won with a birdie on the second extra hole.

"Call it an air ball," Irwin said. "I would have never believed anything like this would happen. What a day."

The day started with Irwin and Watson trailing local favorite Tom Kite by a single shot. Irwin caught Kite with a birdie at the second hole, but he hit a tee shot on the fifth that found a clump of pampas grass and forced him to hit his second shot left-handed. He didn't do well and walked away with a double bogey. He didn't calm down until he made a birdie at the 10th to pull within four strokes of the lead. "I hit a boiling point," Irwin said. "I got carried away."

Kite's lead over Irwin stayed at four until Irwin birdied the 14th, 17th and 18th while Kite stumbled with bogeys on those same holes. Meanwhile, Watson hung within a shot of the lead with one to play. He joined the playoff after rolling in an eight-footer for birdie at the 18th. Watson shot 73, while Kite limped in with a 76 to tie for fourth with Jim Thorpe at 210, one behind Bob Gilder, who finished with a 68. "I feel bad," said Kite, who lived only a few miles from the course. "I feel like I let the whole town down."

Watson almost won his first event of the year on the first hole of the playoff, the par-five 18th. His second shot landed in a greenside bunker, and he hit a beautiful pitch that hit the hole before spinning out. Both players birdied the 18th and rode back to the par-three 16th. There Irwin made an eight-footer for birdie after Watson's birdie effort missed from 12 feet.

Watson said of Irwin, "If he can whiff it from inches and still win the tournament, that shows you he's the best on the tour."

Bayer Advantage Celebrity Pro-Am—$1,600,000
Winner: Jay Sigel

It seemed appropriate that Jay Sigel's ailing back would heal at a tournament sponsored by an aspirin company. For most of the year the 59-year-old Sigel was having trouble righting himself out of bed in the morning. It was one of the reasons he hadn't had a top-10 finish all year, and why he was forced to withdraw after one round of the Bruno's Memorial Classic only two weeks before arriving for the Bayer Advantage Celebrity Pro-Am. So no one was more surprised than Sigel when he shot a closing 65 for an 11-under-par 205 total, and won by one stroke over Mike McCullough.

"I couldn't put one foot in front of the other for a while," Sigel said. "I've been doing some special exercises, and it really freed my back up."

His health improved just in time to become the 12th different winner in 12 events in 2003, this one coming on a new Tom Watson-designed golf course that had everybody talking. Wind made the 6,900-yard National Golf Club of Kansas City the toughest test of the year in the opening round. The field averaged 75.38, with only six players managing to break par. "I'm grinning from ear to ear," Watson said. "The golf course proved itself." Then he added, "If we don't have any wind, there will be a lot of birdies."

Watson was right. The wind died down on Saturday and 15 players broke 70. Sigel was among them, shooting 68 to pull within two strokes of the leader, Vicente Fernandez, who followed his opening 71 with a 67. McCullough was two shots back after rounds of 73 and 67, and Des Smyth and Allen Doyle were also in the hunt at two back.

The complexion of the tournament changed quickly on Sunday. Sigel birdied his first three holes and turned in 31 to take a one-stroke lead over McCullough, who shot 32, and Fernandez, who shot 34. After a fabulous up-and-down for par from a bunker on the 11th, Sigel extended his lead to two with a 10-footer for birdie at the 12th. He made another short birdie at the 13th while McCullough was making bogey at the 12th. Suddenly, the lead was four.

McCullough came back with birdies at the 13th, 14th and 15th while Sigel was taking an unplayable lie and struggling to make bogey at the 15th. The two remained tied until Sigel hit his second shot at the par-five 18th into a greenside bunker, blasted out to nine feet, and made the putt for birdie. McCullough, playing one group behind Sigel, had a chance at the 18th, but after pulling his tee shot into the rough, he hit his second shot 108 yards from the hole. His third shot came up 20 feet short, and he missed his birdie chance.

"I hit the ball just like I wanted to," McCullough said of his shot at the 18th. "But it got awfully high into the wind. It was right on line." McCullough shot 66 and finished in second at 206, one behind Sigel, but one better than Fernandez, who shot 69 to finish third.

Columbus Southern Open—$1,500,000
Winner: Morris Hatalsky

The Champions Tour still had plenty of critics through the spring of 2003, but no one could complain about a lack of diversity. Through 13 events, the former Senior PGA Tour produced 13 different winners, the 13th coming in Columbus, Georgia, when Morris Hatalsky closed out the weekend with eight straight pars to edge local favorite Allen Doyle by one stroke in the Columbus Southern Open.

Hatalsky shared the 36-hole lead with Jim Thorpe before making three birdies in his first 10 holes on Sunday and closing out the day with a four-footer for par on the 18th to shoot 67 and finish the week at 12-under-par 198. Doyle, who lives less than 20 miles away in LaGrange, had a chance to force a playoff, but his 12-footer for birdie at the 18th slid low. That prompted a great groan from the crowd, who were biased in favor of the local boy who became something of a *Tin Cup* legend after running a mat-and-dirt driving range for 20 years before bursting onto the Champions Tour.

"I didn't do too, too bad," Doyle said after tapping in for par on the 18th and finishing alone in second with 67 for a 199 total. "I won over $100,000, and I know my family still loves me."

Hatalsky, the 2002 Champions Tour Rookie of the Year, made birdies on the fourth, seventh and 10th holes before reeling off his string of pars. He not only finished the week without a bogey, he extended his streak to 79 consecutive holes at par or better. "Don't wake me up," he said afterward. "I've never had a streak like that."

He also hadn't had a victory that required such conservative play down the stretch. "I was basically coaxing 20-, 25-footers for two putts," he said. "I saw Allen didn't make birdies, so I was just playing to the middle of the greens."

The hottest player of the day was Bruce Fleisher, who birdied seven of the final 13 holes for a 62 which moved him into a four-way tie for third with Dana Quigley, Des Smyth and Doug Tewell at 200. Larry Nelson shot 63 on Sunday for a 201 total and a share of fourth with Dave Barr and Hubert Green.

Music City Championship at Gaylord Opryland—$1,400,000
Winner: Jim Ahern

With gray hair waving like a fan beneath a blue-and-white Ford cap and words like "dadgum" rolling off his Okie tongue like sorghum syrup, Nashville, Tennessee, couldn't have created a better winner for its Music City Championship than Jim Ahern. Throw in the fact that Ahern's journeyman career was like a Merle Haggard song — long, hard, sorrowful, and only one five-footer away from redemption — and he was a perfect fit.

The redemption came in the form of a wire-to-wire victory at Springhouse Golf Club at Opryland that included two lightning rounds of 64 and 63 to open up a seven-stroke lead over Jose Maria Canizares. With 18 holes to play, Ahern's only worry was becoming too complacent. "If you go out there at the beginning of the day to protect your lead, you're going to have problems," the winner said. "My goal was to double (the lead). I wanted to stay aggressive, and keep making birdies. I didn't want to back off."

He didn't back down, even after missing a five-foot putt for eagle on the first hole. The tap-in birdie kept the lead intact, but not for long. Rodger Davis almost made an ace at the par-three third. His tap-in birdie cut the lead to five shots, but Davis never mounted a charge after that. Canizares fared a little better. When he birdied the 12th, 13th and 14th while Ahern struggled with his putter, the lead was cut to two shots. "When it got down to two strokes you never know," Ahern said. "Two strokes can disappear like that out here."

But at the par-three 15th, Canizares missed the green, chipped to four feet, and missed his par putt. "I hit a nice chip, but missed the putt," Canizares said. "Without making that shot, it was impossible to win the tournament." When Ahern birdied the 16th, it was essentially over. Pars on the final two holes gave the winner a closing round of 69 and a 20-under total of 196, four better than Canizares, who was second, one clear of Larry Nelson (the designer of the Springhouse golf course), who finished with six consecutive birdies for 64.

Senior PGA Championship—$2,000,000
Winner: John Jacobs

It wasn't supposed to be this way. If anyone in the Jacobs family was supposed to win a major championship, it was the eldest son, Tommy, who finished second to Ken Venturi in the 1964 U.S. Open and lost in a playoff to Jack Nicklaus in the 1966 Masters. Younger brother John, a larger-than-life talent who was said to have squandered the best years of his career on good wine and fine women, was never expected to win one of the big ones.

Something strange happened on the way to the awards ceremony at the

Senior PGA Championship. John Jacobs, in his 58th year and four senior victories into a resurrected career, shot 68 on Sunday at Aronimink Golf Club in suburban Philadelphia for a four-under-par 276 total and a two-stroke victory over Bobby Wadkins, the younger brother of another major champion, Lanny, who was spending his senior days in the CBS broadcast booth.

"I had a hard time keeping it together," Jacobs said of his thoughts coming up to the last hole when he knew he had a victory in the bag. "Nicklaus beat Tommy in a playoff, and Venturi beat him in the Open, which he should have won. I know how sad he was in those days, and I started thinking, 'Dammit, Tommy, I'm going to take this thing home somehow, and there's going to be a Jacobs on one of these trophies.'"

Back home in Southern California, Tommy Jacob, age 68, watched his little brother become the oldest winner of a major since 61-year-old Pete Cooper won the Senior PGA Championship in 1976. "I played a practice round with him Monday, and he loved the course at first sight," Tommy said. "Johnny kept saying, 'This is my golf tournament to lose.' I've never seen him so focused as he was this week. One day after his round he was sitting in front of his locker, quiet, and in deep thought. During the rain delays, he would go sit in his car. He didn't want any interference. He was concentrating totally all week."

That concentration was never more evident than in the final round when Jacobs, who started two shots behind Des Smyth, rolled in a 25-footer for birdie on the 15th to move to three under par for the week and into possession of the lead, one stroke ahead of Wadkins with three holes to play. "I told my caddie, 'I just want to lag it on the left, make par, and get out of there,'" Jacobs said. When the putt went in, Jacobs raised his arms to the crowd. He knew a win was within his grasp.

One hole later, Jacobs reached the par-five with a huge drive and a five iron. When he two-putted for birdie, the lead was two. Wadkins, playing one group behind, also reached the 16th in two, but he three-putted for par. "It wasn't the first time I three-putted," said Wadkins, who finished with 70 and a 278 total. "And it won't be the last. But it might have come at the worst time ever."

Armed with a two-stroke lead, Jacobs made routine pars on the final two holes for the emotional win. "I was as good as anybody at 13," the winner said. "I was as good as anybody at 18. When I went on tour, I was as good as anybody. It just didn't work out. But I've got a wonderful wife and a wonderful life. I might have had some regrets at 40, but not at 58."

Tommy Jacobs had no regrets either. "It makes me feel as if I won it," Tommy said. "Johnny could have won a lot of tournaments, but he just never got focused. He always had a happy-go-lucky attitude."

Farmers Charity Classic—$1,500,000
Winner: Doug Tewell

Another week, another different winner. For the 16th time in as many events, the Champions Tour produced a different champion. This time it was Doug Tewell who overcame a bad back and low expectations to win the Farmers

Charity Classic in Grand Rapids, Michigan, with a birdie on the third hole of a playoff. Tewell shot 66 for a 15-under-par 201 total to tie Eamonn Darcy. He then rolled in a 14-foot birdie putt to capture his first title in more than a year.

"This game is so crazy," Tewell said. "When you least expect it is when you play well." He played just well enough. Trailing Ed Dougherty by two strokes at the beginning of the final round, Tewell never held the lead until the 17th hole. After a bogey on the 16th dropped him two behind Darcy, Tewell hit a perfect drive and a solid four iron to within 15 feet on the 518-yard par-five hole. An eagle putt moved him into a tie with Darcy, who closed with 65 for his 201. Dougherty shot 72 and finished in a tie for fourth at 204.

Tewell called the shot at the 17th, "one of the best I've hit in that situation in a long time. Then I hit the putt really soft, which surprised me, because I knew I had to make it."

He made the putt, but almost lost the tournament on the first hole of the playoff. Playing the 18th for a second time, Tewell flew his second shot over the green and into the high grass.

Darcy was on the green and chose to chip with a five wood, an odd choice under the circumstances. When he ran his chip shot six feet past and he missed the putt for par, Tewell had new life. A flop shot and two putts for bogey kept the playoff going. On the second extra hole Darcy made a slippery eight-footer for par to extend the match one more hole. That's when Tewell hit his second shot at the 18th to within 14 feet and made the putt for birdie.

"I had low expectations, and now I'm wondering if that might have helped me," Tewell said. "I've had back trouble all my life. I just played along, and all of a sudden I'm on the back nine with a chance to win." As for his yearlong winless streak, Tewell tried to dismiss it. "You think about it," he said. "But then this happens. I've been doing the right things all along, and it means I can still do it."

U.S. Senior Open—$2,600,000
Winner: Bruce Lietzke

Given Bruce Lietzke's passion for working on his collection of antique muscle cars, it seemed appropriate when Tom Watson used an automotive metaphor in describing Lietzke's final round at the U.S. Senior Open. "Bruce's nickname today was Leaky," Watson said. "He was leaking a lot of oil and smoke, blowing that blue smoke out of his pipes, but the engine still worked. He came in on two pistons, but he was still moving."

Lietzke limped in with a 73 on a day when he couldn't find the fairway, but the score was good enough. He finished with a seven-under-par 277 at the Inverness Club in Toledo, Ohio, enough for a two-shot victory over Watson, who was handed his second consecutive Senior Open disappointment.

Finally, in the year's 17th tournament, the Champions Tour had a repeat winner. Lietzke earlier won the Liberty Mutual Legends of Golf.

A year ago, Watson battled Don Pooley to a playoff before losing in extra holes. This time around, the crowd was clearly behind Watson, in part because of the one that got away the year before and in part because of Watson's caddie, Bruce Edwards, and the saga of his battle with ALS. Edwards was offered a cart by the USGA, but just as he did in the U.S. Open at Olympia Fields, he respectfully declined. "He is struggling," Watson said of Edwards. "His legs hurt him. The problem with ALS is you don't want to get exhausted. Exhaustion will make your muscles deteriorate much faster. If you exhaust them, they won't come back."

Tired or not, Edwards and Watson were buoyed by the support of a gallery that cheered their every step. They had a lot to cheer about early on. Watson rolled in putt after crucial putt on his way to a 66 and a three-shot lead in the first round. "I turned a 71 into a 66 with good long putts and chipping, a 'Watson Roll,'" Watson said. "I used to break a lot of peoples' hearts making a lot of putts."

Unfortunately for Watson and his followers, the Watson Roll didn't last. He came back with 72 and 70 to trail Lietzke by four strokes thanks to Lietzke's 64 on Saturday. "That was the best round of my life," Lietzke said. "I feel like a NASCAR driver and they've taken fourth gear out of my car," he said. He was referring to the tight fairways at Inverness that took the driver, Lietzke's most proficient club, out of his hands. He also said he wasn't concerned about leading a major championship by four shots with 18 to play. "I've seen what happens to people who win majors," he said. "And I've always liked to stay low on the radar screen. It really brought Bill (Rogers) down. I never purposely lost a major, but I was never in position to win that many. It seems to mean more to other guys. To me it is another tournament on my schedule."

Lietzke swore the pressure of leading a major didn't get to him, but he certainly didn't put together a very Lietzke-like final round. He found only five fairways on Sunday, but hit enough great iron shots to hold off Watson, who finished with 71 for a 279 total, a score the eight-time major champion thought would be good enough. "I thought five under would be a lock-cinch win," Watson said. He was off by two.

Despite his struggles, destiny seemed to be on Lietzke's side at the par-five eighth when he hit a 360-yard drive and a 195-yard five iron to within seven feet for eagle. When that putt fell, the lead was six shots, and Lietzke held on. He made another birdie from the rough at the 16th, which gave him enough leeway to bogey the 17th and 18th and still win by two.

"The opportunity was there today," Watson said. "I didn't do my job and Bruce did his job. I'm not going to cry about that. I played well enough to put pressure on him, and he played bad enough to give me the golf tournament. But it wasn't to be."

Lietzke agreed. "It's not the person who finished second or third, or the strength of the field," he said, "it's did you survive a week on a golf course that tests every part of your game. I'm not sure I feel like a champion as much as a survivor."

Ford Senior Players Championship—$2,500,000
Winner: Craig Stadler

Only one month after reaching 50 and in his fourth start on the Champions Tour, Craig Stadler broke into the club with a three-stroke win over Tom Watson, Tom Kite and Jim Thorpe in the seniors' third major of the year, the Ford Senior Players Championship in Dearborn, Michigan. Stadler got the victory on the strength of a putter that seemed to know no wrong. He took only 51 putts in the final two rounds, 10 fewer than his tour average. The result was a 65-66 weekend that put this one away early.

"This is one of those rare weeks in the last 10 years that I've putted well all week," Stadler said. "You have no idea how good that feels."

Tom Watson knew how it felt, for a couple of days at least. Watson shot 64 on a windy Friday when only five players broke 70 and the next lowest score was 68. Just as he had done when he shot a similar number in the U.S. Senior Open, Watson rolled in putts from everywhere. His lead was two at the halfway mark. "When the conditions get tough, that's when you can separate yourself," Watson said. "You can make a statement. I think at times when you don't have the wind, you don't focus quite as well, and you may take risks sometimes on shots you shouldn't."

As if foretelling his own fortune, Watson didn't play as well on Saturday when the conditions were relatively calm. His 71 allowed Stadler (who had 24 putts) to tie him for the lead. The big man grabbed the lead early on Sunday with a birdie on the first hole and a lip-out for birdie on the second. The turning point, however, was the par-five third. Watson hit his second shot into the greenside bunker while Stadler played tree-tag with some pines on his way to a bogey. But when Watson failed to get his third shot out of the bunker, he too made bogey, and Stadler walked to the fourth tee thinking he had stolen one.

Stadler proceeded to hit his approach at the fifth hole to an inch, and then rolled in a 45-footer for birdie at the sixth. When he made his third consecutive birdie at the par-five seventh, this one was effectively over. When he chipped in from 30 feet at the 12th while Watson was making bogey, Stadler's lead was five. His only three-putt of the week came at the par-five 13th where he ran an eagle putt well past the hole and missed the birdie effort coming back. By then it didn't matter. Stadler cruised in with a series of pars for a 17-under-par 271 total and a three-shot edge over Watson, who birdied the last hole, Thorpe, who shot 65 on Sunday, and Kite, who started the day six shots back and shot a course-record 63 that included eight birdies, one eagle and a bogey.

"That was really a fun day," Kite said. "Going into the round, I felt that if I shot something like 64 I'd have a really good shot. As it turned out, I shot 63 and didn't come close."

Watson wasn't quite as thrilled about his final round. "I can't complain too much," he said. "I had my opportunities to do well, and Craig just outplayed me, straight-up outplayed me. I feel like Tommy Aaron. Tommy had a history of finishing second. I've finished second too many times out here on the Champions Tour."

Stadler hadn't experienced that frustration, at least not yet. Winning in his fourth start was important. "I wanted to win early," he said. "I wanted to come out and just tell myself — and pretty much a lot of people — that I can still play good, still play well consistently."

Senior British Open—€1,422,297
Winner: Tom Watson

See PGA European Tour section.

FleetBoston Classic—$1,500,000
Winner: Allen Doyle

In an speech that would have made Yogi Berra proud, Allen Doyle left a lot of people scratching their heads when he said of his three-stroke victory at the FleetBoston Classic in Concord, Massachusetts, "I wasn't going to let not having won recently prevent me from winning sooner."

The Doyle-ism was meant to convey his determination of not letting the 61 starts since last cashing a winner's check prohibit him from winning this one, which he did with relative ease. Rounds of 67 and a course-record 63 gave Doyle a two-shot edge over Bob Gilder going into the final round. He extended that lead with an eagle at the par-five fifth after hitting a 261-yard three wood to within 18 inches of the hole. He made another birdie at the eighth to extend the lead to four.

After that, Doyle cruised in with 10 straight pars for a 67 and an 18-under-par 198 total. Gilder shot 68 to tie Bruce Fleisher for second at 201. "I wish I could have put some pressure on him," Gilder said. "He just wasn't accepting it. I wish I could have made it a little more interesting. But nothing was going to rattle him today."

Fleisher, who was the first-round leader after a 64, made it interesting when he ran off six birdies in his first 14 holes on Sunday. But the birdie well ran dry after that, and he finished with 66 to tie Gilder, one clear of fourth-place finishers D.A. Weibring and Tom Purtzer.

Doyle wasn't concerned about Fleisher, or anyone else for that matter. He grew up in Concord and was a member of the local sports Hall of Fame (for hockey, not golf), so this was a home game for him, even though he had resided in LaGrange, Georgia, for decades. Once he had the lead, he wasn't going to let it go. "I knew that someone was going to have to come get me," Doyle said. "A lot of time, if you put it in cruise control, there's time to put it in a higher gear. But I didn't need to. I don't like playing that conservative, but there was no way I was going to let it slip away."

3M Championship—$1,750,000
Winner: Wayne Levi

If Wayne Levi were a stock, as a Wall Street investor, Levi would have advised you to sell. All the trends were pointing downward, as they had since Levi won four times and earned PGA Tour Player of the Year honors in 1990. He had been on the Champions Tour for the better part of two years, and a bad back and even shakier putter had kept him off almost everyone's chart. "Stock in Wayne Levi just kept going down," Levi said.

That's what made Levi's victory so special at the 3M Championship at the TPC of the Twin Cities in Blaine, Minnesota. Nobody expected it, not even Levi. After rolling in a four-footer for birdie at the final hole for a 68 and an 11-under-par 205 total, Levi walked into the scorer's tent unaware that he had won the tournament by one stroke over Morris Hatalsky and Gil Morgan. "I thought, 'What are they talking about?'" Levi said. "I thought there was going to be a playoff."

That might have been the case if Morgan had been able to make a birdie on the second nine. After four birdies to take the lead, Morgan made nine pars on the second nine. "I had plenty of chances, but I couldn't make anything happen," Morgan said. "I couldn't make any birdies down the stretch." His best chance was on the 18th when he hit his second shot at the par-five hole under the scoreboard, and then hit a perfect pitch to seven feet before missing the putt. Both Morgan and Hatalsky finished with 68s.

Hatalsky also had more than a fighting chance, but his birdie putt at the 18th hit the hole and spun out. Tom Purtzer, who was tied for the lead at 10 under par through 16 holes, chunked a seven iron into the water at the par-three 17th. He re-teed, and promptly hit another seven iron into the same spot in the creek. The quadruple bogey dropped Purtzer into a tie for 10th at 209. "I hadn't made a putt all day," Purtzer said. "I was trying to hit in there close. That's what can happen when you try to do too much."

The final contender with a shot at forcing a playoff was second-round co-leader Ben Crenshaw, who had his best tournament since joining the Champions Tour. Crenshaw was one under par with one to play and needed an eagle to force a playoff. After missing the green with his second shot, he hit a deft pitch, but the ball rolled past the hole and he missed the subsequent birdie putt for a 71 and a tie for fourth with Graham Marsh and Bob Murphy at 207.

The last man standing was Levi, who made five birdies and two bogeys in his closing round, the final one on the 18th hole putting him over the top. "It really comes down to what you think of yourself, and I knew it was just a matter of time for me," the winner said. "It just took a little longer than I thought it would. This is what you practice all your life to achieve — to be the guy holding the trophy at the end."

Long Island Classic—$1,500,000
Winner: Jim Thorpe

On the strength of a record-tying round of 60, Jim Thorpe held on with a birdie at the 17th hole on Sunday to win the Long Island Classic in East Meadow, New York, by one shot over Bob Gilder. Thorpe, who matched Isao Aoki's mark for the low round in Champions Tour history, carried a two-shot lead into the final round, but gave up the lead with a double bogey at the fourth. Gilder, who shot 64 and 66 in the first two rounds, took the lead and held it until Thorpe's 10-footer at the 17th found the hole. That shifted the lead back to Thorpe, which is where it remained. The winner shot 67 for a 15-under-par 195 total, one better than Gilder, who closed with 66.

"I knew my game was sharp today, and that Gilder was going to be a tough competitor," Thorpe said. "You need things like that fourth hole to happen. It was a rude awakening, and it took the pressure off me and put it on him."

After the fiasco at the fourth, Thorpe never missed a fairway and had five birdies, the final one coming at the 17th. Gilder had one last chance at the 455-yard, par-four 18th. He hit a 201-yard five iron to within six feet, setting up a perfect uphill putt for birdie to force a playoff. But the ball rolled past the hole. Gilder tapped in for his second consecutive 66 and second place at 196, three clear of third-place finisher Des Smyth, who shot 67.

"I read that last putt to go straight," Gilder said. "The ball was in a little hole, and just seemed to jump away. Obviously, I'm disappointed. I seemed to make all the putts except the last one. Jim made shots when he needed them, and his birdie on the 17th was big."

The win was Thorpe's sixth career title, but his first win in 42 starts. He also became the 21st different winner in 22 events in the 2003 season.

Allianz Championship—$1,500,000
Winner: Don Pooley

Noticeably absent from the drama of the 2003 U.S. Senior Open was the 2002 champion. He had a good excuse. Don Pooley tore a ligament in his shoulder on January 3, and had to undergo surgery. His five-month recovery was arduous, painful and often frustrating. Pooley had made only four starts on the Champions Tour by the middle of August. He felt good about a 10th-place finish at the 3M Championship where he shot a second-round 63, but the depth of the recovery was still in question when he traveled to Des Moines, Iowa, for the Allianz Championship.

At the week's end, Pooley announced that he was officially back. "This is huge, it really is," he said after breaking away from a pack of competitors in the final nine holes and closing with 67 for a 13-under-par 200 total and a three-stroke victory. "To prove to myself that I came back and can win again, there were a lot of doubts there not too long ago."

Pooley led by one over Bruce Lietzke, Bruce Fleisher and Jim Thorpe going into the final round, but on the first nine there were as many as 10 players within two of the lead. Among them was former Los Angeles Dodgers pitcher Rick Rhoden, playing in his second Champions Tour event on a sponsor's exemption. Rhoden started the final round two shots back after rounds of 69 and 66, and he quickly took a share of the lead with three birdies on the front nine. When he rolled in a long birdie putt at the 11th, Rhoden took a one-shot lead.

"I thought he did a fabulous job," Pooley said of Rhoden's performance. "I was a big fan of his when he was pitching for the Dodgers. On the 11th green, I was thinking, 'You know, I wish he was still pitching.'"

Moments after Rhoden made his birdie, Pooley rolled in a 25-foot eagle putt from the fringe at the 11th to reclaim the lead for good. "That putt on 11 was one of the best putts under pressure I've ever made," Pooley said. "It was a slick left-to-right putt, and it ended up right in the heart. I felt real good about it."

By the time Pooley hit it to six feet on the par-three 14th and made that one for birdie, the tournament was effectively over. His lead was four thanks to some shaky putting down the stretch by Rhoden, who three-putted the 12th, 13th and 14th after the birdie at the 11th. "My putter just got to feeling like a sledgehammer for three holes," Rhoden said. He finished the day with a 69, which left him tied for fifth with Doug Tewell and Tom Kite at 204. "I'm just proud I hung in there and played well," Rhoden said. "Other than the three holes, I couldn't have asked for a better day."

Pooley couldn't have asked for much more, either. After his birdie at the 14th, he coasted in with four pars for 67. "I was just trying to avoid disaster the rest of the way and enjoy it," he said. "This is a huge turnaround pretty quickly for me. It's a wonderful game now."

Lietzke, Thorpe and Fleisher all shot 69 to share second at 203, but the way the 2003 season had gone it made sense that none of them won. All three had already hoisted a trophy in 2003, and this was the year of a different winner every week. Pooley made it 22 different champions in 23 weeks. Only Lietzke had two wins through mid-August. "It just shows you how many capable winners there are on this tour," Pooley said.

JELD-WEN Tradition—$2,200,000
Winner: Tom Watson

There aren't many absolutes in golf, but one thing remained unchanged in 2003: If Tom Watson putted well, there weren't many people who could beat him. The eight-time major champion and Hall of Famer made an Oregon apple basket full of birdie putts during the four rounds of the JELD-WEN Tradition, the Champions Tour's final major held at the Reserve Vineyards in Aloha, Oregon. The last birdie putt was from four feet on the 72nd hole and gave Watson a one-stroke victory over Gil Morgan, Jim Ahern and Tom Kite. In the process, Watson brought even more attention to the cause that had reinvigorated him: ALS, Lou Gehrig's disease, which had afflicted Watson's caddie, Bruce Edwards.

"I promised Bruce I was going to win for him before it was over," Watson said after posting a 70 for a 15-under-par 273 total. "Today, as he said, it was the first of many. I hope he's right."

Watson was the second repeat winner on the 2003 Champions Tour. Edwards was unable to travel with him with he won the Senior British Open.

This one was the perfect combination of heartfelt emotion and good old-fashioned drama, with the results uncertain until both Ahern and Kite missed birdie putts on the final hole with Watson watching on the television monitor in the scorer's trailer. "I was ready for a playoff," Watson said. "I was given a gift, and I was very happy, obviously."

It was Watson who provided the gift earlier in the week. He jumped out to an early lead by virtue of a 62 on Friday to go with an opening-round 68. The lead was four strokes at the halfway mark. "I had the door pretty well shut and locked if I played a decent round on Saturday," he said, but it was not to be. He shot 73 and lost the lead to Ahern, who opened with 66 and followed with a pair of 68s.

"With that 62 I used up most of my good shots," Watson said. "That 62 was easy. Everything was under control. So why does it change? The last two days I struggled. Fortunately, my putter worked for me."

He hit two shots in the water on Sunday, the first coming at the 10th, which resulted in bogey, and the second coming at the 16th after he had clawed his way back into the lead with birdies at the 12th and 15th. "After bogeying 16, I said, 'Well, I lost it here," Watson said.

There was still a chance if he could birdie the 18th, the third consecutive par-five to finish the Reserve Vineyard, a unique design that Kite called "quite spectacular." Watson hit a perfect drive, but pulled his three wood into the left greenside bunker. He hit a great shot to four feet and made the putt for birdie to shoot 70 and be first in the clubhouse at 15-under-par 273. Morgan made par on the 18th to shoot 68 and finish at 274.

That left it to Kite and Ahern, both playing in the final group behind Watson. Ahern was first, but he missed his six-footer and finished with 72, tied with Morgan at 274. Kite was next. He hit his third shot to five feet, leaving what appeared to be an easy uphill effort to force a playoff. But he also missed, just as he had from seven feet two holes before, finishing with 71 for his 274. "I let the tournament get away," Kite said. "You've got to make those putts."

"You didn't know what was going to happen until the very last putt," Watson said. "It could have gone to a number of different players. But I made a lot of four- to six-footers, like the Watson of old."

Kroger Classic—$1,500,000
Winner: Gil Morgan

Armed with a new driver and confidence that he could find more than 70 percent of the fairways, Gil Morgan finally won again after a passel of near-misses. He birdied two of the last four holes including a two-putt birdie at the final hole of the Kroger Classic to shoot 16-under-par 200 and beat his best friend, Doug Tewell, by two strokes.

"My driver has been holding me back," Morgan said. "It cost me at least two tournaments this year." Two weeks before making the trek to Maineville, Ohio, Morgan abandoned his old driver and went to a new Callaway ERC Fusion with 7.5 degrees of loft and a 44-inch shaft. "It's something I can control and have confidence in," he said. "This time I won with driving."

Morgan took a two-shot lead into the final round after an opening 65 and a five-under 67 on Saturday. Tewell was two strokes back, and Graham Marsh and Larry Nelson trailed by three and four shots respectively. As had happened too many times in 2003, Morgan lost the lead with a couple of early bogeys at the third and fourth holes. "I only made one bogey in two days, and then I made two in a row today," Morgan said. "I don't like that concept."

He made up for it with birdies at the fifth, eighth and ninth to regain a one-shot advantage, but another bogey at the 13th where he missed the green with a sand wedge dropped him into a three-way tie with Marsh and Nelson. Tewell joined the hunt with a birdie at the 15th while Marsh was making bogey on the same hole after hitting his tee shot so wildly he had to declare a lost ball.

The three-way knot between Morgan, Tewell and Nelson was broken when Morgan split the middle of the 15th fairway and hit a nine iron to 10 feet. Making that putt gave Morgan a lead that he wouldn't relinquish. Nelson made bogey at the 16th to drop two back, and Morgan clinched the victory when he reached the par-five 18th with his second shot and two-putted for birdie to extend the final margin to two.

"That birdie at 15 was critical," Morgan said after signing for a 68. "I was concerned after I made bogey at 13. That was a real detriment." It also conjured some bad memories of the many lost opportunities of 2003. "I had played well several times and finished second four times. It was getting pretty late in the year. I had started to think I might not win this year."

Tewell finished with 68 after failing to get up-and-down for birdie at the 18th. His 202 total left him in second place, one better than Nelson, who shot 67, and Jim Thorpe, who came roaring out of the pack with a 64. "It was a pretty good shootout, but Gil played well," Tewell said. "I was hitting some great golf shots. It just wasn't my day to win. Gil kept us all at bay. He deserved to win."

Constellation Energy Classic—$1,500,000
Winner: Larry Nelson

Statistics have shown that seniors tend to play well between ages 50 and 55, and then show an accelerated decline. Could Larry Nelson be an exception? Five days after his 56th birthday, Nelson capped a wire-to-wire victory with a 70 for a nine-under-par 207 total at the Constellation Energy Classic in Baltimore, Maryland. It was Nelson's first victory in almost two years after the former Champions Tour Player of the Year suffered a series of back and neck injuries that had many wondering if he would ever win again.

"You never really know when the last event is going to be that you win, and for a long time you think, well, maybe you've already had your last one," Nelson said. He lost the lead to Doug Tewell early in the final round, regained it with a couple of birdies in the middle, lost it again at the 15th, then regained it with a birdie at the par-five 16th, all while suffering from a bee sting on his right index finger that caused his hand to swell up like a balloon. "I've never been stung during a round before," he said. "It kind of ticked me off."

The bee sting came as Nelson was lining up a 12-foot putt for par on the ninth hole. His hand went numb and he said it hurt at impact through the remainder of the round. "Had it been my left hand, it would've really been rough," he said. "The right one, you probably don't need anyway." Nelson converted the 12-footer at the ninth after the sting and a 25-footer for birdie at the 11th to regain a share of the lead with Tewell, who trailed Nelson by three after two rounds, but birdied the 10th and 13th to gain a share of the lead.

Tewell sank a 15-footer at the 15th to take the lead again, but Nelson caught him with a 15-footer for birdie at the 16th. Tewell, playing a group ahead of Nelson, hit his only bad shot of the round at the 17th, which led to an ill-timed bogey. One back with one to play, Tewell tried to make a birdie at the 18th, but he charged his 15-footer and missed. When he tapped in for bogey, Tewell shot 69 for the day, 209 for the week, and shared second place with Jim Dent, who finished with 71.

"I've got a bad taste right now," Tewell said. "I've gotten the best of Larry a lot the last couple of years. I guess it was my turn to give it back today and make it easy for him."

Nelson parred the 17th and 18th to take home his first title since 2001. "I've been playing well, and I've been close," he said. "I just hit a lot of good shots and outlasted everybody."

SAS Championship—$1,800,000
Winner: D.A. Weibring

The worst part was the wait. After struggling with his putter for most of the week, Tom Kite needed only 22 putts on Sunday and only nine on the final nine holes as he shot a course-record and career-low 61 in the final round of the SAS Championship at Prestonwood Country Club in Cary, North Carolina. That 11-under-par score gave Kite a 12-under 204 total and a one-stroke lead as the final group made the turn. That meant Kite had to wait more than two hours to see if his score would hold.

When Doug Tewell, who started the final round at seven under and got to 12 under through 16 holes, failed to convert a birdie putt on the par-five 17th and missed the green and failed to get up and down at the 18th, Kite appeared to have survived his biggest threat. What no one expected was an eagle-birdie finish from D.A. Weibring.

Weibring, playing in only his sixth Champions Tour event since turning age 50 in May, also started the final round at seven under but was suffering from flu symptoms. After he wobbled off the fourth green, his caddie insisted that he ride on a golf cart. "I felt uncomfortable using the cart, but it saved me," Weibring said. "I'm a traditionalist. I wanted to walk. But he was right. If you start running out of steam on the fourth hole, there's a long way to go. We work as a team and I try to pay attention to him."

With a little more energy, Weibring played the first 15 holes four under par, but lost his concentration on the 16th. Staring at a two-footer for par, he got out of his rhythm and pushed the putt out of the hole. That left him two strokes behind Kite with two holes to play. "That disappointed me a lot," Weibring said. "I've always been pretty good under the gun."

Meanwhile Bobby Wadkins was also putting on a charge. Two second-nine birdies put Wadkins at 12 under par through 16 holes with the par-five 17th and the birdie-friendly 18th ahead. On both holes, Wadkins pushed his tee shots. At the 17th, it cost him a chance to go for the green with his second shot. He hit his third to 15 feet and failed to convert the birdie. At the 18th, his tee shot landed in a fairway bunker. From there he hit his approach to 30 feet and failed to convert. Wadkins finished the round at 69 and tied with Kite at 204.

That left Weibring, who appeared to be out of the hunt after his short miss at the 16th. He hit a perfect drive and a huge four wood to within seven feet at the 17th. When the eagle putt found the hole, Weibring was at 12 under. On the last hole, he hit it to 14 feet and made that putt for a 66 and a 203 total.

"I couldn't have hit it better if I stood there all my life," Weibring said of his closing two holes. The victory made Weibring the seventh first-time winner of the year, and the 24th different champion in 26 events, one shy of the Champions Tour record of 25 different winners in 1995.

Greater Hickory Classic at Rock Barn—$1,500,000
Winner: Craig Stadler

No one has ever confused Craig Stadler with a Renaissance Man, but it was hard to come up with a more apt description for the resurgence Stadler experienced after reaching age 50. Not only did he win on the Champions Tour in only his fourth start, he became the only Champions Tour member ever to win a PGA Tour event when he captured the B.C. Open. This week in Hickory, North Carolina, he became only the third person of 2003 to win more than one Champions Tour event. The victory came when Stadler shot 66 at the Greater Hickory Classic at Rock Barn with birdies on his first four holes and five of his first seven, to overtake leader Larry Nelson and win by two strokes.

So how did Stadler explain his success? "I haven't thought too much about it, and frankly, I don't care to," he said after posting a six-birdie, no-bogey round for a 15-under-par 201 total. "The game is just different for me right now. I know I'm playing well."

He held the best final-round scoring average of any senior (68.82) heading into the event and proved why when he rolled in putts from five, 45 and 10 feet on the first three holes. After another birdie at the fourth from 15 feet and a two-putt birdie at the par-five seventh for a first-nine 31, Stadler had leapt ahead of Nelson. An eight-footer for birdie at the 11th got him to 15 under par and four clear of Nelson, who three-putted the 11th for bogey.

Eight pars followed, the final one coming with a two-putt for the victory. "The game isn't tough to figure out when you're hitting it good, and tee to green I'm probably playing as well as I ever have," Stadler said. "Even so, I still can think about the shots that got away. I really haven't made the putts out there, not nearly as many as I should have made."

He joined Bruce Lietzke and Tom Watson as the only multiple winners of the year so far on the Champions Tour. "The last six rounds I've really hit the ball close," Stadler said. "I'm hitting it so well, but I'm not making near as many putts as I should be making. If I ever get the putter figured out, well, who knows what could happen."

Nelson finished second at 203 after a final-round 70.

Turtle Bay Championship—$1,500,000
Winner: Hale Irwin

It had only been a month since Hale Irwin lamented the summer as one he would "ruefully remember." Struggling with an uncooperative putter and a back that was giving him fits, Irwin said, "It has been a different, unsettling and disappointing year." The crux of his problem, or so he claimed, was an injury he sustained when he made a swing correction after winning the

Kinko's Classic in Austin, Texas. "Three mornings later I nearly fell face first into the sink," he said. "I guess my body didn't take well to making the correct golf swing. It's just going to require rest and then strengthening those muscles. The only thing that bothers it is playing golf."

Four weeks later, Irwin shot a final-round 67 for an eight-under-par 208 total and a two-stroke victory in the Turtle Bay Championship in Kahuku, Hawaii, becoming the first player in Champions Tour history to win the same tournament four times in a row and five times overall.

There was nothing rueful or unsettling about Irwin's performance. He birdied the fifth, third, fourth and ninth holes to turn in 32 with three birdie putts coming from outside 15 feet. While he bogeyed the 11th, he came back with one more birdie, an18-footer at the 17th that found the hole just minutes after second-round leader Tom Kite rolled in a 40-footer for birdie at the 16th to reclaim a share of the lead.

Irwin's birdie at the 17th forced Kite to play the par-five 18th more aggressively than he might have liked. After a good drive, Kite needed to carry a three wood 242 yards. The shot came up one foot short and rolled back into a water hazard guarding the front of the green. Kite made bogey for an even-par 72 final round, a 210 total, and his fourth runner-up finish of the year without a victory.

"When you make three sixes on the par-fives, you are not going to do well," Kite said. "That was the tournament for me. I knew I needed to make a four at 18. I hit a solid shot, but I didn't get the height I needed."

Irwin made par at the 18th, which was enough. He admitted to being nervous in the closing stretch, but he also enjoyed the adrenalin rush of being back in the hunt. "That's a good thing," he said of the jitters he experienced on the last few holes. "It's the fight. It's the thrill. It's the chase. If I don't feel that, then I'm gone."

As for his back, Irwin called it "80 percent" saying, "This is the first week when my back didn't give me an issue."

SBC Championship—$1,500,000
Winner: Craig Stadler

Who would have believed that the only player on the Champions Tour with three or more victories would be a guy who also won a PGA Tour event after turning 50 and after putting on an additional 15 pounds? Certainly not Craig Stadler, who was as surprised as anyone by the success, his best since 1982, when he won four events including the Masters and was named Player of the Year. "I probably had more confidence in 1982 than I do now," the winner of the SBC Championship said after firing a final-round 67 for a 15-under-par 198 total and a four-stroke victory. "That was a magical year. Winning breeds winning. The more you win, the more you expect to be there. It's fun now, that's for sure."

Stadler led Bob Gilder by two going into the final round on the strength of a seven-under-par 64 on Saturday. Despite having some trouble finding the fairways, Stadler never let anyone get close. He made an eagle, three birdies and one bogey on the final hole that didn't matter, cruising in for a four-stroke win over Gilder, who finished second after a 69.

"I struggled with my driver all week," Stadler said. "But I seemed to hit it square on the face on the hard holes. I kind of kept it mistake-free until the end. The eagle at the 10th was a boost. I made virtually all of my putts within six feet this week."

Gilder agreed with that assessment. "Craig's really on his game right now," he said. "I didn't quite have it today. I could not birdie a par-five. I had it in perfect position on all of them. He was really on his game, and I was not."

Allen Doyle had the low round on Sunday, shooting a 66 to finish third at 204, one shot clear of Tom Kite, Hale Irwin, Fuzzy Zoeller, Walter Hall and Tom Watson.

Charles Schwab Cup Championship—$2,500,000
Winner: Jim Thorpe

It's not often that the winner and the runner-up are equally happy with the outcome. But then it's not often that both the winner and the runner-up walk away with so much to be thankful for. In this case Jim Thorpe was the wire-to-wire winner at the season-ending Charles Schwab Cup Championship. He smoked his traditional victory cigar long before strolling up the final fairway and tapping in for a closing round of 68, a 20-under-par 268 total and $440,000, the biggest paycheck of his career.

The runner-up, and the man who played alongside Thorpe in the final group, was Tom Watson, who trailed by four going into Sunday's finale, but could only shave one shot off Thorpe's lead. Watson shot 67 for total of 271. He also won the Champions Tour money title, edging Thorpe out by $23,000. Watson also won the Charles Schwab Cup, a new award given to the tour's most consistent performer. Moments after being presented with the Cup, Watson announced that he would donate the $1 million annuity that went with it to charities fighting ALS, the disease that afflicted Watson's caddie, Bruce Edwards.

"This is the cream," Watson said. "When you play well for a year, you make a heck of a lot of money. It's just going to allow me to give a lot more money to the charities I normally give to."

Watson gave it his all on Sunday, but Thorpe wasn't budging. Having led by at least three strokes at the end of every day after an opening 63, Thorpe hit every green in regulation on Sunday and didn't let anyone get close. "The thing that means something to me is just coming out here and playing with the best golfers in the world," he said. "This week, I probably pushed myself to the absolute limit. I don't think I can play any harder."

Despite his stellar ball-striking, Thorpe was only one under par through 15 holes. He made a 67-footer for eagle at the par-five 16th and added another birdie putt on the 17th, taking all the mystery out of the outcome, allowing himself and Watson a chance to bask in what they both knew was a special moment. "The door was open all day, until the loud slam at 16," Watson said. "Jim deserved it, because of the way he played. He was better than me today."

European Seniors Tour

Digicel Jamaica Classic—€233,099
Winner: Ray Carrasco

Ray Carrasco, a golfing epitome of a rags-to-riches lifetime, surprised himself when he won the season-opening Digicel Jamaica Classic. The 55-year-old Californian came to the Half Moon Resort in Jamaica's Montego Bay in late March with a game that was "really rusty" from a shortage of practice in the three months since undergoing shoulder surgery for an old baseball injury. The rust dissolved quickly as Carrasco proved he was no "one-win wonder" with a closing two-under-par 70 to edge Spain's Manuel Pinero by a stroke with his 211 total. Carrasco, the eldest of 15 children in a working-class family, had broken the victory ice nine months earlier at Wentworth in the Travis Perkins Senior Masters.

"It was fantastic to win at Wentworth," Carrasco said, "but in some ways this is even better because the conditions were so tough." The players faced winds up to 30 miles an hour in tropical 90 degree heat in the first of three events in the Caribbean opening of the 2003 European Seniors Tour.

Australian Terry Gale and American Jeff Van Wagenen, both previous winners on the circuit, jumped off in front the first day with four-under-par 68s, a shot ahead of England's Nick Job and American David Oakley. Carrasco had a 71 and followed with 70 Saturday to move within a stroke of the lead, then held by the quartet of Spanish veteran Manuel Pinero, England's John Morgan, Australian standout Noel Ratcliffe and newcomer Bob Larratt, a qualifying tournament graduate from Leicestershire, who fired the day's best round of 66 for his 140.

The tide turned in Carrasco's favor at the 12th hole Sunday. At that point, Carrasco trailed Morgan by two shots. However, the Englishman double-bogeyed that par-three hole and the American then produced five birdies and an incoming 33 to finish with 70–211, a shot ahead of Pinero, two ahead of Guillermo Encina and four in front of Morgan and Alan Tapie.

Royal Westmoreland Barbados Open—€185,632
Winner: Terry Gale

The time warp wasn't as great this time. Australian Terry Gale had won twice on the European Seniors Tour, first in his debut year on the circuit at the 1996 Senior PGA Championship and second six years later in the GIN Monte Carlo Invitational late in the 2002 season. Only six months elapsed before Gale scored a decisive third triumph in the Royal Westmoreland Barbados Open, rolling to a six-stroke victory at Royal Westmoreland Golf Club.

He blew things open in Saturday's second round with an eight-under-par 64 that he described as "one of the best rounds of golf I have ever put together and something I will remember for a long time to come." That sparkling effort on a windy day, when only one other player broke 70, included an eagle and eight birdies. It rushed him to a six-stroke lead after starting the day five shots behind Denis Durnian, Order of Merit runner-up the previous two seasons, who opened in front with 65. When all the returns were in, Gale was at 134 and his nearest pursuers were Durnian, who slumped to a 75, Brian Jones (71) and David Oakley (69) at 140.

Gale, 56, who won nearly 30 tournaments in his younger days on the Australasian, Far East and Japan Tours, was nonetheless a bit shaky on his front nine Sunday, turning one over par after three bogeys and two birdies. He shifted into gear when he birdied the 12th hole and finished with a par round when he dropped a 10-footer for a final birdie at the 18th hole. That gave him a 206 total and reestablished the six-stroke margin he had at the start of the day. Jones also shot 72 and shared second place with American Jerry Bruner, who closed with 69 for his 212. Durnian and Oakley, with 74s, fell back into a five-way tie for fourth with Nick Job, Denis O'Sullivan and John Chillas.

Tobago Plantations Seniors Classic—€182,041
Winner: Terry Gale

Terry Gale probably would be the last person to criticize the incongruity of tournaments on the European Seniors Tour being played a hemisphere away in the Caribbean after the trio of events there was over in early April. After all, he won twice and finished sixth in the other tournament that launched the 2003 season, defying windy conditions at all three stops with a 24-under-par overall performance.

The 56-year-old Australian capped it all at the Tobago Plantations Golf and Beach Club with the circuit's first back-to-back victories in three years. He produced a seven-under-par 65 in the final round of the Tobago Plantations Seniors Classic that gave him a three-stroke triumph over John Chillas, the second-round leader. He finished the tournament 13 under par at 203. Delroy Cambridge and Guillermo Encina tied for third six strokes behind the winner.

Gale was poised for the victory from the start. He trailed David Creamer, the 60-year-old Englishman who won the Super Senior auxiliary events in Jamaica and Barbados, by a single stroke after the first round. Creamer, better known in Britain as a table tennis champion, opened with 67. Gale (70) and Cambridge (69-69) remained a shot back after John Chillas fired a torrid 65 and took over first place Saturday with a seven-under-par 137.

On Sunday, the Australian overtook Chillas with a birdie-eagle finish to the front nine and ticked off three more birdies on the back nine for the 65. He had only one bogey over the 54 holes and remarked, "This is the best golf I have played for a long time. I just wish we could keep on playing."

AIB Irish Seniors Open—€330,000
Winner: Noel Ratcliffe

After a six-week hiatus, the European Seniors Tour moved into the meat of its 2003 schedule in Ireland and another Australian veteran came to the fore. Noel Ratcliffe, the 2000 Order of Merit leader, took over where Terry Gale left off in the Caribbean, surviving a final-round scare to win the AIB Irish Seniors Open by a stroke with his five-under-par 211. It was his seventh victory as a senior, coming after an off season in 2002.

Jamaican Delroy Cambridge, a three-time winner in 2002, was Ratcliffe's strongest opponent at Adara Manor Hotel and Golf Resort in County Limerick. Cambridge shared the first-round lead at 68 with Americans Gary Wintz and Jeff Van Wagenen, a shot ahead of Ratcliffe and fellow Australians David Good and Brian Jones. Then, on Saturday, Cambridge overcame tough playing conditions — rain and gusty winds — to take solo position of first place with 69 for 137. Ratcliffe matched the 69 and had the runner-up spot to himself just a stroke off the pace entering the final round. American Bob Lendzion was at 140.

Ratcliffe moved ahead Sunday after Delroy three-putted the first hole, and the lead changed hands three times in the tight finish. Ratcliffe seemed to have it wrapped up in the stretch, but lost his tee shot on the short 17th and needed the par he made at the 18th for 73 to nip Cambridge (75), Lendzion (72) and Scotland's Martin Gray (70). Japan's Seiji Ebihara, who was trying to win the Irish Seniors for a third year in a row, finished another shot back with 72 for 213. "It was tough out there," said Ratcliffe. "The wind was swirling, which made club selection very difficult. Not a great day to play golf."

Wallonia Open—€130,000
Winner: Hank Woodrome

Hank Woodrome arrived in Belgium for the Wallonia Open virtually and understandably unnoticed, but left to the applause accorded him as a winner, his first on the European Seniors Tour. With the victory, the Californian, whose ranking was so low beforehand that he had only played in two of the first four events, gained exempt status for two years. As he said, "Now I can start to plan my life sensibly again."

The win did not come easily. In fact, it came in the first playoff of the season when Woodrome defeated Ulsterman Eddie Polland on the first extra hole. The two men had tied after 54 holes with six-under-par 210s.

Neither man drew much attention as they shot 71s in the first round. That focus was on South Africa's Robbie Stewart, who had turned 50 two days earlier and took the lead with 68. He faded Saturday, however, and American Steve Stull and Englishman Denis Durnian forged in front with 138s. Stull, who won in 2002 at Tobago, shot 67 and Durnian 68. Polland was in a group of five at 140, while Woodrome had another 71 for 142.

Woodrome finished strongly Sunday with an eagle at the par-five 11th and birdies at the 14th and 16th, but missed an eight-footer at the 18th that would have won the tournament. He shot 68. Polland also had a chance to end it in regulation moments later. After making three birdies and a bogey through 17 holes, he missed from 12 feet for the win. On the playoff hole, the 18th, Woodrome reached the green in regulation, but Polland came up short. He took three to get down, missing a four-foot par putt. Woodrome two-putted from 10 feet for the victory, denying Polland his first victory on the circuit since 1999. Four players — Terry Gale, a two-time 2003 victor; Bob Larratt, David Oakley and Denis O'Sullivan — missed the playoff by one stroke.

Irvine Whitlock Jersey Seniors Classic—€143,025
Winner: Malcolm Gregson

Experience paid off for Malcolm Gregson on the final day of the Irvine Whitlock Jersey Seniors Classic. Gregson, a Ryder Cup player and seven-time winner in Europe and Africa in his younger days, was locked in a tight battle with European Seniors Tour rookie Bob Cameron and was coming off a lackluster, front-nine 37. But he knew how to win and did so by running off four birdies on the next five holes. He shot 70 for a 13-under-par 203, finishing three strokes ahead of Cameron.

"This is a dream come true for me," said the 59-year-old Gregson, whose last of three Seniors Tour victories came in 1998 in the Is Molas Seniors Open. "To be honest, at my age, I didn't think I would ever win again."

The first round belonged to Bill Longmuir, launching what was to be one of the best showings of the season. Longmuir, a journeyman on the European Tour for nearly two decades who just turned 50 earlier in the week, began his senior career with an eight-under-par 64 at the La Moye Golf Club in Jersey. He credited the performance to a winter in Florida practicing under the watchful eye of his good friend Greg Norman. He had a three-stroke lead over four players — Gregson, David Good, Paul Leonard and David Oakley.

Longmuir didn't have it Saturday, though. He slipped to 75 and Gregson and Denis Durnian took charge. Durnian posted a 65 early for 133 and the lead, but Gregson came in late in the round with an eagle at the 16th and a birdie at the 18th for 66 and a matching 133. It was four strokes back to Denis O'Sullivan in third place.

Cameron, the former Sundridge Park professional in Kent who started the round six off the pace, moved into contention on the front nine Sunday as Gregson and, more extremely, Durnian struggled. Durnian eventually shot 75 and tied for third at 208 with Guillermo Encina. Although he couldn't outplay Gregson, Cameron shot 67 to nail down second place.

De Vere Northumberland Seniors Classic—€211,445
Winner: Jerry Bruner

Jerry Bruner did not have fond memories of past experiences at the Slaley Hall course when he arrived at the site of the De Vere Northumberland Seniors Classic in late June, but he didn't let it interfere with one of his best showing in four years on the European Seniors Tour. Two years earlier, the

American seemingly had the De Vere title in his pocket until Noel Ratcliffe picked it when he holed a 100-yard wedge shot at the final hole for his second eagle of the round and won by a stroke.

"It took a while to get over that that one," Bruner admitted in the glow of his strong, four-stroke victory, his second on the European circuit. The 56-year-old Californian won the European Seniors Tour Championship in 2001 and had nine second-place finishes during his previous four years overseas.

Bruner took charge in Friday's opening round and was never challenged as he rolled to the wire-to-wire victory. He opened with a four-under-par 68 on a day in which he said "the wind was strong enough to blow the roof off our house in California." It gave him a one-shot lead over Spaniard Manuel Pinero. Bruner stretched his lead to five strokes Saturday with a dazzling 65, ringing up eight birdies and taking a single bogey. Scot John Chillas also shot 65 and moved up into a second-place tie with Pinero (69) at 138.

A lightning storm early Sunday delayed play for two hours, but it didn't bother Bruner. Birdies at the fourth and seventh holes gave him a comfort level that kept him in control, even when Chillas made a mid-round challenge with four birdies in five holes. Bruner finished with 69 for 202 and the four-stroke margin over Chillas. It was the Scot's second runner-up finish and fourth top-10 of the year. Rookie Bob Cameron, second the week before, placed third at 208.

Ryder Cup Wales Seniors Open—€725,917
Winner: Bill Longmuir

Talk about making an instant impact! Playing in just his third event on the European Seniors Tour, Bill Longmuir not only walked off with his first victory but also soared into the top position on the Order of Merit. This happened because the tournament — the Ryder Cup Wales Seniors Open — sported the biggest purse of the 2003 season other than the Senior British Open itself and prize money converts into Order of Merit points.

Longmuir, who had hinted at things to come when, less than a month earlier, he shot 64 in his very first senior round at the Jersey Seniors and finished eighth, got better every day in his victory quest at Royal St. David's Golf Club in Wales. Ultimately, he posted an eight-under-par 199 on the par-69 course and won by three strokes over American David Oakley. As he mentioned in Jersey, the victorious Scot attributed his success to his winter of practice in Florida as the guest of Greg Norman, a good friend from their contemporary days on the European Tour.

The story the first day, though, was yet another remarkable performance by Neil Coles, one of the game's most enduring players. Coles, the record-holder as senior golf's oldest winner and runner-up to Des Smyth in that category on the regular European Tour, shot 65 less than three months before his 69th birthday and shared the lead with Chile's Guillermo Encina. Longmuir opened with 68.

Coles had a 70 Saturday, dropping back as Encina, a frequent contender in earlier 2003 tournaments, duplicated his 65 and assumed a two-stroke lead over Oakley and Australia's Brian Jones. Longmuir improved by two shots with 66 and moved into fourth place, but trailed by four shots going into the final round.

Encina's hopes for his initial tour victory fizzled as he struggled to a 73, and Longmuir took advantage of the opening. Even par through six holes, Longmuir moved in front to stay with birdies on three of the next four holes. Playing the 202-yard 18th hole, Longmuir thought that he was tied with Oakley, who was in the final group behind him, but he clinched the victory with a final birdie off a six-iron tee shot to five feet. Not vital, it turned out, because the American bogeyed the last two holes for 70–202. Encina finished third at 203.

The Mobile Cup—€181,670
Winner: Carl Mason

A copycat scenario unfolded in The Mobile Cup tournament at Stoke Park, Buckinghamshire. A week after Bill Longmuir won within a month of his 50th birthday, Carl Mason duplicated the feat. In fact, the Englishman was making just his second start when he edged Bob Cameron, another first-year man, by a stroke with his 10-under-par 203. It was his first victory since he won twice on the European Tour in 1994 and it launched a top-ranking season. He won three more times before the end of the year.

Simon Owen, of near-miss fame in the 1978 Open Championship won by Jack Nicklaus, set the first-round pace with 66, one stroke in front of Denis O'Sullivan and two ahead of the again contending Guillermo Encina and Cameron. Mason shot 69 and Longmuir 70. The next day, Mason claimed first place with 66, parring in after eagling the 13th hole, as Encina and Cameron both shot 69s for 137s, two back.

Sunday's round did not start well for Mason. He bogeyed the first hole, Cameron birdied, and they were tied for the lead. The two senior rookies battled evenly until Mason racked up successive birdies at the 13th and 14th holes for a two-stroke lead. Cameron struck back with a birdie at the 16th but couldn't make up the other shot. Mason shot 68 and Cameron 69 for his 204. Italian Guiseppe Cali took third place at 208.

Mason might have known he would win. His wife, Beryl, wasn't there, just as she had missed his two European Tour victories in 1994 and three other wins in Africa. She broke an ankle while following him the preceding week in Wales.

Senior British Open—€1,422,297
Winner: Tom Watson

Tom Watson's love affair with the British Isles added a chapter in late July when the 53-year-old Hall of Famer captured the Senior British Open on the same Scottish grounds of Turnberry where he defeated Jack Nicklaus for the 1977 Open Championship in one of the most transfixing duels in the history of the game. The victory, coupled with Watson's run of five Open Championship triumphs in eight years in the 1970s and 1980s, accentuated the success he has enjoyed in Scotland and England, far greater than any other American in history.

Even though he fashioned a potent 64 in the final round, Watson gained new life when Carl Mason, the neophyte senior riding the crest of a victory in his second start the previous week, stumbled with a double-bogey six at the 72nd hole and dropped into a tie with him at 17-under-par 263. Watson won the title, his second senior major (2001 Senior PGA), on the second hole of the subsequent playoff.

With its handsome purse and newly accepted status on America's Champions Tour as a bona fide major, the Senior British Open drew its strongest field ever with its return to Turnberry, where it came into existence in 1987. Two of the standouts — Watson and Tom Kite — shared the first-round lead with four-under 66s, one stroke ahead of seven others, including Mason. The Englishman, who was grouped with Watson and Jack Nicklaus the first two days, outscored them both when he unleashed a 64 Friday for a 131 that moved him into the lead, one stroke ahead of American D.A. Weibring (69-63) and two in front of Watson (67).

Mason and Weibring both carded 65s Saturday as Watson slipped three off the pace with a 66–199 that put him in a tie for third with Kite and Bruce Summerhays. Watson closed the gap on the Englishman Sunday, the big jump coming when he holed a 112-yard sand wedge shot at the par-four 10th hole. Playing ahead of Mason, Watson reached the 18th hole seven under par for the round, but bogeyed there. "To be honest, I thought I lost it there. Carl played so great all week," Watson reflected. However, Mason drove into a fairway bunker and took the six that sent the decision to the playoff. After both parred the first extra hole, Watson won with another par after Mason again found sand off the tee.

Amid the disappointment, Mason had the consolation of knowing that second-place money vaulted him into first place on his tour's Order of Merit. Summerhays shot 65 Sunday and missed the playoff by a stroke.

De Vere PGA Seniors Championship—€283,608
Winner: Bill Longmuir

The domination of the 50-year-olds continued when the long-established De Vere PGA Seniors Championship was played again at the De Vere Carden Park course. Bill Longmuir, who reached the age minimum in June, scored his second victory in a month the first weekend of August at Carden Park, and Carl Mason, the equally hot newcomer, tied for second with Irishman Denis O'Sullivan, two behind the winner.

The victorious Scot was a model of consistency in the PGA Seniors. He laced together four rounds in the 60s in shooting his 17-under-par 271, starting it off with a 68 in the Thursday round. That left him three shots off the lead as O'Sullivan opened with 65. The next day, Longmuir shot 67 and was joined in first place at 135 by Nick Job, who counted his first-ever competitive hole-in-one in his 65. His unique prize for the ace: 180 bottles of Australian wine. O'Sullivan took a 71 to drop a stroke behind the leaders, joined at 136 by Denis Durnian and American Dick McClean, who shot 64, then disappeared from view over the weekend.

It was Mason's turn to shoot 64 Saturday and it elevated him into a tie for the lead at 204 with Job and Longmuir. Mason eagled the first hole, then, after being stung by a wasp at the fourth tee, ran off three birdies and another eagle. Meanwhile, Longmuir was getting through a shaky round with a 69 that also included two eagles, six birdies and seven bogeys, among them a missed 12-incher at the last hole. Job had four birdies and a bogey in his 69 round.

Longmuir more than made up for his embarrassing missed putt in the final round as he notched the victory and joined Terry Gale as a double 2003 winner. Longmuir led by just a stroke after bogeying the 17th, but finished in fine style when he fired a nine-iron approach to seven feet and dropped the birdie putt for 67 and the winning 271. He became the first rookie to win twice since John Grace did it in 2000 and the youngest two-time winner in tour history, bagging the PGA Seniors 54 days into his 50th year. Mason shot 69 and O'Sullivan 67 with a birdie at the last hole in tying for second place.

Bad Ragaz PGA Seniors Open—€160,000
Winner: Horacio Carbonetti

After moving around Great Britain for two months, the European Seniors Tour set up shop in Switzerland for the Bad Ragaz PGA Seniors Open. It proved to be a week of sensational scoring by many in the field, but most particularly by Horacio Carbonetti. The Argentinean rang up his first victory, winning by three strokes with a 13-under-par 197.

Birdies were flying everywhere right from the start in oppressive heat at the Bad Ragaz Golf Club. England's David Creamer and South Africa's Neville Clarke had 15 birdies between them as they shot 63s to take the first-round lead, one stroke ahead of the 55-year-old Carbonetti, who led the qualifying tournament in 2002 in acquiring his playing privileges.

The Argentinean had to shake off three early bogeys in gathering in his 64 Friday, but was much more solid Saturday when he duplicated the score and set a European Seniors Tour 36-hole record with his 128. He had seven birdies and a bogey as he moved two strokes in front of Clarke, who shot 67, and three ahead of Priscillo Diniz, who tied the course record with 62. Bill Longmuir, shooting for his third victory in his first seven starts, kept his hopes alive when he finished strongly for a 64, but he trailed by five strokes at 133.

Carbonetti was never challenged Sunday as he rolled to the first tour victory ever by an Argentinean. Two early birdies and a bogey at the 15th produced a modest 69 and his 197 total, which was just two strokes off the all-time 54-hole record. "I didn't play as well as I did during the first two rounds, but I ground out the pars and that proved enough," commented Carbonetti afterward. David Good of Australia climbed into second place Sunday with 66–200, and Diniz (70) tied for third at 201 with Longmuir (68) and John Irwin of Canada (69).

Travis Perkins Senior Masters—€320,720
Winner: John Chillas

Scotland's John Chillas, who had been knocking at the door frequently during the season, became the fifth first-time winner of 2003 when he took a one-stroke victory in the Travis Perkins Senior Masters on the Edinburgh course at England's famed Wentworth Club. Chillas, twice a runner-up earlier in his third season on the circuit, closed with 69 for 209, seven under par, on a warm day in which the hottest player was Neil Coles, the oldest on site at age 68.

The Irish took charge in the opening round with a pair of 67s as Chillas began quietly with 70. Eamonn Darcy, just back from America and competition on the Champions Tour there, and David Jones were the surprise leaders, Darcy because of jet lag and Jones because of inactivity on the circuit. Jones is heavily into the course design business and hadn't played a competitive round in six weeks. A miracle three, when he holed out a difficult pitch shot after winding up unplayable in a bush at a par-three hole, saved him from early disaster.

Chillas' chances seemed a bit bleak after Saturday's round when the two top positions were held by Bill Longmuir and Terry Gale, the season's only double winners. Longmuir shot 68 for 137 and Gale 70 for 139 to pace the field. Gale, making his best showing since his pair of victories in the Caribbean at the start of the season, made two late bogeys, though. Chillas, with another 70, was tied for third at 140 with Order of Merit leader Carl Mason (69), Jeff Van Wagenen (69) and Darcy (72).

Sunday was a showing of extremes, but not by the winner. Chillas made four birdies on the back nine, then bogeyed the 18th for his 69–209. Longmuir made the victory possible when his game failed him for the first time on the senior tour. He suffered a pair of double bogeys on the front nine and wound up shooting 78. On the other hand, the remarkable Coles charged up the standings. After a bogey at the second hole, Coles amassed 10 birdies, shot 64, the low round of the week by two strokes, and finished in third place.

Nigel Mansell Classic—€212,677
Winner: Mike Miller

Perhaps he drew inspiration from the maiden victory of fellow Scot John Chillas the week before. Something brought out the best in Mike Miller at the Nigel Mansell Classic. Miller's best showings all year had been sixth- and ninth-place finishes early in the season before he joined Chillas and four others as a first-time winner on the European Seniors Tour with a two-stroke victory. It was the third straight week that a previously winless player broke the ice. He shook off a potentially unnerving shanked iron shot on the 71st hole with a regulation par at the last hole for 72 and an 11-under-par 205.

Perhaps, too, it was a new putting grip that propelled Miller to victory. Coming off a run of poor putting, the Scot seized the lead the first day and never let go. He opened with a five-under-par 67 at Mansell's Woodbury Park course in Devon and led by a stroke over Neville Clarke, Guillermo Encina, England's Ian Mosey and Australian Ian Stanley. His five-birdie round included one 50-foot putt and three others of between 15 and 25 feet.

Miller's game remained solid Saturday. He again went without a bogey and remarked that "I played beautifully out there today. I don't think I made a single mistake." He had an eagle on the par-five 14th and four birdies for 66 to go 11 under par at 133. Terry Gale, a two-time winner in 2003, played his last 10 holes in seven under for 65–135.

On Sunday, Miller was sailing toward an easy victory when near disaster struck at the 17th tee. "I tried to drive a low iron down the fairway, but I completely miscued it and shanked it straight into the trees." He double-bogeyed the hole and his lead was down to one. But he regrouped, fired his six-iron tee shot across the water onto the green at the par-three finishing hole, and two-putted from 40 feet for the victory. Gale finished in a tie for second at 207 with Delroy Cambridge, Denis Durnian, Denis O'Sullivan and Stanley.

Mansell, the Formula One racing great and tournament host, is a two-handicap amateur, played in the event and shot 73-72 before he blew a piston with a 78 Sunday. Still, with 223, he finished ahead of 13 professionals in the field.

Charles Church Scottish Seniors Open—€217,390
Winner: Terry Gale

Australian Terry Gale became the first player to win three times on the 2003 European Seniors Tour and he had a pretty good idea that victory was in the cards for him at the Charles Church Scottish Seniors Open.

"This has been coming for a few weeks now," Gale observed after scoring his overall fifth senior victory at The Roxburgh Golf Club near Kelso, Scotland. He had played in the final group in the previous three tournaments, "but I didn't quite do it."

The tournament drew particular attention in Scotland because it marked the senior debut of popular native son Sam Torrance. While he was opening with a 73 that proved to be his undoing in the long run, Englishman Nick Job took the lead with a five-under-par 67, his round highlighted by a 243-yard, three-wood second shot at the par-five 11th that set up a 10-foot eagle putt.

Gale was two back at 69, then took the lead Saturday. He blew up a storm early with three birdies and an eagle on the first six holes and added another birdie on the back nine for 66–135. Fellow Australian David Good shot a tournament record-tying 65 and moved into second place at 137. Job slipped back to 138 with 71.

It looked as though Gale might let another chance escape Sunday when he bogeyed the second hole, but he rebounded with four birdies on the next five holes and was never threatened after that. He went on to shoot two-under-par 70 for an 11-under-par 205 total that gave him a two-stroke victory over Job (69) and Barry Vivian (68). Torrance shot 74 Sunday and tied for 15th place.

Bovis Lend Lease European Senior Masters—€323,041
Winner: Paul Leonard

Paul Leonard finally got the Irish into the winner's circle of the 2003 European Seniors Tour, but the victory in the Bovis Lend Lease European Senior Masters came as a bit of a shocker, especially to the 58-year-old veteran from Northern Ireland. "This was so unexpected," said Leonard, whose only victory in almost nine years came in the Efteling European Trophy in 1998. "I haven't been playing well in recent weeks because I've been suffering with a virus."

There was nothing sick about his game Sunday in the final round at Woburn Golf and Country Club in England. He came from six strokes off the lead with a six-under-par 66 for 208, then waited and watched as, one by one, the likely contenders fell short on Woburn's Duke's course. Nick Job and Bill Longmuir finished a stroke back and tied for second at 209.

It was a constantly changing scene from the start at Woburn. The first day saw two unlikely players — Englishman Keith Ashdown and South Africa's John Mashego — lead with 67s, then fall out of the picture after that. On Saturday, 60-year-old Irishman Liam Higgins, who hadn't won since the mid-1990s, shot into the lead with a 66 for 136, three shots ahead of his nearest pursuers — John Chillas and Brian Jones — and four ahead of Sam Torrance, playing in his second senior event.

Higgins suffered the same fate as Ashdown and Mashego Sunday, shooting 76 and eventually falling to ninth place. Leonard went the other way with four front-nine birdies, stumbled with a drive into the trees and a double bogey at the seventh, and reeled off four more birdies on the incoming nine. Job got to seven under at the 14th hole, but couldn't muster a birdie on the last four holes. For Longmuir, it was too little too late, as two birdies on the last three holes didn't quite reach.

Ian Mosey was eight under at one point but took two bogeys on the last three holes, and John Chillas had a last-ditch chance for a tie but needed and failed to hole out from the fairway at the 18th. They tied for fourth at 210 with Torrance and Jerry Bruner.

Daily Telegraph/Turismo Andaluz Seniors Match Play—€142,054
Winner: Carl Mason

Carl Mason became the European Seniors Tour's third multiple winner and strengthened his hold on the Order of Merit lead when he waded through five duels in four days to win the Daily Telegraph/Turismo Andaluz Seniors Match Play at Los Flamingos Golf Club near Malaga, Spain, in mid-September. Mason completed his march to his second title of the season with an exciting, 1-up victory over Ireland's Denis O'Sullivan on the final Saturday.

The lead changed hands six times in that final match. After the last switch, Mason opened a two-hole lead with three to play, only to have the Irishman square the match again with birdies at the 16th and 17th holes. At the 18th, Mason got up and down from a bunker, but O'Sullivan hit a poor wedge to the front edge of the green and three-putted. "What a dreadful way to finish," O'Sullivan mourned. Mason concurred, "The match was so good it deserved a better finish than that."

Mason, playing in a match play event for the first time in 15 years, had his toughest battle with Spaniard Manuel Pinero, who took him to the 20th hole before losing in the second round. Mason won his other matches — over Martin Gray in the first round, Noel Ratcliffe in the quarter-finals and Denis Durnian in the semi-finals — by 3-and-2 scores.

O'Sullivan's toughest match came against Delroy Cambridge, the defending champion, in the semi-finals, O'Sullivan winning on the 18th hole. He took out Eddie Polland, 2 and 1, in the first round, and John Chillas in the second round and Jim Rhodes, the 2001 winner, in the quarter-finals by 3-and-2 counts.

Merseyside English Seniors Open—€215,692
Winner: Carl Mason

Carl Mason took any suspense that there might have been out of the race for the end-of-season No. 1 spot on the Order of Merit when he followed his Seniors Match Play triumph in Spain with an equally tight win in the Merseyside English Seniors Open at Hillside Golf Club in Southport. The one-stroke victory, his third, gave Mason enough points to clinch the victory, a noteworthy achievement considering that he didn't qualify for the tour until the eighth tournament. His closest pursuer, Bill Longmuir, finished in a second-place tie at Hillside with Denis O'Sullivan, whose "luck of the Irish" was all bad during the 2003 season so far as victory near-misses were concerned.

Yet another first-year man made his mark there when Alan Mew, a Trinidad and Tobago native who lives in Southampton, shot 67 in the opening round of the new tournament and took a two-stroke lead over Simon Owen and David Oakley. Australian David Good grabbed first place Saturday with a sparkling, seven-under-par 65 for 136, but the 56-year-old from Tasmania had no comfort zone with Mason just a stroke behind him after shooting 66 and Longmuir (140) and O'Sullivan (141) next in line.

When Good faded in the early going Sunday, it all came down to a tense 18th hole. Mason led Longmuir and O'Sullivan by a stroke, but drove into a fairway bunker, reminiscent of the mishap that cost him the title at Turnberry in the Senior British Open. This time, though, he played a wonderful seven iron onto the green and two-putted for 71 and 208 total. Longmuir had 69 and O'Sullivan 68 for their 209s.

Tunisian Seniors Open—€180,685
Winner: David Good

It was a complete turnabout for David Good at the Tunisian Seniors Open. The week before at the Merseyside English Open, the 56-year-old Australian took the lead into the final round and imploded with a 74, finishing fourth. At Port El Kantaoui Golf Club in Tunisia, though, he raced from a share of the second-round lead to a five-stroke victory with a course-record 64. "I waited for this for quite a while," said Good, whose only previous victory came in the Legends of Golf event in 2001.

Two 2003 winners — Bill Longmuir and Horacio Carbonetti — started fast in the beastly heat of North Africa Friday, turning 12 birdies and an eagle into a pair of 65s. Good started with 66, sharing third place with Geoff Tickell of Wales. Good and Carbonetti posted 134 totals the second day to lead by one stroke over Italy's Guiseppe Cali and two over Longmuir (71). The day's big excitement came from the 354-yard hole-in-one recorded by Guillermo Encina at the dogleg par-four 11th hole, the longest ace by far in tour history. As was the case when Nick Job made an hole-in-one earlier in the season, Encina's prize was wine, 354 bottles of it, and he doesn't drink. That same day, Delroy Cambridge also achieved another rarity — eagles on two par-fours.

Good was on top of his game Sunday and gave no one a chance from his first-hole birdie on. He was out in 31 with an eagle at the par-five ninth and put it away by following with four consecutive birdies for the 64. "Today I came close to playing as well as I have ever have," he evaluated after signing for his 64 that gave him an 18-under-par 198. Encina followed his ace and 67 with a 65 Sunday to snatch second place with 203. Carbonetti shot 70 and finished third with 204.

Estoril Seniors Tour Championship—€240,000
Winner: Carl Mason

Carl Mason put an exclamation point on what was a remarkable rookie season when he totally dominated the Estoril Seniors Tour Championship. Not only did he lead the season-ending tournament at Quinta da Marinha near Lisbon, Portugal, from start to finish, but he left the field eight strokes in his dust.

Consider what Mason did in 2003: Not turning 50 until June 25, the Englishman played in just 11 tournaments, yet the Tour Championship was his fourth victory, and he ran away with the Order of Merit with a record €350,242. Not to mention how close he came to winning the Senior British Open in July.

"It's hard to believe what I have managed to do," summed up the Englishman. "I thought that with a bit of luck I might be able to win once before the end of the season, but to win four times is beyond my wildest dreams." In fact, only Tommy Horton, the European Seniors Tour's all-time champion, won as many tournaments in a single season. He did that four times.

Mason was off and running Friday with a seven-under-par 64, staking himself to a three-stroke lead over American Steve Stull and four over Terry Gale. He ran off six birdies and a bogey on the first 15 holes, then knocked a 240-yard, five-wood shot four feet from the hole at the par-five 16th and dropped the eagle putt. Mason maintained a two-shot lead Saturday despite a two-over-par 73 in a round played in a heavy rainstorm. Actually, it appeared he was turning the competition into a rout until he bogeyed his last four holes. Gale shot 71 and joined Keith MacDonald in second place at 139.

Mason quickly eliminated all opposition in the early going Sunday as he went four ahead with birdies at the third and fifth holes and established the huge final margin with birdies on four of the last six holes for 65 and 11-under-par 202 total. MacDonald, Noel Ratcliffe and Dragon Taki were distant seconds at 210.

Japan Senior Tour

Castle Hill Open—¥30,000,000
Winner: Chen Tze-ming

Chen Tze-ming overcame a slow start and staggered to his second victory on the Japan Senior Tour in the season-launching Castle Hill Open in May at Castle Hill Country Club in Aichi Prefecture. Despite an opening 73 and a closing 75, Chen managed a one-stroke victory with his two-under-par 214.

The first-round 73 left the Taiwanese player virtually miles out of the lead, as Toshiharu Morimoto fired a 66 and led by three strokes over Kazuo Kanayama and by four over Katsunari Takahashi and Kunio Yamashita. Then, in a complete turning of the tables, Chen matched Morimoto's 66 and soared all the way into first place, three strokes in front of Morimoto (76) and Takahashi (72). Kanayama disappeared with an 81 and finished 46th with 80–230.

Chen's final-round 75 for 214 total was just enough to edge Morimoto and his 73–215.

Aderans Wellness Open—¥60,000,000
Winner: Takashi Miyoshi

Three weeks later, Takashi Miyoshi took a somewhat different route to his second victory on the Japan Senior Tour. Miyoshi trailed only two players after the first round of the Aderans Wellness Open in Niigata Prefecture, led after two days and snagged the win in a playoff after finishing the 54 holes tied with Kinpachi Yoshimura at six-under-par 210.

Mikio Ichikawa put a sparkling 66 on the board on opening day and led by three over Hiroshi Fujita. Miyoshi was among eight players who started with 70s and, when he followed with 68, he slipped into a one-stroke lead at 138. Ichikawa skidded to 73 for 139, joined in the runner-up position by Yoshimura, who added the week's best round of 65 to his opening 74. Yoshimura shot 71 in the final round to overtake Miyoshi, who had a par round for his 210. Seiji Ebihara and Terry Gale both shot 68s but missed the playoff by a stroke.

Fancl Senior Classic—¥60,000,000

Winner: Katsunari Takahashi

Katsunari Takahashi began his domination of the 2003 Japan Senior Tour with his usual victory in the Fancl Senior Classic. Takahashi picked up his first victory of the season and sixth of his senior career at Susono Country Club, outlasting Takashi Miyoshi by one stroke with his six-under-par 210. It was his third consecutive victory in the Fancl Classic.

Seiichi Kanai, the leading all-time winner on the circuit with 10 victories, shot the only round in the 60s the first day, his 68 giving him a two-stroke lead over Miyoshi, the Aderans Wellness winner in the last previous tournament two months earlier in the season, and four others – Hsieh Min-nan, Koji Okuno, Tadami Ueno and Mitsuo Iwata.

Takahashi began with 71, then followed with 68 for 139, tying Miyoshi (69) for the lead. Kenjiro Iwama and Teruo Nakamura were next in the standings at 141, but never challenged the leaders. Takahashi shot 71 to Miyoshi's 72 in the last round to lock up the victory.

Japan PGA Senior Championship—¥30,000,000

Winner: Noboru Fujiike

Noboru Fujiike, who last won a professional tournament in 1983, ended the victory drought in fine style, winning the Japan PGA Senior Championship, one of the two most prestigious events on the Japan Senior Tour and the first of three October tournaments concluding the light season. Fujiike won by two strokes over Katsunari Takahashi, preventing him from sweeping the final four events of the year.

The lead changed hands every day at Yamada Golf Club in Chiba Prefecture. Shinsaku Maeda was in front the first day with his five-under-par 67, one stroke ahead of Takahashi and Tadeo Furuichi and two on top of Fujiike and Toru Nakamura.

Shoichi Sato took over the next day when he blistered the course with 64 for 138. Takahashi remained just a stroke off the lead with 71–139, and Fujiike (71) came in with 140 with Seiji Ono, who had a pair of 70s. Takahashi moved ahead in the third round, shooting 69 for 208 and a two-shot lead over Fujiike (70). Ono (70) was the runner-up at 209. Fujiike secured the victory with his 68–278 as Takahashi slipped to a par 72 and 280. Yoshitaka Yamamoto was another three shots back in third place.

PGA Philanthropy Biglayzac Senior—¥30,000,000

Winner: Katsunari Takahashi

Katsunari Takahashi became the Japan Senior Tour's first multiple winner of 2003 when he came from behind to win the PGA Philanthropy Biglayzac Senior at Biglayzac Country Club in Miyagi Prefecture. On a day when 70 was the best score, Takahashi shot 72 and took the title by three strokes with his five-under-par 283. It was his seventh senior victory in four years.

Toyotake Nakao had a 67 on opening Thursday to lead Takanori Sekura, Koji Nakajima and Tatsuo Fujima by a stroke. Takahashi began with 71, then grabbed a share of the lead the next day with a 69–140, tied with Nakao, who dropped off to a 73. Sekura shot 67 Saturday for 210 and edged a stroke ahead of Takahashi before Takahashi closed it out Sunday.

Japan Senior Open Championship—¥50,000,000
Winner: Katsunari Takahashi

Katsunari Takahashi landed his first title on the Japan Senior Tour in 2000 when he won the Japan Senior Open Championship, the No. 1 event on the circuit each year. Three years later, he repeated that Senior Open victory at Takarazuka Golf Club in Hyogo Prefecture to climax his fine season with his third title of the year and eighth of his senior career.

It took a strong weekend finish for Takahashi to get to the front at the end. He started 72-71 as Yukio Noguchi opened with 66 and led by three strokes. Noguchi skied to 75 the next day, though, and Yoshitaka Yamamoto took over the lead with 70-66–136. He led Toru Nakamura by three.

Then Nakamura turned the tables, shooting 68 to Noguchi's 73, and went two shots in front Saturday. Takahashi shot 68 and climbed into third place at 210 and followed with his winning 67–277, five under par. With his eight victories, Takahashi trails only Seiichi Kanai (10) and Fujio Kobayashi (nine) on the all-time victory list.

14. Women's Tours

The winningest professional golfer in the world in 2003 was a woman, which should come as no surprise, given the dominance we have come to expect from Annika Sorenstam. But Sorenstam didn't win the most events of the year. Her seven victories missed the mark by three. Yuri Fudoh won 10 titles on the Japan LPGA Tour and none outside her country. She tied for 20th in the U.S. Women's Open. Fudoh's dominance in Japan and nowhere else could be compared to that of Jumbo Ozaki.

Fudoh, just 26 years old but on the Japan LPGA Tour since 1996, compiled record earnings of ¥149,328,679 to lead the money list for the fourth year in a row. She had two runner-up and seven other top-five finishes. That's 19 of her 24 tournaments. Her figure on the Women's World Money List was $1,278,228 for fourth place.

Perhaps the most telling statistic about Fudoh's season: Her earnings total exceeded that of No. 1 Toshimitsu Izawa on the men's Japan Tour by almost ¥14 million.

Sorenstam's game traveled well. The 33-year-old Swede won once in Japan (Nichirei Cup World Ladies), once in England (Weetabix Women's British Open), and five times in the United States including another major title (McDonald's LPGA Championship). She also was one four-wood shot away from possibly capturing her third U.S. Women's Open and one wedge shot away from victory in the Kraft Nabisco Championship, which would have been a calendar-year Grand Slam. As it was, she became only the fourth woman to win the career Grand Slam, and in October she was inducted into the World Golf Hall of Fame.

You probably heard that Sorenstam took her game to the PGA Tour. The Bank of America Colonial, once a stately event on the men's circuit, had fallen on hard times, stuck in the schedule between the Masters and the Memorial and looking for a boost to attract fans and ratings. They found it when Sorenstam accepted an invitation to play. In what was the biggest newsmaking event in golf and one of the biggest in all of sports, Sorenstam became the first woman in 58 years to play in a PGA Tour event. Her 71 and 74 scores missed the cut, but for five days in May, Sorenstam provided one of the biggest news events in the world.

Sorenstam's goal was to see how she stacked up against the best players in the game and to draw attention to the women's game. She accomplished both. She drew a great deal of attention to the women's professional game, which had a pretty good year.

In addition to Sorenstam's seven wins, Korea's Ji-Hee Lee won four times in Japan and Korea's Se Ri Pak and Taiwan's Candie Kung had three victories apiece in America. Sophie Gustafson of Sweden won once in America and captured three titles in Europe on the Evian Ladies European Tour, putting her tied for third, along with Lee, in line behind Fudoh and Sorenstam among the winningest women golfers.

American Juli Inkster came away with a couple of victories — one in the United States and one at the Evian Masters in France. Other two-time winners were Australia's Rachel Teske and Korea's Hee-Won Han in America,

Michiko Hattori and Miho Koga in Japan, and Laurette Maritz in South Africa.

The Women's World Money List was led by Sorenstam with $2,159,050, followed by Koreans Pak with $1,611,928 and Grace Park with $1,417,702, then Fudoh and Korea's Han with $1,111,860. The leading American was Inkster, in sixth place with $1,028,205.

The one thing LPGA Tour commissioner Ty Votaw emphasized to his players in 2003 was the importance of personality and congeniality to the ongoing success of the LPGA Tour. In that respect he found some naturals in players like Angela Stanford, a bubbly Fort Worth, Texas, native who won her first event at the ShopRite Classic and made two long bombs in the U.S. Women's Open, one on the 18th hole in regulation to get into a playoff and the second on the last hole of the playoff to force Hilary Lunke to make an eight-footer to win. Lunke, another example of what Votaw had been preaching, made the putt in the playoff to become an unlikely major champion.

The women's year ended much the way it began, with Sorenstam making headlines. This time it was over Thanksgiving weekend, and Sorenstam was once again playing with the boys. Her 39-yard sand shot found the hole for eagle in the Skins Game and was the talk at many dinner tables over the holidays. That she finished second to Fred Couples in the two-day event was, in her words, "the perfect ending to a special year."

U.S. LPGA Tour

Welch's/Fry's Championship—$800,000
Winner: Wendy Doolan

On a week when the attention-starved LPGA Tour wanted to make a positive splash after a four-month hiatus, the biggest news coming out the Welch's/Fry's Championship in Tucson, Arizona, concerned the emerging affair between the commissioner, Ty Votaw, and one the players, Sophie Gustafson. The LPGA board of directors met the week before the start of the season in what should have been a strategy session. Instead, the board's No. 1 agenda item was the dalliance of the commissioner.

"We had a meeting and the matter was discussed openly and honestly," said board chairwoman Marguerite Sallee. "There is 100 percent support for Ty. It is one of those matters that is certainly gray. It would be different if he were seeing one of his reports at the office of the LPGA. What matters is how it is handled, and I think Ty has behaved with grace and dignity."

Votaw graciously declined comment, saying only that he was "not going to comment on matters concerning my personal life," while his tour was trying to recapture a few column inches and a headline or two. Fortunately, the players put on a good show. Australian Wendy Doolan shot 65 on a soggy Sunday to run down a crop of greats including Lorie Kane, Betsy King and Grace Park. It was Doolan's second 65 of the week (the first coming on Thursday) and her second-best score. She shot 62 on Friday as part of an assault on par that made the tour's comeback look less like a warm-up and more like the unleashing of a lot of pent-up birdies. Meg Mallon shot 60 on Friday and 64 on Thursday. Kane shot 61 on Thursday. A.J. Eathorn shot 62 on Thursday, and Christina Kim matched that score on Saturday. Grace Park shot 63 on Friday after a 65 on Thursday and trailed the leader by four shots.

It was that kind of week, and that kind of course. The field averaged 68.53, which was lower than the Annika Sorenstam's average for all of 2002 when she won the Vare Trophy. Two under par missed the cut.

"We talked about whether there was a 59 out here, and I thought there was," Mallon said. She had an 18-footer on her final hole on Friday to break 60 and left the putt short. "I couldn't tell which way it was going to break, right or left. I was pretty relaxed, joking around. I said, 'I'd like my whole group to read this putt for me,' because it truly was the first one I couldn't get a good line and good pace on. I got so focused on the line I didn't hit it hard enough."

Mallon finished the weekend with a pair of 70s, which would have been good enough on most weeks. This time around it earned her a sixth-place finish. The weekend looked to belong to Kane, who shot 65 on Saturday after rounds of 61 and 64. That was enough for a two-shot edge over Mallon and Doolan, three clear of Kim and four ahead of Park. But this was a week when a score in the 70s wasn't good enough, as Kane found out when she shot even-par 70 on Sunday to fall three shots short.

"I got a little out of my routine with the rain coming and going," Kane said. "Basically, I didn't get the job done. But I did a lot of good things this week. I'm comfortable with the way I'm thinking and feeling. I really have the fire in the belly to have a really great year."

Doolan reached 20 under par through eight holes on Sunday, at which point she seemed in control. A seven-birdie day that including one from five feet on the 15th to go to 21 under while Park was making a double bogey on the 17th gave Doolan a comfortable margin. She finished at 21-under-par 259, three clear of Kane, King and Park.

"I've seen girls shoot 20-plus under par, but I never thought I could do it," Doolan said. "But I guess I can, because it happened."

Safeway Ping—$1,000,000
Winner: Se Ri Pak

After opting out of the season opener to work with her coach, Henri Reis, Annika Sorenstam appeared in Phoenix for the Safeway Ping tournament rested and ready to pick up where she left off in 2002. After all, Moon Valley was the course where Sorenstam shot her historic 59, and where she seemed to be running away from the field in 2002 before fading with a 76 on Sunday and then losing in a playoff to Rachel Teske.

This time Sorenstam shot 67 and 66 and shared the lead at the halfway mark with Patricia Meunier-Lebouc and Se Ri Pak. A 65 on Saturday gave Sorenstam a two-shot edge over Meunier-Lebouc and a three-shot margin over Pak and Grace Park. Three clear with one round to play was a position Sorenstam loved, and one from which she rarely lost. But just as happened in 2002, Sorenstam's putter failed her in the final round. After missing short birdie putts on the first three holes, she left her birdie efforts short on the fourth and fifth, and the frustration bubbled to the surface. Her only birdie of the day was a two-putt effort after hitting the par-five 10th with her second shot. Sorenstam shot 71 for a 19-under-par 269 and finished tied for third with Hee-Won Han and Meunier-Lebouc.

"I thought I had to shoot a low score, like eight under, to have a chance, because I knew Annika would go low again," Pak said. Her instincts were right, even if she got the player wrong. Pak rolled in eagles on the fourth and eighth holes to take the outright lead, but it turned out to be Park, not Sorenstam, she needed to watch.

Park made six birdies in her final 10 holes to close with a 65 and pull within a shot of Pak's lead. Then the leader made a crucial mistake. Debating between a three wood and five wood for her tee shot at the 17th, Pak chose the longer club and pulled her tee shot into the water. She took a drop and a penalty, and hit her third shot into the middle of the green some 45 feet from the hole. "I was just thinking about two putts and going to a playoff," Pak said. Imagine her surprise when the ball fell in the hole. When she finally made eye contact with her caddie, Colin Cann, they both erupted in laughter.

"I couldn't even look at her," Cann said. "What was there to say?"

Pak ended the drama when she hit her approach to the 18th to three feet for her final birdie of the tournament. She shot 64 on Sunday and 265 for the week, one better than Park and three clear of the trio that included Sorenstam.

Kraft Nabisco Championship—$1,600,000
Winner: Patricia Meunier-Lebouc

This was the kind of marquee final round the LPGA needed to get the public thinking about women's golf again. Folks in the desert couldn't wait to see big hitting, 13-year-old Michelle Wie, who not only became the youngest player ever to make the cut in a major, she made it into the last group on Sunday. Annika Sorenstam, who was looking to win an unprecedented four straight Kraft Nabisco Championship titles, was also in the group, along with a vibrant, attractive Frenchwoman named Patricia Meunier-Lebouc that no one knew much about, but who seemed to add a charming complement to this major finish. Had it not taken place on the same day Davis Love was shooting 64 to win The Players Championship, this final round in Palm Springs might have been the most watched and talked about pre-Masters golf day of the year.

Meunier-Lebouc held the lead going into the final round thanks to a 68 on Friday bracketed by two 70s. Sorenstam was second, three strokes back, and Wie, after 66 on Saturday, rounded out the final threesome, four behind the leader. Meunier-Lebouc finished with 73 for a 281 total, seven under par, to edge Sorenstam, who had 71, by one stroke. Wie shot 76 and tied for ninth place at 288.

Sorenstam came out swinging and Wie came out pounding tee shots, but Meunier-Lebouc remained steady throughout. After Sorenstam hit her approach on the first hole to one foot, the lead was down to two. When she hit the second green in two and was faced with a 19-foot eagle putt, it appeared as though the lead might evaporate completely. But the wonderfully tempered Frenchwoman hit her second shot 10 yards short of the hole and chipped in for an eagle. When Sorenstam's putt hit the lip (a theme that would be repeated numerous times), the lead was back to three.

That changed on the next tee when Meunier-Lebouc hit a left-center tee shot that took a wicked left bounce and ended up two feet out of bounds. The subsequent double bogey cut her lead to one over Sorenstam and two over Wie. "I was moving too fast," Meunier-Lebouc said. "It was not a swing in my time."

All three players bogeyed the eighth and parred the ninth, which meant that with nine holes to play, Meunier-Lebouc was seven under par, Sorenstam was six, and Wie was four. No one else was making a run, so it would come down to this threesome.

Sorenstam birdied the 10th to capture a share of the lead, and at that point a lot of prognosticators figured the outcome was inevitable. The winner of 11 titles in 2002 and defending champion in the season's first major rarely gave up leads in the final nine. When Sorenstam rolled in a birdie putt from 12 feet on the 12th, a putt she accentuated by going down on one knee and giving a fist-pump that would have made Tiger Woods proud, a lot of folks figured this one was over.

"I was feeling shy until she made the birdie on 12 and took the lead," Meunier-Lebouc said. "Suddenly, I looked and said to myself, 'Okay, what, so she's got the lead? Now you can play golf maybe.' I just relaxed and let it go, and suddenly I found my vision and my attitude from the first two days."

Meunier-Lebouc rolled in a 15-footer for birdie at the 13th, which she followed with a healthy fist-pump of her own. A moment later, Sorenstam missed a three-footer for par and Meunier-Lebouc's one-shot lead was restored. One hole later, Sorenstam made another critical error, pulling her tee shot into a hazard. She was fortunate to make bogey. The lead was back to two, which is where it stayed for the next three holes thanks to Sorenstam's ability to find the lip of the hole, but not the bottom.

With the margin still at two as the players reached the 18th tee, Sorenstam went after a drive and pulled it in the fairway bunker. Meunier-Lebouc followed her into the same trap. Wie outdrove them both by 20 yards, which was about standard for the week. After the round Sorenstam's caddie said of Wie: "She hits it better than any woman out here, including Annika." Unfortunately, Wie putted like a 13-year-old. After reaching the par-five 11th green in two, she three-putted for par, and followed it up with another three-putt at the 15th, and a third at the 18th. The disappointing 76 left her tied for ninth place with Jennifer Rosales, the best finish by a 13-year-old in the history of major championship play.

Meunier-Lebouc three-putted the final green as well, but by that point the final bogey was moot. Sorenstam missed her birdie try from 25 feet. The affable Frenchwoman had her first major title. "It's wonderful," she said. "I really was feeling that maybe it's my day. I deserve it."

The Office Depot—$1,500,000
Winner: Annika Sorenstam

It said a lot about Annika Sorenstam's dominance that she could, in three starts, have a third, a second and a victory, and still have to answer questions about the state of her game. But at least she was honest. "My game hasn't been on top," she said after shooting 68, 72 and 71 at El Caballero Country Club in Tarzana, California, for a 211 total, five under par, to win The Office Depot by four strokes. "But I fought through it. What wears on me more than anything is I'm not playing my best. I hit a lot of good shots, then I hit something out of the blue. That's not a very comfortable feeling on this golf course, where you have to be so precise."

Only four players broke par for the week on a course Sorenstam described as "U.S. Open-type," and the scoring average for the week was 75.889, higher than the previous week's Kraft Nabisco, which is a major. "In the afternoon the poa annua starts to grow," Sorenstam said of the new and treacherous greens at El Caballero. "You are going to have to hit your putts firm, but when they are fast it's tough to be aggressive. You have to judge when it's a good time to be aggressive and when it's not."

Sorenstam was aggressive on Friday, posting one of only five rounds in the 60s. That gave her a four-shot lead over Heather Bowie. The lead was two on Saturday after Sorenstam struggled on the greens for a 72 and Bowie managed a two-under-par 70. Pat Hurst stood three back after 68 on Saturday, and Mi-Hyun Kim was also three back after scores of 74 and 69.

Sorenstam struggled early on Sunday, making bogeys on her first two holes to fall into a tie with Bowie. A birdie by Sorenstam at the fifth coupled with a bogey by Bowie restored the Swede's two-shot lead. The lead dipped to one shot when Sorenstam bogeyed the 13th while Pak, playing two groups ahead, birdied the 14th. But Pak bogeyed the 15th from the right trees, and the lead was back to two. Twenty minutes later, Sorenstam made a great bogey from deep in the right trees at the 15th. That allowed Bowie and Pak to inch a little closer, but it could have been a lot worse.

"She made a great bogey," Bowie said. "That could have been a great turnaround for one of us."

Instead, Sorenstam finished with a couple of birdies at the 17th and 18th to increase the margin of victory to four over Pak (71), Bowie (73) and Hurst (72), who tied at 215. Kim shot 75 and finished tied for eighth at 218.

Sorenstam admitted she wasn't as sharp as she was last year. "I know this sounds funny, because it's only April, but I'm very, very tired," she said. "A lot has been going on, and I feel it in my head. I'm worn out mentally."

She took the next week for a vacation with her husband in Las Vegas, venue for the next event in two weeks. "I hope that's going to be enough," she said. "My muscles are not real tired, but just mentally, the way I think on the golf course, is very uncharacteristic. It's not the way I normally think, and I can't really control it."

Takefuji Classic—$1,100,000

Winner: Candie Kung

For the fifth time in as many starts in 2003, and the 15th consecutive event dating back to the previous year, a foreign-born, foreign-bred, American-enriched winner emerged on the LPGA Tour. This time it was Candie Kung (Taiwan), who bogeyed the final hole at Las Vegas Country Club to win the Takefuji Classic by two shots over Annika Sorenstam (Sweden), Soo-Yun Kang (South Korea), and the lone contending American, Cristie Kerr.

"Obviously the LPGA is well-represented internationally," said Laura Diaz, who led after the first day with a 66, but struggled over the final 36 holes. "We have some phenomenal young players from all over, including America. More than few of us can carry the flag."

Kerr was the only U.S. flag-waver in the hunt late in this one. Rounds of 67 and 68 put the American one shot back going into the final 18 holes. But she was only that close because of Kung's seeming inability to play the 18th. In the first round, Kung laid up on the par-five and chunked a wedge into the water for a double bogey. On Friday, she made bogey after shanking her third shot. Those shots left Kung tied with Catriona Matthew at 134 going into the final round.

Matthew was never a factor, shooting 74 to finish tied for sixth at 208, and Kerr could not hang on despite grabbing a one-shot lead early with two birdies in the first eight holes. Kung took charge in the middle of the round with birdies at the ninth (to regain a share of the lead), 10th (to retake it outright) and 12th (to extend it to the final margin of two shots). Kerr made another bogey on the second nine to extend the margin to three, which is where it remained when Kung stood on the tee at her nemesis hole: the par-five 18th.

"I was just trying to hit a green and walk out of there with a par," Kung said. Instead, she missed a meaningless four-footer for par, shot 70 for a 12-under-par 204 total, and walked out with a $165,000 winner's check.

Sorenstam and Kang had the low rounds of the day (67) to tie Kerr (71) for second at 206, while Hee-Won Han also shot 67 to finish alone in fifth at 207. "I've been playing catch-up the last two rounds," said Sorenstam, who had two 67s after opening with an even-par 72. "I've always been in favor of four-day tournaments, but I knew this one was 54 holes going in. I'm very pleased with the way I played the last two days. I had a chance at the end."

Kerr also felt she had a chance. "If one of my putts goes in, it kind of changes the momentum of the tournament," the lone American contender said. "But it was just Candie's day. She's a solid young player. She has a bright future."

Chick-fil-A Charity Championship—$1,350,000

Winner: Se Ri Pak

Despite sinking an 18-foot putt on the fourth playoff hole to win her second tournament of the year, 25-year-old Se Ri Pak wasn't the most popular youngster in the field at the Chick-fil-A Charity Championship in Stockbridge, Georgia. That was because every man, woman and child in attendance, including tournament host Nancy Lopez, wanted to see 13-year-old phenomenon Michelle Wie.

Wie flew from Honolulu to Atlanta and played her only practice round on less than three hours' sleep. She then upstaged the professional in her pro-am group. Pamela Karrigan was all but ignored by the three amateurs who were so excited about playing with Wie that they posed for their group picture without Karrigan. There were quick apologies when Karrigan said, "What about me?"

A lot of other professionals were saying the same thing before the week was over. "Yeah, it's difficult, but it's great to see," said Kris Tschetter, who played in the group immediately ahead of Wie on Saturday. "I'm supportive of anything that creates this kind of buzz out here."

The buzz continued throughout the weekend. With rounds of 72 and 70, Wie made her second consecutive cut on the LPGA Tour and dazzled everyone with her length and precise ball-striking. On Saturday, Wie outdrove her playing partners, Lorena Ochoa and Barb Mucha, by as much as 40 yards. By the 18th, Mucha had seen enough. After Wie hit her tee shot 301 yards on the fly (the ball backed up a foot on the wet fairway), Mucha handed her driver to Wie and said, "I can't watch this anymore. Here, you hit it for me."

Wie shot 71 on Sunday and finished in a respectable tie for 33rd. Meg Mallon said, "We're witnessing a once-in-a-lifetime phenomenon with her. She hits the ball incredible now, and you've got to figure she's only going to be better as she matures." Beth Daniel called her "Amazing," saying, "When I came out, the idea of a 13-year-old playing out here was unheard of." Rosie Jones joined the chorus, saying of Wie, "When she's 18, I'm out of here. She doesn't look 13, and she doesn't play like she's 13. She may talk like she's 13, but she's got the most beautiful swing I've ever seen. You think you're looking at Tiger Woods. Just a huge arc. It's pretty awesome."

Once the Wie-envy died down, this one had a stellar finish. Pak trailed Karrie Webb by three strokes at the beginning of the final round, but those positions changed on the first nine when Pak birdied her first three holes and Webb struggled to find the fairway. A flurry of closing birdies gave Pak a final-round 64, which looked as though it would be enough until Shani Waugh birdied the last three holes to shoot 65 and share the lead at the end of regulation at 19-under-par 200.

The playoff started on the 18th and was halved with birdies. They moved to the 10th, where both players made par. The second time down the 18th — a par-five of 492 yards — Pak hit her second shot into the scorer's tent 20 yards right of the green. From there she took relief and then hit a pitch to 10 feet and made the putt for birdie to extend the playoff to a fourth hole.

This time, Waugh stumbled, pulling her tee shot into a lake. But Pak missed the green again and had to make the 18-footer for par to win. No one, including Waugh, was surprised when the putt fell. "She putted incredible," Waugh said. "I was not surprised at all when she made that putt."

Pak wasn't surprised either, but she was relieved. "Those were some amazing up-and-downs," she said. "Putting saved my day. I impressed myself."

Michelob Light Open—$1,600,000
Winner: Grace Park

For a while it looked as though the American victory drought on the LPGA Tour was about to end. Even though she had trailed by a shot at the beginning of the day, Cristie Kerr played 14 solid holes, and when a birdie putt fell at the 14th, she had a two-shot lead at the Michelob Light Open at Kingsmill in Williamsburg, Virginia, with four holes to play. Her closest pursuers were Karrie Webb, who had the best round of the day (67), but who was sitting in the clubhouse at eight-under-par 276, and Lorena Ochoa, who shot 69 and was tied with Webb. The other pursuer was Grace Park of Korea, who held the lead at the end of the day on Saturday, but gave it up immediately with a double bogey on her first hole and two more bogeys before she reached the fifth tee.

Park had said on Saturday, "I have never — knock on wood before I say it — I have never lost a tournament with the lead going into the final round, from junior golf on." By the fifth tee she was looking for a tree or two to knock on in order to turn things around.

She must have found one, because Park birdied the fifth, sixth and seventh to pull within one of Kerr, which is where it remained until Kerr made the birdie at the 14th to pull ahead by two. Just as quickly as the tide had turned on the first nine, it turned back in Park's favor on the next. Kerr missed the fairway at the 15th and 16th and made bogey on both holes. When Park rolled in a 35-footer for birdie at the 16th, the lead and the momentum had changed for good.

Kerr parred the 17th and 18th for a final round of 71 and a 276 total. She then stood to the side of the green and watched as Park, a good friend from their junior golf days together and a bridesmaid in Kerr's wedding, studied the 18-footer for par. If she missed, there would be a four-way playoff. The putt found the center of the hole for 71 and a winning 275 total, and Park leapt into the arms of her caddie as the two of them celebrated.

"She got off to a horrible start," Kerr said. "I was trying not to watch. A lot of people would have given up, but not Grace. She's a great competitor and a great friend. She deserved it." Kerr's disappointment was obvious, but she tried to put a brave face on it. "I view myself as one of the hardest working players on tour," she said. "Maybe I'm to win a major this year, or maybe win next week."

Park also views herself as a hard worker. When asked about the dominance of foreign players on the LPGA (her win put the streak of consecutive non-American winners at 17, dating back to August of 2002), Park said, "We are good, aren't we? I know that Korean players work very hard. They are the first ones on the range, the last ones to leave. I think that's why we are seeing more and more Korean players at the top."

Asahi Ryokuken International—$1,300,000
Winner: Rosie Jones

For the first time in what was quickly approaching a calendar year, age, guile and American grit beat youth, talent and a beige passport, as 43-year-old Rosie Jones put a stop to the foreign winning steak on the LPGA Tour. Jones led wire-to-wire at the Asahi Ryokuken International in North Augusta, South Carolina. It was the second time she ended a winless streak for the Americans, the first coming in 2001 when her victory at the Kathy Ireland Invitational made her first American to win in 10 events. This year she ended the American drought after nine months and 17 consecutive tournaments.

"I was talking about that on the drive over here," she said. "It's just kind of funny that two years ago it was 10 wins before an American hit one, and I got it there. And I'm just glad to do it here."

She did it with the game that has been her bread-and-butter for 20 years. She hit every fairway for the first two days and shot 66 and 68 to lead Wendy Ward by one stroke going into the weekend. A steady 69 on Saturday extended the lead to two over Laura Diaz, who also had 69, and three over Ward, who shot 71 in the third round.

In the final round, Jones hit a perfect approach to five feet on the first hole and rolled in the putt for birdie to extend the lead to three. At the fourth, she extended the lead further with an eight-footer for birdie. When that putt fell, Jones swept her arms across her body and charged to the edge of the green in what could have passed for a 43-year-old's victory lap.

The only hiccups in her round came when she missed birdie putts of five and eight feet on the sixth and seventh holes. She gave another leg kick and fist pump after a 12-footer for par fell on the eighth. By then the lead was six, as Diaz had taken double bogey from the woods on the fifth hole. Jones mis-hit one shot, chunking a sand shot at the par-three 15th and having to make a 15-footer for bogey. When that putt fell, the lead was three, which was where it remained. Jones tapped in for par at the 18th for a final round of 70, a 273 total and her first victory in two years.

"My game feels really strong," she said. "I hit a lot of good irons, and that has been really lacking the last couple of years. I knew I could win again. I take a lot of time off in the winter, and sometimes when you come back in March you wonder if you have lost a step. It takes me a few tournaments to get my game going."

Ward finished alone in second at 273 after shooting 70 on Sunday, while Diaz shot 73 and fell into a tie for third with Patricia Meunier-Lebouc and Lorena Ochoa at 278.

Corning Classic—$1,000,000
Winner: Juli Inkster

On a week when the eyes of the world were on women's golf, the LPGA actually had a tournament that went largely unnoticed. That was a shame, given how well Juli Inkster played to win the Corning Classic in Corning, New York, but with Annika Sorenstam playing in Fort Worth, Texas, at the Bank of American Colonial, no one on the ladies' tour minded taking a backseat.

"It's a great week for golf, of which the LPGA is a part and Corning is a part," commissioner Ty Votaw said. "There were people on the golf course who wanted to know what Annika was doing, and there were people on the golf course watching the players. In terms of television remotes back down at Colonial, there's an enormous amount of exposure for Corning, and as a result, the LPGA Tour."

When players like Inkster weren't shooting 62s, they were in the locker room or media center watching Sorenstam. Lorie Kane came into the media center as the second round co-leader, but she asked the first question. "How's Annika doing?" The answer was that Sorenstam shot 71 and 74 and missed the cut, but no one at Corning seemed to mind.

"I don't think there are any negatives, at least not from where I stand," Kane said. "I think the most exciting thing is it's going to bring more people out here to watch her, and in turn that means watching us."

If they had watched in Corning, they would have seen a low-scoring birdie-fest that wasn't finished until course and tournament records were shattered. Kane and Catriona Matthew were tied for the lead at the halfway mark at 12-under-par 132. Meg Mallon was one shot further back after rounds of 67 and 66, and Inkster was two off the pace after following her opening 68 with a 66 on Friday.

"I figured somebody would go low," Kane said, "There was a number out there for someone, and I tried my best to have it."

On Saturday Matthew took the lead with a 67, and Kane stayed two back after shooting 69. Inkster fell to three back with a 68 of her own, and Beth Daniel pulled to four off the pace with a 67.

Inkster came out knowing she needed to make birdies on Sunday in order to have a chance, and she did exactly that. After a par at the first hole, she birdied the second, third, fourth, fifth and seventh to tie Kane for the lead. Then Inkster hit a sand wedge to four feet at the eighth and made that putt to reach the old tournament-record mark of 20 under. She also took a one-shot lead. Turning with a first-nine score of 30, Inkster kept up the pressure. She birdied the 10th, 11th and lipped out an 18-foot eagle effort at the 12th. Her only bogey came when she missed the fairway at the 14th and tried to hit a miracle shot from under a tree rather than chipping back to the fairway and taking her medicine. She also flew the green at the 15th, but made a great up-and-down for par.

She got it back on track after pulling her tee shot into the fairway bunker at the 17th. From a perfect lie, Inkster hit a nine iron to four feet and rolled in her 10th birdie of the day. She made it an even 11 when another nine-iron approach at the 18th stopped 20 feet below the hole and she rolled that putt in for a 62, the lowest final-round score by a winner in LPGA history.

"I was just really calm today," Inkster said after signing for a tournament-record 24-under-par 264 and a four-shot win over Kane. "I felt like I was playing well enough to go out there and shoot a good score. The key for me this week was I got the ball in the fairway off the tee most of the time, and from there I played very well. I got on a roll early and made some great par putts coming down the stretch. Sometimes they just go in."

Kane was left shaking her head. She finished with 67 and 20-under-par 268, tying the old tournament record, only to lose by four strokes. "That doesn't happen every day," she said. "We had an elite field here this week, and I think there might have been some motivation for all of us in what Annika did. I thought somebody would go low, and I just didn't go low enough."

Kellogg-Keebler Classic—$1,200,000
Winner: Annika Sorenstam

So nine days after missing the cut at the Bank of America Colonial and saying she was "going back to my tour where I belong," Annika Sorenstam proved that, while she wasn't quite as good as the men, she was far, far better than all of the women.

On a week when a lesser player would have put her game on cruise control, Sorenstam came to the Kellogg-Keebler Classic at Stonebridge Country Club in Aurora, Illinois, site of her 11-stroke victory in 2002, and promptly lapped the field again. This time she opened with 62 for a three-shot lead and never looked back. A 66 on Saturday kept the lead at two over Mhairi McKay, and an easy 71 on Sunday for a 17-under-par 199 total proved good enough for a three-stroke win over McKay.

"No, no letdown at all," Sorenstam said. "On the contrary, when I came back here, I thought everybody was so positive and energetic that I was back, especially the fans. I thought they were pulling for me all week. It was great."

Despite five three-putts in 54 holes, and a nagging tendency to leave makeable birdie putts short, Sorenstam appeared on her way to breaking the tournament-record 21-under-par total that she set the year before. She closed out Saturday's round with three consecutive birdies and came out Sunday with two more to start her day. "I was thinking last year I was 21 under, and my goal was to get to 23 this year," she said.

Then she missed a three-footer for birdie at the third and failed to get up and down from beyond the green at the seventh. But by then the mystery and drama were gone. McKay made a triple bogey at the seventh to shoot herself out of contention.

McKay, who was runner-up to Sorenstam in 2002 as well, played well down the stretch with four birdies on the second nine for an even-par 72 final round and a 202 total, which left her alone in second place. "I sort of had not the best start," she said, "so to finish this way is a great feeling. I'm kind of a bit disappointed at the same time, because I really wanted to push Annika today, but I'm proud of myself for hanging in there and finishing strong."

Sorenstam chipped her third shot to two inches on the par-five 14th and tapped in to go to 19 under, which put her on track to break her old record. But she missed another short birdie putt at the 15th and three-putted for bogey at the 17th. With the record out of the question and victory all but assured, she lost focus on the final tee and hit it into an unplayable lie. After a poor drop, a poor approach and an outstanding greenside bunker shot that almost went in the hole, Sorenstam tapped in for bogey, a 199 total and a three-shot win.

"I always feel so welcome here," Sorenstam said. "That plays a big part, just to come to a place where you like it, so you can play your best. And then I got off to such a great start again, 10 under. I was just on a roll after that."

McDonald's LPGA Championship—$1,600,000
Winner: Annika Sorenstam

As a mark of Annika Sorenstam's dominance of women's golf, consider the following: With a par on the first extra hole at DuPont Country Club in Wilmington, Delaware, Sorenstam won her 45th title and fifth major championship five months before her 33rd birthday. The victory at the McDonald's LPGA Championship placed her on track to best her record 11 wins in 2002, and she did all this a mere two weeks after becoming the first woman in 58 years to play in a PGA Tour event.

"Winning is what it's all about," Sorenstam said after letting a seven-shot lead slip away to a charging Grace Park on Sunday and then coming back with a crucial par to win on the first extra hole. "I thought Colonial was a great experience and, who knows, maybe all the pressure I experienced then helped me to pull through today."

To pull through, she had to play 34 grueling holes in soggy conditions after the third round was postponed due to rain. She began that day by rolling in a 14-footer for birdie at the eighth hole to extend her lead over Park to eight. But that was where the birdies would stop. Although she rarely missed the fairway, Sorenstam's short game began showing signs of fatigue as she missed a number of short putts the rest of the morning. She finished the third round with a 72.

That was in stark contrast to Friday when she hit every fairway and every green on her way to a tournament-low 64 and a seven-shot edge over Park. For a while it looked like this would be a runaway. Then Park came out swinging, and Sorenstam's putter became a bit shaky. Always the bane of her game, the Swede missed short putts on the 10th, 13th and 15th in the third round, while Park charged in with 70 to pull within five.

By the time Sorenstam teed off in the final round, Park had inched one shot closer with a birdie on her first hole. When the 24-year-old South Korean hit a three wood to within four feet at the par-five 11th, she knew it could be the shot of the tournament. She made the eagle putt and was tied for the lead with seven holes to play. Then Park made the best par of the week when she pulled her tee shot into the thick rough at the par-five 16th. The ball nestled so deep in the wet rough that Park could barely see it, and she failed to get it out of the high stuff in her first attempt. The lie for her third shot was worse than it was for her second. This time, however, she managed to hack it back to the fairway where she hit her fourth shot to six feet and made the tricky downhill putt for par. One hole later Park took the outright lead with a six-footer for birdie.

Sorenstam kept it close by making some spectacular up-and-downs late in the final round. None was bigger than the play at the 14th when her tee shot hit a tree and bounced into the left rough. With a tree limiting her backswing, Sorenstam hit a six iron short of the green, pitched to three feet, and made the crucial putt to stay close. One hole later she regained a share of the lead when she hit her second shot into the greenside bunker at the par-five and blasted out to two feet.

Park, playing two groups ahead, continued to make pars and ended the day with a four-under-par 67, her lowest round in a major as a professional. For a moment it looked as though her six-under-par 278 total would be good enough for the win. She and Sorenstam were the only two players under par — Rosie Jones, Rachel Teske and Beth Daniel tied for third at even-par 284 — and Sorenstam hit a short drive in the right cut of rough on the 18th. But the Swede hit a spectacular seven-wood approach into the final hole and made a crucial par to shoot 72 and tie Park at six under.

The playoff was anticlimactic. Park missed the green at the 18th and failed to get up and down, while Sorenstam hit a six iron into the center of the green and two-putted for the win. "I am proud of myself today," Park said. "I played very well. I am a little disappointed that I didn't play well in the playoff, but you know, with Annika I am, to be honest, quite jealous. She is the No. 1 player in the world, and she deserves all the attention. I just wish I was No. 1."

Sorenstam admitted that Park wasn't far behind. "She kept the pressure on me," she said. "I'm just glad that I made it when I needed to."

Giant Eagle Classic—$1,000,000
Winner: Rachel Teske

After the month Annika Sorenstam had been through, the last thing she needed was another playoff. She had just come off two consecutive victories, one in the LPGA's second major of the season that required one hole of overtime. One week before that she had been the biggest news item in America when she teed off in the Bank of America Colonial. So you could forgive her a little letdown at the Giant Eagle Classic in Vienna, Ohio, especially after watching Rachel Teske make a 35-footer on the last hole of regulation to become the fourth member of the playoff, and then standing by as Teske did it again from 18 feet on the third extra hole.

"I just felt like I walked straight into a wall," Sorenstam said after missing a seven-footer for birdie on the final hole of regulation that would have won outright, and a 10-footer on the first extra hole to win. "I kept eating my carrots, energy bars, bananas, and I tried to drink everything I could. My knees have been shaking for three hours. I'm ready to go home and take a break."

Teske was just getting started. After finishing tied for third in the McDonald's LPGA Championship the week before, she came out with a hot putter and a renewed determination. She entered the final round tied with Jean Bartholomew at 135, with Sorenstam and Jennifer Rosales one shot back. But Sorenstam soon joined Teske atop the leaderboard with a birdie on her first hole. The Swede looked poised to move well ahead of the pack when she hit a three-wood second shot at the par-five fifth that stopped six feet from the hole. But Sorenstam missed the eagle putt and had to settle for birdie. Still, she was one ahead at that point and would stretch the lead to two with a 20-foot birdie putt at the sixth, and keep it there with a downhill five-footer for birdie at the ninth.

The biggest charge of the day came from Lorie Kane, who started six shots back but made five birdies between the 10th and 16th holes to post a 63 and a 204 total. Bartholomew had a rough go on Sunday, shooting 74 to fall into a five-way tie for 12th at 209, but Rosales played well, shooting 68 to join Kane at 204. Teske was next in with a 69 for her 204, which left

Sorenstam with the seven-footer to win. She missed, finishing with 68.

"I had a chance and blew it," Sorenstam said. "It's not the end of the world."

All four players parred the first two extra holes, but the third time down the 18th hole, Kane and Sorenstam missed the fairway with their tee shots and hit their approaches to 20 and 50 feet respectively. From the fairway, Rosales hit her approach to 16 feet, and Teske, also in the fairway and the longest of the four off the tee, hit her second shot to 18 feet.

Sorenstam thrilled the crowd by rolling her 50-footer just over the right edge of the hole. Then Kane missed. Teske rolled her putt in the center of the hole, and Rosales, looking for her first win, missed badly.

"It feels great to come out on top," Teske said. "Any time you can win against these great players, it's a plus."

Wegmans Rochester LPGA—$1,200,000
Winner: Rachel Teske

As Rachel Teske will readily admit, sometimes ignorance is truly bliss. Teske started the final round at the Wegmans Rochester LPGA with a four-stroke lead and seemed to be playing well. When she missed a par putt on the 14th, she walked to the 15th tee blissfully ignorant of the fact that hard-charging Lorena Ochoa had whittled her lead to a single shot.

"I didn't know," Teske admitted. "I really wasn't watching the leaderboard at all. You usually get a feeling for whether you're ahead or behind. I felt in control most of the day, so I guess it really wasn't an issue."

It certainly wasn't an issue after Teske hit a perfect nine iron to the 135-yard par-three that stopped 12 feet from the hole. When that birdie putt fell, the lead was back to two, and would grow to the original four before the round was complete.

"That's just what my plan was for that hole," Teske said of her birdie at the 15th. "To be able to switch it on and come back with a birdie when I wanted to, that just made me feel good."

A solid par at the 16th kept the lead at two. Then Teske hit a perfect seven wood from 198 yards at the par-five 17th hole. When the ball stopped 15 feet from the hole, victory seemed secure. Making the eagle putt was gravy. Her round included birdies at the seventh and eighth in addition to the crucial one at the 15th and the eagle at the 17th.

"I hit the ball really well on the front nine, so to make the birdies gave me confidence going to the back nine," Teske said after tapping in for par on the 18th for a round of 68 and an 11-under-par 277 total. "I knew there would be some good scores out there."

She was right on that. Grace Park also shot 68 to finish alone in third at 282, but it was Ochoa who provided most of the final-round drama. The highly touted 21-year-old rookie from Guadalajara, Mexico, made two birdies and an eagle on the first nine to pull within a two shots of Teske. The margin dwindled to one when Teske missed the fairway at the 14th and had to punch out. Ochoa made a couple of additional birdies on the back for a tournament-low score of 66, but it wasn't enough to catch the leader.

"I'm very happy with the way I finished," Ochoa said after taking second place at 281. "I did very good and I'm very excited. I was trying to go for all the pins, tried to be really aggressive on all my putts for birdie, and it worked. Early in the morning I thought if I could go six under par I could at least get into a playoff. But Rachel just played very, very solid."

It was the second time in Teske's career that she had won back-to-back events, the first coming in 1998 when she went by her maiden name of Hetherington. This time, a little older and wiser, she wasn't going to make any future predictions for the upcoming U.S. Open or any other event. "I don't have any expectations for the Open," she said. "I know I'm playing well, and I'll get there and see how the course is playing, see how I can improve my game to adapt to the course, and then just play it as well as I can."

ShopRite Classic—$1,300,000
Winner: Angela Stanford

With all the media attention on players like Annika Sorenstam, Juli Inkster and 13-year-old Michele Wie one week before the U.S. Women's Open, it was easy to overlook a 25-year-old winless Texan in her third year on tour. That was before Angela Stanford shot 65, 67 and 65 for a 197 total and a wire-to-wire victory in the ShopRite Classic in Galloway Township, New Jersey. Her margin of victory was three strokes over Becky Morgan and four clear of Inkster and Lorie Kane, another Open favorite. For Stanford, a four-time All-American from TCU, flying under the media radar was just fine as long as she got the trophy and the check.

"I believe if you want to be the best, you have to beat the best," Stanford said. She did all of the above, shooting 65 on Friday to share the lead with Laura Diaz and Kris Lindstrom. Her 67 on Saturday gave her a one-shot lead over Inkster, Diana D'Alessio and Michele Redman.

"It was the same feeling I had when I teed it up for the first time in an LPGA event," Stanford said of her nerves going into the final round. "I was thinking to myself, 'I can't believe I'm here.' I was in tears on the first tee just because I knew it was happening. I have no idea how I was able to take the club back."

She took it back very well, striping a drive off the first tee and hitting her approach five feet beyond the hole. When that putt fell for the first birdie of the day, the nerves seemed to disappear with the ball. At the second hole, she rolled in a 30-footer for birdie to extend the lead to three. One hole later, she hit a five iron from 190 yards into the par-five, and the ball stopped five feet below the hole. When that putt fell, Stanford's lead seemed secure.

No one got within two shots after that. Inkster tried to apply a little pressure with an eagle of her own at the third, but she followed it up with two consecutive bogeys and never challenged. Morgan and Kane tried to make a game of it with some later birdies on the back nine, but it was too little too late. "I noticed toward the end that they were creeping up on me," Stanford said. "I thought, 'Hmm, maybe I should get back to playing one shot at a time.'"

Stanford made 12 consecutive pars before rolling in birdie putts at the 16th and 17 to reach 16 under, which is where she finished. "I wish I could remember some of the round," she said. "I heard it was great."

A few people in the crowd wished they had seen it as well. At times Stanford's gallery was no more than 50 people, as most of those came to see Sorenstam (who finished tied for 14th and never contended) or Wie, who hadn't fully recovered from her Women's Public Links Championship win. The teenager shot 71-72-72 and showed signs of a short game that needed attention. "I played really bad," Wie said. "I'm really bummed."

Morgan finished with 66 for second place at 200, while Kane and Inkster shot 66 and 68 respectively to share third at 201.

U.S. Women's Open—$3,100,000
Winner: Hilary Lunke

In a year of upsets that saw Ben Curtis win the Open Championship and Shaun Micheel win the PGA Championship, no story was more surprising than Hilary Lunke in the U.S. Women's Open. The second-year professional and pride of Edina, Minnesota, didn't hit the ball much farther than the women's club champion at Pumpkin Ridge Golf Club, but she managed to make every crucial putt she needed over the four days and then an 18-footer on the 18th hole of a playoff to come away from North Plains, Oregon, as the year's most unlikely major champion.

In addition to holding off Kelly Robbins in the playoff, Lunke sank the winning putt after watching Angela Stanford roll in a 30-footer for birdie to move into a tie for the lead at even par. One minute later Lunke did what she had done all week — put a perfect stroke on a 15-footer and watched the ball disappear into the cup. "I can't believe it," Lunke said. "I just tried to trust my stroke, concentrated on the line, and I finally got the speed right." Later she added, "I didn't have 100 percent of my ball-striking, but I had 155 percent of my putting."

She needed every bit of it. The shortest hitter in the field (averaging 222 yards off the tee) on the second-longest course in U.S. Women's Open history, Lunke wore out her seven and nine woods all week. After rounds of 71, 69 and 68, where she averaged 27.5 putts per round, Lunke led by a shot over Stanford and by three over Annika Sorenstam. With Sorenstam in the final group, Stanford coming off her first win as a professional the week before in Rochester, and never-won-before Lunke looking more like a crosswalk marshal and carpool mom than the leader in the most prestigious tournament in women's golf, Sorenstam was the odds-on favorite in the final round.

Sorenstam remained the favorite through 71 holes. With Lunke struggling in the final round, Robbins in the clubhouse at one-under-par 283 and Stanford needing birdie to shoot 74 and finish the week in red figures, Sorenstam needed only a par on the reachable par-five 18th to insure a playoff berth. A birdie would likely guarantee a victory. Standing in the middle of the fairway, she had only 236 yards to the flag, perfect four-wood distance.

When Sorenstam came out of the shot, the gasp could be heard two holes over. The ball flew right, beyond the trees and the scorer's tent and next to the portable toilets. That set up the most dramatic moments of the week as Sorenstam pleaded her case for a favorable drop. None was forthcoming, and she was left with a 40-yard shot under some trees and over a bunker.

"There was hardly any grass. It was dirt," she said. "I didn't expect the ball to shoot so high, and it hit the branch and then went into the bunker." From there, Sorenstam hit a poor bunker shot to 15 feet and missed her par putt badly. The bogey dropped her to two-over 73 for her round and even-par 284 for the championship, one more than she needed to make it a four-way playoff.

"It's going to take a while to get over this," the Swede said. "But at the end of the day it's just a golf tournament. Right now, I just want to forget this week. I'll charge my batteries and be ready when I need to. But right now, I feel like being grumpy."

While Sorenstam considered her drop options, Lunke and Stanford were waiting in the middle of the 18th fairway. After a while, Lunke sat on her bag and opened her umbrella to keep the sun off her face. "It was definitely frustrating to wait so long," Lunke said. "I thought when we got there the wait would only be two or three minutes, and she would take her drop and move on."

After the wait, Lunke hit her second shot into a bunker and Stanford hit a lay-up short of the green. Stanford played first, pitching the ball to 20 feet, and Lunke hit a beautiful bunker shot from 102 yards to 12 feet. Stanford needed to make the putt to have a shot at a playoff. Lunke needed it for an outright victory.

When Stanford's putt when in for her 74 and 283 total, the crowd erupted. Lunke took her time and hit a great putt that stopped one roll short of the hole, as she finished with 75 and 283.

In the 18-hole playoff, Robbins was the favorite until she bogeyed three of her first four holes. Stanford bogeyed her first two holes on Monday morning, which gave Lunke an early two-shot lead. But Stanford got back into things with birdies at the 11th and 12th, and an unlikely chip-in for birdie at the 14th to pull even with Lunke, who missed her first six greens and managed to get up and down on all but one of them. When Stanford failed to get up and down on the 17th, Lunke seemed in control with a one-shot lead.

Both players hit great tee shots and great lay-ups. Lunke played first to the par-five and hit it 15 feet. Stanford hit her shot left and 30 feet away. That set up Stanford's improbable putt. For the second day in a row, she made a long one at the 18th in a do-or-die situation. "I knew she was going to make it," Lunke said. "I was just trying to focus on my line and pretend it was match play."

Lunke did just that, rolling the ball perfectly into the center of the hole for a birdie and the win. Lunke shot 70, while Stanford posted 71 and Robbins, 73. "I can barely remember hitting the putt," Lunke said. "I heard that roar from the gallery two times for Angela, and I wanted to hear it for me."

Stanford was the first person over to congratulate Lunke. "She put it on top of me," the runner-up said. "That's just awesome. It's unfortunate. I wanted to win. But it was so much fun."

BMO Financial Group Canadian Women's Open—$1,300,000

Winner: Beth Daniel

Beth Daniel overcame the elements and a charging Juli Inkster to shoot 68 in a downpour and become, at age 46, the oldest winner in LPGA Tour history. Her 13-under-par 275 in the BMO Financial Group Canadian Women's Open at Vancouver's Point Grey Country Club included a three-footer for birdie on the 17th and a six-footer on the 18th that was the difference.

When that putt fell and Inkster's 12-footer for birdie failed to find the hole, Daniel, 46 years, eight months and 29 days young, edged out JoAnne Carner's oldest-winner record by three and a half months. Carner won the 1985 Safeco Classic at 46.

This was Daniel's first win since 1995, and she hoped it would not be her last. "You go through a spell that long and you start wondering if you're ever going to win again, and if you're too old to be out here," Daniel said. "But I've always had confidence in myself. I've had a lot of disappointments in those eight years. I've been close and didn't win. Today I was able to come through and won it."

After three 69s, Daniel started the final round tied with Inkster. Birdies on the first and third holes gave the elder statesman a two-shot advantage at the turn. That changed when Daniel missed short birdie efforts at the 10th and 11th and opened the door for Inkster, who made up one shot with a birdie at the par-five 10th.

The turning point seemed to be the 12th. Daniel hit her tee shot into the right rough and struggled to make a bogey, while Inkster hit her approach to two feet and rolled the putt in for birdie. "The only time I derailed was the two-shot swing at 12," Daniel said. "All of a sudden I didn't have the lead anymore, so I had to dig in deep and get it back."

Both players parred the 13th through 16th, which set up the dramatics at the par-three 17th. Inkster hit a great tee shot to eight feet, but Daniel hit her shot three feet to the left of the flag. Inkster thought she had made her birdie putt, and so did Daniel. "Juli should have made that putt on 17," the winner said. "I don't know what happened. It went right at the hole."

That miss provided the opening Daniel needed. She made her birdie to regain a share of the lead, and hit her third shot at the par-five 18th to six feet. Inkster's third looked like it might go in the hole for eagle. The ball hit inches from the flag, but spun back 12 feet, leaving her a straightforward uphill putt for birdie. But when Inkster missed, Daniel "dug deep" and made the six-footer for the win. Daniel shot 68 for a 275 total, while Inkster shot 69 for 276.

"Seventeen was in the heart," Inkster said of the gut-wrenching loss. "It wasn't short, it was in the heart. It kept going left, and then it just went to the right. I don't know how it does that."

The 43-year-old Inkster finished alone in second, three clear of Grace Park and Kim Saiki, whose combined age was only one year older than Daniel.

"I look at the teenagers and young players, and I think there is a great future for women's golf," Daniel said. "But there's one thing Juli, Betsy King and myself have in common: We're all in our 40s, and we all love to practice and work on our games. Any time you have a good work ethic, it has a tendency to eventually pay off."

Sybase Big Apple Classic—$950,000
Winner: Hee-Won Han

After some bad memories from a year ago when Hee-Won Han missed a six-footer at the final hole of the Sybase Big Apple Classic for her first win on the LPGA Tour and then lost in a playoff to Gloria Park, the 2001 Rookie of the Year rolled in a four-footer on the 18th at Wykagyl Country Club in New Rochelle, New York, for a two-shot victory over Meg Mallon.

Mallon birdied the 16th and 17th, and stroked a 60-foot eagle putt on the 18th that looked good all the way. When that putt stopped two inches short of the hole and Mallon tapped in for a closing 73 and a 275 total, Han breathed easier. Her lead was one with one to play. She could handle that.

"I just focused on the last thee holes with no bogeys," Han said. The five-footer for birdie gave Han an even-par 71, good enough for an 11-under-par 273 total and a two-shot margin over Mallon, who struggled with her ball-striking right up to the 16th tee.

Han took the lead on the fifth with a five-foot birdie putt while Mallon was making bogey from the right rough. The big swing came three holes later. According to Mallon, "The point when I really needed to take off was when she was making double on eight." When Mallon's birdie putt to pull back into a tie for the lead came up short, her shoulders sagged and she seemed resigned to her fate. One hole later, she hit her drive in the rough and made another bogey. "I tried to put a little pressure on her, but she responded well," Mallon said.

When Mallon bogeyed the 12th, Han's lead was four. But Han appeared to let Mallon back into the game with consecutive bogeys on the 13th and 14th, which brought back memories of 2002 when Han missed short birdie putts on the 16th, 17th and 18th and again in the playoff with Park. But this time, Han played the final four holes in two under, good enough for a two-shot margin.

Grace Park shot 68, equaling the day's low round, to finish tied for third with second-round leader Cindy Figg-Currier at 279, while Michele Redman made birdie on the final hole to shoot 69 and finish fifth at 280.

Evian Masters—€2,222,073
Winner: Juli Inkster

See Evian Ladies European Tour section.

Weetabix Women's British Open—€1,670,445
Winner: Annika Sorenstam

See Evian Ladies European Tour section.

Wendy's Championship for Children—$1,100,000
Winner: Hee-Won Han

A Korean won the LPGA Wendy's Championship for Children, which wasn't news. Koreans had been winning for years. What was news was that a Korean, Hee-Won Han, won in a week when allegations that Koreans might have fudged the rules plagued the LPGA Tour.

"There are many of us coming over here, and we're good," said Han, who shot 66 for a 17-under-par 199 total, and then made a 20-foot birdie putt to beat Wendy Ward on the third playoff hole. "I don't think about the controversy. I just play my own game."

The alleged infractions — which the LPGA ruled moot since there was "no corroborating evidence" to support the claims — included accusations that Korean players received advice from their parents (mostly their fathers) who spoke only Korean, and that one father improved his daughter's lie. Minny Yao, a four-year veteran said, "There are many good things in Korean culture, but in America, playing golf, some things are not the right way. Some players really don't know what they're doing. They're realizing some of the things they've done are wrong."

Commissioner Ty Votaw would not elaborate on the right or wrong of his meeting with Korean players during the tournament. "This was simply a dialogue, that's all I can say," Votaw said. "The case is now closed."

Some of the Koreans, like Soo-Yan Kang, were angry at being grouped with anyone accused of cheating, but the controversy didn't effect Han, who shot 68 and 65 and led by one over Michele Redman going into the final round. Redman shot a respectable 67 and never came close. Han jumped out to a solid lead with a 30 on the front nine in soggy conditions.

Ward, who started the final round three shots back, caught fire early. She had five birdies and an eagle in her first nine holes and had no putts outside of seven feet. Her outward 29 pulled her within two of Han's lead. Ward slowed down a little on the second nine, but still birdied two of her last four holes to shoot a course-record 63 and be the first at 199.

Han held a one-shot lead with two holes to play, but a three-putt at the 17th and a failure to convert a birdie at the 18th left her tied with Ward. This was a bad sign for Han, who lost a playoff in 2002 to Gloria Park after failing to convert similar birdie opportunities. This time, however, Han was confident in her putting, and rightfully so: She ranked third for the week in putting with 81 putts for 54 holes.

She one-putted each of the three playoff holes, the first for par, the second for birdie and the third from seven feet for the victory after Ward left her birdie effort on the par-three 17th on the lip. "All I could do was keep putting birdies on the board and see if she'd make a mistake," Ward said. "Hee-Won played great."

Jamie Farr Kroger Classic—$1,000,000
Winner: Se Ri Pak

They haven't erected a statue of Se Ri Pak in Sylvania, Ohio. That comes after five victories. Her 13-under-par 271 that included a rain-delayed 64 in the third round and a 71 on Sunday was only Pak's fourth win at the suburban Toledo event. Already the holder of the course record — a 61, shot in her victory in 1998, that was at the time an LPGA scoring record — Pak appeared to be on track to break that number on Saturday. She birdied eight of her first 13 holes before lightning moved in and play was suspended. When play resumed on Sunday morning, Pak couldn't find her rhythm and played the final five holes in one over par.

That was still good enough for a one-stroke lead over Hee-Won Han and a three-shot edge over Marisa Baena. The lead quickly expanded to two strokes when Han pushed her opening tee shot and struggled to make bogey. But Han rallied with birdies at the fifth and sixth to temporarily gain a share of the lead, until Pak, playing alongside her compatriot, rolled in a six-footer for birdie at the sixth to regain a one-shot advantage.

One hole later Pak extended the lead again when she hit her third shot to the par-five to within a foot of the hole. Six straight pars by Pak expanded the lead to three shots, which is where it stayed until Han rolled in an eight-footer for birdie at the 14th while Pak failed to get up and down and walked away with bogey. The two-shot swing cut the lead to a single stroke with four holes to play.

At the 15th Pak salvaged par after missing the green, and Han, who also missed the green, wasn't as fortunate. When her par putt slid by the hole, the lead was back to two. The lead seesawed again on the next hole when Pak pushed her tee shot, failed to find the fairway from the rough, and walked away with a double bogey. Han made par, and the two were tied with two to play.

At the par-five 17th, Pak hit a perfect tee shot, but pulled her second shot into the rough left of the green. From there she hit a great pitch that stopped four feet from the hole. Pak's birdie at the 17th proved to be the difference. At the final hole Han hit her tee shot behind a tree and made bogey to shoot 72 and drop into a tie for second with Baena at 273.

Pak's routine par for a 71 made her only the eighth player in LPGA history to win the same event four times. It was also her third victory of the year, which moved her up to second on the money list behind Annika Sorenstam.

"I guess I'm just relaxed on this course," Pak said. "You have to play smart, and I know what to do. I have a lot of confidence."

Wachovia Classic—$1,200,000
Winner: Candie Kung

Candie Kung never looks at leaderboards; she would rather not know. That strategy worked well for her when she won the Takefuji Classic in Las Vegas earlier in the year. By not knowing how she stood, Kung could relax and play her game. That was harder at the Wachovia Classic in Kutztown, Pennsylvania, where Kung started the final round one stroke ahead of Meg Mallon and Carin Koch and bogeyed two of her first three holes. In the next four holes she had one more bogey and a birdie to lose the lead.

While this was happening, Se Ri Pak was making four birdies on the first nine to take a two-shot lead. Kung also fell behind her playing partners, Mallon and Koch.

"It was hard, but I didn't give up," said Kung, a native of Taiwan and former USC All-American. "There were still 11 holes to play. Anything can happen on those 11 holes. I might birdie all the way in, you never know."

She didn't birdie all the way in, but she did make birdies at the eighth and ninth to move within a shot of Mallon, who assumed sole possession of the lead after Pak bogeyed the 15th. Another birdie at the 10th gave Kung the lead again after Mallon made bogey.

Mallon came back with a birdie at the 11th to regain a share of the lead, but Kung made a great birdie at the 14th to wrest the lead away for good. She was one clear of Mallon and two ahead of Koch and Pak, who fell even further back when she bogeyed the 17th. Mallon also made bogey at the 17th to drop two behind, which is how it finished.

Of course Kung had no idea how any of this was playing out, as she didn't look at any leaderboards and paid very little attention to the other people in her group. "I had no idea how many shots I was up by," she said. "After I signed the scorecard I didn't even know."

With ignorance as her guiding force, Kung stripped a drive down the center of the final fairway, hit a perfect approach just short of the green, chipped to two feet and tapped in for a birdie, a closing round of 70, a 14-under-par 274 total and a two-stroke win over Pak (68) and Mallon (71). Koch shot 70 to finish in fourth at 277.

State Farm Classic—$1,200,000
Winner: Candie Kung

Given how she started her final round the week before, a part of Candie Kung had to be pleased with the way this one was decided. At the Wachovia Classic, Kung took a one-stroke lead into the final round, lost it with three bogeys in her first seven holes, and then rallied to win by two. This time, in the State Farm Classic, she won without finishing a hole on Sunday.

She teed off in the final group at 9:00 a.m. at the Rail Country Club in Springfield, Illinois, in the hopes that the round would be completed before the expected rain arrived. At the time Kung held a one-shot lead over Laura Davies after scores of 64, 67 and 71. Davies had to like her chances given that Kung's scores were trending upward and hers (70, 67 and 66) were headed in the opposite direction. Hee-Won Han was also pleased. After rounds of 66, 69 and 69, she too was in the final group, two strokes behind, and with two recent victories, she felt like her game was on the upswing.

After the final group hit their opening tee shots, the rains came and, after almost four hours of constant downpour with no let-up in sight, officials canceled the final round and declared Kung the winner. It was the first time the final round of an event had been cancelled since the 1997 Chick-fil-A Charity Championship was washed out.

"A win is a win," Kung said. "But everybody out there who made the cut after Friday wanted to finish 72 holes. It just happened to be one of those weeks."

Davies was certainly one of those who hoped to get in all four rounds. "I felt I had a good chance today," she said. "It was anyone's to win, really. Candie had a one-shot lead, but a one-shot lead is nothing."

It's nothing unless you are watching the Weather Channel and realize that it could mean the difference between a win and a runner-up finish, as was the case this week. "I thought there was no way we could play today," Kung said. "I don't like playing in the rain with all the rain gear you have to wear. It's hard to swing the club. In the rain you don't know if the ball will spin. But I practiced with my rain gear, and before I teed off, my caddie told me to be patient. He said it doesn't matter how many times we have to back off a shot, and if there is any water on the green to deal with it. That helped me a lot even if we didn't get to finish the tournament.

"I kind of knew they would cancel it, but I did not want to think so until they said I was the winner. It feels great right now. It still hasn't sunk in yet, and hopefully it will in the next couple of days. Two wins in two weeks. Wow."

John Q. Hammons Hotel Classic—$1,000,000
Winner: Karrie Webb

In a year when most of the buzz on the LPGA Tour centered on Annika Sorenstam, the woman who was the best in women's golf only three short years ago gave notice that she was not to be forgotten. Karrie Webb, long considered one of the best ball-strikers in women's golf, put together a performance in Tulsa, Oklahoma, reminiscent of her glory days in 1999 and 2000 when she won 13 of 47 events and consecutive Player of the Year titles. With a four-under-par 66 on Sunday, Webb cruised to a nine-shot victory at the John Q. Hammons Hotel Classic, her first win since the 2002 Weetabix Women's British Open.

"It's a sense of relief, but also I'm proud because it hasn't been the easiest of years for me," Webb said. "I just wanted to win so badly this year, because I didn't want to be shut out for the first time in my career."

Those worries evaporated early in the final round. Webb started with a three-shot lead over Cristie Kerr, but five quick birdies by Webb on the first nine while Kerr struggled to find the fairways extended the lead to nine. "I was glad I had a nine-shot lead coming down the last, because I didn't have to think about it too much," she said. After tapping in for par and a three-day total of 200, Webb hugged her caddie, Kerr and Kerr's caddie before tossing her ball to a group of fans behind the 18th green.

"You always focus on getting better," Webb said. Her recent slump — if six victories in three seasons could be referred to as a slump — could be traced to swing changes she made after her dominant 2000 season. "I could have gone on the same track just fine," Webb said. "But you never say you've got the game by the tail. I wanted to hit it more like the guys, I guess."

It worked, at least this week. Webb hit 11 of 14 fairways in the final round while Kerr found only six. The winner also found 13 of 18 greens and made only one bogey. "I'm really happy and relieved just to have played well, not necessarily winning by nine strokes, but just playing well enough to win," she said.

Dorothy Delasin also shot 65 on Sunday to move into a tie for second with Candie Kung, Jamie Hullett and Tammie Green at 209, while defending champion Sorenstam shot 68 for a 211 total and a tie for 10th.

Solheim Cup
Winner: Europe

See Evian Ladies European Tour section.

Safeway Classic—$1,200,000
Winner: Annika Sorenstam

In a year that, in her words, "couldn't get much better," Annika Sorenstam won her fifth title when she shot a final-round 68 to win the Safeway Classic in Portland, Oregon, by one stroke over Beth Daniel. In the process, she had back-to-back eagles for the first time in her career. "Obviously, it feels wonderful," Sorenstam said after finishing at 15-under-par 201. "I love coming down the stretch when it's exciting and hitting great shots when you need to. Winning never gets old."

Sorenstam played steady all week, which is what she needed to do after Daniel got off to a blistering start with 62. But the 46-year-old Hall of Famer couldn't keep up the pace on Saturday. She shot 73 and fell into a three-way tie with Sorenstam and Cristie Kerr. "I have a new Korean name," Daniel said. "Everyone writes about me as 'soon-to-be 47,' so just call me Soon To-Bee."

She was not long to be the leader. Sorenstam set the tone early when she pulled her opening tee shot under a tree and, with a restricted swing, punched the ball onto the green 20 feet from the hole. When she made that putt for birdie, the outcome almost seemed assured.

Then came the stretch of eagles. At the par-five fifth, she almost holed an eagle putt and tapped in for birdie. One hole later she holed a wedge shot from 104 yards on the par-four sixth. At the par-five seventh her eagle putt found the hole for a five-under-par, three-hole run. "I was on fire for those three holes for sure," Sorenstam said.

She played the next 11 holes in even par, which gave Daniel and Kerr a chance. Kerr wasn't able to capitalize, despite making four birdies and one bogey for 69 and a 204 total. But Daniel had five birdies and no bogeys through 17 holes to draw within a shot of Sorenstam. When her approach to the 18th stopped 18 feet from the hole, Daniel had one more chance to force a playoff. The putt was struck well, but it skirted the low edge of the hole, leaving Daniel with a closing 67 and a 202 total, but one more than Sorenstam.

"I rolled it well on 18, but I needed to make birdie," Daniel said. "I opened with a 62 and didn't win the golf tournament, so I should be a little disappointed."

For Sorenstam, this was just another chapter in the most memorable season of her career. In addition to capturing the career Grand Slam, participating in the Bank of America Colonial, and anchoring the victorious Solheim Cup team, she was inducted into the Hall of Fame in October, just 11 days after her 33rd birthday. "I've done so many things," Sorenstam said. "I feel like I've been everywhere. I've been to Asia, I've been on the men's tour, and I've been playing Solheim Cup. And later this year, I'm going to play the Skins Game. I've always asked myself why is it happening to me? And then suddenly this year with Colonial and two majors, it's just another memorable year."

Longs Drugs Challenge—$1,000,000
Winner: Helen Alfredsson

It's not often that a winner offers an apology to her playing partner. But then it's not every day that a player like Pat Hurst four-putts the final green to lose by one. That's what happened at the Longs Drugs Challenge, the final full-field event of the 2003 LPGA season. Helen Alfredsson, winless since 1998, was on the receiving end of Hurst's collapse, but the 38-year-old Swede took no joy from the victory. When the drama on the 18th was complete, Alfredsson put her arms around Hurst and said, "I'm sorry."

Alfredsson had already resigned herself to finishing second, which was fine with her. She had only come to Lincoln, California, to bolster her standings on the money list and remain fully exempt for 2004. Shooting 13-under-par 275 was a bonus. "I don't have the spark I usually have," Alfredsson said. "This is a job, but it's not like most jobs. You can't just show up and go through the motions. You have to wake up each morning and say, 'I can't wait to play golf.' I haven't been feeling that this year."

The reflection that comes with age was brought home to Alfredsson earlier in the year when she was the European captain of the Ping Junior Solheim Cup. "I was as childish as they were, singing on the bus at seven in the morning and seven at night," she said. "I miss that. Those kids live for the thrill of hitting a good shot. They don't feel as though they need to do everything perfect."

Saturday was a fairly perfect day for Alfredsson, who shot 64 for a one-stroke lead over a group that included Se Ri Pak, Rachel Teske, Jung Yeon Lee and Hurst. After 14 holes, Pak, Teske, Hurst and Grace Park had all tied Alfredsson's lead. When Hurst rolled in a birdie at the par-five 15th, she broke away from the pack to take the lead outright. That's where it stayed until the final hole.

Hurst's troubles started on her approach. From the fairway at the 378-yard hole, Hurst hit a poor second shot that stopped 80 feet short of the hole. Figuring she needed a birdie to force a playoff, Alfredsson went right at the flag. Her approach stopped 10 feet away, but Hurst, who hadn't won since 2000, hit the worst putt of the week. The ball stopped 20 feet short of the hole. Her second putt wasn't much better. She left herself a shade over four feet for bogey.

Alfredsson didn't make her birdie, but tapped in from a foot for par, which turned out to be enough. Hurst missed the four-footer and walked off with a double bogey. "It's disappointing, obviously," Hurst said. "The bottom line is you want to win tournaments. I didn't close the door and that's tough. All I was trying to do at 18 was two-putt. I never thought I would have been that short."

Alfredsson was happy with the win, but not with the way she won it. "When you haven't been playing well, you want it so much," the winner said. "But I don't like to see anyone finish the way Pat finished. You can't raise your arms and scream, 'Yeah!' in that situation. I know it's the nature of the game, but you wish that you could win outright by making birdie."

Hurst's debacle at the 18th dropped her to 70 and into a five-way tie for second with Park, Lee, Teske and Pak at 276.

Samsung World Championship—$800,000
Winner: Sophie Gustafson

What should have been a showcase event for the LPGA and a showcase victory for Sophie Gustafson, who shot a closing 64 to charge from five strokes back to win the Samsung World Championship by two over Beth Daniel and Rachel Teske, ended in controversy. The question was intent and integrity. Unfortunately, it overshadowed some spectacular play on the part of the winner. At issue was one simple question: Did Gustafson, who made an eagle and eight birdies, cheat?

The incident occurred on the 14th green at the TPC at The Woodlands, near Houston, Texas. Standing over a 30-foot putt that would have given her the lead, Gustafson appeared to take her stance and sole her putter, which is the technical definition of "addressing the ball" in *The Rules of Golf*. When the ball began rolling down an embankment and came to rest eight feet away, many assumed there should have been a one-stroke penalty. But when an official was called to the green, Gustafson claimed she did not ground the club. "The ball had stopped on the top of the slope," she said. "I knew that it could move, and so I never grounded my club. Then it started not to actually move, but to wobble. Probably three to five seconds later, it started to roll down the slope."

Some, including television commentators, said that she grounded her club, but as Juli Inkster, who was playing alongside Gustafson, put it, "If Sophie said she didn't ground her club, then she didn't ground her club. I wasn't really looking at it, but you have to give her the benefit of the doubt. She's a straight arrow."

Given how well Gustafson had played to that point, it seemed a shame that the controversy would overshadow the round. Trailing Teske, Gustafson got off to a great start when she holed a bunker shot at the par-five first hole for eagle. She followed that with birdies on five of her next six holes, the last coming when she rolled in a seven-footer on the par-four seventh to reach 13 under par and take the outright lead.

Teske birdied the first hole, but her putter abandoned her after that, and she reeled off eight straight pars to close out the first nine one under for the day and 12 under for the tournament. That proved to be enough to reclaim the lead after Gustafson flubbed a chip shot at the ninth and took a double bogey to drop back to 11 under. The Swede rebounded with a birdie at the 10th to reclaim a share of the lead. She and Teske swapped birdies a few minutes later when Gustafson rolled in a five-footer at the 13th while Teske made a 15-footer for birdie at the 12th.

Teske, playing one group behind Gustafson, reclaimed the lead when she, too, birdied the par-five 13th while Gustafson was calling an official out to the 14th green. To her credit, Gustafson put any whiff of controversy behind her when she rolled in a birdie putt at the 15th to regain a share of the lead at 14 under.

It looked like a playoff might be imminent, but then Teske, who looked fatigued in the closing holes, bogeyed the 16th and 17th, which allowed Gustafson to cruise in with three pars for a closing 64 and a 274 total, for a two-shot win over Teske, who finished with 71, and Daniel, who shot 70.

CJ Nine Bridges Classic—$1,250,000
Winner: Shi Hyan Ahn

No one was surprised when a Korean won the CJ Nine Bridges Classic, a late-season event held on Korea's Jeju Island in the South China Sea. Everyone was shocked by which Korean took the title. Shi Hyun Ahn, a 19-year-old playing in her first LPGA event and who had yet to compete outside her country, led wire-to-wire and won by three strokes over Gloria Park, Grace Park, Se Ri Pak and Laura Davies.

"I am so happy," Ahn said through an interpreter after following her 65-71 start with a closing 68 that included an eagle on the last hole. "I was obsessed with winning the tournament, and I think that helped me win."

She also appeared undaunted by playing with a national hero like Pak or an LPGA legend like Davies, both of whom (along with Grace Park) began the final round three shots off Ahn's lead. "I was very nervous today," the winner admitted. "I did not expect to win, but I'm very happy I did. My plan was to shoot three under, and I did even better."

The eagle at the 18th, a short par-five with water guarding the green, where Ahn hit a booming drive and a six iron to six feet, was icing on this teenager's cake. It wasn't the only great hole she played. Ahn birdied her first hole after watching Pak drain a solid putt for birdie. "When Se Ri birdied the first, I thought she would win," Ahn said. "But then I also made birdie. That helped settle me down."

Ahn's only bogey came at the par-three 13th, but she made up for it with a birdie at the 14th to keep the lead at two. That's where it remained until the last hole when Ahn put together two great swings in a clutch situation to finish the week at 12-under-par 204.

"I think Ahn is a great player," Pak said. "It is the first time I have played with her, but I'm sure she is a star of the future. It must have been tough for her playing with Laura and me, but she hung in there and seemed really comfortable with her game."

Gloria Park had the low round of the tournament, shooting a course-record 62 to move into a tie for second with Grace Park, Pak and Davies.

Mizuno Classic—¥135,600,000
Winner: Annika Sorenstam

See Japan LPGA Tour section.

Mobile Tournament of Champions—$750,000
Winner: Dorothy Delasin

On a sunny Sunday in Semmes, Alabama, where the course named Magnolia was anything but sweet and genteel, Dorothy Delasin sank an eight-footer on her 19th hole of the day to win the Mobile Tournament of Champions in a playoff with Hee-Won Han.

"It was a downhiller with a cup or cup and a half of break to the left," Delasin said of the winning putt. "I had been stroking the ball good and I just told myself to put a good stroke on it, and if it goes in, it goes in. If it doesn't, we go to No. 17 for another hole. It looked like it might break away, and then it went in the side door. It was just a rush of emotion that was all built up. It just came out."

Delasin started the final round with a one-shot lead over Han, which she maintained through 16 holes. On the difficult par-three 17th, Delasin pushed her tee shot into trees on a hillside guarding the right edge of the green. She was fortunate the ball didn't bounce back into a marsh-like hazard. Still, it looked as though bogey was going to be a probable score on the hole. That presented a problem for the leader, since Han hit her tee shot 10 feet away and was staring at a simple birdie putt to go four under on the back nine and seven under for the tournament.

Delasin hit the best pitch she could, but still had 12 feet for par. When that putt fell, the best Han could do was tie for the lead, which she did by making the 10-footer for birdie. "Her putt on 17 was a good one," Han said. "That was big."

Both players reached the 18th hole in regulation and had reasonable birdie putts to win. But Han's 30-footer slid past the hole and Delasin's 15-footer stopped one roll short. Both players tapped in for par and 280 totals, Han having shot 68 (32 on the second nine) and Delasin, 69.

The playoff started back on the 18th where both players hit the fairway on the uphill, dogleg-right par-four. From there they both fired at the flag. Han hit her approach to 10 feet, and Delasin stuck it inside her ball, leaving a straightforward eight-footer for the win. For a moment it looked as though a birdie would be needed to halve. Han hit a great putt that was right on line, but stopped a fraction of an inch short. "It was just a little short," she said. "It was downhill, but not as fast as it looked."

That set up Delasin's putt to win.

"Dorothy played well," Han said afterward. "She made the putt in the playoff, and I missed. That was it."

ADT Championship—$1,000,000
Winner: Meg Mallon

In a year when she won five tournaments, two majors, low stroke average and Player of the Year honors for the third straight year and, in her spare time, made history by playing in a men's event, Annika Sorenstam would rather forget her first week and last week of the season. The first week out she blew a three-shot lead in Phoenix and the last week she did the same thing in the ADT Championship at Trump International Golf Club in West

Palm Beach, Florida. In March it was Se Ri Pak that took advantage of Sorenstam's late-round blunders. In November it was Meg Mallon who rose to the occasion.

"She's setting the standard," Mallon said of constantly hearing about Sorenstam's dominance. "I need to play better to beat her, and I did it today. I need to do that more often next year. But, yeah, you get a little bit of a burr in your side, but you know, there's something you can do about it — play better."

Mallon did just that, reeling off six birdies in a 10-hole stretch while Sorenstam missed putt after crucial putt. On the sixth, the Swede left an eight-footer short. She then missed a six-footer on the ninth and three-putted for par after reaching the par-five 12th in two. The difference in the rounds could be summed up very simply: Mallon had 26 putts; Sorenstam had 33.

Mallon's final birdie came at the famous par-three 17th, the hole where Donald Trump built the largest manmade waterfall on any golf course in the world. She hit her tee shot to 15 feet and made it. Sorenstam, playing one group behind, hit it to 20 feet and missed. That proved to be a microcosm of the day.

Still the two were tied with one hole to play. Mallon played the final hole safely and made a routine par for a five-under-par 67 and a 281 total. But Sorenstam, who made few bad swings during the week, saved her worst for last. She pull-hooked her tee shot into the high rough. From there she hacked it back to the fairway, hit her third to 12 feet, and missed the par putt that would have forced a playoff. Sorenstam shot 71 for a 282 total.

"I figured if I shot three under today, I would be fine," Sorenstam said, correctly predicting the score she needed to win outright. "I had my chances, I really did. I just didn't execute well today. But I'm going to let go of this in a heartbeat. This year has been too great to look back and say that this was a big disappointment. I'm very happy with my year. It's been fabulous in so many ways. Tomorrow's a big day for me. I've got my induction into the LPGA Hall of Fame, so not a lot of things are going to make me unhappy right now."

Nothing could spoil Mallon's mood either. "I saw all your faces yesterday," the winner said, chiding reporters about their assumption that Sorenstam was going to win. "No one's going to beat her tomorrow. That's what you all were thinking." She was right, and the reporters who spoke with her afterward admitted it. "You guys act like it's the first time," she said. "I've beaten her before. You know what? I'm sure they're saying, 'Geez, if Meg can do it, anybody can do it.' But it's not necessarily about facing down the No. 1 player. Facing down your own demons is far more difficult."

Evian Ladies European Tour

ANZ Ladies Masters—A$800,000
Winner: Laura Davies

See Australian Women's Tour section.

AAMI Women's Australian Open—A$500,000
Winner: Mhairi McKay

See Australian Women's Tour section.

Tenerife Ladies Open—€200,000
Winner: Elisabeth Esterl

After five runner-up finishes and 22 top-10s, Elisabeth Esterl of Germany won her first professional title at the Tenerife Ladies Open. A final round of 69 for a 276 total helped the 26-year-old to a one-stroke win over Becky Brewerton, a 21-year-old Welsh amateur. Brewerton led after the second and third rounds after scores of 69, 67 and 68, but closed with 73.

Twice during the final round Esterl caught Brewerton, only to drop a shot and fall back. But as Brewerton bogeyed the 17th, Esterl birdied the same hole and then the 18th from eight feet. "It's been a long time coming and I am now so relieved," said Esterl, who finished at 12 under par. "Everyone has been saying I should have won so many times and I am glad I handled the pressure today."

Only two weeks previously, Brewerton had beaten the Bavarian in the Weetabix Challenge between a team of amateurs and the tour professionals. "Becky is such a good player, a wonderful ball-striker, and she has a great future ahead of her. I was very impressed with her," said Esterl. Ana Belen Sanchez and Karine Icher shared third place, and Iben Tinning and Corinne Dibnah tied for fifth.

La Perla Italian Open—€190,000
Winner: Ludivine Kreutz

With the lead changing virtually every hole and five players topping the leaderboard at different times during the final round, Ludivine Kreutz got on with simply playing golf. Her method was so successful the 29-year-old from France won her first title after five years on tour in which her best result was a sixth-place finish.

A closing 70 gave Kreutz a 10-under-par total of 282 in the La Perla

Italian Open at Poggio dei Medici in Tuscany and left her one stroke ahead of Anne-Marie Knight, Karen Lunn and Tenerife champion Elisabeth Esterl. Kreutz birdied three of the last four holes to claim the title, from 12 feet at the 15th, from two feet at the 17th, and safely two-putting at the final hole. At that point only Knight could catch her, but the Australian's chip for eagle was not quite close enough.

"I still can't believe it," said Kreutz, who was as surprised as anyone at the result. "I don't quite realize what has happened. I've always dreamed of winning on tour, but I've not had a great record in five years. This is just superb."

Lancia Ladies Open of Portugal—€165,000
Winner: Alison Munt

Alison Munt collected her third title but her first in three years at the Lancia Ladies Open of Portugal after beating Elisabeth Esterl at the first extra hole at Aroeira. Munt, a 37-year-old from Australia, started the final round two strokes behind 36-hole leader Vicky Uwland, but after Esterl had come through the field with a closing 66, Munt needed two birdies over the last four holes to tie.

Munt duly birdied the 15th and 16th holes, but had to save par from 10 feet at the 17th before her birdie attempt from six feet for victory at the 18th slid past. The pair tied at 209, seven under par, but in the playoff at the par-five 18th, Esterl went into a lake with her third shot and had to concede defeat.

Uwland shared third place with Spaniard Ana Belen Sanchez at six under par, while Italian Open winner Ludivine Kreutz claimed fifth place. Two 13-year-old British juniors, Henrietta Brockway and Florentyna Parker, were given invitations for the event and impressed their playing partners despite each missing the cut.

Open de Espana Feminino—€250,000
Winner: Federica Dassu

Federica Dassu won the sixth title of her 19-year-old career at the Open de Espana and promptly announced her retirement at the end of the season. Dassu had not won for seven years, but at age 44 became the oldest winner in the history of the Ladies European Tour. It was an emotional victory because her mother had recently died of cancer. "I dedicate this victory to her and I would have loved for her to be here to share it with me," said Dassu. "This victory is more special than all of my others."

Dassu began the final round three strokes off the lead, but a closing 70 at Salamanca gave the Italian victory at six-under-par 282, by two strokes over compatriot Sophie Sandolo, Ana Belen Sanchez of Spain, and Australia's Corinne Dibnah. Virginie Auffret, a 25-year-old from France, maintained her lead through 12 holes, but dropped seven shots in the last five holes as she slipped into a tie for fifth place with Elisabeth Esterl and Iben Tinning.

Dassu suddenly inherited the lead and saved par from a bunker at the 17th and then parred the 18th. "I made three huge putts today and that kept me going," Dassu said. "The save on 17 was incredible, especially for me, I'm not very good out of bunkers! When I saw Virginie had double-bogeyed the 16th, I knew I was in the lead and I started panicking, but now I am absolutely relieved."

Ladies Irish Open—€165,000
Winner: Sophie Gustafson

A brilliant 10-under-par round of 63 in the second round on the Mahoney's Point course at the beautiful Killarney Club helped Sophie Gustafson to her third Ladies Irish Open title. Gustafson, a 29-year-old Swede, opened up a five-stroke lead over Laura Davies, and although she closed with 73 to the English golfer's 71, she was not threatened on the final day. Gustafson claimed a three-stroke victory at 17-under-par 293, with Davies taking second place and Trish Johnson third, with Alison Nicholas and Kirsty Taylor sharing fourth place.

Gustafson had won the Irish Open in 1998 and 2000, and this was her ninth European win and the 14th of her career. "Ireland always brings me a bit of luck," Gustafson said. "I have been playing better in America than the scores suggest, and after I holed a few putts on the first two days, the confidence came flooding back." With the Solheim Cup to be played in Sweden later in the season, Gustafson had returned to Europe to try to secure her place in the match.

Arras Open de France Dames—€275,000
Winner: Lynnette Brooky

Lynnette Brooky retained her title at the Arras Open de France Dames, but only after an exciting final day. Brooky shared the lead after three rounds with Norway's Vibeke Stensrud with Trish Johnson of England a stroke behind. In the final round, Brooky and Johnson returned five-under-par rounds of 67 and Stensrud a 68.

It gave the 35-year-old from New Zealand her third European title and she became the first player on tour to defend a title successfully for four years. At 14 under par, with a total of 274, Brooky won by one over Johnson and Stensrud, who birdied the 18th after falling behind the other two contenders. Carin Koch, in her second event since giving birth to her second child two months before, took fourth place.

Brooky and Johnson both went to the turn in 32. Johnson tied for the lead with a birdie at the 10th, but Brooky went ahead at the 11th. After going over the green at the 13th, a penalty drop cost Johnson a bogey while Brooky birdied to lead by three. At the 14th, there was a two-stroke swing the other way and Brooky had to par in from the 15th, where she holed from eight feet after visiting a bunker, to stay in front.

Evian Masters—€2,222,073
Winner: Juli Inkster

Juli Inkster eased to her 30th career victory with a superb display over the final two rounds of the Evian Masters. In the third round the 43-year-old Californian set a new course record with a round of 64, while the following day, on her wedding anniversary, she added a 65 in which she did not drop a shot. At 21 under par, with a total of 267, Inkster set a new tournament record, two strokes better than Annika Sorenstam's old mark, while also becoming the first American to win in the 10-year history of the tournament.

High above Lake Geneva, Inkster ran away from a strong field of both LPGA and European Tour stars to win by six strokes over Korea's Hee-Won Han. Young Mexican Lorena Ochoa shared third place with Rosie Jones, two strokes further back, while Karrie Webb was fifth and Se Ri Pak sixth.

Sharing the lead with Jones overnight, Inkster went to the turn in 32 and finished off the tournament in style by birdieing the last three holes. "It was tough starting out, as there were many players in the hunt, but I managed to pull away a little," said Inkster. "Coming down the back nine was a lot of fun and I had the chance to soak up the atmosphere. It's an honor to become the first American to win the event."

Weetabix Women's British Open—€1,670,445
Winner: Annika Sorenstam

What was already an incredible season for Annika Sorenstam, following her appearance on the men's PGA Tour at Colonial, got even better here when, just as at the McDonald's LPGA Championship, the 32-year-old Swede won a major championship that had previously eluded her. In the case of the Weetabix Women's British Open, it was a tournament in which she had been a runner-up three times and in which she had missed the cut the previous year, the only time she had endured that in four seasons.

This victory, her fifth of the season and the 56th of her career, gave Sorenstam a career Grand Slam. But it was only at the 72nd hole of the historic Royal Lytham and St. Annes that the Sorenstam finally defeated her playing partner, Se Ri Pak. Sorenstam's accuracy was in evidence over the closing nine holes as she perfectly plotted her way around a links that caused everyone else, including all her closest rivals, severe headaches. Only one player, an early starter, bettered the final-round 70 that ensured Sorenstam won with a 278 total, 10 under par, by one stroke over Pak. Karrie Webb and Grace Park were a further stroke behind, with overnight leader Patricia Meunier-Lebouc, 12 weeks pregnant and suffering from morning sickness, falling back to finish fifth.

"I am thrilled," Sorenstam said. "I have wanted this tournament for so long and been so close. I believe I have become better since playing at the Colonial. There were times today when I felt the pressure and then I thought it was not as bad as the Colonial. This was not about a dominating performance. There were so many great players pushing themselves to play better on a tough course. But that's what motivates me. This was the one I really wanted."

Around the turn, Sorenstam, three-time champion Webb, the 2001 winner Pak, and Meunier-Lebouc, the Kraft Nabisco champion from March, were all tied for the lead. Webb bogeyed the 10th and the 11th holes, so the attention was quickly concentrated on the Swedish-Korean pairing. Sorenstam birdied the par-five 11th to go one ahead, but Pak responded with a two at the short 12th. Pak, who hated her first experience of links golf five years ago on this same course, has since developed a creative flair, and her tee shot was a superbly executed three-quarter punch shot to three feet.

The par-five 15th had troubled Sorenstam all week, but now she chipped to a foot for a birdie. Not even a streaker could disturb her concentration, even if her caddie went after him with his boot. "I've never seen that before at a women's event," Sorenstam said. "He was ugly so it wasn't worth it." Pak failed to get up and down from a bunker for her birdie, and although she birdied the next hole to draw even, only a fine recovery from another pot bunker at the 17th green saved her from falling one behind.

Pak then drove into a fairway bunker at the 18th and could not reach the green in two, while Sorenstam, apparently nerveless, hit a magnificent drive down the fairway. Pak bogeyed and the Swede two-putted for her sixth major victory.

Sorenstam, who dropped only one stroke in the last 38 holes, was wearing a necklace that she had been sent by a woman claiming it was for "performance." She said it would work in 10 days and she had put it on 10 days before. Another was for "grounding" which she gave to her husband. "I need the performance and he needs to calm down," she said.

HP Open—€517,042
Winner: Sophie Gustafson

As if holding off the best player in the game was not enough, Sophie Gustafson had to deal with a charging Suzann Pettersen as well as suffering an unfortunate incident with a photographer on the final green at the HP Open. Gustafson led by two over Sorenstam after 54 holes and both scored final rounds of 68 at Drottningholm. But Pettersen scored a superb 62, 10 under par, to set the target at 269, 19 under par.

Even so, victory looked assured for Gustafson, five under for her round playing the last hole. She was 30 feet away from the hole on the 18th green and putted up to 18 inches, but as she attempted to tap in, a photographer's camera let off a volley of clicks on her backswing and the putt shaved the hole and stayed out. Gustafson, upset at the incident, was now in a playoff with Pettersen, who hit into the crowd at the first extra hole but saved par from the drop zone for a half. The second hole was also halved, but the third time around Pettersen again missed the green and could not make her par.

Gustafson had to two-putt from 10 feet to win and duly tapped in from 18 inches, safely this time. "It definitely disturbed me on my backswing," said Gustafson of the original incident. "I was very upset during the playoff and I have to thank my caddie for calming me down. This win means so much to me. To win in Sweden and to beat the world's best player on the final day makes me feel so proud. This is a very important moment in my career."

While Gustafson won for the second time this season, Pettersen's round, which tied the European Tour's lowest ever, had included a stretch of eight under for six holes from the seventh. At the short par-four ninth, measuring 275 yards, she drove to 10 inches for an eagle. Sorenstam finished in third place, with Laura Davies and Becky Morgan tying for fourth.

BT Ladies Open—€238,635
Winner: Sophie Gustafson

Sophie Gustafson won for the second week in a row, and for the second time in Ireland this season, in another dramatic conclusion to the BT Ladies Open at Warrenpoint. Gustafson managed only four pars during her final round of 72 which left the Swede with a 275 total, 13 under par and one stroke ahead of Alison Nicholas, who closed with 73.

Nicholas, the former U.S. Open champion who was looking for her first win in Europe since 1996, led for much of a final day played in strong winds beneath the Mountains of Mourne. But at the 17th hole, Gustafson's power brought her an eagle after she holed from 40 feet to jump into the lead by one. Both were short of the green at the 18th, and while Gustafson thinned her chip through the green, Nicholas missed her par putt from 12 feet.

The Swede then holed from 10 feet for her bogey and the victory. "It was absolutely unbelievable," said Gustafson. "I knew I needed something special down the last few holes and to make an eagle when I did was just extraordinary, I couldn't believe it."

Wales WPGA Championship of Europe—€636,360
Winner: Shani Waugh

Shani Waugh, seven years after her only other victory, won the Wales WPGA Championship after holing a putt from 70 feet on the final green at Royal Porthcawl. Birdies at the last two holes gave Waugh a two-stroke victory over Welsh amateur Becky Brewerton. Though the birdie at the 18th was not required, the putt was tricky enough to suggest a three-putt could not be ruled out, which would have led to a playoff.

Brewerton finished runner-up for the second time and confirmed she would turn professional at the end of the season. She finished one stroke ahead of Stephanie Arricau from France, who had led after three rounds, with Elisabeth Esterl finishing in fourth place and Sophie Gustafson in fifth. Waugh closed with a four-under-par 69 to finish at 286, six under par.

Her week had not included a lot of sleep as she accompanied Catrin Nilsmark, who was sharing the same accommodation, to an emergency room at a local hospital where they spent all night after the second round. Nilsmark had injured her back during the first round, but her main role for the week was as Solheim Cup captain. After Mhairi McKay took the seventh and final automatic place on the qualifying list, along with Annika Sorenstam, Sophie Gustafson, Elisabeth Esterl, Laura Davies, Iben Tinning and Ana Belen Sanchez, Nilsmark selected Patricia Meunier-Lebouc, Carin Koch, Suzann Pettersen, Catriona Matthew and Janice Moodie as her wild cards.

Solheim Cup
Winner: Europe

While the perfect script might have been for Annika Sorenstam to secure the winning point for Europe as they claimed their third victory in the Solheim Cup, such Hollywood-like touches were not necessary as Catrin Nilsmark's team swept to an overwhelming win at Barseback on the southwest coast of Sweden. Leading by three points after two days of foursomes and fourballs, Europe was not to be overtaken in the singles as happened at Interlachen in 2002. The five points they required came from just the top seven matches with Catriona Matthew's 3-and-1 win over Rosie Jones allowing the celebrations to begin, as Europe coasted to a 17½ points to 10½ points victory over the United States team. Nilsmark, unable to jump or scream due to a ruptured disc, thrust a crutch into the air to mark the triumph.

The Swedish captain's fierce determination throughout the week to carry on regardless of her injury was matched by her team's desire to make sure they completed the job. "We have had a problem in the past closing out the victories," said Nilsmark. "I told my team on Thursday night that we were going on a journey that starts on Friday morning and will not end until Sunday afternoon. But no one could expect to jump in the back of the bus and expect to be driven to the Solheim Cup. Today I can say we had 12 drivers out there."

In front of huge galleries on all three days, Europe went in front on the first morning by winning three of the opening foursomes and halving the other. The United States, led by the experienced pairing of Juli Inkster and Beth Daniel, as well as the talented young pairing of Cristie Kerr and Kelli Kuehne, won three fourballs in afternoon but gave back the ground they had gained in Saturday's foursomes.

The second series of fourballs came down to one of the best matches the event has ever seen. Several holes were halved in birdies and the result was the difference between Europe leading by three points, two or one. At the 17th, Laura Diaz, playing with Kelly Robbins, hit a five iron to five feet and holed the putt, leaving Sorenstam, partnered by Suzann Pettersen, to hole from 22 feet from the fringe for the half. "I've had putts to win majors and other tournaments, but that putt on 17 was very special," Sorenstam said.

At the 18th, Diaz again went close with an eight iron to four feet, but this time the tactic of putting first went awry as she missed the birdie attempt. Europe then had two chances for the victory, and with Sorenstam six feet away, Pettersen made it irrelevant by holing hers from 12 feet.

On Sunday Nilsmark's plan was to get points on the board early and she packed the top half of the draw. Janice Moodie, the week's best putter, led off for Europe, birdied the first hole and was 5 up after 10 holes, before eventually defeating Kuehne 3 and 2. Inkster quickly disposed of Carin Koch 5 and 4, for only the Swede's second loss in 12 Solheim games, but Michele Redman gained the United States' only other win while it mattered.

Sophie Gustafson produced five birdies in beating Heather Bowie, and Iben Tinning, cheered on by the many Danes who had made the journey over the bridge to Malmo from Copenhagen, got 3 up against Wendy Ward at the turn. Though the American fought back strongly, Tinning's superb second shot to two feet at the 17th brought Europe's third win of the morning.

Sorenstam, playing Angela Stanford, again appeared inspired by playing in front of her home gallery. She birdied three of the first six holes and, apart from making a mess of the ninth, played flawlessly. The world No. 1 was expected to lead Europe to victory and never flinched from her task all week.

The glory of holing the winning putt might have been hers had she not holed from 20 feet for a birdie at the 15th and then completed a 3-and-2 win at the 16th. Ahead Matthew had rallied from losing the first two holes to Rosie Jones and did not drop a shot after the first.

Matthew evened the match at the eighth and went 2 up at the 12th, and the end came at the 17th when she put her approach to 10 feet. When Jones failed to save par, the American conceded to the Scot. Matthew had not played in the match since 1998. "It was definitely worth the wait," Matthew said. "I was lucky to be in the winning match, but last time I played, I was in the losing match."

"My players tried as hard as they could but we got outplayed," said the gracious losing captain, Patty Sheehan. Europe got the best out of their strongest players, with Gustafson winning three points, Matthew and Moodie three and a half, and Sorenstam and Pettersen four each. Sorenstam now shares the record of 17½ Solheim Cup points with Laura Davies.

Pettersen lost the chance to become the first player to win all five matches when she conceded to Cristie Kerr at 1 down with three to play. In an unsatisfactory ending, the last four games on the course all walked in once Europe were sure of winning, to leave the home side with a distorted, but nonetheless record, winning margin of 17½ to 10½.

It was also historic as this was the first time Europe's professionals have held both the Ryder and Solheim Cups at the same time, while Great Britain and Ireland's men's amateur team had won the Walker Cup for a third successive time only the previous week.

Biarritz Ladies Classic—€165,000
Winner: Marlene Hedblom

Marlene Hedblom joined her brother Peter as a European Tour winner by claiming the Biarritz Classic with a brilliant final round of 65. Hedblom won for the first time after eight years on tour after finishing two clear of New Zealand's Gina Scott, who could not quite celebrate her 29th birthday in style. Ludivine Kreutz and Marta Prieto shared third place a stroke further back.

Hedblom, who finished with a total of 200, 10 under par, started the final round two strokes off the lead but went to the turn in 31. The 30-year-old from Gavle, whose father Olle is her caddie and coach, birdied the 10th and 15th, and her only blemish was a three-putt at the 18th.

The last official event of the season confirmed Sophie Gustafson as leader of the Order of Merit. The Swede also finished top of the stroke averages and was voted Player of the Year. Rebecca Stevenson was the Rookie of the Year.

Princess Lalla Meriem Cup—US$40,000
Winner: Johanna Head

It took a playoff for Johanna Head to defeat Elisabeth Esterl in the Princess Lalla Meriem Cup, the ladies event held alongside the Hassan II Trophy at Dar-es-Salam Golf Club in Rabat, Morocco. Both had 214 totals, as Head shot rounds of 71, 73 and 70 while Esterl posted 72, 71 and 71. Rebecca Hudson was third at 217.

Japan LPGA Tour

Daikin Orchid Ladies—¥60,000,000
Winner: Yuri Fudoh

Yuri Fudoh wasted no time in putting her mark on the 2003 Japan LPGA Tour. She launched a spectacular season in the Daikin Orchid Ladies, the circuit's traditional opener in early March, capturing her first of 10 victories in a playoff against Aki Nakano after the two players carded matching, eight-under-par 208s at Ryukyu Golf Club in Okinawa. It was the 26-year-old's 16th win in little more than three seasons and second in three years in the Daikin Orchid.

Neither player reached first place until Sunday. Two little-known players — Riko Higashio and Mikiyo Nishizuka — began the tournament on top with 68s, one stroke in front of Kayo Yamada and Nikki Campbell. Fudoh opened with 72, Nakano with 73. Ok-Hee Ku, the South Korean veteran, started weakly with 75, but came up with a record-breaking performance Saturday and surged one stroke into the lead. Ku, winner of 21 titles in Japan over the years, made 11 birdies and shot 62, both new LPGA marks, for 137, one better than Taiwan's Yun-Jye Wei. Fudoh pulled into a third-place tie at 139, but Nakano trailed by eight after a 72.

The South Korean left the door open Sunday when she could only muster a par round. Nakano, a winner eight times in her 14 years on tour, nearly matched Ku's Saturday performance. She put a 63 on the scoreboard early and only Fudoh, with 69, could match it. The subsequent playoff went four holes before Fudoh ended it with a birdie.

Promise Ladies—¥60,000,000
Winner: Ji-Hee Lee

The competition for the Promise Ladies had a strong international flavor when action resumed after the usual month's hiatus following the Daikin Orchid event. Possession of the lead went from a Taiwanese to a Japanese to the South Korean — Ji-Hee Lee — who walked off with the title at Water Hills Golf Club at Tojo. Lee, whose only victory in Japan came near the end of her rookie 2001 season in the Daiohseishi Elleair Open, came from three strokes off the pace Sunday to nail a two-shot victory with her eight-under-par 208.

The Taiwanese leader the first day was Huang Yu-chen, who shot 68 and led Masaki Maeda, Orie Fujino and Rui Kitada by a stroke. The Japanese leader the second day was Fujino, a three-time winner on the circuit. Fujino put up her second 69 to Huang's 71 and went a stroke in front. Maeda (71) and Woo-Soon Ko (70) were at 140, and Lee, who had opened with 70, shot 71, positioned for her Sunday move. After an opening three-putt bogey, the South Korean overtook the leader in mid-round, then wrapped up the victory with a three-birdie run starting at the 14th hole for her clinching 67.

Saishunkan Ladies Hinokuni Open—¥60,000,000
Winner: Ji-Hee Lee

Ji-Hee Lee maintained her winning momentum in Kikuyo for the Saishunkan Ladies Hinokuni Open, but the victory pattern was decidedly different. The South Korean emerged from a group of four leaders in Sunday's final round with no more than a one-under-par round of 71, but it was enough to achieve back-to-back victories with the one-stroke margin her 216 total gave her.

Lee (72-73) shared the lead after Saturday's second round with veteran Kaori Higo (74-71), Kozue Azuma (71-74) and Sae Takamura (70-75) at Kumamoto Kuukou Country Club. The other three fell away Sunday as the 24-year-old plugged away with 17 pars and a single birdie for the 71 that produced her third tour victory.

Rookie Rui Kitada, who led the field on Friday with 69 and skied to a 79 Saturday, came back with another rather erratic 69 Sunday and leaped into second place with the 217. She had six birdies, two bogeys and a double bogey as she made the highest finish of her brief professional career.

Katokichi Queens—¥60,000,000
Winner: Kasumi Fujii

Kasumi Fujii got off to another fast start when she won the Katokichi Queens. It was Fujii's fifth victory and two of the other three came early in the season — the opening Daikin Orchid in 2002 and the Belluna Cup, the second event on the 2001 card. Fujii, the runner-up on the 2002 money list in her seventh season, came from four strokes off the pace in Sunday's final round at Yashima Country Club in Mure to post a one-stroke victory. She closed with a five-under-par 67 for 207.

Lightly regarded Yuka Shiroto held the lead for two days. She opened with 66, the best score of the week, as nearly half the field had to finish their rounds the next morning because of weather delays. That put her on top of the field by a stroke over Rie Mitsuhashi and by two over Kaori Harada and Mihoko Takahashi when all the results were in. Shiroto shot 70 in her second round Saturday and retained her one-shot margin, then over Mie Nakata

(70-67). Two other of the first day's eight 70-shooters were at 138 (Hsiu-Feng Tseng) and 139 (Kumiko Hiyoshi). Fujii had her second 70.

Fujii staged a dazzling finish. Although she gained ground with three birdies against a bogey well through the final round, she carded birdies on the last three holes to wrap up the title.

Nichirei Cup World Ladies—¥60,000,000
Winner: Annika Sorenstam

Annika Sorenstam couldn't have had a greater confidence-builder for her upcoming historic competitive appearance against the leading players on the American PGA Tour. Playing in her final event two weeks before her heralded visit to Fort Worth, the brilliant Swedish star annihilated the field in the Nichirei Cup World Ladies, romping to a nine-stroke victory at Tokyo's Yomiuri Country Club. It was Sorenstam's second win of the year and her career fifth in Japan.

Certainly, everyone at the Nichirei Cup figured Sorenstam was ready for the men. She never trailed at Yomiuri. Despite wind and rain, she opened the 72-hole event with a six-under-par 66, staging a four-birdie run in the middle of the round. She shared the lead with Junko Yasui, who had an eagle in her 66, and they in turn led Michiko Hattori, Sakura Yokomine and Kasumi Fujii, the previous week's winner, by three strokes.

Sorenstam edged a stroke in front of Yasui in another wind-blown round Friday, carding a 70 to Yasui's 71. Still in contention at that point were Yuko Moriguchi at 138 and Kaori Higo and Hattori at 139. On a third straight day in the wind, Sorenstam's one-under-par 71–207 turned the competition into a rout. She swept five strokes ahead of Kaori Suzuki (69), who took the runner-up position, a shot in front of Yasui (76), Fujii (72) and Mayumi Ishii (73).

Two early birdies set the tone for Sorenstam Sunday. She picked up four more and took two bogeys as she shot 68 for 275. Nine distant shots behind in second place at the finish were Suzuki (72), Yasui (71), Hattori (69), Moriguchi (70), Junko Omote (68) and Yuri Fudoh, the defending champion, who killed her chances with 74s in the first and third rounds.

Vernal Ladies—¥100,000,000
Winner: Ok-Hee Ku

It would hardly seem like a proper season on the Japan Tour if Ok-Hee Ku didn't chalk up a victory sometime during the year. The South Korean had missed very few seasons in compiling her wonderful record of 23 wins during a 21-year sojourn in Japan and the pattern was extended in 2003. The 46-year-old Ku landed the Vernal Ladies title at Fukuoka Century Golf Club, surging to a two-stroke victory with a final-round 68. The first-place check of ¥18 million, largest of the early season, jumped her into first place on the money list.

Mayumi Murai, a standout in the 1990s but winless since the 1999 Japan Women's Open, stepped out in front Friday with a four-under-par 68. She led Yuka Shiroto, Shiho Ohyama and Taiwan's Hsiu-Feng Tseng and Yun-

Jye Wei by a stroke. But it proved just a one-day return to glory for Murai, who plummeted from contention Saturday with 77, yielding the lead to Tseng (71) and Toshimi Kimura (70-70). Wei was next at 141, and Ku shared fourth place at 142 with Shiroto, Woo-Soon Ko and Rie Murata.

The best score of the final round, a 68, gave Ku the victory Sunday with a six-under-par 210. Ko shot 70 and seized second place, one stroke in front of Shiroto and Tseng.

Chukyo TV Bridgestone Ladies Open—¥50,000,000
Winner: Yuri Fudoh

It would be ridiculous to hint at a slump, but for a player of Yuri Fudoh's talent, it seemed a bit of a long time before she claimed her second victory of the 2003 season after winning the season opener in early March. Actually, only five tournaments ensued before Fudoh latched on to No. 2 in the Chukyo TV Bridgestone Ladies Open in late May.

She took command the first day and hung on despite a struggling final round Sunday. She got the margin she needed when she opened with a seven-under-par 65 that tied the Ishino course record at Chukyo Golf Club and established a two-stroke lead over Michiko Hattori, a local favorite in Toyota. Fudoh started with two birdies and tapped in a one-foot eagle putt at the sixth in her no-bogey round. Fudoh doubled her margin to four shots Saturday. Continuing to play bogey-free golf, she shot 68 for 133. Hattori took 70 but remained in second place, tied at 137 with Midori Yoneyama (68) and Ok-Hee Ku (67), coming off her Vernal Ladies victory.

In her shaky final round, Fudoh yielded a chunk of her lead when she double-bogeyed the par-five sixth hole, recovered with a pair of birdies, but bogeyed two of the last three holes for 74. The 207 total gave her a one-stroke victory over Toshimi Kimura (70) and Ku (71).

Kosaido Ladies Golf Cup—¥60,000,000
Winner: Michiko Hattori

Yuri Fudoh stood in the way as Michiko Hattori tried and failed to win the Chukyo TV Bridgestone Open in front of her home fans. Fudoh wasn't around the next week at the Kosaido Ladies Golf Cup though, and Hattori brought home the bacon, scoring a one-stroke victory despite a hot closing charge by Taiwan's Yun-Jye Wei at Chiba Kosaido Country Club in Ichihara. Hattori, a popular figure in Japan women's golf since her triumph as a 16-year-old in the prestigious 1985 United States Amateur, improved her professional record to 15 victories with her first win in two years.

Midori Yoneyama, a two-time winner in 2001, launched a bid for her fifth career victory with an opening 67. The 27-year-old, playing in her fifth season on the tour, took a one-stroke lead over Hattori, Wei and Young-Me Lee of South Korea with the bogey-free round. Fierce weather descended on Saturday and scores skyrocketed. Only seven players broke par and Hattori's 72–140 boosted her three strokes into the lead as Yoneyama took a 76 in the wind and rain, but only dropped into second place.

Wei challenged Hattori Sunday, but the 34-year-old veteran held her off with a three-birdie 69 for seven-under-par 209. Wei's 66 left her a stroke short of a tie and playoff. Ok-Hee Ku finished third, four shots behind Wei.

Resort Trust Ladies—¥50,000,000
Winner: Yuri Fudoh

Yuri Fudoh's third win of her spectacular season came much easier than the initial two. Instead of the playoff triumph and one-stroke victory that decided the earlier events, Fudoh raced away from the field in the Resort Trust Ladies, breezing to a seven-shot win just two weeks after the second triumph in the Chukyo TV Bridgestone Open. It was Fudoh's second Resort Trust victory, the first one coming in 2000.

Ji-Hee Lee, right on Fudoh's heels at the top of the money list with her two victories, got a good start toward No. 3 at Okazaki's Tradition Golf Club. She took a one-stroke lead over Kaori Harada and Mikiyo Nishizuka with an opening 70. Fudoh started with a par round, then spurted into a four-stroke lead Saturday when she fashioned a six-under-par 66, the low round of the day. Fuki Kido and Yun-Jye Wei both had 70-72 rounds to share second place.

Fudoh ensured that she would have no problems Sunday by nearly matching the Saturday round. She shot 67 for 205 and the seven-stroke runaway result. Kaori Higo also had a 67 Sunday and climbed into the runner-up spot with Lee, who closed with 69.

We Love Kobe Suntory Ladies Open—¥60,000,000
Winner: Ji-Hee Lee

Ji-Hee Lee continued her hot pursuit of Yuri Fudoh in the victory and money departments of the Japan LPGA Tour at the We Love Kobe Suntory Ladies Open. Lee matched Fudoh in the former category by snatching her third win of the season in the year's second playoff. She birdied the first extra hole to defeat Yun-Jye Wei after both finished the 72-hole tournament with 16-under-par 272s. It moved her within ¥3 million of the standings leader.

The 24-year-old from Seoul seemingly had an easy victory at hand after 54 holes. Starting the tournament with 68, she trailed leader Mayumi Nakajima by two strokes and was one back of Mikiyo Nishizuka and Australian Alison Munt. Lee tore up Japan Memorial Golf Club with a seven-under-par 65 in the second round of the event at Yoshikawa, just outside of Kobe, the Japanese city devastated by an earthquake in the mid-1990s. With 133, she led Hiroko Yamaguchi and rookie Hiromi Takesue by two strokes. Wei loomed another shot back.

Lee doubled her margin Saturday with a 69 for 202. Wei shot 70 and Yamaguchi 71 to hold second place four back at 206. The leader had a 70 Sunday and Wei took advantage of the chink in the Korean's armor. She shot 66 to overtake Lee and force the playoff. Fudoh nearly joined them. Starting the day seven strokes off the lead, Fudoh rolled up a bevy of birdies that produced a 64, but she fell a stroke short of the playoff. She had third place to herself and needed the high finish to retain the No. 1 spot on the money list ahead of Lee. Lee ended the playoff quickly when she ran in a 24-foot birdie putt on the first extra hole.

Apita Circle K Sankus Ladies—¥50,000,000
Winner: Yun-Jye Wei

After several near-misses earlier in the season, Yun-Jye Wei captured the first title in her three-season career in late June, winning the Apita Circle K Sankus Ladies by a stroke with an eight-under-par 208 total. Impressively, the 23-year-old Taiwanese player bounced back from the disappointment of a playoff loss to Ji-Hee Lee the preceding Sunday at Kobe, her second runner-up finish in three weeks.

The rebound began at once at Green Natsugawa Golf Club, Gifu Prefecture. Wei opened with 68 Friday and joined four others — Kaori Suzuki, Mie Nakata, Mayumi Murai and veteran Ikuyo Shiotani — atop the standings. The same score vaulted Wei four strokes in front Friday. She had a bogey-free round — and just one over the first 36 holes — as she settled in ahead of rookie Misato Nishikawa and Eika Otake, who both shot their second 70s of the tournament. Yuri Fudoh was just another shot back after rounds of 73 and 68.

However, it was Miho Koga, 32nd on the money list entering the Apita Circle K, who gave the Taiwanese leader the biggest scare Sunday. Wei managed just a par round and Koga charged to within a stroke with 67 to grab the runner-up slot, one stroke ahead of Fudoh, who had a 69 for 210. Wei was the initial first-time winner of the season.

Belluna Ladies Cup—¥60,000,000
Winner: Shiho Ohyama

When play resumed with the Belluna Ladies Cup after an open week on the schedule, Shiho Ohyama duplicated the ice-breaking feat of Yun-Jye Wei, although she required a final-round rally and a playoff to do it at Obatago Golf Club. By coincidence, both Ohyama and Wei began their careers in 2001 at the age of 21.

The Belluna Ladies Cup's first-round leader was Taiwan's Hsiu-Feng Tseng, who had eight birdies, including a five-in-a-row stretch on her back nine, and shot 66. She was one stroke ahead of Hiroko Yamaguchi. Far back at 73 was Ohyama. She made up three of those seven strokes Saturday, when rookie Hiromi Takesue produced a 66–136 and edged a shot ahead of Yamaguchi (70) and Shin Sora of South Korea (70-67), who had a chip-in eagle and two bogeys in her round. Ohyama also shot 67 for 140.

Ohyama birdied her last two holes and repeated her 67 Sunday, then watched as Sora and Yamaguchi were finishing with 70s for their nine-under-par 207 totals that brought about the playoff. The overtime work ended at the second extra hole, where Ohyama made the only par on the par-four 18th with a six-foot putt.

Toyo Suisan Ladies Hokkaido—¥50,000,000
Winner: Kaori Suzuki

It was going to be three in a row, no matter who won the playoff that climaxed the Toyo Suisan Ladies Hokkaido tournament in mid-July. Neither Kaori Suzuki nor Junko Omote had won on the Japan LPGA Tour. So when Suzuki bumped off Omote on the first extra hole at Sapporo Kitahiroshima Prince Golf Course, she became the third consecutive first-time winner.

The outcome was particularly disappointing to Omote, who held the lead the first two days and entered the final round four strokes up on the field. Omote set a course record Friday when she birdied five of her last seven holes, took no bogeys and shot 65. That gave her a four-stroke advantage over Toshimi Kimura and Megumi Higuchi. Suzuki was at 71.

Omote preserved her four-stroke lead with a two-under-par 70 Saturday, but the runner-up then at 139 was Fumiko Muraguchi, who shot 68. Suzuki advanced to third place with 69–140. Omote let her lead slip away when she floundered to a 75 Sunday, enabling Suzuki to catch her with 70 for her 210 and then win the playoff.

Stanley Ladies—¥60,000,000
Winner: Yuri Fudoh

Yuri Fudoh extended her mastery over her peers and her grip on the money list lead with her fourth victory of the season, taking the Stanley Ladies by three strokes. It came five weeks after her last previous win and she had two third-place finishes in the three events in which she played in the interim.

Yuka Shiroto, who is winless in her 11 seasons on the circuit, made her second bid of the season in the Stanley. Shiroto, who led for two days before dropping back in the Katokichi Queens in April, birdied the last two holes of her opening round at Tomei Country Club for a seven-under-par 65. That gave her a two-stroke lead over newcomer Hiromi Takesue and 17-year-veteran Rie Fujiwara. Shiroto's game crashed Saturday as she shot 75 and fell four strokes off the pace. Fumiko Muraguchi, who took a run at a victory the previous week in the Toyo Suisan, seized the top spot Saturday. She paired 68s and seized a three-stroke lead as she sought her first win since her three-victory season in 1999 when she was the leading money winner. Woo-Soon Ko (69-70) and Takesue (67-72) were at 139, and Fudoh was with Shiroto and Michiko Mitsui (69-71).

It was all Fudoh Sunday. She banged out three early birdies to take charge of the competition as Muraguchi faded toward 75. Fudoh went on to a 68 to wrap up the three-shot triumph with 208. Mitsui (71), Ko (72) and Mihoko Takahashi (69) tied for second with Muraguchi at 211.

Golf 5 Ladies—¥50,000,000
Winner: Mihoko Takahashi

Mihoko Takahashi gave a hint of things to come when she fired 69 and jumped into a second-place tie in the Sunday finale of the Stanley tournament that preceded the Golf 5 Ladies event at Mizunami Country Club. She came out blazing in the Golf 5 and led all the way to her third career victory on the Japan LPGA Tour. She won twice in 2002.

Takahashi blistered the course with eight birdies on the first 11 holes in the opening round, finishing with a 67 and a one-stroke lead over Mie Nakata, two over Ji-Hee Lee, the only other players who broke 70 that day. The 24-year-old maintained her one-stroke lead Saturday with a one-under-par 71. Nakata blew to a 78, and Chihiro Nakajima moved into second place with 69–139 and Kozue Azuma was alone at 140 after a 68.

Takahashi polished off her victory in fine style with a 66 Sunday for a 12-under-par 204. Nakajima shot 67 for 206 to hold the runner-up slot, two in front of Yuriko Ohtsuka (67) and the ever-present Yuri Fudoh, who closed with 65 to jump into the third-place tie.

NEC Karuizawa 72—¥60,000,000
Winner: Akiko Fukushima

No wonder Akiko Fukushima returns to Japan from her forays on the U.S. LPGA Tour in mid-August. She wouldn't want to miss the NEC Karuizawa 72, which she won in 1996 and 2002. Fukushima did it again in 2003, emerging from a four-player cluster of week-long contenders in Sunday's final round to post a four-stroke victory. It was Fukushima's 16th victory on the Japan LPGA Tour since her initial win as a 20-year-old in 1994, a record that would no doubt be more gaudy had she not decided to play full-time in America in 1999 and done so ever since.

The NEC Karuizawa 72 had an unusual leaderboard throughout the competition. Five players — Fukushima, Ikuyo Shiotani, Kaori Suzuki, Yuri Fudoh and Rie Fujiwara — all shot 69 in Friday's first round, and four of them finished 1-2-3-4 Sunday afternoon. Fujiwara fell away with 76 in the second round, when Fudoh and Shiotani shot 71s and led with 140s, a stroke in front of Fukushima (72) and two ahead of Suzuki (73).

Fukushima put away her third NEC title handily when she came up with the best round of the week, a 67, to finish with an eight-under-par 208, four ahead of Shiotani (72) and five in front of Suzuki (71) and Fudoh (73).

New Caterpillar Mitsubishi Ladies—¥60,000,000
Winner: Yuri Fudoh

Yuri Fudoh's remarkable 2003 run continued at the New Caterpillar Mitsubishi Ladies tournament as she registered her fifth victory of the season. So dominant was the 26-year-old star that, in the two tournaments between the fourth and fifth wins, she tied for third place twice and, with the New Caterpillar victory, built her earnings close to ¥75 million.

Miho Koga, another young player making her mark, shot a course-record, seven-under-par 66 to take the lead in the first round at Daihakone Country Club, but Fudoh was right behind her at 67 on the par-73 course. The 21-year-old Koga, already in her third year on the tour, had never led before. And she didn't after 36 holes. Fudoh took over Saturday, shooting a bogey-free 68 for 135 and a comfortable five-stroke lead over Koga (74) and Junko Omote (68-72).

Fudoh had some discomfort Sunday, though, before racking up the title. The Kumamoto native had to overcome an early double bogey and wound up shooting a par 73 for 208. Omote took second place three back at 71-211, and Koga, with 73, tied for third at 213 with Toshimi Kimura.

Yonex Ladies—¥60,000,000
Winner: Miho Koga

The Japan LPGA Tour got its newest and youngest winner at the Yonex Ladies at the end of August. Miho Koga, the 21-year-old who had made her presence felt on several occasions earlier in the season as she rose to 18th on the money list, landed her first title in her third season on the circuit.

The week before, Koga led after the first round and finished third. At the Yonex Ladies, Koga made her move later. The first day, she shot 69, two behind tri-leaders Hsiu-Feng Tseng, Hiromi Takesue and Yoko Tsuchiya. She and 18-year-old amateur Ai Miyazato trailed Kaori Higo and Mayumi Hagaki by a shot.

Koga followed with 66 Saturday and took a one-stroke lead over Takesue (69) and two over Miyazato. Enter Yuri Fudoh, carrying a 140 score into the final round. The leading money winner put the pressure on with a 69, but Koga kept her, Higo (70) and Miyazato (72) at bay with her closing par 72 for 207 and a two-stroke victory margin over those three players. She became the fourth first-time winner of the 2003 season.

Fujisankei Ladies Classic—¥60,000,000
Winner: Ikuyo Shiotani

It was a veteran's turn to shine the following week in the Fujisankei Ladies Classic at Fujizakura Country Club. Ikuyo Shiotani, with 19 victories in her two decades on the circuit, was on top of her game as she led outright from wire to wire and won No. 20 going away. The 41-year-old has scored victories in each of the past three seasons.

Shiotani began her title run with a five-under-par 66, and Fuki Kido, a six-time winner playing in her 19th season, occupied the runner-up position at the end of the first round with 68. A host of 69 shooters were next and two of them supplanted Kido in second place after 36 holes. Woo-Soon Ko and Toshimi Kimura carded 68s for 137, but were three strokes behind Shiotani, who added 68 to her opening score for 134.

Shiotani repeated the 68 Sunday for her final 202 and a five-stroke victory as only two other players broke 70 that day. One was Kido, who returned to the runner-up slot with 69–207. Ko and Kimura, with 73s, finished tied for third at 210.

Japan LPGA Championship —¥70,000,000
Winner: Yuri Fudoh

As impressive as Yuri Fudoh's brilliant five-season record was, one important ingredient was missing. The talented 26-year-old did not have a major
title among the 20 victories she had compiled since 1999. Fudoh rectified
that situation nicely in mid-September by scoring a decisive triumph in the
Japan LPGA Championship and acquiring its Konika Minolta Cup. She put
together four solid rounds for an 11-under-par 277 and a four-stroke victory
over Michie Ohba and Miho Koga, the Yonex winner two weeks earlier. It
was her sixth win in 2003.

Ohba was the first-round leader. With 66, she led Fudoh, Kyoko Ono and
Hiromi Mogi by a stroke. Fudoh went ahead to stay on Friday. She shot 68
for 135 to move three strokes in the lead over Ohba (72) and Ji-Yeon Han
(67). Fudoh gave up a stroke of her lead Saturday when she shot a par round
for 207, and Woo-Soon Ko took over second place with 70–209. Koga (70-
69-71) and Yasuko Satoh (72-69-69) were at 210. Fudoh served up a solid,
unspectacular 70 Sunday for her 277 and she went unthreatened. Ohba (68)
and Koga (71) finished tied for second at 281.

Munsingwear Ladies Tokai Classic—¥60,000,000
Winner: Yuri Fudoh

By late September, Yuri Fudoh seemed to be becoming unstoppable. Fudoh
put the Munsingwear Ladies Tokai Classic back to back with her Japan
LPGA Championship, making it three victories in four consecutive starts.
The win, her seventh of the season, wasn't quite as sturdy as were the
previous two, a final-round 69 giving her a 10-under-par 206 and a one-
stroke victory over Kaori Harada.

Fudoh couldn't break free of the other contenders until the very end as she
won the Munsingwear Tokai for a second time. She opened the tournament
at Ryosan Golf Club with a five-under-par 67, but had to share first place
with Norimi Tarasawa, who was playing in her first tournament of the season. Five players — Hiroko Yamaguchi, Hsiu-Feng Tseng, Seiko Watanabe,
Woo-Soon Ko and Rie Murata — trailed by a stroke. Tarasawa fell from
contention with 74-76 but got her first check at week's end.

Harada and Yamaguchi joined Fudoh at the top Saturday. Fudoh shot 70
for her 137, Harada 70-67 for hers, and Yamaguchi 69-68 for hers. Junko
Omote, runner-up to Fudoh in the New Caterpillar Mitsubishi, and Hisao-
Chuan Lu had their second 69s for 138s. Fudoh's Sunday 69 was just enough
to edge Harada, who shot 70. Yamaguchi had 71 and tied Junko Yasui (69)
for third at 208.

Miyagi TV Cup Dunlop Ladies Open—¥60,000,000
Winner: Ai Miyazato

Youth was served — in spades — at the Miyagi TV Cup Dunlop Ladies
Open. For the first time in 30 years, an amateur won on the Japan LPGA

Tour and, in this case, the amateur was Ai Miyazato, 18 years old and a high school senior. The only previous amateur winner was Chikako Kiyomoto, now an LPGA executive. Miyazato's one-stroke victory was not a huge surprise, though. A girl whose has two older brothers — Kiyoshi and Yusaku — on the men's tour, she was the Japan Women's Amateur Champion and Asian Games individual gold medalist at the time.

Miyazato, who admitted that "my hands were trembling and I was shaking in my shoes," sank a clutch birdie putt on the 18th green Sunday to put the victory out of reach of Mari Katayama and Hiroko Yamaguchi, who had led for two days. The birdie gave Miyazato a one-under-par 71 and a five-under-par total of 211. Yamaguchi shot 73 and Katayama 70 Sunday to tie for second at 212.

Yamaguchi, who was a co-leader going into the final round the previous week in the Munsingwear Tokai Classic but finished third, rebounded at Rifu Golf Club with a potent 66 in the first round, staking herself to a three-stroke lead over Hisako Takada. Miyazato shot 70 and shared third place with Woo-Soon Ko and Mikiyo Nishizuka. Yamaguchi, in her fourth season on tour, lost ground Saturday. She took a 73 for 139 and led then by just a stroke over Miyazato and Nishizuka, who had 70s again, and Junko Yoshida (71-69).

The victory started Miyazato thinking about turning professional, according to her father and golf mentor, Masaru Miyazato.

Japan Women's Open—¥70,000,000
Winner: Michiko Hattori

Michiko Hattori's spangled career record gained another sparkling bauble the first week of October when she won her second Japan Women's Open nine years after the first one. The 34-year-old Hattori, who now has 16 wins scattered over 12 seasons in Japan, also counts another major — the 1998 LPGA Championship — among her top achievements since winning the U.S. Women's Amateur as a 16-year-old in 1985.

While Hattori was sitting on top of the world after her playoff victory over Ji-Hee Lee of Taiwan, Yuri Fudoh was down in the dumps. She encountered a huge hiccup at the Open in what had been a dream season to that point. Seeking to land her first Japan Open title to go with the LPGA Championship she had won earlier in the year, Fudoh began the week on Chiba Country Club's Noda course with a two-under-par 70, placed comfortably with Shiho Ohyama and Hiromi Kobayashi a stroke behind leader Hattori. But the roof caved in on her Friday. Fudoh took a double bogey and six bogeys, shot 79 and was out of the picture, eventually tying for 30th place.

Ohyama slipped a stroke into the lead that day with 71 for 141 as Hattori carded a 73 and joined Ayako Uehara (71-71) at 142. Woo-Soon Ko was at 143, and five others, including Ji-Hee Lee, were at 144. Ohyama suffered the same fate as Fudoh Saturday, only worse. She took an 82 and Hattori took over first place with 71–213, one stroke ahead of Uehara (72) and two in front of Lee and Hiroko Yamaguchi, who had 71s.

Par was hard to come by Sunday. Hattori struggled to a two-over-par 74 and Lee forced a playoff with her 72. They finished a stroke ahead of Uehara

(74) and Nikki Campbell (72), who had the tournament's best score of 67 Saturday. The playoff wasn't exactly a classic, either. The coveted title went to the 35-year-old Hattori, even though she bogeyed the second extra hole. Lee's hopes disappeared with a double bogey.

Sankyo Ladies Open—¥60,000,000
Winner: Ji-Hee Lee

Credit Ji-Hee Lee with a sizeable portion of intestinal fortitude to go with her fine golf game. Surely bitterly downcast after suffering a playoff-ending double bogey with the Japan Ladies Open title on the line just a few days past, the 24-year-old Taiwanese newcomer marched to her fourth victory of the season in the Sankyo Ladies Open at Niisato.

It took a round of action for Lee to shake off the disappointment, though. She opened the Sankyo at Akagi Country Club with a par 72 and found herself seven strokes behind Toshimi Kimura, the defending champion, who banged out eight birdies en route to a 65 and a two-stroke lead over Kasumi Fujii, who had six birdies on her card.

Lee made up a lot of ground Saturday. She fired a 67 for 139 and was three strokes off the pace after Kimura posted a 71–136. Only Mari Nishi (70-68) sat between the two and she proved no factor Sunday. Lee conjured up a sizzling 65, the day's best score, to soar in front. Her 12-under-par 204 gave her a three-stroke victory over Mie Nakata, who closed with 67–207. Kimura took a 72 and finished third. Yuri Fudoh showed that her failure in the Women's Open was just a bump in an otherwise smooth road when she shot 67 Sunday and tied for fourth place.

Fujitsu Ladies—¥60,000,000
Winner: Yuri Fudoh

Rolling again, Yuri Fudoh scored one of the easiest of her array of 2003 victories when she won the Fujitsu Ladies for a second time and put her eighth triumph of the year into the books. Fudoh led outright from start to finish at the Tokyu Seven Hundred Club in Chiba in mid-October, ultimately winning by two strokes with her 12-under-par 204.

Fudoh's first-round 67 put her a stroke in the lead, ahead of Mineko Nasu by one stroke and four others by two. Then she gave herself a big cushion Saturday when she added a 68 for 135. Five strokes separated her from runner-up Ok-Hee Ku, who had rounds of 71 and 69 for her 140. Another stroke back were Masaki Maeda (70-71), Mihoko Takahashi (69-72) and Fumiko Muraguchi (71-70).

Only Ok-Hee Ku mounted any sort of threat to Fudoh Sunday. She shot a sterling 66, but Fudoh kept her at bay with a 69 to establish the winning two-shot margin. Fudoh won the Fujitsu the first time in 2001, her fourth and last victory that season.

Masters Golf Club Ladies—¥50,000,000
Winner: Hiromi Takesue

The complement of first-time winners on the 2003 Japan LPGA Tour rose to six at the inaugural Masters Golf Club Ladies tournament. Hiromi Takesue was the new inductee and, unlike the other professionals, was playing in her first season on the circuit. She had made noises several times earlier in the campaign, presaging the victory at the Masters Golf Club at Miki in Hyogo Prefecture.

International star Karrie Webb flew in for the tournament and made her presence felt early. She shot an opening-round 69, one stroke off the lead of Ai-Yu Tu, the 48-year-old Taiwan veteran with 58 victories to her credit. Takesue started with 70 and jumped ahead of the rest Saturday when she followed with 66 for 136. Miho Koga, the Yonex winner, moved into second place with 71-66–137. Ai-Yu Tu and Webb had 70s and stood at 138 and 139, respectively, going into the final round.

A two-under-par 70 brought Takesue her maiden victory in comfortable fashion. With her 206 total, she finished four strokes in front of Webb, who shot 71, and Michie Ohba, who came from well back with a 67 for her 210. Koga slumped to 74 and Tu to 76 Sunday.

Mizuno Classic—¥135,600,000
Winner: Annika Sorenstam

It proved to be a momentous occasion when Annika Sorenstam returned to Japan for the second time in 2003, this time to play in the Mizuno Classic, an event on the schedules of both the U.S. and Japan LPGA Tours. Just as she did in June when she ran away with the Nichirei Cup tournament in Tokyo, Sorenstam raced wire to wire to win the Mizuno Classic by the same nine-stroke margin and clinched the U.S. LPGA's points-based Player of the Year Award.

It was her third consecutive Mizuno triumph, which, coupled with her three straight wins in the Michelob Light Classic, made her the first LPGA player ever to win more than one tournament three years in a row. Furthermore, it was her sixth victory of the year and her sixth in Japan overall.

The rout started the first day when the 33-year-old Swede hammered out a nine-under-par 63 on the North course of Seta Golf Club, taking a two-stroke lead over Grace Park and Jung-Yeon Lee, both regulars on the American circuit. When Sorenstam repeated the feat Saturday, she widened the gap to six strokes with her 126. Lee (67) and Se Ri Pak (67-65) were at 132. Park (68) was another stroke back with Rachel Teske (65) and Yuri Fudoh (66), the top player on the Japan LPGA circuit.

Sorenstam concluded her record-breaking performance with a 66 Sunday, her 192 breaking the old mark by two strokes and establishing the nine-shot final margin. Park, Pak and Sophie Gustafson tied for second at 201, and Fudoh led the Japanese circuit players with 69–202.

Sorenstam took special pride in pointing out that it was the first time she had ever played 54 holes without a three-putt or a bogey. Remarkable golf.

Itoen Ladies—¥60,000,000
Winner: Yuri Fudoh

Not surprisingly, Yuri Fudoh successfully defended her championship in the Itoen Ladies in mid-November. She had won her first title on the Japan LPGA Tour in the Itoen event in 1999, so the 2003 victory at the Great Island Club was her third in that late-season tournament, the only one she had tripled among her first 24 victories.

Kasumi Fujii, who won the early season Katokichi Queens tournament, was on track for another win for the first two days of the Itoen. She opened in a four-way tie for the lead at 69 with Hiroko Yamaguchi, Masaki Maeda and Ji-Yeon Han of South Korea, then seized the lead for herself with 68 for 137. Fudoh was right on her trail, though, two behind at 139 after rounds of 70 and 69. She was tied there with Mizue Igarashi (71-68) and Han (69-70).

On a miserable Sunday when the best score shot was 71, Fudoh notched her ninth victory of the season via a playoff. The best she could do was a two-over-par 74 for 213 and she was overtaken by Junko Omote, who carded scores of 67-71 after starting the tournament with a 75. The playoff went three extra holes before Fudoh won with a birdie.

Daiohseishi Elleair Ladies Open—¥80,000,000
Winner: Miho Koga

Miho Koga, who won her first tournament on the Japan LPGA Tour at the end of August, became the fourth multiple winner of the season when she added the Daiohseishi Elleair Ladies Open to her record in the season's penultimate event. The 21-year-old did it the hard way, coming from six strokes off the pace in the final round and winning a playoff.

Hsiu-Feng Tseng of Taiwan, a frequent contender but a non-winner during 2003, launched another bid at Elleair Golf Club at Matsuyama and led for two days. She opened with 67 and led by two over Kaori Higo, Mitsuko Kawasaki and Hiromi Kobayashi, the defending champion. Tseng's margin was just one after 36 holes. She shot 71 for 138. Riko Higashio, who had started weakly with 74, shot 65 Saturday and jumped into second place, a stroke ahead of Hiromi Takesue, the Masters Golf Club winner three weeks earlier.

Koga seemed out of contention with her 73-71 scores the first two days. But her final-round 65 and Tseng's 76 enabled Koga to finish in a first-place tie with Higashio at 209, seven under par. In the ensuing playoff, Koga birdied the first extra hole to secure her second 2003 triumph.

Japan LPGA Tour Championship—¥60,000,000
Winner: Yuri Fudoh

The Japan LPGA Tour season ended just as it started nine months earlier — with Yuri Fudoh accepting winner's accolades. Fudoh finished what was by far her finest season and one of the tour's most dynamic seasons ever with her 10th victory in the climactic, limited-field Japan LPGA Tour Championship. She did it impressively, recovering from a seven-shot deficit after the first round to close it out Sunday five strokes ahead of the 22-player field at Miyazaki Country Club.

The lead changed hands three times during the tournament. Akiko Fukushima, the NEC Karuizawa winner in August after returning from America, held it first with an opening 68. She was two shots in front of Ji-Hee Lee, a four-time winner in 2003, and three ahead of Miho Koga, who won twice during the season. When Fukushima floundered Friday and took 76, Kasumi Fujii took over first place with 73-69–142. Lee was one back with Fudoh, who had rebounded from her opening 75 with a 68. Fukushima was two behind, sitting at 144.

Fudoh then followed with 66 for 209 to go two strokes in front of Fujii (69), four ahead of Lee (70) and seven on top of Fukushima (72). A modest 70 Sunday moved Fudoh to seven-under-par 279 and her final margin over runner-up Fukushima, who shot 68, the day's only round in the 60s.

First prize money of ¥15 million raised Fudoh's money winning total for the year to ¥149,325,679. That gave her the tour's No. 1 position for the fourth year in a row and her 2003 winnings were nearly double the total accumulated by No. 2 Ji-Hee Lee. Fudoh accomplished this in 24 tournaments, in which, in addition to her 10 victories, she had two seconds, four thirds, a fourth and two fifths. That's 19 of the 24 starts. She never missed a cut and ran her victory total to 25 in eight seasons. What's the definition of domination?

Australian Women's Tour

Contrabart ALPG Players Championship—A$100,000
Winner: Tamara Hyett

Tamara Hyett, a 25-year-old from Melbourne, won her first career title at the Contrabart ALPG Players Championship, but only after withstanding a remarkable charge from Laura Davies. Hyett was three ahead going into the final round at Horizons Golf Resort, but returned a 76, while Davies, who started nine behind, set a new course record with a 67 that included two eagles and four birdies. Hyett birdied the 16th and the 18th to tie Davies at 281, 11 under par, and then birdied the 18th again on the first extra hole to win the playoff.

Another Englishwoman, Georgina Simpson, led by three strokes after 10 holes, but faded to finish in third place, one stroke out of the playoff. A hole-in-one with a seven iron from 150 yards at the sixth hole helped Trish Johnson to share fourth place with Maria Hjorth.

"I battled hard all day long," said Hyett. "I had a slump in the middle but fought back with those two birdies at the end. It was great playing with Laura, she was encouraging all day long. It was a dream for me to be playing alongside her, and to win as well, it doesn't get any better than that."

ANZ Ladies Masters—A$800,000
Winner: Laura Davies

Laura Davies continued the fine form she had shown the previous week to win the ANZ Ladies Masters by overtaking local favorite Karrie Webb with a final-round 68 and 203 total at the Royal Pines Golf Club in Surfers Paradise. In the first European Tour co-sanctioned event of the season, the 39-year-old Davies also made sure her streak of winning every year since 1985 continued.

With Webb, a four-time former champion at the event, bogeying the final hole, fellow Australian Rebecca Stevenson joined Davies at 12 under par by holing a 70-foot putt across the final green for 68 and a 204 total. Davies then needed to hole a right-to-left putt from 12 feet to prevent another playoff.

"I'm feeling confident with my game again and to beat Karrie in Australia is great," Davies said. "Over the last couple of seasons, I've been struggling. I just couldn't hit the driver, and my caddies, Paul and Terry, have been tortured into watching me hit three irons off the tee when I should be hitting driver.

"I got the win out of the way early this year," she added. "Last year, I left it until late in the season and this could be the springboard for a good year."

Lorena Ochoa, a 21-year-old Mexican, finished in fourth place two strokes behind Davies. The tournament was shortened to 54 holes by rain on the third day.

AAMI Women's Australian Open—A$500,000
Winner: Mhairi McKay

Mhairi McKay's parents, at home in Scotland, got an early Sunday morning wake-up call, but it was worth it to hear about their 27-year-old daughter's first professional victory in the AAMI Women's Australian Open. A runner-up four times in six years as a professional, McKay's closing round of 67 left her with an 11-under-par total of 277 and one ahead of the previous week's winner, Laura Davies, who was not out of the top two in her three weeks in Australia.

After Davies birdied the first two holes, McKay found herself six behind but birdied the eighth and ninth. As Davies began to drop shots, the Scot claimed four birdies in a row from the 13th to the 16th, where she got up and down from 50 yards short of the green. Davies also birdied the 16th to get within one, but could not close the gap at the last two holes. Rachel Teske took third place, another stroke back, with Marnie McGuire and Samantha Head sharing fourth.

"I can't believe it, it's all I ever wanted to do," McKay said. "It's such a great feeling, I'm absolutely ecstatic. I had no idea how things stood until after I holed my putt on the 18th and saw I was one ahead. I had to wait for Laura to finish, but as soon as I knew I had won, I phoned home. My parents brought me up and encouraged me all the way and I owe them everything."

Nedbank Women's Tour of South Africa

Acer South African Women's Open—R200,000
Winner: Helena Svensson

Just five months after turning professional, Swedish rookie Helena Svensson won her first title at the Acer South African Women's Open. Svensson started playing the game at the age of nine, but worked as a staff nurse before turning to golf full time. A week after her 24th birthday, she closed with 71 at Royal Johannesburg and Kensington Golf Clubs to finish with a 54-hole total of five-under-par 211. Svensson won R30,000 and finished one stroke ahead of South African Caryn Louw after a final round of 69, with Elisabeth Esterl, Marlene Hedblom and Anna Becker sharing third place two strokes further back.

Pam Golding Ladies International—R200,000
Winner: Laurette Maritz

South Africa's Laurette Maritz won her first tournament in five years with a three-stroke victory in the Pam Golding Ladies International at Parkview in Johannesburg. The 39-year-old, who recorded the seventh victory of her career, hit a wedge to three feet at the 16th and holed a 40-footer at the 17th for two crucial birdies after Elisabeth Esterl, twice, and Mandy Adamson both got within a shot of the lead on the back nine. Maritz won R30,000 after a closing 69 gave her a seven-under total of 209. Esterl finished second after a 71, with Adamson and Denmark's Carina Vagner sharing third place four strokes behind.

Telkom Women's Classic—R200,000
Winner: Cherry Moulder

Cherry Moulder earned her first victory on her home tour the hard way in the Telkom Women's Classic. Leading by two strokes entering the last round, Moulder went to the turn in 40 and had to birdie three of the last four holes to get into a playoff. Moulder, after a 73, tied with Denmark's Rikke Rassmussen at 212, four under par, and then holed a 12-foot par putt at the first extra hole before Rasmussen missed from 10 feet. Scandinavians were well to the fore with another Dane, Amanda Moltke-Leth, third, and Swede Johanna Westerberg fourth and Cecilia Ekelundh and Jessica Krantz sharing fifth place.

Nedbank Women's South African Masters—R200,000
Winner: Laurette Maritz

Laurette Maritz claimed her second victory in three weeks at the Nedbank Women's South African Masters at Houghton. The R30,000 first prize also left Maritz at the top of the Order of Merit with R72,450. A final-round 68, in which she did not drop a shot, for a 10-under-par total of 206, gave her a four-stroke victory over Mandy Adamson. Sarah Heath of England was third a further two strokes behind, while tied for sixth place at one under par was 13-year-old amateur Ashleigh Simon.

"This is a sweet day," said Maritz, a professional for 15 years. "It's like a dream come true — to win twice at home and win the Order of Merit. It had been a while since I'd won, and then to win twice is wonderful. As long as I kept fit and keep playing good golf, I feel I can carry on for a long time."

APPENDIXES

Official World Golf Ranking
(As of December 31, 2003)

Ranking		Player	Country	Points Average	Total Points	No. of Events	01/02 Points Lost	2003 Points Gained
1	(1)	Tiger Woods	USA	14.58	583.08	40	-578.52	+501.37
2	(8)	Vijay Singh	Fiji	9.77	556.70	57	-320.56	+550.87
3	(3)	Ernie Els	SAf	8.41	445.85	53	-400.76	+477.13
4	(9)	Davis Love	USA	7.53	368.76	49	-265.34	+412.39
5	(11)	Jim Furyk	USA	6.81	353.99	52	-243.62	+392.70
6	(46)	Mike Weir	Can	6.54	300.63	46	-208.78	+390.81
7	(5)	Retief Goosen	SAf	5.92	349.44	59	-323.91	+303.62
8	(7)	Padraig Harrington	Ire	5.28	258.95	49	-235.06	+217.92
9	(6)	David Toms	USA	5.09	269.62	53	-308.60	+247.10
10	(28)	Kenny Perry	USA	5.08	269.08	53	-194.22	+301.42
11	(23)	Darren Clarke	NIr	4.26	238.65	56	-186.13	+245.69
12	(13)	Nick Price	Zim	4.06	162.32	40	-166.54	+158.91
13	(165)	Chad Campbell	USA	3.84	238.27	62	-85.80	+269.37
14	(32)	Stuart Appleby	Aus	3.84	230.55	60	-139.41	+200.37
15	(2)	Phil Mickelson	USA	3.83	195.24	51	-314.52	+131.59
16	(25)	Robert Allenby	Aus	3.67	213.02	58	-180.73	+190.35
17	(83)	Fredrik Jacobson	Swe	3.60	165.54	46	-76.20	+157.30
18	(20)	Charles Howell	USA	3.39	220.33	65	-175.67	+184.95
19	(35)	Thomas Bjorn	Den	3.31	165.60	50	-122.61	+147.80
20	(17)	Justin Leonard	USA	3.28	164.21	50	-185.56	+149.80
21	(41)	K.J. Choi	Kor	3.28	210.09	64	-132.47	+193.32
22	(48)	Brad Faxon	USA	3.24	171.64	53	-137.23	+182.05
23	(104)	Paul Casey	Eng	3.08	160.36	52	-89.77	+179.74
24	(33)	Scott Verplank	USA	3.07	159.82	52	-148.89	+166.55
25	(40)	Adam Scott	Aus	3.04	179.46	59	-138.16	+162.70
26	(12)	Chris DiMarco	USA	3.04	169.99	56	-224.83	+152.37
27	(44)	Chris Riley	USA	2.94	167.33	57	-126.84	+146.09
28	(43)	Peter Lonard	Aus	2.91	191.81	66	-138.50	+169.19
29	(126)	Jay Haas	USA	2.88	141.29	49	-91.56	+178.48
30	(88)	Bob Tway	USA	2.87	154.98	54	-99.10	+162.91
31	(60)	Stephen Leaney	Aus	2.86	140.10	49	-98.76	+135.82
32	(137)	Jonathan Kaye	USA	2.85	156.82	55	-82.84	+173.20
33	(27)	Jerry Kelly	USA	2.84	167.77	59	-170.63	+143.49
34	(1268T)	Ben Curtis	USA	2.74	109.49	40	-15.98	+125.47
35	(26)	Rocco Mediate	USA	2.72	127.60	47	-135.17	+117.54
36	(4)	Sergio Garcia	Spn	2.71	143.64	53	-253.93	+75.60
37	(145)	Fred Couples	USA	2.71	108.25	40	-61.59	+128.87
38	(34)	Fred Funk	USA	2.67	173.47	65	-155.13	+151.48
39	(29)	Shigeki Maruyama	Jpn	2.57	133.52	52	-127.90	+100.70
40	(24)	Bob Estes	USA	2.50	127.48	51	-168.33	+121.73
41	(10)	Colin Montgomerie	Sco	2.46	135.07	55	-170.69	+77.52
42	(76)	Ian Poulter	Eng	2.42	135.72	56	-87.52	+123.86
43	(55)	Alex Cejka	Ger	2.42	135.44	56	-85.75	+118.09
44	(18)	Michael Campbell	NZl	2.41	120.73	50	-138.30	+78.18
45	(19)	Eduardo Romero	Arg	2.39	105.02	44	-94.93	+61.31
46	(245)	Shaun Micheel	USA	2.36	139.25	59	-51.06	+150.91
47	(21)	Rich Beem	USA	2.36	141.43	60	-144.58	+70.30
48	(127)	Phillip Price	Wal	2.31	113.02	49	-64.65	+118.66
49	(49)	Toshimitsu Izawa	Jpn	2.29	105.56	46	-100.16	+98.40
50	(123)	Tim Herron	USA	2.25	132.97	59	-78.17	+138.71

( ) Ranking in brackets indicates position as of December 31, 2002.

Ranking		Player	Country	Points Average	Total Points	No. of Events	01/02 Points Lost	2003 Points Gained
51	(53)	Loren Roberts	USA	2.24	109.68	49	-90.87	+92.28
52	(37)	Justin Rose	Eng	2.22	130.99	59	-129.37	+103.72
53	(71)	Stewart Cink	USA	2.19	124.66	57	-108.38	+130.24
54	(89)	Steve Flesch	USA	2.16	140.64	65	-104.91	+143.43
55	(101)	Trevor Immelman	SAf	2.14	137.01	64	-102.89	+142.56
56	(85)	Kirk Triplett	USA	2.13	106.39	50	-96.09	+119.41
57	(68)	John Huston	USA	2.10	103.09	49	-82.62	+101.06
58	(39)	Niclas Fasth	Swe	2.10	109.16	52	-116.99	+103.52
59	(47)	Shingo Katayama	Jpn	2.09	117.00	56	-103.03	+90.38
60	(147)	Brian Davis	Eng	2.08	118.31	57	-59.44	+123.13
61	(45)	Jeff Sluman	USA	2.07	132.58	64	-135.57	+110.31
62	(22)	Scott Hoch	USA	2.06	82.28	40	-150.21	+75.89
63	(77)	John Rollins	USA	2.05	127.39	62	-88.79	+112.34
64	(30)	Scott McCarron	USA	2.04	111.95	55	-126.41	+89.41
65	(182)	Lee Westwood	Eng	2.00	116.00	58	-46.46	+119.69
66	(14)	Angel Cabrera	Arg	1.99	91.62	46	-129.04	+54.13
67	(56)	Tim Clark	SAf	1.99	119.40	60	-79.85	+116.86
68	(158)	Briny Baird	USA	1.97	129.98	66	-73.32	+142.15
69	(73)	Jonathan Byrd	USA	1.96	119.46	61	-74.33	+97.52
70	(51)	Len Mattiace	USA	1.93	105.96	55	-123.44	+98.55
71	(31)	Craig Parry	Aus	1.86	98.75	53	-110.73	+50.40
72	(136)	Mathias Gronberg	Swe	1.82	78.04	43	-55.18	+86.82
73	(63)	Nick Faldo	Eng	1.77	70.92	40	-72.60	+63.10
74	(42)	Paul Lawrie	Sco	1.77	86.86	49	-108.03	+61.44
75	(90)	Rory Sabbatini	SAf	1.77	92.01	52	-85.87	+99.89
76	(131)	Geoff Ogilvy	Aus	1.76	105.90	60	-66.51	+100.33
77	(177)	J.L. Lewis	USA	1.76	109.30	62	-63.23	+119.08
78	(100)	Dan Forsman	USA	1.75	90.84	52	-63.85	+80.95
79	(36)	Steve Lowery	USA	1.75	99.54	57	-113.53	+64.08
80	(203)	Robert Gamez	USA	1.72	94.33	55	-48.78	+107.03
81	(74)	Ricardo Gonzalez	Arg	1.68	70.76	42	-62.08	+54.56
82	(288)	Todd Hamilton	USA	1.68	67.02	40	-31.11	+78.26
83	(64)	Bradley Dredge	Wal	1.67	85.37	51	-80.89	+65.98
84	(233)	Ignacio Garrido	Spn	1.65	77.40	47	-40.74	+86.43
85	(142)	Duffy Waldorf	USA	1.62	84.41	52	-59.53	+86.21
86	(237)	Tim Petrovic	USA	1.61	104.39	65	-52.15	+120.15
87	(118)	Gary Evans	Eng	1.57	84.71	54	-63.68	+71.69
88	(54)	Tom Lehman	USA	1.55	74.48	48	-100.53	+74.50
89	(16)	Bernhard Langer	Ger	1.53	78.25	51	-147.64	+46.84
90	(253)	Tetsuji Hiratsuka	Jpn	1.53	88.75	58	-31.30	+87.04
91	(58)	Mark Calcavecchia	USA	1.53	74.74	49	-98.99	+75.40
92	(157)	Ben Crane	USA	1.51	87.64	58	-59.23	+93.17
93	(38)	Jose Maria Olazabal	Spn	1.49	86.57	58	-133.05	+64.90
94	(168)	Miguel A. Jimenez	Spn	1.49	75.99	51	-50.51	+73.57
95	(103)	Lee Janzen	USA	1.46	78.74	54	-82.16	+77.46
96	(163)	Carlos Rodiles	Spn	1.45	73.87	51	-32.24	+60.40
97	(65)	Kevin Sutherland	USA	1.45	79.48	55	-108.59	+78.61
98	(80)	David Smail	NZl	1.41	76.00	54	-68.15	+44.09
99	(70)	Phil Tataurangi	NZl	1.38	55.17	40	-65.67	+24.08
100	(222)	Alastair Forsyth	Sco	1.37	72.80	53	-42.00	+75.17

( ) Ranking in brackets indicates position as of December 31, 2002.

Ranking		Player	Country	Points Average	Total Points	No. of Events	01/02 Points Lost	2003 Points Gained
101	(133)	Andre Stolz	Aus	1.35	56.77	42	-45.03	+57.13
102	(167)	Brendan Jones	Aus	1.34	76.13	57	-37.74	+62.23
103	(180)	Nick O'Hern	Aus	1.33	70.66	53	-44.88	+70.85
104	(50)	Toru Taniguchi	Jpn	1.30	66.53	51	-97.77	+28.53
105	(106)	Stephen Ames	T&T	1.30	71.44	55	-75.40	+69.86
106	(298)	Peter Jacobsen	USA	1.30	55.79	43	-21.69	+58.60
107	(184)	Maarten Lafeber	Hol	1.29	76.18	59	-37.44	+63.27
108	(169)	Aaron Baddeley	Aus	1.29	69.61	54	-48.45	+72.59
109	(98)	Matt Gogel	USA	1.26	64.25	51	-69.92	+56.84
110	(175)	Rodney Pampling	Aus	1.26	79.32	63	-58.92	+78.69
111	(150)	David Howell	Eng	1.26	62.84	50	-58.66	+69.93
112	(107)	Hiroyuki Fujita	Jpn	1.25	69.01	55	-52.71	+43.33
113	(156)	Mark McNulty	Zim	1.25	53.92	43	-36.65	+47.90
114	(370)	Woody Austin	USA	1.25	83.98	67	-40.61	+101.33
115	(125)	Greg Owen	Eng	1.25	64.79	52	-64.29	+61.58
116	(105)	Hidemichi Tanaka	Jpn	1.24	79.66	64	-68.47	+66.63
117	(62)	Robert Karlsson	Swe	1.24	61.87	50	-68.61	+43.80
118	(114)	Carl Pettersson	Swe	1.23	67.83	55	-74.11	+66.73
119	(138)	Katsumasa Miyamoto	Jpn	1.23	65.36	53	-49.46	+56.26
120	(132)	Brandt Jobe	USA	1.20	59.87	50	-52.59	+47.33
121	(130)	Taichi Teshima	Jpn	1.19	67.65	57	-66.06	+67.36
122	(144)	Tom Pernice, Jr.	USA	1.17	72.47	62	-72.84	+77.58
123	(196)	Raphael Jacquelin	Frn	1.16	66.19	57	-48.85	+70.24
124	(79)	Thomas Levet	Frn	1.16	69.65	60	-74.76	+48.63
125	(141)	Jarrod Moseley	Aus	1.16	70.50	61	-49.22	+55.95
126	(59)	Anders Hansen	Den	1.15	60.96	53	-77.62	+34.60
127	(115)	Frank Lickliter	USA	1.13	67.99	60	-79.66	+68.88
128	(269)	Hennie Otto	SAf	1.12	59.61	53	-28.36	+59.91
129	(152)	Joe Durant	USA	1.12	62.75	56	-62.86	+73.15
130	(93)	Luke Donald	Eng	1.11	65.41	59	-48.80	+52.81
131	(449)	Peter Hedblom	Swe	1.10	44.11	40	-18.43	+52.47
132	(120)	Jeff Maggert	USA	1.10	56.97	52	-66.54	+54.68
133	(211)	Jyoti Randhawa	Ind	1.09	48.92	45	-19.97	+40.39
134	(72)	Billy Andrade	USA	1.09	65.13	60	-87.01	+48.26
135	(691)	Hideto Tanihara	Jpn	1.08	48.50	45	-9.12	+53.59
136	(178)	Skip Kendall	USA	1.08	65.64	61	-61.18	+72.16
137	(384)	Tommy Armour	USA	1.07	57.83	54	-23.40	+61.22
138	(57)	Dean Wilson	USA	1.07	54.57	51	-76.66	+36.71
139	(215)	Soren Kjeldsen	Den	1.07	56.57	53	-47.15	+61.43
140	(236)	Peter Fowler	Aus	1.06	62.79	59	-41.12	+62.24
141	(110)	Masashi Ozaki	Jpn	1.05	56.87	54	-54.90	+40.85
142	(186)	Stephen Allan	Aus	1.04	60.29	58	-33.51	+43.97
143	(173)	Andrew Coltart	Sco	1.04	65.30	63	-49.10	+60.40
144	(212)	Hirofumi Miyase	Jpn	1.03	50.69	49	-35.57	+48.00
145	(86)	Billy Mayfair	USA	1.03	64.11	62	-90.12	+56.77
146	(95)	Soren Hansen	Den	1.03	57.71	56	-66.76	+35.74
147	(154)	John Bickerton	Eng	1.03	57.69	56	-48.88	+48.70
148	(128)	S.K. Ho	Kor	1.01	44.59	44	-33.46	+32.24
149	(299)	Hank Kuehne	USA	1.01	48.27	48	-25.17	+54.58
150	(204)	Thongchai Jaidee	Tha	1.01	42.23	42	-31.94	+39.05

( ) Ranking in brackets indicates position as of December 31, 2002.

Ranking		Player	Country	Points Average	Total Points	No. of Events	01/02 Points Lost	2003 Points Gained
151	(171)	Hal Sutton	USA	1.00	50.19	50	-55.03	+58.10
152	(302)	Daisuke Maruyama	Jpn	1.00	53.09	53	-19.31	+49.04
153	(235)	Keiichiro Fukabori	Jpn	1.00	53.00	53	-30.12	+49.23
154	(102)	Nobuhito Sato	Jpn	0.99	54.66	55	-62.73	+30.69
155	(652)	Brenden Pappas	SAf	0.98	59.94	61	-19.30	+72.11
156	(149)	David Gossett	USA	0.98	57.90	59	-58.52	+55.60
157	(99)	Paul McGinley	Ire	0.98	52.76	54	-83.60	+54.62
158	(241)	Paul Sheehan	Aus	0.98	43.89	45	-19.87	+38.78
159	(75)	Peter O'Malley	Aus	0.97	51.31	53	-78.08	+31.62
160	(146)	Zhang Lian-wei	Chi	0.94	54.75	58	-39.95	+47.71
161	(129)	Yasuharu Imano	Jpn	0.93	52.25	56	-36.91	+27.36
162	(160)	Glen Day	USA	0.90	57.89	64	-48.06	+49.16
163	(318)	Paul Goydos	USA	0.90	41.56	46	-23.57	+44.57
164	(67)	Dudley Hart	USA	0.90	43.21	48	-78.82	+27.44
165	(331T)	Tsuyoshi Yoneyama	Jpn	0.89	48.90	55	-22.80	+50.74
166	(112)	David Peoples	USA	0.89	53.18	60	-70.54	+41.53
167	(423)	Kenneth Ferrie	Eng	0.88	44.01	50	-22.14	+51.26
168	(109)	Pierre Fulke	Swe	0.87	34.96	40	-44.75	+22.02
169	(199)	Craig Barlow	USA	0.87	44.40	51	-26.52	+35.85
170	(155)	Kim Jong-duck	Kor	0.87	40.77	47	-29.35	+23.40
171	(162)	Harrison Frazar	USA	0.85	46.97	55	-50.30	+47.61
172	(170)	Tom Byrum	USA	0.85	45.73	54	-38.01	+39.31
173	(194)	Brent Geiberger	USA	0.84	37.92	45	-42.09	+37.93
174	(69)	Tsuneyuki Nakajima	Jpn	0.84	33.66	40	-53.12	+10.07
175	(82)	Ian Woosnam	Wal	0.84	34.40	41	-62.03	+20.35
176	(94)	Bob Burns	USA	0.84	48.59	58	-56.37	+14.60
177	(190)	Craig Stadler	USA	0.84	33.48	40	-28.96	+28.09
178	(134)	J.P. Hayes	USA	0.83	40.91	49	-46.39	+35.13
179	(52)	John Cook	USA	0.83	33.17	40	-83.59	+ 5.30
180	(122)	Barry Lane	Eng	0.83	47.26	57	-59.55	+33.16
181	(81)	Jesper Parnevik	Swe	0.82	47.41	58	-79.59	+37.32
182	(192)	Naomichi Ozaki	Jpn	0.81	42.10	52	-29.80	+28.61
183	(143)	Joey Sindelar	USA	0.81	49.26	61	-55.46	+44.17
184	(78)	Steve Elkington	Aus	0.80	32.17	40	-56.27	+10.36
185	(232)	David Lynn	Eng	0.80	46.58	58	-41.96	+49.96
186	(287)	Prayad Marksaeng	Tha	0.80	44.93	56	-24.63	+42.65
187	(84)	Chris Smith	USA	0.80	48.09	60	-74.68	+23.42
188	(108)	Pat Perez	USA	0.80	50.38	63	-65.83	+39.26
189	(231)	Kiyoshi Murota	Jpn	0.80	44.68	56	-34.50	+41.88
190	(1268T)	Marcus Fraser	Aus	0.79	31.75	40	-5.52	+37.26
191	(350)	Cliff Kresge	USA	0.79	44.11	56	-24.99	+49.69
192	(414)	Steven Conran	Aus	0.79	42.47	54	-16.93	+43.79
193	(230)	Paul Stankowski	USA	0.79	40.84	52	-37.29	+39.37
194	(161)	Heath Slocum	USA	0.78	49.90	64	-46.14	+41.63
195	(181)	Carlos Franco	Par	0.77	47.54	62	-45.37	+43.36
196	(296)	Arron Oberholser	USA	0.76	34.99	46	-23.49	+39.43
197	(113)	Cameron Beckman	USA	0.76	40.16	53	-71.37	+36.17
198	(116)	Mark O'Meara	USA	0.75	38.39	51	-54.04	+30.42
199	(276)	Richard S. Johnson	Swe	0.75	42.75	57	-30.74	+45.01
200	(537)	Gary Murphy	Ire	0.74	31.86	43	-10.68	+34.82

( ) Ranking in brackets indicates position as of December 31, 2002.

Age Groups of Current Top 100 World Ranked Players

Under 25	25-28	29-30	31-32	33-34	35-36	37-38	39-42	Over 43
				Els				
				Furyk				
				Weir				
				Goosen				K.Perry
				Mickelson				N.Price
				K.J.Choi				Haas
				Leaney				Tway
				Kaye				Couples
	Woods			Maruyama			Singh	Funk
	Casey			Cejka			Love	Romero
	Curtis		Harrington	M.Campbell			Faxon	Roberts
	Poulter		Appleby	Micheel			Verplank	Sluman
	Rollins	Campbell	Allenby	Beem	Toms	Kelly	Mediate	Hoch
	T.Clark	Jacobson	Bjorn	Herron	Clarke	Estes	Montgomerie	Faldo
	Byrd	C.Riley	Leonard	Cabrera	DiMarco	P.Price	Triplett	Lewis
Howell	Sabbatini	Cink	Fasth	Gronberg	Lonard	McCarron	Huston	Forsman
Scott	Ogilvy	Katayama	Baird	Lawrie	Izawa	Parry	Waldorf	Lowery
Garcia	Crane	B.Davis	Garrido	R.Gonzalez	Flesch	Hamilton	Jimenez	Lehman
Rose	Rodiles	Westwood	Hiratsuka	Evans	Mattiace	Petrovic	Janzen	Langer
Immelman	Forsyth	Dredge	Tataurangi	Smail	Gamez	Olazabal	Sutherland	Calcavecchia

2003 World Ranking Review

Major Movements

Upward				Downward			
	Net Points	Position			Net Points	Position	
Name	Gained	2002	2003	Name	Lost	2002	2003
Vijay Singh	230	8	2	Phil Mickelson	183	2	15
Chad Campbell	184	165	13	Sergio Garcia	178	4	36
Mike Weir	182	46	6	David Duval	142	15	242
Jim Furyk	149	11	5	Bernhard Langer	101	16	89
Davis Love	147	9	4	Colin Montgomerie	93	10	41
Ben Curtis	109	1269	34	John Cook	78	52	179
Kenny Perry	107	28	10	Tiger Woods	77	1	1
Shaun Micheel	100	245	46	Angel Cabrera	75	14	66
Jonathan Kaye	90	137	32	Rich Beem	74	21	47
Paul Casey	90	104	23	Chris DiMarco	72	12	26
Jay Haas	87	126	29	Toru Taniguchi	69	50	104
Fredrik Jacobson	81	83	17	Jose Maria Olazabal	68	38	93
Ernie Els	76	3	3	John Daly	64	91	281
Lee Westwood	73	182	65	Craig Parry	60	31	71
Briny Baird	69	158	68	Michael Campbell	60	18	44
Tim Petrovic	68	237	86				
Fred Couples	67	145	37				
Bob Tway	64	88	30				
Brian Davis	64	147	60				

Highest-Rated Events of 2003

Event		No. of World Ranked Players Participating				World Rating Points
	Top 5	Top 15	Top 30	Top 50	Top 100	
1 PGA Championship	5	14	29	48	96	796
2 U.S. Open Championship	5	15	30	50	77	758
3 The Open Championship	5	15	29	47	76	738
4 Masters Tournament	5	15	30	49	68	720
5 The Players Championship	3	12	27	46	76	673
6 WGC NEC Invitational	5	15	30	50	68	736
7 WGC Accenture Match Play	4	14	29	49	64	705
8 WGC American Express	5	14	29	48	61	696
9 Nissan Open	1	10	25	39	65	557
10 Memorial Tournament	3	10	18	29	54	498
11 Bay Hill Invitational	3	5	17	35	57	494
12 The Tour Championship	5	13	24	26	31	462
13 Volvo PGA Championship	1	2	4	13	24	190
14 The International	3	10	18	27	46	431
15 Wachovia Championship	2	9	18	29	52	436
16 Western Open	3	7	14	23	46	396
17 Chrysler Championship	3	8	14	24	44	387
18 Buick Classic	3	7	15	21	42	384
19 Phoenix Open	3	8	13	21	50	378
20 Sony Open	2	6	13	22	44	369
21 EDS Byron Nelson Champ.	1	9	16	24	41	352
22 Funai Classic at Disney	4	7	12	18	41	358
23 Ford Championship	0	7	15	24	46	350
24 MCI Heritage	2	6	15	24	41	347
25 Bank of America Colonial	0	6	14	21	46	329
26 Mercedes Championships	3	8	15	19	32	311
27 HP Classic of New Orleans	2	6	13	20	34	303
28 Las Vegas Invitational	2	3	13	20	42	300
29 Buick Invitational	2	3	10	18	39	299
30 Bob Hope Chrysler Classic	1	4	10	18	37	282
31 Dunhill Links Championship	2	5	7	16	28	256
32 Deutsche Bank Championship	3	4	7	17	35	282
33 Honda Classic	0	3	12	20	36	263
34 Barclays Scottish Open	1	3	7	16	31	230
35 Chrysler Greater Greensboro	2	6	13	15	20	257
36 FBR Capital Open	1	4	9	17	32	257
37 Buick Open	2	4	10	14	23	246
38 Shell Houston Open	2	5	8	13	30	245
39 AT&T Pebble Beach Pro-Am	2	5	9	12	32	243
40 Deutsche Bank SAP Open	1	3	5	12	25	203

World Golf Rankings 1968-2003

Year	No. 1	No. 2	No. 3	No. 4	No. 5
1968	Nicklaus	Palmer	Casper	Player	Charles
1969	Nicklaus	Player	Casper	Palmer	Charles
1970	Nicklaus	Player	Casper	Trevino	Charles
1971	Nicklaus	Trevino	Player	Palmer	Casper
1972	Nicklaus	Player	Trevino	Crampton	Palmer
1973	Nicklaus	Weiskopf	Trevino	Player	Crampton
1974	Nicklaus	Miller	Player	Weiskopf	Trevino
1975	Nicklaus	Miller	Weiskopf	Irwin	Player
1976	Nicklaus	Irwin	Miller	Player	Green
1977	Nicklaus	Watson	Green	Irwin	Crenshaw
1978	Watson	Nicklaus	Irwin	Green	Player
1979	Watson	Nicklaus	Irwin	Trevino	Player
1980	Watson	Trevino	Aoki	Crenshaw	Nicklaus
1981	Watson	Rogers	Aoki	Pate	Trevino
1982	Watson	Floyd	Ballesteros	Kite	Stadler
1983	Ballesteros	Watson	Floyd	Norman	Kite
1984	Ballesteros	Watson	Norman	Wadkins	Langer
1985	Ballesteros	Langer	Norman	Watson	Nakajima
1986	Norman	Langer	Ballesteros	Nakajima	Bean
1987	Norman	Ballesteros	Langer	Lyle	Strange
1988	Ballesteros	Norman	Lyle	Faldo	Strange
1989	Norman	Faldo	Ballesteros	Strange	Stewart
1990	Norman	Faldo	Olazabal	Woosnam	Stewart
1991	Woosnam	Faldo	Olazabal	Ballesteros	Norman
1992	Faldo	Couples	Woosnam	Olazabal	Norman
1993	Faldo	Norman	Langer	Price	Couples
1994	Price	Norman	Faldo	Langer	Olazabal
1995	Norman	Price	Langer	Els	Montgomerie
1996	Norman	Lehman	Montgomerie	Els	Couples
1997	Norman	Woods	Price	Els	Love
1998	Woods	O'Meara	Duval	Love	Els
1999	Woods	Duval	Montgomerie	Love	Els
2000	Woods	Els	Duval	Mickelson	Westwood
2001	Woods	Mickelson	Duval	Els	Love
2002	Woods	Mickelson	Els	Garcia	Goosen
2003	Woods	Singh	Els	Love	Furyk

(*The World of Professional Golf* 1968-1985; World Ranking 1986-2003)

Year	No. 6	No. 7	No. 8	No. 9	No. 10
1968	Boros	Coles	Thomson	Beard	Nagle
1969	Beard	Archer	Trevino	Barber	Sikes
1970	Devlin	Coles	Jacklin	Beard	Huggett
1971	Barber	Crampton	Charles	Devlin	Weiskopf
1972	Jacklin	Weiskopf	Oosterhuis	Heard	Devlin
1973	Miller	Oosterhuis	Wadkins	Heard	Brewer
1974	M. Ozaki	Crampton	Irwin	Green	Heard
1975	Green	Trevino	Casper	Crampton	Watson
1976	Watson	Weiskopf	Marsh	Crenshaw	Geiberger
1977	Marsh	Player	Weiskopf	Floyd	Ballesteros
1978	Crenshaw	Marsh	Ballesteros	Trevino	Aoki
1979	Aoki	Green	Crenshaw	Ballesteros	Wadkins
1980	Pate	Ballesteros	Bean	Irwin	Player
1981	Ballesteros	Graham	Crenshaw	Floyd	Lietzke
1982	Pate	Nicklaus	Rogers	Aoki	Strange
1983	Nicklaus	Nakajima	Stadler	Aoki	Wadkins
1984	Faldo	Nakajima	Stadler	Kite	Peete
1985	Wadkins	O'Meara	Strange	Pavin	Sutton
1986	Tway	Sutton	Strange	Stewart	O'Meara
1987	Woosnam	Stewart	Wadkins	McNulty	Crenshaw
1988	Crenshaw	Woosnam	Frost	Azinger	Calcavecchia
1989	Kite	Olazabal	Calcavecchia	Woosnam	Azinger
1990	Azinger	Ballesteros	Kite	McNulty	Calcavecchia
1991	Couples	Langer	Stewart	Azinger	Davis
1992	Langer	Cook	Price	Azinger	Love
1993	Azinger	Woosnam	Kite	Love	Pavin
1994	Els	Couples	Montgomerie	M. Ozaki	Pavin
1995	Pavin	Faldo	Couples	M. Ozaki	Elkington
1996	Faldo	Mickelson	M. Ozaki	Love	O'Meara
1997	Mickelson	Montgomerie	M. Ozaki	Lehman	O'Meara
1998	Price	Montgomerie	Westwood	Singh	Mickelson
1999	Westwood	Singh	Price	Mickelson	O'Meara
2000	Montgomerie	Love	Sutton	Singh	Lehman
2001	Garcia	Toms	Singh	Clarke	Goosen
2002	Toms	Harrington	Singh	Love	Montgomerie
2003	Weir	Goosen	Harrington	Toms	Perry

World's Winners of 2003

SPECIAL EVENTS

CVS Charity Classic	Jeff Sluman/Rocco Mediate
Franklin Templeton Shootout	Jeff Sluman (2)/Hank Kuehne
Callaway Golf Pebble Beach Invitational	John Daly (2)
UBS Cup	Tied
PGA Grand Slam of Golf	Jim Furyk (3)
Office Depot Father-Son Challenge	Hale Irwin (3)/Steve Irwin
Target World Challenge	Davis Love (5)

NATIONWIDE TOUR

Chitimacha Louisiana Open	Brett Wetterich
First Tee Arkansas Classic	Ted Purdy
Rheem Classic	Zach Johnson
BMW Charity Pro-Am at The Cliffs	Tripp Isenhour
Virginia Beach Open	Michael Long
SAS Carolina Classic	David Morland
LaSalle Bank Open	Andre Stolz (2)
Northeast Pennsylvania Classic	Blaine McCallister
Lake Erie Charity Classic	Guy Boros
Knoxville Open	Vaughn Taylor
Samsung Canadian PGA Championship	Tom Carter
Reese's Cup Classic	Joe Ogilvie (2)
Henrico County Open	Mark Hensby
Dayton Open	Guy Boros (2)
Chattanooga Classic	Jason Bohn
Omaha Classic	Bo Van Pelt
Price Cutter Charity Championship	Tom Carter (2)
Preferred Health Systems Wichita Open	Jeff Klauk
Alberta Calgary Classic	Tom Carter (3)
Envirocare Utah Classic	Zach Johnson (2)
Oregon Classic	Chris Couch
Albertsons Boise Open	Roger Tambellini
Mark Christopher Charity Classic	James Oh
Monterey Peninsula Classic	Scott Gutschewski
Gila River Classic at Wild Horse Pass Resort	Lucas Glover
Permian Basin Charity Golf Classic	D.J. Brigman
Miccosukee Championship	Craig Bowden
Nationwide Tour Championship	Chris Couch (2)

CANADIAN TOUR

TravelTex.com Canadian Tour Classic	Anders Hultman
TravelTex.com Canadian Tour Challenge	Rob Johnson
Michelin Guadalajara Classic	Erik Compton
Corona Ixtapa Classic	Derek Gillespie
Northern Ontario Open	Mario Tiziani
MTS Classic	Jon Mills
Telus Edmonton Open	Rob Johnson (2)
Victoria Open	Patrick Damron
Greater Vancouver Classic	*James Lepp
Lewis Chitengwa Memorial Championship	Nick Watney
Bay Mills Open Players Championship	Rodney Butcher
Casino de Charlevoix Cup	Bryn Parry/Alex Rocha

TOUR DE LAS AMERICAS (SOUTH AMERICA)

Caribbean Open	Rafael Gomez
Samsung Panama Open	Charles Warren
Cable & Wireless Panama Masters	Andres Romero
Costa Rica Open	Sebastian Fernandez
Telefonica CA Guatemala Open	Daniel Vancsik
Amex Los Encinos Open	James Hepworth
Acapulco Fest Invitational	Octavio Gonzalez

Bancolombia American Express Open	Angel Romero
Medellin Open	Andres Romero (2)
American Express Trump Brazil Open	Carlos Franco
Mexican Open	Eduardo Herrera

PGA EUROPEAN TOUR

Dubai Desert Classic	Robert-Jan Derksen
Qatar Masters	Darren Fichardt
Madeira Island Open	Bradley Dredge
Algarve Open de Portugal	Fredrik Jacobson
Canarias Open de Espana	Kenneth Ferrie
Italian Open Telecom Italia	Mathias Gronberg
Benson and Hedges International Open	Paul Casey (2)
Deutsche Bank - SAP Open	Padraig Harrington
Volvo PGA Championship	Ignacio Garrido
Celtic Manor Resort Wales Open	Ian Poulter
Daily Telegraph Damovo British Masters	Greg Owen
Aa St. Omer Open	Brett Rumford
Diageo Championship at Gleneagles	Soren Kjeldsen
Open de France	Philip Golding
Smurfit European Open	Phillip Price
Barclays Scottish Open	Ernie Els (5)
The Open Championship	Ben Curtis
Nissan Irish Open	Michael Campbell
Scandic Carlsberg Scandinavian Masters	Adam Scott
Nordic Open	Ian Poulter (2)
BMW Russian Open	Marcus Fraser (3)
BMW International Open	Lee Westwood
Omega European Masters	Ernie Els (6)
Trophee Lancome	Retief Goosen
Linde German Masters	K.J. Choi (2)
Dunhill Links Championship	Lee Westwood (2)
Dutch Open	Maarten Lafeber
HSBC World Match Play	Ernie Els (7)
Turespana Mallorca Classic	Miguel Angel Jimenez
Telefonica Open de Madrid	Ricardo Gonzalez
Volvo Masters Andalucia	Fredrik Jacobson (2)
The Seve Trophy	Great Britain & Ireland

CHALLENGE TOUR

Panalpina Banque Commerciale du Maroc Classic	Greig Hutcheon
Tessali - Metaponto Open di Puglia e Basilicata	Martin LeMesurier
Izki Challenge de Espana	Martin Erlandsson
Fortis Challenge Open	Johan Edfors (2)
Nykredit Danish Open	Marcus Fraser
Clearstream International Luxembourg Open	Martin LeMesurier (2)
Galeria Kaufhof Pokal Challenge	Michael Jonzon
Volvo Finnish Open	Jamie Elson
Open des Volcans Challenge de France	Ivo Giner
Kitzbuhel Golf Alpin Open	David Geall
Terme Euganee International Open	Ivo Giner (2)
Talma Finnish Challenge	Marcus Fraser (2)
Rolex Trophy	Michael Jonzon (2)
Skandia PGA Open	Titch Moore
BA CA Golf Open	Robert Coles
Benmore Developments N. Ireland Masters	Darren Clarke (2)
Telia Grand Prix	Euan Little
Open de Toulouse	Scott Drummond
Ryder Cup Wales Challenge	Craig Willaims
Challenge Tour Grand Final	Jose Manuel Carriles

ASIAN PGA TOUR

Caltex Masters	Zhang Lian-wei
Carlsberg Malaysian Open	Arjun Atwal
Myanmar Open	Lin Keng-chi
Phoenix Dynasty Cup	Asia
Royal Challenge Indian Open	Mike Cunning
Thailand Open	Edward Loar
Maekyung Open	Chung Joon
SK Telecom Open	K.J. Choi
Mercuries Masters	Lin Wen-ko
Kolon Cup Korean Open	John Daly
Macau Open	Colin Montgomerie
Sanya Open	Marcus Both
Hero Honda Masters	Arjun Atwal (2)
Volvo China Open	Zhang Lian-wei (2)
Acer Taiwan Open	Jason Dawes
Omega Hong Kong Open	Padraig Harrington (2)
Volvo Masters of Asia	Thongchai Jaidee

JAPAN TOUR

Token Homemate Cup	Andre Stolz
Tsuruya Open	Hirofumi Miyase
The Crowns	Hidemasa Hoshino
Fujisankei Classic	Todd Hamilton
Japan PGA Championship	Shingo Katayama
Munsingwear Open KSB Cup	Hirofumi Miyase (2)
Diamond Cup	Todd Hamilton (2)
JCB Classic Sendai	Katsuyoshi Tomori
Mandom Lucido Yomiuri Open	Hideto Tanihara
Gateway to the Open Mizuno Open	Todd Hamilton (3)
Japan Tour Championship	Toshimitsu Izawa
Woodone Open	Toshimitsu Izawa (2)
Sato Foods NST Niigata Open	Katsumasa Miyamoto
Aiful Cup	Taichi Teshima
Sun Chlorella Classic	Brendan Jones
Hisamitsu-KBC Augusta	Soushi Tajima
Japan PGA Match Play	Todd Hamilton (4)
Suntory Open	Jyoti Randhawa
ANA Open	Yeh Wei-tze
Acom International	Masahiro Kuramoto
Georgia Tokai Classic	Nozomi Kawahara
Japan Open	Keiichiro Fukabori
Bridgestone Open	Naomichi Ozaki
ABC Championship	Shingo Katayama (2)
Mitsui Sumitomo Visa Taiheiyo Masters	Kiyoshi Murota
Dunlop Phoenix	Thomas Bjorn
Casio World Open	Katsumune Imai
Golf Nippon Series JT Cup	Tetsuji Hiratsuka
Asia/Japan Okinawa Open	Hideto Tanihara (2)

AUSTRALASIAN TOUR

Holden New Zealand Open	Mahal Pearce
Heineken Classic	Ernie Els (3)
ANZ Championship	Paul Casey
Johnnie Walker Classic	Ernie Els (4)
Jacob's Creek Open	Joe Ogilvie
Clearwater Classic	Ryan Palmer
MasterCard Masters	Robert Allenby
Australian PGA Championship	Peter Senior
Australian Open	Peter Lonard

AFRICAN TOURS

South African Airways Open	Trevor Immelman
Dunhill Championship	Mark Foster
Dimension Data Pro-Am	Trevor Immelman (2)
Southern Africa Tour Championship	Hennie Otto
Stanbic Zambia Open	Johan Edfors
FNB Botswana Open	Trevor Fisher
Limpopo Industrelek Classic	Marc Cayeux
Capital Alliance Royal Swazi Sun Open	Des Terblanche
Devonvale Championship	Hendrik Buhrmann
Canon Classic	Tyrol Auret
Royal Swazi Sun Classic	Nic Henning
Parmalat Classic	Desvonde Botes
Seekers Travel Pro-Am	Chris Williams
Bearing Man Highveld Classic	Dion Fourie
Platinum Classic	Doug McGuigan
Nelson Mandela Invitational	Lee Westwood (3)/Simon Hobday
Presidents Cup	Tied
Nedbank Golf Challenge	Sergio Garcia
Hassan II Trophy	Santiago Luna
Ernie Els Invitational	Ernie Els (8)

CHAMPIONS TOUR

MasterCard Championship	Dana Quigley
Royal Caribbean Golf Classic	Dave Barr
ACE Group Classic	Vicente Fernandez
Verizon Classic	Bruce Fleisher
MasterCard Classic	David Eger
SBC Classic	Tom Purtzer
Toshiba Senior Classic	Rodger Davis
Emerald Coast Classic	Bob Gilder
Liberty Mutual Legends of Golf	Bruce Lietzke
Bruno's Memorial Classic	Tom Jenkins
Kinko's Classic of Austin	Hale Irwin
Bayer Advantage Celebrity Pro-Am	Jay Sigel
Columbus Southern Open	Morris Hatalsky
Music City Championship at Gaylord Opryland	Jim Ahern
Senior PGA Championship	John Jacobs
Farmers Charity Classic	Doug Tewell
U.S. Senior Open	Bruce Lietzke (2)
Ford Senior Players Championship	Craig Stadler
FleetBoston Classic	Allen Doyle
3M Championship	Wayne Levi
Long Island Classic	Jim Thorpe
Allianz Championship	Don Pooley
JELD-WEN Tradition	Tom Watson (2)
Kroger Classic	Gil Morgan
Constellation Energy Classic	Larry Nelson
SAS Championship	D.A. Weibring
Greater Hickory Classic at Rock Barn	Craig Stadler (3)
Turtle Bay Championship	Hale Irwin (2)
SBC Championship	Craig Stadler (4)
Charles Schwab Cup Championship	Jim Thorpe (2)

EUROPEAN SENIORS TOUR

Digicel Jamaica Classic	Ray Carrasco
Royal Westmoreland Barbados Open	Terry Gale
Tobago Plantations Seniors Classic	Terry Gale (2)
AIB Irish Seniors Open	Noel Ratcliffe
Wallonia Open	Hank Woodrome
Irvine Whitlock Jersey Seniors Classic	Malcolm Gregson
De Vere Northumberland Seniors Classic	Jerry Bruner
Ryder Cup Wales Seniors Open	Bill Longmuir
The Mobile Cup	Carl Mason
Senior British Open	Tom Watson
De Vere PGA Seniors Championship	Bill Longmuir (2)
Bad Ragaz PGA Seniors Open	Horacio Carbonetti
Travis Perkins Senior Masters	John Chillas
Nigel Mansell Classic	Mike Miller
Charles Church Scottish Seniors Open	Terry Gale (3)
Bovis Lend Lease European Senior Masters	Paul Leonard
Daily Telegraph/Turismo Andaluz Match Play	Carl Mason (2)
Merseyside English Seniors Open	Carl Mason (3)
Tunisian Seniors Open	David Good
Estoril Seniors Tour Championship	Carl Mason (4)

JAPAN SENIOR TOUR

Castle Hill Open	Chen Tze-ming
Aderans Wellness Open	Takashi Miyoshi
Fancl Senior Classic	Katsunari Takahashi
Japan PGA Senior Championship	Noboru Fujiike
PGA Philanthropy Biglayzac Senior	Katsunari Takahashi (2)
Japan Senior Open Championship	Katsunari Takahashi (3)

U.S. LPGA TOUR

Welch's/Fry's Championship	Wendy Doolan
Safeway Ping	Se Ri Pak
Kraft Nabisco Championship	Patricia Meunier-Lebouc
The Office Depot	Annika Sorenstam
Takefuji Classic	Candie Kung
Chick-fil-A Charity Championship	Se Ri Pak (2)
Michelob Light Open	Grace Park
Asahi Ryokuken International	Rosie Jones
Corning Classic	Juli Inkster
Kellogg-Keebler Classic	Annika Sorenstam (3)
McDonald's LPGA Championship	Annika Sorenstam (4)
Giant Eagle Classic	Rachel Teske
Wegmans Rochester LPGA	Rachel Teske (2)
ShopRite Classic	Angela Stanford
U.S. Women's Open	Hilary Lunke
BMO Financial Group Canadian Women's Open	Beth Daniel
Sybase Big Apple Classic	Hee-Won Han
Wendy's Championship for Children	Hee-Won Han (2)
Jamie Farr Kroger Classic	Se Ri Pak (3)
Wachovia Classic	Candie Kung (2)
State Farm Classic	Candie Kung (3)
John Q. Hammons Hotel Classic	Karrie Webb
Safeway Classic	Annika Sorenstam (6)
Longs Drugs Challenge	Helen Alfredsson
Samsung World Championship	Sophie Gustafson (4)
CJ Nine Bridges Classic	Shi Hyun Ahn
Mobile Tournament of Champions	Dorothy Delasin
ADT Championship	Meg Mallon

EVIAN LADIES EUROPEAN TOUR

Tenerife Ladies Open	Elisabeth Esterl
La Perla Italian Open	Ludivine Kreutz
Lancia Ladies Open of Portugal	Alison Munt
Open de Espana Feminino	Federica Dassu
Ladies Irish Open	Sophie Gustafson
Arras Open de France Dames	Lynnette Brooky
Evian Masters	Juli Inkster (2)
Weetabix Women's British Open	Annika Sorenstam (5)
HP Open	Sophie Gustafson (2)
BT Ladies Open	Sophie Gustafson (3)
Wales WPGA Championship of Europe	Shani Waugh
Solheim Cup	Europe
Biarritz Ladies Classic	Marlene Hedblom
Princess Lalla Meriem Cup	Johanna Head

JAPAN LPGA TOUR

Daikin Orchid Ladies	Yuri Fudoh
Promise Ladies	Ji-Hee Lee
Saishunkan Ladies Hinokuni Open	Ji-Hee Lee (2)
Katokichi Queens	Kasumi Fujii
Nichirei Cup World Ladies	Annika Sorenstam (2)
Vernal Ladies	Ok-Hee Ku
Chukyo TV Bridgestone Ladies Open	Yuri Fudoh (2)
Kosaido Ladies Golf Cup	Michiko Hattori
Resort Trust Ladies	Yuri Fudoh (3)
We Love Kobe Suntory Ladies Open	Ji-Hee Lee (3)
Apita Circle K Sankus Ladies	Yun-Jye Wei
Belluna Ladies Cup	Shiho Ohyama
Toyo Suisan Ladies Hokkaido	Kaori Suzuki
Stanley Ladies	Yuri Fudoh (4)
Golf 5 Ladies	Mihoko Takahashi
NEC Karuizawa 72	Akiko Fukushima
New Caterpillar Mitsubishi Ladies	Yuri Fudoh (5)
Yonex Ladies	Miho Koga
Fujisankei Ladies Classic	Ikuyo Shiotani
Japan LPGA Championship	Yuri Fudoh (6)
Munsingwear Ladies Tokai Classic	Yuri Fudoh (7)
Miyagi TV Cup Dunlop Ladies Open	*Ai Miyazato
Japan Women's Open	Michiko Hattori (2)
Sankyo Ladies Open	Ji-Hee Lee (4)
Fujitsu Ladies	Yuri Fudoh (8}
Masters Golf Club Ladies	Hiromi Takesue
Mizuno Classic	Annika Sorenstam (7)
Itoen Ladies	Yuri Fudoh (9)
Daiohseishi Elleair Ladies Open	Miho Koga (2)
Japan LPGA Tour Championship	Yuri Fudoh (10)

AUSTRALIAN WOMEN'S TOUR

Contrabart ALPG Players Championship	Tamara Hyett
ANZ Ladies Masters	Laura Davies
AAMI Women's Australian Open	Mhairi McKay

NEDBANK WOMEN'S TOUR OF SOUTH AFRICA

Acer South African Women's Open	Helena Svensson
Pam Golding Ladies International	Laurette Maritz
Telkom Women's Classic	Cherry Moulder
Nedbank Women's South African Masters	Laurette Maritz (2)

Multiple Winners of 2003

PLAYER	WINS	PLAYER	WINS
Yuri Fudoh	10	Ivo Giner	2
Ernie Els	8	Retief Goosen	2
Annika Sorenstam	7	Hee-Won Han	2
Davis Love	5	Padraig Harrington	2
Tiger Woods	5	Michiko Hattori	2
Sophie Gustafson	4	Juli Inkster	2
Todd Hamilton	4	Toshimitsu Izawa	2
Ji-Hee Lee	4	Fredrik Jacobson	2
Carl Mason	4	Rob Johnson	2
Vijay Singh	4	Zach Johnson	2
Craig Stadler	4	Michael Jonzon	2
Tom Carter	3	Shingo Katayama	2
Marcus Fraser	3	Miho Koga	2
Jim Furyk	3	Martin LeMesurier	2
Terry Gale	3	Bruce Lietzke	2
Trevor Immelman	3	Bill Longmuir	2
Hale Irwin	3	Laurette Maritz	2
Candie Kung	3	Hirofumi Miyase	2
Se Ri Pak	3	Joe Ogilvie	2
Kenny Perry	3	Ian Poulter	2
Katsunari Takahashi	3	Andres Romero	2
Mike Weir	3	Rory Sabbatini	2
Lee Westwood	3	Adam Scott	2
Arjun Atwal	2	Jeff Sluman	2
Guy Boros	2	Andre Stolz	2
Paul Casey	2	Hideto Tanihara	2
K.J. Choi	2	Rachel Teske	2
Darren Clarke	2	Jim Thorpe	2
Chris Couch	2	David Toms	2
John Daly	2	Tom Watson	2
Johan Edfors	2	Zhang Lian-wei	2

World Money List

This list of the 400 leading money winners in the world of professional golf in 2003 was compiled from the results of men's (excluding seniors) tournaments carried in the Appendixes of this edition. This list includes tournaments with a minimum of 36 holes and four contestants and does not include such competitions as skins games, pro-ams and shootouts.

In the 38 years during which World Money Lists have been compiled, the earnings of the player in the 200th position have risen from a total of $3,326 in 1966 to $476,645 in 2003. The top 200 players in 1966 earned a total of $4,680,287. In 2003, the comparable total was $286,722,615.

The world money list of the International Federation of PGA Tours was used for the official money list events of the U.S. PGA Tour, PGA European Tour, PGA Tour of Japan, Asian PGA Tour, Southern Africa Tour and PGA Tour of Australasia. The conversion rates used for 2003 for other events and other tours were: Euro = US$1.13; British pound = US$1.62; Japanese yen = US$0.00856; South African rand = US$0.145; Australian dollar = US$0.73; Canadian dollar = US$0.72.

POS.	PLAYER, COUNTRY	TOTAL MONEY
1	Vijay Singh, Fiji	$8,499,611
2	Ernie Els, South Africa	7,604,342
3	Tiger Woods, USA	7,400,288
4	Davis Love, USA	7,333,146
5	Jim Furyk, USA	5,650,365
6	Mike Weir, Canada	5,636,710
7	Kenny Perry, USA	4,815,122
8	Retief Goosen, South Africa	4,434,918
9	Chad Campbell, USA	4,204,864
10	David Toms, USA	3,757,155
11	Darren Clarke, N. Ireland	3,664,447
12	Padraig Harrington, Ireland	3,196,597
13	Brad Faxon, USA	3,070,945
14	Stuart Appleby, Australia	2,928,558
15	K.J. Choi, Korea	2,917,831
16	Jay Haas, USA	2,848,545
17	Justin Leonard, USA	2,835,525
18	Chris DiMarco, USA	2,735,630
19	Robert Allenby, Australia	2,729,339
20	Charles Howell, USA	2,658,955
21	Thomas Bjorn, Denmark	2,638,202
22	Nick Price, Zimbabwe	2,622,097
23	Bob Tway, USA	2,601,600
24	Adam Scott, Australia	2,583,799
25	Shaun Micheel, USA	2,521,849
26	Jonathan Kaye, USA	2,474,837
27	Jerry Kelly, USA	2,392,092
28	Fred Funk, USA	2,382,153
29	Scott Verplank, USA	2,306,714
30	Rory Sabbatini, South Africa	2,304,701
31	Fredrik Jacobson, Sweden	2,276,341

POS.	PLAYER, COUNTRY	TOTAL MONEY
32	Steve Flesch, USA	2,275,430
33	Sergio Garcia, Spain	2,225,863
34	Tim Herron, USA	2,218,890
35	Briny Baird, USA	2,202,519
36	Paul Casey, England	2,184,013
37	Chris Riley, USA	2,178,133
38	Rocco Mediate, USA	2,147,656
39	Fred Couples, USA	2,056,745
40	Ben Curtis, USA	2,053,348
41	J.L. Lewis, USA	2,039,259
42	Kirk Triplett, USA	2,006,311
43	Jeff Sluman, USA	1,999,748
44	Trevor Immelman, South Africa	1,942,093
45	Peter Lonard, Australia	1,926,539
46	Ian Poulter, England	1,896,457
47	Lee Westwood, England	1,836,555
48	Bob Estes, USA	1,824,414
49	Justin Rose, England	1,799,059
50	Stewart Cink, USA	1,786,043
51	Alex Cejka, Germany	1,761,367
52	Tim Petrovic, USA	1,753,855
53	Shigeki Maruyama, Japan	1,720,542
54	Phillip Price, Wales	1,696,030
55	Tim Clark, South Africa	1,666,952
56	Phil Mickelson, USA	1,658,031
57	Stephen Leaney, Australia	1,650,840
58	John Huston, USA	1,631,369
59	John Rollins, USA	1,625,431
60	Brian Davis, England	1,573,365
61	Robert Gamez, USA	1,519,804
62	Woody Austin, USA	1,518,707
63	Geoff Ogilvy, Australia	1,497,807
64	Scott McCarron, USA	1,439,599
65	Jonathan Byrd, USA	1,430,538
66	Ben Crane, USA	1,419,070
67	Scott Hoch, USA	1,400,750
68	Len Mattiace, USA	1,386,726
69	Niclas Fasth, Sweden	1,343,012
70	Frank Lickliter, USA	1,340,436
71	Brenden Pappas, South Africa	1,307,809
72	Loren Roberts, USA	1,297,739
73	Peter Jacobsen, USA	1,285,226
74	Raphael Jacquelin, France	1,231,092
75	Mark Calcavecchia, USA	1,221,069
76	Hank Kuehne, USA	1,212,571
77	Tom Pernice, Jr., USA	1,210,541
78	Duffy Waldorf, USA	1,208,305
79	Lee Janzen, USA	1,207,001
80	Colin Montgomerie, Scotland	1,188,607
81	Rodney Pampling, Australia	1,175,703
82	Tom Lehman, USA	1,175,147
83	Toshimitsu Izawa, Japan	1,172,184
84	David Howell, England	1,169,232
85	Dan Forsman, USA	1,140,209

POS.	PLAYER, COUNTRY	TOTAL MONEY
86	Rich Beem, USA	1,121,586
87	Joe Durant, USA	1,119,002
88	Kevin Sutherland, USA	1,101,418
89	Hidemichi Tanaka, Japan	1,101,304
90	Ignacio Garrido, Spain	1,096,718
91	Hal Sutton, USA	1,064,719
92	Carl Pettersson, Sweden	1,055,839
93	Michael Campbell, New Zealand	1,041,958
94	Shingo Katayama, Japan	1,039,682
95	Stephen Ames, Trinidad & Tobago	1,029,959
96	Tetsuji Hiratsuka, Japan	1,022,620
97	Skip Kendall, USA	1,022,244
98	Aaron Baddeley, Australia	1,003,317
99	Todd Hamilton, USA	1,000,942
100	Alastair Forsyth, Scotland	994,690
101	Miguel Angel Jimenez, Spain	983,160
102	Tommy Armour, USA	932,984
103	Steve Lowery, USA	932,293
104	Greg Owen, England	926,837
105	Mathias Gronberg, Sweden	919,537
106	Thomas Levet, France	911,050
107	Matt Gogel, USA	899,710
108	Carlos Rodiles, Spain	894,228
109	Eduardo Romero, Argentina	884,976
110	Jose Maria Olazabal, Spain	873,079
111	Paul Lawrie, Scotland	872,745
112	David Gossett, USA	865,458
113	Brett Quigley, USA	846,044
114	Billy Mayfair, USA	842,186
115	Luke Donald, England	835,679
116	Glen Day, USA	829,589
117	Bernhard Langer, Germany	826,974
118	Soren Kjeldsen, Denmark	823,823
119	Heath Slocum, USA	815,812
120	Taichi Teshima, Japan	793,057
121	Paul McGinley, Ireland	780,023
122	Harrison Frazar, USA	778,956
123	Gary Evans, England	772,640
124	Nick Faldo, England	755,677
125	Jeff Maggert, USA	747,166
126	Billy Andrade, USA	744,694
127	Nick O'Hern, Australia	741,676
128	Cliff Kresge, USA	737,600
129	Maarten Lafeber, Netherlands	735,168
130	Paul Goydos, USA	734,284
131	Philip Golding, England	733,627
132	Carlos Franco, Paraguay	725,855
133	Andrew Coltart, Scotland	721,247
134	Paul Stankowski, USA	719,436
135	Brendan Jones, Australia	718,401
136	Steve Allan, Australia	708,932
137	Peter Fowler, Australia	696,324
138	Peter Hedblom, Sweden	696,018
139	Jarrod Moseley, Australia	693,598

POS.	PLAYER, COUNTRY	TOTAL MONEY
140	Brandt Jobe, USA	691,604
141	Joey Sindelar, USA	691,328
142	Kenneth Ferrie, England	689,286
143	David Peoples, USA	674,222
144	John Bickerton, England	665,089
145	Richard Johnson, Sweden	660,933
146	J.J. Henry, USA	660,341
147	Dean Wilson, USA	656,645
148	Jeff Brehaut, USA	655,819
149	Mark O'Meara, USA	654,977
150	Darren Fichardt, South Africa	648,820
151	Craig Barlow, USA	638,721
152	Mark McNulty, Zimbabwe	632,070
153	Bradley Dredge, Wales	628,732
154	Jay Williamson, USA	628,332
155	Todd Fischer, USA	627,198
156	John Senden, Australia	624,950
157	Barry Lane, England	624,574
158	Arron Oberholser, USA	619,865
159	Patrick Sheehan, USA	618,019
160	Angel Cabrera, Argentina	616,080
161	David Lynn, England	613,380
162	Cameron Beckman, USA	608,981
163	Robert-Jan Derksen, Netherlands	606,741
164	Marco Dawson, Germany	601,729
165	Kiyoshi Murota, Japan	599,487
166	Hideto Tanihara, Japan	598,822
167	Daisuke Maruyama, Japan	596,942
168	Tom Byrum, USA	590,720
169	Neal Lancaster, USA	590,627
170	Brent Geiberger, USA	588,533
171	J.P. Hayes, USA	585,331
172	David Frost, South Africa	584,377
173	Ricardo Gonzalez, Argentina	580,223
174	Robert Damron, USA	580,087
175	Andrew Magee, USA	578,558
176	Pat Perez, USA	578,141
177	Jesper Parnevik, Sweden	570,587
178	Tsuyoshi Yoneyama, Japan	567,044
179	Andre Stolz, Australia	566,297
180	Notah Begay, USA	565,572
181	Hirofumi Miyase, Japan	562,506
182	Robert Karlsson, Sweden	561,841
183	Stephen Gallacher, Scotland	542,417
184	Olin Browne, USA	542,092
185	Kent Jones, USA	541,257
186	Zhang Lian-wei, China	526,405
187	Katsumasa Miyamoto, Japan	526,220
188	Craig Parry, Australia	520,796
189	Dicky Pride, USA	508,619
190	Hiroyuki Fujita, Japan	506,169
191	Esteban Toledo, Mexico	504,895
192	David Smail, New Zealand	503,446
193	Pat Bates, USA	496,978

POS.	PLAYER, COUNTRY	TOTAL MONEY
194	Zach Johnson, USA	494,882
195	Glen Hnatiuk, Canada	488,429
196	Per-Ulrik Johansson, Sweden	484,577
197	Spike McRoy, USA	483,073
198	Mark Wilson, USA	482,502
199	Chris Smith, USA	479,523
200	Anders Hansen, Denmark	476,645
201	Peter O'Malley, Australia	474,296
202	Keiichiro Fukabori, Japan	473,986
203	Peter Lawrie, Ireland	469,064
204	Garrett Willis, USA	467,213
205	Tom Carter, USA	466,133
206	Dennis Paulson, USA	463,809
207	Jyoti Randhawa, India	462,013
208	Katsumune Imai, Japan	461,398
209	Hennie Otto, South Africa	460,508
210	David Sutherland, USA	451,442
211	Mesashi Ozaki, Japan	450,176
212	Dudley Hart, USA	449,235
213	Jamie Donaldson, Wales	448,890
214	Brian Gay, USA	447,647
215	Steven Conran, Australia	438,055
216	Gary Murphy, Ireland	437,160
217	Soren Hansen, Denmark	436,428
218	John E. Morgan, England	434,673
219	Nick Dougherty, England	434,339
220	Mike Heinen, USA	432,417
221	Tom Gillis, USA	432,100
222	Aaron Barber, USA	425,277
223	Ian Woosnam, Wales	422,232
224	Souchi Tajima, Japan	417,562
225	Naomichi Ozaki, Japan	417,125
226	Arjun Atwal, India	416,796
227	Paul Sheehan, New Zealand	413,184
228	Greg Chalmers, Australia	412,053
229	Prayad Marksaeng, Thailand	410,978
230	Joe Ogilvie, USA	407,823
231	Hidemasa Hoshino, Japan	392,372
232	Marten Olander, Sweden	383,954
233	S.K. Ho, Korea	383,637
234	Corey Pavin, USA	383,598
235	James Kingston, South Africa	380,365
236	David Park, Wales	370,908
237	Mike Grob, USA	369,231
238	Steven Scahill, New Zealand	368,965
239	Craig Perks, New Zealand	368,163
240	John Daly, USA	366,190
241	Carl Paulson, USA	365,177
242	Phil Tataurangi, New Zealand	357,109
243	Scott Laycock, Australia	352,105
244	Marcel Siem, Germany	350,189
245	Darron Stiles, USA	348,107
246	Santiago Luna, Spain	347,194
247	Henrik Stenson, Sweden	343,633

POS.	PLAYER, COUNTRY	TOTAL MONEY
248	Chris Anderson, USA	343,501
249	Chris Couch, USA	342,874
250	Christian Cevaer, France	342,232
251	Mark Foster, England	339,201
252	Nozomi Kawahara, Japan	337,772
253	Jose Coceres, Argentina	337,682
254	Raymond Russell, Scotland	333,256
255	Yeh Wei-tze, Taiwan	332,860
256	Katsuyoshi Tomori, Japan	331,243
257	Charl Schwartzel, South Africa	329,277
258	Masahiro Kuramoto, Japan	324,127
259	Rolf Muntz, Netherlands	323,334
260	Richard Sterne, South Africa	323,181
261	John Riegger, USA	320,430
262	Kenichi Kuboya, Japan	320,340
263	Nicolas Colsaerts, Belgium	319,903
264	Thongchai Jaidee, Thailand	319,135
265	Nobuhito Sato, Japan	318,001
266	Jean-Francois Remesy, France	316,463
267	Bo Van Pelt, USA	314,668
268	Richard Green, Australia	312,070
269	Kim Jong-duck, Korea	309,276
270	John Maginnes, USA	308,928
271	Guy Boros, USA	306,073
272	Ryan Palmer, USA	305,916
273	Tadahiro Takayama, Japan	305,655
274	Toru Taniguchi, Japan	302,936
275	Mathew Goggin, Australia	299,238
276	Bob Burns, USA	293,974
277	Dinesh Chand, Fiji	291,407
278	Paul Gow, Australia	290,580
279	Blaine McCallister, USA	289,052
280	Fredrik Andersson, Sweden	287,500
281	Martin Maritz, South Africa	286,485
282	Takashi Kanemoto, Japan	286,033
283	Mark Hensby, Australia	285,399
284	Paul Azinger, USA	285,143
285	Hideki Kase, Japan	280,910
286	Jonathan Lomas, England	279,093
287	Gene Sauers, USA	278,644
288	Stephen Dodd, Wales	277,011
289	Shigemasa Higaki, Japan	276,497
290	Mike Sposa, USA	276,447
291	Simon Khan, England	275,348
292	Tsukasa Watanabe, Japan	274,446
293	Gary Orr, Scotland	273,735
294	Ian Leggatt, Canada	271,014
295	Lin Keng-chi, Taiwan	269,400
296	Anthony Wall, England	268,042
297	Mark Roe, England	265,809
298	Paul Broadhurst, England	265,170
299	Jason Bohn, USA	264,876
300	Graeme McDowell, N. Ireland	263,920
301	Kevin Na, Korea	263,701

POS.	PLAYER, COUNTRY	TOTAL MONEY
302	Tripp Isenhour, USA	262,646
303	Pierre Fulke, Sweden	261,945
304	Simon Yates, Scotland	261,892
305	Steven Alker, New Zealand	261,359
306	Miles Tunnicliff, England	256,276
307	Donnie Hammond, USA	255,414
308	Kazuhiko Hosokawa, Japan	253,850
309	Jose Manuel Lara, Spain	252,067
310	Brett Rumford, Australia	250,599
311	Daniel Chopra, Sweden	249,678
312	Gregory Havret, France	249,587
313	Shinichi Yokota, Japan	247,684
314	Matt Kuchar, USA	247,297
315	Steve Webster, England	245,161
316	Emanuele Canonica, Italy	244,820
317	Matthew Blackey, England	244,580
318	Bill Glasson, USA	244,507
319	Toru Suzuki, Japan	244,202
320	Peter Senior, Australia	243,414
321	Mark Brooks, USA	240,489
322	Simon Wakefield, England	239,519
323	Jason Dufner, USA	237,637
324	Paul Sjoland, Sweden	237,023
325	David Gilford, England	235,362
326	Brent Schwartzrock, USA	233,067
327	Ted Purdy, USA	232,373
328	Steve Elkington, Australia	231,809
329	Anthony Painter, Australia	230,953
330	Tomohiro Kondo, Japan	227,704
331	Azuma Yano, Japan	224,670
332	Doug Barron, USA	224,589
333	Vaughn Taylor, USA	223,988
334	Andy Oldcorn, Scotland	222,958
335	Yasuharu Imano, Japan	221,526
336	Jarmo Sandelin, Sweden	221,366
337	Kiyoshi Maita, Japan	221,288
338	Chris Downes, Australia	220,378
339	Jim Carter, USA	220,361
340	Tjaart van der Walt, South Africa	220,327
341	Mitsuhiro Tateyama, Japan	219,301
342	Yusaku Miyazato, Japan	219,153
343	Julien Clement, Switzerland	217,690
344	Brian Bateman, USA	217,150
345	Michael Clark, USA	216,322
346	Dave Stockton, Jr., USA	214,876
347	Mikko Ilonen, Finland	212,878
348	Jason Gore, USA	210,214
349	Charles Warren, USA	209,901
350	Charlie Wi, Korea	209,700
351	Andrew Marshall, England	208,935
352	Henrik Bjornstadt, Norway	206,537
353	Roger Chapman, England	203,574
354	Steve Pate, USA	203,427
355	Greg Norman, Australia	202,665

POS.	PLAYER, COUNTRY	TOTAL MONEY
356	Klas Eriksson, Sweden	202,053
357	David Morland, Canada	200,535
358	Markus Brier, Austria	198,802
359	Lucas Glover, USA	197,639
360	Deane Pappas, South Africa	196,740
361	D.J. Brigman, USA	195,941
362	Hisayuki Sasaki, Japan	195,309
363	Jamie Spence, England	194,455
364	Jay Don Blake, USA	194,293
365	Go Higaki, Japan	193,110
366	Robert Rock, England	192,886
367	Nobuhiro Masuda, Japan	192,407
368	Terry Price, Australia	190,551
369	Roger Tambellini, USA	189,723
370	Mads Vibe-Hastrup, Denmark	188,067
371	Shaun Webster, England	187,467
372	Brad Kennedy, Australia	184,215
373	Zaw Moe, Myanmar	183,839
374	Grant Waite, New Zealand	183,774
375	David Carter, England	182,047
376	Marcus Fraser, South Africa	181,678
377	Iain Pyman, England	181,300
378	Jeff Gallagher, USA	180,360
379	Craig Bowden, USA	180,238
380	Tommy Tolles, USA	179,963
381	Peter Baker, England	177,517
382	Russ Cochran, USA	175,905
383	Jay Delsing, USA	175,126
384	Miguel Angel Martin, Spain	175,025
385	Brett Wetterich, USA	174,805
386	Kyle Thompson, USA	174,008
387	Jason Caron, USA	172,292
388	Scott Gutschewski, USA	172,103
389	Paul Claxton, USA	171,594
390	Brian Henninger, USA	171,255
391	Simon Dyson, England	171,003
392	Gary Emerson, England	170,905
393	John Cook, USA	170,866
394	Michael Long, New Zealand	168,143
395	Steen Tinning, Denmark	167,712
396	Koki Idoki, Japan	166,328
397	Paul Eales, England	163,831
398	Jeev Milkha Singh, India	163,755
399	Greg Turner, New Zealand	162,463
400	Shigeru Nonaka, Japan	161,769

World Money List Leaders

YEAR	PLAYER, COUNTRY	TOTAL MONEY
1966	Jack Nicklaus, USA	$168,088
1967	Jack Nicklaus, USA	276,166
1968	Billy Casper, USA	222,436
1969	Frank Beard, USA	186,993
1970	Jack Nicklaus, USA	222,583
1971	Jack Nicklaus, USA	285,897
1972	Jack Nicklaus, USA	341,792
1973	Tom Weiskopf, USA	349,645
1974	Johnny Miller, USA	400,255
1975	Jack Nicklaus, USA	332,610
1976	Jack Nicklaus, USA	316,086
1977	Tom Watson, USA	358,034
1978	Tom Watson, USA	384,388
1979	Tom Watson, USA	506,912
1980	Tom Watson, USA	651,921
1981	Johnny Miller, USA	704,204
1982	Raymond Floyd, USA	738,699
1983	Seve Ballesteros, Spain	686,088
1984	Seve Ballesteros, Spain	688,047
1985	Bernhard Langer, Germany	860,262
1986	Greg Norman, Australia	1,146,584
1987	Ian Woosnam, Wales	1,793,268
1988	Seve Ballesteros, Spain	1,261,275
1989	David Frost, South Africa	1,650,230
1990	Jose Maria Olazabal, Spain	1,633,640
1991	Bernhard Langer, Germany	2,186,700
1992	Nick Faldo, England	2,748,248
1993	Nick Faldo, England	2,825,280
1994	Ernie Els, South Africa	2,862,854
1995	Corey Pavin, USA	2,746,340
1996	Colin Montgomerie, Scotland	3,071,442
1997	Colin Montgomerie, Scotland	3,366,900
1998	Tiger Woods, USA	2,927,946
1999	Tiger Woods, USA	7,681,625
2000	Tiger Woods, USA	11,034,530
2001	Tiger Woods, USA	7,771,562
2002	Tiger Woods, USA	8,292,188
2003	Vijay Singh, Fiji	8,499,611

Career World Money List

Here is a list of the 50 leading money winners for their careers through the 2003 season. It includes players active on both the regular and senior tours of the world. The World Money List from this and the 37 previous editions of the annual and a table prepared for a companion book, *The Wonderful World of Professional Golf* (Atheneum, 1973) form the basis for this compilation. Additional figures were taken from official records of major golf associations, although shortcomings in records-keeping outside the United States in the 1950s and 1960s and a few exclusions from U.S. records during those years prevent these figures from being completely accurate, although the careers of virtually all of these top 50 players began after that time. Conversion of foreign currency figures to U.S. dollars is based on average values during the particular years involved.

POS.	PLAYER, COUNTRY	TOTAL MONEY
1	Tiger Woods, USA	$48,383,030
2	Ernie Els, South Africa	40,454,383
3	Vijay Singh, Fiji	34,916,013
4	Davis Love, USA	34,126,444
5	Nick Price, Zimbabwe	28,796,599
6	Hale Irwin, USA	28,510,620
7	Colin Montgomerie, Scotland	27,603,143
8	Phil Mickelson, USA	26,038,919
9	Bernhard Langer, Germany	24,692,680
10	Fred Couples, USA	23,892,151
11	Greg Norman, Australia	23,768,395
12	Scott Hoch, USA	21,751,606
13	Masashi Ozaki, Japan	21,547,953
14	Jim Furyk, USA	21,389,893
15	Tom Kite, USA	20,360,828
16	Mark Calcavecchia, USA	20,036,645
17	David Duval, USA	19,623,515
18	Gil Morgan, USA	19,609,590
19	Nick Faldo, England	19,545,549
20	Tom Lehman, USA	19,422,511
21	Raymond Floyd, USA	19,070,410
22	Tom Watson, USA	18,679,539
23	Mark O'Meara, USA	18,361,227
24	Jose Maria Olazabal, Spain	18,257,601
25	David Toms, USA	18,218,585
26	Justin Leonard, USA	18,107,813
27	Brad Faxon, USA	17,465,403
28	Ian Woosnam, Wales	17,279,896
29	Darren Clarke, N. Ireland	17,232,493
30	Isao Aoki, Japan	17,120,253
31	Larry Nelson, USA	17,010,975
32	Lee Trevino, USA	16,994,228
33	Retief Goosen, South Africa	16,983,003
34	Jeff Sluman, USA	16,834,402
35	David Frost, South Africa	16,110,773
36	Hal Sutton, USA	16,024,218
37	Sergio Garcia, Spain	15,639,855

POS.	PLAYER, COUNTRY	TOTAL MONEY
38	Jim Colbert, USA	15,161,466
39	Kenny Perry, USA	14,955,240
40	Paul Azinger, USA	14,928,813
41	Lee Westwood, England	14,891,323
42	Payne Stewart, USA	14,617,674
43	Craig Stadler, USA	14,443,207
44	Padraig Harrington, Ireland	14,253,686
45	Fred Funk, USA	14,218,858
46	Mike Weir, Canada	14,167,769
47	Naomichi Ozaki, Japan	14,031,173
48	Loren Roberts, USA	13,982,165
49	Bob Tway, USA	13,884,604
50	Corey Pavin, USA	13,795,345

These 50 players have won $1,007,192,464 in their careers.

Senior World Money List

This list includes official earnings from the world money list of the International Federation of PGA Tours, U.S. Senior PGA Tour, European Seniors Tour and Japan Senior Tour, along with other winnings in established unofficial events when reliable figures could be obtained.

POS.	PLAYER, COUNTRY	TOTAL MONEY
1	Tom Watson, USA	$2,086,125
2	Craig Stadler, USA	2,028,108
3	Hale Irwin, USA	1,932,391
4	Jim Thorpe, USA	1,854,606
5	Bruce Lietzke, USA	1,735,826
6	Tom Kite, USA	1,670,819
7	Gil Morgan, USA	1,620,206
8	Larry Nelson, USA	1,445,973
9	Tom Jenkins, USA	1,415,503
10	Dana Quigley, USA	1,358,304
11	Allen Doyle, USA	1,349,272
12	Bruce Fleisher, USA	1,310,013
13	Bob Gilder, USA	1,278,247
14	Doug Tewell, USA	1,237,681
15	Vicente Fernandez, Argentina	1,163,339
16	Morris Hatalsky, USA	1,150,584
17	Des Smyth, Ireland	1,084,600
18	Tom Purtzer, USA	1,043,977
19	Rodger Davis, Australia	1,015,844
20	Bobby Wadkins, USA	942,109
21	Wayne Levi, USA	935,241
22	Mike McCullough, USA	887,434
23	David Eger, USA	851,217

POS.	PLAYER, COUNTRY	TOTAL MONEY
24	John Jacobs, USA	785,181
25	D.A. Weibring, USA	747,141
26	Graham Marsh, Australia	745,152
27	Fuzzy Zoeller, USA	741,830
28	Dave Barr, Canada	731,726
29	Jay Sigel, USA	721,989
30	Jose Maria Canizares, Spain	680,895
31	Isao Aoki, Japan	656,665
32	Jim Ahern, USA	626,958
33	Walter Hall, USA	578,806
34	Ed Dougherty, USA	565,146
35	Mike Hill, USA	563,235
36	Eamonn Darcy, Ireland	557,179
37	Stewart Ginn, Australia	553,941
38	Dave Stockton, USA	529,801
39	Carl Mason, England	520,772
40	Hubert Green, USA	514,575
41	Bruce Summerhays, USA	509,194
42	Tom Wargo, USA	496,614
43	Don Pooley, USA	491,012
44	Raymond Floyd, USA	490,275
45	Hugh Baiocchi, South Africa	475,512
46	Mark McCumber, USA	475,021
47	James Mason, USA	465,985
48	Jim Colbert, USA	443,303
49	Bill Longmuir, Scotland	411,643
50	Jim Dent, USA	408,020
51	Jerry McGee, USA	386,565
52	Leonard Thompson, USA	372,079
53	J.C. Snead, USA	358,175
54	Katsunari Takahashi, Japan	348,450
55	John Bland, South Africa	344,150
56	Jack Nicklaus, USA	328,706
57	Bobby Walzel, USA	328,129
58	John Harris, USA	324,304
59	Bob Murphy, USA	321,583
60	Seiji Ebihara, Japan	292,556
61	John Schroeder, USA	284,121
62	Terry Gale, Australia	261,646
63	Ed Fiori, USA	260,810
64	Terry Dill, USA	254,917
65	Mike Smith, USA	252,274
66	Pat McDonald, USA	249,604
67	Andy Bean, USA	239,043
68	Bob Charles, New Zealand	233,746
69	Ben Crenshaw, USA	231,512
70	Andy North, USA	227,741
71	John Chillas, Scotland	227,450
72	Bill Rogers, USA	222,039
73	Dave Eichelberger, USA	211,239
74	Bob Eastwood, USA	207,867
75	Steven Veriato, USA	204,386
76	Dick Mast, USA	198,308
77	Gibby Gilbert, USA	197,448

POS.	PLAYER, COUNTRY	TOTAL MONEY
78	Lanny Wadkins, USA	193,453
79	Jim Holtgrieve, USA	191,945
80	Dale Douglass, USA	189,989
81	Arnold Palmer, USA	188,311
82	Joe Inman, USA	184,471
83	Lee Trevino, USA	183,642
84	Jay Overton, USA	181,199
85	Jim Albus, USA	180,835
86	Gary Koch, USA	178,321
87	Takashi Miyoshi, Japan	171,594
88	Ted Goin, USA	171,202
89	Denis Durnian, England	170,504
90	Guillermo Encina, Chile	164,288
91	Rocky Thompson, USA	161,890
92	David Oakley, USA	161,513
93	Howard Twitty, USA	151,555
94	Denis O'Sullivan, Ireland	147,383
95	Delroy Cambridge, Jamaica	146,305
96	Jerry Bruner, USA	144,684
97	David Good, Australia	141,607
98	Nick Job, England	140,851
99	Sam Torrance, Scotland	137,561
100	Sammy Rachels, USA	137,340
101	Noel Ratcliffe, Australia	135,758
102	Bill Kratzert, USA	135,686
103	Danny Edwards, USA	132,152
104	Tony Jacklin, England	129,000
105	Yoshitaka Yamamoto, Japan	127,303
106	Brian Jones, Australia	125,971
107	Bob Cameron, England	123,546
108	Horacio Carbonetti, Argentina	117,836
109	Toru Nakamura, Japan	115,048
110	Giuseppe Cali, Italy	114,541
111	Gary Player, South Africa	113,898
112	Rex Caldwell, USA	108,862
113	Charles Coody, USA	107,372
114	Mark Pfeil, USA	105,730
115	Larry Ziegler, USA	105,413
116	Jim Rhodes, England	100,578
117	Gary McCord, USA	98,176
118	T.M. Chen, Taiwan	95,189
119	Keith MacDonald, England	94,553
120	John Morgan, England	92,975
121	Alan Tapie, USA	88,480
122	Walter Morgan, USA	87,427
123	Paul Leonard, N. Ireland	84,197
124	R.W. Eaks, USA	83,607
125	Butch Sheehan, USA	83,570

Women's World Money List

This list includes official earnings on the U.S. LPGA Tour, Evian Ladies European Tour and Japan LPGA Tour, along with other winnings in established unofficial events when reliable figures could be obtained.

POS.	PLAYER, COUNTRY	TOTAL MONEY
1	Annika Sorenstam, Sweden	$2,159,050
2	Se Ri Pak, Korea	1,611,928
3	Grace Park, Korea	1,417,702
4	Yuri Fudoh, Japan	1,278,228
5	Hee-Won Han, Korea	1,111,860
6	Juli Inkster, USA	1,028,205
7	Rachel Teske, Australia	971,322
8	Candie Kung, Taiwan	938,079
9	Beth Daniel, USA	917,654
10	Karrie Webb, Australia	864,754
11	Lorena Ochoa, Mexico	858,478
12	Sophie Gustafson, Sweden	825,585
13	Rosie Jones, USA	808,785
14	Meg Mallon, USA	775,780
15	Patricia Meunier-Lebouc, France	701,346
16	Laura Davies, England	698,878
17	Cristie Kerr, USA	696,097
18	Lorie Kane, Canada	682,752
19	Ji-Hee Lee, Korea	668,788
20	Hilary Lunke, USA	654,660
21	Angela Stanford, USA	643,192
22	Becky Morgan, Wales	522,784
23	Catriona Matthew, Scotland	515,905
24	Mi-Hyun Kim, Korea	511,188
25	Miho Koga, Japan	487,226
26	Dorothy Delasin, USA	486,970
27	Michele Redman, USA	468,918
28	Suzann Pettersen, Norway	454,123
29	Jeong Jang, Korea	452,778
30	Wendy Ward, USA	445,244
31	Ok-Hee Ku, Korea	443,577
32	Michiko Hattori, Japan	440,693
33	Kelly Robbins, USA	440,058
34	Laura Diaz, USA	436,592
35	Pat Hurst, USA	419,125
36	Heather Bowie, USA	398,659
37	Kasumi Fujii, Japan	387,530
38	Woo-Soon Ko, Korea	386,760
39	Jennifer Rosales, Philippines	373,118
40	Soo-Yan Kang, Korea	363,341
41	Mhairi McKay, Scotland	343,827
42	Shiho Ohyama, Japan	341,325
43	Akiko Fukushima, Japan	336,621
44	Gloria Park, Korea	332,295
45	Hiroko Yamaguchi, Japan	326,786

POS.	PLAYER, COUNTRY	TOTAL MONEY
46	Karen Stupples, England	325,774
47	Yun-Jye Wei, Taiwan	324,066
48	Shani Waugh, Australia	301,727
49	Toshimi Kimura, Japan	299,684
50	Junko Omote, Japan	295,034
51	Helen Alfredsson, Sweden	281,028
52	Hsiu-Feng Tseng, Taiwan	262,820
53	Natalie Gulbis, USA	262,204
54	Jung Yeon Lee, Korea	261,587
55	Hiromi Takesue, Japan	259,656
56	Danielle Ammaccapane, USA	258,476
57	Midori Yoneyama, Japan	258,187
58	Ikuyo Shiotani, Japan	254,571
59	Wendy Doolan, Australia	248,591
60	Leta Lindley, USA	239,722
61	Kaori Higo, Japan	239,370
62	Janice Moodie, Scotland	238,310
63	Kaori Suzuki, Japan	237,087
64	Mihoko Takahashi, Japan	230,601
65	Tammie Green, USA	224,507
66	Young Kim, Korea	223,866
67	Kim Saiki, USA	222,804
68	Kate Golden, USA	220,602
69	Vicki Goetze-Ackerman, USA	219,711
70	Christina Kim, USA	215,632
71	Donna Andrews, USA	211,242
72	Kelli Kuehne, USA	203,306
73	Yuka Shiroto, Japan	197,552
74	Emilee Klein, USA	197,289
75	Elisabeth Esterl, Germany	192,033
76	Marisa Baena, Colombia	189,338
77	Aki Nakano, Japan	189,248
78	Michelle Ellis, Australia	188,997
79	Yasuko Satoh, Japan	188,320
80	Fuki Kido, Japan	184,062
81	Carin Koch, Sweden	183,872
82	Nikki Campbell, Canada	180,739
83	Samantha Head, England	179,773
84	Michie Ohba, Japan	177,525
85	Tina Barrett, USA	174,821
86	Brandie Burton, USA	170,036
87	Kaori Harada, Japan	167,629
88	Mikiyo Nishizuka, Japan	167,521
89	Joanne Mills, Australia	160,406
90	Mie Nakata, Japan	156,240
91	Moira Dunn, USA	153,927
92	Johanna Head, England	150,488
93	Kyoko Ono, Japan	148,750
94	Betsy King, USA	148,586
95	Yuriko Ohtsuka, Japan	148,024
96	Junko Yasui, Japan	145,299
97	Masaki Maeda, Japan	140,391
98	Shin Sora, Korea	139,217
99	Rui Kitada, Japan	137,119

POS.	PLAYER, COUNTRY	TOTAL MONEY
100	Yu Ping Lin, Taiwan	136,538
101	Orie Fujino, Japan	135,868
102	Paula Marti, Spain	134,681
103	Beth Bauer, USA	133,146
104	Jamie Hullett, USA	132,965
105	Catrin Nilsmark, Sweden	131,641
106	Chieko Amanuma, Japan	129,826
107	Iben Tinning, Denmark	129,742
108	Maria Hjorth, Sweden	127,369
109	Stephanie Louden, USA	118,880
110	Jill McGill, USA	118,239
111	Lynnette Brooky New Zealand	117,935
112	Chihiro Nakajima, Japan	116,277
113	Tracy Hanson, USA	116,064
114	Young-Me Lee, Korea	115,665
115	Kayo Yamada, Japan	111,476
116	Alison Nicholas, England	110,652
117	Mineko Nasu, Japan	110,628
118	Liselotte Neumann, Sweden	108,379
119	Yuko Motoyama, Japan	108,323
120	Angela Jerman, USA	106,082
121	Miriam Nagl, Germany	105,947
122	Dottie Pepper, USA	105,607
123	Fumiko Muraguchi, Japan	104,857
124	Trish Johnson, England	103,965
125	Anna Acker-Macosko, USA	102,915
126	Amy Fruhwirth, USA	102,252
127	Young-A Yang, Korea	100,566
128	Cindy Figg-Currier, USA	100,337
129	Heather Daly-Donofrio, USA	99,955
130	Mitsuko Kawasaki, Japan	97,967
131	Hiromi Kobayashi, Japan	96,311
132	Stephanie Arricau, France	95,304
133	Ana Belen Sanchez, Spain	92,627
134	Michiko Mitsui, Japan	90,692
135	Mari Katayama, Japan	90,587
136	Ludivine Kreutz, France	88,611
137	Silvia Cavalleri, Italy	87,891
138	Deb Richard, USA	86,824
139	Junko Yoshida, Japan	85,269
140	Riko Higashio, Japan	84,533
141	Denise Killeen, USA	84,463
142	Hiromi Mogi, Japan	83,289
143	Joanne Morley, England	82,874
144	Ji-Yeon Han, Korea	82,489
145	Dawn Coe-Jones, Canada	82,100
146	Seiko Watanabe, Japan	81,707
147	Kumiko Hiyoshi, Japan	81,104
148	Rebecca Stevenson, Australia	80,995
149	Rie Murata, Japan	80,351
150	Marnie McGuire, New Zealand	80,304

American Tours

Mercedes Championships

Plantation Course at Kapalua, Lahaina, Maui, Hawaii
Par 36-37–73; 7,263 yards

January 9-12
purse, $5,000,000

	SCORES				TOTAL	MONEY
Ernie Els	64	65	65	67	261	$1,000,000
Rocco Mediate	72	69	65	63	269	450,000
K.J. Choi	67	67	62	73	269	450,000
Vijay Singh	68	70	67	65	270	224,000
Retief Goosen	70	65	66	69	270	224,000
Bob Estes	66	66	70	69	271	155,000
Jim Furyk	64	72	67	68	271	155,000
Chris Riley	65	70	67	69	271	155,000
Jonathan Byrd	68	69	71	63	271	155,000
Gene Sauers	65	72	69	66	272	125,000
Jerry Kelly	65	70	67	70	272	125,000
Jeff Sluman	72	67	70	64	273	105,000
Kevin Sutherland	71	66	69	67	273	105,000
Loren Roberts	68	70	67	69	274	90,000
Luke Donald	68	72	69	66	275	85,000
Charles Howell	73	66	67	70	276	82,000
Craig Perks	69	71	67	70	277	79,000
Phil Tataurangi	68	70	69	70	277	79,000
Chris Smith	69	71	69	69	278	75,000
Justin Leonard	71	68	71	68	278	75,000
Dan Forsman	69	71	69	70	279	70,000
Nick Price	69	69	75	66	279	70,000
J.P. Hayes	72	67	70	70	279	70,000
Len Mattiace	75	68	69	68	280	66,000
Craig Parry	71	69	71	70	281	61,250
Shigeki Maruyama	66	72	70	73	281	61,250
Sergio Garcia	71	73	66	71	281	61,250
Matt Kuchar	70	70	73	68	281	61,250
Chris DiMarco	70	75	69	68	282	56,500
Spike McRoy	72	71	73	66	282	56,500
Ian Leggatt	69	67	79	67	282	56,500
John Rollins	72	72	69	69	282	56,500
Jose Maria Olazabal	74	71	69	69	283	53,500
Bob Burns	71	72	74	66	283	53,500
Matt Gogel	69	75	73	69	286	52,000
Rich Beem	74	71	70	75	290	51,000

Sony Open in Hawaii

Waialae Country Club, Honolulu, Hawaii
Par 35-35–70; 7,060 yards

January 16-19
purse, $4,500,000

	SCORES				TOTAL	MONEY
Ernie Els	66	65	66	67	264	$810,000
Aaron Baddeley	66	64	65	69	264	486,000
(Els defeated Baddeley on second playoff hole.)						
Chris DiMarco	65	66	69	66	266	306,000

	SCORES				TOTAL	MONEY
Jerry Kelly	68	68	67	65	268	198,000
Robert Allenby	68	69	65	66	268	198,000
Stuart Appleby	68	71	67	63	269	162,000
Fred Funk	66	68	69	67	270	130,950
Joe Durant	67	69	67	67	270	130,950
Shigeki Maruyama	66	66	69	69	270	130,950
Chris Riley	65	69	69	67	270	130,950
Briny Baird	68	65	67	70	270	130,950
Dan Forsman	68	70	69	64	271	94,500
Robert Gamez	66	69	65	71	271	94,500
Peter Lonard	66	65	72	68	271	94,500
Corey Pavin	67	68	68	69	272	72,000
Tim Petrovic	68	67	68	69	272	72,000
Cameron Beckman	69	69	68	66	272	72,000
Carl Paulson	70	69	68	65	272	72,000
Charles Howell	70	66	68	68	272	72,000
Andrew Magee	71	65	68	69	273	46,928.57
David Peoples	71	69	66	67	273	46,928.57
Loren Roberts	67	68	70	68	273	46,928.57
Vijay Singh	67	70	68	68	273	46,928.57
Retief Goosen	64	66	72	71	273	46,928.57
Jason Gore	70	67	68	68	273	46,928.57
Pat Perez	70	70	69	64	273	46,928.58
Dudley Hart	70	68	68	68	274	31,275
Rodney Pampling	68	69	72	65	274	31,275
Yasuharu Imano	67	69	71	67	274	31,275
Tag Ridings	70	65	69	70	274	31,275
Ben Crane	68	70	66	70	274	31,275
Rory Sabbatini	70	69	69	66	274	31,275
Jeff Sluman	68	68	67	72	275	23,271.42
Jim Furyk	67	67	70	71	275	23,271.43
Brenden Pappas	65	69	71	70	275	23,271.43
Steven Alker	71	66	71	67	275	23,271.43
Sergio Garcia	67	70	69	69	275	23,271.43
Harrison Frazar	67	67	69	72	275	23,271.43
Mark Wilson	72	66	70	67	275	23,271.43
John Cook	67	68	69	72	276	15,363
Tom Lehman	68	70	70	68	276	15,363
Steve Lowery	68	69	67	72	276	15,363
Dicky Pride	66	71	71	68	276	15,363
Vance Veazey	73	67	67	69	276	15,363
Tim Herron	68	66	75	67	276	15,363
Anthony Painter	69	66	69	72	276	15,363
Scott Laycock	70	70	70	66	276	15,363
Arron Oberholser	70	68	69	69	276	15,363
John Rollins	68	69	70	69	276	15,363
John Huston	68	69	71	69	277	10,770
Kenny Perry	64	71	71	71	277	10,770
John Maginnes	71	69	67	70	277	10,770
Chad Campbell	66	70	71	70	277	10,770
Brian Gay	72	67	71	67	277	10,770
Jonathan Byrd	68	70	69	70	277	10,770
Jeff Brehaut	70	69	71	68	278	10,215
K.J. Choi	67	71	72	68	278	10,215
Alex Cejka	70	70	70	69	279	10,035
Andy Miller	67	72	76	64	279	10,035
Olin Browne	69	70	69	72	280	9,675
Bart Bryant	72	67	72	69	280	9,675
Chris Smith	66	70	74	70	280	9,675
Esteban Toledo	71	69	71	69	280	9,675

	SCORES				TOTAL	MONEY
Craig Perks	68	70	72	70	280	9,675
Notah Begay	70	69	73	68	280	9,675
Jeff Maggert	68	72	70	71	281	9,315
Shaun Micheel	69	70	72	70	281	9,315
Brent Geiberger	70	66	75	71	282	9,135
Thomas Levet	70	70	74	68	282	9,135
Brad Faxon	70	70	74	69	283	8,955
Hidemichi Tanaka	71	68	70	74	283	8,955
Chris Anderson	70	69	72	73	284	8,775
Yusaku Miyazato	68	71	73	72	284	8,775
Jason Buha	69	69	74	74	286	8,595
Akio Sadakata	68	72	78	68	286	8,595
J.L. Lewis	68	71	75	73	287	8,460
Robin Freeman	70	69	73	77	289	8,370

Phoenix Open

TPC of Scottsdale, Scottsdale, Arizona
Par 35-36–71; 7,089 yards

January 23-26
purse, $4,000,000

	SCORES				TOTAL	MONEY
Vijay Singh	67	66	65	63	261	$720,000
John Huston	64	67	66	67	264	432,000
Robert Gamez	70	65	64	66	265	192,000
Tim Petrovic	66	63	68	68	265	192,000
Retief Goosen	65	68	65	67	265	192,000
Harrison Frazar	62	67	67	69	265	192,000
Joe Durant	69	65	66	66	266	129,000
Alex Cejka	67	65	70	64	266	129,000
Phil Mickelson	69	67	67	64	267	112,000
Mike Weir	70	66	65	66	267	112,000
David Toms	64	72	63	69	268	92,000
Scott McCarron	66	65	68	69	268	92,000
John Rollins	65	66	70	67	268	92,000
Dan Forsman	66	69	67	67	269	70,000
Kirk Triplett	66	69	63	71	269	70,000
Chris DiMarco	69	69	62	69	269	70,000
Chad Campbell	67	65	68	69	269	70,000
Steve Stricker	69	62	68	71	270	50,400
Matt Gogel	68	66	67	69	270	50,400
Jesper Parnevik	68	68	66	68	270	50,400
Charles Howell	66	69	68	67	270	50,400
Rory Sabbatini	69	66	67	68	270	50,400
Luke Donald	65	66	70	69	270	50,400
Olin Browne	67	68	66	70	271	34,100
Jay Haas	69	65	67	70	271	34,100
Justin Leonard	69	69	64	69	271	34,100
Cameron Beckman	69	64	69	69	271	34,100
Rocco Mediate	69	67	67	69	272	27,800
Tom Pernice, Jr.	69	67	71	65	272	27,800
Stephen Ames	70	68	67	67	272	27,800
Hidemichi Tanaka	70	66	65	71	272	27,800
Jim Carter	69	65	68	71	273	22,640
Brandel Chamblee	69	65	69	70	273	22,640
Scott Verplank	69	66	70	68	273	22,640
Carl Paulson	68	66	70	69	273	22,640
James McLean	65	72	68	68	273	22,640
Fred Funk	68	69	69	68	274	17,600

	SCORES				TOTAL	MONEY
Lee Janzen	69	69	69	67	274	17,600
Pat Bates	68	70	70	66	274	17,600
Spike McRoy	68	70	67	69	274	17,600
Carlos Franco	70	67	68	69	274	17,600
J.J. Henry	65	67	72	70	274	17,600
Paul Azinger	68	69	69	69	275	12,826.67
Steve Elkington	66	70	70	69	275	12,826.67
Tom Lehman	67	70	70	68	275	12,826.66
David Peoples	69	69	68	69	275	12,826.66
Woody Austin	70	66	69	70	275	12,826.67
Rodney Pampling	68	65	69	73	275	12,826.67
Fulton Allem	68	69	71	68	276	9,691.43
Mark Calcavecchia	70	64	66	76	276	9,691.43
Skip Kendall	69	69	72	66	276	9,691.42
Gene Sauers	68	69	66	73	276	9,691.43
Per-Ulrik Johansson	71	67	67	71	276	9,691.43
Robert Allenby	67	71	69	69	276	9,691.43
Patrick Moore	68	68	73	67	276	9,691.43
Tim Herron	70	66	66	75	277	9,080
Peter Lonard	69	65	74	69	277	9,080
Shaun Micheel	66	67	71	74	278	8,880
Paul Stankowski	69	68	72	69	278	8,880
Mark Hensby	70	67	70	71	278	8,880
Billy Mayfair	69	68	71	71	279	8,600
Chris Smith	67	70	71	71	279	8,600
Jonathan Kaye	72	64	75	68	279	8,600
Sergio Garcia	69	67	70	73	279	8,600
Jose Maria Olazabal	67	71	74	69	281	8,320
Jay Williamson	68	70	71	72	281	8,320
Craig Barlow	69	69	74	69	281	8,320
Andrew Magee	73	65	73	72	283	8,040
Dudley Hart	70	68	70	75	283	8,040
Notah Begay	69	69	70	75	283	8,040
Arron Oberholser	72	66	69	76	283	8,040
Bill Glasson	71	67	76	79	293	7,840

Bob Hope Chrysler Classic

PGA West, Palmer Course: Par 36-36–72; 6,950 yards
Indian Wells CC: Par 36-36–72; 6,478 yards
Bermuda Dunes CC: Par 36-36–72; 6,927 yards
La Quinta CC: Par 36-36–72; 7,060 yards
La Quinta, California

January 29-February 2
purse, $4,500,000

	SCORES					TOTAL	MONEY
Mike Weir	67	64	65	67	67	330	$810,000
Jay Haas	67	61	67	68	69	332	486,000
Chris DiMarco	64	68	66	66	70	334	261,000
Tim Herron	69	64	61	65	75	334	261,000
David Gossett	69	67	62	66	72	336	180,000
Phil Mickelson	70	68	63	69	67	337	156,375
Pat Perez	69	61	70	66	71	337	156,375
Stephen Ames	63	67	64	71	73	338	126,000
Justin Leonard	66	67	69	66	70	338	126,000
Jonathan Kaye	66	71	64	70	67	338	126,000
Harrison Frazar	67	62	72	66	71	338	126,000
Davis Love	67	64	68	69	71	339	91,125
Scott Verplank	70	69	64	66	70	339	91,125

	SCORES					TOTAL	MONEY
Jerry Kelly	71	66	64	67	71	339	91,125
Frank Lickliter	65	72	63	67	72	339	91,125
J.L. Lewis	67	65	65	72	71	340	67,500
Steve Lowery	68	68	62	68	74	340	67,500
Joey Sindelar	69	69	65	68	69	340	67,500
Kirk Triplett	68	67	70	66	69	340	67,500
Cliff Kresge	67	65	67	68	73	340	67,500
Skip Kendall	69	68	66	66	72	341	43,521.43
Jeff Maggert	70	66	68	70	67	341	43,521.43
Jeff Sluman	68	69	69	65	70	341	43,521.43
John Maginnes	71	64	67	64	75	341	43,521.42
Doug Barron	66	67	66	67	75	341	43,521.43
Todd Fischer	68	66	66	67	74	341	43,521.43
Rodney Pampling	65	66	65	71	74	341	43,521.43
Tom Pernice, Jr.	69	66	70	64	73	342	31,275
Dudley Hart	69	69	67	68	69	342	31,275
Kevin Sutherland	70	66	67	69	70	342	31,275
Chad Campbell	68	68	65	64	77	342	31,275
Dan Forsman	66	71	67	65	74	343	25,470
John Huston	66	66	70	66	75	343	25,470
David Peoples	70	65	71	65	72	343	25,470
Kenny Perry	69	69	65	63	77	343	25,470
Briny Baird	71	66	66	65	75	343	25,470
Duffy Waldorf	68	66	73	65	72	344	19,800
Esteban Toledo	66	69	69	71	69	344	19,800
Paul Stankowski	72	68	66	64	74	344	19,800
Matt Gogel	65	70	64	70	75	344	19,800
Scott McCarron	70	62	71	67	74	344	19,800
Chris Riley	67	71	63	70	73	344	19,800
John Cook	64	71	66	69	75	345	13,702.50
Fred Couples	69	65	69	66	76	345	13,702.50
Steve Jones	68	70	69	66	72	345	13,702.50
Andrew Magee	72	69	65	66	73	345	13,702.50
Tim Petrovic	68	67	68	67	75	345	13,702.50
Joe Durant	67	63	74	69	72	345	13,702.50
Stewart Cink	68	68	67	68	74	345	13,702.50
Alex Cejka	69	66	69	65	76	345	13,702.50
Mark Calcavecchia	66	66	71	72	71	346	10,656
Robert Gamez	65	70	65	68	78	346	10,656
Hal Sutton	72	70	64	69	71	346	10,656
David Toms	70	66	69	69	72	346	10,656
Geoff Ogilvy	67	69	70	65	75	346	10,656
John Daly	69	73	64	66	75	347	10,260
Tom Lehman	67	68	73	67	73	348	10,035
David Sutherland	69	67	69	67	76	348	10,035
Glen Hnatiuk	68	65	70	68	77	348	10,035
John Senden	69	68	74	64	73	348	10,035
Fred Funk	70	71	67	66	75	349	9,720
Patrick Moore	67	68	65	72	77	349	9,720
Ben Crane	69	66	69	66	79	349	9,720
Peter Jacobsen	67	67	68	65	83	350	9,495
Bob Burns	67	69	68	71	75	350	9,495
Olin Browne	68	70	73	64	76	351	9,180
Corey Pavin	69	68	69	65	80	351	9,180
Shaun Micheel	65	68	70	69	79	351	9,180
Jeff Brehaut	68	65	69	73	76	351	9,180
Cameron Beckman	69	70	70	66	76	351	9,180
Spike McRoy	69	68	72	66	79	354	8,910
Donnie Hammond	69	70	63	73	81	356	8,820

AT&T Pebble Beach National Pro-Am

Pebble Beach GL: Par 36-36–72; 6,799 yards
Poppy Hills GC: Par 36-36–72; 6,861 yards
Spyglass Hill GC: Par 36-36–72; 6,817 yards
Pebble Beach, California

February 6-9
purse, $5,000,000

	SCORES				TOTAL	MONEY
Davis Love	72	67	67	68	274	$900,000
Tom Lehman	68	70	70	67	275	540,000
Mike Weir	67	74	67	68	276	290,000
Tim Herron	69	69	72	66	276	290,000
Rocco Mediate	70	71	68	70	279	190,000
Jim Furyk	71	66	73	69	279	190,000
Brad Faxon	70	70	70	70	280	155,833.33
Paul Stankowski	71	67	73	69	280	155,833.33
Phil Tataurangi	68	73	70	69	280	155,833.34
Rodney Pampling	70	68	70	73	281	125,000
Tim Clark	74	66	70	71	281	125,000
Rory Sabbatini	71	69	70	71	281	125,000
Tim Petrovic	70	72	70	71	283	100,000
Paul Goydos	71	75	67	70	283	100,000
J.L. Lewis	70	71	71	72	284	75,000
Mark O'Meara	71	68	74	71	284	75,000
Tom Pernice, Jr.	69	74	70	71	284	75,000
Marco Dawson	68	76	71	69	284	75,000
Kevin Sutherland	66	72	73	73	284	75,000
Dicky Pride	70	71	69	74	284	75,000
Jason Caron	68	74	71	71	284	75,000
Kenny Perry	69	74	70	72	285	52,000
Brian Watts	72	71	72	70	285	52,000
Dave Stockton, Jr.	69	71	74	71	285	52,000
Ken Green	68	75	72	71	286	40,833.33
Frank Lickliter	75	69	71	71	286	40,833.34
Patrick Sheehan	75	71	68	72	286	40,833.33
David Edwards	74	71	73	69	287	30,500
Donnie Hammond	68	75	73	71	287	30,500
Lee Janzen	72	74	70	71	287	30,500
Loren Roberts	71	69	76	71	287	30,500
Greg Kraft	68	75	73	71	287	30,500
Bob May	70	76	70	71	287	30,500
Vijay Singh	70	71	72	74	287	30,500
Dudley Hart	76	69	69	73	287	30,500
Brenden Pappas	74	73	71	69	287	30,500
Steven Alker	74	72	67	74	287	30,500
Fred Couples	69	76	73	70	288	22,000
Grant Waite	74	68	73	73	288	22,000
Brett Quigley	73	74	70	71	288	22,000
Jay Williamson	72	72	71	73	288	22,000
Brian Claar	72	71	74	72	289	17,500
Robert Gamez	67	76	73	73	289	17,500
Skip Kendall	71	74	72	72	289	17,500
Craig Stadler	70	73	72	74	289	17,500
Richard S. Johnson	73	75	69	72	289	17,500
Olin Browne	75	71	72	72	290	13,016.66
Gary Hallberg	74	71	73	72	290	13,016.66
Brian Henninger	72	74	70	74	290	13,016.67
Scott Laycock	74	72	70	74	290	13,016.67
John Rollins	71	71	73	75	290	13,016.67
Pat Perez	69	75	74	72	290	13,016.67

	SCORES				TOTAL	MONEY
Scott Simpson	74	71	71	75	291	11,700
Hal Sutton	73	74	70	74	291	11,700
Willie Wood	68	74	72	79	293	11,450
K.J. Choi	72	73	72	76	293	11,450
Mark Brooks	70	75	73	76	294	11,100
Woody Austin	74	71	71	78	294	11,100
Anthony Painter	70	72	75	77	294	11,100
Andy Miller	75	72	71	76	294	11,100
Todd Rose	75	69	74	76	294	11,100
Robin Freeman	73	73	72	77	295	10,750
Jonathan Byrd	72	73	73	77	295	10,750
Phil Mickelson	72	71	73	80	296	10,600

Buick Invitational

Torrey Pines Golf Course, La Jolla, California
South Course: Par 36-36–72; 7,568 yards
North Course: Par 36-36–72; 6,874 yards

February 13-16
purse, $4,500,000

	SCORES				TOTAL	MONEY
Tiger Woods	70	66	68	68	272	$810,000
Carl Pettersson	69	68	70	69	276	486,000
Brad Faxon	70	64	71	72	277	306,000
Phil Mickelson	69	68	69	72	278	186,000
Briny Baird	70	65	72	71	278	186,000
Arron Oberholser	65	70	72	71	278	186,000
Mark Calcavecchia	71	68	71	69	279	130,950
Marco Dawson	68	66	76	69	279	130,950
Jonathan Kaye	68	67	72	72	279	130,950
Charles Howell	74	68	68	69	279	130,950
Luke Donald	69	70	71	69	279	130,950
Tim Clark	70	70	73	67	280	103,500
Fred Couples	69	68	70	74	281	84,375
Dennis Paulson	68	67	73	73	281	84,375
Craig Perks	70	71	69	71	281	84,375
Ben Crane	71	68	70	72	281	84,375
Steven Alker	69	67	70	76	282	72,000
Joey Sindelar	70	71	73	69	283	63,000
Spike McRoy	67	71	72	73	283	63,000
Cameron Beckman	68	74	72	69	283	63,000
Jay Haas	73	69	70	72	284	43,521.43
Skip Kendall	66	73	72	73	284	43,521.43
Tom Lehman	71	71	69	73	284	43,521.43
Dave Stockton, Jr.	72	69	70	73	284	43,521.42
Per-Ulrik Johansson	72	68	75	69	284	43,521.43
Brent Geiberger	72	69	72	71	284	43,521.43
Shigeki Maruyama	73	70	70	71	284	43,521.43
Bob Estes	74	69	69	73	285	28,050
Fred Funk	71	64	74	76	285	28,050
Len Mattiace	74	67	68	76	285	28,050
Kirk Triplett	69	71	71	74	285	28,050
Bob Tway	68	68	74	75	285	28,050
Brett Quigley	70	69	74	72	285	28,050
Paul Stankowski	71	69	71	74	285	28,050
Doug Barron	69	72	74	70	285	28,050
Rory Sabbatini	73	65	72	75	285	28,050
Ken Green	74	67	73	72	286	19,350

		SCORES			TOTAL	MONEY
Neal Lancaster	71	65	75	75	286	19,350
Cliff Kresge	69	72	74	71	286	19,350
Chris Riley	72	67	72	75	286	19,350
Alex Cejka	73	70	70	73	286	19,350
Mathew Goggin	69	72	73	72	286	19,350
Joel Kribel	69	71	71	75	286	19,350
Brian Watts	69	71	72	75	287	13,605
Paul Goydos	74	67	72	74	287	13,605
David Berganio, Jr.	73	70	73	71	287	13,605
Dean Wilson	66	71	75	75	287	13,605
Brenden Pappas	73	70	75	69	287	13,605
J.J. Henry	75	67	70	75	287	13,605
Donnie Hammond	70	70	76	72	288	10,697.14
Woody Austin	73	69	75	71	288	10,697.14
Jeff Brehaut	70	73	70	75	288	10,697.14
Todd Fischer	72	70	73	73	288	10,697.14
Kenichi Kuboya	72	67	74	75	288	10,697.15
Pat Perez	69	71	73	75	288	10,697.15
Jonathan Byrd	72	71	73	72	288	10,697.14
Larry Mize	68	73	72	76	289	9,945
Corey Pavin	75	68	70	76	289	9,945
Thomas Levet	69	72	74	74	289	9,945
Anthony Painter	73	69	75	72	289	9,945
John Senden	72	68	75	74	289	9,945
John E. Morgan	67	72	74	76	289	9,945
Kevin Sutherland	74	69	74	73	290	9,495
Tom Gillis	71	71	75	73	290	9,495
Scott Laycock	77	66	72	75	290	9,495
Greg Chalmers	71	71	77	71	290	9,495
Geoff Ogilvy	75	68	74	74	291	9,270
Gene Sauers	74	68	78	72	292	9,135
Jose Coceres	72	68	73	79	292	9,135
Steve Flesch	71	69	75	78	293	8,955
Heath Slocum	71	72	73	77	293	8,955
Steve Jones	71	69	75	79	294	8,775
Aaron Baddeley	73	70	78	73	294	8,775
Notah Begay	75	67	74	84	300	8,640

Nissan Open

Riviera Country Club, Pacific Palisades, California
Par 35-36–71; 7,148 yards

February 20-23
purse, $4,500,000

		SCORES			TOTAL	MONEY
Mike Weir	72	68	69	66	275	$810,000
Charles Howell	69	65	68	73	275	486,000
(Weir defeated Howell on second playoff hole.)						
Fred Funk	65	74	70	68	277	261,000
Nick Price	68	67	70	72	277	261,000
Tiger Woods	72	68	73	65	278	171,000
K.J. Choi	70	69	67	72	278	171,000
Fred Couples	74	68	69	68	279	150,750
Len Mattiace	69	67	71	73	280	135,000
Chad Campbell	73	70	66	71	280	135,000
Bob Estes	69	71	68	73	281	96,428.57
Dan Forsman	76	66	70	69	281	96,428.57
Duffy Waldorf	70	69	70	72	281	96,428.57

	SCORES				TOTAL	MONEY
Marco Dawson	72	73	66	70	281	96,428.57
Shaun Micheel	74	69	72	66	281	96,428.58
Darren Clarke	71	74	68	68	281	96,428.57
Rich Beem	73	65	69	74	281	96,428.57
Steve Elkington	68	73	67	74	282	58,885.71
Stephen Ames	70	69	72	71	282	58,885.72
Brandt Jobe	74	67	67	74	282	58,885.71
Stewart Cink	73	67	69	73	282	58,885.71
Niclas Fasth	75	66	73	68	282	58,885.72
Brenden Pappas	74	67	72	69	282	58,885.72
Angel Cabrera	75	68	65	74	282	58,885.71
Olin Browne	72	73	70	68	283	38,362.50
Lee Janzen	70	71	72	70	283	38,362.50
Jeff Sluman	68	74	69	72	283	38,362.50
Hidemichi Tanaka	72	68	72	71	283	38,362.50
Corey Pavin	72	68	70	74	284	31,275
Loren Roberts	72	70	70	72	284	31,275
Brian Gay	71	74	67	72	284	31,275
Aaron Baddeley	69	71	72	72	284	31,275
Skip Kendall	71	71	72	71	285	25,470
Jim Furyk	74	70	71	70	285	25,470
Cameron Beckman	68	73	68	76	285	25,470
Arron Oberholser	73	69	71	72	285	25,470
Pat Perez	74	69	68	74	285	25,470
Craig Parry	76	66	74	70	286	20,250
Kevin Sutherland	72	70	71	73	286	20,250
Steve Flesch	74	70	71	71	286	20,250
Phil Tataurangi	72	70	74	70	286	20,250
Carl Pettersson	77	68	71	70	286	20,250
Jay Haas	73	69	74	71	287	14,875.71
Scott Verplank	75	70	69	73	287	14,875.72
Steve Stricker	72	69	74	72	287	14,875.72
Pat Bates	72	73	72	70	287	14,875.71
David Duval	69	70	73	75	287	14,875.71
Robert Allenby	72	69	73	73	287	14,875.72
Peter Lonard	75	69	73	70	287	14,875.71
Davis Love	76	69	71	72	288	11,520
Jeff Brehaut	73	72	70	73	288	11,520
Scott Hoch	74	71	73	71	289	10,732.50
Billy Mayfair	72	71	77	69	289	10,732.50
Chris Smith	74	69	70	76	289	10,732.50
Jerry Kelly	73	71	73	72	289	10,732.50
Rocco Mediate	73	72	70	75	290	10,215
Esteban Toledo	75	70	73	72	290	10,215
Glen Hnatiuk	69	74	72	75	290	10,215
Alex Cejka	73	71	73	73	290	10,215
John Cook	74	70	74	73	291	9,765
Bernhard Langer	72	72	73	74	291	9,765
David Berganio, Jr.	75	69	71	76	291	9,765
Paul Stankowski	75	70	76	70	291	9,765
Shigeki Maruyama	74	70	72	75	291	9,765
Joe Acosta, Jr.	71	72	73	75	291	9,765
Jeff Maggert	72	73	72	75	292	9,315
Per-Ulrik Johansson	74	71	75	72	292	9,315
Greg Chalmers	72	72	72	76	292	9,315
David Gossett	75	70	74	73	292	9,315
Tom Byrum	76	69	74	74	293	9,045
Ben Crane	71	74	72	76	293	9,045
Craig Barlow	72	71	73	78	294	8,910

	SCORES				TOTAL	MONEY
J.J. Henry	72	73	73	78	296	8,820
Craig Stadler	76	69	76	76	297	8,730
Bob Burns	73	70	79	76	298	8,640

WGC Accenture Match Play

La Costa Resort and Spa, Carlsbad, California
Par 36-36–72; 7,278 yards

February 26-March 2
purse, $6,000,000

FIRST ROUND

Tiger Woods defeated Carl Pettersson, 2 and 1.
K.J. Choi defeated Fred Funk, 1 up.
Justin Leonard defeated Jose Maria Olazabal, 2 up.
Stephen Leaney defeated Bob Estes, 2 and 1.
Padraig Harrington defeated John Cook, 4 and 3.
Scott Hoch defeated Tom Lehman, 3 and 1.
Toshimitsu Izawa defeated Chris DiMarco, 2 and 1.
Eduardo Romero defeated John Huston, 2 and 1.
Jay Haas defeated Retief Goosen, 5 and 3.
Shigeki Maruyama defeated Scott McCarron, 4 and 3.
Nick Price defeated Paul Lawrie, 4 and 3.
Niclas Fasth defeated Charles Howell, 1 up.
Kevin Sutherland defeated Sergio Garcia, 2 and 1.
Justin Rose defeated David Duval, 20 holes.
Rocco Mediate defeated Shingo Katayama, 1 up.
Adam Scott defeated Bernhard Langer, 3 and 2.
Phil Tataurangi defeated Ernie Els, 20 holes.
Peter Lonard defeated Kenny Perry, 2 and 1.
Robert Allenby defeated Trevor Immelman, 4 and 2.
Jeff Sluman defeated Michael Campbell, 3 and 2.
Davis Love defeated Paul Casey, 5 and 4.
Darren Clarke defeated Tim Clark, 4 and 3.
Jim Furyk defeated Len Mattiace, 2 and 1.
Steve Lowery defeated Rich Beem, 2 up.
Phil Mickelson defeated Robert Karlsson, 1 up.
Brad Faxon defeated Craig Parry, 2 and 1.
Mike Weir defeated Loren Roberts, 26 holes.
Jerry Kelly defeated Thomas Bjorn, 5 and 4.
David Toms defeated Anders Hansen, 3 and 1.
Chris Riley defeated Stuart Appleby, 1 up.
Alex Cejka defeated Colin Montgomerie, 4 and 2.
Angel Cabrera defeated Scott Verplank, 3 and 2.

(Each losing player received $30,000.)

SECOND ROUND

Woods defeated Choi, 5 and 3.
Leaney defeated Leonard, 6 and 5.
Hoch defeated Harrington, 3 and 2.
Izawa defeated Romero, 3 and 1.
Haas defeated Maruyama, 1 up.
Price defeated Fasth, 2 and 1.
Sutherland defeated Rose, 1 up.
Scott defeated Mediate, 1 up.
Lonard defeated Tataurangi, 5 and 4.
Allenby defeated Sluman, 1 up.

Clarke defeated Love, 7 and 6.
Furyk defeated Lowery, 6 and 5.
Mickelson defeated Faxon, 3 and 2.
Kelly defeated Weir, 2 and 1.
Toms defeated Riley, 1 up.
Cejka defeated Cabrera, 4 and 2.

(Each losing player received $60,000.)

THIRD ROUND

Woods defeated Leaney, 7 and 6.
Hoch defeated Izawa, 4 and 3.
Haas defeated Price, 20 holes.
Scott defeated Sutherland, 2 and 1.
Lonard defeated Allenby, 1 up.
Clarke defeated Furyk, 2 up.
Kelly defeated Mickelson, 3 and 2
Toms defeated Cejka, 1 up.

(Each losing player received $95,000.)

QUARTER-FINALS

Woods defeated Hoch, 5 and 4.
Scott defeated Haas, 2 and 1.
Lonard defeated Clarke, 2 up.
Toms defeated Kelly, 4 and 3.

(Each losing player received $200,000.)

SEMI-FINALS

Woods defeated Scott, 19 holes.
Toms defeated Lonard, 1 up.

PLAYOFF FOR THIRD-FOURTH PLACE

Scott defeated Lonard, 1 up.

(Scott earned $480,000; Lonard earned $390,000.)

FINAL

Woods defeated Toms, 2 and 1.

(Woods earned $1,050,000; Toms earned $600,000.)

Chrysler Classic of Tucson

Omni Tucson National Resort, Tucson, Arizona
Par 36-36–72; 7,109 yards

February 27-March 2
purse, $3,000,000

	SCORES				TOTAL	MONEY
Frank Lickliter	67	63	70	69	269	$540,000
Chad Campbell	70	71	63	67	271	324,000
Brenden Pappas	71	66	67	68	272	204,000
Bob Tway	71	67	68	67	273	132,000
Aaron Barber	71	71	66	65	273	132,000

	SCORES				TOTAL	MONEY
Andrew Magee	68	74	64	68	274	97,125
Dean Wilson	68	69	71	66	274	97,125
Stewart Cink	72	69	67	66	274	97,125
Arron Oberholser	69	67	70	68	274	97,125
Steve Flesch	70	70	64	71	275	75,000
Mike Sposa	73	70	66	66	275	75,000
Carlos Franco	72	66	68	69	275	75,000
Tom Byrum	69	69	67	71	276	54,600
Chris Smith	70	70	69	67	276	54,600
Kirk Triplett	70	67	72	67	276	54,600
Jeff Brehaut	68	69	69	70	276	54,600
Kent Jones	68	69	69	70	276	54,600
Brian Gay	67	66	76	68	277	40,500
Hidemichi Tanaka	75	69	67	66	277	40,500
Aaron Baddeley	66	71	68	72	277	40,500
*Ricky Barnes	69	70	68	70	277	
James McLean	71	70	68	68	277	40,500
Steve Elkington	73	71	67	67	278	31,200
Duffy Waldorf	71	69	68	70	278	31,200
Anthony Painter	71	73	67	67	278	31,200
Hal Sutton	69	71	71	68	279	23,400
Mike Heinen	70	73	67	69	279	23,400
Todd Barranger	72	64	72	71	279	23,400
Tim Herron	73	66	67	73	279	23,400
Carl Paulson	70	71	68	70	279	23,400
Dan Forsman	68	69	71	72	280	19,500
Jeff Klein	69	71	67	73	280	19,500
Gary Nicklaus	73	65	70	72	280	19,500
David Frost	73	70	68	70	281	14,550
David Peoples	71	68	70	72	281	14,550
David Berganio, Jr.	74	67	68	72	281	14,550
Brian Bateman	67	73	72	69	281	14,550
Woody Austin	70	73	69	69	281	14,550
Deane Pappas	72	68	72	69	281	14,550
Dicky Pride	65	72	73	71	281	14,550
Jonathan Kaye	72	72	69	68	281	14,550
J.J. Henry	70	71	67	73	281	14,550
Jeff Quinney	71	70	70	70	281	14,550
Glen Day	72	69	69	72	282	9,620
Notah Begay	71	71	68	72	282	9,620
Geoff Ogilvy	68	70	70	74	282	9,620
Joel Kribel	70	69	71	72	282	9,620
Andy Miller	71	66	68	77	282	9,620
Graeme McDowell	71	72	64	75	282	9,620
Jeff Gallagher	72	68	72	71	283	7,485
Cliff Kresge	70	72	66	75	283	7,485
Kenneth Staton	72	68	70	73	283	7,485
Richard S. Johnson	75	68	69	71	283	7,485
Esteban Toledo	71	70	68	75	284	6,912
John Maginnes	70	70	73	71	284	6,912
Mathew Goggin	73	70	70	71	284	6,912
Darron Stiles	74	70	69	71	284	6,912
Patrick Sheehan	73	69	71	71	284	6,912
Jim Carter	72	72	69	72	285	6,570
Corey Pavin	72	72	71	70	285	6,570
Brandt Jobe	69	72	74	70	285	6,570
Thomas Levet	73	71	70	71	285	6,570
Doug Barron	71	73	69	72	285	6,570
Mark Wilson	71	69	71	74	285	6,570
Neal Lancaster	75	69	72	70	286	6,300

	SCORES				TOTAL	MONEY
Brett Quigley	70	71	70	75	286	6,300
Rory Sabbatini	68	74	72	72	286	6,300
Billy Mayfair	72	71	74	70	287	6,030
David Sutherland	76	66	71	74	287	6,030
Jay Williamson	73	69	74	71	287	6,030
Cameron Beckman	74	69	73	71	287	6,030
Kenichi Kuboya	68	76	71	72	287	6,030
Cameron Yancey	73	71	72	71	287	6,030
Steve Pate	71	72	74	71	288	5,700
Dave Stockton, Jr.	72	72	71	73	288	5,700
Glen Hnatiuk	72	71	76	69	288	5,700f
David Gossett	71	71	68	78	288	5,700
John E. Morgan	77	63	77	71	288	5,700
Garrett Willis	69	68	72	80	289	5,490
Heath Slocum	72	72	68	77	289	5,490
Donnie Hammond	74	68	72	77	291	5,310
Grant Waite	67	73	73	78	291	5,310
Mike Grob	74	70	73	74	291	5,310
Jason Caron	69	74	74	74	291	5,310
Gabriel Hjertstedt	72	72	73	76	293	5,160
Jeff Maggert	67	75	77	75	294	5,070
Tim Petrovic	73	71	72	78	294	5,070
Bob May	70	74	80	72	296	4,980

Ford Championship at Doral

Doral Golf Resort & Spa, Blue Course, Miami, Florida
Par 36-36–72; 7,125 yards
(Playoff extended to Monday due to darkness.)

March 6-10
purse, $5,000,000

	SCORES				TOTAL	MONEY
Scott Hoch	66	70	66	69	271	$900,000
Jim Furyk	68	66	69	68	271	540,000
(Hoch defeated Furyk on third playoff hole.)						
Bob Tway	65	68	69	71	273	340,000
Tim Petrovic	70	72	65	67	274	240,000
Kenny Perry	69	71	71	64	275	182,500
Heath Slocum	68	71	69	67	275	182,500
Jonathan Byrd	75	68	66	66	275	182,500
Skip Kendall	68	74	65	69	276	140,000
Shaun Micheel	67	72	70	67	276	140,000
Cliff Kresge	71	66	68	71	276	140,000
Rodney Pampling	64	71	70	71	276	140,000
Davis Love	69	73	67	68	277	110,000
Mark Wilson	71	71	68	67	277	110,000
John Huston	74	68	68	68	278	77,500
Tom Pernice, Jr.	70	68	72	68	278	77,500
Mike Weir	70	67	67	74	278	77,500
Dean Wilson	75	66	67	70	278	77,500
Carlos Franco	67	68	68	75	278	77,500
Aaron Barber	72	71	67	68	278	77,500
Patrick Sheehan	72	69	69	68	278	77,500
J.J. Henry	69	70	72	67	278	77,500
Jeff Sluman	70	69	68	72	279	48,000
Brian Watts	69	71	71	68	279	48,000
Neal Lancaster	69	69	70	71	279	48,000
Woody Austin	71	68	70	70	279	48,000

	SCORES				TOTAL	MONEY
Glen Day	69	72	68	70	279	48,000
Steve Elkington	69	69	71	71	280	29,961.54
Robert Gamez	70	68	68	74	280	29,961.54
Billy Mayfair	68	72	65	75	280	29,961.53
Stephen Ames	68	69	73	70	280	29,961.54
Matt Peterson	68	70	70	72	280	29,961.54
Paul Goydos	69	71	68	72	280	29,961.54
Pat Bates	71	70	67	72	280	29,961.54
Mike Heinen	70	71	68	71	280	29,961.54
Brent Geiberger	67	70	71	72	280	29,961.54
Jose Coceres	68	71	70	71	280	29,961.54
Garrett Willis	76	67	70	67	280	29,961.54
John Senden	69	68	69	74	280	29,961.53
Ben Crane	69	69	72	70	280	29,961.54
Mark Calcavecchia	73	68	68	72	281	18,000
Loren Roberts	74	67	69	71	281	18,000
Marco Dawson	67	71	74	69	281	18,000
Esteban Toledo	68	74	68	71	281	18,000
Brett Quigley	71	69	68	73	281	18,000
Spike McRoy	72	69	69	71	281	18,000
J.P. Hayes	71	68	69	73	281	18,000
K.J. Choi	73	68	69	71	281	18,000
Jay Haas	73	69	67	73	282	12,566.66
Lee Janzen	72	67	72	71	282	12,566.67
Nick Price	70	73	69	70	282	12,566.67
Scott Verplank	72	71	71	68	282	12,566.67
Tim Herron	71	70	70	71	282	12,566.66
Greg Chalmers	73	70	68	71	282	12,566.67
Billy Andrade	70	73	69	71	283	11,150
Fred Funk	69	74	72	68	283	11,150
Peter Jacobsen	74	66	71	72	283	11,150
Gene Sauers	71	72	70	70	283	11,150
Glen Hnatiuk	75	67	72	69	283	11,150
John Maginnes	69	69	75	70	283	11,150
Per-Ulrik Johansson	69	70	70	74	283	11,150
Thomas Levet	66	74	71	72	283	11,150
Stuart Appleby	69	71	70	73	283	11,150
David Gossett	69	71	73	70	283	11,150
Olin Browne	69	69	70	76	284	10,150
Nick Faldo	71	70	69	74	284	10,150
Donnie Hammond	70	73	67	74	284	10,150
Len Mattiace	71	67	74	72	284	10,150
Mike Sposa	74	67	67	76	284	10,150
Carl Paulson	68	71	71	74	284	10,150
Scott Laycock	72	71	74	67	284	10,150
Brenden Pappas	73	69	73	69	284	10,150
Joel Kribel	71	72	69	72	284	10,150
Luke Donald	71	72	70	71	284	10,150
Hal Sutton	75	67	71	72	285	9,500
Chris Anderson	69	73	74	69	285	9,500
Hank Kuehne	70	71	72	72	285	9,500
Mark Brooks	69	74	71	72	286	9,200
Craig Barlow	71	72	75	68	286	9,200
Hidemichi Tanaka	71	67	73	75	286	9,200
John E. Morgan	72	69	72	74	287	9,000
Chris DiMarco	76	67	71	75	289	8,900
Craig Perks	70	71	74	75	290	8,800
Steven Alker	72	70	73	76	291	8,700
Steve Stricker	70	73	75	75	293	8,550
Brian Gay	72	71	76	74	293	8,550

Honda Classic

The Country Club of Mirasol, Palm Beach Gardens, Florida   March 13-16
Par 36-36–72; 7,157 yards   purse, $5,000,000

	SCORES				TOTAL	MONEY
Justin Leonard	63	70	64	67	264	$900,000
Davis Love	66	65	65	69	265	440,000
Chad Campbell	69	65	66	65	265	440,000
Tim Herron	69	63	70	64	266	240,000
Billy Mayfair	70	65	64	68	267	182,500
Jim Furyk	64	69	69	65	267	182,500
Notah Begay	63	67	69	68	267	182,500
Chris DiMarco	69	68	65	66	268	130,000
Brett Quigley	68	66	66	68	268	130,000
Woody Austin	66	70	63	69	268	130,000
Jerry Kelly	70	62	67	69	268	130,000
Brian Gay	67	67	67	67	268	130,000
John Rollins	71	65	65	67	268	130,000
Tom Byrum	67	64	68	70	269	80,000
Mark Calcavecchia	69	66	69	65	269	80,000
Bob Estes	66	67	70	66	269	80,000
Carlos Franco	67	67	65	70	269	80,000
Chris Riley	65	68	65	71	269	80,000
Geoff Ogilvy	70	64	69	66	269	80,000
Carl Pettersson	70	67	65	67	269	80,000
David Peoples	65	65	71	69	270	56,000
J.P. Hayes	69	68	68	65	270	56,000
Doug Barron	70	66	65	69	270	56,000
Peter Jacobsen	69	65	71	66	271	42,625
Brandt Jobe	67	67	69	68	271	42,625
Jay Williamson	67	66	68	70	271	42,625
Stewart Cink	67	68	69	67	271	42,625
Fred Funk	67	66	69	70	272	29,250
Robert Gamez	66	67	69	70	272	29,250
John Huston	68	64	71	69	272	29,250
Esteban Toledo	64	67	71	70	272	29,250
Neal Lancaster	69	64	68	71	272	29,250
Shaun Micheel	67	67	66	72	272	29,250
Joe Durant	67	68	68	69	272	29,250
Bob Burns	70	64	70	68	272	29,250
Jeff Brehaut	63	68	69	72	272	29,250
Hidemichi Tanaka	68	66	68	70	272	29,250
Arron Oberholser	70	64	70	68	272	29,250
Aaron Barber	69	65	67	71	272	29,250
Bernhard Langer	68	65	71	69	273	18,000
Mark O'Meara	68	66	66	73	273	18,000
Kenny Perry	69	68	68	68	273	18,000
Dudley Hart	70	68	70	65	273	18,000
Glen Day	69	64	71	69	273	18,000
Robert Allenby	71	67	69	66	273	18,000
Briny Baird	67	70	66	70	273	18,000
J.J. Henry	70	65	71	67	273	18,000
Billy Andrade	71	65	67	71	274	12,211.11
Mark Brooks	67	69	68	70	274	12,211.12
Skip Kendall	70	67	69	68	274	12,211.11
Per-Ulrik Johansson	68	70	68	68	274	12,211.11
Cameron Beckman	67	70	69	68	274	12,211.11
Carl Paulson	67	70	67	70	274	12,211.11
John Senden	64	70	71	69	274	12,211.11

	SCORES				TOTAL	MONEY
Charles Howell	69	68	69	68	274	12,211.11
Ben Crane	71	67	69	67	274	12,211.11
Hal Sutton	67	66	72	70	275	10,950
Duffy Waldorf	70	65	73	67	275	10,950
Mike Heinen	70	67	69	69	275	10,950
Brent Geiberger	68	70	67	70	275	10,950
Rodney Pampling	71	67	68	69	275	10,950
Aaron Baddeley	66	69	74	66	275	10,950
Justin Rose	70	65	71	69	275	10,950
Akio Sadakata	67	68	71	69	275	10,950
Ken Green	67	69	68	72	276	10,450
Adam Scott	71	67	76	62	276	10,450
Jesper Parnevik	68	67	71	71	277	10,150
Todd Fischer	68	70	72	67	277	10,150
Garrett Willis	72	66	70	69	277	10,150
Alan Morin	70	68	72	67	277	10,150
Mathew Goggin	73	65	71	69	278	9,850
Matt Kuchar	70	67	72	69	278	9,850
Brad Faxon	69	68	69	73	279	9,700
Pat Bates	69	69	71	71	280	9,600
Glen Hnatiuk	70	68	72	71	281	9,500
Robert Damron	70	68	72	72	282	9,400
Richard S. Johnson	70	66	76	74	286	9,300

Bay Hill Invitational

Bay Hill Club & Lodge, Orlando, Florida
Par 36-36–72; 7,239 yards

March 20-23
purse, $4,500,000

	SCORES				TOTAL	MONEY
Tiger Woods	70	65	66	68	269	$810,000
Brad Faxon	70	71	65	74	280	297,000
Kenny Perry	72	68	69	71	280	297,000
Kirk Triplett	73	69	68	70	280	297,000
Stewart Cink	69	69	70	72	280	297,000
Aaron Baddeley	69	70	70	72	281	162,000
J.L. Lewis	69	73	73	67	282	140,250
Jeff Sluman	75	69	68	70	282	140,250
Jerry Kelly	76	66	70	70	282	140,250
Billy Andrade	72	71	69	71	283	93,375
Stephen Ames	73	70	66	74	283	93,375
Steve Flesch	72	72	68	71	283	93,375
Jeff Brehaut	75	70	69	69	283	93,375
Jonathan Kaye	69	70	73	71	283	93,375
Ben Crane	70	73	68	72	283	93,375
Pat Perez	74	69	69	71	283	93,375
Ty Tryon	73	67	74	69	283	93,375
Tim Petrovic	73	70	72	69	284	65,250
Scott Verplank	71	72	67	74	284	65,250
Robert Gamez	70	71	70	74	285	50,580
John Huston	73	70	66	76	285	50,580
Duffy Waldorf	72	68	73	72	285	50,580
Vijay Singh	75	67	74	69	285	50,580
J.P. Hayes	77	69	70	69	285	50,580
Nick Faldo	70	74	68	74	286	34,350
Skip Kendall	74	70	67	75	286	34,350
Marco Dawson	70	70	72	74	286	34,350

	SCORES				TOTAL	MONEY
Stephen Leaney	73	68	69	76	286	34,350
Adam Scott	75	72	72	67	286	34,350
Carl Pettersson	75	68	71	72	286	34,350
Craig Parry	75	72	69	71	287	25,521.42
Colin Montgomerie	75	70	70	72	287	25,521.43
Niclas Fasth	72	68	76	71	287	25,521.43
Arron Oberholser	75	71	68	73	287	25,521.43
Peter Lonard	71	69	75	72	287	25,521.43
K.J. Choi	75	69	71	72	287	25,521.43
Jonathan Byrd	76	71	67	73	287	25,521.43
Jeff Maggert	69	72	70	77	288	19,800
Ernie Els	74	65	72	77	288	19,800
Darren Clarke	74	68	72	74	288	19,800
Alex Cejka	73	70	70	75	288	19,800
Dan Forsman	72	70	71	76	289	14,130
Steve Lowery	73	67	76	73	289	14,130
Len Mattiace	71	76	71	71	289	14,130
Shaun Micheel	73	71	72	73	289	14,130
Matt Gogel	73	72	70	74	289	14,130
Rodney Pampling	72	67	74	76	289	14,130
Charles Howell	75	72	71	71	289	14,130
Ben Curtis	75	70	71	73	289	14,130
David Gossett	71	71	72	75	289	14,130
Mark O'Meara	72	74	70	75	291	10,656
Eduardo Romero	72	72	73	74	291	10,656
Greg Kraft	75	72	73	71	291	10,656
Matt Kuchar	71	73	74	73	291	10,656
Andy Miller	73	72	72	74	291	10,656
Rocco Mediate	76	70	73	73	292	9,990
Joey Sindelar	74	72	73	73	292	9,990
Dudley Hart	75	72	70	75	292	9,990
Tim Herron	75	71	71	75	292	9,990
Angel Cabrera	75	70	72	75	292	9,990
Justin Rose	75	71	70	76	292	9,990
Tim Clark	76	68	71	77	292	9,990
John Daly	71	73	70	79	293	9,585
Chris Smith	74	73	72	74	293	9,585
Cameron Beckman	76	69	71	78	294	9,405
Stuart Appleby	74	71	72	77	294	9,405
Jose Maria Olazabal	75	72	71	77	295	9,090
Dean Wilson	75	71	76	73	295	9,090
Robert Damron	76	70	72	77	295	9,090
Lee Westwood	72	74	71	78	295	9,090
Harrison Frazar	75	70	72	78	295	9,090
Mark Brooks	75	72	68	81	296	8,775
Peter Jacobsen	74	70	72	80	296	8,775
Larry Mize	74	73	72	79	298	8,595
Chad Campbell	76	70	73	79	298	8,595
Tom Pernice, Jr.	77	70	74	79	300	8,460
Paul Goydos	75	72	75	79	301	8,370
Geoff Ogilvy	74	72	80	76	302	8,280
Scott Hoch	78	69	76	82	305	8,190

The Players Championship

TPC at Sawgrass, Stadium Course,
Ponte Vedra Beach, Florida
Par 36-36–72; 7,093 yards

March 27-30
purse, $6,000,000

	SCORES				TOTAL	MONEY
Davis Love	70	67	70	64	271	$1,170,000
Jay Haas	68	70	67	72	277	572,000
Padraig Harrington	67	68	70	72	277	572,000
Jim Furyk	73	68	68	69	278	286,000
Robert Allenby	70	71	72	65	278	286,000
Chad Campbell	72	66	71	70	279	225,875
Darren Clarke	71	70	67	71	279	225,875
Kirk Triplett	72	70	71	67	280	195,000
Scott Verplank	71	72	68	69	280	195,000
Fred Couples	67	71	69	74	281	175,500
Mark Calcavecchia	73	68	72	69	282	133,250
Brad Faxon	73	69	71	69	282	133,250
Jeff Maggert	71	70	68	73	282	133,250
Duffy Waldorf	70	72	68	72	282	133,250
Tiger Woods	72	70	68	72	282	133,250
Briny Baird	76	68	68	70	282	133,250
Bob Tway	68	73	69	73	283	94,250
Stephen Ames	73	69	71	70	283	94,250
Craig Perks	68	69	70	76	283	94,250
Adam Scott	69	69	74	71	283	94,250
Chris DiMarco	77	67	70	70	284	65,000
Justin Leonard	73	70	68	73	284	65,000
Stuart Appleby	71	72	71	70	284	65,000
Niclas Fasth	68	73	71	72	284	65,000
Geoff Ogilvy	71	68	72	73	284	65,000
Tim Clark	69	72	69	74	284	65,000
Neal Lancaster	70	72	69	74	285	47,125
Glen Day	72	67	73	73	285	47,125
Mike Weir	72	71	69	73	285	47,125
Jay Williamson	74	69	68	74	285	47,125
Bob Estes	71	68	72	75	286	42,250
Skip Kendall	68	69	73	77	287	35,192.85
Corey Pavin	70	69	69	79	287	35,192.85
Kenny Perry	70	73	69	75	287	35,192.86
Jeff Sluman	72	72	70	73	287	35,192.86
Brandt Jobe	72	70	70	75	287	35,192.86
Jonathan Kaye	73	70	70	74	287	35,192.86
Charles Howell	72	71	72	72	287	35,192.86
Nick Faldo	74	68	72	74	288	26,000
Tom Lehman	69	72	75	72	288	26,000
Steve Flesch	71	68	70	79	288	26,000
Glen Hnatiuk	71	72	71	74	288	26,000
Stewart Cink	69	71	73	75	288	26,000
Justin Rose	72	71	69	76	288	26,000
Fred Funk	70	70	75	74	289	20,150
Rocco Mediate	68	70	73	78	289	20,150
Shigeki Maruyama	76	65	74	74	289	20,150
Billy Andrade	71	72	73	74	290	16,336.67
Bernhard Langer	72	70	71	77	290	16,336.66
Kevin Sutherland	69	73	72	76	290	16,336.67
Per-Ulrik Johansson	73	70	75	72	290	16,336.67
Jesper Parnevik	76	68	69	77	290	16,336.66
Carlos Franco	71	71	72	76	290	16,336.67

	SCORES				TOTAL	MONEY
Shaun Micheel	71	73	71	76	291	15,015
Tim Herron	71	73	72	75	291	15,015
John Daly	70	70	72	80	292	14,495
Esteban Toledo	74	69	72	77	292	14,495
David Berganio, Jr.	75	69	72	76	292	14,495
Paul Lawrie	71	73	74	74	292	14,495
Notah Begay	77	67	76	72	292	14,495
Peter Lonard	73	68	71	80	292	14,495
Mark Brooks	73	70	75	75	293	13,845
Steve Jones	68	75	76	74	293	13,845
Dudley Hart	75	69	75	74	293	13,845
Joe Durant	75	67	75	76	293	13,845
Bob Burns	74	70	72	78	294	13,455
Matt Gogel	70	71	77	76	294	13,455
Lee Janzen	73	69	70	83	295	13,260
Jim Carter	69	73	77	80	299	13,065
Robert Gamez	71	73	74	81	299	13,065
Loren Roberts	75	69	78	78	300	12,870

BellSouth Classic

TPC at Sugarloaf, Duluth, Georgia
Par 36-36–72; 7,293 yards

April 3-6
purse, $4,000,000

	SCORES				TOTAL	MONEY
Ben Crane	73	72	64	63	272	$720,000
Bob Tway	70	66	69	71	276	432,000
Jay Williamson	68	72	70	67	277	208,000
Retief Goosen	68	70	74	65	277	208,000
Hank Kuehne	71	69	67	70	277	208,000
Tom Pernice, Jr.	70	70	66	72	278	134,000
Stewart Cink	72	70	67	69	278	134,000
John Rollins	72	69	68	69	278	134,000
Chris DiMarco	67	72	72	68	279	104,000
Paul Lawrie	72	68	71	68	279	104,000
Brenden Pappas	71	69	69	70	279	104,000
J.J. Henry	70	71	67	71	279	104,000
Billy Andrade	68	71	69	72	280	70,666.66
Fred Couples	69	73	69	69	280	70,666.67
Lee Janzen	69	67	67	77	280	70,666.66
Skip Kendall	72	69	71	68	280	70,666.67
Esteban Toledo	71	68	70	71	280	70,666.67
Kevin Sutherland	72	71	70	67	280	70,666.67
Olin Browne	70	71	68	72	281	50,200
Deane Pappas	75	69	68	69	281	50,200
Briny Baird	72	68	71	70	281	50,200
Scott Laycock	72	72	67	70	281	50,200
Mark Calcavecchia	69	75	71	68	283	35,600
Donnie Hammond	73	70	75	65	283	35,600
David Sutherland	74	69	71	69	283	35,600
Mike Sposa	71	70	72	70	283	35,600
Hidemichi Tanaka	73	70	70	70	283	35,600
Jim Carter	71	72	69	72	284	27,200
David Toms	73	71	69	71	284	27,200
Brandt Jobe	70	71	70	73	284	27,200
Todd Barranger	73	71	71	69	284	27,200
James McLean	72	70	70	72	284	27,200

	SCORES				TOTAL	MONEY
John Huston	70	72	70	73	285	21,133.33
Steve Jones	71	70	70	74	285	21,133.33
Larry Mize	71	72	72	70	285	21,133.34
Mike Grob	76	69	71	69	285	21,133.33
Brent Geiberger	73	71	68	73	285	21,133.33
Carlos Franco	72	70	73	70	285	21,133.34
Blaine McCallister	75	71	69	71	286	16,400
Joey Sindelar	69	71	71	75	286	16,400
Brad Lardon	68	72	76	70	286	16,400
Brian Bateman	75	68	73	70	286	16,400
Michael Clark	71	75	72	68	286	16,400
J.L. Lewis	74	71	71	71	287	11,342.22
Jeff Gallagher	71	69	71	76	287	11,342.22
Steve Stricker	73	70	74	70	287	11,342.22
Brett Quigley	73	72	70	72	287	11,342.23
Jesper Parnevik	74	72	70	71	287	11,342.22
Thomas Levet	73	67	75	72	287	11,342.22
Garrett Willis	77	68	73	69	287	11,342.22
Brent Schwarzrock	72	71	72	72	287	11,342.23
John E. Morgan	69	71	75	72	287	11,342.22
Bob May	75	68	73	72	288	9,260
Mathew Goggin	71	74	71	72	288	9,260
Kenichi Kuboya	73	68	73	74	288	9,260
Akio Sadakata	71	72	71	74	288	9,260
Bob Burns	68	77	73	71	289	8,960
Mike Heinen	70	73	75	71	289	8,960
Cameron Yancey	72	68	74	75	289	8,960
Doug Barron	74	69	74	73	290	8,800
Dan Forsman	74	70	75	72	291	8,560
Corey Pavin	72	74	73	72	291	8,560
Glen Day	73	71	74	73	291	8,560
Darron Stiles	72	71	72	76	291	8,560
Andy Miller	71	75	69	76	291	8,560
Andrew Magee	74	69	77	73	293	8,240
Todd Fischer	73	71	73	76	293	8,240
Steve Allan	75	71	69	78	293	8,240
Nolan Henke	76	69	73	76	294	8,000
Harrison Frazar	76	70	75	73	294	8,000
Carl Pettersson	71	68	75	80	294	8,000
Mark Wilson	74	71	76	74	295	7,800
Ben Curtis	72	72	76	75	295	7,800
Scott Dunlap	72	71	80	74	297	7,600
Glen Hnatiuk	72	71	80	74	297	7,600
Ryuji Imada	76	70	73	78	297	7,600

Masters Tournament

Augusta National Golf Club, Augusta, Georgia
Par 36-36–72; 7,290 yards

April 10-13
purse, $6,000,000

	SCORES				TOTAL	MONEY
Mike Weir	70	68	75	68	281	$1,080,000
Len Mattiace	73	74	69	65	281	648,000
(Weir defeated Mattiace on first playoff hole.)						
Phil Mickelson	73	70	72	68	283	408,000
Jim Furyk	73	72	71	68	284	288,000
Jeff Maggert	72	73	66	75	286	240,000

	SCORES				TOTAL	MONEY
Ernie Els	79	66	72	70	287	208,500
Vijay Singh	73	71	70	73	287	208,500
Mark O'Meara	76	71	70	71	288	162,000
David Toms	71	73	70	74	288	162,000
Scott Verplank	76	73	70	69	288	162,000
Jose Maria Olazabal	73	71	71	73	288	162,000
Jonathan Byrd	74	71	71	72	288	162,000
Retief Goosen	73	74	72	70	289	120,000
Tim Clark	72	75	71	71	289	120,000
Davis Love	77	71	71	71	290	93,000
Tiger Woods	76	73	66	75	290	93,000
Paul Lawrie	72	72	73	73	290	93,000
Angel Cabrera	76	71	71	72	290	93,000
Rich Beem	74	72	71	73	290	93,000
K.J. Choi	76	69	72	73	290	93,000
*Ricky Barnes	69	74	75	73	291	
Bob Estes	76	71	74	71	292	72,000
Brad Faxon	73	71	79	70	293	57,600
Nick Price	70	75	72	76	293	57,600
Scott McCarron	77	71	72	73	293	57,600
Chris Riley	76	72	70	75	293	57,600
Adam Scott	77	72	74	70	293	57,600
Fred Couples	73	75	69	77	294	43,500
Darren Clarke	66	76	78	74	294	43,500
Sergio Garcia	69	78	74	73	294	43,500
Charles Howell	73	72	76	73	294	43,500
*Hunter Mahan	73	72	73	76	294	
Nick Faldo	74	73	75	73	295	36,375
Rocco Mediate	73	74	73	75	295	36,375
Loren Roberts	74	72	76	73	295	36,375
Kevin Sutherland	77	72	76	70	295	36,375
Billy Mayfair	75	70	77	74	296	31,650
Shingo Katayama	74	72	76	74	296	31,650
Craig Parry	74	73	75	75	297	27,000
Kenny Perry	76	72	78	71	297	27,000
Robert Allenby	76	73	74	74	297	27,000
Phil Tataurangi	75	70	74	78	297	27,000
Justin Rose	73	76	71	77	297	27,000
Jeff Sluman	75	72	76	75	298	23,400
Pat Perez	74	73	79	75	301	22,200
*Ryan Moore	73	74	75	79	301	
John Rollins	74	71	80	77	302	21,000
Jerry Kelly	72	76	77	79	304	19,800
Craig Stadler	76	73	79	77	305	18,600

Out of Final 36 Holes

			TOTAL	
Scott Hoch	77	73	150	
Eduardo Romero	74	76	150	
Shigeki Maruyama	75	75	150	
Padraig Harrington	77	73	150	
Toru Taniguchi	71	79	150	
Steve Elkington	75	76	151	
Lee Janzen	78	73	151	
Tom Lehman	75	76	151	
Larry Mize	78	74	152	
Tom Watson	75	77	152	
Miguel Angel Jimenez	76	77	153	
Stuart Appleby	77	76	153	
Steve Lowery	78	76	154	

	SCORES			TOTAL	
Kirk Triplett	82	72		154	
Ian Woosnam	80	74		154	
Colin Montgomerie	78	76		154	
Toshimitsu Izawa	78	76		154	
Chad Campbell	77	77		154	
Niclas Fasth	81	73		154	
Ben Crenshaw	79	76		155	
Fred Funk	79	76		155	
Jay Haas	79	76		155	
Bernhard Langer	79	76		155	
Sandy Lyle	82	73		155	
Fuzzy Zoeller	77	78		155	
Justin Leonard	82	73		155	
Craig Perks	80	75		155	
Michael Campbell	78	77		155	
John Cook	78	78		156	
John Huston	73	83		156	
Thomas Levet	79	77		156	
Tom Byrum	82	75		157	
Raymond Floyd	77	80		157	
Peter Lonard	78	82		160	
Seve Ballesteros	77	85		162	
Jack Nicklaus	85	77		162	
Gary Player	82	80		162	
David Duval	79	83		162	
Alejandro Larrazabal	82	81		163	
Charles Coody	83	81		164	
Arnold Palmer	83	83		166	
George Zahringer	82	85		167	
Tommy Aaron	92	80		172	
Chris DiMarco	82			WD	

(Professionals who did not complete 72 holes received $5,000.)

MCI Heritage

Harbour Town Golf Links, Hilton Head Island, South Carolina   April 17-20
Par 36-35–71; 6,916 yards   purse, $4,500,000

	SCORES				TOTAL	MONEY
Davis Love	66	69	69	67	271	$810,000
Woody Austin	68	70	65	68	271	486,000
(Love defeated Austin on fourth playoff hole.)						
Hal Sutton	67	66	71	68	272	216,000
Chris Riley	69	70	66	67	272	216,000
Geoff Ogilvy	68	67	70	67	272	216,000
David Gossett	71	67	68	66	272	216,000
Tom Pernice, Jr.	67	70	68	68	273	140,250
Steve Flesch	68	69	67	69	273	140,250
Matt Gogel	69	67	69	68	273	140,250
Bob Estes	69	72	66	67	274	93,375
Peter Jacobsen	69	69	67	69	274	93,375
Jeff Sluman	68	70	64	72	274	93,375
Ernie Els	69	66	70	69	274	93,375
Glen Hnatiuk	69	68	69	68	274	93,375
Jim Furyk	70	66	69	69	274	93,375
Stewart Cink	67	65	69	73	274	93,375

		SCORES			TOTAL	MONEY
Rodney Pampling	67	72	67	68	274	93,375
Kenny Perry	67	69	67	72	275	60,750
Glen Day	70	70	71	64	275	60,750
Chad Campbell	67	67	70	71	275	60,750
Tim Clark	68	69	69	69	275	60,750
Tom Lehman	69	73	68	66	276	50,400
Skip Kendall	72	68	68	69	277	41,400
Corey Pavin	69	68	69	71	277	41,400
Jay Williamson	68	72	71	66	277	41,400
Dean Wilson	74	66	70	67	277	41,400
Fred Funk	72	69	68	69	278	29,953.13
Nick Price	68	66	71	73	278	29,953.12
Scott Simpson	67	71	70	70	278	29,953.13
Brandt Jobe	68	74	68	68	278	29,953.13
Paul Goydos	69	69	68	72	278	29,953.12
Briny Baird	69	70	72	67	278	29,953.13
John Senden	66	71	69	72	278	29,953.12
Trevor Immelman	72	69	67	70	278	29,953.12
Mark Calcavecchia	69	66	72	72	279	23,175
Darren Clarke	70	69	71	69	279	23,175
Doug Barron	71	67	67	74	279	23,175
Bernhard Langer	71	70	70	69	280	17,550
Len Mattiace	68	73	68	71	280	17,550
Rocco Mediate	67	70	70	73	280	17,550
Scott Verplank	70	68	73	69	280	17,550
Joe Durant	70	70	74	66	280	17,550
Jesper Parnevik	73	69	74	64	280	17,550
Cliff Kresge	70	70	67	73	280	17,550
Robert Damron	69	72	69	70	280	17,550
Garrett Willis	69	72	69	70	280	17,550
Billy Andrade	70	71	73	67	281	11,300
Robert Gamez	72	68	70	71	281	11,300
Donnie Hammond	74	63	72	72	281	11,300
Steve Jones	74	68	69	70	281	11,300
Bob Tway	71	67	72	71	281	11,300
Pat Bates	71	69	69	72	281	11,300
Justin Leonard	71	71	68	71	281	11,300
Kelly Mitchum	68	72	74	67	281	11,300
Craig Barlow	65	76	71	69	281	11,300
Per-Ulrik Johansson	73	69	69	71	282	10,215
Jonathan Byrd	70	71	69	72	282	10,215
David Edwards	72	67	70	74	283	9,945
Lee Janzen	70	69	73	71	283	9,945
Gene Sauers	70	72	70	71	283	9,945
Greg Chalmers	67	72	69	75	283	9,945
Billy Mayfair	70	69	73	72	284	9,540
Loren Roberts	71	70	72	71	284	9,540
Ian Leggatt	72	68	72	72	284	9,540
Tim Herron	72	70	72	70	284	9,540
Patrick Sheehan	71	71	72	70	284	9,540
Andrew Magee	74	67	72	72	285	9,225
D.A. Weibring	69	72	71	73	285	9,225
Mark O'Meara	70	71	70	75	286	8,910
Dudley Hart	73	68	72	73	286	8,910
Todd Barranger	68	72	69	77	286	8,910
Luke Donald	73	68	75	70	286	8,910
Carl Pettersson	69	71	74	72	286	8,910
Tom Byrum	70	72	71	74	287	8,595
Thomas Levet	70	71	73	73	287	8,595

	SCORES				TOTAL	MONEY
Shaun Micheel	72	70	71	75	288	8,370
John Maginnes	73	69	73	73	288	8,370
Carl Paulson	69	73	73	73	288	8,370
Joel Edwards	69	72	74	74	289	8,190

Shell Houston Open

Redstone Golf Club, Humble, Texas
Par 36-36–72; 7,508 yards

April 24-27
purse, $4,500,000

	SCORES				TOTAL	MONEY
Fred Couples	65	68	67	67	267	$810,000
Mark Calcavecchia	68	65	68	70	271	336,000
Stuart Appleby	66	70	66	69	271	336,000
Hank Kuehne	69	64	72	66	271	336,000
Jay Haas	67	67	70	68	272	180,000
Jeff Maggert	71	66	72	64	273	162,000
John Daly	69	69	67	70	275	145,125
Geoff Ogilvy	70	69	68	68	275	145,125
Peter Jacobsen	67	71	69	69	276	117,000
Vijay Singh	67	68	70	71	276	117,000
Kevin Sutherland	69	70	67	70	276	117,000
Steve Flesch	72	66	67	71	276	117,000
John Riegger	70	68	67	72	277	84,375
David Sutherland	69	67	68	73	277	84,375
Scott McCarron	69	68	67	73	277	84,375
Carlos Franco	73	67	68	69	277	84,375
Robert Gamez	71	66	67	74	278	65,250
Ernie Els	69	69	69	71	278	65,250
Briny Baird	67	71	68	72	278	65,250
Trevor Immelman	70	68	65	75	278	65,250
Bob May	69	68	69	73	279	43,521.43
Paul Stankowski	69	66	71	73	279	43,521.43
Chad Campbell	68	72	67	72	279	43,521.43
Garrett Willis	72	68	69	70	279	43,521.43
Alex Cejka	70	70	66	73	279	43,521.43
Greg Chalmers	73	68	64	74	279	43,521.42
Darron Stiles	70	70	67	72	279	43,521.43
Olin Browne	67	70	69	74	280	31,950
Jim Carter	71	69	68	72	280	31,950
Phil Mickelson	70	69	68	73	280	31,950
Tom Pernice, Jr.	66	70	71	74	281	24,975
Shaun Micheel	70	69	69	73	281	24,975
Jerry Kelly	69	69	71	72	281	24,975
Jeff Brehaut	69	71	67	74	281	24,975
Thomas Levet	72	68	70	71	281	24,975
Arron Oberholser	69	69	71	72	281	24,975
Ben Curtis	72	69	70	70	281	24,975
Kenneth Staton	69	70	70	72	281	24,975
Tom Byrum	71	70	72	69	282	18,450
Marco Dawson	71	70	66	75	282	18,450
Cameron Beckman	69	72	69	72	282	18,450
Heath Slocum	70	70	73	69	282	18,450
Ben Crane	69	69	69	75	282	18,450
Fred Funk	69	69	70	75	283	13,986
Brian Bateman	74	67	70	72	283	13,986
Ian Leggatt	68	69	71	75	283	13,986

		SCORES			TOTAL	MONEY
John Senden	71	70	70	72	283	13,986
Patrick Sheehan	68	73	70	72	283	13,986
David Peoples	66	70	75	73	284	10,750
David Toms	70	66	73	75	284	10,750
Paul Goydos	69	72	69	74	284	10,750
David Berganio, Jr.	67	73	72	72	284	10,750
Deane Pappas	68	71	68	77	284	10,750
Justin Leonard	71	67	72	74	284	10,750
Robert Damron	70	70	73	71	284	10,750
Hidemichi Tanaka	70	71	71	72	284	10,750
Richard S. Johnson	70	70	73	71	284	10,750
Tom Gillis	71	70	68	76	285	10,035
Rory Sabbatini	68	70	69	78	285	10,035
Andrew Magee	68	69	73	76	286	9,810
Neal Lancaster	69	71	69	77	286	9,810
Brandt Jobe	68	71	69	78	286	9,810
Dan Forsman	72	69	73	73	287	9,495
Brian Henninger	70	70	73	74	287	9,495
Woody Austin	69	70	69	79	287	9,495
Harrison Frazar	70	68	75	74	287	9,495
Phil Blackmar	70	71	72	77	290	9,225
David Frost	73	68	73	76	290	9,225
Carl Paulson	67	74	73	78	292	9,090
Jose Coceres	67	71	74	85	297	9,000

HP Classic of New Orleans

English Turn Golf & Country Club, May 1-4
New Orleans, Louisiana purse, $5,000,000
Par 36-36–72; 7,116 yards

		SCORES			TOTAL	MONEY
Steve Flesch	67	70	65	65	267	$900,000
Bob Estes	66	66	66	69	267	540,000
(Flesch defeated Estes on first playoff hole.)						
Scott Verplank	65	63	67	74	269	340,000
Mark Wilson	65	67	69	69	270	240,000
J.L. Lewis	68	68	65	70	271	190,000
Jerry Kelly	67	69	65	70	271	190,000
Woody Austin	66	72	65	69	272	167,500
David Frost	70	65	71	67	273	145,000
Chris DiMarco	69	68	65	71	273	145,000
Briny Baird	68	71	66	68	273	145,000
Jeff Sluman	65	69	66	74	274	106,000
Vijay Singh	67	68	69	70	274	106,000
Brian Bateman	66	70	70	68	274	106,000
Paul Stankowski	64	69	71	70	274	106,000
Patrick Sheehan	68	69	72	65	274	106,000
Skip Kendall	68	69	67	71	275	65,666.67
Davis Love	65	67	71	72	275	65,666.67
Steve Lowery	71	64	73	67	275	65,666.67
John Riegger	66	68	68	73	275	65,666.67
Kirk Triplett	66	66	67	76	275	65,666.66
Scott McCarron	70	67	66	72	275	65,666.67
Mike Sposa	73	63	71	68	275	65,666.67
Brian Gay	65	66	68	76	275	65,666.66
Stuart Appleby	71	68	63	73	275	65,666.66

	SCORES				TOTAL	MONEY
Tom Pernice, Jr.	67	70	69	70	276	39,000
Esteban Toledo	69	70	67	70	276	39,000
Pat Bates	68	68	71	69	276	39,000
Greg Chalmers	70	66	68	72	276	39,000
Geoff Ogilvy	67	67	69	73	276	39,000
Stephen Ames	65	68	70	74	277	29,714.28
Shaun Micheel	69	68	71	69	277	29,714.29
David Sutherland	68	68	70	71	277	29,714.29
Jay Williamson	69	65	69	74	277	29,714.28
Brent Geiberger	68	68	72	69	277	29,714.29
Stewart Cink	65	72	68	72	277	29,714.28
Jason Caron	70	68	69	70	277	29,714.29
Kent Jones	72	67	69	70	278	22,000
Cameron Beckman	69	69	69	71	278	22,000
Todd Barranger	66	65	76	71	278	22,000
Lee Westwood	69	67	69	73	278	22,000
Darron Stiles	66	68	73	71	278	22,000
K.J. Choi	65	70	73	70	278	22,000
Mark Brooks	69	69	71	70	279	15,600
Dan Forsman	71	67	75	66	279	15,600
Jeff Brehaut	70	67	68	74	279	15,600
Cliff Kresge	70	69	68	72	279	15,600
Chris Riley	68	70	68	73	279	15,600
Hank Kuehne	70	68	71	70	279	15,600
Akio Sadakata	64	68	72	75	279	15,600
Gene Sauers	69	70	72	69	280	11,966.67
Bob May	69	67	71	73	280	11,966.67
Carlos Franco	71	65	73	71	280	11,966.67
Hidemichi Tanaka	70	69	69	72	280	11,966.67
Mathew Goggin	70	69	68	73	280	11,966.66
Charles Howell	68	70	69	73	280	11,966.66
Billy Andrade	73	66	66	76	281	11,000
Joel Edwards	69	70	70	72	281	11,000
Billy Mayfair	66	71	71	73	281	11,000
Mike Heinen	71	68	70	72	281	11,000
Michael Clark	70	67	73	71	281	11,000
Jesper Parnevik	70	68	68	75	281	11,000
John Senden	71	67	70	73	281	11,000
Brent Schwarzrock	67	70	68	76	281	11,000
Cameron Yancey	66	68	68	79	281	11,000
Craig Perks	69	70	74	69	282	10,450
Heath Slocum	70	69	69	74	282	10,450
Kelly Gibson	71	68	73	71	283	10,100
Phil Mickelson	70	69	67	77	283	10,100
Hal Sutton	69	70	72	72	283	10,100
Brian Watts	70	68	72	73	283	10,100
John Rollins	69	70	75	69	283	10,100
Rich Beem	69	68	72	75	284	9,800
Chris Smith	71	68	70	76	285	9,650
Chris Anderson	68	71	65	81	285	9,650
Ben Curtis	68	69	73	76	286	9,500
Todd Fischer	66	73	70	78	287	9,400

Wachovia Championship

Quail Hollow Club, Charlotte, North Carolina
Par 36-36–72; 7,360 yards

May 8-11
purse, $5,600,000

	SCORES				TOTAL	MONEY
David Toms	70	69	66	73	278	$1,008,000
Robert Gamez	72	67	71	70	280	418,133.33
Vijay Singh	73	72	67	68	280	418,133.34
Brent Geiberger	71	69	71	69	280	418,133.33
Nick Price	66	71	74	70	281	212,800
Kirk Triplett	69	74	67	71	281	212,800
Tom Pernice, Jr.	73	67	74	68	282	168,700
Dean Wilson	70	72	70	70	282	168,700
Greg Chalmers	71	71	71	69	282	168,700
Charles Howell	70	69	72	71	282	168,700
Fred Funk	71	70	70	72	283	111,200
Tim Petrovic	73	68	71	71	283	111,200
Duffy Waldorf	69	71	73	70	283	111,200
Joe Durant	70	73	71	69	283	111,200
Woody Austin	72	71	70	70	283	111,200
J.P. Hayes	72	66	72	73	283	111,200
J.J. Henry	71	72	71	69	283	111,200
Chris DiMarco	70	72	70	72	284	78,400
Mike Weir	72	70	73	69	284	78,400
Brenden Pappas	73	70	72	69	284	78,400
David Frost	71	73	70	71	285	62,720
Billy Mayfair	71	74	71	69	285	62,720
Rich Beem	67	72	74	72	285	62,720
Larry Mize	72	71	72	71	286	46,480
Spike McRoy	70	74	67	75	286	46,480
Chad Campbell	71	72	69	74	286	46,480
Garrett Willis	72	72	71	71	286	46,480
David Gossett	72	70	70	74	286	46,480
Tom Lehman	72	72	71	72	287	36,400
Davis Love	73	72	74	68	287	36,400
Blaine McCallister	72	70	72	73	287	36,400
Brandt Jobe	70	69	75	73	287	36,400
Justin Leonard	71	71	74	71	287	36,400
Fred Couples	66	72	74	76	288	28,280
Brad Faxon	73	68	74	73	288	28,280
Stephen Ames	69	75	74	70	288	28,280
Paul Goydos	68	72	74	74	288	28,280
Jeff Brehaut	68	73	78	69	288	28,280
Mathew Goggin	75	67	71	75	288	28,280
Jim Carter	71	73	72	73	289	18,663.27
Jay Haas	73	70	73	73	289	18,663.27
Steve Lowery	74	68	72	75	289	18,663.27
Frank Lickliter	73	67	74	75	289	18,663.27
Carlos Franco	73	69	74	73	289	18,663.27
Stewart Cink	72	69	74	74	289	18,663.27
Alex Cejka	73	71	73	72	289	18,663.28
Peter Lonard	72	71	73	73	289	18,663.27
John Senden	69	74	73	73	289	18,663.27
Rory Sabbatini	73	71	75	70	289	18,663.28
Jason Caron	72	72	74	71	289	18,663.28
Andrew Magee	71	74	72	73	290	13,104
Kevin Sutherland	71	69	74	76	290	13,104
Glen Day	71	74	73	72	290	13,104
Craig Barlow	75	70	75	70	290	13,104

	SCORES				TOTAL	MONEY
Patrick Sheehan	72	71	77	70	290	13,104
Matt Kuchar	71	71	72	76	290	13,104
K.J. Choi	73	72	70	75	290	13,104
Kenny Perry	72	73	71	75	291	12,488
Hidemichi Tanaka	74	71	72	74	291	12,488
Len Mattiace	75	67	76	74	292	12,264
Ben Crane	71	73	74	74	292	12,264
Chris Smith	70	72	77	74	293	11,984
Ian Leggatt	71	74	72	76	293	11,984
Charles Warren	72	72	76	73	293	11,984
Olin Browne	73	72	73	76	294	11,536
Neal Lancaster	72	73	76	73	294	11,536
John Maginnes	72	73	74	75	294	11,536
Michael Muehr	72	73	76	73	294	11,536
Jason Gore	73	67	80	74	294	11,536
Donnie Hammond	74	71	74	79	298	11,200

EDS Byron Nelson Championship

TPC Four Seasons Resort at Las Colinas: May 15-18
Par 35-35–70; 7,017 yards purse, $5,600,000
Cottonwood Valley Course: Par 34-36–70; 6,846 yards
Irving, Texas

	SCORES				TOTAL	MONEY
Vijay Singh	65	65	69	66	265	$1,008,000
Nick Price	66	70	66	65	267	604,800
Robert Allenby	67	67	69	65	268	380,800
Scott Verplank	69	63	72	65	269	268,800
Jim Furyk	64	70	70	66	270	224,000
Hal Sutton	68	69	66	68	271	187,600
David Toms	68	70	65	68	271	187,600
Per-Ulrik Johansson	66	69	67	69	271	187,600
Andrew Magee	68	68	67	69	272	140,000
Jerry Kelly	65	69	70	68	272	140,000
Justin Leonard	67	70	69	66	272	140,000
Briny Baird	65	69	69	69	272	140,000
Peter Lonard	68	67	68	69	272	140,000
Lee Janzen	68	66	70	69	273	95,200
Jeff Sluman	63	69	68	73	273	95,200
Brandt Jobe	66	72	68	67	273	95,200
Cameron Beckman	66	68	67	72	273	95,200
Anthony Painter	68	68	70	67	273	95,200
Olin Browne	70	67	69	68	274	60,900
Robert Gamez	66	66	74	68	274	60,900
Tim Petrovic	65	66	74	69	274	60,900
David Berganio, Jr.	67	73	68	66	274	60,900
J.P. Hayes	66	68	71	69	274	60,900
Hidemichi Tanaka	66	69	68	71	274	60,900
John Rollins	66	70	71	67	274	60,900
Luke Donald	69	65	67	73	274	60,900
Bob Estes	66	71	68	70	275	41,440
Bob Tway	69	67	70	69	275	41,440
Kevin Sutherland	64	68	73	70	275	41,440
Mark O'Meara	67	70	71	68	276	34,020
Chris DiMarco	70	65	73	68	276	34,020
Bob May	67	69	76	64	276	34,020
Dean Wilson	66	71	69	70	276	34,020

	SCORES				TOTAL	MONEY
Carlos Franco	70	67	71	68	276	34,020
Brenden Pappas	73	65	71	67	276	34,020
Tommy Armour	65	75	69	68	277	26,950
Dudley Hart	68	67	70	72	277	26,950
John Senden	69	67	69	72	277	26,950
Jason Gore	71	68	71	67	277	26,950
Billy Mayfair	66	71	72	69	278	22,400
Chad Campbell	69	69	69	71	278	22,400
Rich Beem	68	69	69	72	278	22,400
Richard S. Johnson	66	72	69	71	278	22,400
Jim Carter	65	73	73	68	279	16,184
Brad Faxon	67	67	70	75	279	16,184
Phil Mickelson	65	72	71	71	279	16,184
Steve Stricker	69	70	71	69	279	16,184
Spike McRoy	65	72	72	70	279	16,184
Brent Geiberger	66	71	71	71	279	16,184
Ben Curtis	66	71	74	68	279	16,184
K.J. Choi	67	69	75	68	279	16,184
Corey Pavin	69	71	71	69	280	13,132
Gene Sauers	68	71	72	69	280	13,132
Esteban Toledo	69	69	72	70	280	13,132
Arron Oberholser	67	70	73	70	280	13,132
Robert Damron	69	66	74	72	281	12,600
Harrison Frazar	68	70	69	74	281	12,600
Michael Flynn	68	71	68	74	281	12,600
Hank Kuehne	67	72	74	68	281	12,600
Jay Don Blake	67	70	77	68	282	12,096
Tom Byrum	66	71	75	70	282	12,096
Donnie Hammond	69	71	67	75	282	12,096
Greg Chalmers	70	69	68	75	282	12,096
Charles Howell	70	70	70	72	282	12,096
Greg Norman	67	72	74	70	283	11,536
Mike Grob	68	72	75	68	283	11,536
Glen Hnatiuk	71	69	72	71	283	11,536
Mark Walker	65	70	76	72	283	11,536
Akio Sadakata	66	73	74	70	283	11,536
Doug Barron	67	72	73	72	284	11,144
Jason Caron	69	70	73	72	284	11,144
Patrick Sheehan	72	64	80	69	285	10,976
Alex Cejka	70	70	75	71	286	10,864
Rory Sabbatini	69	71	70	77	287	10,752
Jay Williamson	70	70	78	70	288	10,472
Mark Wilson	71	68	74	75	288	10,472
Darron Stiles	68	72	75	73	288	10,472
David Gossett	69	71	75	73	288	10,472
James McLean	69	71	79	70	289	10,192
Dave Stockton, Jr.	67	73	75	77	292	10,080

Bank of America Colonial

Colonial Country Club, Fort Worth, Texas
Par 35-35–70; 7,080 yards

May 22-25
purse, $5,000,000

	SCORES				TOTAL	MONEY
Kenny Perry	68	64	61	68	261	$900,000
Justin Leonard	68	72	66	61	267	540,000
Jeff Sluman	68	68	67	65	268	340,000
Brandt Jobe	67	70	68	64	269	240,000

	SCORES				TOTAL	MONEY
Hal Sutton	71	67	65	67	270	175,625
Pat Bates	69	66	69	66	270	175,625
Jim Furyk	68	65	69	68	270	175,625
Rory Sabbatini	64	70	67	69	270	175,625
Dan Forsman	66	66	73	67	272	130,000
Fred Funk	70	67	69	66	272	130,000
Esteban Toledo	68	68	69	67	272	130,000
Harrison Frazar	69	69	66	68	272	130,000
Phil Mickelson	67	70	68	68	273	91,000
Loren Roberts	67	69	70	67	273	91,000
Marco Dawson	68	70	71	64	273	91,000
Steve Flesch	69	66	69	69	273	91,000
Stewart Cink	67	70	66	70	273	91,000
Olin Browne	67	71	68	68	274	70,000
Jay Haas	69	70	67	68	274	70,000
Lee Janzen	71	67	70	66	274	70,000
Brandel Chamblee	70	69	70	66	275	48,357.15
Billy Mayfair	69	70	68	68	275	48,357.14
Tim Petrovic	68	66	72	69	275	48,357.14
Nick Price	70	70	65	70	275	48,357.14
Dean Wilson	71	67	69	68	275	48,357.14
Briny Baird	70	68	68	69	275	48,357.14
John Senden	71	70	68	66	275	48,357.15
Corey Pavin	68	70	69	69	276	32,535.71
Gene Sauers	69	68	70	69	276	32,535.72
Jay Williamson	67	67	73	69	276	32,535.71
Frank Lickliter	68	66	70	72	276	32,535.71
Shigeki Maruyama	70	68	70	68	276	32,535.72
Patrick Sheehan	65	72	68	71	276	32,535.71
Carl Pettersson	71	69	68	68	276	32,535.72
Billy Andrade	68	68	71	70	277	24,650
Dudley Hart	70	71	68	68	277	24,650
Bob Burns	69	70	70	68	277	24,650
Jesper Parnevik	66	68	73	70	277	24,650
Alex Cejka	70	70	65	72	277	24,650
Kirk Triplett	69	71	70	68	278	19,500
Spike McRoy	67	72	71	68	278	19,500
Glen Day	67	70	75	66	278	19,500
Chad Campbell	67	67	74	70	278	19,500
Tim Herron	71	68	69	70	278	19,500
J.L. Lewis	72	69	70	68	279	14,014.29
Rocco Mediate	68	72	68	71	279	14,014.29
Stephen Ames	67	72	74	66	279	14,014.28
Shaun Micheel	71	69	72	67	279	14,014.28
Brett Quigley	67	73	68	71	279	14,014.29
Woody Austin	70	67	72	70	279	14,014.29
Brian Gay	68	69	76	66	279	14,014.28
Craig Parry	67	70	72	71	280	11,725
Bob Tway	69	70	73	68	280	11,725
Joe Durant	70	70	71	69	280	11,725
J.P. Hayes	70	71	71	68	280	11,725
Mark Calcavecchia	65	75	72	69	281	11,200
Duffy Waldorf	67	70	71	73	281	11,200
Brian Watts	67	71	72	71	281	11,200
Mike Sposa	67	69	74	71	281	11,200
Greg Chalmers	68	71	72	70	281	11,200
Len Mattiace	69	69	75	69	282	10,900
David Frost	69	71	75	68	283	10,650
Scott Verplank	69	69	71	74	283	10,650
Brian Henninger	70	69	71	73	283	10,650

	SCORES				TOTAL	MONEY
Brenden Pappas	70	68	74	71	283	10,650
Steve Elkington	72	68	70	74	284	10,200
Peter Jacobsen	72	68	71	73	284	10,200
Joey Sindelar	69	71	71	73	284	10,200
Jonathan Kaye	73	67	72	72	284	10,200
Rich Beem	68	69	76	71	284	10,200
Brent Geiberger	71	70	72	72	285	9,800
Cliff Kresge	68	70	73	74	285	9,800
Luke Donald	68	71	73	73	285	9,800
Tom Byrum	70	71	72	73	286	9,550
Jeff Brehaut	68	70	74	74	286	9,550
Fulton Allem	75	66	74	78	293	9,400

Memorial Tournament

Muirfield Village Golf Club, Dublin, Ohio
Par 36-36–72; 7,221 yards

May 29-June 1
purse, $5,000,000

	SCORES				TOTAL	MONEY
Kenny Perry	65	68	70	72	275	$900,000
Lee Janzen	67	67	71	72	277	540,000
Mike Weir	72	70	71	65	278	340,000
Vijay Singh	67	69	72	71	279	220,000
Tiger Woods	67	71	76	65	279	220,000
Stewart Cink	70	69	72	69	280	180,000
Chad Campbell	67	70	74	70	281	161,250
Retief Goosen	67	67	74	73	281	161,250
Mark Calcavecchia	69	70	70	73	282	145,000
Jose Maria Olazabal	73	69	66	75	283	135,000
Justin Leonard	71	69	76	69	285	120,000
John Rollins	70	69	74	72	285	120,000
Robert Gamez	70	68	75	73	286	91,000
Ernie Els	73	70	70	73	286	91,000
Jesper Parnevik	70	71	73	72	286	91,000
Padraig Harrington	70	71	73	72	286	91,000
K.J. Choi	70	70	73	73	286	91,000
John Huston	66	74	78	69	287	70,000
Jeff Sluman	70	72	72	73	287	70,000
Stuart Appleby	71	71	76	69	287	70,000
Jay Haas	75	69	71	73	288	56,000
Peter Lonard	72	72	75	69	288	56,000
Ben Crane	73	68	73	74	288	56,000
Jim Furyk	68	70	75	76	289	44,000
Shigeki Maruyama	69	75	72	73	289	44,000
Tim Herron	72	68	77	72	289	44,000
Jay Williamson	73	73	70	74	290	37,750
Charles Howell	64	74	77	75	290	37,750
Spike McRoy	68	68	84	71	291	32,500
Lee Westwood	72	68	75	76	291	32,500
Rory Sabbatini	71	71	75	74	291	32,500
Adam Scott	67	72	79	73	291	32,500
Jonathan Byrd	74	72	71	74	291	32,500
Jeff Maggert	68	73	71	80	292	25,250
Bob Tway	69	72	74	77	292	25,250
J.P. Hayes	73	72	73	74	292	25,250
Glen Day	73	73	74	72	292	25,250
Stephen Leaney	73	72	73	74	292	25,250

	SCORES				TOTAL	MONEY
Carl Pettersson	70	70	77	75	292	25,250
Brad Faxon	67	77	74	75	293	19,500
Steve Lowery	70	76	73	74	293	19,500
Gene Sauers	70	75	70	78	293	19,500
Ian Leggatt	70	76	74	73	293	19,500
Hidemichi Tanaka	70	72	79	72	293	19,500
Mark O'Meara	76	69	72	77	294	15,050
Tim Petrovic	70	71	78	75	294	15,050
Kevin Sutherland	73	71	73	77	294	15,050
Luke Donald	70	69	80	75	294	15,050
Gary Nicklaus	69	75	77	74	295	12,800
David Gossett	72	74	75	74	295	12,800
Dudley Hart	69	72	76	79	296	12,300
Billy Andrade	69	75	79	74	297	11,725
Len Mattiace	70	72	80	75	297	11,725
David Peoples	77	68	77	75	297	11,725
Tim Clark	74	72	79	72	297	11,725
John Daly	68	73	83	74	298	11,350
Craig Perks	70	72	76	80	298	11,350
Keith Fergus	69	76	79	75	299	11,050
Peter O'Malley	72	71	76	80	299	11,050
Bob Burns	75	68	82	74	299	11,050
Jerry Kelly	70	72	84	73	299	11,050
Woody Austin	68	74	76	82	300	10,750
Frank Lickliter	72	72	81	75	300	10,750
David Duval	73	72	78	78	301	10,550
Jonathan Kaye	73	73	76	79	301	10,550
David Edwards	72	73	81	77	303	10,350
Peter Jacobsen	73	71	80	79	303	10,350
Chris Smith	73	72	84	75	304	10,200
J.L. Lewis	77	69	85	76	307	10,100

FBR Capital Open

TPC at Avenel, Potomac, Maryland
Par 36-35–71; 7,005 yards
(Event extended to Monday due to rain.)

June 5-9
purse, $4,500,000

	SCORES				TOTAL	MONEY
Rory Sabbatini	68	66	68	68	270	$810,000
Fred Funk	70	70	66	68	274	336,000
Duffy Waldorf	71	68	66	69	274	336,000
Joe Durant	69	70	69	66	274	336,000
Bernhard Langer	70	68	69	68	275	171,000
J.L. Lewis	71	67	68	69	275	171,000
Davis Love	70	71	68	67	276	140,250
Tom Gillis	68	68	70	70	276	140,250
Niclas Fasth	68	68	67	73	276	140,250
Chris DiMarco	71	68	67	71	277	112,500
Todd Fischer	73	68	67	69	277	112,500
Scott Laycock	71	67	70	69	277	112,500
Marco Dawson	72	68	67	71	278	84,375
Cliff Kresge	70	69	70	69	278	84,375
Padraig Harrington	70	70	66	72	278	84,375
Patrick Sheehan	68	69	71	70	278	84,375
Robert Gamez	66	74	75	64	279	67,500
Hal Sutton	68	69	70	72	279	67,500

	SCORES				TOTAL	MONEY
Rich Beem	67	70	69	73	279	67,500
Dan Forsman	72	72	67	69	280	56,250
Brett Quigley	74	67	70	69	280	56,250
John Riegger	71	73	69	68	281	46,800
Woody Austin	71	67	70	73	281	46,800
John Maginnes	72	66	72	71	281	46,800
Pat Bates	71	73	68	70	282	36,750
Glen Hnatiuk	68	70	70	74	282	36,750
Notah Begay	67	69	71	75	282	36,750
Jay Don Blake	69	72	71	71	283	29,282.15
Joel Edwards	69	71	73	70	283	29,282.14
John Huston	69	72	67	75	283	29,282.14
David Peoples	74	70	73	66	283	29,282.14
Mike Grob	70	74	67	72	283	29,282.15
David Duval	74	62	73	74	283	29,282.14
Brad Elder	72	69	70	72	283	29,282.14
Bob Estes	72	70	70	72	284	23,175
Danny Ellis	70	69	72	73	284	23,175
Tim Herron	73	69	69	73	284	23,175
Scott Simpson	71	72	71	71	285	19,800
Mike Sposa	71	72	76	66	285	19,800
Jonathan Kaye	72	70	71	72	285	19,800
Hidemichi Tanaka	69	70	70	76	285	19,800
Bob Burns	71	72	76	67	286	14,478.75
Craig Barlow	72	70	70	74	286	14,478.75
Paul Lawrie	68	71	70	77	286	14,478.75
Jason Gore	70	72	71	73	286	14,478.75
Brent Schwarzrock	71	67	75	73	286	14,478.75
Jonathan Byrd	74	70	72	70	286	14,478.75
Andy Miller	74	68	74	70	286	14,478.75
Richard S. Johnson	70	72	72	72	286	14,478.75
Bill Glasson	75	69	74	69	287	10,854
Craig Parry	70	71	71	75	287	10,854
Joey Sindelar	71	72	71	73	287	10,854
Stuart Appleby	74	70	78	65	287	10,854
Garrett Willis	69	75	69	74	287	10,854
Andrew Magee	70	70	74	74	288	10,215
Mark O'Meara	73	70	68	77	288	10,215
Robert Allenby	71	73	72	72	288	10,215
John Senden	74	70	72	72	288	10,215
Chip Sullivan	72	72	71	74	289	9,675
Jose Maria Olazabal	72	69	74	74	289	9,675
Per-Ulrik Johansson	73	70	73	73	289	9,675
Cameron Beckman	76	67	71	75	289	9,675
Alex Cejka	69	74	66	80	289	9,675
Briny Baird	70	73	75	71	289	9,675
Charles Howell	69	69	74	77	289	9,675
Troy Matteson	69	71	75	74	289	9,675
Aaron Barber	71	70	75	74	290	9,225
Darron Stiles	69	71	79	71	290	9,225
Brandt Jobe	74	70	70	77	291	9,045
Carlos Franco	71	70	71	79	291	9,045
Kirk Triplett	70	71	74	77	292	8,910
Harrison Frazar	70	72	77	74	293	8,775
Kenneth Staton	75	69	73	76	293	8,775
Frank Lickliter	73	70	76	75	294	8,640
Matt Kuchar	73	71	76	75	295	8,505
Tim Clark	75	69	72	79	295	8,505
Todd Barranger	71	72	79	75	297	8,325
Steven Alker	69	71	79	78	297	8,325

U.S. Open Championship

Olympia Fields Country Club (North Course),
Olympia Fields, Illinois
Par 36-34–70; 7,188 yards

June 12-15
purse, $6,000,000

	SCORES				TOTAL	MONEY
Jim Furyk	67	66	67	72	272	$1,080,000
Stephen Leaney	67	68	68	72	275	650,000
Kenny Perry	72	71	69	67	279	341,367
Mike Weir	73	67	68	71	279	341,367
Justin Rose	70	71	70	69	280	185,934
Fredrik Jacobson	69	67	73	71	280	185,934
David Toms	72	67	70	71	280	185,934
Ernie Els	69	70	69	72	280	185,934
Nick Price	71	65	69	75	280	185,934
Padraig Harrington	69	72	72	68	281	124,936
Jonathan Kaye	70	70	72	69	281	124,936
Cliff Kresge	69	70	72	70	281	124,936
Scott Verplank	76	67	68	70	281	124,936
Billy Mayfair	69	71	67	74	281	124,936
Hidemichi Tanaka	69	71	71	71	282	93,359
Tom Byrum	69	69	71	73	282	93,359
Tim Petrovic	69	70	70	73	282	93,359
Jonathan Byrd	69	66	71	76	282	93,359
Eduardo Romero	70	66	70	76	282	93,359
Peter Lonard	72	69	74	68	283	64,170
Tiger Woods	70	66	75	72	283	64,170
Robert Damron	69	68	73	73	283	64,170
Jay Williamson	72	69	69	73	283	64,170
Justin Leonard	66	70	72	75	283	64,170
Mark Calcavecchia	68	72	67	76	283	64,170
Ian Leggatt	68	70	68	77	283	64,170
Vijay Singh	70	63	72	78	283	64,170
John Maginnes	72	70	72	70	284	41,254
Kevin Sutherland	71	71	72	70	284	41,254
Tom Watson	65	72	75	72	284	41,254
Kirk Triplett	71	68	73	72	284	41,254
Stewart Cink	70	68	72	74	284	41,254
Brett Quigley	65	74	71	74	284	41,254
Dicky Pride	71	69	66	78	284	41,254
Brandt Jobe	70	68	76	71	285	32,552
Sergio Garcia	69	74	71	71	285	32,552
Chris DiMarco	72	71	71	71	285	32,552
Fred Funk	70	73	71	71	285	32,552
Angel Cabrera	72	68	73	72	285	32,552
Chad Campbell	70	70	69	76	285	32,552
Mark O'Meara	72	68	67	78	285	32,552
Retief Goosen	71	72	73	70	286	25,002
Loren Roberts	69	72	74	71	286	25,002
Colin Montgomerie	69	74	71	72	286	25,002
Bernhard Langer	70	70	73	73	286	25,002
Steve Lowery	70	72	70	74	286	25,002
Darren Clarke	70	69	72	75	286	25,002
Marco Dawson	72	71	75	69	287	19,025
Niclas Fasth	75	68	73	71	287	19,025
Woody Austin	74	64	76	73	287	19,025
Daniel Forsman	71	67	73	76	287	19,025
Darron Stiles	71	68	72	76	287	19,025
Charles Howell	70	73	74	71	288	17,004

	SCORES				TOTAL	MONEY
John Rollins	73	70	68	77	288	17,004
Phil Mickelson	70	70	75	74	289	16,199
Lee Janzen	72	68	72	77	289	16,199
Len Mattiace	69	73	77	71	290	15,643
*Trip Kuehne	74	67	76	73	290	
*Ricky Barnes	71	71	79	70	291	
Olin Browne	72	70	74	75	291	15,347
Chris Anderson	72	70	78	72	292	14,810
Brian Davis	71	72	74	75	292	14,810
Alex Cejka	73	66	76	77	292	14,810
J.P. Hayes	70	73	79	71	293	14,200
Jay Don Blake	66	77	75	75	293	14,200
Brian Henninger	76	67	76	76	295	13,711
Fred Couples	70	72	73	80	295	13,711
Ryan Dillon	72	68	81	80	301	13,334

Out of Final 36 Holes

Tim Clark	69	75	144
Steve Flesch	73	71	144
Jose Maria Olazabal	74	70	144
Tom Gillis	68	76	144
Rob Bradley	73	71	144
Joe Durant	72	72	144
Stuart Appleby	75	69	144
Neal Lancaster	72	72	144
Craig Parry	70	74	144
Adam Scott	72	72	144
Spike McRoy	71	73	144
Joe Ogilvie	70	74	144
Dudley Hart	72	73	145
Paul Casey	76	69	145
Richard S. Johnson	71	74	145
Geoff Ogilvy	74	71	145
Craig Bowden	76	69	145
Jeff Sluman	74	71	145
Jesper Parnevik	74	71	145
Thomas Bjorn	71	74	145
*John Bradley Holmes	76	69	145
Geoffrey Sisk	76	70	146
Grant Waite	74	72	146
Jeff Maggert	74	72	146
Roland Thatcher	73	73	146
Hiroshi Matsuo	72	74	146
Trevor Immelman	72	74	146
*Hunter Mahan	74	72	146
Brian Gay	77	69	146
Scott Hoch	70	76	146
Bryce Molder	74	72	146
Dean Wilson	76	70	146
Robert Allenby	75	71	146
David Smail	74	72	146
*Chris Baryla	72	74	146
Jerry Kelly	75	72	147
Bob Estes	70	77	147
Doug Dunakey	73	74	147
Toru Taniguchi	79	68	147
Bob Tway	74	73	147
Sean McCarty	78	69	147
Jay Haas	75	72	147

	SCORES				TOTAL
Bill Lunde	74	73			147
Rocco Mediate	73	74			147
Doug Labelle	72	76			148
Warren Schutte	77	71			148
Corey Pavin	72	76			148
Tom Kite	72	76			148
Shigeki Maruyama	75	73			148
Mark Wurtz	76	72			148
Larry Mize	76	72			148
Bret Guetz	75	73			148
Chris Riley	76	72			148
Rory Sabbatini	73	75			148
Maarten Lafeber	75	73			148
Paul Lawrie	75	74			149
Bob Burns	78	71			149
*Bill Haas	73	76			149
Brad Elder	75	74			149
Rodney Pampling	72	77			149
Kent Jones	76	73			149
*Luke List	75	74			149
Tommy Armour	76	73			149
Sean Murphy	78	71			149
Billy Andrade	78	72			150
Nick Faldo	75	75			150
David Duval	78	72			150
Rich Beem	74	76			150
Brad Faxon	73	77			150
Davis Love	76	75			151
Matt Seppanen	76	76			152
*Rick Reinsberg	76	76			152
Steve Gotsche	76	76			152
*Chez Reavie	75	78			153
Alan Morin	79	74			153
Scott McCarron	74	79			153
Cortney Brisson	75	78			153
Anthony Arvidson	75	78			153
K.J. Choi	79	74			153
Chris Smith	77	77			154
Michael Campbell	74	80			154
Greg Hiller	78	77			155
Jason Knutzon	75	81			156
Joey Sindelar	76	81			157
Don Pooley	81	76			157
Roy Biancalana	75	84			159
*Tom Glissmeyer	80	79			159
Hale Irwin					WD

(Professionals who did not complete 72 holes received $5,000.)

Buick Classic

Westchester Country Club, Harrison, New York   June 19-22
Par 36-35–71; 6,722 yards   purse, $5,000,000

	SCORES				TOTAL	MONEY
Jonathan Kaye	70	66	68	67	271	$900,000
John Rollins	70	67	67	67	271	540,000

(Kaye defeated Rollins on first playoff hole.)

	SCORES				TOTAL	MONEY
Joey Sindelar	66	69	70	68	273	340,000
Fred Funk	71	70	64	69	274	196,875
Jay Haas	74	68	67	65	274	196,875
Skip Kendall	68	66	70	70	274	196,875
Sergio Garcia	70	69	66	69	274	196,875
Brad Faxon	69	67	74	65	275	145,000
Tom Lehman	71	70	68	66	275	145,000
J.L. Lewis	68	68	70	69	275	145,000
Scott Verplank	70	68	68	70	276	120,000
Ernie Els	68	71	68	69	276	120,000
Fred Couples	69	68	69	71	277	91,000
Shaun Micheel	69	68	73	67	277	91,000
Woody Austin	74	64	70	69	277	91,000
Tiger Woods	67	69	71	70	277	91,000
Brenden Pappas	74	67	68	68	277	91,000
David Toms	75	65	71	67	278	67,500
Vijay Singh	70	68	71	69	278	67,500
Tom Gillis	71	65	70	72	278	67,500
Retief Goosen	67	66	73	72	278	67,500
David Peoples	72	68	69	70	279	45,071.43
Loren Roberts	71	71	71	66	279	45,071.42
Per-Ulrik Johansson	71	70	72	66	279	45,071.43
Jim Furyk	66	73	71	69	279	45,071.43
Alex Cejka	70	69	66	74	279	45,071.43
Peter Lonard	72	66	71	70	279	45,071.43
John E. Morgan	72	68	70	69	279	45,071.43
Dudley Hart	70	69	73	68	280	35,500
Kent Jones	71	67	73	70	281	31,750
Shigeki Maruyama	67	69	74	71	281	31,750
Briny Baird	63	69	72	77	281	31,750
Carl Pettersson	71	67	71	72	281	31,750
Steve Flesch	69	68	71	74	282	27,625
Cliff Kresge	69	71	72	70	282	27,625
Billy Mayfair	71	69	70	73	283	22,535.72
Jeff Brehaut	73	65	75	70	283	22,535.71
J.P. Hayes	73	66	71	73	283	22,535.71
Rodney Pampling	70	70	71	72	283	22,535.72
Fredrik Jacobson	70	70	70	73	283	22,535.72
Luke Donald	71	71	71	70	283	22,535.71
Jonathan Byrd	72	70	69	72	283	22,535.71
Donnie Hammond	70	72	73	69	284	16,033.33
Andrew Magee	71	71	71	71	284	16,033.33
John Senden	73	68	73	70	284	16,033.34
Paul Gow	73	69	72	70	284	16,033.33
Matt Kuchar	69	71	70	74	284	16,033.34
Rory Sabbatini	71	71	73	69	284	16,033.33
Deane Pappas	68	74	73	70	285	12,340
Matt Gogel	71	70	73	71	285	12,340
Cameron Beckman	75	67	70	73	285	12,340
Jesper Parnevik	69	72	71	73	285	12,340
Kenichi Kuboya	72	67	73	73	285	12,340
Billy Andrade	70	72	69	75	286	11,450
John Riegger	71	68	75	72	286	11,450
Robert Damron	72	68	72	74	286	11,450
Richard S. Johnson	74	67	72	73	286	11,450
Steve Elkington	69	69	77	72	287	11,050
Mathew Goggin	71	71	71	74	287	11,050
Heath Slocum	73	68	76	70	287	11,050
Chris Anderson	72	68	70	77	287	11,050
Brandel Chamblee	70	72	73	73	288	10,650

	SCORES				TOTAL	MONEY
Lee Janzen	74	66	72	76	288	10,650
Richard Zokol	73	69	75	71	288	10,650
Darron Stiles	72	69	71	76	288	10,650
Tommy Armour	71	71	73	74	289	10,300
Mike Grob	73	67	74	75	289	10,300
Ben Curtis	70	72	74	73	289	10,300
Brett Quigley	74	67	74	75	290	10,050
J.J. Henry	69	72	76	73	290	10,050
Joe Durant	74	67	76	75	292	9,850
Craig Perks	74	68	75	75	292	9,850

FedEx St. Jude Classic

TPC at Southwind, Memphis, Tennessee
Par 36-35–71; 7,006 yards

June 26-29
purse, $4,500,000

	SCORES				TOTAL	MONEY
David Toms	68	67	65	64	264	$810,000
Nick Price	73	67	65	62	267	486,000
Bob Estes	67	70	66	65	268	234,000
Fredrik Jacobson	66	67	68	67	268	234,000
Richard S. Johnson	64	66	69	69	268	234,000
Lee Janzen	68	66	67	68	269	156,375
Ben Crane	70	68	64	67	269	156,375
David Peoples	65	66	70	69	270	139,500
Fred Funk	71	69	65	66	271	112,500
Jay Haas	64	70	69	68	271	112,500
Kirk Triplett	67	67	69	68	271	112,500
Chris DiMarco	68	70	65	68	271	112,500
Hank Kuehne	68	68	69	66	271	112,500
Stephen Ames	68	71	68	65	272	81,000
Tim Herron	68	68	65	71	272	81,000
John Senden	71	68	66	67	272	81,000
John Huston	67	63	73	70	273	67,500
Robert Allenby	70	70	67	66	273	67,500
Robert Damron	65	73	70	65	273	67,500
Dicky Pride	69	67	67	71	274	46,928.57
Scott McCarron	69	70	67	68	274	46,928.57
Vance Veazey	69	67	70	68	274	46,928.57
Notah Begay	68	71	64	71	274	46,928.57
Chris Riley	69	66	68	71	274	46,928.57
Matt Kuchar	72	68	67	67	274	46,928.58
David Gossett	66	67	71	70	274	46,928.57
Pat Bates	68	67	70	70	275	33,300
Craig Barlow	70	68	67	70	275	33,300
Ben Curtis	72	67	71	65	275	33,300
Brandel Chamblee	72	65	68	71	276	27,945
Willie Wood	71	69	68	68	276	27,945
Mike Grob	68	70	69	69	276	27,945
Glen Day	71	69	65	71	276	27,945
J.J. Henry	70	70	69	67	276	27,945
Esteban Toledo	71	70	65	71	277	22,185
Kevin Sutherland	71	68	67	71	277	22,185
Jose Coceres	69	69	68	71	277	22,185
Garrett Willis	68	70	71	68	277	22,185
Greg Chalmers	68	71	69	69	277	22,185
Tommy Armour	69	68	72	69	278	17,100

	SCORES				TOTAL	MONEY
Jim Carter	69	68	70	71	278	17,100
Joel Edwards	69	69	65	75	278	17,100
Tim Petrovic	70	68	73	67	278	17,100
Loren Roberts	72	69	66	71	278	17,100
Mike Heinen	70	71	67	70	278	17,100
Anthony Painter	69	72	68	70	279	12,757.50
Aaron Barber	70	69	68	72	279	12,757.50
Brad Elder	68	71	68	72	279	12,757.50
Kenneth Staton	69	71	70	69	279	12,757.50
Andrew Magee	68	71	67	74	280	11,070
Cameron Beckman	68	71	70	71	280	11,070
Darron Stiles	64	74	68	74	280	11,070
Dennis Paulson	66	70	73	72	281	10,368
Dean Wilson	68	73	71	69	281	10,368
Thomas Levet	73	67	67	74	281	10,368
Danny Ellis	70	68	74	69	281	10,368
Aaron Baddeley	67	74	74	66	281	10,368
Len Mattiace	67	71	72	72	282	9,945
Scott Simpson	69	67	73	73	282	9,945
Kent Jones	67	69	75	71	282	9,945
Heath Slocum	69	70	72	71	282	9,945
Jay Williamson	69	71	70	73	283	9,630
Jason Gore	71	70	73	69	283	9,630
Brent Schwarzrock	69	72	71	71	283	9,630
Keith Fergus	69	72	74	69	284	9,405
Kelly Gibson	70	69	73	72	284	9,405
Neal Lancaster	73	67	72	73	285	9,180
Doug Barron	73	68	72	72	285	9,180
Chris Anderson	68	71	75	71	285	9,180
Robert Gamez	73	68	75	70	286	8,955
Steven Alker	69	72	70	75	286	8,955
David Edwards	68	71	70	78	287	8,820
Paul Azinger	67	72	70	79	288	8,685
John E. Morgan	69	71	79	69	288	8,685
Andy Bean	69	69	71	80	289	8,550
Troy Matteson	74	67	75	74	290	8,460
Frank Lickliter	71	70	76	75	292	8,370
Duffy Waldorf	68	71	80	75	294	8,280

100th Western Open

Cog Hill Golf & Country Club, Lemont, Illinois
Par 36-36–72; 7,073 yards

July 3-6
purse, $4,500,000

	SCORES				TOTAL	MONEY
Tiger Woods	63	70	65	69	267	$810,000
Rich Beem	69	71	65	67	272	486,000
Jerry Kelly	66	72	68	68	274	234,000
Mike Weir	67	70	69	68	274	234,000
Jim Furyk	71	66	72	65	274	234,000
Robert Allenby	69	67	68	71	275	156,375
Cliff Kresge	67	68	69	71	275	156,375
Dudley Hart	73	65	70	68	276	130,500
Chad Campbell	67	73	69	67	276	130,500
Fredrik Jacobson	69	74	67	66	276	130,500
Vijay Singh	71	70	70	66	277	112,500
Scott McCarron	69	71	68	70	278	103,500

	SCORES				TOTAL	MONEY
Skip Kendall	70	72	70	67	279	79,500
David Toms	65	69	74	71	279	79,500
Kirk Triplett	69	69	71	70	279	79,500
Charles Howell	70	69	71	69	279	79,500
Ben Curtis	71	71	69	68	279	79,500
Luke Donald	73	65	72	69	279	79,500
Tom Byrum	70	70	67	73	280	54,540
Chris Smith	71	69	70	70	280	54,540
Scott Verplank	70	65	73	72	280	54,540
Robert Damron	68	69	70	73	280	54,540
Jose Coceres	72	69	71	68	280	54,540
Ian Leggatt	70	69	73	69	281	39,600
Carlos Franco	68	72	72	69	281	39,600
Craig Barlow	72	71	72	66	281	39,600
Glen Day	69	71	66	76	282	33,300
John Senden	71	72	69	70	282	33,300
Heath Slocum	67	70	74	71	282	33,300
Tommy Armour	72	68	74	69	283	26,742.86
Dan Forsman	69	73	68	73	283	26,742.86
Billy Mayfair	71	69	70	73	283	26,742.86
Phil Mickelson	70	69	68	76	283	26,742.85
Joey Sindelar	71	71	73	68	283	26,742.85
Jeff Brehaut	74	69	70	70	283	26,742.86
David Gossett	71	70	71	71	283	26,742.86
Duffy Waldorf	69	74	68	73	284	19,800
Stephen Ames	70	72	72	70	284	19,800
Steve Flesch	70	72	69	73	284	19,800
Craig Perks	73	66	70	75	284	19,800
Peter Lonard	74	66	68	76	284	19,800
J.J. Henry	69	73	71	71	284	19,800
Bob Estes	70	73	70	72	285	14,430
J.L. Lewis	68	72	76	69	285	14,430
Andrew Magee	71	71	71	72	285	14,430
Mike Small	73	70	73	69	285	14,430
Justin Leonard	70	70	71	74	285	14,430
Hidemichi Tanaka	70	69	72	74	285	14,430
David Frost	71	71	72	72	286	11,700
Pat Bates	73	70	68	76	287	10,770
Carl Paulson	70	71	73	73	287	10,770
Kenichi Kuboya	69	71	73	74	287	10,770
Jason Gore	67	70	78	72	287	10,770
Tim Clark	71	71	72	73	287	10,770
Jonathan Byrd	71	71	70	75	287	10,770
Darron Stiles	69	73	75	71	288	10,260
Tom Lehman	69	73	74	73	289	10,080
David Sutherland	70	70	75	74	289	10,080
Jesper Parnevik	73	70	73	73	289	10,080
Donnie Hammond	68	71	76	75	290	9,720
Vance Veazey	64	75	78	73	290	9,720
Anthony Painter	70	72	73	75	290	9,720
Matt Kuchar	70	72	73	75	290	9,720
Hunter Mahan	75	68	73	74	290	9,720
Thomas Levet	70	72	78	72	292	9,405
Shigeki Maruyama	69	72	76	75	292	9,405
Paul Goydos	73	70	72	78	293	9,225
Dean Wilson	75	67	76	75	293	9,225
Pat Perez	69	74	74	77	294	9,090
Andy Miller	74	68	79	74	295	9,000

Greater Milwaukee Open

Brown Deer Park Golf Course, Milwaukee, Wisconsin
Par 35-35–70; 6,739 yards

July 10-13
purse, $3,500,000

	SCORES				TOTAL	MONEY
Kenny Perry	69	67	66	66	268	$630,000
Steve Allan	69	66	68	66	269	308,000
Heath Slocum	72	63	68	66	269	308,000
Brett Quigley	66	67	72	65	270	168,000
Billy Mayfair	67	72	67	66	272	118,650
Dennis Paulson	68	69	69	66	272	118,650
Chris Smith	72	69	67	64	272	118,650
Jeff Gallagher	73	66	67	66	272	118,650
Brenden Pappas	72	68	63	69	272	118,650
Hal Sutton	69	70	67	67	273	91,000
Spike McRoy	69	70	69	65	273	91,000
Grant Waite	70	72	67	65	274	68,600
Jerry Kelly	66	67	70	71	274	68,600
Shigeki Maruyama	66	69	69	70	274	68,600
Todd Fischer	69	68	68	69	274	68,600
Richard S. Johnson	69	69	69	67	274	68,600
Tommy Armour	67	68	70	70	275	52,500
Loren Roberts	69	66	70	70	275	52,500
Kent Jones	67	71	69	68	275	52,500
Joel Edwards	66	69	70	71	276	36,500
Paul Goydos	70	69	70	67	276	36,500
J.P. Hayes	71	67	69	69	276	36,500
Dicky Pride	72	69	70	65	276	36,500
Notah Begay	67	72	68	69	276	36,500
Jason Gore	69	72	72	63	276	36,500
Hunter Mahan	70	70	68	68	276	36,500
Robert Gamez	69	68	73	67	277	24,850
Rocco Mediate	69	69	68	71	277	24,850
David Peoples	70	72	67	68	277	24,850
Danny Ellis	72	68	68	69	277	24,850
Arron Oberholser	69	68	70	70	277	24,850
Jay Don Blake	64	68	71	75	278	17,780
Olin Browne	72	70	69	67	278	17,780
David Sutherland	69	69	71	69	278	17,780
Mike Heinen	73	69	74	62	278	17,780
Frank Lickliter	70	69	70	69	278	17,780
Mario Tiziani	73	69	66	70	278	17,780
Carlos Franco	70	67	70	71	278	17,780
Michael Muehr	68	70	69	71	278	17,780
Harrison Frazar	71	68	66	73	278	17,780
K.J. Choi	70	68	72	68	278	17,780
Mark Calcavecchia	67	70	71	71	279	10,752
Donnie Hammond	71	68	71	69	279	10,752
Scott Hoch	73	65	71	70	279	10,752
Corey Pavin	71	70	69	69	279	10,752
Joey Sindelar	67	68	76	68	279	10,752
Stan Utley	71	68	68	72	279	10,752
Stephen Ames	70	71	71	67	279	10,752
Pat Bates	69	70	71	69	279	10,752
Greg Chalmers	70	70	66	73	279	10,752
Patrick Sheehan	68	65	70	76	279	10,752
Billy Andrade	68	70	70	72	280	8,041.25
Jim Carter	69	70	69	72	280	8,041.25
Dan Forsman	70	70	69	71	280	8,041.25

	SCORES				TOTAL	MONEY
Skip Kendall	73	69	67	71	280	8,041.25
John Morse	69	70	71	70	280	8,041.25
Kenneth Staton	66	72	74	68	280	8,041.25
J.J. Henry	73	68	70	69	280	8,041.25
Pat Perez	71	71	69	69	280	8,041.25
Peter Jacobsen	68	72	72	69	281	7,525
Kirk Triplett	65	74	70	72	281	7,525
Willie Wood	68	72	71	70	281	7,525
Greg Kraft	71	69	71	70	281	7,525
Brian Henninger	70	72	71	68	281	7,525
Andy Miller	71	70	69	71	281	7,525
Mark Brooks	71	71	70	70	282	7,140
Jay Delsing	70	69	71	72	282	7,140
Doug Barron	69	71	68	74	282	7,140
Hidemichi Tanaka	73	68	70	71	282	7,140
John Senden	69	73	70	70	282	7,140
Deane Pappas	69	71	72	71	283	6,930
Tom Pernice, Jr.	73	68	70	73	284	6,825
John Maginnes	72	70	70	72	284	6,825
Steven Alker	69	71	76	69	285	6,720
Gene Sauers	69	73	74	70	286	6,580
Tom Scherrer	70	70	74	72	286	6,580
Gavin Coles	71	70	74	71	286	6,580
Kenichi Kuboya	72	70	72	73	287	6,440
Bill Glasson	71	71	75	72	289	6,370
Mike Hulbert	69	73	81	71	294	6,300

B.C. Open

En-Joie Golf Club, Endicott, New York
Par 37-35–72; 6,994 yards

July 17-20
purse, $3,000,000

	SCORES				TOTAL	MONEY
Craig Stadler	67	69	68	63	267	$540,000
Steve Lowery	64	64	68	72	268	264,000
Alex Cejka	66	66	69	67	268	264,000
Rodney Pampling	67	70	66	66	269	144,000
Mike Grob	68	69	70	64	271	98,250
John Maginnes	66	69	67	69	271	98,250
Glen Day	68	68	69	66	271	98,250
Steve Allan	68	65	71	67	271	98,250
Hank Kuehne	70	68	67	66	271	98,250
John E. Morgan	68	65	68	70	271	98,250
Brett Quigley	67	65	70	70	272	72,000
David Gossett	69	65	68	70	272	72,000
Dicky Pride	67	69	70	67	273	58,000
Carlos Franco	68	68	69	68	273	58,000
Notah Begay	68	69	70	66	273	58,000
Michael Bradley	67	67	72	68	274	49,500
David Frost	67	71	66	70	274	49,500
Barry Cheesman	66	69	73	67	275	32,910
Joel Edwards	69	68	67	71	275	32,910
Robert Gamez	68	66	70	71	275	32,910
Esteban Toledo	68	69	71	67	275	32,910
Jim McGovern	67	70	69	69	275	32,910
Brian Henninger	69	67	67	72	275	32,910
Spike McRoy	68	67	70	70	275	32,910

	SCORES				TOTAL	MONEY
Tom Gillis	70	69	71	65	275	32,910
Aaron Barber	68	69	70	68	275	32,910
Chris Downes	70	71	64	70	275	32,910
Guy Boros	69	69	67	71	276	21,300
Neal Lancaster	68	72	66	70	276	21,300
Harrison Frazar	66	71	70	69	276	21,300
David Peoples	69	68	72	68	277	16,650
Mike Springer	69	68	71	69	277	16,650
Pat Bates	69	63	75	70	277	16,650
Per-Ulrik Johansson	70	66	69	72	277	16,650
Deane Pappas	72	66	69	70	277	16,650
Andy Miller	72	68	67	70	277	16,650
James McLean	67	72	68	70	277	16,650
Ty Tryon	67	69	70	71	277	16,650
Jay Delsing	68	69	70	71	278	11,400
Jeff Maggert	68	70	68	72	278	11,400
Joey Sindelar	72	69	68	69	278	11,400
Marco Dawson	71	68	69	70	278	11,400
Doug Barron	71	67	69	71	278	11,400
Todd Fischer	68	70	71	69	278	11,400
Pat Perez	67	74	68	69	278	11,400
Akio Sadakata	69	69	70	70	278	11,400
Kelly Gibson	67	70	71	71	279	7,705.71
Dennis Paulson	70	70	69	70	279	7,705.72
Mike Heinen	70	70	69	70	279	7,705.72
Carl Paulson	69	68	70	72	279	7,705.71
Arron Oberholser	67	69	71	72	279	7,705.71
Brent Schwarzrock	72	66	70	71	279	7,705.71
Jason Buha	73	68	70	68	279	7,705.72
Jim Carter	69	69	71	71	280	6,720
Trevor Dodds	71	69	70	70	280	6,720
Jim Gallagher, Jr.	71	69	67	73	280	6,720
Blaine McCallister	70	71	70	69	280	6,720
Pete Jordan	67	70	73	70	280	6,720
Brian Gay	69	66	73	72	280	6,720
Hidemichi Tanaka	69	69	70	72	280	6,720
Brad Elder	69	72	71	68	280	6,720
Richard S. Johnson	69	72	72	67	280	6,720
Dave Stockton, Jr.	71	68	73	69	281	6,360
Gavin Coles	71	67	71	72	281	6,360
Chris Anderson	70	69	72	70	281	6,360
Michael Clark	76	65	69	72	282	6,210
Todd Barranger	69	71	70	72	282	6,210
Michael Muehr	71	68	73	71	283	6,060
Anthony Painter	74	67	73	69	283	6,060
Steven Alker	71	70	70	72	283	6,060
Willie Wood	70	71	72	71	284	5,940
Stan Utley	72	67	73	73	285	5,850
Kaname Yokoo	67	70	78	70	285	5,850
John Morse	71	70	73	74	288	5,760
Gary Hallberg	67	70	71	81	289	5,700
Dan Halldorson	69	72	75	77	293	5,640

Greater Hartford Open

TPC at River Highlands, Cromwell, Connecticut
Par 35-35–70; 6,820 yards

July 24-27
purse, $4,000,000

		SCORES			TOTAL	MONEY
Peter Jacobsen	63	67	69	67	266	$720,000
Chris Riley	72	65	63	68	268	432,000
Todd Fischer	66	69	69	65	269	272,000
Steve Pate	67	68	68	67	270	165,333.34
Kenny Perry	66	68	67	69	270	165,333.33
Craig Barlow	65	68	68	69	270	165,333.33
Joe Durant	68	69	66	68	271	124,666.67
Robert Damron	69	64	69	69	271	124,666.66
Briny Baird	72	65	68	66	271	124,666.67
Shaun Micheel	71	68	68	65	272	108,000
Jay Delsing	69	68	68	68	273	79,428.57
Bill Glasson	70	68	69	66	273	79,428.58
Kevin Sutherland	68	68	68	69	273	79,428.57
Mike Heinen	67	67	70	69	273	79,428.57
Glen Hnatiuk	70	69	67	67	273	79,428.57
Rodney Pampling	70	64	69	70	273	79,428.57
Darron Stiles	69	63	70	71	273	79,428.57
Willie Wood	66	66	68	74	274	56,000
Heath Slocum	69	66	68	71	274	56,000
K.J. Choi	66	72	65	71	274	56,000
Mark Brooks	67	68	70	70	275	41,600
Joey Sindelar	68	67	71	69	275	41,600
Frank Lickliter	71	67	69	68	275	41,600
Stewart Cink	72	67	71	65	275	41,600
J.J. Henry	66	67	69	73	275	41,600
Robin Freeman	69	69	67	71	276	28,400
Jay Haas	63	68	75	70	276	28,400
Steve Lowery	69	68	70	69	276	28,400
Stan Utley	71	67	68	70	276	28,400
Mathew Goggin	67	71	67	71	276	28,400
Patrick Sheehan	70	67	71	68	276	28,400
Jonathan Byrd	67	71	69	69	276	28,400
Jay Williamson	72	66	65	74	277	22,600
Notah Begay	73	66	69	69	277	22,600
Paul Gow	71	69	68	69	277	22,600
Brad Faxon	67	73	72	66	278	18,433.34
Dennis Paulson	64	70	72	72	278	18,433.33
Tim Petrovic	68	70	72	68	278	18,433.33
Tom Gillis	71	67	72	68	278	18,433.34
Mike Sposa	68	71	67	72	278	18,433.33
Jonathan Kaye	66	72	67	73	278	18,433.33
Neal Lancaster	67	72	73	67	279	14,000
Brian Bateman	67	71	71	70	279	14,000
Per-Ulrik Johansson	69	68	68	74	279	14,000
Danny Ellis	68	70	68	73	279	14,000
Carl Paulson	72	66	71	70	279	14,000
Jay Don Blake	72	68	69	71	280	10,576
Tom Pernice, Jr.	70	65	71	74	280	10,576
Paul Goydos	67	65	74	74	280	10,576
Mike Grob	68	70	70	72	280	10,576
Chris Anderson	73	67	70	70	280	10,576
Billy Andrade	68	69	74	70	281	9,280
Mark Calcavecchia	70	69	71	71	281	9,280
Brian Henninger	69	64	70	78	281	9,280

	SCORES				TOTAL	MONEY
Matt Gogel	67	71	74	69	281	9,280
Brian Gay	68	69	73	71	281	9,280
Garrett Willis	67	72	75	67	281	9,280
Olin Browne	69	70	74	69	282	8,800
Robert Gamez	70	69	70	73	282	8,800
Phil Mickelson	67	73	70	72	282	8,800
Hidemichi Tanaka	72	67	73	70	282	8,800
Akio Sadakata	68	69	68	77	282	8,800
Joel Edwards	69	70	71	73	283	8,400
Deane Pappas	69	70	75	69	283	8,400
Tom Scherrer	70	70	72	71	283	8,400
Brenden Pappas	71	68	72	72	283	8,400
Hank Kuehne	72	67	75	69	283	8,400
Gavin Coles	70	67	73	74	284	8,080
Aaron Baddeley	67	72	70	75	284	8,080
John E. Morgan	69	71	71	73	284	8,080
Brett Quigley	68	69	73	75	285	7,880
D.J. Trahan	73	67	74	71	285	7,880
Mike Standly	67	73	74	72	286	7,680
Steve Allan	71	68	72	75	286	7,680
Jason Caron	69	70	70	77	286	7,680
Richard S. Johnson	69	70	69	79	287	7,520

Buick Open

Warwick Hills Golf & Country Club,
Grand Blanc, Michigan
Par 36-36–72; 7,127 yards

July 31-August 3
purse, $4,000,000

	SCORES				TOTAL	MONEY
Jim Furyk	68	66	65	68	267	$720,000
Chris DiMarco	67	64	71	67	269	264,000
Tiger Woods	69	65	69	66	269	264,000
Briny Baird	70	68	65	66	269	264,000
Geoff Ogilvy	70	65	69	65	269	264,000
Neal Lancaster	67	68	66	69	270	139,000
Paul Goydos	68	68	66	68	270	139,000
Andrew Magee	71	64	71	66	272	112,000
Kenny Perry	69	67	66	70	272	112,000
Vijay Singh	69	67	70	66	272	112,000
Paul Gow	66	67	69	70	272	112,000
Paul Azinger	71	66	68	68	273	88,000
Jeff Sluman	71	68	67	67	273	88,000
John Huston	69	67	73	65	274	68,000
David Sutherland	66	67	74	67	274	68,000
Dicky Pride	70	69	67	68	274	68,000
Garrett Willis	67	68	70	69	274	68,000
Heath Slocum	67	71	67	69	274	68,000
Jay Delsing	71	67	67	70	275	48,480
Hal Sutton	72	64	70	69	275	48,480
Woody Austin	69	66	68	72	275	48,480
Mike Heinen	70	69	69	67	275	48,480
Todd Barranger	71	66	71	67	275	48,480
Fred Funk	68	68	69	71	276	30,950
Tom Pernice, Jr.	70	67	71	68	276	30,950
Scott Verplank	69	70	66	71	276	30,950
Shaun Micheel	67	68	72	69	276	30,950
Ian Leggatt	71	69	70	66	276	30,950

	SCORES				TOTAL	MONEY
Scott McCarron	70	70	70	66	276	30,950
Stuart Appleby	67	72	68	69	276	30,950
Hank Kuehne	69	68	68	71	276	30,950
Bob Estes	72	66	66	73	277	22,133.33
Stephen Ames	69	70	70	68	277	22,133.34
Esteban Toledo	72	68	69	68	277	22,133.34
Jerry Kelly	69	72	69	67	277	22,133.33
Craig Perks	66	71	68	72	277	22,133.33
Thomas Levet	67	69	74	67	277	22,133.33
John Daly	68	69	69	72	278	16,400
Jeff Brehaut	70	69	69	70	278	16,400
Mike Sposa	65	76	72	65	278	16,400
Robert Damron	68	70	69	71	278	16,400
Carl Paulson	66	69	65	78	278	16,400
Alex Cejka	72	69	70	67	278	16,400
Charles Howell	71	66	69	72	278	16,400
Danny Briggs	72	64	73	70	279	11,712
Skip Kendall	72	68	70	69	279	11,712
Rocco Mediate	68	69	70	72	279	11,712
Kent Jones	67	71	69	72	279	11,712
Darron Stiles	68	72	70	69	279	11,712
Olin Browne	72	67	74	67	280	9,508.57
Grant Waite	68	71	69	72	280	9,508.57
Steve Flesch	70	68	68	74	280	9,508.57
Spike McRoy	68	71	70	71	280	9,508.58
Craig Barlow	72	69	71	68	280	9,508.57
Doug Barron	69	72	69	70	280	9,508.57
Mathew Goggin	71	68	74	67	280	9,508.57
Tom Scherrer	70	69	72	70	281	8,920
Carlos Franco	70	68	71	72	281	8,920
Greg Chalmers	72	67	71	71	281	8,920
Kenneth Staton	70	69	73	69	281	8,920
Tom Byrum	68	71	73	70	282	8,560
Bob Tway	70	71	72	69	282	8,560
Brian Henninger	70	71	68	73	282	8,560
Ben Curtis	68	71	76	67	282	8,560
Ty Tryon	70	69	71	72	282	8,560
Kaname Yokoo	69	68	72	74	283	8,280
Jason Buha	67	71	71	74	283	8,280
Brian Bateman	70	69	73	72	284	8,120
Todd Fischer	72	69	71	72	284	8,120
Hidemichi Tanaka	72	69	73	71	285	7,960
Steven Alker	71	69	73	72	285	7,960
Jay Don Blake	69	72	72	73	286	7,840
Stan Utley	70	70	77	71	288	7,760
Jeff Klein	69	71	78	72	290	7,680
Dean Wilson	69	72	73	78	292	7,600

The International

Castle Pines Golf Club, Castle Rock, Colorado
Par 36-36–72; 7,559 yards

August 6-10
purse, $5,000,000

	POINTS				TOTAL	MONEY
Davis Love	19	17	5	5	46	$900,000
Vijay Singh	4	15	9	6	34	440,000
Retief Goosen	2	15	9	8	34	440,000
Chris DiMarco	8	7	11	7	33	240,000

	POINTS				TOTAL	MONEY
John Rollins	11	15	5	0	31	200,000
Phil Mickelson	8	14	1	3	26	173,750
Ernie Els	4	5	4	13	26	173,750
Geoff Ogilvy	9	3	8	5	25	155,000
Charles Howell	14	4	3	3	24	145,000
Bob Tway	12	6	0	5	23	125,000
Robert Allenby	7	3	5	8	23	125,000
Paul Casey	7	9	-2	9	23	125,000
Matt Gogel	-3	7	11	6	21	100,000
Stuart Appleby	9	4	-1	9	21	100,000
Briny Baird	6	2	8	4	20	87,500
K.J. Choi	3	5	6	6	20	87,500
Stewart Cink	5	11	1	2	19	80,000
J.J. Henry	6	10	6	-4	18	75,000
Kent Jones	5	14	-1	-1	17	70,000
Jose Maria Olazabal	1	6	5	4	16	58,250
Mathew Goggin	4	10	4	-2	16	58,250
John Senden	1	10	6	-1	16	58,250
Steve Allan	5	6	2	3	16	58,250
Tom Lehman	-3	9	6	3	15	40,500
Tim Petrovic	2	11	3	-1	15	40,500
Eduardo Romero	0	8	11	-4	15	40,500
David Sutherland	7	2	6	0	15	40,500
Chris Riley	10	1	1	3	15	40,500
Rodney Pampling	2	6	9	-2	15	40,500
Steve Lowery	9	3	3	-1	14	32,500
Bob Burns	6	6	3	-1	14	32,500
Brett Quigley	0	6	9	-1	14	32,500
Aaron Baddeley	5	4	3	1	13	29,500
Fred Couples	-3	12	4	-1	12	27,000
Duffy Waldorf	3	4	8	-3	12	27,000
Alex Cejka	4	6	4	-2	12	27,000
Scott McCarron	4	6	2	-2	10	24,500
Sergio Garcia	2	8	4	-9	5	23,500

Out of Final 18 Holes

Tom Pernice, Jr.	2	2	7		11	21,000
David Toms	-1	11	1		11	21,000
Woody Austin	3	2	6		11	21,000
Chad Campbell	0	9	2		11	21,000
John Riegger	2	7	1		10	17,500
Neal Lancaster	4	3	3		10	17,500
Glen Hnatiuk	5	4	1		10	17,500
Brian Bateman	2	7	0		9	14,175
Pat Bates	2	5	2		9	14,175
Todd Barranger	3	4	2		9	14,175
Harrison Frazar	-5	10	4		9	14,175
Mark Brooks	3	2	3		8	12,175
Justin Leonard	1	12	-5		8	12,175
Greg Chalmers	8	-1	1		8	12,175
Darron Stiles	3	6	-1		8	12,175
Mike Weir	9	-2	0		7	11,550
Heath Slocum	8	-1	0		7	11,550
Esteban Toledo	1	7	-2		6	11,250
Steve Stricker	1	4	1		6	11,250
Jonathan Kaye	12	-6	0		6	11,250
Gavin Coles	2	4	0		6	11,250
Shaun Micheel	1	7	-3		5	10,950

	POINTS			TOTAL	MONEY
Jason Caron	-1	5	1	5	10,950
Ian Leggatt	-1	5	0	4	10,750
Darren Clarke	2	8	-6	4	10,750
Paul Goydos	-1	5	-1	3	10,550
Tom Gillis	5	3	-5	3	10,550
Craig Perks	-4	9	-3	2	10,400
Jeff Brehaut	0	5	-4	1	10,100
Frank Lickliter	1	7	-7	1	10,100
Cameron Beckman	6	6	-11	1	10,100
Brian Gay	1	3	-3	1	10,100
Phillip Price	9	-4	-4	1	10,100
Jason Buha	-2	8	-7	-1	9,800
Lee Janzen	1	3	-6	-2	9,700
Olin Browne	-2	6	-11	-7	9,600

PGA Championship

Oak Hill Country Club, Rochester, New York
Par 35-35–70; 7,134 yards

August 14-17
purse, $6,000,000

	SCORES				TOTAL	MONEY
Shaun Micheel	69	68	69	70	276	$1,080,000
Chad Campbell	69	72	65	72	278	648,000
Tim Clark	72	70	68	69	279	408,000
Alex Cejka	74	69	68	69	280	288,000
Jay Haas	70	74	69	69	282	214,000
Ernie Els	71	70	70	71	282	214,000
Fred Funk	69	73	70	72	284	175,666.67
Loren Roberts	70	73	70	71	284	175,666.67
Mike Weir	68	71	70	75	284	175,666.67
Billy Andrade	67	72	72	74	285	135,500
Kenny Perry	75	72	70	68	285	135,500
Niclas Fasth	76	70	71	68	285	135,500
Charles Howell	70	72	70	73	285	135,500
Robert Gamez	70	73	70	73	286	98,250
Scott McCarron	74	70	71	71	286	98,250
Tim Herron	69	72	74	71	286	98,250
Rodney Pampling	66	74	73	73	286	98,250
Rocco Mediate	72	74	71	70	287	73,000
Kevin Sutherland	69	74	71	73	287	73,000
Jim Furyk	72	74	69	72	287	73,000
Toshimitsu Izawa	71	72	71	73	287	73,000
Carlos Franco	73	73	69	72	287	73,000
Phil Mickelson	66	75	72	75	288	52,000
Stuart Appleby	74	73	71	70	288	52,000
Luke Donald	73	72	71	72	288	52,000
Adam Scott	72	69	72	75	288	52,000
Woody Austin	72	73	69	75	289	43,000
Geoff Ogilvy	71	71	77	70	289	43,000
Todd Hamilton	70	74	73	73	290	36,600
David Toms	75	72	71	72	290	36,600
Frank Lickliter	71	72	71	76	290	36,600
Peter Lonard	74	74	69	73	290	36,600
Padraig Harrington	72	76	69	73	290	36,600
Fred Couples	74	71	72	74	291	29,000
Lee Janzen	68	74	72	77	291	29,000
J.L. Lewis	71	75	71	74	291	29,000

		SCORES			TOTAL	MONEY
Vijay Singh	69	73	70	79	291	29,000
Jesper Parnevik	73	72	72	74	291	29,000
Mark Calcavecchia	73	71	76	72	292	22,000
Hal Sutton	75	71	67	79	292	22,000
Joe Durant	71	76	75	70	292	22,000
Tiger Woods	74	72	73	73	292	22,000
Robert Allenby	70	77	73	72	292	22,000
Briny Baird	73	71	67	81	292	22,000
Tom Pernice, Jr.	70	71	72	80	293	17,500
Duffy Waldorf	70	75	72	76	293	17,500
Angel Cabrera	71	76	72	74	293	17,500
Shigeki Maruyama	75	72	73	74	294	14,733.33
Trevor Immelman	74	70	77	73	294	14,733.33
Ben Crane	73	73	76	72	294	14,733.33
Len Mattiace	74	70	75	76	295	13,320
Jose Maria Olazabal	74	74	76	71	295	13,320
Brian Gay	74	74	75	72	295	13,320
Gary Evans	74	74	71	76	295	13,320
Jose Coceres	73	68	78	76	295	13,320
Chris DiMarco	74	71	78	73	296	12,700
Bob Estes	71	76	73	77	297	12,450
Scott Hoch	75	72	73	77	297	12,450
Bernhard Langer	75	72	75	75	297	12,450
Aaron Baddeley	69	77	73	78	297	12,450
Billy Mayfair	76	72	78	72	298	12,000
Eduardo Romero	77	71	76	74	298	12,000
Phil Tataurangi	72	71	78	77	298	12,000
Jonathan Kaye	74	73	72	79	298	12,000
Ian Poulter	72	75	72	79	298	12,000
Paul Casey	79	69	75	76	299	11,700
Bob Burns	72	76	70	82	300	11,600
Rory Sabbatini	71	75	75	81	302	11,500
Michael Campbell	74	71	80	79	304	11,350
K.J. Choi	74	74	80	76	304	11,350

Out of Final 36 Holes

Paul Azinger	73	76	149
Dan Forsman	75	74	149
Davis Love	74	75	149
Greg Norman	79	70	149
Gene Sauers	72	77	149
Scott Verplank	77	72	149
Steve Flesch	79	70	149
Thomas Bjorn	78	71	149
Paul McGinley	73	76	149
Darren Clarke	79	70	149
Stephen Leaney	73	76	149
Sergio Garcia	72	77	149
Peter Jacobsen	73	77	150
Tom Lehman	75	75	150
Steve Lowery	75	75	150
Tom Watson	75	75	150
Don Berry	74	76	150
Shingo Katayama	75	75	150
Mathias Gronberg	76	74	150
Greg Owen	77	73	150
Fredrik Jacobson	76	74	150
Bradley Dredge	75	75	150
Carl Pettersson	74	76	150

	SCORES		TOTAL
Mark Brooks	77	74	151
John Daly	76	75	151
Bob Tway	78	73	151
Kevin Burton	78	73	151
Chris Riley	73	78	151
Retief Goosen	77	74	151
Lee Westwood	73	78	151
Ignacio Garrido	75	76	151
Brian Davis	73	78	151
Ben Curtis	75	76	151
John Rollins	78	73	151
Hank Kuehne	70	81	151
Alastair Forsyth	73	78	151
Rob Labritz	76	75	151
Jeff Maggert	79	73	152
Chip Sullivan	74	78	152
J.C. Anderson	76	76	152
Stewart Cink	79	73	152
Phillip Price	77	75	152
Scott Porter	80	72	152
Jerry Kelly	78	75	153
Jeffrey Lankford	78	76	154
Ken Schall	80	74	154
Jeff Sluman	75	79	154
Tim Thelen	75	79	154
Justin Leonard	79	75	154
Robert Karlsson	75	79	154
Mark O'Meara	73	82	155
David Tentis	79	76	155
Dean Wilson	78	77	155
Anders Hansen	78	77	155
Justin Rose	77	78	155
Stephen Ames	82	74	156
Colin Montgomerie	82	74	156
Craig Parry	79	78	157
Tim Petrovic	82	75	157
Steve Schneiter	77	80	157
Dino Lucchesi	79	78	157
Rich Beem	82	75	157
Mike Schuchart	77	81	158
Michael Combs	79	79	158
Andre Stolz	75	83	158
Cary Sciorra	76	82	158
Skip Kendall	80	79	159
Rick Schuller	79	80	159
Bob Sowards	81	78	159
Jonathan Byrd	80	79	159
Ron Philo, Jr.	82	78	160
Ricardo Gonzalez	77	83	160
Sean Farren	79	81	160
Brad Faxon	82	79	161
Dave Spengler	81	80	161
Pierre Fulke	81	80	161
Toru Taniguchi	82	79	161
John Guyton	80	81	161
Alan Morin	84	79	163
Terry Hatch	84	81	165
Tim Fleming	84	83	167
John Huston	79		WD
Kirk Triplett	76		WD

	SCORES	TOTAL
John Jacobs	87	WD
David Duval	80	WD
Wayne Defrancesco	79	WD

(Professionals who did not complete 72 holes received $2,000.)

WGC NEC Invitational

Firestone Country Club, South Course, Akron, Ohio
Par 35-35–70; 7,139 yards

August 21-24
purse, $6,000,000

	SCORES				TOTAL	MONEY
Darren Clarke	65	70	66	67	268	$1,050,000
Jonathan Kaye	68	69	65	70	272	550,000
Davis Love	66	70	68	69	273	360,000
Tiger Woods	65	72	67	70	274	235,000
Chris Riley	66	67	70	71	274	235,000
Vijay Singh	69	65	72	69	275	163,333.34
Jim Furyk	69	69	68	69	275	163,333.33
Robert Allenby	69	69	68	69	275	163,333.33
Brad Faxon	68	67	70	71	276	116,750
Trevor Immelman	70	68	70	68	276	116,750
Dan Forsman	69	68	70	70	277	91,666.67
Bernhard Langer	71	73	65	68	277	91,666.67
Steve Flesch	71	67	67	72	277	91,666.66
Fred Funk	72	62	72	72	278	75,000
Peter Jacobsen	73	64	71	70	278	75,000
Toshimitsu Izawa	70	71	68	69	278	75,000
Jay Haas	72	69	73	65	279	59,250
Ernie Els	67	70	71	71	279	59,250
Retief Goosen	67	69	69	74	279	59,250
Paul Casey	72	66	71	70	279	59,250
Fred Couples	67	71	71	71	280	52,500
Charles Howell	72	68	74	66	280	52,500
Phil Mickelson	68	73	70	70	281	48,000
Shaun Micheel	71	69	70	71	281	48,000
Colin Montgomerie	68	70	70	73	281	48,000
Mike Weir	71	72	69	69	281	48,000
Justin Leonard	75	69	69	68	281	48,000
Peter Lonard	70	73	72	66	281	48,000
Angel Cabrera	70	71	70	70	281	48,000
Len Mattiace	72	69	69	72	282	43,000
Sergio Garcia	64	76	69	73	282	43,000
Ben Curtis	64	76	72	70	282	43,000
Eduardo Romero	70	74	68	71	283	38,583.33
Hal Sutton	68	69	68	78	283	38,583.33
David Toms	66	67	76	74	283	38,583.33
Chris DiMarco	71	68	73	71	283	38,583.34
Justin Rose	72	73	69	69	283	38,583.34
Ian Poulter	73	68	67	75	283	38,583.33
Paul Azinger	72	69	67	76	284	35,500
Jeff Sluman	67	74	75	68	284	35,500
Padraig Harrington	73	71	70	70	284	35,500
Nick Price	73	67	71	74	285	33,750
Alex Cejka	72	68	71	74	285	33,750
Robert-Jan Derksen	73	70	70	72	285	33,750
Ben Crane	71	75	68	71	285	33,750

	SCORES				TOTAL	MONEY
Bob Estes	68	74	70	74	286	31,500
Scott Verplank	66	73	70	77	286	31,500
Stuart Appleby	70	75	68	73	286	31,500
Lee Westwood	70	70	73	73	286	31,500
Steve Allan	74	68	76	68	286	31,500
Scott Hoch	69	72	72	74	287	29,750
Rory Sabbatini	73	72	70	72	287	29,750
Mark Calcavecchia	70	68	73	77	288	28,150
Kenny Perry	72	76	68	72	288	28,150
Jerry Kelly	68	71	76	73	288	28,150
Chad Campbell	73	71	72	72	288	28,150
K.J. Choi	73	71	71	73	288	28,150
Paul McGinley	70	71	73	75	289	27,000
Kaname Yokoo	73	71	70	75	289	27,000
Niclas Fasth	67	76	74	72	289	27,000
Thomas Bjorn	72	72	75	71	290	26,250
Stewart Cink	70	71	74	75	290	26,250
Philip Golding	76	69	73	72	290	26,250
Craig Parry	69	75	71	76	291	25,500
Tim Clark	73	69	73	76	291	25,500
Adam Scott	72	70	69	80	291	25,500
Phillip Price	68	75	75	74	292	24,625
Pierre Fulke	72	72	75	73	292	24,625
John Rollins	75	72	71	74	292	24,625
Rich Beem	69	69	78	76	292	24,625
Steen Tinning	71	74	76	72	293	23,375
Jesper Parnevik	69	72	75	77	293	23,375
Stephen Leaney	75	69	72	77	293	23,375
Michael Campbell	74	71	70	78	293	23,375
Jonathan Byrd	71	77	73	72	293	23,375
Kevin Na	71	80	69	73	293	23,375
Rocco Mediate	78	73	69	74	294	22,000
Bob Burns	74	70	75	75	294	22,000
Robert Karlsson	72	72	77	73	294	22,000
Ignacio Garrido	74	74	72	74	294	22,000
Hennie Otto	72	69	75	78	294	22,000
Nick Faldo	74	67	79	75	295	21,125
Jarrod Moseley	76	74	72	73	295	21,125
Fredrik Jacobson	75	71	77	73	296	20,750
Gene Sauers	73	76	77	82	308	20,500

Reno-Tahoe Open

Montreux Golf & Country Club, Reno, Nevada
Par 36-36–72; 7,577 yards

August 21-24
purse, $3,000,000

	SCORES				TOTAL	MONEY
Kirk Triplett	67	68	73	63	271	$540,000
Tim Herron	69	65	69	71	274	324,000
Dennis Paulson	68	66	73	68	275	174,000
Rodney Pampling	67	73	67	68	275	174,000
Harrison Frazar	69	72	70	66	277	120,000
Craig Barlow	70	65	68	75	278	104,250
Hidemichi Tanaka	71	71	67	69	278	104,250
J.P. Hayes	68	68	71	72	279	93,000
David Sutherland	70	67	72	71	280	87,000
Guy Boros	71	66	70	74	281	66,500

	SCORES				TOTAL	MONEY
Mike Grob	69	74	68	70	281	66,500
Paul Stankowski	67	72	69	73	281	66,500
Dicky Pride	71	68	72	70	281	66,500
Scott McCarron	71	72	70	68	281	66,500
Nick Watney	72	66	70	73	281	66,500
David Peoples	70	71	69	72	282	45,000
Paul Goydos	72	70	70	70	282	45,000
Thomas Levet	71	70	73	68	282	45,000
Brian Gay	69	69	73	71	282	45,000
J.J. Henry	66	75	68	73	282	45,000
Billy Mayfair	69	72	71	71	283	30,000
Chris Smith	69	72	72	70	283	30,000
Duffy Waldorf	71	69	71	72	283	30,000
Neal Lancaster	72	69	72	70	283	30,000
Tom Scherrer	72	71	72	68	283	30,000
Cameron Beckman	68	69	70	76	283	30,000
Jeff Maggert	70	72	71	71	284	19,550
John Riegger	71	70	70	73	284	19,550
Bob Tway	67	73	70	74	284	19,550
Grant Waite	74	69	74	67	284	19,550
Kevin Sutherland	72	71	73	68	284	19,550
Woody Austin	69	72	69	74	284	19,550
Paul Gow	69	69	74	72	284	19,550
Jason Gore	70	74	72	68	284	19,550
Jason Buha	71	72	71	70	284	19,550
Garrett Willis	70	73	70	72	285	14,750
Patrick Sheehan	70	75	73	67	285	14,750
Luke Donald	68	75	71	71	285	14,750
Mark Brooks	71	71	72	72	286	11,700
David Frost	69	73	71	73	286	11,700
Shigeki Maruyama	70	69	72	75	286	11,700
Carl Paulson	66	76	76	68	286	11,700
Arron Oberholser	71	71	72	72	286	11,700
Darron Stiles	75	70	72	69	286	11,700
Andy Miller	67	73	74	72	286	11,700
Richard Zokol	72	71	69	75	287	8,505
Todd Fischer	73	72	72	70	287	8,505
John Senden	69	73	71	74	287	8,505
Chris Anderson	75	69	74	69	287	8,505
Tommy Armour	74	71	72	71	288	7,131.43
Bart Bryant	70	69	72	77	288	7,131.43
Robin Freeman	67	75	74	72	288	7,131.43
Mike Standly	74	70	74	70	288	7,131.42
Mike Heinen	73	71	74	70	288	7,131.43
Cliff Kresge	71	74	70	73	288	7,131.43
Brad Elder	69	75	72	72	288	7,131.43
Jay Don Blake	72	70	76	71	289	6,690
Steve Pate	67	73	79	70	289	6,690
Pat Bates	71	74	70	74	289	6,690
Aaron Barber	69	74	74	72	289	6,690
Jay Delsing	70	72	74	74	290	6,450
Greg Kraft	72	71	72	75	290	6,450
Jose Coceres	73	68	76	73	290	6,450
Richard S. Johnson	73	68	77	72	290	6,450
Corey Pavin	72	72	75	72	291	6,240
Deane Pappas	70	73	75	73	291	6,240
Jason Caron	69	73	73	76	291	6,240
Gavin Coles	70	71	74	77	292	6,060
Pat Perez	69	76	74	73	292	6,060
Akio Sadakata	72	69	78	73	292	6,060

	SCORES				TOTAL	MONEY
Jeff Klein	75	69	75	74	293	5,940
Frank Lickliter	72	71	73	78	294	5,880
Mathew Goggin	73	71	80	71	295	5,820
Gary Hallberg	70	75	80	72	297	5,700
David Ogrin	71	74	75	77	297	5,700
Steven Alker	72	73	76	76	297	5,700
Anthony Painter	71	72	80	75	298	5,580

Deutsche Bank Championship

TPC of Boston, Norton, Massachusetts
Par 36-35–71; 7,145 yards

August 29-September 1
purse, $5,000,000

	SCORES				TOTAL	MONEY
Adam Scott	69	62	67	66	264	$900,000
Rocco Mediate	67	70	66	65	268	540,000
Justin Rose	63	71	68	67	269	340,000
Vijay Singh	65	68	71	66	270	240,000
Tim Herron	67	68	68	68	271	190,000
Geoff Ogilvy	68	66	68	69	271	190,000
Steve Flesch	66	69	69	69	273	161,250
Tiger Woods	70	69	67	67	273	161,250
Darren Clarke	67	68	67	73	275	140,000
Jonathan Kaye	71	67	63	74	275	140,000
Tim Clark	71	69	66	70	276	120,000
Carl Pettersson	71	71	67	67	276	120,000
Glen Day	68	68	72	69	277	88,333.33
Kent Jones	68	69	72	68	277	88,333.33
Jim Furyk	74	68	69	66	277	88,333.34
Phillip Price	67	72	72	66	277	88,333.34
John Senden	74	64	69	70	277	88,333.33
Jonathan Byrd	70	71	67	69	277	88,333.33
Tim Petrovic	66	70	72	70	278	60,600
Robert Allenby	74	64	72	68	278	60,600
Dean Wilson	70	70	71	67	278	60,600
Briny Baird	71	67	70	70	278	60,600
Darron Stiles	71	68	68	71	278	60,600
Brad Faxon	75	66	68	70	279	41,500
Greg Norman	69	67	70	73	279	41,500
Mike Grob	71	70	70	68	279	41,500
Peter Lonard	70	70	69	70	279	41,500
Paul Gow	73	68	68	70	279	41,500
Dan Forsman	73	69	69	69	280	34,000
Glen Hnatiuk	69	72	67	72	280	34,000
Stewart Cink	72	67	70	71	280	34,000
Paul Azinger	69	73	70	69	281	25,400
David Frost	69	71	71	70	281	25,400
Andrew Magee	70	68	76	67	281	25,400
Billy Mayfair	68	73	70	70	281	25,400
Tom Pernice, Jr.	73	69	71	68	281	25,400
Neal Lancaster	71	71	69	70	281	25,400
Joe Durant	71	71	72	67	281	25,400
Todd Fischer	72	66	72	71	281	25,400
Arron Oberholser	66	73	70	72	281	25,400
K.J. Choi	67	68	68	78	281	25,400
Joey Sindelar	72	68	70	72	282	17,500
Jeff Sluman	71	71	68	72	282	17,500
Carl Paulson	68	69	71	74	282	17,500

		SCORES			TOTAL	MONEY
Harrison Frazar	72	68	73	69	282	17,500
Richard S. Johnson	71	70	71	70	282	17,500
Olin Browne	70	70	70	73	283	12,440
Jim Carter	69	71	70	73	283	12,440
Corey Pavin	69	72	73	69	283	12,440
Pat Bates	66	75	74	68	283	12,440
Tom Gillis	70	70	72	71	283	12,440
Jay Williamson	72	67	71	73	283	12,440
Carlos Franco	74	68	71	70	283	12,440
Garrett Willis	66	72	68	77	283	12,440
Kenichi Kuboya	71	67	73	72	283	12,440
Patrick Sheehan	73	69	72	69	283	12,440
Paul Stankowski	74	68	75	67	284	11,200
Jesper Parnevik	72	68	72	72	284	11,200
Mark Wilson	71	70	74	69	284	11,200
Spike McRoy	74	68	72	71	285	10,900
Cliff Kresge	65	75	72	73	285	10,900
Heath Slocum	67	71	72	75	285	10,900
Jeff Maggert	71	69	74	72	286	10,600
Brian Henninger	67	73	73	73	286	10,600
Frank Lickliter	70	70	70	76	286	10,600
John Maginnes	71	69	73	74	287	10,400
Cameron Yancey	72	68	77	71	288	10,300
Robert Damron	70	72	75	72	289	10,200
Doug Barron	69	71	75	75	290	10,100
Brent Schwarzrock	66	74	76	76	292	10,000
Tim Wilkinson	74	68	74	77	293	9,900

Bell Canadian Open

Hamilton Golf & Country Club, Ancaster,
Ontario, Canada
Par 35-35–70; 6,986 yards

September 4-7
purse, $4,200,000

		SCORES			TOTAL	MONEY
Bob Tway	70	70	66	66	272	$756,000
Brad Faxon	67	72	66	67	272	453,600
(Tway defeated Faxon on third playoff hole.)						
Tom Pernice, Jr.	68	72	65	68	273	285,600
Hidemichi Tanaka	66	70	67	71	274	184,800
K.J. Choi	71	70	67	66	274	184,800
Fred Funk	69	68	68	70	275	145,950
Vijay Singh	75	67	65	68	275	145,950
Loren Roberts	70	67	71	68	276	126,000
Matt Gogel	69	70	70	67	276	126,000
Mike Weir	69	69	70	69	277	113,400
Tommy Armour	68	71	70	69	278	96,600
Garrett Willis	70	69	69	70	278	96,600
Steve Allan	72	66	69	71	278	96,600
Jay Don Blake	71	72	71	65	279	63,093.34
Tom Byrum	67	69	73	70	279	63,093.33
Bob Estes	70	69	71	69	279	63,093.33
Len Mattiace	71	69	70	69	279	63,093.33
Jeff Sluman	72	69	71	67	279	63,093.34
Paul Goydos	71	70	67	71	279	63,093.33
Thomas Levet	72	70	70	67	279	63,093.33
Peter Lonard	71	69	72	67	279	63,093.34

	SCORES				TOTAL	MONEY
Charles Howell	67	68	70	74	279	63,093.33
David Edwards	71	69	70	70	280	35,400
Tom Lehman	68	69	74	69	280	35,400
Stephen Ames	72	69	69	70	280	35,400
Glen Day	67	73	73	67	280	35,400
Chris Riley	69	70	69	72	280	35,400
Mathew Goggin	69	72	68	71	280	35,400
Patrick Sheehan	68	73	69	70	280	35,400
Mike Standly	75	67	70	69	281	27,930
Dicky Pride	70	72	70	69	281	27,930
Kelly Gibson	67	70	75	70	282	21,336
Dennis Paulson	74	69	65	74	282	21,336
John Riegger	71	70	74	67	282	21,336
Scott Verplank	72	70	73	67	282	21,336
Neal Lancaster	75	65	73	69	282	21,336
Jeff Brehaut	68	71	70	73	282	21,336
Deane Pappas	72	70	70	70	282	21,336
Aaron Barber	75	68	67	72	282	21,336
Pat Perez	71	72	68	71	282	21,336
Adam Scott	74	69	68	71	282	21,336
Donnie Hammond	72	71	68	72	283	14,280
Dave Rummells	73	70	69	71	283	14,280
David Sutherland	71	71	73	68	283	14,280
Steven Alker	72	68	73	70	283	14,280
Aaron Baddeley	71	69	71	72	283	14,280
Hunter Mahan	73	69	70	71	283	14,280
Paul Azinger	70	68	76	70	284	10,342.50
David Frost	73	66	71	74	284	10,342.50
Joey Sindelar	74	68	71	71	284	10,342.50
Mike Springer	72	67	69	76	284	10,342.50
Kent Jones	71	68	72	73	284	10,342.50
Carlos Franco	74	67	70	73	284	10,342.50
Chris Anderson	71	71	72	70	284	10,342.50
Jason Buha	70	70	70	74	284	10,342.50
Mark Wilson	74	68	70	73	285	9,450
Michael Harris	71	72	71	71	285	9,450
Andy Miller	69	73	70	73	285	9,450
John E. Morgan	71	72	71	71	285	9,450
Jim Carter	70	72	69	75	286	8,988
Jim McGovern	71	68	75	72	286	8,988
Steve Stricker	74	68	72	72	286	8,988
Brett Quigley	71	72	72	71	286	8,988
Kaname Yokoo	73	70	73	70	286	8,988
Derek Gillespie	69	74	73	70	286	8,988
Jon Mills	71	72	72	71	286	8,988
Corey Pavin	73	70	72	72	287	8,442
Mike Grob	71	69	73	74	287	8,442
Glen Hnatiuk	71	70	74	72	287	8,442
Todd Fischer	70	73	68	76	287	8,442
Briny Baird	71	66	78	72	287	8,442
Paul Gow	73	67	74	73	287	8,442
Olin Browne	70	71	72	75	288	8,022
Mike Sposa	72	71	73	72	288	8,022
David Morland	71	70	71	76	288	8,022
Kenichi Kuboya	69	67	74	78	288	8,022
*Christopher Baryla	71	68	77	72	288	
Guy Boros	72	69	74	74	289	7,812
Bill Glasson	68	71	78	76	293	7,686
Esteban Toledo	72	70	75	76	293	7,686
Jeff Klein	71	72	76	78	297	7,560

John Deere Classic

TPC at Deere Run, Silvis, Illinois
Par 35-36–71; 7,183 yards
(Event extended to Monday—rain.)

September 12-15
purse, $3,500,000

		SCORES			TOTAL	MONEY
Vijay Singh	66	68	69	65	268	$630,000
J.L. Lewis	65	65	71	71	272	261,333.33
Chris Riley	66	69	66	71	272	261,333.34
Jonathan Byrd	65	67	72	68	272	261,333.33
Kevin Sutherland	69	67	71	66	273	127,750
Paul Stankowski	70	65	68	70	273	127,750
Hidemichi Tanaka	70	67	67	69	273	127,750
Jerry Kelly	71	70	68	65	274	105,000
Notah Begay	67	71	65	71	274	105,000
Bernhard Langer	71	65	70	69	275	91,000
Glen Day	72	65	70	68	275	91,000
Joe Durant	70	68	68	70	276	73,500
Tom Gillis	75	65	68	68	276	73,500
Pat Perez	69	68	71	68	276	73,500
Mathias Gronberg	71	69	69	68	277	61,250
Carl Pettersson	71	70	73	63	277	61,250
Billy Mayfair	67	71	69	71	278	50,750
Scott McCarron	70	68	69	71	278	50,750
Aaron Barber	68	70	70	70	278	50,750
Brent Schwarzrock	73	67	70	68	278	50,750
Stephen Ames	72	69	72	66	279	37,800
Bob Burns	67	73	69	70	279	37,800
Niclas Fasth	73	68	68	70	279	37,800
Harrison Frazar	69	69	72	69	279	37,800
Jeff Maggert	68	72	71	69	280	29,400
Steven Alker	69	73	67	71	280	29,400
Mark Brooks	71	70	71	69	281	22,808.33
Tom Byrum	70	69	72	70	281	22,808.33
Peter Jacobsen	72	69	73	67	281	22,808.33
Davis Love	70	70	70	71	281	22,808.34
Steve Lowery	72	68	75	66	281	22,808.34
Paul Goydos	71	71	71	68	281	22,808.33
Brian Gay	72	68	70	71	281	22,808.33
Garrett Willis	67	73	69	72	281	22,808.34
Brenden Pappas	69	73	71	68	281	22,808.33
Skip Kendall	67	74	72	69	282	15,069.44
John Riegger	73	69	68	72	282	15,069.44
Chris Smith	67	72	72	71	282	15,069.45
Shaun Micheel	73	66	73	70	282	15,069.45
Jeff Brehaut	70	72	68	72	282	15,069.44
Craig Barlow	69	70	70	73	282	15,069.45
Kenichi Kuboya	69	70	70	73	282	15,069.45
Chris Anderson	69	69	71	73	282	15,069.44
Luke Donald	70	72	70	70	282	15,069.44
Paul Azinger	69	72	70	72	283	10,850
Robert Gamez	69	73	71	70	283	10,850
Dennis Paulson	67	72	71	73	283	10,850
Jim Carter	72	69	71	72	284	8,904
Joey Sindelar	68	73	70	73	284	8,904
Stan Utley	73	66	73	72	284	8,904
Greg Chalmers	71	70	74	69	284	8,904
Akio Sadakata	70	68	74	72	284	8,904
Tom Lehman	72	69	76	68	285	8,064

	SCORES				TOTAL	MONEY
Loren Roberts	70	70	73	72	285	8,064
D.A. Weibring	69	69	73	74	285	8,064
Deane Pappas	72	70	74	69	285	8,064
Tom Scherrer	67	74	71	73	285	8,064
Kirk Triplett	72	69	73	72	286	7,805
Steve Allan	72	70	74	70	286	7,805
Tommy Armour	68	74	73	73	288	7,700
Esteban Toledo	68	72	76	73	289	7,595
Andy Miller	69	72	72	76	289	7,595
Mike Grob	72	69	76	73	290	7,490
*Tyler Swanson	71	71	76	73	291	
Bart Bryant	72	70	76	74	292	7,420

84 Lumber Classic of Pennsylvania

Nemacolin Woodlands Resort & Spa, Mystic Rock Course, Farmington, Pennsylvania
Par 36-36–72; 7,329 yards
(Due to rain delays, 36 holes played on Sunday.)

September 18-21
purse, $4,000,000

	SCORES				TOTAL	MONEY
J.L. Lewis	69	67	68	62	266	$720,000
Tim Petrovic	67	69	65	67	268	298,666.66
Frank Lickliter	70	67	65	66	268	298,666.67
Stuart Appleby	69	68	64	67	268	298,666.67
Rocco Mediate	68	70	67	66	271	146,000
Cameron Beckman	67	66	64	74	271	146,000
Jesper Parnevik	68	66	70	67	271	146,000
Craig Barlow	67	68	68	69	272	120,000
Robert Damron	67	66	66	73	272	120,000
Chris DiMarco	70	65	67	71	273	100,000
Shigeki Maruyama	68	70	67	68	273	100,000
Rory Sabbatini	68	70	64	71	273	100,000
Brett Quigley	67	67	70	70	274	77,333.33
Jerry Kelly	67	68	69	70	274	77,333.34
Kenichi Kuboya	71	68	70	65	274	77,333.33
Skip Kendall	68	69	71	67	275	47,566.67
Chris Smith	71	68	68	68	275	47,566.66
Tom Gillis	69	68	71	67	275	47,566.67
Tom Scherrer	71	64	74	66	275	47,566.67
Michael Clark	66	71	68	70	275	47,566.67
Carl Paulson	68	69	66	72	275	47,566.67
Arron Oberholser	68	71	71	65	275	47,566.67
Heath Slocum	70	64	72	69	275	47,566.66
Ben Curtis	69	67	70	69	275	47,566.67
David Gossett	69	69	69	68	275	47,566.67
Luke Donald	67	72	72	64	275	47,566.66
Jonathan Byrd	69	68	68	70	275	47,566.67
Len Mattiace	68	70	69	69	276	29,000
Steve Stricker	69	70	68	69	276	29,000
Grant Waite	66	71	69	71	277	26,000
Mathew Goggin	69	70	68	70	277	26,000
Chris Anderson	70	69	69	69	277	26,000
Billy Andrade	73	64	68	73	278	20,250
David Edwards	69	69	72	68	278	20,250
David Peoples	67	69	67	75	278	20,250
Mike Springer	71	68	71	68	278	20,250

	SCORES				TOTAL	MONEY
Mike Standly	67	69	70	72	278	20,250
Jim McGovern	72	66	69	71	278	20,250
Pat Bates	67	71	69	71	278	20,250
Harrison Frazar	69	68	70	71	278	20,250
Donnie Hammond	65	72	69	73	279	15,600
Jeff Gallagher	71	68	71	69	279	15,600
Glen Day	71	65	73	70	279	15,600
David Frost	67	71	72	70	280	12,432
Joe Durant	71	68	72	69	280	12,432
Rodney Pampling	70	69	71	70	280	12,432
Brent Schwarzrock	66	72	69	73	280	12,432
Kenneth Staton	69	66	71	74	280	12,432
Jay Don Blake	71	68	72	70	281	9,980
Jeff Maggert	69	68	69	75	281	9,980
Joey Sindelar	68	69	74	70	281	9,980
Scott Laycock	67	68	77	69	281	9,980
Jeff Brehaut	68	71	70	73	282	9,360
J.J. Henry	73	66	72	71	282	9,360
Tom Pernice, Jr.	67	71	72	74	284	9,200
Brandel Chamblee	70	68	75	72	285	9,120
Cliff Kresge	68	70	71	77	286	9,040

The following players made the 36-hole cut, but field was reduced for Sunday's double round:

			TOTAL	MONEY
John Riegger	70	70	140	8,560
Neal Lancaster	71	69	140	8,560
David Sutherland	71	69	140	8,560
John Morse	70	70	140	8,560
Spike McRoy	70	70	140	8,560
Glen Hnatiuk	70	70	140	8,560
Per-Ulrik Johansson	70	70	140	8,560
Gavin Coles	65	75	140	8,560
Darron Stiles	71	69	140	8,560
Jason Buha	74	66	140	8,560
Andy Miller	69	71	140	8,560
Tommy Armour	70	71	141	7,560
Mark Calcavecchia	73	68	141	7,560
Jim Gallagher, Jr.	68	73	141	7,560
Larry Mize	69	72	141	7,560
Mark O'Meara	68	73	141	7,560
Brian Henninger	74	67	141	7,560
Steve Flesch	68	73	141	7,560
Paul Stankowski	74	67	141	7,560
Robert Allenby	73	68	141	7,560
Gabriel Hjertstedt	73	68	141	7,560
Patrick Sheehan	73	68	141	7,560
Jason Gore	71	70	141	7,560
Hank Kuehne	70	71	141	7,560
Jason Caron	70	71	141	7,560

Valero Texas Open

LaCantera Golf Club, Resort Course, San Antonio, Texas
Par 35-35–70; 7,001 yards

September 25-28
purse, $3,500,000

	SCORES				TOTAL	MONEY
Tommy Armour	64	62	63	65	254	$630,000
Loren Roberts	64	66	69	62	261	308,000
Bob Tway	61	69	67	64	261	308,000
Duffy Waldorf	64	69	62	67	262	168,000
Aaron Baddeley	62	70	69	62	263	140,000
Dan Forsman	64	63	70	67	264	126,000
Paul Goydos	65	64	68	68	265	98,291.66
Steve Flesch	67	66	68	64	265	98,291.67
Glen Hnatiuk	65	68	64	68	265	98,291.66
Frank Lickliter	68	69	64	64	265	98,291.67
K.J. Choi	67	62	69	67	265	98,291.67
Richard S. Johnson	66	67	66	66	265	98,291.67
Kent Jones	68	65	66	67	266	67,666.67
Stewart Cink	65	66	67	68	266	67,666.66
Arron Oberholser	66	66	66	68	266	67,666.67
Tom Lehman	66	63	70	68	267	59,500
Neal Lancaster	65	70	65	68	268	45,800
Mike Heinen	67	65	69	67	268	45,800
Chad Campbell	71	66	67	64	268	45,800
Carl Paulson	66	69	68	65	268	45,800
Garrett Willis	67	65	68	68	268	45,800
Ben Crane	66	69	68	65	268	45,800
Hunter Mahan	70	67	67	64	268	45,800
Olin Browne	67	64	71	67	269	29,050
Tom Byrum	63	71	69	66	269	29,050
David Peoples	65	67	69	68	269	29,050
Tim Petrovic	67	68	65	69	269	29,050
Tim Clark	65	63	71	70	269	29,050
Marco Dawson	67	68	70	65	270	22,750
Cameron Beckman	63	67	71	69	270	22,750
Rodney Pampling	65	68	67	70	270	22,750
Scott Laycock	66	66	69	69	270	22,750
J.J. Henry	68	66	66	70	270	22,750
Billy Andrade	68	67	68	68	271	16,931.25
Robert Gamez	65	72	66	68	271	16,931.25
John Huston	64	68	69	70	271	16,931.25
David Toms	66	66	70	69	271	16,931.25
Shigeki Maruyama	69	68	69	65	271	16,931.25
John Senden	67	69	68	67	271	16,931.25
Paul Gow	70	67	69	65	271	16,931.25
Luke Donald	65	66	69	71	271	16,931.25
Mark Brooks	66	70	70	66	272	13,300
Patrick Sheehan	66	68	71	67	272	13,300
Mark Calcavecchia	68	69	68	68	273	10,115
John Riegger	70	66	69	68	273	10,115
Hal Sutton	66	63	69	75	273	10,115
Greg Kraft	66	71	69	67	273	10,115
Notah Begay	71	63	72	67	273	10,115
Heath Slocum	61	70	70	72	273	10,115
Rory Sabbatini	63	68	72	70	273	10,115
Akio Sadakata	67	64	71	71	273	10,115
Andrew Magee	67	69	69	69	274	8,080
Brandt Jobe	67	67	71	69	274	8,080
Jay Williamson	68	69	68	69	274	8,080

	SCORES				TOTAL	MONEY
Scott McCarron	66	68	68	72	274	8,080
Craig Perks	71	65	69	69	274	8,080
Briny Baird	67	70	69	68	274	8,080
Charles Howell	65	64	70	75	274	8,080
David Edwards	68	69	70	68	275	7,595
Jeff Maggert	69	68	71	67	275	7,595
Corey Pavin	68	69	69	69	275	7,595
Scott Verplank	68	66	67	74	275	7,595
Brian Henninger	67	68	72	68	275	7,595
Bob Burns	69	67	68	71	275	7,595
David Frost	65	69	70	72	276	7,280
J.L. Lewis	65	71	68	72	276	7,280
Stan Utley	70	67	69	70	276	7,280
Dennis Paulson	69	68	68	72	277	6,930
John Maginnes	72	65	68	72	277	6,930
Per-Ulrik Johansson	68	67	71	71	277	6,930
Ian Leggatt	67	69	68	73	277	6,930
Danny Ellis	67	67	71	72	277	6,930
Jose Coceres	67	68	70	72	277	6,930
Jason Gore	65	68	72	72	277	6,930
Cliff Kresge	63	72	72	71	278	6,650
Donnie Hammond	69	68	70	72	279	6,510
Tim Herron	69	67	71	72	279	6,510
Hank Kuehne	67	69	66	77	279	6,510
Sergio Garcia	68	69	68	75	280	6,370
Blaine McCallister	65	71	73	73	282	6,300
Mike Grob	69	67	75	72	283	6,230

WGC American Express Championship

Capital City Club, Crabapple Course, Woodstock, Georgia
Par 35-35–70; 7,137 yards

October 2-5
purse, $6,000,000

	SCORES				TOTAL	MONEY
Tiger Woods	67	66	69	72	274	$1,050,000
Vijay Singh	70	70	64	72	276	405,000
Tim Herron	66	72	67	71	276	405,000
Stuart Appleby	71	68	69	68	276	405,000
David Toms	73	72	67	65	277	235,000
Padraig Harrington	71	73	69	66	279	182,500
K.J. Choi	67	71	68	73	279	182,500
Retief Goosen	73	69	67	72	281	137,500
Paul Casey	73	71	66	71	281	137,500
Fred Couples	71	73	70	68	282	111,250
Ignacio Garrido	68	71	69	74	282	111,250
Ernie Els	71	74	71	67	283	89,375
Jim Furyk	70	74	69	70	283	89,375
Alex Cejka	70	76	72	65	283	89,375
Sergio Garcia	65	73	70	75	283	89,375
Brad Faxon	75	71	66	72	284	71,000
Rocco Mediate	66	72	73	73	284	71,000
Loren Roberts	69	75	70	70	284	71,000
Niclas Fasth	68	76	70	70	284	71,000
Jonathan Kaye	73	69	73	70	285	65,000
Steve Flesch	71	75	72	68	286	60,000
Jerry Kelly	70	72	69	75	286	60,000
Robert Allenby	72	76	73	65	286	60,000
Charles Howell	76	75	65	70	286	60,000

	SCORES				TOTAL	MONEY
Bob Estes	77	74	68	68	287	53,000
Eduardo Romero	72	74	68	73	287	53,000
Toshimitsu Izawa	70	74	72	71	287	53,000
Kenny Perry	70	74	70	74	288	46,071.43
Mike Weir	69	73	72	74	288	46,071.43
Thomas Bjorn	74	73	67	74	288	46,071.42
Chris Riley	74	73	70	71	288	46,071.43
David Howell	74	75	71	68	288	46,071.43
Fredrik Jacobson	75	74	70	69	288	46,071.43
Justin Rose	75	69	74	70	288	46,071.43
Lee Westwood	72	71	71	75	289	41,500
Brian Davis	71	77	68	73	289	41,500
Peter Lonard	75	74	70	71	290	40,000
Phil Mickelson	73	77	70	71	291	38,500
Darren Clarke	69	82	72	68	291	38,500
Fred Funk	73	74	69	76	292	36,250
Davis Love	74	77	70	71	292	36,250
Alastair Forsyth	71	77	71	73	292	36,250
Adam Scott	70	73	75	74	292	36,250
Peter O'Malley	69	74	70	80	293	34,250
Shaun Micheel	72	75	71	75	293	34,250
Trevor Immelman	70	77	71	75	293	34,250
Ian Poulter	73	74	68	78	293	34,250
Nick Price	71	73	73	77	294	32,500
Arjun Atwal	76	72	72	74	294	32,500
Hennie Otto	76	73	73	72	294	32,500
Scott Verplank	75	75	68	77	295	31,083.33
Colin Montgomerie	74	75	70	76	295	31,083.33
Taichi Teshima	77	75	70	73	295	31,083.34
Jay Haas	74	72	75	75	296	30,000
Len Mattiace	70	74	74	78	296	30,000
Craig Parry	76	72	75	73	296	30,000
Phillip Price	70	79	72	75	296	30,000
Jyoti Randhawa	69	77	74	76	296	30,000
J.L. Lewis	72	74	77	74	297	28,625
Bob Tway	73	80	70	74	297	28,625
Chad Campbell	74	76	73	74	297	28,625
Raphael Jacquelin	77	80	68	72	297	28,625
Soren Kjeldsen	70	75	74	78	297	28,625
Rich Beem	76	75	73	73	297	28,625
Kirk Triplett	74	72	70	82	298	27,750
Ben Curtis	76	76	72	75	299	27,375
Thongchai Jaidee	73	72	72	82	299	27,375
Michael Campbell	82	76	75	67	300	26,875
Mark Foster	76	77	73	74	300	26,875
Scott Hoch	75	79	75	72	301	26,375
Chris DiMarco	76	74	76	75	301	26,375
Todd Hamilton	78	81	72	71	302	26,000

Southern Farm Bureau Classic

Annandale Golf Club, Madison, Mississippi
Par 36-36–72; 7,199 yards

October 2-5
purse, $3,000,000

	SCORES				TOTAL	MONEY
John Huston	66	66	68	68	268	$540,000
Brenden Pappas	72	69	66	62	269	324,000
Shigeki Maruyama	68	68	68	66	270	204,000

	SCORES				TOTAL	MONEY
Paul Stankowski	68	68	66	70	272	124,000
Hidemichi Tanaka	66	68	68	70	272	124,000
Chris Anderson	69	66	67	70	272	124,000
Glen Day	72	69	66	66	273	93,500
Jose Coceres	71	67	70	65	273	93,500
Tim Clark	69	66	69	69	273	93,500
Russ Cochran	71	69	68	66	274	75,000
Luke Donald	69	67	67	71	274	75,000
John E. Morgan	73	65	68	68	274	75,000
Bill Glasson	76	67	67	65	275	53,000
Bernhard Langer	71	71	66	67	275	53,000
David Peoples	73	67	67	68	275	53,000
Jim McGovern	68	69	69	69	275	53,000
Kent Jones	68	70	68	69	275	53,000
Craig Barlow	71	71	67	66	275	53,000
Billy Andrade	71	68	70	67	276	35,100
David Frost	68	69	69	70	276	35,100
Neal Lancaster	73	67	68	68	276	35,100
Brian Henninger	72	70	69	65	276	35,100
Brett Quigley	68	69	71	68	276	35,100
Jeff Brehaut	74	68	67	67	276	35,100
Joe Durant	72	67	72	66	277	22,900
Per-Ulrik Johansson	72	70	65	70	277	22,900
Stewart Cink	74	66	69	68	277	22,900
Patrick Sheehan	67	73	67	70	277	22,900
Ben Crane	70	69	70	68	277	22,900
Carl Pettersson	69	73	70	65	277	22,900
Corey Pavin	69	68	71	70	278	17,400
Brandt Jobe	72	69	66	71	278	17,400
Woody Austin	71	67	72	68	278	17,400
Mike Heinen	71	71	69	67	278	17,400
Thomas Levet	72	71	70	65	278	17,400
Scott Laycock	71	72	69	66	278	17,400
Esteban Toledo	75	67	69	68	279	14,400
Danny Ellis	71	71	70	67	279	14,400
Bart Bryant	69	70	72	69	280	12,900
Tom Scherrer	72	67	71	70	280	12,900
Brian Gay	74	67	68	71	280	12,900
Olin Browne	71	69	69	72	281	9,420
Joey Sindelar	69	70	70	72	281	9,420
Willie Wood	71	66	73	71	281	9,420
Brian Bateman	71	70	70	70	281	9,420
Spike McRoy	69	72	69	71	281	9,420
Tom Gillis	70	70	68	73	281	9,420
Mike Sposa	71	71	72	67	281	9,420
Vance Veazey	75	66	75	65	281	9,420
Paul Gow	70	68	74	69	281	9,420
Kelly Gibson	71	69	69	73	282	7,104
John Riegger	70	73	71	68	282	7,104
Ian Leggatt	70	71	73	68	282	7,104
Greg Chalmers	70	70	73	69	282	7,104
David Gossett	73	70	67	72	282	7,104
Brad Bryant	73	70	67	73	283	6,780
Skip Kendall	71	72	70	70	283	6,780
Pat Bates	73	70	68	72	283	6,780
David Edwards	67	72	72	73	284	6,510
Hal Sutton	71	72	71	70	284	6,510
Greg Kraft	73	70	72	69	284	6,510
Kenichi Kuboya	71	71	73	69	284	6,510

	SCORES				TOTAL	MONEY
Heath Slocum	71	71	73	69	284	6,510
Akio Sadakata	76	66	73	69	284	6,510
Carlos Franco	66	72	69	78	285	6,300
Mike Springer	72	68	71	76	287	6,210
John Maginnes	69	71	77	70	287	6,210
Dave Stockton, Jr.	71	68	76	73	288	6,090
Anthony Painter	72	71	69	76	288	6,090
Nolan Henke	74	69	74	72	289	5,970
Kaname Yokoo	72	71	75	71	289	5,970

Las Vegas Invitational

TPC at Summerlin: Par 36-36–72; 7,243 yards
TPC at The Canyons: Par 36-35–71; 7,063 yards
Southern Highlands GC: Par 36-36–72; 7,381 yards
Las Vegas, Nevada

October 8-12
purse, $4,000,000

	SCORES					TOTAL	MONEY
Stuart Appleby	62	68	63	66	69	328	$720,000
Scott McCarron	69	62	64	67	66	328	432,000
(Appleby defeated McCarron on first playoff hole.)							
Steve Lowery	65	64	70	65	67	331	272,000
Scott Verplank	64	62	66	73	67	332	192,000
David Frost	67	65	71	65	65	333	160,000
Steve Flesch	62	64	66	68	74	334	139,000
Woody Austin	65	65	65	72	67	334	139,000
Billy Andrade	66	71	65	66	67	335	124,000
Phil Mickelson	67	64	69	68	68	336	104,000
Jerry Kelly	65	67	65	73	66	336	104,000
Robert Allenby	66	66	65	66	73	336	104,000
Rory Sabbatini	66	64	71	68	67	336	104,000
Jim Furyk	65	67	67	70	68	337	84,000
Paul Goydos	67	65	68	67	71	338	70,000
Frank Lickliter	70	64	69	66	69	338	70,000
Dean Wilson	67	63	73	69	66	338	70,000
Patrick Sheehan	66	67	68	69	68	338	70,000
Mark Brooks	68	65	64	70	72	339	47,000
Brad Faxon	70	71	65	63	70	339	47,000
Kirk Triplett	68	69	67	68	67	339	47,000
Glen Day	68	63	71	69	68	339	47,000
Matt Gogel	71	68	66	67	67	339	47,000
Stewart Cink	67	66	69	67	70	339	47,000
Mark Wilson	64	68	68	72	67	339	47,000
Charles Howell	63	65	70	69	72	339	47,000
Tom Byrum	69	67	69	70	65	340	28,400
Russ Cochran	64	67	70	72	67	340	28,400
Bill Glasson	67	67	63	71	72	340	28,400
Tim Petrovic	64	67	66	70	73	340	28,400
Kent Jones	69	65	66	69	71	340	28,400
John Senden	63	67	69	71	70	340	28,400
Kenichi Kuboya	71	65	67	66	71	340	28,400
Donnie Hammond	67	67	69	69	69	341	19,400
Skip Kendall	69	68	65	69	70	341	19,400
Tom Lehman	71	65	66	71	68	341	19,400
Andrew Magee	66	71	69	67	68	341	19,400
Duffy Waldorf	69	67	67	70	68	341	19,400
Chris DiMarco	68	67	68	68	70	341	19,400

		SCORES				TOTAL	MONEY
Pat Bates	69	70	64	70	68	341	19,400
Jeff Brehaut	64	68	69	71	69	341	19,400
Chris Riley	65	68	73	67	68	341	19,400
Phillip Price	69	66	70	69	67	341	19,400
Dan Forsman	62	69	75	69	67	342	13,600
Robert Gamez	66	71	67	68	70	342	13,600
Stephen Ames	66	69	68	73	66	342	13,600
Todd Fischer	67	70	65	70	70	342	13,600
John Riegger	68	68	67	67	73	343	10,576
Jeff Sluman	68	67	69	71	68	343	10,576
Paul Stankowski	68	65	72	66	72	343	10,576
Craig Barlow	62	67	68	73	73	343	10,576
Richard S. Johnson	66	65	68	75	69	343	10,576
Bart Bryant	68	68	70	73	65	344	9,440
Brian Bateman	68	68	70	71	67	344	9,440
Mike Heinen	67	68	65	72	72	344	9,440
Bob Estes	69	68	67	76	65	345	9,000
Len Mattiace	72	68	65	71	69	345	9,000
Bob Burns	64	67	67	78	69	345	9,000
Deane Pappas	65	72	68	69	71	345	9,000
Tim Herron	67	62	66	78	72	345	9,000
Rich Beem	63	67	73	71	71	345	9,000
Darren Clarke	63	71	68	73	71	346	8,720
Paul Azinger	66	69	71	72	69	347	8,400
Joe Durant	67	68	70	73	69	347	8,400
Dicky Pride	67	68	70	70	72	347	8,400
Chad Campbell	64	71	70	71	71	347	8,400
Jesper Parnevik	66	69	70	70	72	347	8,400
Cliff Kresge	67	70	69	74	67	347	8,400
Ben Crane	67	68	68	72	72	347	8,400
Steve Pate	66	74	66	69	73	348	8,040
Jonathan Byrd	65	70	71	69	73	348	8,040
Vance Veazey	69	67	68	74	71	349	7,880
Greg Chalmers	72	66	65	72	74	349	7,880
Peter Jacobsen	69	66	71	72	72	350	7,680
Billy Mayfair	71	68	67	72	72	350	7,680
Tom Pernice, Jr.	67	66	72	76	69	350	7,680
Cameron Yancey	70	65	70	74	72	351	7,520
Spike McRoy	68	69	68	70	77	352	7,400
Aaron Barber	63	67	73	77	72	352	7,400
Edward Fryatt	69	69	68	74	76	356	7,280
Notah Begay	68	70	68	79	75	360	7,200

Chrysler Classic of Greensboro

Forest Oaks Country Club, Greensboro, North Carolina
Par 36-36–72; 7,246 yards

October 16-19
purse, $4,500,000

		SCORES			TOTAL	MONEY
Shigeki Maruyama	65	64	70	67	266	$810,000
Brad Faxon	67	67	68	69	271	486,000
Matt Gogel	70	67	68	68	273	306,000
Robert Allenby	70	70	66	68	274	216,000
Jay Haas	69	68	70	68	275	142,392.86
Stephen Ames	64	71	71	69	275	142,392.85
Jeff Brehaut	69	70	68	68	275	142,392.86
Brenden Pappas	71	68	70	66	275	142,392.86
K.J. Choi	68	69	68	70	275	142,392.85

		SCORES			TOTAL	MONEY
Jonathan Byrd	66	70	71	68	275	142,392.86
John E. Morgan	66	72	70	67	275	142,392.86
Dave Stockton, Jr.	68	69	71	68	276	91,125
Mike Heinen	73	66	73	64	276	91,125
Stuart Appleby	68	70	68	70	276	91,125
Briny Baird	69	72	67	68	276	91,125
Robert Gamez	71	70	67	69	277	74,250
Kevin Sutherland	72	70	69	66	277	74,250
John Huston	67	71	70	70	278	60,750
Jeff Sluman	73	66	70	69	278	60,750
Per-Ulrik Johansson	71	66	70	71	278	60,750
Chris Anderson	68	75	68	67	278	60,750
Skip Kendall	69	70	72	68	279	39,487.50
Tom Lehman	70	72	69	68	279	39,487.50
David Sutherland	71	66	69	73	279	39,487.50
Kent Jones	73	68	70	68	279	39,487.50
Jesper Parnevik	70	72	72	65	279	39,487.50
Scott Laycock	72	70	70	67	279	39,487.50
Peter Lonard	68	70	67	74	279	39,487.50
Steven Alker	70	68	68	73	279	39,487.50
Billy Andrade	71	69	70	70	280	26,742.86
Peter Jacobsen	63	74	70	73	280	26,742.85
Corey Pavin	69	73	66	72	280	26,742.86
Joey Sindelar	70	71	70	69	280	26,742.86
Tom Carter	70	66	72	72	280	26,742.86
Brian Gay	71	72	68	69	280	26,742.86
David Gossett	70	72	66	72	280	26,742.85
Tom Pernice, Jr.	69	72	69	71	281	18,450
Tim Petrovic	74	68	67	72	281	18,450
David Toms	65	74	68	74	281	18,450
Brandt Jobe	70	70	72	69	281	18,450
Carl Paulson	68	70	72	71	281	18,450
Retief Goosen	68	73	72	68	281	18,450
Kenichi Kuboya	67	73	69	72	281	18,450
Paul Gow	66	69	72	74	281	18,450
Brad Elder	68	72	70	71	281	18,450
Tom Byrum	68	68	72	74	282	13,110
Jim Furyk	69	69	74	70	282	13,110
Cliff Kresge	70	71	70	71	282	13,110
David Frost	71	71	71	70	283	10,822.50
Jeff Gallagher	73	70	67	73	283	10,822.50
Jerry Kelly	68	75	72	68	283	10,822.50
Dicky Pride	66	70	71	76	283	10,822.50
Todd Fischer	70	73	69	71	283	10,822.50
Mathew Goggin	72	70	72	69	283	10,822.50
Darron Stiles	70	69	72	72	283	10,822.50
Brent Schwarzrock	71	71	73	68	283	10,822.50
Mark Brooks	71	72	73	68	284	10,035
Bernhard Langer	69	73	75	67	284	10,035
Loren Roberts	70	71	71	72	284	10,035
Ben Crane	70	72	73	69	284	10,035
Olin Browne	72	70	68	75	285	9,495
Jim Carter	69	73	70	73	285	9,495
Fred Funk	70	72	72	71	285	9,495
Deane Pappas	73	70	67	75	285	9,495
Kelly Mitchum	68	74	72	71	285	9,495
Robert Damron	71	72	70	72	285	9,495
Greg Chalmers	72	71	72	70	285	9,495
Geoff Ogilvy	68	69	74	74	285	9,495
Andrew Magee	74	69	70	73	286	9,000

	SCORES				TOTAL	MONEY
Neal Lancaster	75	68	69	74	286	9,000
Pat Perez	72	71	72	71	286	9,000
Donnie Hammond	70	72	72	73	287	8,685
Kenny Perry	69	70	73	75	287	8,685
J.P. Hayes	72	70	68	77	287	8,685
Hidemichi Tanaka	70	73	69	75	287	8,685
Gavin Coles	70	73	72	73	288	8,460
Glen Hnatiuk	71	69	75	74	289	8,370
Esteban Toledo	71	72	71	76	290	8,190
Anthony Painter	67	75	74	74	290	8,190
Heath Slocum	69	70	78	73	290	8,190
Jim Gallagher, Jr.	72	70	76	73	291	7,965
Hank Kuehne	72	70	71	78	291	7,965
Thomas Levet	74	69	75	74	292	7,785
Aaron Barber	69	74	76	73	292	7,785
Vance Veazey	70	73	79	71	293	7,650
Carl Pettersson	70	70	79	75	294	7,560
Aaron Baddeley	71	71	76	77	295	7,470
Brandel Chamblee	70	73	77	76	296	7,380
Ty Tryon	73	70	80	74	297	7,290

FUNAI Classic at the Walt Disney World Resort

Walt Disney World Resort, Lake Buena Vista, Florida   October 23-26
Magnolia Course: Par 36-36–72; 7,243 yards   purse, $4,000,000
Palm Course: Par 36-36–72; 7,193 yards

	SCORES				TOTAL	MONEY
Vijay Singh	64	65	69	67	265	$720,000
Scott Verplank	66	66	66	71	269	298,666.67
Tiger Woods	66	67	71	65	269	298,666.67
Stewart Cink	67	65	66	71	269	298,666.66
Davis Love	67	65	69	69	270	152,000
John Rollins	66	65	67	72	270	152,000
Bob Estes	67	63	72	69	271	129,000
Michael Clark	72	66	68	65	271	129,000
Rocco Mediate	65	67	69	71	272	108,000
Bob Tway	67	65	71	69	272	108,000
Geoff Ogilvy	66	70	66	70	272	108,000
Fred Couples	68	66	68	71	273	78,400
David Peoples	65	66	69	73	273	78,400
Jim Furyk	70	67	71	65	273	78,400
Tom Carter	67	67	71	68	273	78,400
Brent Schwarzrock	67	65	72	69	273	78,400
Briny Baird	72	62	70	70	274	64,000
Tommy Armour	69	67	71	68	275	50,400
Dan Forsman	65	69	73	68	275	50,400
Tom Pernice, Jr.	71	67	67	70	275	50,400
Retief Goosen	70	64	68	73	275	50,400
Charles Howell	68	68	70	69	275	50,400
Ben Crane	66	71	71	67	275	50,400
Bart Bryant	68	68	70	70	276	32,400
Tom Lehman	68	70	68	70	276	32,400
Woody Austin	73	63	72	68	276	32,400
Spike McRoy	68	70	70	68	276	32,400
John Senden	70	69	69	68	276	32,400
Tim Clark	69	65	74	68	276	32,400

	SCORES			TOTAL	MONEY
Jay Don Blake	69	66	71	71	277	22,755.56
Brad Bryant	70	66	72	69	277	22,755.56
Phil Mickelson	71	67	72	67	277	22,755.55
Jeff Sluman	67	70	72	68	277	22,755.56
Duffy Waldorf	68	67	70	72	277	22,755.55
Jesper Parnevik	70	69	67	71	277	22,755.55
Peter Lonard	69	69	70	69	277	22,755.56
Brenden Pappas	63	72	72	70	277	22,755.56
Aaron Barber	69	67	70	71	277	22,755.55
Robert Gamez	68	71	68	71	278	16,000
Kirk Triplett	67	69	71	71	278	16,000
Stephen Ames	72	64	71	71	278	16,000
Deane Pappas	66	73	66	73	278	16,000
David Gossett	69	70	72	67	278	16,000
Richard S. Johnson	68	71	69	70	278	16,000
John Huston	64	71	70	74	279	11,712
Joe Durant	67	68	72	72	279	11,712
Brett Quigley	69	69	72	69	279	11,712
Craig Barlow	69	70	71	69	279	11,712
Hidemichi Tanaka	69	66	68	76	279	11,712
Corey Pavin	66	69	72	73	280	9,508.57
Gene Sauers	70	66	73	71	280	9,508.57
Shaun Micheel	69	70	72	69	280	9,508.57
Kevin Sutherland	68	70	70	72	280	9,508.57
Notah Begay	69	69	70	72	280	9,508.58
Anthony Painter	73	65	75	67	280	9,508.57
Mathew Goggin	71	67	71	71	280	9,508.57
Steve Flesch	70	68	72	71	281	8,840
Cliff Kresge	69	69	73	70	281	8,840
Harrison Frazar	67	70	73	71	281	8,840
Heath Slocum	69	70	73	69	281	8,840
Rory Sabbatini	68	71	73	69	281	8,840
Pat Perez	64	71	74	72	281	8,840
Nick Price	70	68	67	77	282	8,320
Paul Goydos	67	69	72	74	282	8,320
Glen Day	69	69	74	70	282	8,320
Aaron Baddeley	69	70	72	71	282	8,320
Jason Gore	71	66	77	68	282	8,320
Hank Kuehne	69	70	74	69	282	8,320
Carl Pettersson	70	67	70	75	282	8,320
Skip Kendall	69	70	75	70	284	7,920
Dicky Pride	66	71	73	74	284	7,920
Carl Paulson	72	67	73	72	284	7,920
Paul Azinger	66	69	77	73	285	7,720
Danny Ellis	68	69	73	75	285	7,720
Steve Lowery	70	67	75	74	286	7,560
Neal Lancaster	68	69	75	74	286	7,560
Vance Veazey	71	68	75	74	288	7,440
Chris Anderson	68	71	77	73	289	7,360

Chrysler Championship

Westin Innisbrook Resort, Copperhead Course, October 30-November 2
Palm Harbor, Florida purse, $4,800,000
Par 36-35–71; 7,295 yards

		SCORES			TOTAL	MONEY
Retief Goosen	69	66	67	70	272	$864,000
Vijay Singh	70	70	65	70	275	518,400
Briny Baird	72	66	66	72	276	326,400
Tim Petrovic	71	69	66	72	278	211,200
Chad Campbell	68	69	72	69	278	211,200
Dan Forsman	67	75	69	68	279	160,800
Davis Love	69	72	72	66	279	160,800
Thomas Levet	71	67	71	70	279	160,800
Brad Faxon	72	71	68	69	280	124,800
Stephen Ames	74	67	72	67	280	124,800
Peter Lonard	71	71	70	68	280	124,800
Geoff Ogilvy	71	71	68	70	280	124,800
Jeff Sluman	71	70	68	72	281	90,000
Mike Weir	71	73	70	67	281	90,000
Justin Leonard	74	71	66	70	281	90,000
Jonathan Byrd	72	67	72	70	281	90,000
Tom Byrum	70	71	71	71	283	62,811.43
Robert Gamez	68	72	74	69	283	62,811.43
Kenny Perry	73	69	70	71	283	62,811.43
Loren Roberts	71	69	68	75	283	62,811.43
Duffy Waldorf	69	73	70	71	283	62,811.43
Jose Coceres	68	68	72	75	283	62,811.42
Pat Perez	70	70	70	73	283	62,811.43
Mark Calcavecchia	72	70	71	71	284	35,520
Skip Kendall	72	71	72	69	284	35,520
Neal Lancaster	72	70	68	74	284	35,520
Brett Quigley	71	74	67	72	284	35,520
Jerry Kelly	68	69	73	74	284	35,520
Jesper Parnevik	74	69	70	71	284	35,520
Robert Damron	71	73	68	72	284	35,520
Kenichi Kuboya	73	69	69	73	284	35,520
Charles Howell	66	71	74	73	284	35,520
J.J. Henry	69	67	73	75	284	35,520
Bob Estes	72	69	74	70	285	24,240
John Huston	72	72	70	71	285	24,240
Ernie Els	70	74	70	71	285	24,240
Brandt Jobe	71	71	69	74	285	24,240
Jeff Brehaut	72	69	69	75	285	24,240
Jay Williamson	74	69	69	73	285	24,240
Steve Lowery	69	72	73	72	286	19,200
Chris Riley	72	73	71	70	286	19,200
Aaron Baddeley	71	71	70	74	286	19,200
K.J. Choi	71	74	71	70	286	19,200
Paul Azinger	73	71	73	70	287	14,918.40
David Peoples	72	72	72	71	287	14,918.40
Joe Durant	75	68	71	73	287	14,918.40
Woody Austin	75	65	76	71	287	14,918.40
Aaron Barber	71	72	71	73	287	14,918.40
Donnie Hammond	70	74	74	70	288	11,976
Lee Janzen	74	70	71	73	288	11,976
Glen Hnatiuk	74	68	72	74	288	11,976
John Rollins	70	73	73	72	288	11,976
Olin Browne	74	71	69	75	289	11,059.20

	SCORES				TOTAL	MONEY
Jeff Maggert	70	75	71	73	289	11,059.20
Brian Bateman	73	72	68	76	289	11,059.20
Pat Bates	74	69	73	73	289	11,059.20
Craig Barlow	71	71	71	76	289	11,059.20
Steve Flesch	72	72	72	74	290	10,608
Stewart Cink	72	72	73	73	290	10,608
David Gossett	72	72	74	72	290	10,608
Luke Donald	76	69	72	73	290	10,608
Len Mattiace	70	73	75	73	291	10,320
Brenden Pappas	73	72	73	73	291	10,320
Bernhard Langer	71	74	73	74	292	10,176
Billy Andrade	75	70	76	72	293	9,984
Mark Wilson	73	72	76	72	293	9,984
Hank Kuehne	71	69	71	82	293	9,984
Mike Grob	72	72	75	77	296	9,792
Jason Gore	70	75	78	76	299	9,648
Rory Sabbatini	74	71	79	75	299	9,648
Carl Paulson	70	74	74	82	300	9,504

Tour Championship

Champions Golf Club, Houston, Texas
Par 36-35–71; 7,295 yards

November 6-9
purse, $6,000,000

	SCORES				TOTAL	MONEY
Chad Campbell	70	69	61	68	268	$1,080,000
Charles Howell	67	67	67	70	271	648,000
Retief Goosen	69	67	67	69	272	414,000
Chris Riley	69	68	66	70	273	288,000
Davis Love	73	67	67	69	276	228,000
Vijay Singh	73	68	67	68	276	228,000
Jonathan Kaye	69	70	68	70	277	204,000
Jim Furyk	71	71	67	69	278	192,000
Fred Funk	68	67	71	73	279	163,650
Kenny Perry	67	73	70	69	279	163,650
Scott Verplank	71	71	69	68	279	163,650
Steve Flesch	71	68	67	73	279	163,650
Bob Tway	72	68	72	68	280	131,850
Jerry Kelly	68	74	70	68	280	131,850
Robert Allenby	69	73	68	70	280	131,850
Briny Baird	69	72	71	68	280	131,850
Ernie Els	70	69	73	69	281	120,000
Darren Clarke	74	68	67	73	282	117,000
Mike Weir	72	73	67	71	283	112,500
K.J. Choi	77	68	70	68	283	112,500
Brad Faxon	76	71	71	66	284	103,200
David Toms	69	69	74	72	284	103,200
Kirk Triplett	70	71	72	71	284	103,200
Chris DiMarco	68	70	71	75	284	103,200
Justin Leonard	69	69	73	73	284	103,200
Tiger Woods	70	70	71	74	285	96,000
Stuart Appleby	71	76	69	70	286	94,800
J.L. Lewis	75	68	71	74	288	93,600
Jay Haas	77	71	70	71	289	92,400
Nick Price	73	69	75	76	293	91,200
Tim Herron	79	69	74	77	299	90,000

WGC World Cup

Kiawah Island Resort, Ocean Course,
Kiawah Island, South Carolina
Par 36-36–72; 7,443 yards

November 13-16
purse, $4,000,000

	INDIVIDUAL SCORES				TOTAL
SOUTH AFRICA—$1,400,000 Trevor Immelman/Rory Sabbatini	70	69	63	73	275
ENGLAND—$700,000 Justin Rose/Paul Casey	73	73	66	67	279
FRANCE—$400,000 Thomas Levet/Raphael Jacquelin	69	72	68	71	280
GERMANY—$200,000 Alex Cejka/Marcel Siem	67	77	67	71	282
UNITED STATES—$135,000 Jim Furyk/Justin Leonard	71	70	68	75	284
IRELAND—$135,000 Paul McGinley/Padraig Harrington	74	77	66	67	284
JAPAN—$102,500 Shigeki Maruyama/Hidemichi Tanaka	74	71	71	69	285
SWEDEN—$102,500 Niclas Fasth/Fredrik Jacobson	72	72	67	74	285
PARAGUAY—$71,667 Carlos Franco/Marco Ruiz	70	75	70	71	286
SCOTLAND—$71,667 Paul Lawrie/Alastair Forsyth	71	73	68	74	286
S. KOREA—$71,667 K.J. Choi/S.K. Ho	71	75	71	69	286
WALES—$60,000 Ian Woosnam/Bradley Dredge	68	74	71	75	288
ARGENTINA—$55,000 Eduardo Romero/Angel Cabrera	70	73	70	76	289
SPAIN—$50,000 Miguel Angel Jimenez/Ignacio Garrido	71	75	66	81	293
TRINIDAD & TOBAGO—$48,000 Stephen Ames/Robert Ames	75	81	67	71	294
AUSTRALIA—$48,000 Stuart Appleby/Stephen Leaney	72	76	71	75	294
NEW ZEALAND—$48,000 Michael Campbell/David Smail	71	74	72	77	294
MEXICO—$46,000 Alex Quiroz/Antonio Maldonado	71	78	70	79	298

	INDIVIDUAL SCORES				TOTAL
DENMARK—$45,000					
Anders Hansen/Soren Kjeldsen	72	84	72	73	301
MYANMAR—$44,000					
Kyi Hla Han/Aung Win	72	83	73	74	302
HONG KONG—$43,000					
Derek Fung/James Stewart	76	80	69	78	303
INDIA—$42,000					
Gaurav Ghei/Digvijay Singh	81	83	70	70	304
THAILAND—$41,000					
Jamnian Chitprasong/Pornsakon Tipsanit	76	78	76	84	314
CHILE—WD					
Roy MacKenzie/Felipe Aguilar					

Special Events

CVS Charity Classic

Rhode Island Country Club, Barrington, Rhode Island
Par 36-35–71; 6,694 yards

July 23-24
purse $1,200,000

	SCORES		TOTAL	MONEY (Team)
Jeff Sluman/Rocco Mediate	63	57	120	$230,000
Brad Faxon/Billy Andrade	63	58	121	170,000
Dudley Hart/Chris DiMarco	63	59	122	135,000
Dana Quigley/Brett Quigley	62	61	123	110,000
Jerry Kelly/Peter Jacobsen	62	62	124	102,500
Davis Love/Fred Couples	62	62	124	102,500
David Toms/Fred Funk	66	61	127	92,500
Nick Price/Scott McCarron	61	66	127	92,500
Tim Herron/Rich Beem	63	65	128	85,000
Len Mattiace/Mark Calcavecchia	63	66	129	80,000

Franklin Templeton Shootout

Tiburon Golf Course, Naples, Florida
Par 36-36–72; 7,193 yards

November 14-16
purse, $2,400,000

	SCORES			TOTAL	MONEY (Each)
Jeff Sluman/Hank Kuehne	65	68	60	193	$275,000
Brad Faxon/Scott McCarron	67	63	63	193	$142,500
Shaun Micheel/Chad Campbell	69	63	61	193	$142,500
(Sluman and Kuehne won on second extra hole.)					
Mark O'Meara/John Cook	68	64	63	195	$90,000

	SCORES			TOTAL	MONEY
					(Each)
Kenny Perry/Scott Hoch	66	63	67	196	$77,500
Rocco Mediate/Lee Janzen	69	66	63	198	$75,000
Matt Kuchar/Fred Funk	67	68	64	199	$71,250
Craig Stadler/Peter Jacobsen	69	68	62	199	$71,250
Greg Norman/Steve Elkington	72	69	60	201	$66,250
Tom Kite/John Huston	72	64	65	201	$66,250
Paul Azinger/Olin Browne	68	70	65	203	$62,500
Rich Beem/Mark Calcavecchia	72	70	63	205	$60,000

Callaway Golf Pebble Beach Invitational

Pebble Beach GL: Par 36-36–72; 6,840 yards
Spyglass Hills GC: Par 36-36–72; 6,859 yards
Del Monte GC: Par 36-36–72; 6,278 yards
Pebble Beach, California

November 20-23
purse, $300,000

	SCORES				TOTAL	MONEY
John Daly	69	68	73	69	279	$60,000
Jim Thorpe	67	77	67	69	280	24,300
Bo Van Pelt	74	64	73	69	280	24,300
Michael Muehr	69	69	72	71	281	10,600
James McLean	72	72	67	71	282	8,500
Kevin Sutherland	73	70	69	70	282	8,500
Janice Moodie	70	68	73	72	283	7,000
Todd Fischer	69	73	68	74	284	5,800
Steve Flesch	68	74	71	71	284	5,800
Jeff Brehaut	74	69	71	70	284	5,800
Jeff Gallagher	71	72	71	70	284	5,800
Kirk Triplett	72	69	72	72	285	4,750
Brett Quigley	75	71	69	70	285	4,750
Bruce Fleisher	69	71	72	74	286	4,000
Andy Miller	70	71	75	70	286	4,000
Mark Brooks	68	71	78	69	286	4,000
Curt Byrum	72	67	72	76	287	3,500
Dave Cunningham	72	70	72	74	288	3,300
Rob Oppenheim	65	73	75	76	289	2,933
Cliff Kresge	70	72	72	75	289	2,933
Shawn McEntee	73	74	71	71	289	2,933
Carin Koch	71	71	71	77	290	2,650
Stewart Cink	72	72	71	75	290	2,650
Matt Gogel	72	71	71	77	291	2,300
Spike McRoy	77	71	67	76	291	2,300
Dean Wilson	67	73	75	76	291	2,300
Jim Carter	70	73	74	74	291	2,300
Duffy Waldorf	79	71	67	74	291	2,300
Todd Barranger	69	74	75	73	291	2,300
Harrison Frazar	72	68	73	79	292	2,080
Jeff Gove	71	70	75	76	292	2,080
Charles Warren	68	75	73	76	292	2,080
Roger Tambellini	69	71	75	78	293	2,040
Sean Farren	71	73	72	78	294	2,020
Brad Martin	70	73	70	82	295	2,000
Emilee Klein	70	75	72	79	296	1,970
Natalie Gulbis	71	70	77	78	296	1,970
Charlotta Sorenstam	73	69	76	81	299	1,970
Tom Lehman	70	69	74		WD	1,910
Scott Miller	68	80	71		WD	1,910

UBS Cup

Sea Island Golf Club, Seaside Course, St. Simons Island, Georgia   November 21-23
Par 35-35–70; 6,945 yards   purse, $3,000,000

FIRST DAY
Alternate Shot

Tony Jacklin and Nick Faldo (World) defeated Arnold Palmer and Rocco Mediate, 1 up.
Bernhard Langer and Colin Montgomerie (World) defeated Raymond Floyd and Hale Irwin, 5 and 3.
Scott Hoch and Hal Sutton (US) defeated Carl Mason and Bill Longmuir, 1 up.
Mark O'Meara and Craig Stadler (US) defeated Barry Lane and Ian Woosnam, 1 up.
Eduardo Romero and Vicente Fernandez (World) defeated Tom Watson and Curtis Strange, 4 and 3.
Brad Faxon and Bruce Lietzke (US) halved with Roger Davis and Des Smyth.

POINTS: Rest of the World 3½, United States 2½

SECOND DAY
Best-Ball

Sutton and Irwin (US) defeated Smyth and Davis, 5 and 3.
Palmer and Strange (US) defeated Jacklin and Faldo, 4 and 3.
Romero and Fernandez (World) defeated Watson and Mediate, 5 and 3.
Mason and Longmuir (World) defeated O'Meara and Stadler, 1 up.
Faxon and Hoch (US) defeated Woosnam and Lane, 1 up.
Montgomerie and Langer (World) defeated Floyd and Lietzke, 2 and 1.

POINTS: Rest of the World 3, United States 3
TWO-DAY TOTAL: Rest of the World 6½, United States 5½

THIRD DAY
Singles

Irwin (US) defeated Langer, 7 and 5.
Lietzke (US) defeated Lane, 6 and 5.
O'Meara (US) defeated Woosnam, 6 and 5.
Jacklin (World) defeated Palmer, 1 up.
Faldo (World) defeated Strange, 2 up.
Watson (US) halved with Montgomerie.
Smyth (World) defeated Stadler, 1 up.
Longmuir (World) defeated Mediate, 1 up.
Faxon (US) defeated Mason, 2 and 1.
Floyd (US) halved with Davis.
Sutton (US) defeated Fernandez, 2 and 1.
Hoch (US) halved with Romero.

POINTS: Rest of the World 5½, United States 6½
TOTAL POINTS: Rest of the World 12, United States 12 (US retains the Cup.)

(Each member of each team received $125,000.)

PGA Grand Slam of Golf

Poipu Bay Resort, Kauai, Hawaii
Par 36-36–72; 7,081 yards

December 5-6
purse, $1,000,000

	SCORES		TOTAL	MONEY
Jim Furyk	67	68	135	$400,000
Mike Weir	72	71	143	250,000
Shaun Micheel	75	70	145	200,000
Ben Curtis	73	73	146	150,000

Office Depot Father-Son Challenge

Champions Gate Golf Resort, Orlando, Florida
Par 37-35–72; 7,069 yards

December 6-7
purse, $1,000,000

	SCORES		TOTAL	MONEY
				(Won by professional)
Hale/Steve Irwin	62	61	123	$200,000
Jack/Jack Nicklaus II	62	62	124	105,000
Larry/Josh Nelson	63	62	125	80,000
Vijay/Qass Singh	66	60	126	54,750
Craig/Kevin Stadler	65	61	126	54,750
Tom/David Kite	64	62	126	54,750
Bernhard/Stefan Langer	61	65	126	54,750
Raymond/Robert Floyd	66	62	128	47,500
Dave/Ron Stockton	66	62	128	47,500
Johnny/Scott Miller	66	64	130	46,000
Mark/Shaun O'Meara	63	68	131	45,000
Arnold Palmer/Sam Saunders	65	67	132	44,000
Lee/Tony Trevino	67	67	134	42,500
Lanny/Travis Wadkins	70	64	134	42,500
Jerry/Wesley Pate	66	70	136	41,000
Seve/Javier Ballesteros	70	72	142	40,000

Target World Challenge

Sherwood Country Club, Thousand Oaks, California
Par 36-35–71; 7,206 yards

December 11-14
purse, $5,000,000

	SCORES				TOTAL	MONEY
Davis Love	70	72	63	72	277	$1,200,000
Tiger Woods	71	71	72	65	279	700,000
Padraig Harrington	74	67	70	71	282	500,000
Justin Leonard	71	72	70	71	284	317,500
Mike Weir	75	68	69	72	284	317,500
K.J. Choi	72	71	65	77	285	225,000
Vijay Singh	74	69	73	70	286	205,000
Robert Allenby	72	71	72	74	289	195,000
Fred Couples	73	72	69	76	290	185,000
Nick Price	74	69	75	73	291	177,500
Chris DiMarco	74	68	72	77	291	177,500
Shaun Micheel	76	69	73	75	293	170,000
Jay Haas	76	72	75	72	295	165,000
Ben Curtis	78	74	72	72	296	160,000
Kenny Perry	71	77	75	74	297	155,000
Darren Clarke	81	73	70	75	299	150,000

Nationwide Tour

Jacob's Creek Open
See Australasian Tour chapter.

Clearwater Classic
See Australasian Tour chapter.

Chitimacha Louisiana Open

Le Triomphe Country Club, Broussard, Louisiana
Par 36-36–72; 7,004 yards

March 27-30
purse, $475,000

	SCORES				TOTAL	MONEY
Brett Wetterich	62	68	64	70	264	$85,500
Ken Duke	62	66	68	71	267	51,300
Russ Cochran	69	66	66	68	269	27,550
Steve Allan	65	63	68	73	269	27,550
Tom Carter	64	65	72	69	270	19,000
Wes Short	66	61	73	71	271	16,506.25
Brent Schwarzrock	69	66	70	66	271	16,506.25
Robin Freeman	64	68	68	72	272	13,300
Scott Sterling	65	67	70	70	272	13,300
Andrew McLardy	68	64	72	68	272	13,300
Kyle Thompson	67	65	72	68	272	13,300
Lee Porter	67	68	70	68	273	10,450
Rob McKelvey	63	69	70	71	273	10,450
Blaine McCallister	70	65	71	68	274	7,600
Fran Quinn	69	67	71	67	274	7,600
Mark Wurtz	69	67	69	69	274	7,600
Zoran Zorkic	67	67	71	69	274	7,600
Tripp Isenhour	66	72	70	66	274	7,600
Joe Ogilvie	66	67	71	70	274	7,600
James Driscoll	70	65	72	67	274	7,600
Shane Bertsch	70	65	70	70	275	5,700
Ben Bates	67	70	68	71	276	4,342.86
Kelly Gibson	68	64	73	71	276	4,342.86
Mike Grob	67	65	67	77	276	4,342.85
Deane Pappas	70	64	70	72	276	4,342.85
Bo Van Pelt	65	69	71	71	276	4,342.86
Stephen Gangluff	66	67	72	71	276	4,342.86
George McNeill	67	67	71	71	276	4,342.86
Brian Kamm	65	72	69	71	277	3,154
Kris Cox	69	68	66	74	277	3,154
Bob Heintz	67	71	69	70	277	3,154
Jimmy Green	67	70	73	67	277	3,154
Doug LaBelle	68	64	73	72	277	3,154

First Tee Arkansas Classic

Diamante Golf Club, Hot Springs Village, Arkansas
Par 36-36–72; 7,519 yards

April 17-20
purse, $475,000

	SCORES				TOTAL	MONEY
Ted Purdy	69	67	68	71	275	$85,500
Chris Tidland	69	70	68	68	275	51,300
(Purdy defeated Tidland on third playoff hole.)						
Vance Veazey	70	70	67	69	276	24,700
Tjaart van der Walt	68	66	72	70	276	24,700
Zach Johnson	65	65	74	72	276	24,700
Mike Grob	69	71	69	68	277	15,912.50
Danny Ellis	72	67	68	70	277	15,912.50
Bo Van Pelt	70	68	67	72	277	15,912.50
Bob Heintz	67	73	67	71	278	12,825
D.A. Points	71	72	67	68	278	12,825
Lucas Glover	69	67	74	68	278	12,825
Grant Waite	71	69	68	71	279	9,975
Scott Gump	74	67	66	72	279	9,975
Mark Hensby	71	70	66	72	279	9,975
Russ Cochran	71	71	71	67	280	7,600
Steve Haskins	70	69	71	70	280	7,600
Jeff Gallagher	71	72	67	70	280	7,600
Lee Porter	73	68	69	70	280	7,600
James Driscoll	69	70	72	69	280	7,600
Willie Wood	70	70	71	70	281	5,145.83
Dicky Pride	68	73	70	70	281	5,145.84
Joe Ogilvie	74	65	72	70	281	5,145.83
Craig Lile	68	74	68	71	281	5,145.83
Ben Curtis	74	68	71	68	281	5,145.83
Brett Wetterich	71	70	70	70	281	5,145.84
Brian Henninger	70	69	71	72	282	3,800
Scott Petersen	69	70	69	74	282	3,800
Ryan Palmer	72	70	71	69	282	3,800
Mike Standly	68	72	71	72	283	3,053.58
Michael Allen	69	73	70	71	283	3,053.57
Zoran Zorkic	72	69	69	73	283	3,053.57
Ron Whittaker	71	69	72	71	283	3,053.57
Bryce Molder	71	69	72	71	283	3,053.57
Doug Garwood	72	68	71	72	283	3,053.57
Boo Weekley	70	69	71	73	283	3,053.57

Rheem Classic

Hardscrabble Country Club, Fort Smith, Arkansas
Par 35-35–70; 6,619 yards

April 24-27
purse, $475,000

	SCORES				TOTAL	MONEY
Zach Johnson	65	70	71	66	272	$85,500
Steve Haskins	69	70	63	70	272	51,300
(Johnson defeated Haskins on first playoff hole.)						
Mike Sullivan	67	67	70	69	273	27,550
Scott Petersen	64	75	68	66	273	27,550
Emlyn Aubrey	67	69	67	71	274	17,337.50
Michael Muehr	69	67	70	68	274	17,337.50
Jason Dufner	69	67	66	72	274	17,337.50
Omar Uresti	70	70	68	67	275	13,300

	SCORES				TOTAL	MONEY
Tom Carter	68	70	66	71	275	13,300
Hunter Haas	67	70	69	69	275	13,300
Boo Weekley	66	69	69	71	275	13,300
Willie Wood	70	69	68	69	276	9,975
Franklin Langham	65	68	67	76	276	9,975
Ryuji Imada	66	69	70	71	276	9,975
Trevor Dodds	70	70	71	66	277	7,837.50
Shane Bertsch	70	72	67	68	277	7,837.50
Bubba Watson	70	66	69	72	277	7,837.50
Josh Broadaway	70	69	71	67	277	7,837.50
Chip Beck	68	69	71	70	278	5,557.50
Michael Bradley	70	70	70	68	278	5,557.50
David Edwards	67	68	72	71	278	5,557.50
Eric Meeks	67	71	69	71	278	5,557.50
Tripp Isenhour	69	67	70	72	278	5,557.50
Tjaart van der Walt	68	71	68	71	278	5,557.50
Dave Rummells	68	73	71	67	279	3,895
Rick Price	68	66	74	71	279	3,895
Tom Scherrer	71	68	74	66	279	3,895
David Morland	72	65	68	74	279	3,895
Jeff Hart	70	72	72	66	280	3,206.25
Jeff Gove	73	67	73	67	280	3,206.25
Bo Van Pelt	69	68	69	74	280	3,206.25
Jess Daley	72	70	70	68	280	3,206.25

BMW Charity Pro-Am at The Cliffs

The Cliffs Golf & Country Club, Travelers Rest, South Carolina   May 1-4
Valley Course: Par 36-36–72; 7,023 yards   purse, $575,000
Cliffs at Keowee Vineyards: Par 36-35–71; 7,006 yards

	SCORES				TOTAL	MONEY
Tripp Isenhour	64	70	66	69	269	$103,500
Kyle Thompson	70	69	66	66	271	62,100
Paul Claxton	68	72	66	66	272	39,100
Joe Ogilvie	70	68	69	67	274	22,640.63
John Paul Curley	67	72	69	66	274	22,640.63
Zach Johnson	66	70	69	69	274	22,640.62
Jason Dufner	71	68	67	68	274	22,640.62
Emlyn Aubrey	69	68	67	71	275	16,675
Tommy Tolles	72	65	69	69	275	16,675
Lucas Glover	69	70	69	67	275	16,675
Rick Price	66	68	69	73	276	13,225
Shane Bertsch	72	69	66	69	276	13,225
Bo Van Pelt	68	68	71	69	276	13,225
Mark Wurtz	69	68	67	73	277	10,925
Stan Utley	69	67	72	70	278	8,912.50
Scott Sterling	71	69	72	66	278	8,912.50
Steve Runge	69	70	67	72	278	8,912.50
Chris Zambri	66	69	73	70	278	8,912.50
Jason Schultz	69	65	75	69	278	8,912.50
Andy Sanders	73	68	66	71	278	8,912.50
Robin Freeman	68	73	66	72	279	5,788.33
Scott Gump	68	72	68	71	279	5,788.34
Bobby Gage	72	67	69	71	279	5,788.33
Jeff Freeman	67	72	69	71	279	5,788.33
Tom Scherrer	67	69	71	72	279	5,788.33
Michael Long	68	69	73	69	279	5,788.34

	SCORES				TOTAL	MONEY
Eric Meeks	65	68	73	74	280	4,163
Mike Sullivan	70	68	70	72	280	4,163
Keoke Cotner	67	70	73	70	280	4,163
Rich Barcelo	69	68	70	73	280	4,163
Kevin Pendley	69	68	72	71	280	4,163

Virginia Beach Open

TPC of Virginia Beach, Virginia Beach, Virginia   May 15-18
Par 36-36–72; 7,432 yards   purse, $450,000

	SCORES				TOTAL	MONEY
Michael Long	72	65	70	70	277	$81,000
Vaughn Taylor	71	69	70	69	279	48,600
Omar Uresti	68	73	69	71	281	26,100
Tripp Isenhour	75	66	66	74	281	26,100
Eduardo Herrera	65	73	71	73	282	16,425
John Elliott	69	69	76	68	282	16,425
Jason Dufner	73	70	69	70	282	16,425
Russ Cochran	70	69	71	73	283	13,950
Blaine McCallister	70	68	71	75	284	12,600
Craig Lile	70	67	71	76	284	12,600
Fran Quinn	67	69	74	75	285	10,350
Daniel Chopra	76	68	68	73	285	10,350
Bubba Watson	69	68	74	74	285	10,350
Zach Johnson	69	70	69	78	286	8,100
Hunter Haas	69	73	74	70	286	8,100
Roland Thatcher	72	69	69	76	286	8,100
Dicky Pride	72	68	73	74	287	6,300
Ken Duke	72	72	69	74	287	6,300
Ted Purdy	73	66	73	75	287	6,300
Charles Warren	73	68	75	71	287	6,300
Paul Dickinson	73	70	72	72	287	6,300
Dennis Paulson	73	68	76	71	288	4,356
Dan Pohl	68	71	76	73	288	4,356
Jeff Freeman	69	69	74	76	288	4,356
Zoran Zorkic	71	70	71	76	288	4,356
Todd Rose	73	70	74	71	288	4,356
Tim Thelen	73	71	73	72	289	3,082.50
Kevin Johnson	72	68	73	76	289	3,082.50
Todd Demsey	70	74	73	72	289	3,082.50
Rob McKelvey	70	73	75	71	289	3,082.50
Paul Claxton	69	72	73	75	289	3,082.50
David Branshaw	68	76	71	74	289	3,082.50
John Paul Curley	75	68	72	74	289	3,082.50
Lucas Glover	71	69	73	76	289	3,082.50

SAS Carolina Classic

TPC at Wakefield Plantation, Raleigh, North Carolina   May 22-25
Par 35-36–71; 7,257 yards   purse, $500,000

	SCORES				TOTAL	MONEY
David Morland	66	68	66	68	268	$90,000
Rob Bradley	72	67	68	62	269	44,000

	SCORES				TOTAL	MONEY
Vaughn Taylor	65	72	66	66	269	44,000
Tripp Isenhour	70	70	64	67	271	18,850
Paul Claxton	70	68	65	68	271	18,850
Brett Wetterich	68	68	66	69	271	18,850
D.J. Brigman	67	66	69	69	271	18,850
Lucas Glover	67	71	67	66	271	18,850
Eduardo Herrera	70	67	67	68	272	14,000
Kevin Johnson	64	71	68	69	272	14,000
Mike Reid	71	66	66	70	273	10,250
Dicky Pride	72	67	67	67	273	10,250
Keoke Cotner	72	66	68	67	273	10,250
Rich Barcelo	70	70	67	66	273	10,250
Todd Rose	66	71	67	69	273	10,250
Jason Dufner	65	66	76	66	273	10,250
Daniel Chopra	71	67	71	65	274	7,250
Joe Ogilvie	65	68	71	70	274	7,250
Charles Warren	66	71	69	68	274	7,250
Bubba Watson	73	67	66	68	274	7,250
Paul Gow	69	66	70	70	275	5,600
Craig Lile	66	70	68	71	275	5,600
Bo Van Pelt	72	68	69	66	275	5,600
Blaine McCallister	70	65	73	68	276	4,240
Steve Pate	69	68	72	67	276	4,240
Dennis Paulson	70	68	64	74	276	4,240
Scott Petersen	70	69	68	69	276	4,240
Shane Bertsch	66	69	73	68	276	4,240
Michael Bradley	70	68	69	70	277	3,060
Russ Cochran	70	68	70	69	277	3,060
Dave Rummells	70	69	70	68	277	3,060
Jeff Gallagher	67	69	70	71	277	3,060
Rick Price	70	66	71	70	277	3,060
Mark Wurtz	69	66	72	70	277	3,060
Jeff Freeman	70	70	69	68	277	3,060
Mark Hensby	68	70	73	66	277	3,060
Nick Cassini	70	68	71	68	277	3,060
Johnson Wagner	69	68	71	69	277	3,060

LaSalle Bank Open

The Glen Club, Glenview, Illinois
Par 36-36–72; 7,149 yards

June 5-8
purse, $500,000

	SCORES				TOTAL	MONEY
Andre Stolz	70	65	68	68	271	$90,000
Tommy Tolles	68	67	66	72	273	54,000
D.A. Points	68	69	64	73	274	29,000
Daniel Chopra	68	66	68	72	274	29,000
Victor Schwamkrug	66	69	67	73	275	19,000
Jimmy Green	69	69	66	71	275	19,000
Todd Demsey	72	69	69	67	277	15,583.34
Scott Sterling	72	67	69	69	277	15,583.33
Vaughn Taylor	71	66	69	71	277	15,583.33
Gary Nicklaus	74	67	67	70	278	12,500
David Branshaw	69	68	68	73	278	12,500
Wes Short	70	65	70	73	278	12,500
David Morland	69	71	70	69	279	10,500
Chris Downes	70	68	71	71	280	8,500

	SCORES				TOTAL	MONEY
Bubba Watson	71	70	71	68	280	8,500
Zach Johnson	68	69	71	72	280	8,500
Ted Purdy	66	72	70	72	280	8,500
Joe Ogilvie	68	70	69	73	280	8,500
John Elliott	74	66	72	69	281	6,750
Jeff Gove	69	71	67	74	281	6,750
Omar Uresti	71	71	68	72	282	5,200
Rob Bradley	70	70	71	71	282	5,200
Nolan Henke	70	70	69	73	282	5,200
Ryan Palmer	69	70	69	74	282	5,200
Ty Armstrong	68	70	68	76	282	5,200
Kevin Durkin	71	67	72	73	283	3,575
Emlyn Aubrey	72	69	70	72	283	3,575
Kevin Johnson	68	71	70	74	283	3,575
Jess Daley	69	71	72	71	283	3,575
Craig Lile	71	71	70	71	283	3,575

Northeast Pennsylvania Classic

Glenmaura National Golf Club, Scranton, Pennsylvania
Par 36-35–71; 6,990 yards

June 12-15
purse, $450,000

	SCORES				TOTAL	MONEY
Blaine McCallister	68	64	64	69	265	$81,000
Bill Glasson	65	68	67	68	268	48,600
Omar Uresti	67	63	69	70	269	23,400
Ryuji Imada	67	69	66	67	269	23,400
Zach Johnson	65	69	68	67	269	23,400
Paul Gow	75	65	61	69	270	15,075
Charles Warren	67	67	70	66	270	15,075
Jason Dufner	65	66	71	68	270	15,075
Tommy Tolles	70	66	70	65	271	13,050
Brian Wilson	65	73	67	67	272	10,800
Shane Bertsch	70	66	66	70	272	10,800
Chris Tidland	67	70	65	70	272	10,800
Daniel Chopra	66	72	68	66	272	10,800
Mike Brisky	72	68	67	66	273	8,325
Stephen Gangluff	68	66	68	71	273	8,325
Gary Nicklaus	69	66	69	70	274	6,975
Kenichi Kuboya	68	67	67	72	274	6,975
D.A. Points	72	67	69	66	274	6,975
Boo Weekley	68	70	70	66	274	6,975
Stan Utley	70	66	72	67	275	4,875
Willie Wood	72	68	68	67	275	4,875
Franklin Langham	68	70	69	68	275	4,875
Chris Couch	68	72	66	69	275	4,875
Brett Wetterich	71	68	67	69	275	4,875
Jason Bohn	66	74	69	66	275	4,875
Jeff Hart	66	72	69	69	276	3,345
David Morland	69	70	67	70	276	3,345
Ken Duke	68	71	69	68	276	3,345
Gavin Coles	67	70	70	69	276	3,345
Ryan Palmer	68	70	73	65	276	3,345
Lucas Glover	64	74	73	65	276	3,345

Lake Erie Charity Classic

Peek'n Peak Resort, Upper Course, Findley Lake, New York
Par 36-36–72; 6,888 yards

June 19-22
purse, $450,000

		SCORES			TOTAL	MONEY
Guy Boros	69	67	69	70	275	$81,000
Bob Heintz	66	70	69	71	276	39,600
Chris Couch	71	68	70	67	276	39,600
Stan Utley	68	66	66	77	277	18,600
Scott Sterling	68	67	71	71	277	18,600
Roland Thatcher	65	73	70	69	277	18,600
Bo Van Pelt	67	70	68	73	278	14,025
Zach Johnson	67	71	68	72	278	14,025
Bubba Watson	66	70	71	71	278	14,025
Tom Scherrer	70	71	67	71	279	11,250
Paul Claxton	72	66	68	73	279	11,250
Hunter Haas	74	67	70	68	279	11,250
Tommy Tolles	72	68	67	73	280	7,250
Craig Bowden	71	66	74	69	280	7,250
Franklin Langham	71	67	70	72	280	7,250
Shane Bertsch	67	69	67	77	280	7,250
Todd Demsey	69	67	71	73	280	7,250
Rob McKelvey	68	72	69	71	280	7,250
Jeff Gove	68	72	68	72	280	7,250
Michael Long	66	71	74	69	280	7,250
Vaughn Taylor	68	67	70	75	280	7,250
Gary Hallberg	66	70	73	72	281	4,680
David Branshaw	71	70	72	68	281	4,680
Jason Dufner	68	69	72	72	281	4,680
Sonny Skinner	68	70	74	70	282	3,182.73
Michael Allen	64	74	73	71	282	3,182.73
Matt Peterson	69	72	73	68	282	3,182.73
Tripp Isenhour	69	71	70	72	282	3,182.72
Stiles Mitchell	67	69	74	72	282	3,182.72
Steve Allan	70	68	73	71	282	3,182.73
Joe Ogilvie	68	72	70	72	282	3,182.72
Chad Lydiatt	69	73	72	68	282	3,182.73
Han Lee	73	69	70	70	282	3,182.73
Jason Bohn	71	71	72	68	282	3,182.73
Kevin Muncrief	72	67	73	70	282	3,182.73

Knoxville Open

Fox Den Country Club, Knoxville, Tennessee
Par 36-36–72; 7,142 yards

June 26-29
purse, $475,000

		SCORES			TOTAL	MONEY
Vaughn Taylor	68	69	67	64	268	$85,500
Joe Ogilvie	65	71	66	66	268	51,300
(Taylor defeated Ogilvie on first playoff hole.)						
Doug LaBelle	67	67	68	68	270	32,300
John Elliott	68	65	67	71	271	22,800
Chris Couch	68	69	67	69	273	19,000
Lucas Glover	70	70	69	65	274	17,100
Danny Briggs	73	66	68	68	275	13,822.50
Chris Tidland	68	70	68	69	275	13,822.50
Charles Warren	70	69	70	66	275	13,822.50

	SCORES				TOTAL	MONEY
Kevin Pendley	68	70	68	69	275	13,822.50
Roland Thatcher	65	68	69	73	275	13,822.50
Kevin Durkin	70	69	68	69	276	10,925
David Ogrin	70	68	68	71	277	8,142.86
Mark Wurtz	70	67	71	69	277	8,142.86
Craig Bowden	68	67	69	73	277	8,142.85
Tripp Isenhour	71	69	68	69	277	8,142.85
Paul Claxton	68	68	72	69	277	8,142.85
Jeff Gove	71	69	68	69	277	8,142.86
Bo Van Pelt	69	68	72	68	277	8,142.86
Tjaart van der Walt	70	68	71	69	278	6,175
Scott Gump	70	71	70	68	279	4,275
Guy Boros	68	67	70	74	279	4,275
Rocky Walcher	71	65	70	73	279	4,275
Scott Sterling	71	68	71	69	279	4,275
Bob Heintz	68	71	70	70	279	4,275
Mike Brisky	68	71	68	72	279	4,275
Iain Steel	71	66	72	70	279	4,275
Tyler Williamson	69	72	69	69	279	4,275
George McNeill	69	68	73	69	279	4,275
Jeff Klauk	70	71	72	66	279	4,275

Samsung Canadian PGA Championship

DiamondBack Golf Club, Richmond Hill, Ontario, Canada
Par 35-36–71; 7,067 yards

July 3-6
purse, $450,000

	SCORES				TOTAL	MONEY
Tom Carter	70	69	66	70	275	$81,000
Jason Bohn	70	65	68	72	275	48,600
(Carter defeated Bohn on first playoff hole.)						
Blaine McCallister	72	67	69	68	276	30,600
Kelly Gibson	69	70	66	72	277	16,965
Scott Dunlap	71	68	66	72	277	16,965
Jaxon Brigman	71	71	67	68	277	16,965
Steve Ford	71	69	68	69	277	16,965
Derek Gillespie	70	69	69	69	277	16,965
Michael Allen	68	67	69	74	278	12,600
Andy Sanders	68	70	67	73	278	12,600
Danny Briggs	68	71	68	72	279	9,540
Tripp Isenhour	70	70	70	69	279	9,540
Michael Long	73	68	67	71	279	9,540
Roger Tambellini	67	74	69	69	279	9,540
Ryan Palmer	72	67	70	70	279	9,540
P.J. Cowan	70	68	69	73	280	6,750
Todd Demsey	69	73	70	68	280	6,750
Rob McMillan	70	71	68	71	280	6,750
Daniel Chopra	69	73	71	67	280	6,750
Han Lee	75	68	70	67	280	6,750
Jim McGovern	66	74	69	72	281	4,275
John Elliott	68	75	71	67	281	4,275
Ron Ewing	68	70	71	72	281	4,275
David McKenzie	72	71	70	68	281	4,275
Terry Hatch	68	71	69	73	281	4,275
Zach Johnson	73	68	66	74	281	4,275
Mark Walker	70	69	71	71	281	4,275
Scott Gibson	69	71	72	69	281	4,275

	SCORES				TOTAL	MONEY
Jim Rutledge	73	69	72	68	282	3,037.50
Brad Sutterfield	69	70	71	72	282	3,037.50
Charles Warren	69	72	69	72	282	3,037.50
Brian Payne	69	70	71	72	282	3,037.50

Reese's Cup Classic

Country Club of Hershey, East Course,
Hershey, Pennsylvania
Par 36-35–71; 7,154 yards

July 10-13
purse, $450,000

	SCORES				TOTAL	MONEY
Joe Ogilvie	71	67	66	70	274	$81,000
Wes Short	72	71	65	69	277	29,700
Paul Claxton	71	66	71	69	277	29,700
David McKenzie	68	72	67	70	277	29,700
Zach Johnson	68	69	70	70	277	29,700
Michael Christie	74	66	69	69	278	15,637.50
Anthony Rodriguez	70	65	72	71	278	15,637.50
Scott Gump	71	67	70	71	279	13,500
Charles Warren	67	73	69	70	279	13,500
Steve Ford	68	68	74	70	280	11,250
Bo Van Pelt	72	67	72	69	280	11,250
Jason Bohn	70	72	70	68	280	11,250
Sean Murphy	71	65	70	75	281	8,437.50
Chris Tidland	71	69	71	70	281	8,437.50
Lucas Glover	71	69	73	68	281	8,437.50
Boo Weekley	70	70	69	72	281	8,437.50
Russ Cochran	69	71	68	74	282	6,090
Mark Wurtz	69	68	71	74	282	6,090
Omar Uresti	71	71	72	68	282	6,090
Franklin Langham	72	70	70	70	282	6,090
Tom Carter	72	70	69	71	282	6,090
Rob McKelvey	69	74	68	71	282	6,090
Brian Kamm	70	70	73	70	283	3,960
Guy Boros	71	67	72	73	283	3,960
Matt Peterson	69	74	67	73	283	3,960
Mike Brisky	68	71	72	72	283	3,960
Ryan Howison	72	68	71	72	283	3,960
Roger Tambellini	69	68	74	72	283	3,960
Andy Morse	72	71	66	75	284	2,846.25
Kevin Johnson	68	71	70	75	284	2,846.25
Zoran Zorkic	69	67	73	75	284	2,846.25
Craig Bowden	70	71	74	69	284	2,846.25
Chris Zambri	68	72	70	74	284	2,846.25
David Branshaw	64	72	74	74	284	2,846.25
Jason Schultz	69	71	72	72	284	2,846.25
Kyle Thompson	69	70	70	75	284	2,846.25

Henrico County Open

The Dominion Club, Richmond, Virginia
Par 36-36–72; 6,987 yards

July 17-20
purse, $450,000

	SCORES				TOTAL	MONEY
Mark Hensby	71	67	67	63	268	$81,000
Zach Johnson	67	68	68	65	268	48,600
(Hensby defeated Johnson on first playoff hole.)						
Tom Carter	64	71	67	67	269	30,600
Sonny Skinner	66	66	68	70	270	18,600
Daniel Chopra	66	69	69	66	270	18,600
Bo Van Pelt	66	66	68	70	270	18,600
Tripp Isenhour	69	70	69	63	271	15,075
Fran Quinn	69	70	66	67	272	11,700
Bobby Gage	67	69	64	72	272	11,700
Mike Brisky	68	70	66	68	272	11,700
Chris Zambri	67	68	71	66	272	11,700
Charles Warren	68	66	71	67	272	11,700
Bubba Dickerson	68	67	67	70	272	11,700
Wes Short	68	67	68	70	273	7,425
Craig Bowden	67	66	68	72	273	7,425
Keoke Cotner	70	68	69	66	273	7,425
David Branshaw	67	69	68	69	273	7,425
Stephen Gangluff	69	70	69	65	273	7,425
Jimmy Walker	68	69	70	66	273	7,425
Sean Murphy	73	67	67	67	274	5,242.50
Matt Peterson	71	67	70	66	274	5,242.50
Chris Tidland	68	69	68	69	274	5,242.50
Hunter Haas	66	70	69	69	274	5,242.50
Brian Wilson	70	69	66	70	275	3,720
David Morland	68	71	69	67	275	3,720
Brad Adamonis	71	68	73	63	275	3,720
D.J. Brigman	66	71	71	67	275	3,720
D.A. Points	67	70	69	69	275	3,720
Josh Broadaway	69	71	67	68	275	3,720
Ben Bates	70	69	68	69	276	2,925
Scott Gump	71	69	67	69	276	2,925
Ken Duke	70	69	65	72	276	2,925
Erik Compton	71	67	66	72	276	2,925

Dayton Open

Golf Club at Yankee Trace, Centerville, Ohio
Par 36-36–72; 7,139 yards

July 24-27
purse, $450,000

	SCORES				TOTAL	MONEY
Guy Boros	64	64	70	67	265	$81,000
Zach Johnson	66	68	67	67	268	48,600
Ryan Palmer	66	68	65	71	270	30,600
Andy Morse	68	69	67	68	272	19,800
Daniel Chopra	72	67	70	63	272	19,800
Bart Bryant	70	69	65	69	273	14,085
Bobby Gage	67	66	70	70	273	14,085
Rick Price	66	66	70	71	273	14,085
Andrew McLardy	67	69	68	69	273	14,085
Kevin Pendley	68	70	68	67	273	14,085
Craig Bowden	68	70	66	70	274	10,350

	SCORES				TOTAL	MONEY
Joe Ogilvie	67	65	65	77	274	10,350
Greg Boyette	72	66	70	66	274	10,350
Zoran Zorkic	65	68	73	69	275	7,200
Ty Armstrong	67	70	70	68	275	7,200
Chris Couch	66	72	68	69	275	7,200
David Morland	69	65	68	73	275	7,200
Paul Claxton	69	69	70	67	275	7,200
D.A. Points	71	62	68	74	275	7,200
Boo Weekley	69	67	67	72	275	7,200
Russ Cochran	67	70	68	71	276	4,680
Lee Porter	69	69	69	69	276	4,680
Bob Heintz	67	67	74	68	276	4,680
Bo Van Pelt	68	69	71	68	276	4,680
Josh Broadaway	70	67	71	68	276	4,680
Wes Short	69	67	72	69	277	3,600
Tom Carter	68	70	70	69	277	3,600
Stephen Gangluff	68	66	69	74	277	3,600
Danny Briggs	71	66	69	72	278	3,090
John Elliott	72	65	71	70	278	3,090
Jin Park	67	68	71	72	278	3,090

Chattanooga Classic

Black Creek Club, Chattanooga, Tennessee
Par 36-36–72; 7,044 yards

July 31-August 3
purse, $450,000

	SCORES				TOTAL	MONEY
Jason Bohn	65	67	69	64	265	$81,000
Kyle Thompson	67	66	65	68	266	48,600
Ryan Palmer	65	68	65	69	267	30,600
Tom Carter	66	67	67	68	268	19,800
Jimmy Walker	71	67	64	66	268	19,800
Bart Bryant	69	68	69	63	269	14,085
Ted Purdy	64	70	70	65	269	14,085
Rob Bradley	66	66	69	68	269	14,085
Vaughn Taylor	67	69	65	68	269	14,085
Lucas Glover	70	69	66	64	269	14,085
Johnson Wagner	70	69	66	65	270	11,250
Kevin Johnson	66	69	68	68	271	8,550
Jeff Freeman	68	67	69	67	271	8,550
Tjaart van der Walt	69	69	67	66	271	8,550
Jason Dufner	68	69	67	67	271	8,550
Kevin Durkin	67	71	68	65	271	8,550
Matt Weibring	69	70	68	64	271	8,550
Tommy Tolles	67	67	67	71	272	5,868
Omar Uresti	68	71	65	68	272	5,868
Ken Duke	69	65	68	70	272	5,868
Mark Hensby	70	70	66	66	272	5,868
James Driscoll	65	72	68	67	272	5,868
Franklin Langham	69	69	64	71	273	4,500
Chad Wilfong	64	71	70	68	273	4,500
Sung Man Lee	69	71	67	67	274	3,960
Jim Benepe	67	67	71	70	275	3,278.57
Steve Haskins	69	69	64	73	275	3,278.57
Fran Quinn	69	70	68	68	275	3,278.57
Scott Dunlap	70	66	70	69	275	3,278.58
Bradley Hughes	66	71	68	70	275	3,278.57

	SCORES				TOTAL	MONEY
Paul Claxton	69	68	70	68	275	3,278.57
Tommy Biershenk	65	66	74	70	275	3,278.57

Omaha Classic

The Champions Club, Omaha, Nebraska
Par 36-36–72; 7,099 yards

August 7-10
purse, $550,000

	SCORES				TOTAL	MONEY
Bo Van Pelt	64	67	69	62	262	$99,000
Craig Lile	70	60	69	65	264	59,400
Tjaart van der Walt	70	64	64	67	265	37,400
Steve Ford	66	67	68	65	266	24,200
Todd Demsey	65	66	70	65	266	24,200
Blaine McCallister	69	69	65	64	267	18,425
Ted Purdy	68	65	66	68	267	18,425
Roland Thatcher	67	69	64	67	267	18,425
Victor Schwamkrug	65	73	65	65	268	15,950
Guy Boros	68	63	68	70	269	14,300
Todd Rose	66	64	70	69	269	14,300
Sean Murphy	66	68	67	69	270	11,137.50
Scott Petersen	67	65	71	67	270	11,137.50
Steve Runge	68	63	72	67	270	11,137.50
Paul Claxton	67	67	65	71	270	11,137.50
Grant Waite	68	69	67	67	271	7,975
Michael Allen	70	68	67	66	271	7,975
Craig Bowden	67	67	69	68	271	7,975
David Branshaw	70	65	69	67	271	7,975
John Paul Curley	67	69	68	67	271	7,975
Scott Gutschewski	65	67	70	69	271	7,975
Danny Briggs	68	70	67	67	272	5,170
Eric Meeks	67	70	68	67	272	5,170
Fran Quinn	66	70	62	74	272	5,170
Sonny Skinner	67	69	68	68	272	5,170
Omar Uresti	65	66	72	69	272	5,170
Jimmy Walker	65	70	68	69	272	5,170
Michael Bradley	72	65	70	66	273	3,740
Kelly Gibson	70	67	71	65	273	3,740
Scott Dunlap	68	67	67	71	273	3,740
Bob Heintz	65	68	72	68	273	3,740
Daniel Chopra	70	65	66	72	273	3,740
Jason Bohn	67	70	65	71	273	3,740

Price Cutter Charity Championship

Highland Springs Country Club, Springfield, Missouri
Par 36-36–72; 7,060 yards

August 14-17
purse, $525,000

	SCORES				TOTAL	MONEY
Tom Carter	66	68	68	65	267	$94,500
Roland Thatcher	66	67	71	64	268	46,200
Doug LaBelle	65	66	68	69	268	46,200
Keoke Cotner	67	70	66	66	269	20,672
Trevor Dodds	66	70	66	67	269	20,672
Craig Bowden	66	66	69	68	269	20,672

	SCORES				TOTAL	MONEY
Stephen Gangluff	64	67	68	70	269	20,672
David Branshaw	67	69	72	62	270	14,175
Franklin Langham	66	68	70	66	270	14,175
Scott Gutschewski	63	72	68	67	270	14,175
Jason Dufner	69	65	69	67	270	14,175
Richard Barcelo	66	64	71	69	270	14,175
P.J. Cowan	68	67	69	67	271	9,844
Chris Tidland	66	70	66	69	271	9,844
Guy Boros	69	66	66	70	271	9,844
Zach Johnson	71	66	64	70	271	9,844
Rob McKelvey	68	69	70	65	272	7,613
Eduardo Herrera	68	70	68	66	272	7,613
D.A. Points	69	70	67	66	272	7,613
Scott Petersen	73	66	66	67	272	7,613
Tjaart van der Walt	67	69	69	68	273	5,670
Jeff Hart	66	71	68	68	273	5,670
Ryan Howison	69	66	69	69	273	5,670
Blaine McCallister	70	67	65	71	273	5,670
Mark Wurtz	68	70	69	67	274	4,410
Charles Warren	70	65	70	69	274	4,410
Joe Ogilvie	65	63	74	72	274	4,410
Scott Dunlap	74	65	69	67	275	3,510
Danny Briggs	69	69	68	69	275	3,510
Willie Wood	67	67	71	70	275	3,510
Jimmy Walker	70	69	67	69	275	3,510
Todd Demsey	70	66	69	70	275	3,510
Boo Weekley	68	68	68	71	275	3,510
Scott Gump	67	67	66	75	275	3,510

Preferred Health Systems Wichita Open

Crestview Country Club, Wichita, Kansas
Par 36-35–71; 6,913 yards

August 21-24
purse, $475,000

	SCORES				TOTAL	MONEY
Jeff Klauk	66	69	64	66	265	$85,500
Mike Brisky	64	68	70	64	266	41,800
Mark Hensby	65	66	66	69	266	41,800
Blaine McCallister	65	67	68	67	267	20,900
Wil Collins	67	71	64	65	267	20,900
Omar Uresti	65	70	66	67	268	15,378.12
Brad Ott	69	67	65	67	268	15,378.13
Ryan Palmer	69	68	68	63	268	15,378.13
Tag Ridings	66	67	65	70	268	15,378.12
Bob Friend	69	70	63	67	269	10,178.57
Ken Duke	69	66	67	67	269	10,178.57
Andre Stolz	67	73	64	65	269	10,178.57
Jason Schultz	70	65	67	67	269	10,178.57
Rich Barcelo	69	66	68	66	269	10,178.57
Hunter Haas	70	68	66	65	269	10,178.58
Nick Cassini	67	68	67	67	269	10,178.57
Tom Carter	70	70	66	64	270	7,362.50
Jimmy Walker	70	65	70	65	270	7,362.50
Eduardo Herrera	66	69	70	66	271	5,557.50
Jeff Freeman	66	69	68	68	271	5,557.50
Joe Ogilvie	67	68	71	65	271	5,557.50
Ted Purdy	67	67	71	66	271	5,557.50
Victor Schwamkrug	69	70	69	63	271	5,557.50

	SCORES				TOTAL	MONEY
Roger Tambellini	68	69	67	67	271	5,557.50
Mike Austin	69	63	72	68	272	3,990
Todd Demsey	74	66	66	66	272	3,990
Scott Gutschewski	69	67	68	68	272	3,990
Jim Benepe	71	66	68	68	273	3,348.75
Jeev Milkha Singh	67	72	68	66	273	3,348.75
Ryuji Imada	70	69	69	65	273	3,348.75
Ned Michaels	68	69	67	69	273	3,348.75

Alberta Calgary Classic

The Links at GlenEagles, Cochrane, Alberta, Canada
Par 36-36–72; 7,019 yards

August 28-31
purse, $450,000

	SCORES				TOTAL	MONEY
Tom Carter	68	68	62	65	263	$81,000
Nick Cassini	70	67	65	66	268	48,600
Mike Standly	65	68	63	73	269	26,100
Mario Tiziani	68	67	63	71	269	26,100
Jeff Freeman	69	66	69	66	270	16,425
John Morse	70	64	67	69	270	16,425
David Branshaw	67	67	69	67	270	16,425
Blaine McCallister	69	66	69	68	272	12,600
Jeev Milkha Singh	65	68	70	69	272	12,600
Daniel Chopra	66	69	68	69	272	12,600
Wade Ormsby	72	67	70	63	272	12,600
Scott Dunlap	72	67	67	67	273	9,112.50
Scott Hend	67	70	68	68	273	9,112.50
Wes Martin	68	67	66	72	273	9,112.50
Rob Johnson	69	70	66	68	273	9,112.50
Jim Benepe	73	66	68	67	274	4,950
Mike Springer	70	67	70	67	274	4,950
Michael Allen	68	69	70	67	274	4,950
Rick Price	66	68	71	69	274	4,950
Matt Bettencourt	70	68	66	70	274	4,950
Ken Duke	71	66	68	69	274	4,950
Shane Tait	73	66	67	68	274	4,950
David McKenzie	68	70	68	68	274	4,950
Terry Hatch	68	68	69	69	274	4,950
Wes Heffernan	68	67	67	72	274	4,950
Jeff Klauk	70	68	67	69	274	4,950
Dave Christensen	70	67	67	70	274	4,950
Scott Gutschewski	67	68	70	69	274	4,950
Lee Williamson	68	70	67	69	274	4,950
Patrick Damron	71	66	68	69	274	4,950

Envirocare Utah Classic

Willow Creek Country Club, Sandy, Utah
Par 35-37–72; 7,104 yards

September 4-7
purse, $450,000

	SCORES				TOTAL	MONEY
Zach Johnson	68	69	65	65	267	$81,000
Bobby Gage	67	68	66	67	268	48,600
Scott Gutschewski	65	71	64	69	269	30,600

	SCORES				TOTAL	MONEY
Mark Hensby	69	66	68	68	271	21,600
Joe Ogilvie	68	71	67	67	273	18,000
Scott Gump	71	63	70	70	274	15,637.50
Franklin Langham	69	69	70	66	274	15,637.50
Jeff Freeman	65	69	66	75	275	11,700
Shane Bertsch	68	69	69	69	275	11,700
Ted Purdy	72	70	66	67	275	11,700
Roger Tambellini	71	66	66	72	275	11,700
Jimmy Walker	69	67	69	70	275	11,700
Nick Cassini	69	70	71	65	275	11,700
Barry Cheesman	73	66	71	66	276	6,975
Lee Porter	65	71	70	70	276	6,975
Jason Schultz	66	70	73	67	276	6,975
Andrew McLardy	73	67	67	69	276	6,975
Scott Hend	73	65	68	70	276	6,975
Bo Van Pelt	69	70	65	72	276	6,975
Bryce Molder	69	70	70	67	276	6,975
Bubba Watson	67	72	69	68	276	6,975
Rick Price	71	66	69	71	277	4,860
Scott Piercy	66	74	71	66	277	4,860
Tommy Tolles	68	72	66	72	278	3,915
Matt Bettencourt	71	67	69	71	278	3,915
Daniel Chopra	68	73	68	69	278	3,915
Roland Thatcher	67	66	72	73	278	3,915
Chris Couch	74	67	70	68	279	3,114
Chris Zambri	71	71	69	68	279	3,114
Keoke Cotner	68	71	69	71	279	3,114
Iain Steel	74	65	70	70	279	3,114
Brett Wetterich	68	69	72	70	279	3,114

Oregon Classic

Shadow Hills Country Club, Junction City, Oregon
Par 36-36–72; 7,007 yards

September 11-14
purse, $450,000

	SCORES				TOTAL	MONEY
Chris Couch	66	68	71	69	274	$81,000
Jason Bohn	68	66	69	71	274	48,600
(Couch defeated Bohn on first playoff hole.)						
Brett Wetterich	69	70	72	65	276	26,100
Jimmy Walker	69	71	70	66	276	26,100
Hunter Haas	70	68	72	68	278	18,000
Ryuji Imada	69	69	68	73	279	15,637.50
Ted Purdy	68	73	67	71	279	15,637.50
Jason Dufner	68	67	71	74	280	13,050
Bubba Watson	69	68	68	75	280	13,050
Kevin Durkin	72	66	72	70	280	13,050
Jaxon Brigman	71	70	68	72	281	9,540
Mark Wurtz	68	66	72	75	281	9,540
Andrew McLardy	69	73	67	72	281	9,540
Bo Van Pelt	66	72	71	72	281	9,540
Boo Weekley	70	73	72	66	281	9,540
Emlyn Aubrey	71	71	66	74	282	6,108.75
Barry Cheesman	68	74	68	72	282	6,108.75
Craig Bowden	67	72	71	72	282	6,108.75
Scott Petersen	70	72	70	70	282	6,108.75
Mark Hensby	70	74	72	66	282	6,108.75

	SCORES				TOTAL	MONEY
Andre Stolz	67	73	72	70	282	6,108.75
Roger Tambellini	67	75	71	69	282	6,108.75
Mark Walker	70	71	73	68	282	6,108.75
Scott Gump	68	73	69	73	283	4,020
Michael Allen	70	71	71	71	283	4,020
Stephen Gangluff	73	71	68	71	283	4,020
Russ Cochran	71	73	73	67	284	2,929.10
Tommy Tolles	72	70	72	70	284	2,929.09
Jeff Freeman	68	70	74	72	284	2,929.09
Steve Ford	72	70	70	72	284	2,929.09
Shane Bertsch	71	70	71	72	284	2,929.09
Ryan Howison	72	69	68	75	284	2,929.09
Michael Long	72	72	71	69	284	2,929.09
Tag Ridings	70	73	71	70	284	2,929.09
Tommy Biershenk	73	71	70	70	284	2,929.09
Scott Piercy	70	71	74	69	284	2,929.09
Nick Cassini	70	74	67	73	284	2,929.09

Albertsons Boise Open

Hillcrest Country Club, Boise, Idaho
Par 36-35–71; 6,698 yards

September 18-21
purse, $600,000

	SCORES				TOTAL	MONEY
Roger Tambellini	68	65	66	68	267	$108,000
Tripp Isenhour	73	69	67	64	273	52,800
Charles Warren	65	71	67	70	273	52,800
Tjaart van der Walt	68	67	70	69	274	23,625
John Paul Curley	66	74	69	65	274	23,625
Ryan Palmer	69	67	71	67	274	23,625
Jeff Quinney	69	70	68	67	274	23,625
Brian Wilson	66	67	70	72	275	17,400
Todd Demsey	67	71	69	68	275	17,400
Mark Hensby	70	68	69	68	275	17,400
Danny Briggs	69	67	70	71	277	12,720
Tommy Tolles	72	69	70	66	277	12,720
Brad Ott	72	66	65	74	277	12,720
Bobby Kalinowski	68	69	71	69	277	12,720
Bo Van Pelt	68	73	69	67	277	12,720
Michael Allen	71	71	68	68	278	9,000
Jimmy Green	67	71	69	71	278	9,000
Michael Muehr	67	71	70	70	278	9,000
Kyle Thompson	67	72	69	70	278	9,000
Brett Wetterich	70	67	69	72	278	9,000
Fran Quinn	68	68	69	74	279	6,720
Charles Raulerson	71	70	70	68	279	6,720
Franklin Langham	69	69	68	73	279	6,720
Omar Uresti	70	71	71	68	280	5,088
Daniel Chopra	71	66	75	68	280	5,088
Ryuji Imada	69	69	70	72	280	5,088
Jason Schultz	67	68	70	75	280	5,088
Kyle Kovacs	70	71	71	68	280	5,088
Jeff Gove	68	70	75	68	281	3,984
Stephen Gangluff	69	69	70	73	281	3,984
Jason Bohn	67	70	71	73	281	3,984
Scott Gutschewski	69	70	67	75	281	3,984
Jason Dufner	71	67	72	71	281	3,984

Mark Christopher Charity Classic

Empire Lakes Golf Club, Rancho Cucamonga, California
Par 36-35–71; 6,972 yards

September 25-28
purse, $450,000

		SCORES			TOTAL	MONEY
James Oh	65	66	66	71	268	$81,000
Jess Daley	69	62	67	70	268	48,600
(Oh defeated Daley on third playoff hole.)						
Chris Starkjohann	68	67	70	64	269	30,600
Danny Briggs	69	67	68	67	271	19,800
Jason Dufner	65	69	71	66	271	19,800
Ryuji Imada	69	69	68	66	272	15,075
Robert Conrad	67	68	70	67	272	15,075
Jimmy Walker	69	70	67	66	272	15,075
Daniel Chopra	70	66	67	70	273	12,600
Joe Ogilvie	66	70	71	66	273	12,600
Chris Tidland	68	65	69	72	274	10,800
Ted Purdy	68	71	70	65	274	10,800
Ron Skayhan	69	69	68	69	275	9,000
Jason Bohn	67	73	68	67	275	9,000
Steve Haskins	69	67	70	70	276	7,200
Fran Quinn	70	67	72	67	276	7,200
Ryan Howison	67	70	71	68	276	7,200
Brad Ott	67	67	69	73	276	7,200
Keoke Cotner	68	70	70	68	276	7,200
Bob Heintz	68	68	68	73	277	5,242.50
Doug LaBelle	67	68	71	71	277	5,242.50
Bryce Molder	70	66	70	71	277	5,242.50
Jason Higton	69	69	73	66	277	5,242.50
Scott Gump	68	69	70	71	278	3,470
Jaxon Brigman	68	69	69	72	278	3,470
Jeff Freeman	69	71	64	74	278	3,470
Mike Brisky	68	67	74	69	278	3,470
Todd Demsey	69	71	68	70	278	3,470
Casey Martin	67	71	67	73	278	3,470
Kyle Thompson	72	67	71	68	278	3,470
Hunter Haas	67	71	70	70	278	3,470
Sung Man Lee	68	70	70	70	278	3,470

Monterey Peninsula Classic

Bayonet and Black Horse Golf Courses, Seaside, California
Bayonet Course: Par 36-36–72; 7,117 yards

October 2-5
purse, $450,000

		SCORES			TOTAL	MONEY
Scott Gutschewski	68	69	67	72	276	$81,000
Michael Allen	69	74	70	67	280	33,600
Rich Barcelo	73	69	66	72	280	33,600
Zach Johnson	69	71	72	68	280	33,600
Ryuji Imada	68	73	72	69	282	17,100
Joe Ogilvie	69	73	66	74	282	17,100
Wes Short	70	73	69	71	283	15,075
Trevor Dodds	70	77	68	69	284	13,500
Chris Couch	72	74	67	71	284	13,500
Zoran Zorkic	69	68	74	74	285	10,800
Andre Stolz	72	69	72	72	285	10,800
John Paul Curley	71	68	72	74	285	10,800

	SCORES				TOTAL	MONEY
Boo Weekley	70	71	73	71	285	10,800
Eduardo Herrera	74	68	71	73	286	7,875
Casey Martin	69	77	70	70	286	7,875
Kyle Thompson	68	70	76	72	286	7,875
Jason Bohn	69	76	69	72	286	7,875
Steve Haskins	70	72	72	73	287	5,868
Blaine McCallister	74	71	73	69	287	5,868
Scott Dunlap	73	72	69	73	287	5,868
Charles Raulerson	73	71	67	76	287	5,868
John Elliott	71	73	71	72	287	5,868
Boyd Summerhays	72	73	71	72	288	4,185
Robert Conrad	72	71	73	72	288	4,185
Mark Worthington	73	74	71	70	288	4,185
Troy Matteson	75	69	71	73	288	4,185
Franklin Langham	74	71	71	73	289	3,195
Shane Bertsch	71	73	71	74	289	3,195
Paul Claxton	76	71	72	70	289	3,195
Roger Tambellini	72	71	75	71	289	3,195
Vaughn Taylor	76	70	74	69	289	3,195
Kevin Pendley	72	75	71	71	289	3,195

Gila River Classic at Wild Horse Pass Resort

Whirlwind Golf Club, Cattail Course, Chandler, Arizona   October 9-12
Par 36-36–72; 7,017 yards   purse, $475,000

	SCORES				TOTAL	MONEY
Lucas Glover	67	69	67	67	270	$85,500
Robin Freeman	69	68	65	69	271	35,466.66
John Elliott	66	71	65	69	271	35,466.67
Tommy Tolles	70	66	65	70	271	35,466.67
Jeff Freeman	68	68	66	70	272	18,050
Jason Dufner	69	72	65	66	272	18,050
Fran Quinn	70	64	72	67	273	14,804.17
Mark Hensby	73	66	66	68	273	14,804.16
Scott Gutschewski	69	66	70	68	273	14,804.17
Wes Short	68	67	72	67	274	12,350
Tjaart van der Walt	67	69	68	70	274	12,350
Scott Sterling	67	71	67	70	275	10,450
Ryuji Imada	68	66	71	70	275	10,450
Eduardo Herrera	68	68	70	70	276	8,550
Brian Wilson	67	66	69	74	276	8,550
Jeff Gove	66	70	67	73	276	8,550
Mike Sullivan	69	68	71	69	277	7,125
Ryan Howison	69	71	67	70	277	7,125
Brad Ott	69	70	70	68	277	7,125
Ted Purdy	71	69	74	64	278	5,533.75
Bo Van Pelt	72	67	68	71	278	5,533.75
Jimmy Walker	72	69	68	69	278	5,533.75
Roland Thatcher	69	68	73	68	278	5,533.75
Craig Bowden	71	66	72	70	279	3,827.14
Todd Demsey	69	69	68	73	279	3,827.14
Bradley Hughes	69	70	71	69	279	3,827.15
Chris Couch	69	70	71	69	279	3,827.14
Andrew Tschudin	68	69	68	74	279	3,827.14
Stephen Gangluff	70	70	68	71	279	3,827.14
Zach Johnson	70	67	73	69	279	3,827.15

Permian Basin Charity Golf Classic

Midland Country Club, Midland, Texas
Par 36-36–72; 7,354 yards

October 16-19
purse, $450,000

	SCORES				TOTAL	MONEY
D.J. Brigman	71	68	67	66	272	$81,000
Mark Hensby	69	65	69	70	273	33,600
Jimmy Walker	74	68	64	67	273	33,600
Jason Dufner	69	66	70	68	273	33,600
Daniel Chopra	71	69	66	68	274	18,000
Wes Short	70	67	68	70	275	16,200
Charles Warren	70	70	67	69	276	14,025
Stephen Gangluff	73	68	66	69	276	14,025
George McNeill	72	69	68	67	276	14,025
Ben Bates	72	71	67	67	277	9,975
Mark Wiebe	71	70	68	68	277	9,975
Scott Gump	69	70	68	70	277	9,975
Sonny Skinner	69	67	68	73	277	9,975
Ryuji Imada	71	72	67	67	277	9,975
Jeremy Wilkinson	71	67	70	69	277	9,975
Kevin Johnson	72	67	71	68	278	6,312.86
Bob Heintz	69	72	68	69	278	6,312.86
Todd Demsey	71	70	70	67	278	6,312.86
Ryan Howison	69	71	69	69	278	6,312.86
Ryan Palmer	68	74	67	69	278	6,312.85
Jess Daley	68	70	67	73	278	6,312.85
Mark Walker	71	69	70	68	278	6,312.86
Steve Haskins	71	69	69	70	279	3,857.14
Sean Murphy	68	68	71	72	279	3,857.14
Brian Wilson	73	67	68	71	279	3,857.14
Brad Ott	72	67	72	68	279	3,857.14
Rich Barcelo	66	74	71	68	279	3,857.15
Doug Garwood	72	70	67	70	279	3,857.14
Nick Cassini	75	66	71	67	279	3,857.15
Mike Standly	69	72	70	69	280	2,880
Guy Boros	71	71	70	68	280	2,880
Tjaart van der Walt	72	70	64	74	280	2,880
David Branshaw	69	69	75	67	280	2,880
Roland Thatcher	70	73	66	71	280	2,880

Miccosukee Championship

Miccosukee Golf & Country Club, Miami, Florida
Par 36-35–71; 7,200 yards

October 23-26
purse, $500,000

	SCORES				TOTAL	MONEY
Craig Bowden	69	65	65	71	270	$90,000
Chris Couch	71	67	68	65	271	54,000
Ryan Palmer	70	68	66	68	272	29,000
Bo Van Pelt	68	68	70	66	272	29,000
Dave Schreyer	70	69	67	67	273	19,000
Jason Dufner	71	62	71	69	273	19,000
Kelly Gibson	68	67	68	71	274	15,062.50
Blaine McCallister	73	63	70	68	274	15,062.50
Jason Schultz	72	67	70	65	274	15,062.50
Ted Purdy	67	69	71	67	274	15,062.50

	SCORES				TOTAL	MONEY
Barry Cheesman	71	66	68	70	275	11,500
Jeff Freeman	68	70	69	68	275	11,500
Paul Claxton	65	66	73	71	275	11,500
Jim McGovern	68	68	72	68	276	8,250
Bob Heintz	70	68	70	68	276	8,250
Mark Hensby	64	68	72	72	276	8,250
Roger Tambellini	69	66	67	74	276	8,250
Brett Wetterich	67	67	70	72	276	8,250
Jeff Klauk	67	72	69	68	276	8,250
Scott Sterling	67	67	73	70	277	6,033.33
Bradley Hughes	70	68	72	67	277	6,033.34
Jason Bohn	70	67	69	71	277	6,033.33
Chris Starkjohann	71	68	65	74	278	4,400
Grant Waite	64	68	72	74	278	4,400
Willie Wood	70	66	71	71	278	4,400
Mark Wurtz	69	69	72	68	278	4,400
Keoke Cotner	70	67	73	68	278	4,400
Jess Daley	67	68	70	73	278	4,400
Steve Pate	69	69	72	69	279	3,320
Omar Uresti	69	68	71	71	279	3,320
Shane Bertsch	70	66	71	72	279	3,320
Rich Barcelo	68	66	75	70	279	3,320
Erik Compton	66	71	71	71	279	3,320

Nationwide Tour Championship

Robert Trent Jones Golf Trail at Capitol Hill,
Senator Course, Prattville, Alabama
Par 36-36–72; 7,656 yards

October 30-November 2
purse, $625,000

	SCORES				TOTAL	MONEY
Chris Couch	66	67	65	72	270	$112,500
D.J. Brigman	66	68	71	68	273	67,500
Zach Johnson	65	72	69	68	274	42,500
Ken Duke	67	66	70	72	275	30,000
Bo Van Pelt	66	70	74	66	276	23,750
Jason Bohn	73	68	65	70	276	23,750
Jess Daley	68	69	70	70	277	20,937.50
Jeff Freeman	71	68	72	67	278	17,500
Wes Short	70	68	67	73	278	17,500
Chris Tidland	71	64	71	72	278	17,500
Mark Hensby	73	69	67	69	278	17,500
Tommy Tolles	71	72	65	71	279	12,656.25
Tjaart van der Walt	67	70	65	77	279	12,656.25
Jeff Klauk	71	70	69	69	279	12,656.25
Jason Dufner	66	70	72	71	279	12,656.25
Scott Gutschewski	70	69	73	68	280	10,625
Andre Stolz	69	71	69	73	282	9,375
Daniel Chopra	68	71	67	76	282	9,375
Roger Tambellini	68	72	71	71	282	9,375
Doug LaBelle	69	66	72	77	284	7,583.33
Ryan Palmer	76	70	68	70	284	7,583.34
Jimmy Walker	70	70	68	76	284	7,583.33
Blaine McCallister	71	71	69	74	285	6,281.25
Bobby Gage	70	69	73	73	285	6,281.25
David Morland	72	69	71	73	285	6,281.25
David Branshaw	72	69	73	71	285	6,281.25

	SCORES				TOTAL	MONEY
Charles Warren	69	72	72	73	286	5,625
Guy Boros	72	72	68	75	287	5,015.62
Paul Claxton	72	74	71	70	287	5,015.63
Craig Lile	68	73	72	74	287	5,015.62
Roland Thatcher	67	74	75	71	287	5,015.63

Canadian Tour

TravelTex.com Canadian Tour Classic

Barton Creek, Crenshaw Cliffside Course, Austin, Texas
Par 36-36–72; 6553 yards

February 13-16
purse, C$150,000

	SCORES				TOTAL	MONEY
Anders Hultman	67	68	68	69	272	C$24,000
Michael Harris	66	69	68	71	274	9,150
Craig Kanada	70	67	68	69	274	9,150
Joe Ogilvie	67	64	69	74	274	9,150
Roger Tambellini	64	67	71	72	274	9,150
Jason Bohn	66	71	68	70	275	5,175
James Driscoll	68	68	69	70	275	5,175
Adam Short	67	69	69	71	276	4,650
Rob McMillan	67	67	74	69	277	4,200
Jimmy Walker	70	67	69	71	277	4,200
Derrick Centers	69	67	73	69	278	3,300
Scott Gibson	70	69	68	71	278	3,300
Clint Jensen	73	65	68	72	278	3,300
Jon Mills	70	71	70	67	278	3,300
Lee Williamson	66	72	69	72	279	2,700
Rafael Gemoets	68	66	73	73	280	2,325
Darren Griff	70	67	72	71	280	2,325
Josh Habig	68	67	71	74	280	2,325
Omar Uresti	69	66	70	75	280	2,325
Rodney Butcher	69	72	72	68	281	1,725
Erik Compton	69	70	70	72	281	1,725
Jess Daley	66	68	71	76	281	1,725
Kevin Jones	69	70	68	74	281	1,725
David Ogrin	73	65	69	74	281	1,725
Chris Parra	70	70	71	70	281	1,725
Jason Schultz	73	67	70	71	281	1,725
Dave Christensen	67	70	74	71	282	1,315
Craig Matthew	67	69	72	74	282	1,315
Kris Mikkelsen	70	65	72	75	282	1,315
Jeff Quinney	69	70	68	75	282	1,315
Adam Speirs	70	70	71	71	282	1,315
Chris Wisler	70	67	70	75	282	1,315

TravelTex.com Canadian Tour Challenge

Barton Creek, Fazio Foothills Course, Austin, Texas
Par 36-36–72; 6,956 yards
(Event shortened to 36 holes—rain.)

February 20-23
purse, C$150,000

	SCORES		TOTAL	MONEY
Rob Johnson	65	69	134	C$24,000
Michael Harris	69	67	136	11,700
Mark Johnson	72	64	136	11,700
James Driscoll	67	71	138	6,600
Hank Kuehne	70	68	138	6,600
Brad Sutterfield	66	73	139	5,175
Lee Williamson	67	72	139	5,175
Philip Jonas	68	72	140	4,350
Stephen Woodard	69	71	140	4,350
Iain Steel	67	73	140	4,350
Chris Wall	71	70	141	3,600
Craig Kanada	69	72	141	3,600
Vic Wilk	74	68	142	2,362.50
David Ogrin	73	69	142	2,362.50
Derek Gillespie	75	67	142	2,362.50
Conrad Ray	71	71	142	2,362.50
Jason Enloe	71	71	142	2,362.50
Chris Greenwood	71	71	142	2,362.50
Rich Massey	70	72	142	2,362.50
Robert Hamilton	70	72	142	2,362.50
Ben Pettitt	69	73	142	2,362.50
Patrick Damron	74	68	142	2,362.50
David Patrick	74	69	143	1,385.63
Jason Bohn	74	69	143	1,385.63
Bobby Kalinowski	71	72	143	1,385.63
Bryn Parry	72	71	143	1,385.63
Adam Speirs	74	69	143	1,385.63
Jon Mills	73	70	143	1,385.63
Steve Scott	71	72	143	1,385.63
Michael Standly	72	71	143	1,385.63
Chris Locker	70	73	143	1,385.63
David Howser	67	76	143	1,385.63
Jason Allred	71	72	143	1,385.63
Craig Taylor	72	71	143	1,385.63

Michelin Guadalajara Classic

Guadalajara Country Club, Guadalajara, Mexico
Par 71; 6,815 yards

May 8-11
purse, C$150,000

	SCORES				TOTAL	MONEY
Erik Compton	67	71	69	63	270	C$24,000
David Hearn	70	67	73	64	274	11,700
Antonio Maldonado	67	71	67	69	274	11,700
Derek Gillespie	68	72	69	66	275	5,887
Cory Jones	70	69	67	69	275	5,887
Alejandro Quiroz	69	71	68	67	275	5,887
Conrad Ray	74	69	69	63	275	5,887
Josh Habig	68	73	69	66	276	4,350
Alexandre Rocha	62	77	68	69	276	4,350
Roger Tambellini	70	69	66	71	276	4,350

	SCORES				TOTAL	MONEY
Steve Marino	67	71	70	70	278	3,750
Jason Bohn	68	72	69	70	279	2,940
Michael Harris	71	68	71	69	279	2,940
Clint Jensen	69	68	72	70	279	2,940
Mauricio Molina	70	69	69	71	279	2,940
Chris Wisler	69	69	73	68	279	2,940
Darren Griff	67	72	74	67	280	2,250
Jose Trauwitz	70	71	71	68	280	2,250
Julio Zapata	67	70	72	71	280	2,250
Jorge Corral	67	69	67	78	281	1,800
Octavio Gonzalez	69	74	68	70	281	1,800
Rob Johnson	73	68	69	71	281	1,800
Chris Wall	68	74	69	70	281	1,800
Eric Woods	69	73	72	67	281	1,800
Robert Hamilton	71	72	69	70	282	1,474
Jim Salinetti	72	68	72	70	282	1,474
Zoltan Veress	71	70	71	70	282	1,474
Bryan Wright	70	70	73	69	282	1,474
Paul Devenport	68	72	73	70	283	1,268
Miguel Fernandez	70	72	72	69	283	1,268
Carlos Pelaez	65	72	72	74	283	1,268
Adam Short	66	72	74	71	283	1,268

Corona Ixtapa Classic

Palma Real Golf Club, Ixtapa, Mexico
Par 36-36–72; 6,875 yards

May 15-18
purse, C$150,000

	SCORES				TOTAL	MONEY
Derek Gillespie	66	67	67	65	265	C$24,000
Jim Salinetti	65	70	67	71	273	14,400
Clint Jensen	67	67	69	71	274	6,900
Brad Sutterfield	69	68	68	69	274	6,900
Chris Wall	66	70	69	69	274	6,900
Pablo Del Olmo	67	65	70	72	274	6,900
Paul Devenport	71	69	66	69	275	4,500
Miguel Fernandez	69	66	68	72	275	4,500
Scott Ford	66	70	70	69	275	4,500
Miguel Guzman	68	66	70	71	275	4,500
Octavio Gonzalez	71	68	70	67	276	3,180
Michael Harris	68	69	71	68	276	3,180
Alan McLean	68	70	71	67	276	3,180
Conrad Ray	69	70	69	68	276	3,180
David Tentis	69	66	69	72	276	3,180
Jason Bohn	65	71	71	70	277	2,400
Bob Jacobsen	67	69	67	74	277	2,400
Brian Payne	64	71	73	69	277	2,400
Eduardo Argiro	72	68	70	68	278	1,975
Kris Mikkelsen	66	71	71	70	278	1,975
Jon Mills	71	68	69	70	278	1,975
Bryan DeCorso	70	71	68	70	279	1,688
David Hearn	65	71	71	72	279	1,688
Jim Lemon	72	69	72	66	279	1,688
Dan Olsen	70	69	68	72	279	1,688
Richie Coughlan	70	66	71	73	280	1,414
Rodolfo Gonzalez	67	73	70	70	280	1,414
Anders Hultman	68	71	69	72	280	1,414
Alejandro Quiroz	74	65	70	71	280	1,414

	SCORES				TOTAL	MONEY
Mark Johnson	70	71	69	71	281	1,245
Joshua Lower	73	66	71	71	281	1,245
Jose Trauwitz	71	69	70	71	281	1,245

Northern Ontario Open

Saute Ste. Marie Golf Club, Saute Ste. Marie, Ontario   June 26-29
Par 35-35–70; 6,767 yards   purse, C$175,000

	SCORES				TOTAL	MONEY
Mario Tiziani	69	67	67	68	271	C$28,000
Tony Carolan	67	73	68	69	277	13,650
David McKenzie	67	69	71	70	277	13,650
Darren Griff	69	70	69	71	279	7,233
Michael Hospodar	69	73	68	69	279	7,233
Kris Mikkelsen	69	71	68	71	279	7,233
John Bachman	72	72	69	67	280	4,725
Dave Christensen	73	71	69	67	280	4,725
Michael Harris	72	70	68	70	280	4,725
David Hearn	72	71	67	70	280	4,725
Craig Matthew	74	68	71	67	280	4,725
Sal Spallone	71	73	73	63	280	4,725
Bryan Wright	75	68	70	67	280	4,725
Dirk Ayers	72	68	69	72	281	2,975
Scott Ford	72	72	66	71	281	2,975
Josh Habig	73	72	67	69	281	2,975
Lee Williamson	72	69	67	73	281	2,975
Chris Wisler	68	71	72	70	281	2,975
Martin Price	71	71	72	68	282	2,362
Alex Quiroz	73	69	68	72	282	2,362
Scott Gibson	71	71	70	71	283	2,056
Derek Gillespie	74	66	70	73	283	2,056
Matt McQuillan	71	70	69	73	283	2,056
Danny Paniccia	74	69	68	72	283	2,056
Wes Heffernan	69	74	70	71	284	1,687
Steve Marino	67	72	74	71	284	1,687
John Patterson	72	70	72	70	284	1,687
Tim Turpen	75	69	71	69	284	1,687
Chris Wollmann	73	71	70	70	284	1,687
Matt Bettencourt	72	69	73	71	285	1,382
Brett Bingham	73	72	73	67	285	1,382
Brad Fritsch	74	70	70	71	285	1,382
Eddie Maunder	69	76	69	71	285	1,382
Ben Pettitt	73	71	72	69	285	1,382
Jarrod Warner	73	72	70	70	285	1,382

MTS Classic

Pine Ridge Golf Club, Winnipeg, Manitoba   July 10-13
Par 36-35–71; 6,522 yards   purse, C$150,000

	SCORES				TOTAL	MONEY
Jon Mills	67	65	72	71	275	C$24,000
Bryan DeCorso	67	73	70	68	278	14,400
Lee Williamson	69	73	69	68	279	9,000

	SCORES				TOTAL	MONEY
Anders Hultman	70	71	69	70	280	6,600
Mark Johnson	72	68	67	73	280	6,600
Dave Christensen	67	68	71	75	281	4,837
Wes Heffernan	70	70	68	73	281	4,837
Wes Martin	68	68	72	73	281	4,837
Rob McMillan	68	72	65	76	281	4,837
Doug McGuigan	69	69	69	75	282	3,900
Chris Wisler	65	72	68	77	282	3,900
Dirk Ayers	71	68	71	73	283	2,940
John Bachman	68	74	69	72	283	2,940
David Faught	67	74	66	76	283	2,940
Nathan Green	67	70	75	71	283	2,940
Craig Taylor	66	71	72	74	283	2,940
Dean North	63	71	74	76	284	2,400
Brett Bingham	64	72	77	72	285	2,044
Josh Habig	72	70	69	74	285	2,044
Bryn Parry	66	68	79	72	285	2,044
Jim Salinetti	72	71	65	77	285	2,044
David Hearn	67	76	66	77	286	1,725
Scotty Kral	68	71	75	72	286	1,725
Ben Pettitt	69	71	74	72	286	1,725
Tony Carolan	71	71	72	73	287	1,325
Richie Coughlan	68	70	70	79	287	1,325
Brad Fritsch	70	69	79	69	287	1,325
Michael Harris	66	73	76	72	287	1,325
Jesse Hibler	73	70	69	75	287	1,325
Jason Higton	67	73	71	76	287	1,325
Cory Jones	72	68	72	75	287	1,325
Brian McCann	69	69	74	75	287	1,325
Alex Quiroz	76	67	70	74	287	1,325
Shawn Walsh	70	69	72	76	287	1,325

Telus Edmonton Open

Windermere Golf Club, Edmonton, Alberta
Par 36-35–71; 6,756 yards

July 17-20
purse, C$150,000

	SCORES				TOTAL	MONEY
Rob Johnson	69	64	71	69	273	C$24,000
Dustin Risdon	70	68	69	68	275	14,400
Stuart Anderson	70	71	69	66	276	6,900
Dave Christensen	72	69	69	66	276	6,900
Jason Enloe	70	65	70	71	276	6,900
Scott Hend	73	70	64	69	276	6,900
Michael Harris	68	72	70	67	277	4,650
Arden Knoll	67	67	71	72	277	4,650
Chris Wall	67	67	70	73	277	4,650
Richie Coughlan	72	67	69	70	278	3,600
Todd Fanning	74	66	71	67	278	3,600
Jason Higton	64	73	71	70	278	3,600
Chris Wisler	70	69	72	67	278	3,600
Ben Ferguson	73	70	67	69	279	2,550
Rafael Gemoets	72	70	68	69	279	2,550
Michael Sabo	69	68	73	69	279	2,550
Chris Wollmann	74	66	70	69	279	2,550
Stephen Woodard	68	67	70	74	279	2,550
Eduardo Argiro	69	68	74	69	280	1,850

	SCORES				TOTAL	MONEY
David Faught	71	70	68	71	280	1,850
Mark Johnson	69	71	69	71	280	1,850
Bobby Kalinowski	72	71	69	68	280	1,850
*Mike Mezei	71	67	68	74	280	
Danny Paniccia	72	70	69	69	280	1,850
James Stewart	74	67	69	70	280	1,850
Tony Carolan	70	71	67	73	281	1,348
Matt Donovan	75	64	73	69	281	1,348
Steve Marino	69	73	68	71	281	1,348
Jon Mills	71	67	71	72	281	1,348
Chris Parra	71	71	67	72	281	1,348
Conrad Ray	70	71	67	73	281	1,348
Zoltan Veress	72	68	70	71	281	1,348
Tele Wightman	68	74	71	68	281	1,348
Jeff Wood	67	76	67	71	281	1,348

Victoria Open

Royal Colwood Golf Club, Victoria, British Columbia
Par 35-35–70; 6,656 yards

July 24-27
purse, C$175,000

	SCORES				TOTAL	MONEY
Patrick Damron	63	67	71	68	269	C$28,000
Robert Hamilton	67	69	67	67	270	13,650
Richard Zokol	65	68	72	65	270	13,650
David McKenzie	72	67	68	64	271	7,700
Steve Schneiter	65	67	73	66	271	7,700
Jason Enloe	68	68	69	67	272	6,038
Stephen Woodard	67	68	71	66	272	6,038
Wes Martin	71	65	69	68	273	5,425
Paul Devenport	70	70	68	67	275	4,550
Ben Ferguson	68	71	68	68	275	4,550
Michael Harris	66	68	68	73	275	4,550
David Hearn	72	66	71	66	275	4,550
Chris Greenwood	68	72	69	67	276	3,383
Brad Sutterfield	70	70	68	68	276	3,383
Chris Wollmann	67	69	73	67	276	3,383
Dave Christensen	67	70	73	67	277	2,372
*Craig Doell	69	70	68	70	277	
Brad Fritsch	72	69	69	67	277	2,372
Rafael Gemoets	69	68	68	72	277	2,372
Wes Heffernan	70	69	68	70	277	2,372
Philip Jonas	71	69	70	67	277	2,372
Alex Quiroz	69	68	71	69	277	2,372
Alex Rocha	71	66	72	68	277	2,372
Adam Short	70	68	69	70	277	2,372
Neale Smith	70	71	69	67	277	2,372
Eduardo Argiro	73	67	70	68	278	1,719
Josh Habig	70	68	68	72	278	1,719
Kris Mikkelsen	68	68	71	71	278	1,719
James Stewart	70	70	70	68	278	1,719
Richie Coughlan	69	68	76	66	279	1,505
Joshua Lower	69	70	70	70	279	1,505
Alan McLean	69	69	72	69	279	1,505

Greater Vancouver Classic

Swan-e-set Bay Resort, Vancouver, British Columbia
Par 36-36–72; 7,000 yards

July 31-August 3
purse, C$175,000

	SCORES				TOTAL	MONEY
*James Lepp	66	70	66	67	269	
Nathan Fritz	66	72	68	68	274	C$22,400
Mark Johnson	69	67	69	69	274	22,400
Scott Hend	73	66	70	66	275	9,450
Chris Wall	71	71	68	65	275	9,450
Jason Allred	70	68	71	67	276	6,650
Jesse Hibler	74	64	66	72	276	6,650
Erik Compton	66	73	69	69	277	5,425
Patrick Damron	70	70	68	69	277	5,425
David Mathis	71	71	68	67	277	5,425
Matt Bettencourt	66	70	75	67	278	4,725
Billy Noon	71	71	65	72	279	4,025
Brad Sutterfield	68	71	70	70	279	4,025
Mario Tiziani	67	69	71	72	279	4,025
Derek Crawford	73	70	71	66	280	2,975
Paul Devenport	68	69	74	69	280	2,975
Jason Enloe	70	69	72	69	280	2,975
Bobby Kalinowski	71	71	70	68	280	2,975
Lee Williamson	69	70	74	67	280	2,975
Tony Carolan	68	72	71	70	281	1,983
Brad Fritsch	72	69	71	69	281	1,983
Darren Griff	71	71	68	71	281	1,983
Josh Habig	64	72	73	72	281	1,983
Robert Hamilton	72	70	67	72	281	1,983
Gene Jones	71	72	68	70	281	1,983
Conrad Ray	72	67	70	72	281	1,983
Michael Sabo	73	66	71	71	281	1,983
Sal Spallone	70	72	70	69	281	1,983
James Stewart	70	70	70	71	281	1,983
Eduardo Argiro	69	73	70	70	282	1,479
Michael Harris	67	74	71	70	282	1,479
Andrew Smeeth	71	68	73	70	282	1,479
Drew Symons	71	69	71	71	282	1,479

Lewis Chitengwa Memorial Championship

Stoney Creek at Wintergreen, Wintergreen, Virginia
Par 36-36–72; 7,004 yards

August 14-17
purse, C$150,000

	SCORES				TOTAL	MONEY
Nick Watney	66	67	68	67	268	C$24,000
Derek Gillespie	67	67	70	69	273	10,200
Alan McLean	72	68	69	64	273	10,200
Alex Quiroz	70	67	68	68	273	10,200
Robert Hamilton	71	72	65	67	275	5,700
Chris Wisler	66	76	68	65	275	5,700
Ryan Dillon	70	68	71	67	276	4,650
Scott Hend	69	72	67	68	276	4,650
Craig Matthew	71	70	67	68	276	4,650
Ted Brown	66	72	69	70	277	3,600
Jim Lemon	65	70	70	72	277	3,600
Jeff McCammon	67	70	72	68	277	3,600

	SCORES				TOTAL	MONEY
Chris Wall	68	65	72	72	277	3,600
Matt Bettencourt	73	67	67	71	278	2,850
Mark Johnson	69	71	72	67	279	2,700
Eduardo Argiro	74	69	69	68	280	2,250
Mike Capone	72	70	70	68	280	2,250
Mario Tiziani	69	69	71	71	280	2,250
Lee Williamson	73	68	71	68	280	2,250
Justin Young	72	66	73	69	280	2,250
Chris Locker	71	73	67	70	281	1,838
Alex Rocha	69	73	70	69	281	1,838
Ryan Ellis	72	69	69	72	282	1,545
Nathan Fritz	74	68	69	71	282	1,545
Jesse Hibler	72	71	67	72	282	1,545
Kevin Jones	69	70	71	72	282	1,545
Joshua Lower	69	73	68	72	282	1,545
Stephen Woodard	73	70	68	71	282	1,545
Dirk Ayers	72	69	72	70	283	1,206
Kent Fukushima	73	67	72	71	283	1,206
Ramiro Goti	75	69	70	69	283	1,206
Chris Greenwood	71	69	71	72	283	1,206
Matt Kilgo	68	68	73	74	283	1,206
Scotty Kral	69	74	68	72	283	1,206
Tele Wightman	69	68	73	73	283	1,206

Bay Mills Open Players Championship

Wild Bluff Golf Club, Brimley, Michigan
Par 36-36–72; 7,101 yards

August 21-24
purse, C$235,000

	SCORES				TOTAL	MONEY
Rodney Butcher	69	72	67	70	278	C$37,600
Jon Mills	71	74	68	70	283	22,560
David McKenzie	73	74	68	70	285	14,100
Brad Sutterfield	70	74	70	72	286	11,280
Jim Lemon	75	71	69	72	287	8,225
Doug McGuigan	69	72	71	75	287	8,225
Mario Tiziani	73	72	68	74	287	8,225
Chris Wall	70	71	72	74	287	8,225
Matt Bettencourt	72	72	74	70	288	6,110
Robert Hamilton	76	70	73	69	288	6,110
Kevin Jones	72	74	70	72	288	6,110
Bryan Wright	70	73	71	74	288	6,110
*Lindsay Bernakevitch	73	71	71	74	289	
Anders Hultman	73	72	73	71	289	4,406
Wes Martin	73	72	72	72	289	4,406
Alan McLean	73	72	71	73	289	4,406
Bryan Saltus	76	70	71	72	289	4,406
Michael Harris	67	75	72	76	290	3,313
Rob Johnson	77	70	71	72	290	3,313
Rich Massey	73	73	73	71	290	3,313
Rob Oppenheim	76	71	70	73	290	3,313
Drew Symons	70	77	72	71	290	3,313
Dirk Ayers	72	75	69	75	291	2,384
Dave Christensen	71	76	73	71	291	2,384
Derek Gillespie	69	73	76	73	291	2,384
Danny Paniccia	70	72	74	75	291	2,384
Alex Quiroz	70	72	76	73	291	2,384

	SCORES				TOTAL	MONEY
Michael Sabo	72	70	72	77	291	2,384
Paul Scaletta	75	71	75	70	291	2,384
Brennan Webb	74	74	71	72	291	2,384
Jeff Wood	72	74	73	72	291	2,384

Casino de Charlevoix Cup

Le Manoir Richelieu Golf Club, Pointe-au-Pic, Quebec   August 28-31
Par 71; 6,225 yards   purse, C$100,000

FIRST DAY
Canadian Tour
Michael Sabo and Adam Speirs defeated Scott Hawley and Rob Oppenheim, 20 holes.
Matt Donovan and Tele Wightman defeated Dean North and Adam Short, 19 holes.
Alex Rocha and Bryn Parry defeated David Burbidge and Josh Lower, 2 and 1.
Nathan Green and Kevin Jones defeated John Colwell and Matt McQuillan, 3 and 2.
Michael Hospodar and Cory Jones defeated Nick Davey and Ben Gallie, 1 up.
Julian James and Craig Matthew defeated Brian Flugstad and Walter Keating, 5 and 3.
Doug McGuigan and Alan McLean defeated Dean Kennedy and Dave Levesque,
2 and 1.
Brennan Webb and Chris Wisler defeated Mark Wilson and unknown.

Quebec Tour
Carl Desjardins and Luc Rochefort defeated Serge Thivierge and Claude Tremblay,
2 and 1.
Mathieu Belanger and Andre NolsStephane defeated Cartier and Eric Gauthier,
4 and 3.
Michel Boyer and Stephane L'Ecuyer defeated Carlo Blanchard and Benoit
Boudreault, 1 up.
Gregg Cuthill and Jason Morin defeated Jerome Blais and Dave Kelly, 2 and 1.
Phillipe Gariepy and Pierre St. Jacques defeated Derek Ackford and Jeff McDonald,
2 and 1.
Patrick McGuigan and Alan Palmer defeated Remi Bouchard and Kevin Senecal, 1 up.
Michel Lapointe and Jean Marc Tourangeau defeated Christian Manegre and David
Simard, 3 and 2.
Pete Bousquet and Jean Louis Lamarre defeated Sylvain Allaire and Jacques
Deschenes, 3 and 2.

(Each losing team received C$1,000.)

SECOND DAY
Canadian Tour
Parry and Rocha defeated James and Matthew, 4 and 3.
McGuigan and McLean defeated Donovan and Wightman, 6 and 5.
Green and Kevin Jones defeated Hospodar and Cory Jones, 5 and 4.
Webb and Wisler defeated Sabo and Speirs, 1 up.

Quebec Tour
Boyer and L'Ecuyer defeated McGuigan and Palmer, 2 and 1.
Lapointe and Tourangeau defeated Belanger and NolsStephane, 6 and 5.
Cuthill and Morin defeated Gariepy and St. Jacques, 4 and 3.
Lamarre and Bousquet defeated Desjardins and Rochefort, 2 and 1.

(Each losing team received C$2,000.)

QUARTER-FINALS
Webb and Wisler defeated Green and Jones, 2 and 1.
Parry and Rocha defeated McGuigan and McLean, 2 and 1.

Boyer and L'Ecuyer defeated Lapointe and Tourangeau, 5 and 4.
Lamarre and Bousquet defeated Cuthill and Morin, 2 and 1.

(Each losing team received C$4,000.)

SEMI-FINALS
Parry and Rocha defeated Webb and Wisler, 1 up.
Bousquet and Lamarre defeated Boyer and L'Ecuyer, 4 and 3.

(Each losing team received C$8,000.)

FINAL

Parry and Rocha defeated Bousquet and Lamarre, 2 and 1.

(Parry and Rocha received C$20,000; Bousquet and Lamarre received C$16,000.)

Tour de las Americas (South America)

Caribbean Open

Our Lucaya Golf Resort, Freeport, Bahamas
Par 36-36—72; 6,824 yards

January 8-11
purse, US$50,000

	SCORES				TOTAL	MONEY
Rafael Gomez	71	66	69	69	275	US$9,000
John Bloomfield	64	71	71	72	278	5,700
Eduardo Argiro	71	73	68	68	280	3,600
Richard Terga	66	67	74	73	280	3,600
Alexandre Rocha	77	71	67	66	281	2,600
Jimmy Delancey	69	69	71	73	282	1,900
Tim Conley	72	69	68	73	282	1,900
Julio Zapata	74	74	67	68	283	1,520
Gustavo Acosta	76	71	72	66	285	1,420
Gregory Boyette	74	70	75	67	286	1,120
Hernan Rey	72	74	71	69	286	1,120
Shannon Sykora	69	74	72	71	286	1,120
Geoffry Schacher	74	70	70	72	286	1,120
Bob Heintz	70	71	71	74	286	1,120
Bo Van Pelt	70	71	71	74	286	1,120
Tee McCabe	74	71	74	68	287	820
Oscar Serna	73	74	72	68	287	820
Pedro Martinez	70	72	75	70	287	820
Juan Abbate	71	72	71	73	287	820
Victor Leoni	71	70	70	76	287	820
Arthur Hafemann	74	72	71	71	288	622.50
Jaime Acevedo	73	73	70	72	288	622.50
Matt Mocniak	68	71	74	75	288	622.50
Mauricio Molina	72	69	67	80	288	622.50
P.J. Cowan	74	72	76	68	290	570

	SCORES				TOTAL	MONEY
John Pitt	69	75	75	72	291	540
Itamar Cohen	74	72	73	72	291	540
Ryan Grant	77	71	73	71	292	505
Michael Sims	72	76	73	71	292	505
Miguel Fernandez	73	71	71	78	293	490

Samsung Panama Open

Coronado Golf Resort, Coronado, Panama
Par 36-36–72; 6,983 yards

January 15-18
purse, US$200,000

	SCORES				TOTAL	MONEY
Charles Warren	70	73	70	71	284	US$40,000
Ken Duke	71	69	74	71	285	21,000
Juan Abbate	72	68	74	72	286	13,000
Steve Haskins	75	71	69	72	287	7,200
Alejandro Quiroz	74	75	67	71	287	7,200
Jeff Klauk	71	73	70	73	287	7,200
Rafael Gomez	74	72	73	69	288	6,000
Mario Tiziani	73	71	77	68	289	5,033.33
Victor Schwamkrug	73	72	75	69	289	5,033.33
Jaxon Brigman	76	75	67	71	289	5,033.33
Javier Sanchez	72	70	72	76	290	4,200
Eduardo Argiro	72	72	75	72	291	3,650
Lucas Glover	66	75	75	75	291	3,650
Sonny Skinner	75	71	74	72	292	3,200
Miguel Fernandez	71	78	74	70	293	2,228.57
Ramon Franco	74	77	72	70	293	2,228.57
Pedro Martinez	74	77	70	72	293	2,228.57
Marion Dantzler	73	74	74	72	293	2,228.57
John Engler	70	73	77	73	293	2,228.57
David Morland	72	70	77	74	293	2,228.57
Chris Rieve	72	76	70	75	293	2,228.57
Rodolfo Gonzalez	77	76	70	70	293	2,228.57
Roger Tambellini	78	72	73	71	294	1,500
Robert Bradley	79	69	74	72	294	1,500
Roland Thatcher	72	77	72	73	294	1,500
Julio Zapata	72	74	73	75	294	1,500
Matt Mocniak	79	71	73	72	295	1,116.66
Steve Runge	75	80	72	68	295	1,116.66
Gregory Boyette	74	71	75	75	295	1,116.66
Jason Bohn	71	74	75	75	295	1,116.66

Cable & Wireless Panama Masters

Summit Golf & Resort, Panama City, Panama
Par 36-36–72; 6,676 yards

January 23-26
purse, US$40,000

	SCORES				TOTAL	MONEY
Andres Romero	66	70	72	66	274	US$7,200
Juan Abbate	68	69	72	69	278	4,560
Miguel Guzman	71	65	73	70	279	2,880
Jose Trauwitz	72	64	72	71	279	2,880
Raul Fretes	66	72	74	68	280	1,494.40
Miguel Fernandez	70	67	73	70	280	1,494.40

	SCORES				TOTAL	MONEY
Johnson Wagner	66	69	73	72	280	1,494.40
Jesus Amaya	70	71	67	72	280	1,494.40
Cesar Monasterio	69	64	74	73	280	1,494.40
Alvaro Pinedo	70	72	71	68	281	1,016
Hernan Rey	70	73	70	68	281	1,016
Shannon Sykora	72	72	68	70	282	876
Clodomiro Carranza	69	69	70	74	282	876
Rigoberto Velasquez	67	72	75	69	283	796
Marco Ruiz	71	72	69	71	283	796
Pedro Martinez	73	68	74	69	284	696
Ramon Franco	69	70	75	70	284	696
Sebastian Fernandez	67	70	72	75	284	696
Dan Stone	69	70	76	70	285	596
Pablo Del Grosso	69	67	75	74	285	596
Carl Meares	68	73	75	72	288	498
Daniel Vancsik	72	70	74	72	288	498
Diego Vanegas	69	69	76	74	288	498
Julio Zapata	71	69	70	78	288	498
Patricio Vilaclara	69	73	75	72	289	456
Adam Spring	72	74	77	67	290	424
Eduardo Argiro	72	71	75	72	290	424
Gustavo Mendoza	72	72	73	73	290	424
Walker Layne	71	69	78	73	291	392
Manuel Merizalde	72	71	75	73	291	392
Rodolfo Gonzalez	75	71	72	73	291	392

Costa Rica Open

Cariari Country Club, San Jose, Costa Rica
Par 36-35–71; 6,577 yards

January 30-February 2
purse, US$100,000

	SCORES				TOTAL	MONEY
Sebastian Fernandez	70	68	69	71	278	US$18,000
Cesar Monasterio	67	68	69	74	278	11,400
(Fernandez defeated Monasterio on first playoff hole.)						
Alex Balicki	68	70	71	70	279	8,000
Gustavo Mendoza	66	70	70	74	280	6,400
Pedro Martinez	71	70	68	72	281	5,200
Jon Levitt	69	75	71	69	284	3,800
Sean Bebb	71	71	72	70	284	3,800
Juan Abbate	73	70	73	70	286	2,700
Martin Erlandsson	77	69	70	70	286	2,700
Rodolfo Gonzalez	75	72	72	68	287	2,200
Benoit Teilleria	72	75	71	69	287	2,200
Marc Pendaries	77	70	71	69	287	2,200
Rafael Gomez	71	74	74	69	288	1,850
Geoffry Schacher	75	72	70	71	288	1,850
Angel Romero	69	75	72	73	289	1,700
Jesus Amaya	75	69	75	71	290	1,350
Peter Hanson	72	71	74	73	290	1,350
Julio Zapata	73	72	72	73	290	1,350
Alvaro Ortiz	68	69	78	75	290	1,350
Carl Meares	72	70	73	75	290	1,350
Andre Bossert	77	71	67	75	290	1,350
Steven O'Hara	73	75	70	73	291	1,020
Paul Dwyer	74	72	77	69	292	880
Christophe Hanell	71	73	73	75	292	880
Andres Romero	75	73	69	75	292	880

Ernie Els was No. 1 on the European Order of Merit, including four of his eight victories.

The highlight for Darren Clarke was his victory in the WGC NEC Invitational.

Padraig Harrington won twice.

Fredrik Jacobson climbed from No. 83 to No. 17.

Stuart Franklin/Getty Images

Stuart Franklin/Getty Images

Stuart Franklin/Getty Images

Andrew Redington/Getty Images

Adam Scott won in Europe and America.

Stuart Franklin/Getty Images

Ian Poulter had two European Tour victories.

Phil Inglis

Thomas Bjorn was ranked 19th.

Ross Kinnaird/Getty Images

Paul Casey had victories in Australasia and Europe.

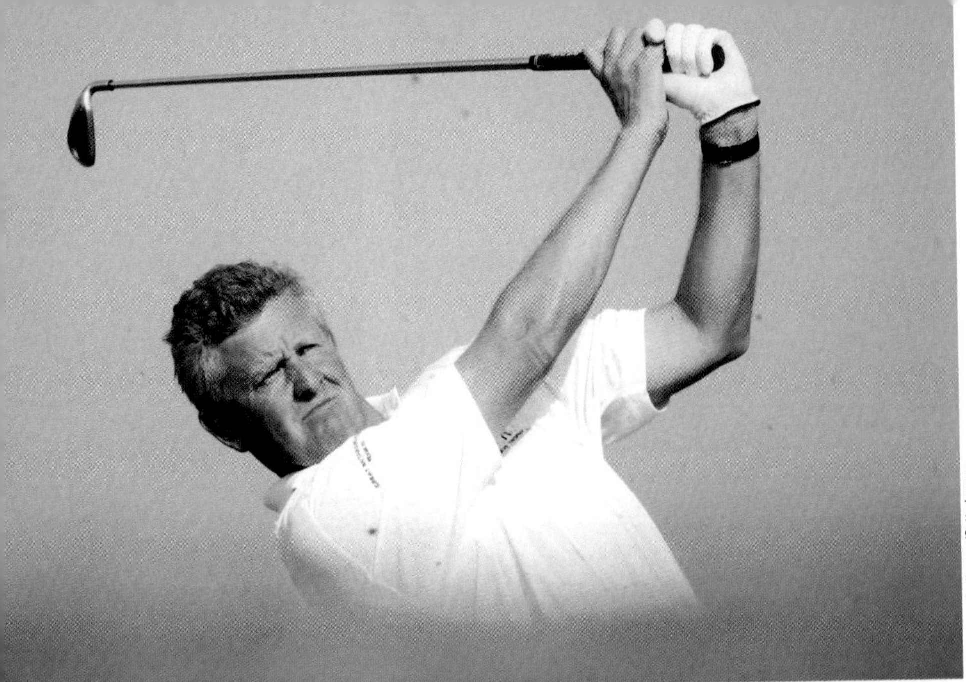

Andrew Redington/Getty Images

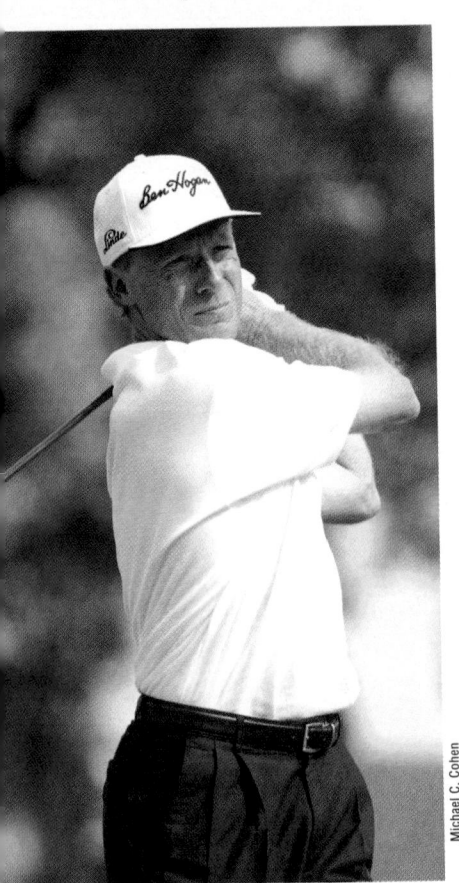

Colin Montgomerie's only victory came in the Macau Open.

Michael C. Cohen

Bernhard Langer fell to No. 89.

Stuart Franklin/Getty Images

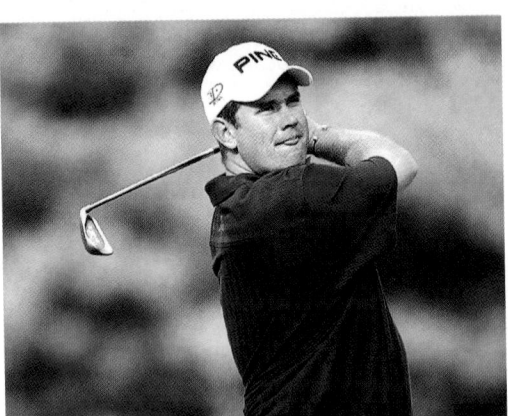

Lee Westwood rebounded with two European wins.

Phil Inglis

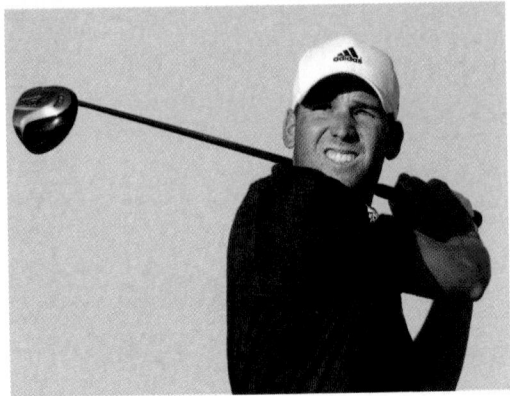

Sergio Garcia didn't win in Europe or America.

Warren Little/Getty Images

Trevor Immelman won the S.A. Airways Open.

Stuart Franklin/Getty Images

Brian Davis was ninth in Europe.

Ross Kinnaird/Getty Images

Phillip Price was European Open champion.

Ross Kinnaird/Getty Images

Stephen Leaney was ranked No. 31.

Stuart Franklin/Getty Images

Retief Goosen took the Trophee Lancome.

Ignacio Garrido won the Volvo PGA.

Michael Campbell won in Ireland.

Peter Lonard took the Australian Open.

Alastair Forsyth was second at Gleneagles.

David Howell was 16th in Europe.

Greg Owen won the British Masters.

HSBC World Match Play

Ernie Els received the first Mark McCormack Trophy with his fifth HSBC World Match Play title.

Vijay Singh lost 5 & 4 to Els in the semis.

Thomas Bjorn lost 4 & 3 in the final.

Ben Curtis was beaten 2 up by Bjorn.

Asia/Japan

Zhang Lian-wei won twice, including the Caltex Masters over Ernie Els.

Arjun Atwal had two Asian Tour victories.

Thongchai Jaidee won the Volvo Masters.

Harry How/Getty Images

Phil Inglis

Paul Lakatos/AFP/Getty Images

K.J. Choi won the SK Telecom Open.

Toshimitsu Izawa led the Japan Tour.

Todd Hamilton won four in Japan.

Shigeki Maruyama won in America.

Shingo Katayama had two victories.

In addition to holding the Solheim Cup, Annika Sorenstam had seven victories.

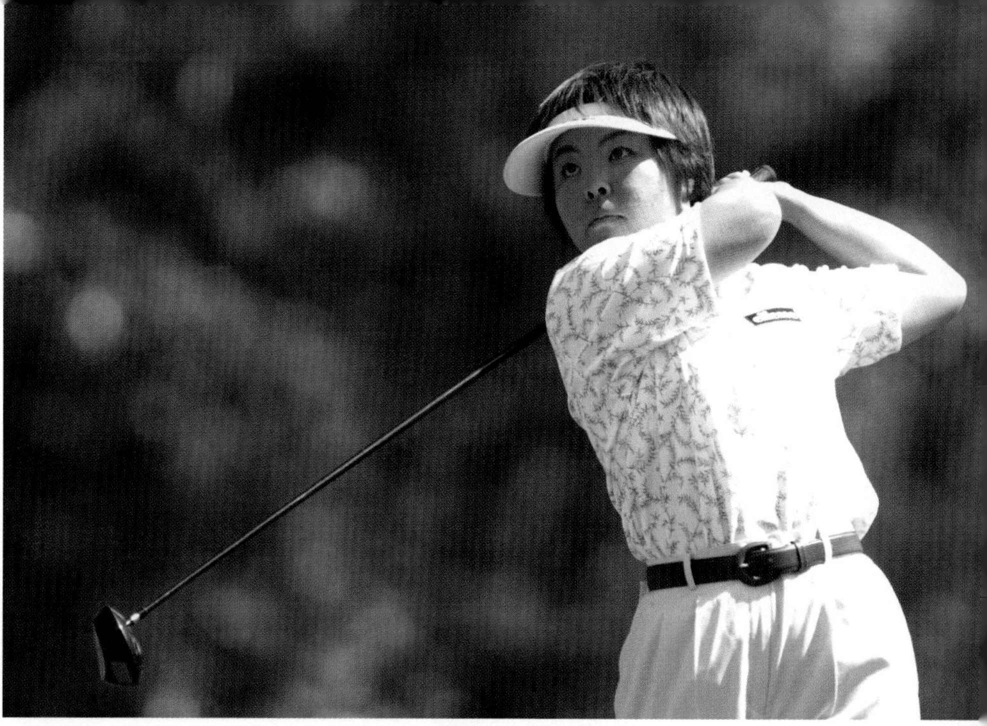
Scott Halleran/Getty Images

Japan's Yuri Fudoh was the worldwide leader with 10 victories.

Scott Halleran/Getty Images

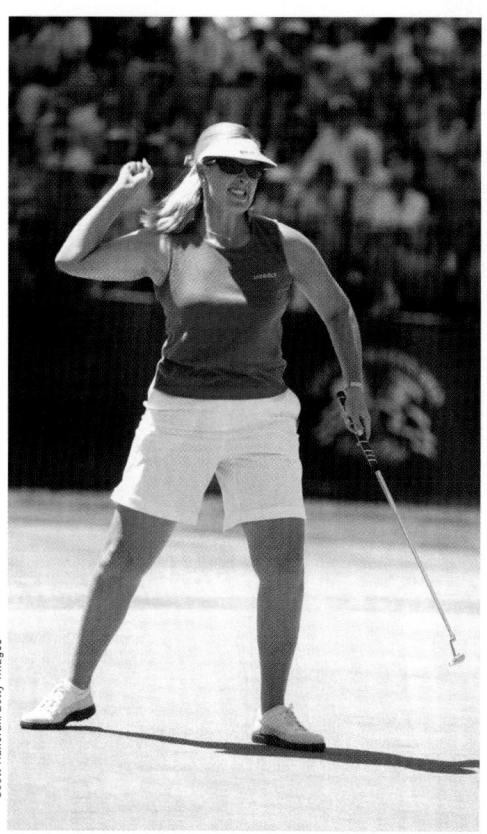

Hilary Lunke won the U.S. Women's Open.

Scott Halleran/Getty Images

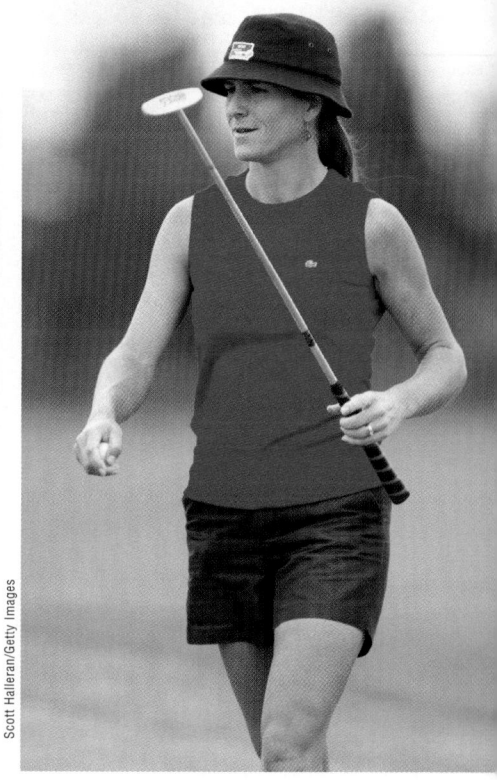

Patricia Meunier-Lebouc won a major.

Andy Lyons/Getty Images

Se Ri Pak had three LPGA victories.

Scott Halleran/Getty Images

Rachel Teske won twice.

Scott Halleran/Getty Images

Hee-Won Han had back-to-back wins.

Andy Lyons/Getty Images

Grace Park was third in money.

Candie Kung took three trophies.

Meg Mallon won the year-end ADT Championship.

Karrie Webb was 10th in earnings.

Juli Inkster was the leading American woman.

Michelle Wie, age 13, was a sensation.

Senior Tours

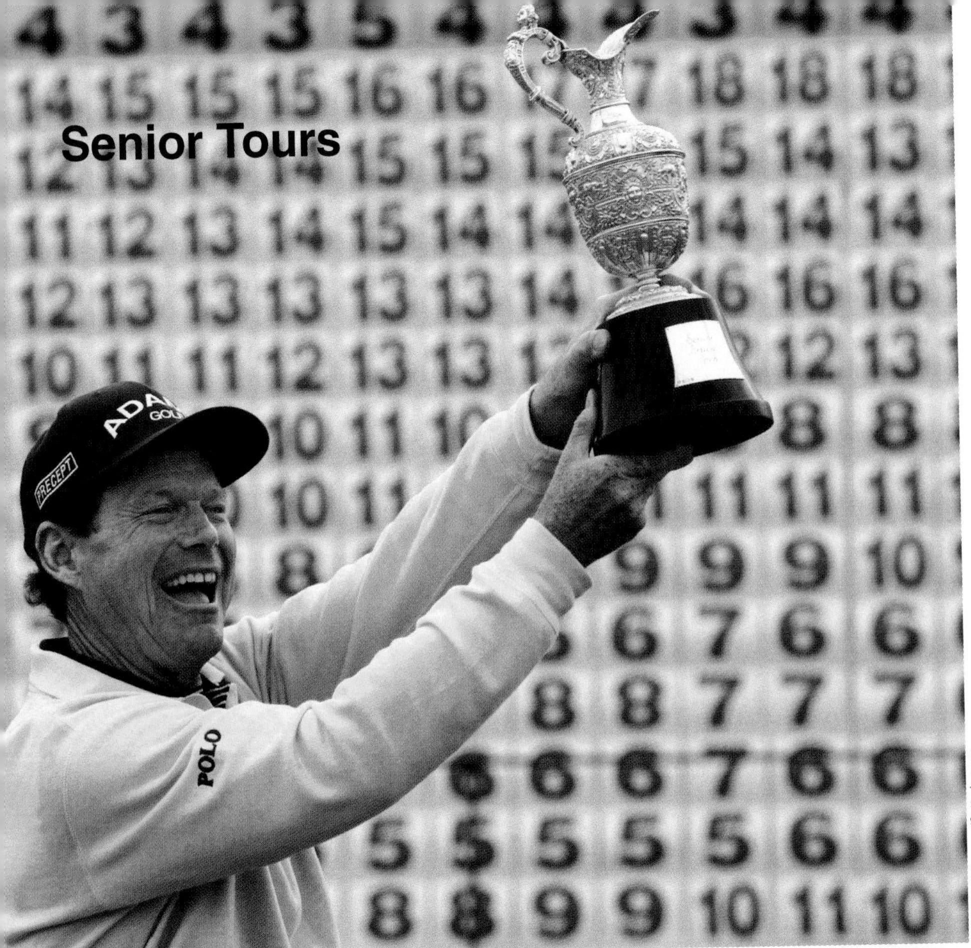

David Cannon/Getty Images

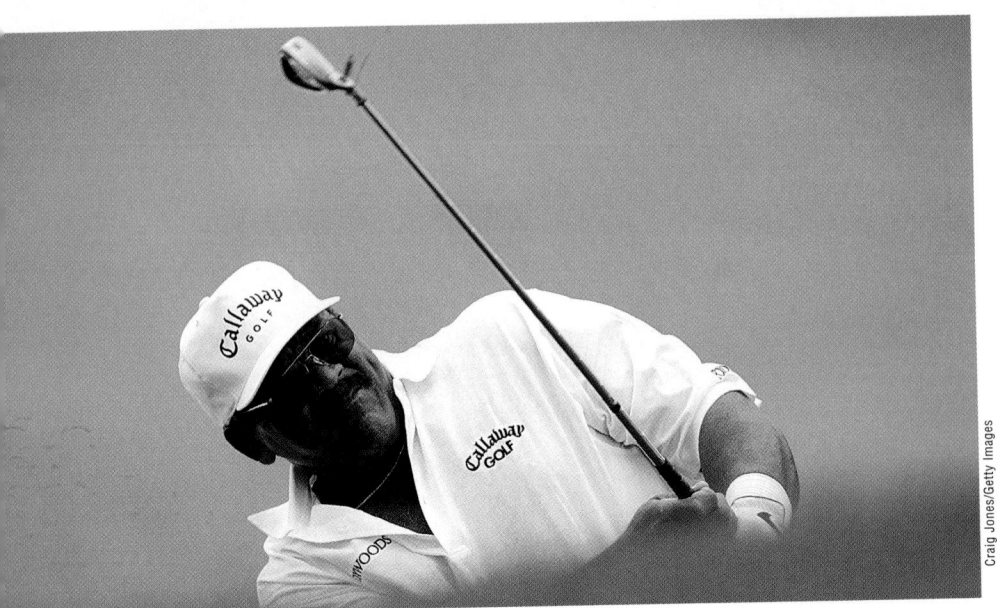

Tom Watson won the Senior British Open at Turnberry, where he also won the 1977 Open.

Craig Jones/Getty Images

Jim Thorpe was the winner of the season-ending Charles Schwab Cup Championship.

Gil Morgan was the Kroger Classic winner.

Bruce Lietzke won the U.S. Senior Open.

Hale Irwin took two victories.

Tom Jenkins won at Bruno's Memorial.

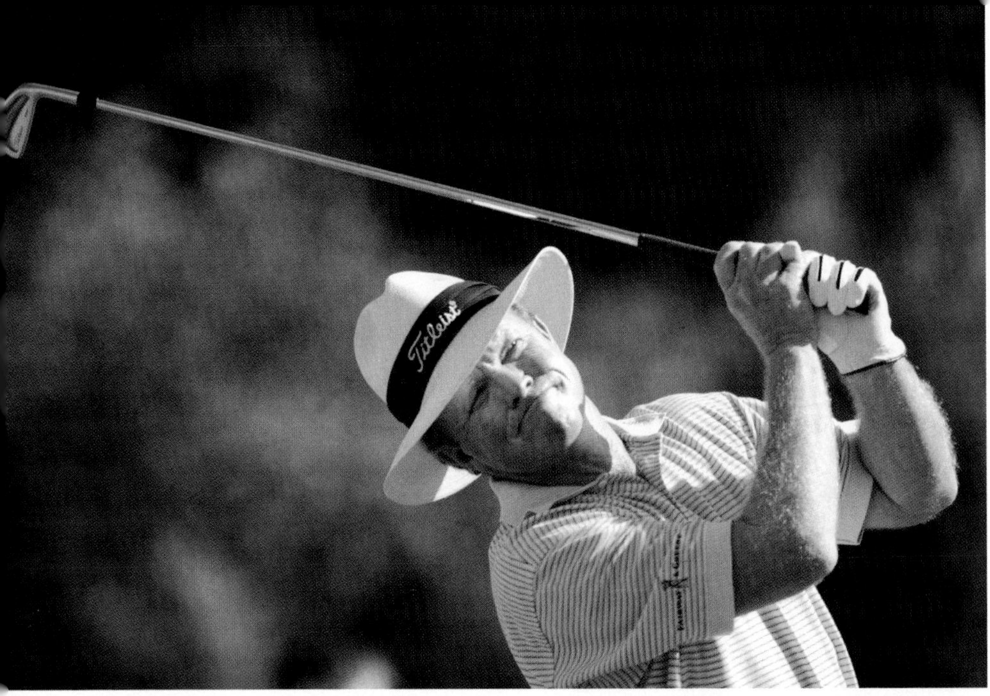

Jonathan Ferrey/Getty Images

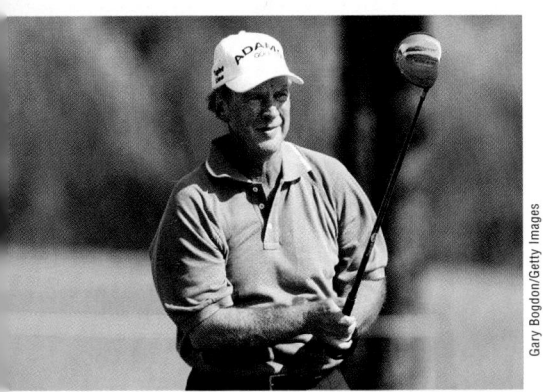

Although Tom Kite did not have a victory, he finished sixth on the money list.

Gary Bogdon/Getty Images

Larry Nelson stayed in the top 10.

Scott Halleran/Getty Images

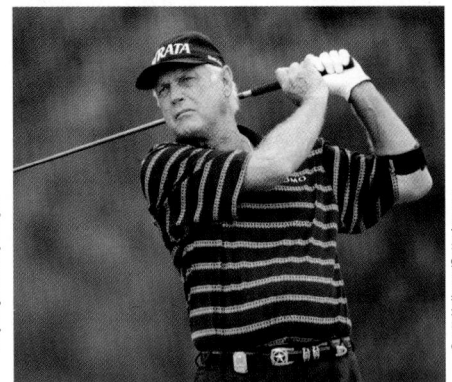

John Jacobs was Senior PGA champion.

Scott Halleran/Getty Images

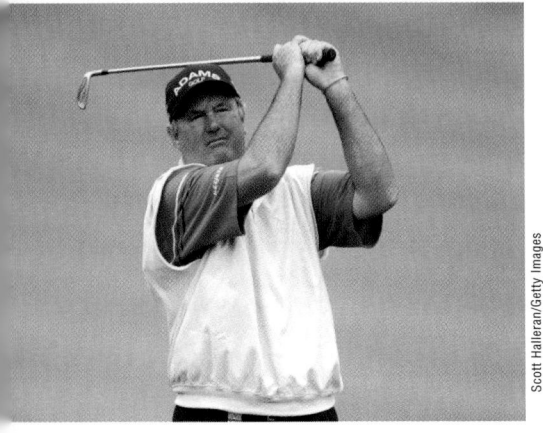

Allen Doyle won at FleetBoston.

Craig Jones/Getty Images

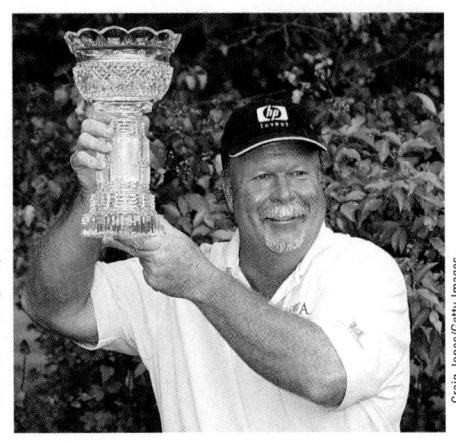

Craig Stadler won the Ford Seniors.

	SCORES				TOTAL	MONEY
Marc Warren	73	70	73	76	292	880
James Hepworth	70	76	68	78	292	880
Ilya Goroneskoul	69	76	74	74	293	750
Ryan Dillon	76	70	67	80	293	750
Frederic Cupillard	75	72	75	72	294	700
Damien McGrane	72	75	75	72	294	700
Lionel Alexandre	73	73	73	75	294	700

Telefonica CA Guatemala Open

Hacienda Neuva Country Club, Guatemala City, Guatemala
Par 36-35–71; 7,082 yards

February 6-9
purse, US$100,000

	SCORES				TOTAL	MONEY
Daniel Vancsik	68	68	70	68	274	US$18,000
Juan Abbate	68	69	66	71	274	11,400
(Vancsik defeated Abbate on first playoff hole.)						
Michael Kirk	69	69	66	71	275	7,200
Damien McGrane	69	61	73	72	275	7,200
Julio Zapata	70	69	69	68	276	5,200
Ilya Goroneskoul	67	72	70	68	277	3,466.66
Pedro Martinez	71	68	68	70	277	3,466.66
Johan Edfors	67	67	71	72	277	3,466.66
Sam Little	74	67	68	69	278	2,300
Richard Terga	68	70	70	70	278	2,300
Michael Jonzon	68	68	71	71	278	2,300
Hernan Rey	67	69	69	73	278	2,300
Peter Hanson	66	73	76	64	279	1,750
Shannon Sykora	71	68	70	70	279	1,750
Christophe Hanell	68	69	71	71	279	1,750
Jose Trauwitz	70	68	69	72	279	1,750
Jon Levitt	72	71	69	68	280	1,500
Miguel Guzman	70	68	72	71	281	1,400
Ben Mason	71	69	76	66	282	1,116
Marco Bernardini	68	73	74	67	282	1,116
Rodolfo Gonzalez	70	69	74	69	282	1,116
Diego Vanegas	73	69	69	71	282	1,116
Rafael Gomez	72	71	67	72	282	1,116
Cesar Monasterio	73	69	72	69	283	860
Mark Sanders	71	66	76	70	283	860
Sebastian Fernandez	71	69	73	70	283	860
James Hepworth	73	67	69	74	283	860
Massimo Florioli	70	71	74	69	284	730
Jesus Amaya	70	71	73	70	284	730
Mauricio Molina	69	74	71	70	284	730
Alex Balicki	74	69	71	70	284	730

Amex Los Encinos Open

Los Encinos Golf Club, Toluta, Mexico
Par 36-36–72; 7,100 yards

February 12-15
purse, US$100,000

	SCORES				TOTAL	MONEY
James Hepworth	71	67	71	66	275	US$18,000
Francesco Guermani	72	69	70	67	278	8,600

	SCORES				TOTAL	MONEY
Jose Trauwitz	72	66	70	70	278	8,600
Sam Walker	70	69	67	72	278	8,600
Stuart Little	72	71	73	63	279	4,266.66
Richard McEvoy	68	71	72	68	279	4,266.66
Mauricio Molina	72	64	72	71	279	4,266.66
Greig Hutcheon	70	70	71	69	280	2,600
Steven O'Hara	75	68	67	70	280	2,600
Jamie Little	68	71	70	71	280	2,600
Sebastian Fernandez	69	73	72	67	281	1,866.66
Markus Westerberg	76	68	70	67	281	1,866.66
Michael Jonzon	72	71	70	68	281	1,866.66
Rafael Alarcon	73	67	72	69	281	1,866.66
Erol Simsek	74	69	69	69	281	1,866.66
Rodolfo Gonzalez	72	70	67	72	281	1,866.66
Daniel Vancsik	71	69	74	68	282	1,211.42
Juan Abbate	72	68	73	69	282	1,211.42
David Dupart	69	72	71	70	282	1,211.42
Antonio Pilar	72	71	69	70	282	1,211.42
John Bloomfield	73	67	71	71	282	1,211.42
Massimo Florioli	72	66	72	72	282	1,211.42
Guido Van Der Valk	72	69	69	72	282	1,211.42
Hernan Rey	74	65	71	73	283	900
Kariem Baraka	69	69	71	74	283	900
Miguel Fernandez	72	65	76	71	284	820
Juan Salazar	71	71	69	73	284	820
Julio Zapata	70	74	71	70	285	750
Richard Terga	70	73	69	73	285	750
Paul Dwyer	75	68	73	70	286	640
Christophe Hanell	70	69	76	71	286	640
Peter Gustafsson	73	67	75	71	286	640
Wolfgang Huget	74	70	71	71	286	640
Pedro Martinez	67	70	77	72	286	640
Luis Arechiga	70	70	73	73	286	640
Ryan Grant	72	72	69	73	286	640
Cesar Monasterio	70	70	72	74	286	640
Chris Gane	70	74	68	74	286	640

Acapulco Fest Invitational

Acapulco Princess Resort, Acapulco, Mexico
Par 35-35–70; 6,355 yards

May 22-25
purse, US$50,000

	SCORES				TOTAL	MONEY
Octavio Gonzalez	66	66	64	67	263	US$9,000
Raul Fretes	67	68	66	64	265	4,850
Miguel Fernandez	69	64	64	68	265	4,850
Rafael Gomez	67	70	66	63	266	3,200
Pedro Martinez	70	69	66	64	269	2,133
Rodolfo Gonzalez	69	66	69	65	269	2,133
John Bloomfield	65	67	70	67	269	2,133
Richard Terga	72	66	65	67	270	1,520
Bob Jacobson	65	69	70	71	275	1,420
Kent Fukushima	67	71	64	74	276	1,270
Julio Zapata	68	74	70	64	276	1,270
Jorge Corral	71	68	73	65	277	1,120
Alan McLean	73	67	66	72	278	1,070
Mauricio Asbun	78	68	68	65	279	1,020

	SCORES				TOTAL	MONEY
Jesus Torres	69	71	69	72	281	945
Jose Trauwitz	67	70	69	75	281	945
Manuel Bermudez	72	69	68	73	282	845
Hernan Rey	73	65	69	75	282	845
Rafael Ponce	66	73	69	75	283	745
Charles Wyatt	70	71	72	70	283	745
Manuel Inman	72	72	65	75	284	633
Jerome Valentin	72	71	71	70	284	633
Victor Leoni	75	69	68	72	284	633
Pablo Del Olmo	67	68	75	75	285	570
Martin Stanovich	69	74	71	71	285	570
Daniel Barbetti	68	70	76	71	285	570
Ken Wertzberger	74	69	75	69	287	530
Julian James	70	72	71	75	288	510
Pablo Fernandez	76	73	74	68	291	490
Esteban Isasi	81	73	66	71	291	490
Henrique Lavie	73	71	75	72	291	490

Bancolombia American Express Open

Serrezuela Golf Club, Bogata, Colombia
Par 36-36–72; 7,325 yards

November 13-16
purse, US$35,000

	SCORES				TOTAL	MONEY
Angel Romero	66	67	71	69	273	US$6,300
Juan Salazar	70	69	72	67	278	3,990
Miguel Guzman	69	72	69	70	280	2,800
Juan Abbate	70	70	71	70	281	2,030
Gustavo Mendoza	67	74	68	72	281	2,030
Ariel Canete	72	70	71	69	282	1,082.66
Jose Garrido	71	68	73	70	282	1,082.66
Carlos Larrain	71	69	71	71	282	1,082.66
Manuel Merizalde	70	71	70	71	282	1,082.66
Clodomiro Carranza	72	68	70	72	282	1,082.66
Omar Beltran	72	65	72	73	282	1,082.66
Miguel Fernandez	73	68	73	69	283	766.50
Julio Zapata	68	72	71	72	283	766.50
Raul Fretes	68	73	73	70	284	661.50
Rodolfo Gonzalez	76	68	69	71	284	661.50
Rodrigo Castaneda	70	70	71	73	284	661.50
Mario Hurtado	76	66	69	73	284	661.50
Michael Sims	70	71	74	70	285	539
Luis Arechiga	72	71	71	71	285	539
Alvaro Pinedo	73	70	70	72	285	539
Marcelo Soria	74	70	71	71	286	469
Andres Rodriguez	71	73	71	72	287	418.25
Fernando Posada	72	72	71	72	287	418.25
Pedro Martinez	72	70	72	73	287	418.25
Rigoberto Velasquez	70	71	72	74	287	418.25
Ramon Franco	71	72	72	73	288	378
Geoffry Schacher	77	67	71	73	288	378
Ricardo Ferrin	75	69	74	71	289	346.50
Andres Romero	76	67	73	73	289	346.50
Efren Cubillos	72	71	73	73	289	346.50
Omar Suarez	70	74	72	73	289	346.50

Medellin Open

Campestre Llano Grande, Medellin, Colombia
Par 36-36–72; 7,022 yards

November 20-23
purse, US$50,000

	SCORES				TOTAL	MONEY
Andres Romero	69	68	67	65	269	US$9,000
Carlos Larrain	69	70	65	66	270	5,700
Mario Hurtado	71	71	68	62	272	4,000
Ariel Canete	67	67	70	70	274	3,200
Angel Romero	71	70	66	68	275	2,350
Miguel Fernandez	69	69	66	71	275	2,350
Clodomiro Carranza	70	69	70	67	276	1,383.33
Miguel Rodriguez	67	71	70	68	276	1,383.33
Jose Garrido	70	69	68	69	276	1,383.33
Jesus Osmar	70	68	68	70	276	1,383.33
Raul Fretes	66	72	68	70	276	1,383.33
Julio Zapata	64	74	67	71	276	1,383.33
Jesus Amaya	72	68	71	66	277	1,045
Miguel Guzman	66	70	71	70	277	1,045
Manuel Merizalde	69	73	69	67	278	945
Victor Varona	70	69	70	69	278	945
Rafael Echenique	73	67	68	71	279	870
Miguel Carballo	69	69	72	70	280	770
Ramon Franco	71	69	70	70	280	770
Ricardo Ferrin	74	69	66	71	280	770
Sergio Acevedo	74	69	72	66	281	650
Rodolfo Gonzalez	69	70	70	72	281	650
Marcelo Soria	73	70	70	69	282	595
Fabian Gomez	70	73	70	69	282	595
Pablo Benzadon	70	69	74	70	283	560
Juan Salazar	74	69	68	72	283	560
Michael Sims	71	70	71	72	284	530
Mauricio Molina	73	69	76	67	285	500
Patricio Vilaclara	69	74	75	67	285	500
Martin Velazquez	71	71	74	69	285	500

American Express Trump Brazil Open

San Fernando Golf Club, San Paulo, Brazil
Par 35-36–71; 6,733 yards

November 27-30
purse, US$100,000

	SCORES				TOTAL	MONEY
Carlos Franco	70	71	69	71	281	US$18,000
Eduardo Argiro	73	71	68	69	281	11,400
(Franco defeated Argiro on second playoff hole.)						
Alexandre Rocha	72	71	70	69	282	5,950
Miguel Carballo	73	68	71	70	282	5,950
Sebastian Fernandez	69	70	72	71	282	5,950
Raul Fretes	68	72	69	73	282	5,950
Joao Corteiz	73	72	68	70	283	3,400
Diego Vanegas	69	74	72	69	284	2,800
Daniel Vancsik	75	71	71	68	285	2,600
Ariel Canete	73	71	71	71	286	2,400
Alvaro Pinedo	74	73	75	66	288	1,975
Gustavo Acosta	74	72	72	70	288	1,975
Andres Romero	74	73	70	71	288	1,975
Miguel Fernandez	70	73	72	73	288	1,975

	SCORES				TOTAL	MONEY
Julio Zapata	74	75	73	67	289	1,500
Fabiano Dos Santos	75	75	71	68	289	1,500
Mauricio Molina	73	72	75	69	289	1,500
Rodolfo Gonzalez	69	77	74	69	289	1,500
Erik Andersson	70	71	74	74	289	1,500
Mario Hurtado	74	73	75	68	290	988.57
Luis Rueda	76	74	71	69	290	988.57
Clodomiro Carranza	76	70	73	71	290	988.57
Kevin Haefner	71	76	72	71	290	988.57
Manuel Bermudez	72	76	71	71	290	988.57
Miguel Rodriguez	72	78	69	71	290	988.57
Jose Aderbal	73	73	72	72	290	988.57
Carlos Larrain	76	74	73	68	291	744
Vinicius Muller	75	75	72	69	291	744
Carlos Benedetti	73	75	71	72	291	744
Armando Saavedra	72	73	71	75	291	744
Pedro Martinez	71	74	70	76	291	744

Mexican Open

Moon Palace Resort, Cancun, Mexico
Par 36-36–72; 7,201 yards

December 11-14
purse, US$300,000

	SCORES				TOTAL	MONEY
Eduardo Herrera	69	68	71	70	278	$54,000
Eduardo Argiro	70	72	69	68	279	29,100
Jeff Burns	70	69	70	70	279	29,100
Esteban Toledo	73	66	70	73	282	17,400
Omar Uresti	74	67	66	75	282	17,400
Christian Reimbold	73	73	65	72	283	11,400
Ariel Canete	70	71	67	75	283	11,400
Brad Sutterfield	70	73	69	72	284	8,400
Jorge Berendt	74	69	70	72	285	7,500
Gregory Boyette	70	71	67	77	285	7,500
Clodomiro Carranza	74	70	74	68	286	5,925
Jaime Gomez	74	70	71	71	286	5,925
Pedro Martinez	69	75	71	71	286	5,925
Patricio Vilaclara	75	71	68	72	286	5,925
Antonio Maldonado	69	77	71	70	287	4,950
Rafael Echenique	72	68	69	78	287	4,950
Brad Adamonis	75	68	76	69	288	3,634.28
Raul Fretes	75	72	72	69	288	3,634.28
Jose Trauwitz	71	71	75	71	288	3,634.28
Rafael Gomez	73	69	74	72	288	3,634.28
Antonio Serna	73	70	72	73	288	3,634.28
D.J. Fiese	73	72	68	75	288	3,634.28
Hernan Rey	77	69	67	75	288	3,634.28
Daniel De Leon	74	70	74	71	289	2,346.66
Daniel Vancsik	70	74	73	72	289	2,346.66
Rafael Alarcon	78	65	72	74	289	2,346.66
David Hearn	70	73	72	74	289	2,346.66
Manuel Inman	70	72	72	75	289	2,346.66
Carlos Larrain	74	70	70	75	289	2,346.66
Cesar Monasterio	70	70	73	76	289	2,346.66
David Ogrin	69	74	70	76	289	2,346.66
Alexandre Rocha	71	68	73	77	289	2,346.66

European Tours

South African Airways Open
See African Tours chapter.

Dunhill Championship
See African Tours chapter.

Caltex Masters
See Asia/Japan Tours chapter.

Heineken Classic
See Australasian Tour chapter.

ANZ Championship
See Australasian Tour chapter.

Johnnie Walker Classic
See Australasian Tour chapter.

Carlsberg Malaysian Open
See Asia/Japan Tours chapter.

Dubai Desert Classic

Emirates Golf Club, Dubai, United Arab Emirates
Par 35-37–72; 7,201 yards

March 6-9
purse, €1,778,110

	SCORES				TOTAL	MONEY
Robert-Jan Derksen	67	72	67	65	271	€291,994
Ernie Els	66	68	69	69	272	194,657.80
David Lynn	68	66	69	71	274	90,518.14
Alastair Forsyth	65	69	69	71	274	90,518.14
Ian Woosnam	69	66	70	69	274	90,518.14
Mikko Ilonen	67	67	73	68	275	52,558.92
Thomas Bjorn	69	66	71	69	275	52,558.92
Kevin Na	68	69	68	70	275	52,558.92
Phillip Price	71	67	68	70	276	37,141.64
Thongchai Jaidee	70	68	67	71	276	37,141.64
Darren Clarke	70	69	72	66	277	31,184.96
Brian Davis	68	72	70	67	277	31,184.96
Mark Foster	73	66	68	72	279	26,921.85
Jyoti Randhawa	70	72	69	68	279	26,921.85
Jamie Donaldson	67	71	72	69	279	26,921.85
David Park	71	69	72	68	280	23,169.72
Fredrik Andersson	68	73	72	67	280	23,169.72
Gary Orr	71	69	68	72	280	23,169.72
Soren Kjeldsen	71	72	71	66	280	23,169.72
Richard Bland	72	67	70	72	281	19,030.71
Peter Lawrie	72	69	67	73	281	19,030.71

	SCORES				TOTAL	MONEY
Paul Lawrie	70	72	69	70	281	19,030.71
Bradley Dredge	73	69	69	70	281	19,030.71
John Bickerton	69	71	70	71	281	19,030.71
David Carter	70	73	70	68	281	19,030.71
Mikael Lundberg	69	69	72	71	281	19,030.71
Nick Dougherty	67	69	73	72	281	19,030.71
Shingo Katayama	70	68	75	69	282	14,383.62
Tobias Dier	69	69	76	68	282	14,383.62
Greg Owen	67	69	74	72	282	14,383.62
Rolf Muntz	73	67	74	68	282	14,383.62
Ignacio Garrido	72	69	68	73	282	14,383.62
Trevor Immelman	71	68	73	70	282	14,383.62
Soren Hansen	72	71	71	68	282	14,383.62
Charlie Wi	70	72	70	70	282	14,383.62
Simon Yates	69	72	68	73	282	14,383.62
Steve Webster	71	71	70	70	282	14,383.62
Maarten Lafeber	71	69	73	70	283	11,387.77
Henrik Bjornstad	70	72	71	70	283	11,387.77
Miguel Angel Jimenez	68	69	71	75	283	11,387.77
Stephen Gallacher	69	70	71	73	283	11,387.77
Lee Westwood	70	73	69	71	283	11,387.77
Henrik Nystrom	70	70	70	74	284	9,811
Miles Tunnicliff	70	72	74	68	284	9,811
Jarrod Moseley	74	68	74	68	284	9,811
Mark Roe	71	71	71	71	284	9,811
Padraig Harrington	73	70	71	71	285	8,234.23
Paul Broadhurst	71	70	74	70	285	8,234.23
Robert Karlsson	76	67	72	70	285	8,234.23
Paul McGinley	72	69	77	67	285	8,234.23
Jarmo Sandelin	73	69	70	73	285	8,234.23
Patrik Sjoland	68	74	73	71	286	6,022.38
Ian Garbutt	73	63	73	77	286	6,022.38
Jonathan Lomas	69	70	74	73	286	6,022.38
Euan Little	71	71	73	71	286	6,022.38
Mark O'Meara	68	72	75	71	286	6,022.38
Paul Eales	73	69	71	73	286	6,022.38
Richard Green	72	70	73	71	286	6,022.38
Peter Fowler	72	71	71	72	286	6,022.38
Marten Olander	70	71	71	75	287	4,730.30
Shaun Webster	71	72	72	72	287	4,730.30
Simon Wakefield	71	70	73	73	287	4,730.30
Roger Wessels	68	72	73	75	288	3,854.32
Francois Delamontagne	75	68	72	73	288	3,854.32
Jamie Elson	72	68	74	74	288	3,854.32
Raul Ballesteros	70	72	75	71	288	3,854.32
Darren Fichardt	74	69	73	72	288	3,854.32
Carlos Rodiles	72	71	71	74	288	3,854.32
Peter Baker	71	72	76	69	288	3,854.32
Nicolas Vanhootegem	69	74	76	70	289	3,197.33
Henrik Stenson	70	72	72	76	290	2,626.50
Ian Poulter	68	70	78	74	290	2,626.50
Barry Lane	74	67	78	72	291	2,616
Raphael Jacquelin	69	74	78	70	291	2,616
Sven Struver	67	69	78	77	291	2,616
Anders Forsbrand	73	70	75	73	291	2,616
Christian Cevaer	72	71	72	76	291	2,616
Mark McNulty	72	70	76	75	293	2,616
Klas Eriksson	70	71	79	73	293	2,616
Warren Bennett	69	74	79	75	297	2,601

Qatar Masters

Doha Golf Club, Doha, Qatar
Par 36-36–72; 7,110 yards

March 13-16
purse, €1,400,200

		SCORES			TOTAL	MONEY
Darren Fichardt	71	69	66	69	275	€226,983.50
James Kingston	68	67	71	69	275	151,316.30
(Fichardt defeated Kingston on first playoff hole.)						
Paul McGinley	68	72	70	67	277	85,254.98
David Howell	66	72	72	68	278	68,095.04
Peter Fowler	71	67	71	72	281	52,705.56
Peter Hedblom	71	71	73	66	281	52,705.56
David Park	70	71	71	70	282	40,857.02
Gary Evans	73	70	70	70	283	30,597.37
John Bickerton	73	70	68	72	283	30,597.37
Richard Green	71	69	70	73	283	30,597.37
Padraig Harrington	70	73	76	65	284	23,470.09
Roger Chapman	71	69	73	71	284	23,470.09
Gary Birch, Jr.	70	74	71	69	284	23,470.09
David Dixon	70	68	73	74	285	18,463.48
Greg Owen	72	71	73	69	285	18,463.48
Marten Olander	69	74	74	68	285	18,463.48
Paul Broadhurst	69	73	70	73	285	18,463.48
Philip Golding	68	74	72	71	285	18,463.48
Andrew Marshall	73	71	70	71	285	18,463.48
Soren Hansen	71	69	74	71	285	18,463.48
Jose Manuel Lara	69	73	71	73	286	15,389.48
Jean-Francois Remesy	70	68	75	73	286	15,389.48
Richard Sterne	70	74	72	70	286	15,389.48
Nick Dougherty	73	71	71	72	287	13,550.91
Raymond Russell	73	69	71	74	287	13,550.91
Phillip Price	73	71	68	75	287	13,550.91
Miles Tunnicliff	70	74	72	71	287	13,550.91
Mark Foster	72	70	74	71	287	13,550.91
Julien Clement	73	70	74	70	287	13,550.91
Gregory Havret	69	75	72	72	288	11,508.06
Henrik Stenson	71	71	74	72	288	11,508.06
Kenneth Ferrie	71	70	75	72	288	11,508.06
Francois Delamontagne	70	75	67	76	288	11,508.06
Stuart Little	74	69	76	70	289	10,214.26
Damien McGrane	73	72	71	73	289	10,214.26
Kevin Na	73	72	76	68	289	10,214.26
Roger Wessels	71	74	72	73	290	9,669.50
Mikael Lundberg	74	69	75	73	291	9,124.74
Fredrik Widmark	72	73	73	73	291	9,124.74
Michael Archer	71	74	75	71	291	9,124.74
Soren Kjeldsen	72	73	72	75	292	8,171.40
Ed Stedman	70	75	73	74	292	8,171.40
Paul Dwyer	71	73	73	75	292	8,171.40
Steven Bowditch	70	70	74	78	292	8,171.40
Lee S. James	72	73	75	73	293	7,490.45
Sebastien Delagrange	71	74	77	72	294	7,081.88
Massimo Florioli	72	73	75	74	294	7,081.88
Barry Lane	72	73	79	71	295	6,264.74
Malcolm Mackenzie	72	72	77	74	295	6,264.74
Nicolas Colsaerts	71	73	80	71	295	6,264.74
Peter Lawrie	73	70	79	73	295	6,264.74
Alvaro Salto	73	72	78	73	296	5,583.79
Marc Farry	69	75	75	78	297	5,311.41
Julien Van Hauwe	71	74	80	82	307	5,039.03

Madeira Island Open

Santo da Serra Golf Club, Madeira, Portugal

Par 36-36–72; 6,826 yards

March 20-23

purse, €600,000

	SCORES				TOTAL	MONEY
Bradley Dredge	69	72	60	71	272	€100,000
Fredrik Andersson	73	68	70	69	280	44,740
Brian Davis	74	70	68	68	280	44,740
Andrew Marshall	71	70	69	70	280	44,740
Sam Little	76	68	68	69	281	25,440
Robert-Jan Derksen	67	79	68	68	282	21,000
Santiago Luna	71	72	70	70	283	18,000
Julien Clement	68	76	69	71	284	13,480
Andrew Coltart	74	69	70	71	284	13,480
Mikko Ilonen	73	70	71	70	284	13,480
Van Phillips	68	74	67	76	285	10,340
Jesus Maria Arruti	66	74	74	71	285	10,340
Marcel Siem	70	74	71	70	285	10,340
Stuart Little	77	71	72	66	286	8,460
Paul Broadhurst	70	72	70	74	286	8,460
Shaun Webster	71	75	68	72	286	8,460
Henrik Stenson	72	69	71	74	286	8,460
Simon Hurd	71	75	72	68	286	8,460
Damien McGrane	72	76	69	70	287	7,440
Fredrik Orest	71	75	70	72	288	6,792
Andrew Sherborne	68	77	71	72	288	6,792
Marcello Santi	69	73	72	74	288	6,792
Christopher Hanell	72	73	72	71	288	6,792
Matthew Cort	71	72	72	73	288	6,792
Ivo Giner	74	75	67	73	289	6,060
Robert Coles	79	71	71	68	289	6,060
Diego Borrego	75	73	71	70	289	6,060
Christian Cevaer	73	77	72	68	290	5,520
Lucas Parsons	75	76	68	71	290	5,520
Carlos Rodiles	71	78	72	69	290	5,520
Peter Baker	74	72	71	74	291	4,671.43
Nicolas Colsaerts	73	77	71	70	291	4,671.43
Gary Murphy	72	74	73	72	291	4,671.43
Alessandro Tadini	73	76	72	70	291	4,671.43
Erol Simsek	73	77	70	71	291	4,671.43
Ben Mason	73	72	72	74	291	4,671.43
Nicolas Vanhootegem	72	77	70	72	291	4,671.43
Mark Sanders	75	76	74	67	292	4,020
Sebastien Delagrange	72	72	76	72	292	4,020
Philip Golding	73	74	75	70	292	4,020
Johan Rystrom	76	76	70	71	293	3,540
Jean-Francois Lucquin	72	74	72	75	293	3,540
Renaud Guillard	71	80	70	72	293	3,540
Miguel Angel Martin	71	76	70	76	293	3,540
Fernando Roca	73	73	71	76	293	3,540
David Drysdale	73	77	69	75	294	2,880
Stuart Cage	73	76	71	74	294	2,880
Markus Brier	71	75	74	74	294	2,880
Daniel Silva	76	76	72	70	294	2,880
Knud Storgaard	73	75	74	72	294	2,880
Jean Hugo	73	78	74	69	294	2,880
Chris Gane	73	79	72	71	295	2,160
Philip Walton	74	74	73	74	295	2,160
Jarmo Sandelin	71	77	69	78	295	2,160

	SCORES				TOTAL	MONEY
James Hepworth	73	77	70	75	295	2,160
Neil Cheetham	74	75	73	73	295	2,160
Daren Lee	74	75	73	73	295	2,160
Alberto Binaghi	70	77	80	69	296	1,800
Gary Emerson	73	72	73	79	297	1,530
Peter Mitchell	72	79	72	74	297	1,530
Julien Van Hauwe	68	78	73	78	297	1,530
Ilya Goroneskoul	72	80	72	73	297	1,530
Marco Bernardini	73	74	79	71	297	1,530
Stephen Browne	73	77	76	71	297	1,530
Pehr Magnebrant	73	74	75	75	297	1,530
Raimo Sjoberg	71	77	73	76	297	1,530
Richard McEvoy	76	76	75	71	298	1,175
Fredrik Widmark	74	74	73	77	298	1,175
Seve Ballesteros	76	75	71	76	298	1,175
Gordon Brand, Jr.	79	73	74	72	298	1,175
Alvaro Salto	72	80	72	75	299	895.50
Jan-Are Larsen	73	79	73	74	299	895.50
David Dixon	73	77	75	74	299	895.50
Simon Wakefield	76	74	76	73	299	895.50
Raul Ballesteros	78	73	72	78	301	888
Edward Rush	71	78	75	78	302	885
Carl Suneson	79	72	76	77	304	882

Algarve Open de Portugal

Vale do Lobo Golf Club, Faro, Portugal
Par 37-35–72; 7,125 yards

April 17-20
purse, €1,250,000

	SCORES				TOTAL	MONEY
Fredrik Jacobson	64	76	71	72	283	€208,330
Bradley Dredge	69	73	74	68	284	93,210
Jamie Donaldson	72	71	73	68	284	93,210
Brian Davis	70	71	71	72	284	93,210
Greg Owen	66	70	76	73	285	53,000
James Kingston	72	75	72	68	287	40,625
Richard Sterne	73	73	69	72	287	40,625
David Lynn	71	72	74	72	289	26,812.50
Jarmo Sandelin	75	67	79	68	289	26,812.50
Carlos Rodiles	69	71	76	73	289	26,812.50
Marcel Siem	71	68	76	74	289	26,812.50
Steve Webster	72	73	73	73	291	20,250
Jose Manuel Lara	73	72	74	72	291	20,250
*Richard Walker	73	73	74	71	291	
Gustavo Rojas	70	75	74	72	291	20,250
Rolf Muntz	72	70	78	72	292	16,285.71
Graeme McDowell	70	75	76	71	292	16,285.71
Ben Mason	75	69	74	74	292	16,285.71
Terry Price	76	71	76	69	292	16,285.71
Maarten Lafeber	73	73	71	75	292	16,285.71
Kenneth Ferrie	74	72	74	72	292	16,285.71
Charl Schwartzel	72	70	74	76	292	16,285.71
Soren Kjeldsen	76	72	73	72	293	12,812.50
Jonathan Lomas	72	72	75	74	293	12,812.50
Paul Eales	77	69	76	71	293	12,812.50
Matthew Blackey	74	71	73	75	293	12,812.50
Mikael Lundberg	75	71	72	75	293	12,812.50

	SCORES				TOTAL	MONEY
Alastair Forsyth	72	72	76	73	293	12,812.50
Van Phillips	70	77	75	71	293	12,812.50
Phillip Price	73	71	72	77	293	12,812.50
Fredrik Andersson	73	73	73	75	294	10,053.57
Simon Khan	74	74	73	73	294	10,053.57
Simon Dyson	74	72	76	72	294	10,053.57
Patrik Sjoland	73	73	73	75	294	10,053.57
David Carter	72	72	75	75	294	10,053.57
Soren Hansen	74	75	76	69	294	10,053.57
Barry Lane	72	77	76	69	294	10,053.57
Gordon Brand, Jr.	72	71	78	74	295	8,125
Malcolm Mackenzie	74	75	73	73	295	8,125
Jamie Spence	77	71	73	74	295	8,125
Jean-Francois Lucquin	76	71	75	73	295	8,125
Charlie Wi	74	75	75	71	295	8,125
Andrew Raitt	74	70	76	75	295	8,125
Andrew Coltart	71	71	75	78	295	8,125
Miles Tunnicliff	73	75	76	72	296	7,000
David Drysdale	76	69	78	73	296	7,000
Mikko Ilonen	73	72	75	77	297	6,375
Robert Karlsson	73	73	73	78	297	6,375
Miguel Angel Martin	73	75	72	77	297	6,375
Jesus Maria Arruti	72	77	75	74	298	5,750
*Zane Scotland	75	72	80	71	298	
Richard McEvoy	77	72	74	75	298	5,750
Nick Dougherty	74	75	77	73	299	4,875
Lee S. James	71	73	81	74	299	4,875
Ignacio Garrido	78	71	77	73	299	4,875
Benn Barham	75	71	78	75	299	4,875
Jan-Are Larsen	73	72	77	77	299	4,875
Anders Hansen	71	75	80	74	300	4,000
Euan Little	70	79	78	73	300	4,000
Santiago Luna	74	75	77	75	301	3,625
Philip Golding	72	76	77	76	301	3,625
Raymond Russell	76	72	80	73	301	3,625
Henrik Nystrom	74	72	81	75	302	3,250
Mads Vibe-Hastrup	78	71	73	80	302	3,250
Warren Bennett	74	73	78	77	302	3,250
David Gilford	75	74	77	77	303	2,812.50
Andrew Oldcorn	75	72	79	77	303	2,812.50
Roger Chapman	73	75	80	75	303	2,812.50
Fredrik Widmark	74	74	78	77	303	2,812.50
Federico Bisazza	74	72	83	76	305	2,437.50
Marten Olander	73	75	78	79	305	2,437.50
Simon Wakefield	75	72	79	81	307	2,290

Canarias Open de Espana

Golf Costa Adeje, Tenerife, Canary Islands
Par 36-36–72; 6,816 yards

April 24-27
purse, €1,750,000

	SCORES				TOTAL	MONEY
Kenneth Ferrie	67	65	65	69	266	€291,660
Peter Lawrie	67	64	69	66	266	151,995
Peter Hedblom	64	70	65	67	266	151,995
(Ferrie defeated Lawrie and Hedblom on second playoff hole.)						
Brian Davis	66	67	65	69	267	80,850

	SCORES				TOTAL	MONEY
Mads Vibe-Hastrup	69	68	65	65	267	80,850
Gary Evans	67	69	67	65	268	49,175
Santiago Luna	67	64	66	71	268	49,175
Paul Casey	64	65	68	71	268	49,175
Charl Schwartzel	63	70	67	68	268	49,175
Peter Fowler	69	65	65	70	269	27,650
Jose Maria Olazabal	64	67	69	69	269	27,650
Marten Olander	63	69	67	70	269	27,650
Richard Green	67	66	68	68	269	27,650
Anthony Wall	68	68	65	68	269	27,650
Phillip Price	66	68	69	66	269	27,650
Paul McGinley	66	66	67	70	269	27,650
Simon Khan	66	65	66	72	269	27,650
Markus Brier	68	68	67	66	269	27,650
Ricardo Gonzalez	68	70	65	67	270	21,000
Miguel Angel Jimenez	66	67	67	70	270	21,000
Sergio Garcia	69	67	66	68	270	21,000
Julien Van Hauwe	65	69	69	68	271	19,250
Jamie Spence	69	69	68	65	271	19,250
Raymond Russell	67	67	67	70	271	19,250
*Pablo Martin-Benavides	67	66	64	74	271	
Jarmo Sandelin	64	70	70	68	272	16,887.50
Ivo Giner	66	69	67	70	272	16,887.50
Mikko Ilonen	67	65	68	72	272	16,887.50
Carlos Quevedo	69	65	71	67	272	16,887.50
Shaun Webster	64	70	67	71	272	16,887.50
Soren Hansen	64	68	65	75	272	16,887.50
Nicolas Colsaerts	65	68	68	72	273	12,687.50
Marcel Siem	67	71	64	71	273	12,687.50
Miles Tunnicliff	64	65	70	74	273	12,687.50
Philip Golding	68	67	72	66	273	12,687.50
David Gilford	72	65	63	73	273	12,687.50
Anders Hansen	68	70	69	66	273	12,687.50
Steve Webster	67	69	66	71	273	12,687.50
Klas Eriksson	67	67	71	68	273	12,687.50
James Kingston	69	67	68	69	273	12,687.50
Stephen Scahill	67	68	68	70	273	12,687.50
David Park	67	69	70	67	273	12,687.50
Martin Maritz	68	68	67	70	273	12,687.50
Bradley Dredge	67	66	68	73	274	9,450
Julien Clement	69	63	66	76	274	9,450
Gary Murphy	68	67	70	69	274	9,450
Jose Rivero	67	68	69	70	274	9,450
Roger Chapman	68	70	65	71	274	9,450
Warren Bennett	66	68	71	69	274	9,450
Mattias Eliasson	66	70	68	71	275	7,175
Miguel Angel Martin	70	66	70	69	275	7,175
Mathias Gronberg	67	66	72	70	275	7,175
Andrew Raitt	67	70	67	71	275	7,175
Nicolas Vanhootegem	67	65	72	71	275	7,175
Fredrik Widmark	66	67	67	75	275	7,175
Jamie Donaldson	68	66	67	74	275	7,175
Fredrik Andersson	64	71	66	75	276	5,191.67
Mark Pilkington	67	69	72	68	276	5,191.67
Fredrik Orest	71	66	70	69	276	5,191.67
Andrew Marshall	65	67	70	74	276	5,191.67
Gary Emerson	71	67	74	64	276	5,191.67
Jarrod Moseley	71	66	72	67	276	5,191.67
Robert-Jan Derksen	68	70	69	70	277	4,200
Mark Roe	72	65	69	71	277	4,200

	SCORES				TOTAL	MONEY
Soren Kjeldsen	68	69	70	70	277	4,200
Richard Sterne	67	70	68	72	277	4,200
Graeme McDowell	65	68	68	76	277	4,200
*Alvaro Quiros	70	68	70	69	277	
Roger Wessels	68	68	72	70	278	3,500
Eduardo Fernandez	69	67	69	73	278	3,500
Gordon Brand, Jr.	65	70	71	72	278	3,500
Knud Storgaard	68	70	69	72	279	2,766.50
Francisco Cea	68	70	66	75	279	2,766.50
Dean Robertson	69	66	73	71	279	2,766.50
John Bickerton	66	69	71	73	279	2,766.50
Andrew Oldcorn	64	72	69	75	280	2,614.50
Manuel Moreno	67	69	74	70	280	2,614.50
Nick Dougherty	71	67	70	73	281	2,610
Federico Bisazza	70	67	69	76	282	2,607
Fredrik Jacobson	70	68	74	71	283	2,604
Malcolm Mackenzie	70	68	71	75	284	2,601
Tomas Jesus Munoz	68	70	75	72	285	2,598

Italian Open Telecom Italia

Gardagolf Country Club, Brescia, Italy
Par 36-36–72; 7,112 yards

May 1-4
purse, €1,100,000

	SCORES				TOTAL	MONEY
Mathias Gronberg	71	67	68	65	271	€183,330
Ricardo Gonzalez	67	70	66	70	273	82,026.66
Colin Montgomerie	70	67	71	65	273	82,026.66
Jose Manuel Lara	69	68	71	65	273	82,026.66
Simon Khan	70	72	64	68	274	42,570
Martin Maritz	71	71	66	66	274	42,570
Fredrik Widmark	69	65	72	69	275	30,250
Pierre Fulke	68	70	66	71	275	30,250
Rolf Muntz	69	66	69	72	276	20,702
Gustavo Rojas	70	68	68	70	276	20,702
Marc Farry	72	66	68	70	276	20,702
Peter O'Malley	64	70	70	72	276	20,702
Emanuele Canonica	72	70	68	66	276	20,702
Roger Wessels	70	71	70	66	277	16,500
James Hepworth	73	70	67	67	277	16,500
Marcel Siem	73	68	67	70	278	15,180
Barry Lane	71	68	69	70	278	15,180
Steen Tinning	72	64	70	73	279	13,244
Ian Poulter	74	66	71	68	279	13,244
Jarrod Moseley	74	64	73	68	279	13,244
Stephen Scahill	71	69	68	71	279	13,244
Erol Simsek	68	69	69	73	279	13,244
Matthew Cort	71	68	71	70	280	11,770
Philip Golding	70	70	72	68	280	11,770
Peter Fowler	71	71	67	71	280	11,770
Nicolas Colsaerts	72	67	73	69	281	10,615
Gianluca Baruffaldi	71	71	70	69	281	10,615
Tobias Dier	68	71	72	70	281	10,615
David Dixon	73	69	68	71	281	10,615
Terry Price	74	67	69	72	282	8,983.33
Julien Clement	70	71	70	71	282	8,983.33
Sven Struver	70	67	74	71	282	8,983.33
Richard Green	73	68	66	75	282	8,983.33

	SCORES				TOTAL	MONEY
Anthony Wall	69	70	71	72	282	8,983.33
Philip Walton	73	69	70	70	282	8,983.33
Andrew Sherborne	68	71	71	73	283	7,260
Mattias Eliasson	68	69	74	72	283	7,260
Roger Chapman	67	76	69	71	283	7,260
Denny Lucas	73	66	71	73	283	7,260
Steven Bowditch	74	67	72	70	283	7,260
Richard Sterne	68	70	71	74	283	7,260
Pehr Magnebrant	71	65	68	79	283	7,260
Gary Clark	66	70	69	78	283	7,260
Andrew Coltart	72	70	69	73	284	6,050
Andrew Marshall	72	70	68	74	284	6,050
Gary Emerson	73	69	74	68	284	6,050
Hennie Otto	73	70	69	73	285	5,610
Raul Ballesteros	69	73	72	72	286	4,950
Marcello Santi	71	71	70	74	286	4,950
Neil Cheetham	70	67	77	72	286	4,950
Matthew Blackey	68	73	73	72	286	4,950
Fredrik Orest	67	72	76	71	286	4,950
Alvaro Salto	73	67	72	75	287	3,677.14
Ben Mason	70	71	70	76	287	3,677.14
Brett Rumford	71	70	78	68	287	3,677.14
Michele Reale	71	71	72	73	287	3,677.14
Sam Little	70	73	74	70	287	3,677.14
Jean-Francois Remesy	71	71	72	73	287	3,677.14
Damien McGrane	73	68	74	72	287	3,677.14
Gregory Havret	72	71	74	71	288	2,970
Ivo Giner	72	68	74	74	288	2,970
David Geall	68	70	70	80	288	2,970
Charl Schwartzel	72	68	78	71	289	2,640
Stuart Little	68	72	73	76	289	2,640
Gary Murphy	69	73	70	77	289	2,640
Andrea Maestroni	71	69	77	73	290	2,365
Federico Bisazza	69	69	78	74	290	2,365
*Edoardo Molinari	71	71	74	75	291	
Jesus Maria Arruti	70	72	75	74	291	2,200
Jean Hugo	72	70	75	75	292	2,090
Simon Wakefield	70	72	73	78	293	2,010

Benson and Hedges International Open

The De Vere Belfry, Sutton Coldfield, England
Par 36-36—72; 7,118 yards

May 8-11
purse, €1,596,860

	SCORES				TOTAL	MONEY
Paul Casey	71	69	66	71	277	€262,227.90
Padraig Harrington	67	68	71	75	281	174,818.60
Rolf Muntz	70	71	69	72	282	81,292.13
Paul Lawrie	71	72	70	69	282	81,292.13
Stephen Scahill	71	70	65	76	282	81,292.13
Richard S. Johnson	73	68	79	64	284	55,068.86
Brian Davis	70	74	69	72	285	40,593.62
Angel Cabrera	68	69	70	78	285	40,593.62
David Park	72	70	74	69	285	40,593.62
Simon Khan	72	70	71	73	286	28,203.12
Matthew Blackey	71	76	69	70	286	28,203.12
Nick O'Hern	73	74	68	71	286	28,203.12

	SCORES				TOTAL	MONEY
David Dixon	66	78	68	74	286	28,203.12
Jose Manuel Lara	72	68	73	74	287	23,128.92
Klas Eriksson	75	72	73	67	287	23,128.92
Bradley Dredge	73	69	72	73	287	23,128.92
Ricardo Gonzalez	70	72	70	76	288	19,635.98
Arjun Atwal	71	73	76	68	288	19,635.98
Jamie Spence	72	71	72	73	288	19,635.98
Soren Hansen	77	70	70	71	288	19,635.98
Jean Van de Velde	75	70	70	73	288	19,635.98
Gary Emerson	75	70	70	74	289	16,835.34
Paul McGinley	73	72	71	73	289	16,835.34
Niclas Fasth	75	73	66	75	289	16,835.34
Robert Rock	71	73	72	73	289	16,835.34
Jamie Elson	71	69	78	71	289	16,835.34
Daniel Greenwood	79	66	70	75	290	14,711.25
Lee Westwood	72	73	73	72	290	14,711.25
Colin Montgomerie	72	70	72	76	290	14,711.25
Peter Lawrie	74	71	72	73	290	14,711.25
Henrik Stenson	68	76	72	75	291	12,429.83
Richard Bland	76	71	70	74	291	12,429.83
Roger Chapman	71	71	73	76	291	12,429.83
John Bickerton	74	71	72	74	291	12,429.83
Markus Brier	74	72	71	74	291	12,429.83
Julien Clement	71	70	74	76	291	12,429.83
Mikko Ilonen	75	67	73	77	292	10,227.07
Gordon Brand, Jr.	69	74	75	74	292	10,227.07
Jean-Francois Remesy	71	70	74	77	292	10,227.07
David Gilford	69	75	74	74	292	10,227.07
Raphael Jacquelin	73	72	72	75	292	10,227.07
Stephen Leaney	69	72	77	74	292	10,227.07
John E. Morgan	73	75	72	72	292	10,227.07
Nick Dougherty	73	75	72	73	293	8,024.32
Richard Sterne	70	75	73	75	293	8,024.32
Justin Rose	72	75	75	71	293	8,024.32
Henrik Bjornstad	71	77	73	72	293	8,024.32
Gary Murphy	74	73	70	76	293	8,024.32
Bernhard Langer	71	71	74	77	293	8,024.32
Stephen Dodd	74	73	73	73	293	8,024.32
Terry Price	73	71	74	76	294	5,443.95
Mads Vibe-Hastrup	72	76	67	79	294	5,443.95
Tobias Dier	69	76	73	76	294	5,443.95
David Lynn	74	74	72	74	294	5,443.95
David Drysdale	75	72	75	72	294	5,443.95
Eduardo Romero	73	71	74	76	294	5,443.95
Santiago Luna	73	75	74	72	294	5,443.95
Anthony Wall	73	72	76	73	294	5,443.95
Shaun Webster	71	74	73	76	294	5,443.95
Martin Maritz	71	74	74	75	294	5,443.95
Emanuele Canonica	69	72	75	79	295	4,248.17
Phillip Price	73	72	72	79	296	3,618.81
Miles Tunnicliff	70	75	78	73	296	3,618.81
Marcel Siem	70	78	73	75	296	3,618.81
Andrew Coltart	70	73	75	78	296	3,618.81
Retief Goosen	74	73	74	75	296	3,618.81
Malcolm Mackenzie	72	74	74	76	296	3,618.81
Peter Fowler	72	72	77	75	296	3,618.81
Mark Roe	72	72	76	77	297	2,645.37
David Carter	72	73	79	73	297	2,645.37
Johan Rystrom	74	72	77	74	297	2,645.37

	SCORES				TOTAL	MONEY
Ian Garbutt	70	77	77	73	297	2,645.37
Peter Hedblom	75	69	76	78	298	2,352.50
Sandy Lyle	75	67	75	81	298	2,352.50
Jorge Berendt	71	74	77	77	299	2,348
Peter Mitchell	72	74	74	80	300	2,345
Alastair Forsyth	73	75	81	72	301	2,342
Charl Schwartzel	72	70	80	80	302	2,339
Costantino Rocca	71	77	77	78	303	2,336
Peter Senior	74	74	80	80	308	2,333

Deutsche Bank - SAP Open

Gut Kaden Golf Club, Hamburg, Germany
Par 36-36–72; 7,215 yards

May 15-18
purse, €2,700,000

	SCORES				TOTAL	MONEY
Padraig Harrington	65	66	70	68	269	€450,000
Thomas Bjorn	71	70	65	63	269	300,000
(Harrington defeated Bjorn on first playoff hole.)						
Retief Goosen	65	69	70	66	270	169,020
Niclas Fasth	68	69	68	66	271	135,000
Justin Rose	72	68	67	65	272	96,660
Paul Casey	70	66	69	67	272	96,660
Graeme McDowell	70	65	68	69	272	96,660
Greg Owen	70	69	67	67	273	60,660
Paul Lawrie	70	66	69	68	273	60,660
Darren Clarke	67	69	69	68	273	60,660
Thomas Levet	71	67	68	68	274	49,680
Peter Lawrie	67	69	71	68	275	42,727.50
Marc Farry	70	70	69	66	275	42,727.50
Nick Faldo	70	67	70	68	275	42,727.50
David Park	71	70	70	64	275	42,727.50
Andrew Coltart	68	67	70	71	276	35,707.50
Alastair Forsyth	70	67	72	67	276	35,707.50
Anthony Wall	71	70	64	71	276	35,707.50
Gregory Havret	70	70	68	68	276	35,707.50
Nicolas Colsaerts	70	70	69	68	277	28,920
Peter Baker	67	69	71	70	277	28,920
Soren Kjeldsen	71	68	71	67	277	28,920
Robert-Jan Derksen	70	69	68	70	277	28,920
Mads Vibe-Hastrup	71	67	66	73	277	28,920
Stephen Gallacher	71	67	68	71	277	28,920
John Bickerton	72	69	68	68	277	28,920
David Carter	69	70	68	70	277	28,920
Miles Tunnicliff	69	68	70	70	277	28,920
Robert Karlsson	68	67	71	72	278	23,220
Gustavo Rojas	69	69	72	68	278	23,220
Tiger Woods	69	71	70	68	278	23,220
Stephen Leaney	72	70	68	68	278	23,220
Carlos Rodiles	72	69	69	68	278	23,220
Jean Van de Velde	72	67	69	71	279	18,360
Colin Montgomerie	69	69	68	73	279	18,360
Peter Fowler	72	68	70	69	279	18,360
Klas Eriksson	72	65	72	70	279	18,360
Raphael Jacquelin	68	68	73	70	279	18,360
Stephen Scahill	72	70	69	68	279	18,360
Henrik Bjornstad	70	72	67	70	279	18,360

	SCORES				TOTAL	MONEY
Johan Rystrom	71	68	72	68	279	18,360
Emanuele Canonica	71	71	69	68	279	18,360
Simon Wakefield	70	69	69	71	279	18,360
Nick Dougherty	73	68	69	70	280	15,120
Anders Hansen	68	70	69	73	280	15,120
David Howell	71	71	69	70	281	12,960
Fredrik Widmark	70	71	66	74	281	12,960
David Drysdale	74	68	70	69	281	12,960
Martin Maritz	71	71	68	71	281	12,960
Jamie Elson	71	70	69	71	281	12,960
Kevin Na	69	68	71	73	281	12,960
Fredrik Jacobson	71	68	74	69	282	10,260
Mark Pilkington	74	68	72	68	282	10,260
Peter O'Malley	69	66	74	73	282	10,260
Nick O'Hern	69	73	68	72	282	10,260
Steen Tinning	72	70	68	73	283	8,010
Miguel Angel Jimenez	68	71	71	73	283	8,010
Warren Bennett	68	69	76	70	283	8,010
Jarrod Moseley	72	66	74	71	283	8,010
Benn Barham	68	70	75	70	283	8,010
Mikael Lundberg	70	71	72	70	283	8,010
Stuart Little	74	68	69	73	284	6,885
Gary Emerson	73	68	72	71	284	6,885
Richard Green	74	67	73	71	285	6,075
Ronan Rafferty	74	68	74	69	285	6,075
Bernhard Langer	72	70	70	73	285	6,075
Nicolas Vanhootegem	71	69	73	72	285	6,075
Christian Cevaer	68	71	75	73	287	5,150
Mikko Ilonen	72	70	74	71	287	5,150
Marcel Siem	72	69	75	71	287	5,150
Philip Golding	74	67	70	77	288	4,045.50
Steve Webster	76	66	72	74	288	4,045.50
Markus Brier	69	72	73	74	288	4,045.50
Simon Khan	72	70	69	77	288	4,045.50
Jonathan Lomas	70	72	76	73	291	4,038
Jochen Lupprian	70	70	74	78	292	4,035
Gary Birch, Jr.	71	69	78	80	298	4,032

Volvo PGA Championship

Wentworth Club, Surrey, England
Par 35-37–72; 7,072 yards

May 22-25
purse, €3,500,000

	SCORES				TOTAL	MONEY
Ignacio Garrido	70	69	66	65	270	€583,330
Trevor Immelman	69	69	64	68	270	388,880
(Garrido defeated Immelman on first playoff hole.)						
Mathias Gronberg	72	67	67	67	273	219,100
Ernie Els	69	69	67	69	274	175,000
Kenneth Ferrie	70	67	70	68	275	135,450
Barry Lane	72	68	68	67	275	135,450
Soren Kjeldsen	68	72	69	67	276	96,250
Thomas Levet	74	69	66	67	276	96,250
Nick Faldo	71	68	68	70	277	65,870
Phillip Price	71	69	67	70	277	65,870
Colin Montgomerie	69	70	69	69	277	65,870
Gary Orr	69	72	66	70	277	65,870

	SCORES				TOTAL	MONEY
Paul Casey	70	72	64	71	277	65,870
Kevin Na	69	70	68	71	278	48,358.33
Darren Clarke	66	69	72	71	278	48,358.33
Niclas Fasth	69	67	68	74	278	48,358.33
Eduardo Romero	72	71	65	70	278	48,358.33
David Gilford	70	69	71	68	278	48,358.33
Paul Eales	74	69	67	68	278	48,358.33
Stephen Leaney	69	73	65	72	279	40,716.67
Peter Fowler	70	71	70	68	279	40,716.67
Adam Scott	68	73	71	67	279	40,716.67
Martin Maritz	71	71	68	70	280	36,400
Sandy Lyle	75	68	67	70	280	36,400
Henrik Bjornstad	71	71	71	67	280	36,400
John Bickerton	72	69	71	68	280	36,400
Robert Rock	69	68	70	73	280	36,400
Mikko Ilonen	69	70	72	70	281	31,675
Stephen Dodd	71	72	69	69	281	31,675
Peter Hedblom	69	74	69	69	281	31,675
Marten Olander	73	67	69	72	281	31,675
Mark McNulty	69	71	68	74	282	26,031.25
Ronan Rafferty	69	72	72	69	282	26,031.25
Justin Rose	68	73	70	71	282	26,031.25
Miles Tunnicliff	69	73	71	69	282	26,031.25
Emanuele Canonica	71	69	69	73	282	26,031.25
Paul McGinley	70	69	71	72	282	26,031.25
Fredrik Jacobson	72	69	70	71	282	26,031.25
Andrew Coltart	68	71	70	73	282	26,031.25
Alastair Forsyth	67	71	71	74	283	21,700
Henrik Stenson	71	72	70	70	283	21,700
Gordon Brand, Jr.	68	70	68	77	283	21,700
Jamie Donaldson	69	71	68	75	283	21,700
Ian Woosnam	68	69	72	75	284	18,900
Jean Van de Velde	71	70	70	73	284	18,900
Raymond Russell	74	67	73	70	284	18,900
James Kingston	67	76	67	74	284	18,900
David Drysdale	72	71	71	71	285	15,750
Michael Campbell	69	74	69	73	285	15,750
Matthew Blackey	70	73	71	71	285	15,750
Ricardo Gonzalez	69	73	70	73	285	15,750
Jose Maria Olazabal	68	71	74	72	285	15,750
Jean-Francois Remesy	73	69	75	69	286	12,250
Sam Torrance	70	71	70	75	286	12,250
Peter Baker	68	73	70	75	286	12,250
Anders Hansen	70	72	70	74	286	12,250
Henrik Nystrom	73	69	74	70	286	12,250
Greg Owen	68	71	73	75	287	9,625
Pierre Fulke	71	72	70	74	287	9,625
Steen Tinning	74	69	70	74	287	9,625
Roger Chapman	71	69	79	68	287	9,625
Santiago Luna	72	71	71	73	287	9,625
Greg Turner	72	70	71	74	287	9,625
Peter Senior	68	73	76	71	288	7,700
Darren Fichardt	69	73	77	69	288	7,700
Nick O'Hern	73	69	71	75	288	7,700
Mikael Lundberg	72	69	73	74	288	7,700
Thongchai Jaidee	67	72	76	73	288	7,700
Carlos Rodiles	70	73	73	73	289	6,520
Soren Hansen	69	68	77	75	289	6,520
Arjun Atwal	68	74	72	77	291	5,250
David Orr	72	71	75	74	292	5,245.50

	SCORES				TOTAL	MONEY
Barry Austin	73	68	77	74	292	5,245.50
Christian Cevaer	73	70	77	75	295	5,241
Ben Willman	73	68	77	79	297	5,238

Celtic Manor Resort Wales Open

Celtic Manor Resort, Newport, Wales
Par 36-36–72; 7,355 yards

May 29-June 1
purse, €2,112,185

	SCORES				TOTAL	MONEY
Ian Poulter	65	67	68	70	270	€347,360
Darren Fichardt	68	67	70	68	273	155,413.50
Jarrod Moseley	74	67	63	69	273	155,413.50
Jonathan Lomas	66	71	68	68	273	155,413.50
Andrew Coltart	68	69	67	71	275	80,656.99
Mark McNulty	69	67	69	70	275	80,656.99
Santiago Luna	68	69	70	69	276	53,771.32
Peter Fowler	67	72	68	69	276	53,771.32
Phillip Price	68	66	68	74	276	53,771.32
Jarmo Sandelin	67	73	68	70	278	36,264.38
Bradley Dredge	71	69	67	71	278	36,264.38
Fredrik Jacobson	71	68	64	75	278	36,264.38
Iain Pyman	73	67	68	70	278	36,264.38
Jamie Donaldson	68	71	68	71	278	36,264.38
Roger Chapman	74	68	67	70	279	29,386.65
Jean-Francois Remesy	68	72	69	70	279	29,386.65
Richard Green	67	70	72	70	279	29,386.65
Peter Lawrie	68	75	67	70	280	25,913.05
Terry Price	71	71	68	70	280	25,913.05
Christian Cevaer	71	72	65	72	280	25,913.05
Stephen Gallacher	70	72	69	70	281	22,925.76
David Drysdale	68	70	73	70	281	22,925.76
Arjun Atwal	75	68	72	66	281	22,925.76
Barry Lane	69	71	66	75	281	22,925.76
Graeme McDowell	70	72	72	67	281	22,925.76
Sven Struver	68	72	71	71	282	19,799.52
Nick O'Hern	65	72	70	75	282	19,799.52
Steve Webster	70	70	69	73	282	19,799.52
Paul Broadhurst	72	70	72	68	282	19,799.52
Stephen Dodd	70	71	71	70	282	19,799.52
Diego Borrego	71	72	69	71	283	16,226.67
Greg Owen	74	68	70	71	283	16,226.67
Patrik Sjoland	72	69	69	73	283	16,226.67
Philip Golding	72	69	69	73	283	16,226.67
Alessandro Tadini	69	70	73	71	283	16,226.67
David Howell	70	69	71	73	283	16,226.67
Nick Dougherty	72	70	72	69	283	16,226.67
Martin Maritz	74	68	70	72	284	13,963.87
Malcolm Mackenzie	67	73	70	74	284	13,963.87
Carlos Rodiles	68	70	76	70	284	13,963.87
Anthony Wall	72	70	72	71	285	11,879.71
David Park	70	72	74	69	285	11,879.71
Emanuele Canonica	71	70	70	74	285	11,879.71
Jean-Francois Lucquin	69	74	68	74	285	11,879.71
Julien Clement	71	72	70	72	285	11,879.71
Alastair Forsyth	67	73	75	70	285	11,879.71
Robert Rock	70	71	73	71	285	11,879.71

	SCORES				TOTAL	MONEY
Julien Van Hauwe	68	75	72	71	286	8,545.06
Ricardo Gonzalez	67	71	72	76	286	8,545.06
Ian Garbutt	72	71	77	66	286	8,545.06
Stephen Scahill	71	69	72	74	286	8,545.06
Simon Wakefield	69	71	72	74	286	8,545.06
Richard Bland	72	69	71	74	286	8,545.06
Gregory Havret	68	73	74	71	286	8,545.06
Marten Olander	74	67	70	75	286	8,545.06
Marc Farry	73	70	73	70	286	8,545.06
Klas Eriksson	68	72	74	73	287	5,731.44
Fredrik Orest	70	73	70	74	287	5,731.44
Sandy Lyle	70	70	76	71	287	5,731.44
Anders Hansen	73	70	71	73	287	5,731.44
Maarten Lafeber	72	70	73	72	287	5,731.44
Peter Baker	74	69	73	71	287	5,731.44
Jesus Maria Arruti	68	69	76	74	287	5,731.44
David Dixon	72	69	74	72	287	5,731.44
Michael Campbell	69	73	70	76	288	4,585.15
Barry Austin	68	74	73	73	288	4,585.15
Philip Archer	67	73	70	78	288	4,585.15
Henrik Bjornstad	73	67	72	77	289	3,978.43
Simon Hurd	70	72	74	73	289	3,978.43
Miles Tunnicliff	70	70	74	75	289	3,978.43
Nicolas Colsaerts	69	73	69	79	290	3,124.50
Euan Little	73	70	74	73	290	3,124.50
Shaun Webster	72	71	74	74	291	3,115.50
Jamie Spence	71	71	71	78	291	3,115.50
Robert-Jan Derksen	70	73	72	76	291	3,115.50
Raphael Jacquelin	74	69	75	73	291	3,115.50
Gary Murphy	69	74	77	74	294	3,106.50
Fredrik Widmark	69	73	80	72	294	3,106.50
Benn Barham	73	69	78	76	296	3,102

Daily Telegraph Damovo British Masters

Marriott Forest of Arden Hotel, Warwickshire, England
Par 36-36–72; 7,213 yards

June 5-8
purse, €2,105,520

	SCORES				TOTAL	MONEY
Greg Owen	68	68	67	71	274	€348,312.50
Ian Poulter	71	73	63	70	277	181,512.60
Christian Cevaer	73	70	66	68	277	181,512.60
Anthony Wall	72	70	67	71	280	88,750.02
Darren Clarke	71	71	72	66	280	88,750.02
Robert Rock	73	69	70	68	280	88,750.02
Raphael Jacquelin	70	72	72	67	281	50,888.46
Jorge Berendt	72	72	67	70	281	50,888.46
David Lynn	66	71	71	73	281	50,888.46
Stephen Gallacher	69	71	71	70	281	50,888.46
Soren Kjeldsen	70	73	70	69	282	34,148.56
Richard Green	70	66	71	75	282	34,148.56
Henrik Stenson	69	74	70	69	282	34,148.56
Mathias Gronberg	73	71	66	72	282	34,148.56
Fredrik Andersson	74	70	68	70	282	34,148.56
Mark Roe	71	70	69	73	283	25,809.96
Darren Fichardt	72	66	71	74	283	25,809.96
Nick O'Hern	72	70	70	71	283	25,809.96

	SCORES				TOTAL	MONEY
Philip Golding	69	73	69	72	283	25,809.96
Marcel Siem	66	71	74	72	283	25,809.96
Robert Karlsson	75	69	69	70	283	25,809.96
Ignacio Garrido	67	72	73	71	283	25,809.96
Mikael Lundberg	69	69	71	74	283	25,809.96
David Howell	72	71	67	74	284	20,794.26
Barry Lane	73	68	68	75	284	20,794.26
Justin Rose	69	75	73	67	284	20,794.26
Jarrod Moseley	70	73	70	71	284	20,794.26
Gary Orr	72	72	72	68	284	20,794.26
Andrew Coltart	68	73	70	73	284	20,794.26
Peter Fowler	65	75	69	76	285	17,067.31
David Gilford	70	73	71	71	285	17,067.31
Peter Baker	69	74	68	74	285	17,067.31
Gregory Havret	73	71	70	71	285	17,067.31
Markus Brier	71	72	70	72	285	17,067.31
Patrik Sjoland	70	72	71	72	285	17,067.31
Sandy Lyle	72	71	73	70	286	13,584.19
Marten Olander	75	67	71	73	286	13,584.19
Philip Archer	71	73	72	70	286	13,584.19
Miguel Angel Jimenez	72	70	71	73	286	13,584.19
Charlie Wi	72	72	68	74	286	13,584.19
Stephen Scahill	73	71	67	75	286	13,584.19
Simon Wakefield	71	71	73	71	286	13,584.19
Matthew Blackey	70	68	70	78	286	13,584.19
Lee Westwood	67	76	73	70	286	13,584.19
Gordon Brand, Jr.	71	73	71	72	287	10,240.39
Santiago Luna	70	74	71	72	287	10,240.39
Costantino Rocca	69	72	73	73	287	10,240.39
Brian Davis	72	70	69	76	287	10,240.39
Henrik Bjornstad	73	71	69	74	287	10,240.39
Iain Pyman	71	72	73	71	287	10,240.39
Jamie Donaldson	70	71	68	78	287	10,240.39
Mark James	71	72	67	78	288	7,941.52
Peter Lawrie	69	74	70	75	288	7,941.52
Euan Little	72	71	72	73	288	7,941.52
Jean-Francois Lucquin	69	71	73	75	288	7,941.52
Mark Mouland	74	70	69	76	289	6,090.49
Robert-Jan Derksen	70	73	73	73	289	6,090.49
Gary Emerson	71	72	78	68	289	6,090.49
James Kingston	72	70	70	77	289	6,090.49
Matthew Cort	69	72	75	73	289	6,090.49
Mikko Ilonen	75	67	72	75	289	6,090.49
Brett Rumford	71	70	69	79	289	6,090.49
Fernando Roca	73	70	72	75	290	4,911.21
Adam Mednick	72	69	74	75	290	4,911.21
Bradley Dredge	72	72	70	76	290	4,911.21
Robert Coles	76	68	76	70	290	4,911.21
Fredrik Orest	71	73	75	72	291	4,089.19
Damien McGrane	75	67	74	75	291	4,089.19
Paul Eales	72	72	74	73	291	4,089.19
Raymond Russell	66	77	75	73	291	4,089.19
Klas Eriksson	71	71	74	76	292	3,132
Jarmo Sandelin	67	76	68	81	292	3,132
Gary Birch, Jr.	72	69	76	75	292	3,132
Jesus Maria Arruti	66	76	76	76	294	3,126
Ivo Giner	73	69	73	83	298	3,123

Aa St. Omer Open

Aa St. Omer Golf Club, St. Omer, France
Par 36-35–71; 6,799 yards

June 12-15
purse, €400,000

	SCORES				TOTAL	MONEY
Brett Rumford	64	70	68	67	269	€66,660
Ben Mason	70	69	66	69	274	44,440
Federico Bisazza	68	72	68	70	278	25,040
Mattias Eliasson	66	73	69	71	279	15,740
Damien McGrane	72	70	69	68	279	15,740
Peter Hanson	69	69	70	71	279	15,740
James Hepworth	70	72	70	67	279	15,740
Alvaro Salto	68	67	74	71	280	8,240
Cesar Monasterio	66	73	72	69	280	8,240
Garry Houston	68	69	68	75	280	8,240
Stuart Little	71	68	71	70	280	8,240
Martin Lemesurier	72	73	68	67	280	8,240
Martin Erlandsson	70	69	70	72	281	6,146.67
Sebastien Branger	69	69	72	71	281	6,146.67
Bjorn Pettersson	68	74	68	71	281	6,146.67
Neil Cheetham	71	72	74	65	282	5,400
Erol Simsek	71	70	71	70	282	5,400
Lucas Parsons	72	69	73	68	282	5,400
Pasi Purhonen	73	70	73	67	283	4,960
Philip Walton	74	70	71	69	284	4,405.71
Marc Pendaries	69	72	71	72	284	4,405.71
Paul Broadhurst	69	69	73	73	284	4,405.71
Michele Reale	70	69	72	73	284	4,405.71
Sion Bebb	69	72	72	71	284	4,405.71
Raphael Pellicioli	74	71	68	71	284	4,405.71
Allan Hogh	71	72	70	71	284	4,405.71
Marco Soffietti	72	72	70	71	285	3,444.44
Philip Golding	74	67	73	71	285	3,444.44
Pehr Magnebrant	71	74	69	71	285	3,444.44
Robert Coles	70	71	73	71	285	3,444.44
Gary Clark	72	70	71	72	285	3,444.44
Marco Bernardini	70	71	73	71	285	3,444.44
Mark Sanders	70	70	74	71	285	3,444.44
Michael Kirk	69	69	75	72	285	3,444.44
Gregory Bourdy	74	70	69	72	285	3,444.44
Greig Hutcheon	73	72	70	71	286	2,760
Titch Moore	71	70	74	71	286	2,760
Johan Edfors	71	71	73	71	286	2,760
Joakim Rask	68	74	71	73	286	2,760
Philippe Lima	68	74	71	73	286	2,760
Lionel Alexandre	70	70	77	70	287	2,360
Michael Archer	70	71	77	69	287	2,360
Jamie Little	72	70	76	69	287	2,360
Gianluca Baruffaldi	70	71	70	76	287	2,360
Oskar Bergman	72	71	71	73	287	2,360
Fredrik Orest	74	71	74	69	288	1,960
Scott Drummond	72	73	73	70	288	1,960
Denny Lucas	67	75	75	71	288	1,960
Christopher Hanell	70	73	71	74	288	1,960
Simon Dyson	69	75	72	72	288	1,960
Marcel Haremza	70	73	74	72	289	1,520
Jean Hugo	71	74	72	72	289	1,520
Paul Dwyer	72	72	71	74	289	1,520
Edward Rush	72	71	73	73	289	1,520

	SCORES				TOTAL	MONEY
Brad Kennedy	72	71	73	73	289	1,520
Marcus Fraser	70	71	74	74	289	1,520
Alessandro Tadini	71	74	73	72	290	1,120
Massimo Florioli	71	72	74	73	290	1,120
David Dupart	71	74	74	71	290	1,120
Kariem Baraka	73	72	73	72	290	1,120
Thomas Norret	74	70	75	71	290	1,120
Peter Gustafsson	74	70	75	71	290	1,120
Paul McKechnie	70	75	73	72	290	1,120
Sam Little	68	76	74	73	291	940
Andrew Beal	70	75	72	74	291	940
Nicolas Vanhootegem	74	71	71	76	292	840
Michael Jonzon	71	73	74	74	292	840
Nicolas Marin	71	73	75	73	292	840
Dominique Nouailhac	74	71	73	75	293	760
Raimo Sjoberg	71	74	73	76	294	670
Daniel Vancsik	74	70	77	73	294	670
Mark Mouland	75	70	77	73	295	594
Olivier David	74	71	73	77	295	594
David Geall	71	71	77	76	295	594
Stefano Reale	74	71	74	77	296	587
Lee S. James	75	70	77	74	296	587
*Jerome Guillain	74	70	76	79	299	
Gary David Cullen	70	75	78	77	300	582

Diageo Championship at Gleneagles

Gleneagles Hotel, Perthshire, Scotland
Par 36-36–72; 7,060 yards

June 19-22
purse, €1,719,309

	SCORES				TOTAL	MONEY
Soren Kjeldsen	72	68	67	72	279	€281,928
Alastair Forsyth	70	73	69	69	281	187,947.30
Paul Broadhurst	73	68	71	70	282	105,892.20
Colin Montgomerie	72	73	69	69	283	84,578.40
Miguel Angel Martin	74	70	70	71	285	60,558.13
Rolf Muntz	72	70	73	70	285	60,558.13
Stephen Gallacher	76	71	67	71	285	60,558.13
John Bickerton	74	71	71	70	286	40,090.16
Adam Scott	72	75	66	73	286	40,090.16
Raphael Jacquelin	74	72	71	70	287	31,350.39
Richard Green	74	75	68	70	287	31,350.39
Stephen Dodd	72	71	75	69	287	31,350.39
Nicolas Colsaerts	76	73	71	68	288	26,557.62
Paul Casey	76	71	68	73	288	26,557.62
Steve Webster	77	71	68	73	289	23,851.11
Andrew Raitt	75	71	72	71	289	23,851.11
Brad Kennedy	70	72	74	73	289	23,851.11
Sandy Lyle	73	71	74	72	290	20,679.42
Philip Golding	75	75	69	71	290	20,679.42
Paul Eales	74	74	73	69	290	20,679.42
Nicolas Vanhootegem	73	73	71	73	290	20,679.42
Peter Fowler	77	73	69	72	291	17,084.84
David Gilford	76	74	70	71	291	17,084.84
Shaun Webster	76	72	69	74	291	17,084.84
Hennie Otto	74	77	67	73	291	17,084.84
Gary Orr	75	68	72	76	291	17,084.84

		SCORES			TOTAL	MONEY
Iain Pyman	71	74	73	73	291	17,084.84
Francois Delamontagne	72	76	70	73	291	17,084.84
David Orr	76	74	72	69	291	17,084.84
Graeme McDowell	74	77	68	72	291	17,084.84
David Howell	77	70	73	72	292	13,363.39
Peter Baker	75	74	71	72	292	13,363.39
Julien Clement	78	74	68	72	292	13,363.39
Miles Tunnicliff	78	69	72	73	292	13,363.39
Peter O'Malley	76	74	71	71	292	13,363.39
Gustavo Rojas	71	75	74	72	292	13,363.39
Mark Mouland	75	74	75	69	293	11,164.35
Jean-Francois Remesy	74	77	71	71	293	11,164.35
Jean-Francois Lucquin	73	77	75	68	293	11,164.35
Ian Garbutt	76	76	69	72	293	11,164.35
Simon Wakefield	73	75	70	75	293	11,164.35
David Park	75	75	71	72	293	11,164.35
Mark McNulty	75	75	72	72	294	9,980.25
Mark James	76	75	70	74	295	8,796.15
Alvaro Salto	77	72	75	71	295	8,796.15
Barry Lane	74	75	73	73	295	8,796.15
Darren Fichardt	77	75	70	73	295	8,796.15
Lee Westwood	74	74	75	72	295	8,796.15
Martin Maritz	74	74	73	74	295	8,796.15
Sam Torrance	74	71	73	78	296	6,597.11
Neil Cheetham	73	71	79	73	296	6,597.11
Christian Cevaer	75	75	71	75	296	6,597.11
Roger Wessels	74	77	68	77	296	6,597.11
Fredrik Andersson	78	74	70	74	296	6,597.11
Mads Vibe-Hastrup	76	75	71	74	296	6,597.11
Ben Mason	76	76	73	71	296	6,597.11
Philip Walton	74	74	72	77	297	4,990.13
Paul Lawrie	77	71	76	73	297	4,990.13
Gary Clark	79	70	72	76	297	4,990.13
Zane Scotland	72	78	71	76	297	4,990.13
Gary Murphy	73	76	72	77	298	4,398.08
Julien Van Hauwe	79	73	71	75	298	4,398.08
Russell Claydon	73	79	73	73	298	4,398.08
Ross Drummond	78	73	75	73	299	3,890.61
Ivo Giner	71	72	75	81	299	3,890.61
Thomas Norret	78	73	71	77	299	3,890.61
Andrew Marshall	79	73	73	75	300	3,309.13
Jean Hugo	75	75	72	78	300	3,309.13
Jesus Maria Arruti	76	76	73	75	300	3,309.13
Pierre Fulke	78	74	75	73	300	3,309.13
Gregory Havret	72	75	78	76	301	2,534
Matthew Blackey	74	77	78	72	301	2,534
Marc Warren	70	75	75	81	301	2,534
Santiago Luna	75	75	72	80	302	2,526.50
Mark Roe	77	75	72	78	302	2,526.50
Titch Moore	76	75	74	78	303	2,520.50
Sebastien Delagrange	73	78	75	77	303	2,520.50
Philip Archer	74	78	78	75	305	2,516
Fraser Mann	74	76	84	77	311	2,511.50
Adam Mednick	74	75	78	84	311	2,511.50
Scott Kammann	75	77	79	81	312	2,507

Open de France

Le Golf National, Paris, France
Par 36-36–72; 7,105 yards

June 26-29
purse, €2,500,000

	SCORES				TOTAL	MONEY
Philip Golding	66	70	68	69	273	€416,660
David Howell	71	65	69	69	274	277,770
Justin Rose	68	69	73	65	275	140,750
Peter O'Malley	70	69	66	70	275	140,750
Andrew Oldcorn	69	70	69	68	276	89,500
Brian Davis	68	72	68	68	276	89,500
Simon Wakefield	70	70	70	66	276	89,500
Barry Lane	70	68	67	72	277	53,625
Pierre Fulke	70	68	67	72	277	53,625
Bradley Dredge	67	72	70	68	277	53,625
Stephen Gallacher	68	69	69	71	277	53,625
Jose Maria Olazabal	70	68	69	71	278	40,500
Raphael Jacquelin	70	68	68	72	278	40,500
Thomas Bjorn	70	64	71	73	278	40,500
Robert-Jan Derksen	68	74	66	71	279	35,250
Stephen Leaney	70	70	71	68	279	35,250
Matthew Blackey	71	71	68	69	279	35,250
Santiago Luna	70	70	70	70	280	30,100
Miguel Angel Martin	70	68	70	72	280	30,100
Jose Manuel Lara	67	69	71	73	280	30,100
Andrew Marshall	69	74	70	67	280	30,100
Graeme McDowell	70	68	73	69	280	30,100
Carlos Rodiles	70	69	71	71	281	25,250
Miguel Angel Jimenez	67	74	69	71	281	25,250
Nicolas Colsaerts	66	70	73	72	281	25,250
Marcel Siem	74	69	64	74	281	25,250
Stephen Dodd	72	67	71	71	281	25,250
Stephen Scahill	74	67	72	68	281	25,250
Martin Maritz	73	70	67	71	281	25,250
Ian Poulter	75	68	67	72	282	20,107.14
Jarrod Moseley	69	72	73	68	282	20,107.14
Paul McGinley	71	72	69	70	282	20,107.14
Ignacio Garrido	71	72	68	71	282	20,107.14
Raymond Russell	71	70	69	72	282	20,107.14
John Bickerton	69	71	68	74	282	20,107.14
David Carter	71	69	70	72	282	20,107.14
Gordon Brand, Jr.	70	73	67	73	283	16,000
Marc Farry	68	73	70	72	283	16,000
Soren Kjeldsen	71	71	67	74	283	16,000
Ilya Goroneskoul	76	67	69	71	283	16,000
Richard Bland	72	67	70	74	283	16,000
Julien Van Hauwe	74	68	70	71	283	16,000
Alastair Forsyth	68	73	71	71	283	16,000
Richard Sterne	71	71	69	72	283	16,000
*Jean-Baptiste Gonnet	70	71	72	70	283	
Gary Murphy	68	74	74	68	284	13,250
Peter Lawrie	69	73	67	75	284	13,250
Francois Delamontagne	69	69	73	73	284	13,250
Olivier Edmond	70	72	72	71	285	11,750
Jean Louis Guepy	71	72	72	70	285	11,750
Simon Dyson	70	69	69	77	285	11,750
Peter Fowler	72	69	70	75	286	9,750
Kenneth Ferrie	71	72	73	70	286	9,750
Trevor Immelman	71	72	71	72	286	9,750

	SCORES				TOTAL	MONEY
Jonathan Lomas	69	74	74	69	286	9,750
Mathias Gronberg	72	70	68	76	286	9,750
Anders Hansen	70	66	75	76	287	7,833.33
Gustavo Rojas	71	69	73	74	287	7,833.33
Gary Birch, Jr.	67	74	71	75	287	7,833.33
Ronan Rafferty	70	72	71	75	288	6,375
Eduardo Romero	75	68	70	75	288	6,375
Greg Turner	73	69	69	77	288	6,375
Arjun Atwal	72	71	69	76	288	6,375
Henrik Stenson	71	70	72	75	288	6,375
Miles Tunnicliff	74	69	68	77	288	6,375
Emanuele Canonica	69	74	74	71	288	6,375
Fredrik Widmark	73	69	74	72	288	6,375
Gary Orr	71	72	74	72	289	5,125
David Park	72	69	73	75	289	5,125
Darren Fichardt	71	68	75	76	290	4,750
Sven Struver	70	72	71	78	291	4,160
Ian Garbutt	71	71	72	77	291	4,160
*Eric Chaudouet	66	77	69	79	291	
Per Nyman	72	69	75	76	292	3,742.50
Mark Pilkington	72	71	74	75	292	3,742.50
Mikko Ilonen	73	70	74	75	292	3,742.50
Charl Schwartzel	70	68	74	80	292	3,742.50
Gary Evans	72	69	71	82	294	3,735

Smurfit European Open

The K Club, Dublin, Ireland
Par 35-37–72; 7,337 yards

July 3-6
purse, €2,887,500

	SCORES				TOTAL	MONEY
Phillip Price	66	69	67	70	272	€481,245.20
Mark McNulty	68	69	68	68	273	250,793.80
Alastair Forsyth	66	70	69	68	273	250,793.80
Gary Evans	68	70	69	68	275	144,375
Eduardo Romero	69	68	71	68	276	111,746.30
Darren Clarke	67	68	70	71	276	111,746.30
Jarmo Sandelin	72	66	67	73	278	79,406.25
Andrew Coltart	67	70	70	71	278	79,406.25
Barry Lane	70	70	69	70	279	58,520
Angel Cabrera	70	69	66	74	279	58,520
Lee Westwood	70	71	69	69	279	58,520
Colin Montgomerie	68	71	73	68	280	49,665
Carlos Rodiles	73	70	70	68	281	44,371.25
Raymond Russell	71	73	67	70	281	44,371.25
Paul Casey	73	71	68	69	281	44,371.25
Mark Roe	71	70	71	70	282	38,981.25
Raphael Jacquelin	72	70	71	69	282	38,981.25
Thomas Bjorn	71	71	72	68	282	38,981.25
Roger Chapman	70	73	72	68	283	34,144.69
Nick O'Hern	70	72	70	71	283	34,144.69
David Lynn	71	71	70	71	283	34,144.69
Mikko Ilonen	69	71	73	70	283	34,144.69
Mark James	72	69	68	75	284	30,463.13
Bernhard Langer	73	67	71	73	284	30,463.13
Brian Davis	76	66	74	68	284	30,463.13
Matthew Blackey	73	69	71	71	284	30,463.13

	SCORES				TOTAL	MONEY
Gary Murphy	67	75	71	72	285	25,698.75
Shaun Webster	70	76	65	74	285	25,698.75
Soren Hansen	67	75	69	74	285	25,698.75
Rolf Muntz	73	69	71	72	285	25,698.75
John Bickerton	71	73	71	70	285	25,698.75
Retief Goosen	66	74	68	77	285	25,698.75
Charl Schwartzel	72	64	76	73	285	25,698.75
Nick Faldo	75	70	69	72	286	21,656.25
Mathias Gronberg	73	65	77	71	286	21,656.25
David Carter	73	73	67	73	286	21,656.25
Klas Eriksson	69	72	67	79	287	18,191.25
Anders Hansen	73	73	71	70	287	18,191.25
Darren Fichardt	74	71	69	73	287	18,191.25
Miguel Angel Jimenez	74	72	73	68	287	18,191.25
Paul McGinley	72	73	70	72	287	18,191.25
Stephen Scahill	69	71	74	73	287	18,191.25
Bradley Dredge	75	70	71	71	287	18,191.25
Fredrik Andersson	67	74	69	77	287	18,191.25
Niclas Fasth	70	75	73	69	287	18,191.25
Richard Green	73	73	68	74	288	14,437.50
Andrew Raitt	69	73	74	72	288	14,437.50
Richard Sterne	74	70	71	73	288	14,437.50
Jamie Donaldson	71	70	77	70	288	14,437.50
Sandy Lyle	72	73	70	74	289	11,550
Steve Webster	73	71	73	72	289	11,550
Anthony Wall	74	72	73	70	289	11,550
Julien Clement	73	72	74	70	289	11,550
Miles Tunnicliff	74	68	76	71	289	11,550
Stephen Gallacher	71	74	70	74	289	11,550
David Gilford	73	73	69	75	290	8,720.25
Stephen Leaney	74	71	73	72	290	8,720.25
Nicolas Colsaerts	75	69	70	76	290	8,720.25
Nicolas Vanhootegem	74	71	72	73	290	8,720.25
Brett Rumford	75	71	72	72	290	8,720.25
David Howell	71	74	74	72	291	6,504.09
Padraig Harrington	73	73	73	72	291	6,504.09
Marten Olander	71	71	73	76	291	6,504.09
Damien McGrane	73	72	73	73	291	6,504.09
Arjun Atwal	76	70	74	71	291	6,504.09
Greg Owen	70	74	72	75	291	6,504.09
David Drysdale	74	72	69	76	291	6,504.09
Mark Pilkington	72	72	77	70	291	6,504.09
Ben Mason	72	72	74	73	291	6,504.09
Graeme McDowell	69	73	73	76	291	6,504.09
Andrew Oldcorn	73	72	73	74	292	4,326.50
Ian Woosnam	74	70	75	73	292	4,326.50
Michael Campbell	70	75	70	77	292	4,326.50
Mikael Lundberg	73	73	68	78	292	4,326.50
Stephen Dodd	70	73	75	75	293	4,319
Gustavo Rojas	71	75	78	71	295	4,316
Andrew Marshall	75	71	71	79	296	4,313
Costantino Rocca	72	73	77	75	297	4,310
Peter Hedblom	72	73	75	79	299	4,307

Barclays Scottish Open

Loch Lomond Golf Club, Glasgow, Scotland
Par 36-35–71; 7,095 yards

July 10-13
purse, €3,240,447

	SCORES				TOTAL	MONEY
Ernie Els	64	67	67	69	267	€532,888.90
Phillip Price	67	68	68	69	272	277,708
Darren Clarke	69	70	64	69	272	277,708
Gary Murphy	70	69	68	67	274	159,869.60
Ian Poulter	70	68	68	69	275	114,466.60
Gary Evans	71	71	68	65	275	114,466.60
Peter Lonard	70	68	68	69	275	114,466.60
Mark Roe	72	68	71	65	276	75,778.19
Iain Pyman	69	71	67	69	276	75,778.19
Bradley Dredge	69	68	70	70	277	57,313.25
Alastair Forsyth	72	69	66	70	277	57,313.25
Paul Casey	69	74	68	66	277	57,313.25
Charl Schwartzel	75	68	67	67	277	57,313.25
David Howell	66	73	70	69	278	44,177.30
Anders Hansen	72	69	72	65	278	44,177.30
Kenneth Ferrie	72	72	68	66	278	44,177.30
Nick O'Hern	72	72	65	69	278	44,177.30
David Lynn	70	70	70	68	278	44,177.30
Lee Westwood	71	72	67	68	278	44,177.30
Brian Davis	71	70	69	69	279	36,690.07
Raphael Jacquelin	72	70	68	69	279	36,690.07
Paul McGinley	73	71	67	68	279	36,690.07
Rolf Muntz	72	70	72	65	279	36,690.07
Eduardo Romero	72	73	68	67	280	32,293.66
Peter O'Malley	67	76	62	75	280	32,293.66
Benn Barham	72	70	69	69	280	32,293.66
Tim Clark	68	68	71	73	280	32,293.66
Martin Maritz	67	71	70	72	280	32,293.66
Jose Manuel Lara	73	69	72	67	281	27,017.96
Jean-Francois Remesy	71	71	72	67	281	27,017.96
Soren Hansen	74	71	67	69	281	27,017.96
Marcel Siem	69	73	69	70	281	27,017.96
Thomas Bjorn	72	70	67	72	281	27,017.96
Niclas Fasth	73	71	71	66	281	27,017.96
Maarten Lafeber	74	69	69	70	282	22,701.48
Shaun Webster	72	68	67	75	282	22,701.48
Scott Henderson	70	71	71	70	282	22,701.48
Phil Mickelson	76	68	70	68	282	22,701.48
Raymond Russell	70	72	71	69	282	22,701.48
Andrew Oldcorn	71	71	72	69	283	19,184.35
Greg Turner	71	71	75	66	283	19,184.35
Stephen Leaney	74	70	72	67	283	19,184.35
Nicolas Colsaerts	69	71	71	72	283	19,184.35
Simon Khan	73	70	70	70	283	19,184.35
Fredrik Andersson	70	72	72	69	283	19,184.35
Jose Maria Olazabal	73	72	71	68	284	15,986.96
Paul Eales	68	73	71	72	284	15,986.96
Julien Clement	69	74	69	72	284	15,986.96
Robert Karlsson	71	69	69	75	284	15,986.96
Robert-Jan Derksen	71	72	68	74	285	11,606.53
Colin Montgomerie	71	70	72	72	285	11,606.53
Gregory Havret	70	74	70	71	285	11,606.53
Richard Bland	72	71	69	73	285	11,606.53
Stephen Dodd	72	73	72	68	285	11,606.53

	SCORES				TOTAL	MONEY
Andrew Coltart	75	68	70	72	285	11,606.53
Henrik Nystrom	73	71	73	68	285	11,606.53
Terry Price	67	68	72	78	285	11,606.53
Brett Rumford	67	72	72	74	285	11,606.53
John Rollins	70	75	76	64	285	11,606.53
Roger Chapman	73	70	68	75	286	8,153.35
Miguel Angel Jimenez	72	72	71	71	286	8,153.35
Ian Garbutt	70	69	75	72	286	8,153.35
Gary Orr	73	72	70	71	286	8,153.35
David Carter	74	70	72	70	286	8,153.35
Carl Pettersson	69	72	68	77	286	8,153.35
Klas Eriksson	70	74	68	75	287	6,714.52
Richard Green	71	74	72	70	287	6,714.52
Stephen Gallacher	73	70	74	70	287	6,714.52
Steve Webster	70	73	73	72	288	5,571.18
Jarmo Sandelin	71	68	75	74	288	5,571.18
Graeme McDowell	71	71	72	74	288	5,571.18
Emanuele Canonica	71	71	77	70	289	4,791.50
Tobias Dier	71	74	69	75	289	4,791.50
Sandy Lyle	73	72	74	74	293	4,787
Julien Van Hauwe	69	76	74	75	294	4,784
Gordon Brand, Jr.	71	72	74	78	295	4,781
Ricardo Gonzalez	72	73	77	74	296	4,778

The Open Championship

Royal St. George's Golf Club, Sandwich, England
Par 36-35–71; 7,106 yards

July 17-20
purse, €5,685,750

	SCORES				TOTAL	MONEY
Ben Curtis	72	72	70	69	283	€1,010,800
Vijay Singh	75	70	69	70	284	498,180
Thomas Bjorn	73	70	69	72	284	498,180
Tiger Woods	73	72	69	71	285	267,140
Davis Love	69	72	72	72	285	267,140
Brian Davis	77	73	68	68	286	194,218
Fredrik Jacobson	70	76	70	70	286	194,218
Nick Faldo	76	74	67	70	287	141,151
Kenny Perry	74	70	70	73	287	141,151
Hennie Otto	68	76	75	69	288	98,192
Retief Goosen	73	75	71	69	288	98,192
Gary Evans	71	75	70	72	288	98,192
Phillip Price	74	72	69	73	288	98,192
Sergio Garcia	73	71	70	74	288	98,192
Chad Campbell	74	71	72	72	289	71,237.34
Stuart Appleby	75	71	71	72	289	71,237.34
Pierre Fulke	77	72	67	73	289	71,237.34
Greg Norman	69	79	74	68	290	60,648
Tom Watson	71	77	73	69	290	60,648
Mathias Gronberg	71	74	73	72	290	60,648
Ernie Els	78	68	72	72	290	60,648
Padraig Harrington	75	73	74	69	291	47,531.67
K.J. Choi	77	72	72	70	291	47,531.67
J.L. Lewis	78	70	72	71	291	47,531.67
Peter Fowler	77	73	70	71	291	47,531.67
Thomas Levet	71	73	74	73	291	47,531.67
Angel Cabrera	75	73	70	73	291	47,531.67

	SCORES				TOTAL	MONEY
Mike Weir	74	76	71	71	292	37,544
Andrew Oldcorn	72	74	73	73	292	37,544
Paul McGinley	77	73	69	73	292	37,544
Nick Price	74	72	72	74	292	37,544
Mark Foster	73	73	72	74	292	37,544
S.K. Ho	70	73	72	77	292	37,544
Stewart Cink	75	75	75	68	293	27,115.11
Bob Estes	77	71	76	69	293	27,115.11
Adam Mednick	76	72	76	69	293	27,115.11
Shingo Katayama	76	73	73	71	293	27,115.11
Gary Murphy	73	74	73	73	293	27,115.11
Duffy Waldorf	76	73	71	73	293	27,115.11
Marco Ruiz	73	71	75	74	293	27,115.11
Jose Coceres	77	70	72	74	293	27,115.11
Scott McCarron	71	74	73	75	293	27,115.11
Rich Beem	76	74	75	69	294	20,577
Robert Allenby	73	75	74	72	294	20,577
Tom Byrum	77	72	71	74	294	20,577
Tom Lehman	77	73	72	73	295	17,132.03
Markus Brier	76	71	74	74	295	17,132.03
Anthony Wall	75	74	71	75	295	17,132.03
Brad Faxon	77	73	70	75	295	17,132.03
Ian Poulter	78	72	70	75	295	17,132.03
Mathew Goggin	76	72	70	77	295	17,132.03
Fred Couples	71	75	71	78	295	17,132.03
Mark McNulty	79	71	77	69	296	14,728.80
Rory Sabbatini	79	71	75	71	296	14,728.80
Michael Campbell	78	72	74	72	296	14,728.80
Trevor Immelman	77	73	72	74	296	14,728.80
Raphael Jacquelin	77	71	72	76	296	14,728.80
David Lynn	73	76	71	76	296	14,728.80
Alastair Forsyth	74	70	78	75	297	13,790.20
Craig Parry	73	73	76	75	297	13,790.20
Skip Kendall	73	76	73	75	297	13,790.20
Darren Clarke	75	75	71	76	297	13,790.20
Phil Mickelson	74	72	73	78	297	13,790.20
Peter Lonard	73	73	70	81	297	13,790.20
Stephen Leaney	74	76	78	70	298	13,068.20
Mark O'Meara	73	77	77	71	298	13,068.20
Charles Howell	71	76	77	74	298	13,068.20
Len Mattiace	74	75	74	75	298	13,068.20
Katsuyoshi Tomori	72	77	75	76	300	12,707.20
John Rollins	72	76	78	75	301	12,562.80
Chris Smith	74	73	76	79	302	12,418.40
Ian Woosnam	73	75	80	75	303	12,201.80
John Daly	75	74	74	80	303	12,201.80
Mark Roe	77	70			DQ	11,913
Jesper Parnevik	72	75			DQ	11,913

Out of Final 36 Holes

Mark Calcavecchia	78	73			151	4,332
Anders Hansen	76	75			151	4,332
Lee Janzen	76	75			151	4,332
Justin Leonard	74	77			151	4,332
Jose Maria Olazabal	74	77			151	4,332
Eduardo Romero	75	76			151	4,332
Steen Tinning	78	73			151	4,332
Lee Westwood	76	75			151	4,332
Bradley Dredge	80	72			152	4,332

	SCORES		TOTAL	MONEY
Niclas Fasth	76	76	152	4,332
Jim Furyk	74	78	152	4,332
Ignacio Garrido	80	72	152	4,332
Jay Haas	80	72	152	4,332
Soren Kjeldsen	74	78	152	4,332
Bernhard Langer	76	76	152	4,332
Sandy Lyle	73	79	152	4,332
Nick O'Hern	82	70	152	4,332
Corey Pavin	74	78	152	4,332
Andrew Raitt	74	78	152	4,332
Hal Sutton	76	76	152	4,332
Scott Verplank	78	74	152	4,332
*Ricky Barnes	79	74	153	
Steven Bowditch	77	76	153	3,610
Joe Durant	77	76	153	3,610
Todd Hamilton	76	77	153	3,610
Jarrod Moseley	74	79	153	3,610
Rolf Muntz	82	71	153	3,610
Cameron Percy	76	77	153	3,610
Chris Riley	78	75	153	3,610
Jeff Sluman	78	75	153	3,610
David Toms	80	73	153	3,610
Chris DiMarco	79	75	154	3,610
Soren Hansen	80	74	154	3,610
Cliff Kresge	81	73	154	3,610
Hirofumi Miyase	81	73	154	3,610
Peter O'Malley	78	76	154	3,610
Marten Olander	79	75	154	3,610
Luke Donald	76	79	155	3,610
Kenneth Ferrie	74	81	155	3,610
Fred Funk	75	80	155	3,610
Dudley Hart	76	79	155	3,610
Paul Lawrie	81	74	155	3,610
Craig Perks	78	77	155	3,610
Nobuhito Sato	72	83	155	3,610
Charl Schwartzel	78	77	155	3,610
Christopher Smith	77	78	155	3,610
Paul Casey	85	71	156	3,249
Robert-Jan Derksen	78	78	156	3,249
Steve Flesch	73	83	156	3,249
David Howell	77	79	156	3,249
Jonathan Kaye	75	81	156	3,249
Shigeki Maruyama	83	73	156	3,249
Greg Owen	79	77	156	3,249
Adam Scott	82	74	156	3,249
Simon Wakefield	82	74	156	3,249
*Gary Wolstenholme	74	82	156	
Gary Emerson	77	80	157	3,249
Euan Little	80	77	157	3,249
Jyoti Randhawa	80	77	157	3,249
Mark Smith	80	77	157	3,249
Hideto Tanihara	79	78	157	3,249
Paul Wesselingh	79	78	157	3,249
Ben Crane	78	80	158	3,249
Iain Pyman	81	77	158	3,249
Justin Rose	79	80	159	3,249
*Scott Godfrey	82	78	160	
David Smail	77	83	160	3,249
David Duval	83	78	161	3,249
Philip Golding	83	78	161	3,249

	SCORES				TOTAL	MONEY
Malcolm Mackenzie	82	79			161	3,249
Robert Coles	85	77			162	2,888
Adam Le Vesconte	82	80			162	2,888
Anthony Sproston	83	80			163	2,888
Andrew George	79	85			164	2,888
Noboru Sugai	83	82			165	2,888
Toru Taniguchi	82	87			169	2,888
Charles Challen	86	87			173	2,888
Steve Elkington					WD	2,888
Colin Montgomerie					WD	2,888
Jerry Kelly					WD	2,888
Paul Azinger					WD	2,888

Nissan Irish Open

Portmarnock Golf Club, Dublin, Ireland
Par 36-36–72; 7,363 yards

July 24-27
purse, €1,800,000

	SCORES				TOTAL	MONEY
Michael Campbell	66	69	71	71	277	€300,000
Peter Hedblom	70	71	68	68	277	156,340
Thomas Bjorn	64	74	68	71	277	156,340
(Campbell defeated Hedblom and Bjorn on first playoff hole.)						
David Lynn	69	65	72	73	279	83,160
Greg Owen	68	71	68	72	279	83,160
Sven Struver	71	71	69	69	280	63,000
Robert Karlsson	69	69	69	75	282	49,500
Peter Lonard	71	68	69	74	282	49,500
Greg Turner	71	71	69	72	283	38,160
Raymond Russell	71	73	68	71	283	38,160
Gary Murphy	74	68	70	72	284	28,740
Paul Broadhurst	67	74	71	72	284	28,740
Miguel Angel Jimenez	73	68	71	72	284	28,740
Peter O'Malley	70	69	72	73	284	28,740
Lee Westwood	70	72	69	73	284	28,740
John Bickerton	71	72	72	69	284	28,740
Shaun Webster	72	71	67	75	285	22,110
Gary Emerson	68	71	72	74	285	22,110
Simon Khan	68	73	70	74	285	22,110
Mark Pilkington	76	67	69	73	285	22,110
Brett Rumford	72	71	70	72	285	22,110
Charl Schwartzel	71	71	70	73	285	22,110
Peter Fowler	70	73	70	73	286	17,370
Alvaro Salto	70	72	71	73	286	17,370
Jose Maria Olazabal	70	73	72	71	286	17,370
Peter Lawrie	70	68	71	77	286	17,370
Ian Poulter	70	71	69	76	286	17,370
Jarrod Moseley	70	72	71	73	286	17,370
Christian Cevaer	72	71	70	73	286	17,370
James Kingston	73	69	71	73	286	17,370
Luke Donald	68	74	69	75	286	17,370
Ben Mason	69	71	70	76	286	17,370
Malcolm Mackenzie	70	72	73	72	287	13,920
Paul McGinley	74	66	76	71	287	13,920
Andrew Raitt	70	72	70	75	287	13,920
Jean-Francois Remesy	69	75	71	73	288	11,700
Maarten Lafeber	72	69	71	76	288	11,700

	SCORES				TOTAL	MONEY
Arjun Atwal	70	74	70	74	288	11,700
Jean Hugo	70	73	71	74	288	11,700
Jean-Francois Lucquin	72	68	70	78	288	11,700
Nicolas Colsaerts	72	72	73	71	288	11,700
Ian Garbutt	72	70	71	75	288	11,700
Markus Brier	71	71	69	77	288	11,700
Matthew Blackey	75	67	71	75	288	11,700
Mark Roe	69	74	72	74	289	9,720
Peter Baker	72	70	71	76	289	9,720
Damien McGrane	72	70	76	72	290	8,460
Jesus Maria Arruti	73	71	72	74	290	8,460
Phillip Price	68	76	71	75	290	8,460
Darren Clarke	75	68	72	75	290	8,460
Fredrik Andersson	71	73	73	73	290	8,460
David Gilford	70	74	75	72	291	6,840
Didier de Vooght	71	73	74	73	291	6,840
Patrik Sjoland	73	70	73	75	291	6,840
Terry Price	73	70	77	71	291	6,840
Carlos Rodiles	69	75	72	76	292	5,340
Simon Wakefield	70	73	77	72	292	5,340
David Park	71	72	70	79	292	5,340
Lee S. James	71	72	72	77	292	5,340
Damian Mooney	70	74	75	73	292	5,340
Stephen Gallacher	68	73	76	75	292	5,340
Henrik Bjornstad	74	70	72	77	293	4,590
Soren Hansen	72	72	71	78	293	4,590
Klas Eriksson	72	68	77	77	294	4,230
Euan Little	72	71	72	79	294	4,230
Ian Woosnam	72	70	75	78	295	3,690
Steve Webster	71	73	72	79	295	3,690
Jamie Spence	71	71	77	76	295	3,690
Nick Dougherty	71	71	77	76	295	3,690
Robert Coles	74	69	78	75	296	3,280
Sandy Lyle	72	71	75	79	297	2,697
Jonathan Lomas	74	69	76	78	297	2,697
Simon Dyson	69	72	74	82	297	2,697
Robert Rock	73	71	76	78	298	2,691
Pierre Fulke	74	70	81	80	305	2,688

Scandic Carlsberg Scandinavian Masters

Barseback Golf & Country Club, Malmo, Sweden
Par 36-36–72; 7,365 yards

July 31-August 3
purse, €1,900,000

	SCORES				TOTAL	MONEY
Adam Scott	70	71	67	69	277	€316,660
Nick Dougherty	67	69	74	69	279	211,110
Robert Karlsson	71	69	71	69	280	98,166.66
Andrew Coltart	67	76	69	68	280	98,166.66
Luke Donald	71	68	71	70	280	98,166.66
Miguel Angel Jimenez	73	70	71	67	281	61,750
Carl Pettersson	69	75	66	71	281	61,750
Jamie Spence	74	70	69	69	282	42,686.67
Peter Hedblom	70	70	71	71	282	42,686.67
Fredrik Jacobson	71	70	72	69	282	42,686.67
Maarten Lafeber	68	71	69	75	283	34,960
Philip Archer	71	70	71	72	284	30,067.50

	SCORES				TOTAL	MONEY
Richard S. Johnson	71	71	69	73	284	30,067.50
Adam Mednick	73	69	71	71	284	30,067.50
Michael Campbell	70	72	71	71	284	30,067.50
Mark Roe	71	70	71	73	285	23,465
Robert-Jan Derksen	73	71	67	74	285	23,465
Mark Foster	74	67	73	71	285	23,465
Sven Struver	72	71	70	72	285	23,465
Soren Kjeldsen	71	70	70	74	285	23,465
Carlos Rodiles	69	72	73	71	285	23,465
Jamie Donaldson	76	69	70	70	285	23,465
Charl Schwartzel	72	72	69	72	285	23,465
Gordon Brand, Jr.	73	71	73	69	286	17,765
Bernhard Langer	70	71	72	73	286	17,765
Barry Lane	71	75	71	69	286	17,765
Damien McGrane	73	73	69	71	286	17,765
Henrik Stenson	73	72	73	68	286	17,765
Gary Orr	71	71	69	75	286	17,765
Fredrik Andersson	74	68	75	69	286	17,765
Raymond Russell	72	70	71	73	286	17,765
Jean Louis Guepy	75	71	69	71	286	17,765
Ben Mason	72	72	73	69	286	17,765
Mark James	69	70	72	76	287	14,250
Steve Webster	70	72	68	77	287	14,250
Simon Wakefield	70	71	74	72	287	14,250
David Gilford	67	74	75	72	288	12,730
Marten Olander	72	72	72	72	288	12,730
Paul Broadhurst	71	74	74	69	288	12,730
Tobias Dier	72	71	73	72	288	12,730
Kevin Na	68	74	74	72	288	12,730
Richard Bland	71	75	69	74	289	10,830
Nicolas Colsaerts	73	73	73	70	289	10,830
Roger Wessels	72	75	72	70	289	10,830
Andrew Raitt	74	72	72	71	289	10,830
Terry Price	71	73	73	72	289	10,830
Jean-Francois Remesy	72	71	75	72	290	8,740
Trevor Immelman	73	74	74	69	290	8,740
Jonathan Lomas	72	73	76	69	290	8,740
Ignacio Garrido	72	72	70	76	290	8,740
Stephen Scahill	68	74	78	70	290	8,740
Henrik Nystrom	73	72	76	69	290	8,740
Brian Davis	71	73	75	72	291	6,840
Paul McGinley	75	72	74	70	291	6,840
Jarmo Sandelin	71	73	73	74	291	6,840
Graeme McDowell	73	72	75	71	291	6,840
Greg Turner	69	74	76	73	292	5,605
Andrew Marshall	72	74	74	72	292	5,605
Ian Garbutt	72	71	73	76	292	5,605
Bradley Dredge	75	71	76	70	292	5,605
Ronan Rafferty	73	72	73	75	293	4,750
Philip Golding	75	72	75	71	293	4,750
Johan Rystrom	77	70	72	74	293	4,750
Christopher Hanell	75	72	73	73	293	4,750
Aaron Baddeley	72	74	72	75	293	4,750
Marc Farry	74	71	76	73	294	3,895
Gary Emerson	78	69	76	71	294	3,895
Peter Baker	73	73	76	72	294	3,895
Julien Clement	75	71	75	73	294	3,895
Gregory Havret	70	75	76	74	295	3,055.67
Simon Hurd	69	73	73	80	295	3,055.67
Greg Owen	71	73	74	77	295	3,055.67

	SCORES				TOTAL	MONEY
Joakim Haeggman	73	74	78	71	296	2,842.50
Rolf Muntz	76	71	74	75	296	2,842.50
Arjun Atwal	73	68	76	80	297	2,836.50
Zane Scotland	73	73	77	74	297	2,836.50
Andrew Oldcorn	73	74	76	75	298	2,832
Roger Chapman	74	73	76	76	299	2,829
Warren Bennett	74	73	76	77	300	2,826
Mark Pilkington	70	77	85	80	312	2,823

Nordic Open

Simon's Golf Club, Copenhagen, Denmark
Par 35-37–72; 7,027 yards

August 7-10
purse, €1,600,000

	SCORES				TOTAL	MONEY
Ian Poulter	68	67	65	66	266	€266,660
Colin Montgomerie	70	65	64	68	267	177,770
Gregory Havret	68	63	69	68	268	82,666.66
Soren Hansen	71	66	62	69	268	82,666.66
Stephen Gallacher	71	65	69	63	268	82,666.66
Brian Davis	66	68	67	68	269	56,000
David Gilford	66	67	67	70	270	48,000
Marten Olander	66	73	65	67	271	34,320
Steve Webster	66	71	69	65	271	34,320
Miguel Angel Jimenez	65	70	68	68	271	34,320
Patrik Sjoland	69	64	68	70	271	34,320
Julien Clement	70	70	68	64	272	27,520
Peter Lawrie	69	66	73	65	273	24,586.67
Henrik Bjornstad	72	69	66	66	273	24,586.67
Andrew Coltart	66	69	69	69	273	24,586.67
Peter Hedblom	70	68	69	67	274	22,080
Miles Tunnicliff	73	64	68	69	274	22,080
Mark Foster	69	68	67	71	275	19,560
Maarten Lafeber	72	69	66	68	275	19,560
Thomas Bjorn	67	69	72	67	275	19,560
Kevin Na	70	64	69	72	275	19,560
Soren Kjeldsen	68	72	69	67	276	17,600
Peter Jespersen	68	68	71	69	276	17,600
David Park	67	71	68	70	276	17,600
Raphael Jacquelin	62	72	74	69	277	14,254.55
Greg Turner	67	72	68	70	277	14,254.55
Alessandro Tadini	72	67	70	68	277	14,254.55
Nicolas Colsaerts	73	68	67	69	277	14,254.55
Peter O'Malley	70	70	67	70	277	14,254.55
Jorge Berendt	70	71	68	68	277	14,254.55
Stephen Scahill	70	68	74	65	277	14,254.55
John Bickerton	67	70	67	73	277	14,254.55
Fredrik Widmark	67	70	67	73	277	14,254.55
Francois Delamontagne	67	70	69	71	277	14,254.55
Marcus Fraser	68	70	72	67	277	14,254.55
Malcolm Mackenzie	72	67	67	72	278	10,720
Jamie Spence	69	72	68	69	278	10,720
Peter Baker	67	72	70	69	278	10,720
Gustavo Rojas	72	69	71	66	278	10,720
Benn Barham	72	66	73	67	278	10,720
Simon Dyson	71	70	66	71	278	10,720
David Dixon	70	69	71	68	278	10,720

	SCORES				TOTAL	MONEY
Mattias Eliasson	72	69	67	71	279	8,480
Damien McGrane	71	69	71	68	279	8,480
Jonathan Lomas	69	65	73	72	279	8,480
Christian Cevaer	68	71	69	71	279	8,480
David Lynn	67	66	73	73	279	8,480
Terry Price	71	69	69	70	279	8,480
Matthew Cort	68	70	69	72	279	8,480
David Howell	72	68	70	70	280	6,240
Philip Archer	65	69	71	75	280	6,240
Philip Golding	67	69	72	72	280	6,240
Andrew Raitt	66	68	74	72	280	6,240
Fredrik Andersson	70	68	73	69	280	6,240
Raymond Russell	65	72	71	72	280	6,240
Jean Louis Guepy	69	72	70	69	280	6,240
Barry Lane	72	66	72	71	281	4,640
Shaun Webster	69	68	72	72	281	4,640
Steen Tinning	72	68	71	70	281	4,640
Jean Hugo	71	69	72	69	281	4,640
David Carter	69	70	70	72	281	4,640
Roger Chapman	68	70	75	69	282	3,680
Miguel Angel Martin	70	70	71	71	282	3,680
Robert-Jan Derksen	68	72	72	70	282	3,680
Chris Gane	70	68	71	73	282	3,680
Marcel Siem	73	68	72	69	282	3,680
Per Nyman	73	68	70	71	282	3,680
Fernando Roca	70	71	74	67	282	3,680
Klas Eriksson	68	69	76	70	283	2,562.86
Sven Struver	68	73	72	70	283	2,562.86
Michael Archer	69	69	70	75	283	2,562.86
Jan-Are Larsen	68	70	70	75	283	2,562.86
Robert Karlsson	67	72	71	73	283	2,562.86
Matthew Blackey	72	69	69	73	283	2,562.86
Tobias Dier	67	67	73	76	283	2,562.86
Jose Manuel Lara	73	68	69	74	284	2,382
Stuart Little	69	70	71	74	284	2,382
Jamie Donaldson	69	69	77	69	284	2,382
Titch Moore	71	70	74	70	285	2,373
Rolf Muntz	73	67	75	70	285	2,373
Graeme McDowell	73	68	73	71	285	2,373
Emanuele Canonica	72	67	71	76	286	2,365.50
Nick Dougherty	71	70	71	74	286	2,365.50
Jean-Francois Lucquin	71	70	75	71	287	2,359.50
Johan Rystrom	69	72	76	70	287	2,359.50
Ben Mason	73	68	75	72	288	2,355

BMW Russian Open

Le Meridien Moscow Golf & Country Club, Moscow, Russia   August 14-17
Par 36-36–72; 7,174 yards   purse, €400,000

	SCORES				TOTAL	MONEY
Marcus Fraser	68	65	68	68	269	€66,660
Martin Wiegele	68	66	67	68	269	44,440
(Fraser defeated Wiegele on second playoff hole.)						
Peter Hanson	71	68	67	66	272	25,040
Jose Manuel Carriles	68	67	70	69	274	15,740
Tim Milford	72	68	67	67	274	15,740

	SCORES				TOTAL	MONEY
Andrew Coltart	69	67	69	69	274	15,740
Graeme Storm	71	69	69	65	274	15,740
Mads Vibe-Hastrup	70	70	67	68	275	10,000
Kalle Brink	69	66	71	70	276	8,480
Robert Rock	68	69	70	69	276	8,480
Jesus Maria Arruti	68	69	69	71	277	6,893.33
Michele Reale	72	68	71	66	277	6,893.33
Richard McEvoy	70	68	71	68	277	6,893.33
Damien McGrane	70	68	69	71	278	5,422.86
Garry Houston	74	66	66	72	278	5,422.86
Shaun Webster	73	66	68	71	278	5,422.86
Johan Edfors	67	68	72	71	278	5,422.86
Ian Garbutt	69	70	69	70	278	5,422.86
David Orr	68	72	67	71	278	5,422.86
Steven O'Hara	67	72	70	69	278	5,422.86
Alvaro Salto	72	68	70	69	279	4,400
Jamie Little	71	68	72	68	279	4,400
Sion Bebb	69	69	69	72	279	4,400
Markus Brier	72	68	71	68	279	4,400
Sebastian Fernandez	69	69	71	70	279	4,400
Michael Archer	68	71	71	70	280	3,800
Richard Dinsdale	69	70	71	70	280	3,800
James Hepworth	73	65	72	70	280	3,800
Erol Simsek	70	68	73	69	280	3,800
Oskar Bergman	68	71	71	70	280	3,800
Renaud Guillard	70	66	71	74	281	3,160
Nicolas Vanhootegem	66	72	68	75	281	3,160
Andrew Raitt	70	72	68	71	281	3,160
Joakim Rask	67	69	73	72	281	3,160
Ivo Giner	70	71	72	68	281	3,160
Jamie Elson	69	65	78	69	281	3,160
Chris Gane	73	69	70	70	282	2,680
Massimo Florioli	71	70	67	74	282	2,680
Didier de Vooght	71	71	69	71	282	2,680
Ben Mason	73	69	71	69	282	2,680
David Ryles	68	66	68	80	282	2,680
Fredrik Orest	69	72	71	71	283	2,200
Mark Davis	67	69	74	73	283	2,200
Sven Struver	70	70	73	70	283	2,200
Pasi Purhonen	71	66	71	75	283	2,200
Benoit Teilleria	71	70	72	70	283	2,200
Marco Bernardini	68	72	72	71	283	2,200
Steven Bowditch	71	69	66	77	283	2,200
Euan Little	70	72	73	69	284	1,640
Stuart Little	74	66	71	73	284	1,640
Jan-Are Larsen	71	69	70	74	284	1,640
Mark Pilkington	69	73	71	71	284	1,640
Jean Louis Guepy	67	73	72	72	284	1,640
John Mellor	73	68	70	73	284	1,640
Brad Kennedy	69	70	70	75	284	1,640
Kalle Vainola	70	71	74	70	285	1,165.71
Scott Drummond	71	71	70	73	285	1,165.71
Ilya Goroneskoul	70	68	73	74	285	1,165.71
Stefano Reale	71	70	71	73	285	1,165.71
Thomas Besancenez	68	70	74	73	285	1,165.71
Pehr Magnebrant	67	74	74	70	285	1,165.71
Sebastien Delagrange	71	71	73	70	285	1,165.71
Mark Mouland	69	72	72	73	286	960
Dominique Nouailhac	73	69	72	72	286	960
Bjorn Pettersson	70	70	74	72	286	960

	SCORES				TOTAL	MONEY
Paul Dwyer	69	70	75	73	287	820
Federico Bisazza	71	71	70	75	287	820
Thomas Norret	70	72	70	75	287	820
Paul McKechnie	71	69	73	74	287	820
Philip Archer	69	71	73	75	288	618.33
Marcello Santi	67	72	74	75	288	618.33
Gianluca Baruffaldi	67	73	73	75	288	618.33
Lee S. James	69	70	75	74	288	618.33
Sam Walker	73	69	75	71	288	618.33
Regis Gustave	70	71	71	76	288	618.33
Lionel Alexandre	71	71	74	75	291	585
Hennie Walters	71	70	77	75	293	582

BMW International Open

Golfclub Munchen Nord-Eichenreid, Munich, Germany
Par 36-36–72; 6,963 yards

August 28-31
purse, €1,800,000

	SCORES				TOTAL	MONEY
Lee Westwood	65	68	70	66	269	€300,000
Alex Cejka	69	66	70	67	272	200,000
Raphael Jacquelin	62	69	71	71	273	79,200
Peter Hedblom	66	66	74	67	273	79,200
Gary Evans	66	68	68	71	273	79,200
Andrew Coltart	70	70	65	68	273	79,200
Paul Casey	65	69	70	69	273	79,200
Marcel Siem	64	70	68	72	274	40,440
Robert Karlsson	65	64	71	74	274	40,440
John Bickerton	67	68	68	71	274	40,440
David Howell	64	71	70	70	275	29,412
Brian Davis	68	69	65	73	275	29,412
Trevor Immelman	69	67	72	67	275	29,412
Gary Emerson	64	68	73	70	275	29,412
Stephen Gallacher	67	66	72	70	275	29,412
Carlos Rodiles	71	69	69	67	276	25,380
Soren Kjeldsen	69	67	71	70	277	22,110
Miguel Angel Jimenez	71	65	68	73	277	22,110
Paul McGinley	69	66	70	72	277	22,110
Ernie Els	68	71	74	64	277	22,110
Thomas Bjorn	64	70	70	73	277	22,110
Andrew Raitt	70	69	68	70	277	22,110
Bernhard Langer	67	72	72	67	278	18,180
Robert-Jan Derksen	75	65	68	70	278	18,180
Maarten Lafeber	68	72	68	70	278	18,180
Soren Hansen	68	67	74	69	278	18,180
Stephen Dodd	71	69	67	71	278	18,180
Charl Schwartzel	70	64	74	70	278	18,180
Kevin Na	71	69	71	67	278	18,180
Peter Fowler	74	66	70	69	279	14,940
Alessandro Tadini	73	67	68	71	279	14,940
Ignacio Garrido	71	68	69	71	279	14,940
Markus Brier	68	71	69	71	279	14,940
Jamie Donaldson	74	65	68	72	279	14,940
Marten Olander	69	69	70	72	280	12,420
Joakim Haeggman	71	65	71	73	280	12,420
Ian Garbutt	69	67	72	72	280	12,420
Gary Orr	71	68	70	71	280	12,420

	SCORES				TOTAL	MONEY
Stephen Scahill	68	68	71	73	280	12,420
Simon Dyson	69	68	70	73	280	12,420
Martin Maritz	66	71	69	74	280	12,420
Malcolm Mackenzie	69	66	72	74	281	10,260
Barry Lane	72	65	71	73	281	10,260
Simon Hurd	70	69	74	68	281	10,260
Raymond Russell	69	68	70	74	281	10,260
Lee S. James	71	69	68	73	281	10,260
Gordon Brand, Jr.	69	70	70	73	282	8,280
Roger Chapman	71	68	73	70	282	8,280
Darren Fichardt	71	67	71	73	282	8,280
Andrew Marshall	72	67	74	69	282	8,280
Charlie Wi	69	70	69	74	282	8,280
Nicolas Vanhootegem	69	70	70	73	282	8,280
Steen Tinning	67	72	71	73	283	6,840
David Lynn	69	71	70	73	283	6,840
Tobias Dier	69	68	70	77	284	6,300
Greg Owen	69	70	69	77	285	5,760
Brett Rumford	70	67	72	76	285	5,760
Shaun Webster	68	70	76	72	286	5,220
Johan Rystrom	68	70	74	74	286	5,220
Miles Tunnicliff	70	70	69	77	286	5,220
*Martin Kaymer	69	69	76	72	286	
Santiago Luna	71	68	75	73	287	4,680
Paul Broadhurst	72	67	73	75	287	4,680
Russell Claydon	70	69	73	75	287	4,680
Klas Eriksson	67	73	75	73	288	4,140
David Park	74	66	76	72	288	4,140
Fredrik Andersson	66	70	75	77	288	4,140
Gustavo Rojas	69	69	72	79	289	3,780
Benn Barham	68	71	76	79	294	3,600
Simon Wakefield	71	68	83	74	296	3,420
Jose Manuel Lara	68	66	78		WD	3,280

Omega European Masters

Crans-sur-Sierre Golf Club, Crans Montana, Switzerland
Par 36-35–71; 6,857 yards

September 4-7
purse, €1,600,000

	SCORES				TOTAL	MONEY
Ernie Els	65	69	68	65	267	€266,660
Michael Campbell	67	67	73	66	273	177,770
Eduardo Romero	66	67	67	74	274	100,160
Robert Karlsson	65	67	71	72	275	67,946.66
Emanuele Canonica	70	68	67	70	275	67,946.66
Andrew Coltart	70	72	66	67	275	67,946.66
Peter Hedblom	67	68	71	70	276	48,000
David Howell	68	69	67	73	277	30,720
Brian Davis	70	66	68	73	277	30,720
Miguel Angel Jimenez	69	69	72	67	277	30,720
Paul Eales	66	69	75	67	277	30,720
Jarrod Moseley	71	68	68	70	277	30,720
David Lynn	70	69	69	69	277	30,720
Paul Casey	68	70	67	72	277	30,720
Marc Farry	66	73	66	73	278	22,080
Raphael Jacquelin	69	67	68	74	278	22,080
Marten Olander	70	70	70	68	278	22,080

		SCORES			TOTAL	MONEY
Nathan Fritz	70	66	74	68	278	22,080
Mark Foster	71	70	67	71	279	18,920
Sergio Garcia	67	70	72	70	279	18,920
Mattias Eliasson	68	71	72	68	279	18,920
Erol Simsek	70	70	67	72	279	18,920
Carlos Rodiles	68	74	69	69	280	17,120
Henrik Bjornstad	66	72	71	71	280	17,120
Richard Bland	67	71	71	71	280	17,120
Andrew Oldcorn	74	68	68	71	281	14,480
Alvaro Salto	71	70	67	73	281	14,480
Shaun Webster	69	72	70	70	281	14,480
Trevor Immelman	68	66	75	72	281	14,480
Colin Montgomerie	70	68	72	71	281	14,480
Miles Tunnicliff	70	69	68	74	281	14,480
Patrik Sjoland	67	68	73	73	281	14,480
Matthew Cort	68	71	71	71	281	14,480
Roger Chapman	71	68	72	71	282	11,680
Ronan Rafferty	69	71	73	69	282	11,680
Jean-François Lucquin	71	67	71	73	282	11,680
Eduardo De La Riva	70	70	70	72	282	11,680
Richard Sterne	71	64	73	74	282	11,680
Jesus Maria Arruti	72	70	71	70	283	9,600
Mathias Gronberg	75	67	72	69	283	9,600
Christian Cevaer	71	71	72	69	283	9,600
Simon Hurd	69	73	70	71	283	9,600
Iain Pyman	71	70	72	70	283	9,600
Simon Dyson	69	69	74	71	283	9,600
Felipe Aguilar	73	67	71	72	283	9,600
Marcus Fraser	69	72	68	74	283	9,600
Barry Lane	68	74	72	70	284	7,200
Jamie Spence	68	70	76	70	284	7,200
Joakim Haeggman	69	73	69	73	284	7,200
Benn Barham	72	69	71	72	284	7,200
Fredrik Andersson	72	70	69	73	284	7,200
Henrik Nystrom	73	68	72	71	284	7,200
Mikael Lundberg	70	71	73	70	284	7,200
Malcolm Mackenzie	70	72	70	73	285	5,000
Philip Walton	71	69	74	71	285	5,000
Bradford Vaughan	69	69	74	73	285	5,000
Hennie Otto	72	68	71	74	285	5,000
Soren Hansen	72	69	73	71	285	5,000
Ricardo Gonzalez	67	73	70	75	285	5,000
Adam Mednick	68	70	72	75	285	5,000
Nick Dougherty	73	65	76	71	285	5,000
Maarten Lafeber	67	74	69	76	286	3,760
Titch Moore	72	69	74	71	286	3,760
Ian Garbutt	72	68	72	74	286	3,760
Gustavo Rojas	70	72	69	75	286	3,760
Paul Lawrie	68	72	74	72	286	3,760
Tobias Dier	72	70	72	72	286	3,760
Jarmo Sandelin	71	71	71	74	287	3,200
Charl Schwartzel	69	71	68	80	288	3,040
Alessandro Tadini	67	72	78	72	289	2,930
Klas Eriksson	70	71	79	71	291	2,398.50
Darren Fichardt	70	72	74	75	291	2,398.50
Alexandre Chopard	73	68	78	74	293	2,394
Gary Emerson	70	72	73	79	294	2,391
Miguel Angel Martin	67	74	75	79	295	2,388

Trophee Lancome

Saint-Nom-la-Breteche, Paris, France
Par 36-35–71; 6,903 yards

September 11-14
purse, €1,800,000

	SCORES				TOTAL	MONEY
Retief Goosen	63	65	68	70	266	€300,000
Paul McGinley	66	67	66	71	270	200,000
Raphael Jacquelin	69	67	68	67	271	101,340
Ian Poulter	67	69	65	70	271	101,340
Hennie Otto	69	65	70	68	272	69,660
Nicolas Colsaerts	66	66	68	72	272	69,660
Jean-Francois Remesy	72	65	70	66	273	54,000
David Howell	69	70	67	68	274	42,660
Carlos Rodiles	66	66	73	69	274	42,660
Peter Fowler	67	69	73	66	275	33,360
Marten Olander	71	66	67	71	275	33,360
Damien McGrane	68	68	67	72	275	33,360
Ian Woosnam	70	67	70	69	276	25,980
Padraig Harrington	68	68	71	69	276	25,980
Maarten Lafeber	68	70	70	68	276	25,980
Euan Little	71	69	69	67	276	25,980
Richard Bland	68	71	68	69	276	25,980
Simon Wakefield	65	74	70	67	276	25,980
Eduardo Romero	68	67	70	72	277	20,988
Steve Webster	69	71	68	69	277	20,988
Nick O'Hern	69	70	69	69	277	20,988
Gary Evans	73	68	66	70	277	20,988
David Lynn	69	69	66	73	277	20,988
Mark McNulty	68	67	72	71	278	17,640
Henrik Stenson	70	68	68	72	278	17,640
Peter Baker	71	66	72	69	278	17,640
Jarrod Moseley	68	71	71	68	278	17,640
Jesus Maria Arruti	70	68	73	67	278	17,640
Markus Brier	68	70	69	71	278	17,640
John Bickerton	71	67	68	72	278	17,640
Robert-Jan Derksen	68	73	71	67	279	14,940
Nicolas Vanhootegem	69	70	69	71	279	14,940
Marcus Fraser	67	73	71	68	279	14,940
Gary Murphy	71	69	72	68	280	13,320
Ricardo Gonzalez	69	69	71	71	280	13,320
Stephen Gallacher	71	68	69	72	280	13,320
Mikael Lundberg	64	70	73	73	280	13,320
Mark Foster	71	69	67	74	281	11,520
Soren Kjeldsen	70	71	72	68	281	11,520
Philip Golding	69	70	69	73	281	11,520
Jorge Berendt	67	73	69	72	281	11,520
Gustavo Rojas	70	70	69	72	281	11,520
David Drysdale	72	69	67	73	281	11,520
Titch Moore	68	72	71	71	282	9,000
Colin Montgomerie	68	72	70	72	282	9,000
Patrik Sjoland	70	70	69	73	282	9,000
Mads Vibe-Hastrup	72	68	68	74	282	9,000
Fredrik Widmark	71	65	71	75	282	9,000
Simon Dyson	71	67	77	67	282	9,000
Charl Schwartzel	68	70	69	75	282	9,000
Hunter Mahan	73	68	71	70	282	9,000
Andrew Raitt	70	71	70	72	283	6,660
Terry Price	66	73	74	70	283	6,660
Brett Rumford	68	70	72	73	283	6,660

	SCORES				TOTAL	MONEY
Jamie Donaldson	68	69	70	76	283	6,660
Martin Maritz	71	70	70	72	283	6,660
Peter O'Malley	69	72	70	73	284	5,400
Murray Urquhart	74	63	74	73	284	5,400
Mark Pilkington	67	71	74	72	284	5,400
Santiago Luna	68	73	75	69	285	4,410
Darren Fichardt	68	71	74	72	285	4,410
Kenneth Ferrie	68	73	73	71	285	4,410
Ian Garbutt	71	70	74	70	285	4,410
Bradley Dredge	68	70	72	75	285	4,410
Henrik Nystrom	72	68	69	76	285	4,410
David Carter	69	70	74	72	285	4,410
Thomas Norret	75	66	73	71	285	4,410
Stephen Scahill	70	71	75	70	286	3,510
Matthew Blackey	71	70	72	73	286	3,510
Klas Eriksson	71	68	74	74	287	2,812.40
Shaun Webster	70	71	72	74	287	2,812.40
Raymond Russell	70	71	72	74	287	2,812.40
Eddie Lee	70	71	75	71	287	2,812.40
Ben Curtis	69	72	74	72	287	2,812.40
Gregory Havret	71	69	73	75	288	2,688
Jonathan Lomas	69	71	71	78	289	2,683.50
Matthew Cort	71	69	71	78	289	2,683.50
Philip Archer	70	71	73	76	290	2,679
Marc Farry	71	70	72	78	291	2,674.50
Fernando Roca	69	71	75	76	291	2,674.50
Andrew Coltart	68	73	78	76	295	2,670

Linde German Masters

Gut Larchenhof, Cologne, Germany
Par 36-36—72; 7,289 yards

September 18-21
purse, €3,000,000

	SCORES				TOTAL	MONEY
K.J. Choi	63	68	64	67	262	€500,000
Miguel Angel Jimenez	67	62	67	68	264	333,330
Ian Poulter	65	63	69	68	265	168,900
Niclas Fasth	68	67	65	65	265	168,900
Anders Hansen	69	62	72	65	268	107,400
Carlos Rodiles	65	65	67	71	268	107,400
Darren Clarke	65	71	65	67	268	107,400
David Howell	66	69	69	65	269	64,350
Jarrod Moseley	68	65	67	69	269	64,350
Mathias Gronberg	68	69	68	64	269	64,350
Michael Campbell	69	67	66	67	269	64,350
Gary Orr	65	66	70	69	270	51,600
Henrik Stenson	72	65	68	66	271	46,100
Alex Cejka	70	69	67	65	271	46,100
Lee Westwood	71	67	70	63	271	46,100
Justin Rose	69	66	70	67	272	40,500
Retief Goosen	68	67	66	71	272	40,500
Adam Scott	66	69	67	70	272	40,500
Mark McNulty	68	67	66	73	274	32,640
Nick O'Hern	67	70	72	65	274	32,640
Thomas Levet	70	68	68	68	274	32,640
Joakim Haeggman	72	68	64	70	274	32,640
Paul McGinley	67	72	69	66	274	32,640

	SCORES				TOTAL	MONEY
Ricardo Gonzalez	71	67	68	68	274	32,640
Fredrik Jacobson	60	71	70	73	274	32,640
Raymond Russell	68	71	69	66	274	32,640
Paul Casey	65	67	67	75	274	32,640
Marcus Fraser	66	70	72	66	274	32,640
Maarten Lafeber	67	69	69	70	275	26,700
Miles Tunnicliff	67	63	71	74	275	26,700
Mikael Lundberg	69	67	70	69	275	26,700
Eduardo Romero	69	69	74	64	276	23,280
Darren Fichardt	69	67	72	68	276	23,280
Ian Garbutt	69	70	66	71	276	23,280
Bradley Dredge	67	69	69	71	276	23,280
David Park	67	70	68	71	276	23,280
Hennie Otto	72	66	69	70	277	20,400
Emanuele Canonica	69	68	70	70	277	20,400
Stephen Dodd	68	69	69	71	277	20,400
David Lynn	74	65	71	67	277	20,400
Trevor Immelman	71	69	70	68	278	18,600
Paul Lawrie	69	67	72	70	278	18,600
Ian Woosnam	67	67	71	74	279	15,900
Philip Golding	71	69	70	69	279	15,900
Marcel Siem	71	66	70	72	279	15,900
Charlie Wi	69	71	70	69	279	15,900
Jonathan Lomas	69	71	71	68	279	15,900
Brett Rumford	66	72	68	73	279	15,900
Richard Sterne	69	69	68	73	279	15,900
Peter Fowler	69	67	73	71	280	11,400
David Gilford	66	71	69	74	280	11,400
Brian Davis	71	69	71	69	280	11,400
Anthony Wall	67	70	71	72	280	11,400
Robert Karlsson	68	68	72	72	280	11,400
Simon Dyson	70	67	73	70	280	11,400
Martin Maritz	73	66	71	70	280	11,400
Charl Schwartzel	72	66	67	75	280	11,400
Santiago Luna	72	66	71	72	281	8,700
Jose Maria Olazabal	72	68	72	69	281	8,700
John Bickerton	67	68	72	74	281	8,700
Sandy Lyle	67	72	73	70	282	7,950
Greg Owen	72	68	75	67	282	7,950
Jamie Spence	68	70	74	71	283	7,500
Peter Hedblom	68	65	80	71	284	7,050
Graeme McDowell	70	70	69	75	284	7,050
Raphael Jacquelin	71	67	77	70	285	6,600
Andrew Oldcorn	69	69	75	73	286	5,867.50
Klas Eriksson	72	68	73	73	286	5,867.50
Barry Lane	70	70	78	68	286	5,867.50
Richard Porter	70	70	73	73	286	5,867.50
Tobias Dier	71	68	75	73	287	4,500
Henrik Nystrom	69	71	78	73	291	4,597

Dunhill Links Championship

St. Andrews Old Course: Par 36-36–72; 7,115 yards   September 25-28
Carnoustie Championship Course: Par 36-36–72; 7,112 yards   purse, €4,281,240
Kingsbarns Golf Links: Par 36-36–72; 7,059 yards
St. Andrews, Scotland

	SCORES				TOTAL	MONEY
Lee Westwood	70	68	62	67	267	€705,093.48
Ernie Els	72	65	67	64	268	470,059.38
Raphael Jacquelin	69	68	64	69	270	264,833.11
Maarten Lafeber	68	69	67	67	271	195,451.91
Darren Clarke	67	68	66	70	271	195,451.91
David Howell	67	68	69	68	272	112,025.25
Brian Davis	74	70	66	62	272	112,025.25
Nick O'Hern	73	67	67	65	272	112,025.25
Henrik Stenson	71	66	67	68	272	112,025.25
Richard Sterne	71	67	65	69	272	112,025.25
Michael Campbell	68	68	66	71	273	77,842.32
Mark McNulty	71	66	68	69	274	66,948.63
Peter Lawrie	67	68	71	68	274	66,948.63
Simon Yates	66	71	66	71	274	66,948.63
Phillip Price	68	71	66	69	274	66,948.63
Ian Poulter	69	69	68	69	275	57,112.57
Charlie Wi	71	70	66	68	275	57,112.57
Vijay Singh	72	66	69	68	275	57,112.57
Mark James	70	71	67	68	276	49,328.34
Julien Clement	72	68	70	66	276	49,328.34
Paul Lawrie	69	67	68	72	276	49,328.34
Stephen Scahill	70	73	67	66	276	49,328.34
Fredrik Jacobson	71	68	65	72	276	49,328.34
Kenneth Ferrie	71	72	68	66	277	42,728.66
Trevor Immelman	71	71	68	67	277	42,728.66
Joakim Haeggman	69	73	69	66	277	42,728.66
David Park	70	70	66	71	277	42,728.66
John Bickerton	70	70	70	67	277	42,728.66
Nick Faldo	71	70	70	67	278	35,748.24
Ian Woosnam	72	69	70	67	278	35,748.24
Nick Price	68	70	70	70	278	35,748.24
Richard Green	74	72	64	68	278	35,748.24
Glen Day	69	73	67	69	278	35,748.24
Jamie Donaldson	67	74	69	68	278	35,748.24
Santiago Luna	73	68	70	68	279	27,921.70
Padraig Harrington	72	69	67	71	279	27,921.70
Klas Eriksson	69	69	69	72	279	27,921.70
Robert-Jan Derksen	70	72	65	72	279	27,921.70
Anders Hansen	74	67	69	69	279	27,921.70
Darren Fichardt	73	70	67	69	279	27,921.70
Angel Cabrera	73	70	67	69	279	27,921.70
Nick Dougherty	70	70	67	72	279	27,921.70
David Gleeson	70	71	67	71	279	27,921.70
Shaun Micheel	73	69	67	70	279	27,921.70
Gary Evans	70	69	68	73	280	21,998.92
Mathias Gronberg	71	73	66	70	280	21,998.92
Raymond Russell	73	70	66	71	280	21,998.92
Patrik Sjoland	70	70	70	70	280	21,998.92
Ricardo Gonzalez	69	70	66	76	281	17,345.30
Thomas Bjorn	71	73	65	72	281	17,345.30
James Kingston	70	69	70	72	281	17,345.30
Fredrik Andersson	72	72	66	71	281	17,345.30

	SCORES				TOTAL	MONEY
Terry Price	71	70	68	72	281	17,345.30
Simon Dyson	68	70	70	73	281	17,345.30
Adam Scott	72	67	70	72	281	17,345.30
Henrik Bjornstad	68	68	68	78	282	13,537.79
Peter O'Malley	69	70	70	73	282	13,537.79
Steen Tinning	74	71	65	73	283	11,845.57
Thomas Levet	73	67	70	73	283	11,845.57
Soren Hansen	66	71	74	72	283	11,845.57
Miles Tunnicliff	72	72	66	73	283	11,845.57
Mark Pilkington	72	71	67	73	283	11,845.57
Miguel Angel Martin	69	72	70	74	285	10,364.87
Andrew Coltart	73	69	69	74	285	10,364.87
Alastair Forsyth	69	72	70	75	286	9,730.29

Dutch Open

Hilversumsche Golf Club, Hilversum, Netherlands — October 9-12
Par 35-35–70; 6,634 yards — purse, €1,000,000

	SCORES				TOTAL	MONEY
Maarten Lafeber	67	69	64	67	267	€166,660
Soren Hansen	68	65	66	69	268	86,855
Mathias Gronberg	70	66	67	65	268	86,855
Steen Tinning	66	67	69	68	270	46,200
Jamie Donaldson	64	70	67	69	270	46,200
Gary Murphy	64	70	67	70	271	30,000
Gary Evans	70	68	65	68	271	30,000
Alastair Forsyth	64	72	68	67	271	30,000
Kenneth Ferrie	70	67	68	67	272	18,233.33
Gary Emerson	68	68	67	69	272	18,233.33
Miguel Angel Jimenez	69	69	68	66	272	18,233.33
Stephen Dodd	67	70	68	67	272	18,233.33
Adam Mednick	68	67	73	64	272	18,233.33
Fredrik Andersson	67	66	69	70	272	18,233.33
Brian Davis	69	71	67	66	273	14,100
David Carter	65	70	72	66	273	14,100
Simon Dyson	69	66	69	69	273	14,100
Santiago Luna	69	70	66	69	274	11,537.50
Marten Olander	70	68	66	70	274	11,537.50
Steve Webster	67	73	67	67	274	11,537.50
Jamie Spence	69	69	65	71	274	11,537.50
Pierre Fulke	68	69	72	65	274	11,537.50
Christian Cevaer	70	69	67	68	274	11,537.50
David Lynn	65	69	71	69	274	11,537.50
Markus Brier	68	65	70	71	274	11,537.50
Anthony Wall	67	70	68	70	275	10,100
Mark Roe	67	72	67	70	276	9,350
Warren Bennett	70	70	71	65	276	9,350
Gary Orr	71	67	68	70	276	9,350
Benn Barham	69	66	72	69	276	9,350
Gordon Brand, Jr.	67	66	72	72	277	7,900
Malcolm Mackenzie	68	70	68	71	277	7,900
Nicolas Colsaerts	67	69	66	75	277	7,900
David Park	68	67	67	75	277	7,900
Patrik Sjoland	67	71	70	69	277	7,900
Brad Kennedy	68	71	69	69	277	7,900
Andrew Oldcorn	71	67	74	66	278	6,800

		SCORES			TOTAL	MONEY
Henrik Stenson	66	71	70	71	278	6,800
Ian Garbutt	70	67	71	70	278	6,800
Andrew Coltart	69	70	71	68	278	6,800
Costantino Rocca	70	65	73	71	279	5,500
Ian Woosnam	70	70	72	67	279	5,500
Marc Farry	70	70	69	70	279	5,500
Jean-Francois Remesy	71	68	67	73	279	5,500
Carlos Rodiles	70	69	67	73	279	5,500
Peter Hedblom	70	68	71	70	279	5,500
Raymond Russell	70	70	68	71	279	5,500
John Bickerton	67	71	71	70	279	5,500
Tobias Dier	69	71	70	69	279	5,500
Roger Chapman	71	68	69	72	280	3,711.11
Mark James	67	72	70	71	280	3,711.11
David Howell	70	69	70	71	280	3,711.11
Barry Lane	69	71	69	71	280	3,711.11
Andrew Marshall	68	67	73	72	280	3,711.11
Robert Karlsson	70	70	69	71	280	3,711.11
Bradley Dredge	67	70	68	75	280	3,711.11
Stephen Gallacher	72	68	71	69	280	3,711.11
Richard Sterne	71	65	69	75	280	3,711.11
Peter Baker	67	72	70	72	281	2,600
Paul Eales	69	65	72	75	281	2,600
Jonathan Lomas	67	72	73	69	281	2,600
Rolf Muntz	66	73	73	69	281	2,600
Stephen Scahill	66	71	71	73	281	2,600
Fredrik Widmark	65	66	75	75	281	2,600
Martin Maritz	73	67	70	71	281	2,600
Simon Wakefield	70	69	72	72	283	2,200
Tony Johnstone	66	70	71	77	284	2,050
Mark Pilkington	67	72	68	77	284	2,050
*Jan-Willem Van Hoof	74	65	73	72	284	
Soren Kjeldsen	72	68	73	72	285	1,681.75
Jean-Francois Lucquin	71	66	75	73	285	1,681.75
Nicolas Vanhootegem	67	71	75	72	285	1,681.75
Nick Dougherty	70	68	73	74	285	1,681.75
Inder Van Weerelt	70	70	74	72	286	1,494
Joost Steenkamer	67	72	73	76	288	1,491

HSBC World Match Play

Wentworth Club, West Course, Surrey, England   October 16-19
Par 434 534 444–35; 345 434 455–37–72; 7,072 yards   purse, £2,300,000

FIRST ROUND

Tim Clark defeated Stephen Leaney, 3 and 2

Leaney	4 3 4	4 4 4	3 4 5	35	3 4 5	3 3 5	4 5 5	37	72
Clark	4 3 4	5 3 5	4 4 3	35	2 4 5	4 3 5	4 5 4	36	71

Match all-square

Leaney	4 3 3	4 3 4	4 5 5	35	4 4 4	4 3 5	4		
Clark	4 3 5	4 3 5	4 4 4	36	3 4 4	4 3 4	3		

Vijay Singh defeated Alex Cejka, 8 and 7

Singh	3 2 4	4 3 4	5 4 4	33	3 4 4	5 3 4	4 4 4	35	68
Cejka	4 3 5	4 4 4	4 4 4	36	3 5 5	4 3 4	4 5 5	38	74

Singh leads, 6 up

Singh	4 4 4	4 3 3	4 4 5	35	3 4
Cejka	4 5 4	5 3 4	4 3 4	36	4 4

Chad Campbell defeated Fredrik Jacobson, 6 and 5

Campbell	4 2 3	3 3 4	6 4 3	32	2 4 5	5 3 5	4 5 4	37	69
Jacobson	4 3 4	4 3 5	4 4 4	35	3 4 4	4 4 5	4 5 5	38	73

Campbell leads, 5 up

Campbell	4 2 4	4 3 4	3 4 5	33	4 4 5	4
Jacobson	5 3 4	5 4 4	3 4 4	36	4 3 4	4

Thomas Bjorn defeated Len Mattiace, 4 and 3

Mattiace	4 3 4	4 3 4	4 4 3	33	3 4 4	5 4 5	4 4 5	38	71
Bjorn	4 3 4	4 3 4	5 5 4	36	3 3 5	5 3 4	4 5 6	38	74

Mattiace leads, 3 up

Mattiace	5 4 4	4 4 5	4 4 5	39	3 5 4	5 3 5
Bjorn	4 3 4	5 3 4	4 3 4	34	3 4 4	3 4 4

SECOND ROUND

Ernie Els defeated Tim Clark, 2 up

Els	4 3 4	4 3 5	4 4 4	35	3 4 3	4 3 5	4 5 4	35	70
Clark	4 4 4	4 4 3	4 3 4	34	3 4 4	4 3 5	5 5 4	37	71

Els leads, 2 up

Els	4 3 4	5 2 3	3 4 4	32	3 4 4	5 3 5	4 4 4	36	68
Clark	5 3 4	4 3 4	4 4 4	35	3 4 4	4 2 4	3 4 5	33	68

Vijay Singh defeated Shaun Micheel, 1 up, 38th hole

Micheel	4 3 4	4 2 4	4 4 4	33	2 4 4	4 2 5	5 6 5	37	70
Singh	4 3 4	4 3 4	4 4 4	34	4 4 4	4 4 5	5 6 4	40	74

Micheel leads, 2 up

Micheel	4 3 4	3 3 4	5 4 4	34	4 4 4	4 2 4	3 C 4	X	X
Singh	4 3 4	4 3 3	3 4 3	31	2 4 4	4 3 4	4 W 4	X	X

Match all-square

Micheel	4 4
Singh	4 3

Ben Curtis defeated Chad Campbell, 5 and 3

Curtis	5 2 4	5 3 4	5 4 4	36	3 3 4	4 3 4	4 4 3	32	68
Campbell	4 3 3	4 4 4	4 4 4	34	4 3 4	5 3 4	4 4 4	35	69

Curtis leads, 1 up

Curtis	4 3 4	4 3 3	4 3 4	32	3 4 4	4 3 3
Campbell	4 2 4	5 3 4	3 4 4	33	3 4 5	4 4 5

Thomas Bjorn defeated Mike Weir, 5 and 4

Weir	4 3 5	4 3 4	4 3 4	34	3 4 4	5 4 4	3 6 4	37	71
Bjorn	4 3 4	3 3 4	4 5 4	34	4 3 4	5 2 4	3 5 4	34	68

Bjorn leads, 3 up

Weir	4 3 4	5 3 5	4 5 3	36	3 3 3	5 4
Bjorn	4 2 4	5 3 4	4 4 4	34	3 4 4	4 2

SEMI-FINALS

Ernie Els defeated Vijay Singh, 5 and 4

Els	4 3 4	4 3 4	4 4 3	33	3 4 4	5 3 5	3 4 4	35	68
Singh	4 3 4	4 2 4	3 4 4	32	2 4 3	4 4 4	4 5 5	35	67

Singh leads, 1 up

Els	4 2 4	4 3 4	4 4 4	33	2 4 3	3 3
Singh	5 3 5	5 4 4	5 3 4	38	2 3 3	4 4

Thomas Bjorn defeated Ben Curtis, 2 up

Curtis	4 3 4	4 3 3	4 4 5	34	3 4 5	3 3 6	3 4 4	35	69
Bjorn	4 3 4	4 2 5	4 4 4	34	2 4 4	3 3 4	4 4 5	33	67

Bjorn leads, 2 up

Curtis	5 2 4	6 2 4	4 4 4	35	3 4 5	5 4 4	3 5 5	38	73
Bjorn	5 3 4	4 3 4	4 3 5	35	4 3 5	3 5 3	C 5 3	X	X

FINAL

Ernie Els defeated Thomas Bjorn, 4 and 3

Els	4 3 3	4 3 4	3 4 4	32	4 4 5	4 4 5	4 4 4	38	70
Bjorn	4 3 4	4 4 4	4 5 4	36	4 4 4	4 3 3	5 5 4	36	72

Els leads, 3 up

Els	4 3 4	4 3 4	4 4 W	X	3 4 4	4 2 4
Bjorn	4 3 4	4 4 4	4 4 C	X	4 4 3	4 1 4

PRIZE MONEY: Els £1,000,000; Bjorn £400,000; Curtis, Singh £120,000 each; Campbell, Clark, Micheel, Weir £90,000 each; Cejka, Jacobson, Leaney, Mattiace £75,000 each.

LEGEND: C—conceded hole to opponent; W—won hole by concession without holing out; X—no total score.

Turespana Mallorca Classic

Pula Golf Club, Majorca, Spain
Par 35-35—70; 6,568 yards
(Event shortened to 54 holes—rain.)

October 16-19
purse, €400,000

	SCORES			TOTAL	MONEY
Miguel Angel Jimenez	72	67	65	204	€66,660
Jose Maria Olazabal	66	69	70	205	44,440
Jamie Spence	71	66	69	206	22,520
Gary Emerson	73	64	69	206	22,520
Paul Broadhurst	68	70	69	207	12,384
Tomas Jesus Munoz	72	66	69	207	12,384
Simon Khan	69	72	66	207	12,384
James Hepworth	70	67	70	207	12,384
Benn Barham	68	68	71	207	12,384
Miguel Angel Martin	70	67	71	208	6,960
Klas Eriksson	74	65	69	208	6,960
Jose Manuel Lara	69	68	71	208	6,960
Maarten Lafeber	68	68	72	208	6,960
Marcel Siem	68	68	72	208	6,960
Mark Foster	69	68	72	209	5,211.43
Jose Manuel Carriles	68	68	73	209	5,211.43
Mattias Eliasson	74	69	66	209	5,211.43

	SCORES			TOTAL	MONEY
Damien McGrane	64	71	74	209	5,211.43
Jonathan Lomas	71	69	69	209	5,211.43
Gustavo Rojas	68	70	71	209	5,211.43
David Carter	71	70	68	209	5,211.43
Andrew Marshall	73	70	67	210	4,280
Ricardo Gonzalez	70	66	74	210	4,280
Sion Bebb	68	69	73	210	4,280
Markus Brier	71	66	73	210	4,280
Michael Jonzon	67	71	72	210	4,280
Euan Little	72	70	69	211	3,620
Charlie Wi	71	66	74	211	3,620
David Park	70	64	77	211	3,620
Francois Delamontagne	70	69	72	211	3,620
Simon Dyson	72	69	70	211	3,620
Jamie Elson	73	70	68	211	3,620
Santiago Luna	68	75	69	212	2,885
Titch Moore	72	69	71	212	2,885
Henrik Stenson	68	68	76	212	2,885
Fernando Roca	71	71	70	212	2,885
Christian Cevaer	71	71	70	212	2,885
Lee S. James	71	70	71	212	2,885
Michael Kirk	70	71	71	212	2,885
Louis Oosthuizen	71	67	74	212	2,885
Marc Farry	75	68	70	213	2,320
Jan-Are Larsen	72	71	70	213	2,320
Eduardo De La Riva	69	73	71	213	2,320
Gary Clark	69	74	70	213	2,320
Patrik Sjoland	71	68	74	213	2,320
Mads Vibe-Hastrup	71	71	71	213	2,320
Jose Rivero	73	70	71	214	1,720
Shaun Webster	71	70	73	214	1,720
Paul Eales	71	71	72	214	1,720
Jorge Berendt	72	69	73	214	1,720
James Kingston	72	68	74	214	1,720
Simon Hurd	69	73	72	214	1,720
Matthew Blackey	68	72	74	214	1,720
Lee Westwood	72	69	73	214	1,720
Fredrik Widmark	72	69	73	214	1,720
Mark Mouland	72	69	74	215	1,124.44
Alvaro Salto	72	70	73	215	1,124.44
Warren Bennett	71	66	78	215	1,124.44
Stuart Little	67	72	76	215	1,124.44
Jean-Francois Lucquin	70	70	75	215	1,124.44
Olivier David	72	70	73	215	1,124.44
David Geall	76	67	72	215	1,124.44
Christopher Hanell	69	71	75	215	1,124.44
Ben Mason	69	74	72	215	1,124.44
Roger Chapman	77	66	73	216	823.33
Scott Drummond	68	72	76	216	823.33
Michael Archer	73	70	73	216	823.33
Jesus Maria Arruti	73	69	74	216	823.33
David Drysdale	70	71	75	216	823.33
Matthew Cort	73	70	73	216	823.33
Adam Mednick	71	72	74	217	598.50
Martin Lemesurier	68	72	77	217	598.50
Sam Walker	70	70	78	218	594
Johan Edfors	75	68	77	220	591
Mark Pilkington	71	71	79	221	588
Didier de Vooght	66	74	83	223	585

Telefonica Open de Madrid

Club de Campo, Madrid, Spain
Par 36-35–71; 6,967 yards

October 23-26
purse, €1,400,000

	SCORES				TOTAL	MONEY
Ricardo Gonzalez	69	70	66	65	270	€233,330
Padraig Harrington	65	73	68	65	271	93,137.50
Marten Olander	69	65	70	67	271	93,137.50
Nick O'Hern	67	67	69	68	271	93,137.50
Paul Casey	63	65	71	72	271	93,137.50
Peter Fowler	67	66	70	70	273	39,340
Sergio Garcia	64	71	71	67	273	39,340
Paul Lawrie	69	64	70	70	273	39,340
Matthew Blackey	70	70	68	65	273	39,340
Pierre Fulke	71	65	70	68	274	26,880
Adam Scott	72	69	68	65	274	26,880
*Gonzalo Fernandez-Castan	67	70	70	67	274	
Jose Maria Olazabal	70	68	70	67	275	23,310
Patrik Sjoland	69	70	69	67	275	23,310
Anders Hansen	71	67	70	68	276	19,740
Jarrod Moseley	70	69	68	69	276	19,740
Greg Owen	72	66	71	67	276	19,740
Niclas Fasth	71	71	69	65	276	19,740
Alastair Forsyth	70	71	69	66	276	19,740
Brian Davis	70	68	70	69	277	16,100
Maarten Lafeber	69	67	69	72	277	16,100
Thomas Levet	66	71	72	68	277	16,100
Miguel Angel Jimenez	70	67	71	69	277	16,100
Robert Karlsson	65	67	74	71	277	16,100
Andrew Coltart	69	68	68	72	277	16,100
Jose Manuel Lara	69	70	72	67	278	13,090
Jamie Spence	71	70	70	67	278	13,090
Carlos Rodiles	72	70	68	68	278	13,090
Gregory Havret	67	70	70	71	278	13,090
Ignacio Garrido	68	71	68	71	278	13,090
Bradley Dredge	69	71	68	70	278	13,090
David Park	74	63	68	73	278	13,090
Stephen Gallacher	69	64	72	73	278	13,090
Andrew Oldcorn	71	69	68	71	279	10,826.67
Klas Eriksson	71	70	69	69	279	10,826.67
Stephen Dodd	68	73	69	69	279	10,826.67
Jean-Francois Remesy	71	71	70	68	280	9,660
Raphael Jacquelin	71	68	71	70	280	9,660
Christian Cevaer	76	66	69	69	280	9,660
Angel Cabrera	67	68	71	74	280	9,660
David Lynn	73	69	68	70	280	9,660
Miguel Angel Martin	69	70	68	74	281	7,980
Ian Woosnam	68	72	70	71	281	7,980
David Howell	71	69	70	71	281	7,980
Jesus Maria Arruti	71	68	74	68	281	7,980
Miles Tunnicliff	67	70	73	71	281	7,980
Simon Dyson	74	66	72	69	281	7,980
Martin Maritz	69	70	70	72	281	7,980
Warren Bennett	69	71	72	70	282	6,580
Barry Lane	67	74	69	72	282	6,580
Gary Orr	72	67	72	71	282	6,580
Mark Roe	68	74	72	69	283	5,320
Kenneth Ferrie	72	66	70	75	283	5,320
Richard Bland	71	69	70	73	283	5,320

	SCORES				TOTAL	MONEY
Soren Hansen	69	70	74	70	283	5,320
Peter O'Malley	70	68	74	71	283	5,320
David Drysdale	72	69	70	72	283	5,320
Santiago Luna	71	71	71	71	284	4,130
Jean-Francois Lucquin	72	70	73	69	284	4,130
Rolf Muntz	71	68	73	72	284	4,130
Jarmo Sandelin	67	73	72	72	284	4,130
Soren Kjeldsen	69	69	74	73	285	3,780
Eduardo De La Riva	73	69	73	71	286	3,570
Nick Dougherty	69	71	72	74	286	3,570
Gary Murphy	71	68	74	74	287	3,360
Costantino Rocca	75	67	71	76	289	3,150
Gary Emerson	74	68	75	72	289	3,150
Carlos Balmaseda Sanchez	72	69	71	78	290	2,940
Raymond Russell	71	70	74	76	291	2,800
Mikko Ilonen	73	68	75	75	291	2,800
Ian Poulter	72	70	76		WD	1,280
Lee Westwood	68	68	77		WD	1,280

Volvo Masters Andalucia

Club de Golf Valderrama, Sotegrande, Spain
Par 36-36–72; 7,006 yards

October 30-November 2
purse, €3,500,000

	SCORES				TOTAL	MONEY
Fredrik Jacobson	64	71	71	70	276	€583,330
Carlos Rodiles	68	69	69	70	276	388,880
(Jacobsen defeated Rodiles on fourth playoff hole.)						
Brian Davis	71	73	69	66	279	227,500
John Bickerton	71	72	70	69	282	175,000
Stephen Leaney	77	72	67	68	284	142,000
Greg Owen	73	67	73	71	284	142,000
Sergio Garcia	71	71	73	71	286	105,000
Michael Campbell	75	69	74	68	286	105,000
Ian Poulter	74	72	73	68	287	87,500
Jose Maria Olazabal	70	75	70	73	288	67,313.34
Colin Montgomerie	71	74	70	73	288	67,313.34
Adam Scott	72	75	68	73	288	67,313.34
Nick O'Hern	70	78	69	72	289	50,925
Jarrod Moseley	73	72	70	74	289	50,925
Darren Clarke	77	72	68	72	289	50,925
Angel Cabrera	71	74	73	71	289	50,925
Bradley Dredge	72	73	71	73	289	50,925
Paul Casey	77	70	73	69	289	50,925
Padraig Harrington	76	74	70	70	290	45,150
Anders Hansen	66	73	73	78	290	45,150
Peter Fowler	72	79	70	70	291	41,650
Darren Fichardt	73	72	74	72	291	41,650
Miguel Angel Jimenez	75	72	73	71	291	41,650
David Howell	73	77	72	71	293	37,275
Raphael Jacquelin	74	75	72	72	293	37,275
Phillip Price	75	71	75	72	293	37,275
Thomas Bjorn	71	73	74	75	293	37,275
Barry Lane	75	76	71	72	294	33,600
Ricardo Gonzalez	77	70	74	73	294	33,600
Stephen Gallacher	71	75	76	72	294	33,600
Nick Faldo	74	71	73	77	295	28,350

	SCORES				TOTAL	MONEY
Mark McNulty	74	75	71	75	295	28,350
Trevor Immelman	77	70	76	72	295	28,350
Philip Golding	76	73	76	70	295	28,350
Paul McGinley	75	73	76	71	295	28,350
Gary Evans	74	75	69	77	295	28,350
Niclas Fasth	71	77	74	73	295	28,350
Eduardo Romero	73	73	72	78	296	23,625
Robert Karlsson	74	75	73	74	296	23,625
Robert-Jan Derksen	74	71	73	79	297	21,525
Paul Lawrie	75	75	72	75	297	21,525
Peter Lawrie	72	77	77	72	298	19,950
Lee Westwood	75	72	76	75	298	19,950
Maarten Lafeber	77	75	71	77	300	18,200
Justin Rose	73	74	77	76	300	18,200
Ignacio Garrido	79	76	75	70	300	18,200
Peter Hedblom	78	72	73	78	301	16,100
Alastair Forsyth	82	75	71	73	301	16,100
Jamie Donaldson	81	74	74	72	301	16,100
Gary Murphy	74	78	76	75	303	14,750
Mathias Gronberg	73	80	78	73	304	14,300
Kenneth Ferrie	74	77	74	80	305	13,850
David Lynn	82	82	70	72	306	13,175
Andrew Coltart	82	82	70	72	306	13,175
Soren Kjeldsen	75	73	78	82	308	12,600
Nick Dougherty	78	78	80	76	312	12,250
Soren Hansen	74				WD	11,900

The Seve Trophy

Campo de Golf Parador El Saler, Valencia, Spain
Par 36-36–72; 6,355 yards

November 6-9
purse, €2,200,000

FIRST DAY
Fourballs

Lee Westwood and David Howell (Great Britain & Ireland) defeated Jose Maria Olazabal and Seve Ballesteros, 2 up.
Brian Davis and Paul Casey (GB&I) defeated Ignacio Garrido and Miguel Angel Jimenez, 2 and 1.
Alex Cejka and Raphael Jacquelin (Continental Europe) defeated Justin Rose and Ian Poulter, 4 and 3.
Fredrik Jacobson and Niclas Fasth (Cont.) halved with Paul Lawrie and Colin Montgomerie.
Phillip Price and Padraig Harrington (GB&I) defeated Thomas Bjorn and Sergio Garcia, 2 up.

POINTS: Great Britain & Ireland 3½, Continental Europe 1½

SECOND DAY
Fourballs

Westwood and Howell (GB&I) defeated Bjorn and Garcia, 5 and 3.
Cejka and Jacquelin (Cont.) defeated Lawrie and Montgomerie, 2 and 1.
Davis and Casey (GB&I) defeated Garrido and Jimenez, 2 up.
Jacobson and Fasth (Cont.) defeated Price and Harrington, 1 up.
Rose and Poulter (GB&I) defeated Olazabal and Ballesteros, 3 and 1.

POINTS: Great Britain & Ireland 3, Continental Europe 2

THIRD DAY
Greensomes

Fasth and Jacobson (Cont.) defeated Harrington and Lawrie, 5 and 4.
Bjorn and Olazabal (Cont.) halved with Rose and Montgomerie.
Cejka and Jacquelin (Cont.) defeated Casey and Davis, 3 and 2.
Westwood and Poulter (GB&I) defeated Garcia and Ballesteros, 3 and 1.

POINTS: Great Britain & Ireland 1½, Continental Europe 2½

Foursomes

Harrington and Montgomerie (GB&I) defeated Jimenez and Garrido, 2 and 1.
Fasth and Jacobson (Cont.) defeated Lawrie and Casey, 3 and 2.
Cejka and Jacquelin (Cont.) defeated Howell and Westwood, 5 and 3.
Rose and Poulter (GB&I) defeated Garcia and Bjorn, 2 and 1.

POINTS: Great Britain & Ireland 2, Continental Europe 2

FOURTH DAY
Singles

Montgomerie (GB&I) defeated Ballesteros, 5 and 4.
Howell (GB&I) defeated Cejka, 1 up.
Garrido (Cont.) defeated Lawrie, 3 and 2.
Jacobson (Cont.) defeated Westwood, 2 and 1.
Harrington (GB&I) halved with Olazabal.
Poulter (GB&I) halved with Fasth.
Casey (GB&I) defeated Bjorn (withdrew due to injury).
Rose (GB&I) defeated Jacquelin, 3 and 2.
Jimenez (Cont.) defeated Davis, 2 and 1.
Garcia (Cont.) defeated Price, 4 and 3.

POINTS: Great Britain & Ireland 5, Continental Europe 5

TOTAL POINTS: Great Britain & Ireland 15, Continental Europe 13

(Each member of the Great Britain & Ireland team received €150,000; each member of
the Continental Europe team received €70,000.)

Omega Hong Kong Open

See Asia/Japan Tours chapter.

Challenge Tour

MasterCard Costa Rica Open
See American Tours chapter.

Telefonica Guatemala Open
See American Tours chapter.

Los Encinos Open
See American Tours chapter.

Stanbic Zambia Open
See African Tours chapter.

Madeira Island Open
See PGA European Tour section.

Panalpina Banque Commerciale du Maroc Classic

Royal Golf Dar-es-Salam, Rabat, Morocco
Par 36-37–73; 7,359 yards

April 10-13
purse, €130,000

	SCORES				TOTAL	MONEY
Greig Hutcheon	72	70	72	70	284	€21,660
Scott Drummond	71	74	72	69	286	14,440
Jamie Little	68	75	72	74	289	7,313
Sebastian Fernandez	72	71	74	72	289	7,313
Steven O'Hara	74	70	72	74	290	5,284.50
Charl Schwartzel	73	73	71	73	290	5,284.50
Martin Erlandsson	73	73	70	75	291	4,298.67
Johan Edfors	75	72	72	72	291	4,298.67
Michele Reale	73	70	72	76	291	4,298.67
Didier de Vooght	74	71	73	74	292	3,640
Philip Archer	72	72	74	75	293	3,072.33
Hennie Otto	77	69	74	73	293	3,072.33
Gary Clark	71	75	74	73	293	3,072.33
Robert Coles	73	71	77	73	294	2,161.25
Murray Urquhart	73	73	76	72	294	2,161.25
Sebastien Delagrange	71	76	72	75	294	2,161.25
Wolfgang Huget	78	69	74	73	294	2,161.25
Garry Houston	71	75	73	76	295	1,547
Elvis Galera	74	72	76	73	295	1,547
Thomas Besancenez	71	74	75	75	295	1,547
Mark Sanders	72	75	72	76	295	1,547
Robert Johansen	72	72	71	80	295	1,547
Philip Walton	71	73	76	76	296	1,256.67
Bradford Vaughan	72	72	76	76	296	1,256.67
Marcel Haremza	72	76	75	73	296	1,256.67
Kariem Baraka	74	71	74	77	296	1,256.67
Daniel Vancsik	74	74	70	78	296	1,256.67
Louis Oosthuizen	70	78	74	74	296	1,256.67
Stuart Little	69	74	74	80	297	1,069.25

	SCORES				TOTAL	MONEY
Stefano Reale	77	71	76	73	297	1,069.25
Erol Simsek	72	74	75	76	297	1,069.25
David Dupart	75	73	73	76	297	1,069.25

Tessali - Metaponto Open di Puglia e Basilicata

Riva dei Tessali: Par 35-36–71; 6,502 yards   May 8-11
Metaponto: Par 36-36–72; 6,873 yards   purse, €120,000
Taranto, Italy

	SCORES				TOTAL	MONEY
Martin LeMesurier	68	66	69	70	273	€20,000
Sam Walker	67	67	73	66	273	10,412
Andre Bossert	70	67	69	67	273	10,412
(LeMesurier defeated Walker on first and Bossert on second playoff hole.)						
Ryan Reid	67	70	68	69	274	5,544
Marcello Santi	73	69	66	66	274	5,544
Stuart Little	70	68	71	66	275	4,482
Scott Drummond	66	72	67	70	275	4,482
Marc Pendaries	68	72	65	71	276	3,516
Marco Soffietti	62	75	73	66	276	3,516
Richard McEvoy	74	67	69	66	276	3,516
David Ryles	72	67	68	69	276	3,516
Tim Milford	71	68	69	69	277	2,832
Raphael Pellicioli	70	68	72	68	278	2,460
Gregory Bourdy	68	72	70	68	278	2,460
Ed Stedman	68	71	70	70	279	1,597.50
Sebastian Fernandez	69	71	68	71	279	1,597.50
Brett Rumford	72	68	69	70	279	1,597.50
Dominique Nouailhac	71	69	71	68	279	1,597.50
Erol Simsek	69	69	71	70	279	1,597.50
Andrea Maestroni	70	68	72	69	279	1,597.50
Cesar Monasterio	71	70	71	67	279	1,597.50
Emmanuele Lattanzi	72	70	67	70	279	1,597.50
Didier de Vooght	71	71	69	69	280	1,141.71
Carlos Quevedo	73	66	71	70	280	1,141.71
Gary Clark	72	70	72	66	280	1,141.71
Wolfgang Huget	71	69	71	69	280	1,141.71
Kariem Baraka	69	72	70	69	280	1,141.71
Juan Abbate	71	71	71	67	280	1,141.71
Allan Hogh	67	73	69	71	280	1,141.71
Johan Edfors	69	72	70	70	281	960
Greig Hutcheon	62	71	75	73	281	960
Alessandro Tadini	70	66	74	71	281	960
Kalle Brink	68	68	72	73	281	960

Izki Challenge de Espana

Izki Golf Urturi, Vittoria, Spain   May 15-18
Par 36-36–72; 7,162 yards   purse, €135,000

	SCORES				TOTAL	MONEY
Martin Erlandsson	64	68	70	71	273	€22,500
Jose Manuel Carriles	69	65	69	73	276	8,975.25
Scott Drummond	71	70	67	68	276	8,975.25

	SCORES				TOTAL	MONEY
Peter Hanson	70	69	68	69	276	8,975.25
Martin LeMesurier	73	66	68	69	276	8,975.25
Gary Clark	69	72	70	66	277	5,042.25
Mark Sanders	70	68	69	70	277	5,042.25
Alvaro Salto	72	71	65	70	278	4,455
Johan Edfors	70	72	68	69	279	4,104
Alex Balicki	72	69	69	70	280	3,631.50
Michael Kirk	73	71	68	68	280	3,631.50
Paolo Terreni	70	72	65	74	281	2,907
Marco Soffietti	67	72	72	70	281	2,907
Pasi Purhonen	71	69	68	73	281	2,907
Garry Houston	74	69	69	70	282	1,957.50
Greig Hutcheon	71	70	67	74	282	1,957.50
Ryan Reid	69	72	69	72	282	1,957.50
Adam Crawford	70	74	70	68	282	1,957.50
Sebastian Fernandez	69	71	73	69	282	1,957.50
Paul McKechnie	72	71	70	70	283	1,593
Manuel Moreno	71	72	69	72	284	1,444.50
James Hepworth	72	68	70	74	284	1,444.50
Tuomas Tuovinen	70	67	73	74	284	1,444.50
Stephen Browne	71	68	72	73	284	1,444.50
Jose Rivero	73	70	68	74	285	1,221.75
Neil Cheetham	71	70	73	71	285	1,221.75
Ivo Giner	72	72	71	70	285	1,221.75
Scott Gardiner	68	75	70	72	285	1,221.75
Richard McEvoy	71	71	71	72	285	1,221.75
Marcus Fraser	69	72	71	73	285	1,221.75

Fortis Challenge Open

Burggolf Purmerend, Purmerend, Netherlands
Par 36-36–72; 6,686 yards

May 22-25
purse, €135,000

	SCORES				TOTAL	MONEY
Johan Edfors	67	67	69	70	273	€22,500
Kalle Brink	72	70	68	65	275	15,000
Mark Sanders	69	70	67	70	276	8,427
Stuart Little	69	71	68	70	278	6,750
Jose Manuel Carriles	70	74	69	66	279	5,269.50
Ryan Reid	71	68	66	74	279	5,269.50
Brett Rumford	71	69	66	73	279	5,269.50
Cesar Monasterio	71	71	70	68	280	4,279.50
Louis Oosthuizen	72	67	70	71	280	4,279.50
Peter Hanson	67	72	70	72	281	3,483
Didier de Vooght	71	74	65	71	281	3,483
Andre Bossert	70	74	66	71	281	3,483
Scott Drummond	73	73	66	70	282	2,902.50
Robert Coles	70	71	69	74	284	2,497.50
Gary Clark	69	75	69	71	284	2,497.50
Kalle Vainola	73	71	68	73	285	1,803.60
Birgir Hafthorsson	69	78	68	70	285	1,803.60
Wolfgang Huget	73	71	69	72	285	1,803.60
Juan Abbate	72	71	71	71	285	1,803.60
Tuomas Tuovinen	71	75	68	71	285	1,803.60
Ilya Goroneskoul	74	69	69	74	286	1,471.50
Jean Louis Guepy	73	69	69	75	286	1,471.50
Gareth Paddison	69	73	70	74	286	1,471.50

	SCORES				TOTAL	MONEY
Joost Steenkamer	74	70	74	69	287	1,282.50
Denny Lucas	73	71	70	73	287	1,282.50
Richard Porter	72	71	69	75	287	1,282.50
Jean Hugo	71	73	68	75	287	1,282.50
Thomas Norret	74	73	71	69	287	1,282.50
Titch Moore	73	73	72	70	288	1,096.20
Marco Soffietti	69	69	77	73	288	1,096.20
Olivier David	73	74	69	72	288	1,096.20
Pehr Magnebrant	72	72	69	75	288	1,096.20
Mads Iversen	70	72	73	73	288	1,096.20

Nykredit Danish Open

Gilleleje Golf Club, Helsingor, Denmark
Par 36-36–72; 6,736 yards

June 5-8
purse, €125,000

	SCORES				TOTAL	MONEY
Marcus Fraser	70	71	69	66	276	€20,830
Joakim Rask	68	75	68	68	279	10,847.50
Gregory Bourdy	72	73	65	69	279	10,847.50
Martin Erlandsson	72	70	68	71	281	5,775
Martin LeMesurier	72	70	73	66	281	5,775
Scott Drummond	73	72	69	68	282	4,668.75
Allan Hogh	72	73	70	67	282	4,668.75
Peter Hanson	74	72	69	69	284	3,662.50
Jimmy Kawalec	73	70	74	67	284	3,662.50
Pasi Purhonen	74	70	66	74	284	3,662.50
Louis Oosthuizen	71	74	71	68	284	3,662.50
Cesar Monasterio	76	68	73	68	285	2,565.63
Neil Cheetham	73	71	74	67	285	2,565.63
James Hepworth	71	75	69	70	285	2,565.63
Peter Gustafsson	72	73	71	69	285	2,565.63
Garry Houston	73	71	70	72	286	1,718.75
Michele Reale	73	71	70	72	286	1,718.75
Carlos Quevedo	72	71	74	69	286	1,718.75
Mark Loftus	73	71	73	69	286	1,718.75
Magnus Persson Atlevi	76	67	68	76	287	1,341.67
Kalle Brink	71	72	75	69	287	1,341.67
Marco Soffietti	79	67	71	70	287	1,341.67
Massimo Florioli	71	71	73	72	287	1,341.67
Daren Lee	72	75	72	68	287	1,341.67
Christopher Hanell	76	70	70	71	287	1,341.67
Stuart Little	70	77	70	71	288	1,150
Niklas Bruzelius	73	74	70	71	288	1,150
Martin Wiegele	72	70	70	76	288	1,150
Peter Malmgren	75	68	74	72	289	1,041.67
Tim Milford	72	71	73	73	289	1,041.67
Oskar Bergman	67	73	80	69	289	1,041.67

Aa St. Omer Open

See PGA European Tour section.

Clearstream International Luxembourg Open

Kikuoka Golf & Country Club, Canach, Luxembourg
Par 36-36–72; 7,067 yards

June 19-22
purse, €115,000

	SCORES				TOTAL	MONEY
Martin LeMesurier	64	64	66	71	265	€19,160
Greig Hutcheon	63	68	66	70	267	12,770
Jimmy Kawalec	68	70	67	65	270	5,939.67
Regis Gustave	67	68	66	69	270	5,939.67
Adam Crawford	69	67	67	67	270	5,939.67
Magnus Persson Atlevi	69	66	69	67	271	4,295.25
Richard McEvoy	69	69	66	67	271	4,295.25
Edward Rush	69	70	66	67	272	3,795
Ulf Wendling	72	66	67	68	273	2,973.90
Fredrik Henge	71	69	70	63	273	2,973.90
Erol Simsek	67	69	67	70	273	2,973.90
Sam Walker	69	71	65	68	273	2,973.90
Gareth Paddison	69	70	68	66	273	2,973.90
Alex Balicki	70	67	66	71	274	1,830.80
Leif Westerberg	68	66	70	70	274	1,830.80
Alexander Renard	69	69	71	65	274	1,830.80
Jamie Elson	69	67	68	70	274	1,830.80
Louis Oosthuizen	68	67	68	71	274	1,830.80
Peter Malmgren	69	71	68	67	275	1,360.83
Peter Hanson	69	65	67	74	275	1,360.83
Kariem Baraka	71	68	67	69	275	1,360.83
Scott Drummond	73	67	67	69	276	1,150
Michele Reale	72	67	66	71	276	1,150
Carlos Quevedo	70	67	71	68	276	1,150
Tony Edlund	68	71	68	69	276	1,150
Magnus Carlsson	68	70	69	69	276	1,150
Steven O'Hara	70	67	67	72	276	1,150
Alan McLean	71	64	71	71	277	989
Benoit Teilleria	68	72	69	68	277	989
Daniel Vancsik	70	68	69	70	277	989

Galeria Kaufhof Pokal Challenge

Rittergut Birkhof Golf Club, Dusseldorf, Germany
Par 36-36–72; 6,807 yards

June 26-29
purse, €110,000

	SCORES				TOTAL	MONEY
Michael Jonzon	63	63	69	68	263	€18,330
Philip Archer	63	67	69	66	265	8,197.33
Christopher Hanell	64	67	63	71	265	8,197.33
David Ryles	68	65	66	66	265	8,197.33
Alex Cejka	69	67	69	61	266	4,664
Jose Manuel Carriles	66	66	68	67	267	4,108.50
Martin Erlandsson	67	69	65	66	267	4,108.50
Hennie Otto	71	67	63	67	268	3,487
Martin Wiegele	67	70	65	66	268	3,487
Tim Milford	72	66	67	64	269	2,719.75
Ivo Giner	70	67	67	65	269	2,719.75
Jamie Elson	65	70	67	67	269	2,719.75
Marcus Fraser	70	66	65	68	269	2,719.75
Gregory Bourdy	68	67	67	68	270	2,145
Mark Mouland	70	67	66	68	271	1,595

	SCORES				TOTAL	MONEY
Johan Edfors	68	65	71	67	271	1,595
Carlos Quevedo	70	69	67	65	271	1,595
Michael Kirk	66	71	70	64	271	1,595
Louis Oosthuizen	67	67	70	67	271	1,595
Steven O'Hara	70	68	68	66	272	1,298
Pasi Purhonen	68	67	69	69	273	1,199
Graeme Storm	68	65	71	69	273	1,199
Steven Bowditch	70	64	70	69	273	1,199
David Geall	68	67	68	71	274	1,045
Andrew Butterfield	70	69	69	66	274	1,045
Euan McIntosh	66	68	70	70	274	1,045
Marco Bernardini	69	68	69	68	274	1,045
Kariem Baraka	66	67	70	71	274	1,045
Niki Zitny	69	69	68	69	275	859.38
Younes El Hassani	68	68	69	70	275	859.38
Bradford Vaughan	69	65	69	72	275	859.38
Jimmy Kawalec	67	70	73	65	275	859.38
Christoph Gunther	67	69	72	67	275	859.38
Massimo Florioli	69	69	71	66	275	859.38
Ben Mason	70	67	68	70	275	859.38
Mark Sanders	69	69	69	68	275	859.38

Volvo Finnish Open

Espoon Golfseura, Espoo, Finland
Par 36-36–72; 6,773 yards

July 3-6
purse, €100,000

	SCORES				TOTAL	MONEY
Jamie Elson	67	65	66	66	264	€16,660
Martin Wiegele	65	69	65	67	266	11,110
Marcus Fraser	68	67	65	67	267	6,250
Hennie Otto	68	67	69	64	268	4,620
Joachim Larsen	67	65	69	67	268	4,620
Johan Edfors	71	65	68	65	269	3,735
David Ryles	65	69	67	68	269	3,735
Ari Pasanen	66	65	72	69	272	3,300
Scott Drummond	70	68	66	69	273	2,920
Sam Little	69	70	68	66	273	2,920
Mattias Eliasson	70	65	68	71	274	2,260
Ilya Goroneskoul	70	64	70	70	274	2,260
Craig Cowper	67	69	69	69	274	2,260
James Hepworth	67	69	72	66	274	2,260
Ulf Wendling	68	69	68	70	275	1,566.67
Marcel Haremza	67	71	69	68	275	1,566.67
Daren Lee	70	70	69	66	275	1,566.67
Kalle Brink	66	70	71	69	276	1,310
Cesar Monasterio	66	71	69	71	277	1,097.14
Fredrik Henge	68	70	70	69	277	1,097.14
David Geall	66	68	72	71	277	1,097.14
Johan Skold	70	68	73	66	277	1,097.14
Joakim Rask	70	69	69	69	277	1,097.14
Juan Abbate	69	69	71	68	277	1,097.14
Steven O'Hara	67	70	69	71	277	1,097.14
Jonas Torines	69	69	72	68	278	876.67
Jamie Little	72	68	69	69	278	876.67
Carlos Quevedo	68	70	71	69	278	876.67
Sandeep Grewal	69	70	71	68	278	876.67

	SCORES	TOTAL	MONEY
Craig Williams	71 68 71 68	278	876.67
Ed Stedman	70 68 71 69	278	876.67

Open des Volcans Challenge de France

Golf des Volcans, Orcines, France
Par 36-35–71; 7,093 yards

July 10-13
purse, €125,000

	SCORES	TOTAL	MONEY
Ivo Giner	68 67 67 67	269	€20,830
David Patrick	68 70 64 70	272	13,880
Marc Pendaries	73 69 66 65	273	7,032.50
Peter Gustafsson	68 67 70 68	273	7,032.50
Jose Manuel Carriles	70 69 70 66	275	4,879.17
Marcus Higley	67 69 69 70	275	4,879.17
Peter Hanson	69 69 66 71	275	4,879.17
Alessandro Napoleoni	68 72 69 67	276	3,520
Scott Drummond	73 69 67 67	276	3,520
Chris Gane	70 70 70 66	276	3,520
Graeme Storm	69 71 68 68	276	3,520
Richard McEvoy	69 71 67 69	276	3,520
Pehr Magnebrant	68 69 69 71	277	2,312.50
Johan Skold	71 70 70 66	277	2,312.50
Michael Jonzon	71 69 70 67	277	2,312.50
Oskar Bergman	67 68 70 72	277	2,312.50
Mark Mouland	65 70 73 70	278	1,645.83
Jacques Thalamy	70 71 70 67	278	1,645.83
Sebastien Delagrange	70 71 67 70	278	1,645.83
*Jean-Baptiste Gonnet	71 70 70 67	278	
Cesar Monasterio	70 70 69 70	279	1,341.67
Garry Houston	69 68 71 71	279	1,341.67
Lionel Alexandre	68 72 68 71	279	1,341.67
Paul Dwyer	71 70 68 70	279	1,341.67
Benoit Teilleria	67 72 70 70	279	1,341.67
Juan Abbate	72 69 72 66	279	1,341.67
Greig Hutcheon	71 69 73 67	280	1,131.25
David Geall	73 68 67 72	280	1,131.25
Sion Bebb	72 69 68 71	280	1,131.25
Edward Rush	69 71 68 72	280	1,131.25

Kitzbuhel Golf Alpin Open

Kitzbuhel-Schwarzsee, Kitzbuhel, Austria
Par 35-36–71; 6,571 yards

July 17-20
purse, €110,000

	SCORES	TOTAL	MONEY
David Geall	61 67 70 63	261	€18,330
Michael Kirk	63 69 66 66	264	12,220
Michael Jonzon	66 68 62 69	265	6,186
Kariem Baraka	64 67 65 69	265	6,186
Peter Hanson	69 66 64 67	266	4,471.50
Louis Oosthuizen	66 70 65 65	266	4,471.50
Peter Gustafsson	62 64 70 71	267	3,938
Jamie Little	68 67 66 67	268	3,223
Federico Bisazza	67 65 69 67	268	3,223

	SCORES				TOTAL	MONEY
Ivo Giner	67	70	65	66	268	3,223
Richard McEvoy	64	71	67	66	268	3,223
Christopher Hanell	67	70	69	63	269	2,368.67
Steven O'Hara	66	67	69	67	269	2,368.67
Raphael Pellicioli	68	69	64	68	269	2,368.67
Scott Drummond	68	66	65	71	270	1,723.33
Lewis Atkinson	69	69	70	62	270	1,723.33
Sebastian Fernandez	69	67	66	68	270	1,723.33
Daren Lee	69	65	69	68	271	1,441
Peter Jespersen	67	71	64	70	272	1,276
Massimo Florioli	68	70	64	70	272	1,276
Christophe Pottier	70	66	68	68	272	1,276
Sion Bebb	70	68	69	65	272	1,276
Marc Pendaries	67	65	70	71	273	1,114.67
Olivier David	71	64	70	68	273	1,114.67
Andrew Butterfield	70	66	68	69	273	1,114.67
Marcel Haremza	68	69	68	69	274	979
Marco Soffietti	74	64	67	69	274	979
Carlos Quevedo	67	71	65	71	274	979
Massimo Scarpa	65	72	71	66	274	979
Gareth Paddison	68	69	70	67	274	979

Terme Euganee International Open

Padova Golf Club, Valsansibio, Italy
Par 36-36–72; 6,612 yards

July 24-27
purse, €108,000

	SCORES				TOTAL	MONEY
Ivo Giner	63	68	64	64	259	€18,000
Martin Erlandsson	65	67	66	62	260	12,000
Pasi Purhonen	72	64	63	66	265	6,070.80
Gianluca Baruffaldi	68	64	68	65	265	6,070.80
Marcel Haremza	65	69	65	68	267	4,579.20
Rafael Gomez	65	67	65	71	268	4,033.80
Regis Gustave	68	68	65	67	268	4,033.80
Marco Soffietti	69	69	66	65	269	3,164.40
Massimo Florioli	71	67	63	68	269	3,164.40
Carlos Quevedo	68	68	67	66	269	3,164.40
Peter Gustafsson	71	63	67	68	269	3,164.40
Stuart Little	68	68	68	66	270	2,216.70
Marcello Santi	67	71	66	66	270	2,216.70
John Mellor	66	68	69	67	270	2,216.70
Paul McKechnie	67	68	67	68	270	2,216.70
Benoit Teilleria	68	69	69	65	271	1,485
Juan Abbate	68	64	70	69	271	1,485
Daniel Vancsik	67	66	70	68	271	1,485
Steven O'Hara	67	68	68	68	271	1,485
David Patrick	69	65	66	72	272	1,274.40
Paolo Terreni	64	67	72	70	273	1,117.80
Neil Cheetham	68	69	70	66	273	1,117.80
Zane Scotland	65	68	74	66	273	1,117.80
Sebastian Fernandez	69	68	70	66	273	1,117.80
Raphael Pellicioli	70	66	66	71	273	1,117.80
Steven Bowditch	66	69	66	72	273	1,117.80
Marc Pendaries	68	70	68	68	274	918
Peter Hanson	64	67	71	72	274	918
Andrea Maestroni	70	67	68	69	274	918

	SCORES				TOTAL	MONEY
Sam Little	69	69	64	72	274	918
Euan McIntosh	67	66	69	72	274	918
Barry Hume	72	66	68	68	274	918

Talma Finnish Challenge

Talma Golf Club, Finland
Par 36-36–72; 6,897 yards

July 31-August 3
purse, €150,000

	SCORES				TOTAL	MONEY
Marcus Fraser	67	66	71	71	275	€25,000
Tony Edlund	73	64	70	68	275	16,660
(Fraser defeated Edlund on third playoff hole.)						
Martin Wiegele	66	71	71	68	276	9,370
Pasi Purhonen	66	71	72	68	277	6,565
Benoit Teilleria	70	67	71	69	277	6,565
Daniel Vancsik	68	70	69	70	277	6,565
Paolo Terreni	70	70	72	66	278	5,160
Christophe Pottier	72	69	69	68	278	5,160
Cesar Monasterio	70	70	70	69	279	4,210
Joakim Kristiansson	70	70	71	68	279	4,210
Oskar Bergman	69	72	69	69	279	4,210
Peter Malmgren	70	70	71	69	280	2,790
Titch Moore	67	68	72	73	280	2,790
Chris Gane	73	67	71	69	280	2,790
Johan Skold	70	68	72	70	280	2,790
Sebastian Fernandez	66	71	73	70	280	2,790
Richard McEvoy	68	67	72	73	280	2,790
Mark Mouland	69	72	71	69	281	1,685.63
Kalle Vainola	70	69	74	68	281	1,685.63
Marco Soffietti	69	69	73	70	281	1,685.63
John Mellor	74	67	72	68	281	1,685.63
Tuomas Tuovinen	69	72	70	70	281	1,685.63
Craig Williams	68	73	72	68	281	1,685.63
David Patrick	70	70	72	69	281	1,685.63
Stephen Browne	69	70	70	72	281	1,685.63
Sam Little	72	68	73	69	282	1,228.64
Massimo Florioli	71	68	73	70	282	1,228.64
Gianluca Baruffaldi	70	71	73	68	282	1,228.64
Andrew Butterfield	70	71	71	70	282	1,228.64
Erol Simsek	68	72	70	72	282	1,228.64
Leif Westerberg	70	71	72	69	282	1,228.64
Kariem Baraka	71	68	74	69	282	1,228.64
Janne Mommo	67	71	71	73	282	1,228.64
Regis Gustave	66	71	76	69	282	1,228.64
Ed Stedman	72	68	73	69	282	1,228.64
David Ryles	72	68	70	72	282	1,228.64

BMW Russian Open

See PGA European Tour section.

Rolex Trophy

Geneva Golf Club, Geneva, Switzerland
Par 36-36–72; 6,875 yards

August 21-24
purse, €169,450

		SCORES			TOTAL	MONEY
Michael Jonzon	66	67	67	67	267	€17,000
Martin Wiegele	71	70	63	66	270	11,000
Jose Manuel Carriles	68	68	66	69	271	8,500
Peter Gustafsson	65	69	68	69	271	8,500
Richard McEvoy	68	71	67	65	271	8,500
Johan Edfors	68	66	73	65	272	6,750
Martin LeMesurier	73	65	69	65	272	6,750
Marc Pendaries	66	68	70	69	273	5,800
Martin Erlandsson	62	67	71	73	273	5,800
Jamie Elson	69	70	69	65	273	5,800
Garry Houston	67	70	72	65	274	5,200
Andrew Marshall	67	69	69	69	274	5,200
Stuart Little	67	73	68	66	274	5,200
Mark Sanders	70	67	70	68	275	4,800
Cesar Monasterio	71	72	67	67	277	4,650
Sebastian Fernandez	66	74	70	67	277	4,650
Gregory Bourdy	66	70	71	71	278	4,500
Ivo Giner	72	71	67	70	280	4,350
Michael Kirk	69	68	72	71	280	4,350
Peter Hanson	70	68	72	72	282	4,200
Christopher Hanell	72	70	67	73	282	4,200

Skandia PGA Open

Falsterbo Golf Club, Sweden
Par 34-37–71; 6,684 yards

August 28-31
purse, €110,000

		SCORES			TOTAL	MONEY
Titch Moore	72	68	65	68	273	€18,330
Sebastian Fernandez	67	70	71	67	275	12,220
Peter Hanson	67	73	68	68	276	6,186
Olivier David	70	72	65	69	276	6,186
Marc Pendaries	69	71	69	68	277	3,971
Cesar Monasterio	72	69	70	66	277	3,971
Christian Nilsson	67	72	70	68	277	3,971
Daren Lee	71	69	70	67	277	3,971
Gregory Bourdy	72	70	70	65	277	3,971
Kalle Brink	66	73	70	69	278	2,838
James Hepworth	68	69	71	70	278	2,838
Steven Bowditch	72	66	68	72	278	2,838
Johan Skold	67	73	70	69	279	2,255
Steven O'Hara	70	70	71	68	279	2,255
*Steven Jeppesen	69	72	67	71	279	
Eric Carlberg	70	66	76	68	280	1,815
Garry Houston	71	68	69	72	280	1,815
Mattias Eliasson	69	66	73	73	281	1,377.20
Martin Erlandsson	69	71	72	69	281	1,377.20
Jimmy Kawalec	71	71	74	65	281	1,377.20
Dennis Edlund	69	74	71	67	281	1,377.20
Leif Westerberg	70	72	68	71	281	1,377.20
Mark Mouland	73	70	69	70	282	1,082.71
Euan Little	74	66	72	70	282	1,082.71

	SCORES				TOTAL	MONEY
Sam Little	72	71	69	70	282	1,082.71
Paul Dwyer	71	68	68	75	282	1,082.71
Sion Bebb	73	70	72	67	282	1,082.71
Kariem Baraka	71	72	69	70	282	1,082.71
Stephen Browne	74	68	69	71	282	1,082.71
Marco Soffietti	71	70	67	75	283	848.22
Stefano Reale	69	72	75	67	283	848.22
Neil Cheetham	67	75	70	71	283	848.22
Joakim Rask	71	71	67	74	283	848.22
Magnus Carlsson	72	69	66	76	283	848.22
Linus Pettersson	70	72	72	69	283	848.22
Hampus Von Post	69	72	70	72	283	848.22
Daniel Vancsik	70	69	71	73	283	848.22
Michael Kirk	68	72	71	72	283	848.22

BA CA Golf Open

Fontana Golf Club, Vienna, Austria
Par 36-36–72; 7,040 yards

September 4-7
purse, €150,000

	SCORES				TOTAL	MONEY
Robert Coles	70	67	70	68	275	€25,000
Steven Bowditch	67	67	68	73	275	16,660
(Coles defeated Bowditch on first playoff hole.)						
Sion Bebb	75	64	67	71	277	7,266.25
Joakim Rask	68	70	70	69	277	7,266.25
Edward Rush	65	67	74	71	277	7,266.25
Louis Oosthuizen	72	66	67	72	277	7,266.25
Martin Erlandsson	69	66	71	72	278	5,160
Peter Gustafsson	70	69	70	69	278	5,160
Cesar Monasterio	72	67	70	70	279	4,210
Graeme Storm	69	69	69	72	279	4,210
Richard McEvoy	66	73	69	71	279	4,210
Markus Brier	73	67	71	69	280	3,540
Mark Mouland	74	68	65	74	281	2,432.14
Kalle Brink	69	68	72	72	281	2,432.14
Thomas Besancenez	70	68	70	73	281	2,432.14
Gianluca Baruffaldi	70	68	70	73	281	2,432.14
Richard Finch	64	69	78	70	281	2,432.14
Martin LeMesurier	72	67	72	70	281	2,432.14
Jamie Elson	73	67	69	72	281	2,432.14
Magnus Persson Atlevi	70	69	73	70	282	1,770
Marc Pendaries	67	69	69	78	283	1,527.86
Jose Manuel Carriles	72	66	70	75	283	1,527.86
Marcel Haremza	73	69	69	72	283	1,527.86
Scott Drummond	71	70	72	70	283	1,527.86
Massimo Florioli	70	72	67	74	283	1,527.86
James Hepworth	71	71	73	68	283	1,527.86
Kariem Baraka	69	70	69	75	283	1,527.86
Ulf Wendling	71	69	69	75	284	1,159.09
Steve Collins	72	70	72	70	284	1,159.09
Garry Houston	71	67	71	75	284	1,159.09
Richard Porter	67	72	67	78	284	1,159.09
Stefano Reale	71	71	73	69	284	1,159.09
Johan Edfors	69	72	73	70	284	1,159.09
Michele Reale	69	72	70	73	284	1,159.09
Pehr Magnebrant	66	72	72	74	284	1,159.09

	SCORES			TOTAL	MONEY
Daren Lee	72	68 72 72		284	1,159.09
David Orr	68	72 74 70		284	1,159.09
Ryan Grant	74	68 69 73		284	1,159.09

Benmore Developments Northern Ireland Masters

Clandeboye Golf Club, Belfast, N. Ireland
Par 35-36–71; 6,771 yards

September 11-14
purse, €220,648

	SCORES				TOTAL	MONEY
Darren Clarke	72	66	65	70	273	€35,877.75
Stuart Little	69	69	68	69	275	23,908.93
Jamie Elson	68	71	70	67	276	13,446.98
Sion Bebb	71	67	69	70	277	8,992.76
Michael Jonzon	69	63	75	70	277	8,992.76
Leif Westerberg	74	68	68	67	277	8,992.76
Stephen Browne	71	70	66	70	277	8,992.76
Martin LeMesurier	70	72	68	68	278	6,823.95
Jon Lupton	64	67	73	74	278	6,823.95
Greig Hutcheon	68	69	70	72	279	5,790.67
Graeme Storm	71	69	69	70	279	5,790.67
Paul Dwyer	73	67	72	68	280	4,635.41
Marc Warren	66	73	72	69	280	4,635.41
Louis Oosthuizen	71	67	76	66	280	4,635.41
Michael Hoey	69	72	72	68	281	3,234.38
Sandeep Grewal	73	68	70	70	281	3,234.38
Peter Gustafsson	71	70	71	69	281	3,234.38
Jack Doherty	67	70	76	68	281	3,234.38
Magnus Persson Atlevi	69	69	73	71	282	2,497.09
Jose Manuel Carriles	69	69	74	70	282	2,497.09
Ryan Reid	73	69	72	68	282	2,497.09
Sebastian Fernandez	68	69	77	68	282	2,497.09
Mark Mouland	71	70	72	70	283	2,181.37
Mark Sanders	71	71	71	70	283	2,181.37
Andrew Johnson	70	70	73	70	283	2,181.37
Marcus Higley	72	70	73	69	284	1,835.15
Martin Erlandsson	72	70	71	71	284	1,835.15
Paul Nilbrink	72	70	74	68	284	1,835.15
Chris Gane	70	68	74	72	284	1,835.15
Marco Bernardini	68	72	72	72	284	1,835.15
Craig Williams	70	70	75	69	284	1,835.15
Gareth Paddison	70	72	76	66	284	1,835.15
David Ryles	72	69	72	71	284	1,835.15

Telia Grand Prix

Ljunghusens Golf Club, Stockholm, Sweden
Par 35-36–71; 6,719 yards

September 18-21
purse, €132,419

	SCORES				TOTAL	MONEY
Euan Little	65	71	71	69	276	€22,069.86
Robert Coles	65	72	69	72	278	14,712.87
Fredrik Henge	69	71	69	70	279	7,443.61
Jamie Elson	70	68	68	73	279	7,443.61
Peter Gustafsson	72	69	63	77	281	5,382.84

	SCORES				TOTAL	MONEY
Ari Savolainen	72	70	70	69	281	5,382.84
*Mikael Detterberg	71	70	70	70	281	
Sam Little	69	72	70	71	282	4,740.61
Robert McGuirk	73	70	71	69	283	3,728.92
Dennis Edlund	70	69	74	70	283	3,728.92
Joakim Kristiansson	67	71	70	75	283	3,728.92
Fredrik Widmark	69	72	70	72	283	3,728.92
Martin LeMesurier	68	70	70	75	283	3,728.92
Magnus Persson Atlevi	69	71	73	71	284	2,231.26
Jose Manuel Carriles	73	69	69	73	284	2,231.26
Philip Archer	68	71	67	78	284	2,231.26
Murray Urquhart	74	67	72	71	284	2,231.26
Alan McLean	64	68	73	79	284	2,231.26
Leif Westerberg	70	69	69	76	284	2,231.26
Kalle Brink	74	68	68	75	285	1,405.12
Mattias Eliasson	74	69	70	72	285	1,405.12
Cesar Monasterio	68	72	72	73	285	1,405.12
Scott Drummond	69	73	66	77	285	1,405.12
Markus Westerberg	72	68	69	76	285	1,405.12
Mads Iversen	70	71	72	72	285	1,405.12
Graeme Storm	70	66	77	72	285	1,405.12
Daniel Vancsik	68	75	73	69	285	1,405.12
Steven O'Hara	71	71	69	74	285	1,405.12
Marc Pendaries	73	70	71	72	286	1,078.27
Paul Nilbrink	71	72	70	73	286	1,078.27
Olivier David	70	72	71	73	286	1,078.27
Pehr Magnebrant	67	69	69	81	286	1,078.27
Paul Dwyer	73	68	70	75	286	1,078.27
Michael Jonzon	69	70	68	79	286	1,078.27
Oskar Bergman	74	68	69	75	286	1,078.27

Open de Toulouse

Toulouse-Palmola Golf Club, Toulouse, France October 2-5
Par 36-36–72; 6,732 yards purse, €110,000

	SCORES				TOTAL	MONEY
Scott Drummond	66	67	65	71	269	€18,330
Mark Mouland	67	65	67	70	269	9,546
Alex Balicki	67	67	66	69	269	9,546
(Drummond defeated Mouland and Balicki on first playoff hole.)						
David Geall	67	66	70	68	271	5,500
Richard McEvoy	69	66	67	70	272	4,664
Euan Little	69	65	68	72	274	3,949
Jesus Maria Arruti	66	67	71	70	274	3,949
Thomas Norret	66	66	72	70	274	3,949
Cesar Monasterio	66	67	68	74	275	3,344
Chris Gane	68	70	68	70	276	2,838
Sion Bebb	72	67	69	68	276	2,838
Jamie Elson	69	67	68	72	276	2,838
John Mellor	69	68	70	70	277	2,255
Nicolas Marin	66	72	70	69	277	2,255
Alvaro Salto	69	70	70	69	278	1,595
Fredrik Orest	69	67	74	68	278	1,595
Robert Coles	68	68	70	72	278	1,595
Fredrik Widmark	66	67	70	75	278	1,595
Sebastian Fernandez	66	68	75	69	278	1,595

	SCORES				TOTAL	MONEY
Jose Manuel Carriles	72	64	68	75	279	1,201.20
Paul Dwyer	67	70	69	73	279	1,201.20
Benoit Teilleria	67	70	71	71	279	1,201.20
Graeme Storm	70	66	72	71	279	1,201.20
Craig Williams	70	68	70	71	279	1,201.20
Marc Pendaries	69	70	65	76	280	1,028.50
Philip Archer	67	70	70	73	280	1,028.50
Didier de Vooght	70	68	72	70	280	1,028.50
Dominique Nouailhac	69	69	70	72	280	1,028.50
Stuart Little	69	67	74	71	281	870.57
Jan-Are Larsen	65	70	72	74	281	870.57
Christopher Hanell	72	66	72	71	281	870.57
Tuomas Tuovinen	71	68	69	73	281	870.57
Bruno-Teva Lecuona	68	71	68	74	281	870.57
Gareth Paddison	71	67	72	71	281	870.57
Gregory Bourdy	68	68	70	75	281	870.57

Ryder Cup Wales Challenge

De Vere Northop Country Park Golf Club, Wales
Par 35-36–71; 6,521 yards

October 9-12
purse, €120,000

	SCORES				TOTAL	MONEY
Craig Williams	70	64	66	67	267	€20,000
Robert Coles	65	66	67	69	267	8,941.33
Robert Rock	64	67	65	71	267	8,941.33
Sam Walker	67	68	66	66	267	8,941.33
(Williams won on first playoff hole.)						
Sion Bebb	69	67	69	65	270	4,878
Kariem Baraka	67	68	65	70	270	4,878
Titch Moore	71	68	65	67	271	3,968
Olivier David	69	66	68	68	271	3,968
Edward Rush	70	68	65	68	271	3,968
Mattias Eliasson	67	67	65	73	272	2,967
Johan Edfors	68	69	70	65	272	2,967
Gary Clark	65	67	71	69	272	2,967
Marc Warren	68	71	66	67	272	2,967
Garry Houston	69	68	67	69	273	1,840
Liam Bond	70	66	68	69	273	1,840
Sebastien Delagrange	70	68	67	68	273	1,840
Ben Mason	67	68	69	69	273	1,840
Tuomas Tuovinen	67	71	65	70	273	1,840
Martin LeMesurier	68	70	65	70	273	1,840
Marc Pendaries	67	72	65	70	274	1,310.40
Jesus Maria Arruti	69	66	68	71	274	1,310.40
Linus Pettersson	69	70	67	68	274	1,310.40
Steven O'Hara	69	66	68	71	274	1,310.40
Gareth Paddison	68	66	72	68	274	1,310.40
Kalle Brink	68	71	66	70	275	1,086
Alex Balicki	72	67	70	66	275	1,086
Greig Hutcheon	69	68	69	69	275	1,086
David Geall	68	70	68	69	275	1,086
John Mellor	69	65	69	72	275	1,086
Steven Bowditch	68	68	69	70	275	1,086

Challenge Tour Grand Final

Golf du Medoc, Bordeaux, France
Par 35-36–71; 6,917 yards

October 23-26
purse, €150,000

	SCORES				TOTAL	MONEY
Jose Manuel Carriles	72	65	70	66	273	€25,600
Johan Edfors	68	69	66	70	273	17,100
(Carriles defeated Edfors on first playoff hole.)						
Jamie Elson	70	71	67	67	275	9,700
Martin Erlandsson	71	71	69	66	277	7,700
Damien McGrane	69	72	68	69	278	6,033.33
Stuart Little	71	72	70	65	278	6,033.33
Sebastian Fernandez	66	72	71	69	278	6,033.33
Sion Bebb	72	68	73	67	280	4,320
Ben Mason	71	70	71	68	280	4,320
Steven O'Hara	70	73	68	69	280	4,320
Martin LeMesurier	69	72	71	68	280	4,320
Gregory Bourdy	68	68	75	69	280	4,320
Cesar Monasterio	74	67	72	68	281	3,300
Greig Hutcheon	75	66	71	70	282	3,000
Marc Pendaries	70	71	68	74	283	2,700
Euan Little	68	70	74	72	284	2,200
Titch Moore	72	69	71	72	284	2,200
Martin Wiegele	71	73	76	64	284	2,200
Scott Drummond	75	71	69	70	285	1,780
Jamie Little	71	75	68	71	285	1,780
Graeme Storm	71	76	65	73	285	1,780
Peter Gustafsson	76	69	69	71	285	1,780
Alex Balicki	71	70	72	73	286	1,620
Sam Little	72	78	73	64	287	1,506.67
Craig Williams	74	69	76	68	287	1,506.67
Richard McEvoy	74	68	73	72	287	1,506.67
Pasi Purhonen	76	75	67	70	288	1,342.50
Robert Coles	73	71	76	68	288	1,342.50
Michael Jonzon	71	74	74	69	288	1,342.50
Ivo Giner	73	70	73	72	288	1,342.50

Asian PGA Tour

Caltex Masters

Laguna National Golf & Country Club, Singapore
Par 36-36–72; 7,145 yards

January 23-26
purse, US$900,000

	SCORES				TOTAL	MONEY
Zhang Lian-wei	68	71	69	70	278	US$150,000
Ernie Els	69	67	70	73	279	100,000
Prayad Marksaeng	73	67	69	71	280	56,340
Simon Khan	66	73	72	70	281	41,580
Maarten Lafeber	70	72	69	70	281	41,580
Rick Gibson	68	76	71	68	283	27,000
Andrew Marshall	67	73	73	70	283	27,000
Per Nyman	68	76	67	72	283	27,000
Fran Quinn	71	70	71	72	284	20,160
Dean Robertson	70	72	75	68	285	15,255
Thongchai Jaidee	73	71	71	70	285	15,255
Markus Brier	69	71	74	71	285	15,255
Jean-Francois Lucquin	73	69	72	71	285	15,255
Arjun Atwal	67	70	76	72	285	15,255
Simon Yates	68	69	72	76	285	15,255
Daniel Chopra	65	77	72	72	286	12,150
James Kingston	70	70	72	74	286	12,150
Jean-Francois Remesy	73	69	70	74	286	12,150
Ted Purdy	69	71	74	73	287	10,350
Kenneth Ferrie	71	73	70	73	287	10,350
Mads Vibe-Hastrup	71	72	71	73	287	10,350
Thammanoon Srirot	70	69	73	75	287	10,350
Nick O'Hern	71	72	69	75	287	10,350
Mark Pilkington	70	72	69	76	287	10,350
Mardan Mamat	70	70	76	72	288	8,550
Kang Wook-soon	71	69	74	74	288	8,550
Jan Are Larsen	71	70	73	74	288	8,550
Lin Keng-chi	71	71	72	74	288	8,550
David Lynn	73	72	74	69	288	8,550
John Bickerton	68	73	73	74	288	8,550
Fredrik Widmark	69	72	72	75	288	8,550
Yeh Wei-tze	69	72	75	73	289	6,885
Brad Kennedy	75	70	72	72	289	6,885
Eddie Lee	74	68	73	74	289	6,885
Chung Joon	72	72	73	72	289	6,885
Stephen Leaney	70	75	73	71	289	6,885
Paul Broadhurst	66	79	75	69	289	6,885
David Park	67	75	74	74	290	5,670
Lu Wen-teh	67	77	72	74	290	5,670
Jyoti Randhawa	70	69	78	73	290	5,670
Gustavo Rojas	67	74	76	73	290	5,670
Kyi Hla Han	70	73	72	75	290	5,670
Gary Murphy	70	68	81	71	290	5,670
Stephen Dodd	70	71	73	76	290	5,670
James Oh	71	69	76	75	291	4,410
Hendrik Buhrmann	72	73	72	74	291	4,410
Philip Archer	73	72	73	73	291	4,410
Anthony Kang	71	73	75	72	291	4,410

	SCORES				TOTAL	MONEY
Santiago Luna	72	71	78	70	291	4,410
Richard Green	72	72	78	69	291	4,410
Lam Chih-bing	69	70	72	80	291	4,410
Nick Dougherty	68	74	76	74	292	3,510
Benn Barham	65	78	75	74	292	3,510
Jason Knutzon	69	74	76	73	292	3,510
Gregory Hanrahan	66	75	74	78	293	2,970
Des Terblanche	72	73	73	75	293	2,970
Kevin Na	70	72	78	73	293	2,970
Craig Kamps	72	72	73	77	294	2,655
Matthew Blackey	72	72	78	72	294	2,655
Gerry Norquist	71	70	76	78	295	2,385
Andrew Pitts	72	72	76	75	295	2,385
Amandeep Johl	72	73	75	75	295	2,385
Marten Olander	71	72	80	72	295	2,385
Henrik Bjornstad	70	72	76	78	296	2,115
Soren Kjeldsen	75	69	75	77	296	2,115
Jeev Milkha Singh	66	71	80	80	297	1,890
Euan Little	69	74	75	79	297	1,890
Simon Wakefield	75	69	78	75	297	1,890
Chris Williams	68	76	73	82	299	1,566.52
Julien Van Hauwe	70	74	77	78	299	1,566.52
Gary Evans	73	71	81	74	299	1,566.52
Klas Eriksson	74	71	75	80	300	1,343.16
Lee S. James	68	74	81	77	300	1,343.16
Jarrod Moseley	76	68	79	77	300	1,343.16
Thaworn Wiratchant	73	72	80	77	302	1,336.76
Pablo Del Olmo	71	74	78	80	303	1,333.56
Poh Eng Wah	71	72	84	79	306	1,330.37
Edward Loar	75	70	78	84	307	1,327.17

Carlsberg Malaysian Open

Mines Resort & Golf Club, Kuala Lumpur, Malaysia
Par 35-36–71; 6,785 yards

February 20-23
purse, US$1,100,000

	SCORES				TOTAL	MONEY
Arjun Atwal	62	65	67	66	260	US$183,330
Brad Kennedy	68	66	66	64	264	95,540
Retief Goosen	66	64	66	68	264	95,540
Dean Robertson	66	70	64	66	266	55,000
Thammanoon Srirot	63	69	70	65	267	46,640
Daniel Chopra	65	68	66	69	268	38,500
Ted Oh	64	67	70	68	269	33,000
Patrik Sjoland	68	66	70	66	270	27,500
Simon Khan	69	67	67	68	271	20,702
Gerald Rosales	72	68	66	65	271	20,702
Simon Dyson	65	70	68	68	271	20,702
Yeh Wei-tze	65	69	72	65	271	20,702
Liang Wen-chong	68	66	66	71	271	20,702
Boonchu Ruangkit	69	70	69	64	272	16,170
Chawalit Plaphol	70	71	64	67	272	16,170
Padraig Harrington	66	66	67	73	272	16,170
Martin Maritz	70	69	69	65	273	13,970
Andrew Marshall	71	66	66	70	273	13,970
Paul McGinley	67	69	70	67	273	13,970
Emanuele Canonica	67	66	68	72	273	13,970

		SCORES			TOTAL	MONEY
Terry Price	70	70	68	66	274	12,100
Thongchai Jaidee	68	68	70	68	274	12,100
Mathias Gronberg	72	64	71	67	274	12,100
Arjun Singh	67	69	70	68	274	12,100
Fredrik Andersson	62	69	71	72	274	12,100
Jan Are Larsen	73	65	69	68	275	10,780
Kang Wook-soon	66	72	70	67	275	10,780
Gary Rusnak	66	69	70	70	275	10,780
Zaw Moe	70	69	67	70	276	9,625
Mike Cunning	70	69	70	67	276	9,625
Charl Schwartzel	71	69	67	69	276	9,625
Pablo Del Olmo	70	67	74	65	276	9,625
Soren Kjeldsen	70	68	71	68	277	8,045.71
Sung Mao-chang	69	70	70	68	277	8,045.71
Thaworn Wiratchant	68	69	73	67	277	8,045.71
Alastair Forsyth	71	70	68	68	277	8,045.71
Kim Felton	74	67	68	68	277	8,045.71
Prayad Marksaeng	68	66	70	73	277	8,045.71
David Gleeson	73	68	71	65	277	8,045.71
Simon Yates	66	73	68	71	278	6,380
Mardan Mamat	69	70	68	71	278	6,380
Marcus Fraser	67	71	70	70	278	6,380
Kyi Hla Han	70	68	71	69	278	6,380
Chris Williams	68	69	70	71	278	6,380
Jean-Francois Lucquin	70	70	69	69	278	6,380
Stephen Scahill	68	68	71	71	278	6,380
Anthony Kang	67	68	73	70	278	6,380
Harmeet Kahlon	66	75	72	66	279	5,280
Eddie Lee	73	68	69	69	279	5,280
Charlie Wi	72	67	71	70	280	4,290
Ian Woosnam	70	68	74	68	280	4,290
Andrew Pitts	68	72	70	70	280	4,290
Rick Gibson	69	68	70	73	280	4,290
Chung Joon	67	69	73	71	280	4,290
Des Terblanche	72	69	71	68	280	4,290
Brian Davis	73	68	70	69	280	4,290
Jason Knutzon	70	68	67	76	281	3,300
Per Nyman	73	67	70	71	281	3,300
Rafael Ponce	75	66	72	68	281	3,300
Tobias Dier	73	66	75	68	282	2,805
Alessandro Tadini	65	75	74	68	282	2,805
Robert-Jan Derksen	69	71	70	72	282	2,805
Gerry Norquist	71	69	71	71	282	2,805
Periasamy Gunasagaran	66	70	73	73	282	2,805
V. Arumugam	72	69	70	71	282	2,805
Lee S. James	70	69	69	75	283	2,255
Maarten Lafeber	73	67	71	72	283	2,255
Jorge Berendt	69	72	70	72	283	2,255
Hendrik Buhrmann	72	69	67	75	283	2,255
Sushi Ishigaki	71	68	73	72	284	1,830.05
Simon Wakefield	70	71	75	68	284	1,830.05
S. Murthy	67	69	77	72	285	1,643.61
*S. Sivachandran	71	69	71	74	285	
Amandeep Johl	68	68	72	77	285	1,643.61
Ben Mason	68	73	71	73	285	1,643.61
Stephen A. Lindskog	67	73	73	73	286	1,633.89
Knud Storgaard	69	72	73	72	286	1,633.89
Hsieh Yu-shu	68	73	72	73	286	1,633.89
Shaaban Hussin	68	72	75	72	287	1,624.17

		SCORES			TOTAL	MONEY
Mark James	72	69	72	74	287	1,624.17
Angleo Que	72	69	71	75	287	1,624.17
Mads Vibe-Hastrup	73	67	71	80	291	1,617.69
David Dixon	71	70	79	76	296	1,614.45

Myanmar Open

Yangon Golf Club, Yangon, Myanmar
Par 36-36–72; 7,011 yards

February 27-March 2
purse, US$200,000

		SCORES			TOTAL	MONEY
Lin Keng-chi	67	69	70	69	275	US$32,300
Thongchai Jaidee	69	68	72	69	278	22,260
James Kingston	67	72	70	70	279	11,200
Aung Win	68	74	67	70	279	11,200
Daniel Chopra	76	68	67	69	280	7,500
Arjun Singh	70	72	69	69	280	7,500
Mardan Mamat	71	72	69	70	282	5,153.33
Lin Wen-tang	71	71	69	71	282	5,153.33
Chris Rodgers	71	73	68	70	282	5,153.33
Rafael Ponce	73	68	72	70	283	3,701.33
Terry Pilkadaris	71	70	71	71	283	3,701.33
Rick Gibson	69	70	71	73	283	3,701.33
Simon Yates	75	68	73	68	284	3,072
Harmeet Kahlon	69	72	72	71	284	3,072
Jason Knutzon	73	66	67	78	284	3,072
Thammanoon Srirot	73	73	71	68	285	2,645
Edward Loar	72	76	68	69	285	2,645
Prayad Marksaeng	70	73	72	70	285	2,645
Mukesh Kumar	68	69	76	72	285	2,645
James Oh	76	73	67	70	286	2,370
Dean Alaban	74	70	69	73	286	2,370
*Prom Meesawat	71	74	74	69	288	
Soe Kyaw Naing	73	70	74	71	288	2,190
Clay Devers	75	70	71	72	288	2,190
Aaron Meeks	69	72	72	75	288	2,190
Chawalit Plaphol	70	72	70	76	288	2,190
Gary Rusnak	74	74	68	73	289	2,040
Scott Barr	71	72	78	69	290	1,730
Kevin Na	73	75	74	68	290	1,730
Michael Hoey	74	72	75	69	290	1,730
Johan Skold	75	74	71	70	290	1,730
Lin Chie-hsiang	73	74	70	73	290	1,730
Dong Yi	71	71	75	73	290	1,730
Thaworn Wiratchant	73	73	72	72	290	1,730
Boonchu Ruangkit	72	73	73	72	290	1,730
*Zaw Zin Win	74	74	70	72	290	
Scott Taylor	76	69	71	74	290	1,730
Muhammad Munir	72	71	72	75	290	1,730

Phoenix Dynasty Cup

Mission Hills Golf Club, World Cup Course, Shenzhen, China   March 14-16
Par 36-36–72; 7,102 yards

FIRST DAY
Foursomes

Zhang Lian-wei and Liang Wen-chong (Asia) defeated Hajime Meshiai and Nobuhito Sato, 1 up.
Hiroyuki Fujita and Katsumasa Miyamoto (Japan) defeated Arjun Atwal and Jeev Milkha Singh, 3 and 1.
Taichi Teshima and Keiichiro Fukabori (Japan) defeated Lin Keng-chi and Kang Wook-soon, 1 up.
Thongchai Jaidee and Prayad Marksaeng (Asia) defeated Toru Suzuki and Katsunori Kuwabara, 2 and 1.
Tsuneyuki Nakajima and Tomohiro Kondo (Japan) defeated Thammanoon Srirot and Thaworn Wiratchant, 2 and 1.
Charlie Wi and Jyoti Randhawa (Asia) defeated Kiyoshi Murota and Yasuharo Imano, 2 and 1.

FIRST-DAY POINTS: Asia 3, Japan 3

SECOND DAY
Fourballs

Nakajima and Meshiai (Japan) defeated Srirot and Wiratchant, 3 and 2.
Jaidee and Marksaeng (Asia) defeated Miyamoto and Suzuki, 2 and 1.
Lin and Kang (Asia) defeated Sato and Imano, 4 and 3.
Atwal and Singh (Asia) defeated Fujita and Fukabori, 2 and 1.
Zhang and Liang (Asia) defeated Murota and Kondo, 2 and 1.
Randhawa and Wi (Asia) defeated Teshima and Kuwabara, 5 and 4.

SECOND-DAY POINTS: Asia 5, Japan 1
TOTAL POINTS: Asia 8, Japan 4

THIRD DAY
Singles

Marksaeng (Asia) defeated Teshima, 2 and 1.
Kang (Asia) defeated Suzuki, 4 and 2.
Randhawa (Asia) defeated Miyase, 2 up.
Kuwabara (Japan) defeated Wiratchant, 2 up.
Wi (Asia) defeated Meshiai, 4 and 3.
Liang (Asia) defeated Imano, 1 up.
Murota (Japan) defeated Lin, 6 and 5.
Srirot (Asia) defeated Fujita, 4 and 3.
Nakajima (Japan) defeated Atwal, 4 and 2.
Jaidee (Asia) halved with Kondo.
Singh (Asia) defeated Miyamoto, 2 and 1.
Zhang (Asia) defeated Sato, 4 and 3.

THIRD-DAY POINTS: Asia 8½, Japan 3½
TOTAL POINTS: Asia 16½, Japan 7½

Royal Challenge Indian Open

Delhi Golf Club, New Delhi, India
Par 36-36–72; 6,835 yards

March 27-30
purse, US$300,000

		SCORES			TOTAL	MONEY
Mike Cunning	69	69	68	64	270	US$50,000
Rick Gibson	65	72	69	69	275	33,090
James Kingston	69	67	71	69	276	16,537.50
Adam Groom	67	69	69	71	276	16,537.50
Zaw Moe	63	73	70	71	277	11,775
Arjun Atwal	69	72	67	70	278	9,562.50
Jyoti Randhawa	66	71	67	74	278	9,562.50
Aung Win	71	68	71	69	279	7,032.50
Mo Joong-kyung	69	71	67	72	279	7,032.50
Craig Kamps	73	69	69	69	280	5,752.50
Digvijay Singh	69	73	67	71	280	5,752.50
Amritinder Singh	69	74	69	69	281	4,987.50
Thammanoon Srirot	70	71	71	69	281	4,987.50
Richard Backwell	70	73	69	70	282	4,410
David Gleeson	70	72	70	70	282	4,410
Anura Rohana	73	70	69	70	282	4,410
Brad Kennedy	72	72	71	68	283	3,695
Steve Friesen	70	74	72	67	283	3,695
Yusof Ali	70	72	71	70	283	3,695
Mardan Mamat	70	72	70	71	283	3,695
Kim Felton	67	73	72	71	283	3,695
Chen Yuan-chi	69	71	71	72	283	3,695
Shiv Prakash	70	72	73	69	284	3,195
Zai Kipgen	74	67	73	70	284	3,195
Chan Yih-shin	72	72	69	71	284	3,195
Pablo Del Olmo	67	72	71	74	284	3,195
Firoz Ali	71	71	74	69	285	2,630
Olle Nordberg	69	71	74	71	285	2,630
Chris Williams	67	73	74	71	285	2,630
Clay Devers	69	71	74	71	285	2,630
Soe Kyaw Naing	68	75	70	72	285	2,630
Pappan	71	70	71	73	285	2,630
Gaurav Ghei	72	66	73	74	285	2,630
Terry Pilkadaris	69	71	71	74	285	2,630
Kyi Hla Han	70	71	70	74	285	2,630

Thailand Open

Krisada City Golf Hills, Thailand
Par 36-36–72; 6,975 yards

April 3-6
purse, US$150,000

		SCORES			TOTAL	MONEY
Edward Loar	67	66	67	69	269	US$24,225
Jason Dawes	68	65	70	71	274	16,695
Chen Yuan-chi	71	69	70	65	275	8,400
Lin Wen-tang	70	68	71	66	275	8,400
Boonchu Ruangkit	71	68	66	71	276	5,625
Aung Win	67	69	68	72	276	5,625
Jason Knutzon	68	70	70	69	277	3,865
Thaworn Wiratchant	70	69	69	69	277	3,865
Gaurav Ghei	70	70	65	72	277	3,865
*Prom Meesawat	72	66	71	69	278	

	SCORES				TOTAL	MONEY
Lam Chih-bing	70	65	72	71	278	2,685
Amandeep Johl	71	67	68	72	278	2,685
Andrew Pitts	71	65	70	72	278	2,685
Thongchai Jaidee	67	66	71	74	278	2,685
Bobby Lincoln	71	69	71	68	279	2,115
Chris Williams	71	69	71	68	279	2,115
Sushi Ishigaki	72	66	71	70	279	2,115
Rick Gibson	69	66	72	72	279	2,115
Shannon Jones	68	71	67	73	279	2,115
Chung Chun-hsing	68	72	70	70	280	1,758
Alex Rodger	68	71	71	70	280	1,758
Unho Park	71	68	69	72	280	1,758
Adam Groom	67	67	73	73	280	1,758
Rashid Ismail	70	72	64	74	280	1,758
Anthony Kang	67	69	74	71	281	1,507.50
Hong Chia-yuh	69	70	72	70	281	1,507.50
Kao Bo-Song	70	72	68	71	281	1,507.50
Aaron Meeks	68	68	73	72	281	1,507.50
Lu Wei-lan	72	70	67	72	281	1,507.50
Firoz Ali	69	68	71	73	281	1,507.50

Maekyung Open

Nam Seoul Country Club, Seoul, Korea
Par 36-36–72; 6,796 yards

May 1-4
purse, US$400,000

	SCORES				TOTAL	MONEY
Chung Joon	70	68	68	69	275	US$81,037
Amandeep Johl	70	70	69	67	276	50,648
Thongchai Jaidee	74	68	69	67	278	24,311
Choi Yoon-soo	71	70	68	70	279	20,259
Choi Sang-ho	73	72	69	66	280	12,938
Shin Yong-jin	74	71	66	69	280	12,938
*Kim Kyung-tae	74	68	70	68	280	
Choi Gwang-soo	71	73	66	70	280	12,938
Eddie Lee	72	73	69	67	281	8,995
Jang Ik-jae	71	73	74	65	283	7,029
Unho Park	73	70	73	67	283	7,029
Sushi Ishigaki	73	69	72	69	283	7,029
Ted Oh	71	70	71	71	283	7,029
*Kim Sang-ho	76	70	71	67	284	
Yoo Jong-koo	73	72	72	67	284	5,510
Richard Backwell	69	73	70	72	284	5,510
Suk Jong-ryul	69	71	73	71	284	5,510
Kim Hyung-tae	71	71	70	72	284	5,510
Chris Williams	75	69	73	68	285	4,943
Andrew Pitts	71	74	71	69	285	4,943
Park No-seok	72	75	69	69	285	4,943
Lee Kun-hee	72	73	72	69	286	4,477
Brad Kennedy	74	71	71	70	286	4,477
Yang Yong-eun	74	70	71	71	286	4,477
Lim Hyung-soo	73	71	71	71	286	4,477
Hong Chia-yuh	72	75	71	69	287	3,869
Arjun Singh	71	73	73	70	287	3,869
Lin Wen-tang	73	72	71	71	287	3,869
Gerald Rosales	72	71	73	71	287	3,869
Chung Jae-hoon	70	72	71	74	287	3,869
Lee In-woo	70	74	70	73	287	3,869

SK Telecom Open

Baekahmvista Country Club, Seoul, Korea
Par 36-36–72; 7,079 yards
(Second round cancelled—rain.)

June 26-29
purse, US$400,000

	SCORES			TOTAL	MONEY
K.J. Choi	64	69	68	201	US$82,290
Shin Yong-jin	68	64	69	201	41,145
(Choi defeated Shin on second playoff hole.)					
Corey Pavin	67	68	68	203	24,687
Kim Tae-bok	66	70	69	205	16,842
Park Young-soo	70	64	71	205	16,842
Yang Yong-eun	67	66	72	205	16,842
Liang Wen-chong	69	67	71	207	11,850
Lee In-woo	69	68	70	207	11,850
Choi Gwang-soo	68	72	68	208	9,216
Joon Chung	70	66	72	208	9,216
Daniel Chopra	68	69	71	208	9,216
Katsuhiko Yamazaki	66	73	70	209	7,900
*Kim Seung-hyuk	67	69	73	209	
Kim Felton	71	71	68	210	6,320
James Oh	71	69	70	210	6,320
Cho Do-hyun	68	71	71	210	6,320
Kang Wook-soon	66	69	75	210	6,320
Thongchai Jaidee	69	66	75	210	6,320
Choi Sang-ho	69	70	72	211	5,102
Thaworn Wiratchant	69	70	72	211	5,102
Sung Mao-chang	71	71	70	212	4,197
Sushi Ishigaki	71	71	70	212	4,197
*Sung Si-woo	71	71	70	212	
Kyi Hla Han	68	72	72	212	4,197
Gerald Rosales	70	70	72	212	4,197
Kim Wan-tae	69	69	74	212	4,197
Kevin Na	67	72	73	212	4,197
Ahmad Bateman	69	73	71	213	3,162
Bae Sung-chul	71	71	71	213	3,162
Hong Chia-yuh	66	75	72	213	3,162
Kong Young-joon	69	71	73	213	3,162
Gleeson David	66	71	76	213	3,162
Harmeet Kahlon	69	69	75	213	3,162
Moon Choong-hwan	71	68	74	213	3,162

Mercuries Masters

Taiwan Golf & Country Club, Taipei, Taiwan
Par 36-36–72; 6,950 yards

September 11-14
purse, US$300,000

	SCORES				TOTAL	MONEY
Lin Wen-ko	70	69	68	73	280	US$76,878.28
Thongchai Jaidee	68	70	67	76	281	46,126.97
Thammanoon Srirot	74	69	66	73	282	26,907.40
Arjun Singh	75	71	67	71	284	19,219.57
Lu Wen-teh	73	73	67	72	285	14,414.68
Yeh Chang-ting	70	70	70	75	285	14,414.68
Thaworn Wiratchant	74	71	69	72	286	10,570.76
Stephen Lindskog	73	70	69	74	286	10,570.76
Boonchu Ruangkit	70	76	70	71	287	7,303.44

	SCORES				TOTAL	MONEY
Hsieh Dong-shu	72	69	72	74	287	7,303.44
Danny Chia	75	70	72	71	288	5,958.07
Chen Tsang-te	73	72	72	71	288	5,958.07
Chung Chun-hsing	73	71	72	72	288	5,958.07
Gerald Rosales	72	75	68	73	288	5,958.07
Lin Keng-chi	71	72	74	72	289	4,804.89
Lin Wen-tang	69	74	72	74	289	4,804.89
Chawalit Plaphol	73	73	70	73	289	4,804.89
Danny Zarate	74	74	73	69	290	4,161.04
Chan Yih-shin	73	73	72	72	290	4,161.04
Andrew Pitts	71	75	72	72	290	4,161.04
Kyi Hla Han	74	73	70	73	290	4,161.04
Wang Ter-chang	72	69	81	69	291	3,738.21
Lin Chien-bing	73	75	73	70	291	3,738.21
Hsieh Yu-shu	74	74	73	70	291	3,738.21
Hsieh Min-nan	72	72	73	74	291	3,738.21
Su Chin-jung	72	71	75	74	292	3,459.52
Gary Rusnak	75	72	70	75	292	3,459.52
Sung Mao-chang	76	72	69	75	292	3,459.52
Des Terblanche	72	70	77	74	293	3,267.33
Brad Kennedy	74	69	73	77	293	3,267.33

Kolon Cup Korean Open

Woo Jung Hills Country Club, Cheonan, Korea
Par 36-36–72

October 9-12
purse, US$400,000

	SCORES				TOTAL	MONEY
John Daly	73	69	72	68	282	US$85,543
Thaworn Wiratchant	70	72	71	70	283	42,771
Simon Yates	74	76	66	68	284	29,084
Shin Yong-jin	74	70	71	70	285	20,530
Kim Jong-duck	76	66	74	70	286	16,253
Kim Dae-sub	74	73	72	68	287	13,601
Yang Yong-eun	76	71	71	69	287	13,601
S.K. Ho	75	70	69	73	287	13,601
Kevin Na	73	72	72	73	290	9,431
Lee Sun-ho	68	72	75	75	290	9,431
Clay Devers	71	72	72	75	290	9,431
Liang Wen-chong	71	72	70	77	290	9,431
Cho Hyun-jun	70	77	73	71	291	6,458
Jason Dawes	73	73	74	71	291	6,458
Gerald Rosales	73	75	74	70	292	5,089
*Kim Kyung-tae	71	75	75	71	292	
Lu Wen-teh	72	76	76	68	292	5,089
Park Nam-sin	78	68	73	73	292	5,089
Ted Oh	67	74	76	75	292	5,089
Lee Jun-young	75	72	69	76	292	5,089
Jang Ik-jae	70	76	69	77	292	5,089
*Lee Dong-hwan	78	73	73	69	293	
Harmeet Kahlon	75	76	68	74	293	4,319
Kim Felton	74	71	71	77	293	4,319
Chung Jae-hoon	74	72	70	77	293	4,319
Hendrik Buhrmann	74	76	71	73	294	4,020
*Sung Si-woo	70	72	73	79	294	
Kim Tae-hoon	74	74	74	73	295	3,555
Kang Ji-man	72	76	73	74	295	3,555
Pablo Del Olmo	75	73	73	74	295	3,555

	SCORES				TOTAL	MONEY
Choi Gwang-soo	74	73	73	75	295	3,555
Lee In-woo	79	72	77	67	295	3,555
Choi Sang-ho	73	69	76	77	295	3,555
Robert Jacobson	71	70	77	77	295	3,555
Park Boo-won	75	72	70	78	295	3,555

Macau Open

Macau Golf & Country Club, Macau
Par 35-36–71; 6,622 yards

October 16-19
purse, US$250,000

	SCORES				TOTAL	MONEY
Colin Montgomerie	66	72	67	68	273	US$40,375
Scott Barr	66	67	69	71	273	27,825
(Montgomerie defeated Barr on first playoff hole.)						
Arjun Atwal	70	69	68	68	275	15,500
Kevin Na	69	71	69	68	277	10,416.67
Lu Wei-lan	67	70	70	70	277	10,416.67
Jason Knutzon	66	70	69	72	277	10,416.67
Kyi Hla Han	70	70	72	66	278	6,081.25
Chawalit Plaphol	70	70	70	68	278	6,081.25
Robert Jacobson	70	69	70	69	278	6,081.25
Hendrik Buhrmann	72	65	72	69	278	6,081.25
Hong Chia-yuh	70	73	72	65	280	4,299.67
Andrew Pitts	73	68	70	69	280	4,299.67
Thaworn Wiratchant	68	67	72	73	280	4,299.67
Simon Yates	69	68	74	70	281	3,600
Lin Wen-tang	69	71	69	72	281	3,600
Adam Le Vesconte	72	69	68	72	281	3,600
Derek Fung	66	75	68	72	281	3,600
Glenn Joyner	70	67	71	74	282	3,162.50
Sushi Ishigaki	69	68	69	76	282	3,162.50
Terry Pilkadaris	70	70	74	69	283	2,887.50
Brad Kennedy	71	74	69	69	283	2,887.50
Chris Williams	67	74	71	71	283	2,887.50
Unho Park	71	71	69	72	283	2,887.50
Soe Kyaw Naing	71	72	70	71	284	2,700
Derek Crawford	70	69	77	69	285	2,475
Troy Kennedy	73	67	75	70	285	2,475
Ahmad Bateman	70	70	75	70	285	2,475
Jason Dawes	71	70	73	71	285	2,475
Wang Ter-chang	71	74	68	72	285	2,475
Chung Chun-hsing	71	72	73	70	286	2,175
Jim Johnson	72	71	71	72	286	2,175
Marcus Both	72	72	69	73	286	2,175

Sanya Open

Yalong Bay Golf Club, Sanya, China
Par 36-36–72

October 23-26
purse, US$200,000

	SCORES				TOTAL	MONEY
Marcus Both	68	70	70	67	275	US$32,300
Mardan Mamat	68	71	72	65	276	14,887
Hendrik Buhrmann	69	70	71	66	276	14,887

	SCORES				TOTAL	MONEY
Chen Yuan-chi	68	69	71	68	276	14,887
Danny Chia	75	70	69	63	277	7,000
Lin Wen-ko	69	69	70	69	277	7,000
Brad Kennedy	69	69	70	69	277	7,000
Stephen Lindskog	67	68	72	71	278	5,000
Scott Strange	70	66	74	69	279	3,891
Lin Wen-tang	69	75	67	68	279	3,891
Jason Dawes	71	67	69	72	279	3,891
Simon Yates	70	67	70	72	279	3,891
Andrew Pitts	71	64	72	73	280	3,072
Chawalit Plaphol	68	71	69	72	280	3,072
Greg Hanrahan	66	70	69	75	280	3,072
Gerry Norquist	71	71	71	68	281	2,596
Arjun Singh	71	69	72	69	281	2,596
Kyi Hla Han	73	71	66	71	281	2,596
Thaworn Wiratchant	74	69	67	71	281	2,596
Terry Pilkadaris	70	69	70	72	281	2,596
Angelo Que	73	70	71	68	282	2,310
Gerald Rosales	70	69	71	72	282	2,310
Anthony Kang	72	69	74	68	283	2,010
Lu Wei-lan	70	67	76	70	283	2,010
Adam Le Vesconte	69	71	73	70	283	2,010
Boonchu Ruangkit	68	72	73	70	283	2,010
Jim Johnson	69	70	73	71	283	2,010
Lin Chien-bing	71	68	72	72	283	2,010
Keith Horne	68	69	73	73	283	2,010
Hsu Mong-nan	72	70	68	73	283	2,010

Hero Honda Masters

Delhi Golf Club, New Delhi, India
Par 36-35–71; 6,831 yards

November 6-9
purse, US$300,000

	SCORES				TOTAL	MONEY
Arjun Atwal	69	71	70	71	281	US$48,450
Pablo Del Olmo	68	74	72	68	282	22,330
Jyoti Randhawa	71	70	68	73	282	22,330
Gary Rusnak	73	71	65	73	282	22,330
Kim Felton	77	68	69	69	283	10,500
Rafiq Ali	71	70	71	71	283	10,500
Unho Park	72	70	69	72	283	10,500
Simon Yates	73	69	73	69	284	7,095
Jeev Milkha Singh	66	72	73	73	284	7,095
Mukesh Kumar	73	69	72	71	285	5,552
Rafael Ponce	74	69	67	75	285	5,552
Digvijay Singh	71	68	68	78	285	5,552
Uttam Singh Mundy	72	71	73	70	286	4,420.80
Scott Barr	72	72	70	72	286	4,420.80
Sung Mao-chang	75	70	68	73	286	4,420.80
Ashok Kumar	70	74	68	74	286	4,420.80
Anthony Kang	70	70	71	75	286	4,420.80
Terry Pilkadaris	72	70	73	72	287	3,675
Gaurav Ghei	72	72	70	73	287	3,675
Chawalit Plaphol	73	72	69	73	287	3,675
Vijay Kumar	68	71	73	75	287	3,675
Akinori Tani	71	75	74	68	288	3,015
Hendrik Buhrmann	73	71	75	69	288	3,015

	SCORES				TOTAL	MONEY
Pat Giles	69	73	75	71	288	3,015
Jason Dawes	73	73	71	71	288	3,015
Stephen Lindskog	72	70	73	73	288	3,015
Boonchu Ruangkit	74	71	71	72	288	3,015
Jason Knutzon	75	71	69	73	288	3,015
Firoz Ali	72	70	72	74	288	3,015
David Gleeson	71	73	70	74	288	3,015
Thaworn Wiratchant	72	73	68	75	288	3,015

Volvo China Open

Shanghai Silport Golf Club, Shanghai, China
Par 36-36–72; 7,062 yards

November 13-16
purse, US$500,000

	SCORES				TOTAL	MONEY
Zhang Lian-wei	67	69	69	72	277	US$90,000
Thaworn Wiratchant	68	69	73	69	279	55,500
Unho Park	70	70	67	74	281	30,900
Adam Fraser	68	67	75	72	282	24,000
Chawalit Plaphol	70	71	70	72	283	17,750
Choi Gwang-soo	71	64	75	73	283	17,750
Pat Giles	70	74	71	69	284	14,000
David Gleeson	70	67	75	73	285	9,995
Ross Bain	71	65	74	75	285	9,995
Scott Strange	70	67	71	77	285	9,995
Simon Yates	72	68	69	76	285	9,995
Jason Knutzon	71	74	71	71	287	7,730
Des Terblanche	70	72	73	72	287	7,730
Greg Hanrahan	73	67	73	74	287	7,730
Soe Kyaw Naing	74	71	68	74	287	7,730
Gary Rusnak	73	69	76	70	288	6,575
Nico van Rensburg	70	73	71	74	288	6,575
Rafael Ponce	71	67	75	75	288	6,575
Angelo Que	67	73	72	76	288	6,575
Vijay Kumar	73	73	72	71	289	5,680
Andrew Pitts	74	73	69	73	289	5,680
Scott Barr	70	69	76	74	289	5,680
Park No-seok	74	70	69	76	289	5,680
Danny Zarate	67	71	74	77	289	5,680
Anura Rohana	75	72	72	71	290	5,066.67
Hong Chia-yuh	68	72	78	72	290	5,066.67
Kim Sang-ki	70	73	72	75	290	5,066.67
Uttam Singh Mundy	73	71	74	73	291	4,550
Liang Wen-chong	69	76	73	73	291	4,550
Craig Kamps	72	72	72	75	291	4,550
Fran Quinn	74	69	71	77	291	4,550

Acer Taiwan Open

Sunrise Golf & Country Club, Tao Yuan, Taiwan
Par 36-36–72; 7,062 yards

November 20-23
purse, US$300,000

	SCORES				TOTAL	MONEY
Jason Dawes	68	70	73	73	284	US$50,000
Jeev Milkha Singh	65	80	77	70	292	33,090

	SCORES				TOTAL	MONEY
Lin Wen-tang	69	77	75	74	295	18,325
Hendrik Buhrmann	68	76	80	72	296	14,750
Simon Yates	72	72	72	81	297	11,775
Pat Giles	68	74	76	80	298	8,833.33
Chen Chung-cheng	70	70	80	78	298	8,833.33
Kim Felton	70	77	78	73	298	8,833.33
Wang Ter-chang	70	73	78	78	299	5,836.50
Stephen Lindskog	73	76	75	75	299	5,836.50
Chang Tse-peng	75	72	78	74	299	5,836.50
Thaworn Wiratchant	71	76	79	73	299	5,836.50
Terry Pilkadaris	74	73	77	76	300	4,824
Andrew Pitts	74	75	74	78	301	4,320
Justin Rose	70	79	75	77	301	4,320
David Gleeson	72	78	74	77	301	4,320
Scott Taylor	69	81	75	76	301	4,320
Dong Yi	74	73	80	75	302	3,870
Adam Le Vesconte	75	78	75	75	303	3,720
Vijay Kumar	71	81	78	74	304	3,600
Amandeep Johl	69	81	77	78	305	3,465
Chen Jung-hsin	72	78	79	76	305	3,465
Anthony Kang	71	76	79	81	307	3,195
Su Chin-jung	70	76	81	80	307	3,195
Glenn Joyner	75	79	77	76	307	3,195
Chris Williams	72	74	87	74	307	3,195
Jang Ik-jae	70	74	83	81	308	2,745
Lee Lien-fu	71	78	79	80	308	2,745
Danny Zarate	71	80	78	79	308	2,745
Hsu Mong-nan	73	77	80	78	308	2,745
Kao Bo-song	67	84	79	78	308	2,745
Harmeet Kahlon	71	75	86	76	308	2,745

Omega Hong Kong Open

Hong Kong Golf Club, Hong Kong
Par 34-36–70; 6,768 yards

December 4-7
purse, US$700,000

	SCORES				TOTAL	MONEY
Padraig Harrington	67	69	67	66	269	US$113,000
Hennie Otto	68	68	69	65	270	77,870
Chris Gane	70	67	67	69	273	32,685
Darren Clarke	68	69	69	67	273	32,685
Thomas Bjorn	69	71	65	68	273	32,685
Fredrik Jacobson	68	65	71	69	273	32,685
James Kingston	69	70	68	67	274	17,996.67
Prayad Marksaeng	67	69	67	71	274	17,996.67
Christopher Hanell	68	69	65	72	274	17,996.67
Jose Maria Olazabal	68	71	70	66	275	12,125
David Carter	70	71	65	69	275	12,125
Michael Campbell	67	71	71	66	275	12,125
Gary Rusnak	68	70	68	69	275	12,125
Rob Rashell	70	67	67	71	275	12,125
Nick Faldo	69	72	67	68	276	9,090
Marc Pendaries	70	71	68	67	276	9,090
Nobuhito Sato	68	72	68	68	276	9,090
Stephen Dodd	69	72	68	67	276	9,090
Henrik Nystrom	69	66	73	68	276	9,090
Richard McEvoy	62	68	74	72	276	9,090

	SCORES				TOTAL	MONEY
Steven Jeppesen	68	73	69	66	276	9,090
Anthony Kang	71	70	67	69	277	7,730
Wang Ter-chang	68	70	70	69	277	7,730
Kim Felton	67	73	69	68	277	7,730
Kyi Hla Han	69	70	71	68	278	6,995
Barry Lane	67	72	67	72	278	6,995
Derek Fung	68	71	69	70	278	6,995
K.J. Choi	70	68	70	70	278	6,995
Shaun Webster	68	70	75	66	279	5,980
Gary Emerson	73	69	72	65	279	5,980
Andrew Raitt	73	68	70	68	279	5,980
Danny Zarate	71	70	70	68	279	5,980
Amandeep Johl	66	71	72	70	279	5,980
Edward Loar	67	73	72	67	279	5,980
Zhang Lian-wei	67	72	72	69	280	5,000
Ian Garbutt	69	72	70	69	280	5,000
Johan Skold	70	71	73	66	280	5,000
Peter Gustafsson	72	64	73	71	280	5,000
Adam Fraser	69	68	69	74	280	5,000
Harmeet Kahlon	68	72	70	70	280	5,000
Daniel Gaunt	69	73	66	72	280	5,000
Andrew Pitts	74	67	71	69	281	4,230
Arjun Singh	69	71	70	71	281	4,230
Lu Wen-teh	71	70	68	72	281	4,230
Michael Jonzon	75	67	69	70	281	4,230
Soren Hansen	74	68	67	73	282	3,810
Jamie Elson	72	67	68	75	282	3,810
Simon Dyson	73	67	67	76	283	3,320
Paul Marantz	71	71	70	71	283	3,320
Steven O'Hara	66	71	74	72	283	3,320
Pablo Del Olmo	70	70	73	70	283	3,320
Tyrol Auret	71	68	71	73	283	3,320
Mike Cunning	70	72	69	73	284	2,490
Desvonde Botes	67	71	74	72	284	2,490
Peter Hanson	68	73	73	70	284	2,490
Chris Williams	69	73	72	70	284	2,490
Joakim Haeggman	72	70	74	68	284	2,490
Michael Kirk	72	70	69	73	284	2,490
Robert Jacobson	71	71	72	70	284	2,490
Rick Gibson	72	70	69	74	285	1,815
Tsai Chi-huang	68	70	75	72	285	1,815
Jamie Spence	71	69	72	73	285	1,815
Des Terblanche	70	68	74	73	285	1,815
Mads Vibe-Hastrup	70	71	70	74	285	1,815
Tobias Dier	72	69	70	74	285	1,815
Chen Yuan-chi	70	71	73	71	285	1,815
Louis Oosthuizen	71	69	71	74	285	1,815
Simon Yates	73	69	73	72	287	1,465
Sion Bebb	74	68	72	73	287	1,465
Clay Devers	71	70	73	74	288	1,204.18
Sam Walker	69	72	73	74	288	1,204.18
Tom Whitehouse	69	72	75	75	291	1,042.19
M. Sasidaran	70	72	76	73	291	1,042.19
Boonchu Ruangkit	70	72	77	74	293	1,035.78
Scott Strange	72	68	73	80	293	1,035.78

Volvo Masters of Asia

Bangkok Golf Club, Bangkok, Thailand
Par 35-36–71; 6,731 yards

December 11-14
purse, US$500,000

	SCORES			TOTAL	MONEY
Thongchai Jaidee	71	64	65	65	265	US$90,000
Lin Keng-chi	65	69	65	67	266	50,000
Jyoti Randhawa	67	67	70	65	269	30,000
Boonchu Ruangkit	67	74	68	63	272	20,000
Andrew Raitt	71	68	68	65	272	20,000
Thammanoon Srirot	68	67	65	72	272	20,000
Pablo Del Olmo	65	71	69	68	273	10,316.66
Gary Rusnak	66	68	71	68	273	10,316.66
Harmeet Kahlon	69	70	66	68	273	10,316.66
Jason Knutzon	70	64	70	69	273	10,316.66
Andrew Marshall	72	63	69	69	273	10,316.66
Ted Purdy	62	66	71	74	273	10,316.66
Jason Dawes	68	68	72	67	275	6,971.42
Mardan Mamat	68	67	71	69	275	6,971.42
Prayad Marksaeng	68	70	67	70	275	6,971.42
Thaworn Wiratchant	69	67	68	71	275	6,971.42
Des Terblanche	68	70	66	71	275	6,971.42
Amandeep Johl	69	69	66	71	275	6,971.42
Matthew Cort	69	67	66	73	275	6,971.42
Stephen Dodd	68	69	70	69	276	5,800
Gerald Rosales	73	68	67	68	276	5,800
Lin Wen-tang	71	67	68	70	276	5,800
Ted Oh	67	71	72	67	277	5,171.42
Craig Kamps	69	71	70	67	277	5,171.42
Kyi Hla Han	73	68	68	68	277	5,171.42
Chawalit Plaphol	68	68	72	69	277	5,171.42
David Gleeson	72	68	68	69	277	5,171.42
Simon Yates	69	68	67	73	277	5,171.42
Unho Park	67	66	70	74	277	5,171.42
Andrew Pitts	69	71	70	68	278	4,650
Hendrik Buhrmann	71	70	69	68	278	4,650

Asia/Japan Okinawa Open

See Japan Tour section.

Japan Tour

Token Homemate Cup

Token Tado Country Club, Mie
Par 35-36–71; 7,047 yards

April 3-6
purse, ¥100,000,000

	SCORES				TOTAL	MONEY
Andre Stolz	65	71	71	71	278	¥20,000,000
Tsuyoshi Yoneyama	63	72	71	73	279	7,200,000
Tadahiro Takayama	71	66	73	69	279	7,200,000
Nobuhiro Masuda	70	67	72	70	279	7,200,000
Toru Suzuki	64	73	76	67	280	3,487,500
Tetsuji Hiratsuka	70	69	71	70	280	3,487,500
Prayad Marksaeng	67	70	73	70	280	3,487,500
Zhang Lian-wei	70	67	74	69	280	3,487,500
Yasuharu Imano	68	68	74	71	281	2,820,000
Yeh Wei-tze	68	73	72	69	282	2,620,000
Tetsu Nishikawa	68	68	74	73	283	2,220,000
Nobuhito Sato	70	66	74	73	283	2,220,000
Craig Jones	66	69	78	70	283	2,220,000
Yoshitaka Yamamoto	68	73	71	72	284	1,670,000
Masayoshi Yamazoe	69	70	75	70	284	1,670,000
Taichi Teshima	68	71	72	73	284	1,670,000
Yusaku Miyazato	70	68	75	71	284	1,670,000
Mamoru Osanai	68	70	71	76	285	1,300,000
Go Higaki	69	72	70	74	285	1,300,000
Ryuichi Oda	68	72	72	73	285	1,300,000
Hideto Tanihara	68	71	70	76	285	1,300,000
Naomichi Ozaki	68	71	73	74	286	917,142
Masahiro Kuramoto	68	71	76	71	286	917,142
Takenori Hiraishi	72	69	73	72	286	917,142
Daisuke Maruyama	69	69	72	76	286	917,142
Katsumune Imai	70	71	72	73	286	917,142
Kim Jong-duck	72	70	72	72	286	917,142
Makoto Sueoka	67	73	75	71	286	917,142
Hiroya Kamide	68	72	73	74	287	720,000
Todd Hamilton	70	67	74	76	287	720,000

Tsuruya Open

Sports Shinko Country Club, Kawanishi, Hyogo
Par 35-36–71; 6,759 yards

April 24-27
purse, ¥100,000,000

	SCORES				TOTAL	MONEY
Hirofumi Miyase	68	62	70	70	270	¥20,000,000
Hisayuki Sasaki	65	71	69	65	270	8,400,000
Takashi Kanemoto	67	67	69	67	270	8,400,000
(Miyase defeated Sasaki and Kanemoto on first playoff hole.)						
Tetsuji Hiratsuka	67	72	68	66	273	4,400,000
Zhang Lian-wei	67	69	73	64	273	4,400,000
Shinichi Akiba	68	68	66	73	275	3,078,000

	SCORES				TOTAL	MONEY
Nobuhito Sato	72	69	67	67	275	3,078,000
Hirodai Kawai	71	67	69	68	275	3,078,000
Hideto Tanihara	68	68	73	66	275	3,078,000
Brendan Jones	67	68	66	74	275	3,078,000
Keiichiro Fukabori	69	68	71	68	276	2,120,000
Shingo Katayama	67	72	67	70	276	2,120,000
Richard Lee	68	71	69	68	276	2,120,000
Andre Stolz	68	70	73	65	276	2,120,000
Paul Sheehan	75	67	65	70	277	1,720,000
Tsukasa Watanabe	70	68	70	70	278	1,432,000
Katsuyoshi Tomori	71	67	68	72	278	1,432,000
Toshimitsu Izawa	69	69	69	71	278	1,432,000
Yoshiaki Mano	72	68	67	71	278	1,432,000
Hidemasa Hoshino	66	71	70	71	278	1,432,000
Satoshi Higashi	69	72	69	69	279	1,100,000
Koki Idoki	68	73	67	71	279	1,100,000
Steve Conran	72	69	68	70	279	1,100,000
Tateo Ozaki	67	72	69	72	280	800,000
Kiyoshi Maita	67	73	71	69	280	800,000
Tsuyoshi Yoneyama	69	71	70	70	280	800,000
Mitsunori Harakawa	66	71	71	72	280	800,000
Shinichi Yokota	67	72	68	73	280	800,000
David Smail	72	69	71	68	280	800,000
Masanori Kobayashi	69	73	70	68	280	800,000
Yoshinobu Tsukada	67	72	72	69	280	800,000

The Crowns

Nagoya Golf Club, Wago Course, Togo, Aichi
Par 35-35–70; 6,547 yards

May 1-4
purse, ¥120,000,000

	SCORES				TOTAL	MONEY
Hidemasa Hoshino	69	64	70	67	270	¥24,000,000
Toshimitsu Izawa	68	67	71	67	273	8,640,000
Taichi Teshima	64	68	70	71	273	8,640,000
Zaw Moe	66	67	72	68	273	8,640,000
Tsukasa Watanabe	67	68	68	71	274	4,360,000
Toru Taniguchi	67	67	69	71	274	4,360,000
Shigemasa Higaki	69	64	73	68	274	4,360,000
Hiroyuki Fujita	63	70	69	73	275	3,396,000
Steve Conran	69	66	69	71	275	3,396,000
Paul Sheehan	66	68	70	71	275	3,396,000
Hiroshi Goda	69	66	70	71	276	2,544,000
Shingo Katayama	69	69	69	69	276	2,544,000
Christian Pena	67	71	69	69	276	2,544,000
Zhang Lian-wei	71	68	70	67	276	2,544,000
Seiki Okuda	67	69	70	71	277	1,724,571
Tadahiro Takayama	69	71	71	66	277	1,724,571
Jeev Milkha Singh	71	69	67	70	277	1,724,571
Peter Teravainen	67	65	73	72	277	1,724,571
Brendan Jones	69	69	70	69	277	1,724,571
Justin Rose	73	66	70	68	277	1,724,571
S.K. Ho	68	65	74	70	277	1,724,571
Nobuhito Sato	67	68	75	68	278	1,128,000
Kazuhiko Hosokawa	70	68	70	70	278	1,128,000
Nozomi Kawahara	66	71	66	75	278	1,128,000
Kazumasa Sakaitani	66	70	71	71	278	1,128,000

	SCORES				TOTAL	MONEY
Tomohiro Kondo	62	70	75	71	278	1,128,000
Soushi Tajima	68	66	73	71	278	1,128,000
Katsunari Takahashi	72	69	68	70	279	842,400
Takenori Hiraishi	71	69	69	70	279	842,400
Koki Idoki	70	69	72	68	279	842,400
Lin Keng-chi	69	71	70	69	279	842,400
Kevin Na	68	69	72	70	279	842,400

Fujisankei Classic

Kawana Hotel Golf Course, Fuji Course, Ito, Shizuoka
Par 35-36–71; 6,694 yards

May 8-11
purse, ¥110,000,000

	SCORES				TOTAL	MONEY
Todd Hamilton	67	67	65	68	267	¥22,000,000
Shigeru Nonaka	68	68	67	69	272	9,240,000
Tetsuji Hiratsuka	71	65	68	68	272	9,240,000
Masashi Ozaki	64	73	67	70	274	4,840,000
Zhang Lian-wei	72	66	66	70	274	4,840,000
Kazuhiko Hosokawa	71	68	68	68	275	3,648,333
Prayad Marksaeng	71	68	66	70	275	3,648,333
Paul Sheehan	69	70	69	67	275	3,648,333
Shigemasa Higaki	72	70	67	67	276	2,882,000
Go Higaki	71	65	69	71	276	2,882,000
Hideto Tanihara	70	69	66	71	276	2,882,000
Mitsunori Harakawa	70	69	66	72	277	2,222,000
David Smail	67	71	68	71	277	2,222,000
Kim Jong-duck	72	69	68	68	277	2,222,000
Hsieh Chin-sheng	70	71	68	69	278	1,837,000
Shinichi Yokota	71	70	66	71	278	1,837,000
Satoshi Higashi	69	73	70	67	279	1,433,666
Kiyoshi Maita	75	66	67	71	279	1,433,666
Hiroyuki Fujita	72	66	67	74	279	1,433,666
Steve Conran	68	68	70	73	279	1,433,666
Mitsuhiro Tateyama	72	72	70	65	279	1,433,666
Katsumune Imai	73	66	69	71	279	1,433,666
Tsuneyuki Nakajima	69	69	68	74	280	1,078,000
Keiichiro Fukabori	70	70	68	72	280	1,078,000
Tsuyoshi Yoneyama	71	69	71	70	281	946,000
Ryoken Kawagishi	64	71	71	75	281	946,000
Chen Tze-chung	67	74	66	74	281	946,000
Kiyoshi Murota	65	70	72	75	282	668,250
Tsukasa Watanabe	68	71	73	70	282	668,250
Takenori Hiraishi	70	71	71	70	282	668,250
Hisayuki Sasaki	73	70	72	67	282	668,250
Yasunori Ida	70	70	70	72	282	668,250
Toru Suzuki	72	71	70	69	282	668,250
Hirofumi Miyase	73	69	69	71	282	668,250
Lin Keng-chi	73	71	67	71	282	668,250
Naotoshi Nakamura	71	72	67	72	282	668,250
Masanori Kobayashi	73	69	69	71	282	668,250
Soushi Tajima	73	71	68	70	282	668,250
Frankie Minoza	71	72	72	67	282	668,250

Japan PGA Championship

Miho Golf Club, Ibaragi
Par 36-36–72; 7,010 yards

May 15-18
purse, ¥110,000,000

		SCORES			TOTAL	MONEY
Shingo Katayama	71	66	66	68	271	¥22,000,000
S.K. Ho	71	66	66	69	272	11,000,000
Tsukasa Watanabe	72	66	67	68	273	7,480,000
Toru Suzuki	67	66	67	75	275	4,840,000
Hiroyuki Fujita	69	68	68	70	275	4,840,000
Yoshiaki Mano	69	71	66	70	276	3,795,000
Makoto Inoue	70	68	69	69	276	3,795,000
Todd Hamilton	68	70	69	70	277	3,355,000
Toru Taniguchi	70	68	69	72	279	2,992,000
Nobuhito Sato	73	69	69	68	279	2,992,000
Prayad Marksaeng	76	68	69	67	280	2,662,000
Kiyoshi Maita	73	69	70	69	281	2,222,000
Azuma Yano	71	70	69	71	281	2,222,000
Kim Jong-duck	72	72	68	69	281	2,222,000
Shigeru Nonaka	77	69	68	68	282	1,628,000
Kaname Yokoo	74	71	69	68	282	1,628,000
Kazuhiro Shimizu	76	70	67	69	282	1,628,000
Tomohiro Kondo	72	71	69	70	282	1,628,000
Christian Pena	73	67	73	69	282	1,628,000
Zhang Lian-wei	77	68	67	70	282	1,628,000
Kazuhiko Hosokawa	75	69	69	70	283	1,130,800
Taichi Teshima	73	71	67	72	283	1,130,800
David Smail	74	69	67	73	283	1,130,800
Hideto Tanihara	71	71	71	70	283	1,130,800
Brendan Jones	76	65	71	71	283	1,130,800
Tsuneyuki Nakajima	74	70	67	73	284	858,000
Kiyoshi Murota	76	68	68	72	284	858,000
Hajime Meshiai	69	74	69	72	284	858,000
Shinichi Yokota	77	69	67	71	284	858,000
Chen Tze-chung	72	70	72	70	284	858,000

Munsingwear Open KSB Cup

Rokko Kokusai Golf Club, Hyogo
Par 36-36–72; 7,206 yards

May 22-25
purse, ¥120,000,000

		SCORES			TOTAL	MONEY
Hirofumi Miyase	67	71	69	68	275	¥24,000,000
S.K. Ho	66	73	67	72	278	12,000,000
Taichi Teshima	66	69	71	73	279	6,960,000
Mitsuhiro Tateyama	70	67	72	70	279	6,960,000
Tadahiro Takayama	69	71	69	71	280	4,800,000
Takashi Kanemoto	66	70	74	71	281	3,980,000
Dinesh Chand	68	72	71	70	281	3,980,000
Masanori Kobayashi	68	74	68	71	281	3,980,000
Toru Taniguchi	70	73	69	70	282	3,264,000
Kazuhiko Hosokawa	66	74	71	71	282	3,264,000
Keiichiro Fukabori	72	71	70	70	283	2,544,000
Katsumasa Miyamoto	64	74	72	73	283	2,544,000
Steve Conran	72	70	70	71	283	2,544,000
Go Higaki	64	75	73	71	283	2,544,000
Tsukasa Watanabe	70	73	71	70	284	1,944,000

	SCORES				TOTAL	MONEY
Shigeru Nonaka	74	71	70	69	284	1,944,000
Hidemasa Hoshino	72	67	73	72	284	1,944,000
Nobuo Serizawa	71	74	71	69	285	1,512,000
Hidezumi Shirakata	68	71	72	74	285	1,512,000
Zaw Moe	69	75	68	73	285	1,512,000
Toshihiro Aizawa	71	74	70	70	285	1,512,000
Todd Hamilton	67	71	74	73	285	1,512,000
Naomichi Ozaki	68	72	71	75	286	1,176,000
Jun Kikuchi	71	72	71	72	286	1,176,000
Toshimitsu Izawa	71	70	72	74	287	984,000
Takuya Ogawa	66	72	76	73	287	984,000
Tomohiro Kondo	70	72	73	72	287	984,000
Zhang Lian-wei	76	66	69	76	287	984,000
Jyoti Randhawa	70	72	73	72	287	984,000
Shigemasa Higaki	70	71	76	71	288	816,000
Tatsuhiko Ichihara	72	71	72	73	288	816,000

Diamond Cup

Oarai Golf Club, Ibaragi
Par 36-36–72; 7,200 yards

May 29-June 1
purse, ¥110,000,000

	SCORES				TOTAL	MONEY
Todd Hamilton	67	72	72	65	276	¥22,000,000
Steve Conran	68	71	74	66	279	11,000,000
Katsuyoshi Tomori	73	67	71	69	280	6,380,000
Daisuke Maruyama	67	74	70	69	280	6,380,000
Kiyoshi Maita	70	67	72	72	281	3,996,666
Katsuya Nakagawa	73	68	74	66	281	3,996,666
Yeh Wei-tze	67	73	72	69	281	3,996,666
Nozomi Kawahara	73	72	71	66	282	3,355,000
Katsunori Kuwabara	70	68	74	71	283	2,882,000
Shingo Katayama	72	71	72	68	283	2,882,000
Taichiro Kiyota	70	71	75	67	283	2,882,000
Takashi Kanemoto	70	69	77	68	284	2,442,000
Tsukasa Watanabe	66	72	74	73	285	2,112,000
Zhang Lian-wei	71	71	70	73	285	2,112,000
Masashi Ozaki	69	70	75	72	286	1,488,666
Ryoken Kawagishi	71	73	71	71	286	1,488,666
Takeshi Sakiyama	73	73	72	68	286	1,488,666
Shinichi Akiba	71	71	72	72	286	1,488,666
Shinichi Yokota	68	73	74	71	286	1,488,666
Mamoru Osanai	67	74	75	70	286	1,488,666
Yoshiaki Mano	73	69	71	73	286	1,488,666
Tadahiro Takayama	68	71	78	69	286	1,488,666
Azuma Yano	71	73	75	67	286	1,488,666
Toshimitsu Izawa	69	73	75	70	287	946,000
Keiichiro Fukabori	72	74	70	71	287	946,000
Tetsuji Hiratsuka	72	73	72	70	287	946,000
Kiyoshi Miyazato	70	73	74	70	287	946,000
Brendan Jones	73	67	73	74	287	946,000
Hidezumi Shirakata	73	69	75	71	288	716,833
Nobuhito Sato	72	72	73	71	288	716,833
Zaw Moe	76	67	72	73	288	716,833
Dinesh Chand	69	75	75	69	288	716,833
Nobuhiro Masuda	73	71	72	72	288	716,833
Jyoti Randhawa	73	73	71	71	288	716,833

JCB Classic Sendai

Omotezao Kokusai Golf Club, Shibata, Miyagi
Par 36-35–71; 6,625 yards

June 5-8
purse, ¥100,000,000

	SCORES				TOTAL	MONEY
Katsuyoshi Tomori	64	68	64	68	264	¥20,000,000
Yusaku Miyazato	68	68	65	65	266	10,000,000
Shingo Katayama	70	66	68	65	269	6,800,000
Dinesh Chand	68	66	70	66	270	4,800,000
Tsuyoshi Yoneyama	71	64	69	67	271	3,800,000
Tadahiro Takayama	67	70	64	70	271	3,800,000
Masayuki Kawamura	69	66	70	67	272	3,175,000
Tadahisa Inoue	70	70	65	67	272	3,175,000
Shigemasa Higaki	69	68	69	67	273	2,720,000
Yui Ueda	68	70	69	66	273	2,720,000
Hideki Kase	71	68	69	66	274	1,970,000
Kazuhiko Hosokawa	72	66	69	67	274	1,970,000
Takashi Kanemoto	72	68	66	68	274	1,970,000
Katsumune Imai	70	71	69	64	274	1,970,000
Rick Gibson	70	67	68	69	274	1,970,000
S.K. Ho	70	65	71	68	274	1,970,000
Satoshi Higashi	69	69	67	70	275	1,303,333
Tetsuji Hiratsuka	69	68	71	67	275	1,303,333
Yoshiaki Mano	67	71	69	68	275	1,303,333
Kazuhiro Shimizu	70	65	70	70	275	1,303,333
Kiyoshi Miyazato	74	65	71	65	275	1,303,333
Brendan Jones	70	65	70	70	275	1,303,333
Kiyoshi Murota	69	71	66	70	276	980,000
Katsuya Nakagawa	70	65	74	67	276	980,000
Nobuo Serizawa	69	70	67	71	277	800,000
Yasunori Ida	68	68	70	71	277	800,000
Keiichiro Fukabori	68	70	66	73	277	800,000
Masanori Kobayashi	73	66	71	67	277	800,000
Hideto Tanihara	70	68	68	71	277	800,000
Jyoti Randhawa	63	75	71	68	277	800,000

Mandom Lucido Yomiuri Open

Yomiuri Country Club, Nishinomiya, Hyogo
Par 36-36–72; 7,073 yards
(Event shortened to 54 holes—rain.)

June 19-22
purse, ¥100,000,000

	SCORES			TOTAL	MONEY
Hideto Tanihara	65	71	64	200	¥15,000,000
Nobuhito Sato	69	69	65	203	7,500,000
Azuma Yano	69	69	66	204	5,100,000
Masashi Ozaki	66	68	71	205	3,100,000
Kiyoshi Maita	68	67	70	205	3,100,000
Kaname Yokoo	68	69	68	205	3,100,000
Shingo Katayama	72	66	68	206	2,292,500
Satoru Hirota	68	69	69	206	2,292,500
Kim Jong-duck	67	73	66	206	2,292,500
Katsunori Kuwabara	72	69	66	207	1,965,000
Naomichi Ozaki	71	64	73	208	1,665,000
Kazuhiro Kinjo	72	70	66	208	1,665,000
Todd Hamilton	69	68	71	208	1,665,000
Satoshi Higashi	68	73	68	209	990,000

	SCORES	TOTAL	MONEY
Kiyoshi Murota	69 72 68	209	990,000
Yoshitaka Yamamoto	69 71 69	209	990,000
Tatsuo Takasaki	71 68 70	209	990,000
Tsuyoshi Yoneyama	73 69 67	209	990,000
Toshimitsu Izawa	66 70 73	209	990,000
Keiichiro Fukabori	76 66 67	209	990,000
Kazuhiko Hosokawa	69 70 70	209	990,000
Taichi Teshima	73 67 69	209	990,000
Tetsuji Hiratsuka	71 66 72	209	990,000
Kazuhiro Shimizu	72 70 67	209	990,000
Paul Sheehan	68 71 70	209	990,000
Katsuyoshi Tomori	73 69 68	210	585,000
Shinichi Akiba	70 68 72	210	585,000
Shinichi Yokota	67 72 71	210	585,000
Tomohiro Kondo	71 69 70	210	585,000
Hidehisa Shikata	68 68 74	210	585,000

Gateway to the Open Mizuno Open

Setonaikai Golf Club, Kasaoka, Okayama
Par 36-36–72; 7,256 yards

June 26-29
purse, ¥100,000,000

	SCORES	TOTAL	MONEY
Todd Hamilton	70 66 73 69	278	¥20,000,000
Brendan Jones	69 72 69 69	279	10,000,000
Toshimitsu Izawa	67 71 68 74	280	5,200,000
Nobuhito Sato	70 69 71 70	280	5,200,000
Tetsuji Hiratsuka	69 68 72 71	280	5,200,000
Tsuneyuki Naka	71 71 69 70	281	3,316,666
Go Higaki	72 70 72 67	281	3,316,666
Tatsuya Mitsuhashi	75 70 67 69	281	3,316,666
Tsukasa Watanabe	69 72 70 71	282	2,620,000
Hiroya Kamide	71 69 73 69	282	2,620,000
Yeh Wei-tze	72 67 69 74	282	2,620,000
Kiyoshi Maita	70 67 74 72	283	2,120,000
Kim Jong-duck	72 70 71 70	283	2,120,000
Toru Taniguchi	72 72 71 69	284	1,670,000
Yeh Chang-ting	70 69 73 72	284	1,670,000
Steve Conran	68 69 74 73	284	1,670,000
Koushi Yokoyama	75 69 69 71	284	1,670,000
Takashi Kanemoto	74 70 73 68	285	1,220,000
Taichi Teshima	71 71 73 70	285	1,220,000
Satoru Hirota	73 66 73 73	285	1,220,000
Tadahiro Takayama	66 75 71 73	285	1,220,000
Ryuichi Oda	76 69 72 68	285	1,220,000
Paul Sheehan	73 71 73 68	285	1,220,000
Katsumasa Miyamoto	71 72 73 70	286	860,000
Mamoru Osanai	71 70 75 70	286	860,000
David Smail	72 73 69 72	286	860,000
Yoshinobu Tsukada	70 70 73 73	286	860,000
Jeev Milkha Singh	71 71 72 72	286	860,000
Kiyoshi Murota	72 71 73 71	287	651,666
Toru Nakamura	74 69 73 71	287	651,666
Yuji Igarashi	73 72 72 70	287	651,666
Shinichi Akiba	73 69 75 70	287	651,666
Hideto Tanihara	71 70 73 73	287	651,666
Kaneyori Aramoto	73 69 75 70	287	651,666

Japan Tour Championship

Shishido Hills Country Club, Tomobe, Ibaragi
Par 36-35–71; 7,030 yards

July 3-6
purse, ¥120,000,000

	SCORES				TOTAL	MONEY
Toshimitsu Izawa	70	63	68	69	270	¥24,000,000
David Smail	66	69	67	69	271	10,080,000
Tadahiro Takayama	68	66	69	68	271	10,080,000
Taichi Teshima	68	65	70	71	274	5,280,000
Katsumasa Miyamoto	66	71	71	66	274	5,280,000
Naomichi Ozaki	68	71	69	67	275	4,140,000
Hajime Meshiai	68	70	67	70	275	4,140,000
Daisuke Maruyama	68	68	71	70	277	3,522,000
Tetsuji Hiratsuka	68	69	68	72	277	3,522,000
Yoshinori Mizumaki	71	69	68	70	278	2,664,000
Keiichiro Fukabori	68	72	69	69	278	2,664,000
Kazuhiko Hosokawa	72	70	69	67	278	2,664,000
Koumei Oda	71	71	69	67	278	2,664,000
Craig Parry	69	70	71	68	278	2,664,000
Toru Taniguchi	67	71	72	69	279	1,944,000
Yoshiaki Mano	70	70	71	68	279	1,944,000
Paul Sheehan	68	73	71	67	279	1,944,000
Go Higaki	70	73	68	69	280	1,704,000
Tateo Ozaki	69	73	74	65	281	1,326,857
Kiyoshi Murota	69	71	70	71	281	1,326,857
Shinichi Yokota	73	68	72	68	281	1,326,857
Mitsuhiro Tateyama	70	72	70	69	281	1,326,857
Todd Hamilton	68	73	73	67	281	1,326,857
Zhang Lian-wei	69	70	71	71	281	1,326,857
Brendan Jones	71	70	68	72	281	1,326,857
Takashi Kanemoto	69	72	71	70	282	1,008,000
Masanori Kobayashi	71	69	73	69	282	1,008,000
Hideki Kase	72	71	70	70	283	864,000
Tsukasa Watanabe	70	72	68	73	283	864,000
Toru Suzuki	71	73	71	68	283	864,000
Hsieh Chin-sheng	68	69	75	71	283	864,000

Woodone Open

Hiroshima Country Club, Higashi, Hiroshima
Par 36-36–72; 7,010 yards

July 10-13
purse, ¥100,000,000

	SCORES				TOTAL	MONEY
Toshimitsu Izawa	66	68	69	72	275	¥20,000,000
Kiyoshi Murota	70	71	64	70	275	10,000,000
(Izawa defeated Murota on second playoff hole.)						
Toru Suzuki	70	67	67	72	276	6,800,000
Masayuki Kawamura	69	68	71	69	277	4,133,333
Katsunori Kuwabara	74	63	67	73	277	4,133,333
Azuma Yano	71	72	66	68	277	4,133,333
Tomohiro Kondo	70	72	64	72	278	3,300,000
Taichi Teshima	69	70	70	70	279	2,935,000
Daisuke Maruyama	73	66	69	71	279	2,935,000
Mitsunori Harakawa	74	69	67	70	280	2,136,666
Keiichiro Fukabori	68	70	71	71	280	2,136,666
Jun Kikuchi	68	72	66	74	280	2,136,666
Katsumune Imai	68	70	68	74	280	2,136,666

	SCORES				TOTAL	MONEY
Nobuhiro Masuda	72	69	71	68	280	2,136,666
Kazuhiro Nagatani	69	70	71	70	280	2,136,666
Hiroshi Goda	73	70	71	67	281	1,390,000
Hajime Meshiai	72	69	69	71	281	1,390,000
Tetsuji Hiratsuka	73	68	68	72	281	1,390,000
Mitsuhiro Tateyama	68	72	73	68	281	1,390,000
Koumei Oda	71	71	70	69	281	1,390,000
Prayad Marksaeng	68	70	70	73	281	1,390,000
Shigeru Nonaka	71	67	69	75	282	1,020,000
Tatsuhiko Takahashi	69	66	74	73	282	1,020,000
Brendan Jones	69	70	76	67	282	1,020,000
Tsuyoshi Yoneyama	71	68	68	76	283	840,000
Kazumasa Sakaitani	70	71	72	70	283	840,000
Dinesh Chand	66	75	69	73	283	840,000
Hisao Ahara	72	71	67	73	283	840,000
Hidezumi Shirakata	69	69	73	73	284	666,000
Shinichi Akiba	74	69	71	70	284	666,000
Lin Keng-chi	70	72	71	71	284	666,000
Soushi Tajima	68	71	70	75	284	666,000
Chen Tze-chung	70	71	70	73	284	666,000

Sato Foods NST Niigata Open

Nakamine Golf Club, Toyoura, Niigata
Par 36-36–72; 7,023 yards

July 24-27
purse, ¥50,000,000

	SCORES				TOTAL	MONEY
Katsumasa Miyamoto	65	71	69	66	271	¥10,000,000
Gregory Meyer	69	70	67	66	272	5,000,000
Yoshiaki Mano	68	66	69	70	273	3,400,000
Tetsuji Hiratsuka	73	67	66	68	274	2,200,000
Hideto Tanihara	66	71	68	69	274	2,200,000
Hideki Kase	69	66	68	72	275	1,539,000
Jun Kikuchi	68	69	71	67	275	1,539,000
Dinesh Chand	74	66	70	65	275	1,539,000
Nobuhiro Masuda	70	69	67	69	275	1,539,000
Unho Park	70	71	67	67	275	1,539,000
Tsuyoshi Yoneyama	69	69	65	73	276	985,000
Mitsunori Harakawa	72	69	67	68	276	985,000
Tetsuya Haraguchi	67	70	72	67	276	985,000
Masanori Kobayashi	67	72	69	68	276	985,000
Yoshinobu Tsukada	71	70	67	68	276	985,000
Keishiro Nakata	73	68	71	64	276	985,000
Hideki Haraguchi	73	68	66	70	277	672,000
Shinichi Akiba	70	67	70	70	277	672,000
Kazuhiro Kinjo	69	70	66	72	277	672,000
Daisuke Maruyama	73	64	70	70	277	672,000
Kaneyori Aramoto	70	71	65	71	277	672,000
Takenori Hiraishi	68	69	69	72	278	495,000
Koki Idoki	73	68	69	68	278	495,000
Takuya Ogawa	69	72	68	69	278	495,000
Satoru Hirota	67	70	68	73	278	495,000
Mitsutaka Kusakabe	69	69	72	69	279	380,000
Shinichi Yokota	71	68	72	68	279	380,000
Kazumasa Sakaitani	71	69	70	69	279	380,000
Kazuhiro Shimizu	69	69	72	69	279	380,000
Ryuichi Oda	68	70	70	71	279	380,000
Koumei Oda	66	72	69	72	279	380,000

Aiful Cup

Twinfields Golf Club, Komatsu, Ishikawa
Par 36-36–72; 7,125 yards

July 31-August 3
purse, ¥120,000,000

		SCORES			TOTAL	MONEY
Taichi Teshima	67	64	70	68	269	¥24,000,000
Katsumasa Miyamoto	68	64	72	65	269	12,000,000
(Teshima defeated Miyamoto on first playoff hole.)						
Tetsuji Hiratsuka	66	68	67	69	270	8,160,000
Soushi Tajima	68	67	72	66	273	5,760,000
Toshimitsu Izawa	68	69	68	69	274	4,360,000
Jun Kikuchi	71	66	69	68	274	4,360,000
Wayne Perske	67	69	67	71	274	4,360,000
Masanori Kobayashi	68	67	75	65	275	3,522,000
Takuya Taniguchi	69	69	66	71	275	3,522,000
Hidehisa Shikata	65	68	68	75	276	2,784,000
Nobuo Serizawa	70	70	67	69	276	2,784,000
Mitsuhiro Tateyama	67	73	67	69	276	2,784,000
Hidemasa Hoshino	70	66	72	68	276	2,784,000
Toshihiro Aizawa	70	69	69	69	277	2,064,000
Katsuya Nakagawa	71	68	69	69	277	2,064,000
Yeh Wei-tze	72	63	70	72	277	2,064,000
Kazuhiko Hosokawa	71	69	71	67	278	1,824,000
Craig Jones	71	66	69	73	279	1,512,000
Steve Conran	70	68	69	72	279	1,512,000
Koki Idoki	65	70	72	72	279	1,512,000
Hideto Tanihara	72	67	70	70	279	1,512,000
Hsieh Chin-sheng	69	70	70	70	279	1,512,000
Takashi Kanemoto	72	67	72	69	280	1,116,000
Mamoru Osanai	67	73	69	71	280	1,116,000
Tatsuo Takasaki	69	70	70	71	280	1,116,000
Prayad Marksaeng	71	66	71	72	280	1,116,000
Hiroyuki Fujita	68	68	71	74	281	845,142
Hideki Kase	70	68	70	73	281	845,142
Seiki Okuda	71	68	71	71	281	845,142
Ryuichi Oda	69	70	70	72	281	845,142
Paul Sheehan	67	69	73	72	281	845,142
Zaw Moe	72	67	72	70	281	845,142
Frankie Minoza	69	70	71	71	281	845,142

Sun Chlorella Classic

Sapporo Bay Golf Club, Ishikari, Hokkaido
Par 36-36–72; 7,039 yards

August 7-10
purse, ¥130,000,000

		SCORES			TOTAL	MONEY
Brendan Jones	71	73	68	68	280	¥26,000,000
Taichi Teshima	71	69	70	70	280	10,920,000
Daisuke Maruyama	71	69	68	72	280	10,920,000
(Jones defeated Teshima and Maruyama on first playoff hole.)						
Kazuhiro Kinjo	70	71	69	73	283	4,875,000
Shigemasa Higaki	73	69	72	69	283	4,875,000
Azuma Yano	75	67	66	75	283	4,875,000
Soushi Tajima	75	68	70	70	283	4,875,000
Takuya Taniguchi	73	72	71	67	283	4,875,000
Takashi Kanemoto	74	69	73	68	284	3,406,000
Hideto Tanihara	74	67	70	73	284	3,406,000

	SCORES				TOTAL	MONEY
Frankie Minoza	76	69	68	71	284	3,406,000
Kiyoshi Murota	71	69	72	73	285	2,223,000
Masahiro Kuramoto	72	73	69	71	285	2,223,000
Tsuyoshi Yoneyama	72	75	66	72	285	2,223,000
Hiroyuki Fujita	77	68	66	74	285	2,223,000
Shinichi Yokota	74	67	71	73	285	2,223,000
Tetsuji Hiratsuka	72	72	68	73	285	2,223,000
Tomohiro Kondo	74	70	72	69	285	2,223,000
Chen Tze-chung	75	70	70	70	285	2,223,000
Hajime Meshiai	77	66	67	76	286	1,430,000
Lin Keng-chi	76	71	69	70	286	1,430,000
Go Higaki	73	74	67	72	286	1,430,000
Yoshikazu Haku	74	70	69	73	286	1,430,000
Richard Lee	75	71	72	68	286	1,430,000
Keiichiro Fukabori	75	69	75	68	287	1,040,000
Mitsuhiro Tateyama	74	70	69	74	287	1,040,000
Hirokazu Kuniyoshi	71	72	69	75	287	1,040,000
Jeev Milkha Singh	74	68	71	74	287	1,040,000
Zhang Lian-wei	72	71	69	75	287	1,040,000
Paul Sheehan	75	69	75	68	287	1,040,000

Hisamitsu-KBC Augusta

Keya Golf Club, Shima, Fukuoka
Par 36-36–72; 7,154 yards

August 28-31
purse, ¥100,000,000

	SCORES				TOTAL	MONEY
Soushi Tajima	64	70	68	67	269	¥20,000,000
Hisayuki Sasaki	70	68	66	69	273	8,400,000
Dinesh Chand	66	68	69	70	273	8,400,000
Kiyoshi Murota	69	69	69	67	274	4,400,000
Katsumune Imai	68	70	68	68	274	4,400,000
Tetsuji Hiratsuka	69	68	68	70	275	3,600,000
Masashi Ozaki	70	71	67	68	276	2,947,500
Tsukasa Watanabe	71	68	69	68	276	2,947,500
Daisuke Maruyama	69	69	69	69	276	2,947,500
Mamoru Osanai	71	69	68	68	276	2,947,500
Takenori Hiraishi	71	64	70	72	277	2,420,000
Hideki Kase	70	68	69	71	278	1,880,000
Nobuhito Sato	70	70	72	66	278	1,880,000
Yoshinobu Tsukada	75	67	69	67	278	1,880,000
Tomohiro Kondo	73	68	68	69	278	1,880,000
Kiyoshi Miyazato	71	68	69	70	278	1,880,000
Satoshi Higashi	67	69	70	73	279	1,262,857
Hajime Meshiai	69	69	71	70	279	1,262,857
Shigemasa Higaki	71	69	71	68	279	1,262,857
Tadahiro Takayama	69	70	70	70	279	1,262,857
Nobuhiro Masuda	70	69	71	69	279	1,262,857
Frankie Minoza	72	70	67	70	279	1,262,857
Paul Sheehan	69	72	67	71	279	1,262,857
Takuya Taniguchi	71	70	68	71	280	940,000
Hiroya Kamide	67	72	68	74	281	780,000
Hiroshi Tominaga	70	71	68	72	281	780,000
Nozomi Kawahara	69	70	68	74	281	780,000
Mitsuhiro Tateyama	75	67	70	69	281	780,000
Katsuya Nakagawa	69	70	67	75	281	780,000
Koumei Oda	75	67	70	69	281	780,000
Thammanoon Srirot	72	68	71	70	281	780,000

Japan PGA Match Play

Nidom Classic Course, Tomakomai, Hokkaido
Par 36-36–72; 6,957 yards

September 4-7
purse, ¥80,000,000

FIRST ROUND

Shingo Katayama defeated Steve Conran, 3 and 2.
Hidemasa Hoshino defeated Katsuyoshi Tomori, 6 and 5.
Taichi Teshima defeated Takashi Kanemoto, 5 and 4.
Hirofumi Miyase defeated Kazuhiko Hosokawa, 1 up.
Toru Taniguchi defeated Keiichiro Fukabori, 3 and 2.
Kim Jong-duck defeated Katsunori Kuwabara, 4 and 3.
Todd Hamilton defeated Kiyoshi Murota, 3 and 2.
Katsumasa Miyamoto defeated Hideto Tanihara, 3 and 2.
Shinichi Yokota defeated Brendan Jones, 2 and 1.
S.K. Ho defeated Tadahiro Takayama, 20 holes.
Yasuharu Imano defeated Nobuhito Sato, 2 up.
Tetsuji Hiratsuka defeated Daisuke Maruyama, 3 and 2.
David Smail defeated Dinesh Chand, 19 holes.
Tsukasa Watanabe defeated Tomohiro Kondo, 2 and 1.
Hiroyuki Fujita defeated Shigemasa Higaki, 4 and 3.
Zaw Moe defeated Tsuneyuki Nakajima, 3 and 2.

(Each losing player received ¥400,000.)

SECOND ROUND

Hoshino defeated Katayama, 1 up.
Miyase defeated Teshima, 20 holes.
Taniguchi defeated Kim, 3 and 1.
Hamilton defeated Miyamoto, 5 and 4.
Ho defeated Yokota, 2 and 1.
Hiratsuka defeated Imano, 2 and 1.
Smail defeated Watanabe, 2 up.
Fujita defeated Moe, 5 and 4.

(Each losing player received ¥800,000.)

QUARTER-FINALS

Miyase defeated Hoshino, 21 holes.
Hamilton defeated Taniguchi, 5 and 3.
Hiratsuka defeated Ho, 3 and 2.
Smail defeated Fujita, 2 and 1.

(Each losing player received ¥1,800,000.)

SEMI-FINALS

Hamilton defeated Miyase, 1 up.
Smail defeated Hiratsuka, 4 and 3.

THIRD-FOURTH PLACE PLAYOFF

Hiratsuka defeated Miyase, 22 holes.

(Hiratsuka received ¥9,000,000; Miyase received ¥6,000,000.)

FINAL

Hamilton defeated Smail, 3 and 2.

(Hamilton received ¥30,000,000; Smail received ¥15,000,000.)

Suntory Open

Sobu Country Club, Inzai, Chiba
Par 35-36–71; 7,155 yards

September 11-14
purse, ¥100,000,000

	SCORES				TOTAL	MONEY
Jyoti Randhawa	68	68	71	69	276	¥20,000,000
Paul Sheehan	69	67	73	69	278	10,000,000
Hiroyuki Fujita	67	66	78	69	280	6,800,000
Tsuyoshi Yoneyama	72	67	74	68	281	4,800,000
Hideki Kase	71	68	74	69	282	4,000,000
Shingo Katayama	70	71	71	72	284	3,078,000
Tomohiro Kondo	73	73	74	64	284	3,078,000
Tetsuji Hiratsuka	70	71	72	71	284	3,078,000
Katsuyoshi Tomori	74	67	71	72	284	3,078,000
Masayuki Kawamura	65	69	75	75	284	3,078,000
Shigemasa Higaki	73	72	68	72	285	1,905,714
Frankie Minoza	70	70	73	72	285	1,905,714
Hirokazu Kuniyoshi	72	72	71	70	285	1,905,714
Katsumasa Miyamoto	70	70	75	70	285	1,905,714
Hiroya Kamide	73	72	73	67	285	1,905,714
Steve Conran	68	73	74	70	285	1,905,714
David Smail	72	69	72	72	285	1,905,714
Takenori Hiraishi	74	71	69	72	286	1,084,000
David Ishii	73	70	74	69	286	1,084,000
Tatsuo Takasaki	70	67	76	73	286	1,084,000
Keiichiro Fukabori	74	70	74	68	286	1,084,000
Takashi Kanemoto	75	68	77	66	286	1,084,000
Masayoshi Yamazoe	73	68	76	69	286	1,084,000
Phil Mickelson	71	75	71	69	286	1,084,000
Toru Suzuki	75	69	72	70	286	1,084,000
Masashi Ozaki	69	71	73	73	286	1,084,000
Tadahisa Inoue	70	69	72	75	286	1,084,000
Kiyoshi Murota	73	69	75	70	287	740,000
Naomichi Ozaki	71	67	79	70	287	740,000
Gregory Meyer	70	73	71	73	287	740,000

ANA Open

Sapporo Golf Club, Wattsu Course,
Kitahiroshima, Hokkaido
Par 36-36–72; 7,063 yards

September 18-21
purse, ¥100,000,000

	SCORES				TOTAL	MONEY
Yeh Wei-tze	67	66	72	72	277	¥20,000,000
Masashi Ozaki	70	71	67	70	278	8,400,000
Tsuyoshi Yoneyama	67	72	69	70	278	8,400,000
Kiyoshi Maita	68	70	71	70	279	4,400,000
Shinichi Yokota	69	72	69	69	279	4,400,000
Toru Taniguchi	71	70	68	71	280	3,450,000
Steve Conran	70	69	71	70	280	3,450,000

	SCORES				TOTAL	MONEY
Taichi Teshima	65	72	72	72	281	2,830,000
David Smail	69	71	72	69	281	2,830,000
Hidemasa Hoshino	67	72	73	69	281	2,830,000
Hirofumi Miyase	70	68	71	73	282	2,220,000
Daisuke Maruyama	71	71	72	68	282	2,220,000
Paul Sheehan	66	71	72	73	282	2,220,000
Dinesh Chand	71	71	70	71	283	1,820,000
Hiroyuki Fujita	71	71	74	68	284	1,524,000
Shingo Katayama	73	68	74	69	284	1,524,000
Tatsuhiko Takahashi	72	71	69	72	284	1,524,000
Koumei Oda	70	72	72	70	284	1,524,000
Yusaku Miyazato	70	73	70	71	284	1,524,000
Hideki Kase	72	72	73	68	285	1,100,000
Toshimitsu Izawa	71	74	71	69	285	1,100,000
Shigeru Nonaka	70	75	72	68	285	1,100,000
Kazuhiro Kinjo	70	71	68	76	285	1,100,000
Kiyoshi Miyazato	70	71	75	69	285	1,100,000
Tsukasa Watanabe	72	70	72	72	286	820,000
Masanori Kobayashi	71	72	73	70	286	820,000
Christian Pena	70	71	74	71	286	820,000
Brendan Jones	70	74	71	71	286	820,000
Wayne Perske	69	72	70	75	286	820,000
Jun Kikuchi	71	74	73	69	287	680,000
Craig Jones	71	72	68	76	287	680,000

Acom International

Ishioka Golf Club, Ogawa, Ibaraki   September 25-28
Par 36-35–71; 7,046 yards   purse, ¥120,000,000

	SCORES				TOTAL	MONEY
Masahiro Kuramoto	59	69	70	73	271	¥24,000,000
Masashi Ozaki	68	67	68	68	271	10,080,000
Katsumasa Miyamoto	69	69	68	65	271	10,080,000
(Kuramoto defeated Ozaki and Miyamoto on first playoff hole.)						
Richard Lee	68	68	68	68	272	5,760,000
Hirofumi Miyase	66	68	69	70	273	4,560,000
Lin Keng-chi	67	68	69	69	273	4,560,000
Naomichi Ozaki	67	69	67	71	274	3,668,000
Prayad Marksaeng	65	70	68	71	274	3,668,000
Paul Sheehan	73	67	67	67	274	3,668,000
Shingo Katayama	70	68	69	68	275	3,024,000
Yusaku Miyazato	69	64	69	73	275	3,024,000
Kiyoshi Maita	67	70	69	70	276	2,424,000
Toru Taniguchi	70	66	67	73	276	2,424,000
Mitsuhiro Tateyama	67	67	73	69	276	2,424,000
Koki Idoki	66	68	70	73	277	1,944,000
Steve Conran	68	65	71	73	277	1,944,000
Nibuhiro Masuda	70	69	67	71	277	1,944,000
Toru Suzuki	66	68	73	71	278	1,656,000
Shinichi Yokota	67	64	74	73	278	1,656,000
Go Higaki	70	70	69	70	279	1,464,000
Hidemasa Hoshino	68	69	71	71	279	1,464,000
Katsunari Takahashi	66	67	75	72	280	1,188,000
Taichi Teshima	67	67	72	74	280	1,188,000
Kiyoshi Miyazato	66	73	71	70	280	1,188,000
Brendan Jones	70	64	72	74	280	1,188,000

	SCORES			TOTAL	MONEY
Kiyoshi Murota	69	70	69 73	281	912,000
Mitsunori Harakawa	64	72	72 73	281	912,000
Kazuhiko Hosokawa	69	68	73 71	281	912,000
Kazuhiro Kinjo	69	71	70 71	281	912,000
Jeev Milkha Singh	64	73	67 77	281	912,000
Wayne Perske	67	71	72 71	281	912,000

Georgia Tokai Classic

Miyoshi Country Club, Miyoshi, Aichi
Par 36-36–72; 7,125 yards

October 9-12
purse, ¥120,000,000

	SCORES				TOTAL	MONEY
Nozomi Kawahara	69	68	69	69	275	¥24,000,000
Tsuyoshi Yoneyama	73	67	68	68	276	10,080,000
Shingo Katayama	69	69	69	69	276	10,080,000
Kazuhiko Hosokawa	74	68	70	66	278	4,960,000
Daisuke Maruyama	68	66	73	71	278	4,960,000
Katsumune Imai	70	72	69	67	278	4,960,000
Ryoken Kawagishi	71	67	69	72	279	3,960,000
Zhang Lian-wei	69	73	70	68	280	3,660,000
Masashi Ozaki	71	73	70	67	281	3,024,000
Koki Idoki	71	74	69	67	281	3,024,000
Shigeru Harimoto	71	69	71	70	281	3,024,000
Hideto Tanihara	68	72	72	69	281	3,024,000
Yoshinori Mizumaki	69	72	70	71	282	2,224,000
Hirofumi Miyase	69	70	76	67	282	2,224,000
Jeev Milkha Singh	69	75	67	71	282	2,224,000
Naomichi Ozaki	72	68	72	71	283	1,770,000
Hideki Kase	73	69	72	69	283	1,770,000
Keiichiro Fukabori	71	70	71	71	283	1,770,000
Katsunori Kuwabara	69	73	69	72	283	1,770,000
Toru Taniguchi	71	70	71	72	284	1,416,000
Nobuhito Sato	73	71	70	70	284	1,416,000
Tetsuji Hiratsuka	73	71	71	69	284	1,416,000
Hidezumi Shirakata	70	73	69	73	285	1,038,857
Shinichi Yokota	69	71	75	70	285	1,038,857
Katsumasa Miyamoto	70	71	74	70	285	1,038,857
Satoru Hirota	68	76	70	71	285	1,038,857
Tadahisa Inoue	73	70	68	74	285	1,038,857
Katsuya Nakagawa	69	75	73	68	285	1,038,857
Tomohiro Kondo	70	71	72	72	285	1,038,857
Gregory Meyer	69	73	74	70	286	796,000
Shinichi Akiba	69	69	78	70	286	796,000
Takashi Kanemoto	68	73	70	75	286	796,000

Japan Open

Nikko Country Club, Tochigi
Par 36-35–71; 6,867 yards

October 16-19
purse, ¥120,000,000

	SCORES			TOTAL	MONEY
Keiichiro Fukabori	66	75	71 64	276	¥24,000,000
Yasuharu Imano	69	72	66 71	278	13,200,000
Prayad Marksaeng	74	69	69 69	281	9,300,000

	SCORES				TOTAL	MONEY
Brendan Jones	70	71	72	69	282	5,080,000
Toru Taniguchi	73	72	69	68	282	5,080,000
Ryoken Kawagishi	66	72	72	72	282	5,080,000
Steve Conran	71	70	72	70	283	3,090,000
Daisuke Maruyama	70	68	72	73	283	3,090,000
Craig Parry	68	71	71	73	283	3,090,000
Tatsuhiko Takahashi	67	70	75	72	284	2,376,000
Yusaku Miyazato	72	73	69	71	285	1,956,000
Hajime Meshiai	74	68	71	72	285	1,956,000
Satoshi Oide	68	74	73	71	286	1,644,000
Katsumasa Miyamoto	73	72	69	72	286	1,644,000
Tetsuji Hiratsuka	69	77	69	72	287	1,374,000
Hirofumi Miyase	71	70	71	75	287	1,374,000
Toru Suzuki	71	70	71	75	287	1,374,000
Taichi Teshima	72	70	70	75	287	1,374,000
*Yuta Ikeda	69	73	73	73	288	
Hiroyuki Fujita	72	71	73	72	288	1,143,200
Shingo Katayama	71	72	74	71	288	1,143,200
Shinichi Yokota	72	71	70	75	288	1,143,200
Katsuyoshi Tomori	70	72	71	75	288	1,143,200
Hiroshi Goda	71	71	70	76	288	1,143,200
Jun Kikuchi	71	70	75	73	289	982,750
Masashi Ozaki	71	72	75	71	289	982,750
Nakata Norihiko	75	72	73	69	289	982,750
Tsuyoshi Yoneyama	73	69	72	75	289	982,750
Hidemasa Hoshino	66	73	75	75	289	982,750
Nobuhito Sato	70	72	72	75	289	982,750
Hideto Tanihara	70	74	70	75	289	982,750
Hideki Kase	71	71	70	77	289	982,750

Bridgestone Open

Phoenix Country Club, Miyazaki
Par 36-36–72; 7,208 yards

October 23-26
purse, ¥110,000,000

	SCORES				TOTAL	MONEY
Naomichi Ozaki	66	69	67	65	267	¥22,000,000
Paul Sheehan	66	67	66	68	267	11,000,000
(Ozaki defeated Sheehan on second playoff hole.)						
Lin Keng-chi	69	73	64	65	271	5,280,000
Shingo Katayama	69	68	67	67	271	5,280,000
Hiroyuki Fujita	66	66	71	68	271	5,280,000
Hideto Tanihara	70	68	63	70	271	5,280,000
Brendan Jones	70	70	66	66	272	3,492,500
Tetsuji Hiratsuka	65	73	67	67	272	3,492,500
Daisuke Maruyama	65	67	67	74	273	3,102,000
Koki Idoki	69	70	69	66	274	2,882,000
Masashi Ozaki	70	71	66	68	275	2,552,000
Hidemasa Hoshino	66	70	70	69	275	2,552,000
Taichi Teshima	70	72	68	66	276	2,222,000
Steve Conran	70	70	69	68	277	1,586,444
Tsuyoshi Yoneyama	71	69	68	69	277	1,586,444
Todd Hamilton	70	70	68	69	277	1,586,444
Hajime Meshiai	71	63	73	70	277	1,586,444
Hirofumi Miyase	71	68	67	71	277	1,586,444
Tim Petrovic	67	70	68	72	277	1,586,444
Nobuhito Sato	70	69	66	72	277	1,586,444

	SCORES				TOTAL	MONEY
Zhang Lian-wei	67	71	71	68	277	1,586,444
Nobuhiro Masuda	71	69	71	66	277	1,586,444
Scott Laycock	68	72	68	70	278	998,800
Shigemasa Higaki	72	70	65	71	278	998,800
Kiyoshi Maita	68	70	66	74	278	998,800
Takashi Kanemoto	72	70	67	69	278	998,800
Taichiro Kiyota	71	68	72	67	278	998,800
Toru Taniguchi	71	69	69	70	279	772,200
Shinichi Yokota	70	70	68	71	279	772,200
Kim Jong-duck	69	67	71	72	279	772,200
*Yuta Ikeda	67	75	65	72	279	
Takashi Iwamoto	69	70	66	74	279	772,200
Katsuyoshi Tomori	69	73	68	69	279	772,200

ABC Championship

ABC Golf Club, Tojo, Hyogo
Par 36-36–72; 7,176 yards

October 30-November 2
purse, ¥120,000,000

	SCORES				TOTAL	MONEY
Shingo Katayama	64	69	68	64	265	¥24,000,000
Katsumasa Miyamoto	70	69	64	71	274	12,000,000
Tsuyoshi Yoneyama	71	68	68	68	275	6,240,000
Toshimitsu Izawa	70	72	66	67	275	6,240,000
Tetsuji Hiratsuka	69	63	72	71	275	6,240,000
Hiroyuki Fujita	67	70	66	73	276	4,140,000
Zaw Moe	72	65	71	68	276	4,140,000
Masashi Ozaki	69	71	69	68	277	3,151,200
Hideki Kase	70	71	69	67	277	3,151,200
Toru Suzuki	67	69	69	72	277	3,151,200
Ryoken Kawagishi	69	68	71	69	277	3,151,200
Taichi Teshima	68	68	71	70	277	3,151,200
Tsuneyuki Nakajima	70	68	71	69	278	2,154,000
Mitsuhiro Tateyama	72	68	67	71	278	2,154,000
Katsuya Nakagawa	69	70	71	68	278	2,154,000
Brendan Jones	69	69	71	69	278	2,154,000
Katsunori Kuwabara	70	70	67	72	279	1,764,000
Prayad Marksaeng	70	70	70	69	279	1,764,000
Kiyoshi Maita	68	71	70	71	280	1,512,000
Nobumitsu Yuhara	69	69	73	69	280	1,512,000
Nozomi Kawahara	73	73	66	68	280	1,512,000
Masahiro Kuramoto	72	71	68	70	281	1,128,000
Toshiaki Odate	69	73	70	69	281	1,128,000
Shinichi Yokota	68	74	70	69	281	1,128,000
Satoru Hirota	73	69	68	71	281	1,128,000
Jeev Milkha Singh	69	67	71	74	281	1,128,000
Jyoti Randhawa	70	71	72	68	281	1,128,000
Naomichi Ozaki	69	72	71	70	282	864,000
Keiichiro Fukabori	75	68	72	67	282	864,000
Kazuhiko Hosokawa	71	71	70	70	282	864,000
Steve Conran	71	68	71	72	282	864,000

Mitsui Sumitomo Visa Taiheiyo Masters

Taiheiyo Club, Gotemba Course, Gotemba, Shizuoka
Par 36-36–72; 7,246 yards

November 13-16
purse, ¥150,000,000

	SCORES				TOTAL	MONEY
Kiyoshi Murota	66	71	62	73	272	¥30,000,000
Hiroyuki Fujita	69	71	68	70	278	10,800,000
Kim Jong-duck	72	69	66	71	278	10,800,000
Ben Curtis	65	69	71	73	278	10,800,000
Hideki Kase	69	70	68	72	279	6,000,000
Azuma Yano	67	69	72	72	280	5,400,000
Dinesh Chand	70	71	68	72	281	4,762,500
Tomohiro Kondo	68	68	70	75	281	4,762,500
Tsuyoshi Yoneyama	67	71	68	76	282	4,080,000
Toshimitsu Izawa	67	69	70	76	282	4,080,000
Tsuneyuki Nakajima	68	70	69	76	283	3,480,000
Shingo Katayama	72	71	69	71	283	3,480,000
Tetsuji Hiratsuka	71	73	71	69	284	2,780,000
Todd Hamilton	72	69	71	72	284	2,780,000
Jyoti Randhawa	70	73	71	70	284	2,780,000
Tsukasa Watanabe	74	70	71	70	285	2,212,500
Shigemasa Higaki	73	67	71	74	285	2,212,500
Go Higaki	69	70	69	77	285	2,212,500
Brendan Jones	68	71	75	71	285	2,212,500
Masashi Ozaki	66	70	76	74	286	1,710,000
Takashi Kanemoto	71	68	74	73	286	1,710,000
Katsumune Imai	68	74	74	70	286	1,710,000
Henrik Bjornstad	72	71	70	73	286	1,710,000
Mamoru Osanai	69	74	69	75	287	1,350,000
Daisuke Maruyama	69	74	70	74	287	1,350,000
Steve Conran	72	72	66	77	287	1,350,000
Koki Idoki	67	73	72	76	288	1,082,500
Taichi Teshima	68	73	70	77	288	1,082,500
Lin Keng-chi	71	71	72	74	288	1,082,500
Zaw Moe	71	69	74	74	288	1,082,500
Katsuya Nakagawa	68	74	71	75	288	1,082,500
Nobuhiro Masuda	70	75	69	74	288	1,082,500

Dunlop Phoenix

Phoenix Country Club, Miyazaki
Par 36-35–71; 6,917 yards

November 20-23
purse, ¥200,000,000

	SCORES				TOTAL	MONEY
Thomas Bjorn	67	65	69	71	272	¥40,000,000
Daisuke Maruyama	67	65	72	70	274	20,000,000
Tetsuji Hiratsuka	68	65	74	68	275	10,400,000
Lee Westwood	69	72	68	66	275	10,400,000
David Gossett	69	71	67	68	275	10,400,000
Sergio Garcia	66	65	67	78	276	7,200,000
Hank Kuehne	66	75	64	73	278	6,600,000
Kenichi Kuboya	67	70	70	72	279	6,100,000
Toshimitsu Izawa	67	69	67	77	280	5,640,000
Hideki Kase	69	69	69	74	281	4,640,000
David Smail	68	73	71	69	281	4,640,000
Craig Parry	67	72	73	69	281	4,640,000
Prayad Marksaeng	68	69	69	75	281	4,640,000

	SCORES				TOTAL	MONEY
Masahiro Kuramoto	69	70	71	72	282	3,340,000
Keiichiro Fukabori	72	70	68	72	282	3,340,000
Toru Taniguchi	69	71	70	72	282	3,340,000
Brendan Jones	70	72	67	73	282	3,340,000
Hidemichi Tanaka	71	73	69	70	283	2,760,000
Trevor Immelman	69	71	71	72	283	2,760,000
Kiyoshi Murota	72	72	67	73	284	2,520,000
Ryoken Kawagishi	68	73	74	70	285	2,200,000
Kim Jong-duck	71	66	77	71	285	2,200,000
Peter Teravainen	68	75	70	72	285	2,200,000
Tsuneyuki Nakajima	76	70	72	68	286	1,840,000
Jyoti Randhawa	71	68	75	72	286	1,840,000
Gregory Meyer	69	71	72	75	287	1,640,000
Todd Hamilton	71	72	71	73	287	1,640,000
Zhang Lian-wei	68	73	73	73	287	1,640,000
Hisayuki Sasaki	72	68	77	71	288	1,365,000
Shinichi Yokota	69	72	69	78	288	1,365,000
Jun Kikuchi	66	70	73	79	288	1,365,000
Dinesh Chand	71	74	68	75	288	1,365,000

Casio World Open

Ibusuki Golf Club, Kaimon, Kagoshima
Par 36-36–72; 7,151 yards

November 27-30
purse, ¥140,000,000

	SCORES				TOTAL	MONEY
Katsumune Imai	65	65	67	67	264	¥28,000,000
Shingo Katayama	73	66	66	66	271	11,760,000
Brendan Jones	73	67	64	67	271	11,760,000
Tsuneyuki Nakajima	72	68	65	67	272	5,786,666
Soushi Tajima	67	71	64	70	272	5,786,666
Kim Jong-duck	71	67	68	66	272	5,786,666
Shigemasa Higaki	69	71	67	67	274	4,445,000
Jyoti Randhawa	68	66	69	71	274	4,445,000
Mamoru Osanai	69	66	69	71	275	3,948,000
Naomichi Ozaki	71	70	68	67	276	3,528,000
Taichi Teshima	74	67	67	68	276	3,528,000
Nobuhiro Masuda	74	66	67	71	278	2,968,000
Takuya Taniguchi	73	67	70	68	278	2,968,000
Koki Idoki	67	72	69	71	279	2,140,000
Toshimitsu Izawa	73	67	67	72	279	2,140,000
Shinichi Akiba	72	67	70	70	279	2,140,000
Nobuhito Sato	71	73	65	70	279	2,140,000
Tetsuji Hiratsuka	70	67	69	73	279	2,140,000
Mitsuhiro Tateyama	70	71	69	69	279	2,140,000
Ryuichi Oda	72	69	69	69	279	2,140,000
Tsuyoshi Yoneyama	68	69	71	72	280	1,652,000
Hiroyuki Fujita	74	70	67	70	281	1,386,000
Takashi Kanemoto	69	71	69	72	281	1,386,000
Tomohiro Kondo	72	65	71	73	281	1,386,000
Christian Pena	70	71	69	71	281	1,386,000
Hideki Kase	73	71	68	70	282	1,064,000
Takenori Hiraishi	73	70	70	69	282	1,064,000
Go Higaki	69	72	70	71	282	1,064,000
Yui Ueda	71	69	72	70	282	1,064,000
Frankie Minoza	68	70	74	70	282	1,064,000
Prayad Marksaeng	68	71	72	71	282	1,064,000

Golf Nippon Series JT Cup

Tokyo Yomiuri Country Club, Tokyo
Par 35-35–70; 6,961 yards

December 4-7
purse, ¥100,000,000

	SCORES				TOTAL	MONEY
Tetsuji Hiratsuka	66	68	63	67	264	¥30,000,000
Toshimitsu Izawa	67	65	68	67	267	13,800,000
Hiroyuki Fujita	69	67	66	66	268	7,400,000
David Smail	66	66	71	66	269	5,400,000
Taichi Teshima	66	65	70	70	271	4,150,000
Steve Conran	71	70	67	66	274	3,433,333
Keiichiro Fukabori	69	69	67	69	274	3,433,333
Kiyoshi Murota	66	69	69	70	274	3,433,333
Soushi Tajima	68	68	69	70	275	2,950,000
Hideto Tanihara	67	69	70	70	276	2,750,000
Katsumune Imai	69	68	70	70	277	2,550,000
Hidemasa Hoshino	69	71	73	65	278	2,250,000
Masashi Ozaki	68	69	70	71	278	2,250,000
Nozomi Kawahara	72	66	69	72	279	1,850,000
Naomichi Ozaki	71	70	66	72	279	1,850,000
Brendan Jones	67	72	69	73	281	1,650,000
Yeh Wei-tze	74	69	69	70	282	1,500,000
Jyoti Randhawa	70	70	70	72	282	1,500,000
Tsuyoshi Yoneyama	68	68	73	74	283	1,350,000
Masahiro Kuramoto	70	74	70	70	284	1,250,000
Shingo Katayama	68	73	70	73	284	1,250,000
Paul Sheehan	70	71	75	70	286	1,100,000
Katsuyoshi Tomori	76	71	70	73	290	980,000
Daisuke Maruyama	70	70	74	76	290	980,000
Katsumasa Miyamoto	68	83	70	72	293	940,000

Asia/Japan Okinawa Open

Southern Links Golf Club, Naha
Par 36-36–72, 7,002 yards

December 18-21
purse, ¥100,000,000

	SCORES				TOTAL	MONEY
Hideto Tanihara	66	76	68	69	279	¥20,000,000
Chung Joon	67	73	72	70	282	5,078,571
Charlie Wi	72	73	73	64	282	5,078,571
Yusaku Miyazato	67	75	75	65	282	5,078,571
Simon Yates	68	76	70	68	282	5,078,571
Ted Oh	66	74	71	71	282	5,078,571
Tsuyoshi Yoneyama	67	73	68	74	282	5,078,571
Hiroshi Goda	65	74	68	75	282	5,078,571
Masashi Ozaki	63	79	67	74	283	2,820,000
Thongchai Jaidee	69	73	73	69	284	2,420,000
Shinichi Yokota	71	75	69	69	284	2,420,000
Rick Gibson	73	72	69	70	284	2,420,000
Yasuharu Imano	71	73	73	68	285	1,590,000
S.K. Ho	69	77	71	68	285	1,590,000
Taichi Teshima	67	78	70	70	285	1,590,000
Kiyoshi Murota	70	75	69	71	285	1,590,000
Terry Pilkadaris	71	74	69	71	285	1,590,000
Tadahiro Takayama	69	72	72	72	285	1,590,000
Hirokazu Kuniyoshi	66	73	72	74	285	1,590,000
Shigemasa Higaki	69	73	68	75	285	1,590,000

	SCORES				TOTAL	MONEY
Tetsuji Hiratsuka	68	77	71	70	286	1,180,000
Yoshiaki Mano	72	69	73	73	287	1,060,000
Hidemasa Hoshino	72	70	73	72	287	1,060,000
Go Higaki	70	76	73	69	288	840,000
Keiichiro Fukabori	68	77	72	71	288	840,000
Soushi Tajima	71	74	72	71	288	840,000
Katsumune Imai	70	73	72	73	288	840,000
Lam Chih-bing	65	77	73	73	288	840,000
Jun Kikuchi	66	76	73	73	288	840,000
Katsunori Kuwabara	69	75	72	73	289	663,333
Nobuhito Sato	67	75	76	71	289	663,333
Lin Wen-ko	67	76	72	74	289	663,333

Australasian Tour

Holden New Zealand Open

Auckland Golf Club, Auckland, New Zealand
Par 37-35–72; 6,788 yards

January 16-19
purse, NZ$700,000

	SCORES				TOTAL	MONEY
Mahal Pearce	69	70	69	70	278	A$122,353.85
Brett Rumford	68	73	71	68	280	69,333.85
Nathan Green	73	72	69	67	281	39,255.19
Chris Downes	67	70	69	75	281	39,255.19
Eddie Lee	68	76	70	69	283	23,281.22
Scott Gardiner	73	74	66	70	283	23,281.22
Wade Ormsby	70	74	68	71	283	23,281.22
Darrell Kestner	68	74	68	73	283	23,281.22
Michael Pearson	72	73	73	66	284	14,080.40
Grant Waite	71	69	75	69	284	14,080.40
Richard Lee	75	69	70	70	284	14,080.40
Brendan Jones	69	70	72	73	284	14,080.40
*Chris Johns	72	70	69	73	284	
Wayne Grady	68	75	67	74	284	14,080.40
Michael Campbell	69	73	67	75	284	14,080.40
Gareth Paddison	69	69	70	76	284	14,080.40
Marcus Norgren	72	74	70	69	285	7,821.30
Alastair Sidford	71	71	73	70	285	7,821.30
Murray Poje	73	74	68	70	285	7,821.30
Craig Jones	66	72	76	71	285	7,821.30
David Smail	69	70	74	72	285	7,821.30
Marcus Fraser	70	72	70	73	285	7,821.30
Alan Patterson	66	71	74	74	285	7,821.30
Kix Kawahara	73	72	66	74	285	7,821.30
Wayne Perske	71	73	73	69	286	6,321.61
Paul Sheehan	74	69	71	72	286	6,321.61
Ed Stedman	68	76	73	70	287	5,111.67
*Brad Heaven	68	72	76	71	287	
*Mark Smith	71	73	72	71	287	
Phil Tataurangi	71	73	71	72	287	5,111.67
Martin Doyle	72	74	69	72	287	5,111.67
Stephen Scahill	74	70	70	73	287	5,111.67
Peter Fowler	72	72	69	74	287	5,111.67

Heineken Classic

Royal Melbourne Golf Club, Melbourne, Victoria
Par 36-36–72; 6,995 yards

January 30-February 2
purse, A$2,000,000

	SCORES				TOTAL	MONEY
Ernie Els	70	72	66	65	273	A$378,947.36
Peter Lonard	67	72	67	68	274	178,421.05
Nick Faldo	69	71	65	69	274	178,421.05
Stephen Gallacher	70	70	71	65	276	77,894.74
Gary Evans	67	73	70	66	276	77,894.74
Soren Kjeldsen	71	67	71	67	276	77,894.74

	SCORES			TOTAL	MONEY
David Lynn	69	65	73	69	276	77,894.74
Paul Casey	65	67	74	70	276	77,894.74
Bob Friend	70	73	69	66	278	54,736.84
Peter Fowler	67	72	70	69	278	54,736.84
David Bransdon	74	67	71	67	279	42,105.26
John Bickerton	68	70	72	69	279	42,105.26
Steve Allan	68	68	73	70	279	42,105.26
Jarrod Moseley	70	72	73	65	280	29,350.88
Nick O'Hern	71	71	71	67	280	29,350.88
Thomas Bjorn	70	68	71	71	280	29,350.88
Richard Green	69	71	69	71	280	29,350.88
Brian Davis	70	74	65	71	280	29,350.88
David Smail	71	68	69	72	280	29,350.88
Darren Fichardt	70	74	69	68	281	21,473.68
Greg Turner	68	73	70	70	281	21,473.68
Richard Lee	69	69	72	71	281	21,473.68
Stephen Collins	69	72	69	71	281	21,473.68
Stephen Scahill	71	69	69	72	281	21,473.68
Eddie Lee	70	71	72	69	282	15,605.26
Steven Bowditch	72	72	69	69	282	15,605.26
Jorge Berendt	73	68	70	71	282	15,605.26
Patrik Sjoland	73	69	69	71	282	15,605.26
Greg Norman	73	69	69	71	282	15,605.26
Soren Hansen	72	71	68	71	282	15,605.26
Simon Khan	72	72	67	71	282	15,605.26
Ian Poulter	74	64	71	73	282	15,605.26
Lucas Parsons	68	73	73	69	283	11,578.94
Paul Sheehan	72	70	72	69	283	11,578.94
Jyoti Randhawa	71	73	69	70	283	11,578.94
Cameron Percy	71	71	70	71	283	11,578.94
Santiago Luna	66	74	71	72	283	11,578.94
Steve Webster	68	69	70	76	283	11,578.94
Michael Long	74	68	73	69	284	8,842.10
Robert Karlsson	69	73	73	69	284	8,842.10
Jamie Donaldson	74	66	74	70	284	8,842.10
Fredrik Andersson	72	68	73	71	284	8,842.10
Andrew Tschudin	69	73	71	71	284	8,842.10
David Park	75	68	70	71	284	8,842.10
Charlie Wi	74	70	68	72	284	8,842.10
Euan Walters	74	70	70	71	285	6,736.84
Kenneth Ferrie	70	72	71	72	285	6,736.84
Niclas Fasth	68	70	68	79	285	6,736.84
Brad Kennedy	71	70	76	69	286	5,368.42
Scott Hend	72	70	75	69	286	5,368.42
Scott Laycock	73	70	73	70	286	5,368.42
Tony Carolan	70	74	69	73	286	5,368.42
Ricardo Gonzalez	68	72	76	71	287	4,602.10
Brett Rumford	71	70	74	72	287	4,602.10
Ian Garbutt	68	71	75	73	287	4,602.10
Warren Bennett	67	74	71	75	287	4,602.10
Mahal Pearce	71	69	71	76	287	4,602.10
Nick Dougherty	72	72	74	70	288	4,421.05
Anthony Wall	70	70	76	72	288	4,421.05
Paul Lawrie	71	71	74	72	288	4,421.05
Gary Simpson	72	72	72	73	289	4,294.74
David Diaz	73	70	72	74	289	4,294.74
Nathan Green	70	73	71	75	289	4,294.74
Arjun Atwal	69	70	75	76	290	4,231.58
Lee S. James	73	70	74	74	291	4,157.89
Jean-Francois Remesy	70	73	73	75	291	4,157.89

	SCORES				TOTAL	MONEY
Mathias Gronberg	72	69	74	77	292	4,084.21
Scott Gardiner	73	71	73	76	293	4,021.05
Dean Robertson	72	72	72	77	293	4,021.05
Chris Downes	72	72	76	76	296	3,957.89

ANZ Championship

New South Wales Golf Club, Sydney, New South Wales
Par 36-36–72; 6,955 yards

February 6-9
purse, A$1,750,000

	POINTS				TOTAL	MONEY
Paul Casey	8	10	21	6	45	A$331,578.94
Nick O'Hern	10	12	8	11	41	156,118.42
Stuart Appleby	16	2	15	8	41	156,118.42
Peter Lonard	15	0	8	16	39	81,052.63
Jarrod Moseley	3	18	3	15	39	81,052.63
Greg Turner	4	9	7	18	38	66,315.80
Martin Doyle	4	7	7	19	37	56,184.21
Scott Hend	4	8	17	8	37	56,184.21
Peter Senior	10	9	9	7	35	47,894.73
Robert Karlsson	11	9	11	4	35	47,894.73
Peter Fowler	17	2	10	5	34	40,526.31
Paul Marantz	8	11	1	13	33	32,697.37
Klas Eriksson	4	12	5	12	33	32,697.37
Soren Kjeldsen	5	7	12	9	33	32,697.37
Jamie Donaldson	4	10	11	8	33	32,697.37
Richard Lee	7	14	4	7	32	25,236.84
Nick Dougherty	(-2)	15	17	2	32	25,236.84
Brendan Jones	8	14	1	8	31	21,414.48
Terry Price	10	12	4	5	31	21,414.48
Andre Stolz	5	12	7	6	30	19,894.74
Richard Bland	3	10	6	10	29	18,513.16
Arjun Atwal	3	14	3	9	29	18,513.16
Craig Parry	14	7	1	7	29	18,513.16
Stephen Scahill	11	0	11	7	29	18,513.16
Mahal Pearce	7	12	(-1)	10	28	15,059.21
Ricardo Gonzalez	6	6	7	9	28	15,059.21
Steve Conran	11	2	8	7	28	15,059.21
Gregory Havret	0	13	13	2	28	15,059.21
David Carter	10	9	(-1)	9	27	12,526.31
Soren Hansen	4	15	1	7	27	12,526.31
Nathan Green	9	13	3	2	27	12,526.31
Michael Pearson	10	6	4	6	26	11,236.84
Steve Webster	10	2	11	3	26	11,236.84
Stephen Gallacher	0	12	(-1)	14	25	9,947.37
David Drysdale	10	9	(-3)	9	25	9,947.37
Mark Foster	8	9	1	7	25	9,947.37
Gary Evans	7	14	(-2)	6	25	9,947.37
David Howell	11	6	9	(-1)	25	9,947.37
Brad Kennedy	10	1	8	5	24	8,289.47
Cameron Percy	5	11	5	3	24	8,289.47
Stephen Collins	12	3	6	3	24	8,289.47
Jean-Francois Remesy	10	3	8	3	24	8,289.47
Jyoti Randhawa	4	10	3	6	23	6,631.58
Matthew Ecob	5	13	1	4	23	6,631.58
Bradley Hughes	7	9	5	2	23	6,631.58
Stephen Leaney	11	3	7	2	23	6,631.58

	POINTS				TOTAL	MONEY
Marcus Cain	10	5	10	(-2)	23	6,631.58
Peter O'Malley	4	7	1	10	22	5,019.73
Matthew Blackey	12	2	5	3	22	5,019.73
Paul Sheehan	5	7	8	2	22	5,019.73
Ignacio Garrido	4	12	10	(-4)	22	5,019.73
Henrik Bjornstad	10	1	5	5	21	4,144.73
David Lynn	6	6	5	4	21	4,144.73
Mike Clayton	9	8	4	0	21	4,144.73
Adam Le Vesconte	6	6	4	4	20	3,997.37
Patrik Sjoland	(-1)	15	3	3	20	3,997.37
Raphael Jacquelin	9	8	(-3)	5	19	3,923.68
Doug LaBelle	(-1)	12	3	5	19	3,923.68
Shannon Jones	8	5	3	2	18	3,850
Paul Lawrie	4	7	9	(-2)	18	3,850
Mikko Ilonen	(-2)	19	(-4)	4	17	3,776.32
Leigh McKechnie	1	11	6	(-1)	17	3,776.32
Jorge Berendt	6	7	(-3)	6	16	3,696.49
Raymond Russell	6	10	(-4)	4	16	3,696.49
Ian Garbutt	2	10	6	(-2)	16	3,696.49
Dean Robertson	0	14	(-6)	7	15	3,573.68
Adam Mednick	4	9	0	2	15	3,573.68
Wayne Riley	2	11	0	2	15	3,573.68
Carlos Rodiles	7	4	5	(-3)	13	3,500
Martin Maritz	6	5	(-3)	3	11	3,444.73
Adrian Percey	4	10	(-3)	0	11	3,444.73
Tony Carolan	7	4	0	(-2)	9	3,389.47
David Gleeson	3	8	(-2)	(-6)	3	3,352.63

Johnnie Walker Classic

Lake Karrinyup Country Club, Perth, Western Australia
Par 36-36–72; 7,011 yards

February 13-16
purse, £1,000,000

	SCORES				TOTAL	MONEY
Ernie Els	64	65	64	66	259	A$459,118.45
Stephen Leaney	68	67	68	66	269	239,269.97
Andre Stolz	68	68	67	66	269	239,269.97
Justin Rose	68	69	69	65	271	100,495.87
Robert Allenby	69	64	72	66	271	100,495.87
Retief Goosen	72	65	66	68	271	100,495.87
David Smail	68	71	64	68	271	100,495.87
Jean-Francois Remesy	68	67	67	69	271	100,495.87
Niclas Fasth	74	65	66	67	272	58,402.21
Craig Kamps	71	67	64	70	272	58,402.21
Ignacio Garrido	69	69	68	68	274	46,143.25
Michael Long	71	66	68	69	274	46,143.25
Nathan Green	73	68	64	69	274	46,143.25
Craig Spence	73	68	63	70	274	46,143.25
Craig Parry	68	69	72	66	275	38,842.97
Chris Downes	67	73	68	67	275	38,842.97
Robert Karlsson	69	71	66	69	275	38,842.97
Paul Casey	71	70	67	68	276	33,677.69
David Howell	71	69	67	69	276	33,677.69
Paul McGinley	67	71	68	70	276	33,677.69
Simon Yates	72	68	65	71	276	33,677.69
Brett Rumford	67	73	67	70	277	30,303.03
Trevor Immelman	73	68	66	70	277	30,303.03

	SCORES				TOTAL	MONEY
Terry Price	66	71	69	71	277	30,303.03
Peter O'Malley	67	75	68	68	278	26,170.80
Charlie Wi	72	71	66	69	278	26,170.80
Scott Gardiner	74	69	65	70	278	26,170.80
Jamie Donaldson	68	71	69	70	278	26,170.80
Greg Owen	69	64	74	71	278	26,170.80
Bradley Hughes	75	67	65	71	278	26,170.80
David Lynn	65	72	68	73	278	26,170.80
Tony Carolan	72	70	68	69	279	22,038.57
Jarrod Moseley	70	71	68	70	279	22,038.57
Paul Sheehan	68	71	69	71	279	22,038.57
Steen Tinning	72	70	69	69	280	20,110.19
Clay Devers	70	72	66	72	280	20,110.19
Henrik Bjornstad	69	71	66	74	280	20,110.19
Arjun Singh	68	71	71	71	281	17,079.89
Arjun Atwal	73	69	68	71	281	17,079.89
Marcus Norgren	70	71	70	70	281	17,079.89
Alastair Forsyth	73	69	70	69	281	17,079.89
Ian Woosnam	67	71	75	68	281	17,079.89
Nick Dougherty	73	66	74	68	281	17,079.89
David Gilford	71	72	71	67	281	17,079.89
Nick O'Hern	74	68	72	67	281	17,079.89
Andrew Bonhomme	71	70	69	72	282	11,845.73
Raphael Jacquelin	68	74	67	73	282	11,845.73
Soren Kjeldsen	73	67	71	71	282	11,845.73
Raymond Russell	70	70	71	71	282	11,845.73
Kevin Na	71	72	69	70	282	11,845.73
Marcus Cain	69	72	67	74	282	11,845.73
Gary Evans	70	71	71	70	282	11,845.73
Jonathan Lomas	73	70	70	69	282	11,845.73
Adam Crawford	71	72	70	69	282	11,845.73
Nick Faldo	68	74	71	69	282	11,845.73
Jyoti Randhawa	72	69	73	68	282	11,845.73
James Kingston	72	69	69	73	283	7,713.49
Peter Fowler	70	73	68	72	283	7,713.49
Thomas Bjorn	68	74	67	74	283	7,713.49
Santiago Luna	70	69	72	72	283	7,713.49
Brian Davis	71	70	70	72	283	7,713.49
Warren Bennett	71	68	73	71	283	7,713.49
Stephen Scahill	70	73	71	69	283	7,713.49
Grant Dodd	71	71	70	72	284	6,336.08
Richard Green	71	69	72	72	284	6,336.08
Patrik Sjoland	75	67	72	70	284	6,336.08
Darren Fichardt	70	72	68	75	285	5,392.57
Andrew Pitts	74	69	70	72	285	5,392.57
Ian Poulter	74	69	70	72	285	5,392.57
John Bickerton	70	68	75	72	285	5,392.57
Andrew Tschudin	70	72	70	74	286	4,125.91
Barry Lane	74	68	72	72	286	4,125.91
Eddie Lee	73	70	73	70	286	4,125.91
Matthew Ecob	72	71	71	73	287	4,112.20
Edward Loar	72	68	76	71	287	4,112.20
Mardan Mamat	69	72	73	74	288	4,103.98
Ted Oh	71	72	74	72	289	4,098.50
*Michael Sim	72	71	71	76	290	*
Mark Allen	73	69	72	76	290	4,090.28
David Gleeson	71	72	72	75	290	4,090.28
Anthony Wall	72	71	71	77	291	4,082.06
Gary Simpson	72	70	76	73	291	4,082.06

Jacob's Creek Open

Kooyonga Golf Club, Adelaide, South Australia
Par 36-36–72; 6,711 yards

February 27-March 2
purse, A$1,000,000

	SCORES				TOTAL	MONEY
Joe Ogilvie	66	70	71	72	279	A$198,947.36
Shane Tait	70	72	67	71	280	112,736.84
Peter Senior	72	71	70	69	282	57,289.47
David Morland	75	72	67	68	282	57,289.47
Mahal Pearce	72	68	76	66	282	57,289.47
Peter Fowler	69	74	71	69	283	32,936.84
Peter O'Malley	68	70	74	71	283	32,936.84
Andre Stolz	70	71	71	71	283	32,936.84
Tjaart van der Walt	73	71	71	68	283	32,936.84
Andrew McLardy	69	73	74	67	283	32,936.84
Craig Carmichael	74	72	72	66	284	22,105.26
D.J. Brigman	73	71	71	69	284	22,105.26
Roland Thatcher	65	72	74	73	284	22,105.26
Cameron Percy	70	71	71	73	285	18,236.85
Nathan Green	71	72	73	69	285	18,236.85
Paul Claxton	71	73	73	69	286	14,515.78
Kim Felton	69	70	75	72	286	14,515.78
Hunter Haas	72	72	71	71	286	14,515.78
Scott Gump	73	71	75	68	287	11,250
Jarrod Moseley	65	74	71	77	287	11,250
Adrian Percey	72	71	71	73	287	11,250
Craig Spence	72	74	73	68	287	11,250
Nick O'Hern	71	71	73	72	287	11,250
Chris Downes	73	71	70	73	287	11,250
D.A. Points	70	75	68	74	287	11,250
Eric Meeks	76	71	71	70	288	9,394.74
Kevin Johnson	75	71	69	74	289	8,215.78
Ron Ewing	74	73	70	72	289	8,215.78
Terry Price	71	71	76	71	289	8,215.78
Wes Short	75	69	74	72	290	6,918.94
Shane Bertsch	72	70	71	77	290	6,918.94
Doug LaBelle	72	72	71	75	290	6,918.94
Jason Dawes	75	72	69	74	290	6,918.94
Andrew Buckle	73	73	70	74	290	6,918.94

Clearwater Classic

Clearwater Resort, Christchurch, New Zealand
Par 36-36–72; 7,137 yards

March 6-9
purse, A$1,000,000

	SCORES				TOTAL	MONEY
Ryan Palmer	69	63	71	68	271	A$189,473.68
Andre Stolz	70	68	68	68	274	107,368.42
Kevin Johnson	73	70	66	67	276	71,052.63
David Branshaw	71	71	69	67	278	50,526.32
Nick O'Hern	74	68	68	69	279	42,105.26
David Morland	70	70	71	69	280	34,035.09
Chris Downes	72	71	68	69	280	34,035.09
Peter O'Malley	72	64	73	71	280	34,035.09
Jess Daley	73	70	70	68	281	25,964.91
Rick Price	71	67	73	70	281	25,964.91
Kyle Thompson	74	69	69	69	281	25,964.91

	SCORES				TOTAL	MONEY
Pete Jordan	73	70	70	69	282	19,298.24
Jason Dawes	73	69	70	70	282	19,298.24
Joe Ogilvie	67	73	71	71	282	19,298.24
Trevor Dodds	73	70	71	69	283	12,637.42
Brendan Jones	70	72	71	70	283	12,637.42
Lee Porter	70	71	73	69	283	12,637.42
Brian Wilson	70	69	73	71	283	12,637.42
Mark Hensby	68	74	73	68	283	12,637.42
David McKenzie	69	73	73	68	283	12,637.42
Bradley Hughes	72	69	71	71	283	12,637.42
Zoran Zorkic	70	71	75	67	283	12,637.42
D.J. Brigman	70	70	72	71	283	12,637.42
Brad Kennedy	74	69	71	70	284	8,666.66
Rob McKelvey	72	72	69	71	284	8,666.66
Shane Bertsch	70	70	74	70	284	8,666.66
Sonny Skinner	68	70	74	72	284	8,666.66
Tjaart van der Walt	71	70	74	69	284	8,666.66
Stephen Collins	70	71	68	75	284	8,666.66
Roland Thatcher	72	69	72	72	285	6,473.68
Brett Rumford	71	69	73	72	285	6,473.68
Jason King	73	71	70	71	285	6,473.68
Keoke Cotner	70	71	71	73	285	6,473.68
Eric Meeks	72	70	70	73	285	6,473.68
Jeff Freeman	67	73	71	74	285	6,473.68

MasterCard Masters

Huntingdale Golf Club, Melbourne, Victoria
Par 36-36–72; 6,996 yards

December 4-7
purse, A$1,250,000

	SCORES				TOTAL	MONEY
Robert Allenby	67	67	72	71	277	A$225,000
Adam Scott	71	69	73	64	277	90,625
Craig Parry	70	72	68	67	277	90,625
Jarrod Moseley	67	72	69	69	277	90,625
(Allenby defeated Parry and Moseley on first and Scott on second playoff hole.)						
Peter Lonard	66	73	72	68	279	47,500
Rodney Pampling	69	72	68	70	279	47,500
Steve Allan	72	71	70	67	280	40,000
Peter O'Malley	69	74	69	69	281	35,000
Andrew Buckle	70	72	68	71	281	35,000
*James Nitties	70	72	66	73	281	
Geoff Ogilvy	67	76	74	65	282	27,916.66
Euan Walters	71	70	73	68	282	27,916.66
Peter Senior	67	69	75	71	282	27,916.66
Richard Green	71	73	70	69	283	21,875
Jason Dawes	72	70	71	70	283	21,875
Matthew Ecob	69	73	74	68	284	17,312.50
Michael Pearson	71	74	68	71	284	17,312.50
Adam Crawford	69	74	69	72	284	17,312.50
Craig Carmichael	70	73	69	72	284	17,312.50
Jens Nilsson	72	69	71	73	285	13,781.25
Scott Gardiner	71	71	70	73	285	13,781.25
Steve Elkington	72	68	79	68	287	12,300
Brett Rumford	75	70	72	70	287	12,300
Leigh McKechnie	75	71	70	71	287	12,300
Adam Groom	70	70	74	73	287	12,300

	SCORES				TOTAL	MONEY
Gareth Paddison	70	70	74	73	287	12,300
John Senden	68	79	70	71	288	9,625
Peter Fowler	69	71	76	72	288	9,625
Nick O'Hern	68	70	76	74	288	9,625
Brad Lamb	68	70	72	78	288	9,625

Australian PGA Championship

Hyatt Regency Coolum Resort, Coolum, Queensland
Par 36-36–72; 6,852 yards

December 11-14
purse, A$1,000,000

	SCORES				TOTAL	MONEY
Peter Senior	64	65	69	73	271	A$180,000
Rodney Pampling	65	69	69	69	272	102,000
Craig Parry	67	68	68	70	273	67,500
Scott Laycock	71	69	67	67	274	48,000
Peter Lonard	68	72	67	68	275	40,000
Euan Walters	71	67	71	67	276	36,000
Wade Ormsby	67	73	63	74	277	32,000
Peter Fowler	69	69	69	71	278	28,000
Peter O'Malley	68	67	69	74	278	28,000
Steve Allan	70	67	71	71	279	25,000
Steve Conran	72	71	70	67	280	20,000
Andrew Bonhomme	72	66	71	71	280	20,000
Scott Gardiner	68	71	65	76	280	20,000
Chip Beck	71	73	69	68	281	13,941.66
David McKenzie	77	66	69	69	281	13,941.66
Nick O'Hern	67	68	74	72	281	13,941.66
Matthew Ecob	67	72	70	72	281	13,941.66
Adam Crawford	69	70	68	74	281	13,941.66
Ryan Palmer	69	69	68	75	281	13,941.66
Adam Le Vesconte	70	69	74	69	282	10,000
Kurt Barnes	76	68	69	69	282	10,000
David Diaz	71	73	69	69	282	10,000
Jens Nilsson	67	73	71	71	282	10,000
Jean Van de Velde	69	69	69	75	282	10,000
Greg Norman	67	74	66	75	282	10,000
Jarrod Moseley	74	67	71	71	283	7,900
Anthony Gilligan	73	70	69	71	283	7,900
Adam Scott	68	69	74	72	283	7,900
Steve Collins	64	73	77	70	284	6,520
Scott Hend	69	71	74	70	284	6,520
Aaron Byrnes	71	69	73	71	284	6,520
Richard Moir	75	68	70	71	284	6,520
Andrew Buckle	71	72	70	71	284	6,520

Australian Open

Moonah Links, Rye, Victoria
Par 36-36–72; 7,466 yards

December 18-21
purse, A$1,500,000

	SCORES				TOTAL	MONEY
Peter Lonard	68	72	70	69	279	A$270,000
Stephen Leaney	71	70	68	71	280	127,125
Chris Downes	67	70	71	72	280	127,125

	SCORES				TOTAL	MONEY
Peter Fowler	70	71	70	70	281	66,000
Craig Jones	69	71	70	71	281	66,000
Robert Allenby	72	70	70	70	282	48,500
Martin Doyle	73	69	69	71	282	48,500
Steve Conran	73	69	68	72	282	48,500
Matthew Ecob	72	68	71	72	283	39,000
Ricky Barnes	69	69	72	73	283	39,000
Craig Spence	71	75	73	65	284	26,850
Nathan Green	69	70	74	71	284	26,850
Scott Hend	71	71	70	72	284	26,850
Steve Allan	72	66	72	74	284	26,850
Matthew Millar	72	69	69	74	284	26,850
Stuart Appleby	69	73	68	74	284	26,850
Wade Ormsby	74	72	67	72	285	19,500
Peter Senior	71	68	74	73	286	17,437.50
John Senden	71	70	71	74	286	17,437.50
Euan Walters	72	72	74	69	287	15,300
Craig Parry	69	71	74	73	287	15,300
Jens Nilsson	72	72	70	73	287	15,300
Scott Gardiner	74	70	69	74	287	15,300
Jarrod Moseley	71	69	71	76	287	15,300
Aaron Baddeley	71	74	74	69	288	11,940
Marcus Fraser	73	71	73	71	288	11,940
Nick O'Hern	72	72	73	71	288	11,940
Andrew Webster	74	72	71	71	288	11,940
Greg Chalmers	71	70	75	72	288	11,940
Anthony Painter	75	69	74	71	289	9,975
Paul Marantz	77	69	72	71	289	9,975
*James Nitties	71	71	72	75	289	

African Tours

South African Airways Open

Erinvale Golf Club, Cape Town, South Africa
Par 36-36–72; 7,087 yards

January 9-12
purse, £500,000

	SCORES				TOTAL	MONEY
Trevor Immelman	70	71	66	67	274	R1,073,254.50
Tim Clark	67	67	71	69	274	781,166.25
(Immelman defeated Clark on first playoff hole.)						
Charl Schwartzel	75	69	68	65	277	305,402.04
Tjaart van der Walt	69	76	64	68	277	305,402.04
Bobby Lincoln	71	68	69	69	277	305,402.04
Bradford Vaughan	69	71	68	69	277	305,402.04
Jean Hugo	66	73	65	73	277	305,402.04
Stephen Dodd	71	73	67	67	278	131,439.71
Andrew Coltart	68	69	73	68	278	131,439.71
Gary Murphy	71	67	71	69	278	131,439.71
Rolf Muntz	68	70	69	71	278	131,439.71
Brian Davis	71	69	67	71	278	131,439.71
Justin Rose	72	69	66	71	278	131,439.71
Louis Oosthuizen	73	70	70	66	279	96,457.05
David Howell	69	72	67	71	279	96,457.05
Ian Hutchings	75	68	64	72	279	96,457.05
Hennie Otto	72	72	67	69	280	87,966.11
James Kingston	67	72	71	70	280	87,966.11
Bradley Dredge	71	72	69	69	281	77,844.91
Raphael Jacquelin	72	72	68	69	281	77,844.91
Alastair Forsyth	73	67	71	70	281	77,844.91
Per Nyman	69	73	69	70	281	77,844.91
Philip Golding	71	70	64	76	281	77,844.91
Richard Sterne	74	72	68	68	282	68,267.14
Brett Liddle	72	72	69	69	282	68,267.14
Paul Lawrie	72	72	69	69	282	68,267.14
Steve Webster	72	72	67	71	282	68,267.14
Peter Baker	75	67	70	71	283	62,267.14
Nick Dougherty	72	66	73	72	283	62,267.14
Jean-Francois Remesy	71	70	74	69	284	55,700.55
Ryan Reid	72	74	69	69	284	55,700.55
Simon Hurd	71	68	75	70	284	55,700.55
Scott Dunlap	70	74	69	71	284	55,700.55
Graeme McDowell	75	71	67	71	284	55,700.55
Mark McNulty	74	67	71	72	284	55,700.55
David Park	73	70	73	69	285	47,549.25
David Drysdale	68	72	75	70	285	47,549.25
Andre Cruse	76	68	71	70	285	47,549.25
Scott Drummond	70	76	67	72	285	47,549.25
Craig Lile	75	71	67	72	285	47,549.25
Ian Garbutt	69	77	66	73	285	47,549.25
Markus Brier	72	73	73	68	286	38,039.40
Nicolas Colsaerts	73	70	73	70	286	38,039.40
Peter Lawrie	68	69	77	72	286	38,039.40
Marcel Siem	72	70	72	72	286	38,039.40
Gary Birch, Jr.	73	70	70	73	286	38,039.40
Keith Horne	74	69	70	73	286	38,039.40

	SCORES				TOTAL	MONEY
Iain Pyman	68	73	69	76	286	38,039.40
Steve van Vuuren	71	70	68	77	286	38,039.40
Marc Farry	74	68	74	71	287	26,567.20
Roger Wessels	74	72	70	71	287	26,567.20
Dean van Staden	73	73	70	71	287	26,567.20
Lewis Atkinson	71	72	72	72	287	26,567.20
Matthew Blackey	78	67	70	72	287	26,567.20
Tony Johnstone	73	72	70	72	287	26,567.20
Des Terblanche	71	71	72	73	287	26,567.20
Anders Hansen	71	71	71	74	287	26,567.20
Ian Poulter	72	70	70	75	287	26,567.20
Simon Dyson	75	66	75	72	288	20,038.61
Ian Keenan	70	72	74	72	288	20,038.61
Jaco Van Zyl	72	73	71	72	288	20,038.61
Andrew Butterfield	73	72	71	72	288	20,038.61
Mark Pilkington	73	71	73	72	289	17,661.15
Ulrich van den Berg	75	71	68	75	289	17,661.15
Jamie Donaldson	75	67	70	77	289	17,661.15
Sandeep Grewal	75	67	75	73	290	15,623.32
Lee S. James	75	70	70	75	290	15,623.32
David Carter	75	70	70	75	290	15,623.32
*Peter Karmas	75	71	76	69	291	
Nic Henning	72	71	70	78	291	14,264.78
Nico Le Grange	72	72	74	74	292	11,887.31
Titch Moore	74	71	65	82	292	11,887.31
John Bele	73	73	73	74	293	10,148.64
Grant Muller	70	72	75	76	293	10,148.64
Padraig Dooley	70	76	72	76	294	10,082.48
Johan Rystrom	75	71	70	78	294	10,082.48
Mark Mouland	75	70	70	79	294	10,082.48
Tim Rice	75	71	72	77	295	10,029.50
Warren Abery	74	68	78	76	296	9,989.89
Callie Swart	75	70	73	78	296	9,989.89
Benn Barham	77	68	78	77	300	9,950.16

Dunhill Championship

Houghton Golf Club, Johannesburg, South Africa   January 16-19
Par 36-36–72; 7,284 yards   purse, £500,000

	SCORES				TOTAL	MONEY
Mark Foster	70	66	69	68	273	R1,079,535
Paul Lawrie	68	73	67	65	273	424,024.95
Trevor Immelman	69	67	70	67	273	424,024.95
Doug McGuigan	69	67	69	68	273	424,024.95
Anders Hansen	70	65	69	69	273	424,024.95
Bradford Vaughan	70	66	66	71	273	424,024.95
(Foster won on second playoff hole.)						
Justin Rose	73	67	70	65	275	184,819.12
Richard Sterne	68	67	70	70	275	184,819.12
Steen Tinning	72	69	68	67	276	134,600.25
Paul Casey	67	76	65	68	276	134,600.25
Ian Poulter	70	68	68	70	276	134,600.25
Tim Clark	68	70	72	67	277	107,270.25
Per Nyman	71	69	69	68	277	107,270.25
Bradley Dredge	65	68	70	74	277	107,270.25
Gary Murphy	71	67	71	69	278	95,313.37

	SCORES				TOTAL	MONEY
Scott Dunlap	67	72	69	70	278	95,313.37
Mads Vibe-Hastrup	71	71	69	68	279	82,445.50
David Howell	72	71	68	68	279	82,445.50
Michael Kirk	68	74	68	69	279	82,445.50
Andrew Marshall	71	71	68	69	279	82,445.50
Andrew McLardy	68	74	66	71	279	82,445.50
Stephen Dodd	65	71	71	72	279	82,445.50
Jean Hugo	68	70	72	70	280	68,666.62
Andrew Butterfield	71	69	70	70	280	68,666.62
Chris Williams	67	72	70	71	280	68,666.62
Philip Golding	72	70	67	71	280	68,666.62
Hennie Otto	69	69	70	72	280	68,666.62
Raphael Jacquelin	69	71	68	72	280	68,666.62
Lee Westwood	71	67	71	72	281	57,506.87
David Lynn	69	73	67	72	281	57,506.87
Louis Oosthuizen	66	75	72	68	281	57,506.87
David Park	75	68	71	67	281	57,506.87
Michiel Bothma	69	73	66	73	281	57,506.87
Mark Roe	67	67	70	77	281	57,506.87
Ian Hutchings	71	72	68	71	282	49,877.25
Hendrik Buhrmann	73	69	68	72	282	49,877.25
Francois Delamontagne	74	69	70	69	282	49,877.25
Iain Pyman	71	67	70	74	282	49,877.25
Richard Bland	69	65	72	76	282	49,877.25
Dean van Staden	71	71	69	72	283	40,995
David Dixon	75	65	70	73	283	40,995
Callie Swart	66	74	70	73	283	40,995
Nicolas Vanhootegem	72	64	73	74	283	40,995
Bobby Lincoln	71	70	71	71	283	40,995
Simon Khan	71	71	71	70	283	40,995
Alastair Forsyth	69	72	67	75	283	40,995
Simon Hurd	72	71	72	68	283	40,995
Fredrik Orest	73	70	69	72	284	30,063
Mark McNulty	74	68	70	72	284	30,063
Kenneth Ferrie	69	73	70	72	284	30,063
Markus Brier	69	68	72	75	284	30,063
Martin Maritz	70	71	71	72	284	30,063
Jean-Francois Remesy	72	67	73	72	284	30,063
Jamie Donaldson	70	72	71	71	284	30,063
Andrew Raitt	70	72	74	68	284	30,063
Mark Mouland	68	75	69	73	285	23,230.50
Craig Lile	67	73	72	73	285	23,230.50
Tjaart van der Walt	70	72	67	77	286	19,472.62
Scott Drummond	68	70	74	74	286	19,472.62
Matthew Blackey	69	73	72	72	286	19,472.62
Nick Dougherty	71	72	71	72	286	19,472.62
Simon Wakefield	72	69	74	71	286	19,472.62
Ryan Reid	71	72	72	71	286	19,472.62
Peter Baker	71	69	75	71	286	19,472.62
John Bele	73	70	73	70	286	19,472.62
Paul Broadhurst	71	70	70	76	287	16,056.37
Donald Gammon	74	69	70	74	287	16,056.37
Bradley Davison	71	69	72	76	288	12,702.95
Mark Pilkington	71	68	73	76	288	12,702.95
Dean Robertson	72	71	71	74	288	12,702.95
Bafana Hlophe	71	72	72	73	288	12,702.95
Mikael Lundberg	73	70	76	69	288	12,702.95
Justin Hobday	69	70	71	79	289	10,141.48
Nic Henning	72	69	70	78	289	10,141.48

	SCORES				TOTAL	MONEY
Wallie Coetsee	73	68	75	73	289	10,141.48
Tony Johnstone	73	67	77	72	289	10,141.48
Simon Dyson	68	70	80	71	289	10,141.48
Johan Rystrom	76	67	71	78	292	10,061.68
Ben Mason	67	76	78	73	294	10,035.03
Julien Clement	72	71	77	75	295	10,008.38

Dimension Data Pro-Am

Gary Player Country Club: Par 36-36–72; 6,958 yards
Lost City Golf Course: Par 36-36–72; 6,983 yards
Sun City, South Africa

January 23-26
purse, R2,000,000

	SCORES				TOTAL	MONEY
Trevor Immelman	67	68	65	71	271	R317,000
Andrew McLardy	69	70	68	65	272	184,100
Bruce Vaughan	68	66	69	69	272	184,100
Nick Price	69	70	69	66	274	98,200
Hennie Otto	70	72	71	66	279	64,700
Craig Lile	72	70	69	68	279	64,700
Titch Moore	72	68	71	68	279	64,700
Scott Dunlap	68	69	73	69	279	64,700
Don Gammon	71	72	69	68	280	38,533.33
Ian Hutchings	70	72	71	67	280	38,533.33
Darren Clarke	63	72	69	76	280	38,533.33
Tjaart van der Walt	72	72	67	71	282	32,200
Jean Hugo	72	73	67	70	282	32,200
Mark Mouland	69	76	69	69	283	28,200
Louis Oosthuizen	74	67	72	70	283	28,200
Michael Kirk	71	69	73	70	283	28,200
Marc Cayeux	72	73	70	69	284	25,700
Andrew Butterfield	72	69	73	70	284	25,700
Dean van Staden	74	73	71	67	285	23,800
Andre Cruse	69	77	69	70	285	23,800
Malcolm Mackenzie	70	73	73	70	286	21,400
Justin Rose	69	73	76	68	286	21,400
Deane Pappas	70	75	72	69	286	21,400
Bradford Vaughan	72	69	71	74	286	21,400
Andre Bossert	68	72	72	74	286	21,400
Wallie Coetsee	76	69	70	72	287	18,700
Vaughn Groenewald	78	69	71	69	287	18,700
Darren Fichardt	74	70	71	72	287	18,700
Mark Murless	69	71	74	73	287	18,700
Michael Green	73	74	70	71	288	16,200
Chris Davison	68	75	75	70	288	16,200
Callie Swart	70	73	73	72	288	16,200
John Bele	72	70	75	71	288	16,200
Ulrich van den Berg	72	73	74	69	288	16,200
Patrick O'Brien	69	70	73	76	288	16,200

Southern Africa Tour Championship

Leopard Creek Country Club, Malelane, South Africa
Par 36-36–72; 7,352 yards

January 30-February 2
purse, R2,000,000

	SCORES				TOTAL	MONEY
Hennie Otto	71	64	68	68	271	R317,000
Trevor Immelman	71	70	69	63	273	230,000
Craig Lile	73	67	69	70	279	138,200
Mark McNulty	70	73	69	70	282	90,200
Mark Mouland	74	64	73	71	282	90,200
James Kingston	71	68	74	70	283	64,200
Titch Moore	67	71	73	72	283	64,200
Nic Henning	68	72	76	69	285	42,866.66
Vaughn Groenewald	72	70	73	70	285	42,866.66
Alan McLean	70	72	72	71	285	42,866.66
Charl Schwartzel	70	73	72	71	286	34,200
Marco Gortana	72	67	74	73	286	34,200
Brett Liddle	73	75	71	68	287	29,533.33
Wayne Bradley	71	77	69	70	287	29,533.33
Scott Dunlap	70	67	76	74	287	29,533.33
Keith Horne	72	72	75	69	288	24,800
Doug McGuigan	74	70	74	70	288	24,800
Wallie Coetsee	76	72	70	70	288	24,800
Bradley Davison	75	71	70	72	288	24,800
Bradford Vaughan	70	70	75	73	288	24,800
Desvonde Botes	72	75	65	76	288	24,800
Bruce Vaughan	70	73	77	69	289	20,200
Scott Drummond	75	70	74	70	289	20,200
Louis Oosthuizen	71	78	69	71	289	20,200
Andre Cruse	72	71	74	72	289	20,200
Bobby Lincoln	71	74	72	72	289	20,200
Michiel Bothma	74	72	71	72	289	20,200
Mark Foster	74	75	67	73	289	20,200
Grant Muller	75	74	71	70	290	17,266.66
Alan Michell	73	75	71	71	290	17,266.66
Roger Wessels	71	71	74	74	290	17,266.66

Stanbic Zambia Open

Lusaka Golf Club, Lusaka, Zambia
Par 35-38–73; 7,226 yards
(Shortened to 54 holes—rain.)

March 6-9
purse, €100,000

	SCORES			TOTAL	MONEY
Johan Edfors	70	70	66	206	R134,664.33
Michael Kirk	68	72	70	210	95,815.50
Scott Drummond	65	72	74	211	69,684
Bobby Lincoln	69	70	73	212	52,263
Hennie Otto	71	72	70	213	39,197.25
Louis Oosthuizen	73	70	70	213	39,197.25
Dismas Indiza	73	72	69	214	21,253.62
Mark Murless	74	70	70	214	21,253.62
Ciaran McMonagle	70	73	71	214	21,253.62
Sean Ludgater	72	69	73	214	21,253.62
Jamie Little	72	68	74	214	21,253.62
Peter Whiteford	76	68	71	215	14,807.85
Rafael Gomez	74	70	71	215	14,807.85

	SCORES			TOTAL	MONEY
Thomas Norret	70	72	73	215	14,807.85
Sandeep Grewal	73	69	73	215	14,807.85
Sebastian Fernandez	69	68	78	215	14,807.85
Steven O'Hara	73	73	70	216	10,452.60
David Ryan	70	72	74	216	10,452.60
Sammy Daniels	71	71	74	216	10,452.60
Keith Horne	68	73	75	216	10,452.60
Desvonde Botes	70	67	79	216	10,452.60
Bradford Vaughan	74	74	69	217	8,013.66
Wallie Coetsee	71	76	70	217	8,013.66
Nasho Kamungeremu	73	73	71	217	8,013.66
Cesar Monasterio	74	71	72	217	8,013.66
Thabang Simon	75	69	73	217	8,013.66
James Hepworth	70	73	74	217	8,013.66
Ulrich van den Berg	70	71	76	217	8,013.66
Nic Henning	73	75	70	218	6,881.29
Magnus Carlsson	73	75	70	218	6,881.29
Warren Abery	75	72	71	218	6,881.29
Chris Carney	71	74	73	218	6,881.29
Michiel Bothma	72	70	76	218	6,881.29
Oliver Seno	70	69	79	218	6,881.29

FNB Botswana Open

Phakalane Golf Club, Gaborone, Botswana
Par 36-36–72; 7,446 yards

March 27-29
purse, R250,000

	SCORES			TOTAL	MONEY
Trevor Fisher	67	68	66	201	R39,250
Des Terblanche	67	69	67	203	28,750
Sean Farrell	66	69	69	204	20,000
Ulrich van den Berg	70	69	67	206	14,750
Andre Cruse	70	70	67	207	9,166.66
Adilson da Silva	71	69	67	207	9,166.66
Sean Ludgater	68	70	69	207	9,166.66
Nic Henning	74	68	66	208	5,114.28
Shaun Norris	67	74	67	208	5,114.28
Grant Muller	68	72	68	208	5,114.28
Jaco Van Zyl	70	70	68	208	5,114.28
Brett Liddle	71	68	69	208	5,114.28
Richard Sterne	69	69	70	208	5,114.28
Peter Banda	70	68	70	208	5,114.28
Mark Murless	73	68	68	209	4,000
Wickus Myburgh	70	71	68	209	4,000
Justin Hobday	70	73	67	210	3,441.66
Ian Kennedy	70	72	68	210	3,441.66
Chris Davison	68	74	68	210	3,441.66
Richard Fulford	71	70	69	210	3,441.66
Ashley Roestoff	70	70	70	210	3,441.66
Charl Schwartzel	69	68	73	210	3,441.66
Hanno de Weerd	74	69	68	211	2,750
Ian Hutchings	72	71	68	211	2,750
Louis Oosthuizen	69	73	69	211	2,750
Jason Lipshitz	72	70	69	211	2,750
Callie Swart	68	72	71	211	2,750
Alex Baillie	69	71	71	211	2,750
Mike Lamb	73	70	69	212	2,350

	SCORES			TOTAL	MONEY
Bafana Hlophe	73	69	70	212	2,350
Barry Painting	68	72	72	212	2,350

Limpopo Industrelek Classic

Pietersburg Golf Club, Pietersburg, South Africa   May 8-10
Par 36-36–72; 7,090 yards   purse, R300,000

	SCORES			TOTAL	MONEY
Marc Cayeux	68	64	65	197	R47,100
Tyrol Auret	67	66	67	200	34,500
Sean Ludgater	66	71	65	202	24,000
Sean Farrell	64	70	69	203	17,700
Bobby Lincoln	66	72	66	204	10,200
Thomas Aiken	72	65	67	204	10,200
Adilson da Silva	67	69	68	204	10,200
Grant Muller	68	67	69	204	10,200
Andre Cruse	71	68	66	205	6,012
Des Terblanche	67	68	70	205	6,012
Alex Baillie	70	64	71	205	6,012
Ryan Dreyer	65	69	71	205	6,012
Hanno de Weerd	67	66	72	205	6,012
Steve Basson	73	68	65	206	4,900
Shaun Norris	68	72	66	206	4,900
Mike Lamb	68	71	67	206	4,900
Brett Liddle	71	70	66	207	4,130
Trevor Fisher	67	72	68	207	4,130
Titch Moore	67	72	68	207	4,130
Chris Williams	68	70	69	207	4,130
Desvonde Botes	70	68	69	207	4,130
Richard Fulford	66	71	70	207	4,130
Thabang Simon	72	67	69	208	3,360
Patrick O'Brien	71	68	69	208	3,360
Ted Hendriks	69	70	69	208	3,360
Omar Sandys	66	70	72	208	3,360
Derek Scullard	68	67	73	208	3,360
Nico van Rensburg	71	71	67	209	2,955
Chris Davison	69	66	74	209	2,955
Joe Nawanga	69	72	69	210	2,600
Divan van den Heever	72	68	70	210	2,600
Vaughn Groenewald	72	68	70	210	2,600
Callie Swart	69	70	71	210	2,600
Ian Kennedy	69	70	71	210	2,600
Dean Lambert	69	69	72	210	2,600

Capital Alliance Royal Swazi Sun Open

Royal Swazi Sun Country Club, Mbabane, Swaziland   May 16-18
Par 36-36–72; 6,156 yards   purse, R250,000

	POINTS			TOTAL	MONEY
Des Terblanche	13	18	5	36	R39,250
Adilson da Silva	1	20	15	36	28,750
(Terblanche defeated da Silva on first playoff hole.)					
Keith Horne	9	11	11	31	20,000

	POINTS			TOTAL	MONEY
Hendrik Buhrmann	7	13	10	30	10,562.50
Desvonde Botes	8	12	10	30	10,562.50
Trevor Fisher	6	21	3	30	10,562.50
James Kingston	13	15	2	30	10,562.50
Ashley Roestoff	2	14	13	29	6,500
Patrick O'Brien	8	5	15	28	5,750
Titch Moore	14	5	8	27	5,250
Sean Farrell	13	6	6	25	4,800
Andre van Staden	10	13	2	25	4,800
Josef Fourie	7	11	5	23	4,450
Alex Baillie	5	6	11	22	4,250
Nic Henning	13	2	6	21	4,075
Thabang Simon	7	5	8	20	3,850
Bradley Davison	9	7	4	20	3,850
Bobby Lincoln	6	6	7	19	3,437.50
John Bele	3	10	6	19	3,437.50
Chris Williams	8	5	6	19	3,437.50
Dougie McCabe	7	10	2	19	3,437.50
Justin Hobday	2	7	9	18	2,956.25
Wallie Coetsee	10	4	4	18	2,956.25
Ian Kennedy	14	3	1	18	2,956.25
Mike Lamb	5	12	1	18	2,956.25
Joe Nawanga	3	4	10	17	2,700
Callie Swart	4	4	8	16	2,508.33
Lindani Ndwandwe	0	9	7	16	2,508.33
Grant Muller	6	9	1	16	2,508.33
Richard Fulford	-1	10	6	15	2,312.50
Chris Davison	11	4	0	15	2,312.50

Devonvale Championship

Devonvale Conference & Golf Estate, Koelenhof May 28-30
Par 36-36–72; 6,444 yards purse, R200,000

	SCORES			TOTAL	MONEY
Hendrik Buhrmann	66	65	67	198	R31,400
Marc Cayeux	66	68	65	199	19,500
Shaun Norris	66	68	65	199	19,500
Justin Hobday	68	65	67	200	10,400
Des Terblanche	67	66	67	200	10,400
Brett Liddle	65	71	66	202	6,066.66
Ian Kennedy	65	69	68	202	6,066.66
Warren Abery	64	68	70	202	6,066.66
Sean Farrell	71	68	65	204	4,400
Adilson da Silva	69	69	66	204	4,400
Desvonde Botes	70	67	68	205	3,840
Richard Fulford	65	68	72	205	3,840
Bobby Lincoln	67	71	68	206	3,213.33
Nico van Rensburg	71	66	69	206	3,213.33
Warrick Druian	70	66	70	206	3,213.33
Keith Horne	67	69	70	206	3,213.33
Bradley Davison	66	69	71	206	3,213.33
Andre Cruse	69	65	72	206	3,213.33
Cliffie Howes	66	71	70	207	2,750
Ulrich van den Berg	69	67	71	207	2,750
Alan Michell	73	68	67	208	2,500
Steve Basson	72	67	69	208	2,500

	SCORES			TOTAL	MONEY
Thabang Simon	71	66	71	208	2,500
Dean Lambert	69	70	70	209	2,240
Grant Muller	68	70	71	209	2,240
Alain Norris	67	68	74	209	2,240
Michael Green	72	69	69	210	2,040
Patrick O'Brien	69	70	71	210	2,040
Mark Murless	74	67	70	211	1,850
Roux Burger	73	66	72	211	1,850
Dean Nysschen	70	68	73	211	1,850
Nico Le Grange	67	71	73	211	1,850

Canon Classic

Bramble Hill Golf Club, Fancourt   June 5-7
Par 35-36–71; 6,291 yards   purse, R200,000

	SCORES			TOTAL	MONEY
Tyrol Auret	65	68	67	200	R31,400
Warren Abery	64	70	66	200	23,000
(Auret defeated Abery on first playoff hole.)					
Grant Muller	67	69	65	201	13,900
Justin Hobday	73	62	66	201	13,900
Brett Liddle	69	69	64	202	9,000
Ian Kennedy	68	68	68	204	5,700
Ian Hutchings	70	66	68	204	5,700
Richard Fulford	66	70	68	204	5,700
Alan Michell	68	66	70	204	5,700
Roux Burger	66	70	71	207	4,200
Henk Alberts	68	75	65	208	3,506.66
Mike Michell	71	68	69	208	3,506.66
Bafana Hlophe	70	68	70	208	3,506.66
Adilson da Silva	67	71	70	208	3,506.66
Ryan Dreyer	67	71	70	208	3,506.66
Ashley Roestoff	68	69	71	208	3,506.66
Keith Horne	71	70	69	210	2,960
Nic Henning	72	67	71	210	2,960
Chris Davison	73	69	69	211	2,750
Andre Cruse	69	71	71	211	2,750
Hanno de Weerd	72	71	69	212	2,412
Vaughn Groenewald	69	74	69	212	2,412
Nico Le Grange	70	72	70	212	2,412
Desvonde Botes	71	69	72	212	2,412
Hendrik Buhrmann	68	70	74	212	2,412
Des Terblanche	69	74	70	213	2,160
Gerlou Roux	73	70	71	214	1,975
Jayde Tannous	69	74	71	214	1,975
Andre van Staden	70	73	71	214	1,975
Jeff Inglis	68	72	74	214	1,975

Royal Swazi Sun Classic

Royal Swazi Sun Country Club, Mbabane, Swaziland
Par 36-36–72; 6,156 yards

June 20-22
purse, R200,000

	SCORES			TOTAL	MONEY
Nic Henning	65	66	67	198	R31,400
Mark Murless	65	66	69	200	23,000
Andre Cruse	70	65	66	201	13,900
Andre van Staden	65	68	68	201	13,900
Nico van Rensburg	69	67	67	203	7,333.33
Sean Farrell	66	69	68	203	7,333.33
Tyrol Auret	66	65	72	203	7,333.33
Wallie Coetsee	69	70	65	204	4,900
Desvonde Botes	70	69	65	204	4,900
Mike Lamb	68	71	67	206	3,960
Ian Kennedy	69	69	68	206	3,960
Justin Hobday	67	67	72	206	3,960
Shane Pringle	72	67	68	207	3,480
Keith Horne	67	68	72	207	3,480
Richard Fulford	74	67	67	208	3,080
Hanno de Weerd	69	71	68	208	3,080
Des Terblanche	72	67	69	208	3,080
Wayne de Haas	69	66	73	208	3,080
Brett Liddle	72	69	68	209	2,650
Barry Painting	66	75	68	209	2,650
Callie Swart	69	68	72	209	2,650
Sammy Daniels	67	68	74	209	2,650
Vaughn Groenewald	73	69	68	210	2,200
Hendrik Buhrmann	69	72	69	210	2,200
Warren Abery	71	70	69	210	2,200
Ashley Roestoff	70	70	70	210	2,200
Trevor Fisher	68	71	71	210	2,200
Ryan Dreyer	72	65	73	210	2,200
Bradley Davison	73	71	67	211	1,910
Bafana Hlophe	70	70	71	211	1,910
Jeff Inglis	70	74	68	212	1,730
Ian Hutchings	71	73	68	212	1,730

Parmalat Classic

Silver Lakes Golf Club, Mbabane, Swaziland
Par 36-36–72; 7,189 yards

June 25-27
purse, R200,000

	SCORES			TOTAL	MONEY
Desvonde Botes	68	69	70	207	R31,400
James Kingston	67	70	72	209	23,000
Nic Henning	70	69	72	211	13,900
Andre Cruse	71	64	76	211	13,900
Michael du Toit	75	67	72	214	9,000
Hendrik Buhrmann	68	78	69	215	7,000
Shaun Norris	74	70	72	216	5,600
Ryan Dreyer	72	69	75	216	5,600
Callie Swart	80	66	71	217	4,246.66
Ulrich van den Berg	75	69	73	217	4,246.66
Warren Abery	69	72	76	217	4,246.66
Wallie Coetsee	74	70	74	218	3,740
Steve van Vuuren	75	73	71	219	3,154.28

	SCORES			TOTAL	MONEY
Sammy Daniels	79	69	71	219	3,154.28
Des Terblanche	73	71	75	219	3,154.28
Brett Liddle	71	72	76	219	3,154.28
Hennie Walters	70	73	76	219	3,154.28
Sean Farrell	71	71	77	219	3,154.28
Vaughn Groenewald	71	71	77	219	3,154.28
Adilson da Silva	73	74	73	220	2,550
Omar Sandys	78	67	75	220	2,550
Justin Hobday	72	70	78	220	2,550
Alain Norris	72	70	78	220	2,550
Grant Muller	75	70	76	221	2,240
Mike Lamb	74	68	79	221	2,240
Jeff Inglis	74	66	81	221	2,240
Nico van Rensburg	80	69	73	222	1,852.50
Bafana Hlophe	75	74	73	222	1,852.50
Ian Kennedy	79	69	74	222	1,852.50
Keith Horne	73	73	76	222	1,852.50
Patrick O'Brien	72	74	76	222	1,852.50
Shane Pringle	76	70	76	222	1,852.50
Warrick Druian	73	71	78	222	1,852.50
Eddie Lombard	72	72	78	222	1,852.50

Seekers Travel Pro-Am

Dainfern Country Club, Sandton, South Africa
Par 36-36–72; 6,813 yards

October 2-4
purse, R200,000

	SCORES			TOTAL	MONEY
Chris Williams	71	67	65	203	R31,400
Jason Jackson	69	68	66	203	19,500
Ashley Roestoff	64	71	68	203	19,500
(Williams defeated Roestoff on second and Jackson on sixth playoff hole.)					
Alan Michell	70	67	67	204	11,800
Albert Kruger	71	66	69	206	8,000
Dion Fourie	64	70	72	206	8,000
Wallie Coetsee	69	70	68	207	5,000
Doug McGuigan	70	69	68	207	5,000
Andre Cruse	68	69	70	207	5,000
Patrick O'Brien	67	69	71	207	5,000
Des Terblanche	67	71	70	208	3,747
Gary Thain	69	69	70	208	3,747
Marc Cayeux	68	69	71	208	3,747
Ryan Dreyer	72	68	69	209	3,330
Michiel Bothma	71	68	70	209	3,330
James Kingston	73	69	68	210	2,860
Justin Hobday	68	73	69	210	2,860
Ulrich van den Berg	69	71	70	210	2,860
Adilson da Silva	73	67	70	210	2,860
Grant Muller	70	66	74	210	2,860
Thabang Simon	71	61	78	210	2,860
Bradford Vaughan	72	71	68	211	2,365
Ian Kennedy	73	69	69	211	2,365
Tyrol Auret	67	72	72	211	2,365
Thomas Aiken	67	71	73	211	2,365
Nic Henning	72	72	68	212	1,949
Michael Green	75	69	68	212	1,949
Nico van Rensburg	71	71	70	212	1,949

	SCORES			TOTAL	MONEY
Michael du Toit	71	71	70	212	1,949
Nico Le Grange	73	68	71	212	1,949
Warrick Druian	69	71	72	212	1,949
Ian Hutchings	71	69	72	212	1,949

Bearing Man Highveld Classic

Witbank Golf Club, Witbank, South Africa
Par 36-36–72; 6,641 yards

October 10-12
purse, R200,000

	SCORES			TOTAL	MONEY
Dion Fourie	66	67	68	201	R31,400
Desvonde Botes	68	69	65	202	19,500
Divan van den Heever	67	63	72	202	19,500
Tyrol Auret	71	66	66	203	9,267
Albert Kruger	68	68	67	203	9,267
Doug McGuigan	68	64	71	203	9,267
Adilson da Silva	69	68	67	204	5,267
Nic Henning	67	68	69	204	5,267
Ashley Roestoff	68	65	71	204	5,267
Thabang Simon	69	68	68	205	4,070
Warrick Druian	67	67	71	205	4,070
Alan Michell	67	72	67	206	3,567
Ian Hutchings	66	70	70	206	3,567
Wallie Coetsee	69	66	71	206	3,567
Lindani Ndwandwe	70	72	65	207	2,865
Ian Kennedy	73	68	66	207	2,865
Hennie Otto	71	69	67	207	2,865
Steve Basson	69	70	68	207	2,865
Vaughn Groenewald	72	67	68	207	2,865
Travis Fraser	65	73	69	207	2,865
Ulrich van den Berg	69	68	70	207	2,865
Kevin Stone	70	66	71	207	2,865
Jason Jackson	73	68	67	208	2,320
Thomas Aiken	65	74	69	208	2,320
Henk Alberts	67	68	73	208	2,320
Callie Swart	70	71	68	209	2,080
Gary Thain	70	69	70	209	2,080
Mark Murless	71	66	72	209	2,080
Mike Lamb	73	68	69	210	1,910
Nico van Rensburg	73	68	69	210	1,910

Platinum Classic

Mooi Nooi Golf Club, Rustenburg, South Africa
Par 36-36–72; 6,936 yards

October 30-November 1
purse, R500,000

	SCORES			TOTAL	MONEY
Doug McGuigan	68	64	67	199	R79,000
Ashley Roestoff	68	66	66	200	57,500
Richard Sterne	65	70	68	203	34,600
Mike Lamb	69	67	68	204	24,550
Nico van Rensburg	67	70	68	205	19,175
Clinton Whitelaw	66	69	70	205	19,175
Ulrich van den Berg	72	69	65	206	11,913

	SCORES			TOTAL	MONEY
Steve van Vuuren	69	69	68	206	11,913
David Ryan	69	68	69	206	11,913
Dean van Staden	65	72	69	206	11,913
Marc Cayeux	69	71	67	207	8,125
Charl Schwartzel	70	70	67	207	8,125
Nic Henning	71	68	68	207	8,125
Alan Michell	65	67	75	207	8,125
Bradford Vaughan	69	70	69	208	6,975
Justin Hobday	67	72	69	208	6,975
Chris Davison	70	68	71	209	6,600
Warren Abery	71	70	69	210	6,013
Sean Farrell	72	68	70	210	6,013
Trevor Fisher, Jr.	70	69	71	210	6,013
Titch Moore	69	69	72	210	6,013
James Kingston	67	75	69	211	5,475
Des Terblanche	72	69	70	211	5,475
Bafana Hlophe	69	73	70	212	5,025
Wallie Coetsee	70	72	70	212	5,025
Dion Fourie	65	74	73	212	5,025
Sean Ludgater	68	70	74	212	5,025
Mike Michell	71	75	67	213	4,500
Thabang Simon	70	72	71	213	4,500
Omar Sandys	70	70	73	213	4,500

Nelson Mandela Invitational

Arabella Country Club, Hermanus, South Africa   November 15-16
Par 36-36–72

	SCORES		TOTAL
Lee Westwood/Simon Hobday	65	64	129
Tim Clark/Hugh Baiocchi	64	67	131
Andrew Coltart/John Mashego	65	67	132
Omar Sandys/John Bland	68	65	133
Hennie Otto/John Fourie	67	67	134
Charl Schwartzel/Gary Player	68	68	136
Richard Sterne/Vincent Tshabalala	71	67	138
Irvin Mosate/Bob Charles	73	67	140

Presidents Cup

Fancourt Hotel & Country Club Estate, George, South Africa   November 20-23
Par 36-36–73; 7,234 yards

FIRST DAY
Foursomes

Nick Price and Mike Weir (Int'l) defeated David Toms and Phil Mickelson, 1 up.
Retief Goosen and Vijay Singh (Int'l) defeated Chris DiMarco and Jerry Kelly, 3 and 2.
Davis Love and Kenny Perry (US) defeated Peter Lonard and Tim Clark, 4 and 2.
Ernie Els and Adam Scott (Int'l) defeated Justin Leonard and Jim Furyk, 1 up.
Jay Haas and Fred Funk (US) halved with Robert Allenby and Stephen Leaney.
Tiger Woods and Charles Howell (US) defeated Stuart Appleby and K.J. Choi, 4 and 3.

POINTS: International Team 3½, United States Team 2½

SECOND DAY
Morning Fourballs

Allenby and Weir (Int'l) defeated Mickelson and Toms, 3 and 1.
Perry and Love (US) defeated Goosen and Choi, 2 and 1.
Furyk and Haas (US) defeated Appleby and Scott, 6 and 5.
DiMarco and Leonard (US) defeated Singh and Price, 2 up.
Els and Clark (Int'l) defeated Woods and Howell, 5 and 3.

Afternoon Foursomes

Perry and Kelly (US) defeated Choi and Lonard, 2 and 1.
Funk and Toms (US) defeated Allenby and Leaney, 4 and 3.
Woods and Howell (US) defeated Clark and Goosen, 1 up.
Els and Scott (Int'l) defeated DiMarco and Mickelson, 1 up.
Furyk and Leonard (US) defeated Singh and Weir, 5 and 4.

POINTS: International Team 3, United States Team 7
TWO-DAY TOTAL: International Team 6½, United States Team 9½

THIRD DAY
Fourballs

Lonard and Leaney (Int'l) defeated Funk and Mickelson, 2 and 1.
Els and Clark (Int'l) defeated Furyk and Haas, 3 and 2.
Scott and Choi (Int'l) defeated Perry and Kelly, 5 and 4.
Singh and Goosen (Int'l) defeated Woods and Howell, 2 and 1.
Weir and Allenby (Int'l) defeated DiMarco and Leonard, 1 up.
Appleby and Price (Int'l) defeated Love and Toms, 2 and 1.

POINTS: International Team 6, United States Team 0
THREE-DAY TOTAL: International Team 12½, United States Team 9½

FOURTH DAY
Singles

Furyk (US) defeated Weir, 3 and 1.
Kelly (US) defeated Clark, 1 up.
Perry (US) defeated Price, 1 up.
Choi (Int'l) defeated Leonard, 4 and 2.
Howell (US) defeated Scott, 5 and 4.
Haas (US) defeated Leaney, 4 and 3.
Goosen (Int'l) defeated Mickelson, 2 and 1.
Lonard (Int'l) defeated Funk, 4 and 3.
DiMarco (US) defeated Appleby, 1 up.
Singh (Int'l) defeated Toms, 4 and 3.
Woods (US) defeated Els, 4 and 3.
Love (US) halved with Robert Allenby.

POINTS: International Team 4½, United States Team 7½
TOTAL POINTS: International Team 17, United States Team 17
(The Presidents Cup was called a draw after regulation play ended in a tie followed by three playoff holes between Woods and Els.)

Nedbank Golf Challenge

Gary Player Country Club, Sun City, South Africa
Par 36-36–72; 7,769 yards

November 27-30
purse, US$4,060,000

	SCORES				TOTAL	MONEY
Sergio Garcia	68	66	70	70	274	$1,200,000
Retief Goosen	70	67	68	69	274	500,000
(Garcia defeated Goosen on first playoff hole.)						
Vijay Singh	65	72	71	69	277	400,000
Darren Clarke	66	71	74	67	278	300,000
Jerry Kelly	67	67	76	71	281	182,500
Kenny Perry	65	68	73	75	281	182,500
Chris DiMarco	66	71	74	71	282	140,000
Adam Scott	66	74	74	68	282	140,000
Stuart Appleby	67	75	70	72	284	130,000
Jay Haas	70	72	71	72	285	120,000
Tim Clark	68	71	73	73	285	120,000
Fred Funk	71	71	71	72	285	120,000
Padraig Harrington	72	70	74	70	286	100,000
Charles Howell	73	67	75	72	287	90,000
Robert Allenby	66	78	69	74	287	90,000
Stephen Leaney	68	72	70	77	287	90,000
Ernie Els	72	75	74	69	290	80,000
Nick Price	69	75	75	73	292	75,000

Hassan II Trophy

Dar-es-Salam Golf Club, Red Course, Rabat, Morocco
Par 36-37–73; 7,600 yards

December 11-14
purse, US$350,100

	SCORES				TOTAL	MONEY
Santiago Luna	68	70	69	70	277	US$50,000
Joakim Haeggman	71	73	69	68	281	25,000
Mark Roe	70	73	73	66	282	22,000
Nicolas Colsaerts	70	71	72	70	283	19,500
Miguel Angel Martin	72	74	73	67	286	15,500
Peter Baker	74	65	75	72	286	15,500
Soshi Tajima	72	70	71	73	286	15,500
Gregory Havret	71	74	73	69	287	14,000
Younes El Hassani	71	72	73	72	288	13,250
Roger Chapman	76	70	69	73	288	13,250
Mustapha El Kherraz	73	72	71	73	289	12,500
Henrik Nystrom	75	72	72	71	290	12,000
Alberto Binaghi	76	72	75	70	293	11,500
Bobby Casper	76	75	73	70	294	10,600
Olivier Edmond	74	76	72	72	294	10,600
Emanuele Canonica	75	73	70	76	294	10,600
Abdelhaq Sabi	75	76	73	72	296	10,150
Jerome Theunis	72	75	74	75	296	10,150
Ty Tryon	79	75	71	72	297	10,000
Mark Davis	79	76	71	73	299	9,900
Greig Hutcheon	70	78	79	73	300	9,800
Marwane Chemssedine	76	74	75	77	302	9,700
Rachid El Hali	74	80	77	77	308	9,600
Butch Baird	79	78	73	79	309	9,500

Ernie Els Invitational

Fancourt Golf Club, George, South Africa
Outeniqua Course: Par 36-36–72; 6,496 yards
Montagu Course: Par 36-36–72; 6,479 yards

December 16-17
purse, R234,280

	SCORES		TOTAL	MONEY
Ernie Els	65	60	125	R25,000
Bobby Lincoln	65	68	133	19,000
Louis Oosthuizen	68	68	136	17,300
Bradford Vaughan	70	69	139	13,500
Charl Schwartzel	72	67	139	13,500
Richard Sterne	72	67	139	13,500
Ulrich van den Berg	69	71	140	6,500
Trevor Immelman	68	72	140	6,500
Omar Sandys	69	72	141	3,660
Chris Davison	71	70	141	3,660
Nic Henning	73	68	141	3,660
Michiel Bothma	70	72	142	3,500
Titch Moore	71	71	142	3,500
Nico van Rensburg	72	71	143	3,500
Richard Kaplan	71	73	144	3,500
Sammy Daniels	74	70	144	3,500
Robbie Stewart	75	69	144	3,500
Don Gammon	71	74	145	3,500
Ian Hutchings	71	74	145	3,500
Marc Cayeux	75	70	145	3,500
Darren Fichardt	75	70	145	3,500
John Bland	72	74	146	3,500
Mark Wiltshire	71	76	147	3,500
Brett Liddle	72	75	147	3,500
Dean van Staden	72	75	147	3,500
Ian Palmer	73	74	147	3,500
Gavin Levenson	74	73	147	3,500
Doug McGuigan	74	74	148	3,500
Kevin Stone	76	72	148	3,500
Wayne Bradley	75	74	149	3,500

Senior Tours

MasterCard Championship

Hualalai Golf Club, Kaupulehu-Kona, Hawaii
Par 36-36–72; 6,850 yards

January 31-February 2
purse, $1,500,000

	SCORES			TOTAL	MONEY
Dana Quigley	66	65	67	198	$250,000
Larry Nelson	67	64	69	200	150,000
Fuzzy Zoeller	68	63	70	201	120,000
Tom Watson	70	66	67	203	89,500
Stewart Ginn	68	66	69	203	89,500
Steven Veriato	66	68	70	204	67,000
Bruce Fleisher	68	65	72	205	49,750
Tom Jenkins	70	66	69	205	49,750
Bruce Lietzke	68	65	72	205	49,750
Allen Doyle	70	66	69	205	49,750
Ed Dougherty	68	69	69	206	35,250
Tom Kite	69	67	70	206	35,250
Jack Nicklaus	68	72	66	206	35,250
John Jacobs	72	65	69	206	35,250
Jay Sigel	67	69	71	207	30,000
Isao Aoki	71	67	70	208	25,500
Hale Irwin	66	71	71	208	25,500
Gil Morgan	74	68	66	208	25,500
Jim Thorpe	70	66	72	208	25,500
James Mason	70	67	71	208	25,500
Leonard Thompson	70	68	71	209	21,000
Sammy Rachels	72	67	71	210	19,500
Lee Trevino	68	71	71	210	19,500
Jose Maria Canizares	68	71	72	211	17,500
Doug Tewell	70	69	72	211	17,500
Jim Colbert	74	67	71	212	14,300
Hubert Green	71	71	70	212	14,300
Gary Player	70	67	75	212	14,300
John Schroeder	76	67	69	212	14,300
Bobby Wadkins	72	70	70	212	14,300
Walter Hall	74	69	70	213	12,500
Dave Eichelberger	74	72	68	214	11,875
Mike McCullough	70	73	71	214	11,875
Bob Gilder	74	67	76	217	11,375
J.C. Snead	74	73	70	217	11,375
Arnold Palmer	73	76	77	226	11,000

Royal Caribbean Golf Classic

Crandon Park Golf Course, Key Biscayne, Florida
Par 36-36–72; 6,953 yards

February 7-9
purse, $1,450,000

	SCORES			TOTAL	MONEY
Dave Barr	70	70	67	207	$217,500
Gil Morgan	70	68	70	208	116,000
Bobby Wadkins	66	74	68	208	116,000

	SCORES			TOTAL	MONEY
Rodger Davis	69	70	70	209	86,275
Hubert Green	72	68	71	211	68,875
Isao Aoki	71	72	69	212	49,300
Mike McCullough	70	73	69	212	49,300
Tom Purtzer	71	69	72	212	49,300
Allen Doyle	70	71	71	212	49,300
Billy Kratzert	71	72	70	213	36,250
Dana Quigley	73	70	70	213	36,250
Jim Colbert	74	71	69	214	27,840
Bruce Lietzke	74	72	68	214	27,840
Jerry McGee	69	73	72	214	27,840
Leonard Thompson	71	73	70	214	27,840
James Mason	75	70	69	214	27,840
Gary Koch	69	72	74	215	20,416
Wayne Levi	75	73	67	215	20,416
Larry Nelson	73	73	69	215	20,416
Christy O'Connor, Jr.	68	73	74	215	20,416
Vicente Fernandez	73	71	71	215	20,416
Mike Hill	71	75	70	216	13,952.22
Mark McCumber	72	70	74	216	13,952.22
Doug Tewell	71	75	70	216	13,952.22
Howard Twitty	72	71	73	216	13,952.22
Bobby Walzel	72	73	71	216	13,952.22
John Jacobs	71	75	70	216	13,952.22
Tom Wargo	73	72	71	216	13,952.22
Hugh Baiocchi	74	73	69	216	13,952.23
Pat McDonald	74	73	69	216	13,952.23
Jim Dent	71	74	72	217	9,183.33
Bob Eastwood	75	74	68	217	9,183.34
David Eger	69	74	74	217	9,183.33
Dave Eichelberger	73	69	75	217	9,183.33
Bruce Fleisher	71	75	71	217	9,183.34
Tom Kite	74	72	71	217	9,183.33
Jay Sigel	74	70	73	217	9,183.33
Stewart Ginn	73	73	71	217	9,183.33
Walter Hall	70	76	71	217	9,183.34
Ed Dougherty	72	73	73	218	6,960
Dale Douglass	73	70	75	218	6,960
Bob Gilder	74	72	72	218	6,960
Andy North	75	73	70	218	6,960

ACE Group Classic

TwinEagles Golf Club, Naples, Florida
Par 36-36–72; 7,134 yards

February 14-16
purse, $1,600,000

	SCORES			TOTAL	MONEY
Vicente Fernandez	66	68	68	202	$240,000
Tom Watson	68	68	69	205	128,000
Des Smyth	70	69	66	205	128,000
Gil Morgan	68	70	68	206	78,400
Jay Overton	71	63	72	206	78,400
Tom Purtzer	70	67	69	206	78,400
Hale Irwin	69	70	68	207	46,720
Tom Jenkins	68	69	70	207	46,720
Tom Kite	70	70	67	207	46,720
Leonard Thompson	71	68	68	207	46,720

	SCORES			TOTAL	MONEY
Jim Thorpe	67	68	72	207	46,720
Dave Barr	68	65	75	208	33,600
Larry Nelson	72	67	69	208	33,600
Isao Aoki	68	70	71	209	28,800
Bruce Lietzke	71	66	72	209	28,800
Walter Hall	71	67	71	209	28,800
Morris Hatalsky	73	70	67	210	23,240
Mike McCullough	67	69	74	210	23,240
Doug Tewell	71	66	73	210	23,240
Jim Ahern	72	65	73	210	23,240
Jose Maria Canizares	72	67	72	211	18,613.33
Mike Smith	70	68	73	211	18,613.33
Bobby Walzel	68	71	72	211	18,613.34
David Eger	68	74	70	212	15,640
Bruce Fleisher	67	74	71	212	15,640
Gary Koch	68	71	73	212	15,640
Dick Mast	72	69	71	212	15,640
Terry Dill	68	74	71	213	12,400
Dale Douglass	74	70	69	213	12,400
Mark McCumber	74	69	70	213	12,400
Bill Rogers	72	69	72	213	12,400
Tom Wargo	73	70	70	213	12,400
Allen Doyle	73	69	71	213	12,400
Rodger Davis	70	65	79	214	9,632
Ed Dougherty	71	69	74	214	9,632
J.C. Snead	72	71	71	214	9,632
Howard Twitty	71	71	72	214	9,632
Hugh Baiocchi	72	73	69	214	9,632
Jim Dent	68	69	78	215	7,840
Bob Gilder	71	74	70	215	7,840
Graham Marsh	74	70	71	215	7,840
Bruce Summerhays	68	75	72	215	7,840
Jay Sigel	70	72	73	215	7,840

Verizon Classic

TPC of Tampa Bay, Lutz, Florida
Par 35-36–71; 6,783 yards

February 21-23
purse, $1,600,000

	SCORES			TOTAL	MONEY
Bruce Fleisher	68	70	67	205	$240,000
Hale Irwin	68	69	69	206	140,800
Mike Hill	69	74	66	209	115,200
Mike McCullough	67	74	70	211	78,400
Mark McCumber	68	75	68	211	78,400
Jim Thorpe	71	72	68	211	78,400
Dave Barr	72	73	67	212	51,200
Gil Morgan	71	74	67	212	51,200
Dana Quigley	70	73	69	212	51,200
Tom Jenkins	72	73	68	213	38,400
Allen Doyle	70	73	70	213	38,400
Des Smyth	72	71	70	213	38,400
Tom Watson	72	74	68	214	31,200
Fuzzy Zoeller	73	71	70	214	31,200
David Graham	69	78	68	215	24,826.67
Hubert Green	71	79	65	215	24,826.67
Wayne Levi	72	70	73	215	24,826.66

	SCORES			TOTAL	MONEY
Gary McCord	73	75	67	215	24,826.67
Jack Nicklaus	71	75	69	215	24,826.66
Tom Purtzer	74	74	67	215	24,826.67
Rodger Davis	71	74	71	216	18,160
Bob Gilder	73	75	68	216	18,160
Tom Kite	68	75	73	216	18,160
John Mahaffey	73	71	72	216	18,160
Isao Aoki	75	72	70	217	13,942.86
Terry Dill	76	70	71	217	13,942.86
Andy North	69	77	71	217	13,942.86
Mark Pfeil	70	77	70	217	13,942.86
John Jacobs	70	74	73	217	13,942.85
James Mason	70	75	72	217	13,942.85
Hugh Baiocchi	77	72	68	217	13,942.86
David Eger	72	79	67	218	10,800
Doug Tewell	70	75	73	218	10,800
Bobby Wadkins	72	74	72	218	10,800
Tom Wargo	70	77	71	218	10,800
Jose Maria Canizares	77	75	67	219	8,832
Bob Eastwood	71	76	72	219	8,832
Danny Edwards	72	73	74	219	8,832
Jerry McGee	73	74	72	219	8,832
Jim Holtgrieve	70	76	73	219	8,832

MasterCard Classic

Bosque Real Country Club, Col. Lomas Altas, Mexico
Par 36-36–72; 7,204 yards

March 7-9
purse, $2,000,000

	SCORES			TOTAL	MONEY
David Eger	69	70	65	204	$300,000
Hale Irwin	70	69	66	205	133,500
Tom Jenkins	70	65	70	205	133,500
Bruce Lietzke	67	68	70	205	133,500
Eamonn Darcy	67	68	70	205	133,500
Walter Hall	71	68	67	206	80,000
Steven Veriato	73	65	70	208	72,000
Isao Aoki	68	69	72	209	57,333.33
Dana Quigley	71	69	69	209	57,333.34
Seiji Ebihara	68	71	70	209	57,333.33
Allen Doyle	65	75	70	210	48,000
Danny Edwards	69	73	69	211	39,500
Tom Kite	72	65	74	211	39,500
Graham Marsh	70	73	68	211	39,500
Bobby Walzel	70	69	72	211	39,500
Bob Gilder	73	67	72	212	32,000
Jerry McGee	68	72	72	212	32,000
Doug Tewell	71	71	70	212	32,000
Jose Maria Canizares	72	70	71	213	26,266.67
Bruce Summerhays	69	73	71	213	26,266.66
Hugh Baiocchi	74	69	70	213	26,266.67
Dave Barr	72	69	73	214	21,040
Gary Player	71	70	73	214	21,040
John Schroeder	72	70	72	214	21,040
Howard Twitty	69	75	70	214	21,040
Stewart Ginn	71	72	71	214	21,040
Bruce Fleisher	68	73	74	215	17,000

	SCORES			TOTAL	MONEY
Billy Kratzert	71	69	75	215	17,000
John Mahaffey	70	71	74	215	17,000
John Harris	71	72	72	215	17,000
Jim Albus	73	71	72	216	13,800
Ed Dougherty	71	73	72	216	13,800
Hubert Green	74	70	72	216	13,800
Jay Overton	72	72	72	216	13,800
Fuzzy Zoeller	70	70	76	216	13,800
Bob Eastwood	72	69	76	217	11,250
Dave Eichelberger	72	76	69	217	11,250
Mike McCullough	74	75	68	217	11,250
John Bland	74	75	68	217	11,250
Morris Hatalsky	72	73	73	218	9,000
Joe Inman	69	75	74	218	9,000
Wayne Levi	72	74	72	218	9,000
Mike Smith	73	73	72	218	9,000
Jim Holtgrieve	73	72	73	218	9,000
Jay Sigel	75	69	74	218	9,000
Des Smyth	75	75	68	218	9,000

SBC Classic

Valencia Country Club, Valencia, California
Par 36-36–72; 6,905 yards
(Shortened to 36 holes—rain.)

March 14-16
purse, $1,500,000

	SCORES		TOTAL	MONEY
Tom Purtzer	67	68	135	$225,000
Gil Morgan	65	71	136	132,000
Sammy Rachels	69	69	138	98,625
John Schroeder	66	72	138	98,625
Hubert Green	71	69	140	58,312.50
Jim Thorpe	71	69	140	58,312.50
Allen Doyle	69	71	140	58,312.50
Des Smyth	70	70	140	58,312.50
Raymond Floyd	71	70	141	39,000
Tom Wargo	73	68	141	39,000
John Bland	71	70	141	39,000
Tom Jenkins	74	68	142	28,000
Dana Quigley	74	68	142	28,000
Mike Smith	70	72	142	28,000
Doug Tewell	72	70	142	28,000
James Mason	67	75	142	28,000
Hugh Baiocchi	70	72	142	28,000
Jose Maria Canizares	70	73	143	17,018.18
Ed Dougherty	74	69	143	17,018.18
Dale Douglass	73	70	143	17,018.18
Bruce Fleisher	73	70	143	17,018.18
Bob Gilder	74	69	143	17,018.18
Ted Goin	73	70	143	17,018.18
Hale Irwin	73	70	143	17,018.19
Mark McCumber	71	72	143	17,018.18
Bill Rogers	71	72	143	17,018.18
J.C. Snead	72	71	143	17,018.18
Walter Hall	74	69	143	17,018.19
Jim Colbert	72	72	144	10,864.28
Rodger Davis	73	71	144	10,864.29

	SCORES			TOTAL	MONEY
Danny Edwards	72	72		144	10,864.29
Wayne Levi	71	73		144	10,864.28
Gary McCord	71	73		144	10,864.28
Jim Ahern	73	71		144	10,864.29
Bertus Smit	75	69		144	10,864.29
George Archer	71	74		145	7,971.42
Terry Dill	75	70		145	7,971.43
Tom Kite	74	71		145	7,971.43
Bruce Lietzke	73	72		145	7,971.43
Graham Marsh	75	70		145	7,971.43
Larry Nelson	75	70		145	7,971.43
Stewart Ginn	74	71		145	7,971.43

Toshiba Senior Classic

Newport Beach Country Club, Newport Beach, California
Par 35-36–71; 6,584 yards

March 21-23
purse, $1,550,000

	SCORES			TOTAL	MONEY
Rodger Davis	65	64	68	197	$232,500
Larry Nelson	70	64	67	201	136,400
Jose Maria Canizares	66	66	70	202	92,483.34
Hale Irwin	67	66	69	202	92,483.33
John Jacobs	67	66	69	202	92,483.33
Bruce Lietzke	67	68	68	203	58,900
Gil Morgan	69	68	66	203	58,900
Ed Dougherty	68	69	67	204	40,920
Hubert Green	72	65	67	204	40,920
Wayne Levi	66	68	70	204	40,920
Allen Doyle	68	68	68	204	40,920
Jim Ahern	64	67	73	204	40,920
David Eger	66	66	73	205	27,125
Dave Stockton	68	68	69	205	27,125
Doug Tewell	68	70	67	205	27,125
Jim Thorpe	68	67	70	205	27,125
Tom Wargo	69	67	69	205	27,125
Vicente Fernandez	69	69	67	205	27,125
George Archer	69	71	66	206	18,267.86
Bob Gilder	69	69	68	206	18,267.86
Tom Kite	70	68	68	206	18,267.86
Mike McCullough	72	65	69	206	18,267.85
Jerry McGee	68	67	71	206	18,267.85
Tom Purtzer	68	69	69	206	18,267.86
Walter Hall	70	70	66	206	18,267.86
Andy Bean	71	70	66	207	13,485
Mark McCumber	66	71	70	207	13,485
Howard Twitty	68	70	69	207	13,485
Jay Sigel	69	68	70	207	13,485
Hugh Baiocchi	69	70	68	207	13,485
Tom Jenkins	73	67	68	208	10,927.50
Dana Quigley	69	68	71	208	10,927.50
Lanny Wadkins	65	73	70	208	10,927.50
Tom Watson	69	69	70	208	10,927.50
Jim Colbert	71	70	68	209	9,300
Terry Dill	68	69	72	209	9,300
Leonard Thompson	68	73	68	209	9,300
Terry Mauney	73	68	69	210	8,525

	SCORES			TOTAL	MONEY
Jim Dent	69	72	70	211	7,750
Dale Douglass	70	71	70	211	7,750
Billy Kratzert	70	69	72	211	7,750
Sammy Rachels	73	65	73	211	7,750

Emerald Coast Classic

The Moors Golf Club, Milton, Florida
Par 35-35–70; 6,832 yards

April 18-20
purse, $1,450,000

	SCORES			TOTAL	MONEY
Bob Gilder	66	64	63	193	$217,500
Larry Nelson	66	65	66	197	106,091.67
Leonard Thompson	63	68	66	197	106,091.67
Vicente Fernandez	65	66	66	197	106,091.66
Tom Purtzer	66	66	67	199	63,437.50
Dana Quigley	66	66	67	199	63,437.50
Graham Marsh	68	66	66	200	49,300
Bobby Wadkins	70	61	69	200	49,300
Gil Morgan	63	68	70	201	40,600
Mike Smith	66	67	69	202	36,250
Bobby Walzel	66	67	69	202	36,250
Dave Barr	67	68	68	203	29,483.33
Bruce Fleisher	64	74	65	203	29,483.34
Mike McCullough	69	68	66	203	29,483.33
Wayne Levi	69	67	68	204	24,650
Tom Watson	64	66	74	204	24,650
Eamonn Darcy	69	68	67	204	24,650
Terry Dill	70	65	70	205	18,125
Billy Kratzert	68	70	67	205	18,125
Mark McCumber	69	66	70	205	18,125
Jerry McGee	70	66	69	205	18,125
Fuzzy Zoeller	68	68	69	205	18,125
Jay Sigel	68	69	68	205	18,125
John Harris	72	67	66	205	18,125
Rodger Davis	68	69	69	206	13,224
Morris Hatalsky	67	64	75	206	13,224
Jay Overton	67	66	73	206	13,224
James Mason	67	67	72	206	13,224
Pat McDonald	71	65	70	206	13,224
Allen Doyle	69	67	71	207	11,455
Mike Hill	69	69	70	208	10,005
Mark Pfeil	67	67	74	208	10,005
John Jacobs	67	70	71	208	10,005
Tom Wargo	71	67	70	208	10,005
Stewart Ginn	69	68	71	208	10,005
Charles Coody	71	68	70	209	7,854.17
Dale Douglass	72	68	69	209	7,854.17
David Eger	67	74	68	209	7,854.16
Tom Kite	68	68	73	209	7,854.16
Jim Holtgrieve	65	71	73	209	7,854.17
Hugh Baiocchi	71	68	70	209	7,854.17

Liberty Mutual Legends of Golf

Westin Savannah Harbor Golf Resort & Spa,
Savannah, Georgia
Par 36-36–72; 6,627 yards

April 25-27
purse, $2,250,000

	SCORES			TOTAL	MONEY
Bruce Lietzke	70	65	71	206	$354,000
David Eger	71	69	67	207	189,500
Dana Quigley	69	67	71	207	189,500
Bob Gilder	70	69	69	208	126,000
Hubert Green	70	67	71	208	126,000
Morris Hatalsky	68	70	71	209	84,000
Doug Tewell	71	72	66	209	84,000
Bobby Wadkins	75	69	65	209	84,000
Rodger Davis	70	70	70	210	58,750
Raymond Floyd	70	71	69	210	58,750
Fuzzy Zoeller	68	71	71	210	58,750
Vicente Fernandez	67	73	70	210	58,750
Tom Jenkins	72	71	68	211	46,250
John Jacobs	75	70	66	211	46,250
Jim Colbert	73	68	71	212	36,083.33
Bruce Fleisher	75	69	68	212	36,083.33
Hale Irwin	70	69	73	212	36,083.33
Graham Marsh	73	72	67	212	36,083.34
Mark McCumber	69	72	71	212	36,083.33
James Mason	71	74	67	212	36,083.34
Larry Nelson	70	74	69	213	27,100
Allen Doyle	73	71	69	213	27,100
Stewart Ginn	73	72	68	213	27,100
Dave Barr	71	71	72	214	20,683.33
Andy Bean	70	74	70	214	20,683.34
Ed Dougherty	71	70	73	214	20,683.33
Wayne Levi	74	72	68	214	20,683.34
Gil Morgan	73	71	70	214	20,683.33
Dave Stockton	74	69	71	214	20,683.33
Mike McCullough	74	70	71	215	16,300
J.C. Snead	73	69	73	215	16,300
Bob Murphy	73	71	72	216	14,125
Andy North	71	72	73	216	14,125
Tom Purtzer	72	71	73	216	14,125
Leonard Thompson	76	70	70	216	14,125
Ben Crenshaw	73	71	73	217	11,950
Dave Eichelberger	74	70	73	217	11,950
Tom Wargo	72	72	73	217	11,950
Jay Sigel	72	75	70	217	11,950
Jim Thorpe	77	72	69	218	10,800

Bruno's Memorial Classic

Greystone Golf & Country Club, Hoover, Alabama
Par 36-36–72; 7,092 yards

May 2-4
purse, $1,400,000

	SCORES			TOTAL	MONEY
Tom Jenkins	67	66	67	200	$210,000
Bruce Fleisher	66	67	70	203	123,200
Jim Colbert	69	67	69	205	92,050
Hale Irwin	65	67	73	205	92,050

	SCORES			TOTAL	MONEY
Rodger Davis	70	67	69	206	66,500
Bob Gilder	68	67	72	207	47,600
Graham Marsh	68	70	69	207	47,600
Bruce Summerhays	70	69	68	207	47,600
John Jacobs	69	68	70	207	47,600
Mike Hill	69	72	67	208	36,400
Dave Barr	70	68	72	210	27,200
Mark McCumber	71	70	69	210	27,200
Bob Murphy	69	69	72	210	27,200
Tom Purtzer	70	69	71	210	27,200
Doug Tewell	72	69	69	210	27,200
Jim Holtgrieve	71	71	68	210	27,200
Seiji Ebihara	71	69	70	210	27,200
Tom Kite	73	68	70	211	20,300
Tom Wargo	68	70	73	211	20,300
Ben Crenshaw	70	73	69	212	15,983.34
Ed Dougherty	70	72	70	212	15,983.34
Gary Koch	69	71	72	212	15,983.33
Gil Morgan	72	70	70	212	15,983.33
Dana Quigley	69	71	72	212	15,983.33
Des Smyth	68	72	72	212	15,983.33
Bob Charles	71	65	77	213	11,900
Wayne Levi	72	71	70	213	11,900
John Schroeder	69	74	70	213	11,900
Bobby Wadkins	71	69	73	213	11,900
James Mason	70	71	72	213	11,900
Allen Doyle	72	71	70	213	11,900
Jim Dent	72	70	72	214	9,240
Dave Eichelberger	71	71	72	214	9,240
Gibby Gilbert	73	73	68	214	9,240
Leonard Thompson	69	71	74	214	9,240
Walter Hall	74	68	72	214	9,240
Andy Bean	73	71	71	215	7,560
Hubert Green	73	71	71	215	7,560
Morris Hatalsky	67	74	74	215	7,560
Larry Ziegler	66	76	73	215	7,560

Kinko's Classic of Austin

The Hills Country Club, Austin, Texas
Par 36-36–72; 6,651 yards

May 9-11
purse, $1,600,000

	SCORES			TOTAL	MONEY
Hale Irwin	69	66	73	208	$240,000
Tom Watson	66	69	73	208	140,800
(Irwin defeated Watson on second playoff hole.)					
Bob Gilder	71	70	68	209	115,200
Tom Kite	69	65	76	210	85,600
Jim Thorpe	72	68	70	210	85,600
Jose Maria Canizares	70	70	71	211	64,000
Morris Hatalsky	72	66	74	212	51,200
Bruce Lietzke	69	67	76	212	51,200
Jack Nicklaus	71	69	72	212	51,200
Graham Marsh	70	69	74	213	38,400
Allen Doyle	69	68	76	213	38,400
Des Smyth	72	68	73	213	38,400
Andy Bean	69	70	75	214	28,000

	SCORES			TOTAL	MONEY
Gil Morgan	72	70	72	214	28,000
Dana Quigley	76	68	70	214	28,000
John Schroeder	72	66	76	214	28,000
Dave Stockton	71	71	72	214	28,000
Walter Hall	73	70	71	214	28,000
Rodger Davis	73	70	72	215	19,840
Bruce Fleisher	77	69	69	215	19,840
Doug Tewell	75	72	68	215	19,840
Leonard Thompson	73	69	73	215	19,840
Vicente Fernandez	74	67	74	215	19,840
Jim Colbert	75	67	74	216	15,296
Wayne Levi	74	70	72	216	15,296
Larry Nelson	74	72	70	216	15,296
Andy North	72	67	77	216	15,296
James Mason	73	67	76	216	15,296
Ben Crenshaw	75	68	74	217	11,840
Hubert Green	72	71	74	217	11,840
Tom Jenkins	72	70	75	217	11,840
Dick Mast	75	72	70	217	11,840
Steven Veriato	73	72	72	217	11,840
Hugh Baiocchi	75	68	74	217	11,840
Ed Fiori	75	69	74	218	9,040
Joe Inman	65	74	79	218	9,040
Mike McCullough	73	75	70	218	9,040
Bill Rogers	75	69	74	218	9,040
Bobby Wadkins	73	75	70	218	9,040
Tom Wargo	73	74	71	218	9,040

Bayer Advantage Celebrity Pro-Am

National Golf Club of Kansas City, Parkville, Missouri
Par 36-36–72; 6,955 yards

May 16-18
purse, $1,600,000

	SCORES			TOTAL	MONEY
Jay Sigel	72	68	65	205	$240,000
Mike McCullough	73	67	66	206	142,000
Vicente Fernandez	71	67	69	207	116,000
Hale Irwin	74	68	68	210	86,250
Pat McDonald	77	65	68	210	86,250
Tom Jenkins	71	71	69	211	54,675
Fuzzy Zoeller	74	71	66	211	54,675
Allen Doyle	72	68	71	211	54,675
Des Smyth	73	67	71	211	54,675
Jerry McGee	75	68	69	212	36,800
Tom Watson	72	71	69	212	36,800
John Jacobs	75	68	69	212	36,800
James Mason	70	71	71	212	36,800
Gil Morgan	75	70	68	213	29,600
Dave Stockton	73	69	71	213	29,600
Jose Maria Canizares	69	75	70	214	24,800
Ed Fiori	72	73	69	214	24,800
Hugh Baiocchi	73	73	68	214	24,800
Eamonn Darcy	73	71	70	214	24,800
Danny Edwards	73	74	68	215	18,266.67
Morris Hatalsky	81	69	65	215	18,266.67
Wayne Levi	72	75	68	215	18,266.67
Roger Maltbie	73	71	71	215	18,266.66

	SCORES			TOTAL	MONEY
Jay Overton	77	72	66	215	18,266.67
Bobby Wadkins	73	73	69	215	18,266.66
Andy Bean	71	72	73	216	14,315
Ben Crenshaw	76	70	70	216	14,315
Ed Dougherty	74	70	72	216	14,315
John Bland	74	69	73	216	14,315
Joe Inman	73	74	70	217	11,406.67
Andy North	72	72	73	217	11,406.66
Bobby Walzel	77	70	70	217	11,406.67
Jim Holtgrieve	75	71	71	217	11,406.67
Stewart Ginn	73	72	72	217	11,406.66
Walter Hall	75	72	70	217	11,406.67
Dave Barr	80	71	67	218	8,700
Dave Eichelberger	70	75	73	218	8,700
Hubert Green	77	68	73	218	8,700
Graham Marsh	75	75	68	218	8,700
Lee Trevino	76	72	70	218	8,700
Butch Sheehan	72	69	77	218	8,700

Columbus Southern Open

Green Island Country Club, Columbus, Georgia
Par 35-35–70; 6,418 yards

May 23-25
purse, $1,500,000

	SCORES			TOTAL	MONEY
Morris Hatalsky	66	65	67	198	$225,000
Allen Doyle	66	66	67	199	132,000
Bruce Fleisher	68	70	62	200	82,125
Dana Quigley	66	67	67	200	82,125
Doug Tewell	68	64	68	200	82,125
Des Smyth	66	66	68	200	82,125
Dave Barr	70	65	66	201	48,000
Hubert Green	73	64	64	201	48,000
Larry Nelson	70	68	63	201	48,000
Tom Jenkins	67	65	70	202	37,500
Stewart Ginn	70	67	65	202	37,500
Tom Kite	66	68	69	203	29,625
Jim Holtgrieve	68	68	67	203	29,625
John Bland	68	69	66	203	29,625
Jim Ahern	68	65	70	203	29,625
Jim Dent	70	69	65	204	24,000
Ed Dougherty	65	69	70	204	24,000
Walter Hall	66	70	68	204	24,000
Andy Bean	70	71	64	205	17,678.58
Rik Massengale	69	67	69	205	17,678.57
Tom Purtzer	68	70	67	205	17,678.57
Jim Thorpe	67	64	74	205	17,678.57
Bobby Wadkins	65	71	69	205	17,678.57
Larry Ziegler	67	69	69	205	17,678.57
Eamonn Darcy	71	69	65	205	17,678.57
Jose Maria Canizares	67	70	69	206	12,750
Dave Eichelberger	68	69	69	206	12,750
Jerry McGee	67	72	67	206	12,750
Jack Spradlin	72	68	66	206	12,750
Bobby Walzel	70	68	68	206	12,750
John Jacobs	69	69	68	206	12,750
Bob Gilder	67	75	65	207	9,675

	SCORES			TOTAL	MONEY
Lon Hinkle	69	69	69	207	9,675
Joe Inman	69	71	67	207	9,675
Wayne Levi	72	64	71	207	9,675
John Harris	70	71	66	207	9,675
Vicente Fernandez	67	72	68	207	9,675
Steven Veriato	70	70	68	208	7,950
Butch Sheehan	68	70	70	208	7,950
Hugh Baiocchi	72	67	69	208	7,950

Music City Championship at Gaylord Opryland

Springhouse Golf Club, Nashville, Tennessee
Par 36-36–72; 6,808 yards

May 30-June 1
purse, $1,400,000

	SCORES			TOTAL	MONEY
Jim Ahern	64	63	69	196	$210,000
Jose Maria Canizares	68	65	67	200	123,200
Larry Nelson	69	68	64	201	100,800
Ed Dougherty	70	67	66	203	74,900
Tom Jenkins	67	67	69	203	74,900
Hale Irwin	68	70	67	205	53,200
Hugh Baiocchi	68	67	70	205	53,200
Rodger Davis	67	66	73	206	38,500
Dave Stockton	69	69	68	206	38,500
Jim Holtgrieve	69	65	72	206	38,500
Stewart Ginn	72	69	65	206	38,500
Vicente Fernandez	67	72	68	207	30,800
R.W. Eaks	73	64	71	208	26,600
Mike Hill	68	71	69	208	26,600
Butch Sheehan	69	70	69	208	26,600
Ed Fiori	69	69	71	209	20,393.33
Bruce Fleisher	73	68	68	209	20,393.33
Gary Koch	75	69	65	209	20,393.34
Wayne Levi	75	67	67	209	20,393.33
Allen Doyle	74	71	64	209	20,393.34
John Harris	68	71	70	209	20,393.33
Dave Barr	71	67	72	210	13,471.11
Gibby Gilbert	71	70	69	210	13,471.11
Morris Hatalsky	68	69	73	210	13,471.11
Tom Purtzer	71	69	70	210	13,471.11
Dana Quigley	69	73	68	210	13,471.11
Doug Tewell	65	73	72	210	13,471.11
Jim Thorpe	71	68	71	210	13,471.11
Bobby Wadkins	71	68	71	210	13,471.11
Des Smyth	73	70	67	210	13,471.12
Dick Mast	70	73	68	211	9,450
J.C. Snead	67	70	74	211	9,450
D.A. Weibring	71	73	67	211	9,450
Tom Wargo	71	70	70	211	9,450
Jay Sigel	69	73	69	211	9,450
John Bland	71	71	69	211	9,450
Ted Goin	72	67	73	212	7,420
Mike McCullough	68	75	69	212	7,420
Bobby Walzel	73	70	69	212	7,420
James Mason	74	67	71	212	7,420
Seiji Ebihara	72	72	68	212	7,420

Senior PGA Championship

Aronimink Golf Club, Newtown Square, Pennsylvania June 5-8
Par 35-35–70; 7,152 yards purse, $2,000,000

	SCORES				TOTAL	MONEY
John Jacobs	68	69	71	68	276	$360,000
Bobby Wadkins	68	72	68	70	278	216,000
Bruce Lietzke	75	67	70	67	279	116,000
Fuzzy Zoeller	69	70	70	70	279	116,000
Doug Tewell	69	73	69	69	280	71,000
Des Smyth	71	70	65	74	280	71,000
Gil Morgan	70	66	73	72	281	58,000
Allen Doyle	69	67	73	72	281	58,000
Vicente Fernandez	69	71	72	69	281	58,000
Bruce Fleisher	71	71	74	66	282	42,600
Bob Gilder	77	67	70	68	282	42,600
Tom Kite	70	68	74	70	282	42,600
Mark McCumber	71	71	72	68	282	42,600
Larry Nelson	69	74	69	70	282	42,600
Craig Stadler	70	69	75	69	283	33,000
John Irwin	73	73	72	65	283	33,000
David Eger	74	70	70	70	284	24,000
Raymond Floyd	71	72	70	71	284	24,000
Wayne Levi	70	69	73	72	284	24,000
Dick Mast	73	68	70	73	284	24,000
Dana Quigley	71	70	75	68	284	24,000
Tom Watson	71	73	73	67	284	24,000
Jay Sigel	73	68	72	71	284	24,000
Seiji Ebihara	72	66	75	72	285	16,500
John Harris	69	74	69	73	285	16,500
Jose Maria Canizares	71	68	73	74	286	14,500
Bill Rogers	72	71	74	69	286	14,500
Morris Hatalsky	69	71	75	72	287	12,750
John Bland	72	71	72	72	287	12,750
Stewart Ginn	71	74	71	71	287	12,750
John Chillas	71	70	75	71	287	12,750
Andy Bean	70	73	74	71	288	11,250
Tom Jenkins	71	71	77	69	288	11,250
Jim Dent	76	70	73	70	289	9,300
Ted Goin	71	73	74	71	289	9,300
Mike McCullough	71	72	76	70	289	9,300
Mike San Filippo	68	70	78	73	289	9,300
John Schroeder	73	72	72	72	289	9,300
Tom Wargo	75	70	74	70	289	9,300
Ed Dougherty	70	76	73	71	290	7,350
Gary McCord	73	73	71	73	290	7,350
Eamonn Darcy	76	69	73	72	290	7,350
Pat McDonald	73	72	74	71	290	7,350

Farmers Charity Classic

Egypt Valley Country Club, Ada, Michigan June 20-22
Par 36-36–72; 6,909 yards purse, $1,500,000

	SCORES			TOTAL	MONEY
Doug Tewell	69	66	66	201	$225,000
Eamonn Darcy	67	69	65	201	132,000

(Tewell defeated Darcy on third playoff hole.)

	SCORES			TOTAL	MONEY
Morris Hatalsky	65	71	67	203	108,000
Ed Dougherty	66	66	72	204	68,625
Hubert Green	66	67	71	204	68,625
Bruce Lietzke	68	70	66	204	68,625
Mike McCullough	71	65	68	204	68,625
Gil Morgan	70	68	67	205	43,000
Dave Stockton	68	69	68	205	43,000
Allen Doyle	68	71	66	205	43,000
Mark Pfeil	71	64	71	206	31,875
Mike Smith	66	72	68	206	31,875
Bobby Walzel	72	68	66	206	31,875
D.A. Weibring	69	68	69	206	31,875
Tom Purtzer	73	70	64	207	27,000
Bob Eastwood	72	69	67	208	24,750
Bruce Fleisher	66	69	73	208	24,750
Isao Aoki	73	71	65	209	19,800
Bob Murphy	70	72	67	209	19,800
Craig Stadler	73	72	64	209	19,800
Tom Wargo	66	70	73	209	19,800
Stewart Ginn	68	73	68	209	19,800
Bob Gilder	73	67	70	210	15,375
Tom Jenkins	76	69	65	210	15,375
Wayne Levi	71	72	67	210	15,375
Graham Marsh	69	72	69	210	15,375
Rodger Davis	71	75	65	211	12,450
Jim Dent	69	73	69	211	12,450
David Eger	68	68	75	211	12,450
Christy O'Connor, Jr.	72	74	65	211	12,450
James Mason	69	71	71	211	12,450
Tom Kite	72	70	70	212	9,675
Bobby Wadkins	68	72	72	212	9,675
Jay Sigel	70	76	66	212	9,675
John Bland	72	68	72	212	9,675
John Harris	71	74	67	212	9,675
Walter Hall	71	71	70	212	9,675
Raymond Floyd	71	71	71	213	7,650
Dick Mast	74	72	67	213	7,650
Bruce Summerhays	70	72	71	213	7,650
Jim Holtgrieve	71	70	72	213	7,650
Luis Carbonetti	74	74	65	213	7,650

U.S. Senior Open

Inverness Club, Toledo, Ohio
Par 35-36–71; 7,255 yards

June 26-29
purse, $2,600,000

	SCORES				TOTAL	MONEY
Bruce Lietzke	69	71	64	73	277	$470,000
Tom Watson	66	72	70	71	279	280,000
Vicente Fernandez	73	64	71	72	280	176,651
Fuzzy Zoeller	71	71	74	69	285	111,387
Allen Doyle	72	69	71	73	285	111,387
Wayne Levi	73	73	71	70	287	83,877
Mike McCullough	70	73	72	72	287	83,877
Andy North	77	70	70	71	288	70,360
Lanny Wadkins	75	73	71	69	288	70,360
Tom Jenkins	74	71	75	69	289	60,117
Craig Stadler	78	69	70	72	289	60,117

	SCORES				TOTAL	MONEY
Jose Maria Canizares	76	70	73	71	290	48,553
Jim Dent	74	71	75	70	290	48,553
Morris Hatalsky	73	76	73	68	290	48,553
Tom Kite	72	73	74	71	290	48,553
Gil Morgan	73	74	70	73	290	48,553
Ed Dougherty	74	71	75	71	291	39,831
Bob Murphy	74	73	75	69	291	39,831
Rodger Davis	73	71	72	76	292	31,697
R.W. Eaks	76	69	77	70	292	31,697
Raymond Floyd	75	74	71	72	292	31,697
Dan Halldorson	73	73	72	74	292	31,697
Des Smyth	73	74	74	71	292	31,697
Stewart Ginn	76	72	72	72	292	31,697
Gary Groh	74	75	75	69	293	23,904
Mark McCumber	75	72	71	75	293	23,904
Jack Nicklaus	77	73	74	69	293	23,904
Fred Gibson	76	73	72	73	294	19,961
Graham Marsh	71	72	73	78	294	19,961
Isao Aoki	74	75	74	72	295	17,371
Hubert Green	76	75	69	75	295	17,371
J.C. Snead	70	77	76	72	295	17,371
Jim Thorpe	76	74	73	72	295	17,371
Jay Sigel	73	75	72	75	295	17,371
Bill Rogers	75	75	74	72	296	14,801
Bobby Wadkins	76	72	76	72	296	14,801
Pete Oakley	77	72	75	72	296	14,801
John Harris	75	72	76	73	296	14,801
Jim Ahern	74	74	76	72	296	14,801
Joe Inman	76	74	69	78	297	12,760
Larry Nelson	71	75	76	75	297	12,760
John Bland	77	73	74	73	297	12,760

Ford Senior Players Championship

TPC of Michigan, Dearborn, Michigan
Par 36-36–72; 6,876 yards

July 10-13
purse, $2,500,000

	SCORES				TOTAL	MONEY
Craig Stadler	67	73	65	66	271	$375,000
Tom Kite	66	72	73	63	274	183,000
Jim Thorpe	68	72	69	65	274	183,000
Tom Watson	70	64	71	69	274	183,000
Tom Jenkins	70	70	69	69	278	97,500
Mike McCullough	66	71	68	73	278	97,500
Gil Morgan	64	73	72	69	278	97,500
Tom Purtzer	67	74	72	65	278	97,500
Ed Dougherty	71	71	67	71	280	67,500
Dave Stockton	69	71	69	71	280	67,500
Dana Quigley	67	75	68	71	281	60,000
Isao Aoki	72	72	73	67	284	50,833.34
Bruce Fleisher	71	74	70	69	284	50,833.33
Hale Irwin	72	71	74	67	284	50,833.33
Dave Barr	74	72	72	68	286	41,250
Mark McCumber	72	73	69	72	286	41,250
Allen Doyle	66	76	72	72	286	41,250
Stewart Ginn	73	70	73	70	286	41,250
Terry Mauney	69	68	75	75	287	32,025

	SCORES				TOTAL	MONEY
Andy North	67	69	76	75	287	32,025
James Mason	72	75	71	69	287	32,025
John Harris	70	73	73	71	287	32,025
Mike Hill	69	71	75	73	288	24,500
Dick Mast	70	71	73	74	288	24,500
Doug Tewell	66	76	76	70	288	24,500
Fuzzy Zoeller	67	73	79	69	288	24,500
Bruce Summerhays	73	76	69	70	288	24,500
John Bland	74	75	71	68	288	24,500
Larry Nelson	69	71	75	74	289	20,750
Rodger Davis	73	71	75	71	290	18,833.34
Bob Gilder	71	78	71	70	290	18,833.33
Graham Marsh	72	71	74	73	290	18,833.33
Bruce Lietzke	70	74	73	74	291	16,875
Vicente Fernandez	68	74	74	75	291	16,875
David Eger	74	75	69	74	292	14,400
Ted Goin	71	76	74	71	292	14,400
Morris Hatalsky	74	73	71	74	292	14,400
Butch Sheehan	73	69	75	75	292	14,400
Jay Sigel	75	70	73	74	292	14,400
Jose Maria Canizares	72	75	75	71	293	11,250
Jim Dent	73	73	72	75	293	11,250
R.W. Eaks	73	73	78	69	293	11,250
Wayne Levi	75	73	74	71	293	11,250
Jack Nicklaus	74	76	71	72	293	11,250
Don Pooley	68	79	71	75	293	11,250
Bobby Wadkins	71	79	73	70	293	11,250

Senior British Open

See PGA European Tour section.

FleetBoston Classic

Nashawtuc Country Club, Concord, Massachusetts
Par 35-36–71; 6,729 yards

August 1-3
purse, $1,500,000

	SCORES			TOTAL	MONEY
Allen Doyle	68	63	67	198	$225,000
Bruce Fleisher	64	71	66	201	120,000
Bob Gilder	68	65	68	201	120,000
Tom Purtzer	65	70	67	202	80,250
D.A. Weibring	68	69	65	202	80,250
Ed Fiori	68	67	68	203	57,000
Doug Tewell	69	66	68	203	57,000
Morris Hatalsky	71	67	66	204	43,000
James Mason	67	66	71	204	43,000
Jay Sigel	67	71	66	204	43,000
Dave Barr	68	67	70	205	33,000
Bobby Wadkins	68	69	68	205	33,000
John Harris	67	70	68	205	33,000
David Eger	67	69	70	206	26,250
Billy Kratzert	70	69	67	206	26,250
Bruce Lietzke	73	68	65	206	26,250
Dana Quigley	68	71	67	206	26,250
Terry Dill	71	67	69	207	19,800

	SCORES			TOTAL	MONEY
Tom Jenkins	71	67	69	207	19,800
Dick Mast	67	69	71	207	19,800
Mike McCullough	70	66	71	207	19,800
Dave Stockton	68	68	71	207	19,800
Mike Hill	73	66	69	208	15,375
Jerry McGee	69	72	67	208	15,375
Craig Stadler	69	68	71	208	15,375
Tom Wargo	72	71	65	208	15,375
Jim Albus	69	72	68	209	11,175
Ben Crenshaw	73	68	68	209	11,175
Bob Eastwood	71	65	73	209	11,175
Tom Kite	73	70	66	209	11,175
Wayne Levi	72	68	69	209	11,175
J.C. Snead	69	71	69	209	11,175
Jim Thorpe	73	66	70	209	11,175
Lee Trevino	71	70	68	209	11,175
Jim Ahern	71	72	66	209	11,175
Eamonn Darcy	69	70	70	209	11,175
Ted Goin	68	71	71	210	8,100
Graham Marsh	69	72	69	210	8,100
Mark Pfeil	72	69	69	210	8,100
John Bland	71	70	69	210	8,100

3M Championship

TPC of the Twin Cities, Blaine, Minnesota
Par 36-36–72; 7,100 yards

August 8-10
purse, $1,750,000

	SCORES			TOTAL	MONEY
Wayne Levi	68	68	69	205	$262,500
Morris Hatalsky	67	71	68	206	140,000
Gil Morgan	70	68	68	206	140,000
Ben Crenshaw	69	67	71	207	85,750
Graham Marsh	70	71	66	207	85,750
Bob Murphy	68	71	68	207	85,750
Bill Rogers	70	70	68	208	56,000
Des Smyth	72	70	66	208	56,000
Eamonn Darcy	74	67	67	208	56,000
Don Pooley	73	63	73	209	37,625
Tom Purtzer	69	66	74	209	37,625
Dana Quigley	73	70	66	209	37,625
Jim Thorpe	67	71	71	209	37,625
D.A. Weibring	70	70	69	209	37,625
Hugh Baiocchi	69	67	73	209	37,625
Jose Maria Canizares	72	70	68	210	25,491.67
Ed Dougherty	74	68	68	210	25,491.66
Ted Goin	72	71	67	210	25,491.67
Bruce Lietzke	71	71	68	210	25,491.67
Dave Stockton	72	70	68	210	25,491.67
James Mason	70	68	72	210	25,491.66
Tom Kite	73	70	68	211	17,215.63
Mike Smith	68	70	73	211	17,215.62
Leonard Thompson	69	70	72	211	17,215.62
Bruce Summerhays	74	69	68	211	17,215.62
John Jacobs	72	71	68	211	17,215.63
Jay Sigel	72	71	68	211	17,215.63
Walter Hall	71	72	68	211	17,215.63

	SCORES			TOTAL	MONEY
Scott Masingill	69	70	72	211	17,215.62
Terry Dill	73	70	69	212	12,906.25
Gary Koch	75	70	67	212	12,906.25
Larry Nelson	74	67	71	212	12,906.25
Bobby Walzel	74	66	72	212	12,906.25
Bob Eastwood	75	66	72	213	10,325
Tom Jenkins	72	70	71	213	10,325
Mike McCullough	70	71	72	213	10,325
Mike San Filippo	72	72	69	213	10,325
J.C. Snead	75	70	68	213	10,325
Jim Ahern	75	69	69	213	10,325
Jim Colbert	73	72	69	214	7,875
David Eger	68	73	73	214	7,875
Bruce Fleisher	73	70	71	214	7,875
Joe Inman	72	73	69	214	7,875
Hale Irwin	68	75	71	214	7,875
John Harris	70	72	72	214	7,875
Tom Herzan	74	70	70	214	7,875

Long Island Classic

Eisenhower Park, Red Course, East Meadow, New York
Par 34-36–70; 6,806 yards

August 15-17
purse, $1,500,000

	SCORES			TOTAL	MONEY
Jim Thorpe	68	60	67	195	$225,000
Bob Gilder	64	66	66	196	132,000
Des Smyth	66	66	67	199	108,000
Mike McCullough	68	65	67	200	89,250
Jose Maria Canizares	70	67	65	202	58,312.50
Rodger Davis	66	69	67	202	58,312.50
Mike Hill	68	67	67	202	58,312.50
Jerry McGee	67	69	66	202	58,312.50
Dave Barr	68	69	66	203	36,000
Gibby Gilbert	71	67	65	203	36,000
Tom Jenkins	70	70	63	203	36,000
Andy North	68	68	67	203	36,000
Vicente Fernandez	65	70	68	203	36,000
Wayne Levi	70	65	69	204	27,750
Bobby Wadkins	68	71	65	204	27,750
Bruce Fleisher	62	72	71	205	24,000
Bobby Walzel	69	66	70	205	24,000
James Mason	67	69	69	205	24,000
Jim Albus	72	65	69	206	18,600
Ed Fiori	71	68	67	206	18,600
Stewart Ginn	70	67	69	206	18,600
John Harris	67	70	69	206	18,600
Pat McDonald	69	70	67	206	18,600
Bob Eastwood	69	69	69	207	13,714.29
Danny Edwards	68	69	70	207	13,714.29
Mark Hayes	69	69	69	207	13,714.29
Gary Koch	66	69	72	207	13,714.28
Dana Quigley	67	71	69	207	13,714.29
Craig Stadler	68	68	71	207	13,714.28
Hugh Baiocchi	67	69	71	207	13,714.28
Seiji Ebihara	66	73	69	208	11,025
Walter Hall	71	68	69	208	11,025

	SCORES			TOTAL	MONEY
George Burns	69	71	69	209	9,675
Morris Hatalsky	68	68	73	209	9,675
Larry Ziegler	69	71	69	209	9,675
John Bland	66	72	71	209	9,675
Mike San Filippo	73	69	68	210	7,950
J.C. Snead	70	69	71	210	7,950
Bruce Summerhays	74	67	69	210	7,950
Terry Florence	69	70	71	210	7,950
Allen Doyle	68	75	67	210	7,950

Allianz Championship

Glen Oaks Country Club, West Des Moines, Iowa
Par 35-36–71; 6,864 yards

August 22-24
purse, $1,500,000

	SCORES			TOTAL	MONEY
Don Pooley	66	67	67	200	$225,000
Bruce Fleisher	70	64	69	203	109,750
Bruce Lietzke	65	69	69	203	109,750
Jim Thorpe	67	67	69	203	109,750
Tom Kite	67	69	68	204	61,750
Doug Tewell	72	66	66	204	61,750
Rick Rhoden	69	66	69	204	61,750
John Bland	69	69	67	205	45,000
Walter Hall	67	70	68	205	45,000
Ben Crenshaw	68	70	68	206	34,500
Rodger Davis	69	68	69	206	34,500
Hale Irwin	67	71	68	206	34,500
Tom Purtzer	68	69	69	206	34,500
Bob Gilder	67	69	71	207	25,500
Morris Hatalsky	68	67	72	207	25,500
Mark McCumber	68	70	69	207	25,500
Des Smyth	70	71	66	207	25,500
Stewart Ginn	70	71	66	207	25,500
George Burns	68	71	69	208	18,125
Rex Caldwell	68	69	71	208	18,125
Doug Johnson	69	70	69	208	18,125
Mike McCullough	70	68	70	208	18,125
Jay Sigel	72	68	68	208	18,125
Pat McDonald	71	69	68	208	18,125
David Eger	66	72	71	209	13,987.50
Graham Marsh	72	68	69	209	13,987.50
Jim Holtgrieve	67	72	70	209	13,987.50
Hugh Baiocchi	70	70	69	209	13,987.50
Andy Bean	73	66	71	210	11,340
Dave Eichelberger	70	69	71	210	11,340
Mark Lye	69	73	68	210	11,340
Jay Overton	68	73	69	210	11,340
Allen Doyle	67	68	75	210	11,340
Bob Charles	73	69	69	211	8,850
Dale Douglass	72	69	70	211	8,850
Dana Quigley	73	70	68	211	8,850
Bobby Wadkins	68	70	73	211	8,850
D.A. Weibring	69	72	70	211	8,850
Larry Ziegler	71	70	70	211	8,850
Terry Dill	71	73	68	212	6,900
Ed Dougherty	69	71	72	212	6,900

	SCORES			TOTAL	MONEY
Joe Inman	71	69	72	212	6,900
Tom Jenkins	70	72	70	212	6,900
Bobby Walzel	73	73	66	212	6,900
Fuzzy Zoeller	68	71	73	212	6,900

JELD-WEN Tradition

Reserve Vineyards & Golf Club, Aloha, Oregon
Par 36-36–72; 7,172 yards

August 28-31
purse, $2,200,000

	SCORES				TOTAL	MONEY
Tom Watson	68	62	73	70	273	$330,000
Tom Kite	68	68	67	71	274	161,333.33
Gil Morgan	69	70	67	68	274	161,333.34
Jim Ahern	66	68	68	72	274	161,333.33
Morris Hatalsky	68	68	67	72	275	96,800
Bruce Summerhays	73	68	68	66	275	96,800
Dana Quigley	74	71	64	67	276	70,400
Jim Thorpe	69	68	68	71	276	70,400
Hugh Baiocchi	72	69	69	66	276	70,400
Hale Irwin	67	67	70	73	277	50,600
Jack Nicklaus	72	67	68	70	277	50,600
Craig Stadler	71	70	69	67	277	50,600
D.A. Weibring	70	68	70	69	277	50,600
Don Pooley	73	71	70	64	278	40,700
Des Smyth	69	70	71	68	278	40,700
Bob Eastwood	69	73	66	71	279	35,200
Wayne Levi	68	71	70	70	279	35,200
Tom Purtzer	71	73	68	67	279	35,200
Stewart Ginn	71	71	67	71	280	31,020
Isao Aoki	70	75	64	72	281	24,007.50
Dave Barr	69	69	71	72	281	24,007.50
Jim Colbert	70	73	70	68	281	24,007.50
Bruce Fleisher	68	70	70	73	281	24,007.50
Graham Marsh	67	70	69	75	281	24,007.50
Mike McCullough	69	69	71	72	281	24,007.50
Fuzzy Zoeller	66	70	74	71	281	24,007.50
Vicente Fernandez	70	68	69	74	281	24,007.50
Rodger Davis	72	73	70	67	282	17,424
Ed Fiori	73	68	70	71	282	17,424
Bob Gilder	70	69	70	73	282	17,424
Jay Sigel	71	71	68	72	282	17,424
Walter Hall	73	67	68	74	282	17,424
Ben Crenshaw	73	72	67	71	283	13,566.67
Ted Goin	71	70	69	73	283	13,566.66
Larry Nelson	69	71	70	73	283	13,566.67
Bobby Walzel	75	67	69	72	283	13,566.67
John Harris	70	70	70	73	283	13,566.66
Eamonn Darcy	71	73	70	69	283	13,566.67
Mike Smith	69	72	74	69	284	11,220
Lanny Wadkins	72	67	75	70	284	11,220
James Mason	74	70	68	72	284	11,220

Kroger Classic

TPC at River's Bend, Maineville, Ohio
Par 36-36–72; 7,145 yards

September 5-7
purse, $1,500,000

	SCORES			TOTAL	MONEY
Gil Morgan	65	67	68	200	$225,000
Doug Tewell	68	66	68	202	132,000
Jim Thorpe	67	72	64	203	98,625
Larry Nelson	66	70	67	203	98,625
Graham Marsh	68	67	69	204	71,250
Don Pooley	69	70	66	205	54,000
D.A. Weibring	69	70	66	205	54,000
Hugh Baiocchi	69	69	67	205	54,000
Bruce Fleisher	70	68	68	206	40,500
Tom Jenkins	68	69	69	206	40,500
Des Smyth	70	70	67	207	34,500
Isao Aoki	69	68	70	207	34,500
Wayne Levi	69	73	66	208	27,750
Gary Koch	68	73	67	208	27,750
Jay Sigel	69	74	65	208	27,750
Pat McDonald	71	70	67	208	27,750
Leonard Thompson	69	72	68	209	23,250
Rex Caldwell	69	68	72	209	23,250
J.C. Snead	68	70	72	210	20,325
Jerry McGee	66	71	73	210	20,325
John Harris	69	71	71	211	17,450
Walter Hall	71	69	71	211	17,450
Ed Dougherty	71	69	71	211	17,450
Jay Overton	74	68	70	212	13,406.25
Allen Doyle	70	72	70	212	13,406.25
Steven Veriato	70	72	70	212	13,406.25
Dana Quigley	71	71	70	212	13,406.25
Andy Bean	72	72	68	212	13,406.25
John Schroeder	73	68	71	212	13,406.25
Bobby Wadkins	74	71	67	212	13,406.25
Bobby Walzel	70	70	72	212	13,406.25
Raymond Floyd	72	70	71	213	8,925
Jim Colbert	69	73	71	213	8,925
Jim Ahern	72	70	71	213	8,925
Jose Maria Canizares	70	73	70	213	8,925
Seiji Ebihara	68	72	73	213	8,925
Mike Hill	69	71	73	213	8,925
Joe Inman	72	68	73	213	8,925
Ed Fiori	72	68	73	213	8,925
Vicente Fernandez	74	72	67	213	8,925
Bruce Summerhays	66	71	76	213	8,925

Constellation Energy Classic

Hayfields Country Club, Hunt Valley, Maryland
Par 36-36–72; 7,031 yards

September 12-14
purse, $1,500,000

	SCORES			TOTAL	MONEY
Larry Nelson	67	70	70	207	$225,000
Jim Dent	73	65	71	209	120,000
Doug Tewell	71	69	69	209	120,000
Sam Torrance	74	68	68	210	73,500

	SCORES			TOTAL	MONEY
Jay Sigel	67	70	73	210	73,500
Des Smyth	67	71	72	210	73,500
Isao Aoki	71	70	70	211	40,285.71
Wayne Levi	74	68	69	211	40,285.71
Tom Purtzer	70	71	70	211	40,285.71
Dana Quigley	74	70	67	211	40,285.72
Bobby Wadkins	73	69	69	211	40,285.72
Bobby Walzel	72	70	69	211	40,285.71
Walter Hall	72	70	69	211	40,285.72
Bruce Fleisher	73	68	71	212	27,750
Tom Jenkins	70	70	72	212	27,750
Ed Fiori	69	70	74	213	24,750
John Bland	71	69	73	213	24,750
Dave Barr	71	73	70	214	21,750
Allen Doyle	74	72	68	214	21,750
Bob Eastwood	76	70	69	215	19,050
Craig Stadler	76	71	68	215	19,050
Andy Bean	72	69	75	216	15,425
David Eger	75	72	69	216	15,425
Ted Goin	74	70	72	216	15,425
Graham Marsh	74	68	74	216	15,425
Leonard Thompson	73	70	73	216	15,425
James Mason	74	72	70	216	15,425
Mark Lye	72	74	71	217	12,750
John Harris	73	71	73	217	12,750
Jim Albus	74	74	70	218	11,300
Rex Caldwell	74	72	72	218	11,300
Morris Hatalsky	77	69	72	218	11,300
Dave Eichelberger	77	73	69	219	9,250
Joe Inman	74	72	73	219	9,250
Tom Kite	76	69	74	219	9,250
Gary McCord	69	76	74	219	9,250
Jim Thorpe	73	72	74	219	9,250
Pat McDonald	80	72	67	219	9,250
Bob Charles	74	77	69	220	6,900
Ben Crenshaw	76	68	76	220	6,900
Terry Dill	75	73	72	220	6,900
Ed Dougherty	72	72	76	220	6,900
Don Pooley	73	74	73	220	6,900
Mike Smith	70	76	74	220	6,900
J.C. Snead	75	73	72	220	6,900
Eamonn Darcy	77	69	74	220	6,900

SAS Championship

Prestonwood Country Club, Cary, North Carolina
Par 36-36–72; 7,129 yards

September 19-21
purse, $1,800,000

	SCORES			TOTAL	MONEY
D.A. Weibring	65	72	66	203	$270,000
Tom Kite	70	73	61	204	144,000
Bobby Wadkins	67	68	69	204	144,000
Tom Jenkins	71	67	67	205	82,350
Wayne Levi	68	69	68	205	82,350
Doug Tewell	68	69	68	205	82,350
Jim Thorpe	73	66	66	205	82,350
Andy Bean	72	66	69	207	49,500

	SCORES			TOTAL	MONEY
Jose Maria Canizares	66	75	66	207	49,500
Mike Hill	69	71	67	207	49,500
Craig Stadler	72	68	67	207	49,500
Bob Charles	73	67	68	208	34,560
Don Pooley	70	70	68	208	34,560
Stewart Ginn	72	70	66	208	34,560
Jim Ahern	65	67	76	208	34,560
Walter Hall	69	66	73	208	34,560
David Eger	71	65	73	209	26,145
Bruce Fleisher	67	69	73	209	26,145
Allen Doyle	73	65	71	209	26,145
John Harris	72	68	69	209	26,145
Hale Irwin	70	71	70	211	19,944
Dana Quigley	70	69	72	211	19,944
Bruce Summerhays	72	71	68	211	19,944
John Jacobs	71	71	69	211	19,944
Eamonn Darcy	68	71	72	211	19,944
Ed Dougherty	72	70	70	212	14,965.71
Graham Marsh	73	70	69	212	14,965.71
John Schroeder	70	75	67	212	14,965.71
J.C. Snead	70	73	69	212	14,965.72
Leonard Thompson	69	75	68	212	14,965.71
Howard Twitty	75	69	68	212	14,965.72
Jay Sigel	70	73	69	212	14,965.72
Gil Morgan	75	69	69	213	11,100
Larry Nelson	72	71	70	213	11,100
Mike Smith	77	68	68	213	11,100
Rocky Thompson	72	72	69	213	11,100
Lanny Wadkins	74	68	71	213	11,100
Bobby Walzel	73	67	73	213	11,100
Mike McCullough	76	68	70	214	8,640
Tom Purtzer	70	71	73	214	8,640
Bill Rogers	71	69	74	214	8,640
Fuzzy Zoeller	68	73	73	214	8,640
Jim Holtgrieve	74	69	71	214	8,640
John Bland	72	68	74	214	8,640

Greater Hickory Classic at Rock Barn

Rock Barn Golf & Country Club, Conover, North Carolina
Par 36-36–72; 6,553 yards

September 26-28
purse, $1,500,000

	SCORES			TOTAL	MONEY
Craig Stadler	66	69	66	201	$225,000
Larry Nelson	64	69	70	203	132,000
Jim Thorpe	67	71	66	204	108,000
Tom Jenkins	66	70	69	205	89,250
Morris Hatalsky	70	68	68	206	71,250
Gil Morgan	67	74	66	207	60,000
Bob Gilder	65	69	74	208	51,000
Tom Kite	74	64	70	208	51,000
Mark McCumber	70	68	71	209	39,000
Jay Sigel	67	69	73	209	39,000
Walter Hall	72	68	69	209	39,000
Isao Aoki	69	68	73	210	29,625
Dave Eichelberger	69	72	69	210	29,625
Dana Quigley	67	71	72	210	29,625

	SCORES			TOTAL	MONEY
Stewart Ginn	68	67	75	210	29,625
Dave Barr	69	73	69	211	20,083.34
Bruce Fleisher	64	76	71	211	20,083.34
Joe Inman	71	63	77	211	20,083.33
Graham Marsh	73	67	71	211	20,083.33
Doug Tewell	67	70	74	211	20,083.33
D.A. Weibring	70	70	71	211	20,083.33
Tom Wargo	69	69	73	211	20,083.33
Allen Doyle	70	72	69	211	20,083.34
John Harris	68	72	71	211	20,083.33
Jim Dent	73	68	71	212	13,987.50
Wayne Levi	72	69	71	212	13,987.50
Bob Murphy	72	68	72	212	13,987.50
James Mason	66	69	77	212	13,987.50
Jose Maria Canizares	70	74	69	213	11,587.50
David Eger	71	68	74	213	11,587.50
Ed Fiori	72	69	72	213	11,587.50
Gary Player	73	68	72	213	11,587.50
Bob Eastwood	68	75	71	214	9,450
Bruce Lietzke	69	73	72	214	9,450
Fuzzy Zoeller	71	75	68	214	9,450
John Jacobs	71	69	74	214	9,450
Hugh Baiocchi	69	73	72	214	9,450
Mike Hill	68	76	71	215	6,900
Hale Irwin	69	73	73	215	6,900
Don Pooley	71	72	72	215	6,900
Tom Purtzer	72	71	72	215	6,900
Leonard Thompson	70	74	71	215	6,900
Steven Veriato	71	71	73	215	6,900
Bobby Wadkins	68	75	72	215	6,900
Lanny Wadkins	68	70	77	215	6,900
Bruce Summerhays	73	72	70	215	6,900
John Bland	71	72	72	215	6,900

Turtle Bay Championship

Palmer Course at Turtle Bay Resort, Kahuku, Hawaii
Par 36-36–72; 7,044 yards

October 10-12
purse, $1,500,000

	SCORES			TOTAL	MONEY
Hale Irwin	68	73	67	208	$225,000
Tom Kite	71	67	72	210	132,000
Graham Marsh	73	73	65	211	98,625
Bruce Summerhays	74	71	66	211	98,625
Rodger Davis	75	70	67	212	71,250
Rex Caldwell	68	72	73	213	54,000
Morris Hatalsky	74	72	67	213	54,000
D.A. Weibring	71	73	69	213	54,000
Ed Fiori	73	70	71	214	36,000
Joe Inman	70	72	72	214	36,000
Tom Purtzer	71	72	71	214	36,000
Dana Quigley	68	73	73	214	36,000
James Mason	72	71	71	214	36,000
Bob Gilder	69	74	72	215	25,500
John Schroeder	77	69	69	215	25,500
Allen Doyle	71	74	70	215	25,500
John Bland	75	72	68	215	25,500

	SCORES			TOTAL	MONEY
Vicente Fernandez	73	72	70	215	25,500
Isao Aoki	72	76	68	216	18,600
Jim Colbert	74	70	72	216	18,600
Dick Mast	69	75	72	216	18,600
Don Pooley	74	72	70	216	18,600
Howard Twitty	76	70	70	216	18,600
Mike Smith	72	76	69	217	14,025
Jim Thorpe	73	73	71	217	14,025
Bobby Walzel	73	75	69	217	14,025
John Harris	74	75	68	217	14,025
Bobby Lincoln	71	77	69	217	14,025
Rick Rhoden	73	73	71	217	14,025
Hugh Baiocchi	71	75	72	218	11,850
Andy Bean	77	73	69	219	10,125
Ed Dougherty	74	71	74	219	10,125
Jerry McGee	69	78	72	219	10,125
Lonnie Nielsen	73	71	75	219	10,125
Butch Sheehan	69	75	75	219	10,125
Jim Ahern	73	75	71	219	10,125
Danny Edwards	73	75	72	220	7,800
Lon Hinkle	79	67	74	220	7,800
Jack Spradlin	74	76	70	220	7,800
Jim Holtgrieve	73	74	73	220	7,800
Stewart Ginn	75	73	72	220	7,800
Pat McDonald	70	82	68	220	7,800

SBC Championship

Oak Hills Country Club, San Antonio, Texas
Par 35-36–71; 6,661 yards

October 17-19
purse, $1,500,000

	SCORES			TOTAL	MONEY
Craig Stadler	67	64	67	198	$225,000
Bob Gilder	66	67	69	202	132,000
Allen Doyle	68	70	66	204	108,000
Hale Irwin	67	71	67	205	64,500
Tom Kite	69	69	67	205	64,500
Tom Watson	70	66	69	205	64,500
Fuzzy Zoeller	67	70	68	205	64,500
Walter Hall	69	67	69	205	64,500
Larry Nelson	70	67	69	206	42,000
Bruce Fleisher	66	70	71	207	36,000
Bill Rogers	68	69	70	207	36,000
Jim Thorpe	65	72	70	207	36,000
Dick Mast	70	70	68	208	28,500
Lanny Wadkins	67	73	68	208	28,500
Eamonn Darcy	71	70	67	208	28,500
Darrell Kestner	74	69	66	209	21,850
Gary Koch	69	73	67	209	21,850
Gary McCord	70	69	70	209	21,850
Mark McCumber	70	70	69	209	21,850
Gil Morgan	73	65	71	209	21,850
Don Pooley	69	72	68	209	21,850
Raymond Floyd	69	70	71	210	16,162.50
Dana Quigley	73	70	67	210	16,162.50
Jim Ahern	69	68	73	210	16,162.50
Hugh Baiocchi	71	67	72	210	16,162.50

	SCORES			TOTAL	MONEY
Mike Hill	70	69	72	211	13,650
Tom Jenkins	69	70	72	211	13,650
Tom Wargo	72	68	71	211	13,650
Rodger Davis	70	70	72	212	11,340
Bob Eastwood	72	67	73	212	11,340
Bruce Lietzke	71	68	73	212	11,340
Sam Torrance	69	72	71	212	11,340
John Harris	74	69	69	212	11,340
Isao Aoki	71	72	70	213	8,850
David Eger	71	71	71	213	8,850
Wayne Levi	74	71	68	213	8,850
Howard Twitty	74	67	72	213	8,850
D.A. Weibring	71	67	75	213	8,850
John Bland	70	77	66	213	8,850
Andy Bean	72	74	68	214	7,350
Dave Eichelberger	74	70	70	214	7,350
James Mason	69	70	75	214	7,350

Charles Schwab Cup Championship

Sonoma Golf Club, Sonoma, California
Par 36-36–72; 6,850 yards

October 23-26
purse, $2,500,000

	SCORES				TOTAL	MONEY
Jim Thorpe	63	67	70	68	268	$440,000
Tom Watson	68	66	70	67	271	254,000
Tom Kite	69	68	69	67	273	213,000
Hale Irwin	73	67	66	68	274	144,333.33
Tom Jenkins	66	67	70	71	274	144,333.33
Gil Morgan	69	70	69	66	274	144,333.34
Larry Nelson	68	71	69	67	275	99,000
Tom Purtzer	70	70	69	66	275	99,000
Craig Stadler	69	68	71	68	276	82,000
David Eger	71	72	67	67	277	73,000
Bruce Fleisher	69	70	69	69	277	73,000
Wayne Levi	70	71	70	67	278	64,000
Rodger Davis	71	68	71	69	279	55,333.34
Graham Marsh	70	67	69	73	279	55,333.33
Vicente Fernandez	69	70	69	71	279	55,333.33
Morris Hatalsky	71	72	69	68	280	47,500
Doug Tewell	74	69	72	65	280	47,500
Dave Barr	69	73	66	74	282	41,750
Bobby Wadkins	69	73	71	69	282	41,750
Bob Gilder	73	73	69	68	283	34,000
Dana Quigley	74	73	68	68	283	34,000
D.A. Weibring	71	73	71	68	283	34,000
Fuzzy Zoeller	72	69	71	71	283	34,000
Des Smyth	72	72	73	66	283	34,000
Bruce Lietzke	71	74	69	71	285	28,000
Allen Doyle	71	73	70	71	285	28,000
Jose Maria Canizares	71	72	76	67	286	26,000
Mike McCullough	75	69	74	71	289	25,000
Jay Sigel	72	71	74	73	290	24,500
John Jacobs	74	75	76	71	296	24,000

European Seniors Tour

Digicel Jamaica Classic

Half Moon Golf Club, Montego Bay, Jamaica
Par 36-36–72; 6,738 yards

March 21-23
purse, €233,099

	SCORES			TOTAL	MONEY
Ray Carrasco	71	70	70	211	€34,965
Manuel Pinero	70	70	72	212	23,310
Guillermo Encina	70	72	71	213	16,317
John Morgan	73	67	74	214	11,678.31
Alan Tapie	70	71	73	214	11,678.31
Christy O'Connor, Jr.	74	69	72	215	8,391.60
Bob Larratt	74	66	75	215	8,391.60
Terry Gale	68	74	73	215	8,391.60
Nick Job	69	73	74	216	6,293.70
Wayne Wright	71	72	73	216	6,293.70
David Creamer	70	73	74	217	5,361.30
Delroy Cambridge	76	71	70	217	5,361.30
Denis Durnian	73	71	74	218	4,428.90
Joe McDermott	71	72	75	218	4,428.90
Steve Stull	75	69	74	218	4,428.90
Keith MacDonald	71	73	75	219	3,510.49
Giuseppe Cali	74	72	73	219	3,510.49
Denis O'Sullivan	70	78	71	219	3,510.49
Hisao Inoue	72	73	74	219	3,510.49
Fred Gibson	72	72	75	219	3,510.49
Noel Ratcliffe	70	70	80	220	2,651.51
John Mashego	75	73	72	220	2,651.51
John Grace	75	71	74	220	2,651.51
David Good	75	71	74	220	2,651.51
Craig Defoy	78	72	71	221	2,125.87
Bob Lendzion	72	75	74	221	2,125.87
John McTear	70	76	75	221	2,125.87
Brian Jones	72	73	76	221	2,125.87
Bob Cameron	75	71	75	221	2,125.87
Bernard Gallacher	77	73	73	223	1,576.34
Simon Owen	79	73	71	223	1,576.34
Bill Brask	70	74	79	223	1,576.34
Eddie Polland	73	73	77	223	1,576.34
Jim Rhodes	73	72	78	223	1,576.34
Jerry Bruner	75	70	78	223	1,576.34
Horacio Carbonetti	70	76	77	223	1,576.34
Gary Wintz	74	75	74	223	1,576.34

Royal Westmoreland Barbados Open

Royal Westmoreland Golf Club, St. James, Barbados
Par 36-36–72; 6,756 yards

March 27-29
purse, €185,632

	SCORES			TOTAL	MONEY
Terry Gale	70	64	72	206	€29,619.52
Jerry Bruner	71	72	69	212	16,785.63

	SCORES			TOTAL	MONEY
Brian Jones	69	71	72	212	16,785.63
Denis Durnian	65	75	74	214	8,223.07
Nick Job	69	72	73	214	8,223.07
David Oakley	71	69	74	214	8,223.07
Denis O'Sullivan	75	72	67	214	8,223.07
John Chillas	68	78	68	214	8,223.07
Keith MacDonald	73	73	69	215	4,936.71
Malcolm Gregson	70	72	73	215	4,936.71
Jim Rhodes	71	75	69	215	4,936.71
David Good	75	70	70	215	4,936.71
Delroy Cambridge	71	75	70	216	3,950.26
Russell Weir	70	74	73	217	3,555.23
Alan Tapie	71	74	72	217	3,555.23
Gary Wintz	71	73	73	217	3,555.23
Bernard Gallacher	73	73	72	218	2,969.13
John Morgan	72	75	71	218	2,969.13
David Creamer	73	72	73	218	2,969.13
George Burns	75	71	73	219	2,606.28
Noel Ratcliffe	73	72	75	220	2,370.16
Ray Carrasco	74	74	72	220	2,370.16
Simon Owen	74	71	76	221	2,122.89
Guillermo Encina	74	78	69	221	2,122.89
Bill Hardwick	74	75	73	222	1,925.38
Priscillo Diniz	71	76	75	222	1,925.38
Ian Stanley	75	74	74	223	1,757.57
John Grace	74	71	78	223	1,757.57
Ian Mosey	74	77	73	224	1,560.30
Eddie Polland	75	79	70	224	1,560.30
Barry Vivian	75	73	76	224	1,560.30

Tobago Plantations Seniors Classic

Tobago Plantations Golf & Beach Resort, Tobago
Par 36-36–72; 6,752 yards

April 3-5
purse, €182,041

	SCORES			TOTAL	MONEY
Terry Gale	68	70	65	203	€27,306.19
John Chillas	72	65	69	206	18,204.13
Guillermo Encina	71	68	70	209	11,377.58
Delroy Cambridge	69	69	71	209	11,377.58
Bob Cameron	73	68	71	212	7,354.47
David Creamer	67	73	72	212	7,354.47
David Good	71	73	68	212	7,354.47
Giuseppe Cali	69	73	71	213	5,825.32
Denis Durnian	72	67	75	214	3,959.40
Mike Miller	70	70	74	214	3,959.40
Horacio Carbonetti	70	74	70	214	3,959.40
John Mashego	72	71	71	214	3,959.40
George Burns	71	69	74	214	3,959.40
Barry Vivian	72	72	70	214	3,959.40
Steve Stull	72	71	71	214	3,959.40
Alan Mew	70	69	75	214	3,959.40
Baldovino Dassu	73	68	74	215	2,301.65
John Morgan	73	71	71	215	2,301.65
Noel Ratcliffe	72	70	73	215	2,301.65
Martin Gray	72	72	71	215	2,301.65
Jerry Bruner	71	73	71	215	2,301.65

	SCORES			TOTAL	MONEY
Jeff Van Wagenen	73	68	74	215	2,301.65
John Benda	71	70	74	215	2,301.65
John Grace	70	74	71	215	2,301.65
Joey Combs	71	69	75	215	2,301.65
Tommy Horton	72	72	72	216	1,619.44
Ian Stanley	73	71	72	216	1,619.44
Jay Horton	73	73	70	216	1,619.44
Gary Wintz	76	69	71	216	1,619.44
Bob Larratt	73	73	71	217	1,370.89
Simon Owen	72	76	69	217	1,370.89
David Oakley	70	76	71	217	1,370.89

AIB Irish Seniors Open

Adare Manor Hotel & Golf Resort, Adare, Ireland
Par 36-36–72; 6,782 yards

May 16-18
purse, €330,000

	SCORES			TOTAL	MONEY
Noel Ratcliffe	69	69	73	211	€49,500
Martin Gray	73	69	70	212	24,750
Bob Lendzion	72	68	72	212	24,750
Delroy Cambridge	68	69	75	212	24,750
Seiji Ebihara	70	71	72	213	14,916
Mike Miller	74	67	73	214	12,540
Jim Rhodes	72	70	72	214	12,540
George Burns	73	72	70	215	10,560
John Chillas	72	71	73	216	8,910
Gary Wintz	68	79	69	216	8,910
Denis Durnian	72	71	74	217	7,920
Baldovino Dassu	71	74	73	218	6,517.50
Alan Tapie	70	73	75	218	6,517.50
Paul Leonard	71	77	70	218	6,517.50
Jerry Bruner	73	70	75	218	6,517.50
Ian Mosey	73	71	75	219	4,969.80
Keith MacDonald	74	73	72	219	4,969.80
Russell Weir	75	74	70	219	4,969.80
Guillermo Encina	74	70	75	219	4,969.80
Steve Stull	70	76	73	219	4,969.80
Terry Gale	74	74	72	220	3,575
David Oakley	71	76	73	220	3,575
Brian Jones	69	73	78	220	3,575
John Mashego	77	72	71	220	3,575
David Good	69	79	72	220	3,575
Alan Mew	73	72	75	220	3,575
John Irwin	77	72	72	221	3,003
Christy O'Connor, Jr.	76	71	75	222	2,673
Malcolm Gregson	73	74	75	222	2,673
Denis O'Sullivan	75	74	73	222	2,673
Jeff Van Wagenen	68	74	80	222	2,673

Wallonia Open

Pierpont Golf Club, Belgium
Par 36-36–72; 6,725 yards

May 23-25
purse, €130,000

	SCORES			TOTAL	MONEY
Hank Woodrome	71	71	68	210	€19,500
Eddie Polland	71	69	70	210	13,000
(Woodrome defeated Polland on first playoff hole.)					
Bob Larratt	73	71	67	211	6,831.50
Terry Gale	73	68	70	211	6,831.50
David Oakley	70	71	70	211	6,831.50
Denis O'Sullivan	71	69	71	211	6,831.50
Noel Ratcliffe	71	71	70	212	3,965
Horacio Carbonetti	70	69	73	212	3,965
Delroy Cambridge	73	72	67	212	3,965
Steve Stull	71	67	74	212	3,965
Giuseppe Cali	73	67	73	213	2,762.50
Bob Cameron	71	71	71	213	2,762.50
David Creamer	70	71	72	213	2,762.50
Robbie Stewart	68	74	71	213	2,762.50
Denis Durnian	70	68	76	214	2,145
John Chillas	70	73	71	214	2,145
Gary Wintz	71	72	71	214	2,145
Tony Allen	71	69	74	214	2,145
John Morgan	69	72	74	215	1,619.80
Keith MacDonald	71	72	72	215	1,619.80
Ray Carrasco	69	72	74	215	1,619.80
Guillermo Encina	69	73	73	215	1,619.80
John Mashego	76	70	69	215	1,619.80
Jay Horton	73	71	72	216	1,365
Bernard Gallacher	73	69	75	217	1,267.50
Geoff Tickell	70	70	77	217	1,267.50
John McTear	73	72	73	218	1,157
Jeff Van Wagenen	75	69	74	218	1,157
Russell Weir	72	73	74	219	962
Peter Dawson	74	69	76	219	962
Alan Tapie	74	71	74	219	962
Steve Wild	74	69	76	219	962
John Grace	70	73	76	219	962
Alan Mew	73	74	72	219	962

Irvine Whitlock Jersey Seniors Classic

La Moye Golf Club, Jersey
Par 36-36–72; 6,581 yards

June 13-15
purse, €143,025

	SCORES			TOTAL	MONEY
Malcolm Gregson	67	66	70	203	€21,657.62
Bob Cameron	68	71	67	206	14,437.46
Denis Durnian	68	65	75	208	9,023.77
Guillermo Encina	68	72	68	208	9,023.77
David Oakley	67	71	71	209	5,832.97
Denis O'Sullivan	70	67	72	209	5,832.97
John Mashego	73	69	67	209	5,832.97
Nick Job	72	72	66	210	4,138.80
Bill Longmuir	64	75	71	210	4,138.80
Paul Leonard	67	72	71	210	4,138.80

	SCORES			TOTAL	MONEY
Alan Tapie	70	69	72	211	3,465.11
Noel Ratcliffe	71	71	70	212	3,032.32
Jim Rhodes	68	71	73	212	3,032.32
Baldovino Dassu	74	70	69	213	2,599.07
Liam Higgins	72	68	73	213	2,599.07
Alberto Croce	69	70	74	213	2,599.07
John Morgan	68	74	72	214	2,237.82
Giuseppe Cali	72	74	68	214	2,237.82
Horacio Carbonetti	70	73	72	215	1,970.62
David Good	67	73	75	215	1,970.62
Bill Hardwick	72	70	74	216	1,732.55
Delroy Cambridge	74	75	67	216	1,732.55
John Chillas	77	74	66	217	1,552.05
Steve Stull	74	73	70	217	1,552.05
Ian Mosey	71	69	78	218	1,346.32
Bob Larratt	70	75	73	218	1,346.32
David Jones	75	71	72	218	1,346.32
Joe McDermott	72	72	74	218	1,346.32
Martin Gray	74	75	70	219	1,045.66
Ray Carrasco	72	79	68	219	1,045.66
David Snell	73	71	75	219	1,045.66
Jerry Bruner	72	76	71	219	1,045.66
John McTear	74	72	73	219	1,045.66
Priscillo Diniz	72	73	74	219	1,045.66
Robbie Stewart	74	76	69	219	1,045.66

De Vere Northumberland Seniors Classic

De Vere Slaley Hall, Hexham, England
Par 36-36–72; 6,838 yards

June 20-22
purse, €211,445

	SCORES			TOTAL	MONEY
Jerry Bruner	68	65	69	202	€31,716.90
John Chillas	73	65	68	206	21,144.60
Bob Cameron	71	69	68	208	14,801.22
Baldovino Dassu	72	68	70	210	10,593.44
Manuel Pinero	69	69	72	210	10,593.44
Nick Job	71	71	70	212	8,034.95
Brian Jones	73	67	72	212	8,034.95
Denis Durnian	74	69	70	213	6,061.45
Maurice Bembridge	74	68	71	213	6,061.45
Steve Stull	74	67	72	213	6,061.45
Simon Owen	75	66	73	214	4,863.26
Delroy Cambridge	74	68	72	214	4,863.26
Neil Coles	72	71	72	215	4,123.20
David Good	75	68	72	215	4,123.20
Eddie Polland	73	73	70	216	3,488.86
Denis O'Sullivan	74	71	71	216	3,488.86
John Fourie	73	70	73	216	3,488.86
David Creamer	75	67	74	216	3,488.86
Guillermo Encina	76	71	70	217	2,711.80
Manuel Velasco	79	64	74	217	2,711.80
John McTear	75	68	74	217	2,711.80
John Irwin	77	70	70	217	2,711.80
Tommy Horton	78	68	72	218	1,938.26
John Morgan	76	70	72	218	1,938.26
Keith MacDonald	75	70	73	218	1,938.26

	SCORES			TOTAL	MONEY
Liam Higgins	74	70	74	218	1,938.26
Peter Townsend	73	72	73	218	1,938.26
Alan Tapie	75	70	73	218	1,938.26
Craig Defoy	72	73	73	218	1,938.26
Horacio Carbonetti	72	75	71	218	1,938.26
Mike Ferguson	71	73	74	218	1,938.26

Ryder Cup Wales Seniors Open

Royal St. David's Golf Club, Harlech, Wales
Par 36-33–69; 6,475 yards

July 4-6
purse, €725,917

	SCORES			TOTAL	MONEY
Bill Longmuir	68	66	65	199	€108,281.30
David Oakley	67	65	70	202	72,187.50
Guillermo Encina	65	65	73	203	50,531.25
Alan Tapie	67	70	67	204	39,703.13
Jim Rhodes	71	65	69	205	32,628.75
Carl Mason	72	68	66	206	24,543.75
John Morgan	69	66	71	206	24,543.75
Giuseppe Cali	69	69	68	206	24,543.75
John Grace	67	70	69	206	24,543.75
Bob Charles	70	68	69	207	14,617.97
Neil Coles	65	70	72	207	14,617.97
Eamonn Darcy	71	69	67	207	14,617.97
Baldovino Dassu	72	67	68	207	14,617.97
Des Smyth	70	68	69	207	14,617.97
John Chillas	66	71	70	207	14,617.97
Barry Vivian	70	68	69	207	14,617.97
Dragon Taki	72	67	68	207	14,617.97
Denis Durnian	67	72	69	208	9,300.16
Terry Gale	70	71	67	208	9,300.16
Bob Cameron	71	68	69	208	9,300.16
Horacio Carbonetti	74	68	66	208	9,300.16
Priscillo Diniz	72	68	68	208	9,300.16
Seiji Ebihara	70	70	68	208	9,300.16
Nick Job	69	69	71	209	6,050.63
Manuel Pinero	70	67	72	209	6,050.63
Russell Weir	68	70	71	209	6,050.63
Malcolm Gregson	68	71	70	209	6,050.63
Ray Carrasco	70	69	70	209	6,050.63
Paul Leonard	73	69	67	209	6,050.63
Bill Hardwick	70	69	70	209	6,050.63
Eddie Polland	69	69	71	209	6,050.63
Jerry Bruner	67	73	69	209	6,050.63
Brian Jones	69	63	77	209	6,050.63
Hank Woodrome	66	70	73	209	6,050.63

The Mobile Cup

Stoke Park, Buckinghamshire, England
Par 36-35–71; 6,720 yards

July 11-13
purse, €181,670

	SCORES			TOTAL	MONEY
Carl Mason	69	66	68	203	€28,158.85
Bob Cameron	68	69	67	204	18,777.41
Giuseppe Cali	70	70	68	208	13,138.37
Bob Charles	71	68	70	209	8,777.81
Terry Gale	69	72	68	209	8,777.81
Guillermo Encina	68	69	72	209	8,777.81
Denis Durnian	69	69	72	210	6,011.10
Noel Ratcliffe	69	71	70	210	6,011.10
Liam Higgins	69	70	71	210	6,011.10
David Oakley	71	69	72	212	4,884.74
Ian Stanley	70	73	70	213	4,320.84
Delroy Cambridge	73	70	70	213	4,320.84
Bill Longmuir	70	71	73	214	3,475.71
Bob Shearer	72	70	72	214	3,475.71
Jim Rhodes	73	71	70	214	3,475.71
David Good	71	73	70	214	3,475.71
Maurice Bembridge	70	73	72	215	2,504.14
Nick Job	72	72	71	215	2,504.14
John Morgan	72	69	74	215	2,504.14
Simon Owen	66	73	76	215	2,504.14
John Chillas	71	72	72	215	2,504.14
Brian Jones	73	69	73	215	2,504.14
John Grace	71	70	74	215	2,504.14
Malcolm Gregson	70	74	72	216	1,926.43
Dragon Taki	74	71	71	216	1,926.43
Jerry Bruner	73	72	72	217	1,747.66
Priscillo Diniz	72	73	72	217	1,747.66
Tommy Horton	74	68	76	218	1,635.03
Ian Mosey	72	74	73	219	1,420.51
Eddie Polland	70	77	72	219	1,420.51
David Huish	72	73	74	219	1,420.51
John Irwin	73	71	75	219	1,420.51
Barry Vivian	76	74	69	219	1,420.51

Senior British Open

Westin Turnberry Resort, Turnberry, Scotland
Par 35-35–70; 6,715 yards

July 24-27
purse, €1,422,297

	SCORES				TOTAL	MONEY
Tom Watson	66	67	66	64	263	€222,778.90
Carl Mason	67	64	65	67	263	147,589.80
(Watson defeated Mason on second playoff hole.)						
Bruce Summerhays	68	65	66	65	264	83,647.97
Tom Kite	66	67	66	67	266	66,847.78
D.A. Weibring	69	63	65	73	270	56,640.61
Mark McCumber	67	69	65	70	271	43,440.47
Brian Jones	69	69	65	68	271	43,440.47
Denis Durnian	67	68	69	68	272	31,673.29
David Eger	71	68	66	67	272	31,673.29
Graham Marsh	71	68	66	68	273	24,734.38
Jim Colbert	72	62	66	73	273	24,734.38

	SCORES				TOTAL	MONEY
Dana Quigley	71	65	70	67	273	24,734.38
Des Smyth	67	75	66	66	274	21,402.58
Jack Nicklaus	70	67	67	71	275	18,819.03
Isao Aoki	69	69	66	71	275	18,819.03
Fuzzy Zoeller	67	69	68	71	275	18,819.03
Stewart Ginn	72	66	67	70	275	18,819.03
Bob Cameron	69	67	68	71	275	18,819.03
Craig Stadler	72	69	69	66	276	16,701.36
Bob Charles	69	68	69	71	277	15,303.70
Bill Longmuir	69	68	71	69	277	15,303.70
Russell Weir	67	67	71	72	277	15,303.70
Terry Gale	70	66	69	72	277	15,303.70
David Good	73	67	68	69	277	15,303.70
Eamonn Darcy	73	68	69	68	278	13,722.50
John Chillas	74	70	66	68	278	13,722.50
Rodger Davis	70	71	71	67	279	12,192.13
Martin Gray	70	70	71	68	279	12,192.13
Don Pooley	72	69	68	70	279	12,192.13
Mark Lye	70	68	72	69	279	12,192.13
Jay Sigel	73	71	65	70	279	12,192.13

De Vere PGA Seniors Championship

De Vere Carden Park, Cheshire, England
Par 36-36–72; 6,583 yards

July 31-August 3
purse, €283,608

	SCORES				TOTAL	MONEY
Bill Longmuir	68	67	69	67	271	€46,892.98
Carl Mason	71	69	64	69	273	23,537.94
Denis O'Sullivan	65	71	70	67	273	23,537.94
Ian Mosey	70	67	71	68	276	11,958.90
Simon Owen	71	72	64	69	276	11,958.90
Horacio Carbonetti	69	68	74	65	276	11,958.90
Denis Durnian	70	66	71	70	277	9,567.12
Alan Mew	68	69	70	71	278	8,863.66
Nick Job	70	65	69	75	279	6,436.70
David Oakley	73	66	67	73	279	6,436.70
Seiji Ebihara	71	72	67	69	279	6,436.70
David Good	67	74	69	69	279	6,436.70
Delroy Cambridge	71	72	67	69	279	6,436.70
Hisao Inoue	71	69	69	70	279	6,436.70
Jerry Bruner	73	71	69	67	280	4,044.92
John Brott	71	69	68	72	280	4,044.92
Maurice Bembridge	75	67	67	72	281	3,130.42
Tommy Horton	75	67	68	71	281	3,130.42
Martin Gray	68	75	69	69	281	3,130.42
Alan Tapie	76	68	69	68	281	3,130.42
Manuel Velasco	75	68	67	71	281	3,130.42
John McTear	73	69	70	69	281	3,130.42
Terry Gale	70	70	67	75	282	2,694.27
Bill Lockie	70	71	70	71	282	2,694.27
John Irwin	71	73	70	68	282	2,694.27
Paul Parajeckas	73	67	69	73	282	2,694.27
John Morgan	72	68	69	74	283	2,412.89
Bob Shearer	67	73	72	71	283	2,412.89
John Chillas	72	69	68	74	283	2,412.89
George Burns	69	70	75	69	283	2,412.89

Bad Ragaz PGA Seniors Open

Bad Ragaz Golf Club, Zurich, Switzerland
Par 35-35–70; 6,098 yards

August 8-10
purse, €160,000

	SCORES			TOTAL	MONEY
Horacio Carbonetti	64	64	69	197	€24,000
David Good	67	67	66	200	16,000
Bill Longmuir	69	64	68	201	9,077.33
Priscillo Diniz	69	62	70	201	9,077.33
John Irwin	66	66	69	201	9,077.33
Maurice Bembridge	70	67	65	202	4,754.29
John Morgan	68	65	69	202	4,754.29
Giuseppe Cali	70	66	66	202	4,754.29
Terry Gale	67	65	70	202	4,754.29
Jerry Bruner	71	66	65	202	4,754.29
Neville Clarke	63	67	72	202	4,754.29
Alan Mew	68	69	65	202	4,754.29
Baldovino Dassu	69	67	67	203	2,960
Guillermo Encina	67	71	65	203	2,960
Manuel Velasco	67	67	69	203	2,960
Noboru Sugai	68	69	66	203	2,960
David Creamer	63	70	71	204	2,480
Dragon Taki	71	66	67	204	2,480
Nick Job	69	66	70	205	2,117.33
Simon Owen	72	65	68	205	2,117.33
Bob Cameron	72	66	67	205	2,117.33
Denis Durnian	69	68	69	206	1,645.33
Tommy Horton	70	65	71	206	1,645.33
Mike Miller	70	65	71	206	1,645.33
John Chillas	71	68	67	206	1,645.33
Brian Jones	66	68	72	206	1,645.33
Steve Stull	71	70	65	206	1,645.33
David Oakley	70	70	67	207	1,328
Denis O'Sullivan	75	65	67	207	1,328
John Grace	68	70	69	207	1,328

Travis Perkins Senior Masters

Wentworth Club, Surrey, England
Par 36-36–72; 6,727 yards

August 15-17
purse, €320,720

	SCORES			TOTAL	MONEY
John Chillas	70	70	69	209	€47,937.49
Eamonn Darcy	68	72	70	210	31,958.32
Neil Coles	73	74	64	211	22,370.83
Carl Mason	71	69	72	212	16,011.12
Terry Gale	69	70	73	212	16,011.12
David Creamer	70	73	70	213	12,783.33
Maurice Bembridge	73	71	70	214	8,269.22
Keith MacDonald	76	72	66	214	8,269.22
Giuseppe Cali	70	74	70	214	8,269.22
Jerry Bruner	72	71	71	214	8,269.22
Jeff Van Wagenen	71	69	74	214	8,269.22
Horacio Carbonetti	69	73	72	214	8,269.22
John Grace	70	71	73	214	8,269.22
Steve Stull	72	71	71	214	8,269.22
Bill Longmuir	69	68	78	215	5,432.92

	SCORES			TOTAL	MONEY
Ray Carrasco	72	72	71	215	5,432.92
Manuel Velasco	71	74	70	215	5,432.92
David Jones	67	74	75	216	4,793.75
Martin Gray	73	73	71	217	4,228.92
David Oakley	71	76	70	217	4,228.92
David Good	69	72	76	217	4,228.92
Ian Mosey	71	78	69	218	3,361.73
Malcolm Gregson	74	72	72	218	3,361.73
Denis O'Sullivan	71	71	76	218	3,361.73
Robbie Stewart	74	73	71	218	3,361.73
Alan Mew	74	73	71	218	3,361.73
Baldovino Dassu	76	73	70	219	2,651.83
Denis Durnian	74	76	69	219	2,651.83
Simon Owen	72	75	72	219	2,651.83
Alan Tapie	75	73	71	219	2,651.83
Delroy Cambridge	76	73	70	219	2,651.83

Nigel Mansell Classic

Woodbury Park Hotel & Country Club, Exeter, England
Par 36-36–72; 6,722 yards

August 22-24
purse, €212,677

	SCORES			TOTAL	MONEY
Mike Miller	67	66	72	205	€31,901.63
Denis Durnian	69	67	71	207	13,194.51
Terry Gale	70	65	72	207	13,194.51
Ian Stanley	68	71	68	207	13,194.51
Denis O'Sullivan	72	65	70	207	13,194.51
Delroy Cambridge	72	67	68	207	13,194.51
Nick Job	74	64	70	208	7,231.04
Ian Mosey	68	68	72	208	7,231.04
Simon Owen	69	69	71	209	5,104.26
Jerry Bruner	71	68	70	209	5,104.26
John Chillas	72	69	68	209	5,104.26
Steve Stull	71	69	69	209	5,104.26
Neville Clarke	68	68	73	209	5,104.26
Keith MacDonald	72	67	71	210	3,934.53
Alan Mew	72	68	70	210	3,934.53
Giuseppe Cali	70	69	72	211	3,402.84
Guillermo Encina	68	69	74	211	3,402.84
Hank Woodrome	69	69	73	211	3,402.84
John Morgan	73	72	67	212	2,814.43
Russell Weir	74	71	67	212	2,814.43
John McTear	74	71	67	212	2,814.43
Bill Longmuir	71	69	73	213	2,187.03
Carl Mason	78	64	71	213	2,187.03
Gery Watine	72	71	70	213	2,187.03
Robbie Stewart	76	68	69	213	2,187.03
David Good	72	69	72	213	2,187.03
Dragon Taki	69	72	72	213	2,187.03
Neil Coles	71	73	70	214	1,765.22
Martin Gray	71	74	69	214	1,765.22
Bob Shearer	71	70	73	214	1,765.22

Charles Church Scottish Seniors Open

The Roxburgh, Kelso, Scotland
Par 36-36–72; 6,845 yards

August 29-31
purse, €217,390

	SCORES			TOTAL	MONEY
Terry Gale	69	66	70	205	€32,608.58
Nick Job	67	71	69	207	18,478.19
Barry Vivian	68	71	68	207	18,478.19
Carl Mason	68	71	70	209	10,891.26
John Chillas	71	71	67	209	10,891.26
Bob Shearer	72	68	70	210	8,695.62
Keith MacDonald	71	70	70	211	6,630.41
Jerry Bruner	71	69	71	211	6,630.41
John McTear	73	67	71	211	6,630.41
David Good	72	65	74	211	6,630.41
Maurice Bembridge	71	72	69	212	4,782.59
Bill Longmuir	70	71	71	212	4,782.59
John Morgan	71	71	70	212	4,782.59
Manuel Velasco	72	69	72	213	4,130.42
Denis Durnian	71	71	72	214	3,482.60
Craig Maltman	68	72	74	214	3,482.60
Sam Torrance	73	67	74	214	3,482.60
Delroy Cambridge	70	70	74	214	3,482.60
Gary Wintz	73	70	71	214	3,482.60
Tommy Horton	71	70	74	215	2,552.17
Malcolm Gregson	74	69	72	215	2,552.17
David Oakley	71	69	75	215	2,552.17
Eddie Polland	75	69	71	215	2,552.17
Bob Cameron	74	73	68	215	2,552.17
Mike Miller	74	69	73	216	2,072.46
Bill Lockie	75	66	75	216	2,072.46
Priscillo Diniz	71	71	74	216	2,072.46
Martin Gray	73	72	72	217	1,847.82
John Mashego	74	70	73	217	1,847.82
Liam Higgins	71	75	72	218	1,503.10
Russell Weir	69	74	75	218	1,503.10
Bob Larratt	72	74	72	218	1,503.10
Bob Lendzion	69	77	72	218	1,503.10
Brian Jones	73	72	73	218	1,503.10
Geoff Tickell	70	71	77	218	1,503.10
Martin Foster	74	71	73	218	1,503.10

Bovis Lend Lease European Senior Masters

Woburn Golf & Country Club, Milton Keynes, England
Par 35-37–72; 6,796 yards

September 5-7
purse, €323,041

	SCORES			TOTAL	MONEY
Paul Leonard	72	70	66	208	€48,456.23
Nick Job	70	72	67	209	27,458.53
Bill Longmuir	70	70	69	209	27,458.53
Ian Mosey	69	71	70	210	14,229.98
Sam Torrance	69	71	70	210	14,229.98
Jerry Bruner	71	71	68	210	14,229.98
John Chillas	71	68	71	210	14,229.98
Brian Jones	70	69	72	211	10,337.33
Christy O'Connor, Jr.	74	69	69	212	8,399.08

	SCORES			TOTAL	MONEY
Liam Higgins	70	66	76	212	8,399.08
Keith Ashdown	67	74	71	212	8,399.08
Noel Ratcliffe	71	72	70	213	6,568.51
Bob Shearer	71	69	73	213	6,568.51
Jim Rhodes	73	70	70	213	6,568.51
John Morgan	70	71	73	214	5,330.19
Eddie Polland	73	67	74	214	5,330.19
Manuel Velasco	74	70	70	214	5,330.19
Delroy Cambridge	71	71	72	214	5,330.19
Carl Mason	74	70	71	215	3,919.33
Keith MacDonald	71	71	73	215	3,919.33
Malcolm Gregson	71	72	72	215	3,919.33
Bob Cameron	68	74	73	215	3,919.33
Gary Wintz	70	71	74	215	3,919.33
Steve Stull	74	71	70	215	3,919.33
Baldovino Dassu	70	76	70	216	3,079.18
Horacio Carbonetti	69	72	75	216	3,079.18
David Creamer	72	74	70	216	3,079.18
Guillermo Encina	73	74	70	217	2,557.91
John Mashego	67	78	72	217	2,557.91
John Grace	70	74	73	217	2,557.91
Barry Vivian	75	71	71	217	2,557.91
Dragon Taki	71	72	74	217	2,557.91

Daily Telegraph/Turismo Andaluz Seniors Match Play

Los Flamingos, Marbella, Spain
Par 36-36–72; 6,386 yards

September 17-20
purse, €142,054

FIRST ROUND

Denis Durnian defeated Mike Miller, 3 and 1.
Giuseppe Cali defeated Paul Leonard, 4 and 3.
Horacio Carbonetti defeated Russell Weir, 1 up.
David Oakley defeated Sebastian Bruna, 1 up.
Carl Mason defeated Martin Gray, 3 and 2.
Manuel Pinero defeated Priscillo Diniz, 6 and 5.
Ian Stanley defeated Baldovino Dassu, 2 and 1.
Noel Ratcliffe defeated Bob Cameron, 2 and 1.
Nick Job defeated Brian Jones, 3 and 2.
Keith MacDonald defeated Gary Wintz, 2 and 1.
Delroy Cambridge defeated Ian Mosey, 5 and 3.
Bill Longmuir defeated Steve Stull, 3 and 2.
John Chillas defeated David Creamer, 1 up.
Denis O'Sullivan defeated Eddie Polland, 2 and 1.
Dragon Taki defeated Hank Woodrome, 1 up.
Jim Rhodes defeated Jerry Bruner, 19 holes.

(Each losing player received €1,598.)

SECOND ROUND

Durnian defeated Cali, 4 and 2.
Oakley defeated Carbonetti, 3 and 1.
Mason defeated Pinero, 20 holes.
Ratcliffe defeated Stanley, 5 and 3.
MacDonald defeated Job, 1 up.
Cambridge defeated Longmuir, 3 and 1.

O'Sullivan defeated Chillas, 3 and 2.
Rhodes defeated Taki, 8 and 7.

(Each losing player received €3,551.)

QUARTER-FINALS

Durnian defeated Oakley, 5 and 4.
Mason defeated Ratcliffe, 3 and 2.
Cambridge defeated MacDonald, 1 up.
O'Sullivan defeated Rhodes, 3 and 2.

(Each losing player received €7,102.)

SEMI-FINALS

Mason defeated Durnian, 3 and 2.
O'Sullivan defeated Cambridge, 1 up.

(Each losing player received €10,654.)

FINALS

Mason defeated O'Sullivan, 1 up.

(Mason received €22,728; O'Sullivan received €15,625.)

Merseyside English Seniors Open

Hillside Golf Club, Southport, England
Par 36-36–72; 6,850 yards

September 26-28
purse, €215,692

	SCORES			TOTAL	MONEY
Carl Mason	71	66	71	208	€32,353.88
Bill Longmuir	71	69	69	209	18,333.86
Denis O'Sullivan	72	69	68	209	18,333.86
David Good	71	65	74	210	11,863.09
Denis Durnian	72	71	71	214	9,188.50
David Oakley	69	73	72	214	9,188.50
Giuseppe Cali	73	71	71	215	7,764.93
Manuel Pinero	75	70	71	216	5,931.54
Simon Owen	69	75	72	216	5,931.54
Brian Jones	73	72	71	216	5,931.54
Gary Wintz	74	69	73	216	5,931.54
Baldovino Dassu	73	72	72	217	4,141.30
Tommy Horton	74	75	68	217	4,141.30
Ian Mosey	78	67	72	217	4,141.30
John Chillas	72	71	74	217	4,141.30
Horacio Carbonetti	75	72	70	217	4,141.30
Martin Gray	75	69	74	218	2,798.61
Paul Leonard	72	71	75	218	2,798.61
Bob Cameron	75	70	73	218	2,798.61
John Mashego	79	67	72	218	2,798.61
Priscillo Diniz	76	71	71	218	2,798.61
John Benda	73	69	76	218	2,798.61
Robbie Stewart	73	73	72	218	2,798.61
Alan Mew	67	79	72	218	2,798.61
Neil Coles	77	72	70	219	1,923.26
Nick Job	76	70	73	219	1,923.26

	SCORES			TOTAL	MONEY
Noel Ratcliffe	74	72	73	219	1,923.26
Russell Weir	77	73	69	219	1,923.26
Manuel Velasco	78	73	68	219	1,923.26
John McTear	78	70	71	219	1,923.26

Tunisian Seniors Open

Port El Kantaoui Golf Club, Tunisia
Par 36-36–72; 6,384 yards

October 2-4
purse, €180,685

	SCORES			TOTAL	MONEY
David Good	66	68	64	198	€27,102.75
Guillermo Encina	71	67	65	203	18,068.50
Horacio Carbonetti	65	69	70	204	12,647.95
Jim Rhodes	69	71	65	205	9,052.32
Delroy Cambridge	69	68	68	205	9,052.32
Eamonn Darcy	69	72	66	207	5,854.19
Bob Larratt	69	67	71	207	5,854.19
Giuseppe Cali	68	67	72	207	5,854.19
Bob Lendzion	69	69	69	207	5,854.19
John Chillas	71	68	68	207	5,854.19
Denis Durnian	67	72	69	208	3,613.70
Terry Gale	71	70	67	208	3,613.70
Alberto Croce	68	69	71	208	3,613.70
Manuel Velasco	70	69	69	208	3,613.70
Jerry Bruner	67	73	68	208	3,613.70
John Mashego	70	69	69	208	3,613.70
Bill Longmuir	65	71	73	209	2,633.30
Noel Ratcliffe	70	69	70	209	2,633.30
Simon Owen	71	70	68	209	2,633.30
Priscillo Diniz	73	71	65	209	2,633.30
Baldovino Dassu	69	69	72	210	2,005.46
Martin Gray	68	72	70	210	2,005.46
Denis O'Sullivan	67	73	70	210	2,005.46
Jeff Van Wagenen	72	73	65	210	2,005.46
Neville Clarke	68	73	69	210	2,005.46
Nick Job	68	70	74	212	1,571.24
Gery Watine	73	68	71	212	1,571.24
Keith MacDonald	72	68	72	212	1,571.24
Eddie Polland	68	70	74	212	1,571.24
Brian Jones	71	73	68	212	1,571.24

Estoril Seniors Tour Championship

Oitavos Golf Club, Lisbon, Portugal
Par 36-35–71; 6,617 yards

October 10-12
purse, €240,000

	SCORES			TOTAL	MONEY
Carl Mason	64	73	65	202	€37,320
Noel Ratcliffe	69	73	68	210	18,658.33
Keith MacDonald	69	70	71	210	18,658.33
Dragon Taki	74	69	67	210	18,658.33
Ian Mosey	70	72	69	211	10,597.50
Terry Gale	68	71	72	211	10,597.50
Nick Job	70	71	71	212	8,461

	SCORES			TOTAL	MONEY
Liam Higgins	75	66	71	212	8,461
Giuseppe Cali	71	72	70	213	6,221.50
Denis O'Sullivan	72	70	71	213	6,221.50
John Irwin	71	70	72	213	6,221.50
Delroy Cambridge	71	74	68	213	6,221.50
Guillermo Encina	69	74	71	214	4,355.17
Manuel Velasco	70	75	69	214	4,355.17
Jerry Bruner	72	76	66	214	4,355.17
Priscillo Diniz	74	72	68	214	4,355.17
David Creamer	72	72	70	214	4,355.17
Steve Stull	67	74	73	214	4,355.17
Maurice Bembridge	72	71	72	215	3,101
John Morgan	71	71	73	215	3,101
Russell Weir	73	73	69	215	3,101
Horacio Carbonetti	70	74	71	215	3,101
John Mashego	69	71	75	215	3,101
Mike Miller	71	73	72	216	2,551
David Oakley	73	75	68	216	2,551
Baldovino Dassu	70	76	71	217	2,069.29
Sam Torrance	76	71	70	217	2,069.29
Malcolm Gregson	73	74	70	217	2,069.29
John Chillas	71	73	73	217	2,069.29
Bob Cameron	79	69	69	217	2,069.29
David Good	74	74	69	217	2,069.29
Alan Mew	74	73	70	217	2,069.29

Japan Senior Tour

Castle Hill Open

Castle Hill County Club, Hoi-gun, Aichi
Par 36-36–72; 6,730 yards

May 23-25
purse, ¥30,000,000

	SCORES			TOTAL	MONEY
Chen Tze-ming	73	66	75	214	¥5,400,000
Toshiharu Morimoto	66	76	73	215	2,700,000
Yoshitaka Yamamoto	75	70	71	216	1,800,000
Yurio Akitomi	72	74	71	217	1,275,000
Katsunari Takahashi	70	72	75	217	1,275,000
Mitsuo Iwata	71	73	74	218	975,000
*M. Siodina	71	72	75	218	
Kinpachi Yoshimura	72	75	72	219	720,000
Yukio Noguchi	74	70	75	219	720,000
Fujio Kobayashi	71	76	73	220	615,000
Kikuo Arai	73	74	73	220	615,000
Minoru Hatsumi	74	73	74	221	525,000

	SCORES			TOTAL	MONEY
Katsuji Hasegawa	75	72	74	221	525,000
Motomasa Aoki	75	71	75	221	525,000
Mikio Ichikawa	75	71	75	221	525,000
Kenichi Tsurumoto	73	77	72	222	393,000
Mitoshi Tomita	73	75	74	222	393,000
Seiichi Kanai	74	73	75	222	393,000
Shuichi Sano	74	72	76	222	393,000
Yasuzo Hagiwara	73	72	77	222	393,000
*Tetsuo Sakata	75	69	78	222	
Hsieh Min-nan	79	69	75	223	300,000
Yoshinari Shikota	76	73	74	223	300,000
*Motohide Yanagi	74	74	75	223	
Noboru Sugai	71	76	76	223	300,000
*Eiji Matsumoto	72	75	76	223	
Norihiko Matsumoto	72	74	77	223	300,000
Takashi Miyoshi	71	74	78	223	300,000
Kenjiro Iwama	74	75	75	224	237,000
Teruo Suzumura	72	76	76	224	237,000
Tadami Ueno	75	72	77	224	237,000
Teruo Nakamura	74	71	79	224	237,000
Toyokake Nakao	74	71	79	224	237,000

Aderans Wellness Open

Nakajo Golf Club, Nakajo, Niigata
Par 36-36–72; 6,876 yards

June 13-15
purse, ¥60,000,000

	SCORES			TOTAL	MONEY
Takashi Miyoshi	70	68	72	210	¥12,000,000
Kinpachi Yoshimura	74	65	71	210	6,000,000
(Miyoshi defeated Yoshimura in playoff.)					
Seiji Ebihara	77	66	68	211	3,300,000
Terry Gale	72	71	68	211	3,300,000
Katsuji Hasegawa	72	70	70	212	2,100,000
Kenjiro Iwama	76	67	70	213	1,376,000
Yoshitaka Yamamoto	71	74	68	213	1,376,000
Toru Nakamura	71	73	69	213	1,376,000
Motomasa Aoki	71	73	69	213	1,376,000
Takaaki Fukuzawa	72	70	71	213	1,376,000
Kouichi Uehara	70	70	73	213	1,376,000
Toyokake Nakao	74	71	69	214	1,050,000
Katsunari Takahashi	70	74	70	214	1,050,000
Toshiharu Morimoto	70	74	71	215	825,000
Seiichi Kanai	72	72	71	215	825,000
Yurio Akitomi	72	72	71	215	825,000
Teruo Nakamura	71	73	71	215	825,000
Mitsuo Iwata	73	70	72	215	825,000
Mikio Ichikawa	66	73	76	215	825,000
Koji Okuno	70	73	73	216	675,000
Kikuo Arai	71	72	73	216	675,000
Eitaro Deguchi	72	75	70	217	570,000
Toshiki Matsui	71	72	74	217	570,000
Masaru Amano	73	70	74	217	570,000
Haruo Yasuda	72	71	74	217	570,000
Takeshi Shibata	74	68	75	217	570,000
Namio Takasu	77	70	71	218	455,000
Kazuo Kanayama	73	71	74	218	455,000

	SCORES			TOTAL	MONEY
Tadami Ueno	73	71	74	218	455,000
Tadao Nakamura	70	71	78	219	397,500
Yasunori Uehara	72	75	72	219	397,500
Shinsaku Maeda	70	76	73	219	397,500
Hiroshi Ishii	74	72	73	219	397,500

Fancl Senior Classic

Susono Country Club, Shizuoka
Par 36-36–72; 6,851 yards

August 22-24
purse, ¥60,000,000

	SCORES			TOTAL	MONEY
Katsunari Takahashi	71	68	71	210	¥15,000,000
Takashi Miyoshi	70	69	72	211	6,900,000
Kenjiro Iwama	72	69	72	213	3,600,000
Toru Nakamura	74	69	71	214	2,400,000
Teruo Nakamura	71	70	74	215	2,100,000
Koji Okuno	70	76	70	216	1,860,000
Fumio Tanaka	71	74	72	217	1,515,000
Chen Tze-ming	76	72	69	217	1,515,000
Seiichi Kanai	68	77	73	218	1,020,857
Shigeru Kawamata	71	73	74	218	1,020,857
Katsuji Hasegawa	72	71	75	218	1,020,857
Mitsunobu Hatsumi	72	73	73	218	1,020,857
Takaaki Fukuzawa	72	70	76	218	1,020,857
Yoshitaka Yamamoto	76	71	71	218	1,020,857
Tadao Furuichi	71	75	72	218	1,020,857
Masaru Amano	73	72	74	219	672,000
Yasunori Uehara	73	76	70	219	672,000
Seiji Ebihara	72	78	69	219	672,000
Tokio Kaneko	73	71	75	219	672,000
Fujio Kobayashi	74	73	72	219	672,000
Eitaro Deguchi	72	74	73	219	672,000
Toru Kurihara	72	70	78	220	516,000
Haruo Yasuda	74	76	70	220	516,000
Kazuo Kanayama	73	75	72	220	516,000
Yasuo Sone	73	74	73	220	516,000
Kunio Yamashita	75	75	70	220	516,000
Toshihiko Ohtsuka	71	76	74	221	406,000
Sadao Sakashita	72	75	74	221	406,000
Hsieh Min-nan	70	75	76	221	406,000
Noboru Sugai	74	73	74	221	406,000
Yurio Akitomi	73	75	73	221	406,000
Toyokake Nakao	74	75	72	221	406,000

Japan PGA Senior Championship

Yamada Golf Club, Chiba
Par 36-36–72; 6,820 yards

October 1-4
purse, ¥30,000,000

	SCORES				TOTAL	MONEY
Noboru Fujiike	69	71	70	68	278	¥5,400,000
Katsunari Takahashi	68	71	69	72	280	2,700,000
Yoshitaka Yamamoto	71	70	70	72	283	1,800,000
Seiji Ebihara	70	73	70	71	284	1,275,000

	SCORES				TOTAL	MONEY
Toru Nakamura	69	72	70	73	284	1,275,000
Takaaki Fukuzawa	70	74	71	70	285	975,000
Tadao Furuichi	68	76	70	71	285	975,000
Takashi Miyoshi	75	72	70	69	286	720,000
Seiji Ono	70	70	69	77	286	720,000
Hsieh Min-nan	71	72	74	70	287	577,500
Chen Tze-ming	76	70	71	70	287	577,500
Junji Hashizoe	73	70	70	74	287	577,500
Shoichi Sato	74	64	73	76	287	577,500
Kikuo Arai	72	71	72	73	288	435,000
Renkyoku Sugiyama	71	73	71	73	288	435,000
Kiyoshi Hinata	70	76	69	73	288	435,000
Seiji Ogawa	72	70	72	74	288	435,000
Toyotake Nakao	72	73	72	72	289	318,000
Katsumi Nanjo	76	69	71	73	289	318,000
Koichi Uehara	70	73	72	74	289	318,000
Tadami Ueno	71	72	70	76	289	318,000
Kazuo Kanayama	72	74	72	72	290	234,375
Toshihiko Kikuichi	73	74	75	68	290	234,375
Reiji Bando	75	69	72	74	290	234,375
Fujio Kobayashi	73	70	73	74	290	234,375
Shuichi Sano	71	74	71	74	290	234,375
Shinsaku Maeda	67	75	73	75	290	234,375
Koji Okuno	70	75	70	75	290	234,375
Kinpachi Yoshimura	71	72	70	77	290	234,375
Minoru Hatsumi	72	75	71	73	291	195,000
Masaru Amano	70	73	74	74	291	195,000
Mitoshi Tomita	71	76	74	70	291	195,000
Norihiko Matsumoto	73	72	76	70	291	195,000

PGA Philanthropy Biglayzac Senior

Biglayzac Country Club, Miyagi
Par 36-36–72; 6,826 yards

October 16-19
purse, ¥30,000,000

	SCORES				TOTAL	MONEY
Katsunari Takahashi	71	69	71	72	283	¥5,400,000
Hisao Inoue	73	70	69	74	286	2,700,000
Tadami Ueno	72	74	71	70	287	1,350,000
Seiji Ebihara	74	72	70	71	287	1,350,000
Yasuzo Hagiwara	73	71	69	74	287	1,350,000
Takanori Sekura	68	75	67	77	287	1,350,000
Chen Tze-ming	77	68	74	70	289	690,000
Yoshitaka Yamamoto	74	70	74	71	289	690,000
Mike Ferguson	71	75	73	70	289	690,000
Koji Nakajima	68	74	73	74	289	690,000
Toyotake Nakao	67	73	74	75	289	690,000
Kunio Yamashita	71	73	69	76	289	690,000
Teruo Nakamura	74	70	71	75	290	495,000
Tadao Furuichi	70	73	71	76	290	495,000
Toshihiko Ohtsuka	73	74	72	72	291	390,000
Toshiharu Morimoto	76	71	71	73	291	390,000
Terry Gale	73	72	71	75	291	390,000
Mitsuo Iwata	72	73	71	75	291	390,000
Toru Nakamura	75	70	71	75	291	390,000
Katsuji Hasegawa	69	74	76	73	292	269,400
Takaaki Fukuzawa	74	75	70	73	292	269,400

	SCORES				TOTAL	MONEY
Kaoru Aoyama	71	74	73	74	292	269,400
Junji Hashizoe	72	73	72	75	292	269,400
Tatsuo Fujima	68	74	71	79	292	269,400
Koji Okuno	74	74	68	77	293	234,000
Yasunori Uehara	74	75	72	73	294	225,000
Masaru Amano	73	72	71	78	294	225,000
Hisashi Nakase	72	76	75	72	295	213,000
Hiroshi Ishii	73	73	72	77	295	213,000
Toshihiko Kikuichi	75	73	73	75	296	198,000
Akira Yabe	73	74	75	74	296	198,000
Fujio Kobayashi	75	71	72	78	296	198,000

Japan Senior Open Championship

Takarazuka Golf Club, Hyogo
Par 36-35–71; 6,630 yards

October 23-26
purse, ¥50,000,000

	SCORES				TOTAL	MONEY
Katsunari Takahashi	72	70	68	67	277	¥10,000,000
Toru Nakamura	71	68	68	71	278	5,500,000
Takeru Shibata	73	69	72	67	281	3,875,000
Seiji Ebihara	69	72	74	67	282	2,325,000
Chen Tze-ming	72	71	69	70	282	2,325,000
Yoshitaka Yamamoto	70	66	73	74	283	1,700,000
Shuichi Sano	72	72	71	69	284	1,287,666
Kazuo Kanayama	73	69	70	72	284	1,287,666
Yurio Akitomi	72	68	70	74	284	1,287,666
Hiroshi Oku	73	71	73	68	285	990,000
Fujio Kobayashi	73	75	70	68	286	750,000
Akira Yabe	73	70	73	70	286	750,000
Motomasa Aoki	72	71	72	71	286	750,000
Eitaro Deguchi	72	70	72	72	286	750,000
Takao Shikage	72	73	72	71	288	597,500
Terry Gale	75	72	70	71	288	597,500
Junji Hashizoe	71	74	77	67	289	535,000
Kenji Togame	69	78	71	71	289	535,000
Yukio Noguchi	66	75	75	73	289	535,000
Koji Nakajima	73	73	72	72	290	485,000
Masaru Amano	76	72	73	70	291	467,500
Mitsuo Iwata	75	71	72	73	291	467,500
*Risaku Hikichi	70	72	71	78	291	
Hiroshi Ishii	74	70	77	71	292	438,000
Takayoshi Nishikawa	77	69	75	71	292	438,000
Toshiharu Morimoto	76	71	72	73	292	438,000
Hisao Inoue	71	75	72	74	292	438,000
Haruo Yasuda	72	75	69	77	293	415,000
Tadao Furuichi	74	74	73	73	294	400,000
Shoichi Kanai	72	74	72	76	294	400,000

Women's Tours

Welch's/Fry's Championship

Randolph Park, Dell Urich Course, Tucson, Arizona
Par 35-35–70; 6,176 yards

March 13-16
purse, $800,000

	SCORES				TOTAL	MONEY
Wendy Doolan	65	62	67	65	259	$120,000
Betsy King	67	65	65	65	262	62,592
Lorie Kane	61	66	65	70	262	62,592
Grace Park	65	63	68	67	263	36,744
Christina Kim	64	67	62	70	263	36,744
Meg Mallon	64	60	70	70	264	26,814
A.J. Eathorne	62	67	69	68	266	21,054
Brandie Burton	66	64	66	70	266	21,054
Karrie Webb	68	66	66	67	267	16,882
Young Kim	63	64	69	71	267	16,882
Juli Inkster	68	62	72	66	268	14,400
Yu Ping Lin	69	64	64	71	268	14,400
Dorothy Delasin	70	65	67	67	269	12,261
Cristie Kerr	68	65	69	67	269	12,261
Laura Davies	65	64	70	70	269	12,261
Stephanie Louden	68	67	71	64	270	9,745
Mi-Hyun Kim	69	67	65	69	270	9,745
Gloria Park	67	67	65	71	270	9,745
Lorena Ochoa	67	66	66	71	270	9,745
Heather Bowie	65	67	67	71	270	9,745
Pat Hurst	63	69	67	71	270	9,745
Karen Stupples	66	66	74	65	271	7,746
Jackie Gallagher-Smith	68	66	70	67	271	7,746
Becky Morgan	68	65	69	69	271	7,746
Deb Richard	64	67	69	71	271	7,746
Jung Yeon Lee	66	67	66	72	271	7,746
Maria Hjorth	67	65	67	72	271	7,746
Patricia Meunier-Lebouc	66	66	69	71	272	6,614
Natalie Gulbis	69	68	63	72	272	6,614
Danielle Ammaccapane	67	68	69	69	273	5,327
Hiromi Kobayashi	66	68	70	69	273	5,327
Candie Kung	68	68	66	71	273	5,327
Ara Koh	68	66	68	71	273	5,327
Akiko Fukushima	65	67	69	72	273	5,327
Soo-Yun Kang	65	66	70	72	273	5,327
Leslie Spalding	71	64	65	73	273	5,327
Hee-Won Han	66	67	67	73	273	5,327
Beth Bauer	71	66	62	74	273	5,327

Safeway Ping

Moon Valley Country Club, Phoenix, Arizona
Par 36-36–72; 6,473 yards

March 20-23
purse, $1,000,000

	SCORES				TOTAL	MONEY
Se Ri Pak	65	68	68	64	265	$150,000
Grace Park	67	67	67	65	266	90,488

	SCORES				TOTAL	MONEY
Hee-Won Han	68	69	66	66	269	52,432
Patricia Meunier-Lebouc	67	66	67	69	269	52,432
Annika Sorenstam	67	66	65	71	269	52,432
Lorena Ochoa	71	70	64	66	271	33,441
Beth Daniel	70	69	65	68	272	27,992
Dorothy Delasin	67	69	69	68	273	24,524
Michele Redman	72	70	68	64	274	21,055
Cristie Kerr	72	65	71	66	274	21,055
Stacy Prammanasudh	71	73	66	65	275	16,857
Kelly Robbins	74	64	70	67	275	16,857
Mi-Hyun Kim	72	68	67	68	275	16,857
Laura Davies	69	66	70	70	275	16,857
Rosie Jones	72	68	68	68	276	13,607
Catriona Matthew	69	70	66	71	276	13,607
Karrie Webb	66	67	68	75	276	13,607
Barb Mucha	72	69	70	66	277	12,038
Liselotte Neumann	72	69	69	67	277	12,038
Kate Golden	72	72	67	67	278	10,412
Miriam Nagl	72	68	70	68	278	10,412
Kris Tschetter	68	71	71	68	278	10,412
Heather Bowie	71	70	67	70	278	10,412
Angela Stanford	68	68	71	71	278	10,412
Laura Diaz	72	68	66	72	278	10,412
Gloria Park	74	66	71	68	279	8,769
Stephanie Louden	71	68	70	70	279	8,769
Suzann Pettersen	70	70	68	71	279	8,769
Shani Waugh	71	70	72	67	280	7,191
Brandie Burton	71	72	68	69	280	7,191
Michelle Ellis	72	69	69	70	280	7,191
Sophie Gustafson	70	70	70	70	280	7,191
Joanne Mills	68	71	71	70	280	7,191
Janice Moodie	72	68	69	71	280	7,191
Sherri Turner	68	68	70	74	280	7,191

Kraft Nabisco Championship

Mission Hills Country Club, Rancho Mirage, California
Par 36-36–72; 6,520 yards

March 27-30
purse, $1,600,000

	SCORES				TOTAL	MONEY
Patricia Meunier-Lebouc	70	68	70	73	281	$240,000
Annika Sorenstam	68	72	71	71	282	146,120
Lorena Ochoa	71	70	74	68	283	106,000
Laura Davies	70	75	69	70	284	82,000
Beth Daniel	75	74	68	70	287	51,200
Catriona Matthew	71	74	72	70	287	51,200
Maria Hjorth	72	72	73	70	287	51,200
Laura Diaz	76	71	69	71	287	51,200
Jennifer Rosales	74	70	72	72	288	35,600
*Michelle Wie	72	74	66	76	288	
Cristie Kerr	74	71	74	71	290	29,160
Rosie Jones	71	75	72	72	290	29,160
Woo-Soon Ko	74	73	70	73	290	29,160
Juli Inkster	75	74	66	75	290	29,160
Catrin Nilsmark	71	78	73	69	291	22,080
Dawn Coe-Jones	72	74	72	73	291	22,080
Dorothy Delasin	71	71	76	73	291	22,080

	SCORES				TOTAL	MONEY
Karen Stupples	71	71	76	73	291	22,080
Se Ri Pak	71	72	71	77	291	22,080
Hee-Won Han	73	74	75	70	292	19,040
Jeong Jang	75	73	76	69	293	17,440
*Aree Song Wongluekiet	72	77	73	71	293	
Danielle Ammaccapane	75	68	78	72	293	17,440
Karrie Webb	70	79	71	73	293	17,440
*Virada Nirapathpongporn	76	72	72	73	293	
Michele Redman	70	72	76	75	293	17,440
Leta Lindley	76	70	75	73	294	15,840
Candie Kung	74	75	74	72	295	14,160
Tammie Green	77	71	73	74	295	14,160
Betsy King	75	74	70	76	295	14,160
Christina Kim	72	76	71	76	295	14,160
Charlotta Sorenstam	73	74	71	77	295	14,160

The Office Depot

El Caballero Country Club, Tarzana, California
Par 36-36–72; 6,394 yards

April 4-6
purse, $1,500,000

	SCORES			TOTAL	MONEY
Annika Sorenstam	68	72	71	211	$225,000
Se Ri Pak	73	71	71	215	104,917
Pat Hurst	75	68	72	215	104,917
Heather Bowie	72	70	73	215	104,917
Michele Redman	76	70	70	216	62,174
Sophie Gustafson	75	72	70	217	46,725
Jeong Jang	75	72	70	217	46,725
Cindy Figg-Currier	70	75	73	218	35,420
Mi-Hyun Kim	74	69	75	218	35,420
Laura Davies	76	74	69	219	28,387
Marisa Baena	74	72	73	219	28,387
Lorie Kane	72	73	74	219	28,387
Jean Bartholomew	77	74	69	220	20,951
Brandie Burton	74	75	71	220	20,951
Catriona Matthew	74	73	73	220	20,951
Jane Crafter	73	74	73	220	20,951
Namika Omata	73	74	73	220	20,951
Beth Daniel	73	71	76	220	20,951
Alison Nicholas	71	72	77	220	20,951
Michelle Ellis	74	77	70	221	16,128
Tracy Hanson	73	77	71	221	16,128
Juli Inkster	73	76	72	221	16,128
Natalie Gulbis	72	76	73	221	16,128
Gloria Park	73	73	75	221	16,128
Young Kim	79	72	71	222	13,339
Grace Park	78	71	73	222	13,339
Christina Kim	76	73	73	222	13,339
Joanne Mills	73	76	73	222	13,339
Kim Williams	74	74	74	222	13,339
Betsy King	75	76	72	223	10,928
Danielle Ammaccapane	72	77	74	223	10,928
Karen Stupples	73	75	75	223	10,928
Dorothy Delasin	73	74	76	223	10,928
Tina Barrett	72	75	76	223	10,928

Takefuji Classic

Las Vegas Country Club, Las Vegas, Nevada
Par 36-36–72; 6,494 yards

April 17-19
purse, $1,100,000

	SCORES			TOTAL	MONEY
Candie Kung	67	67	70	204	$165,000
Annika Sorenstam	72	67	67	206	77,129
Soo-Yun Kang	69	70	67	206	77,129
Cristie Kerr	67	68	71	206	77,129
Hee-Won Han	72	68	67	207	45,707
Akiko Fukushima	69	70	69	208	32,041
Se Ri Pak	69	70	69	208	32,041
Catriona Matthew	66	68	74	208	32,041
Jennifer Rosales	70	71	68	209	22,623
Michele Redman	74	65	70	209	22,623
Kim Saiki	67	70	72	209	22,623
Angela Stanford	71	71	68	210	18,209
Amy Fruhwirth	72	68	70	210	18,209
Kelli Kuehne	68	72	70	210	18,209
Sophie Gustafson	74	70	67	211	14,220
Pat Hurst	73	67	71	211	14,220
Danielle Ammaccapane	72	68	71	211	14,220
Tammie Green	72	68	71	211	14,220
Karen Weiss	71	69	71	211	14,220
Laura Diaz	66	71	74	211	14,220
Vicki Goetze-Ackerman	69	75	68	212	11,424
Karrie Webb	73	69	70	212	11,424
Jackie Gallagher-Smith	69	73	70	212	11,424
Rosie Jones	69	72	71	212	11,424
Kate Golden	70	69	73	212	11,424
Nanci Bowen	71	73	69	213	9,612
Dorothy Delasin	74	69	70	213	9,612
Rachel Teske	71	70	72	213	9,612
Liselotte Neumann	70	71	72	213	9,612
Eva Dahllof	74	72	68	214	7,430
Christina Kim	72	73	69	214	7,430
Marnie McGuire	72	73	69	214	7,430
Diana D'Alessio	74	69	71	214	7,430
Heather Bowie	75	67	72	214	7,430
Tina Barrett	72	70	72	214	7,430
Jane Crafter	71	70	73	214	7,430
Hiromi Kobayashi	70	71	73	214	7,430
Janice Moodie	71	69	74	214	7,430

Chick-fil-A Charity Championship

Eagle's Landing Country Club, Stockbridge, Georgia
Par 36-36–72; 6,368 yards

April 25-27
purse, $1,350,000

	SCORES			TOTAL	MONEY
Se Ri Pak	71	65	64	200	$202,500
Shani Waugh	69	66	65	200	123,000
(Pak defeated Waugh on fourth playoff hole.)					
Suzann Pettersen	69	68	67	204	89,228
Meg Mallon	68	71	66	205	69,026
Sophie Gustafson	66	74	66	206	50,506
Pat Hurst	72	66	68	206	50,506

	SCORES			TOTAL	MONEY
Barb Mucha	70	70	67	207	33,783
Becky Morgan	70	69	68	207	33,783
Karrie Webb	67	66	74	207	33,783
Grace Park	67	72	69	208	26,264
Vicki Goetze-Ackerman	68	70	70	208	26,264
Patricia Meunier-Lebouc	69	71	69	209	20,876
Natalie Gulbis	73	66	70	209	20,876
Donna Andrews	72	67	70	209	20,876
Beth Daniel	72	65	72	209	20,876
Mi-Hyun Kim	69	68	72	209	20,876
Lorena Ochoa	70	74	66	210	15,848
Yu Ping Lin	73	69	68	210	15,848
Helen Alfredsson	73	67	70	210	15,848
Karen Stupples	70	70	70	210	15,848
Catrin Nilsmark	69	70	71	210	15,848
Christina Kim	70	67	73	210	15,848
Angela Jerman	71	73	67	211	12,876
Michelle Ellis	71	71	69	211	12,876
Soo Young Kim	72	69	70	211	12,876
Jan Stephenson	69	72	70	211	12,876
Denise Killeen	68	70	73	211	12,876
Siew-Ai Lim	71	73	68	212	10,586
Kelli Kuehne	70	74	68	212	10,586
Laura Diaz	73	68	71	212	10,586
Tina Barrett	71	69	72	212	10,586
Soo-Yun Kang	66	71	75	212	10,586

Michelob Light Open

Kingsmill River Course, Williamsburg, Virginia
Par 36-35–71; 6,285 yards

May 1-4
purse, $1,600,000

	SCORES				TOTAL	MONEY
Grace Park	67	68	69	71	275	$240,000
Karrie Webb	70	71	68	67	276	110,601
Lorena Ochoa	66	69	72	69	276	110,601
Cristie Kerr	69	68	68	71	276	110,601
Mi-Hyun Kim	69	69	71	68	277	65,542
Annika Sorenstam	68	70	70	70	278	53,625
Jennifer Rosales	69	69	72	69	279	44,886
Juli Inkster	73	69	69	69	280	34,161
Se Ri Pak	69	69	70	72	280	34,161
Patricia Meunier-Lebouc	69	68	71	72	280	34,161
Hee-Won Han	67	72	68	73	280	34,161
Akiko Fukushima	68	68	74	71	281	26,110
Laura Davies	72	69	68	72	281	26,110
Meg Mallon	70	69	70	72	281	26,110
Sophie Gustafson	74	68	71	69	282	22,403
Suzann Pettersen	68	68	71	75	282	22,403
Dorothy Delasin	72	68	73	70	283	19,755
Danielle Ammaccapane	70	71	71	71	283	19,755
Lorie Kane	72	67	73	71	283	19,755
Becky Morgan	70	73	76	65	284	17,001
Rosie Jones	72	71	73	68	284	17,001
Rachel Teske	73	71	70	70	284	17,001
Catriona Matthew	74	69	71	70	284	17,001
Wendy Doolan	73	68	69	74	284	17,001
Jung Yeon Lee	71	68	72	74	285	14,896

	SCORES				TOTAL	MONEY
Natalie Gulbis	69	70	72	74	285	14,896
Moira Dunn	75	67	75	69	286	13,247
Tracy Hanson	73	71	71	71	286	13,247
Denise Killeen	66	76	73	71	286	13,247
Karen Stupples	68	70	76	72	286	13,247

Asahi Ryokuken International

Mount Vintage Plantation, North Augusta, South Carolina
Par 36-36–72; 6,426 yards

May 8-11
purse, $1,300,000

	SCORES				TOTAL	MONEY
Rosie Jones	66	68	69	70	273	$195,000
Wendy Ward	68	67	71	70	276	118,443
Patricia Meunier-Lebouc	70	74	67	67	278	68,630
Lorena Ochoa	68	71	69	70	278	68,630
Laura Diaz	68	68	69	73	278	68,630
Wendy Doolan	70	71	69	69	279	43,772
Danielle Ammaccapane	71	73	70	66	280	34,369
Karen Stupples	72	70	72	66	280	34,369
Dorothy Delasin	69	72	71	69	281	27,560
Hee-Won Han	70	68	73	70	281	27,560
Cristie Kerr	71	73	70	68	282	22,761
Catrin Nilsmark	71	74	68	69	282	22,761
Candie Kung	71	71	69	71	282	22,761
Gloria Park	71	73	73	66	283	17,120
Se Ri Pak	73	69	72	69	283	17,120
Moira Dunn	70	74	69	70	283	17,120
Catriona Matthew	69	73	71	70	283	17,120
Sophie Gustafson	66	73	74	70	283	17,120
Dottie Pepper	70	71	71	71	283	17,120
Pat Hurst	67	69	71	76	283	17,120
Mhairi McKay	75	72	67	70	284	13,877
Kim Saiki	74	73	67	70	284	13,877
Grace Park	73	71	70	70	284	13,877
Diane Irvin	74	72	70	69	285	12,159
Young Kim	74	70	72	69	285	12,159
Shani Waugh	73	73	69	70	285	12,159
Vicki Goetze-Ackerman	72	70	69	74	285	12,159
Meg Mallon	71	74	74	67	286	9,997
Mi-Hyun Kim	74	68	74	70	286	9,997
Karen Weiss	72	73	70	71	286	9,997
Soo-Yun Kang	72	71	71	72	286	9,997
Kelli Kuehne	71	71	70	74	286	9,997
Giulia Sergas	68	70	72	76	286	9,997

Corning Classic

Corning Country Club, Corning, New York
Par 36-36–72; 6,062 yards

May 22-25
purse, $1,000,000

	SCORES				TOTAL	MONEY
Juli Inkster	68	66	68	62	264	$150,000
Lorie Kane	67	65	69	67	268	90,090
Catriona Matthew	68	64	67	70	269	65,354

	SCORES				TOTAL	MONEY
Beth Daniel	69	66	67	68	270	45,625
Meg Mallon	67	66	69	68	270	45,625
Anna Acker-Macosko	71	65	70	66	272	28,527
Rosie Jones	66	70	69	67	272	28,527
Soo-Yun Kang	72	64	68	68	272	28,527
Karrie Webb	71	67	70	65	273	20,963
Wendy Ward	70	66	68	69	273	20,963
Nancy Harvey	71	66	69	68	274	17,881
Helen Alfredsson	66	68	69	71	274	17,881
Christina Kim	70	69	70	66	275	15,685
Karen Stupples	64	70	72	69	275	15,685
Laura Diaz	72	70	71	63	276	12,415
Cristie Kerr	70	68	72	66	276	12,415
Shani Waugh	68	71	69	68	276	12,415
Cindy Schreyer	69	69	69	69	276	12,415
Patricia Meunier-Lebouc	69	67	71	69	276	12,415
Danielle Ammaccapane	69	68	69	70	276	12,415
Natalie Gulbis	67	70	69	70	276	12,415
Michele Redman	66	73	73	65	277	10,359
Moira Dunn	71	68	72	66	277	10,359
Marilyn Lovander	68	70	71	69	278	9,767
Donna Andrews	74	66	72	67	279	8,249
Rachel Teske	75	66	70	68	279	8,249
Maria Hjorth	69	71	71	68	279	8,249
Becky Morgan	71	68	72	68	279	8,249
Eva Dahllof	68	69	74	68	279	8,249
Yu Ping Lin	69	70	71	69	279	8,249
Kris Tschetter	69	70	71	69	279	8,249
Mi-Hyun Kim	67	69	74	69	279	8,249

Kellogg-Keebler Classic

Stonebridge Country Club, Aurora, Illinois
Par 36-36–72; 6,413 yards

May 30-June 1
purse, $1,200,000

	SCORES			TOTAL	MONEY
Annika Sorenstam	62	66	71	199	$180,000
Mhairi McKay	66	64	72	202	109,590
Mi-Hyun Kim	66	71	67	204	70,500
Becky Morgan	67	69	68	204	70,500
Catriona Matthew	69	69	67	205	45,000
Rosie Jones	62	71	72	205	45,000
Hee-Won Han	69	70	67	206	31,800
Angela Stanford	65	71	70	206	31,800
Karrie Webb	72	69	66	207	24,500
Heather Bowie	67	71	69	207	24,500
Juli Inkster	68	67	72	207	24,500
Christina Kim	68	70	70	208	21,000
Sophie Gustafson	72	68	69	209	18,000
Vicki Goetze-Ackerman	70	70	69	209	18,000
Donna Andrews	68	72	69	209	18,000
Natalie Gulbis	72	67	70	209	18,000
Danielle Ammaccapane	68	72	70	210	15,240
Kate Golden	70	69	71	210	15,240
Anna Acker-Macosko	73	70	68	211	13,080
Laura Diaz	70	71	70	211	13,080
Suzanne Strudwick	71	69	71	211	13,080

	SCORES			TOTAL	MONEY
Kelly Robbins	70	70	71	211	13,080
Lorena Ochoa	69	71	71	211	13,080
Tracy Hanson	70	68	73	211	13,080
Gloria Park	72	72	68	212	10,420
Wendy Ward	68	75	69	212	10,420
Laurie Rinker-Graham	69	73	70	212	10,420
Beth Bader	70	71	71	212	10,420
Kelli Kuehne	71	69	72	212	10,420
Laura Davies	68	71	73	212	10,420

McDonald's LPGA Championship

DuPont Country Club, Wilmington, Delaware
Par 35-36–71; 6,408 yards

June 5-8
purse, $1,600,000

	SCORES				TOTAL	MONEY
Annika Sorenstam	70	64	72	72	278	$240,000
Grace Park	69	72	70	67	278	147,934
(Sorenstam defeated Park on first playoff hole.)						
Rosie Jones	73	68	72	71	284	85,718
Rachel Teske	69	70	74	71	284	85,718
Beth Daniel	71	71	70	72	284	85,718
Young-A Yang	73	74	69	69	285	41,873
Joanne Mills	68	73	75	69	285	41,873
Young Kim	70	73	72	70	285	41,873
Becky Morgan	73	70	70	72	285	41,873
Kate Golden	72	70	68	75	285	41,873
Patricia Meunier-Lebouc	75	69	72	70	286	24,037
Jennifer Rosales	74	68	74	70	286	24,037
Suzann Pettersen	70	71	75	70	286	24,037
Angela Jerman	73	72	69	72	286	24,037
Jeong Jang	72	73	69	72	286	24,037
Akiko Fukushima	72	68	74	72	286	24,037
Michele Redman	74	70	69	73	286	24,037
Wendy Ward	68	69	75	74	286	24,037
Hee-Won Han	67	69	74	76	286	24,037
Natalie Gulbis	71	69	78	69	287	16,719
Karen Stupples	73	73	71	70	287	16,719
Tina Barrett	76	69	71	71	287	16,719
Lorena Ochoa	72	72	71	72	287	16,719
Michelle Ellis	73	70	71	73	287	16,719
Donna Andrews	73	70	70	74	287	16,719
Kelli Kuehne	73	73	65	76	287	16,719
Danielle Ammaccapane	74	72	74	68	288	13,769
Angela Stanford	72	73	71	72	288	13,769
Meg Mallon	74	69	70	75	288	13,769
Deb Richard	75	71	74	69	289	11,987
Tracy Hanson	71	77	70	71	289	11,987
Laura Diaz	73	70	75	71	289	11,987
Mi-Hyun Kim	72	72	71	74	289	11,987

Giant Eagle Classic

Squaw Creek Country Club, Vienna, Ohio
Par 37-35–72; 6,446 yards

June 13-15
purse, $1,000,000

	SCORES			TOTAL	MONEY
Rachel Teske	70	65	69	204	$150,000
Lorie Kane	70	71	63	204	69,945
Jennifer Rosales	72	64	68	204	69,945
Annika Sorenstam	71	65	68	204	69,945
(Teske won on third playoff hole.)					
Beth Bauer	71	70	65	206	34,583
Catrin Nilsmark	69	71	66	206	34,583
Se Ri Pak	72	66	68	206	34,583
Meg Mallon	74	69	64	207	22,525
Amy Fruhwirth	70	73	64	207	22,525
Jeong Jang	71	70	66	207	22,525
Grace Park	71	71	66	208	18,841
Loraine Lambert	73	69	67	209	15,575
Candie Kung	71	71	67	209	15,575
Michele Redman	70	71	68	209	15,575
Joanne Mills	70	66	73	209	15,575
Jean Bartholomew	71	64	74	209	15,575
Jenny Lidback	71	70	69	210	12,259
Dottie Pepper	70	70	70	210	12,259
Marisa Baena	69	71	70	210	12,259
Pat Hurst	69	69	72	210	12,259
Dorothy Delasin	73	70	68	211	10,174
Mi-Hyun Kim	73	70	68	211	10,174
Natalie Gulbis	73	69	69	211	10,174
Vicki Goetze-Ackerman	70	72	69	211	10,174
Catriona Matthew	71	70	70	211	10,174
Hilary Lunke	71	69	71	211	10,174
Lisa Kiggens	73	71	68	212	8,541
Helen Alfredsson	72	68	72	212	8,541
Kristal Parker-Manzo	69	70	73	212	8,541
Miriam Nagl	74	69	70	213	7,285
Becky Morgan	73	70	70	213	7,285
Marianne Morris	72	71	70	213	7,285
Giulia Sergas	73	69	71	213	7,285
Lorena Ochoa	71	71	71	213	7,285

Wegmans Rochester LPGA

Locust Hill Country Club, Pittsford, New York
Par 35-37–72; 6,192 yards

June 19-22
purse, $1,200,000

	SCORES				TOTAL	MONEY
Rachel Teske	69	68	72	68	277	$180,000
Lorena Ochoa	73	70	72	66	281	110,392
Grace Park	69	72	73	68	282	80,081
Brandie Burton	74	69	70	70	283	55,906
Se Ri Pak	70	71	72	70	283	55,906
Suzann Pettersen	73	73	69	69	284	40,796
Tammie Green	70	75	71	69	285	32,033
Candie Kung	73	71	71	70	285	32,033
Becky Morgan	75	70	71	70	286	22,272
Michelle Ellis	71	72	73	70	286	22,272

	SCORES				TOTAL	MONEY
Moira Dunn	73	72	70	71	286	22,272
Kelli Kuehne	73	71	71	71	286	22,272
Meg Mallon	73	70	71	72	286	22,272
Soo-Yun Kang	69	72	72	73	286	22,272
Karrie Webb	69	76	73	69	287	16,198
Danielle Ammaccapane	71	74	72	70	287	16,198
Anna Acker-Macosko	69	75	71	72	287	16,198
Stephanie Louden	73	70	70	74	287	16,198
Terry-Jo Myers	73	71	73	71	288	14,143
Wendy Doolan	72	70	73	73	288	14,143
Ashli Bunch	75	73	74	67	289	12,462
Laura Diaz	74	74	73	68	289	12,462
Dorothy Delasin	74	73	72	70	289	12,462
Beth Bader	73	72	74	70	289	12,462
Hilary Lunke	71	73	73	72	289	12,462
Karen Stupples	74	73	74	69	290	9,904
Barb Mucha	73	74	74	69	290	9,904
Amy Fruhwirth	70	73	74	73	290	9,904
Amy Read	69	75	72	74	290	9,904
Hee-Won Han	72	71	73	74	290	9,904
Kristal Parker-Manzo	71	72	72	75	290	9,904
Silvia Cavalleri	70	72	72	76	290	9,904

ShopRite Classic

Marriott Seaview Resort, Bay Course,
Atlantic City, New Jersey
Par 36-35–71; 6,071 yards

June 27-29
purse, $1,300,000

	SCORES			TOTAL	MONEY
Angela Stanford	65	67	65	197	$195,000
Becky Morgan	68	66	66	200	120,196
Lorie Kane	68	67	66	201	77,323
Juli Inkster	66	67	68	201	77,323
Kate Golden	69	67	68	204	54,291
Patricia Meunier-Lebouc	73	63	69	205	40,801
Heather Bowie	67	68	70	205	40,801
Tonya Gill	68	72	66	206	29,503
Jeong Jang	69	68	69	206	29,503
Joanne Morley	67	67	72	206	29,503
Deb Richard	69	69	69	207	23,098
Miriam Nagl	68	69	70	207	23,098
Laura Diaz	65	71	71	207	23,098
Penny Hammel	69	71	68	208	18,623
Angela Jerman	69	69	70	208	18,623
Annika Sorenstam	70	66	72	208	18,623
Michele Redman	67	66	75	208	18,623
Janice Moodie	70	69	70	209	15,706
Soo Young Moon	69	70	70	209	15,706
Johanna Head	68	71	70	209	15,706
Tina Barrett	72	71	67	210	14,083
Catriona Matthew	69	70	71	210	14,083
Mitzi Edge	69	69	72	210	14,083
Marnie McGuire	70	72	69	211	12,108
Brandie Burton	69	72	70	211	12,108
Jeanne-Marie Busuttil	68	72	71	211	12,108
Paula Marti	68	71	72	211	12,108

	SCORES			TOTAL	MONEY
Diana D'Alessio	67	66	78	211	12,108
Nancy Scranton	75	68	69	212	9,016
Marilyn Lovander	74	69	69	212	9,016
Rosie Jones	70	72	70	212	9,016
Jennifer Rosales	74	67	71	212	9,016
Jean Bartholomew	73	68	71	212	9,016
Leigh Ann Mills	72	68	72	212	9,016
Eva Dahllof	68	72	72	212	9,016
Natalie Gulbis	73	66	73	212	9,016
Hiromi Kobayashi	71	68	73	212	9,016
Lori Atsedes	67	72	73	212	9,016

U.S. Women's Open

Pumpkin Ridge Golf Club, North Plains, Oregon   July 3-7
Par 35-36–71; 6,550 yards   purse, $3,100,000

	SCORES				TOTAL	MONEY
Hilary Lunke	71	69	68	75	283	$560,000
Kelly Robbins	74	69	71	69	283	272,004
Angela Stanford	70	70	69	74	283	272,004
(Lunke won 18-hole playoff on Monday with 70 over Stanford (71) and Robbins (73).)						
Annika Sorenstam	72	72	67	73	284	150,994
*Aree Song Wongluekiet	70	73	68	74	285	
Mhairi McKay	66	70	75	75	286	115,333
Jeong Jang	73	69	69	75	286	115,333
Juli Inkster	69	71	74	73	287	97,363
Rosie Jones	70	72	73	73	288	90,241
Grace Park	72	76	73	68	289	79,243
Suzann Pettersen	76	69	69	75	289	79,243
Donna Andrews	69	72	72	77	290	71,362
Jennifer Rosales	74	69	76	73	292	56,500
Cristie Kerr	72	73	73	74	292	56,500
Lorena Ochoa	71	75	72	74	292	56,500
Patricia Meunier-Lebouc	73	69	74	76	292	56,500
Laura Diaz	71	71	74	76	292	56,500
Rachel Teske	71	73	72	76	292	56,500
Natalie Gulbis	73	69	72	78	292	56,500
Yuri Fudoh	74	72	75	72	293	43,491
Beth Daniel	73	69	77	74	293	43,491
Lorie Kane	73	75	73	73	294	36,575
Catriona Matthew	74	70	76	74	294	36,575
Christina Kim	74	74	72	74	294	36,575
Leta Lindley	73	69	77	75	294	36,575
Dorothy Delasin	79	70	76	70	295	28,354
Paula Marti	71	76	76	72	295	28,354
Kelli Kuehne	72	74	75	74	295	28,354
Danielle Ammaccapane	74	74	73	74	295	28,354
*Jane Park	76	73	74	73	296	
Annette DeLuca	71	73	78	74	296	22,678
Ashli Bunch	71	73	77	75	296	22,678
*Elizabeth Janangelo	75	73	73	75	296	
Mi-Hyun Kim	73	73	73	77	296	22,678

BMO Financial Group Canadian Women's Open

Point Grey Golf & Country Club, Vancouver, British Columbia
Par 37-35–72; 6,408 yards

July 10-13
purse, $1,300,000

	SCORES				TOTAL	MONEY
Beth Daniel	69	69	69	68	275	$195,000
Juli Inkster	68	72	67	69	276	118,169
Grace Park	68	75	69	67	279	76,019
Kim Saiki	70	70	69	70	279	76,019
Se Ri Pak	69	75	68	69	281	53,375
Jeong Jang	68	73	73	68	282	43,671
Becky Morgan	71	70	73	69	283	34,290
Donna Andrews	70	73	69	71	283	34,290
Leta Lindley	69	75	72	68	284	27,496
Janice Moodie	71	68	73	72	284	27,496
Chris Johnson	72	71	72	70	285	23,453
Soo-Yun Kang	69	74	71	71	285	23,453
Johanna Head	75	71	67	73	286	20,574
Heather Bowie	66	74	72	74	286	20,574
Tracy Hanson	73	72	71	71	287	18,762
Diana D'Alessio	76	70	74	68	288	15,301
Joanne Morley	72	74	74	68	288	15,301
Amy Fruhwirth	73	75	70	70	288	15,301
Pamela Kerrigan	70	76	71	71	288	15,301
Carin Koch	75	69	73	71	288	15,301
Tina Barrett	71	73	73	71	288	15,301
Silvia Cavalleri	72	71	73	72	288	15,301
Karrie Webb	72	72	71	73	288	15,301
Rachel Teske	76	72	71	70	289	10,837
Catriona Matthew	73	75	71	70	289	10,837
Tina Fischer	71	72	76	70	289	10,837
Kelly Robbins	69	79	70	71	289	10,837
Dawn Coe-Jones	74	73	71	71	289	10,837
Namika Omata	70	73	74	72	289	10,837
Candie Kung	72	74	69	74	289	10,837
Jane Crafter	71	73	71	74	289	10,837
Pat Hurst	68	76	71	74	289	10,837
Laura Davies	69	72	74	74	289	10,837

Sybase Big Apple Classic

Wykagyl Country Club, New Rochelle, New York
Par 35-36–71; 6,161 yards

July 17-20
purse, $950,000

	SCORES				TOTAL	MONEY
Hee-Won Han	68	66	68	71	273	$142,500
Meg Mallon	70	67	65	73	275	85,962
Grace Park	69	69	73	68	279	55,299
Cindy Figg-Currier	69	65	73	72	279	55,299
Michele Redman	72	69	70	69	280	38,827
Kristal Parker-Manzo	70	73	70	68	281	27,219
Denise Killeen	77	68	67	69	281	27,219
Rachel Teske	73	65	74	69	281	27,219
Candie Kung	72	70	70	70	282	19,218
Beth Daniel	68	68	75	71	282	19,218
Kim Williams	69	72	69	72	282	19,218
Kelli Kuehne	71	70	72	70	283	15,469

	SCORES				TOTAL	MONEY
Marilyn Lovander	72	69	71	71	283	15,469
Jennifer Rosales	69	71	69	74	283	15,469
Deb Richard	73	70	70	71	284	13,649
Yu Ping Lin	72	72	74	67	285	11,546
Beth Bader	72	67	75	71	285	11,546
Cindy Schreyer	70	74	69	72	285	11,546
Emilee Klein	68	74	71	72	285	11,546
Laura Diaz	69	70	73	73	285	11,546
Audra Burks	70	71	69	75	285	11,546
Tammie Green	72	72	71	71	286	9,519
Young Kim	69	75	68	74	286	9,519
Tracy Hanson	72	70	70	74	286	9,519
Joanne Mills	70	67	74	75	286	9,519
Jung Yeon Lee	75	70	71	71	287	7,859
Kate Golden	72	72	70	73	287	7,859
Vicki Goetze-Ackerman	68	69	75	75	287	7,859
Gloria Park	73	67	71	76	287	7,859
Stephanie Louden	70	69	72	76	287	7,859
Mi-Hyun Kim	66	71	71	79	287	7,859

Evian Masters
See Evian Ladies European Tour section.

Weetabix Women's British Open
See Evian Ladies European Tour section.

Wendy's Championship for Children

Tartan Fields Golf Club, Dublin, Ohio
Par 37-35–72; 6,517 yards

August 8-10
purse, $1,100,000

	SCORES			TOTAL	MONEY
Hee-Won Han	68	65	66	199	$165,000
Wendy Ward	69	67	63	199	100,221
(Han defeated Ward on third playoff hole.)					
Michele Redman	71	63	67	201	72,704
Juli Inkster	69	69	66	204	56,242
Candie Kung	64	69	72	205	45,268
Michelle Ellis	70	70	66	206	34,020
Lorie Kane	68	68	70	206	34,020
Emilee Klein	70	71	67	208	22,716
Tina Barrett	71	69	68	208	22,716
Nanci Bowen	68	70	70	208	22,716
Catriona Matthew	68	68	72	208	22,716
Jill McGill	67	69	72	208	22,716
Anna Acker-Macosko	71	71	67	209	15,620
Leta Lindley	72	69	68	209	15,620
Jenna Daniels	70	70	69	209	15,620
Tammie Green	71	67	71	209	15,620
Moira Dunn	65	73	71	209	15,620
Mi-Hyun Kim	71	66	72	209	15,620
Suzanne Strudwick	72	66	72	210	13,059
Kim Saiki	72	70	69	211	11,962
Janice Moodie	70	71	70	211	11,962

	SCORES			TOTAL	MONEY
A.J. Eathorne	66	73	72	211	11,962
Angela Buzminski	69	68	74	211	11,962
Jamie Hullett	71	73	68	212	9,364
Dorothy Delasin	71	71	70	212	9,364
Siew-Ai Lim	67	75	70	212	9,364
Jung Yeon Lee	68	73	71	212	9,364
Cristie Kerr	71	69	72	212	9,364
Amy Fruhwirth	70	70	72	212	9,364
Danielle Ammaccapane	71	68	73	212	9,364
Young-A Yang	74	64	74	212	9,364
Heather Bowie	69	69	74	212	9,364

Jamie Farr Kroger Classic

Highland Meadows Golf Club, Sylvania, Ohio
Par 34-37–71; 6,408 yards

August 14-17
purse, $1,000,000

	SCORES				TOTAL	MONEY
Se Ri Pak	69	67	64	71	271	$150,000
Marisa Baena	68	68	67	70	273	79,364
Hee-Won Han	68	67	66	72	273	79,364
Heather Bowie	67	71	70	66	274	46,589
Mi-Hyun Kim	67	73	66	68	274	46,589
Danielle Ammaccapane	70	71	67	67	275	31,227
Janice Moodie	71	69	67	68	275	31,227
Jennifer Rosales	68	70	72	66	276	21,657
Kristal Parker-Manzo	70	71	67	68	276	21,657
Rachel Teske	66	72	70	68	276	21,657
Laura Diaz	65	67	70	74	276	21,657
Beth Daniel	70	73	68	66	277	17,074
Jung Yeon Lee	69	69	64	75	277	17,074
Dottie Pepper	67	71	72	68	278	13,582
Meg Mallon	68	73	68	69	278	13,582
Tina Barrett	73	67	69	69	278	13,582
Kelly Robbins	70	70	67	71	278	13,582
Kelli Kuehne	68	68	70	72	278	13,582
Nicole Jeray	68	68	67	75	278	13,582
Emilee Klein	70	67	72	70	279	11,181
Chris Johnson	74	63	71	71	279	11,181
Carri Wood	67	72	67	73	279	11,181
Jean Bartholomew	71	72	71	66	280	9,452
Michelle Estill	69	71	72	68	280	9,452
Pat Hurst	72	71	68	69	280	9,452
Leta Lindley	71	70	70	69	280	9,452
Joanne Morley	68	72	70	70	280	9,452
Fiona Pike	68	72	69	71	280	9,452
Dawn Coe-Jones	71	72	68	70	281	7,907
Gloria Park	69	72	70	70	281	7,907
Jamie Hullett	70	68	70	73	281	7,907

Wachovia Classic

Berkleigh Country Club, Kutztown, Pennsylvania
Par 35-37–72; 6,381 yards

August 21-24
purse, $1,200,000

	SCORES				TOTAL	MONEY
Candie Kung	71	67	66	70	274	$180,000
Se Ri Pak	70	71	67	68	276	94,323
Meg Mallon	68	66	71	71	276	94,323
Carin Koch	68	72	67	70	277	61,355
Beth Daniel	69	69	71	70	279	49,384
Kim Saiki	72	65	76	67	280	37,113
Karrie Webb	72	70	65	73	280	37,113
Stephanie Louden	73	71	72	65	281	28,134
Grace Park	71	72	68	70	281	28,134
Jeong Jang	74	71	70	67	282	23,345
Gloria Park	73	71	70	68	282	23,345
Emilee Klein	66	74	72	71	283	20,293
Soo-Yun Kang	68	73	70	72	283	20,293
Pat Hurst	73	70	72	69	284	16,142
Mi-Hyun Kim	73	68	74	69	284	16,142
Young Kim	72	69	74	69	284	16,142
Janice Moodie	69	68	77	70	284	16,142
Catriona Matthew	69	74	69	72	284	16,142
Dawn Coe-Jones	68	71	72	73	284	16,142
Betsy King	73	71	70	71	285	13,050
Wendy Ward	70	72	71	72	285	13,050
Karen Stupples	70	74	68	73	285	13,050
Pamela Kerrigan	69	71	69	76	285	13,050
Jackie Gallagher-Smith	70	73	75	68	286	11,014
Laurie Rinker-Graham	69	73	73	71	286	11,014
Jung Yeon Lee	72	71	69	74	286	11,014
Jamie Hullett	69	72	71	74	286	11,014
Kim Williams	71	69	72	74	286	11,014
Angela Stanford	75	71	73	68	287	8,859
Michele Redman	77	69	70	71	287	8,859
Angela Buzminski	70	73	72	72	287	8,859
Nicole Dalkas	71	69	72	75	287	8,859
Sunny Lee	68	72	72	75	287	8,859
Heather Bowie	71	68	71	77	287	8,859

State Farm Classic

Rail Golf Course, Springfield, Illinois
Par 36-36–72; 6,558 yards
(Event shortened to 54 holes—rain.)

August 28-31
purse, $1,200,000

	SCORES			TOTAL	MONEY
Candie Kung	64	67	71	202	$180,000
Laura Davies	70	67	66	203	109,852
Hee-Won Han	66	69	69	204	79,690
Karen Stupples	69	69	68	206	61,647
Kristi Albers	67	74	66	207	38,492
Grace Park	70	69	68	207	38,492
Tammie Green	67	72	68	207	38,492
Rosie Jones	71	65	71	207	38,492
Young Kim	69	72	67	208	22,891
Se Ri Pak	70	69	69	208	22,891

	SCORES			TOTAL	MONEY
Dorothy Delasin	69	70	69	208	22,891
Pat Hurst	67	70	71	208	22,891
Jennifer Rosales	68	67	73	208	22,891
Laurel Kean	74	68	67	209	15,562
Lorie Kane	70	72	67	209	15,562
Jung Yeon Lee	77	64	68	209	15,562
Karen Pearce	72	68	69	209	15,562
Joanne Mills	71	69	69	209	15,562
Nancy Harvey	70	70	69	209	15,562
Eva Dahllof	68	69	72	209	15,562
Jenna Daniels	68	68	73	209	15,562
Cristie Kerr	72	68	70	210	11,944
Kate Golden	72	68	70	210	11,944
Katherine Hull	70	69	71	210	11,944
Kim Williams	70	69	71	210	11,944
Kathryn Marshall	68	71	71	210	11,944
Liselotte Neumann	73	69	69	211	9,468
Jill McGill	72	70	69	211	9,468
Mardi Lunn	69	72	70	211	9,468
Moira Dunn	71	69	71	211	9,468
Penny Hammel	69	71	71	211	9,468
Michelle McGann	67	72	72	211	9,468
Jackie Gallagher-Smith	69	69	73	211	9,468

John Q. Hammons Hotel Classic

Tulsa Country Club, Tulsa, Oklahoma
Par 35-35–70; 6,269 yards

September 5-7
purse, $1,000,000

	SCORES			TOTAL	MONEY
Karrie Webb	65	69	66	200	$150,000
Dorothy Delasin	68	75	66	209	61,541
Candie Kung	71	71	67	209	61,541
Jamie Hullett	70	69	70	209	61,541
Tammie Green	67	72	70	209	61,541
Se Ri Pak	71	72	67	210	26,825
Emilee Klein	70	70	70	210	26,825
Jill McGill	69	70	71	210	26,825
Cristie Kerr	68	69	73	210	26,825
Annika Sorenstam	69	74	68	211	17,384
Audra Burks	71	70	70	211	17,384
Miriam Nagl	71	70	70	211	17,384
Pat Hurst	70	71	70	211	17,384
Rachel Teske	69	71	71	211	17,384
Laura Davies	75	71	66	212	11,714
Vicki Goetze-Ackerman	71	73	68	212	11,714
Kate Golden	70	74	68	212	11,714
Karen Stupples	69	75	68	212	11,714
Lorena Ochoa	73	70	69	212	11,714
Mi-Hyun Kim	71	72	69	212	11,714
Angela Stanford	70	71	71	212	11,714
Rosie Jones	70	71	71	212	11,714
Young-A Yang	68	72	72	212	11,714
Donna Andrews	66	72	74	212	11,714
Beth Bader	70	75	68	213	8,388
Silvia Cavalleri	75	69	69	213	8,388
Dottie Pepper	72	70	71	213	8,388

	SCORES			TOTAL	MONEY
Young Kim	72	70	71	213	8,388
Liselotte Neumann	71	71	71	213	8,388
Nancy Harvey	74	67	72	213	8,388
Stacy Prammanasudh	69	69	75	213	8,388

Solheim Cup

See Evian Ladies European Tour section.

Safeway Classic

Columbia Edgewater Country Club, Portland, Oregon
Par 36-36–72; 6,327 yards

September 26-28
purse, $1,200,000

	SCORES			TOTAL	MONEY
Annika Sorenstam	67	68	66	201	$180,000
Beth Daniel	62	73	67	202	110,950
Cristie Kerr	66	69	69	204	80,487
Leta Lindley	68	69	69	206	62,263
Meg Mallon	70	72	65	207	50,114
Sophie Gustafson	70	70	68	208	35,131
Se Ri Pak	68	71	69	208	35,131
Lorie Kane	71	67	70	208	35,131
Catriona Matthew	70	71	68	209	25,817
Grace Park	66	72	71	209	25,817
Angela Stanford	71	72	67	210	22,020
Jeong Jang	70	73	67	210	22,020
Michelle Ellis	75	68	68	211	18,223
Silvia Cavalleri	69	74	68	211	18,223
Rosie Jones	69	73	69	211	18,223
Jung Yeon Lee	73	68	70	211	18,223
Karrie Webb	69	75	68	212	14,041
Sherri Steinhauer	68	74	70	212	14,041
Mi-Hyun Kim	67	75	70	212	14,041
Heather Bowie	69	71	72	212	14,041
Yu Ping Lin	68	72	72	212	14,041
Hee-Won Han	69	70	73	212	14,041
Soo-Yun Kang	68	69	75	212	14,041
Becky Morgan	73	70	70	213	11,390
Beth Bauer	72	71	70	213	11,390
Suzann Pettersen	71	72	70	213	11,390
Chris Johnson	70	73	70	213	11,390
Emilee Klein	75	70	69	214	10,327
*Michelle Wie	69	72	73	214	
Connie Ross	76	68	71	215	9,355
Kelly Robbins	76	68	71	215	9,355
Vicki Goetze-Ackerman	74	69	72	215	9,355
Tammie Green	67	72	76	215	9,355

Longs Drugs Challenge

Lincoln Hills Club, Lincoln, California
Par 36-36–72; 6,465 yards

October 2-5
purse, $1,000,000

	SCORES				TOTAL	MONEY
Helen Alfredsson	72	69	64	70	275	$150,000
Grace Park	67	73	67	69	276	56,120
Jung Yeon Lee	71	69	66	70	276	56,120
Pat Hurst	70	70	66	70	276	56,120
Rachel Teske	70	70	66	70	276	56,120
Se Ri Pak	71	64	71	70	276	56,120
Karrie Webb	67	73	70	68	278	24,799
Lorena Ochoa	72	69	68	69	278	24,799
Catriona Matthew	72	69	67	70	278	24,799
Gloria Park	68	72	70	69	279	20,020
Liselotte Neumann	73	68	69	70	280	17,351
Suzann Pettersen	69	70	70	71	280	17,351
Sophie Gustafson	66	70	72	72	280	17,351
Soo-Yun Kang	70	73	69	69	281	13,643
Yu Ping Lin	69	72	71	69	281	13,643
Juli Inkster	68	73	71	69	281	13,643
Kelly Robbins	70	72	69	70	281	13,643
Laura Davies	72	70	68	71	281	13,643
Beth Bauer	72	74	69	68	283	11,172
Michelle Ellis	67	72	75	69	283	11,172
Lorie Kane	68	73	70	72	283	11,172
Candie Kung	74	69	66	74	283	11,172
Heather Daly-Donofrio	70	73	71	70	284	9,804
Wendy Ward	68	71	74	71	284	9,804
Kelli Kuehne	77	65	70	72	284	9,804
Ashli Bunch	74	72	68	71	285	8,413
Anna Acker-Macosko	72	73	69	71	285	8,413
Joanne Mills	75	68	70	72	285	8,413
Moira Dunn	71	70	71	73	285	8,413
Michele Redman	70	70	71	74	285	8,413

Samsung World Championship

TPC at The Woodlands, Woodlands, Texas
Par 36-36–72; 6,376 yards

October 9-12
purse, $800,000

	SCORES				TOTAL	MONEY
Sophie Gustafson	72	69	69	64	274	$200,000
Beth Daniel	70	69	67	70	276	105,000
Rachel Teske	70	69	66	71	276	105,000
Annika Sorenstam	70	69	68	70	277	50,000
Se Ri Pak	69	68	69	73	279	40,000
Juli Inkster	71	69	70	70	280	30,000
Grace Park	70	69	73	69	281	24,000
Cristie Kerr	71	70	70	70	281	24,000
Meg Mallon	70	72	70	70	282	21,000
Lorie Kane	74	67	70	72	283	19,000
Karrie Webb	72	73	69	71	285	17,000
Lorena Ochoa	73	73	71	69	286	16,000
Hee-Won Han	73	73	69	73	288	15,000
Rosie Jones	74	71	74	70	289	14,000
Angela Stanford	72	67	75	76	290	13,000

	SCORES				TOTAL	MONEY
Patricia Meunier-Lebouc	73	74	73	71	291	12,000
Hilary Lunke	72	76	75	73	296	11,250
Candie Kung	75	69	76	76	296	11,250
Yun-Jye Wei	77	76	73	76	302	10,500
Mi Na Lee	77	75	76	80	308	10,000

CJ Nine Bridges Classic

Nine Bridges Golf Club, Jeju Island, South Korea
Par 36-36–72; 6,274 yards

October 31-November 2
purse, $1,250,000

	SCORES			TOTAL	MONEY
Shi Hyun Ahn	65	71	68	204	$187,500
Gloria Park	76	69	62	207	79,534
Se Ri Pak	69	70	68	207	79,534
Laura Davies	68	71	68	207	79,534
Grace Park	66	73	68	207	79,534
Suzann Pettersen	74	69	66	209	39,437
Jung Yeon Lee	70	72	67	209	39,437
Rachel Teske	72	70	68	210	29,896
Soo-Yun Kang	69	71	70	210	29,896
Lorie Kane	71	69	71	211	25,761
Marisa Baena	71	69	72	212	23,058
Catriona Matthew	67	72	73	212	23,058
Ok-Hee Ku	70	74	69	213	19,633
Sophie Gustafson	74	69	70	213	19,633
Lorena Ochoa	74	67	72	213	19,633
Becky Morgan	74	71	69	214	16,220
Hyun Ju Shin	69	74	71	214	16,220
Candie Kung	70	72	72	214	16,220
Laura Diaz	72	69	73	214	16,220
Wendy Doolan	74	73	68	215	13,612
Jill McGill	73	72	70	215	13,612
Grace Lee	74	69	72	215	13,612
Mi-Hyun Kim	68	75	72	215	13,612
Jeong Jang	72	68	75	215	13,612
Natalie Gulbis	71	76	69	216	11,481
Ju Mi Kim	73	71	72	216	11,481
Tina Barrett	70	74	72	216	11,481
Joanne Mills	73	70	73	216	11,481
Hilary Lunke	73	77	67	217	10,177
Mi Na Lee	75	68	74	217	10,177

Mizuno Classic

See Japan LPGA Tour section.

Mobile Tournament of Champions

Robert Trent Jones Golf Trail, The Crossings,
Semmes, Alabama
Par 36-36–72; 6,253 yards

November 13-16
purse, $750,000

		SCORES			TOTAL	MONEY
Dorothy Delasin	72	71	68	69	280	$122,000
Hee-Won Han	72	71	69	68	280	75,500
(Delasin defeated Han on first playoff hole.)						
Laura Davies	75	71	70	65	281	54,250
Grace Park	75	72	67	68	282	35,485
Rachel Teske	76	70	67	69	282	35,485
Mi-Hyun Kim	76	68	69	69	282	35,485
Rosie Jones	75	70	71	67	283	24,530
Karrie Webb	71	75	67	70	283	24,530
Lorie Kane	70	74	72	68	284	21,205
Beth Daniel	75	70	73	68	286	19,305
Se Ri Pak	76	73	67	71	287	18,035
Candie Kung	75	72	75	66	288	16,710
Meg Mallon	76	70	70	72	288	16,710
Juli Inkster	76	77	67	69	289	15,310
Wendy Ward	74	72	74	69	289	15,310
Gloria Park	75	73	70	73	291	14,335
Laura Diaz	75	76	71	70	292	13,735
Catriona Matthew	73	76	71	72	292	13,735
Emilee Klein	78	72	72	71	293	13,285
Betsy King	79	69	73	73	294	13,015
Hilary Lunke	75	76	72	72	295	12,302
Kate Golden	77	74	71	73	295	12,302
Janice Moodie	76	75	70	74	295	12,302
Carin Koch	79	73	70	74	296	11,555
Angela Stanford	78	76	67	75	296	11,555
Wendy Doolan	83	74	75	66	298	11,200
Heather Daly-Donofrio	80	74	72	78	304	10,940
Shi Hyun Ahn	79	75	75	77	306	10,700
Tina Fischer	82	80	73	80	315	10,431
Cristie Kerr					WD	
Sophie Gustafson					WD	

ADT Championship

Trump International Golf Club, West Palm Beach, Florida
Par 36-36–72; 6,506 yards

November 20-23
purse, $1,000,000

		SCORES			TOTAL	MONEY
Meg Mallon	71	71	72	67	281	$215,000
Annika Sorenstam	74	70	67	71	282	115,000
Cristie Kerr	74	69	71	71	285	86,000
Beth Daniel	75	72	68	72	287	57,000
Se Ri Pak	73	70	72	73	288	50,000
Grace Park	76	75	69	69	289	43,000
Michele Redman	72	72	72	74	290	33,000
Rosie Jones	76	67	73	74	290	33,000
Laura Diaz	69	77	71	74	291	26,500
Karrie Webb	73	75	73	72	293	21,500
Patricia Meunier-Lebouc	74	73	72	74	293	21,500
Becky Morgan	76	70	73	74	293	21,500

	SCORES				TOTAL	MONEY
Rachel Teske	77	76	70	71	294	15,750
Lorie Kane	70	74	78	72	294	15,750
Juli Inkster	76	75	70	73	294	15,750
Sophie Gustafson	73	77	69	75	294	15,750
Pat Hurst	73	77	77	71	298	13,500
Mi-Hyun Kim	76	73	74	77	300	13,000
Kelly Robbins	82	75	71	73	301	12,250
Laura Davies	73	69	81	79	302	11,500
Candie Kung	82	75	77	69	303	10,800
Lorena Ochoa	76	76	76	75	303	10,800
Dorothy Delasin	74	79	71	79	303	10,800
Hee-Won Han	76	72	76	79	303	10,800
Angela Stanford	76	73	74	81	304	10,000
Heather Bowie	79	76	74	76	305	9,500
Jeong Jang	80	71	78	76	305	9,500
Catriona Matthew	80	78	74	75	307	8,925
Hilary Lunke	81	76	74	76	307	8,925
Wendy Ward	80	79	78	78	315	8,700

Evian Ladies European Tour

ANZ Ladies Masters

See Australian Women's Tour.

AAMI Women's Australian Open

See Australian Women's Tour.

Tenerife Ladies Open

Golf Las Americas, Tenerife, Canary Islands
Par 36-36–72; 6,237 yards

May 1-4
purse, €200,000

	SCORES				TOTAL	MONEY
Elisabeth Esterl	71	69	67	69	276	€30,000
*Becky Brewerton	69	67	68	73	277	
Ana Belen Sanchez	70	67	72	70	279	17,150
Karine Icher	70	69	70	70	279	17,150
Iben Tinning	73	69	68	70	280	9,640
Corinne Dibnah	68	71	68	73	280	9,640
Lara Tadiotto	69	68	72	72	281	6,500
Vibeke Stensrud	69	69	71	72	281	6,500
Kirsty Taylor	72	72	70	68	282	4,740
Trish Johnson	73	72	69	68	282	4,740
Jackie Kebbell	70	67	71	75	283	4,000
Ana Larraneta	69	71	74	70	284	3,446.66
Tina Schneeberger	70	70	71	73	284	3,446.66
Julie Forbes	73	71	67	73	284	3,446.66

	SCORES				TOTAL	MONEY
Marlene Hedblom	72	70	72	71	285	2,980
Lora Fairclough	71	68	74	72	285	2,980
Susan Parry	72	68	71	74	285	2,980
Laurette Maritz	70	75	72	69	286	2,720
Lynnette Brooky	69	76	71	70	286	2,720
Marta Prieto	71	73	68	74	286	2,720
Nicole Stillig	74	73	72	68	287	2,460
Wendy Dicks	72	70	76	69	287	2,460
Pam Sowden	73	73	71	70	287	2,460
*Anna Sanso	71	72	72	72	287	
Rebecca Stevenson	72	72	71	72	287	2,460
Nienke Nijenhuis	67	71	74	75	287	2,460
Xonia Wunsch	71	76	72	69	288	2,190
Karen Lunn	76	72	71	69	288	2,190
Gina Scott	72	73	70	73	288	2,190
Cecilie Lundgreen	71	71	72	74	288	2,190

La Perla Italian Open

Poggio dei Medici Golf Club, Florence, Italy
Par 37-36–73; 6,252 yards

May 15-18
purse, €190,000

	SCORES				TOTAL	MONEY
Ludivine Kreutz	76	68	68	70	282	€26,362.50
Elisabeth Esterl	72	73	67	71	283	13,210.54
Karen Lunn	69	71	70	73	283	13,210.54
Anne-Marie Knight	73	68	69	73	283	13,210.54
Sophie Sandolo	71	73	68	73	285	7,451.80
Lynnette Brooky	69	72	71	74	286	5,711.87
Silvia Cavalleri	71	70	70	75	286	5,711.87
Paula Marti	77	74	70	66	287	3,948.51
Diana Luna	72	72	74	69	287	3,948.51
Veronica Zorzi	73	71	73	70	287	3,948.51
Marina Arruti	73	72	76	68	289	2,882.30
Corinne Dibnah	78	66	75	70	289	2,882.30
Susan Parry	74	74	70	71	289	2,882.30
Marlene Hedblom	74	71	72	72	289	2,882.30
Stephanie Arricau	73	71	72	73	289	2,882.30
*Tullia Calzavara	76	72	72	70	290	
Alison Nicholas	74	70	73	73	290	2,495.65
Ana Belen Sanchez	72	73	70	75	290	2,495.65
Ana Larraneta	75	77	70	69	291	2,355.05
Marie-Laure de Lorenzi	75	70	74	72	291	2,355.05
Federica Dassu	69	76	74	73	292	2,240.81
Riikka Hakkarainen	74	71	74	73	292	2,240.81
Gina Scott	75	77	73	68	293	2,109
Kirsty Taylor	70	77	74	72	293	2,109
Nadina Taylor	74	72	74	73	293	2,109
Laura Cabanillas Gomez	72	77	74	71	294	1,924.46
Mandy Adamson	74	75	73	72	294	1,924.46
Rachel Bailey	74	73	73	74	294	1,924.46
Natascha Fink	73	73	69	79	294	1,924.46
Nina Karlsson	75	73	77	70	295	1,634.47
Carina Vagner	74	78	72	71	295	1,634.47
Maria Blomqvist	75	73	74	73	295	1,634.47
Emma Zackrisson	75	72	74	74	295	1,634.47
Lora Fairclough	73	76	71	75	295	1,634.47

	SCORES				TOTAL	MONEY
Gwladys Nocera	77	73	70	75	295	1,634.47
Iben Tinning	74	73	72	76	295	1,634.47

Lancia Ladies Open of Portugal

Aroeira Golf Club, Aroeira, Portugal
Par 36-36–72; 6,113 yards

May 23-25
purse, €165,000

	SCORES			TOTAL	MONEY
Alison Munt	69	72	68	209	€24,750
Elisabeth Esterl	70	73	66	209	16,747.50
(Munt defeated Esterl on first playoff hole.)					
Ana Belen Sanchez	71	70	69	210	10,230
Vicky Uwland	72	67	71	210	10,230
Ludivine Kreutz	70	72	69	211	6,996
Diana Luna	74	71	67	212	5,362.50
Paula Marti	74	69	69	212	5,362.50
Ana Larraneta	68	72	73	213	4,125
Veronica Zorzi	73	69	72	214	3,696
Cherie Byrnes	72	76	67	215	2,874.30
Gina Scott	70	76	69	215	2,874.30
Rachel Bailey	72	73	70	215	2,874.30
Federica Dassu	71	74	70	215	2,874.30
Christina Kuld	69	72	74	215	2,874.30
Karine Icher	71	72	73	216	2,347.12
Nina Karlsson	73	70	73	216	2,347.12
Lynnette Brooky	69	72	75	216	2,347.12
Marlene Hedblom	70	71	75	216	2,347.12
Lara Tadiotto	70	77	70	217	2,079
Laurette Maritz	76	70	71	217	2,079
Corinne Dibnah	72	74	71	217	2,079
Kirsty Taylor	66	78	73	217	2,079
Karen Margrethe Juul	74	70	73	217	2,079
Trish Johnson	73	77	68	218	1,806.75
Marta Prieto	74	75	69	218	1,806.75
Virginie Auffret	74	73	71	218	1,806.75
Helena Svensson	71	75	72	218	1,806.75
Esther Poburski	73	72	73	218	1,806.75
Iben Tinning	69	75	74	218	1,806.75
Vanessa Vignali	76	72	71	219	1,534.50
Laura Cabanillas Gomez	77	70	72	219	1,534.50
Joanne Oliver	75	71	73	219	1,534.50
Susan Parry	72	72	75	219	1,534.50
Martina Eberl	70	72	77	219	1,534.50

Open de Espana Feminino

Campo de Golf de Salamanca, Salamanca, Spain
Par 36-36–72; 6,201 yards

May 29-June 1
purse, €250,000

	SCORES				TOTAL	MONEY
Federica Dassu	67	73	72	70	282	€37,500
Sophie Sandolo	72	70	71	71	284	18,791.66
Ana Belen Sanchez	71	73	69	71	284	18,791.66
Corinne Dibnah	67	71	73	73	284	18,791.66

	SCORES				TOTAL	MONEY
Iben Tinning	75	72	71	68	286	8,950
Elisabeth Esterl	73	70	72	71	286	8,950
Virginie Auffret	70	70	69	77	286	8,950
Gwladys Nocera	75	72	71	69	287	5,616.66
Linda Ericsson	76	72	68	71	287	5,616.66
Marina Arruti	73	72	67	75	287	5,616.66
Stephanie Arricau	74	68	76	70	288	4,450
Marlene Hedblom	71	73	73	71	288	4,450
Nadina Taylor	69	77	70	73	289	3,866.66
Anne-Marie Knight	75	69	71	74	289	3,866.66
Susan Parry	74	70	71	74	289	3,866.66
Emma Zackrisson	75	72	73	70	290	3,550
Mandy Adamson	72	70	73	75	290	3,550
*Carmen Alonso	74	75	72	70	291	
Ludivine Kreutz	73	73	74	71	291	3,230
Riikka Hakkarainen	74	73	72	72	291	3,230
*Nuria Clau	75	70	73	73	291	
Carina Vagner	75	72	71	73	291	3,230
Anna Becker	76	66	74	75	291	3,230
Lora Fairclough	73	72	71	75	291	3,230
Filippa Helmersson	79	71	72	70	292	2,812.50
Laura Cabanillas Gomez	73	77	72	70	292	2,812.50
Alison Nicholas	74	73	73	72	292	2,812.50
Maria Boden	72	71	74	75	292	2,812.50
Jane Leary	73	71	72	76	292	2,812.50
Tamara Hyett	73	71	71	77	292	2,812.50

Ladies Irish Open

Killarney Golf & Fishing Club, County Kerry, Ireland   June 13-15
Par 36-36–72; 6,101 yards   purse, €165,000

	SCORES			TOTAL	MONEY
Sophie Gustafson	66	63	73	202	€24,750
Laura Davies	66	68	71	205	16,747.50
Trish Johnson	67	71	69	207	11,550
Alison Nicholas	69	70	69	208	7,953
Kirsty Taylor	71	68	69	208	7,953
Cecilia Ekelundh	70	70	69	209	5,775
Cherie Byrnes	69	70	71	210	4,017.75
Vicky Uwland	69	70	71	210	4,017.75
Iben Tinning	69	69	72	210	4,017.75
Virginie Auffret	71	67	72	210	4,017.75
Lara Tadiotto	73	71	67	211	2,767.87
Rebecca Stevenson	69	74	68	211	2,767.87
Marine Monnet	68	74	69	211	2,767.87
Elisabeth Esterl	69	70	72	211	2,767.87
Natascha Fink	70	72	70	212	2,417.25
Corinne Dibnah	70	72	70	212	2,417.25
Isabella Maconi	75	70	68	213	2,215.12
Karine Icher	74	69	70	213	2,215.12
Carin Koch	69	74	70	213	2,215.12
Marlene Hedblom	70	68	75	213	2,215.12
Carina Vagner	75	72	67	214	2,029.50
Lora Fairclough	71	71	72	214	2,029.50
Marta Prieto	71	71	72	214	2,029.50
Asa Gottmo	73	73	69	215	1,806.75
Ana Belen Sanchez	74	72	69	215	1,806.75

	SCORES			TOTAL	MONEY
Filippa Helmersson	69	76	70	215	1,806.75
Julie Forbes	69	72	74	215	1,806.75
Susan Parry	71	70	74	215	1,806.75
Emma Zackrisson	70	70	75	215	1,806.75
Kathryn Marshall	72	75	69	216	1,559.25
Nadina Taylor	73	72	71	216	1,559.25
Gina Scott	75	70	71	216	1,559.25
Diana Luna	74	71	71	216	1,559.25

Arras Open de France Dames

Le Golf d'Arras, St. Aubin, France
Par 36-36–72; 5,800 yards

June 19-22
purse, €275,000

	SCORES				TOTAL	MONEY
Lynnette Brooky	68	70	69	67	274	€41,250
Trish Johnson	71	67	70	67	275	23,581.25
Vibeke Stensrud	72	67	68	68	275	23,581.25
Carin Koch	70	73	67	68	278	14,850
Stephanie Arricau	71	72	71	67	281	9,845
Marlene Hedblom	73	71	69	68	281	9,845
Ana Belen Sanchez	70	69	71	71	281	9,845
Julie Forbes	72	71	71	68	282	5,665
Nadina Taylor	75	70	69	68	282	5,665
Iben Tinning	71	70	72	69	282	5,665
Georgina Simpson	71	75	66	70	282	5,665
Anna Berg	71	72	67	72	282	5,665
Joanne Mills	73	71	72	67	283	4,180
Lora Fairclough	74	72	70	67	283	4,180
Marie-Laure de Lorenzi	73	73	70	67	283	4,180
Diana Luna	72	73	70	68	283	4,180
Marieke Zelsmann	74	73	71	66	284	3,559.28
Ludivine Kreutz	73	73	70	68	284	3,559.28
Paula Marti	77	71	68	68	284	3,559.28
Christina Kuld	73	71	70	70	284	3,559.28
Malin Burstrom	68	75	70	71	284	3,559.28
Helena Svensson	73	72	68	71	284	3,559.28
Kirsty Taylor	69	72	71	72	284	3,559.28
Sophie Sandolo	73	73	70	69	285	3,135
Claire Duffy	71	77	67	70	285	3,135
Rebecca Stevenson	68	73	71	73	285	3,135
Corinne Dibnah	76	72	71	67	286	2,928.75
Samantha Head	72	72	70	72	286	2,928.75
Susan Parry	75	72	72	68	287	2,763.75
Alexandra Armas	72	69	77	69	287	2,763.75

Evian Masters

Evian Masters Golf Club, Evians-les-Bains, France
Par 36-36–72; 6,171 yards

July 23-26
purse, €2,222,073

	SCORES				TOTAL	MONEY
Juli Inkster	66	72	64	65	267	€279,461.70
Hee-Won Han	71	68	65	69	273	182,956.92
Lorena Ochoa	66	70	71	68	275	117,696.85

	SCORES				TOTAL	MONEY
Rosie Jones	67	68	67	73	275	117,696.85
Karrie Webb	70	70	68	68	276	82,639.04
Se Ri Pak	70	72	66	69	277	67,613.76
Cristie Kerr	71	68	70	69	278	53,089.29
Michele Redman	71	71	67	69	278	53,089.29
Soo-Yun Kang	70	78	65	66	279	42,571.33
Lorie Kane	75	68	68	68	279	42,571.33
Leta Lindley	71	72	70	67	280	32,137.50
Wendy Ward	71	69	71	69	280	32,137.50
Carin Koch	72	70	69	69	280	32,137.50
Helen Alfredsson	72	69	69	70	280	32,137.50
Candie Kung	71	69	69	71	280	32,137.50
Sophie Gustafson	71	67	67	75	280	32,137.50
Grace Park	73	73	69	66	281	25,442.99
Annika Sorenstam	72	73	67	69	281	25,442.99
Patricia Meunier-Lebouc	73	67	74	68	282	23,438.84
Janice Moodie	68	71	69	74	282	23,438.84
Johanna Head	73	73	70	67	283	21,035.47
Jeong Jang	68	71	76	68	283	21,035.47
Suzann Pettersen	71	70	69	73	283	21,035.47
Natalie Gulbis	71	70	69	73	283	21,035.47
Betsy King	71	72	70	71	284	19,132.04
Rachel Teske	70	70	74	71	285	18,431.17
Becky Morgan	73	73	70	70	286	17,378.96
Vicki Goetze-Ackerman	74	70	71	71	286	21,035.47
Dorothy Delasin	75	68	74	70	287	16,326.77
Trish Johnson	75	72	72	69	288	14,524.20
Mi-Hyun Kim	72	70	76	70	288	14,524.20
Iben Tinning	71	73	73	71	288	14,524.20
Kirsty Taylor	77	70	69	72	288	14,524.20
Kelly Robbins	70	74	71	73	288	14,524.20

Weetabix Women's British Open

Royal Lytham & St. Annes Golf Club, Lancashire, England
Par 35-37–72; 6,308 yards

July 31-August 3
purse, €1,670,445

	SCORES				TOTAL	MONEY
Annika Sorenstam	68	72	68	70	278	€228,720
Se Ri Pak	69	69	69	72	279	142,950
Grace Park	74	65	71	70	280	89,343.75
Karrie Webb	67	72	70	71	280	89,343.75
Patricia Meunier-Lebouc	70	69	67	76	282	64,327.50
Vicki Goetze-Ackerman	73	71	68	71	283	52,891.50
Wendy Ward	67	71	69	76	283	52,891.50
Sophie Gustafson	73	69	71	71	284	45,744
Young Kim	73	70	72	70	285	41,455.50
Gloria Park	70	75	69	72	286	35,737.50
Candie Kung	73	71	69	73	286	35,737.50
Karen Stupples	69	74	70	74	287	30,019.50
Paula Marti	71	70	70	76	287	30,019.50
Lynnette Brooky	70	74	75	69	288	23,086.42
Laura Diaz	73	74	71	70	288	23,086.42
Jeong Jang	76	69	72	71	288	23,086.42
Cristie Kerr	74	71	71	72	288	23,086.42
Beth Daniel	74	71	67	76	288	23,086.42
Hee-Won Han	75	71	70	73	289	17,868.75

	SCORES				TOTAL	MONEY
Laura Davies	75	70	70	74	289	17,868.75
Lorie Kane	69	75	70	75	289	17,868.75
Becky Morgan	72	70	71	76	289	17,868.75
Heather Bowie	70	66	74	79	289	17,868.75
Hiroko Yamaguchi	72	71	75	72	290	12,859.54
Moira Dunn	70	74	74	72	290	12,859.54
Pat Hurst	73	71	74	72	290	12,859.54
Michiko Hattori	78	69	71	72	290	12,859.54
Jennifer Rosales	69	72	76	73	290	12,859.54
Iben Tinning	71	73	73	73	290	12,859.54
Soo-Yun Kang	70	75	72	73	290	12,859.54
Young-A Yang	71	75	71	73	290	12,859.54
Dottie Pepper	71	75	71	73	290	12,859.54
Lorena Ochoa	74	65	77	74	290	12,859.54
Emilee Klein	72	70	74	74	290	12,859.54
Brandie Burton	76	69	69	76	290	12,859.54

HP Open

Drottningholm Golf Club, Stockholm, Sweden
Par 36-36–72; 6,921 yards

August 7-10
purse, €517,042

	SCORES				TOTAL	MONEY
Sophie Gustafson	67	71	63	68	269	€70,346.25
Suzann Pettersen	70	67	70	62	269	47,600.96
(Gustafson defeated Pettersen on third playoff hole.)						
Annika Sorenstam	68	68	67	68	271	32,828.25
Laura Davies	69	67	70	70	276	22,604.59
Becky Morgan	68	71	67	70	276	22,604.59
Vibeke Stensrud	68	71	66	73	278	16,414.13
Elisabeth Esterl	70	72	70	67	279	12,896.81
Iben Tinning	67	68	72	72	279	12,896.81
Alison Munt	68	71	71	70	280	9,942.27
Ana Larraneta	72	68	69	71	280	9,942.27
Trish Johnson	72	70	69	70	281	7,534.86
Maria Hjorth	68	68	74	71	281	7,534.86
Charlotta Sorenstam	71	70	69	71	281	7,534.86
Alison Nicholas	71	70	69	71	281	7,534.86
Karen Margrethe Juul	69	69	70	73	281	7,534.86
Silvia Cavalleri	69	65	72	75	281	7,534.86
Catrin Nilsmark	69	69	74	70	282	6,378.06
Alexandra Armas	68	72	72	70	282	6,378.06
Lynnette Brooky	73	68	67	74	282	6,378.06
Carin Koch	69	74	69	71	283	6,049.78
Cecilia Ekelundh	74	69	71	70	284	5,698.04
Johanna Head	69	73	71	71	284	5,698.04
Nadina Taylor	69	71	72	72	284	5,698.04
Eleanor Pilgrim	68	70	73	73	284	5,698.04
Karine Icher	68	75	75	67	285	5,135.27
Mandy Adamson	72	71	73	69	285	5,135.27
Helen Alfredsson	70	72	73	70	285	5,135.27
Marlene Hedblom	72	68	69	76	285	5,135.27
Corinne Dibnah	73	69	72	72	286	4,572.50
Ludivine Kreutz	72	73	67	74	286	4,572.50
Raquel Carriedo	66	71	74	75	286	4,572.50
Dale Reid	73	71	66	76	286	4,572.50

BT Ladies Open

Warrenpoint Golf Club, N. Ireland
Par 37-35–72; 5,908 yards

August 14-17
purse, €238,635

	SCORES				TOTAL	MONEY
Sophie Gustafson	66	69	68	72	275	€32,332.50
Alison Nicholas	67	69	67	73	276	21,878.33
Iben Tinning	72	67	67	74	280	15,088.50
Lynnette Brooky	67	70	70	75	282	11,639.70
Elisabeth Esterl	68	72	70	73	283	9,139.32
Johanna Head	71	71	72	72	286	7,544.25
Gina Scott	74	71	69	73	287	6,466.50
Shani Waugh	73	72	70	74	287	6,466.50
Ana Belen Sanchez	68	71	75	75	289	5,108.53
Nina Karlsson	72	76	74	69	291	3,994.86
Jackie Kebbell	70	77	72	72	291	3,994.86
Lora Fairclough	76	68	71	76	291	3,994.86
*Minea Blomqvist	71	75	75	71	292	
Trish Johnson	69	75	76	72	292	3,276.36
Joanne Mills	73	72	74	73	292	3,276.36
Amanda Moltke-Leth	71	71	75	75	292	3,276.36
Rebecca Stevenson	71	67	76	78	292	3,276.36
Karine Icher	75	71	75	72	293	2,858.19
Martina Eberl	75	71	74	73	293	2,858.19
Anne-Marie Knight	72	73	73	75	293	2,858.19
Sophie Sandolo	74	68	74	77	293	2,858.19
Stephanie Arricau	72	69	73	79	293	2,858.19
Emma Zackrisson	75	73	73	73	294	2,521.93
Nadina Taylor	72	74	74	74	294	2,521.93
Johanna Westerberg	75	71	73	75	294	2,521.93
Karen Lunn	74	71	73	76	294	2,521.93
Jane Leary	74	72	71	77	294	2,521.93
Pam Sowden	74	75	75	71	295	2,133.94
Karine Mathiot	73	75	75	72	295	2,133.94
Laurette Maritz	76	70	75	74	295	2,133.94
Marieke Zelsmann	75	72	74	74	295	2,133.94
Alexandra Armas	73	75	72	75	295	2,133.94
Natascha Fink	70	75	74	76	295	2,133.94
Gwladys Nocera	71	77	71	76	295	2,133.94

Wales WPGA Championship of Europe

Royal Porthcawl Golf Club, Bridgend, Wales
Par 36-37–73; 6,183 yards

August 22-25
purse, €636,360

	SCORES				TOTAL	MONEY
Shani Waugh	73	71	73	69	286	€86,190
*Becky Brewerton	73	72	73	70	288	
Stephanie Arricau	69	72	74	74	289	58,321.90
Elisabeth Esterl	76	70	71	73	290	40,222
Sophie Gustafson	76	74	69	72	291	31,028.40
Natascha Fink	75	72	75	70	292	17,789.61
Trish Johnson	70	79	73	70	292	17,789.61
Karen Margrethe Juul	71	71	78	72	292	17,789.61
Karine Icher	75	69	75	73	292	17,789.61
Kirsty Taylor	75	71	72	74	292	17,789.61
Johanna Head	75	72	77	69	293	11,492

	SCORES				TOTAL	MONEY
Paula Marti	79	71	74	70	294	9,423.44
Eleanor Pilgrim	72	74	77	71	294	9,423.44
Becky Morgan	76	71	75	72	294	9,423.44
Nienke Nijenhuis	76	73	72	73	294	9,423.44
Sara Beautell	68	78	72	76	294	9,423.44
Alison Nicholas	78	71	71	75	295	8,044.40
Corinne Dibnah	73	70	76	76	295	8,044.40
Ana Larraneta	73	70	75	77	295	8,044.40
Valerie Van Ryckeghem	78	68	76	74	296	7,412.34
Joanne Mills	79	72	70	75	296	7,412.34
Ludivine Kreutz	76	68	74	78	296	7,412.34
Amanda Moltke-Leth	78	74	73	72	297	6,895.20
Raquel Carriedo	75	70	75	77	297	6,895.20
Gina Scott	74	71	75	77	297	6,895.20
Asa Gottmo	75	77	71	75	298	6,291.87
Veronica Zorzi	74	72	75	77	298	6,291.87
Rachel Bailey	70	77	71	80	298	6,291.87
Rebecca Stevenson	74	72	71	81	298	6,291.87
Martina Eberl	76	70	75	78	299	5,860.92

Solheim Cup

Barseback Golf & Country Club, Malmo, Sweden   September 12-14
Par 36-36–72; 6,470 yards

FIRST DAY
Morning Foursomes

Beth Daniel and Kelly Robbins (USA) halved with Carin Koch and Laura Davies.
Janice Moodie and Catriona Matthew (Europe) defeated Juli Inkster and Wendy Ward, 5 and 3.
Annika Sorenstam and Suzann Pettersen (Europe) defeated Laura Diaz and Heather Bowie, 4 and 3.
Sophie Gustafson and Elisabeth Esterl (Europe) defeated Meg Mallon and Rosie Jones, 3 and 2.

TOTAL: Europe 3½, United States ½

Afternoon Fourballs

Kelli Kuehne and Cristie Kerr (USA) defeated Laura Davies and Catriona Matthew, 2 and 1.
Juli Inkster and Beth Daniel (USA) defeated Annika Sorenstam and Carin Koch, 1 up.
Suzann Pettersen and Patricia Meunier-Lebouc (Europe) defeated Angela Stanford and Meg Mallon, 3 and 2.
Michele Redman and Rosie Jones (USA) defeated Iben Tinning and Sophie Gustafson, 2 up.

TOTAL: Europe 4½, United States 3½

SECOND DAY
Morning Foursomes

Gustafson and Pettersen (Europe) defeated Kuehne and Kerr, 3 and 1.
Stanford and Redman (USA) halved with Esterl and Tinning.
Sorenstam and Koch (Europe) defeated Ward and Bowie, 3 and 2.
Mallon and Robbins (USA) halved with Moodie and Matthew.

TOTAL: Europe 7½, United States 4½

Afternoon Fourballs

Inkster and Daniel (USA) defeated Ana Belen Sanchez and Mhairi McKay, 5 and 4.
Kuehne and Kerr (USA) defeated Gustafson and Davies, 2 and 1.
Moodie and Matthew (Europe) defeated Ward and Jones, 4 and 3.
Sorenstam and Pettersen (Europe) defeated Robbins and Diaz, 1 up.

TOTAL: Europe 9½, United States 6½

THIRD DAY
Singles

Moodie (Europe) defeated Kuehne, 3 and 2.
Inkster (USA) defeated Koch, 5 and 4.
Gustafson (Europe) defeated Bowie, 5 and 4.
Tinning (Europe) defeated Ward, 2 and 1.
Redman (USA) defeated Sanchez, 3 and 1.
Matthew (Europe) defeated Jones, 3 and 1.
Sorenstam (Europe) defeated Stanford, 3 and 2.
Kerr (USA) defeated Pettersen, match conceded.
Davies (Europe) defeated Mallon, match conceded.
Diaz (USA) defeated Esterl, 5 and 4.
McKay (Europe) defeated Daniel, match conceded.
Meunier-Lebouc (Europe) defeated Robbins, match conceded.

TOTAL: Europe 17½, United States 10½

Biarritz Ladies Classic

Biarritz le Phare Golf Club, Biarritz, France
Par 35-35–70; 5,688 yards

September 25-27
purse, €165,000

	SCORES			TOTAL	MONEY
Marlene Hedblom	66	69	65	200	€24,750
Gina Scott	66	68	68	202	16,747.50
Marta Prieto	70	66	67	203	10,230
Ludivine Kreutz	65	68	70	203	10,230
Nina Reis	69	68	68	205	6,385.50
Alexandra Armas	70	66	69	205	6,385.50
*Alexandra Vilatte	67	68	70	205	
Caroline Goasguen	74	67	65	206	3,657.50
Cecilia Ekelundh	71	69	66	206	3,657.50
Karen Lunn	68	71	67	206	3,657.50
Claire Duffy	73	66	67	206	3,657.50
Veronica Zorzi	69	70	67	206	3,657.50
Maria Boden	70	66	70	206	3,657.50
Sarah Heath	72	69	66	207	2,552
Kirsty Taylor	66	74	67	207	2,552
Carina Vagner	70	69	68	207	2,552
Ellen Smets	72	68	68	208	2,310
Stephanie Arricau	70	69	69	208	2,310
Ana Belen Sanchez	70	68	70	208	2,310
Naima Ghilain	69	74	66	209	2,079
Natascha Fink	70	71	68	209	2,079
Diana Luna	70	69	70	209	2,079
Sara Beautell	70	69	70	209	2,079
Johanna Westerberg	68	71	70	209	2,079
Corinne Dibnah	74	70	66	210	1,881
*Virginie Beauchet	73	70	67	210	

	SCORES			TOTAL	MONEY
Ana Larraneta	70	71	69	210	1,881
Nadina Taylor	70	69	71	210	1,881
Trish Johnson	74	70	67	211	1,608.75
Marie-Laure de Lorenzi	73	71	67	211	1,608.75
Laura Cabanillas Gomez	72	71	68	211	1,608.75
Alison Nicholas	71	71	69	211	1,608.75
Valerie Van Ryckeghem	74	68	69	211	1,608.75
*Peggy Fraysse	69	72	70	211	
Laurette Maritz	72	68	71	211	1,608.75
Eva Bjarvall	69	70	72	211	1,608.75
Gwladys Nocera	70	67	74	211	1,608.75

Princess Lalla Meriem Cup

Dar-es-Salam Golf Club, Red Course, Rabat, Morocco
Par 36-37–73; 7,600 yards

December 12-14
purse, US$40,000

	SCORES			TOTAL	MONEY
Johanna Head	71	73	70	214	US$11,000
Elisabeth Esterl	72	71	71	214	7,000
(Head defeated Esterl in playoff.)					
Rebecca Hudson	72	72	73	217	5,000
Sophie Sandolo	75	69	78	222	4,000
Marie-Laure de Lorenzi	75	74	74	223	3,000
Ludivine Kreutz	74	74	76	224	2,000
Xonia Wunsch	78	75	77	230	2,000
Martina Ebrl	72	79	79	230	2,000
Marine Monnet	81	76	75	232	2,000
Mounya Amalou-Sayeh	79	82	78	239	2,000

Japan LPGA Tour

Daikin Orchid Ladies

Ryukyu Golf Club, Okinawa
Par 36-36–72; 6,302 yards

March 7-9
purse, ¥60,000,000

	SCORES			TOTAL	MONEY
Yuri Fudoh	72	67	69	208	¥10,800,000
Aki Nakano	73	72	63	208	5,280,000
(Fudoh defeated Nakano on fourth playoff hole.)					
Ok-Hee Ku	75	62	72	209	4,200,000
Yun-Jye Wei	70	68	73	211	3,000,000
Michiko Hattori	72	69	70	211	3,000,000
Kayo Yamada	69	72	70	211	3,000,000
Yu-Chen Huang	73	70	69	212	1,462,000
Hiromi Kobayashi	73	73	66	212	1,462,000
Mihoko Takahashi	70	69	73	212	1,462,000
Riko Higashio	68	71	73	212	1,462,000
Kaori Higo	70	70	72	212	1,462,000
Kasumi Fujii	74	71	67	212	1,462,000
Woo-Soon Ko	71	71	71	213	996,000
Aiko Hashimoto	71	70	73	214	906,000
Junko Yasui	75	69	70	214	906,000
Ji-Hee Lee	71	69	75	215	696,000
Fumiko Kanoh	71	70	74	215	696,000
Yuka Kuriyama	70	74	71	215	696,000
Yoko Tsuchiya	74	71	70	215	696,000
Seiko Watanabe	72	73	70	215	696,000
Miyuki Shimabukuro	73	72	71	216	540,000
Mie Nakata	73	71	72	216	540,000
Natsuko Noro	69	73	74	216	540,000
Orie Fujino	70	72	74	216	540,000
Junko Yoshida	74	71	71	216	540,000
Michie Ohba	72	75	70	217	486,000
Mikiyo Nishizuka	68	76	73	217	486,000
Nikki Campbell	69	76	72	217	486,000
Yuko Moriguchi	75	72	70	217	486,000
Young-Me Lee	72	72	74	218	426,000
Tomoko Ueda	73	69	76	218	426,000
Ayako Uehara	75	69	74	218	426,000
Mitsuko Kawasaki	72	73	73	218	426,000
Ai-Yu Tu	71	76	71	218	426,000
Chihiro Nakajima	74	72	72	218	426,000
*Mika Miyazato	73	75	70	218	

Promise Ladies

Water Hills Golf Club, Hyogo
Par 36-36–72; 6,433 yards

April 11-13
purse, ¥60,000,000

	SCORES			TOTAL	MONEY
Ji-Hee Lee	70	71	67	208	¥10,800,000
Masaki Maeda	69	71	70	210	5,280,000

	SCORES			TOTAL	MONEY
Kaori Suzuki	72	70	70	212	3,900,000
Orie Fujino	69	69	74	212	3,900,000
Kyoko Ono	76	66	72	214	2,500,000
Harumi Sakagami	73	68	73	214	2,500,000
Woo-Soon Ko	70	70	74	214	2,500,000
Yu-Chen Huang	68	71	76	215	1,800,000
Hsiu-Feng Tseng	73	74	69	216	1,350,000
Fuki Kido	73	71	72	216	1,350,000
Yuri Kawanami	77	71	69	217	888,000
Hisako Ohgane	72	76	69	217	888,000
Yukari Baba	70	76	71	217	888,000
Ikuyo Shiotani	72	74	71	217	888,000
Mineko Nasu	73	73	71	217	888,000
Aki Nakano	73	72	72	217	888,000
Midori Yoneyama	71	72	74	217	888,000
Aki Takamura	71	72	74	217	888,000
Shiho Ohyama	73	76	69	218	548,000
Mayumi Inoue	74	75	69	218	548,000
Kayo Yamada	72	74	72	218	548,000
Mie Nakata	71	73	74	218	548,000
Hiroko Yamaguchi	70	73	75	218	548,000
Chieko Amanuma	71	72	75	218	548,000
Mizue Igarashi	77	72	70	219	462,000
Kayo Segawa	74	73	72	219	462,000
Yuka Kuriyama	71	74	74	219	462,000
Itsumi Okada	77	68	74	219	462,000
Shin Sora	74	71	74	219	462,000
Ji-Yeon Han	71	73	75	219	462,000
Junko Yoshida	73	71	75	219	462,000

Saishunkan Ladies Hinokuni Open

Kumamoto Kuukou Country Club, Kikuyo, Kumamoto
Par 36-36–72; 6,433 yards

April 18-20
purse, ¥60,000,000

	SCORES			TOTAL	MONEY
Ji-Hee Lee	72	73	71	216	¥10,800,000
Rui Kitada	69	79	69	217	5,280,000
Woo-Soon Ko	74	73	72	219	3,300,000
Kumi Yamashita	74	77	68	219	3,300,000
Kaori Higo	74	71	74	219	3,300,000
Sae Takamura	70	75	74	219	3,300,000
Ok-Hee Ku	76	74	70	220	1,800,000
Miho Koga	77	72	71	220	1,800,000
Kozue Azuma	71	74	75	220	1,800,000
Kaori Suzuki	76	76	69	221	1,056,000
Kayo Fukumoto	77	72	72	221	1,056,000
Yuko Moriguchi	76	73	72	221	1,056,000
Chieko Nishida	74	79	68	221	1,056,000
Shiho Ohyama	71	75	75	221	1,056,000
Toshimi Kimura	76	75	71	222	662,000
Yuriko Ohtsuka	77	74	71	222	662,000
Miyuki Shimabukuro	73	77	72	222	662,000
Mitsuko Kawasaki	74	76	72	222	662,000
Yuka Shiroto	76	75	71	222	662,000
Aki Takamura	77	75	70	222	662,000
Kaori Yamamoto	77	73	72	222	662,000

	SCORES			TOTAL	MONEY
Samantha Head	77	73	72	222	662,000
Yuri Fudoh	72	75	75	222	662,000
Masaki Maeda	75	75	73	223	492,000
Midori Yoneyama	76	74	73	223	492,000
Mikiyo Nishizuka	74	75	74	223	492,000
Chihiro Nakajima	75	74	74	223	492,000
Fumiko Muraguchi	73	74	76	223	492,000
Misayo Fujisawa	71	75	77	223	492,000
Kaori Harada	75	75	74	224	414,000
Ikuyo Shiotani	74	77	73	224	414,000
Yun-Jye Wei	75	75	74	224	414,000
Ji-Yeon Han	76	76	72	224	414,000
Kotomi Akiyama	74	75	75	224	414,000
Hiroko Yamaguchi	73	75	76	224	414,000
Ayako Okamoto	74	73	77	224	414,000

Katokichi Queens

Yashima Country Club, Mure, Kagawa
Par 36-36–72; 6,221 yards

April 25-27
purse, ¥60,000,000

	SCORES			TOTAL	MONEY
Kasumi Fujii	70	70	67	207	¥10,800,000
Mie Nakata	70	67	71	208	5,280,000
Samantha Head	70	70	69	209	3,900,000
Yuka Shiroto	66	70	73	209	3,900,000
Kumiko Hiyoshi	70	69	72	211	3,000,000
Shiho Ohyama	71	74	67	212	1,950,000
Chihiro Nakajima	72	71	69	212	1,950,000
Kaori Harada	68	74	70	212	1,950,000
Hsiu-Feng Tseng	70	68	74	212	1,950,000
Mihoko Takahashi	68	72	73	213	1,200,000
Nikki Campbell	71	73	70	214	1,062,000
Orie Fujino	73	71	70	214	1,062,000
Kayo Yamada	74	72	69	215	882,000
Rie Mitsuhashi	67	78	70	215	882,000
Ikuyo Shiotani	76	69	70	215	882,000
Yasuko Satoh	71	72	72	215	882,000
Yuri Kawanami	74	73	69	216	593,142
Miyuki Shimabukuro	72	74	70	216	593,142
Michiko Hattori	73	72	71	216	593,142
Ji-Yeon Han	71	73	72	216	593,142
Azumi Katoh	73	71	72	216	593,142
Hiroko Yamaguchi	71	72	73	216	593,142
Aiko Hashimoto	72	70	74	216	593,142
Toshimi Kimura	75	72	70	217	474,000
Yukiko Itoh	72	74	71	217	474,000
Mikiyo Nishizuka	75	71	71	217	474,000
Miho Koga	72	73	72	217	474,000
Tomo Sakakibara	73	70	74	217	474,000
Yu-Chen Huang	70	71	76	217	474,000
Rie Murata	74	73	71	218	420,000
Yukiyo Haga	73	73	72	218	420,000
Ok-Hee Ku	73	72	73	218	420,000

Nichirei Cup World Ladies

Yomiuri Country Club, Tokyo
Par 36-36–72; 6,424 yards

May 8-11
purse, ¥60,000,000

	SCORES				TOTAL	MONEY
Annika Sorenstam	66	70	71	68	275	¥10,800,000
Junko Omote	72	73	71	68	284	3,430,000
Michiko Hattori	69	70	76	69	284	3,430,000
Yuri Fudoh	74	67	74	69	284	3,430,000
Yuko Moriguchi	71	67	76	70	284	3,430,000
Junko Yasui	66	71	76	71	284	3,430,000
Kaori Suzuki	72	71	69	72	284	3,430,000
Rui Kitada	72	71	72	70	285	1,500,000
Hiroko Yamaguchi	70	74	70	71	285	1,500,000
Kasumi Fujii	69	72	72	72	285	1,500,000
Yasuko Satoh	78	69	70	69	286	1,026,000
*Sakura Yokomine	69	73	74	70	286	
Ji-Hee Lee	72	69	74	71	286	1,026,000
Yuka Kuriyama	72	71	75	70	288	876,000
Mihoko Takahashi	72	73	72	71	288	876,000
Mayumi Ishii	70	70	73	75	288	876,000
Fuki Kido	71	75	73	70	289	726,000
Mayumi Murai	71	74	73	71	289	726,000
Yuriko Ohtsuka	73	75	70	72	290	635,000
Harumi Sakagami	71	72	75	73	291	506,000
Orie Fujino	71	70	76	74	291	506,000
Woo-Soon Ko	75	71	71	74	291	506,000
Kaori Higo	70	69	76	76	291	506,000
Ok-Hee Ku	74	71	70	76	291	506,000
Kayo Yamada	75	67	72	77	291	506,000
Hisako Ohgane	70	72	77	73	292	450,000
Mineko Nasu	74	73	73	72	292	450,000
*Ai Miyazato	70	71	77	74	292	
Hsiu-Feng Tseng	71	72	75	75	293	426,000
Shiho Ohyama	75	66	75	77	293	426,000

Vernal Ladies

Fukuoka Century Golf Club, Amagi, Fukuoka
Par 36-36–72; 6,558 yards

May 16-18
purse, ¥100,000,000

	SCORES			TOTAL	MONEY
Ok-Hee Ku	71	71	68	210	¥18,000,000
Woo-Soon Ko	70	72	70	212	8,800,000
Yuka Shiroto	69	73	71	213	6,500,000
Hsiu-Feng Tseng	69	71	73	213	6,500,000
Yuri Fudoh	73	70	71	214	4,500,000
Toshimi Kimura	70	70	74	214	4,500,000
Nikki Campbell	73	72	70	215	3,500,000
Samantha Head	71	76	69	216	2,500,000
Mineko Nasu	75	72	69	216	2,500,000
Yun-Jye Wei	69	72	75	216	2,500,000
Kasumi Fujii	72	72	73	217	1,790,000
Aki Nakano	76	68	73	217	1,790,000
Shin Sora	76	72	70	218	1,390,000
Michiko Hattori	76	71	71	218	1,390,000
Midori Yoneyama	74	72	72	218	1,390,000

	SCORES			TOTAL	MONEY
Mayumi Murai	68	77	73	218	1,390,000
Mari Katayama	70	74	74	218	1,390,000
Rie Murata	71	71	76	218	1,390,000
Chikako Matsuzawa	71	76	72	219	950,000
Mikiyo Nishizuka	77	70	72	219	950,000
Takayo Bandoh	76	70	73	219	950,000
Ji-Yeon Han	72	71	76	219	950,000
Mayumi Inoue	76	72	72	220	830,000
Fuki Kido	75	72	73	220	830,000
Michie Ohba	74	75	71	220	830,000
Kaori Suzuki	74	72	74	220	830,000
Natsuko Noro	73	77	70	220	830,000
Mie Nakata	75	67	78	220	830,000
Hisako Ohgane	75	73	73	221	700,000
Miho Koga	77	71	73	221	700,000
Shiho Ohyama	69	78	74	221	700,000
Kyoko Ono	75	72	74	221	700,000
Kaori Higo	71	75	75	221	700,000
Yasuko Satoh	72	74	75	221	700,000
Ae-Sook Kim	74	75	72	221	700,000

Chukyo TV Bridgestone Ladies Open

Chukyo Golf Club, Toyota, Aichi
Par 36-36–72; 6,334 yards

May 23-25
purse, ¥50,000,000

	SCORES			TOTAL	MONEY
Yuri Fudoh	65	68	74	207	¥9,000,000
Toshimi Kimura	68	70	70	208	3,950,000
Ok-Hee Ku	70	67	71	208	3,950,000
Michiko Hattori	67	70	73	210	3,000,000
Yuriko Ohtsuka	73	71	67	211	2,250,000
Midori Yoneyama	69	68	74	211	2,250,000
Fuki Kido	71	73	68	212	1,625,000
Natsuko Noro	73	69	70	212	1,625,000
Hsiu-Feng Tseng	73	71	69	213	1,250,000
Yuko Motoyama	72	72	70	214	965,000
Kyoko Ono	72	70	72	214	965,000
Eun-Kyung Chang	72	72	71	215	830,000
Samantha Head	72	74	69	215	830,000
Chieko Amanuma	72	70	73	215	830,000
Shiho Ohyama	73	72	71	216	585,714
Ji-Hee Lee	75	69	72	216	585,714
Azumi Katoh	73	71	72	216	585,714
Michiko Mitsui	71	71	74	216	585,714
Mihoko Takahashi	72	75	69	216	585,714
Miho Koga	72	69	75	216	585,714
Kayo Yamada	72	69	75	216	585,714
Yasuko Satoh	73	72	72	217	430,000
Junko Omote	73	72	72	217	430,000
Michie Ohba	75	69	73	217	430,000
*Ai Miyazato	70	73	74	217	
Ayako Okada	75	72	70	217	430,000
Yoko Inoue	72	70	75	217	430,000
Kaori Harada	77	70	70	217	430,000
Hiroko Yamaguchi	73	69	75	217	430,000
Mie Nakata	74	71	73	218	370,000

	SCORES			TOTAL	MONEY
Masaki Maeda	73	73	72	218	370,000
Junko Yasui	70	73	75	218	370,000
Kumiko Hiyoshi	73	70	75	218	370,000
Orie Fujino	74	69	75	218	370,000

Kosaido Ladies Golf Cup

Chiba Kosaido Country Club, Ichihara, Chiba
Par 36-36–72; 6,260 yards

May 30-June 1
purse, ¥60,000,000

	SCORES			TOTAL	MONEY
Michiko Hattori	68	72	69	209	¥10,800,000
Yun-Jye Wei	68	76	66	210	5,280,000
Ok-Hee Ku	73	71	70	214	4,200,000
Yuriko Ohtsuka	71	74	70	215	3,300,000
Ikuyo Shiotani	72	73	70	215	3,300,000
Kasumi Fujii	70	77	69	216	2,250,000
Hiroko Yamaguchi	73	73	70	216	2,250,000
Mihoko Takahashi	72	74	71	217	1,500,000
Hsiu-Feng Tseng	74	72	71	217	1,500,000
Midori Yoneyama	67	76	74	217	1,500,000
Yuka Shiroto	77	70	71	218	948,000
Miki Nakata	75	71	72	218	948,000
Junko Yasui	70	75	73	218	948,000
Hikaru Kobayashi	72	72	74	218	948,000
Kaori Higo	72	72	74	218	948,000
Yuko Motoyama	75	69	74	218	948,000
Woo-Soon Ko	74	70	74	218	948,000
Mayumi Murai	71	76	72	219	616,800
Kayo Yamada	74	73	72	219	616,800
Young-Me Lee	68	78	73	219	616,800
Mizue Igarasgi	76	72	71	219	616,800
Chieko Amanuma	75	74	70	219	616,800
Seiko Watanabe	73	75	72	220	510,000
Miho Koga	71	76	73	220	510,000
Hiromi Takesue	75	73	72	220	510,000
Misato Nishikawa	73	75	72	220	510,000
Fumiko Muraguchi	69	77	74	220	510,000
Junko Omote	71	77	72	220	510,000
Fuki Kido	71	74	75	220	510,000
Mayumi Inoue	73	76	71	220	510,000

Resort Trust Ladies

The Tradition Golf Club, Aichi
Par 36-36–72; 6,504 yards

June 6-8
purse, ¥50,000,000

	SCORES			TOTAL	MONEY
Yuri Fudoh	72	66	67	205	¥9,000,000
Kaori Higo	77	68	67	212	4,000,000
Ji-Hee Lee	70	73	69	212	4,000,000
Kaori Harada	71	73	72	216	3,000,000
Rie Murata	72	76	69	217	2,250,000
Aki Nakano	71	75	71	217	2,250,000
Yun-Jye Wei	70	72	76	218	1,750,000

	SCORES			TOTAL	MONEY
Ikuyo Shiotani	72	75	72	219	1,250,000
Miho Koga	74	73	72	219	1,250,000
Michiko Hattori	74	71	74	219	1,250,000
*Sakura Yokomine	76	69	75	220	
Kayo Yamada	75	69	76	220	955,000
Hikaru Kobayashi	75	75	71	221	905,000
Riyo Fukuroi	73	77	72	222	730,000
Nikki Campbell	74	75	73	222	730,000
Yuka Shiroto	73	75	74	222	730,000
Kyoko Ono	77	71	74	222	730,000
Yuko Motoyama	77	70	75	222	730,000
Fuki Kido	70	72	80	222	730,000
Young-Me Lee	74	75	74	223	510,000
Takayo Bandoh	76	70	77	223	510,000
Ae-Sook Kim	73	72	78	223	510,000
Ji-Yeon Han	74	70	79	223	510,000
Shin Sora	78	73	73	224	455,000
Yuko Moriguchi	77	74	73	224	455,000
Rie Fujiwara	77	74	73	224	455,000
Kaori Suzuki	76	75	73	224	455,000
Junko Yasui	76	74	74	224	455,000
Yasuko Satoh	73	77	75	225	392,142
Orie Fujino	76	74	75	225	392,142
Michiko Mitsui	72	77	76	225	392,142
Mayumi Ishii	76	73	76	225	392,142
Megumi Higuchi	75	73	77	225	392,142
Junko Yoshida	77	71	77	225	392,142
Yuka Kuriyama	77	71	77	225	392,142

We Love Kobe Suntory Ladies Open

Japan Memorial Golf Club, Yoshikawa, Hyogo
Par 36-36–72; 6,518 yards

June 12-15
purse, ¥60,000,000

	SCORES				TOTAL	MONEY
Ji-Hee Lee	68	65	69	70	272	¥10,800,000
Yun-Jye Wei	69	67	70	66	272	5,280,000
(Lee defeated Wei on first playoff hole.)						
Yuri Fudoh	69	69	71	64	273	4,200,000
Hiroko Yamaguchi	68	67	71	68	274	3,600,000
Hiromi Takesue	68	67	73	68	276	3,000,000
Midori Yoneyama	68	73	70	66	277	2,250,000
Mikiyo Nishizuka	67	73	70	67	277	2,250,000
Megumi Higuchi	68	72	70	68	278	1,650,000
Woo-Soon Ko	70	68	71	69	278	1,650,000
Junko Omote	70	71	71	67	279	1,104,000
Rui Kitada	72	68	71	68	279	1,104,000
Ok-Hee Ku	68	71	68	72	279	1,104,000
Kasumi Fujii	69	73	69	69	280	906,000
*Ai Miyazato	68	72	70	70	280	
Takayo Bandoh	71	70	69	70	280	906,000
Kaori Higo	70	70	69	71	280	906,000
Yuriko Ohtsuka	73	67	73	68	281	786,000
Yuko Motoyama	73	70	72	68	283	615,600
Kaori Yamamoto	72	69	73	69	283	615,600
Kyoko Ono	68	71	74	70	283	615,600
Kaori Suzuki	72	69	72	70	283	615,600

	SCORES				TOTAL	MONEY
*Kyoko Furuya	69	74	70	70	283	
Nikki Campbell	73	70	68	72	283	615,600
Mihoko Takahashi	70	70	74	70	284	522,000
*Sakura Yokomine	68	69	73	74	284	
Shin Sora	70	73	73	69	285	480,000
Mayumi Inoue	69	72	73	71	285	480,000
Junko Yasui	72	70	72	71	285	480,000
Hikaru Kobayashi	73	71	70	71	285	480,000
Hsiao-Chuan Lu	69	72	72	72	285	480,000
Ae-Sook Kim	68	73	72	72	285	480,000

Apita Circle K Sankus Ladies

U Green Golf Club, Natsugawa, Gifu
Par 36-36–72; 6,344 yards

June 20-22
purse, ¥50,000,000

	SCORES			TOTAL	MONEY
Yun-Jye Wei	68	68	72	208	¥9,000,000
Miho Koga	71	71	67	209	4,400,000
Yuri Fudoh	73	68	69	210	3,500,000
Aiko Hashimoto	73	71	67	211	2,312,500
Midori Yoneyama	70	73	68	211	2,312,500
Hiroko Yamaguchi	71	71	69	211	2,312,500
Toshimi Kimura	72	69	70	211	2,312,500
Ok-Hee Ku	70	74	68	212	1,375,000
Kaori Suzuki	68	73	71	212	1,375,000
Mikiyo Nishizuka	73	71	69	213	891,250
Shin Sora	73	69	71	213	891,250
Eika Ohtake	70	70	73	213	891,250
Misato Nishikawa	70	70	73	213	891,250
Kasumi Fujii	69	77	68	214	630,000
Ji-Hee Lee	73	72	69	214	630,000
Ikuyo Shiotani	68	75	71	214	630,000
Michie Ohba	72	70	72	214	630,000
Michiko Hattori	69	72	73	214	630,000
Natsuko Noro	73	68	73	214	630,000
Orie Fujino	72	75	68	215	445,000
Aki Takamura	70	75	70	215	445,000
Hiromi Takesue	71	70	74	215	445,000
Hsiao-Chuan Lu	72	74	70	216	415,000
Mineko Nasu	73	72	71	216	415,000
Kaori Harada	70	72	74	216	415,000
Yu-Chen Huang	70	75	72	217	365,000
Miki Nakata	68	75	74	217	365,000
Yuko Motoyama	71	76	70	217	365,000
Woo-Soon Ko	71	73	73	217	365,000
Masaki Maeda	71	73	73	217	365,000
Aki Nakano	71	76	70	217	365,000
Junko Yasui	72	71	74	217	365,000

Belluna Ladies Cup

Obatago Golf Club, Kanra, Gunma
Par 36-36–72; 6,339 yards

July 4-6
purse, ¥60,000,000

	SCORES			TOTAL	MONEY
Shiho Ohyama	73	67	67	207	¥10,800,000
Hiroko Yamaguchi	67	70	70	207	4,740,000
Shin Sora	70	67	70	207	4,740,000
(Ohyama defeated Yamaguchi and Sora on second playoff hole.)					
Midori Yoneyama	74	66	68	208	3,600,000
Yuko Motoyama	69	73	67	209	2,700,000
Mayumi Inoue	70	68	71	209	2,700,000
Woo-Soon Ko	70	71	69	210	1,950,000
Hiromi Takesue	70	66	74	210	1,950,000
Mie Nakata	76	68	67	211	1,272,000
Hsiu-Feng Tseng	66	72	73	211	1,272,000
Mihoko Takahashi	73	65	73	211	1,272,000
*Kumiko Kaneda	73	72	67	212	
Michiko Hattori	72	73	68	213	906,000
Young-Me Lee	73	70	70	213	906,000
Ji-Hee Lee	73	70	70	213	906,000
Mikiyo Nishizuka	70	72	71	213	906,000
Mitsuko Kawasaki	75	67	71	213	906,000
Keiko Sasaki	73	68	72	213	906,000
Junko Yoshida	70	74	70	214	636,000
Hiromi Mogi	70	71	73	214	636,000
Seiko Watanabe	69	70	75	214	636,000
Chihiro Nakajima	75	72	68	215	516,000
Rena Yamazaki	70	76	69	215	516,000
Megumi Higuchi	76	70	69	215	516,000
Kyoko Ono	72	73	70	215	516,000
Kaori Harada	73	72	70	215	516,000
Kaori Yamamoto	73	72	70	215	516,000
Junko Yasui	71	72	72	215	516,000
Masaki Maeda	73	70	72	215	516,000
Kaori Higo	70	71	74	215	516,000

Toyo Suisan Ladies Hokkaido

Sapporo Kitahiroshima Prince Golf Course, Hokkaido
Par 36-36–72; 6,445 yards

July 11-13
purse, ¥50,000,000

	SCORES			TOTAL	MONEY
Kaori Suzuki	71	69	70	210	¥9,000,000
Junko Omote	65	70	75	210	4,400,000
(Suzuki defeated Omote on first playoff hole.)					
Kyoko Ono	72	71	68	211	3,250,000
Orie Fujino	73	68	70	211	3,250,000
Michie Ohba	74	71	67	212	2,250,000
Samantha Head	70	72	70	212	2,250,000
Midori Yoneyama	70	72	71	213	1,750,000
Yuka Shiroto	72	70	72	214	1,375,000
Fumiko Muraguchi	71	68	75	214	1,375,000
Ikuyo Shiotani	70	74	71	215	1,000,000
Yasuko Satoh	74	73	69	216	910,000
Nobuko Kizawa	74	70	72	216	910,000
Harumi Kawano	72	73	72	217	735,000

	SCORES			TOTAL	MONEY
Rui Kitada	74	71	72	217	735,000
Shin Sora	73	71	73	217	735,000
Chieko Amanuma	70	73	74	217	735,000
Mayumi Murai	72	71	74	217	735,000
Yoko Tsuchiya	74	74	70	218	535,000
Yuko Motoyama	73	72	73	218	535,000
Toshimi Kimura	69	75	74	218	535,000
Kotomi Akiyama	77	71	71	219	445,000
Yoko Inoue	74	74	71	219	445,000
Megumi Higuchi	69	77	73	219	445,000
Seiko Watanabe	73	72	74	219	445,000
Hiromi Takesue	75	70	74	219	445,000
Ji-Hee Lee	75	70	74	219	445,000
Yuri Fudoh	73	70	76	219	445,000
Miho Koga	72	75	73	220	390,000
Nikki Campbell	76	71	73	219	445,000
Kaori Harada	73	73	74	219	445,000
Kaori Higo	70	75	75	219	445,000

Stanley Ladies

Tomei Country Club, Shizuoka
Par 36-36–72; 6,447 yards

July 18-20
purse, ¥60,000,000

	SCORES			TOTAL	MONEY
Yuri Fudoh	70	70	68	208	¥10,800,000
Mihoko Takahashi	71	71	69	211	4,020,000
Michiko Mitsui	69	71	71	211	4,020,000
Woo-Soon Ko	69	70	72	211	4,020,000
Fumiko Muraguchi	68	68	75	211	4,020,000
Yasuko Satoh	73	70	69	212	2,100,000
Kumiko Hiyoshi	72	70	70	212	2,100,000
Hiromi Takesue	67	72	73	212	2,100,000
Keiko Sasaki	73	69	71	213	1,500,000
Midori Yoneyama	72	73	69	214	1,170,000
Yuka Shiroto	65	75	74	214	1,170,000
Michie Ohba	69	76	71	216	1,020,000
Ok-Hee Ku	72	72	72	216	1,020,000
Yu-Chen Huang	73	70	73	216	1,020,000
Kaori Yamamoto	70	75	72	217	708,000
Fumiko Kanoh	71	74	72	217	708,000
Yuko Motoyama	72	73	72	217	708,000
Mikiyo Nishizuka	73	72	72	217	708,000
Nikki Campbell	71	75	71	217	708,000
Shin Sora	74	71	72	217	708,000
Chihiro Nakajima	73	74	70	217	708,000
Misato Nishikawa	71	72	74	217	708,000
Aiko Hashimoto	75	71	72	218	528,000
Aki Nakano	74	72	72	218	528,000
Kozue Azuma	72	74	72	218	528,000
Rie Fujiwara	67	79	72	218	528,000
Michiko Hattori	70	74	74	218	528,000
Fuki Kido	72	75	71	218	528,000
Shiho Ohyama	68	73	77	218	528,000
Seiko Watanabe	75	71	73	219	462,000
Yuko Moriguchi	74	73	72	219	462,000
Yoko Inoue	71	73	75	219	462,000
Hsiao-Chuan Lu	73	71	75	219	462,000

Golf 5 Ladies

Mizunami Country Club, Mizunami, Gifu

July 25-27

Par 36-36–72; 6,469 yards

purse, ¥50,000,000

	SCORES			TOTAL	MONEY
Mihoko Takahashi	67	71	66	204	¥9,000,000
Chihiro Nakajima	70	69	67	206	4,400,000
Yuri Fudoh	71	72	65	208	3,250,000
Yuriko Ohtsuka	71	70	67	208	3,250,000
Fumiko Muraguchi	70	72	67	209	2,250,000
Orie Fujino	70	71	68	209	2,250,000
Shiho Ohyama	71	70	70	211	1,750,000
Kaori Higo	71	72	69	212	1,175,000
Yasuko Satoh	71	71	70	212	1,175,000
Mitsuko Kawasaki	73	68	71	212	1,175,000
Ji-Hee Lee	69	71	72	212	1,175,000
Ok-Hee Ku	74	70	69	213	825,000
Nobuko Kizawa	72	71	70	213	825,000
Miho Koga	73	68	72	213	825,000
Kozue Azuma	72	68	73	213	825,000
Rui Kitada	74	72	68	214	650,000
*Kumiko Kaneda	73	72	69	214	
Megumi Higuchi	70	73	71	214	650,000
Seiko Watanabe	70	71	73	214	650,000
Chizuru Akiyama	71	75	69	215	485,714
Young-Me Lee	72	73	70	215	485,714
Midori Yoneyama	72	73	70	215	485,714
Hiromi Takesue	75	69	71	215	485,714
Misato Nishikawa	71	72	72	215	485,714
Michie Ohba	72	71	72	215	485,714
Rie Murata	72	69	74	215	485,714
Kotomi Akiyama	70	76	70	216	425,000
Junko Yasui	72	74	70	216	425,000
Takayo Bandoh	74	70	72	216	425,000
Kasumi Fujii	74	70	72	216	425,000

NEC Karuizawa 72

Karuizawa 72 Golf Club, Nagano

August 15-17

Par 36-36–72; 6,497 yards

purse, ¥60,000,000

	SCORES			TOTAL	MONEY
Akiko Fukushima	69	72	67	208	¥10,800,000
Ikuyo Shiotani	69	71	72	212	5,280,000
Kaori Suzuki	69	73	71	213	3,900,000
Yuri Fudoh	69	71	73	213	3,900,000
*Sakura Yokomine	73	72	69	214	
Ok-Hee Ku	73	70	71	214	2,700,000
Kasumi Fujii	70	72	72	214	2,700,000
Chieko Amanuma	74	70	71	215	1,950,000
Kaori Harada	74	69	72	215	1,950,000
Toshimi Kimura	72	73	71	216	1,350,000
Mitsuko Kawasaki	70	71	75	216	1,350,000
Michiko Hattori	73	75	69	217	948,000
Rui Kitada	75	73	69	217	948,000
Kotomi Akiyama	71	76	70	217	948,000
Yuka Irie	74	72	71	217	948,000

	SCORES			TOTAL	MONEY
Young-Me Lee	72	73	72	217	948,000
Mikiyo Nishizuka	71	73	73	217	948,000
Kaori Higo	75	69	73	217	948,000
Junko Yoshida	74	73	71	218	616,800
Hsiu-Feng Tseng	74	72	72	218	616,800
Rie Fujiwara	69	76	73	218	616,800
Woo-Soon Ko	73	72	73	218	616,800
Mineko Nasu	71	73	74	218	616,800
Nikki Campbell	75	75	69	219	534,000
Shiho Ohyama	76	73	70	219	534,000
Riko Higashio	71	74	74	219	534,000
Yoko Inoue	74	71	74	219	534,000
Kumiko Hiyoshi	74	75	71	220	486,000
Yumi Kubota	75	74	71	220	486,000
Shin Sora	73	75	72	220	486,000
Hiromi Takesue	74	71	75	220	486,000

New Caterpillar Mitsubishi Ladies

Daihakone Country Club, Hakone, Kanagawa
Par 36-37–73; 6,648 yards

August 22-24
purse, ¥60,000,000

	SCORES			TOTAL	MONEY
Yuri Fudoh	67	68	73	208	¥10,800,000
Junko Omote	68	72	71	211	5,280,000
Toshimi Kimura	70	72	71	213	3,900,000
Miho Koga	66	74	73	213	3,900,000
Chikako Matsuzawa	73	72	69	214	2,160,000
Akiko Fukushima	71	72	71	214	2,160,000
Yun-Jye Wei	71	72	71	214	2,160,000
Nikki Campbell	71	72	71	214	2,160,000
Ae-Sook Kim	70	72	72	214	2,160,000
Shiho Ohyama	71	74	70	215	1,161,000
Yuriko Ohtsuka	71	72	72	215	1,161,000
Hiroko Yamaguchi	73	75	68	216	912,000
Samantha Head	70	76	70	216	912,000
Mikiyo Nishizuka	73	73	70	216	912,000
Nobuko Kizawa	73	73	70	216	912,000
Chieko Amanuma	75	71	70	216	912,000
Fuki Kido	70	75	71	216	912,000
Michiko Hattori	74	70	73	217	702,000
Rui Kitada	71	78	69	218	598,000
Ikuyo Shiotani	74	74	70	218	598,000
Aki Nakano	74	73	71	218	598,000
Mayumi Nakajima	74	75	70	219	540,000
Young-Me Lee	74	72	73	219	540,000
Hiromi Takesue	75	71	73	219	540,000
Kasumi Fujii	75	70	74	219	540,000
Masaki Maeda	74	75	71	220	498,000
Mayumi Murai	75	72	73	220	498,000
Kaori Suzuki	71	72	77	220	498,000
Hikaru Kobayashi	74	75	72	221	438,000
Mie Nakata	73	75	73	221	438,000
Orie Fujino	76	72	73	221	438,000
Aki Takamura	75	73	73	221	438,000
Seiko Watanabe	73	74	74	221	438,000
Hsiao-Chuan Lu	75	72	74	221	438,000
Fumiko Muraguchi	74	73	74	221	438,000

Yonex Ladies

Yonex Country Club, Teradomari, Niigata
Par 36-36–72; 6,302 yards

August 29-31
purse, ¥60,000,000

	SCORES			TOTAL	MONEY
Miho Koga	69	66	72	207	¥10,800,000
Yuri Fudoh	72	68	69	209	4,740,000
Kaori Higo	68	71	70	209	4,740,000
*Ai Miyazato	69	68	72	209	
Young-Me Lee	71	70	70	211	3,000,000
Hsiu-Feng Tseng	67	71	73	211	3,000,000
Yumi Kubota	73	65	73	211	3,000,000
Takayo Bandoh	73	67	72	212	2,100,000
Midori Yoneyama	72	70	71	213	1,500,000
Kasumi Fujii	70	69	74	213	1,500,000
Hiromi Takesue	67	69	77	213	1,500,000
Kyoko Ono	71	73	70	214	972,000
Ayako Okamoto	72	71	71	214	972,000
Chihiro Nakajima	72	70	72	214	972,000
Ae-Sook Kim	73	69	72	214	972,000
Kumi Yamashita	73	68	73	214	972,000
Yoko Tsuchiya	67	73	74	214	972,000
Mineko Nasu	74	70	71	215	702,000
Chieko Amanuma	73	69	73	215	702,000
Hiroko Yamaguchi	70	71	74	215	702,000
Orie Fujino	72	72	72	216	576,000
Mikiyo Nishizuka	73	74	69	216	576,000
Chieko Nishida	70	74	73	217	540,000
Kaori Harada	75	69	73	217	540,000
Mayumi Nakajima	72	71	74	217	540,000
Hikaru Kobayashi	75	67	75	217	540,000
Junko Yasui	73	72	73	218	474,000
Kaori Yamamoto	71	73	74	218	474,000
Fumiko Kano	74	72	72	218	474,000
Woo-Soon Ko	73	71	74	218	474,000
Michie Ohba	72	71	75	218	474,000
Michiko Mitsui	72	74	72	218	474,000
Fuki Kido	71	75	72	218	474,000

Fujisankei Ladies Classic

Fujizakura Country Club, Kawaguchiko, Yamanashi
Par 35-36–71; 6,323 yards

September 5-7
purse, ¥60,000,000

	SCORES			TOTAL	MONEY
Ikuyo Shiotani	66	68	68	202	¥10,800,000
Fuki Kido	68	70	69	207	5,280,000
Woo-Soon Ko	69	68	73	210	3,900,000
Toshimi Kimura	69	68	73	210	3,900,000
Chieko Amanuma	69	72	70	211	3,000,000
Shiho Ohyama	72	73	67	212	2,250,000
Junko Omote	69	69	74	212	2,250,000
Hsiu-Feng Tseng	70	72	71	213	1,650,000
Atsuko Ueno	69	71	73	213	1,650,000
Eika Ohtake	71	72	71	214	1,041,600
Kaori Suzuki	72	71	71	214	1,041,600
Michiko Mitsui	70	72	72	214	1,041,600

	SCORES			TOTAL	MONEY
Hsiao-Chuan Lu	73	69	72	214	1,041,600
Yayoi Arasaki	73	68	73	214	1,041,600
Akiko Fukushima	72	72	71	215	792,000
Mineko Nasu	69	74	72	215	792,000
Keiko Sasaki	72	68	75	215	792,000
Ae-Sook Kim	72	74	70	216	560,571
Ji-Hee Lee	76	70	70	216	560,571
Michie Ohba	72	72	72	216	560,571
Michiko Hattori	74	70	72	216	560,571
Young-Me Lee	72	71	73	216	560,571
Yuka Shiroto	72	71	73	216	560,571
Masaki Maeda	73	70	73	216	560,571
*Ai Miyazato	72	73	72	217	
Hikaru Kobayashi	73	72	72	217	456,000
Kotomi Akiyama	74	71	72	217	456,000
Samantha Head	70	73	74	217	456,000
Kaori Harada	69	73	75	217	456,000
Mayumi Murai	71	71	75	217	456,000
Kozue Azuma	71	71	75	217	456,000
Junko Yasui	74	68	75	217	456,000

Japan LPGA Championship

Taiheiyo Club, Enan Course, Hyogo
Par 36-36–72; 6,487 yards

September 11-14
purse, ¥70,000,000

	SCORES				TOTAL	MONEY
Yuri Fudoh	67	68	72	70	277	¥12,600,000
Michie Ohba	66	72	75	68	281	5,530,000
Miho Koga	70	69	71	71	281	5,530,000
Yasuko Satoh	72	69	69	72	282	4,200,000
Ji-Yeon Han	71	67	74	71	283	2,916,666
Shiho Ohyama	68	72	71	72	283	2,916,666
Woo-Soon Ko	69	70	70	74	283	2,916,666
Shin Sora	72	71	71	70	284	2,100,000
Ji-Hee Lee	70	73	70	72	285	1,470,000
Yun-Jye Wei	71	71	70	73	285	1,470,000
Hikaru Kobayashi	71	71	69	74	285	1,470,000
Rie Fujiwara	70	74	70	72	286	1,085,000
Mitsuko Kawasaki	71	73	70	72	286	1,085,000
Junko Omote	75	66	72	73	286	1,085,000
Fuki Kido	69	71	72	74	286	1,085,000
Kyoko Ono	67	74	72	74	287	770,000
Junko Yasui	70	70	72	75	287	770,000
Hsiu-Feng Tseng	72	69	71	75	287	770,000
Mayumi Nakajima	69	75	68	75	287	770,000
Yuriko Ohtsuka	68	71	72	76	287	770,000
Young-Me Lee	70	71	75	72	288	588,000
Mikiyo Nishizuka	72	70	72	74	288	588,000
Kayo Yamada	71	72	71	74	288	588,000
Akiko Fukushima	69	75	69	75	288	588,000
Ikuyo Shiotani	70	72	71	75	288	588,000
Hsiao-Chuan Lu	69	74	74	72	289	518,000
Michiko Hattori	74	69	73	73	289	518,000
Mari Katayama	72	71	72	74	289	518,000
Hiromi Kobayashi	70	73	70	76	289	518,000
Midori Yoneyama	73	70	69	77	289	518,000

Munsingwear Ladies Tokai Classic

Ryosen Golf Club, Inabe, Mie
Par 36-36–72; 6,402 yards

September 19-21
purse, ¥60,000,000

	SCORES			TOTAL	MONEY
Yuri Fudoh	67	70	69	206	¥10,800,000
Kaori Harada	70	67	70	207	5,400,000
Junko Yasui	71	68	69	208	3,900,000
Hiroko Yamaguchi	68	69	71	208	3,900,000
Hsiu-Feng Tseng	68	71	70	209	2,500,000
Junko Omote	69	69	71	209	2,500,000
Yasuko Satoh	71	69	69	209	2,500,000
Seiko Watanabe	68	74	68	210	1,411,500
Michie Ohba	71	71	68	210	1,411,500
Mikiyo Nishizuka	71	71	68	210	1,411,500
Aki Nakano	75	65	70	210	1,411,500
Midori Yoneyama	70	72	69	211	1,056,000
Nikki Campbell	73	71	67	211	1,056,000
*Kurumi Dohi	69	75	69	213	
Chihiro Nakajima	69	73	71	213	846,000
Young-Me Lee	71	71	71	213	846,000
Ikuyo Shiotani	72	70	71	213	846,000
Woo-Soon Ko	68	72	73	213	846,000
Yuko Motoyama	72	68	73	213	846,000
Miho Koga	70	73	71	214	596,000
Mari Nishi	72	71	71	214	596,000
Rui Kitada	73	70	71	214	596,000
Kaori Yamamoto	73	72	69	214	596,000
Fuki Kido	74	67	73	214	596,000
Hsiao-Chuan Lu	69	69	76	214	596,000
Harumi Sakagami	72	72	71	215	522,000
Hiromi Kobayashi	71	73	71	215	522,000
Shiho Ohyama	71	71	73	215	522,000
Masaki Maeda	71	74	70	215	522,000
Ji-Yeon Han	73	68	74	215	522,000

Miyagi TV Cup Dunlop Ladies Open

Rifu Golf Club, Miyagi
Par 36-36–72; 6,358 yards

September 26-28
purse, ¥60,000,000

	SCORES			TOTAL	MONEY
*Ai Miyazato	70	70	71	211	
Mari Katayama	72	70	70	212	¥8,040,000
Hiroko Yamaguchi	66	73	73	212	8,040,000
Ji-Hee Lee	71	70	72	213	3,900,000
Shiho Ohyama	71	73	69	213	3,900,000
Junko Yoshida	71	69	74	214	1,874,571
Mikiyo Nishizuka	70	70	74	214	1,874,571
Seiko Watanabe	72	71	71	214	1,874,571
Woo-Soon Ko	70	72	72	214	1,874,571
Mihoko Takahashi	72	71	71	214	1,874,571
Rie Murata	73	73	68	214	1,874,571
Miho Koga	71	72	71	214	1,874,571
Aki Takamura	75	71	69	215	942,000
Junko Omote	71	73	71	215	942,000
Hiromi Takesue	72	69	74	215	942,000

	SCORES			TOTAL	MONEY
Junko Yasui	73	73	69	215	942,000
Kaori Harada	71	70	74	215	942,000
Yuko Motoyama	75	68	73	216	702,000
Aki Nakano	72	71	73	216	702,000
Ae-Sook Kim	71	72	73	216	702,000
Ok-Hee Ku	73	74	70	217	564,000
Toshimi Kimura	71	75	71	217	564,000
Mitsuyo Hirata	74	71	72	217	564,000
Hisako Takeda	69	74	74	217	564,000
Kasumi Fujii	76	68	74	218	522,000
Mayumi Murai	72	73	73	218	522,000
Yuka Shiroto	71	72	75	218	522,000
Masaki Maeda	75	72	72	219	462,000
Hsiao-Chuan Lu	74	73	72	219	462,000
Fuki Kido	76	69	74	219	462,000
Hiromi Kobayashi	74	74	71	219	462,000
Yuri Kawanami	74	73	72	219	462,000
Shin Sora	75	70	74	219	462,000
Michiko Mitsui	74	72	73	219	462,000

Japan Women's Open

Chiba Country Club, Noda Course, Chiba
Par 36-36–72; 6,480 yards

October 2-5
purse, ¥70,000,000

	SCORES				TOTAL	MONEY
Michiko Hattori	69	73	71	74	287	¥14,000,000
Ji-Hee Lee	73	71	71	72	287	7,700,000
(Hattori defeated Lee on second playoff hole.)						
Nikki Campbell	75	74	67	72	288	4,497,500
Ayako Uehara	71	71	72	74	288	4,497,500
Hiroko Yamaguchi	75	69	71	76	291	2,940,000
Shiho Ohyama	70	71	82	69	292	2,096,000
Midori Yoneyama	71	77	73	71	292	2,096,000
Kasumi Fujii	71	77	70	74	292	2,096,000
Yasuko Satoh	71	73	73	76	293	1,634,000
*Sakura Yokomine	74	76	73	71	294	
*Akane Iijima	72	75	74	73	294	
Toshimi Kimura	75	73	70	76	294	1,454,000
Woo-Soon Ko	72	71	75	77	295	1,264,000
Ok-Hee Ku	71	73	77	75	296	1,050,666
Hiromi Kobayashi	70	75	76	75	296	1,050,666
Yun-Jye Wei	75	71	75	75	296	1,050,666
*Shinobu Moromizato	77	76	76	68	297	
Rena Yamazaki	78	68	78	73	297	832,333
Kaori Higo	70	75	77	75	297	832,333
Michie Ohba	73	76	72	76	297	832,333
Junko Omote	77	75	73	73	298	686,750
*Ai Miyazato	78	75	75	70	298	
Kyoko Ono	76	71	78	73	298	686,750
Michiko Mitsui	72	76	73	77	298	686,750
Misato Nishikawa	71	74	75	78	298	686,750
Yuriko Ohtsuka	76	77	75	71	299	600,000
Samantha Head	75	71	81	72	299	600,000
Mitsuko Kawasaki	79	72	72	76	299	600,000
Tomoko Kusakabe	73	75	70	81	299	600,000
Mikiyo Nishizuka	74	70	82	74	300	530,714

	SCORES				TOTAL	MONEY
Rebecca Coakley	72	78	76	74	300	530,714
Kumi Yamashita	76	77	73	74	300	530,714
Hsiao-Chuan Lu	75	78	73	74	300	530,714
Kayo Yamada	75	77	73	75	300	530,714
Yuri Fudoh	70	79	75	76	300	530,714
Mari Nishi	74	73	74	79	300	530,714

Sankyo Ladies Open

Akagi Country Club, Niisato, Gunma
Par 36-36–72; 6,398 yards

October 10-12
purse, ¥60,000,000

	SCORES			TOTAL	MONEY
Ji-Hee Lee	72	67	65	204	¥10,800,000
Mie Nakata	73	67	67	207	5,280,000
Toshimi Kimura	65	71	72	208	4,200,000
Yuri Fudoh	71	71	67	209	3,000,000
Mayumi Nakajima	73	69	67	209	3,000,000
Aki Nakano	75	67	67	209	3,000,000
Nikki Campbell	73	68	70	211	2,100,000
Yasuko Satoh	71	73	68	212	1,500,000
Hiromi Mogi	70	72	70	212	1,500,000
Kaori Harada	68	72	72	212	1,500,000
Shin Sora	73	70	70	213	1,074,000
Junko Omote	72	67	74	213	1,074,000
Mari Nishi	70	68	75	213	1,074,000
Shiho Ohyama	72	72	70	214	894,000
Michie Ohba	73	71	70	214	894,000
Michiko Hattori	73	71	70	214	894,000
Akiko Fukushima	71	75	69	215	684,000
Kaori Yamamoto	72	74	69	215	684,000
Hikaru Kobayashi	76	68	71	215	684,000
Hsiu-Feng Tseng	73	71	71	215	684,000
Fuki Kido	76	70	70	216	534,000
Hsiao-Chuan Lu	74	72	70	216	534,000
Miho Koga	74	71	71	216	534,000
Yui Kawahara	69	74	73	216	534,000
Chieko Amanuma	70	73	73	216	534,000
Yuri Kawanami	71	72	73	216	534,000
Mayumi Inoue	72	71	73	216	534,000
Ok-Hee Ku	72	71	73	216	534,000
Kasumi Fujii	67	73	76	216	534,000
Junko Yasui	71	75	71	217	438,000
Hiromi Kobayashi	72	74	71	217	438,000
Orie Fujino	73	72	72	217	438,000
Young-Me Lee	74	71	72	217	438,000
Hiromi Takesue	72	72	73	217	438,000
Kayo Yamada	74	70	73	217	438,000
Ayako Okamoto	71	71	75	217	438,000

Fujitsu Ladies

Tokyu Seven Hundred Club, Chiba
Par 36-36–72; 6,528 yards

October 17-19
purse, ¥60,000,000

	SCORES			TOTAL	MONEY
Yuri Fudoh	67	68	69	204	¥10,800,000
Ok-Hee Ku	71	69	66	206	5,280,000
Mineko Nasu	68	75	67	210	4,200,000
Yuko Motoyama	69	73	69	211	3,300,000
Masaki Maeda	70	71	70	211	3,300,000
Yu-Chen Huang	75	70	67	212	2,400,000
Kaori Higo	69	74	70	213	2,100,000
Seiko Watanabe	72	75	67	214	1,329,600
Yasuko Satoh	71	72	71	214	1,329,600
Yun-Jye Wei	69	76	69	214	1,329,600
Mihoko Takahashi	69	72	73	214	1,329,600
Fumiko Muraguchi	71	70	73	214	1,329,600
Azumi Katoh	72	74	69	215	864,000
Kasumi Fujii	74	70	71	215	864,000
Shiho Ohyama	72	71	72	215	864,000
Kumiko Hiyoshi	74	69	72	215	864,000
Hiromi Mogi	71	71	73	215	864,000
Aki Nakano	75	73	68	216	606,000
Kumi Yamashita	74	73	69	216	606,000
Kayo Yamada	73	72	71	216	606,000
Nikki Campbell	73	69	74	216	606,000
Miho Koga	74	74	69	217	516,000
Michiko Hattori	72	75	70	217	516,000
Mikiyo Nishizuka	76	69	72	217	516,000
Kaori Yamamoto	73	70	74	217	516,000
Hsiu-Feng Tseng	70	72	75	217	516,000
Mitsuko Kawasaki	75	73	70	218	438,000
Kotomi Akiyama	72	75	71	218	438,000
Samantha Head	72	74	72	218	438,000
Mayumi Inoue	72	74	72	218	438,000
Chizuru Akiyama	75	70	73	218	438,000
Harumi Sakagami	75	70	73	218	438,000
Misato Nishikawa	71	73	74	218	438,000
Chihiro Nakajima	71	72	75	218	438,000

Masters Golf Club Ladies

Masters Golf Club, Hyogo
Par 36-36–72; 6,412 yards

October 31-November 2
purse, ¥50,000,000

	SCORES			TOTAL	MONEY
Hiromi Takesue	70	66	70	206	¥9,000,000
Michie Ohba	73	70	67	210	3,950,000
Karrie Webb	69	70	71	210	3,950,000
Miho Koga	71	66	74	211	2,500,000
Chieko Amanuma	70	70	71	211	2,500,000
Michiko Hattori	70	70	71	211	2,500,000
Junko Omote	72	68	72	212	1,750,000
Kasumi Fujii	71	71	71	213	1,375,000
Yuri Fudoh	77	69	67	213	1,375,000
Young-Me Lee	72	74	68	214	960,000
Ai-Yu Tu	68	70	76	214	960,000

	SCORES			TOTAL	MONEY
Yasuko Satoh	72	73	70	215	820,000
Natsuko Noro	72	71	72	215	820,000
Mikiyo Nishizuka	71	74	70	215	820,000
Kayo Yamada	73	71	72	216	670,000
Kelly Robbins	72	73	71	216	670,000
Mayumi Nakajima	71	74	71	216	670,000
Ayako Uehara	76	70	71	217	494,000
Kyoko Ono	71	74	72	217	494,000
Hiromi Mogi	70	73	74	217	494,000
Yukari Baba	72	73	72	217	494,000
Hsiao-Chuan Lu	74	72	71	217	494,000
Aki Nakano	74	72	72	218	415,000
Junko Yasui	75	70	73	218	415,000
Hsiu-Feng Tseng	74	72	72	218	415,000
Riko Higashio	70	74	74	218	415,000
Mari Nishi	72	70	76	218	415,000
Chieko Nishida	70	74	74	218	415,000
Nikki Campbell	75	73	71	219	360,000
Rena Yamazaki	74	72	73	219	360,000
Yukiyo Haga	77	70	72	219	360,000
Nobuko Kizawa	73	71	75	219	360,000
Mihoko Takahashi	73	75	71	219	360,000

Mizuno Classic

Seta Golf Club, North Course, Otsu, Shiga
Par 36-36–72; 6,450 yards

November 7-9
purse, ¥135,600,000

	SCORES			TOTAL	MONEY
Annika Sorenstam	63	63	66	192	¥18,577,200
Sophie Gustafson	68	66	67	201	8,560,966
Grace Park	65	68	68	201	8,560,966
Se Ri Pak	67	65	69	201	8,560,966
Yuri Fudoh	67	66	69	202	6,073,165
Rachel Teske	68	65	70	203	4,150,771
Gloria Park	70	67	67	204	3,259,066
Jung Yeon Lee	65	67	72	204	3,259,066
Soo-Yun Kang	69	68	68	205	2,736,493
Lorena Ochoa	69	71	66	206	2,316,177
Dorothy Delasin	71	64	71	206	2,316,177
Christina Kim	69	66	71	206	2,316,177
Woo-Soon Ko	67	72	68	207	1,844,787
Laura Davies	72	65	70	207	1,844,787
Miho Koga	68	68	71	207	1,844,787
Mi-Hyun Kim	66	69	72	207	1,844,787
Jeong Jang	70	71	67	208	1,473,353
Tina Barrett	69	71	68	208	1,473,353
Junko Omote	74	65	69	208	1,473,353
Lorie Kane	67	71	70	208	1,473,353
Karrie Webb	68	67	73	208	1,473,353
Ji Hee Lee	68	74	67	209	1,199,133
Kelly Robbins	71	70	68	209	1,199,133
Mikiyo Nishizuka	67	72	70	209	1,199,133
Ok-Hee Ku	71	68	70	209	1,199,133
Marisa Baena	74	65	70	209	1,199,133
Laura Diaz	68	69	72	209	1,199,133
Michiko Hattori	71	70	69	210	985,414

	SCORES			TOTAL	MONEY
Karen Stupples	73	67	70	210	985,414
Hee-Won Han	68	71	71	210	985,414
Candie Kung	70	69	71	210	985,414

Itoen Ladies

Great Island Club, Chonan, Chiba
Par 36-36–72; 6,510 yards

November 14-16
purse, ¥60,000,000

	SCORES			TOTAL	MONEY
Yuri Fudoh	70	69	74	213	¥10,800,000
Junko Omote	75	67	71	213	5,280,000
(Fudoh defeated Omote on third playoff hole.)					
Fuki Kido	72	69	74	215	3,600,000
Yuka Shiroto	72	68	75	215	3,600,000
Kasumi Fujii	69	68	78	215	3,600,000
Woo-Soon Ko	70	70	76	216	2,250,000
Mizue Igarashi	71	68	77	216	2,250,000
Hsiu-Feng Tseng	75	68	74	217	1,344,000
Hiroko Yamaguchi	69	72	76	217	1,344,000
Ji-Yeon Han	69	70	78	217	1,344,000
Hiromi Takesue	72	68	77	217	1,344,000
Nikki Campbell	71	72	74	217	1,344,000
Ok-Hee Ku	72	74	72	218	990,000
Kyoko Ono	73	69	76	218	990,000
Akiko Fukushima	72	69	78	219	750,000
Mikiyo Nishizuka	75	71	73	219	750,000
Chieko Amanuma	70	72	77	219	750,000
Yun-Jye Wei	73	72	74	219	750,000
Hsiao-Chuan Lu	70	73	76	219	750,000
Kanna Takanashi	72	74	73	219	750,000
Hiromi Kobayashi	71	76	73	220	570,000
Mie Nakata	74	73	73	220	570,000
Shiho Ohyama	72	74	74	220	570,000
Mitsuko Kawasaki	73	71	76	220	570,000
Miho Koga	72	72	77	221	534,000
Michiko Mitsui	73	73	75	221	534,000
Young-Me Lee	71	73	78	222	486,000
Mayumi Ishii	77	70	75	222	486,000
Junko Yasui	74	72	76	222	486,000
Yoko Tsuchiya	77	71	74	222	486,000
Shiho Katano	76	72	74	222	486,000
Ji-Hee Lee	72	73	77	222	486,000

Daioseishi Elleair Ladies Open

Elleair Golf Club, Matsuyama, Ehime
Par 36-36–72; 6,363 yards

November 21-23
purse, ¥80,000,000

	SCORES			TOTAL	MONEY
Miho Koga	73	71	65	209	¥14,400,000
Riko Higashio	74	65	70	209	7,040,000
(Koga defeated Higashio on first playoff hole.)					
Hiromi Mogi	75	69	66	210	5,600,000
Kasumi Fujii	72	70	69	211	4,400,000

	SCORES			TOTAL	MONEY
Hiromi Takesue	73	67	71	211	4,400,000
Shiho Ohyama	73	72	68	213	2,800,000
Ji-Hee Lee	72	71	70	213	2,800,000
Rui Kitada	72	70	71	213	2,800,000
Kyoko Ono	73	71	70	214	1,569,600
Hsiao-Chuan Lu	72	71	71	214	1,569,600
Kaori Higo	69	73	72	214	1,569,600
Mitsuko Kawasaki	69	72	73	214	1,569,600
Hsiu-Feng Tseng	67	71	76	214	1,569,600
Akiko Fukushima	73	72	70	215	1,096,000
Midori Yoneyama	71	74	70	215	1,096,000
*Sakura Yokomine	74	70	71	215	
Woo-Soon Ko	73	69	73	215	1,096,000
Hiromi Kobayashi	69	73	73	215	1,096,000
Mineko Nasu	71	70	74	215	1,096,000
Chieko Amanuma	73	72	71	216	772,800
Ai Miyazato	70	75	71	216	772,800
Toshimi Kimura	75	71	70	216	772,800
Kayo Yamada	76	70	70	216	772,800
Ji-Yeon Han	72	71	73	216	772,800
Ai Nishikawa	72	73	72	217	696,000
Yoko Tsuchiya	74	73	70	217	696,000
Namika Omata	73	74	70	217	696,000
Norimi Terasawa	73	72	73	218	648,000
Samantha Head	72	73	73	218	648,000
Ok-Hee Ku	71	72	75	218	648,000

Japan LPGA Tour Championship

Miyazaki Country Club, Sadohara, Miyazaki
Par 36-36–72; 6,438 yards

November 27-30
purse, ¥60,000,000

	SCORES				TOTAL	MONEY
Yuri Fudoh	75	68	66	70	279	¥15,000,000
Akiko Fukushima	68	76	72	68	284	7,350,000
Ji-Hee Lee	70	73	70	71	284	7,350,000
Kasumi Fujii	73	69	69	74	285	4,800,000
Toshimi Kimura	76	70	70	71	287	4,140,000
Midori Yoneyama	74	73	69	72	288	3,552,000
Yun-Jye Wei	75	72	70	74	291	2,952,000
Hiroko Yamaguchi	75	73	74	71	293	1,449,600
Kaori Higo	74	74	73	72	293	1,449,600
Michiko Hattori	74	73	73	73	293	1,449,600
Hsiu-Feng Tseng	74	74	72	73	293	1,449,600
Miho Koga	71	74	72	76	293	1,449,600
Hiromi Takesue	74	72	73	76	295	804,000
Mihoko Takahashi	74	73	78	72	297	684,000
Woo-Soon Ko	73	75	74	76	298	564,000
Ok-Hee Ku	76	75	73	75	299	474,000
Junko Omote	76	73	70	80	299	474,000
Shiho Ohyama	77	77	74	72	300	342,000
Kaori Suzuki	75	76	75	74	300	342,000
Ikuyo Shiotani	76	74	75	75	300	342,000
Yuka Shiroto	75	73	77	77	302	294,000
Ai Miyazato	72	79	74	78	303	288,000

Australian Women's Tour

Contrabart ALPG Players Championship

Horizons Golf Resort, Nelson Bay, Australia
Par 36-37–73; 6,243 yards

February 13-16
purse, A$100,000

	SCORES				TOTAL	MONEY
Tamara Hyett	68	68	69	76	281	A$15,000
Laura Davies	71	74	69	67	281	10,000
(Hyett defeated Davies on first playoff hole.)						
Georgina Simpson	69	71	68	74	282	7,000
Trish Johnson	72	72	73	68	285	4,550
Maria Hjorth	72	70	73	70	285	4,550
Nadina Taylor	73	71	72	70	286	3,250
Samantha Head	73	70	72	71	286	3,250
Rebecca Stevenson	74	73	68	72	287	2,500
Johanna Head	74	71	72	71	288	2,100
Rachel Teske	68	77	75	68	288	2,100
Anne-Marie Knight	73	71	76	69	289	1,666.70
Loraine Lambert	69	73	72	75	289	1,666.70
Julie Forbes	69	71	75	74	289	1,666.70
Susie Parry	75	73	70	72	290	1,350
Nicola Moult	72	75	73	71	291	1,206
Stefania Croce	75	72	77	67	291	1,206
Marine Monnet	70	75	74	72	291	1,206
Rebecca Coakley	74	74	71	72	291	1,206
Gwladys Nocera	74	72	74	71	291	1,206
Becky Morgan	73	72	72	75	292	1,065
Shani Waugh	72	76	73	71	292	1,065
Tamie Durdin	72	72	78	70	292	1,065
Joanne Mills	72	71	78	71	292	1,065
Kathryn Marshall	74	72	78	69	293	930
Joanne Morley	74	72	73	74	293	930
Corinne Dibnah	72	77	71	73	293	930
Sophie Gustafson	72	70	73	78	293	930
Riikka Hakkarainen	71	78	71	73	293	930
Catrin Nilsmark	75	72	75	72	294	840
Iben Tinning	73	72	77	73	295	780
Miriam Nagl	72	74	77	72	295	780
Nancy Harvey	76	71	76	72	295	780

ANZ Ladies Masters

Royal Pines Golf Club, Gold Coast, Queensland
Par 37-35–72; 6,397 yards
(Event shortened to 54 holes—rain.)

February 20-23
purse, A$800,000

	SCORES			TOTAL	MONEY
Laura Davies	67	68	68	203	€73,264.21
Rebecca Stevenson	68	68	68	204	41,516.38
Karrie Webb	68	66	70	204	41,516.38
Lorena Ochoa	69	68	68	205	24,421.41

	SCORES			TOTAL	MONEY
Iben Tinning	72	68	66	206	18,193.94
Rachel Teske	71	68	67	206	18,193.94
Gina Scott	70	73	64	207	14,652.84
Samantha Head	70	71	67	208	11,111.74
Paula Marti	69	70	69	208	11,111.74
Shani Waugh	70	71	68	209	7,538.07
Michelle Ellis	67	74	68	209	7,538.07
Anna Becker	73	67	69	209	7,538.07
Corinne Dibnah	69	74	66	209	7,538.07
Kelly Robbins	72	67	70	209	7,538.07
Brenda Ormsby	71	66	72	209	7,538.07
Fiona Pike	71	70	69	210	5,800.08
Sophie Gustafson	70	71	69	210	5,800.08
Mhairi McKay	70	70	70	210	5,800.08
Jennifer Rosales	70	68	72	210	5,800.08
Karen Pearce	73	67	71	211	5,128.48
Rebecca Coakley	70	69	72	211	5,128.48
Natalie Gulbis	69	74	68	211	5,128.48
Johanna Head	72	66	73	211	5,128.48
Janice Moodie	68	69	74	211	5,128.48
Ludivine Kreutz	70	72	70	212	4,235.34
Miriam Nagl	71	69	72	212	4,235.34
Catrin Nilsmark	73	70	69	212	4,235.34
Suzanne Strudwick	71	69	72	212	4,235.34
Suzann Pettersen	69	74	69	212	4,235.34
Nicole Stillig	74	70	68	212	4,235.34
Beth Bauer	73	71	68	212	4,235.34

AAMI Women's Australian Open

Terrey Hills Golf & Country Club,
Sydney, New South Wales
Par 36-36–72; 6,379 yards

February 27-March 2
purse, A$500,000

	SCORES				TOTAL	MONEY
Mhairi McKay	72	67	71	67	277	€46,580.16
Laura Davies	65	68	73	72	278	31,053.44
Rachel Teske	68	72	70	69	279	21,737.41
Samantha Head	70	69	73	69	281	14,129.31
Marnie McGuire	70	71	71	69	281	14,129.31
Rebecca Coakley	67	67	77	71	282	10,402.90
Catriona Matthew	70	70	73	70	283	6,321.59
Suzann Pettersen	73	68	72	70	283	6,321.59
Alison Nicholas	67	72	73	71	283	6,321.59
Patricia Meunier Lebouc	73	67	72	71	283	6,321.59
Beth Bauer	70	66	75	72	283	6,321.59
Lorena Ochoa	67	69	75	72	283	6,321.59
Iben Tinning	68	71	72	72	283	6,321.59
Lynnette Brooky	70	73	70	71	284	3,783.34
Diana Luna	72	72	69	71	284	3,783.34
Silvia Cavalleri	72	68	72	72	284	3,783.34
Karine Icher	71	68	72	73	284	3,783.34
Becky Morgan	67	75	68	74	284	3,783.34
Suzanne Strudwick	72	70	64	78	284	3,783.34
Il-Mi Chung	72	69	72	72	285	3,353.77
Alison Munt	73	68	71	73	285	3,353.77
Karrie Webb	69	67	74	75	285	3,353.77

	SCORES			TOTAL	MONEY
Charlotta Sorenstam	72	68	76	70	286	2,981.13
Janice Moodie	69	70	76	71	286	2,981.13
Nadina Taylor	74	72	69	71	286	2,981.13
Kelly Robbins	68	69	75	74	286	2,981.13
Ludivine Kreutz	74	69	68	75	286	2,981.13
Sophie Gustafson	68	74	73	72	287	2,546.38
Natalie Gulbis	73	70	72	72	287	2,546.38
Miriam Nagl	72	71	70	74	287	2,546.38
Jackie Gallagher-Smith	75	65	70	77	287	2,546.38

Nedbank Women's Tour of South Africa

Acer South African Women's Open

Royal Johannesburg & Kensington Golf Clubs, Johannesburg
Par 37-35–72; 6,186 yards

March 26-28
purse, R200,000

	SCORES			TOTAL	MONEY
Helena Svensson	70	70	71	211	R30,000
Caryn Louw	70	73	69	212	22,000
Marlene Hedblom	73	72	69	214	12,667
Elisabeth Esterl	69	73	72	214	12,667
Anna Becker	69	73	72	214	12,666
Laurette Maritz	75	71	70	216	8,300
Sanet Marais	73	74	70	217	7,100
Mandy Adamson	74	70	75	219	5,700
*Tanika van As	73	72	74	219	
Carina Vagner	74	74	71	219	5,700
Annerie Wessels	74	72	74	220	4,500
Sarah Heath	72	72	76	220	4,500
Cecilie Lundgreen	75	74	72	221	4,000
Judith van Hagen	73	74	75	222	3,900
Kerry Knowles	75	75	73	223	3,800
Andrea Hirschhorn	73	76	75	224	3,550
Johanna Westerberg	76	75	73	224	3,550
Lesley Nicholson	77	74	73	224	3,550
Rikke Rasmussen	77	71	76	224	3,550
Letitia Moses	77	75	73	225	3,250
Gabriella Andren	72	76	77	225	3,250
Vanessa Smith	76	76	74	226	2,954
Amanda Moltke-Leth	76	78	72	226	2,953
Anna Tybring	75	76	75	226	2,953
*Ashleigh Simon	80	76	71	227	
Cherry Moulder	68	80	79	227	2,700
Emma Zackrisson	80	73	75	228	2,600
Nina Reis	74	81	74	229	2,450
*Betty Tsebo Mokoena	76	75	78	229	
Cecilia Ekelundh	78	76	75	229	2,450

Pam Golding Ladies International

Parkview Golf Club, Cape Town
Par 35-37–72; 6,206 yards

April 2-4
purse, R200,000

	SCORES			TOTAL	MONEY
Laurette Maritz	71	69	69	209	R30,000
Elisabeth Esterl	69	72	71	212	22,000
Carina Vagner	74	72	67	213	14,100
Mandy Adamson	74	70	69	213	14,100
Annerie Wessels	73	71	71	215	9,050
Cecilia Ekelundh	73	70	72	215	9,050
Anna Becker	69	74	73	216	6,600
Johanna Westerberg	72	74	70	216	6,600
Stacy Doggett	73	72	72	217	5,000
Caryn Louw	73	73	71	217	5,000
Marlene Hedblom	74	71	73	218	4,150
Anna Tybring	75	72	71	218	4,150
Kerry Knowles	73	71	76	220	3,900
Andrea Hirschhorn	73	73	76	222	3,700
Morgana Robbertze	71	75	76	222	3,700
Amanda Moltke-Leth	72	73	77	222	3,700
Nina Reis	72	78	73	223	3,400
Lesley Nicholson	74	73	76	223	3,500
Helena Svensson	74	74	76	224	3,250
Cecilie Lundgreen	72	75	77	224	3,250
Vanessa Smith	76	74	75	225	2,953
Yvonne Cassidy	77	78	70	225	2,954
Susanne Westling	72	77	76	225	2,953
*Leandri Pieterse	76	75	75	226	
Emma Zackrisson	76	73	78	227	2,650
Sanet Marais	76	76	75	227	2,650
Charlaine Coetzee-Hirst	82	76	70	228	2,300
Judith van Hagen	77	75	76	228	2,300
Sofia Renell	75	77	76	228	2,300
Karen Margrethe Juul	76	79	73	228	2,300
Rikke Rassmussen	75	77	76	228	2,300

Telkom Women's Classic

Johannesburg Country Club, Johannesburg
Par 36-36–72; 6,161 yards

April 9-11
purse, R200,000

	SCORES			TOTAL	MONEY
Cherry Moulder	70	69	73	212	R30,000
Rikke Rassmussen	69	72	71	212	22,000
Amanda Moltke-Leth	73	69	71	213	16,000
Johanna Westerberg	71	70	75	216	12,200
Cecilia Ekelundh	73	74	70	217	9,050
Jessica Krantz	70	74	73	217	9,050
Carina Vagner	69	76	73	218	6,600
*Ashleigh Simon	71	72	75	218	
Lesley Nicholson	75	75	68	218	6,600
Sarah Heath	73	73	73	219	5,000
Emma Zackrisson	73	73	73	219	5,000
Laurette Maritz	74	72	74	220	4,150
Anna Becker	75	75	70	220	4,150
Andrea Hirschhorn	71	75	76	222	3,800

	SCORES			TOTAL	MONEY
Mandy Adamson	71	75	76	222	3,800
Cecilie Lundgreen	74	72	76	222	3,800
Stacy Doggett	74	74	76	224	3,500
Annerie Wessels	78	75	71	224	3,500
Michelle de Vries	72	73	79	224	3,500
Charlaine Coetzee-Hirst	79	74	72	225	3,250
Susanne Westling	71	78	76	225	3,250
Helena Svensson	77	73	76	226	3,030
Vanessa Smith	74	75	77	226	3,030
*Melissa Eaton	75	75	76	226	
Karen Margrethe Juul	73	75	79	227	2,800
*Tanika van As	79	76	73	228	
Fumi Doi	73	74	81	228	2,600
Caryn Louw	75	75	78	228	2,600
Anna Tybring	75	76	77	228	2,600
Nina Reis	79	74	76	229	2,400

Nedbank Women's South African Masters

Houghton Golf Club, Johannesburg
Par 36-36–72; 6,039 yards

April 15-17
purse, R200,000

	SCORES			TOTAL	MONEY
Laurette Maritz	70	68	68	206	R30,000
Mandy Adamson	69	71	70	210	22,000
Sarah Heath	72	69	71	212	16,000
Amanda Moltke-Leth	69	71	73	213	11,000
Andrea Hirschhorn	71	72	70	213	11,000
Deana Rushworth	71	73	71	215	8,300
*Ashleigh Simon	76	69	70	215	
Anna Tybring	71	73	72	216	6,600
Johanna Westerberg	70	74	72	216	6,600
Susanne Westling	74	71	72	217	5,000
Caryn Louw	76	73	68	217	5,000
Annerie Wessels	75	71	72	218	4,300
Charlaine Coetzee-Hirst	74	73	73	220	3,900
Nina Reis	72	75	73	220	3,900
Emma Zackrisson	71	74	75	220	3,900
Helena Svensson	76	73	73	222	3,600
Cherry Moulder	71	76	75	222	3,600
Lesley Nicholson	75	77	70	222	3,600
*Lise Botha	74	73	75	222	
Karen Pringle	73	75	75	223	3,250
Carina Vagner	75	75	73	223	3,250
Rikke Rassmussen	74	74	75	223	3,250
Anna Becker	72	74	77	223	3,250
Kerry Knowles	74	76	75	225	2,880
Zoe Frost	73	77	75	225	2,880
*Gilly Tebbutt	75	78	73	226	
Sofia Renell	74	75	78	227	2,650
Gabriella Andren	72	83	72	227	2,650
Michelle de Vries	76	73	79	228	2,450
*Lindsay Cummings	76	77	75	228	
*Sandra Winter	78	73	77	228	
Letitia Moses	73	82	73	228	2,450